Political Culture, the State, and the Problem of Religious War in Britain and Ireland, 1578–1625

Political Culture, the State, and the Problem of Religious War in Britain and Ireland, 1578–1625

R. MALCOLM SMUTS

Great Clarendon Street, Oxford, OX2 6DP,
United Kingdom

Oxford University Press is a department of the University of Oxford.
It furthers the University's objective of excellence in research, scholarship,
and education by publishing worldwide. Oxford is a registered trade mark of
Oxford University Press in the UK and in certain other countries

© R. Malcolm Smuts 2023

The moral rights of the author have been asserted

First Edition published in 2023

Impression: 1

All rights reserved. No part of this publication may be reproduced, stored in
a retrieval system, or transmitted, in any form or by any means, without the
prior permission in writing of Oxford University Press, or as expressly permitted
by law, by licence or under terms agreed with the appropriate reprographics
rights organization. Enquiries concerning reproduction outside the scope of the
above should be sent to the Rights Department, Oxford University Press, at the
address above

You must not circulate this work in any other form
and you must impose this same condition on any acquirer

Published in the United States of America by Oxford University Press
198 Madison Avenue, New York, NY 10016, United States of America

British Library Cataloguing in Publication Data
Data available

Library of Congress Control Number: 2022943041

ISBN 978-0-19-286313-3

DOI: 10.1093/oso/9780192863133.001.0001

Printed and bound in the UK by
Clays Ltd, Elcograf S.p.A.

Links to third party websites are provided by Oxford in good faith and
for information only. Oxford disclaims any responsibility for the materials
contained in any third party website referenced in this work.

Acknowledgments

This book is the product of many years of reflection and research, during which I have acquired numerous intellectual and personal debts. An invitation from Ronald Asch to participate in a conference in Osnabrück, Germany in 1998, commemorating the 350th anniversary of the Treaty of Westphalia, first stimulated me to think anew about how strategic problems relating to religious war and peace shaped politics and political culture in early Stuart England. A fellowship from the National Endowment for the Humanities at the Folger Shakespeare Library in Washington DC, during the academic year 2005–6, provided an opportunity to investigate the subject more systematically. It was during this fellowship that I began to extend the chronological range of my investigations back into the mid-Elizabethan period, and to incorporate serious attention to Scotland and Ireland. Heather James, Nancy Maguire, and Linda Peck provided especially stimulating collegial company during my year in Washington. Subsequently, the now sadly defunct Center for Interdisciplinary Urban Cultural History at the University of Massachusetts Boston, under the capable directorship of Elizabeth Fay, provided an environment in which to share ideas with colleagues and present an early draft of the book's introduction to a faculty workshop. The late Arthur Kinney's generosity in drawing me into the activities of the "Renaissance Center" he founded at the University of Massachusetts Amherst—since renamed the Arthur F. Kinney Center for Interdisciplinary Renaissance Studies—gave me access to a second, more specialized intellectual community.

Numerous conversations and email exchanges with colleagues in the field, including John Adamson, Jamie Reid Baxter, Pauline Croft, Janet Dickenson, Sue Doran, Luc Duerloo, Alex Gajda, Brendan Kane, Paulina Kewes, Peter Lake, Noah Millstone, Glyn Parry, David Trim, Arthur Williamson, Andy Wood and Neil Younger stimulated and sharpened my thinking about various aspects of the project. At a fairly late stage Simon Adams provided valuable advice about where to find source material relating to the earl of Leicester and his expedition to the Netherlands. Noah Millstone helped guide me to the rich material in the Haus Hof und Staats Archiv in Vienna, while Brendan Kane generously supplied an electronic copy of the Carew manuscripts in Lambeth Palace. Norman Jones alerted me to a relevant collection of documents in the library of Brigham Young University in Salt Lake City. A number of departmental and professional colleagues read and commented helpfully on individual chapters: Jamie Reid Baxter, Sue Doran, Alexandra Courtney, Alex Gajda, David Hunt, Brendan Kane, Paulina Kewes, Glyn Parry, Linda Pollock, Woodruff Smith, David Trim, and Arthur

Williamson. Two anonymous readers of the book proposal for Oxford University Press made several valuable suggestions. Cathryn Steele was a pleasure to work with at OUP. The copy-editor Joanna North did a very professional job.

My wife, MaryBeth, and now-married children, Robert and Felicia, together with their children James Gilbert and Jackson and Wyatt Gulick, provided moral support and welcome distractions from research and writing. The interest in the project of my late mother, the late Alice Smuts, my sister Barbara Smuts, and her partner Michael Abner also helped sustain me. My canine companions Sammie and Wolfij maintained my sanity by constantly insisting on the need for long walks.

Contents

Abbreviations   xi

Introduction: Expanding the Narrative   1
  Making the Past Less Familiar   1
  Kingdoms, Commonwealths, Constitutions, and States: An Historical Note on Political Vocabulary   4
  The State in Britain and Ireland and the Problem of Religious War   16
  Who Controls the State?   18
  The Permeability of States and Dynastic Politics   22
  The Exclusion Crisis of the 1580s   24
  1588–1603: A New Political Landscape?   27
  Peace and the Imperfect Consolidation of a British State, 1603–1625   29

1. Religion, Dynastic Politics, and Public Discourse: The Anjou Match and Its Contexts   33
  Dynastic Politics in a Monarchical Republic   33
  Historical and European Contexts of the Match   36
  English Catholicism and Landed Dynasties   43
  Initial Responses to Anjou's Suit   50
  Print, Public Performance, and the Contest over the Match   55
  John Stubbs and the Rhetoric of Dynastic Libel   64
  Court Politics, Print, and the Public Sphere   72
  Politiques, Protestants, and Jesuits: The Division Hardens   79
  Aftermath: The Sharpening of Confessional and Dynastic Divisions   85

2. The Containment of Militant English Catholicism   90
  The Challenge of the 1580s   90
  Catholic Resiliency and the Protestant State   94
  Dealing with English Catholicism   109
  Imprisonment for Recusancy and Power in the Localities   117
  Assassination, Lynch Law, and Provisions against Civil Chaos   125

3. An Ambiguous Dynastic Threat: James VI and Scotland to 1589   131
  The Scottish Mirror   133
  James's Escape and the Resumption of Conflict, 1583–1585   148
  Patrick Adamson's Appeal to the English Bishops   152
  From Enmity to Fragile Alliance, 1584–1587   157
  How Much Had Really Changed?   160
  James's "Alliance" with the Kirk in Scottish, English, and European Perspectives   169

4. Entrepreneurial Violence and the Protestant State ... 172
   Knight Errantry and Chivalric Policy ... 172
   Military Treatises ... 180
   Conditions of Military Recruitment and Service ... 187
   Privateers and Pirates ... 199
   The Expansion of English Oceanic Enterprise, 1577–1586 ... 207
   The Literature of Oceanic Enterprise ... 214
   War with Spain and the Reshaping of Oceanic Enterprise ... 221
   Conclusions ... 227

5. Defending the State in Ireland ... 229
   Ireland's Complex Social and Cultural Landscape ... 230
   Lordship in Ireland ... 235
   Negotiation or Radical Reform? The Dilemmas of Irish Governance ... 240
   The Religious Dimension ... 251
   The Civil Irish as Enemies of the State ... 260

6. The Earl of Leicester, the Protestant Cause, and the Failure of English State Building in the Netherlands ... 271
   Perspectives on the Crisis of the Mid-1580s ... 273
   The Problem of Sovereignty in the United Provinces ... 278
   Assembling and Paying for Leicester's Expedition ... 283
   The Establishment of Leicester's Governorship ... 286
   Elizabeth Reacts ... 294
   Leicester and the Dutch Politicians ... 302
   Power Struggles, the Buckhurst Embassy, and the Renewed Problem of Sovereignty ... 313
   Leicester's Return and Final Defeat: June–October 1587 ... 322
   Final Assessments ... 329

7. War, Virtue, and the State: Political Culture and the Essex Circle ... 337
   Public Service, the Meanings of Virtue, and Applied Knowledge ... 339
   The Court and Its Politics ... 343
   The Diminished Role of Religion and the Virtue of Noble Races ... 350
   Essex and His Friends ... 355
   The Emotional Economy of the State ... 358
   The Queen and the State ... 365
   Politic History, Tacitus and Essex ... 369
   Disagreements over the Conduct of War and Essex's Revolt ... 377
   Essex's Legacies ... 383

8. The Battle over Erastian Episcopacy in Two British Kingdoms, 1588–1603 ... 388
   The Bill and Book Campaign of 1587, Leicester, and the Dutch Connection ... 390
   Puritans, Popularity, and the State ... 395
   The Scottish Mirror (Again) ... 401

James's "Alliance" with the Kirk 411
The King, the Kirk, and the Catholic Earls 416
From Negotiation to Confrontation and Rupture 426
The Scottish Political Theology of James VI, c. 1597–1603 435
James and the English Conformists 443

9. King James's Peace, the Laws of the Realms, and the Forging of a United Kingdom? 446
The English Invention of *Rex Pacificus* and Its European Context 446
Engendering Peace: Royal Biology and the Refashioning of States 450
The Union of the Crowns, the Concept of Conquest, and the Common Law Mind 457
King James and the Lawyers: A Conflict over Absolutism? 462
Law and Society across Britain and Ireland: The Problem of Diversity 476
Kingship, Law, and Lordship 484

10. The Stuart State and Its Peripheries 489
Frontier Zones: The Borders and Irish Sea 489
Old and New Lordships in the Integration of the Kingdoms 496
Crown Officials, the Old English, and the Contested Role of the Common Law in Ireland 503
Law, State Power, and Religious Resistance in Ireland 516
Presbyterian Resistance in Scotland 529
Conclusions 537

11. Peace Without: The European Policies of James VI and I until 1617 539
Military Exhaustion, Strategic Calculations, and the Pursuit of Peace: The European Context 543
A King of Artifices Who Dissimulates 545
James's Polemical Contest with Jesuits and the Pope 556
Conflict in the Rhineland and the Murder of Henry IV 567
Political Intrigue and Polemic in France, 1610–1619 571
Arminianism, Vorstius, and Dutch Politics 581
Conclusions: James's Motives and Calculations 593

12. Dynastic Politics, Confessional Polarization, and the Challenge of New Religious Wars 597
Marital Diplomacy and Strategic Opportunism 597
Diplomacy and Proxy Conflicts in Central Europe 601
The Origins of the Spanish Match 605
France, Bohemia, and Confessional Polarization, 1617–1620 613
Peace and the Corruption of Religion and Virtue 637

13. The Problem of Religious War and the Structure of Politics at
    the Accession of Charles I   647
    Young Kings, Religious Wars, and the Rule of Favorites   647
    Court Faction, Royal Leadership, and the Problems of Foreign Wars   650
    A New Crisis Seen through Old Ideological Lenses   659
    The Problem of Religious Disharmony, the Militarization of Politics,
    and the Collapse of the State   661

Bibliography of Works Cited   677
Index   719

Abbreviations

Adams, "Protestant Cause"	Simon Adams, "The Protestant Cause: Religious Alliance with the West European Calvinist Communities as a Political Issue in England, 1585–1630," unpublished Oxford DPhil thesis, 1973
AMAE	Archives du ministère des Affairers Etrangère (Paris)
CPA	Correspondance Politique Angleterre
CPH	Correspondance Politique Holland
APC	Acts of the Privy Council of England, ed. John Roche Dasent et al., 42 vols (London, 1890–1974)
Bacon, Works	Works of Francis Bacon, ed. James Spedding, Robert Leslie Ellis, and Denon Heath, 14 vols (London: 1857–74)
BL	British Library
BN	Bibliothèque Nationale de France (Paris)
Bor, Oorsprong	Pieter Bor Christiaenszoon, Oorsprong, Begin, en Vervolgh der Nederlansche Oorlogen, parts 2 and 3 (Amsterdam, 1680–1)
Calderwood	David Calderwood, The true history of the Church of Scotland from the Reformation unto the end of the reign of King James VI (Edinburgh, 1680)
CDIHE	Coleccion de documentos ineditos para la historia de España, 113 vols (Madrid, 1842–95)
Felipe II	Correspondencia de Felipe II con sus embajadores en la corte de Inglaterra, ed. D. José Sancho Rayon and D. Francisco de Zabalburu, vol. 91 (Madrid, 1888)
Gondomar	Correspondencia official de Don Diego Sarmiento de Acuña, Conde de Gondomar, ed. Antonio Balesteros Beretta, vols 1–4 (Madrid, 1936–45)
CSPD	Calendar of State Papers, Domestic Series, of the Reigns of Edward VI, Mary, Elizabeth and James I, 12 vols (London, 1856–1967)
CSPF	Calendar of State Papers, Foreign Series, of the Reign of Elizabeth, 17 vols (London, 1863–1950)
CSPI	Calendar of State Papers Relating to Ireland of the Reigns of Henry VIII, Edward VI, Mary and Elizabeth, 11 vols (London, 1860–1912)
CSPI JI	Calendar of State Papers Relating to Ireland of the Reign of James I, 5 vols (London, 1872–80)

CSPSc	*Calendar of State Papers Relating to Scotland and Mary, Queen of Scots, 1547–1603*, 13 vols (Edinburgh and Glasgow, 1898–1969)
CSPSp	*Calendar of Letters and Papers... Preserved Principally in the Archives of Simancas*, ed. Martin A. S. Hume, 4 vols (London, 1892–9)
CSPV	*Calendar of State Papers, Relating to English Affairs Existing in the Archives of Venice, and in other Libraries of Northern Italy*, ed. G. C. Bentrinck et al., 38 vols (London, 1864–1947)
Hatton	*Memoirs of the Life and Times of Sir Christopher Hatton*, ed. Nicholas Harris Nicolas (London, 1847)
HHStA	Haus- Hof- und Staatsarchiv (Vienna)
HMC Salisbury	Historical Manuscripts Commission, *Calendar of the Manuscripts of the Most Honourable the Marquis of Salisbury... Preserved at Hatfield House*, 24 vols (London, 1883–1976)
Leicester Correspondence	*Correspondence of Robert Dudley Earl of Leicester*, ed. John Bruce, Camden Society Publications, 27 (London, 1844)
Lodge, *Illustrations*	*Illustrations of British History, Biography and Manners in the Reigns of Henry VIII, Edward VI, Mary, Elizabeth and James I*, ed. Edmund Lodge, 3 vols (London, 1791)
LPL	Lambeth Palace Library
McIlwain	*The Political Works of James I*, ed. Charles McIlwain (Cambridge, MA: Harvard University Press, 1918)
NA	Nationaal Archief, The Hague, Netherlands
Nichols, *Elizabeth*	John Nichols, ed., *The Progresses and Public Processions of Queen Elizabeth*, 3 vols (London, 1823)
Nichols, *James I*	John Nichols, ed., *The Progresses, Processions and Magnificent Festivities of King James the First*, 2 vols (London, 1828)
OED	*Oxford English Dictionary*, online edition (www.oed.com)
PPEI	*Proceedings in the Parliaments of Elizabeth I*, ed. T. H. Hartley, 3 vols (Leicester: Leicester University Press, 1981–95)
SNA	Scottish National Archives (Edinburgh)
Spottiswood	John Spottiswood, *The history of the church and state of Scotland beginning in the year of our lord 203 and continued to the end of the reign of James VI* (London, 1655)
SRO	Staffordshire Record Office
STC	English Short Title Catalogue
Teulet, *Relations Politiques*	Alexandre Teulet, ed., *Relations Politiques de la France et de l'Espagne avec l'Ecosse au XVIe siècle*, 5 vols (Paris, 1862)
Teulet, *Papiers d'état*	Alexandre Teulet, ed., *Papiers d'état: Pièces et documents inédits ou peu connus relatifs a l'histoire de l'Écosse*, 3 vols (Paris, 1852–60)
TNA	The National Archives (Kew)

Trumbull Mss. Manuscripts of William Trumbull the elder formerly in the library of the Marquess of Downshire and microfilmed there by the Library of Congress (reference number 041/Camb194/1-Camb215/1), catalogued as Alphabetical vols 1–49. Now deposited in the British Library and recatalogued as Add Mss. 72,242–72,333. References in the text refer to the old alphabetical listing as recorded on the microfilms

Introduction
Expanding the Narrative

Making the Past Less Familiar

Ever since the nineteenth century, historians have depicted the Elizabethan and early Stuart period as an early stage in the development of modern liberal politics. In its most robust Victorian form this approach had strong teleological overtones, as if the constitutional principles and practices of nineteenth-century representative government were a goal toward which past events inexorably advanced. Teleology encouraged a tendency to distinguish between progressive groups, usually identified with radical Protestants and puritans, who pushed developments forward, and conservative or reactionary forces, such as Catholics or supporters of the Stuart court.[1] Efforts during the middle decades of the twentieth century to explain political events as outcomes of economic and social change modified the teleology, while ultimately reinforcing it.[2] A revisionist reaction then began in the 1970s, among historians who demanded that we treat the past on its own terms, without reference to future outcomes of which contemporaries were necessarily ignorant. But because revisionists so often framed their work as a systematic refutation of previous whig and Marxist scholarship, they reinforced older assumptions about the central questions political historians needed to address.[3] Elections, parliamentary politics, and "constitutional" relationships between the king's prerogative, Parliament, and the common law became even more central to historical discussions during the late twentieth-century heyday of revisionism than had been the case a few years earlier.[4]

---

[1] See, for example, Samuel Rawson Gardiner, *The First Two Stuarts and the Puritan Revolution* (New York: Thomas Y. Crowell, 1970), 1 and passim; J. R. Tanner, *English Constitutional Conflicts of the Seventeenth Century, 1603–1689* (Cambridge: Cambridge University Press, 1928 and many later reprints). For a protest against ways in which these biases have marginalized Catholic perspectives see Michael Questier, *Dynastic Politics and the British Reformations, 1558–1630* (Oxford: Oxford University Press, 2019).

[2] See, esp., the many works of Christopher Hill.

[3] Cf. Peter Lake, review article of Conrad Russell, *The Causes of the English Civil War; The Fall of the British Monarchies, 1637–1642*; and *Unrevolutionary England* in *Huntington Library Quarterly* 57 (1994): 167–97.

[4] E.g., Mark Kishlansky, *Parliamentary Selection: Social and Political Choice in Early Modern England* (Cambridge: Cambridge University Press, 1986); Conrad Russell, *Parliaments and English Politics, 1621–1629* (Oxford: Oxford University Press, 1979); Glenn Burgess, *The Politics of the Ancient*

The preoccupation with connections between early modern and fully modern politics never led to an entirely static historiography. Interpretations of the institutional and constitutional structure of English politics expanded considerably in the twentieth century, as research accumulated not only on parliaments, the royal court, and royal administration but also on local politics in counties, towns, and parishes.[5] The sometimes difficult relations between local elites and central authorities emerged in the 1970s as a prominent theme that strongly influenced revisionism.[6] More recently still, an abundance of stimulating work has appeared on political communication and controversy disseminated through print and manuscript texts, including libels and stories of scandal.[7] But valuable as it is, this new work continues to reflect a modern understanding of politics as a deliberative process, involving debates over major policy issues and efforts to rally public support behind contested positions. Historians have accordingly stressed the importance of concepts of counsel used to justify the proffering of controversial advice to the monarch, along with institutions like the privy council, parliament, and county quarter sessions, where policy debates took place.[8] They have

---

Constitution: An Introduction to English Political Thought 1603–1642 (University Park: Pennsylvania State University Press, 1992); Glenn Burgess, *Absolute Monarchy and the Stuart Constitution* (New Haven: Yale University Press, 1996).

[5] See, among studies far too numerous to list in full, Geoffrey Elton, *The Tudor Revolution in Government* (Cambridge: Cambridge University Press, 1953); Alan Everitt, *The Community of Kent and the Great Rebellion* (Leicester: Leicester University Press, 1966); Anne Hughes, *Politics, Society and Civil War in Warwickshire* (Cambridge: Cambridge University Press, 1989); Robert Tittler, *The Reformation and the Towns in England, c. 1540–1640* (Oxford: Clarendon Press, 1998); Keith Wrightson and David Levine, *Poverty and Piety in an English Village, Terling, 1525–1700* (London and New York: Academic Press, 1970).

[6] John Morrill, *Revolt in the Provinces: The People of England and the Tragedies of War 1630–1648* (London: Longman, 2nd ed. 1999), originally published as *The Revolt of the Provinces: Conservatives and Radicals in the English Civil War, 1630–1650* (London: Unwin, 1976).

[7] Central here are several works by Peter Lake, including *Bad Queen Bess? Libels, Secret Histories, and the Politics of Publicity in the Reign of Queen Elizabeth I* (Oxford: Oxford University Press, 2016); *The Politics of the Public Sphere in Early Modern England*, ed. Peter Lake and Steven Pincus (Manchester: Manchester University Press, 2012); and articles that will be cited in the course of this study. For manuscripts see Harold Love, *Scribal Publication in England* (Oxford: Oxford University Press, 1993) and Noah Millstone *Manuscript Circulation and the Invention of Politics in Early Stuart England* (Cambridge: Cambridge University Press, 2016). For scandal-mongering see Alastair Bellany, *The Politics of Court Scandal in Early Modern England: News Culture and the Overbury Affair, 1603–1660* (Cambridge: Cambridge University Press, 2002) and Alastair Bellany and Thomas Cogswell, *The Murder of King James I* (New Haven: Yale University Press, 2015). Treatments of verse libels as political material include Alastair Bellany, "'Raylinge Rymes and Vaunting Verse': Libellous Politics in Early Stuart England, 1603–1628," in *Culture and Politics in Early Stuart England*, ed. Kevin Sharpe and Peter Lake (Basingstoke: Macmillan, 1994), 283–310; Alastair Bellany, 'The Embarrassment of Libels: Perceptions and Representations of Verse Libelling in Early Modern England,' in *Politics of the Public Sphere*, ed. Lake and Pincus, 144–67; and Pauline Croft, "Libels, Popular Literacy and Public Opinion in Early Modern England," *Bulletin of the Institute for Historical Research* 68 (1995): 266–85. Richard Cust, "News and Politics in Early Seventeenth Century England," *Past and Present* 112 (1986): 60–90 was a pioneering discussion that helped initiate the wave of scholarship on the circulation of controversial political material.

[8] John Guy, *Politics, Law and Counsel in Tudor and Early Stuart England* (London: Routledge, 2000); John Guy, "The Rhetoric of Counsel in Early Modern England," in *Tudor Political Thought*, ed. Dale Hoak (Cambridge: Cambridge University Press, 1995), 292–310.

examined the use not only of print but also ceremonial display and visual imagery as tools of persuasion, sometimes drawing explicit comparisons to the media campaigns of modern politicians.[9] Although teleology has fallen out of fashion and historians no longer describe past events as milestones along the road to a contemporary world, much post-revisionist scholarship continues to describe the past in ways that resonate with recent experience.

There is nothing intrinsically wrong with this, since many early modern practices did anticipate later forms of political competition. An expanding use of print and scribal publication as vehicles for controversy, a growing appetite for news, and an increasingly sophisticated exploitation of scandal as a political weapon were all very real features of early modern English society that richly deserve exploration. But focusing attention on such developments can divert attention from other ways of exerting and contesting power in the past that do not resemble forms of politics familiar to us. Twenty-first-century minds easily recognize that reading controversial texts, voting in elections, and engaging in crowd demonstrations amounted to political acts. We may be slower to accord the same status to enlistment in a military company, or participation in a blood feud or cattle raid. But in an age when the majority of adults could not read, the demands of war affected more people, at deeper layers of the social hierarchy, than the consumption of printed and manuscript texts, while in large parts of Ireland, Scotland, and the far North of England cattle raids and feuds remained time-honored ways of contesting power. Although good studies of early modern warfare and blood feuds do exist, these topics tend to be regarded as specialized subfields.[10] But concepts of valor and honor that motivated military service, and forms of kin-solidarity associated with cattle raiding and feuding, deeply shaped the conduct of public affairs and the operation of power. As such they deserve as much recognition from political historians as the bookish preoccupations of humanist scholars and controversialists.

This book proceeds from a conviction that historians sometimes need to make deliberate efforts to recover perspectives on the past that do *not* correspond to modern assumptions or established interpretive models, with the goal not of supplanting established views so much as enlarging them, by recovering new

---

[9] Kevin Sharpe, *Selling the Tudor Monarchy: Authority and Image in Sixteenth-Century England* (New Haven: Yale University Press, 2009) and *Image Wars: Promoting Kings and Commonwealths in England 1603-1660* (New Haven: Yale University Press, 2010). See the dust jacket blurb of the second book for a comparison of early modern practices to "Spin doctors, photo opportunities and 'managing the news'" by modern politicians.

[10] See, for example, Roger Manning, *Swordsmen: The Martial Ethos of the Three Kingdoms* (Oxford: Oxford University Press, 2003); Paul Hammer, *Elizabeth's Wars: War, Government and Society in Tudor England, 1544-1604* (Basingstoke: Palgrave Macmillan, 2003); Charles Carlton, *This Seat of Mars: War and the British Isles, 1485-1746* (New Haven: Yale University Press, 2013); *The Chivalric Ethos and the Development of Military Professionalism*, ed. David Trim (Leiden: Brill, 2003); Keith Brown, *Bloodfeud in Scotland 1573-1625: Violence, Justice and Politics in an Early Modern Society* (Edinburgh: John Donald, 1986). The cattle raid has yet to find its historian.

information and viewing familiar material from unaccustomed angles. Such an enterprise will inevitably raise questions about how we conceptualize the histories of politics and political thought and culture and the relationship between them. Traditionally political history has involved studies of day-to-day events, whereas studies of political thought have tended to focus on theoretical ideas found mainly in printed texts. A whig narrative of constitutional development used to provide ways of connecting these two very different approaches, through the assumption that events led to changes in institutions and institutional relationships that gave rise to theoretical arguments about the structure and guiding principles of the polity. The influence of this older framework remains evident in many recent studies. But revisionist and post-revisionist critiques of whig historiography, along with a broadening of the category of political thought and culture to include less highly theorized forms of expression, have begun to undercut it. The present study pursues an alternative method of seeking to tease out assumptions about the fundamental strategic challenges facing the rulers of Britain and Ireland, found not only in printed texts but also in the working papers of active politicians, including both privy councilors and less exalted royal servants, along with individuals who sought to contest royal policies. It is less concerned with abstract theories of how government ought to work than with the thought processes through which people sought to understand the constantly evolving challenges of their political environment. I will argue that this kind of strategic thinking often involved an emerging discourse about states, as complex and vulnerable political organisms needing protection against specific diseases and threats.

Kingdoms, Commonwealths, Constitutions, and States: An Historical Note on Political Vocabulary

This formulation may invite misunderstandings because, while the concept of a state remains familiar today, its meaning has changed significantly since the late Renaissance. Historians who refer to early modern states often fail to define the word or else adopt a modern definition that differs from contemporary understandings. But similar problems will also arise with respect to other terms—such as kingdom, monarchy, constitution, or commonwealth—used in describing the polities of Tudor and Stuart Britain and Ireland. It therefore makes sense to begin with an historically informed examination of our descriptive terminology, with the twin goals of better understanding how the subjects of Elizabeth I and James VI and I thought about their political world, and how our own choices of vocabulary will shape interpretations of the past.

At first glance the commonplace description of England, Scotland, and Ireland as kingdoms appears relatively straightforward, pointing as it does to the undisputed role of the king (or queen) as the font of authority and key figure around whom the political world revolved. But just what this actually meant—and how far it meant the same or different things in the three kingdoms—has always been less clear. Early modern disagreements arose over whether England was a mixed or pure monarchy, and whether it made a difference if the monarch was a woman.[11] On a practical level, kings and queens always ruled with the assistance of a privy council and cohorts of royal servants and magistrates, who found opportunities to bend royal authority to serve their own purposes. In its daily operation, kingship was therefore something of a collective enterprise, a fact that gave rise to disagreements about how far disrespect or disobedience to the rulers' appointed officers necessarily amounted to disloyalty to himself or herself. The prosecution of a few leading puritans for sedition in the 1590s led to a theoretical claim that Elizabeth possessed a "body politic" that included the bishops she appointed to rule her Church, so that any attack on episcopacy constituted a serious breach of a subject's duty of loyalty to her. The puritan Job Throckmorton accepted the basic premise but qualified it by contending that bishops were merely an "accidental" rather than "essential" part of the queen's "body politic," which was in any case a "fiction" existing merely in "political imagination" rather than "truth or verity." "Therefore, he that defameth her members politic doth defame her majesty only in fiction that is, in plain English, not at all."[12] The subtle complexity of Throckmorton's claim demonstrates just how slippery the concept of royal authority sometimes became.

In two highly influential essays of the 1980s, Patrick Collinson called attention to the inherent ambiguities of such a system by describing Elizabethan England as a *monarchical republic*.[13] Although he coined the phrase, it corresponds fairly closely to a widespread Tudor description of England as a commonwealth under a king or queen, since commonwealth was frequently used to translate the Latin *res publica*.[14] The Elizabethan secretary of state, Sir Thomas Smith, defined a commonwealth as "a multitude of free men collected together and united by common accord and covenants amongst themselves for the conservation of themselves as well in peace as in war."[15] The word therefore implied a government open to

---

[11] A. N. McLaren, *Political Culture in the Reign of Elizabeth I: Queen and Commonwealth, 1558–1585* (Cambridge: Cambridge University Press, 1999).

[12] Job Throckmorton, *A Petition to Her Majesty* (Middleburgh, 1593), 17 and 30.

[13] Patrick Collinson, "The Monarchical Republic of Queen Elizabeth I," *Bulletin of the John Rylands Library* 69 (1987): 394–424 and "De Republica Anglorum: Or, History with the Politics Put Back," inaugural lecture as Regius Professor of History in the University of Cambridge, November 9, 1989 (Cambridge: Cambridge University Press, 1990), both reprinted in Patrick Collinson, *Elizabethan Essays* (London: Hambledon Press, 1994), 1–30 and 31–59; *The Monarchical Republic of Early Modern England: Essays in Response to Patrick Collinson*, ed. John McDiarmid (Aldershot: Ashgate, 2007).

[14] Already in the fifteenth century the word might refer either to a political community (OED definition 1) or the common good or welfare of a community (*OED* definition 2); the conflation of these two senses suggested a government dedicated to promoting the common good.

[15] *De Republica Anglorum* (London, 1583), 10.

reasonably broad participation and activated by an ethos of public service, a view influenced by ancient republican theorists such as Cicero.[16] Most people did not find the idea of a commonwealth under a monarch contradictory. It meant government by a king who ruled in the interest of his people, with the assistance of some sort of political nation, whose members needed to equip themselves with the skills and knowledge required to serve their prince and country. Partly for this reason, it proved especially popular among humanist scholars and pedagogues, who claimed to provide such intellectual equipment, as well as politicians like Smith and William Cecil Lord Burghley, who had received a rigorous humanist education.[17]

Discourse about the commonwealth often involved advocacy of policies intended to benefit the community, by promoting education, rationalizing the distribution of poor relief, promoting economic improvements, and other measures. The term therefore does anticipate aspects of the modern concept of politics as a participatory process involving the formulation of policies that serve public interests, although the parallel should not be oversimplified.[18] Relatively common in the mid-Tudor and early Elizabethan periods, references to England as a commonwealth lost favor in some quarters later in the sixteenth century, as a reaction supporting more authoritarian ideas of royal power gained traction at the court and among certain churchmen.[19] Unlike Smith and Burghley, the second earl of Essex and his circle avoided the word. But James I occasionally employed it, and related concepts of public virtue and public service persisted.[20]

Unlike kingdom and commonwealth, the word constitution, as normally used by historians, is anachronistic for the Elizabethan and early Stuart period, since it only later acquired its modern meaning as "the system or body of fundamental principles according to which a nation, state, or body politic is constituted and

---

[16] See esp. Markku Peltonen, *Classical Humanism and Republicanism in English Political Thought 1570–1640* (Cambridge: Cambridge University Press, 1995).

[17] Winthrop S. Hudson, *The Cambridge Connection and the Elizabethan Settlement of 1559* (Durham, NC: Duke University Press, 1980). Norman Jones, *Governing by Virtue: Lord Burghley and the Management of Elizabethan England* (Oxford: Oxford University Press, 2015) lays particular stress on Burghley's life-long habit of conceiving political and administrative problems in terms of a concept of public virtue that can be related to commonwealth thought.

[18] Among other differences, commonwealth thought was usually embedded within a framework of what might loosely be described as Christian humanist moral values (whether in Catholic or Protestant forms), which differed from the more secular emphases of nineteenth-century political economy. For an acute analysis of the range of ideas associated with the Tudor and early Stuart concept of a commonwealth see Noah Dauber, *State and Commonwealth: The Theory of the State in Early Modern England, 1549–1640* (Princeton: Princeton University Press, 2016). Despite its title the book devotes far less attention to theoretical discussions of states.

[19] John Guy, "Introduction: The 1590s, the Second Reign of Elizabeth I?," in *The Reign of Elizabeth I: Court and Culture in the Last Decade*, ed. John Guy (Cambridge: Cambridge University Press, 1995), 1–19; Peter Lake, "'The Monarchical Republic of Elizabeth I' (and the Fall of Archbishop Grindal) Revisited," in *Monarchical Republic*, ed. McDiarmid, 129–48; Alexandra Gajda, *The Earl of Essex and Late Elizabethan Political Culture* (Oxford: Oxford University Press, 2013), 14–19; Alexandra Gajda, "Political Culture in the 1590s: The 'Second Reign of Elizabeth'," *History Compass* 8 (2009): 88–100.

[20] See esp. Chapter 7. Cf. Gajda, *Earl of Essex*, esp. 21.

governed."[21] According to the *Oxford English Dictionary* "this sense gradually arose" only in the century after the Glorious Revolution, with the earliest example appearing in Scotland in 1689.[22] The failure of most historians to notice the late emergence of the modern concept, and the fact that we still lack a good account of the development of constitutional thought as an eighteenth-century event, indicates the degree to which scholars have taken an English belief in an ancient constitution for granted, rather than investigating rigorously how and when it arose.

What we find in the period covered by this book are discourses about subjects like the common law and parliaments that anticipate aspects of modern constitutional thought, without explicitly referring to a constitution, along with uses of the word that suggest how the later meaning arose, while almost never fully anticipating it.[23] All these uses derived from the verb to constitute, meaning to make or establish.[24] The noun, *constitution*, might therefore refer to the make-up or humoral disposition of an individual's body or a society conceived as a body politic. Alternatively, the word sometimes designated the duties and functions of an office, as in a 1627 reference to the "ancient constitution of the searcher," the officer responsible for identifying plague victims in Westminster. Parliament and other corporate bodies like guilds were also described as having *constitutions*, meaning structures and functions established at their original institution. Very rarely, a use of the word in this last sense comes fairly close to anticipating the modern concept of a body of organizing principles. A memorandum of 1575 on reforms in Ireland, for example, expressed hope that in time "the Irish [may] be brought to be governed either by the law of England or by some constitution to be compounded partly of their own customs and brehon laws that are agreeable to reason."[25] But revealingly, when in the 1650s the English began to compose written documents that redefined how their governing institutions should work, they did not call them constitutions, but instruments of government.[26]

A *constitution* might also mean an ordinance or law, usually of fundamental character. This usage seems to have been especially common in discussions of ecclesiastical affairs, as in an early Elizabethan Catholic description of a rule about the inviolability of clerical vows of celibacy as "the ancient constitution of the

---

[21] *OED*, definition 7 of constitution.
[22] While an exhaustive search might turn up a few earlier examples, we can safely assume that at best they would be vanishingly rare.
[23] For these discourses see, for example, the classic work of John Pocock, *The Ancient Constitution and the Feudal Law: A Study of English Historical Thought in the Seventeenth Century. A Reissue with a Retrospect* (Cambridge: Cambridge University Press, 1987); Burgess, *Politics of the Ancient Constitution*; and the essays collected in *Writing the History of Parliament in Tudor and Early Stuart England*, ed. Paul Cavill and Alexandra Gajda (Manchester: Manchester University Press, 2018).
[24] See *OED* definition 1a. Except where otherwise noted, the following examples derive from word searches in *Early English Books Online* (*EEBO*) and *State Papers Online*.
[25] *CSPI* 3.785.   [26] My thanks to Tim Harris for pointing this out.

church."[27] But examples also occur in secular contexts, such as Robert Phelips's claim in the Parliament of 1625 that "we are the last monarchy in Christendom that retain our original rights and constitutions." The plural form shows that he meant ancient laws rather than a single constitution.[28] Very occasionally the meaning of *constitution* as an ordinance fused with the alternative definition of the word as the composition of a body politic, in phrases that again begin to anticipate the modern concept. In a conference between the two houses of Parliament on the Petition of Right in 1628, John Pym asserted that the laws reaffirmed by that document did not originate "by the grant of princes... but are fundamental from the very original of this kingdom and are part of the essential constitution thereof."[29] Here "the essential constitution" still refers to the basic composition of the English body politic, but in a way that gestures toward belief in "a body of fundamental principles" enshrined in ancient texts like Magna Carta that define how the polity ought to work. On the eve of the Civil War, Charles I pleaded that "albeit we know well that by that constitution of the frame and policy of this kingdom proclamations are not of equal force with laws, nevertheless we think it a duty appertaining to us and inseparably annexed to our crown and regal authority to restrain mischiefs" by issuing them.[30] Although highly suggestive, the king's awkward phrase, "that constitution of the frame and policy of this kingdom," shows that he was trying to express a novel concept that his audience would not readily understand. For modern minds familiar with nineteenth-century constitutional discourse, the step from a belief in numerous ancient "rights and constitutions" to the concept of *the Ancient Constitution* may seem easy and natural. But early modern thinkers were remarkably slow in taking that step, which evidently did not seem obvious to them. By employing a vocabulary of constitutional conflicts to describe early modern politics historians are, often unconsciously, viewing the period through a lens of eighteenth- or early nineteenth-century conceptual assumptions.

[27] Thomas Harding, *A Confutation of a Booke* (1565), sig. 74r. This example is mentioned in the introduction to *Writing the History of Parliament*, ed. Cavill and Gajda, 24. Harding's discussion shows that he is using the word constitution in its restricted early modern sense of an ordinance: "Whosoever hath thus vowed chastity, or by receiving holy orders hath bound themselves to the bond of continency to the same by the ancient constitution of the church annexed, if afterward presuming to marry excuse the satisfying of their carnal lust with the name of wedlock, be they men, be they women, they live in a damnable state." A few lines earlier he had written of "those that have taken holy orders by tradition of the Apostles and the ancient ordinance of the church." Both sentences occur within the context of a specific discussion of whether vows of celibacy can be violated, rather than an account of the general organization and governance of the Church.
[28] *Proceedings in Parliament 1625*, ed. Maija Jansson and William B. Bidwell (New Haven: Yale University Press, 1987), 449. The plural form indicates that Phelips meant ancient laws rather than a single ancient constitution.
[29] *Commons Debates [Proceedings in Parliament] 1628*, vol. 4, ed. Mary Frear Keeler, Maija Jansson Cole, and William Bidwell (New Haven: Yale University Press, 1978), 103.
[30] TNA SP16/476, fol. 237.

When contemporaries wanted to discuss fundamental relationships between laws and institutions, they normally spoke not of *constitutions* but *forms* of government and *states*. Further along in the speech just quoted, Pym declared:

> It is a certain truth that the form of government does actuate and dispose all the parts of the state to the good of the whole; and therefore if a common ligament break, all falls to division, one part against another. This might be proved by history as your lordships know better. True it is that time works alterations in all states, but when on the one side it is endeavored to maintain old laws, and on the other new frames are desired, states fall to confusion; and those states are found to be of best continuance which make the shortest and easiest recourse to their ancient laws.[31]

Where a nineteenth-century orator would have spoken of the need to preserve the Ancient Constitution, Pym warns instead against disruption to the form or frame that prevents confusion in the state. But what exactly did this last term mean? In modern usage the word state can function both as a general term for a government and as a designation for the government's bureaucratic staff of officials.[32] This latter definition has given rise to historical accounts of "state formation" that emphasize the proliferation and expanding functions of local government officers.[33] But although anticipated in a few early modern discussions, these modern definitions correspond only partially and imperfectly to the range of meanings that the word possessed for early modern thinkers.

At first glance those meanings appear so varied as to defy easy classification. All derived from an original definition of a *state* as a condition.[34] Already in the Middle Ages *state* also came to mean, more specifically, an individual's social condition, as determined by age, marital status, vocation, or rank; the specific condition of high rank; behavior befitting a person of rank, along with the dignity and magnificence associated with it; a raised chair under a canopy, employed by nobles and princes to symbolize their pre-eminence; and the particular throne and canopy that always stood in the presence chamber of an English royal palace, known as "*the state*."[35] All these definitions remained current in the early modern period. The plural form, *states* or *estates*, also designated the legislative assemblies of several European countries because they represented the major ranks or conditions of society, the nobility, clergy, and commons.[36] People also began

---

[31] *Commons Debates 1628*, ed. Frear, Cole, and Bidwell, 4.103.
[32] Dauber, *State and Commonwealth*, 1 and 2.
[33] In particular Michael Braddick, *State Formation in Early Modern England, c. 1550–1700* (Cambridge: Cambridge University Press, 2000).
[34] *OED*, definition 1; this meaning existed in root words in both Germanic languages and Latin (Anglo-Saxon *staat*; Latin *status*).
[35] Definitions 14–18.
[36] Definitions 19–21. "State" and "estate" were used more or less interchangeably in the period.

referring to the *state* or *estate* of individuals, particularly lords or kings, comprising their lands and possessions, rights, privileges, and dignity.[37]

This definition shaded in turn into a concept of *the state* as a government, regime, or system of power, which might take the form of a *kingly state*, a republican polity like *the state of Venice*, or even a confederation, like the United Provinces or *United States* of the Netherlands. By a further extension the word sometimes referred to the business of government, often with an emphasis on its specialized and secretive character, as in the phrase *mysteries of state*, or the official title of *secretary of state* given to a minister charged with handling government correspondence, diplomacy, and espionage. The land and people under a government might also be described as a *state*. In all these cases the word retained connotations of its original meaning as a condition.[38] *The state of Ireland* might therefore refer, alternatively or simultaneously, to the kingdom of Ireland, the configuration of social, economic, cultural, and geographic circumstances that determined how power actually worked on the island, or the system of English rule based in Dublin. All these things related to the condition of the Irish as a people under at least the nominal rule of the crown; they were therefore components or facets of an *Irish state*.

This range of meanings might seem to confirm Quentin Skinner's observation that "there has never been any agreed concept to which the word state has answered... As the genealogy of the state unfolds, what it reveals is the contingent and contestable character of the concept, the impossibility of showing that it has any essence or natural boundaries."[39] But as Skinner himself has shown, if we look closely, suggestive patterns of historical usage do emerge. In late medieval Latin treatises on politics, *status* "invariably refers to the condition of a king or kingdom, not a set of institutions."[40] But a more extended range of meanings developed in advice books for princes with their "tradition of practical political reasoning" about how rulers should act to maintain their "state" by fulfilling conditions "of effective government" and maintaining control of "the institutions of government and the means of coercive control that serve to preserve order within political communities."[41] This species of thought gave rise to a concept of *reason of state*—the methods and principles necessary to maintain power in changing political circumstances—which first appeared in Renaissance Italy

---

[37] Definition 1.c. *OED* does not give many instances of this meaning but they are reasonably common in early modern usage.

[38] Definitions 24–8.

[39] "A Genealogy of the Modern State," *Proceedings of the British Academy* 162 (2009): 325–70, at 325.

[40] Quentin Skinner, "From the State of Princes to the Person of the State," in *Visions of Politics*, vol. 2 (Cambridge: Cambridge University Press, 2002), 368–412 at 373–4.

[41] Ibid., 374–8.

before spreading across Europe in the late sixteenth century.[42] Through a process of abstraction it eventually became possible to conceive of *the state* as distinct from both the ruler and the ruled, although Skinner sees this transition as incomplete before the writings of Thomas Hobbes in the mid-seventeenth century.[43] Since it post-dates our period, Hobbes's concept of the state need not concern us.

But the absence before Hobbes of a rigorous theoretical definition of the state as a distinct entity did not prevent individuals from using the word with growing frequency, not just in printed treatises, but also in discussions of contemporary political problems and historic upheavals like the collapse of the Roman Republic or the Norman Conquest. This shows that the association of the word with a "tradition of practical political reasoning" had spread beyond advice manuals to become part of the discursive vocabulary of both scholars and working politicians. In discussions of immediate problems, the term retained a protean quality, often being used in several different senses within a single paragraph, or in ways that seem to hover between alternative definitions. A 1581 memorandum in Burghley's papers about whether Elizabeth should marry the duke of Anjou and join France in a war against Spain provides an example. It begins by asserting that these issues raised "two necessary *questions in state*": whether it was better to ally with France or to risk seeing the French ally with Spain and Scotland in an attack on England; and whether it was better to engage in a foreign war or to risk being assailed at home.[44] The answers appeared obvious. But they raised the additional problem of whether the expense of a foreign war was greater "than your [Elizabeth's] *state or crown* might bear." If so she might prefer "to depend upon God's protection and stand to your own defense." But before adopting this course, the writer exhorted her to "look into *your estate* and think that there can be no peril so great unto you as to have a war break out in your own realm, considering what a number of evil subjects you have." He then concluded by asking the queen to recognize that his frank advice proceeded from his care for "your highness's preservation in that *happy estate* you have lived in these three and twenty years." In the first instance state refers to strategic calculations of political advantage, in the second to the queen's government, while in the third and fourth Elizabeth's "estate" meant her personal circumstances, but in a way that encompassed the condition of her reign as a time of peace overshadowed by threats of treason and foreign aggression.

---

[42] Arlette Jouanna, *Le prince absolu: Apogée et déclin de l'imaginaire monarchique* (Paris: Gallimard, 2014), 75–83. Without citing Skinner, Jouanna describes a broadly similar development of the concept of a state (*état*) from the personal possession of a prince to a more extended and abstract meaning as a system of power.

[43] Skinner, "Genealogy of the Modern State," 340–8 and "State of Princes," 403–4. But cf. Jouanna, *Le prince absolu*, 78: "Avec Botero s'ébauche le long processus d'abstraction qui devait peu à peu conduire le concept d'État à une double distinction, qui le dissocierait tant de la personne du souverain que de la communauté des sujets."

[44] HMC Salisbury 2.413, italics added.

Despite this variety, the meanings cohere within an analysis of a strategic decision about whether or not to conclude a dynastic alliance. Although the queen's state, the state of her kingdom and its subjects, and the state of the political conditions in which she ruled were not quite identical, they were obviously interconnected, and the use of a single word to describe all three tended to bring out this interdependence.

Discussions of problems of state tended to lack the emphasis on collective action in pursuit of specific reforms associated with the term commonwealth. They focused instead on maintaining an existing system of rule against tangible threats.[45] This may explain why Elizabethans seem to have described Ireland as a state more frequently than England: the word appeared more appropriate to a conquered territory where foreign rule had to be imposed on a restive population. Suggestively, Irish common lawyers who opposed arbitrary government policies were an exception, who avoided references to the state, while calling themselves "commonwealthmen."[46] When Elizabethans did refer to an English *state* they often meant a contested system of Protestant rule. Examples include a 1586 pamphlet entitled, *A short declaration of the ende of traytours and false conspirators against the state*; a report by the justices of the peace (JPs) of Norfolk in the following year that they had arrested a group of recusants and committed them "to the custody of such gentlemen as we know to be religious and well affected to the *present state*"; a 1592 complaint by the privy council against gentlemen who sent their sons overseas to be "bred and brought up in the popish religion and corruptness of manners, to the manifest prejudice of the *state here*"; and a set of returns from Kent of young gentlemen studying on the Continent that classified their families as "ill affected" or "well affected" to "*the state.*"[47] Thomas Wilson saw four religious parties or factions in England—religious Protestants, politic Protestants, religious papists, and politic papists—"the first whereof were only found to be sure to *the state*, the other three dangerous."[48] William Lambarde argued for the exclusion not only of Catholics but also "atheists and libertines" from a government commission, because "these Epicureans care not for the

---

[45] For a study arguing that this was the normal meaning of the term *stato* in sixteenth-century Italy, and that discourse about the *stato* differed systematically from republican discourse about politics, see Mauricio Viroli, *From Politics to Reason of State: The Acquisition and Transformation of the Language of Politics, 1250-1600* (Cambridge: Cambridge University Press, 1992).

[46] For discussions see Christopher Maginn, "One State or Two? Ireland and England under the Tudors," in *Frontiers, States and Identity in Early Modern Ireland and Beyond: Essays in Honour of Steven G. Ellis*, ed. Christopher Maginn and Gerald Power (Dublin: Four Courts Press, 2016), 147–64 and Mark Hutchinson, *Calvinism, Reform and the Absolutist State in Elizabethan Ireland* (London: Routledge, 2016).

[47] The pamphlet is by Richard Compton; SP12/208/16; *A Collection of State Papers Relating to Affairs in the Reign of Queen Elizabeth, from the year 1571 to 1596*, ed. William Murden (London, 1740), 667; Staffordshire Record Office Mss. D593/S/4/14/1/9 and DS593/S/4/14/2, italics added.

[48] Thomas Wilson, *The State of England, Anno Dom. 1600, Royal Historical Society Camden*, fifth series, 52 (1936): 1–47 at 41, italics added.

present estate." In all these instances, the choice of *state*, rather than *queen, crown*, or *government*, looks deliberate.⁴⁹ Whereas papists might acknowledge their loyalty to the queen they would have more difficulty professing allegiance to the *state*, and especially to *the present state*, the existing condition of Protestant dominance. Some Catholics protested against this religious definition as a recent innovation. "They will say unto us, howsoever the matter be in itself or was judged in old time, now the case is altered: such men and such doings cannot stand with our state. But (alas) who hath brought the state and form of our commonwealth into these straits?"⁵⁰

In so far as the state was thought to possess a moral significance, this usually had less to do with the pursuit of specific benefits than the protection of society against the evils of foreign conquest or internal disorder. Especially prevalent in France during the wars of religion, this notion of a protective state found its way to England partly through translations of French texts, such as Pierre Charron's *De la sagesse* (1601), published in English translation in 1608. Charron defined *the state* as "rule, dominion, or a certain order in commanding and obeying...the prop, the cement and the soul of humane things...the bond of society, which cannot otherwise subsist."⁵¹ Although he did not explain why the word referred both to political power and social cohesion, his reasoning seems clear. Societies cannot survive without orders "of command and obedience" to settle conflicts and maintain unity, while "rule and dominion" operate most effectively over cohesive civil societies. The social and political orders are therefore inextricably connected and, at base, the same thing. For Charon *the state* thus seems to mean the condition of a people who have become organized into a civil society held together by some form of dominion. He goes on to describe this condition as "difficult, subject to changes," due to "hidden causes," the "corrupt and wicked manners of sovereigns," or the "hatred" that states invariably inspire.⁵² Other writers, who attached adjectives like weak, distracted, torn, and declining to the word state evidently held a similar view.⁵³

This concept of the state as a fragile socio-political order left open a question of priority much debated in the period: do societies create and sustain rulers, or rulers, societies? In theoretical literature that question gave rise to historical myths about the original foundation of nations by primitive kings who gathered people together and gave them laws, or alternatively the establishment of royal governments by sovereign peoples delegating their authority to an individual and his heirs. As Skinner points out, the first concept implied an absolutist state, whereas

---

⁴⁹ SRO Mss. D593/S/4/14/16/14, italics added.
⁵⁰ William Allen, *An Apologie and Declaration of the...Two English Colleges* (Reims, 1581), 93, italics added.
⁵¹ Pierre de Charron, *Of wisdome three books written in French by Peter Charro*, trans. Samson Leonard (London, 1608), 189–90.
⁵² Ibid., 189.   ⁵³ See below for several examples.

the second tended to lead to a belief in the limited, contractual, and revocable nature of sovereignty.[54] But this was again not only a theoretical issue but one of immediate importance in contexts where violent conflict threatened to make civil life impossible.[55] Did the solution lie in the forceful imposition of authority from above, or in more consensual processes? Some English residents of Ireland, notably Richard Beacon and Edmund Spenser, argued that Irish customs and social practices perpetuated conditions of violence, criminality, and oppression that made orderly government impossible. The *state of Ireland* therefore needed to undergo a fundamental transformation imposed by the crown and its soldiers, who were entitled to use as much violence as necessary to complete the task.[56] In 1586 the earl of Leicester justified his decision to accept an appointment as governor general of the United Provinces by arguing that without his supreme command the Dutch *state* would dissolve in chaos through internal bickering. After he returned to England the following winter, another Englishman resident in the Netherlands, Thomas Wilkes, repeatedly complained that the Dutch *state* had indeed begun to fall apart. "The absence of a governor here hath bred many perilous dissensions in and among the provinces, towns and principle members of *the state*"; "*the state here* through the absence of a governor [is] disunited and distracted"; the queen must act to "relieve the *altered and broken estate* of these countries and to stay the disease which doth only begin, by the speedy sending over of some principal man to command here amongst them."[57] Only Leicester's return would restore unity.[58] Whether or not he was aware of the fact, Wilkes effectively saw Leicester as one of Machiavelli's "new princes," a figure who needed to impose a strong *state*—a condition or set of conditions conducive to unity and resistance to foreign aggression—on a people incapable of doing this for themselves.[59] Such assumptions led to an absolutist view of the state grounded not in theoretical principles but a diagnosis of the practical demands arising from immediate historical circumstances.

As orders "of command and obedience" that secured social stability, states were understood to depend on a number of interdependent components that contemporaries often described as "bonds" or "ligaments." This implied an image of connective tissue that held a body politic together, while simultaneously allowing its head to act upon its members. The ligaments included not only institutions,

---

[54] Skinner, "Genealogy of the State," 329–33.
[55] Compare Skinner's highly theoretical discussion to Jouanna, *Le prince absolu. Apogée et déclin de l'imaginaire monarchique* (Paris, Gallimard, 2014), 76–88.
[56] Richard Beacon, *Solon his Follie, or a politique discourse touching the reformation of commonweales conquered, declined or corrupted* (1594); Edmund Spenser, *A View of the Present State of Irelande* (London, 1633 [but written 1595-6]).
[57] *Correspondentie van Robert Dudley, Graf van Leicester, en Andere documenten betreffende zijn Gouvernemente Generaal*, 3 vols, ed. H. Brugmans (Utrecht: Kremink and Sons, 1931), 2.46, 64, 99.
[58] Ibid., 115. Leicester's Dutch adversaries naturally viewed matters differently. See below, pp. 321–2.
[59] The question of whether Leicester or anyone in his entourage had actually read Machiavelli's *The Prince* is an intriguing one that will be briefly discussed later.

laws, and government officials, but also moral beliefs and sentiments, such as loyalty to the prince and love of country; social and economic forms and interests that reinforced political authority; rituals and forms of display; and tangible resources of money and brute force, in the shape of soldiers and fortifications. All of these things acting together, rather than an institutional structure considered in isolation, comprised a *state*. The precise configuration would vary from one state to another, reflecting different local conditions and historical experiences.

The character of a state therefore depended not only on its institutional structure but also on a host of other conditions affecting how power worked on the ground. In England the "order of command and obedience" normally required minimal compulsion, since respect for the law and royal authority assured willing obedience. But in Ireland, whose inhabitants often resented English rule, the state needed an army to support it and regularly resorted to exemplary acts of terror to enforce its control.[60] Although Irish institutions closely resembled those of England, after which they had been patterned, dissimilar environments produced markedly dissimilar states. Ancient states like England had normally formed durable legal, institutional, and customary bonds that rendered them more stable and resilient. As Samuel Daniel argued, "there are so many ligaments in a state that tie it together as it is a hard thing to dissolve them altogether, unless it be by a universal concurrency of causes that produce a general alteration."[61] But even old states might succumb to change, as the Roman Republic did in the early first century. Some contemporaries regarded such alterations as catastrophes but others believed they might at times become beneficial and even necessary. Sir John Hayward and Sir Francis Bacon both argued that England needed to accept an alteration or adjustment in its *state* to accommodate its dynastic unification with Scotland in 1603. Others fiercely resisted this notion.

Contemporaries widely assumed that the ligaments of newly formed states normally remained weak until they had time to mature, necessitating rule by force. Both Daniel and Sir John Hayward believed that the Normans had initially governed England by the sword, until they found ways to settle their authority by causing "the state of England" to undergo a general "alteration of laws, customs, fashion, manner of living, language, writing, with new forms of fights, fortifications, buildings and generally an innovation in most things," to bring it into conformity with Norman customs. The changes affected even fashions in clothing and the way men cut their beards. These seemingly trivial details mattered

---

[60] *Age of Atrocity: Violence and Political Conflict in Early Modern Ireland*, ed. David Edwards, Pádraig Lenihan, and Clodagh Tait (Dublin: Four Courts Press, 2007); Malcolm Smuts, "Organized Violence in the Elizabethan Monarchical Republic," *History* 99 (2014): 418–44; see below pp. 248–50.

[61] *The Complete Works in Verse and Prose of Samuel Daniel*, ed. Alexander Grossart, 5 vols (London, 1896), 5.46.

because, as Hayward explained, "likeness creates liking and love," rendering obedience more natural.[62] The reverse also held true: English officials regarded the survival of bardic poetry and Gaelic dress as inimical to *the state* in Ireland because these things perpetuated a sense of separate identity that fed resistance to English rule. We might summarize in modern language by saying that contemporaries conceived of states as complex configurations of both hard and soft power, shaped through a triangular interaction between sovereign authority, the society over which sovereignty is exercised, and challenging historical contingencies.

The State in Britain and Ireland and the Problem of Religious War

Although this book will give some attention to ideas about commonwealths, it primarily seeks to examine politics and political culture with reference to contemporary understandings of England, Scotland, and the government of Ireland as embattled Protestant states. This will entail both a further examination of contemporary thinking about "problems of state" and a re-examination of political events and processes guided by the early modern concept just described. Rather than viewing politics as something that unfolds primarily within institutions, such as parliament, the privy council, and county quarter sessions, or through public controversies conducted through print and manuscript texts, this book will focus on how a London-based ruling group sought to exert control over the variegated social, cultural, and geographic landscapes of Britain and Ireland, while reacting to religiously inspired challenges to its continuing hold on power. It will also examine responses that government policies provoked. Rather than highlighting the generally optimistic and high-minded values associated with the concept of a commonwealth, or abstract ideas about political rights and duties stressed by constitutional history, I want to explore the often grim and frequently violent patterns of thought and action produced through attempts to secure a Protestant state against rebellions, conspiracies, and foreign invasions.

The problem of religious war in my title is intended as a shorthand descriptor for both actual religious wars and rebellions, and fears that treasonous plots or invasions by foreign powers might ignite civil war in England. To survive these challenges, the state needed not just to maintain itself but to extend and deepen

---

[62] Ibid., 4.133–4; cf. Sir John Hayward, *The Lives of the iii Norman Kings* (London, 1613), 95–6: "In their speech, attire, shaving of the beard, service at the table; in their buildings and household furniture, they [the conquered English] altogether resembled the Normans."

its reach, by attempting to achieve tighter control over religious thought and behavior, stricter surveillance of potential traitors, and increased military capacities. It simultaneously had to deal with problems and controversies that the very expansion of state power produced, since not everyone agreed about the state's needs and the extent to which they justified measures that might have their own unsettling consequences, such as higher taxation or the exclusion of leading families deemed sympathetic to Catholicism from positions of local authority. The degree to which not only Catholics but overly zealous Protestants threatened the state excited considerable controversy. The state's confessional identity therefore had to be not only defended but also constructed, defined, and policed, in ways that involved fierce arguments about what sorts of confessional positions were compatible with political loyalty.

Because this process of construction and definition could never remain entirely confined within England's borders, its examination will also lead to a less insular view of political history. Although religious tensions and conflicts existed at all levels of English society, from local parishes up to the royal court, they were also especially virulent in Scotland, Ireland, and large areas of the European Continent, and confessional politics in all these places constantly threatened to impinge on English affairs. Defending England's Protestant state required the violent suppression of Irish rebellions, efforts to control the state in Scotland, and, for a brief period, experiments in building a more cohesive state in the Netherlands under an English governor general. One result was that English thinking about problems of state was often expansive and cosmopolitan, shaped by strategic challenges beyond the kingdom's frontiers and exchanges with politicians and political theorists in other countries.

The history of the early modern state in Britain and Ireland cannot be adequately told within a framework of national histories, even when expanded to include attention to "foreign policy." It demands attention to the many ways in which English, Scottish, Irish, and European events and ideas became entangled in webs spanning national frontiers, and a narrative that moves back and forth between different geographic locations. Doing this properly, especially over an extended period of time, undeniably presents substantial challenges, while rendering impossible the sort of comprehensive mastery of source materials that studies of more focused topics may hope to achieve. But refusing large-scale analysis risks perpetuating a fragmented view of the past that involves its own kinds of distortions. This book represents one historian's effort to reconstruct processes of change set in motion by challenges of religious conflict that spilled between England, Scotland, Ireland, and the European Continent, between the late 1570s and the mid-1620s. It consists of a series of chapters that are both analytical and narrative in scope, treating separate episodes in the period that connect together through an overarching argument. Before proceeding to a brief summary of that argument, a few more conceptual issues require discussion.

Who Controls the State?

Although early modern thinkers associated states with rule or dominion, usually exercised by sovereign princes, they recognized that a state had needs that went beyond the personal wishes of its head. Even after French theorists developed a concept of the king's absolute will as the soul of the state, they continued to talk about "reasons" and interests of state that existed independently of royal whims.[63] In ruling the state the king needed to subordinate his own desires to its demands, so that not only his political decisions but his recreations and bodily comportment served to uphold it. In embodying the state, he became its servant, perhaps even its slave. All states depended not just on coercive commands but also the willing obedience of most subjects and active cooperation of some in carrying out the ruler's directives. Strong representative assemblies and local institutions might increase a king's need to negotiate power, but even the most absolute sovereigns were never fully autonomous, if only because they had to see through other men's eyes and act through their hands in order to control large kingdoms. This required taking the values and priorities of local oligarchs into account.[64]

States grew not only from the top down but also from the bottom up and middle outward, as people found ways of aligning their own interests and ambitions with sovereign authority, and undertook voluntary initiatives that strengthened orders of command and obedience. This insight lies behind the work of historians like Michael Braddick and Steve Hindle, who have examined what Braddick terms processes of "state formation" that took place primarily at the local level, through the largely uncoordinated efforts of local officials to deal with problems like poor relief, the distribution of taxation, and the enforcement of law and order.[65] The cumulative effect of their activities had the mainly unforeseen consequence of creating tighter and more effective forms of state control. This organic process of "state formation" can be contrasted with efforts by kings and royal ministers to extend their control from the top down, perhaps best described as "state building." Both processes went on continuously, often in symbiotic relationships with each other. Indeed, it is hard to see how things could have been otherwise, especially in a country like England, where a highly centralized monarchy had to rely on unpaid local magistrates to implement its commands. No royal innovation would work unless taken up and developed at the local level, while local experiments in extending order usually needed enabling legislation or

---

[63] Jouanna, *Pouvoir absolu*.
[64] William Beik, *Absolutism and Society in Seventeenth-Century France: State Power and Provincial Society in Languedoc* (Cambridge: Cambridge University Press, 1989).
[65] Braddick, *State Formation*; Steve Hindle, *The State and Social Change in Early Modern England* (Basingstoke: Palgrave Macmillan, 2000).

royal charters to proceed.⁶⁶ Change commonly required initiatives both at the center and in the localities that reinforced each other.

We might expect state formation to primarily affect matters of local concern, such as poor relief, while monarchs and privy councilors determined the conduct of international relations and war. But this was never entirely the case. Until 1585 and again after 1604, the English or British crown relied on companies of volunteer soldiers serving in the pay of foreign states to increase its leverage in European politics, without requiring the kingdom to go to war.⁶⁷ Even after war broke out with Spain in 1588, much of the recruitment of royal armies and a large share of the conduct of war at sea depended on the work of individual captains, ship owners, and aristocratic patrons of military enterprises. Without the aid of voluntary initiatives, the state was no more capable of engaging in European power politics than it was able to collect and distribute poor relief. But it does not follow that voluntarism always meshed harmoniously with royal intentions. Elizabeth's sharp reaction to the preaching campaigns of godly Protestants provides a classic example of how voluntary acts by people who saw themselves as loyal subjects standing in the front lines of the battle against the queen's popish enemies sometimes struck her as insubordinate, disloyal, and dangerous because they threatened her direct control.⁶⁸ Such tensions were by no means confined to arguments over liturgical ceremonies and preaching. Elizabeth and James faced the constant challenge of enlisting energetic service without relinquishing their ability to direct and, when necessary, restrain it. Although they would have liked to turn that energy on and off, as if by a spigot, as their own needs dictated, this rarely proved possible. Privy councilors possessing extensive clientage networks, provincial magnates with ties to the court, and office holders in the royal household who retained strong links to specific localities furnished means by which the ruler might seek to control grass-roots initiatives. But even privy councilors sometimes proved annoyingly independent, especially when sent outside the realm on a military or diplomatic mission, as the earl of Leicester's campaign in the Netherlands in 1586–7, the earl of Essex's expeditions to France in 1592 and Ireland in 1599, and the duke of Buckingham's role during negotiations over the Spanish Match in Madrid all demonstrated.

Because subjects usually had their own ideas about what the defense of the realm and service to their prince required, situations occasionally arose in which individuals equated true loyalty with *disobedience* to official commands. On a few occasions, people accused a king or queen of endangering the state through

---

⁶⁶ Robert Tittler's account of the proliferation of urban corporations in Elizabethan England provides an excellent illustration. See *The Reformation and the Towns in England*.
⁶⁷ See David Trim, "The Context of War and Violence in Sixteenth-Century English Society," *Journal of Early Modern History* 20.2 (2016): 233–55 and below, pp. 177–8.
⁶⁸ Patrick Collinson, *The Elizabethan Puritan Movement* (Berkeley: University of California Press, 1967).

weakness or miscalculation. That was, in effect, the charge that the second earl of Essex lodged against Elizabeth.[69] In 1620 Thomas Scott predicted, in his notorious pamphlet, *Vox Populi*, that if James persisted in his intention of marrying his son to a Spanish princess, disloyal Catholics would "in small time... work so far into the body of the state by buying offices and the like... that with the help of the Jesuits they would undermine it with mere wit."[70] Complaints of this kind, especially when uttered in public, invited the retort that they were themselves crimes against the state because they undermined the respect for royal authority on which it depended. But fears that a ruler's inadequacies might jeopardize the survival of the state over which he presided raised troubling questions about the nature and limits of allegiance.

Some historians have interpreted those tensions as examples of growing resistance to royal absolutism or, more subtly, expressions of a latent conflict between the republican and monarchical sides of the monarchical republic. Up to a point this makes sense. A few writers in both confessional camps argued openly that the paramount need to protect the public good justified forcible resistance to and perhaps even the murder of a ruler who grossly abused his or her powers.[71] Without going nearly that far, members of Elizabeth's council and puritan groups beyond the court sought to pressure her to adopt policies they favored by orchestrating appeals to the public and pressure from parliaments. But we should not allow the use of such tactics to persuade us that efforts to constrain and redirect royal policies necessarily reflected sympathy for republican values. More immediate practical motives were often more important. Even as stalwart a defender of absolute royal authority as James VI and I felt entitled to encourage forceful noble opposition to the regency government of Marie de Médicis after it negotiated a double marriage alliance between the royal families of France and Spain. He believed this treaty threatened not only his own kingdoms and the interests of Protestants throughout Europe but also the future independence of the French crown, by turning it into a satellite of Spain. He therefore claimed to feel "constrained... to prevent the ruin of that state and its principal members" and the absolute authority of the king of France to encourage resistance to a policy carried out in that king's name by the ministers of a legally constituted regency

---

[69] Below, pp. 366–8.
[70] Thomas Scott, *Vox Populi. Or Newes from Spain translated according to the Spanish copies* (London, 1620).
[71] Richard Bancroft, *Dangerous positions and proceedings published and practiced within this island of Brytaine* (London, 1593), 38–9, paraphrased advocates of this position as saying that inferior magistrates had a duty to depose and kill tyrants because "where this justice is not executed the state is most corrupt," leaving the people "as it were without officers," and so compelled to take the sword into their own hands. The underlying premise, of which he strongly disapproved, would seem to be that a proper state required a system of power and authority directed to the administration of justice. If the prince at the head of that system behaved unjustly his powers devolved on the inferior magistrates who normally carried out his commands; if they also failed, the people needed to restore justice through their own violent acts.

government.⁷² The tender age of Louis XIII gave this view some plausibility, since arguably he did not yet have a mature will capable of guiding the French state. But James had earlier almost certainly approved of the earl of Essex's plans to remove Elizabeth's leading ministers by force, after being wrongly convinced that they had conspired to deliver the English crown to the Spanish Infanta Isabella.⁷³ His belief in the divine right of kings notwithstanding, he had few scruples about promoting rebellions or coups to prevent other monarchs from acting in ways that harmed his own interests and what he perceived as the safety of their own states.

Most policy disputes had less to do with tensions between personal monarchy and commonwealth values than choices between alternative strategies for dealing with specific problems, especially threats of religious subversion. The godly and their supporters wanted active preaching campaigns to increase the number of adherents to the faith, robust efforts to suppress popery, and active aid to embattled Protestants abroad. People less sympathetic to godly Protestantism, often including both Elizabeth and James, preferred more moderate and pragmatic policies intended to tamp down confessional animosities. They demanded fairly minimal compliance with a half-reformed Church, while seeking to restrain provocative sermons that fanned religious divisions, continuing to employ Catholic sympathizers in local offices, and trying to avoid open warfare with major European powers. The godly tended to view this pragmatism as at best a set of half-measures that risked provoking God's anger, and at worst a way-station on the road back to popery. They appealed to Parliament and the public to demand more stringent measures, and were stigmatized by opponents, such as John Whitgift, Christopher Hatton, and Richard Bancroft, as "popular" spirits for so doing.⁷⁴

But we should not be fooled by contemporary characterizations of puritanism as a popular movement. The godly never made up anything like a majority of the population and the full implementation of their programs would have required more government repression, along with higher levels of taxation and military conscription. If puritans had gained control they would have used the royal prerogative to initiate expensive military campaigns abroad and socially disruptive forms of religious discipline at home. The state would have become appreciably more intrusive, authoritarian, and burdensome, as an active and zealous minority used its authority to impose its own priorities on the populace. Although that minority would probably have claimed to act on behalf of the commonwealth, to

---

⁷² TNA SP81/15, fol. 26.
⁷³ Alexandra Gajda, "Essex and the 'Popish Plot'," in *Doubtful and Dangerous: The Question of Succession in Late Elizabethan England*, ed. Susan Doran and Paulina Kewes (Manchester: Manchester University Press, 2016), 115–34.
⁷⁴ Peter Lake, "The Politics of 'Popularity' and the Public Sphere: The 'Monarchical Republic' of Elizabeth I Defends Itself," and Paul Hammer, "The Smiling Crocodile: The Earl of Essex and Late Elizabethan Popularity," in *Politics of the Public Sphere*, ed. Lake and Pincus, 59–94 and 95–115.

most people its actions would have seemed more vexatious than the normal operation of royal governance.[75] The godly most often criticized Elizabeth and James not for arbitrary and oppressive rule but excessive tolerance and forbearance toward subjects who deserved harsher treatment. Rather than capricious tyrants in the conventional sense, they looked like weak rulers who failed to exercise their power with sufficient vigor. We need to beware of invoking an overly neat dichotomy between quasi-republican and quasi-absolutist positions, without paying adequate attention to the practical consequences of rival policies, and the ways in which actions carried out in the ruler's name and justified as extensions of the royal prerogative occasionally *conflicted* with royal wishes.

The Permeability of States and Dynastic Politics

An established argument in the historical literature holds that sovereign territorial states consolidated their authority in the early modern period, at the expense of both semi-feudal nobilities and supranational institutions like the Roman Church.[76] But in reality, the sovereign nation state remained, at best, a work in progress well into the seventeenth century, permeable to outside influences in any number of ways. Frontiers were readily crossed by ideas, conveyed through print or by travelers like the seminary priests who began arriving in England, Ireland, and Scotland in the late 1570s. Trade provided a complementary network of exchanges, involving movements not only of goods but also information and people. Commerce facilitated religious and intellectual connections and alliances. Catholic exiles established presses on the Continent that produced tracts smuggled into England hidden in commercial cargoes. Meanwhile an active community of puritan exiles sheltered under the patronage of the Merchant Adventurers Company after it settled in Zeeland in the 1570s. It too had a local press run by a Dutch printer named Richard Schilders, who produced controversial tracts in English that would not have escaped government censorship if printed in London.[77]

The cosmopolitan connections of certain professions, especially clergy, civil lawyers, and academic scholars, provided additional channels of communication, as did communities of English, Irish, and Scottish Catholic exiles living on the Continent and of European Protestant exiles in English towns like Norwich and London.[78] Exiled communities helped connect English puritans to French, Dutch, and Scottish Calvinists, and English and Irish Catholics to the Catholic League in France, the court of Philip II, and the Vatican. The resulting networks had a

---

[75] All of this happened in the 1650s. [76] See, for example, Elton, *Tudor Revolution*.
[77] See below, pp. 391–2.
[78] Katy Gibbons, *English Catholic Exiles in Late Sixteenth-Century Paris* (Woodbridge: Boydell Press, 2011).

political and military as well as a purely religious significance.[79] In Ireland, for example, communications between missionary priests and friars gradually connected remote areas of the island not only to Dublin and other Irish towns but also the European Continent. They played a role in facilitating the rebel earl of Tyrone's negotiations with the court of Philip II.

States also remained permeable to foreign influences at their very centers, due to the dynastic character of royal authority and the importance of dynastic marriages to both domestic and international politics. Elizabeth I was the last English monarch before the nineteenth century to have both an English father and mother, and her unmarried status meant that her court never included a large number of foreign attendants of a royal consort. But her rival and lineal heir, Mary Stuart, was a Scottish queen with a French mother, the widow of the French King François II, and therefore the sister-in-law of his two Valois successors. Questions relating to the English succession therefore inevitably became entangled with French as well as Scottish politics.[80] The possibility that Mary or her son, James VI, might marry into the royal house of Spain, along with negotiations over various possible marriages between Elizabeth and foreign princes created additional entanglements. A generation later, the marriage of James's daughter, Elizabeth, to the Elector Palatine threatened to embroil Britain in the confessional politics of the Holy Roman Empire, while negotiations for Prince Charles's marriage to a Spanish princess caused a major domestic controversy.

Below the level of alliances and rivalries among royal houses, a different but related form of dynastic politics played out among great landed families in the localities, who were always highly conscious of their ancestral connections to their lands and their alliances with other landed dynasties. Like other early modern monarchies, England was a dynastic state not only in the sense that its crown belonged to a ruling family, but also because the dynastic affinities, alliances, and rivalries of its greater families structured politics and social relationships in both court and country, as well as communications between these two poles.[81] This fact allowed confessional conflicts to become entangled with personal and family rivalries, as aristocratic dynasties that remained loyal to Rome sheltered missionary priests, shielded Catholics in their localities, and occasionally flirted with conspiracies to overthrow the Protestant state, while other dynasties patronized godly preachers, while preparing to resist any possible Catholic restoration. In the late 1570s bodies of exiles on the Continent, including some Jesuits, along with the

---

[79] Stuart Carroll, *Martyrs and Murderers: The Guise Family and the Making of Europe* (Oxford: Oxford University Press, 2009), chapter 10.
[80] As has recently been shown by Questier, *Dynastic Politics*.
[81] If anything, this was even more true of Scotland and Ireland than England, both because the nobilities of those kingdoms often effectively controlled the administration of justice and other government functions within their lordships, and because extended ties of kinship played an even more important role in structuring social, economic, and political relationships.

Spanish ambassador in London, Bernardino de Mendoza, attempted to forge links with Catholic aristocratic networks in England, Ireland, and Scotland, in hopes of encouraging more systematic and organized resistance to Protestant rule. The Elizabethan regime had meanwhile constructed its own alliances among the Protestant nobilities of France, the Netherlands, western Germany, and Scotland. In pursuing their own dynastic and confessional goals, rulers of the period invariably tried to infiltrate and ally themselves with aristocratic dynasties in the kingdoms of their rivals, often with significant success. Rather than contests between compact nation states in full control of their own territories, international conflicts involved networks of confessional allies spanning national frontiers.

Chapter 1 examines how the last courtship of Elizabeth I by the duke of Anjou, brother to Henry III of France, came to involve a tangle of religious and dynastic politics on multiple levels, from the international arena down to English localities. Supporters of the match saw it as a way to counter the growing menace of Philip II, and the risk that the Dutch revolt against Spain would allow France to annex the Low Countries. But the match also promised to permit prominent Catholic-leaning families that had been largely excluded from the court after the duke of Norfolk's execution in 1572 to regain entry to it, as Anjou's supporters and clients. This would have had implications for the confessional balance of power not only at the political center but in many localities. The queen's marriage negotiations therefore alarmed many Protestants, giving rise to a controversy that raged both within the court, where it was conducted by oral means and through the dissemination of short manuscript texts, and beyond it through public sermons and printed tracts. The controversy turned partly on opposing efforts to stress Anjou's dignity and power as a French prince, or to smear both him and his family through what amounted to dynastic libels, most notably John Stubbs's *The Discovery of a Gaping Gulf*. But it also involved arguments about whether the English public generally favored the match, as Anjou's supporters claimed, or disliked it so vehemently that its conclusion risked provoking a civil war. Participants in this debate never portrayed the public as a mass of independent citizens forming individual judgments about Anjou, but rather as a population divided into confessional parties or factions ranged under dynastic leaders, including the queen, Anjou, and Mary Stuart. Even when it spilled into a "public" arena the controversy therefore continued to have a marked dynastic character.

The Exclusion Crisis of the 1580s

Negotiations for the match gradually petered out in a climate of sharpening confessional polarization, caused not only by the controversy over Anjou but also by the arrival of a Jesuit mission in England, the outbreak of rebellion in Ireland, and the loss of English control over the government of Scotland. All these events seemed to increase the risk of a religious and dynastic upheaval, especially as it became clear that Elizabeth would never produce an heir of her own body. Mary Stuart, who had the best dynastic claim to succeed Elizabeth, appeared likely to benefit. In another suggestive essay, Collinson argued that the challenge posed by Mary led to an "Elizabethan exclusion crisis," as Protestants tried to bar her from the throne.[82] But he did not attempt to pinpoint the crisis in time or to provide a detailed anatomy, apart from a discussion of the 1584 Bond of Association. Chapters 2–7 attempt a systematic analysis, arguing that the crisis intensified in the early 1580s, reaching its most acute phase between 1584 and early 1587, and that it had not only domestic but important Scottish, Irish, and European dimensions.

The threat of an internal rising in support of Mary had to be taken seriously because, as recent scholarship has shown, English Catholicism remained considerably stronger in this period than historians used to suppose. Chapter 2 begins by reviewing the evidence of Catholic strength in the early 1580s before examining how the council attempted to prevent the emergence of a coordinated religious challenge. It argues that while the authorities had little success in curtailing the arrival of missionary priests and eroding Catholic belief, surveillance by government spies, together with the temporary imprisonment of a large number of prominent Catholics for recusancy, and more permanent restrictions placed on their movements after their release, did create serious obstacles to the formation of an organized network capable of planning and coordinating a serious revolt. The story of the leading Staffordshire recusant, Thomas Lord Paget, will provide a case study of how these defensive measures worked. Beginning in 1584, the development of a stronger system of county militias, largely under the control of strongly Protestant lord and deputy lieutenants, made it easier for supporters of the Protestant state to mobilize forces quickly and seize control in the localities during any sudden crisis.[83] The Bond of Association needs to be viewed not in isolation, but as one important element in this wider array of defensive measures.

While the council moved to contain the threat in England, its control over Scotland collapsed, as the adolescent James VI fell under the influence of his French cousin, Esmé Stuart *seigneur* d'Aubigny, who had ties to the duke of Guise. A major rebellion had also swept across southwestern Ireland. Militant English Catholics, some of whom were in touch with Mendoza, canvassed schemes for destabilizing Elizabeth's rule from multiple directions, not only by fostering more systematic resistance within England but also by encouraging Irish rebellions, turning James VI into an ally, and eventually launching a limited invasion from

---

[82] "The Elizabethan Exclusion Crisis and the Elizabethan Polity," *Proceedings of the British Academy* 84 (1994): 51–92.
[83] On the militias see Neil Younger, *War and Politics in the Elizabethan Counties* (Manchester: Manchester University Press, 2012).

the Continent. Chapter 3 examines the politics of Scotland in the period and English efforts to prevent James from assisting the cause of his mother and her Catholic continental allies. Fear and mistrust of James induced the English crown to support forms of presbyterian radicalism and forcible resistance to royal authority in Scotland that Elizabeth would never have tolerated for a moment in her own kingdom.

Whereas Elizabeth's council tried to deal with Scotland through diplomacy and by supporting noble and clerical allies there, the situation in Ireland and threats of invasion from Europe required more direct military responses. Before turning to them, Chapter 4 surveys cultural attitudes, printed treatises, and practical methods relating to the conduct of warfare on both land and sea. Chapter 5 then turns to the challenges posed by Elizabeth's second kingdom in Ireland. The Tudor state had never established effective control of large parts of the island, where the power of Irish septs or Old English lordships remained dominant.[84] But the localized character of seigneurial power, along with conflicts among Irish lords, had allowed the crown to contain challenges to its rule. From the late 1570s, worrying signs appeared that Catholicism was starting to fuse with Irish resentment of English domination, in ways that had the potential to generate more widespread and organized rebellions, involving not only the Gaelic Irish but also ethnically English populations in the towns and the Pale. This perceived danger imparted a fresh sense of urgency to the pleas of captains and crown servants, who had long wanted to strengthen and extend English governance by forceful methods. It also made those captains and officials mistrustful of the Pale elite that had previously furnished the Dublin administration with most of its officials. Rather than allies in a struggle to overcome Irish "barbarism," the "civil" population of Ireland, mostly descended from medieval English colonists, began to look even more menacing than the "wild" Irish, because it possessed a greater capacity for organized resistance. One result was a substantial, if never entirely complete, replacement of men born in Ireland, who often had considerable familiarity with Irish culture, by newly arrived English Protestants as judges, officials, and military officers, so that the Irish state came to appear even more alien to the island's inhabitants. But since Elizabeth never provided the resources necessary to maintain systematic control over the entire island that state remained vulnerable, as the great rebellion launched by the earls of Tyrone and Tyrconnell in the 1590s graphically demonstrated.

As the English government struggled with problems in Scotland and Ireland, the situation on the Continent grew increasingly menacing, especially after the assassination of the Dutch leader William of Orange in 1584. The following year, after a Spanish offensive had recaptured nearly all the major towns in the southern Netherlands, Elizabeth reluctantly agreed to send a substantial English army,

---

[84] The term Old English refers to the descendants of the medieval English colonists, as opposed to New English officials and planters who had recently arrived.

under the command of the earl of Leicester, to aid the Dutch. But in addition to military assistance, the Dutch clamored for a strong leader to impose order on their decentralized and fractious state, and in 1586 Leicester disobeyed an express royal command by accepting an appointment as governor general of the Netherlands, with nominally absolute powers over both civil and military affairs. This involved him in a bitter dispute with the queen and acrimonious quarrels with Dutch politicians, which are described in Chapter 7.

1588–1603: A New Political Landscape?

By late 1587 Leicester's authority in the Netherlands had collapsed, while Elizabeth's patience with her allies had worn thin. She looked for an exit from the Netherlands through negotiations with Philip's general, the prince of Parma. Several English officials stationed in the Low Countries predicted a disastrous campaigning season the following year. Instead 1588 famously witnessed the defeat of the Spanish Armada, followed in December by the assassination of the duke of Guise and his brother on orders of Henry III, which put an end to fears that the French king would ally himself with the Catholic League and Spain. The following year the murder of Henry III himself made the Protestant Henry of Navarre the hereditary king of France, intensifying a civil war in which Philip decided to intervene directly. By diverting resources, first to the invasion of England and then to France, he relieved pressure on the Dutch, allowing them to recover and ultimately take the offensive. Within Britain, Mary's execution in February 1587 and James's continuing adherence to his English alliance had meanwhile alleviated worries about a Catholic successor to Elizabeth and attacks on England through Scotland.

Although a Catholic threat remained, it now primarily involved the potential for a new Spanish invasion, since without foreign support the internal enemies of Protestant rule appeared too weak and disunited to prevail. The defense of the state had come to resemble more closely a traditional dynastic and international war, especially after Philip II began promoting his daughter, the Infanta Isabella, as claimant to both the French and English thrones. Many Catholics, not only in England but also in France and even in Rome recoiled at this attempt to create a "universal monarchy" by giving the Habsburgs control of all the major crowns of western Europe. Rather than being defined almost exclusively in religious terms, resistance to Spain became associated with support for hereditary legitimacy and the continued independence of European states and churches from Spanish and papal domination.[85]

---

[85] Although France remained Roman Catholic, a Gallican movement defended limited autonomy of the French Church from Rome, while simultaneously asserting the divine right absolute sovereignty of French kings.

After 1588 many of the challenges that had led to the crisis of the previous few years therefore receded, while other problems took their place. In addition to the strains of war, these included a looming generational transition in England, as Elizabeth and the cohort of senior privy councilors that had dominated the court since the early 1570s approached the natural end of their lives. Although the queen exceeded expectations by living until 1603, the deaths of Leicester, Francis Walsingham, and Christopher Hatton between 1588 and 1591 removed three of the four most influential privy councilors, heightening anticipation of the regime change certain to come within a few more years. Although it took some time, the cohesiveness of the privy council eventually broke down in a bitter factional struggle between Leicester's stepson and political heir, Robert Devereux earl of Essex, and most other members of the ruling group. Several historians have followed John Guy in regarding this post-1588 period as a "second reign" of the queen, differing markedly in character from that which had preceded it.[86]

Chapters 8 and 9 re-evaluate and qualify this view by examining elements of both change and continuity between Elizabeth's last years and the previous decade. Chapter 8 builds on previous studies of Essex by Paul Hammer and Alexandra Gajda, while seeking to place the earl's political thinking and behavior within a longer chronological context through comparisons with earlier Elizabethan courtiers who shared his international outlook and strong interest in war. The chapter shows that many features of the earl's outlook, including his dissatisfaction with the queen and her court, were far from novel. Jealousies and rivalries among members of the privy council and other intimates of the queen were also more common before 1588 than some recent work has implied. But Essex and his circle reshaped ideas long present within Elizabethan culture into a more cohesive view of the state—a term he used with great frequency—and the role of specific forms of virtue in upholding it. He also absorbed features of earlier Catholic critiques of the court, partly from figures in his entourage like Lord Henry Howard. Complaints about Elizabeth and older courtiers such as Burghley that had long existed thereby gained a sharper edge, while becoming more detached from confessional polemics.

The looming death of the queen threatened to unsettle not only relations among her councilors but also within the Church, since every royal succession since 1547 had resulted in a new religious settlement. Several members of the council and even some bishops favored significant ecclesiastical reforms, which were vigorously promoted in the Parliament of 1587. But in the immediate aftermath of the Armada, Archbishop Whitgift, Sir Christopher Hatton, and Hatton's chaplain, Richard Bancroft, launched a systematic attack on puritan non-conformity and presbyterian doctrines that gained momentum over the next several years.

---

[86] Guy, "Second Reign of Elizabeth I?"

Although several historians have examined this anti-puritan campaign, they have treated it as a purely English event, with little or no connection to the succession.[87] But there was no guarantee at the time that Elizabeth's successor would not undo the victory over English presbyterianism achieved by Whitgift, Bancroft, and their allies. Although that successor had still not been named, James VI seemed by far the most likely candidate. This fact gave Scottish ecclesiastical politics considerable relevance to the future of the Church of England. Bancroft's determined efforts to discredit Scottish presbyterianism, along with his awkward and unsuccessful attempts to enlist James as an ally in the cause, suggest that he fully understood this fact. Chapter 9 examines how the battle over Erastian episcopacy played out in both British kingdoms. As in the previous decade but in slightly different ways, Scottish religious politics presented a kind of distorted reflection of those in England, refracting similar issues into a distinctly different overall pattern. Whereas the English council tried to reinforce a moderately reformed Church by cracking down simultaneously on Catholic recusancy and puritan non-conformity, James adopted an opposite strategy of cultivating an alliance with the Kirk's presbyterian leaders, while simultaneously extending his favor and protection to several Catholic aristocrats, especially the earl of Huntly. In this way he hoped to manage the factional politics of Scotland, while positioning himself to win both godly Protestant and Catholic support for his eventual succession in England. His favor to Huntly, along with his previous record of dalliances with Jesuits, Guise and Philip II, meant that he had to work especially hard to establish his credentials as a godly king. He did so by accepting legislation that appeared to abolish episcopacy in Scotland, sheltering the English puritans Robert Waldegrave and John Penry, and openly criticizing the English Church and its liturgy. From the perspective of Whitgift and Bancroft, his conduct must have seemed truly alarming. Fortunately for the English conformists, James's always uneasy alliance with the Kirk finally broke down completely in December 1596. The chapter provides a fresh analysis of this rupture, after which James moved considerably closer to the position of Whitgift and Bancroft. It concludes with a brief analysis of James's political theology in the late 1590s, highlighting both similarities and differences to the views of English conformists.

Peace and the Imperfect Consolidation of a British State, 1603–1625

James finally gained the English throne in March 1603, at almost the same moment that the Nine Years War ended in Ireland. Elizabeth's war with Spain

---

[87] See, e.g., Collinson, *Puritan Movement*, part 8; Patrick Collinson, *Richard Bancroft and Elizabethan Anti-Puritanism* (Cambridge: Cambridge University Press, 2013).

had by this time devolved into a costly stalemate, giving each side strong incentives to end it. In addition to bringing Scotland and England under a single crown, James's succession therefore coincided with a transition from war to peace. Protestant rule appeared to have been secured, although exactly what sort of Protestant rule remained unclear, while an unprecedented opportunity presented itself to consolidate royal control over three very different kingdoms, without the distraction of a foreign conflict. Chapters 10 and 11 examine how James and his servants sought to achieve this goal and the reactions that their efforts provoked.

As is well known, the new reign began with an unsuccessful effort to persuade the parliaments of England and Scotland to adopt legislation that would have merged the two kingdoms' laws and institutions. But the project of integrating the Stuart kingdoms needs to be viewed from a broader perspective than a focus on parliamentary debates over formal legal and institutional changes. Debates over the union interacted with sources of tension already present within each of the Stuart kingdoms. In England, proposals to modify the common law intensified a reaction that had already started to develop against a perceived growth of arbitrary government power during the war with Spain that was further intensified by awareness of the growth of absolutist doctrines in France. This combination of circumstances led to the development of an essentially new concept of the common law as the distillation of centuries of English custom that provided a bulwark against unwelcome innovations and abuses. While James did not fully share this view, he recognized that the English system of common law governance generally worked effectively, and although he grumbled about lawyers' quibbles he wisely tried to avoid confrontations pitting the law against his prerogative powers. The growing emphasis on the law nevertheless did render even more difficult the task of finding new sources of revenue that the crown badly needed, by fusing arguments over taxation with disputes over legal principles.

But in addition to formal differences in laws and institutions, England differed from Scotland in having a much stronger system for administering crown authority through royally appointed magistrates. In the northern British kingdom, as in much of Ireland, institutional structures were much weaker and nominally royal offices had often fallen under the control of local lords. These conditions significantly increased the importance of lordship and structures of kin-loyalty in maintaining order in the localities, and accordingly placed greater weight on a king's relationships with his nobles in the governance of his kingdom. Chapter 10 ends with a discussion of these contrasts and a preliminary analysis of how James sought to employ and at times combine both "English" and "Scottish" methods in ruling his three kingdoms.

Chapter 11 continues the analysis by examining more closely James's efforts to bring outlying regions of his kingdoms that had never previously been subjected to strong royal control under firmer governance. These regions included former border districts between England and Scotland, the Scottish Isles and Highlands, and recently conquered regions of Ireland. Ireland, which has normally been overlooked in accounts of British union, represented the most complex case, involving a three-way interaction between royal officials who sought to impose an authoritarian form of English common law governance over the entire island, ethnically English Catholic inhabitants of the island who were developing forms of resistance based on a combination of religion and common law principles, and native Irish who had long lived under very different customs. James generally supported the efforts of his Irish officials to extend common law procedures, but in some regions he also erected new lordships through extensive grants of lands and local authority, or relied on the power of existing lords of both Old English and Irish extraction. The pragmatic and hybrid nature of his approach to governance is again apparent.

In both Ireland and Scotland, James's government made significant progress in reducing disorder and criminality and eliminating or curtailing the seigneurial armies that had obstructed royal control in the past. But it failed to deal effectively with Irish Catholicism, which grew more entrenched and better organized over the course of the reign, while in Scotland the king's efforts after 1616 to impose the English (and Roman Catholic) ceremony of kneeling while receiving communion provoked stiff resistance. These sources of religious disunity, together with the failure of both Elizabeth and James to increase crown revenues significantly, were serious weaknesses. By the end of his reign James presided over a state strong enough to rule all three of his kingdoms with reasonable effectiveness, so long as too much external pressure was not placed upon it. But that state suffered from latent weaknesses that threatened to become crippling if the kingdom ever again became engaged in a major war.

This made the avoidance of war imperative. Chapters 12 and 13 provide an extended re-examination of the neglected subject of James's relations with other European states. The chapters argue that his well-known commitment to peace owed less to philosophical convictions than some historians have supposed and more to calculations of self-interest, camouflaged by high-minded rhetoric. James recognized that he lacked the resources to fight a major war and that in a general European war of religion Calvinists would almost certainly find themselves at a serious disadvantage. He therefore worked to promote cross-confessional alliances based on shared secular interests that would cancel out the normal Catholic advantage. But he remained more worried than historians have commonly appreciated that a revival of militant Catholicism might lead to a renewed assault on Protestant states, not only by Spain but also by France and other Catholic powers. He therefore sought underhanded ways of fomenting difficulties for Spain in the Low Countries, the Holy Roman Empire, and North Italy, while simultaneously seeking to combat any growth of Spanish, Jesuit, and militant Catholic influence within France. He simultaneously sought to mediate disputes among Protestants, partly because he prided himself on his own theological erudition and his role as "defender of the faith," but also from worries that theological controversy would impede unity against any future Catholic aggression.

For a variety of reasons, some beyond his control, his efforts to preserve a European balance of power by playing France and Spain off against each other, while cultivating both Protestant alliances and good relations with the major Catholic powers, began to unravel in the late 1610s. His alarm at what he perceived as a growth of Spanish and Jesuit influence in France drew him into internal political conflicts in that kingdom in ways that antagonized French ministers. He also became involved in a vicious political and religious contest in the United Provinces. As his relations with French and Dutch statesmen worsened he began to pursue a dynastic alliance with Spain, hoping that it would shield his kingdoms, while providing him with additional levers through which to influence European politics. When a new crisis erupted in Bohemia in 1618, he continued to maneuver for advantage, offering to mediate a peaceful settlement while sending ambiguous signals of support to the Protestant protagonists. In the end his equivocations undermined his own credibility with both camps, while failing to prevent the crisis from escalating into a war in which Protestants, led by James's son-in-law, Frederick V of the Palatinate, suffered a crushing defeat.

This turn of events boxed James into a corner, leaving negotiations with Spain as his only means of trying to recover something from the wreckage, short of entering a major war with an empty treasury on the losing side. But since the Spanish had limited control over their Central European allies, they would have found it difficult to assist James even if they had wanted to do so. The debacle disgusted large numbers of Britons who saw their king's actions as a betrayal of the Protestant cause and national humiliation. In addition to religious partisanship, the reaction against his policies was fed by an exaggerated belief in the potency of British valor when not hampered by weak royal leadership, originally promulgated by Essex and other Elizabethan swordsmen like Sir Walter Ralegh. This myth, and a related claim that bold action would quickly expose the hidden weaknesses of Spain's over-extended empire, fed a reaction against James's policy of peace with Spain that was soon taken up by his son and heir, the future Charles I, and the royal favorite, Buckingham. But the new war they launched in 1625 quickly exposed the limits not only of British military power but also the willingness of parliaments to provide adequate war funding, and the solidity of the political coalition that Charles and Buckingham had constructed in their attempt to rally support. The dysfunctional performance of the British state under the pressure of war breathed new life into competing explanations about the sources of failure deriving from earlier polemical campaigns against both papists and puritans. A final chapter discusses how developments traced in the book structured the political and ideological environment that Charles inherited in 1625 and contributed to the collapse of the British state in the early 1640s.

1
Religion, Dynastic Politics, and Public Discourse
The Anjou Match and Its Contexts

Dynastic Politics in a Monarchical Republic

Nearly thirty years ago, Patrick Collinson famously argued that "a dynastic crisis which lasted the entirety of Elizabeth's reign" accentuated implicitly republican tendencies in English political culture.[1] Because "politicians already lived, proleptically, with their queen's death and already imagined the dangerous hiatus which that death would leave behind ... they ... envisaged themselves conducting business in an acephalous commonwealth," in which Parliament, the council, or some other body might need to choose the next king.[2] And because the queen hesitated to take measures needed to assure the continuation of Protestant rule after her death, they also sought to pressure her by encouraging parliamentary and public protests. These circumstances produced an "Elizabethan exclusion crisis" that reached a climax in the mid-1580s, with the Bond of Association, a document drawn up by members of the council and subscribed by hundreds of locally prominent men (and a few women) throughout the realm, pledging that if Mary Stuart or anyone acting on her behalf mounted a violent challenge to the existing regime, Elizabeth's loyal subjects would retaliate with lynch law against the Sottish queen and her supporters.[3]

Collinson saw these measures as reflecting a willingness to act without direct royal command that had both intellectual and institutional roots. Contact with European monarchomach literature, the humanist rediscovery of Greco-Roman republican traditions, and stories of Old Testament prophets all encouraged Protestants to think and behave in independent ways.[4] But in addition the experience of local self-government inherent in the English

---

[1] "The Monarchical Republic of Queen Elizabeth," in *Elizabethan Essays* (London: Hambledon Press, 1994), 51.
[2] Patrick Collinson, "*De Republica Anglorum*: Or, History with the Politics Put Back," in *Elizabethan Essays*, 1–29 at 19.
[3] Patrick Collinson, "The Elizabethan Exclusion Crisis and the Elizabethan Polity," *Proceedings of the British Academy* 84 (1994): 51–92.
[4] See also "The Monarchical Republic of Queen Elizabeth I" and "Puritans, Men of Business and Parliaments," *Elizabethan Essays*, 30–51 and 52–80.

system—a polity consisting "of overlapping, superimposed communities which were also semi-autonomous, self-governing political cultures"—encouraged collective initiative.[5] Anne McLaren's feminist analysis, along with work on print culture by scholars including Markku Peltonen, Michael Questier, Peter Lake, and Natalie Mears, has subsequently reinforced and fleshed out this analysis. McLaren showed how early modern misogyny heightened emphasis on the role of the council and Parliament in tempering the assumed waywardness of a female sovereign.[6] This enlarged the conceptual space in which ideas of engagement in public affairs might develop, encouraging activists to see themselves as members of a masculine political community entitled to counsel and hector the queen when she failed to rule effectively. Peltonen documented the influence of classical republican ideas on discourses concerning local governance and Irish policies during the Elizabethan period, while Lake and Mears have argued for the emergence of a "post-reformation public sphere" in which print and other media spread awareness of controversial issues.[7] Lake and Questier have further stressed the continuing participation of Catholics in the public sphere, as they contested the claims of the regime and its Protestant supporters.[8] While sometimes challenging Collinson's interpretation on points of detail, this subsequent work reinforced his picture of Elizabethan England as a society with a lively and contentious public political culture, in which "citizens were concealed within subjects."[9]

The next several chapters attempt not to refute this view so much as to further complicate it. The starting point will be an examination of the central importance of dynastic authority itself, not only in disputes over title to the throne, but as a fundamental concept operating throughout society, in ways that shaped both thought and action. For all their familiarity with communal self-government, Elizabethans habitually associated legitimate power with claims based on family

---

[5] "De Republica Anglorum," 16.
[6] A. N. McLaren, *Political Culture in the Reign of Elizabeth: Queen and Commonwealth, 1558–1585* (Cambridge: Cambridge University Press, 1999).
[7] Markku Peltonen, *Classical Humanism and Republicanism in English Political Thought 1570–1640* (Cambridge: Cambridge University Press, 1995), chapter 2; Peter Lake and Michael Questier, "Puritans, Papists and the 'Public Sphere' in Early Modern England: The Edmund Campion Affair in Context," *The Journal of Early Modern History* 72 (2000): 587–627; Peter Lake and Stephen Pincus, "Rethinking the Public Sphere in Early Modern England," *Journal of British Studies* 45 (2006): 270–92; *The Politics of the Public Sphere in Early Modern England*, ed. Lake and Pincus (Manchester: Manchester University Press, 2007); Natalie Mears, *Queenship and Political Discourse in the Elizabethan Realms* (Cambridge: Cambridge University Press, 2005). Lake now prefers the term "publicity" to "the public sphere."
[8] See, esp., Peter Lake with Michael Questier, *The Antichrist's Lewd Hat: Protestants, Papists and Players in Post-Reformation England* (New Haven: Yale University Press, 2002) and Peter Lake, *Bad Queen Bess? Libels, Secret Histories, and the Politics of Publicity in the Reign of Queen Elizabeth I* (Oxford: Oxford University Press, 2016).
[9] "The Monarchical Republic of Queen Elizabeth I," 19. See, however, the cautionary note sounded by Mears, *Queenship and Political Discourse*. Collinson's concept of a monarchical republic has been both developed and critiqued in *The Monarchical Republic of Early Modern England: Essays in Response to Patrick Collinson*, ed. John F. McDiarmid (Aldershot: Ashgate, 2007).

position and lineage, and we cannot provide an adequate description of how politics worked without taking this fact into account. It would be hard to find a more representative leader of Collinson's monarchical republic and its Protestant humanist culture than William Cecil Lord Burghley. But the mural Burghley commissioned to represent England in the main gallery of his mansion of Theobalds did not represent the kingdom as a collection of overlapping self-governing parish and county communities. Instead it depicted the realm as a landscape of fields, pastures, and meandering rivers, overshadowed by fifty-two trees, from whose branches dangled the heraldic arms of the leading families of various counties; in other words, as a country sheltered and protected by armigerous lineages literally rooted in its soil.[10]

Every historian of the period is familiar with the sixteenth century's fascination with genealogy, the leading roles that noble and gentry families played in parish and county government, and the lingering importance of tenant loyalty and aristocratic patronage in local society. But the strong emphasis recent studies have placed on the humanist recovery of classical republicanism risks obscuring the continuing importance of more traditional concepts of goodlordship, personal honor, and obligations of loyalty not just to communities but also to leading families. Those concepts underpinned not only the deference accorded to individual landed dynasties in districts around their estates, but also the formation of dynastic networks, often forged and sustained across multiple generations through marriages, gift-giving, and other forms of cooperation that allowed clusters of allied families to dominate entire regions.[11] The central role of dynastic leadership in early modern society also encouraged people to associate public causes with the noble or royal figures who led them, so that conflicts over religion and other major issues sometimes assumed the appearance of quarrels between rival affinities. In 1585 an artisan was arrested for saying that "if the earl of Northumberland were at liberty he is so well loved and of such power and strength as he is able to raise up so many men as could pull the earls of Derby, Leicester and Bedford out of their houses by their ears."[12] Since Northumberland had recently been arrested for involvement in a Catholic plot, while Leicester and Bedford were leading Protestants, this almost certainly amounted to a statement of religious partisanship. But the artisan expressed it without reference to theological beliefs, as a declaration of loyalty to one great nobleman in his rivalry with others. An Elizabethan exclusion crisis developed not only because the queen refused to settle the succession, but also because by doing so she created an environment in which

---

[10] Malcolm Airs, "Pomp and Glory: The Influence of Theobalds," in *Patronage, Culture and Power: The Early Cecils*, ed. Pauline Croft, Yale Studies in British Art 8 (New Haven and London: Yale University Press, 2002), 3–21, esp. 10–11.

[11] For a study of such alliances in several midland counties see Susan Cogan, *Catholic Social Networks in Early Modern England* (Amsterdam: Amsterdam University Press, 2021).

[12] TNA SP12/178/1.

European patterns of religious conflict threatened to link up with opposing networks of kinship and friendship that penetrated deeply into provincial English society. Uncertainty over title to the crown thereby acquired the potential to generate a dynastic and political crisis several layers deep, extending from the international arena down to conflicts at the county and parish level.

Historical and European Contexts of the Match

Henry VIII had sown the seeds of that crisis in the 1530s, when, motivated by his anxiety to produce a male heir, he shook off his kingdom's allegiance to Rome in order to divorce his wife, Katherine of Aragon, and marry Anne Boleyn. Since the Catholic Church never recognized the divorce, the legitimacy of Anne's daughter, Elizabeth, remained questionable. The problem of dynastic insecurity diminished somewhat when Henry's third wife, Jane Seymour, finally gave birth to the coveted male heir, the future Edward VI. Because Katherine had died before his birth, his legitimacy was not in question. But Edward's premature death in 1553 led to a brief crisis as the privy council and its leader, John Dudley duke of Northumberland, tried to divert the succession from Katherine of Aragon's Catholic daughter, Mary Tudor, to a Protestant granddaughter of Henry VII, Jane Gray, who had recently married Northumberland's youngest surviving son. Elizabeth was another intended victim of this coup. In the reign of Queen Jane, she would not only have lost her own claim to the throne but would almost certainly have lived under a cloud of suspicion as a dynastic rival to the monarch, possibly endangering her life.

While we have no direct evidence about how this episode shaped Elizabeth's views of religion and religious politics, she would have had every reason to feel betrayed by Edward's councilors and to have drawn the lesson that she needed to mistrust not only Catholic but also Protestant politicians. Since Northumberland's coup quickly collapsed, the main threat to her safety soon came from her Catholic half-sister, who imprisoned her in the Tower on suspicions of involvement in treasonous plots. Elizabeth survived and mounted the throne after Mary's death without serious opposition, in part because she had the support of the late queen's husband, Philip II of Spain. Philip preferred to overlook her illegitimacy in the eyes of the Catholic Church, along with the possibility that she might again withdraw England from its allegiance to Rome, because the next heir, Mary Stuart queen of Scotland, had married the eldest son of his principal enemy, the king of France. But Mary, with the support of the French crown and her powerful uncle, the duke of Guise, wasted little time in implying that she, rather than Elizabeth, was the rightful queen of England.

By the time of her accession, Elizabeth had therefore already survived a series of potentially lethal disputes with both dynastic and religious dimensions.

Her experiences must have taught her that while dynastic calculations and confessional antagonisms both played central roles in politics, neither operated in altogether straightforward ways. Siblings and co-religionists might become adversaries and near strangers of a rival faith allies, as their own interests dictated. This may help explain her reluctance to marry, since by entertaining multiple suitors while choosing none she kept her options open, allowing her to explore alliances with different dynastic blocs, while she avoided provoking her own Protestant or Catholic subjects by selecting a consort of the rival faith. But her delays increased the risk that she would die without a direct heir, triggering an even more serious crisis than that of 1553. This possibility tempted both foreign princes and her own subjects to take out insurance against the future, by assisting her most plausible heir, Mary Stuart, or alternatively by maneuvering to establish some other rival candidate.

In the late 1570s the queen was fast approaching an age at which she could no longer produce a child. The appearance at this juncture of a serious foreign Catholic suitor, François de Valois duke of Anjou, the younger brother of the king of France, served to crystallize a number of issues relating not only to the succession but also the kingdom's potentially vulnerable position within a Europe dominated by Catholic monarchies.[13] To some, the Anjou match offered a way of resolving those difficulties at a stroke, by giving Elizabeth a husband, an heir, a continental ally, and an opportunity to conciliate powerful but disaffected English families with Catholic sympathies. To others it threatened to subvert the kingdom by erecting a foreign Catholic faction at the epicenter of the polity. Arguments over the Anjou match therefore drew together several wider issues, focusing them with particular intensity.

The nature of foreign Catholic threats to the regime had altered significantly since Elizabeth's accession in 1558. During her early reign the primary menace had come from France and its dynastic satellite Scotland, embodied in the triple dynastic alliance of Mary Stuart, the French royal family, and the staunchly Catholic Guise relatives of Mary's mother. An English-backed Protestant rebellion in Scotland in 1560, the death of Mary's first husband, Francis II, intermittent civil war in France, the collapse of Mary's authority in Scotland and her flight to England in 1567, had combined to alleviate this threat.[14] Although the prospects of a revival of French power continued to worry the English council, for the moment the dangers from that quarter had lessened. But Spain, which had been

[13] Technically this was a reappearance, since he had courted the queen before while he was still duc d'Alençon. He inherited the Anjou title when his brother, who had previously possessed it, mounted the throne as Henry III in 1574. The best survey of Elizabeth's matrimonial diplomacy remains Susan Doran, *Monarchy and Matrimony: The Courtships of Elizabeth I* (London: Routledge, 1996).
[14] Michael Questier, *Dynastic Politics and the British Reformations, 1558-1630* (Oxford: Oxford University Press, 2019), chapter 1, makes a convincing case for the seriousness of the dynastic threat posed by Mary before 1567, and to a degree thereafter. Older accounts include Wallace MacCaffrey, *The Shaping of the Elizabethan Regime* (Princeton: Princeton University Press, 1967), parts 1-3.

relatively supportive of England in the early 1560s, began to look increasingly like an adversary. Following the great victory against the Ottoman fleet at Lepanto in 1572, Philip II redirected his attention and resources away from the Mediterranean, toward the struggle against heresy in the Netherlands and northern Europe. Within a few years the Dutch revolt, which had revived in the year of Lepanto, began to founder, as advances by the Spanish army, under its aggressive commander Don John, accentuated bickering between Catholic and Protestant factions in the rebellious provinces. The Spanish capture of the strategic citadel of Namur in July 1577 and Don John's decisive defeat of the States' army the following January led the Dutch to appeal urgently for French and English help. In March the queen's ambassador to the Dutch rebels, William Davison, strongly urged her to send substantial aid before resistance collapsed. "To cast them off cannot, in my poor judgment, but bring forth a general astonishment in the people, an alteration in the nobility... an advancement of the affairs and hopes of the enemy," without in any way diminishing "the hatred of Spain" toward England. Instead of avoiding war, inaction would only postpone it until "these countries" and "all such as make profession of the Reformed Religion in general" were ruined.[15] The English had learned that Don John aspired to replace Elizabeth on her throne and had obtained papal backing for the project and the provisional support of Philip II, once the Dutch provinces had been conquered.[16] According to Philip's ambassador in London, Don Bernardino de Mendoza, Francis Walsingham and the earl of Leicester took such alarm at the Spanish advances that they sent men to assassinate Don John, whom the Spanish intercepted and executed.[17] Both wanted Elizabeth to send military assistance to the Dutch, although Walsingham realized it would be folly to do so without first winning approval and a substantial grant of supply from Parliament.[18]

Although to varying degrees, the leaders of English Protestantism regarded their own church as part of a larger community of godly communities throughout Europe, with a religious duty to support each other.[19] Failure to assist co-religionists risked inciting God's wrath. But they also knew that Protestants in the Netherlands, Scotland, and France provided buffers protecting England against foreign aggression. The queen had already given enough assistance to

---

[15] Hatton, 47.
[16] Geoffrey Parker, *Imprudent King: A New Life of Philip II* (New Haven: Yale University Press, 2014), 230–1, 238–44.
[17] *CSPSp* 2.583–4, 628. [18] TNA SP12/133/23.
[19] The older view of William Haller, *Foxe's Book of Martyrs and the Elect Nation* (London: Jonathan Cape, 1963), that the English saw themselves as a nation particularly favored by God has been discredited, at least for the sixteenth century. See Richard Bauckham, *Tudor Apocalypse* (Oxford: Sutton Courtney, 1978) and Katherine Firth, *The Apocalyptic Tradition in Reformation Britain* (Oxford: Oxford University Press, 1979), esp. 106–10. See also the argument in Adams, "Protestant Cause," chapter 1 and passim, for an argument that an equation of Catholicism with the cause of Antichrist and consequent sense of solidarity with European reformed churches defined a durable "puritan" outlook on European affairs from the 1570s down to about 1630.

rebels against the kings of France and Spain to provide both with reasons to seek revenge; if France and Spain had not attacked already it was widely assumed that this was because Protestant rebellions kept them too preoccupied to do so. But the fact that England had remained at peace, while French and especially Spanish troops fought prolonged wars, gave these kingdoms a decisive edge in veteran soldiers and seasoned officers, should a war erupt. The queen's council sought to diminish the disadvantage by underhandedly encouraging English volunteers to enlist in Dutch and Huguenot campaigns.[20] But the numbers who did so remained too small to provide more than the nucleus for a national army and Davison therefore hoped to persuade the Dutch to pay for a larger English force.[21] In January 1578 Elizabeth agreed to send an English army of 5,000 foot and 1,000 horse to the Low Countries, which Leicester wanted to lead. A rumor that he was about to do so reached Antwerp in February.[22] But the queen soon had second thoughts and decided instead on the more indirect course of subsidizing prince Johann Casimir of the Palatinate to levy an army to support the Dutch.

A Spanish victory in the Low Countries would have given the best army in Europe control of a base immediately across the North Sea. It would also have left that army idle, consuming Habsburg resources and burdening Habsburg territories with its presence, unless Philip II decided to use it elsewhere, quite possibly against Elizabeth's dominions.[23] Because its Catholic population would likely support an invading force, Ireland remained vulnerable to small incursions even while the Dutch wars lasted. The queen became "very much alarmed," Mendoza reported, when news arrived in the spring of 1578 that the English adventurer and traitor, Thomas Stukeley, had left Tuscany "with six hundred men in a galleon" bound for Ireland. "This alarm has been increased by her being told that his leaving Rome with these forces could only have been with the consent of your Majesty [Philip II]. She has made great preparations all over the country, both to raise men and to reinforce the guards in the ports, as well as ordering the equipment of a large number of ships."[24] Fortunately Stukeley went instead to North Africa, where he died in a Portuguese campaign against the Moors. But the

---

[20] David Trim, "The 'Secret War' of Elizabeth I: England and the Huguenots during the Early Wars of Religion, 1562-1577," *Proceedings of the Huguenot Society of Great Britain and Ireland* 27 (1999): 189-99 and "Fighting 'Jacob's Wars': The Employment of English and Welsh Mercenaries in the European Wars of Religion: France and the Netherlands, 1562-1610," unpublished University of London PhD thesis, 2002, 94-150 and passim. I wish to thank David Trim for many discussions of this and other topics related to Elizabethan military history.

[21] Hatton, 48.

[22] *The Correspondence of Philip Sidney and Hubert Languet*, ed. William Aspenwall Bradley (Boston: Merrymount Press, 1912), 153. Trim, "'Fighting Jacob's Wars'," 140-5 traces the shifts in English policy toward war in the Netherlands in this period.

[23] As Sir Philip Sidney's mentor Hubert Languet pointed out, Spanish troops had grown "accustomed to the sweets of plunder," demonstrating a capacity to loot not just the enemy but friendly civilian populations. If only to spare his own subjects, he predicted, the king of Spain would therefore invade England, *Correspondence of Philip Sidney and Hubert Languet*, 117.

[24] *CSPSp* 2.561-2.

following summer another force of about 600 foreign troops in the pay of the papacy, led by the Irish expatriate James Fitzmaurice, landed in Munster and triggered a rebellion.

Spanish hostility seemed the more worrying because other developments had lately increased Philip II's already formidable resources. The extinction of the ruling Portuguese dynasty in 1579 allowed him to claim Portugal, along with its Asian and African empires and impressive Atlantic fleet. As Richard Topcliffe the priest-hunter remarked, Philip possessed both the East and West Indies, so that "he might (as with his arms) embrace and crush the world; therefore it behoveth his equals to lame him of one of those arms."[25] European trade with the rest of the globe was to a very large degree concentrated in the two great Iberian entrepôts of Lisbon and Seville, while additional commerce with Asia through the Levant had to pass through the Mediterranean, with its choke-point at the Straits of Gibraltar. If Philip regained Antwerp, the main entrepôt of North European commerce in the mid-sixteenth century, he would be in a position to achieve hegemonic control over international commerce, including England's vital cloth trade. That would allow him to blackmail or destabilize the English crown by his ability to cause major economic disruptions in ports and cloth weaving districts.

The French government also appreciated the danger of growing Spanish power and joined Elizabeth in supporting a rival candidate, Dom Antonio, for the Portuguese throne.[26] But a crushing Spanish victory over a predominantly French fleet in the Azores, along with the occupation of Portugal by Philip's army, effectively ended Antonio's hopes. In the same period technological innovations revitalized the mines of Potosi, in modern Bolivia, providing the Spanish crown with annual shipments of silver whose value normally exceeded Elizabeth's entire budget, often by a substantial margin.[27] Modern calculations suggest that total Spanish government resources exceeded those of the English crown by a ratio of more than ten to one. Although contemporaries had only a very imprecise knowledge of these figures, they knew that the king of Spain had far more money to spend on ships and soldiers than Elizabeth, and that his advantage had recently increased.[28]

The growth of Spanish power provided incentives for the English and French to cooperate in the Netherlands. The possibility of an alliance in support of the Dutch had been on the agenda intermittently since 1572. But the prospect of an expansion of French power into the Low Countries seemed in many ways even

---

[25] Lodge, *Illustrations*, 2.225.

[26] Mendoza reported in May of 1579 that a Portuguese representative had met for seven hours with the council over the affairs of his country. See *CDIHE Felipe II*, 382.

[27] Production at Potosi rose by a factor of seven between 1572 and 1585 after the introduction of the silver amalgamation process for extracting ore (Henry Kamen, *Empire: How Spain Became a World Power 1492–1763* [New York: HarperCollins, 2003], 286).

[28] For a modern estimate of Philip's income in the 1570s see Bartolomé Yun, *Marte contra Minerva: El Precio del Imperio Español* (Barcelona: Crítica, 2004), 541, Table 8.4.

more alarming than a Spanish victory. France, rather than Spain, was England's ancient enemy. The St. Bartholomew's Day massacres in August 1572 had graphically shown that France remained a predominantly Catholic kingdom, where violent hatred of Protestantism flourished with the active encouragement of powerful nobles and the collusion of the ruling dynasty. The English still tended to perceive the Low Countries as the medieval dominion of Burgundy, whose enmity with France had for centuries preserved a balance of power in northwest Europe, protecting England's security and facilitating its conquests in France.[29] Although any hostile regime in the Low Countries posed a significant threat, the incorporation of the ancient Burgundian lands into a resurgent France would present a strategic nightmare of colossal proportions. Despite the marriage negotiations with Anjou, Elizabeth and her council grew alarmed when they learned that the Estates General of the Netherlands had considered naming him their sovereign, since this threatened to place Dutch and Flemish ports under French control, tipping the balance in sea power and commerce against England.[30] Elizabeth's senior secretary of state, Thomas Wilson, described the French as both "ancient enemies" and "mighty and dangerous neighbors, who being not our friends will become our foes."[31]

Memories of the Auld Alliance between France and Scotland, and the Guise family's dynastic ties to the Stuarts, made French expansion into the Low Countries even more alarming.[32] Reports that the duke of Guise and his French Catholic following might soon enter the Dutch war on the Spanish side set off additional alarm bells in London.[33] Guise influence had declined at the French court in the late 1570s, while a pro-English regime under the earl of Morton ruled in Edinburgh. But Morton's grip on power briefly collapsed in 1578 and never fully recovered, and worries about a revival of French Catholic influence in Scotland intensified the following year, as James fell under the influence of his French cousin Esmé Stuart *seigneur* d'Aubigny. The Scottish regent had reached out to Elizabeth with an offer of alliance in June 1578 but, to the consternation of councilors like Walsingham and Hatton, she declined it because she did not wish to extend formal recognition to the regime that had deposed Mary.[34] Walsingham thought these scruples more "superstitious than religious." "The Scot is a proud nation," he warned, "if you refuse his friendship when he offereth it, you shall miss it when you would have it: and therefore it greatly importeth her Majesty to look substantially to the matter; for to my judgment it toucheth her as nearly as the

---

[29] See, for example, the comments of the earl of Sussex to Lord Burghley in Lodge, *Illustrations*, 2.88.
[30] *CSPF 1579–80*, 343–7.   [31] TNA SP12/123/17.
[32] Mary was a Guise on her mother's side and had been brought up under the tutelage of her Guise relatives in Paris.
[33] This is a theme of Poulet's dispatches from Paris, particularly in the spring of 1578 in TNA SP78/3/15.
[34] *CSPSc* 5.300.

conservation of the Crown amounteth unto."³⁵ Secretary Wilson thought Scottish poverty compounded the danger: "That young king [James VI]...being not cherished by our most gracious sovereign, must of necessity be forced to seek relief of some other weighty prince, for that he is not able to live of himself, nor his nobility either, who to make their own profit and gain the more, it is to be feared, will seek the support of some foreign prince, either France or Spain. And then what will happen to us by the way of Scotland is to judge by the actions of former ages."³⁶

In April of 1579 Walsingham received intelligence that a dissident group of Scottish nobles had urged James to rely on the French crown rather than Elizabeth.³⁷ Ominous reports circulated the same month of a French fleet assembling for possible intervention in Scotland. Mary anticipated a change in Scottish affairs to her own advantage, while Mendoza and the Scottish queen's agent, John Leslie bishop of Ross, encouraged Philip II to take an interest in Scotland.³⁸ A rebellion against Morton was narrowly forestalled in the summer of 1579, partly through the initiative of Lord Hunsdon, the governor of the garrison at Berwick, who threatened to burn and pillage the estates of Scottish lords adjacent to the English border if they did not submit to Elizabeth's arbitration.³⁹ But although the immediate crisis subsided, the long-term danger remained.⁴⁰ In January, Mendoza reported Elizabeth's anxiety over rumored efforts by Catherine de Médicis to arrange a marriage between the king of Scots and a daughter of the Guise duke of Lorraine. He attempted to drive a wedge between England and France by playing on the queen's fears, warning her that "the greed of Morton and the Scots in general was such as would prompt them to open their arms to anyone, let alone the French, with whom they had such ancient alliances... She pricked up her ears at this and said I was speaking the truth."⁴¹

These developments threatened Elizabeth not only due to Scotland's land border with England but also because so long as she remained childless Mary and James looked like the natural leaders of an English reversionary interest. Knowing this the queen remained acutely suspicious that her own subjects, including seemingly loyal Protestants, might betray her to a Stuart rival, as she believed the duke of Norfolk had done ten years previously by agreeing to marry Mary. The Scottish queen's keeper, the earl of Shrewsbury, lived in constant dread of Elizabeth's jealousy, while at certain moments even Burghley chafed under her suspicions.⁴² Natalie Mears has rightly argued that so long as the issue of the

---

³⁵ Hatton, 66–7, letter dated June 27, 1578.   ³⁶ TNA SP12/123/17.
³⁷ *CSPSc* 5.286; cf. Natalie Mears, "Love-Making and Diplomacy: Elizabeth I and the Anjou Marriage Negotiations," *History* 86 (2001): 442–66 at 460.
³⁸ *CSPSc* 5.285, 288–9, 297; *CDIHE Felipe II*, 91.   ³⁹ *CSPSc* 5.317.
⁴⁰ See the comments of Robert Bowes to the Earl of Leicester on 23 July, ibid., p. 306 paraphrasing BL Cotton Mss. Caligula CIII, fol. 559.
⁴¹ *CSPSp* 2.634.   ⁴² Lodge, *Illustrations*, 2.37–8, 54–5.

succession remained paramount, Scotland and its unmarried king represented an even greater threat to England than Spanish control of the Low Countries.[43] But the two threats were never entirely separable, since Spanish victory in the Netherlands would increase Philip II's opportunities to intervene in Scotland, or in support of any English faction James or Mary managed to attract. This is what made d'Aubigny's rise to favor in Edinburgh so ominous—and so interesting to Elizabeth's Catholic adversaries.

Suspicions that the papacy and the Continent's major Catholic dynasties had entered into a conspiracy to destroy England magnified these worries. Having burgeoned after the St. Bartholomew's Day massacres, these fears never entirely subsided, either in the queen's own mind or among her councilors. Mendoza reported Elizabeth's alarm in March of 1578 after hearing of a meeting between Anjou and the duke of Guise. She told him and the French ambassador, Mauvissière, in separate interviews that she believed their masters had entered into a league to destroy her, which "even some Englishmen" would happily join.[44] She repeated a similar accusation the following January, when Mendoza tried to excite her jealousy of French meddling in Scotland, stating that she knew that the pope had promoted a league against her and that Alba had already reconnoitered the English coast ten years before, to prepare for a future landing in support of a Catholic rebellion.[45] Although she may have made these statements to keep Mendoza and Mauvissière on the defensive, Elizabeth plainly took the threat seriously. She and her councilors knew that they had to worry not just about the Netherlands war, but also the instability of Scottish politics, rebellion in Ireland, domestic recusancy, and the prospect that if any one of these problems worsened it might trigger a chain reaction of adverse events, engulfing the regime in crisis.

English Catholicism and Landed Dynasties

The continuing attachment to Catholicism of many of England's great landed families compounded the government's worries. After the Northern Rebellion of 1569, Elizabeth had broken the regional power of the Percies, Nevilles, and Dacres in the North and weakened the duke of Norfolk's affinity in East Anglia.[46] But remnants of those lords' affinities survived and in some districts continued to wield substantial power.[47] It was by no means certain that the followings of the

---

[43] Mears, "Love-Making and Diplomacy," esp. 450.   [44] *CSPSp* 2.570–1.   [45] Ibid., 632.
[46] See especially A. Hassell-Smith, *County and Court: Government and Politics in Norfolk, 1558–1603* (Oxford: Oxford University Press, 1974).
[47] For these affinities in East Anglia see ibid. and Diarmaid MacCulloch, *Suffolk and the Tudors: Politics and Religion in an English County, 1500–1600* (Oxford: Oxford University Press, 1984) and the discussion below, p. 57. For the remnants of the Neville affinity in the North see Michael Questier,

great northern lords were incapable of revival, especially if defeated nobles who had escaped into exile received backing from the queen's foreign adversaries. Connections forged in exile with Catholic peers in Scotland, Mary Stuart's agents in Paris, and the duke of Guise made this a distinct possibility.[48] As he canvassed schemes to place his niece on the English throne, Guise calculated that he could raise an army of 20,000 horsemen from among the followers of Catholic peers of the North, with Baron Fenhurst alone supplying 4,000 and the earls of Cumberland and Lord Dacre 3,000 each.[49] The exiled earl of Westmoreland, who had entered Spanish service, also figured prominently in his plans.[50] "Westmoreland and other English nobles and gentlemen of the land shall come secretly into the realm and remain in private houses until the army entereth, and then they shall join with the army, which shall come out of Spain."[51] Although Guise was perhaps overly optimistic, the belief that Catholic landowners might mobilize significant bodies of followers seemed plausible, and not only in the North. The council also worried about Sussex, a county boasting five noble families—"more than one shire can well bear"—four of them Catholic or Church papist, in which most of the greater gentry were also "ill affected." The dependence of "weak" lesser gentry on these leading families, a paucity of independent freeholders and the shallow penetration of Protestantism in the county were seen as compounding the security threat that Catholic dynasties represented.[52] Michael Questier has reconstructed one of these Sussex networks, linking the Wriothesley earls of Southampton, the Browne family of Viscount Montague and other local dynasties.[53] In Northamptonshire Catholicism enjoyed the support of Lord Vaux and his neighbor Sir Thomas Tresham, who were both imprisoned for giving hospitality to the Jesuit Edmund Campion in 1581. Vaux had links to leading Catholic families in Leicestershire, while his younger brother, Henry, became active in a national network based in London, dedicated to sheltering priests and coordinating Catholic activities.[54]

The midland county of Warwickshire provides a somewhat different but related picture, painstakingly recovered through the research of Cathryn Enis and

---

"Practical Antipapistry during the Reign of Elizabeth I," *Journal of British Studies* 36 (1997): 371–96, esp. 381–5 and, for a later period, "The Politics of Religious Conformity and the Accession of James I," *Historical Research* 71 (2002): 14–30.

[48] Questier, "Practical Antipapistry," 375–7; Katy Gibbons, *English Catholic Exiles in Late Sixteenth-Century Paris* (Woodbridge: Boydell Press, 2011), 21–2.

[49] *CSPSp* 3.504.   [50] See, e.g., TNA SP12/147/2 and 153/79.

[51] TNA SP12/153/79, summary of an Italian discourse about a planned invasion of England carried by a captured Scottish Jesuit (presumably William Creighton). SP12/173/4 is a second copy.

[52] TNA SP12/165/22.

[53] *Catholicism and Community in Early Modern England* (Cambridge: Cambridge University Press, 2006).

[54] Jessie Childs, *God's Traitors: Terror and Faith in Elizabethan England* (Oxford: Oxford University Press, 2014); Cogan, *Catholic Social Networks*, esp. chapters 3 and 5.

Glyn Parry.[55] Here the affinities of the brothers Ambrose and Robert Dudley, whom Elizabeth had created earls of Warwick and Leicester, eclipsed a gentry network headed by the mostly Catholic Throckmorton family that had previously dominated the county. The Dudleys were essentially upstarts who had risen through the careers of one of Henry VII's notorious new men, Edmund Dudley, and his son John, who dominated the council of Edward VI after 1549. Both had died on the scaffold as convicted traitors, as had John's son, Guildford. But Elizabeth rehabilitated his younger sons, Robert and Ambrose. The Dudley brothers disguised their parvenu status by claiming descent from the Beauchamp earls of Warwick of the late thirteenth and early fourteenth centuries, and through them even more ancient Warwick luminaries going back to the legendary Guy of Warwick in the Saxon period. They adopted the Beauchamp emblem of the bear and ragged staff, purchased manors that had once formed part of the medieval earldom of Warwick, and retained heralds to validate their genealogical claims. Ambrose occupied the Beauchamp seat of Warwick Castle, while his brother established himself nearby in the even more splendid Kenilworth, which had once belonged to John of Gaunt.

But a Catholic member of the Throckmorton network named Robert Arden also engaged heralds, as well as a local antiquarian, in efforts to puncture the Dudleys' claims.[56] Warwickshire politics came to involve a toxic mix of personal and dynastic rivalries, confessional antagonism and contested genealogical claims that Enis describes as elements in a "prevailing ideology of power."[57] The local struggle became linked to the wider politics of the court and kingdom not only because Leicester's rivals at court, notably Thomas Radcliffe earl of Sussex, also questioned his genealogical pretensions, but through the support that Sir Christopher Hatton extended to the Throckmorton network.[58] Among other favors, Hatton procured an appointment as gentleman pensioner at court for William Tresham, younger brother to the ardently Catholic Sir Thomas Tresham, a Throckmorton ally.[59] Leicester and his allies pursued his Warwickshire adversaries with particular vindictiveness. In 1583 Edward Arden was executed for treason on the basis of his association with a kinsman who had made threats

---

[55] Cathryn Enis, "Edward Arden and the Dudley Earls of Warwick and Leicester, c. 1572–1583," *British Catholic History* 33 (2016): 170–210; Cathryn Enis, "The Dudleys, Sir Christopher Hatton and the Justices of Elizabethan Warwickshire," *Midland History* 39 (2014): 1–35; Glyn Parry, "Catholicism and Tyranny in Shakespeare's Warwickshire," in *The Oxford Handbook of the Age of Shakespeare*, ed. R. Malcolm Smuts (Oxford: Oxford University Press, 2016), 121–38; Glyn Parry and Cathryn Enis, *Shakespeare before Shakespeare: Stratford-upon-Avon, Warwickshire & the Elizabethan State* (Oxford: Oxford University Press, 2020); Simon Adams, "'Because I am of that Countrye & Mynde to Plant Myself there': Robert Dudley, Earl of Leicester, and the West Midlands," *Midlands History* 20 (1995): 20–75, reprinted in Simon Adams, *Leicester and the Court: Essays on Elizabethan Politics* (Manchester: Manchester University Press, 2002), 310–73.
[56] Enis, "Edward Arden," 182–4. [57] Ibid., 172. [58] Enis, "Dudleys."
[59] William Tighe, "Five Elizabethan Courtiers, Their Catholic Connections and Their Careers," *British Catholic History* 33 (2016): 211–27.

against Elizabeth, but who also appears to have been demonstrably insane, after a trial that Leicester and his court allies manipulated.[60]

To be sure, religious differences and family alliances did not always coincide as neatly as in these examples. Many families had divided religious allegiances, including even the Throckmortons, who gave their name to a famous plot against Elizabeth's life but who also produced the fervent puritan Job Throckmorton. Most Catholic gentry had Protestant friends in their county and often at court, who shielded them from active prosecution. The confessional allegiances of some landowners remained ambiguous: historians remain unsure of the precise religious views of courtiers like Sir Christopher Hatton, Sir James Croft, and Sir Thomas Sackville baron Buckhurst, and peers such as the earls of Shrewsbury, Derby, and Worcester.[61] Although certainly not forward Protestants, whether they were secret Catholics, conservative conformists, Erastians who put loyalty to their prince ahead of ecclesiastical considerations, or simply men willing to adjust their religion to political circumstances remains unclear.

But networks of noble and gentry families sympathetic to the old religion certainly played a critical role in sustaining English Catholicism, not only as a religion but also as a political force with the potential to reassert itself under the right circumstances, just as the support of landed dynasties like the Russells, Greys, and Dudleys facilitated the spread of Protestant and puritan beliefs.[62] Impropriated benefices gave landed families the ability to influence the religious complexion of entire districts.[63] In Norfolk and Suffolk quarrels over the vetting of clergy nominated by impropriators figured prominently in factional struggles for control of the counties.[64] Local puritans accused the Catholic Sir Thomas Cornwallis of appointing papists to benefices in his possession, probably justifiably, since one of his appointees celebrated mass in Cornwallis's private chapel.[65] Even after the council began purging county magistracies of open Catholics in the 1570s there remained enclaves, like parts of Lancashire or the half-hundred of Lothingland in Suffolk, dominated by networks of conservative gentry, who created safe havens for recusancy, while actively inhibiting Protestant preaching.[66] Elsewhere puritan patrons created pockets of radical Protestantism by appointing effective preachers to impropriated benefices.

---

[60] Parry, "Catholicism and Tyranny"; Parry and Enis, *Shakespeare before Shakespeare*, chapter 4.

[61] For the courtiers see Neil Younger, "How Protestant was the Elizabethan Regime?" *English Historical Review* 133 (2018): 1060–92.

[62] Questier, *Catholicism and Community*. Cf. the reconstruction of the network of partisans of the Jesuit Edmund Campion, stretching into the royal court, in Gerard Kilroy, *Edmund Campion: Memory and Transcription* (Aldershot: Ashgate, 2005).

[63] For the relative stability of the upper levels of gentry society after the mid-sixteenth century see Lawrence Stone, *An Open Elite?* (Oxford: Oxford University Press, 1984).

[64] Hassell-Smith, *Norfolk*; MacCulloch, *Suffolk*.   [65] Gibbons, *Catholic Exiles*, 27.

[66] For Lothingland see Diarmaid MacCulloch, "Catholic and Puritan in Elizabethan Suffolk: A Community Polarises," *Archiv für Reformationsgeschichte* 72 (1981): 232–89, at 241–7.

The private religious beliefs of individual gentlemen in and of themselves posed little danger to the state. But networks of influential Catholic families, cemented by bonds of kinship and friendship as well as religion, were another matter, especially if they became connected to foreign enemies of the queen. The sharpening of European religious polarities across western Europe in the 1560s and 1570s, as the Counter-Reformation gained momentum and wars of religion broke out in France, Scotland and the Low Countries, underlined the danger. So did the departure for continental exile of significant numbers of Catholic gentry and intellectuals, a subject that the next chapter will more fully discuss. A list of English papists residing in Paris in 1580 gives the names of 184 gentlemen, including 40 from "Yorkshire and the north parts," plus 16 doctors, 10 civil lawyers, and 109 students of gentry rank.[67] Other European cities received similar, if smaller communities. In Rome, English civil lawyers, gentlemen, and priests lived as pensioners of the pope.[68] A particularly active clerical exile from Lancashire, William Allen, founded a seminary for training missionary priests, initially in Douay in the Low Countries, whose graduates began arriving in England in 1574. In 1578 the duke of Guise accepted Allen as a client and helped him resettle his seminary in Rouen, after its expulsion from the Netherlands by Dutch Protestants.[69] Through Guise's patronage Allen established relations with other figures who soon emerged as leaders of the Catholic League in Normandy.[70] This makes it plausible to see a fairly direct connection between the growth of organized Catholic militancy in France and Allen's efforts to create a similar movement in Britain. Elizabeth's ambassador in Paris, Sir Henry Cobham, thought so at the time, commenting that "in all the provinces of France there are particular Catholic leagues and certain brotherhoods, which they say is somewhat offered to be framed in England, and to that intent there be diverse hallowed small crosses and medals which are to be worn secretly."[71] In 1579 Allen founded a second English seminary in Rome.

The diary of a spy, Charles Sledd, who infiltrated this institution during the summer, describes feverish talk about schemes to overthrow Elizabeth.[72] He arrived to find his fellow expatriates engaged in fervent discussions of Anjou's

---

[67] TNA SP78/4A/63.   [68] BL Add Mss. 48029, fol. 123v gives a list.
[69] Thomas Francis Knox, *First and Second Diaries of the English College of Douay* (Londo: Sagwan Press, 1977), 139; Stuart Carroll, *Noble Power during the French Wars of Religion: The Guise Affinity and the Catholic Cause in Normandy* (Cambridge: Cambridge University Press, 1998), 176; F. Fabre, "The English College at Eu, 1582–1592," *Catholic Historical Review* 37 (1951): 257–80.
[70] Knox, *College of Douay*, 139; John Bossy, "The Heart of Robert Persons," in *The Reckoned Expense: Edmund Campion and the Early English Jesuits: Essays in Celebration of the First Centenary of Campion Hall, Oxford*, ed. Thomas McCoog (Woodbridge: Boydell Press, 1996), 141–58 at 144.
[71] TNA SP78/4A/22, printed in *CSPF 1579–80*, 29.
[72] BL Add Mss. 48029, fols 128-142v; for a printed edition see Catholic Record Society vol. 53, *Miscellanea Recusant Records*, ed. Claire Talbot (1961), 193–245. Sledd's activities are discussed in Stephen Alford, *The Watchers: A Secret History of the Reign of Elizabeth* (London: Allen Lane, 2012), 69–91 and 113–16.

pursuit of the queen and what it might portend for English Catholics. But they also talked about the recent success of "Sir James Fitzmaurice and Dr. Sander at their being at Rome," in convincing the pope to back projects for challenging the Elizabethan regime in both Ireland and England. Their "persuasions hath taken such deep root and stuck so in the Pope's mind that he promised them to send a power into both the said islands and this is the year that he appointed to do the said business and thereupon sent his legate with Sir James Fitzmaurice and Dr. [Nicholas] Sander into Spain to persuade the King of Spain to be an aider also and to the Emperor, Venetians and Florence."[73] Fitzmaurice and Sander recruited about sixty Italian mercenaries and landed with them at Smerwick in southwestern Ireland in July. By early autumn their exploit had become the talk of the English college, giving rise to exaggerated reports of their progress in driving the English from Ireland. Every man "rejoiced at the Pope's doings and not long after there came news by a messenger from the Pope that all his English pensioners should be ready at two days warning to go on his service."[74]

In November, Allen came to Rome to meet with the pope and coordinate plans for additional challenges to Elizabeth. In a sermon he

> thundered out in speech the arrival of D. Sander in Ireland and Sir James Fitzmorris with 500 Spaniards sent thither by the King of Spain and showed moreover that the Pope and other princes were minded for to aid the said king of Spain and so to send men for Ireland and England from time to time as they could conveniently. He also showed them that it was the Pope's pleasure to send some priests into England for to let the people understand what his holiness was minded to do in those parts ere many months should pass, and that they should not think but the Pope had a care of them being a parcel of his charge. For the sending of these priests every man was willing to further it, so that ... there were diverse appointed to the number of six.[75]

The exiles confidently expected to see a conspiracy against Elizabeth, whom they sarcastically called "the honest woman," begin to unfold within a few months. Allen produced a list of ten peers and several prominent gentlemen—including Lord Henry Howard and the earls of Southampton, Derby, and Northumberland—who allegedly had signed an agreement with the pope and king of Spain to work for a Catholic victory in England.[76] He discussed the color of the beads that would be sent as secret tokens to identify Catholic supporters, and in February he and the pope consecrated a large mass of beads, crucifixes, and other holy tokens for distribution by missionary priests.[77]

---

[73] BL Add Mss. 48029, fol. 133v.   [74] Ibid., fol. 134.   [75] Ibid., fol. 135.
[76] Ibid., fols 136r, 137r.   [77] Ibid., fols 137, 138v.

Rather than moving openly against the English heretics, the exiles believed, the pope and Spain should subvert the regime by more underhanded methods:

> for the king of Spain will not break the league between the queen's majesty himself but will lend men and furniture to the Pope and the Pope's holiness is minded to send some of his English branches as secretly into England as the queen hath into other countries, who shall be more near to her than her grace is aware. They shall also deal so secretly with most of the best nobles and worshipful gentlemen who shall keep in her favor until the very uttermost time, so that when her grace shall think them her trusty subjects they shall [be] as clean against her. In the mean season the nobles and as many gentlemen as please shall be dispensed withal and shall go to church and be sworn to the supremacy as often as the oath shall be ministered but their ladies... shall have mass daily.[78]

Although we always need to treat the uncorroborated testimony of spies with caution, the amount of circumstantial detail in Sledd's diary and the fact that other evidence corroborates several of his assertions encourages confidence in his essential accuracy.[79] Mendoza's correspondence shows that he did discuss schemes to infiltrate and overthrow the Elizabethan state with Lord Henry Howard and other Catholics.[80] Allen's seminary priests had begun arriving in England in greater numbers in 1579, carrying dispensations permitting Catholic landowners to attend Protestant services until such time as a concerted effort to overthrow the Protestant settlement became feasible, in much the way the Roman rumor mill reported. A few of the peers and gentry on Allen's purported list later did become involved in Catholic plots.[81] The papacy supported Fitzmaurice's expedition and Nicholas Sander went to Ireland, where he actively encouraged rebellion, in part by spreading reports that English Catholics would soon rise against Elizabeth and that Spain was preparing to invade the island.[82] He warned an Irish lord in September 1579 to join the Munster rebellion quickly, for "when our aid is come, which daily we look for when the Scottish and English nobility be in arms (as we doubt not they will be shortly) and when strangers begin to invade England itself (as diverse of the English nobility labor and procure), afterward I say it shall be small thanks before God and man to be of our company."[83] Sander, Allen, and their fellow exiles unquestionably underestimated the difficulty of

---

[78] Ibid., fol. 138v.
[79] Alford, *The Watchers*, 75 reaches a similar conclusion. Allen disparaged the accuracy of Sledd's report but he of course had strong motives for doing so.
[80] *CSPSp* 3.236, 316.
[81] For a good concise discussion of these dispensations and their significance in preserving a Catholic community see Robert Zaller, *The Discourses of Legitimacy in Early Modern England* (Stanford: Stanford University Press, 2007), 104–15.
[82] See below, p. 252.
[83] BL Add Mss. 48029, fol. 53v (Sander to Culyke Burke, September 23, 1579).

overwhelming the Protestant state through coordinated rebellions in both of Elizabeth's kingdoms, as the collapse of their schemes would show. But it seems clear that they had some such plan in mind.

Initial Responses to Anjou's Suit

Although the scale of the exiles' planning as yet remained unknown to Elizabeth's council, the danger posed by growing religious division had become increasingly apparent. But the appropriate way of dealing with that danger seemed less obvious. Zealous Protestants saw the suppression of Catholicism as both a religious duty and a political necessity. For Sir Amias Poulet, the queen's ambassador in Paris, every new Catholic provocation reinforced a conviction that vacillation in dealing with popery invited divine retribution. Although his official dispatches discussed politics in secular terms, when writing to close friends he lapsed into religious laments:

> We build upon our own policies; we take not our counsel of the Almighty; we seek not after God, and therefore he turneth his face from us. God only knoweth what will be the end of these things and his will be fulfilled; and grant, if it be his good pleasure that these new and notable examples may yet at the last awake England that lieth lulled in the cradle of dangerous services. I fear our visitation to be near. God grant it be in his mercy![84]

But it was also arguable that the safest course lay in dampening religious animosities and conciliating moderate Catholics who remained loyal to the queen. The debate over the proposed match between Elizabeth and Anjou that developed from the summer of 1578 rapidly became linked to questions about the feasibility of relying on Catholics who seemed prepared to support the Elizabethan state from secular political motives.

Anjou had established a record during the previous several years as an ambitious but pragmatic leader, prepared to ally with Protestants to advance his own interests, but equally to betray them when his interests changed, as he had done in 1577 by taking command of a royal army that sacked two Huguenot strongholds.[85]

---

[84] *Copy-Book of Sir Amias Poulet's Letters Written During his Embassy to France (AD 1577)*, ed. Octavius Ogle (London, 1866), 21.

[85] Until the accession of his brother as Henry III of France in May 1574, François de Valois was known as duke of Alençon. He was still sometimes called by his earlier title later in the decade but will be referred to as Anjou in this study. The best treatment of his career in English is Mack P. Holt, *The Duke of Anjou and the Politique Struggle during the Wars of Religion* (Cambridge: Cambridge University Press, 1986). See also Arlette Jouanna, *Le devoir de révolte: La noblesse française et la gestation de l'État moderne* (Paris: Fayard, 1989), chapter 6.

The following year, after his followers quarreled violently with the *mignons* of Henry III, he left the French court and began raising troops to invade Flanders.[86] On August 13, he concluded a formal agreement with the Dutch to provide an army of 10,000 infantry and 2,000 horse for a period of three months; in return he received assurance that if the rebellious provinces renounced their allegiance to Philip II, he would be their first choice as an alternative sovereign.[87] Unfortunately Anjou's badly paid army soon began to disintegrate, pillaging civilians along both sides of the frontier between Picardy and Flanders, while inflicting little harm on the enemy. It was at this point—and as the Dutch turned again to Elizabeth with urgent pleas for assistance—that he renewed his suit for the queen's hand.[88]

Historians have long recognized that this marriage proposal held out the attractive prospect of an alliance with French *politiques* and the French crown to counter the mounting threat from Spain. But the views of its chief supporter on the council, Thomas Radclyffe earl of Sussex, were considerably subtler than this formulation suggests. Sussex firmly grasped Anjou's ambition and opportunism, describing him as a "man determined to seek to make himself great, either by the marriage of your Majesty or by possession of the Low Countries or by both." This quest for self-aggrandizement might lead him to become either a valuable ally or a dangerous adversary, depending on how Elizabeth treated him.[89] Sussex believed that Henry III and Catherine de Médicis would support Anjou's adventure in the Netherlands, less from loyalty to a member of their own family than because they wanted to remove him from France, where his opportunism threatened to reignite civil war.[90] But without additional English support, Sussex doubted that Anjou would have enough resources to succeed. In that case "he will turn over all his forces to aid Don John and seek his greatness and surety by martial actions that way and by the friendship of the King of Spain," again with the support of a French crown eager to keep him preoccupied.

Although Sussex did not explicitly say so, the fact that Anjou's main territorial base lay in Normandy, where Guise had also been acquiring land and extending his influence, increased the danger. An alliance between the Spanish, Guise, Anjou, and other French Catholics would place virtually the entire coast opposite England, from the ports of Normandy through Picardy and Flanders, under the

---

[86] The *mignons* were a small group of favorites on whom Henry particularly relied.
[87] Holt, *Anjou*, 96–104.   [88] Ibid., 106.
[89] Lodge, *Illustrations*, 2.108. Cf. the abstract of an apparently lost letter by Sussex to the queen, rehearsing similar arguments in *The Egerton Papers*, ed. J. Payne Collier, Camden Society Publications (London, 1840), 74–8.
[90] Lodge, *Illustrations*, 2.108: "the French King and Queen Mother, to deliver him out of France, will by all the possible means that may help to further and advance his greatness in this sort, for their own benefit, quiet and surety, and the avoiding of all fires, troubles and perils at home." In fact, Catherine de Medicis and to a lesser extent Henry III were alarmed by Anjou's invasion of the Netherlands, fearing it might draw them into a war with Spain, although they were more willing to take this risk if they had a sufficiently firm English alliance. Cf. Holt, *Anjou*, 98–101, 111.

control of Elizabeth's enemies.[91] If Dutch resistance to Spain also foundered, the strategic threat would become very grave indeed. By spurning Anjou, Elizabeth therefore risked precipitating precisely the kind of crisis she most dreaded, whereas by marrying him she might hope to turn his restless ambition and his factious French followers into English assets.[92] Anjou would not only supply an army to fight in the Netherlands but also a means of deterring Henry III from future attacks on French Protestants, from fear that his brother's followers, now reinvigorated by English support, would again join forces with the Huguenots to disrupt his kingdom.[93] Elizabeth and her husband would effectively become the arbiters of western European politics, with the power to pacify France while compelling "the King of Spain to take reasonable conditions of his subjects in the Low Countries and the States to take reasonable conditions of their King."[94]

Although Sussex also argued that the marriage might produce an heir and settle the succession, for him this does not appear to have been the principal consideration. His assessment rested instead on the perception that the religious wars of France and the Low Countries were driven not only by confessional animosities, but also by ambitions rooted in a chivalric code of personal and dynastic honor that Elizabeth's marital diplomacy might turn to advantage. It was not simply a question of using the language of courtly love as a diplomatic tool, in the way that Conyers Read and others have depicted Elizabeth doing.[95] Sussex recognized that honor culture impelled junior members of great dynasties to embark on a quest for reputation, power, and glory, to compensate for the disparity between the relatively modest resources afforded them as younger sons and the greatness that their royal birth demanded.[96] Anjou and the self-styled noble "malcontents" who had gathered under his leadership were significant players on the chessboard of international politics.[97]

Sussex acknowledged that Anjou and his supporters might try to create a party in England but he saw this danger as remote, saying it "can never take effect if God take not all senses away both from you [Elizabeth] and all the states of your realm." As for the religious difference between the queen and her husband, this

---

[91] Cf. Poulet's comment in March of 1579, when Anjou and Guise appeared to have reached some kind of accord: "It is supposed that the Province [Normandy] will be appeased and then many of good judgment there are of opinion that the Spaniard will want no assistance from hence" (TNA SP78/3/15). For the expansion of Guise influence in Normandy see Carroll, *Noble Power*, chapters 5 and 6.

[92] This was also the view of Secretary Thomas Wilson. See TNA SP12/123/17. If France was not made an ally through the marriage alliance, Wilson anticipated that it would ally with Spain to attack England.

[93] Lodge, *Illustrations*, 2.109–10. [94] Ibid.

[95] For a criticism of this view see Mears, "Love-Making and Diplomacy."

[96] Mervyn James, "English Politics and the Concept of Honour, 1485–1642," in *Society, Politics and Culture: Studies in Early Modern England* (Cambridge: Cambridge University Press, 1986) remains valuable on honor culture. Jouanna, *Le devoir de révolte* is a longer study of French honor culture and its role in fostering rebellions.

[97] For a discussion see Jouanna, *Le devoir de révolte*, chapter 6.

might be handled through the solution the earl had devised more than a decade before, when negotiating a proposed marriage between Elizabeth and the Archduke Charles of Austria. Anjou should be allowed to practice Catholicism in private with a few of his French attendants but in return he must agree to accompany the queen to public Protestant services.[98] It was an entirely pragmatic solution to the dangers of Catholic subversion and aggression, devised by a man who had loyally served both Mary Tudor and Elizabeth.

So long as it remained unclear how serious the negotiations might become, Sussex's colleagues on the council reacted cautiously to the new proposal. Elizabeth kept her options open, telling Anjou's representative that she was interested but would never marry a man she had not met, so that the duke must come to London. This effectively deferred any decision for at least several months. Walsingham, in a letter to Hatton, showed less concern over the conclusion of the match than the results that might follow its collapse: "No one thing hath procured her [Elizabeth] so much hatred abroad as these wooing matters, for that it is conceived she dallieth therein."[99] Secretary Wilson expressed similar worries: "princes failing of their purposes...can hardly digest the foil but will rather seek a revenge and turn their hearty pretended love to...deadly hatred."[100] But over the course of the winter, with the arrival of Anjou's agent Simier and repeated signs of Elizabeth's inclination to proceed, opposition began to stiffen. Burghley expressed misgivings in January, worrying that an heir to Elizabeth and Anjou might eventually inherit the French as well as the English crown and move to Paris. He seems to have attempted to push Mendoza to persuade Philip II to produce a rival Habsburg suitor.[101]

The strongest resistance came from Hatton and Leicester, whose standing as royal favorites stood in jeopardy. Mendoza reported that their common predicament made them great friends.[102] Opposition from beyond the queen's inner circle also erupted. In January five manuscript tracts by an anonymous "puritan," denouncing the proposed marriage and arguing that as a woman Elizabeth could not be the spiritual head of the Church, were planted in the queen's apartment.[103] Leicester told the French ambassador that many Protestants feared an English repetition of the St. Bartholomew's Day massacres if Elizabeth married Anjou.[104] Sir Francis Knollys saw the marriage proposal as a trap intended to ensnare the queen and her realm in "French bondage," devised "by that holy father the Pope

---

[98] Lodge, *Illustrations*, 2.112, 114–15.   [99] Hatton, 94, letter dated October 9, 1578.
[100] TNA SP12/123/17.
[101] *CSPSp* 2.636. Burghley told Mendoza that he wanted to see the queen married "to a Prince of the House of Austria" and regretted that Spain's unwillingness to renew the treaties of alliance concluded during Mary's reign had forced the English "to seek new friends."
[102] Ibid., 2.659.   [103] Ibid., 2.641.
[104] TNA PRO31/3/27, fol. 275v. Leicester also claimed to have used his influence to quiet these and other Protestant fears, winning over Protestant grandees like the earls of Huntingdon and Pembroke to Anjou's party. We are entitled to our doubts about this last claim.

and plotted out by the serpentine subtlety of the Queen Mother's head... with the intent to erect a French Guisan queen of Scots into the place of her majesty."[105] In March and April, Mendoza and Gilbert Talbot both reported a spate of hostile sermons, including one before the queen that so angered her that she walked out as it was being preached.[106] She then issued a proclamation forbidding the clergy to discuss her marriage. Anjou unwittingly added fuel to the fire by demanding as conditions for the marriage that he be crowned king and granted a pension of £60,000 a year for life, along with possession of an English port and permission to bring with him an entourage of 3,000 French.[107] Although the queen and council promptly rejected them, these demands fed perceptions that he wished to continue in England the sort of factious behavior for which he and his followers had already become notorious.[108]

These early disagreements over the match took place against a background of mounting evidence of a Catholic revival within the court, in London, and in some provincial districts, which Mauvissière had incautiously encouraged. Lord Henry Howard, younger brother of the duke of Norfolk executed in 1572, and Burghley's son-in-law, Edward de Vere earl of Oxford, had both secretly converted to Catholicism in 1577 and entered into a pact to attempt to alter the religious settlement. They had access to the court, where Oxford was a royal favorite, as did another Catholic member of their circle, Charles Arundell. In June of 1577 Oxford approached Mauvissière with an offer to foment a Catholic rebellion in England if the French provided financial assistance. Although Henry III demurred, he instructed his ambassador to encourage Oxford and sent a jewel as a token of respect. As the conflict over the match developed, Mauvissière came to regard Oxford and his Catholic associates as valuable recruits to a court party supportive of Anjou and opposed to Leicester. He saw Sussex, who was Howard's second cousin, as part of this group, along with Elizabeth's new ambassador in Paris, Sir Edward Stafford. Stafford enjoyed valuable connections to the ladies of Elizabeth's bedchamber through his mother, Dorothy, the queen's Mistress of the Robes. Around the fringes of the court network hovered other Catholic and church papist nobles, especially the earls of Surrey, Northumberland, and Rutland.[109]

---

[105] TNA SP12/139/3.
[106] CSPSp 2.658-9; Lodge, Illustrations, 2.150; Peter McCullough, Sermons at Court: Politics and Religion in Elizabethan and Jacobean Preaching (Cambridge: Cambridge University Press, 1998), 67. McCullough speculates that Leicester may have promoted these sermons while protecting those who preached them but he also points out that Hatton's protégé, Bishop John Aylmer of London, was responsible for the roster of court preachers. Although on ecclesiastical policies Hatton's views were closer to those of Sussex than to Leicester's he would have shared an interest in promoting sermons against the match.
[107] Hatton, 110; CDIHE Felipe II, 384-5.
[108] As Mauvissière reported, TNA PRO 31/3/27, fol. 306v.
[109] This paragraph has mainly followed John Bossy, "English Catholics and the French Marriage," Recusant History 5 (1959-60): 2-12. See also James McDermott, 'Sir Edward Strafford' in ODNB.

Although the pact between Howard and Oxford to try to overthrow the current religions settlement remained secret, both English and European observers sensed that English Catholicism had lately grown in strength and assertiveness. Elizabeth may have unwittingly encouraged this impression by restricting prosecution of Catholic non-conformity in an effort to dampen confessional animosities.[110] If so, her strategy backfired by encouraging some Catholics to press for more public concessions. The continuing arrival of Allen's seminarians, followed by the first Jesuit mission to England, in the spring of 1580, contributed to the impression of growing Catholic assertiveness.[111] Thomas McCoog has shown that the General of the Jesuit order, Everard Mercurian, authorized this mission somewhat reluctantly because of the apparent brightening of prospects for English Catholicism that took place as Anjou's suit began to prosper.[112] The Jesuits' European leadership hoped not so much to overthrow the Elizabethan regime as to alter it from within, by stiffening pressure on Anjou's court supporters and the queen herself to grant full religious toleration as the match proceeded.[113]

But as we have seen, Allen and other English exiles had already adopted a much more aggressive strategy. The Suffolk recusant George Gilbert and a nephew of the earl of Southampton named Thomas Pound, who had joined the Jesuit order, created a network of safe houses to shelter priests. Gilbert and Pound recruited more than twenty other wealthy lay Catholics, including some from prominent families like the Northamptonshire Treshams, to pool their resources. In London the group adopted the simple expedient of bribing the chief pursuivant responsible for hunting down priests and directing operations from his house, where Gilbert took up lodgings.[114] Although the council and other Protestants only gradually learned of the extent of this underground network, it was becoming clear in 1579 that a resurgence of Catholic activity was underway.

Print, Public Performance, and the Contest over the Match

In these circumstances, discussion of the Anjou match began to involve calculations about its probable effects not only on England's relations with foreign powers but also on the kingdom's internal stability. If the marriage went forward it would not only create a dynastic alliance between the queen and an opportunistic French Catholic prince, but would almost certainly increase the standing

---

[110] Questier, *Dynastic Politics*, 125.
[111] TNA SP12/123/17 (Wilson's memorandum on the kingdom's perils, 1578; *CSPSp* 2.710); cf. Questier, *Dynastic Politics*, 125–9.
[112] Thomas McCoog, "The English Jesuit Mission and the French Match, 1579–1581," *Catholic Historical Review* 87 (2001): 185–213.
[113] Cf. Lake and Questier, "Campion Affair," 600–12.
[114] Thomas Cooper and rev. Thomas Clancy, "George Gilbert," in *ODNB*.

within the court of a number of English Catholic and church papist nobles who were among Anjou's strongest supporters. Would this help stabilize the regime by broadening its base and dampening religious partisanship, or weaken it by alienating Protestant loyalists, while affording Catholics opportunities to subvert Elizabeth's rule from within? Simon Adams has warned us against seeing Elizabethan court politics as driven by faction.[115] But the potential for factional conflict, not only within the court but beyond it, certainly existed. Sussex and Leicester had been at loggerheads in the 1560s, and although they had since worked harmoniously together a residue of suspicion and ill feeling persisted between them. Some of the Howards nurtured personal grievances against dominant figures on the council, whom they blamed for the duke of Norfolk's demise; they also regarded Leicester, Burghley, and other leading members of the queen's circle as social upstarts, who had wrongfully displaced the old nobility from its rightful place at the center of power.[116] These resentments had little effect on the council's cohesion during the 1570s because Norfolk's close relatives and most of his former allies, apart from Sussex, had been excluded from its ranks. But this might change if the queen chose to strengthen Anjou's support on her council by promoting figures like Norfolk's brother, Lord Henry Howard and the duke's son, Philip Howard earl of Arundel, to it.

Much would obviously depend on Elizabeth's ability or inability to retain the loyalty of her French suitor, her nobility, and her own entourage. But the relative strength of Protestant and Catholic elements among the general population, along with the depth and resilience of public loyalty to the queen, would also be critical. By itself, dissatisfaction and factionalism involving a few noble families posed a limited threat. The real danger was that large bodies of religiously disaffected subjects might rally behind rival aristocratic factions, as had recently happened in France, Scotland, and the Low Countries. Elizabeth and her inner circle knew full well that they could not afford to take the loyalty and docility of ordinary English subjects for granted. But since they had no accurate way of measuring public attitudes or predicting the reactions of the English people if the queen married Anjou, they had to judge such matters impressionistically, by paying attention to outward signs of loyalty or discontent, which interested parties might try to manipulate.

---

[115] "Favourites and Factions at the Elizabethan Court," in *Leicester and the Court: Essays on Elizabethan Politics* (Manchester: Manchester University Press, 2002), 46–67.

[116] A good discussion of the attitudes involved in this struggle during the previous generation can be found in W. A. Sessions, *Henry Howard, the Poet Earl of Surrey: A Life* (Oxford: Oxford University Press, 1999). As Sessions shows, Surrey had been especially antagonistic to Leicester's father, Lord Lisle, the future earl of Warwick and duke of Northumberland. The relationship between the Howards and Dudleys seems to have become almost a simmering family feud. For another discussion that qualifies Adams's argument about the absence of faction at Elizabeth's court see Younger, "How Protestant was the Regime?"

The public controversy that developed around the match needs to be seen in this light, as a debate not simply about Anjou but patterns of loyalty and allegiance throughout English society. In addition to the courtly and international dimensions already explored, it unfolded within a variety of local contexts, as arguments over the marriage resonated with contests already underway in provincial communities. East Anglia provides one example. The diocese of Norwich produced more Catholic recusants than any other see in the province of Canterbury except London, but it also contained areas of vigorous Protestantism, in parts of western Suffolk around the town of Bury, in the Stour Valley and in Norwich itself, where local reformers had been greatly reinforced by an exceptionally large number of religious exiles from the Low Countries.[117] In the recent past the dukes of Norfolk had dominated the region. Although weakened after 1572, the remnants of their religiously conservative affinity had not entirely loosened its grip on local power. They had recently benefited from Elizabeth's determination to suppress radical Protestantism after the suspension of Archbishop Edmund Grindal and suppression of the prophesying movement. Edmund Freke, appointed bishop of Norwich in 1576 with a mandate to crack down on puritanism, allied himself with conservative and crypto-Catholic gentry against forward Protestants. His campaign against puritanism enjoyed additional support from the most forceful judge of the Norfolk circuit, Edmund Anderson, a man who had married into a Catholic family, although he seems himself to have been a strong supporter of royal authority over the Church rather than a committed papist.[118] But the region's Protestants possessed their own links to the court through Nicholas Bacon, whose younger brother Nathaniel lived in Suffolk, and other sympathizers on the council. They tried to discredit Freke and his gentry supporters by accusing them of popery, while simultaneously defending themselves against charges of favoring puritans and anabaptists.[119] East Anglia in the late 1570s provides a classic example of a divided region whose factional alignments had become loosely connected to disagreements within the court.

These conditions lent added significance to a hastily arranged royal progress through Suffolk and Norfolk in the summer of 1578, on which Anjou's representatives accompanied the queen. Progresses were a European institution, used to assert royal authority in outlying areas; they figured prominently, for example, in

---

[117] Hassell-Smith, *Norfolk*; MacCulloch, *Suffolk*; Patrick Collinson, John Craig, and Brett Usher, eds, *Conferences and Combination Lectures in the Elizabethan Church: Dedham and Bury St Edmunds 1582–1590* (Woodbridge: Boydell Press, 2003), esp. xlii–viii.

[118] See Rosemay O'Day's article in *ODNB*.

[119] See, e.g. the letter of John Becom to Nathaniel Bacon about attempts to discredit him at court through false reports of the character of a minister who had catechized his household in H. Smith and G. Baker, eds, *Papers of Nathaniel Bacon*, vol. 2, Norfolk Record Society Publications 49 (1982–3), 8, and Bacon's own comment in January 1578: "The Queen's Majesty having speech touching Norfolk should say she heard there were diverse gentle[men] in that shire anabaptists" (Folger Shakespeare Library Mss. L.d.2).

Catherine de Médicis's efforts to reunite France after periodic episodes of civil war. An English progress gave Elizabeth opportunities not only to show herself and her resplendent entourage to people far from London but also to visit locally prominent landowners and establish or renew personal contacts with them.[120] As during most of her progresses, in 1578 Elizabeth stayed with both Protestant and Catholic landowners.[121] But whereas her visits had previously underlined the queen's impartiality, the East Anglian progress was different. As Diarmaid MacCulloch first noticed, it developed into a demonstration of Elizabeth's favor for Protestants and displeasure with Catholic non-conformity, almost certainly as a result of hidden collaboration between members of the council and local Protestant leaders.[122] Twenty-three prominent recusant gentlemen were summoned before the council at Norwich and interrogated about their refusal to attend the official church. One agreed to conform but the council ordered the imprisonment of the remaining twenty-two. Several recusants and church papists were removed from the commission of the peace, while five stalwart Protestants received knighthoods. Clergy silenced by Freke, including John More, "the apostle of Norwich," received licenses to preach.

Richard Topcliffe gleefully described the discomfiture of one Catholic host, Edward Rookwood, at his seat at Euston in Suffolk:

> My Lord chamberlain, nobly and gravely understanding that Rookwood was excommunicated for papistry, called him before him, demanded of him how he durst presume to attempt her [Elizabeth's] real presence, he, unfit to accompany any Christian person... And to decipher the gentleman to the full, a piece of plate being missed in the court and searched for in his hay house, in the hayrick such an image of Our Lady was there found as for greatness, for gayness and workmanship I did never see a match; and after a sort of country dances ended, in her Majesty's sight the idol was set behind the people, who avoided. She [the statue] rather seemed a beast raised up on a sudden from hell by conjuring than the picture for whom it had been so often and long abused. Her Majesty commanded it to the fire, which in her sight by the country folks was quickly done, to her content, and unspeakable joy of every one but some one or two who had sucked of the idol's poisoned milk.[123]

---

[120] The best study is Mary Hill Cole, *The Portable Queen* (Amherst, MA: University of Massachusetts Press, 1999).

[121] Mary Hill Cole, "Religious Conformity and the Progresses of Elizabeth I," in *Elizabeth I, Always her Own Free Woman*, ed. Carole Levin, Jo Eldridge Carney, and Debra Barrett-Graves (Aldershot: Ashgate, 2003), 63–77.

[122] MacCulloch, *Suffolk*, 195–6. See also Collinson et al., *Conferences*, xlvii–xlviii and Zillah Dovey, *An Elizabethan Progress* (Stroud: Sutton Publishing, 1996).

[123] Lodge, *Illustrations*, 2.120–1; Topcliffe's letter is reproduced in Nichols, *Elizabeth*, 2.216.

Topcliffe saw the whole progress as a triumph of Protestant loyalty: "I did never see her Majesty better received by two countries in one journey than Suffolk and Norfolk now." Elizabeth "hath served God with great zeal and comfortable examples."[124]

Mendoza's dispatches convey exactly the opposite impression. "During her progress in the North [i.e. East Anglia] the Queen has met with more Catholics than she expected... When she entered Norwich large crowds of people came out to receive her and one company of children knelt as she passed and said, as usual, 'God save the Queen'. She turned to them and said, 'Speak up; I know you do not love me here.'" A few months later he reported that Elizabeth had canceled a triumphant "entry" into London from "lack of confidence" in her subjects' loyalty.[125] Although Mendoza probably had little direct knowledge of East Anglia, his dispatches may well reflect reports passed on by English Catholics, and so should not be dismissed out-of-hand. They suggest how stories about the progress, spread by word of mouth, had taken on religious coloration, giving rise to opposing accounts of how the counties had received their queen and her campaign against Catholic non-conformity. These differences mattered, since perceptions of what had happened in East Anglia had considerable relevance to assessments of the regime's strength and stability. If Elizabeth had indeed succeeded in isolating and punishing a recusant faction while inspiring enthusiastic loyalty from most East Anglians, the prospects for any active Catholic resistance in the region would look bleak. But if there remained a large body of sullen and resentful Catholics, awaiting an opportunity to turn the tables on their adversaries, her domestic and foreign enemies might take heart.

It is therefore significant that unlike most English progresses, this one gave rise to at least two and possibly three published accounts. The two that survive were written by a former Norwich schoolmaster and sometime soldier named Thomas Churchyard, and a citizen of London, Bernard Garter.[126] Churchyard's tract purported to describe the *entire* progress, rather than a single episode of pageantry, like the earlier printed accounts of the Kenilworth entertainment that Leicester had provided the queen in 1575, and Elizabeth's visit to the house of Sir Henry Lee shortly thereafter. Although Churchyard described entertainments presented before Elizabeth, he primarily emphasized "the noble receiving... good order, great cheer and charges that her highness's subjects" gave her as she traveled through the region, which he held up as "a mirror and shining glass that all the whole land may look into."[127] He avoided any reference to religious

---

[124] Lodge, *Illustrations*, 2.119–20.
[125] *CSPSp* 2.610–11, 641 (dispatches of November 8, 1578 and January 27, 1579).
[126] Holinshed's *Chronicles* refer to "three half-penny pamphlets" on the progress, although only two appear to have survived. See Nichols, *Elizabeth*, 2.135.
[127] Thomas Churchyard, *A Discourse of the Queen's Majesties Entertainment in Suffolk and Norfolk* (London, 1579), dedicatory epistle to Gilbert Gerard.

confrontations, stressing instead the ways in which local people welcomed the queen through traditional expressions of courtesy, magnificence, and devotion. He stressed the sumptuousness of the cavalcades that greeted Elizabeth as she entered the two East Anglian counties on her route. In Suffolk, although the local gentry had little warning of the queen's approach, "all the velvets and silks were taken up that might be laid hands on and bought for any money, and soon converted to such garments and suits of robes that the show thereof might have beautified the greatest triumph that was in England these many years." Two hundred gentlemen in white velvet and three hundred of the "graver sort" wearing black velvet coats and "fair chains" rode out to meet their queen. In Norfolk the cavalcade numbered 2,500, including 500 gentlemen "so bravely attired and mounted as was worthy the noting."[128] The pamphlet went on to describe the "banquets and feasts," exchanges of gifts, and "triumphs and devices" by which local peers and gentry honored Elizabeth, including an entertainment by Norfolk's heir, Philip Howard earl of Surrey.[129] But Churchyard placed even more stress on the "obedience and love...and courtesy" of the common people, which he pointedly contrasted with "the old haughtiness and stiff necked behavior" and "unmannerly disordered boldness, bred up and fostered on long familiarity" among subjects living near the court.[130]

Churchyard's decision to omit all explicit references to religious disagreements, while stressing the use of traditional visual and behavioral codes to express deference and loyalty to the monarch, must have been a deliberate rhetorical strategy.[131] He reinforced the effect by describing East Anglia's loyalty with a feudal terminology, as "a mere motion of homage and fealty."[132] The tract by Garter describing the queen's entry into Norwich similarly began with a detailed account of the heraldic insignia on the town gate, including the royal arms, a "scutcheon of Saint George his cross," and Elizabeth's badge of a falcon, accompanied by the words: "God and the Queen we serve." On the inside of the gate the Tudor emblem of red and white roses stood above the verse:

---

[128] Ibid., sigs Biii, Biiii.

[129] Soon to become earl of Arundel, father to the famous art patron of the seventeenth century. The ducal title had been lost in 1572. Unfortunately, Churchyard provides little detail about this entertainment.

[130] Churchyard, *Entertainment*, sigs Aiii v, Bii r.

[131] I have discussed this subject at greater length in Malcolm Smuts, "Occasional Events, Literary Texts and Historical Interpretations," in *Neo-Historicism: Studies in Renaissance Literature, History and Politics*, ed. Robin Headlam Wells, Glenn Burgess, and Rowland Wymer (Cambridge: D. S. Brewer, 2001), 179–98. Very rare before 1579, accounts of Elizabeth's interactions with her people become somewhat more frequent but also formulaic thereafter, suggesting the emergence of a cultural trope—no doubt exaggerated and perhaps even semi-mythical—involving the queen's genius at combining magnificence with her "common touch" that became incorporated into her posthumous legend. Modern historians have often been rather uncritical in accepting this trope at face value.

[132] Churchyard, *Entertainment*, Bi.

> Division kindled strife,
>   Blest Union quenched the flame
> Thence sprang our noble Phoenix dear
>   The peerless Prince of Fame.[133]

Both tracts foreshadow the romantic revival of medieval chivalric culture that became such a marked feature of the latter half of the reign.

But while avoiding heavy-handed partisanship, Garter's tract described pageants that hint at Protestant themes and understated resistance to the Anjou match. At her approach to Norwich the queen was to have been greeted by a mythic English king named Gurgunt, the reputed builder of Norwich Castle, who appeared mounted in armor, with silk accessories in the original Tudor livery colors of green and white. His speech recounted the sacking of Rome by an ancient English army.[134] Within the city the queen saw a pageant ably discussed by Susan Doran, in which Venus and Cupid were vanquished by Dame Chastity and her ladies, who confiscated Cupid's arrows and presented them to Elizabeth as a token of her command over her people's hearts.[135] By celebrating the superiority of chastity to erotic love, the pageant implied that the queen should remain single, since her subjects' ardent devotion provided sufficient safeguard for the realm, without the need of a foreign husband. Doran saw this pageant as inventing the trope of Elizabeth as Virgin Queen. Its emphasis on chaste love reinforced and rounded out the central message of both tracts concerning the *mutual* affection binding Elizabeth to her people. As the queen left Norwich "she called Master Mayor and made him knight: and so departing said, 'I have laid up in by breast such good will, as I shall never forget Norwich'; and proceeding onward did shake her riding rod and said, 'farewell Norwich' with water standing in her eyes."[136]

The non-confrontational tone of these treatises and their nostalgic emphasis on a neo-medieval culture of worship—in the sense of giving honor—may in part reflect Churchyard's earlier connections with the Howard family and his more recent ties to Hatton, an opponent of the match but no friend to puritans. Both pamphlets were published by Henry Bynneman, described on Churchyard's title page as a "servant to the right honorable Christopher Hatton, Vice Chamberlain." Churchyard dedicated his tract to the queen's attorney general, Gilbert Gerard, a conformist Protestant with a Catholic wife, but also a close friend of Nicholas Bacon,[137] while Garter chose the Suffolk gentleman and lieutenant of the Tower of London, Sir Owen Hopton, a loyal servant of the queen who also appears to have

---

[133] Bernard Garter, *Joyful Reception... into Norfolk* (1579) in Nichols, *Elizabeth*, 2.143.
[134] Ibid., 138, 142.
[135] Churchyard, *Entertainment*, ci–ciii; Susan Doran, "Juno vs. Diana: The Treatment of Elizabeth I's Marriage in Plays and Entertainments, 1551–1581," *Historical Journal* 38 (1995): 257–74.
[136] Goldingham, *Joyous Reception* in Nichols, *Elizabeth*, 2.166.
[137] See Christopher W. Brooks's article in *ODNB*.

had flexible religious views.[138] The two treatises therefore seem to have emanated from circles opposed to the match but moderate in their religious views. It is easy to overlook their significance because their narratives conform so closely to an image of Elizabeth's triumphant progresses and "love tricks" among her people, endlessly repeated by later generations of historians. But this picture derives largely from printed accounts of Elizabeth's progresses and other public appearances, mainly dating from the latter half of her reign, which cannot safely be treated as objective journalistic reporting. Churchyard and Garter were among the early fabricators of a rhetorically constructed image of Elizabeth's popularity, masquerading as a series of naïve eye-witness reports.[139]

We may compare this image to another rhetorical performance that found its way into print the following year, a Sussex assize sermon preached by an erstwhile protégé of Leicester named William Overton, who shortly afterwards won promotion to the bishopric of Coventry.[140] Sussex was another religiously divided county largely dominated, as we have seen, by Catholic and church papist families, who in some districts impeded the advance of Protestantism by shielding conservative priests from deprivation by Church authorities.[141] Recusancy had begun to develop from the late 1560s, creating "little islands of Catholic worship" in which Marian priests found shelter as they traveled across the county and into Hampshire, building a communications network already in place when the first graduates of continental seminaries arrived.[142] But here the local bishop, Richard Curteys, was an active Protestant who built up a phalanx of Cambridge educated preachers that helped create a local puritan community. In 1577 Curteys overplayed his hand by moving against gentry recusancy so aggressively that he stirred up a storm of protest in which even some conformist Protestants joined, earning a rebuke from the council. Overton, who disliked Curteys, supported his opponents on this occasion. But open non-conformity had begun to reach alarming proportions, with about fifteen leading families and perhaps twice as many among the lesser gentry refusing to attend church. In some cases, the local influence of these families intimidated church wardens from presenting them, while their impropriation of benefices allowed them to install traditionalist clergy as curates and vicars.[143]

Overton's sermon announced a new crackdown, this time carried out through the judicial machinery of the assize rather than by the local ecclesiastical

---

[138] See John Craig's article in *ODNB*. Hopton had presided over the incarceration of the duke of Norfolk but he was rumored to have papists among his subordinates at the Tower and he later befriended Philip Howard earl of Arundel.

[139] For a more extended discussion of these points see Smuts, "Occasional Events."

[140] William Overton, *A Godly and pithie Exhortation made to the Judges and Justices of Sussex* (1579).

[141] Roger B. Manning, *Religion and Society in Elizabethan Sussex: A Study of the Enforcement of the Religious Settlement 1558–1603* (Leicester: Leicester University Press, 1969), 35–45.

[142] Ibid., 45.   [143] Ibid., 82–90, 129–34.

authorities. But he carefully distinguished residual religious traditionalism from outright disloyalty. He began by stressing the inseparability of service to the queen and commonwealth from service to God and the Church, "for Christ is a pattern unto the Prince and the church is a pattern unto the commonwealth to follow."[144] Unfortunately, the "miserable" conditions produced by a proliferation of different religious opinions had destroyed this pattern, so that "the firm and stable word of God is made a flexible nose of wax and every man thinks to writhe it which way he will himself." Sussex's magistrates had a duty to restrain this perverse diversity, since Christ did not come into the world "to rock men asleep and to cry peace, peace, where was no peace" but to wield "a sword... to fight against these things."[145] Overton accused papists and "the books which they write" of causing "all those stirs and troubles that be now in the Church."[146] But he carefully exonerated conservative conformists from this condemnation:

> When I speak of papists, you may not take me that I mean every one that is not thoroughly resolved in every point of religion. For there be many whose eyes God hath not yet opened but will do when it shall please him, and yet in the meantime are good subjects to the queen and necessary members of the commonwealth, whom we must not despise but pray for. But under the name of papists I comprehend those which cleave altogether unto the Pope and papacy, and by open word and writing maintain the usurped authority of the Bishop of Rome.[147]

He especially regretted the hardening of religious divisions since the papal bull excommunicating Elizabeth in 1570:

> Before that time, they could be content to come to the church and hear sermons and to receive the sacraments and to use common prayer with the rest of the congregation of Christ and so forth. They were conformable in all respects... but since they sucked that mad bull they are become even as brainsick calves, forward, stubborn, disobedient in word and deed, not to be led nor ordered by any reason and I would it were no worse. And yet these forsooth cannot be seen nor heard of when time of reformation is: they cannot be heard of at the quarter sessions, nor now at these general sessions, nor when any commission is set upon for redress of such matters... but when the sessions are past, we can both hear and see that they have their open meetings and solemn feastings together, sometimes at one house, sometimes at another house amongst themselves with all freedom and liberty... talking and jousting at their pleasures of the state and of religion.[148]

---

[144] Overton, *Pithie Exhortation*, sig. A viii. [145] Ibid., sigs Bi v, Cii.
[146] Ibid., sig. Cvi.   [147] Ibid., sig. Bv.   [148] Ibid., sigs Dv r–Dvi r.

The problem was not the survival of older religious beliefs but the withdrawal of a factious minority from communion in the parish church and participation in the shire's secular affairs, to form a subversive network of recusant households.

Overton balanced his attack on recusancy with denunciations of "Anabaptists, Libertines and such other like, which would have no commonwealth at all but yet all things in common," adding: "I am afraid lest the Puritans also (as you call them) another sect lately sprung up amongst us, do smell shrewdly of this ill favored smoke."[149] He was advocating Hatton's policy of evenhanded severity toward both religious extremes, more than Leicester's of shielding puritans while suppressing papists. The judges, no doubt prepared in advance, followed up with "a very quick and vehement charge to the grand jury, yea and to the justices themselves and to all others that had any office or authority in the shire, to look more narrowly to matters of religion than heretofore... to conserve the peace and unity of Christ's Church, and to search out and see punished all that were offenders to the contrary."[150]

John Stubbs and the Rhetoric of Dynastic Libel

In their different ways, Overton, Churchyard, and Garter therefore all defined loyalty in terms of participation in communal activities and rituals of devotion to the sovereign, rather than commitment to a doctrinal creed. In principle this outlook was entirely compatible with Sussex's pragmatism, the *politique* tolerance of religious diversity Anjou had displayed in France and the chivalrous language of devotion through which he and his agent, Simier, courted Elizabeth.[151] Although the Norfolk pageant had obliquely protested against the match, nothing in these tracts fundamentally conflicted with a policy of reconciliation between the regime and moderate Catholics willing to engage in minimal public conformity. But was it safe to trust in the appearance of loyalty and deference among community leaders who plainly continued to favor Catholic beliefs? What might happen if Anjou betrayed Elizabeth after their marriage, or if she died before him, leaving a foreign Catholic king consort with a clear field in which to pursue his ambitions? These questions were virtually impossible to address openly without offending both the queen and her suitor, especially after Elizabeth prohibited public discussion of her marriage.

But in October 1579 a London lawyer named John Stubbs faced the issue head-on with his *A Discoverie of a Gaping Gulf Whereinto England is Like to Be Swallowed by an Other French Mariage*. This sensational tract, of which 1,000 copies were printed and distributed through sympathetic figures in localities as

---

[149] Ibid., sigs C viii v–Di. [150] Ibid., sig. A iii.
[151] These have been reproduced in *HMC Salisbury* vol. 2, passim.

distant as Cornwall, expressed its opposition to the match through inflammatory religious rhetoric, anti-French xenophobia, and *ad hominem* attacks on Anjou and his family, in ways transparently intended to inflame partisan feelings.[152] Whereas Churchyard and Garter had obliquely hinted at their opposition to the match, Stubbs forthrightly suggested that Elizabeth had brought her kingdom to the edge of a precipice by succumbing to the blandishments of a man she might soon prove too weak to control. Anjou was nothing less than "the old serpent in shape of a man, whose sting is in his mouth, and who doth his endeavor to seduce our Eve, that she and we may lose this English paradise."[153] Stubbs predicted that the evil example of the queen's Catholic marriage would reverberate through the kingdom as a kind of apostasy: "The prince's fall is like that of a mighty oak which bears down with it many arms and branches; therefore it is often recited in scripture that Jeroboam fell away from God and all Israel with him again."[154]

Whereas Anjou's defenders argued that he would only attend Catholic worship in private with a few French attendants, Stubbs argued that the number of Catholics already practicing their religion, in open defiance of the law, belied this claim. "I pray you, do but go upon the Thames and see what companies go to the French mass, inquire what numbers looked in a backfield gates to the Portugal mass, how the Spanish masses had their customers more than enough, and you shall easily see the loose reckoning of these men." Can anyone doubt, he demanded, whether a "great prince" married to the queen and bearing the title of king, "will not give himself his own conditions for his own religion, to him and his, and so many of ours as will seek it at his hands?"[155] Stubbs refused to believe that the regime might disarm Catholicism by demanding occasional public conformity. This policy had already failed because Catholics refused to accept its terms: limited toleration merely encouraged them to demonstrate their solidarity and push for more concessions.

Having made this point, he launched a vitriolic assault on the French royal family for its record of political manipulation, treachery, and bloodshed. "France is a house of cruelty, especially against Christians, a principal prop of the tottering house of Antichrist."[156] But the well-known vices of the French people paled in comparison to those of their ruling dynasty. In developing this argument Stubbs drew on recent Huguenot and *malcontent*[157] literature, written especially after the 1572 St. Bartholomew's Day massacres that had created a black legend of Valois cruelty and deceit. Catherine de Médicis had become a particular object of abuse, as a foreign queen mother allegedly following the precepts of her countryman,

---

[152] For the print run and distribution see Questier, *Dynastic Politics*, 121 and Collinson, "Elizabethan Exclusion Crisis," 76–7.

[153] *John Stubbs's Gaping Gulf with Letters and Other Relevant Documents*, ed. Lloyd E. Berry (Charlottesville: University of Virginia Press for the Folger Shakespeare Library, 1968), 3–4.

[154] Ibid., 15; cf. 4.   [155] Ibid., 16.   [156] Ibid., 22.

[157] The *malcontents* were an unstable group of discontented Catholics who allied with Huguenots against the crown and the ultra-Catholic followers of the Guise.

Machiavelli, to erect a "Florentine" system of tyranny by cynically playing religious factions off against each other.[158] Ironically, Anjou had himself contributed to these polemics by patronizing Innocent Gentillet, the most famous exponent of the claim that a Machiavellian conspiracy against French liberty had unfolded in the queen mother's entourage.[159]

These tracts contributed to a growing current of dynastic libel emerging in France, England, and other European countries. The libels tacitly accepted the early modern assumption that people of royal and noble birth were normally entitled to rule because they possessed innate virtues lacking in other people. But they depicted specific individuals and families as not only lacking those virtues but infected with a diametrically opposite propensity toward crime and vice. The preservation of a healthy hierarchical society required the *denial* of deference and obedience to such individuals and their lineages. Works of this kind strongly overlapped the genre of "libelous secret histories" purporting to describe sordid political maneuvers, extensively explored in an English context by Peter Lake.[160] A Treatise of Treasons, an anonymous treatise of 1572 often attributed to Mary Stuart's agent, John Leslie bishop of Glasgow, provides a relatively early example. It repeats charges that had been circulating among followers of the duke of Norfolk and other conservative noble families against unnamed Protestant courtiers of base parentage (Burghley and Nicholas Bacon seem to have been the chief targets), whom it accuses of corrupting Elizabeth's judgment with false information intended to poison her mind against the old English nobility, so that she would rely instead on a clique of new men. Although they disguised their maneuvers by claiming to advance Protestantism, these base councilors actually wanted to convert England "from a Christian commonwealth into a Machiavellian state."[161] They manufactured false reports of Catholic conspiracies in order to heighten religious divisions, which they exploited for selfish purposes. Leslie proceeds to portray the contest of noble virtue against ignoble vice in quasi racial terms. The court Machiavels are like the wily Greeks of the Trojan War, especially the figure Sinon, who wormed his way as a spy into the Trojan camp and later released the soldiers from the wooden horse.[162] They have erected "a party

---

[158] See Donald Kelly, "Murd'rous Machiavel in France: A Post-Mortem," *Political Science Quarterly* 85 (1970): 545–59 and more generally Henry Heller, *Anti-Italianism in Sixteenth-Century France* (Toronto: University of Toronto Press, 2003).

[159] Heller, *Anti-Italianism*, 126–30. Gentillet's famous *Discours sur les moyens de bien gourverner et maintenir en bonne paix un royame our autre principauté contre Nicole Marchiavel Florentin* (n.p., 1576), often known as the *Anti-Machiavell*, was dedicated to Anjou. Anjou led a coalition of Huguenots and *malcontents* unhappy with the policies of Henry III and with Guise influence at the French court in the mid-1570s.

[160] *Bad Queen Bess?*. For the term "libelous secret history" see 5.

[161] John Leslie, *A Treatise of Treasons* (Louvain, 1572), sigs E1 v–E2. Cf. Peter Lake's discussion in *Bad Queen Bess?*, chapter 3.

[162] Leslie, *A Treatise of Treasons*, sigs H2–3. The story derives from Virgil's *Aeneid* rather than the *Iliad*.

Protestant" endowed with the "subtlety, falsehood and lewd property of the Greekish nation" that stands opposed to "the Catholic party," whose "modesty and conscience" resembles the "noble nature and royal dealings of the old Trojans."[163]

This was not simply an English or British genre. French tracts attacking Catherine de Médicis developed a similar contrast between French virtue and Italian or Tuscan viciousness, while adding especially pointed accusations against the Medici family and Catherine herself. Henri Estienne's 1574 *Discours merveilleux de la vie, actions et deportements de Catherine de Médicis* is a prime example. This tract, which went through two English editions in 1576, one published in Edinburgh and the other possibly in London,[164] depicts Catherine as a "pattern" of public tyranny and private vice, tainted from birth by the evil stars that presided over her nativity, and even more by her Florentine and Medici blood.[165] "Among all nations in craft and subtlety Italy beareth the name, so in Italy Tuscany, and in Tuscany Florence," while in Florence the Medici had risen from "bondage," "servitude," and "vileness" through exceptional depravity.[166] Descended originally from a wealthy collier, the family's rise to greatness at the expense of more aristocratic lineages had given it an inbred hatred of all nobility.[167] Having come to France as wife of the king's younger son, Estienne alleged, Catherine poisoned the Dauphin to give her husband title to the throne. After her husband's own death, she set about fomenting and manipulating religious factions, engineering the Huguenot conspiracy of Amboise against the Guise, then supporting the Guise in their efforts to exterminate the Huguenots, always with the goal of weakening the strongest party and advancing her own power. When political conspiracy failed she resorted to more poison.[168] Amidst these machinations she met the duke of Alba and concluded a secret agreement with Spain. Since she had married her daughter to Philip II it mattered little to her if Spain conquered a France exhausted by religious war, because her own grandchildren would rule in any case.[169] She cared only about subverting the nobility and preventing a reunification of

---

[163] Ibid.
[164] The title page of the probable London edition listed Heidelberg as the place of publication, while a variant of the 1576 Edinburgh edition that I have used listed Paris, perhaps suggesting clandestine printing. For a discussion of this tract, which credits it with laying down "the foundation of the ongoing and long-lived legend of the wicked Italian queen," see Heller, *Anti-Italianism*, 120–5. There were in all ten international editions in Latin and German as well as French and English (121).
[165] Henri Estienne, *Ane Mervellous discours upon the lyfe, deides and behaviours of Katherine de Medicis, Quene Mother* (Paris [almost certainly for Edinburgh], 1576), 15.
[166] Ibid., 5–6.
[167] Ibid., 7: "Thus it is evident that she is descended from a base progeny and therefore according unto the old proverb, if the mastiff never loved the greyhound then let never the nobility of France attend from Catherine de' Medici no other thing than the abasing and diminishing and utter rooting out of the same."
[168] Ibid., 53.   [169] Ibid., 85.

France across confessional lines that would frustrate her efforts to infiltrate foreigners into positions of power and maintain her tyranny.[170]

Estienne and other writers who wrote in a similar vein wanted to justify a cross-confessional "malcontent" alliance against the court, on the grounds that the differences separating Catholic and Huguenot nobles paled to insignificance compared to the chasm dividing both from the Machiavellian atheists around the queen mother. But it required only minor adjustments for Stubbs to turn their arguments into anti-French and anti-Catholic polemic. He began by associating Medici crimes with the cruelty displayed by the Valois in persecuting Huguenots. Henry II ruled as an implacable enemy of the gospel and his children by Catherine inherited the vices of both parents, growing into a race of tyrants, "even one after another, as a Domition after Nero, as a Trajan after Domitian, as a Julianus after Trajan."[171] The royal family's role in the St. Bartholomew's Day massacres made the Valois "wrathfully marked of God," like the sons of Ahab, as shown by the gruesome deaths of Catherine's two eldest sons: Francis II's ear had rotted off, while Charles IX shed blood from every "vent" in his body.[172] Stubbs likened Catherine's relationship to her family and the pope to that of a bevy of witches with Satan. The queen mother is "the very soul whereby the bodies of the King, of Monsieur, of their sister Margaret and of all the great ones in France do move a hundred hands to affect her purposes. And when we speak of the Queen Mother we must straightways present before us but a body or trunk, wherein the Pope moveth as her soul to devise and have executed whatsoever for the appetite of that see, even as necromancers are said to carry about a dead body by the motion of some unclean spirit."[173]

Stubbs adapted the French argument that Catherine had introduced foreigners into positions of power so they might subvert French liberties by claiming that the dynastic marriage between Elizabeth and Anjou would allow aliens to infiltrate and subvert England's government. The kingdom's laws had long treated the employment of aliens as officers under the crown as "a poison."[174] Stubbs cited historical examples showing the suspicion with which medieval kings regarded foreign ecclesiastics appointed by the pope and the particular troubles caused by marriages between English kings and French princesses. The French practice of selling offices presented another threat. If Anjou should introduce this abuse "after the French manner," the purchasers will become "so many hands and feet" to execute his projects. Even if Anjou himself were barred from sitting on the council, he will "thrust in at the door such counselors in whose mouth he may speak and by them, as by hired spials, to know what is done."[175]

Gentillet had singled out Italians as prime instruments of Catherine de Medicis's Machiavellian plot to establish a "Turkish" system of tyranny. Stubbs's

[170] Ibid., 89. [171] *Gaping Gulf*, ed. Berry, 22. [172] Ibid., 23.
[173] Ibid., 25. [174] Ibid., 34. [175] Ibid., 38.

familiarity with this argument is suggested by his sarcastic reference to "that most Christian court where Machiavelli is their New Testament and atheism is their religion, yea whose whole policy and government seems to set the Turkish tyranny as a pattern," concisely summing up Gentillet's charge.[176] But *Gaping Gulf* again expanded and reoriented the polemic by combining it with xenophobic prejudice against the French—"a people notorious for lying, more perfidious in their dealings with each other than the Moors in their commerce with strangers"— and the Valois, "for what house is more anciently enemy to her Majesty's ancestors and this land?"[177] If the marriage of Marguerite de Valois to Henry of Navarre had served as a pretext for a massacre of French Protestants, what might ensue upon the marriage of Francis de Valois to the queen of England? And how will the English react to Anjou's train, "the scum of the [French] king's court, which is the scum of all France, which is the scum of Europe ... horseleeches," who will suck up English wealth to fill "their beggarly purses," while filling London with their broils.[178]

Having laid these foundations Stubbs went on to develop several subsidiary arguments. He ridiculed the claim that Anjou possessed a strong following from whose support England might derive real benefits. In reality the duke had only a small band of undistinguished followers, as shown by the fact that he had sent a non-entity like Jean de Simier to represent him at the English court, rather than a great nobleman.[179] Anjou's notoriously dissolute life had ruined his reputation, while arousing suspicions that the "vile sins" of his body had entered into his very "bones" and would plague his descendants.[180] The divine curse that God had placed on the Valois had its counterpart in a disease, syphilis, that Anjou might pass to the queen. Stubbs denied that a child conceived by Elizabeth and Anjou would secure the succession. To the contrary, the prospect of offspring offered additional threats. He worked through the various possibilities. The queen and her infant might die in childbirth, producing an immediate crisis. She might give birth to a daughter who would inherit the English but not the French crown. But her father "under color of tutorship" might carry her into France and marry her to a French prince, thus bringing England under foreign control. Alternatively, a son might inherit both kingdoms, whereupon he would undoubtedly move his court to France and place England under the control of a viceroy.[181]

But the gravest danger was the likelihood that Anjou meant to use a marriage with Elizabeth as a ruse to pursue the real French objective of placing Mary Stuart on the throne. Stubbs asserted that Anjou must, "either for love or fear," have a close relationship with the duke of Guise, who in turn strongly favored Mary because of their kinship connection.[182] Mary and her popish allies, including the king of Spain, had attempted to use every available device to overthrow Elizabeth,

[176] Ibid., 76.   [177] Ibid., 38–9 and 39–40.   [178] Ibid., 46.   [179] Ibid., 60.
[180] Ibid., 71.   [181] Ibid., 51–7.   [182] Ibid., 78.

but God had so far frustrated their plans. "Now must some great mean be used and that under cloak of love, which is ever the last popish practice. From no place more fitly than out of France can they fetch this instrument of our woe."[183] "Let other men's squeamish judgments keep them in what temper of suspecting it likes them; I cannot be so blockish but to think that it is more than likely he [Anjou] comes for this Mary."[184] Since it appeared unlikely Henry III would produce heirs, Stubbs pointed out, Anjou represented the last hope for the perpetuation of the Valois dynasty. Would Catherine de Medicis truly risk the survival of her family by marrying him to Elizabeth, whose own prospects for producing children were so uncertain?[185] "No, no, no, the King, his brother and his mother have some other meaning against the church, state and person of our prince, even to have an eye in the head of our court if they can bring it to pass."[186] By intruding "a rabblement of itching, canvassing, discoursing and subtle heads into our court," they mean first to subject England to the rule of "Italianate Frenchmen," and then to exterminate the English nobility, abolish the common law, and introduce a French system of excises and ruinous taxation.[187] "This odd fellow [Anjou], by birth a Frenchman, by profession a papist, an atheist by conversation, an instrument in France of uncleanness, a fly worker in England for Rome and France in this present affair, a sorcerer by common voice and fame" is merely the instrument of a larger conspiracy, spreading throughout Europe under the auspices of the pope and his Valois partners.[188]

What made *Gaping Gulf* so provocative was not just Stubbs's effrontery in lecturing the queen and her council in print on the sensitive issue of her marriage, but his flagrant violation of the decorum that normally protected royalty from crude defamation. The hurriedly prepared proclamation condemning the book and forbidding subjects from reading it makes this clear. It branded Stubbs "a seditious author," whose "fardel of false reports, suggestions and manifest lies, forged against a prince of royal blood" had offended a foreign court in amity with England, while exciting unreasonable fears among Elizabeth's subjects.[189] The claim that the queen's marriage might produce "utter ruin and a change of government," including "alteration of Christian religion," insulted Elizabeth and her council, reflecting its author's seditious design to undermine popular confidence in the state. But it quickly became clear that Stubbs spoke for a significant body of opinion. Mendoza reported in late October that "two pasquins were recently posted on the Lord Mayor's door, saying some very brutal things about

---

[183] Ibid., 79. I have editorially removed a break between paragraphs in the quotation.
[184] Ibid., 80–1.
[185] Ibid., 85. Stubbs raises this extremely delicate point obliquely, asking whether the French royal family would "match here with so far gone hope of having issue," but the point of this phrase seems clear.
[186] Ibid.   [187] Ibid., 88–90.   [188] Ibid., 92.
[189] TNA SP12/132/11; *Tudor Royal Proclamations*, ed. Paul L. Hughes and James F. Larkin, 3 vols (New Haven: Yale University Press, 1969), 3.445–9.

the marriage, amongst which was that when the marriage was attempted there would be 40,000 men collected and ready to prevent it." The proclamation against Stubbs, he reported, "instead of mitigating the public indignation against the French has irritated it and fanned the flame."[190]

By imprisoning Stubbs and his printer and sentencing both to have their right hands severed by the hangman on a public scaffold, the government added fuel to the fire. Mauvissière reported that the queen wanted to execute Stubbs and had postponed the upcoming session of Parliament to prevent it from interfering. But to Elizabeth's fury, several leading figures interceded on his behalf and secretly encouraged him with promises that he would leave prison unharmed and with honor. A judge and a prominent lawyer spoke publicly in his support, provoking the queen to begin imprisoning Stubbs's supporters.[191] Bishop Aylmer of London warned Hatton that although popular auditors had responded well to praises of the queen in the loyalist sermons he had ordered, they reacted angrily whenever preachers denounced Stubbs, "whereby I perceive that any that bend their pen, wit, knowledge or speech against the foreign prince is of them counted a good patriot and *pius subditus*." He hoped to be able to restrain the inhabitants of London from committing "outrages" but felt unable to vouch for parishes beyond the metropolis. Attempting to discipline preachers in these communities by summoning them to London would, he feared, worsen things by making Londoners more aware of the "grudging and groaning abroad" and encouraging further protests. News of the scandal quickly spread to the Continent. The queen's ambassador in Paris, Poulet, vehemently denied having shown a French translation of Stubbs's tract to Anjou. But he admitted having heard a report that an Italian translation had reached the pope.[192] A Dutch politician wrote in alarm to William Davison, worried that the furor over *Gaping Gulf* and its author might do permanent harm to the queen's relations with Englishmen who supported international Protestant causes.[193]

In September, Sussex tried to take advantage of this backlash by arranging an entertainment at his Essex seat at New Hall during a short autumn progress attended by Lord Burghley and a number of Catholic or religiously conservative peers and gentry, including the earls of Northumberland, Surrey and Rutland, and Viscount Montague. As Neil Younger, who discovered a letter describing this previously unknown episode points out, virtually all these peers favored the Anjou match; they also had ties to other Catholic or crypto-Catholic courtiers, notably the earl of Oxford and Lord Henry Howard. Hatton, along with Leicester and other prominent Protestant courtiers (aside from Burghley) stayed away, although whether because they chose to absent themselves or were not invited is not entirely clear. In the entertainment itself Jupiter exhorted Elizabeth to "admit such a

---

[190] Hatton, 133.   [191] TNA PRO31/3/27 fols 404 and 410–11.   [192] *CSPF* 14.79.
[193] Ibid., 95, 99, Villiers (Josse de Zoete) to Davison, November 20 and 28, 1579.

matrimonial conviction as were meet." But as Younger comments, the primary message was "that support for the marriage within the aristocracy was much more broad-based than a relatively small clique of court Catholics," and that if she chose to go ahead with it she might rely on this body of supporters to counter the opposition of her Protestant courtiers and their supporters.[194]

Court Politics, Print, and the Public Sphere

Gaping Gulf intensified a public controversy over the match that infuriated the queen, while threatening not only to sharpen divisions over Anjou within the court but also to bring about a significant alteration in its composition. It is therefore unsurprising that Stubbs's pamphlet figured fairly prominently several years ago, in separate accounts by Natalie Mears and Peter Lake of the emergence an early Elizabethan "public sphere." Some historians dislike this term because of the heavy load of theoretical baggage it carries due to its coinage by the German historical sociologist Jürgen Habermas, in an analysis of changes in eighteenth-century British political culture.[195] But while the desire to avoid getting bogged down in Habermasian theory is understandable, the emergence of some kind of public dimension to conflict over the queen's marriage raises interpretive issues that merit discussion.

One is the relationship between court politics and more public media, including but not limited to print. Habermas drew a sharp distinction between the two, seeing the former as conducted primarily through oral exchanges among a traditional, "feudal" political elite, and the latter as the product of an emerging bourgeois society that exchanged ideas through a commercial printing industry and in commercial venues like coffee houses. Although no one has tried to apply this Marxian model to Elizabethan England, Mears described Stubbs as the product of a milieu centered around the Inns of Court that she saw as detached from the royal court.[196] Lake, on the other hand, argued that members of the privy council at times encouraged the production of printed tracts on controversial issues, in attempts to "bounce" the queen into accepting policies they favored. Although he never put matters so crudely, this suggests a model of printed

---

[194] Neil Younger, "Drama, Politics and News in the Earl of Sussex's Entertainment of Elizabeth at New Hall, 1579," *Historical Journal* 58 (2015): 343–69, quotation at 354.
[195] Lake and Questier, "Campion Affair," esp. 595–9; Natalie Mears, "Counsell, Public Debate and Queenship: John Stubbs's *The Discoverie of a Gaping Gulf*, 1579," *Historical Journal* 44 (2001): 629–50. Cf. Peter Lake, "The Politics of 'Popularity' and the Public Sphere: The 'Monarchical Republic' of Elizabeth I Defends Itself," in *Politics of the Public Sphere*, ed. Lake and Pincus, 59–94 at 70–82. For the original formulation of the concept see Jürgen Habermas, *The Structural Transformation of the Public Sphere: An Inquiry into a Category of Bourgeois Society*, trans. Thomas Burger (Cambridge, MA: MIT Press, 1991), the English edition of a German work that first appeared in 1962.
[196] Mears, "Counsell, Debate and Queenship."

publicity as, at least in part, court politics pursued through alternative methods. This is, in fact, how Elizabeth saw Stubbs's publication, leading her to threaten retaliation against members of her council she blamed for encouraging its appearance.[197]

But while the queen may have been correct, no solid evidence has come to light proving that Stubbs acted at the behest of a court patron, and we need to consider a third possibility. Stubbs may well have acted on his own, or perhaps in consultation with a few close friends, but with an eye on the court's internal debates, which he would have known about from gossip circulating in his environment. The Inns of Court and adjacent districts were already becoming centers for court news and gossip in the 1570s, inhabited not only by lawyers like Stubbs but also men with at least indirect connections to the privy council. As Mears points out, Stubbs's associates included members of Burghley's household, who probably fed him information about council discussions concerning Anjou that seems to have been reflected in his own writing. In the months preceding the publication of *Gaping Gulf*, Anjou's opponents within the court evidently mounted a campaign to persuade Elizabeth of the depth and vehemence of Protestant suspicions of her French suitor. In January 1579, Mendoza reported that "five books" opposing the match had been smuggled into the queen's apartments.[198] A month later Leicester told Mauvissière that he had needed to calm the fears of his Protestant associates that the queen's marriage to Anjou would lead to an English St. Bartholomew's Day massacre.[199] According to Mendoza, councilors hostile to Anjou began gathering "papers" attacking him and arranging for their transmission to the queen.[200] A French follower of Anjou later reminded Elizabeth of how Anjou's adversaries had tried to poison her mind "by the protests of ladies and secret devices."[201] Some courtiers went so far as to tell the queen that "she would die if she did this thing [i.e. married Anjou]."[202]

Whether or not Stubbs knew all these details, he undoubtedly would have heard at least generalized reports of agitation against the match. He must have realized that his vitriolic attack on Anjou would reverberate within the context of an ongoing campaign already being carried out through oral conversations and scribally produced documents. Just what he hoped to achieve remains unclear, but a possibility worth considering is that he intended, not simply to assist Anjou's court opponents but to prod them into adopting more forceful positions. Although Hatton and Leicester wanted to stop the marriage, as courtiers

---

[197] TNA PRO31/3/27, fol. 408v: Elizabeth believed "qu'il [Stubbs] ne l'avait fait sans le consentement de quelques uns de ce conseil, et ladite dame entra en grandes colères et menaces qui durent encore."
[198] *CSPSp* 2.641.   [199] TNA PRO31/3/27, fol. 275v.   [200] Hatton, 163.
[201] Pierre Clausse, Seigneur de Marchaumont to Elizabeth, undated letter of 1580? reproduced in full in *HMC Salisbury* 2.485 ("sollicitant votre majesté par remontrances de dames, par vis secrets, artifice du roi d'Espagne, le tout sortant d'une même boutique").
[202] *CSPSp* 2.701, 702–3.

dependent on royal favor they hesitated to burn their bridges with a man who might soon become their king. This inhibited them from speaking out as forcefully and openly as they might have liked and as some Protestants beyond the court would certainly have preferred. Leicester told Mauvissière that he had worked to *overcome* opposition to the marriage among other Protestant peers, and at about the time that Stubbs's work appeared the earl was lobbying to have himself appointed to head an embassy to Paris, to present the Garter to Henry III and Anjou.[203] Disappointment with his timidity may lie behind a sermon by John Foxe published in 1579, denouncing courtiers as hypocrites: "Thou thinkest it an honorable thing to be conversant among great personages, thou feedest thy fancy with an Italian grace, with the Spanish fashion and the French courtesy, very serviceable in speech, *à votre commandement, Monsieur*."[204] Although on one level a conventional jeremiad against court vanity, Foxe's timing and his reference to serving "Monsieur"—the honorific title by which Anjou was generally known—suggests a more pointed message. If, as seems very likely, the godly had indeed begun to worry that their allies within the court seemed prepared to acquiesce to the queen's marriage rather than risk losing favor, *Gaping Gulf* would have provided a warning that patience was wearing thin.

Regardless of whether that was Stubbs's intention, the appearance of his work unquestionably intensified and further polarized the court debate, in ways that seriously inconvenienced Leicester and Walsingham, who suffered a period of disfavor because of Elizabeth's perception that they sympathized with and may have encouraged his libelous charges.[205] By its crude *ad hominem* attacks, and even more by the notoriety it attracted, *Gaping Gulf* broke through the conventions of courtesy and deference constraining what people normally felt able to say about great princes. That made it more difficult for Anjou's court opponents to dissimulate their opposition to his suit. But Stubbs simultaneously presented the case against Anjou in a register that would have been thoroughly familiar to the general population. The standing of every individual in Elizabethan society depended on maintaining personal reputation or credit that slanderous accusations might easily damage.[206] In a sense every village had its own miniature public sphere, involving the circulation of common knowledge and gossip about its members that affected how their neighbors perceived them. Salacious rumors about disreputable private behavior were a potent weapon in interpersonal quarrels, as social historians have repeatedly shown. By deploying this weapon against

---

[203] TNA PRO31/3/27, fol. 408.   [204] John Foxe, *Christ Jesus Triumphant* (London, 1579).
[205] This, at least, is the impression Mauvissière's's dispatches convey. See, e.g., TNA PRO31/3/31, fol. 417.
[206] For example, Susan Amussen, *An Ordered Society: Gender and Class in Early Modern England* (Oxford: Blackwell, 1988); Martin Ingram, *Church Courts, Sex and Marriage in England* (Cambridge: Cambridge University Press, 1987); Craig Muldrew, *The Economy of Obligation: The Culture of Credit and Social Relations in Early Modern England* (Basingstoke: Palgrave Macmillan, 1998).

the queen's suitor, Stubbs threatened her honor, since in early modern societies a woman's reputation always suffered if she consorted with a disreputable man.

Elizabeth's swift and vehement reaction shows that she recognized what was at stake. She quickly issued a proclamation denouncing *Gaping Gulf* and prohibiting its possession on pain of death, directed that all copies be seized and destroyed, ordered Stubbs and his printer imprisoned, and told her associates that she wanted them executed. Only with difficulty did her councilors persuade her to diminish the punishment to the severing of the offenders' right hands.[207] For good measure she instructed Aylmer to arrange the preaching of multiple sermons that defended her integrity and attacked Stubbs. But these measures backfired by providing opportunities for demonstrations of public sympathy for Stubbs and disapproval of Anjou, which compounded the damage that *Gaping Gulf* had already inflicted. Rather than vindicating herself and her suitor, Elizabeth turned Stubbs into something of a hero among people Aylmer sarcastically but tellingly described as "patriots and *pius subditus*."[208]

Throughout this episode the public was not only repeatedly addressed, by both Stubbs and the proclamations and sermons denouncing him, but also imaginatively constructed and represented. His punishment and attacks on him from the pulpit were also themselves public events that gave people a chance to express their views not as individuals but as groups, in ways that must have given at least some of them a heightened sense that their neighbors shared their view of Stubbs as a patriot and hero. Reports of public sympathy for him bled into narratives of widespread opposition to the match that had already begun to develop before he set pen to paper, reinforcing the warnings previously conveyed to Elizabeth through manuscripts thrust into her chambers and court whispers.[209] While none of the other entertainments and printed tracts we have examined achieved anything like *Gaping Gulf*'s notoriety, if we look closely we may notice that they also tried not only to address public audiences but also to describe them in ways

---

[207] *CSPSp* 2.7; TNA PRO31/3/27, fols 397r–v, 410r. Cf. TNA SP12/132/6, a circular letter to the bishops drawn up by the council but possibly never sent, instructing them to assemble "the special noted preachers and other persons of ecclesiastical good calling" within their dioceses and order them to refute in the pulpit Stubbs's allegations that the queen's receptivity to Anjou's suit endangered the Protestant Church.

[208] Hatton, 133.

[209] Cf. the argument in Mark Knights, *Representation and Misrepresentation in Later Stuart Britain: Partisanship and Political Culture* (New York: Oxford University Press, 2005) that the eighteenth-century British public was as much a fictive construct or representation as an actual body of people. Knights does not deny that some widening of political participation occurred in the period but he contends that the various devices used to express public sentiment—newspaper articles and pamphlets, petitioning campaigns, elections and even riots—were regularly orchestrated and manipulated for partisan purposes, to create an appearance of broad public support for positions that were actually those of a party or interest group. The development of actual bodies of collective opinion cannot be separated from the various devices used to represent these collectivities. Although the tools used in the Elizabethan period were obviously more rudimentary, I am arguing that a similar insight applies even to the late sixteenth century.

that had policy implications. In doing this they never represented the English public as a collection of autonomous individuals, forming independent judgments about public issues through private reading and reflection or discussion in small groups. Instead they invariably focused on the roles played by socially prominent people—the queen, recusant gentry, conservative peers, or Anjou and his allies—in mobilizing and directing bodies of support that would either promote or subvert social and political order. For Churchyard, the warm exchanges between Elizabeth and her subjects during the East Anglian progress expressed emotional bonds and values binding the realm together under its queen. The progress as he described it embodied healthy hierarchical ties of solidarity, through the ways in which the region's gentry and town magistrates arranged resplendent welcoming ceremonies, and the cheers of humbler subjects who turned out to greet their queen. In doing so it not only proclaimed East Anglia's loyalty but used it as a model for subjects in other regions. Although Sussex's entertainment at New Hall ignored the attitudes of the common people, by demonstrating the breadth of noble and gentry support for Anjou it also sought to convey a reassuring message that Elizabeth might rely on the loyalty of her most powerful subjects. By contrast, for Overton the withdrawal of gentry from the collective responsibilities of county governance signaled the dangerous emergence of a fissure that threatened to destroy social and political harmony, while for Stubbs Anjou was not only a Catholic prince but the incarnation of sinister forces of Machiavellianism, popery, and moral corruption, also found in lesser measure among his followers, which threatened to plunge the kingdom into civil war and moral anarchy. None of these tracts or entertainments challenged the principle that queens, princes, nobles, and gentry would guide and rule the common people. Instead they depicted ways in which that principle was either being upheld through the solidarity of the nation with its queen or undermined by the perverse and factious behavior of *certain* people of high rank, who abused their authority to corrupt their inferiors and divide the nation into warring factions.

Two manuscript treatises on the match produced by courtiers in 1580 as memoranda for the queen continued the same pattern of argumentation. These tracts—by Leicester's nephew, Sir Philip Sidney and Lord Henry Howard—were never printed, although Sidney's circulated in manuscript within limited circles. But they continued to focus on the question of whether Elizabeth's marriage to Anjou would preserve or destroy an existing pattern of social and confessional loyalties that underpinned the state or condition of the realm. Sidney, who apparently wrote his letter at the direction of Leicester, began by describing England as a nation "divided into two mighty factions... bound upon the never-ending knot of religion."[210] He then claimed that Elizabeth's "state is so

---

[210] See *Correspondence of Philip Sidney and Hubert Languet*, 187: "you were ordered to write as you did by those whom you were bound to obey."

enwrapped" with the fortunes of the Protestants that it would be extremely perilous for her to withdraw from this "party."[211] Echoing Stubbs, he asserted that a marriage to Anjou will inevitably alienate the "hearts" of all good Protestants, since "the very common people" know him as "the son of the Jezebel of our age," Catherine de Medicis. This awareness, along with Anjou's record of betraying the Huguenots, will cause "all the true religious to abhor such a master and so consequently to diminish much of the hopeful love they have long held to you [Elizabeth]."[212]

Sidney depicted the opposing papist faction as one that would never provide the queen reliable support. It consisted of "men whose spirits are full of anguish; some being forced to oaths they account damnable; some having their ambition stopped...some in prison and disgrace...many thinking you an usurper; many thinking the right you had disannulled by the Pope's excommunication...men of great number, of great riches (because the affairs of state have not lain on them); of united minds, as all men that deem themselves oppressed naturally are." To these "all discontented persons, such as want and disgrace keeps lower than they have set their hearts" have joined themselves. This coalition lacks "nothing so much as a head" to raise an insurrection. Once again, we encounter the assumption that political movements can only succeed by finding a leader of high rank. "If, then, the affectionate side have their affection weakened, and the discontented have a gap to utter their discontentation, I think it will seem an ill preparative for the patient (I mean your estate) to a greater sickness."[213] Anjou is a man who cannot be trusted in such a situation. "As full of light ambition as is possible," his past conduct has shown an utter lack of scruple and he has collected around himself an entourage of factious young men. "With such fancies and favorites is it to be hoped that he will be contained within the limits of your conditions?"[214]

Sidney's letter goes on to consider the reasons why Elizabeth wants the match, which he identifies as "fear of standing alone in respect of foreign dealings, and in home respects, doubt of contempt." As he undoubtedly knew, this summary corresponded closely to a report the council had presented to the queen the previous April.[215] He quickly dismisses the danger of international isolation to concentrate on the argument that Elizabeth will incur contempt among her subjects by failing to produce an heir. He protests that he would have found this argument incredible if he had not heard it from Elizabeth herself, and argues vigorously that her virtues and the benefits of her government will prevent her subjects from turning to worship a rising sun as she ages. While admitting that a few people have defamed her, he dismisses them as a handful of "curs," overlooking his own description a few pages earlier of the queen's enemies as "men of great

---

[211] *Miscellaneous Prose of Sir Philip Sidney*, ed. Katherine Duncan-Jones and Jan van Dorsten (Oxford: Oxford University Press, 1973), 47.
[212] Ibid., 48.   [213] Ibid., 49.   [214] Ibid., 49–50.   [215] HMC Salisbury, 2.240–52.

number, of great riches...of united minds."[216] He goes on to argue, again rather disingenuously, that Elizabeth's experience in the previous reign, when she had provided a rallying point for Protestants unhappy with Mary, offered no true parallel to the current situation. Because Mary was "the oppressor of that religion which lived in many men's hearts," people looked forward to her death; Elizabeth, who favors the gospel, will not suffer from this problem. This passage ignores a danger that one of Burghley's memoranda explicitly recognized: the likelihood that Elizabeth's childlessness would embolden the large body of English Catholics already sympathetic to Mary Stuart to attempt to shorten her reign.[217]

By contrast Howard's manuscript argues vigorously that the failure to produce offspring will lose Elizabeth her subjects' love. He gives numerous historical examples of dynasties overthrown once it became clear they were about to fail biologically. England's conquests in France only became possible, he asserts, because the French royal family's difficulties in producing heirs had already alienated the population; when this dynastic problem ended, so did English victories.[218] He goes on to anticipate a famous trope of the 1590s by warning Elizabeth that if she does not conceive a child, her situation will become like that of Richard II, and "there will not lack a Henry Bolingbroke presumptuously to undertake the usurpation of the royal dignity."[219] Howard points out that some of Anjou's strongest opponents had repeatedly urged the Queen to marry and settle the succession. By resisting the match, he argues, they now intended "to retain Her Majesty in wardship at forty years of age and above," until they have found an alternative husband who will serve as a "fit instrument" for their own "devices" and "perilous practices."[220] He goes on to discuss the dangers that will follow a marriage between the queen and one of her own subjects, and the advantages of a union with an equal from among the royal families of Europe, among whom Anjou is by far the most eligible.

Throughout, Howard shows acute sensitivity to issues of dynastic honor and dignity, which for him take precedence over all other considerations. He argues that if Elizabeth and Anjou produce a son who inherits the crowns of both kingdoms this will enormously enhance royal honor, an outcome the English should welcome.[221] The risk of England's subjection to an absentee king surrounded by French courtiers does not trouble him. What disturbs him instead is the prospect of the queen marrying a "base companion," whose seed will pollute the royal bloodline and whose elevation will engender an "implacable dislike and

---

[216] *Miscellaneous Prose*, ed. Duncan-Jones and van Dorsten, 54–5.
[217] HMC Salisbury, 2.252: "Thirdly, to the contrary sort there must follow an universal inward joy and comfort to all such as bear no devotion to her Majesty, as desire vehemently a change of religion for popery, as are affected and have secretly vowed themselves to the Scottish Queen enemy to the Queen's Majesty and to true Christian religion and friendly to all such as for their public or private respect have been grieved with many accidents during this government."
[218] *Gaping Gulf*, ed. Berry, 162.   [219] Ibid., 164–5.   [220] Ibid., 171.   [221] Ibid., 190–1.

discontentment of all the nobility." The crux of the matter is the need to preserve a social hierarchy rooted in indelible differences between royal, noble, and common lineages, along with the instinctive desire of the common people to see their royal family perpetuate itself through honorable unions.

Howard therefore emphasizes precisely the kind of dynastic honor that Stubbs had so systematically subverted. Unable to suggest openly that the Anjou match would lead to a reversal of the religious settlement, he needed to downplay the significance of confessional differences by focusing on other issues. By contrast Sidney skirted lightly around concepts of dynastic honor, stressing instead that England had become so divided over religion, and Elizabeth so fully identified with Protestantism that her own "state" was now inseparable from the Protestant cause. But even for Sidney religious parties are groupings united by bonds of kinship and political alliance as much as by theological principle: beneath the surface he was warning the queen not to turn away from the Protestant cohort that had served her so well, by embracing recusant and church papist networks whose loyalty remained deeply suspect.

Politiques, Protestants, and Jesuits: The Division Hardens

Although Elizabeth disliked this message she knew better than to dismiss it, especially since her council had declined to endorse the match in the autumn of 1579. A consultation at Greenwich in early October endorsed the view that the marriage would encourage English Catholics and rebels, while raising the danger of Anjou eventually using French military power to subdue England and disinherit all who opposed him, as "at the time of William [the] Conqueror." Unless a remedy could be found for these risks, "no wise man can make this marriage beneficial."[222] Leicester and Hatton seem to have turned up the heat following this meeting, by presenting Elizabeth with papers opposing the match and suggesting, to her intense annoyance, that if she married Anjou the upcoming session of Parliament might demand that she name an heir, since she had brought "their enemies within their own gates." In November a country minister had the temerity to show up at court with a letter opposing the match. After being ushered into the queen's presence by several councilors he began to read his protest but got through only four lines before Elizabeth ordered him imprisoned.[223] Foreign Protestants also began to weigh in. The previous July a relative of the Scottish regent, James Douglas earl of Morton, named James Morray, had arrived in London to express opposition to the match. According to Mauvissière,

---

[222] Hatfield House Cecil Mss. 148, fols 53, 54v, notes on the Consultation at Greenwich on the Queen's marriage dated October 2, 1579.
[223] Ibid., 703; TNA PRO31/3/27 fols 407r–v, 417.

Huguenots residing in the English metropolis also lobbied against it.[224] The brother of the Elector Palatine, Duke Casimir, visited England in October, complaining loudly that Elizabeth had ruined his credit by failing to pay him the money she had promised to support his intervention in the Dutch war the previous year, and proclaiming his resentment over the fact that she had switched her support to Anjou.[225] He asked permission to raise voluntary contributions in English churches for a new army prepared to intervene in France, should a civil war break out there. Mauvissière, who strongly opposed the request, reported that the queen rejected it.[226]

Although some historians have concluded that the resistance of her own council turned Elizabeth against the match in late 1579, this is not the impression she gave to Mauvissière or her own courtiers. Instead she appeared greatly offended by the opposition to Anjou and prepared to shake up her court and council in response. According to Mendoza she felt "greatly irritated" when courtiers argued against the match, squabbling with Hatton and accusing Sir Francis Knollys of personal disloyalty when he "asked her how she could think of marrying a Catholic."[227] In late October she briefly considered adding four prominent Catholics to the council—including Viscount Montagu and the earl of Northumberland—to reinforce Sussex in his support for Anjou.[228] The following month she spent two and a half days in the London house of the late duke of Norfolk's heir, the earl of Arundel, enjoying "a diversity of very expensive entertainments."[229] Mauvissière reported in December that she had become deeply alienated from several of her ancient councilors, although her anger seemed to have cooled by January.[230] She also warmly discussed with him her dislike of Calvinists and puritans, saying that she found "in the Calvinist religion more passion and useless things and nothing for the health of the soul," and that followers of this creed were seditious.[231] Elizabeth may simply have been telling the French ambassador what she thought he wanted to hear, but it is suggestive that he only reported these anti-Calvinist outbursts during a period in late 1579 and early 1580, the high point of the queen's anger at Stubbs and councilors like Leicester and Walsingham. Thereafter Elizabeth alternately warmed and

---

[224] TNA PRO31/3/27 fol. 358v; 28, fol. 123v; *CSPSp 1580-86*, 28. For Huguenot mistrust of Anjou see Hugues Daussy, *Les Huguenots et Le Roi: Le combat politique de Philippe Duplessis-Mornay (1572-1600)* (Geneva: Droz, 2002), 177.
[225] TNA PRO31/3/27, fol. 396.   [226] Ibid., fol. 440.   [227] *CSPSp* 2.704.
[228] McCoog, "English Jesuit Mission," 192-3; TNA PRO31/3/27, fol. 407. Mauvissière reported that during Elizabeth's visit to Sussex's house of New Hall in October, he had treated her to 'mille belles exhortations récitées en latin par personnes doctes et jeunes enfants, le tous proprement accommodé au temps de ce mariage avec grand blâme à ceux qui voudraient contredire une telle alliance' (TNA PRO31/3/27, fol. 392).
[229] *The Venerable Philip Howard, Earl of Arundel, 1557-1559*, ed. William MacMahon and John Hungerford Pollen, Catholic Record Society Publications 21 (London, 1921), 28-9.
[230] TNA PRO31/3/27, fols 426, 28; fol. 9.   [231] Ibid, fols 404; 28 fol. 18.

cooled to the match, keeping both Mauvissière and her own councilors guessing about the outcome.[232]

But events not only in England but also in Spain, France, Ireland, and Scotland had begun to move in directions that further accentuated religious tensions, undercutting the viability of a cross-confessional dynastic alliance. Early in the new year, reports of a great fleet assembling in Spain alarmed the queen and council, causing them to initiate preparations to resist a possible invasion.[233] The episode revived fears about the secret Catholic league that France and Spain were thought to have concluded to exterminate Protestantism.[234] Mendoza, who knew that the Spanish fleet was not intended against England, nevertheless stoked the queen's fears because he thought that Spain's military preparations encouraged English and Irish Catholics to see Elizabeth's rule as vulnerable and step up their resistance.[235] A new religious war erupted in Languedoc after Henry of Navarre's Huguenot troops took the city of Cahors in June, massacring some Catholics. Anticipating a counter-attack, the prince of Condé arrived in London seeking financial assistance. Mauvissière strongly protested and believed he had persuaded the queen to deny the Huguenots support.[236] But the English ambassador in Paris, Lord Cobham, warned of ominous signs of a design to crush French Protestantism, and Walsingham and others on the council wanted to assist Condé.[237] The queen's own suspicions of Henry III's intentions led Mauvissière to warn that a renewed outbreak of serious war in France might scuttle the match. He believed that English "puritans" had attempted to incite the Huguenots in hopes that this would happen. In early July, Sussex complained to Burghley that Leicester, Walsingham, and Hatton had frozen him out of negotiations with Condé, and warned that a "precipitate" decision to assist the Huguenots "would not only overthrow all Monsieur's intentions but also shut up wholly all means for peace and lay the wars fully open, whereof she [Elizabeth] must be the head and in the end is not able to bear the charge."[238] Anjou and Simier also appealed to the queen to restrain Condé from hiring German mercenaries with English money, evidently with success. But Elizabeth then reacted furiously when a Catholic army laid siege to the Huguenot stronghold of La Ferté.[239] Although she blamed Henry III rather than her suitor, the renewed outbreak of religious war across the channel deepened mistrust of the Valois. In October, Mendoza again tried to fan worries about a secret Catholic plot between France and Spain by treating Mauvissière

---

[232] As late as August 1581 Burghley wrote to Walsingham, who had recently departed on an embassy to Paris, "I find her Majesty in words more inclined to the marriage than at your departure." *The Complete Ambassador*, ed. Dudley Digges (London, 1655), 390.
[233] *CSPSp* 3.10–11 and 16–17; Hatton, 159; TNA PRO31/3/28, fol. 32 and SP78/4A/22.
[234] TNA SP78/4A/21. [235] *CSPSp* 3.16–17, 22. Philip II approved of this stratagem (29).
[236] TNA PRO31/3/28, fols 127, 133v, 135.
[237] TNA SP78/4A, fol. 43; *CSPF* 14.296, 473; BL Cotton Mss. Caligula CVI, fol. 54 (Walsingham to Bowes, June 22, 1589).
[238] HMC Salisbury 2.329. [239] Ibid., 335.

"with more cordiality than usual, inviting him to my house and the like, which arouses great suspicion in the queen's mind."[240]

The situation in Scotland had meanwhile become worrying, as the position of the pro-English regent Morton deteriorated and the English council began receiving reports from both Edinburgh and Paris about d'Aubigny's efforts to build a Catholic and Francophile party.[241] Elizabeth feared that d'Aubigny was conspiring to carry James into France, while others suspected a French design, in which Anjou might be complicit, to use Scotland as a base from which to invade England.[242] Mauvissière heard a rumor in February that James VI would soon convert to Catholicism, while a few months later he complained that "those who want to stop the marriage and your friendship [i.e. between France and England] have wanted to give fears and jealousies from the side of Scotland."[243] Morton's execution in June 1581 for complicity in the murder of James's father, Lord Darnley, some thirteen years before, signaled the triumph of d'Aubigny's faction and complete disintegration of English control over Scotland.[244] On the eve of his execution the fallen regent blamed Elizabeth's dalliance with Anjou for the resurgence of Scottish Catholicism, saying it had disheartened her friends and encouraged her enemies. He privately confided to two clergymen that he feared the queen's marriage to Anjou would lead to the total subversion of Protestantism in all of Britain.[245]

Conditions in Ireland also deteriorated as the Munster rebellion continued, drawing in the region's leading magnate, James earl of Desmond.[246] In England sermons critical of the match continued to be preached. One, given during Lent in 1580, somehow found its way into print, complaining of "the danger to the commonwealth where the prince groweth to be insolent and opinative."[247] Shortly thereafter, in June, the first Jesuit missionaries to England—Thomas Campion, Robert Persons, and Ralph Emerson—arrived. As Thomas McCoog has shown, the Order's father general, Everard Mercurian, did not want Jesuits to become entangled in dangerous political activities. But this did not stop the three missionaries. Shortly after his arrival Campion preached a sermon in Lord Paget's London house strongly defending papal authority.[248] In July, he and Persons

---

[240] *CSPSp* 3.62.
[241] See, e.g., BL Cotton Mss. Caligula CVI, fols 11, 12, 29, 69, 72, 82v, 85v, 98v; *CSPF* 14.305, 414, 441. Questier, *Dynastic Politics*, 136–8 also comments on the connection between events in Scotland and religious tensions in England.
[242] *CSPSp* 4.37.   [243] TNA PRO31/3/28, fol. 24v and dispatch of May 27.
[244] These events will be reviewed in greater detail in Chapter 3, below.
[245] TNA PRO31/3/28, fol. 171; BL Harley Mss. 281, fol. 21r–v: "The Monsieur [Anjou] dare not change his religion if he hope for the Crown of France, and therefore you may be assured he will travail to persuade the Queen to his religion and to bring papists into England, which is very easy to be done, the two parts of England being papists. If England and France bind together and be both papists we are left alone... and therefore... in what case shall the religion be with us?"
[246] Below, Chapter 5.   [247] Anonymous, *A Sermon Preached in Lent* (1580), 51.
[248] Questier, *Dynastic Politics*, characterizes this as "virtually a public sermon" (128).

attended an underground synod, in which they argued vigorously against permitting lay Catholics to attend Protestant services. Persons then wrote *A brief discourse containing certayne reasons why Catholiques refuse to go to church* and had it printed on a secret press, while his colleague drew up a challenge to Protestants to engage in a public debate known as "Campion's Brag" that quickly became notorious. As McCoog comments, the circulation of manuscript copies of this last piece removed the religious debate "from ambassadorial chambers to the market place," while instantly turning Campion into "a champion to Catholics and the most wanted priest in England."[249] This alarmed not only strong Protestants but the queen herself, who was described in December as "sharply bent against the papists," to a point at which she contemplated demanding Catholics swear the oath of allegiance and punishing those who twice refused to do so as traitors.[250]

A few months later the earl of Oxford had a falling out with his court allies after seducing Henry Howard's niece, Ann Vavasour. During the Christmas season Leicester persuaded Oxford to reveal the conspiratorial approaches he and his colleagues had made to Mauvissière the previous year. As an investigation began, Henry Howard and two other members of the Catholic network, Francis Southwell and Charles Arundell, panicked and sought refuge with Mendoza, fearing for their lives. They soon surrendered after learning that the queen did not want them executed, but Hatton, Leicester, and Walsingham assembled enough evidence to show that Catholics with access to the court had wanted to use the match to overturn the religious settlement.[251] These revelations compounded the effects of Campion's and Parson's activism, by showing that instead of conciliating these prominent Catholics the marriage negotiations had emboldened them. The council responded by imprisoning and interrogating several leaders, including Lord Howard and his nephew, Philip earl of Arundel, and then launched a broader crackdown on recusancy that will be discussed in the next chapter. Howard's brief refuge in the Spanish embassy led to a more enduring relationship with Mendoza.[252]

Anjou's French partisans tried to counter the effects of this confessional polarization by blaming the conspiracies on Spanish agitation and machinations by the duke of Guise. They warned that English Catholics would continue to plot until they received a leader capable of protecting their interests, while assuring

---

[249] McCoog, "English Jesuit Mission," 201–2.
[250] TNA SP12/144/49, William Herle to Burghley, December 13.
[251] McCoog, "English Jesuit Mission," 202–3.
[252] *Arundel*, ed. Pollen and MacMahon, 31: "Milord Harry, in gratitude for the goodwill with which I had received him, and with a care which I can hardly describe, has informed and informs me of everything he hears, which is of service to your majesty, and recognizes my favor, no little novelty for an Englishman to do. He has very good qualities and intelligence, and much friendship with the ladies of the privy chamber, who inform him exactly what passes indoors. He is also as intimate with the earl of Sussex, as nail with quick."

Elizabeth of their own loyalty.²⁵³ But it did little good. While it is impossible to pinpoint the moment when Elizabeth abandoned her hopes of marrying Anjou or the precise reason she did so, the most plausible explanation is that the accumulating evidence of Catholic intransigence and hostility—in Scotland, Ireland, France, Spain, and in her own kingdom—convinced her that a dynastic alliance with a French Catholic prince had become impracticable. Too many things had happened during the spring and summer of 1580 for her Protestant subjects to accept such an eventuality or for the queen to believe she might rely on Catholic loyalty. In 1581, as a parliament convened and proceeded to stiffen the penalties against recusancy, Elizabeth informed Anjou that the climate of religious opinion in England made it impossible for her to marry him:

> I must tell you that in this assembly of our estates [the parliament] I find the fear and murmuring against our marriage in no way diminished but rather increased, for reasons I have already communicated to you, due to the conduct that the Jesuits, sent in great number to England, so that there are few places in the kingdom that do not have such persuaders to turn people from their obedience, telling them that it is a mortal sin to obey me; and coming at the command of the Pope, to whom they [the English] know that the king [Henry III] and you are obedient. They believe this alliance will plunge us into disorder, the Catholics having the impudence to make trouble under your shadow, the others despairing of aid from my hands, who will not consent to displease you, or if this happens it will produce ill will between us that will torment me worse than death itself.²⁵⁴

Mendoza reported being told by Lord Henry Howard on Christmas Day 1581 that Anjou had responded to the queen's arguments by offering to become a Protestant.²⁵⁵ No one appears to have trusted him enough to take up the offer.

But the gravity of the international situation also made it imperative that Elizabeth maintain a working relationship with French *politiques* and the French crown, since she could not afford to deal with her problems in the Low Countries, Scotland, and Ireland if she also had to defend herself from a hostile France. Although negotiations over the match continued sporadically into 1582,

---

²⁵³ See Marchaumont's letter to Elizabeth, undated but probably 1580 in HMC Salisbury 2.488.
²⁵⁴ HMC Salisbury 2.480: "il faut que je vous dis que en cette assemblée de nos états je trouve la crainte et murmure nullement diminué, ains avancée de ce mariage, pour les raisons que au-devant je vous communiquais, connaissant le menées que les Jésuites, mandées en grand nombre en Angleterre, ont procurés si avant, qu'il y a peu de lieux de ce royaume qui n'ont grand nombre de tels persuadeurs pour leur détourner de mon obéissance, leurs persuadent que c'est mortel péché de m'obéir et eux sortent par commandement du Pape, auquel ils savent que le roi et vous tous obéissent, croient que cette alliance nous mettra tout en brouillerie, les Catholiques prenant hardiesses sous votre ombre à faire assez de trouble, les autre n'espérant d'aide de mes mains, qui ne consentirait à vous déplaire, ou si le fisse, cela se tournerait à malveillance entre nous deux; qui me tourmenterait plus que la mort même."
²⁵⁵ *CSPSp* 3.253.

they now owed more to Elizabeth's desire to keep her options open and English fears of driving Anjou into the arms of Spain and French ultra-Catholics, than a serious belief that a marriage might still occur. Elizabeth turned the negotiations into a cover for bargaining over the conditions under which England subsidized Anjou's army, obliging him to continue in the role of her lover and servant even as his prospects of ever obtaining her hand receded.[256]

Aftermath: The Sharpening of Confessional and Dynastic Divisions

Rather than improving the situation of English Catholics, negotiations over the Anjou match had therefore ended with the consolidation of Protestant control over the council and more strenuous repression of recusancy and missionary activity. The bitterness these setbacks engendered in some circles comes through vividly in a letter of recrimination sent by William Tresham to his erstwhile friend and patron, Hatton, who had declined to intervene to save the writer's brother, Thomas, from imprisonment on suspicion of sedition:

> Sir, remember that the bee gathereth honey of every flower and of many travails frameth a sweet and comfortable being for herself and young ones all the cold winter; but the grasshopper all the summer time joyeth with gallantry in the pleasant meadows and dieth commonly with the cold dew of Bartholomew. You know that the high cedar trees on the tops of huge mountains are most subject to the danger of storms and therefore have most need of many and sure roots. We are all in God's hands, to be raised or pulled down as it shall please Him; and there is none so high now, but may one day, through affliction, stand in as great need of comfort as now my poor brother and your dear friend doth. I beseech you think of him and vouchsafe to bind us and our posterity unto you by the goodness that you may now afford him in furthering his enlargement. The day may come that you may find either him, or his, better able than now they are to acknowledge in all good sort and thankfully to requite your kindness.[257]

Falling in late August, the feast day of St. Bartholomew signaled the end of summer, but Tresham's reference to its killing "cold dew" also hinted unmistakably at the bloody retribution that he wanted to visit on his Protestant tormentors, and possibly also on Hatton. Dashed hopes led to thoughts of violent retribution, while the growing certainty that Elizabeth would die without an heir gave

---

[256] Holt, *Anjou*, chapter 7. His adoption of this role, which in many ways parallels that adopted by loyal Englishmen, is evident in his letters to her, scattered throughout HMC Salisbury vol. 2.
[257] Hatton, 352–3. The letter is undated but must have been written in 1582 or 1583.

Catholics reason to hope for a reversal of fortune in the fairly near future. The same circumstances gave Protestants even stronger incentives to prevent the succession of a Catholic monarch by any and all available means. Losing the confessional and dynastic contest would expose them not only to religious persecution but the penalties for treason: execution, confiscation of their property, and the ruin of their heirs. To avoid that catastrophe, they needed to limit preemptively the ability of Catholics to rally widespread organized support for a candidate of their own choosing in any future contest for the throne.

Since both confessional camps had royal and noble leaders, the conflict between them did not directly imperil the survival of social and political hierarchy. But the intensification of religious conflict nevertheless had potentially unsettling implications. It not only exacerbated rivalries between landed dynasties but encouraged partisans in both camps to try to weaken their opponents' ability to command deference and obedience by attacking their reputations. As the next chapter will show, this was sometimes done through criminal proceedings, the dismissal of individuals from public office, the orchestration of local protests against their conduct, and the deliberate spreading of rumors. Personal and dynastic libels were another weapon. The most notorious Catholic attack on the Elizabethan regime in the 1580s, commonly known as *Leicester's Commonwealth*, is a prime example. Printed on the Continent in 1584, it also circulated widely in manuscript, giving rise to a black legend of Elizabeth's favorite on which Camden and other historians later drew.[258] A recent study has described it as a kind of *Ur-text* for stereotypes of evil councilors down to the reign of Charles I.[259] Lake situates it within a tradition of Catholic polemics going back to the *Treatise of Treasons* and extending forward into the 1590s, while showing how its authors constructed a sophisticated and seemingly plausible account of the ways in which Leicester and his cronies had infiltrated and subverted the Elizabethan state.[260] In doing this, *Leicester's Commonwealth* also portrayed the earl not just as a Machiavellian courtier but the scion of an upstart ignoble family with a long record of deceit, political manipulation, and treason. It pointed out that his grandfather, Edmund Dudley, was executed for treason at the outset of Henry VIII's reign and that his father, John Dudley, had usurped the title of duke of Northumberland from its rightful holder, before marrying Lady Jane Gray to his son and conspiring to place them on the throne by disinheriting the rightful heir. It accused Leicester himself of a host of moral and sexual crimes. He seduced other men's wives and murdered their husbands, along with his political opponents and sometimes his own

---

[258] For a summary of existing knowledge concerning the writing and circulation of this treatise see the introduction to *Leicester's Commonwealth: The Copy of a Letter Written by a Master of Art at Cambridge and Related Documents*, ed. D. C. Peck (Athens, OH: Ohio University Press, 1985).

[259] Curtis Perry, *Literature and Favoritism in Early Modern England* (Cambridge: Cambridge University Press, 2006), chapter 2 and passim.

[260] *Bad Queen Bess?*, esp. chapter 5.

henchmen, often by poison. His ultimate design was to replace Elizabeth on the throne first with his ally, the earl of Huntingdon, and finally with one of his own descendants, thereby accomplishing the work of dynastic subversion his father had unsuccessfully attempted in 1553.[261]

Written by aristocratic exiles living in exile in Paris, *Leicester's Commonwealth* was intended as an occasional piece that would appear during the chaotic situation following the execution of a plan to assassinate Elizabeth and trigger a Catholic rebellion.[262] The goal was not only to defame Leicester and, by extension, the queen's Protestant entourage, but to sow confusion about who the true supporters of Elizabeth, legitimate authority, and social order really were. The tract argued that the only way to preserve hierarchical order under a legitimate queen was to overthrow by violence the ruling group of unprincipled social upstarts at the heart of the Protestant state and replace them by a rival cohort recruited from old Catholic noble families. The argument had a certain plausibility because the dynastic ambitions of the Dudley family and Leicester himself were well-known. The earl's father *had* tried to install his son as Lady Jane's king-consort, and Leicester himself had openly courted the queen earlier in the reign, causing scandal by so doing. Even after she rejected his suit he probably continued to hope that he might somehow find a way to link his own lineage to the royal family.[263] Mendoza's dispatches passed on a series of rumors circulating about Leicester's designs on the throne. The earl allegedly planned to marry his recently born son to Arabella Stuart, with a view to asserting her claim to the throne, after first eliminating Mary and James VI;[264] Elizabeth reportedly believed that Leicester's wife, the former countess of Essex, wanted to marry her daughter to James VI. Mendoza reported that "puritans" discussed justifications for deposing and murdering Elizabeth, so as to replace her with a more rigorous Protestant.[265]

Although printed Catholic polemics generally spared the queen herself from scandalous criticism, salacious stories about her circulated orally,[266] and some Catholics were preparing a systematic campaign of defamation against her, to be unleashed in conjunction with a planned invasion by the duke of Guise. A Scottish Jesuit with some knowledge of the Throckmorton plot, captured and interrogated by the English authorities, reported that the invasion force would have carried a

---

[261] *Leicester's Commonwealth*, ed. Peck, 95.   [262] Ibid., 149–50.
[263] For a discussion of this subject see Michael Brennan, *The Sidneys of Penshurst and the Monarchy, 1500–1700* (Aldershot: Ashgate, 2006).
[264] *CSPSp* 3.426 and 452. Arabella Stuart, a second cousin of James VI, would have inherited his claim if he died without producing heirs and if Mary also died without giving birth to additional children. In addition to this rumor Mendoza reported that the queen believed that Leicester's wife, the former countess of Essex, was planning to marry a daughter from her first marriage to James VI; and that Leicester and Walsingham had reached a secret agreement with the Prince of Orange for Dutch naval support during a succession struggle following the queen's death.
[265] Ibid., 264, 496, 266–7 and 431.
[266] E.g. HMC, *Calendar of the Manuscripts of the Marquis of Bath Preserved at Longleat*, 5 vols (London, 1904–80), 5.58.

number of manuscript libels against the queen in its baggage, along with a press.[267] Upon landing, the invaders planned to print and distribute the libels, along with proclamations denouncing Leicester and Huntingdon, asserting James VI's title to the English throne and threatening all who opposed him with the penalties of treason. Within the realm, the recusant community had assigned Dr. Nicholas Harpsfield the task of preparing works for the press impugning the legitimacy of Elizabeth's birth and title. A printer named William Carter, assigned to work with him, inherited Harpsfield's papers after his death and still had them when caught and interrogated. Harpsfield had written four books, two in English and two in Latin. One in each language attacked the queen's legitimacy directly, while the others did so in the context of historical accounts of the lives of Sir Thomas More and Archbishop Cranmer. Harpsfield defamed not only Elizabeth but "her father, mother, grandmother, aunt, uncle" and other near relations. As ammunition he possessed an archive of documents dating back to the 1530s that had once belonged to Bishop Bonner and Cardinal Pole, perhaps left over from an earlier abortive campaign of defamation prepared during Mary's reign. One his tracts, of which 1,250 copies had been printed, urged ladies of the bedchamber to poison Elizabeth.[268]

Protestants responded in kind with attacks on the "Scottish Jezebel" Mary Stuart and other Catholic leaders both within and beyond the realm. A number of historians, including Alistair Bellany, Alan Bryson, Thomas Cogswell, Pauline Croft, and Adam Fox have demonstrated the widespread use of libels as personal and political weapons in early modern England.[269] Although many earlier specimens exist, Bellany thinks that the number exploded after about 1580. If so this may be one further indication of the importance of the events described in this chapter in producing a more contentious political and social environment.[270] Although libels and slanders did not directly question the hierarchical organization of society, a real danger existed that if left unchecked their proliferation would

---

[267] TNA SP12/173/4: "Then they make an argument that her majesty is not beloved, against whom to bring her highness into slander they have most infamous and slanderous libels already made, but not yet printed, which then shall be published. To which end and for other proclamations which then shall be set forth, they appoint to have a printer with them."

[268] BL Add Mss. 48029, fols 58–59v.

[269] Alistair Bellany, "'Raylinge Rymes and Vaunting Verse': Libellous Politics in Early Stuart England, 1603–1628," in *Culture and Politics in Early Stuart England*, ed. Kevin Sharpe and Peter Lake (Basingstoke: Macmillan, 1994); Alistair Bellany, "Railing Rhymes Revisited: Libels, Scandals and Early Stuart Politics," *History Compass* 5 (2007): 1136–79; Alan Bryson, "Elizabethan Verse Libel," in *Age of Shakespeare*, ed. Smuts, 477–92; Thomas Cogswell, "Underground Verse and the Transformation of Early Stuart Political Culture," in *Political Culture and Cultural Politics in Early Modern England: Essays Presented to David Underdown* (Manchester: Manchester University Press, 1995), 277–300; Pauline Croft, "Libels, Popular Literacy and Public Opinion in Early Modern England," *Bulletin of the Institute for Historical Research* 68 (1995): 265–85; Adam Fox, *Oral and Literate Culture in England, 1500–1700* (Oxford: Oxford University Press, 2000), chapter 6; *Verse Libel in Renaissance England and Scotland*, ed. Steven May and Alan Bryson (Oxford: Oxford University Press, 2016).

[270] Bellany, "Railing Rhymes Revisited."

begin to act as a solvent to normal attitudes of deference among the common people and of courtesy and cooperation among the elite. They had the power to produce local outbreaks of disorder by fanning animosities over religion and other matters, as in King's Lynn in 1582, where a group of malcontents stirred dissension "and almost rebellion in the town, by slanderous libels and rhymes" against the mayor, aldermen, and two ministers.[271]

Recognition of this danger encouraged countervailing efforts to reinforce reverence and loyalty, especially to the queen, through the elaboration of a literary, visual, and ceremonial cult. Although ritualized devotion to English monarchs had existed throughout the Middle Ages, and had been accorded to Elizabeth from the time of her coronation, recent studies have again detected a significant upsurge from about 1580, suggesting once more the pivotal importance of the period of the Anjou courtship.[272] It is simplistic to attribute this development entirely to court "propaganda." Courtiers, along with the poets, writers, and pageant masters they patronized, certainly helped to create the royal cult, but so did people acting on their own initiative, like the hundreds of splendidly clad gentlemen Churchyard described riding out to meet Elizabeth as she entered Suffolk and Norfolk. These individuals knew that the collapse of the queen's authority might harm their own peace and security, by bringing their communities closer to civil war. They had reasons to promote the queen's *state*, in the double sense of her ceremonial dignity and her political power, since her aura of legitimacy protected their *state*, the undisturbed possession of their property and civic peace of their communities.

A few fanatical partisans aside, everyone had an interest in avoiding a descent into religious violence. This fact gave Protestants a certain tactical advantage, since they might claim to be defending not only their religion but the peace of their communities by targeting missionary priests and recusants who willfully defied the law by absenting themselves from parish worship. On the other hand, excessively zealous efforts to target Catholics might also look socially disruptive. Safeguarding the existing state required not just repression but a measure of tact and political finesse, a subject that the next chapter will examine.

---

[271] TNA SP12/150/97. [272] I have discussed this topic in "Occasional Events."

2
The Containment of Militant English Catholicism

The Challenge of the 1580s

In January 1580 Lord Burghley's eldest son, Thomas Cecil, wrote a long memorandum for the queen on the current political situation.[1] Although he may never have sent it, his arguments sufficiently resemble those of Burghley's own memoranda to suggest that they reflect discussions within his father's entourage. Thomas began by asserting that the Anjou match offered the best way of securing the kingdom's future. Without it he saw several "principal perils" threatening Elizabeth and her state, beginning with "the lack of issue of your own body, which will draw all persons to have their eyes bent upon some other successor." He regarded this problem as insoluble, "for it is against natural reason that the subjects of so puissant a realm as this is, being utterly desperate of a successor of your own body should not in their hearts look who should succeed you and rule them with their ... lives, lands and goods."[2] Cecil worried not only that a succession crisis might follow the queen's death but that even during her life her subjects would turn to a rival who seemed capable of securing their futures, in preference to an aging ruler whose power to protect friends and punish enemies might end at any moment. Burghley himself had made a similar point a few months earlier, noting an old saying that the favors of the people are attracted *"potius ad orientem quam occidentem solem,"* more toward the rising than the setting sun. Once it became clear that Elizabeth would never have a child, he predicted, rival candidates to succeed her would start maneuvering, "secretly and yea openly," to the detriment of the kingdom's peace.

In Ireland James Fitzmaurice had reached a similar conclusion, which he saw as an opportunity rather than a danger. Although "Henry VIII left behind him one son and two daughters," he wrote to the earl of Desmond in the spring of 1579, none of them had lawful issue, "because even as King Henry had overthrown many houses in England who bare the ensign of God and, as it were, represented God's majesty towards us, even so God hath determined to root up all them by

---

[1] Hatfield House Cecil Mss. 148, fols 19–21. Cecil enumerated nine concerns but some of these overlap, and I have consolidated his list in what follows.
[2] Ibid., fol. 20.

whom King Henry's name and blazon might have been maintained." That is why even Mary Tudor, "a builder up of God's house for her own part, yet for revenge of her father's fault...left no heir of her own body behind her." It had now become clear that Elizabeth would also leave "no issue of her own body either to reward them that should fight for her or to revenge them that shall fight against her, being a woman that is surely hated of her successor, whosoever he be, and therefore they that seek to please her cannot but be unpleasant to the next heir to the Crown."[3] Considerations not only of religion but also of dynastic pride and self-interest therefore dictated that Desmond should rally to the rebellion now underway, as he soon did. "God forbid the day should ever come wherein it might be said that the earl of Desmond hath forsaken his poor kinsman, his faithful servant the lieutenant of his spiritual father, the banner of his merciful savior, the defense of his ancient faith, the delivery of his dear country and the safeguard of his noble house and posterity."[4] Fitzmaurice sent a similar message to the earl of Kildare, to whom both he and Desmond were distantly related. "Let us consider that our house had continued this many hundred years in honor by keeping the Catholic faith and obeying Catholic princes; being therefore sure of that let us not now put it in hazard whether it shall stand also as long by professing obedience to heretical princes."[5]

Thomas Cecil worried that in addition to encouraging defections among her subjects, the queen's childlessness would furnish opportunities to foreign "popish princes" who wished to punish her for assisting rebels in their own dominions.[6] The prospect of an invasion troubled him less than several domestic problems that foreign princes might exploit. These included the vulnerability of England's economy to a stoppage of trade that would spread distress through the kingdom's maritime and cloth making communities, the incitement of conspiracies focused around Mary Stuart and her son, and the "the stirring of rebellion in Ireland." Cecil noted the "civil" grievances of the Irish, due to the "very hard dealings" that had deprived the native nobility of "their ancient strength, honor and surety," and a "fear of conquest, of late deeply engrafted in the hearts of the wild Irish" by the unwillingness of the Dublin authorities "to wink at some private disorders that do not properly offend the crown."[7] He believed that the aggressive reform campaigns of recent lord deputies like Sussex and Sir Henry Sidney were simply too provocative and too expensive to sustain while the crown faced other urgent challenges. While advising Elizabeth to invest in strategically located forts along Ireland's coast to guard against invading forces, he also urged her to relax pressure on the Irish.[8]

---

[3] TNA SP63/67/32.   [4] Ibid.   [5] Ibid.
[6] Hatfield House Cecil Mss. 148, fol. 20, items 2 and 3 on his list.   [7] Ibid., fol. 20v.
[8] Ibid., fol. 121 for the forts.

Even if it did not produce a serious rebellion, Cecil knew that the mere threat of foreign intervention might distract and weaken the state, since "the charges to resist these attempts by land and sea... your ordinary revenues of your realm will not bear and in time of trouble will hardly be levied by way of subsidies." Burghley also worried that by stirring rebellion in Ireland, a foreign king might exhaust the queen's treasure at minimal cost to himself: "For generally offers of offence being but small do draw persons offended to pay largely for defense... If her Majesty for her defense shall be forced to expend treasure and employ and waste her people, her realm will be wearied therewith... whereto is to be added notably that the realm [of Ireland] already is of late years increased with motives discontented, especially for religion, but the motive also not small for other causes civil."[9] The expense of suppressing Irish discontents threatened to drain the queen's treasure and exhaust her people's patience, leaving England itself more vulnerable to other troubles. Since the crown in fact spent over £230,000—nearly a year's revenues—suppressing Irish rebellions between 1578 and 1582, this analysis had substance.

As Morton's power disintegrated and d'Aubigny's influence rose, Scotland increasingly looked like another source of danger and sinkhole for English treasure. In notes for a council meeting in April 1579, Burghley commented that an enemy "may with three or four thousand soldiers and 100,000 crowns in Scotland force Her Majesty" to spend "above £400,000" guarding her northern frontier.[10] Mendoza recognized the benefits Spain might reap by fomenting trouble in Scotland, as did a number of English Catholics, including Sir Thomas Tresham and members of the Howard family, who thought that a serious missionary campaign might well reverse the progress of the Scottish Reformation.[11] Since English Jesuits would merely face expulsion if caught preaching Catholicism in Scotland, it was suggested that they spearhead the effort.[12] Mendoza hoped that if these plans succeeded, a small invasion force from the Continent, ostensibly of Catholic volunteers, might link up with sympathetic Scots and discontented English Catholics in the North and trigger a large rebellion. Even if Elizabeth survived, he reasoned, she might need to spend so much money guarding against the threats to her north that she would have to withdraw support for the Dutch.[13]

The queen and her council knew or suspected enough of these plans to be seriously alarmed. A discussion by the privy council in November 1580 concluded that James might attempt to enlist foreign assistance and the aid of English malcontents to challenge Elizabeth's hold on the throne. It was pointed out that

---

[9] Ibid., fol. 29v.   [10] Ibid., fol. 35v.

[11] *CSPSp* 3.169, 170–1, 292–3, 363, 372–3, 379, 518–19. For Philip's cautious but interested reaction, ibid., 276, 278, 343, 525. For a discussion see Thomas McCoog, "'Pray to the Lord of the Harvest': Jesuit Missions to Scotland in the Sixteenth Century," *Innes Review* 53 (2002): 127–88.

[12] *CSPSp* 3.287. The story of Spanish, Jesuit, and other Catholic attempts to destabilize England through Scotland will be investigated in detail in the next chapter.

[13] *CSPSp* 3, passim.

civil wars and the service of Scottish volunteers in the Low Countries had substantially improved Scottish military performance since the 1560s, so that in any future war the English must expect to encounter a more formidable enemy than the one they had easily defeated in the past.[14] In February the queen told the French ambassador Castleneau "that Scotland has been perpetually the place from which attempts against England have come and that she had certain information that the King of Spain had that design."[15] Philip II had, in fact, approved a plan devised by Mary's followers to kidnap James and bring him to Spain, so he might be educated in Catholicism and married to a Catholic princess.[16] The deterioration of Anglo-Scots relations led to an increase of criminal violence along the borders, causing English tenants to abandon their holdings and prompting worries that the frontier districts were no longer capable of self-defense.

But in responding to this threat Elizabeth and her council felt hampered by their growing involvement in the Netherlands, to prevent either France or Spain from dominating the region. Thomas Cecil continued to regard the possibility of a French annexation of the Low Countries as the most significant peril. He saw three possible methods of avoiding it, "all dangerous and costly, and none assured." The Queen might take upon herself leadership of the Dutch rebellion, "which will be very chargeable and the sequel doubtful"; she might attempt to "trouble France with foreign wars and civil discord, ... which will also be chargeable and the issue uncertain"; or she might assist Philip II in regaining his sovereignty, "which will also be very chargeable, and perhaps as dangerous as any of the others."[17] While it is clear in retrospect that Cecil overestimated the danger from France while underestimating that from Spain, he correctly perceived that England no longer had a safe exit strategy from the Low Countries. The anticipated demands of the Dutch war help explain why Elizabeth backed away from a military confrontation with Scotland in 1580, as well as her haste in disbanding her Irish army as soon as it appeared to have gotten the better of the Munster rebellion. She needed to conserve resources even if it meant sacrificing her ally Morton, accepting an unfriendly regime in Edinburgh, and failing to finish off her Irish rebels. Burghley regarded the bloodshed caused by civil wars in France and the Low Countries as lamentable "in respect of public and Christian charity," but concluded that since "the law of God and nature doth allow to all princes the defense of their own state and people" the Queen had every right to assist rebels against kings who might otherwise attack her.[18] She "must not spare" in aiding foreign Protestants, "in men, in money or in both." She must also seek an offensive and defensive alliance with Henry of Navarre—who as a king had the

---

[14] BL Cotton Mss. Caligula CVI, fol. 82v: "The Scottish nation is at this day stronger in feats of arms that it was afore time, by reason of their exercise in civil wars at home and their being abroad in the Low Countries."
[15] Teulet, *Relations Politiques*, 3.95.   [16] Teulet, *Papiers d'état*, 3.252.
[17] Hatfield House Cecil Mss. 148, fol. 21r.   [18] BL Cotton Mss. Caligula CVI, fol. 50r.

right to enter into such treaties—as well as the Protestant kings of Denmark and Scotland and several princes in Germany. But since all foreign alliances are "doubtful," England must also prepare to stand alone.[19]

Thomas Cecil's memorandum shows the degree to which people close to the privy council believed in 1580 that Elizabeth and her state faced a looming crisis that derived partly from the certainty that Elizabeth would die without a direct heir, but also from a tangled web of domestic English, Irish, Scottish, and continental European challenges. The vulnerability of the English economy to commercial disruption and the role of New World silver in financing Spanish armies also gave the crisis an Atlantic dimension. It can therefore only be fully understood through a discussion that considers not only the interplay between religious and dynastic politics within England but also English efforts to subjugate Ireland, control Scotland, defend the kingdom's maritime interests, and shape developments on the European Continent. The following several chapters attempt such an analysis. For purposes of clarity it will be necessary to treat the various theaters of operation sequentially, but it needs to be kept in mind that for contemporary statesmen—as well as militant Catholics hoping to overthrow the regime—English, Irish, Scottish, and European challenges were always interconnected.

Catholic Resiliency and the Protestant State

Although the historiography of English Catholicism has undergone major revisions over the last thirty years, reappraisals have only slowly begun to affect political history. Until fairly recently most historians assumed that the old religion was already in steep decline in England by about 1580.[20] Treatments of the subject by Catholic historians generally focused on the heroic resistance to Protestant state power by a relatively small cohort of committed recusants and exiles, who in some cases paid with their lives for their commitment to their faith. While the best study published in the 1970s, John Bossy's *The English Catholic Community 1570–1850*, departed from this approach, it continued to see Elizabeth's reign as the first phase in a transition through which a once dominant faith evolved into a minority dissenting denomination, striving to coexist peacefully with other denominations in a religiously pluralist society.[21] The assumption of Catholic decline led most historians to discount the potential for serious political resistance,

---

[19] Ibid., fols 48, 52.
[20] See in particular A. G. Dickens, *The English Reformation* (University Park: Pennsylvania State University Press, 2nd ed., 1989). A good summary of the more recent evolution of historiographical perspectives away from this older view is chapter 1 of Alexandra Walsham, *Catholic Reformation in Protestant Britain* (Farnham: Ashgate, 2014).
[21] John Bossy, *The English Catholic Community 1570–1850* (London: Longman, 1975).

except perhaps in conservative regions like the North. The great majority of Catholics were seen as loyal and quiescent, more concerned with preserving their ability to worship as their consciences dictated than with reversing the Reformation. The handful who did plot to murder Elizabeth were portrayed as unrepresentative extremists. Thus, one historian admitted that William Allen conspired to overthrow the queen but insisted that the scores of priests Allen trained for the English mission "were not concerned with politics," striving only "to bring their countrymen back to the Roman Church by spiritual means."[22]

Scholarship over the past three decades has gradually modified this picture in ways that suggest that the potential for a serious political challenge to the Protestant ascendancy remained considerably greater, for a much longer period of time, than historians used to suppose.[23] In the 1990s Christopher Haigh vigorously challenged the previously dominant narrative of Protestantism's inexorable advance, portraying the English Reformation instead as weak, sickly, and generally unpopular.[24] In the same decade Eamon Duffy showed that rather than consisting of a mass of decaying popular superstitions, the "traditional religion" of the late Middle Ages retained considerable appeal at all levels of society well into the sixteenth century.[25] If Catholicism eventually declined, as both Haigh and Duffy conceded, this owed more to the repressive activities of the state in banning the mass and destroying the physical paraphernalia of traditional worship than to the appeal of Protestant ideas. Subsequent research has qualified even this modified picture of Catholic decline, at least for the first half of Elizabeth's reign. It has shown that, in addition to lingering attachment to traditional religious practices, English Catholicism produced dynamic reformist impulses, rooted in many of the same Christian humanist traditions that helped inspire Protestantism.[26] Under Mary Tudor, Oxford University became an international center of Catholic scholarship, and as late as 1580 Balliol and New College remained bastions of religious conservatism. William Allen, Thomas Campion, and Robert Persons were all Oxford scholars.[27] Although Cambridge was less infected, it too had its

---

[22] Patrick McGrath, *Papists and Puritans under Elizabeth I: The Early Struggles of the Church of England, the Perils of Moderation* (London: Blandford Press, 1967), 122; cf. 185.
[23] Among the strongest statements of this view is Michael Questier, *Dynastic Politics and the British Reformations, 1558–1630* (Oxford: Oxford University Press, 2019).
[24] Christopher Haigh, *English Reformations: Religion, Politics, and Society under the Tudors* (Oxford: Oxford University Press, 1993).
[25] Eamon Duffy, *The Stripping of the Altars* (New Haven: Yale University Press, 1992).
[26] Compare Duffy, *Stripping of the Altars* to Lucy Wooding *Rethinking Catholicism in Reformation England* (Oxford: Clarendon Press, 2000).
[27] James McConica, "The Catholic Experience in Tudor Oxford," in *The Reckoned Expense: Edmund Campion and the Early English Jesuits: Essays in Celebration of the First Centenary of Campion Hall, Oxford*, ed. Thomas McCoog (Woodbridge: Boydell Press, 1996), 39–65. The council told the vice-chancellor of Oxford in 1581 that most seminary priests were Oxford men (John LaRocca, "Popery and Pounds: The Effect of the Jesuit Mission on Penal Legislation," ibid., 249–63 at 256); for Balliol see TNA SP12/146/10.

share of Catholics and church-papists.[28] Burghley complained in 1582 that two faculty "have maintained covertly in the College a faction against the true religion received, corrupting the youth there with corrupt opinions of popery."[29] The Inns of Court also harbored numerous recusants. In the early 1580s the Middle Temple reported fifteen, of whom three had recently moved to Louvain; Lincoln's Inn sixteen, Grey's Inn fourteen, and the Inner Temple sixty-two.[30] Significant numbers of Old English Catholics from Ireland trained at the Inns of Court, before returning to Dublin and other parts of their homeland.[31] Although weaker than in England, a Catholic minority in Scotland also produced intellectual leaders, like Mary Stewart's agent John Leslie bishop of Ross. As Kristen Kesselring has shown, the 1569 Northern Rebellion had a significant afterlife in Scotland, thanks to the willingness of Scottish Catholic and a few Protestant nobles and lairds to shelter English refugees.[32]

Protestant harassment persuaded numerous Catholic intellectuals from both British kingdoms and Ireland to seek refuge on the Continent, where some tried to lay the groundwork for spiritual and political counter-offensives. During the first decade of Elizabeth's reign approximately 100 senior English academics emigrated to pursue their studies abroad.[33] Allen's seminary at Douai, relocated to Reims in 1578, had already trained and sent approximately 100 missionary priests back to England before the arrival of the first Jesuit mission in 1580. By the end of Elizabeth's reign, the number had grown to 440, while the contribution of other seminaries increased the total to an estimated 600 priests, of whom about half were probably still active.[34] Both the seminarians themselves and alarmed Protestants like Bishop Aylmer believed they had won significant numbers of converts.[35] When the regime cracked down on Catholicism in Oxford more students fled to Allen, who received twenty new recruits within a single fortnight in June 1581. By the following January he had more than 120 seminarians in residence, including many who had fled from Oxford and other English schools.[36] In terms of both new ordinations (forty-three) and missionaries sent back to

---

[28] Ceri Law, *Contested Reformations in the University of Cambridge* (Woodbridge: Boydell Press, 2018), chapter 6.
[29] Burghley to Hatton, July 30, 1582 in Hatton, 261.   [30] Ibid., 256–7.
[31] John Crawford, *A Star Chamber Court in Ireland: The Court of Castle Chamber, 1567–1641* (Dublin: Four Courts Press, 2005), 79, 95, 119–30, 160–1; Brid McGrath, "Ireland and the Third University: Attendance at the Inns of Court, 1603–1649," in *Regions and Rulers in Ireland, 1100–1650*, ed. David Edwards (Dublin: Four Courts Press, 2004), 217–36.
[32] Krista Kesselring, *The Northern Rebellion of 1569: Faith, Politics and Protest in Elizabethan England* (Basingstoke: Palgrave Macmillan, 2007), chapter 3.
[33] Eamon Duffy, "William Allen," in *ODNB*.
[34] Alexandra Walsham, "Translating Trent? English Catholicism and the Counter Reformation," *Historical Research* 78 (2005): 288–310 at 294; Tadhg Ó hAnnracháin, *Catholic Europe, 1592–1648: Centre and Peripheries* (Oxford: Oxford University Press, 2015), 39.
[35] McGrath, *Papists and Puritans*, 112–16.
[36] *The Letters and Memorials of William Cardinal Allen*, ed. Thomas Francis Knox, Records of the English Catholics under the Penal Laws, vol. 2 (London, 1882), 97, 120, 168.

England (forty-two), 1581 was the peak year for his college.[37] Priests and monks trained in continental seminaries had also begun to stiffen recusancy in Ireland.[38] Mary Stuart tried to promote the formation of similar Scottish seminaries.[39]

In addition to men bound for the clergy, substantial numbers of highly literate Catholic laymen went abroad to pursue their education and worship in freedom. Katy Gibbons, who has made a systematic study of such exiles, believes the total number over the course of Elizabeth's reign exceeded 3,000, with over 1,000 resident in France and 400 in Paris.[40] This compares to a total of about 800 Protestant exiles under Mary Tudor. The diaspora of Catholic intellectuals, both priests and laymen, produced a stream of books, pamphlets, poems, plays, and ballads.[41] Active Catholic exile presses already existed in Louvain and Antwerp by 1570, while after 1578 new ones were established at Seville, Valladolid, and Eu in Normandy.[42] A substantial proportion of the literature they produced was in Latin or modern European languages and intended for an international audience,[43] but they also published works in English, as did hidden presses within the realm, like one that Bishop Aylmer's agents discovered in 1579. "Syndicates of scribes" also supplied a flourishing underground trade in Catholic manuscripts.[44] Catholics produced partisan ballads and distributed beads, medallions, and other

---

[37] *The First and Second Diaries of the English College of Douay*, ed. Thomas Francis Knox, Records of English Catholics Under the Penal Laws, vol. I (London, 1877), 10–11, 27–8. Figures for both ordinations and priests sent to England show a sharp rise from the late 1570s to the 1581 peak, followed by a gradual decline over the next few years to considerably lower levels by about 1590.

[38] Colm Lennon, "Taking Sides: The Emergence of Irish Catholic Ideology," in *Taking Sides? Colonial and Confessional Mentalités in Early Modern Ireland: Essays in Honour of Karl S. Bottigheimer*, ed. Vincent Carey and Ute Lotz-Heumann (Dublin: Four Courts Press, 2003), 197–206; Brendan Bradshaw, "The English Reformation and Identity Formation in Ireland and Wales," in *British Consciousness and Identity: The Making of Britain 1533–1707*, ed. Bradshaw and Peter Roberts (Cambridge: Cambridge University Press, 1998), 43–111.

[39] CSPSc 5.290.

[40] Katy Gibbons, *English Catholic Exiles in Late Sixteenth-Century Paris* (Woodbridge: Boydell Press, 2011), 16.

[41] Studies that examine this subject include Alison Shell, *Catholicism, Controversy and the English Literary Imagination, 1558–1660* (Cambridge: Cambridge University Press, 1999); Alison Shell, *Oral Culture and Catholicism in Early Modern England* (Cambridge: Cambridge University Press, 2007); Susannah Brietz Monta, *Martyrdom and Literature in Early Modern England* (Cambridge: Cambridge University Press, 2005); Stefania Tutino, *Law and Conscience in Early Modern England, 1570–1625* (Aldershot: Ashgate, 2007); Victor Houliston, *Catholic Resistance in Elizabethan England* (Aldershot: Ashgate, 2007); Gerard Kilroy, *Edmund Campion: Memory and Transcription* (Aldershot: Ashgate, 2005); Peter Lake and Michael Questier, "Puritans, Papists, and the 'Public Sphere' in Early Modern England: The Edmund Campion Affair in Context," *Journal of Modern History* 72 (2000): 587–627; Peter Lake with Michael Questier, *The Antichrist's Lewd Hat: Protestants, Papists and Players in Post-Reformation England* (New Haven: Yale University Press, 2002), section II; and Walsham, *Catholic Reformation in Protestant Britain*, 235–83.

[42] Walsham, *Catholic Reformation in Protestant Britain*, 245.

[43] Shell, *Catholicism and Literary Imagination*, 13.

[44] McGrath, *Papists and Puritans*, 120; Alexandra Walsham, "'Domme Preachers'? Post-Reformation English Catholicism and the Culture of Print," *Past and Present* 168 (2000): 72–123; Arthur Marrotti, *Religious Ideology and Cultural Fantasy: Catholic and Anti-Catholic Discourses in Early Modern England* (Notre Dame: University of Notre Dame Press, 2005), esp. chapter 3; Shell, *Oral Culture*.

consecrated objects as badges of allegiance to Rome.[45] The old religion shared virtually all the dynamic qualities historians have habitually associated with early Protestantism, including an active reformist intelligentsia, in touch with European currents of religious thought, a strong emphasis on biblically centered piety, an energetic exile community, a skillful use of print and scribal publication, and a willingness to employ ballads and material objects capable of influencing even illiterate audiences.

This vitality demands that we rethink not just our view of Catholicism but the Protestant state's responses to it. If, as historians once assumed, Catholics were declining in number and mostly politically quiescent, the absence of a major rebellion after 1569 requires little explanation and plots against Elizabeth's life can be dismissed as the work of a fanatical fringe. But the evidence compiled by more recent studies that people sympathetic to the old faith remained numerous, probably still more numerous than convinced Protestants in the early 1580s, and that many were prepared to challenge the existing regime if a good opportunity arose, means that we need to re-examine both the potential for a major Catholic uprising and the means by which the state contained the threat.

Unfortunately, we have no way of accurately measuring the distribution of religious attitudes in the period and most of the impressionistic evidence that does survive has obvious biases. Government publicists had every reason to play up the subversive and conspiratorial character of the missionary priests and other Catholics they targeted, whereas Catholic spokesmen like William Allen and Robert Persons had equally strong incentives to deny in their public pronouncements that priests had any interest in politics at all. On the other hand, when appealing for support from wealthy Catholics on the Continent, Allen and Persons sometimes claimed that the seminarians were producing a rising tide of religious resistance that would soon overwhelm the Elizabethan state. Peter Holmes's study of the political thought expressed in English Catholic books identifies similar contrasts. Between 1573 and 1579 authors mostly avoided politics, but starting in 1580 they began to discuss some political questions, as the volume of their output increased substantially. They still avoided advocating open rebellion until 1584, when Allen and others adopted a more aggressive stance in anticipation of a planned invasion of England by the duke of Guise. While Catholic political attitudes probably did evolve over time, these differences also reflect tactical calculations. Holmes concludes that even before 1584, priests probably instructed lay Catholics that so long as the Protestant authorities remained firmly in control they should be obeyed in secular matters, but that

---

[45] Walsham, *Catholic Reformation*, 275–6; APC 12.256.

this might change the moment a real opportunity to install a Catholic regime arrived.⁴⁶

Similar problems arise with respect to communications between English Catholic leaders and foreign allies, especially the court of Spain and the duke of Guise. Because leaders of the exiled community and the most committed Catholics still in England wanted to enlist foreign help, they had every reason to provide optimistic assurances about the amount of support that a foreign invading force would receive once it had landed. In 1582 one Jesuit estimated that "the faction of Catholics in England" comprised two-thirds of the landed elite, who would mostly support an attempt to overthrow Elizabeth. Guise, who was particularly eager to place his Stuart relatives on the English throne, often seems to have taken such assurances more or less at face value, while endorsing them to other European Catholic leaders. In 1583 he sent an agent to Rome who promised that if a Catholic force of a few thousand soldiers landed in Lancashire, 20,000 English horsemen belonging to the affinities of one Scottish and six northern English lords would join them, while another six Catholic peers resident elsewhere in England would also lend support.⁴⁷ Mendoza also tended to believe English Catholic promises of support for invading forces. In 1583 he confidently predicted that "if they saw a strong fleet with foreign troops arrive on the coast" large numbers of Catholics, "schismatics," and even Protestants would rally to support Philip II against the queen.⁴⁸ Philip himself remained more cautious but nevertheless encouraged Catholic activism. Although predictions by committed partisans deserve to be treated with skepticism, they were unlikely to have had no foundation whatever. Parsons, Allen, and Mendoza had high-level contacts within the English Catholic community, such as Lord Henry Howard, who probably did try to canvas support for schemes to overthrow Elizabeth.⁴⁹ Some undertakings undoubtedly had been given, although exactly how many and with what qualifications we have no certain way of knowing.

But since the council would also have had difficulties in identifying disloyal Catholics, this uncertainty is in some ways precisely the point.⁵⁰ The authorities needed to worry not only about the few Catholics already engaged in treasonable activities but the potentially much larger cohort who might join in an attempt to restore the Roman allegiance if Protestant control ever faltered. The papacy had explicitly permitted Catholics to obey Elizabeth in secular matters until such time as a realistic chance of overthrowing her arose. Some priests sanctioned occasional attendance at Protestant worship, in order to preserve Catholic gentlemen's

---

⁴⁶ Peter Holmes, *Resistance and Compromise: The Political Thought of the Elizabethan Catholics* (Cambridge: Cambridge University Press, 1982), 29–30, 33–44, 129–42.
⁴⁷ Teulet, *Papiers d'état*, 3.368.   ⁴⁸ TNA SP12/153/79; *CSPSp* 3.467.
⁴⁹ Teulet, *Papiers d'état*, 3.31, 32.
⁵⁰ For a discussion see "Yielding to the Extremity of the Time: Conformity and Orthodoxy," in Walsham, *Catholic Reformation*, 53–84, esp. 57–62.

property and local influence until an opportune moment to restore the Roman allegiance arrived. These concessions made it difficult to distinguish loyal Catholics and outward conformists from a hidden body of secretly disloyal Catholics quietly awaiting the right opportunity to rebel. Michael Questier has convincingly argued that Catholic loyalty "was always to some degree, and sometimes extremely, conditional."[51] It probably would have been difficult even for many Catholics themselves to identify the exact conditions that would cause it to collapse. Krista Kesselring has shown that the leaders of the 1569 rebellion engaged in lengthy discussions of the legitimacy of taking arms against the crown before actually doing so, but that in many cases an individual's final decision depended on highly contingent circumstances, like pressure from wives and retainers.[52] This sort of outcome was impossible to predict in advance.

Both the number and, in many cases, the identity of potential Catholic rebels was therefore unclear at the time and remains elusive today. In addition to the relative strength of the two confessional camps, the question turns on how many people felt a sufficiently deep commitment to either of them to override their loyalty to the queen and their natural inclination to avoid involvement in dangerous plots. For the theologically informed, the distinction between Protestant and Catholic positions had grown clearer with every passing decade since the 1530s. The fact that all but one of the Marian bishops refused to serve the Elizabethan Church once it had severed its ties with Rome, and that a number of former cathedral clergy played an active role in resisting Protestantism and promoting recusancy under Elizabeth, shows how clear the lines of division had become among the clerical elite.[53] But the behavior of Marian parish priests presents a murkier picture. Many more of them refused to serve in the Elizabethan Church than historians once assumed and, in some dioceses, like Rochester and London, their resignations or deprivations appear to have disrupted at least one parish in five.[54] Others escaped detection while remaining loyal to Rome, often through the protection of sympathetic lay patrons. But the majority did conform, albeit with varying degrees of enthusiasm. A few continued to celebrate mass in private and to criticize Protestant doctrine even while serving as vicars or curates of the official Church, while most ceased to be practicing Catholics in any meaningful sense, although without necessarily absorbing

---

[51] Michael Questier, *Catholicism and Community in Early Modern England* (Cambridge: Cambridge University Press, 2006); Michael Questier, "Elizabeth and the Catholics," in *Catholics and the 'Protestant Nation': Religious Politics and Identity in Early Modern England*, ed. Ethan Shagan (Manchester: Manchester University Press, 2005), quotation at 76.
[52] Kesselring, *Northern Rebellion*, 46–56.
[53] Thomas Mayer, "Not Just the Hierarchy Fought: The Marian Cathedral Chapters, Seminaries of Recusancy," in *Catholic Renewal and Protestant Resistance in Marian England*, ed. Elizabeth Evenden and Vivienne Westbrook (London: Routledge, 2016), 93–126; Frederick E. Smith, "The Origins of Recusancy in Elizabethan England Reconsidered," *Historical Journal* 60 (2017): 301–32.
[54] Peter Marshall and John Morgan, "Clerical Conformity and the Elizabethan Settlement Revisited," *Historical Journal* 59 (2016): 1–22 at 11.

Protestant ideas. For many parish priests the meaning of conformity and allegiance to either religious camp was therefore highly imprecise.[55]

This was undoubtedly even more true among the laity, although our paucity of information about the inner beliefs of most Elizabethans makes it impossible to form a precise picture. Many people must have regarded themselves as English Christians who tried to follow the moral teachings stressed by both rival creeds, without feeling the need to take precise positions on the limits of papal authority, the doctrine of transubstantiation, or the relationship between faith and good works in the process of salvation. Even if they sympathized more with one confession than the other, they would have hesitated to break the law, disrupt the peace of their community, and incur the risk of civil penalties in order to demonstrate their preference.[56] But while we cannot measure the extent to which confessional polarization had taken place, we can identify developments that promoted it. Although primarily intended to save souls, puritan preaching not only enlarged the community of Calvinist believers but also inculcated a sense of solidarity within it, in opposition to "popery." The Jesuit John Gerard admitted that in Norfolk and Suffolk "Catholics were very few" because, "surrounded as they are by most fierce Protestants," they felt too intimidated to express their views in public.[57] As puritans never tired of pointing out, their preaching expanded the number of people prepared to fight to protect the queen and her Church against the Roman enemy, while holding down the numbers of committed papists. But puritanism also tended to produce hostile reactions, not only among committed Catholics but also among people who resented the strict morality and divisive distinctions between the godly and ungodly that puritans promulgated, which disrupted traditional ideals of neighborly solidarity and charity[58]

In a similar way, the most committed and combative Marian priests, reinforced by the seminarians who began arriving in England after 1574, worked assiduously to harden and deepen the attachment of religious conservatives to specifically Catholic doctrines, while encouraging them to withdraw from participation in parish worship. Persons and Campion were particularly insistent on this latter point in 1580.[59] By fostering recusancy they hoped not only to solidify allegiance to Rome but also to demonstrate its strength, both to government authorities and to Catholics themselves. To be sure, some priests resisted this rigorous approach, while even hardliners like Parsons recognized that in some circumstances

---

[55] Ibid., 13–22.
[56] William Sheils, "'Getting On' and 'Getting Along' in Parish and Town: Catholics and Their Neighbours in England," in *Catholic Communities in Protestant States: Britain and the Netherlands c. 1570–1720*, ed. Benjamin Kaplan, Bob Moore, Henk van Nierop, and Judith Pollman (Manchester: Manchester University Press, 2009), 67–83.
[57] John Gerard, *The Autobiography of an Elizabethan* (Oxford: Family Publications, 2006), 32–3.
[58] As recently argued by Andy Wood, *Faith, Hope and Charity: English Neighborhoods, 1500–1640* (Cambridge: Cambridge University Press, 2020), 161–73.
[59] Questier, *Dynastic Politics*, 128; Walsham, *Catholic Reformation in Protestant Britain*, 58.

Catholics might legitimately keep their beliefs hidden, so as to protect their lives, property, or the offices that allowed them to protect co-religionists and advance the cause.[60] But the debate over how far and in what precise circumstances Catholics might attend Protestant services served to emphasize the principle that, even if only through invisible mental reservations, Rome's adherents needed to separate themselves from the official Church and the body of its adherents. The distribution by priests of consecrated beads, *agnus dei* medallions, and similar tokens, by which Catholics might recognize each other, while practicing distinctive forms of ritual devotion, contributed further to the formation of a sense of confessional identity that stood opposed not only to doctrinal Protestantism but also to the casual conformity of the majority of the population.[61]

As John Bossy in particular has shown, before the Reformation the celebration of the eucharist in parish churches had served to reinforce values of communal solidarity and charity.[62] After the break with Rome, communion in one's parish church also came to represent obedience to the crown and the law. But in Elizabeth's reign both puritans and Catholic missionaries turned the eucharist into a mark of division, by refusing to take communion with those who did not share their religious beliefs.[63] In a few communities, Catholics grew sufficiently numerous and assertive to intimidate local Protestants. In 1582 Southampton's ministers were not only "belied and railed upon behind their backs" by "atheists or papists" but also compelled to justify their doctrine before the town's mayor.[64] Four years later in Hereford, "ministers and others" were said to be "put in danger of their lives" by local hostility.[65] This sort of behavior not only demonstrated the strength of a local Catholic faction but in many cases probably helped to increase it, by encouraging more timid sympathizers to express their beliefs openly, and perhaps by fusing Catholicism with a sense of local identity, in opposition to distant government authority. In towns like Colchester, refugees fleeing religious

---

[60] For the internal Catholic debate over such issues see *Recusancy and Conformity in Early Modern England: Manuscript and Printed Sources in Translation*, ed. Ginevra Crosignani, Thomas M. McCoog, and Michael Questier with the assistance of Peter Holmes, Studies and Texts 170 (Toronto: Pontifical Institute of Mediaeval Studies, 2010). See also Tutino, *Law and Conscience* and Peter Lake and Michael Questier, *All Hail the Archpriest: Confessional Conflict, Toleration, and the Politics of Publicity in Post-Reformation England* (Oxford: Oxford University Press, 2019).

[61] For the ritual devotions see Alexandra Walsham, "Beads, Books and Bare Ruined Choirs: Transmutations of Catholic Ritual Life in Protestant England," in *Catholic Communities*, ed. Kaplan et al., 103–22.

[62] John Bossy, "The Mass as a Social Institution, 1500–1700," *Past and Present* 100 (1983): 29–61.

[63] Alexandra Walsham, "Supping with Satan's Disciples: Spiritual and Secular Sociability in Post-Reformation England," in *Getting Along? Religious Identities and Confessional Relations in Early Modern England: Essays in Honour of Professor W. J. Sheils*, ed. Adam Morton and Nadine Lewycky (Aldershot: Ashgate, 2012), 29–55, esp. 30–9. Walsham points out that the survival of secular conventions of hospitality and courtesy mitigated the division, often allowing Catholics and Protestants to coexist as neighbors even while refusing to take communion together, but the religious split must nevertheless have been striking and disturbing for many contemporaries. On popular tolerance for Catholics see Wood, *Faith, Hope and Charity*, 173–6.

[64] TNA SP12/156/43. [65] TNA SP12/195/46.

persecution provoked hostility from laborers and artisans worried about economic competition, but were also defended by the godly and Protestant ministers.⁶⁶ Xenophobia and economic anxiety thus became linked to confessional politics. A process of "confessionalization" proceeded at both ends of the religious spectrum, driven not by the policies of the crown and the official Church, which often sought to blur doctrinal distinctions, but by zealous clergy and their most committed lay supporters.⁶⁷

In addition to winning converts, the itinerate preaching of the missionaries, along with the role of laymen and women in sheltering priests and distributing clandestine literature, forged networks of committed Catholics intent on helping each other evade government authority.⁶⁸ This led to a proliferation of safe houses where priests sheltered, the identification of sympathetic magistrates prepared to protect Catholics from prosecution, and the creation of corridors through which priests and illegal printed material entered and passed through the kingdom in relative safety.⁶⁹ A handful of especially determined Catholics in particular villages created nodal points of resistance. In 1579 Catholics in Northampton were said to "repair in great numbers" to a secret conventicle in the village of Lillingston, a few miles south in Buckinghamshire, organized by a certain Peter Wentworth.⁷⁰ Large aristocratic households, or better yet clusters of such households belonging to allied families, provided especially effective refuges because the social status of their owners inhibited official repression, except when explicitly commanded by the council. Michael Questier has produced a long-term study of one such cluster, centered around the first Viscount Montagu and his heirs in Sussex.⁷¹ In Northamptonshire, Catholics were sheltered by William Lord Vaux, whose friends and relations included other Catholic landowners in his own county, such as Thomas Tresham, and in neighboring Leicestershire.⁷² His eldest son Henry went to London in 1579 and became active in the city's underground Catholic network, along with his neighbor William Tresham and the future conspirator, Francis Throckmorton of Warwickshire. Although imprisoned on suspicion of having harbored the Jesuit Thomas Campion in 1581, Lord Vaux and

---

⁶⁶ For an example see TNA SP12/144/18.
⁶⁷ Peter Marshall, "(Re)defining the English Reformation," *Journal of British Studies* 48 (2009): 564–86.
⁶⁸ Cf. Questier, *Dynastic Politics*, 128–9.
⁶⁹ As examples see TNA SP12/206/74, a list of Catholic safe houses in London in 1587; SP12/240/138, a report to the Council in 1591 of Lancashire JPs with Catholic wives; *The Venerable Philip Howard Earl of Arundel*, ed. John Hungerford Pollen and William MacMahon, Catholic Record Society Publications 21 (London, 1921), 72, a report by a spy in 1585 that priests and Catholic books normally entered England from France around Newcastle because the chief crown officer there was "a papist at heart" with an ardently Catholic wife, who helped them do so safely; and SP12/173/64, the testimony of a Catholic tailor in 1584 that Catholics were able to "pass and repass" between Yarmouth and Norfolk "at their pleasure."
⁷⁰ APC 11.132.   ⁷¹ Questier, *Catholicism and Community*.
⁷² Jessie Childs, *God's Traitors: Terror and Faith in Elizabethan England* (Oxford: Oxford University Press, 2014), 21–39.

his son remained active in raising money to assist their poorer co-religionists and priests four years later.[73] In East Anglia the former Marian privy councilor Sir Henry Bedingfeld sheltered Catholics in his Norfolk house, whom the authorities unsuccessfully tried to arrest in April 1581.[74] In Lincolnshire recusancy benefited from the support of the Tyrwights, an established gentry family whose head had briefly served as the county's lord lieutenant in Mary's reign.[75] Under the very nose of the royal court, in the Middle Temple, the distinguished jurist William Plowden openly espoused his Catholic beliefs, insulted the memory of Henry VIII, and opposed benchers who tried to comply with an order of the council to send in a list of Catholics in their institution. He "practiced that none should be called to the bench but such as will bear with these abuses and this term obtained that three coming in authority before others are kept back without other cause but that they have been and are thought to be too earnest in causes of religion." Through his influence the Middle Temple became "festered with papists and not to be amended" without the council's direct intervention.[76]

Even when directed immediately to spiritual ends, Catholic networks had considerable potential to lay the groundwork for future political activity, as Persons, Allen, and their continental patrons certainly appreciated. Preaching and proselytizing always had political implications, whether or not clergy meddled directly in affairs of state. As one captured priest confessed in 1581, he and his colleagues went about their work not only to save souls but with two other goals in mind: "the one that thereby the Catholic party would grow strong to join if opportunity served either with foreign invasion or tumult at home and the other that Catholics increasing to a great multitude, the Queen's Majesty and her council would thereby be terrified and induced to permit to the Catholics liberty to live according to their consciences."[77] This was a highly provocative strategy, since most people regarded religion as a public duty rather than a purely private matter, which governments therefore had not only the right but the duty to regulate. As Burghley put it, a "law to compel men to serve God is by all men to be thought laudable and necessary, so as no Christian realm is without such law."[78] Withdrawal from a parish community that served both religious and administrative functions looked like an anti-social act.[79] Many people assumed that two religious communities living side by side in the same territory would sooner or later come to blows, as recent events in Ireland, France, and the Netherlands appeared to demonstrate. Grants of toleration, like those extended by the French

---

[73] TNA SP11/178/39; ibid., p. 99.   [74] APC 13.25–6.   [75] APC 12 91–2, 106, 108.
[76] TNA SP12/144/46.
[77] BL Egerton Mss. 2074, fol. 81v, testimony of John Harte, October 3, 1581.
[78] BL Cotton Mss. Titus B III, fol. 63. Cf. Alexandra Walsham, *Charitable Hatred: Tolerance and Intolerance in England, 1500–1700* (Manchester: Manchester University Press, 2006).
[79] Bossy, "Mass as a Social Institution." Although Protestantism abolished the mass, Protestants continued to associate the celebration of the Lord's Supper with bonds between Christian believers and discipline against sins that threatened to disrupt harmonious social relations.

crown to the Huguenots, were normally regarded as provisional measures, intended to last only until the restoration of religious uniformity became feasible. They were hedged about with restrictions and treated as negotiated truces between hostile communities, rather than grants of individual religious freedom. Their enforcement required institutional mechanisms such as *chambres mi-parties*, judicial tribunals with both Catholic and Protestant members, to adjudicate disputes with impartiality.[80] Even the minority of thinkers prepared to defend toleration of private dissent generally condemned public defiance of an established religion as dangerous to civil order.

But in some English districts by the early 1580s such defiance had become entrenched. Although they failed to produce the mass defection from the established Church for which some Catholics had hoped, the missionary priests and Jesuits did galvanize a determined recusant minority that shaded into a larger cohort of Catholic occasional conformists or church-papists—a term revealingly coined around 1582.[81] Catholic ranks included many pillars of the social order. At the apex of the social hierarchy one contemporary counted 21 Catholic peers in 1584, as against 13 Protestants and 14 "indifferent observers of the times," while another listed 26 English and Irish Catholic nobles, as against only 11 Protestants and 14 regarded as neutral.[82] Although we should not place undue confidence in the exact counts, the general impression of a preponderance of Catholic and religiously neutral peers is probably broadly correct, and the picture is unlikely to have been very different for the gentry. A detailed survey of Cheshire gentlemen listed only 23 of 82 as "well affected" or otherwise supportive of the existing regime, variously labeling the rest as "cold," "weak," "worldly," "neuters," or, in a few cases, "recusant."[83] Many districts had significant numbers of Catholic magistrates, even after the regime began weeding them out in the late 1570s.[84]

---

[80] A point demonstrated at length by Olivier Christian, *La paix de religion: l'autonomisation de la raison politique au XVIe siècle* (Paris: Seuil, 1997).

[81] The most systematic treatment is Alexandra Walsham, *Church Papists: Catholicism, Conformity and Confessional Polemic in Early Modern England* (Woodbridge: Boydell Press, 1993).

[82] TNA SP12/168/29 and SP12/157/90. The Catholic peers listed were Northumberland, Shrewsbury, Derby and his son the Lord Strange, Arundel and his two brethren, the Lord Audley and the Lord William Howard, Worcester and his son the Lord Herbert; Westmoreland, Lord Vaux and his sons, Lord Montague Mountjoy and his son, Lord Paget, Windsor and his brethren, Lord Mordaunt, Lord Henry Howard, Lord Dacre of the North, Lord Stockton and his brethren, Lord Lumley, Lord Wharton, Lord Hartley, Lord Sheffield, Lord Morely, Kildare and his son and Lord Cumpton. The Protestants were Leicester, Huntingdon, Warwick, Bedford, Kent, Hunsdon, Buckhurst, and Cromwell, while Rutland, Oxford, Bath, Lincoln, Cumberland, Cobham, Chandos, Montjoy, De La War, Charles Howard, Bromley, Cheney, Dacres of the South, and the Marquess of Southampton were thought indifferent.

[83] TNA SP12/165/23. Twenty-three gentlemen are listed as "well affected," a "good professor," or "an obedient subject" out of a total of 82.

[84] For examples see LaRocca, "Popery and Pounds," 255–9.

According to an early seventeenth-century memorandum, so did the clerical staff of the court of King's Bench.[85]

Catholic officials and clerks used their authority to obstruct prosecutions for recusancy and intimidate Protestants who sought to uncover secret Catholic activities.[86] In an emergency they might conceivably have turned the government's own machinery against it. This had actually happened in 1569, as the Northern earls co-opted local musters to recruit rebel soldiers, and enlisted the support of dozens of constables, who used their authority to draw villagers into the rebellion.[87] Once it had regained control, the crown singled out those constables for particularly brutal punishment, hanging scores of them in their native villages. Catholic conspirators hoped for an even larger defection of royal magistrates during the next rising. Francis Throckmorton confessed in 1584 "that there was a device between the Spanish ambassador and him, how such principal recusants here within the realm as were in the Commission of the Peace in sundry counties might upon the first bruit of the landing of foreign forces, under color and pretext of their authority and the defense of her Majesty levy men, whom they might after join to foreign forces, and convert them against her Majesty."[88] In Sussex, which the duke of Guise planned to invade in 1582 or 1583, landowners of suspect loyalty were accused not only of possessing the best arms and armor in the county but also of impeding local militia exercises and disarming tenant farmers by seizing their fowling pieces.[89] The fact that two Catholic peers, Viscount Montague and the earl of Northumberland, headed a militia commission in 1580 lends credence to the view that men sympathetic to Rome had effectively taken military control of the shire.[90] Proponents of schemes to overthrow Elizabeth anticipated that priests would contribute actively to the mobilization and coordination of efforts to infiltrate and subvert the state from within. One memorandum carried by a captured Jesuit admitted that because of government surveillance, Catholic gentry and townsmen "dared not trust anybody in the world but their priests." But since those priests "are already dispersed through all the shires of the realm," it predicted that they would be able to "dispose of the Catholics as they shall have orders given them" when the time for a great rebellion arrived.[91]

Although it would have been difficult to execute such plans before loyal crown servants became aware of them, pockets of resistance to the enforcement of

---

[85] BL Cotton Mss. Titus B III, fol. 79: "Before it pleased God to place in the King's Bench religious chief justices there was care taken by the Queen's Council for staying of certiorares to remove the indictments out of the shires, because in the King's Bench at that time were a great number of popish clerks and attorneys."

[86] For examples see TNA SP12/129/30 (Bishop William Belthyn of Landaff complains of efforts to obstruct his attempts to arrest priests) and SP12/147/75 (a prominent Catholic intimidates two Protestants who intercepted and opened a letter from a seminarian in Rome).

[87] Kesselring *Northern Rebellion*.   [88] Q. Z., *A Discovery of Treason* (London, 1584), sig. Aiv.
[89] TNA SP12/165/22.   [90] TNA SP12/144.   [91] TNA SP12/153/79.

religious conformity certainly existed within local governing bodies. Robert Jermyn complained in 1582 that a conservative clique had perverted the government of Thetford, displacing good Protestants and stacking the corporation with popish sympathizers.[92] In Norwich in 1570 a pro-Catholic group within the Corporation had attempted to raise the city behind the duke of Norfolk by exploiting resentments against immigrant Protestant craftsmen driven from their homes by the duke of Alva. Although defeated, these dissidents remained waiting in the wings for some time thereafter.[93] In 1586 most of the head constables in Herefordshire were said to be popishly affected, allowing priests to travel unmolested through the county. Constables should be forced to take the oath of allegiance, one Protestant suggested.[94] In most of Lancashire, solid support for the old religion made enforcement of Protestant conformity unworkable.[95] Catholics reportedly harassed and threatened ministers in Southampton and Winchester, where "multitudes" showed "contempt of the preaching of the Word."[96] In Ripple, Worcestershire, two "poor men but very dangerous"—one a former porter of Bishop Bonner—turned their house into a refuge for traveling priests and a Catholic meeting place.[97] Parts of Hampshire were full of papists: "my lord bishop told me he was able to give me a note of 200 in a little corner."[98] In 1583 several Hampshire JPs told the council that many "poor husbandmen and artificers, some wives, servants and young men unmarried in diverse parishes" had recently stopped attending church, claiming that the queen wished only "to bother the wealthier sort" for non-conformity. "Others have boldly affirmed that it is necessary to have mass and they hope to hear it and that they had rather hear bear baiting than the divine service."[99] A priest newly arrived on the Continent from England told Robert Persons in August 1583 that "upwards of four thousand persons" had been reconciled to the Roman Church since the previous Easter.[100] The justices suspected Catholic gentry of secretly fomenting this groundswell of popular religious protest, probably correctly since the Catholic earl of Southampton held great influence in the county.[101] A year later, churchwardens in the county presented about 400 people for recusancy, with as many as 40 or 50 reported in individual parishes. Bishop Cowper believed that many more had

---

[92] TNA SP12/155/63.
[93] Matthew Reynolds, *Godly Reformers and their Opponents in Early Modern England: Religion in Norwich c. 1560–1643* (Woodbridge: Boydell Press, 2005), 49–53.
[94] SP12/195/45 and 46.
[95] Christopher Haigh, *Reformation and Resistance in Tudor Lancashire* (Cambridge: Cambridge University Press, 1975), 271–5 and passim.
[96] SP12/156/43. [97] SP12/156/29. [98] TNA SP12/195/45; TNA SP12/208/75.
[99] BL Cotton Mss. Titus B III, fol. 81.
[100] *The Correspondence and Unpublished Papers of Robert Persons, SJ*, volume 1: *1574–1588*, ed. Victory Houliston, Ginevra Crosignani, and Thomas M. McCoog (Toronto: Pontifical Institute of Mediaeval Studies, 2017), 364.
[101] Questier, *Catholicism and Community*, 63–4 and 159–60.

escaped the net and recommended a special commission to investigate.[102] In 1586 the earl of Sussex believed that a plot to launch a rebellion would soon commence in Hampshire.[103]

Because Catholic networks extended beyond England to exiled communities on the Continent, which in turn had contacts with figures like the prince of Parma and the duke of Guise, they provided a potential means for linking international plots against Elizabeth to resistance within the realm. Guise had become Allen's patron as early as 1578. By 1582 he was actively consulting Allen, Parsons, and Jesuits like William Holt who had gone to Scotland and met secretly with James VI about schemes to invade Britain.[104] The presence of professional soldiers among the continental exiles made these links even more dangerous. The Army of Flanders attracted English émigrés, including 400 who deserted from the Dutch army in 1582. For some time before 1590 the recusant Dorothy Pauncefoot regularly exchanged news about plots to overthrow Elizabeth with the court of the prince of Parma in Flanders, through her husband, a "companion to the earl of Westmoreland" who resided there.[105] Guise tried to recruit some of the young English Catholic gentlemen studying at a seminary he had founded at Eu in Normandy as officers in a force he hoped to use to invade England. In 1583 Philip II agreed to release Englishmen serving in his armies to join a planned invasion of their homeland.[106] Starting around 1582, Guise, Allen, and Persons gave their blessing to a series of plots involving attempted assassinations of Elizabeth and limited invasions from the Continent, intended to trigger and assist a Catholic rebellion. The Spanish were drawn in, initially through Mendoza, who cultivated a number of well-connected English informants, including the courtier and privy councilor Sir James Croft, in addition to Lord Henry Howard.[107] Through Lord Henry, Mendoza hoped to win the cooperation of the entire Howard dynasty. He also developed contacts with other Catholic families, like the Treshams and the Pagets in Staffordshire.[108] Allen and Persons soon came to regard him as indispensable to their cause.[109]

---

[102] John Strype, *Annals of the Reformation*, vol. 3 (London, 1728), Appendix, 98.
[103] Questier, *Catholicism and Community*, 35–7. For a discussion of Catholicism below the ranks of the gentry see Mary B. Rowlands, "Hidden People: Catholic Commoners, 1558–1625," in *English Catholics of Parish and Town 1558–1778*, ed. Rowlands (London: Catholic Record Society, 1999), 36–60.
[104] *Diaries of the English College*, ed. Knox, 139; *Correspondence of Persons*, ed. Houliston et al., 198–301.
[105] TNA SP12/230/34.
[106] Dennis Flynn, "Notes on Jaspar Heywood," in *Reckoned Expense*, ed. McCoog, 179–92 at 186–7; *CSPSp* 3.504–5 (instructions by Guise to Richard Melino, his representative in Rome, August 22).
[107] *CSPSp* 3.128 (for Crofts), 236, 315, 391, 407.
[108] Ibid., 236, 363; *Arundel*, ed. Pollen and MacMahon, 31–2.   [109] *Letters of Allen*, 98.

Dealing with English Catholicism

The government therefore faced a potentially significant but amorphous threat, involving links between foreign powers and conspiratorial English networks of unknown scope. Even in the late 1570s, before the first Jesuit mission to England and the confessional polarization caused by controversy over the Anjou match, the crown had begun to crack down. Mauvissière reported the imprisonment of a "quantity" of Catholics suspected of being partisans of Mary Stuart in November 1577.[110] Five months later Mendoza wrote that 'the queen has sent through all the country fully authorized officers with powers such as never have been granted before, to seize and imprison Catholics."[111] In August Lord Chancellor Nicholas Bacon exhorted the bishops to root out corruption—by which he largely meant covert sympathy for Catholicism—among cathedral deans and chapters.[112] The investigation and punishment of recusants during Elizabeth's East Anglian progress in the same month seems to have presaged a wider campaign that commenced early the following year. In February the council ordered that several Norfolk Catholics who still refused to conform should be turned over to the sheriff for close imprisonment, while commissions were issued to investigate attendance at masses in the Welsh counties of Denbigh and Flint.[113] Several members of the council proposed placing subjects thought to be "evil contented" under legal bonds, while removing them from local offices to diminish their "credit among the people."[114] Over the next few months arrests of recusants or investigations of priests and secret masses were initiated in the town of Northampton, Staffordshire, and the dioceses of Rochester, Gloucester, and London, while the popish conventicle in Llingston was broken up.[115]

In June 1580 the council sent letters to both archbishops, along with the bishops of Durham, Lincoln, and Norwich and the lord president of the Marches of Wales, instructing them to set up ecclesiastical commissions to investigate recusancy.[116] Crackdowns rapidly followed in Lincolnshire, where the Tyrwights were particularly targeted, along with East Anglia, Berkshire, and Wiltshire.[117] The earl of Leicester conferred privately with the earl of Derby about the prosecution of recusants in Cheshire, and the queen also sent Derby a letter exhorting him to proceed energetically.[118] According to Mendoza, the authorities incarcerated sixty individuals in Lancashire alone.[119] On July 26, the council requisitioned several castles and appointed keepers over them, as prisons for

---

[110] TNA PRO31/3/27, fol. 62.　[111] CSPSp 2.577.　[112] HMC Salisbury 2.47.
[113] APC 11.47–8; TNA SP12/129/30.　[114] Hatfield House Cecil Mss. 148, fol. 50.
[115] APC 11.51, 57, 74, 77, 103, 132, 133, 164, 175, 204.　[116] Ibid., 59.
[117] Ibid., 70, 82, 90; BL Lansdowne Mss. 30, fol. 75.
[118] TNA SP12/141/24. Derby claimed the letter and Leicester's advice gave him "great comfort."
[119] CSPSp 3.38.

priests and recusants.[120] Mendoza wrote that the earls of Northampton, Montague, Worcester and Southampton, five barons and 300 gentlemen were then imprisoned.[121] Persons sent the rector of the English College of Rome, Alfonso Aggazari, an even more alarming report in September, claiming that all the prisons in England were crammed with Catholics and that the government had received the names of 50,000 recusants.[122] He no doubt exaggerated but many prominent and some plebeian Catholics were certainly targeted, as the crown attempted to set examples in every shire, in such numbers that the council found it impossible to review their cases in a timely fashion.[123] They eventually included William third baron Vaux and Sir Thomas Tresham, both imprisoned in 1581 for having sheltered Campion; although soon released, both thereafter ceased to play a prominent role in the governance of their native counties. Tresham's courtier brother William also fled the country shortly after Thomas's arrest, allegedly following a quarrel with Leicester, cutting the family off from direct contact with the court.[124]

The campaign continued through the autumn and winter, supplemented by investigations of individuals suspected of having sheltered Campion during his mission, efforts to purge Catholics from the queen's own household and the officers of the corporation of London, an attempt to require the parents of children studying on the Continent to enter into bonds for their future good behavior, and authorization of the use of torture to extract information from a few specific individuals.[125] At least one bishop received instructions in November to deal with conformist gentlemen whose wives refused to attend church. He imposed a fine on these men and compelled them to enter into bonds to make sure their wives would avoid "conference" with "such as are backward in matters of religion."[126] Burghley wanted even stiffer penalties for recusancy enacted and urged the appointment of magistrates prepared to execute the laws "without partiality" by refusing to dispense with penal statutes "for private men's partiality."[127] To prevent rebels and enemies of the queen from rallying behind Mary Stuart, he advocated a law stipulating that if, during the queen's life, "any faction of hers should either move sedition...or any enemy from abroad should move any...matter, either by force or notorious preparation of forces that she [Mary]

---

[120] Ibid., 124; *Recusant Documents from the Ellesmere Manuscripts*, ed. Anthony Petti, Catholic Record Society Publications 60 (St Albans: Fisher Knight, 1968), 3; *The Egerton Papers: A Collection of Public and Private Documents, Chiefly Illustrative of the Times of Elizabeth and James I*, ed. J. Payne Collier (London: Camden Society, 1840), 84.

[121] *CSPSp* 3.50.   [122] *Correspondence of Persons*, ed. Houliston et al., 80.

[123] *APC* 12.156–7.

[124] Susan Cogan, *Catholic Social Networks in Early Modern England* (Amsterdam: University of Amsterdam Press, 2021), 82–7.

[125] *APC* 12.136, 281–3, 294–5 and 315 and 13.37.

[126] TNA SP12/144/36; the bishop in question was John Watson of Rochester.

[127] Hatfield House Cecil Mss. 148, fol. 50.

should be the first that should suffer for it."¹²⁸ He and his colleagues had already begun to contemplate measures later formulated in the Bond of Association.¹²⁹

But both at court and in the provinces, inhibitions remained about prosecuting Catholics who were well integrated within their local communities, and who had done nothing disloyal beyond refusing to attend Protestant services. Despite the view of religion as a public duty, many sympathized with the argument made by Thomas Lord Paget that "faith cannot be forced and if it be it is neither beneficial to the forcers nor to the forced but hurtful to both."¹³⁰ Foxe's *Acts and Monuments* and other polemics against Catholic persecution made it awkward for a Protestant government to punish people for having religious scruples.¹³¹ Rules of courtesy, concepts of neighborliness, and ties of friendship and patronage deterred church wardens from presenting recusants and juries from convicting them. The council had to choose between accepting this inaction or trying to enforce conformity, as it did in Staffordshire in 1581, by ordering the members of a grand jury bound over to appear at the next assizes, to answer for their "contempt" in refusing to indict several known recusants.¹³² Threats to punish local people for treating their Catholic neighbors with charity and forbearance risked creating an impression that the crown's own conduct was dividing communities and turning friends and neighbors against each other. Elizabeth's worries that rigor would stir more resentment than it was worth acted as a brake on the conduct of her more zealous officials. According to Mendoza, in January 1580 she told several bishops "that they were a set of scamps for they were oppressing the Catholics more than she desired."¹³³

Quite apart from such scruples, the practical difficulty of vetting more than a thousand JPs and many thousands of constables and other parish officials—and then finding committed Protestants of sufficient local standing to replace them—strained the council's capacity beyond its limits. Although the council removed some Catholics from commissions of the peace, many soon returned to the bench, while others, especially church-papists, survived the purges altogether.¹³⁴ In some districts, removing all magistrates sympathetic to Catholicism would have

---

¹²⁸ Ibid., fol. 50r-v. Although not explicitly named—Burghley referred instead to a "popish successor"—Mary was clearly intended.
¹²⁹ Cf. the even earlier memorandum of October 1579 reproduced in *A Collection of State Papers Relating to Affairs in the Reign of Queen Elizabeth from the Year 1571 to 1596*, ed. William Murdin (London, 1759), 326.
¹³⁰ SRO D603/K/1/6/1/10/59. On the Catholic side, even Robert Persons conceded the point in principle, writing, for example, that it would be wrong to force a Jew to worship the Trinity because religious acts committed against an individual's conscience always involved mortal sin. He made an exception for Protestants by treating them as apostates from the true faith in which they and their ancestors had been raised: since they had willfully rejected and opposed the Truth, their pleas of conscience lacked validity. See Robert Persons, *A brief discours containing certayne reasons why Catholiques refuse to goe to Church* (1580).
¹³¹ See Walsham, *Charitable Hatred*, 56–64. ¹³² APC 12.270. ¹³³ *CSPSp* 3.22.
¹³⁴ See LaRocca, "Popery and Pounds," 256 for one example.

deprived the crown of magistrates whose local standing made them effective. As Catholics quickly realized, the government's difficulties in proving that people it suspected of disloyalty had committed illegal acts, especially under the constraints imposed by common law rules, put the authorities at a serious disadvantage. Because the law enjoined punishment only for actions an individual had actually committed, rather than beliefs that might lead him to act seditiously at some unspecified point in the future, it provided a very imperfect basis for acting against a nebulous Catholic threat.

The authorities therefore had to fall back on prosecutions of acts that were incontestably illegal, especially refusal to attend Protestant services, attendance at secret celebrations of the mass, and harboring of priests. Elizabeth probably saw these measures as a demonstration of her determination to enforce the law, and perhaps a way of balancing her recent suppression of the puritan prophesying movement by a crackdown on Catholic disobedience. But many of her councilors also saw prosecutions for recusancy, along with the arrest and interrogation of priests, as a way of conducting pre-emptive strikes against the potential formation of organized political resistance to Protestant rule. The wave of prosecutions unfolded during a period of "heightened eschatological anxiety and fear" provoked by perceived threats of Catholic invasion and insurrection that was also fed by reports of abnormal natural events that contemporaries saw as providential warnings.[135] Even some moderate Protestants with no sympathy for puritanism advocated harshness. The conformist cleric and future gentleman of the Chapel Royal, Anthony Anderson, preached a Paul's Cross sermon in 1581 and published it with a dedication to his probable kinsman, Judge Edmund Anderson, the hammer of puritan non-conformity on the Norfolk circuit.[136] It excoriated magistrates who turned a blind eye to recusancy and urged that Catholic non-conformists be prosecuted without mercy: "Your very robes do teach it unto us: you sit in bloody gowns of scarlet hew, as whereby your very apparel doth prognosticate to yourselves and us with what hate to sin and zeal to God you must execute the laws, even to the not only drawing of blood by the sword of equity but even to the dying of the place with the blood of the wicked."[137] In 1581 the council and Parliament considered punishing lay converts to Catholicism as traitors, and those who sheltered or encouraged them with the penalties of praemunire, the loss of property and imprisonment during the queen's pleasure.[138] It eventually dropped these proposals, perhaps because Elizabeth

---

[135] Walsham, *Catholic Reformation*, 331–2.

[136] Anthony Anderson held orthodox Calvinist views on a number of theological points but later opposed puritan ceremonial non-conformity. In the 1590s he was appointed to the Chapel Royal. For a brief account see Henry Patton, "'Of Hir Majesties Chappell': Religious Identities in the Elizabethan Chapel Royal," unpublished Oxford MA thesis, 18–25.

[137] Anthony Anderson, *A Sermon at Paules Cross...23 April 1581 (1581)*, sig. C5v.

[138] See, for example, the notes on proposed legislation in BL Cotton Mss. Titus B III, fol. 64.

considered them too harsh. Capital punishment was instead reserved for priests and the penalties of praemunire for laymen who hid and assisted them, while recusants were subjected to a fine of £20 for each month they refused to attend church.

If strictly enforced this would quickly have ruined all but the wealthiest Catholic families.[139] But consistent enforcement proved difficult. In some places, like Shropshire, accused recusants refused *en masse* to answer summonses to appear before the authorities, preventing the legal penalty from being duly imposed.[140] In Leicestershire the county's dominant magnate, the puritan earl of Huntingdon, appears to have shielded recusants who belonged to his affinity.[141] Catholics who did appear for trial found ways of preventing magistrates from proving that they had broken the law. As a memorandum among Walsingham's papers pointed out, they might refuse to answer the question, "do you or will you go to church," since the common law granted protection against self-incrimination, and the relevant statute provided penalties only for past offenses, not future intentions. If a Catholic had more than one residence he might object when a jury presented him for recusancy that the jurors had no way of knowing whether he attended church while absent from their community.[142] Protestant non-conformity and partial conformity further complicated the picture by allowing Catholics to argue that their refusal to take communion in the required manner was no more illegal than the actions of puritan clerics who dispensed with prescribed ceremonies they disliked. One of the most effective instruments for prosecuting recusancy was through ecclesiastical commissions, ad hoc tribunals empowered to investigate and punish crimes against the Church under procedures not governed by common law that included the tendering of oaths by which individuals were compelled to answer truthfully any questions posed to them before being charged with a specific offense. This was an effective instrument for probing beliefs and forcing people to incriminate themselves. But from 1584 Whitgift began using ecclesiastical commissions—eventually incorporated into a single standing High Commission—to discipline puritan clergy. By the early 1590s over 300 puritan ministers had been suspended. The very people most eager to crack down on recusancy therefore had ample reason to dislike the institution best equipped to do so.[143]

---

[139] LaRocca, "Popery and Pounds," 260–1.
[140] BL Lansdowne Mss. 33, fol. 27: "Of the one hundred that were detected and presented for recusancy [in one part of Shropshire] they could get but four only to be bound."
[141] Cogan, *Catholic Networks*, 164 and 222; the Dudleys also seem to have shielded some Catholic dependants in Warwickshire (ibid., 165–6).
[142] TNA SP12/136/15.
[143] For a good survey of Protestant objections to *ex officio* oaths and Whitgift's use of High Commission see Christopher W. Brooks, *Law, Politics and Society in Early Modern England* (Cambridge: Cambridge University Press, 2009), 97–109.

This conundrum led some Protestants to distinguish between forms of religious disobedience that stemmed only from an excessive zeal for the truth, and those that threatened the state because they involved loyalty to the pope, a foreign prince and the queen's declared enemy. The former seemed essentially harmless and indeed was often characteristic of the queen's most committed supporters, while the latter required severe repression. By this reasoning even some official policies, like Whitgift's efforts to deprive puritan clergy of their stipends and license to preach, looked like acts of *dis*loyalty. Francis Knollys complained to Burghley that Whitgift's actions endangered "the safety and preservation of her majesty's person, crown and dignity," by silencing preachers who spoke out against "Jesuits and their diligent traitorous scholars and soldiers."[144] By carrying out a policy the queen approved, Whitgift had endangered her safety and weakened her "state."[145]

But since the criterion of loyalty to Protestant beliefs had no explicit basis in statute or legal custom, this differential treatment of puritan and popish dissent required careful justification. Parliamentary legislation provided it with some basis by singling out missionary priests for especially harsh punishment because they "withdrew subjects from their allegiance" by inducing them to accept papal authority. The priests were guilty not of spiritual offenses but of "popery" in the strict sense of loyalty to an Italian bishop, who had issued a bull in 1570 absolving Elizabeth's subjects of their allegiance and calling for her deposition. Burghley's pamphlet, *The Execution of Justice in England*, embellished the charge by branding seminarians not only traitors but a "race" of persons "disposed naturally to sedition" and a "kind of vermin."[146] It went on to denounce Catholic exiles as people of dissolute lives cursed by God. The earl of Westmoreland was "bereaved of his children" and "his body [is] now eaten with ulcers of lewd causes," presumably the effects of syphilis.[147] Jesuits received particular opprobrium, not because they were any more active than secular priests but because as a foreign order, associated with Spain and the papacy, they made an especially inviting target.[148] Burghley further refined the rhetorical strategy by impersonating moderate and loyal Catholics disgusted by the appeals of disloyal extremists. "I could wish some expert learned man would feign an answer as from a number of Catholics," he wrote to Walsingham after William Allen had published a tract

---

[144] TNA SP12/171/23.
[145] "I do think it to be a dangerous matter to her majesty's safety that the politic government of matters of state, as well concerning forms and accidents of and to religion, as otherwise, should be taken from all councilors of her majesty's estate and only to be given over to the rule of bishops that are not always indifferent in their own cases of sovereignty" (ibid.).
[146] William Cecil, *The Execution of Justice in England*, ed. Robert Kingdon (Ithaca: Cornell University Press, 1965), 6 and 9.
[147] Ibid., 4.
[148] As Thomas McCoog and others have shown, in the early 1580s Jesuits and secular priests were divided over questions of how far to involve themselves in political action, with cautious moderates and more committed activists in both camps. See, for example, Thomas McCoog, *The Society of Jesus in Ireland, Scotland and England 1541–1588* (Leiden: Brill, 1996).

supporting the Armada "that notwithstanding their evil contentment for religion should profess their obedience and promise with their lives and power against all strange forces offering to land in this realm."[149] He wanted not only to drive a wedge between militant and peaceful Catholics but also to convey an impression of moderation and tolerance on the part of the crown, except with respect to religious beliefs that encouraged acts of treason.

Despite its rhetoric, the council recognized that a bloody persecution might well prove counter-productive by exciting sympathy for the victims. It therefore enforced statutory penalties selectively. Recusancy fines fell disproportionately on a small number of families. Sir Thomas Tresham paid the crippling sum of £1,773 in fines between 1587 and 1592, but most of his co-religionists paid much smaller amounts or escaped altogether. Twenty families paid two-thirds of all fines collected in the same period.[150] The authorities quickly discovered that executing priests risked creating martyrs, moving "many to compassion" and leading "some to affect their religion, upon conceit that an extraordinary contempt of death cannot but proceed from above."[151] While this did not stop the executions entirely it did reduce their number, so that the majority of captured priests received the lighter punishments of banishment or imprisonment, while the death sentence was meted out to those deemed most dangerous or least likely to arouse sympathy. Eleven priests were executed in 1582 but only two (plus two laymen) the following year, despite numerous arrests. Appreciable numbers of priests—Parsons counted thirty in Hull and twenty-six in London—ended up imprisoned, mostly under lax supervision that allowed them to celebrate mass before visitors and conduct other business. Parsons thought that in many cases incarcerated priests were more useful than those who remained free and in hiding, since people knew where to find them and they no longer had as much to lose by undertaking dangerous assignments.[152] He reported a new clamp-down on Catholic communications in the autumn of 1584, a period of heightened tensions involving events in Scotland and revelations about assassination plots against the queen.[153] But the number of executions increased only slightly, to six priests and three Catholic laymen, followed by another two priests and two laymen in 1585.[154] Since these totals included individuals convicted for plotting to murder Elizabeth, they indicate significant restraint. By contrast, in 1588 the government executed twenty-one priests and twenty lay Catholics: during an emergency in which public fear and hatred of the Roman Church increased, inhibitions about shedding blood diminished. In addition to those executed, nearly 100 Catholic missionaries died in prison over the course of the reign.[155]

---

[149] *Arundel*, ed. Pollen and MacMahon, 170. [150] McGrath, *Papists and Puritans*, 198–9.
[151] TNA SP12/195/114. [152] *Correspondence of Persons*, ed. Houliston et al., 365.
[153] Ibid., 505. [154] McGrath, *Papists and Puritans*, 177, n. 2.
[155] Walsham, *Charitable Hatred*, 84.

The executions gave rise to a propaganda contest as Catholic publicists portrayed the victims as courageous martyrs while Protestants sought to discredit them in every way possible.[156] The contest to shape perceptions took place even during executions, as presiding sheriffs cajoled and hectored condemned men to acknowledge their guilt, while priests adopted the role of martyrs eager to die for their faith. Anthony Munday descried one priest facing execution who, upon seeing a colleague hanging from the gallows, "began with holding up his hands" to cry "O sweet Tom, O blessed Tom." Coming to the foot of the gallows he fell on his knees, crying again, "O happy Tom, O blessed Tom, thy sweet soul pray for me," before finally proclaiming to the crowd: "I am brought hitherto this place, to die a death which is both shameful and ignominious, for which I thank thee my Lord God, who framing me to thine own similitude and likeness hath blessed me to this good end."[157] Some priests sought to belie the government's justification for their execution as traitors by affirming their loyalty to the queen on the scaffold and praying for her. But even as an execution commenced, the authorities possessed some leverage over their victims by their ability to shorten or prolong their final agony. They might show mercy by strangling the condemned before proceeding to eviscerate him, or deliberately draw out the torture. In 1586 four of the Babington conspirators were executed serially, so that each had to watch as the hangman castrated and disemboweled his colleagues, knowing his turn would soon come. When one, a priest, asked for a merciful death, the sheriff replied: "it seemeth your religion yieldeth you cold comfort that your mind is on that." The priest confessed his guilt in general terms but the sheriff pressed for details: "you would have killed her majesty... you would have sacked London and overthrown the state," to which the crowd responded "amen, amen." When the priest reaffirmed his belief in the Catholic Church the sheriff warned him against "falling out of the world with the wrong faith"; when he began to pray in Latin, the executioner turned him off the ladder and proceeded with the grisly execution, as the crowd shouted, "God save the queen."[158] Campion's execution gave rise to competing printed narratives, alternately stressing the condemned Jesuit's courage and martyrdom or guilt, and courage or cowardice on the scaffold.[159]

---

[156] This subject has lately given rise to an impressive historical and critical literature. See, for example, Shell, *Catholicism, Controversy*; Lake with Questier, *Antichrist's Lewd Hat*, section II; Anne Dillon, *The Construction of Martyrdom in the English Catholic Community* (Aldershot: Ashgate, 2002); Monta, *Martyrdom and Literature*; Kilroy, *Edmund Campion*; *Martyrs and Martyrdom in England, 1400–1700*, ed. Thomas Freeman and Thomas Mayer (Woodbridge: Boydell Press, 2007); and Tutino, *Law and Conscience*.

[157] A[nthony] M[unday], *A briefe and true report of the execution of certaine traytours at Tiborne* (London, 1582), sigs Bi–ii.

[158] BL Add Mss. 48027.

[159] Lake with Questier, *Antichrist's Lewd Hat*, chapter 7 provides a detailed account of the competing narratives and competition to construct interpretations of the deaths of the regime's Catholic victims.

Imprisonment for Recusancy and Power in the Localities

As so often happened in early modern law enforcement, the authorities therefore used a draconian code to make a few terrifying examples, while deliberately avoiding consistent rigor. But in addition to formal legal proceedings we need to allow for restrictions and penalties imposed on an ad hoc basis, without much due process. Recusants faced imprisonment without trial for periods as long as several months, in county jails, royal castles, or the houses of Protestant neighbors selected as their legal custodians. Although a count of those imprisoned has never been made, they almost certainly numbered in the hundreds if not thousands, as Mendoza claimed. When released, Catholics usually had to enter into bonds restricting their freedom of movement and place of residence. The standard formula, devised in May 1581, required the released prisoner to remain within three miles of a specified residence until he conformed to the Church, to refrain from receiving priests or visiting the houses of other recusants, and to avoid keeping recusant servants.[160] In a few cases the conditions were even more restrictive: the earl of Northumberland, for example, was forbidden to reside in the North. Certificates of individuals who had entered into these bonds were sent to sheriffs and bishops to encourage effective surveillance. Exemptions, even for a limited period, normally required the approval of the nearest bishop, often after the intercession of a member of the council. Enough petitions for such exemptions survive to show that the restrictions remained in force well into the 1590s, when they were enacted by statute, affecting both people who may have been truly dangerous, like the future Gunpowder traitor Sir William Catesby, and others who seem harmless, like two septuagenarians, both poor and one blind, excused in 1594.[161] Even Sir Thomas Cornwallis, the former Steward of Prince Edward's household, was placed under house arrest in 1588.[162] The restraints were not only inconvenient but humiliating, since they branded Catholic landowners as persons of suspect loyalty, subjected them to the oversight of Protestant neighbors, and forced them to beg favors from the very councilors responsible for their incarceration. Sir Thomas Tresham complained bitterly in 1581 that his imprisonment was a disgrace worse than that "afforded brawlers, fighters, unthrifty and loose people," although he felt consoled that other Catholics, "my betters, my equals," received similar treatment. The unpleasantness of his confinement in the house of a Protestant neighbor increased when the man's wife insisted on arguing with him about theology, contrary to the advice of St. Paul "that women should learn in silence," he grumbled. By this and other

---

[160] There are various surviving copies, e.g. *Recusant Documents from the Ellesmere Manuscripts* and *APC* 13.41–2.
[161] LPL Mss. 3470, fols 103, 150 and passim. [162] Ibid., fol. 90.

offenses, she had violated "the rules of Christian charity," he claimed, increasing his "affliction."[163]

By stigmatizing recusants and restricting where they could live or travel, the council undermined their local influence. The case of the Staffordshire magnate, Thomas Lord Paget, provides a notable example. The brother of a Marian privy councilor, Paget probably always favored Catholicism. But until 1580 his religion did not prevent him from exercising his right to place clergy of his choosing in a number of impropriated benefices or serving actively in the governance of his native Staffordshire. His ties to the Cornwallis and Kitson families in East Anglia, where he also controlled impropriated benefices, and to Catholic gentry in the southwest, extended his influence beyond the midlands. In 1580 he allowed Campion to preach to an audience of leading Catholics in his London house.[164] Shortly thereafter, in August, the government ordered Paget imprisoned, along with other Staffordshire gentlemen and two of his own servants, for failing to attend public religious services.[165] He responded with ardent protests of his loyalty and appeals to the queen's mercy, urging that she had always preferred "to bear with the weakness and infirmities of her poor subjects, rather than to execute the force and rigor of her laws."[166] But his plaintiff letters to Burghley, Hatton, Leicester, and Walsingham did him little good. After fourteen weeks of incarceration a compromise was worked out, by which Paget agreed to attend religious services in his own household, and to live in London and attend the court until Elizabeth gave him permission to return to Staffordshire.[167]

He had meanwhile become involved in disputes with several neighbors involving enclosures and iron works erected on his properties in and near Cannock Chase, Staffordshire, which impeded the local inhabitants' ability to graze livestock and otherwise use this wooded area in the accustomed manner.[168] His adversaries included Sir Walter Aston, a justice of the peace who had lately assisted in hunting down Catholic priests in the county.[169] As Paget sat in prison in October he received a letter from the earl of Leicester, asking him to grant "Sir Walter Aston, my good friend," an office in "Cauke Wood," which Aston claimed his ancestors had long held. Aston's "good will and friendship may stand your

---

[163] BL Add Mss. 39828, fols 43, 59, and 60.
[164] Peter Holmes, "Paget, Thomas, fourth Baron Paget," in *ODNB*.
[165] For details see Folger Shakespeare Library Mss. L.a. 709 (unfoliated) for July 12, 1580 and L.a. 713 for April 27, 1581, listing fifteen imprisoned Staffordshire recusants of gentry status; APC 12.30–1, 134, 157, 179, 415.
[166] TNA SRO D603/K/1/6/21.   [167] SRO D603/K/1/6/24 and 38.
[168] The documents refer not to Cannock Chase but variously to Caucke Wood, Cancke Bromley and Buron woods and Cankewood coppice. But Cannock Chase belonged to Lord Paget. It has a long history of industrial use and Canckewood is described in one document as surrounded by settlements whose names correspond to those of villages surrounding Cannock Chase. See TNA STAC5/P29/31, which also supplies the information that Paget's enclosures and iron works were interfering with what local people considered their traditional forest rights.
[169] *APC* 11.57; TNA PC/12, fol. 407.

lordship in as good stead in that country as any others of your neighbors," Leicester urged.[170] Paget refused. Within a year he began receiving reports of attacks on his enclosures, thefts of his timber, and poaching of his game by Aston and others.[171] Some Staffordshire residents circulated a petition complaining against him, for presentation to the privy council. "What they intend or mean to do herein God knoweth," his servant, William Fynney, advised: "for they are a foolish company and maliciously bent [to] do hurt if they can, and therefore very needful to prevent in time such infamy or inconvenience as might ensue."[172] It soon became clear that Aston had encouraged these attacks. When Paget's local agents tried to protect his property, Sir Walter's servants violently assaulted them, leading to three fatalities. "We could not in any wise devise how to make resistance," Fynney advised, "for want of able and meet men for that purpose... and in truth (as we think) it is not four or six men that are able one to assist another to resist Sir Walter Aston and his people, considering how near his house standeth and how he is provided aforehand of a dozen lusty and tall fellows and more that have been and are daily trained in the exercise and knowledge of diverse kinds of weapons for that purpose."[173] While Paget lived in lodgings in a bookbinder's house in Fleet Street, with his friends and servants scattered about the county, his opponent had "the quarrel at his door," the support of the sheriff and the backing of Leicester, who planned to visit the county later that summer.[174] Paget complained to the privy council, which gave him some support, upbraiding the sheriff and fining one of Aston's allies 100 marks.[175] But the penalty may never have been collected and it does not seem to have made much difference in Staffordshire.

As the dispute continued, Aston and his allies inflicted further indignities on Paget. The sheriff not only moved into one of Paget's houses but carted in several loads of bedding and furniture from other Paget residences to make it more comfortable.[176] In addition to a flagrant violation of Paget's property rights this was a public insult meant to show how weak his position had become. In November the dispute led to a Star Chamber case and Paget directed his servants to begin gathering depositions. But Fynney again warned him that unless Paget returned to the county, pursuing the quarrel would likely "do your lordship more hurt than good." Aston had "very many kinsmen and friends within the shire, who cease not as any occasion is offered to travail for him in any case of his by many sinister and indirect ways and means," whereas "our friends [are] few and cold in

---

[170] SRO D603/K/1/6/20. [171] SRO D(w) 1734/2/5/15e.
[172] SRO D603/K/1/6/56, William Fynney to Paget, May 26, 1581.
[173] SRO D603/K/1/7/9 Fynney to Paget, June 9, 1581. Another account of the assault on Paget's enclosures, by a crowd said to number about 30 men armed 'with swords, daggers, long piked staves, foret bills and pitch forks' is in TNA, STAC5/P60/40.
[174] SRO D603/K/1/7/11. [175] Folger Shakespeare Library Mss. L.a. 250 for February 15, 1581.
[176] SRO D(w) 1734/2/5/15j and k.

friendship."¹⁷⁷ Although Fynney may not have known it, Aston had also recently received a letter of thanks from the council "for his good services in furthering her Majesty's service in all things generally within that county of Stafford, and especially in causes of religion," and promising that his efforts would be "remembered" by the queen to "his comfort and benefit."¹⁷⁸ Paget petulantly rejected his servant's advice, writing that if the people of Staffordshire were "so corrupt" as to tolerate Aston's outrages he would not want to live among them.¹⁷⁹

The following January, Paget was threatened with another quarrel in Norfolk, where one of his former household chaplains, whom he had presented to a benefice, came under attack from another clergyman who enjoyed the support of Leicester's ally, Roger Lord North. Paget's protégé claimed that his adversaries merely wanted to appropriate his income and begged his patron "to stand my good lord in mine honest and just causes."¹⁸⁰ But North treated the affair as a religious quarrel, telling the offending vicar that "he would not have any such papists dwell so near him," and gathering testimony about his alleged misdeeds from as far away as Suffolk and Cambridgeshire.¹⁸¹ Paget may also have been cheated of his rights of patronage to a second Norfolk benefice, through the collusion of the incumbent and other nearby inhabitants.¹⁸² In this case the dispute appears to have centered on material interests rather than religion, but Paget's confinement to London and the apparent disfavor of the queen and council crippled his ability to defend his interests and protect his clients.

These humiliations did not deter Paget from speaking out in opposition to legislation against recusants in the Lords in 1581. The following year he found himself further embarrassed by the flight into exile of his younger brother, Charles. He wrote Charles a disapproving letter, urging him to avoid the company of other disloyal exiles and to leave his new residence in Paris for "some other place where you may better avoid the suspicion of being a practiser."¹⁸³ But Charles blatantly ignored this advice by attaching himself to the service of Mary Stuart and allowing himself to be drawn into a scheme of Allen and the duke of Guise for an invasion of England through Sussex. He traveled secretly to Sussex to gather information and consult with the earl of Northumberland and Northumberland's friend Sir William Shelley, who both resided in the county. On his way he visited his brother and evidently told him of Guise's plans. Although Thomas Paget remained skeptical about the scheme, he entertained other landed Catholics at his lodgings in Fleet Street who were apparently far more enthusiastic, and travelled to Northumberland's Sussex seat at Petworth.¹⁸⁴ The council soon got wind of Charles's activities and arrested Northumberland and

---

¹⁷⁷ SRO D603/K/1/7/72 Wm Fynney and Thomas Powntes to Paget, December 22, 1581.
¹⁷⁸ APC 12.270.   ¹⁷⁹ SRO D603/K/1/7/74.   ¹⁸⁰ SRO D603/K/1/7/10.
¹⁸¹ SRO D603/K/1/8/11.   ¹⁸² SRO D603/K/1/7/40.   ¹⁸³ SRO D603/K/1/7/75.
¹⁸⁴ John Bossy, *Under the Molehill: An Elizabethan Spy Story* (New Haven: Yale University Press, 2001), 78 and n. 45, citing TNA SP12/164/26.

Shelley on suspicion of treason; inevitably it would also want to interrogate Lord Paget about how much he knew. To prevent this from happening, Paget fled to France. The crown seized his estates and in 1587 Parliament attainted him of treason. His iron works in Cannock wood ended up in the hands of Sir Philip Sidney's friend, Fulke Greville.[185]

Thomas Lord Paget therefore ended his life as an attainted traitor, supported in exile by a Spanish pension, while other Catholic magnates, like Anthony Browne viscount Montague, continued to serve the crown in their native shires, even being appointed to commissions for detecting recusants.[186] The differences between the two men appear much slighter than their contrasting fates suggest. Paget no doubt exaggerated when he claimed that without Elizabeth's trust he had no desire to live, but he appears to have been only peripherally involved in plots against her. His sheltering of Campion and opposition to legislation against recusancy do indicate a level of political activism, but he was brought into Guise's scheme for an invasion of England by his brother, rather than his own initiative, and he seems to have remained cautious about it. His imprisonment and removal from Staffordshire were caused not by political activities but his conscientious refusal to attend church. By contrast, Montague preserved not only his freedom but also his local influence—and therefore his ability to shield other Catholics—by token conformity. According to a report sent to the Council in 1584 he even managed, by "pretending" to enjoy privileged rights of jurisdiction in the town of Battle, to turn it into a center of popery, where traveling priests found refuge.[187] The second crucial difference was Paget's embarrassing younger brother, whose incautious participation in a genuinely treasonous plot brought down the whole family. But if Guise *had* landed with 6,000 men in Sussex, Lord Paget would have been unable to lend much assistance even if he had wanted to do so, whereas some of Montague's Sussex affinity, if not the viscount himself, would almost certainly have rallied to the invader. The roles of the two peers lends credibility to Sir Walter Ralegh's assertion a few years later that "temperate" Catholics, who sabotaged the queen's government from within, were far more dangerous than obstinate ones, who were more easily rendered harmless.[188]

---

[185] Folger Shakespeare Library Mss. L.a. 321, fol. 2.
[186] For Montagu see Questier, *Catholicism and Community*.
[187] TNA SP12/164/22. Cf. Questier's thorough and subtle discussion in *Catholicism and Community*, 46–78, 118–205.
[188] *The Letters of Sir Walter Ralegh*, ed. Agnes Latham and Joyce Youings (Exeter: University of Exeter Press, 1999), 40, Ralegh to Burleigh, December 21, 1587: "Some other of the commission of Devon (in my conscience before the Lord) being both infected in religion and vehemently malcontent, who by how much the more they are temperate by so much the more [they are] dangerous are secretly great hinderers of all actions tending to the good of her Majesty or safety of the present state. These men make doubt that your honor's instructions alone are not sufficient and safe warrant for their discharge and that if any refuse to contribute they see not by what they should be enforced, with a thousand dilatory cavillations."

Paget's story also illustrates the calibrated nature of the council's responses to recusancy and its reluctance to ruin Catholic families irrevocably. Lord Paget's heir, William, remained behind in England. Shortly after his father's attainder the queen assigned his guardianship to a trusted courtier, Sir George Carey. In 1596 William accompanied Essex to Cadiz; two years later he joined Robert Cecil's entourage on an embassy to France. In 1602 he married Lettice Knollys, the daughter of a solidly Protestant—indeed puritan—court family related by marriage to the Cecils. James I completed his rehabilitation in 1604 by restoring the baronial title, causing grumbling among some Protestants, since William remained a Catholic.[189] Even Charles Paget eventually procured a pardon from James, allowing him to return to England. The Pagets' rehabilitation is reminiscent of the ways in which previous Tudor and Yorkist kings had dealt with disloyal peers since well before the Reformation. Men convicted of treason automatically forfeited their titles and property, but in most cases, if their heirs avoided further missteps they might look forward to eventual rehabilitation and the restoration of at least a portion of their ancestral lands. The possibility of future pardons encouraged families caught up in treasonable acts to reconcile with the victors.

The council's ability to imprison and investigate Catholics on mere suspicion of disloyalty, along with its policies of placing recusants under arrest and seizing their arms during emergencies must, nevertheless, have had chilling effects. It made it clear that even fleeting contact with suspect individuals or other behavior that looked disloyal might lead to serious trouble. This created an atmosphere of fear and caution within the Catholic community that must have inhibited political activism, except among a tiny minority prepared to sacrifice everything for the cause. The government's increasingly extensive network of spies increased the risks. Mendoza complained in 1583 that Elizabeth had so many spies in France dogging the footsteps of Catholic exiles "that it is not possible for their friends to send him a penny without her hearing of it," so that he was compelled to use his privileged diplomatic posts to do so.[190] Even before this the English had infiltrated a spy into his own household, while a mole in the French embassy revealed to Walsingham many details of the conspiracy that became known as the Throckmorton Plot.[191] To be sure, Elizabeth's refusal to move against occasional conformists like Montague, to say nothing of peers who kept their religious views hidden, along with the willingness of staunchly Protestant magnates like Huntingdon and Leicester to shield their own clients regardless of their religious views, meant that many families with Catholic sympathies remained firmly embedded within the structures of local government. Some Protestants continued

---

[189] *ODNB.* [190] *CSPSp* 3.471.
[191] TNA SP12/150/59; Bossy, *Under the Molehill.* For a more general survey of Walsingham's spies see Stephen Alford, *The Watchers: A Secret History of the Reign of Elizabeth* (London: Allen Lane, 2012).

to urge more sweeping measures. But by singling out for punishment Catholics least willing to compromise, while aggressively investigating landowners suspected of harboring priests or having had even fleeting contacts with conspirators, the government created an environment in which organized Catholic resistance became much more difficult. In addition to the direct effects of imprisonment, recusant landowners had strong incentives not only to demonstrate their loyalty to the queen but also to maintain good relations with Protestant neighbors, relatives, and patrons, who might be in a position to help if they got into trouble with the state. They also had ample reason to distance themselves from priests and lay Catholics who continued to engage in illegal and possibly treasonous activities, so as to avoid imputations of guilt-by-association. Fear of jeopardizing their liberty and their estates therefore pushed them to adopt a "loyalist" position and to remain integrated within religiously mixed gentry communities, rather than retreating into networks defined by confessional commitments. On the other hand, Catholics who remained committed to sheltering priests and Jesuits increasingly needed to minimize contacts with conformist and Protestant neighbors, so as to reduce their risk of discovery. This led to a kind of confessional isolation that limited their political effectiveness.[192]

The schemes of Allen, Mendoza, and Guise depended on the assumption that a significant body of English Catholics, led by peers and influential gentlemen, were prepared to rise against the Elizabethan state. Plans for invasions therefore always included provisions for bringing thousands of extra weapons, to arm the supporters expected to come in as a Catholic army marched across the countryside. Although such calculations probably always involved elements of wishful thinking, some potential for the formation of coordinated resistance does seem to have existed around 1580. Executions of priests would have done little to reduce that potential and may actually have increased it, by stoking Catholic anger. But the incarcerations, investigations, and restrictive bonds imposed on lay Catholics would have been another matter. The treatment accorded members of the Howard family, which Mendoza regarded as potentially invaluable allies of Spain, illustrate the relentless government pressure. "My desks and coffers have been six times broken up," Lord Henry Howard complained: "my papers rifled, and sundry books of notes carried away."[193] His nephew, Philip earl of Arundel, suffered two periods of arrest and interrogation, in 1584 and 1585, after he stopped attending Protestant religious services. Like Paget, he found that his imprisonment encouraged a Protestant neighbor, Sir Nicholas Bacon, to begin poaching his deer, spreading defamatory reports and picking quarrels with his

---

[192] For discussions of both tendencies see Cogan, *Catholic Social Networks*, 79, 85, 94, 123–5, 192, 211–13, 219–27, 240–1. Cf. also James E. Kelly, "Counties without Borders? Religious Politics, Kinship Networks and the Formation of Catholic Communities," *Historical Research* 91 (2018): 22–38.

[193] Ibid., fol. 8.

servants.[194] Again like Paget, Arundel finally panicked and attempted to flee abroad, only to be arrested before boarding ship, imprisoned once again and finally convicted of treason.[195] And yet as recently as the autumn of 1580 he had been in high favor at court, participating in jousts accompanied by splendidly liveried servants, and lodging and entertaining the queen for nearly three days in his London mansion. He was, after all, not only one of England's senior nobles but also Elizabeth's cousin, precisely the sort of man who might have led a religiously conservative revival under more propitious circumstances.

Some of Mendoza's comments point to the success of the crown's measures. Whereas in 1581 he received a steady diet of information about affairs at court, by 1582 this had dried up: "things have reached such a point now that no one will speak to me or even to my servants."[196] The one exception was Henry Howard, but even he was worried enough about his future to contemplate exile in Spain.[197] Although "there are many Catholic gentlemen devoted to you, as are all the schismatics and some Protestants," Mendoza told Mary Stuart in 1583, "I find no particularly strong spirit or effort to forward the matter themselves, nor... any close association or league amongst them."[198] The fundamental problem faced by Mendoza and his associates was that any coordinated plan to overthrow Elizabeth required communication among a large number of widely scattered people, on the Continent, in multiple English shires and usually also Scotland, which gave the English authorities multiple opportunities to intercept letters and turn conspirators into cooperative witnesses. Delays in executing plans exacerbated the problem. Guise involved himself repeatedly in schemes to assassinate the queen, invade her realm, and incite a general rebellion, in 1582-3, 1584, and 1586.[199] On every occasion he hesitated to act, often for very good reasons, long enough for the council and its agents to infiltrate his networks of allies and disrupt their activities.

As Catholic attempts to start a coordinated rising faltered, Protestant control strengthened in localities like Staffordshire. In a full-scale civil war, Sir Walter Aston and his dozen or so household thugs would have made little difference. But the freedom with which a man like Aston recruited, trained, and armed his followers and fomented local riots against a Catholic rival who remained confined to London is suggestive. Leicester's previously mentioned persecution of the Ardens and other Catholic families in neighboring Warwickshire and stockpiling of arms in Kenilworth fits the same pattern. If a sudden crisis had erupted in these midland counties, Protestants would have been in a position to mobilize armed force quickly, while most leading Catholics remained disarmed, intimidated, and in Paget's case unable to set foot on his local estates.

---

[194] BL Egerton Mss. 2074, fol. 25.   [195] *Arundel*, ed. Pollen and MacMahon, 22-3, 29.
[196] *CSPSp* 3.406.   [197] Ibid., 316.   [198] Ibid., 467, 471.
[199] Teulet, *Papiers d'état*, 3.240-550 and passim.

Assassination, Lynch Law, and Provisions against Civil Chaos

The government's success in tightening security almost certainly contributed, along with bitterness over the executions of Campion and other priests, to the growing interest of Allen, Persons, and other activists in assassination plots. Only something as dramatic and unexpected as Elizabeth's sudden death, preferably in combination with a landing on the English coast by Guise, Parma, or both, seemed capable of changing the dynamic sufficiently to make the dream of a mass Catholic uprising plausible. Since the issue was never put to the test, we have no sure way of gauging the likely Catholic response to such an eventuality. But the Bond of Association shows how the Protestant regime and its allies would have reacted. Drawn up by Burghley and others on the council in the period following the revelation of the Throckmorton Plot and the murder of the prince of Orange, this document was widely circulated in the counties during the late summer and autumn. It established a voluntary league of loyal subjects who swore to oppose any faction attempting "anything that shall tend to the harm of her majesty's royal person" by armed force, "to the extermination of them and their councilors, aiders and abettors."[200] If the conspiracy took place on behalf of a rival claimant to the throne, that person and her heirs would lose any right to succeed Elizabeth, and were also to be hunted down and killed.[201] Having obtained the seals and signatures of scores of local dignitaries, Burghley set about drafting a statute that would enact the Bond's provisions into law, by authorizing "all natural good and zealous subjects to prosecute" the Queen's enemies "to the death" if a conspiracy against her began to unfold.[202] The statute would also have continued the authority of the privy council and other magistrates after the queen's death by assassination, while the murder was investigated and those responsible punished. It prohibited any subject from proclaiming a successor until the completion of this process.[203]

Although Burghley and his colleagues intended the Bond of Association partly as a deterrent and for that reason publicized it widely,[204] they also made clear that in an emergency they wanted people like Sir Walter Aston to act as Protestant vigilantes with a license to kill. Not surprisingly, this seems to have further increased fear within the Catholic community. In 1588 a rumor spread among Catholics in London "that a sudden massacre of them all was intended upon the first landing of the Spaniards."[205] But the violent and arbitrary provisions of the Bond of Association and Burghley's draft statute troubled the queen and some MPs. Elizabeth, who wanted to conclude an alliance with James VI, objected to

---

[200] TNA SP12/173/81.
[201] The employment of the feminine pronoun left little doubt who was intended.
[202] TNA SP12/176/22 (draft statute in Burghley's hand).   [203] Ibid.
[204] TNA SP12/173/86.   [205] *Arundel*, ed. Pollen and MacMahon, 191.

barring his title to the throne solely because of the actions of his mother.²⁰⁶ By the time she intervened, the Commons was already wrestling with the issue of how to deal with James's possible hostility. With him in mind the House agreed that if "any person pretending title to the Crown do make any invasion" of England he should lose his claim. But someone pointed out the routine occurrence of small raids across the Scottish border and asked how large an encroaching force needed to be to qualify as an invasion. After reviewing various precedents, the House settled on the number of 2,000 soldiers.²⁰⁷ Some MPs objected to disqualifying a possible successor merely on the basis of unproven allegations that he or she had conspired to harm Elizabeth. What if an assassin falsely claimed to act on behalf of a potential successor without that person's knowledge? Surely it was wrong to renounce allegiance to the legitimate successor because of an act for which he or she bore no guilt.²⁰⁸ According to a narrative of the debate, attributed by some historians to the mathematician and Leicester protégé Thomas Digges,²⁰⁹ one MP cited the discussion "of Caesar Borgia in Machiavelli" to argue that a rival claimant who had arranged for the queen's assassination might not only deny all knowledge of the crime but actually punish the murderer. How might the guilt of such a duplicitous criminal be discovered? And what would happen if different factions began contending for the throne, each professing loyalty to the murdered queen and the right, under the proposed statute, to take vengeance on the opposing party? Another MP objected to the arbitrary nature of the punishments envisaged under the act. The question was not whether a crime against the queen deserved to be punished, he argued, but whether the punishment should always be death, and "whether with good conscience every private person *indicta causa* may exterminate or kill" without due process.²¹⁰

Other conundrums added to the Commons' frustration and befuddlement. In January they discussed but rejected a religious test barring any popish successor, partly because they believed Elizabeth did not want the issue discussed, but also from fear of setting a precedent that Catholics might turn against Protestants elsewhere in Europe, like Henry of Navarre.²¹¹ According to Digges, attempts to modify the provisions of the Bond of Association, prompted by the queen's scruples about some of its provisions, touched off an angry debate over whether either the monarch or Parliament had the authority to dispense with solemn oaths:

Some wished the indentures [copies of the Bond] might be extinguished or reformed or new made, with due deliberative reformation. Some thought that

---

²⁰⁶ *PPEI* 2.78. See below, pp. 157–60 for the alliance negotiations. ²⁰⁷ Ibid., 76, 142–3.
²⁰⁸ TNA SP12/176/26.
²⁰⁹ For a discussion of the authorship of this tract, variously ascribed to Digges, Burghley, and Sir Walter Mildmay, see Peter Lake, *Bad Queen Bess? Libels, Secret Histories, and the Politics of Publicity in the Reign of Queen Elizabeth I* (Oxford: Oxford University Press, 2016), 162, n. 24.
²¹⁰ TNA SP12/176/26.   ²¹¹ *PPEI* 2.149–50.

forasmuch as Oath was made only for her Majesty's sake and safety that her Majesty might dispense with such parts of their oath as was grievous to their consciences. And most earnestly desired to have her Majesty moved therein. Others affirmed that the oath was void, for so much as was unlawful, inferring that unlawful oaths bind not. Some thought that was a gap opened to make men careless of all oaths and to swear anything, albeit they meant to perform nothing, and therefore was it affirmed by some that they thought themselves bound to perform their oath plainly and truly as they had made it... and that they were bound to prosecute such for perjured persons... [who] for any color or pretext would desist or separate themselves and that there was no mortal authority could dispense with their oath.[212]

The debate drove a wedge between men who had subscribed to the Bond of Association out of loyalty to the queen, but who disagreed about whether this compelled them to implement its provisions even against her express wishes. A few MPs went so far as to propose a statute forbidding Elizabeth from pardoning any attempt on her own life.[213]

Historians have usually attributed the failure of legislation designed to deal with an interregnum crisis in the 1585 Parliament to Elizabeth's opposition. But although a snap dissolution, which took Burghley by surprise,[214] certainly played a role, it seems clear that many members of the Commons also found the legal and moral problems raised by the proposed acts deeply troubling. By trying to devise a solution to the problem of a succession crisis in which all clear legal authority would cease to exist, Burghley and his colleagues had raised issues about relationships between statute, prerogative authority, natural laws of justice, individual conscience, and solemn oaths that many people evidently found insoluble. The resulting debate drove home the full implications of what an all-out war for the throne, in which armed violence replaced legal procedures, would mean:

> Me thought I did behold a confused company of all parts of the realm of all degrees and estates then rising in arms at such a time as there is no Council of Estate in life, no lawful generals, no lieutenants, no lawful colonels of captains to guide them in any military action, no precedents, no judges, no sheriffs, no justices, briefly no officers in life or authority to maintain justice, preserve peace or with lawful power to command obedience to guide and direct such a distracted chaos of armed men, confusedly rising even at that time when most need should be of greatest government, direction and justice to suppress factions, deride claims and defend the realm from spoil and invasion of strangers, when swarms

---

[212] TNA SP12/176/26; cf. *PPEI* 2.147. [213] *PPEI* 2.177; cf. 147. [214] TNA SP12/180/33.

of needy soldiers abounding in the realms round about us will come flying over to possess and pray upon our felicitous wealth and riches.[215]

Even without the queen's intervention, worries of this kind would have made it difficult to achieve the level of consensus needed to provide a legislative remedy to the threat of her assassination.

But as Neil Younger has shown, the Parliament's dissolution did not end the council's attempt to erect a structure of power capable of surviving Elizabeth's sudden death and assuring the perpetuation of a Protestant regime. On July 3, 1585 it revived the Marian institution of the Lord Lieutenancy in eighteen counties, stretching from the English heartland up to Lancashire. The noblemen appointed as lieutenants—most of them reliable Protestants. including pillars of the government like Burghley, Leicester, and the earl of Warwick—received extensive powers to oversee local militia bands, raise additional forces, and implement police measures in time of emergency. In Staffordshire it comes as little surprise to find Sir Walter Aston acting as an especially energetic deputy lieutenant, who supervised musters and received authority from the council in April 1585 to seize recusants' arms and survey the value of their estates.[216] The following year he assisted in the removal of Mary Stuart from the custody of the religiously conservative earl of Shrewsbury to that of the puritan Sir Amyas Paulet.[217] In 1587 and 1588 he elicited complaints over the taking of an illegal distraint and the behavior of his servants, who assaulted a man at the county quarter sessions.[218] He obviously continued to throw his weight around, probably with the tacit support of his patron, Leicester, but now with the additional authority of his office.

Although the threat of foreign invasion and the decision to send an army into the Netherlands, reached definitively in August 1585, provided part of the context for the erection of the lieutenancy system, Younger has shown that worries about domestic rebellion and threats to the queen's safety were also crucial.[219] In support of this view he cites another Digges treatise, entitled "A Tract against the succession," written after William of Orange's assassination. This called upon Elizabeth "so to establish your estate as no storms shall prevail against it after your death": in other words, to assure the continuation of the present structure of power into the next reign. To that end Digges proposed measures similar to those contained in the failed parliamentary legislation, to extend the authority of the council and other officers of state after the queen's death until a parliament selected her successor, along with the suggestion that the crown appoint seven military

[215] TNA SP12/176/26. [216] Folger Shakespeare Library Mss. L.a. 713.
[217] APC 14.210; CSPSc 8.170. [218] Folger Shakespeare Library Mss., L.a. 791 and 810.
[219] Neil Younger, "Securing the Monarchical Republic: The Remaking of the Lord Lieutenancies in 1585," *Bulletin of the Institute for Historical Research* 88 (2011): 249–65. I wish to thank Dr. Younger for providing me with a copy of this important article before publication.

captains to recruit and command a force of 40,000 soldiers, to deal with any violent resistance.²²⁰ Digges appears to have acted as one of the council's men of business, involved in contingency planning for military as well as procedural measures to be taken in any sudden emergency.

In addition to raising and training militia forces the Lieutenancy was envisaged as an institution capable of administering harsh and arbitrary justice in times of disorder. A 1585 "Abstract of the Authority given to the [Lord] Lieutenants by their Commission" empowered militia commanders to pardon or execute offenders "at their pleasure," to "prescribe orders for the government of the county... execute martial law," and to appoint provost marshals as an auxiliary police force.²²¹ Although no executions appear to have resulted from these measures, the council did issue further grants of arbitrary power to deal with possible trouble from vagabonds and the poor in specific emergencies. During a food shortage in Kent in 1586 it instructed constables to appoint armed assistants to round up and imprison vagabonds without trial.²²² In February 1588 Francis Knollys, John Norreys, Richard Bingham, and Roger Williams advised the council to establish methods for executing by martial law any "papists and malcontents" who attempted to assist a Spanish invasion.²²³ It was imperative, they argued, to deal with such people before foreign troops landed; otherwise "every man shall stand in fear of the firing of his house and destruction of his family" when called out to face the foreign enemy. As summer drew near, the council worried that "false rumors and reports" might "distract the minds of the people and breed confusion" during a military crisis. It therefore ordered the appointment of provost marshals to round up all "vagrant and idle persons," who were to be stocked and imprisoned if they refused to support themselves by honest work.²²⁴ Similar orders were renewed the next year with additional provisions to allow trials of vagrants by martial law.²²⁵ In its instructions to constables in Kent the council elaborated on these provisions by ordering that standing watches be kept at several bridge ferries, as well as along the borders with Sussex and Surrey.²²⁶ These were prudent measures, carried out with restraint: although vagabonds were jailed and occasionally whipped, they were not executed and no Catholic suffered under martial law. But one wonders what might have happened if the Armada had landed.

A review of the treatment of Catholics in England therefore presents a mixed picture. On the one hand it is clear that the regime experimented with a variety of arbitrary measures, ranging from detention without trial to commissions of martial law authorized to carry out summary executions. It seized private papers,

---

[220] TNA SP12/176/26-7, discussed by Younger, "Securing the Monarchical Republic," 251-2.
[221] Lodge, *Illustrations* 2.282.   [222] SRO D593/4/10/4.   [223] TNA SP15/30/94.
[224] BL Add Mss. 48167, "Instructions to lord lieutenants of maritime counties." Identical orders, sent to the magistrates of Kent are in SRO D593/4/11/3/2.
[225] BL Add Mss. 48167, fol. 20v.   [226] SRO D593/4/12/6a.

interrogated prisoners under torture, and held suspects without bail—all violations of common law rules. On the other hand, in dealing with lay landowners it generally proceeded with restraint, except in the case of individuals implicated in genuine plots. Catholic non-conformists had to put up with various forms of surveillance and harassment, including periods of imprisonment that must often have made life very unpleasant. Some were heavily fined. But so long as they steered clear of political conspiracy they had little reason to fear for their lives, and with few exceptions the crown did not seek their financial ruin. Although a few score priests were executed, the backlash this threatened to generate limited the scale of the carnage.

The council's relative restraint probably owed less to its moderation than the fact that a serious rebellion never materialized. If forced to fight for its life, there is little doubt that the Protestant state and its supporters would have acted more ruthlessly. Fortunately, a set of pragmatic measures, intended to deter and disrupt large-scale organized Catholic resistance worked effectively enough to make harsher repression unnecessary. But this success remained fragile because events beyond the kingdom's borders still had the potential to unsettle its internal peace. It is to these contingencies that we must now turn.

3
An Ambiguous Dynastic Threat
James VI and Scotland to 1589

Mary Stuart's dynastic claims posed the most obvious threat to Protestant rule in England, around which every plot to overthrow Elizabeth revolved. But for reasons we have already begun to explore, around 1580 Mary's adolescent son, James VI, emerged as a second, more insidious and dangerous challenge. Born in 1566, he had fallen into the hands of his mother's enemies after her flight from Scotland the following year. They appointed Protestant tutors, including the formidable George Buchanan, to educate him as a godly prince, while successive Protestant regents, especially James Stewart earl of Moray (assassinated in 1570) and James Douglas earl of Morton, ruled Scotland in his name. Morton was regarded as an especially close friend to England. But in 1578 his position collapsed, after he antagonized a number of Scottish lords and factions, including both Catholics and firm Protestants. He partially recovered power a few months later but remained weakened and vulnerable. The arrival in Scotland in 1579 of James's French cousin, Esmé Stuart *seigneur* d'Aubigny, then precipitated a more complete unraveling not only of Morton's position but also English control over Scotland.

D'Aubigny quickly became the king's favored companion. He formed alliances with several of Morton's enemies, including a veteran captain of the Dutch wars named James Stewart, "a young man of a busy brain, a quick taunter with merry conceits and . . . an aspiring brain," who also enjoyed royal favor.[1] They and others began spreading reports that Morton wanted to kidnap James and convey him to England, which the king believed.[2] D'Aubigny consolidated his influence by replacing the small household in which James had spent his childhood with a full royal court. At its core stood a bedchamber filled with d'Aubigny clients, while

---

[1] Sir James Melville of Halhill, *Memoirs of his Own Life* (Edinburgh, 1827; facs. repr. New York: AMS Press, 1973), 263–4. This James Melville, who was a courtier and officer serving various Scottish regimes between the 1560s and 1580s, should not be confused with Andrew Melville's nephew, James, who produced a diary.

[2] See Amy Blakewell, "James VI and James Douglas Earl of Morton," in *James VI and Noble Power in Scotland, 1578–1603*, ed. Miles Kerr-Peterson and Steven J. Reid (London: Routledge, 2017), 12–31, esp. 16–19. According to Blakeway the rumors originated with Argyll and Teulet, *Papiers d'état*, 3.253, 255. The Spanish ambassador in Paris passed on a report that James had accused Morton before the Scottish council of trying to poison and abduct him.

Stewart assumed command of the royal guard.³ The English tried to save Morton and oust d'Aubigny by levying several thousand troops along the border and threatening to invade, but the Scots faced down the threat by raising their own army. Stewart then spearheaded a successful effort to convict the fallen regent of complicity in the murder of James's father, some fourteen years before. Morton's execution in June 1581 confirmed the decisive realignment of power in Edinburgh. Two months later D'Aubigny received the Scottish title of duke of Lennox. Stewart was also later rewarded with the former Hamilton title, earl of Arran.⁴

These events greatly complicated the religious politics of the English succession, but not because they were in any straightforward sense a Catholic coup. Prior to his fall Morton had antagonized leaders of the Kirk, some of whom accused him of presiding over its destruction, and his opponents included strong Protestants, like the earl of Argyll.⁵ James sought to demonstrate his commitment to the Reformation by promulgating an explicitly anti-Catholic "King's Confession" of faith in March 1580. D'Aubigny subscribed to it and asked to receive instruction in Protestant doctrine. But in the fraught conditions of the time, these efforts failed to satisfy the English. D'Aubigny's French Catholic upbringing aroused suspicions that, whatever he might say about his religious beliefs, he intended to revive the Francophile party in Scotland that had previously opposed the Reformation and supported Mary. The fear of Catholic plots to reverse the Reformation by stealth that had developed during negotiations over the Anjou match reinforced this mistrust: understandably, since Mendoza and some English Catholics did hope to co-opt James to serve their plans of dethroning Elizabeth.⁶ Any serious assertion of independence by James, who had now reached adolescence, threatened Elizabeth, by making it more difficult to assure that the "postern gate" to her kingdom would remain permanently shut, and that the Scottish king would not become the center of a reversionary interest among her own subjects. She therefore tried to keep him on a short leash by bullying the Scottish council into removing d'Aubigny and restoring Morton, only to back down when the Scots called her bluff by preparing for war against England. This achieved the worst possible outcome, by antagonizing James and d'Aubigny, giving them ample incentives to destroy Morton and his Anglophile supporters while reaching out to Elizabeth's European enemies for support, without weakening their position.

---

³ The most detailed study of James VI's household is Amy Juhala, "The Household and Court of King James VI of Scotland, 1567–1603," University of Edinburgh PhD thesis, 2000, published online at https://era.ed.ac.uk/handle/1842/1727.

⁴ D'Aubigné's creation as earl of Lennox took place in 1580 and as duke in August 1581, while Stewart received his earldom in April 1581. Additional circumstantial detail about these events is supplied by Melville, *Memoirs*, 266–7.

⁵ Keith Brown, *Noble Society in Scotland: Wealth, Family and Culture from Reformation to Revolution* (Edinburgh: Edinburgh University Press, 2000), 233–4.

⁶ Michael Questier, *Dynastic Politics and the British Reformations, 1558–1630* (Oxford: Oxford University Press, 2019), 136–8.

Relations between the two British courts and monarchs quickly descended in a downward spiral that initially had little to do with religion but that many people soon began to interpret in confessional terms. Events following Morton's execution reinforced the pattern. As a foreigner newly arrived in Scotland, Lennox needed to build a following, which he did by allying with nobles excluded from power under Morton, many of them Catholics or former supporters of Mary.[7] He began secretive consultations with Guise that really did involve schemes to topple Elizabeth, while both he and James met privately with Jesuits who had been sent to assess ways of reversing the progress of Protestantism in Scotland and to overthrow Elizabeth.[8] As rumors of these dealings began to spread, the young king's ultimate allegiances came to appear highly uncertain. This ambiguity did not necessarily disadvantage him in maneuvers over the English succession, since it left him free to seek foreign Catholic support, even while he continued to reassure Scottish and English Protestants that he shared their faith. Schemes developed by some of Mary's confidants for an "association" between mother and son—in effect a form of joint rule—further complicated the picture.[9] For moderates who wanted above all to avoid a civil war of religion, such an arrangement might have provided a compromise offering toleration to both confessions in the future reign of a Catholic queen and Protestant king. It received backing from the French, with whom Elizabeth and her council wanted to maintain good relations as fears of Spanish hostility grew. In May 1583 Mauvissière reported that Elizabeth would favor the scheme, if James and the Scots agreed to it and if she received sufficient assurances that Mary would abide by the conditions to which she had agreed.[10] But the English remained justifiably suspicious that James was dealing with the French and Mary behind their backs, and since the Association would offer no permanent guarantees against an eventual restoration of Catholicism many Protestants found it unacceptable.[11] As had been the case with Anjou, James's religious flexibility and pragmatic willingness to seek political advantage by dealing with partisans of both confessions inspired mistrust that fueled further religious polarization.

The Scottish Mirror

Scottish politics therefore came to provide a kind of distorted mirror in which English Protestants saw threats to the survival of their faith that they had already experienced in their own kingdom not only reflected but magnified. Several other

---

[7] Ruth Grant, "George Gordon, Sixth Earl of Huntly, and the Politics of the Counter-Reformation in Scotland, 1581–1595," University of Edinburgh PhD thesis, 2010, 39–43.
[8] Teulet, *Papiers d'état*, 3.278–9, 280–1.   [9] Questier, *Dynastic Politics*, 137.
[10] Ibid., 567.   [11] For those suspicions see, e.g. BL Harley Mss. 291, 44r–v.

aspects of the relationship between the two kingdoms enhanced and complicated this mirroring effect. Their land border, which lay awkwardly near the most Catholic parts of England and the ancestral lands of several lords exiled in 1569, made Scotland seem an ideal launching pad for an invasion of England. Guise and English Catholic exiles actively canvassed plans for attacking Britain through the border shires, hoping that by doing so they might draw on the assistance of both English and Scottish noble affinities.[12] This strategic threat gave the English government an obvious reason to support Scottish Protestant nobles, especially those whose lands also lay close to the border, as in the case of Morton's nephew, Archibald Douglas earl of Angus. Angus's defeat in the contest over Morton and subsequent flight from Scotland not only further weakened English influence, it also threatened to open a strategic corridor for an attack on England from the north.

The fact that Lowland Scots and English were mutually intelligible dialects of the same language facilitated easy communication and intellectual exchanges. While lodging with Sir Philip Sidney during his English exile in 1582, Angus regularly discussed early drafts of *The Arcadia*.[13] Few French or Dutch nobles would have had sufficient command of English to do this. Scots Protestants employed the English Geneva Bible and read English religious literature, while Edinburgh presses printed English puritan tracts. Scottish clergy who sought refuge in England in 1584 preached to English congregations and were welcomed as brethren by the puritan leader John Field. Revealingly, however, the authorities denied them permission to set up their own London church, unlike French and Walloon exiles who were allowed to do so. Presumably Elizabeth and her bishops feared the presence of a Calvinist congregation worshiping by its own rules in a language that Londoners readily comprehended. Catholics assumed that English missionary priests would have no trouble making themselves understood in Scotland and planned to include them in a campaign to reverse the Reformation there. The similarity of Scottish Gaelic to Irish, along with the proximity of southwestern Scotland to Ulster, generated additional connections. The earliest example of Protestant literature printed in Gaelic was a translation of the English Book of Common Prayer, published in Edinburgh for use in the Highlands.[14] The Protestant earl of Argyll and his Campbell relatives had substantial connections to Ulster, although the English crown was slow to take advantage of them for

---

[12] Thomas Francis Knox, *The Diaries of the English College of Douay*, Records of English Catholics under the Penal Laws, vol. 1 (London, 1877), 337–8; Thomas McCoog, *The Society of Jesus in Ireland, Scotland and Ireland 1541–1588* (Leiden: Brill, 1996), 182–6; Victor Houliston, *Catholic Resistance in Elizabethan England* (Aldershot: Ashgate 2007, 33–4).

[13] David Hume, *History of Scotland* (Edinburgh, 1648), 362. Hume had been a client of Angus's family in the period.

[14] Marc Caball, "Gaelic and Protestant: A Case Study in Early Modern Self-Fashioning, 1567–1608," *Proceedings of the Irish Royal Academy: Archaeology, Culture, History, Literature* 110 (2010): 191–215.

fear of enhancing Scottish influence in Ireland.[15] On the other hand, redshank mercenaries from the Gaelic Isles and Scottish Southwest regularly passed into Ulster to serve Irish rebels. In the 1590s the earl of Tyrone sent agents to negotiate for alliances with Highland clans, under "pretense to confer with the bishop of Argyll for the right translation of the Bible into the Irish tongue."[16]

In the 1540s, the English government had produced literature describing the union of the two British kingdoms under a single crown as providentially ordained, to justify its attempt to force the Scots to marry Mary to Edward VI. Anglophile Scots, including John Knox and eventually James VI, subsequently took up this idea.[17] Although enthusiasm for such a union declined in both kingdoms in the late sixteenth century, the concept of the English and Scots as kindred peoples, destined to join forces in a godly empire, never entirely disappeared. The dynastic connection gave religious partisans in each kingdom a strong incentive to forge bonds with co-religionists in the other. Leading English Catholics believed that a revival of their faith in Scotland would significantly increase their chances of returning England to the Roman allegiance, and therefore promoted a Scottish mission. The English priest William Watts, sent to Scotland by Robert Parsons to investigate conditions there in 1581, returned an optimistic report, which resulted in the dispatch of three Jesuits—the Englishman William Holt and the Scots Edmund Hay and William Creytton or Chrichton—the following year.[18] They received interviews with James VI and Lennox before traveling to Normandy, where they linked up with Persons and the duke of Guise, who were planning a limited invasion of England with the goal of toppling Elizabeth.[19] Mendoza and Mary were also kept informed of their progress. Some English Catholics, notably Sir Thomas Tresham, enthusiastically supported this Scottish strategy.[20]

---

[15] See Jane Dawson, "The Fifth Earl of Argyle, Gaelic Lordship and Political Power in Sixteenth-Century Scotland," *Scottish Historical Review* 67 (1988): 1–27, esp. 3–5 and 17. The earls of Argyle patronized a line of Gaelic bards, the MacEwans, who trained other bards to praise the Campbells (Brown, *Noble Society in Scotland*, 21).

[16] HMC Salisbury 6.60.

[17] A. H. Williamson, *Scottish National Consciousness in the Age of James VI: The Apocalypse, the Union and the Shaping of Scotland's Public Culture* (Edinburgh: John Donald, 1979), chapter 3.

[18] McCoog, *Society of Jesus*, 178–82. Creytton's name is often spelled Chricthon or Chreicton in contemporary documents and modern accounts. On Creytton's own spelling of his name see Francisco de Borja, "Intrigues of a Scottish Jesuit at the Spanish Court: Unpublished Letters of William Crichton to Claudio Aquaviva (Madrid 1590-1592)," in *The Reckoned Expense: Edmund Campion and the Early English Jesuits: Essays in Celebration of the First Centenary of Campion Hall, Oxford*, ed. Thomas McCoog (Woodbridge: Boydell Press, 1996), 215–45.

[19] See the detailed prospectus drawn up in 1582 printed in the original Italian and in English translation in *The Correspondence and Unpublished Papers of Robert Persons, SJ*, volume 1: *1574–1588*, ed. Victory Houliston, Ginevra Crosignani, and Thomas M. McCoog (Toronto: Pontifical Institute of Mediaeval Studies, 2017), 320–40.

[20] Ibid., 183–8. Mendoza reported as early as December 1581 that Thomas and William Tresham "were the first people" to broach the possibility of converting James VI to Catholicism and using

Anxiety about a possible Catholic revival in Scotland and the threat it would pose to their own security gave English Protestants strong incentives to support Scottish Calvinist clergy and lay patrons of the Reformation prepared to oppose Lennox and Arran not only with words but with force. English ambassadors to Scotland and their handlers back in London, especially Walsingham, promoted forms of active resistance to royal and episcopal authority in Scotland that Elizabeth would never have tolerated for a moment in her own kingdom. In many outward respects, Scotland's ecclesiastical politics strongly resembled those of England, involving similar issues concerning the role of bishops and the authority of the crown to govern the Church and suppress Protestant nonconformity. But for a number of reasons, the Scottish disputes had a sharper intensity that tended to force into the open issues that remained half-submerged in the southern kingdom. Unlike its English counterpart, the Scottish Reformation had from the outset depended on insurrectionary violence.[21] Although the Lords of the Congregation who originally brought it about in the late 1550s had various motives for supporting religious change, including self-interest, from the beginning Scottish Protestantism had a more assertive and confrontational character than its English counterpart. But this did not immediately lead to a more radical ecclesiastical polity. As Gordon Donaldson pointed out long ago, the earliest Scottish reformers were never uniformly hostile to episcopacy, partly because even before the Reformation noble families had infiltrated the upper ranks of the kingdom's ecclesiastical hierarchy and in several cases then defected to the Reformation.[22] Calls to abolish bishops and redirect ecclesiastical revenues to support preaching ministers therefore threatened the material interests of powerful lay Protestants.

Doctrinal support for a presbyterian system of church government only developed in the 1570s, appearing in England and Scotland at roughly the same time, through the preaching of Thomas Cartwright in Cambridge in 1572 and of Andrew Melville at Glasgow University after he returned to Scotland in 1574. But the English authorities quickly drove Cartwright into exile, whereas Melville remained Principal at Glasgow before removing to St. Andrews in 1580, allowing his ideas to take root. Equally important, the sort of voluntarist impulses that lay at the heart of the English puritan movement—the determination of enthusiastic reformers to build a better church through their own efforts, without waiting for directives from above—had more opportunities to develop unhindered in Scotland, for the simple reason that Scottish ecclesiastical structures were less

---

Scotland as a base from which to attack Protestantism in England, "and it is with them that I deal, in addition to the priests who have the matter in hand. Although Thomas is a prisoner, I am in constant communication with him by means of priests." *CSPSp* 3.236.

[21] Alec Ryrie, *The Origins of the Scottish Reformation* (Manchester: Manchester University Press, 2006) particularly stresses this violent character.

[22] Gordon Donaldson, *The Scottish Reformation* (Cambridge: Cambridge University Press, 1960), chapters 1–3.

developed and effective.[23] Presbyterianism filled an obvious need for better machinery to govern the Kirk and propagate the gospel than Scottish bishops provided. Although English puritans also argued that the bishops failed to promote preaching and discipline adequately, they faced a more formidable apparatus of episcopal control, backed by a determined queen, whereas Scotland had weaker bishops and a child king.

Secular resistance to royal authority gained greater traction in Scotland for broadly similar reasons. Scottish nobles had long exercised greater control over their localities than their English counterparts, and the minorities first of Mary and then James gave them further opportunities to act independently. The civil war that drove Mary from her throne engendered ideological justifications for resistance to a wayward monarch, most importantly George Buchanan's *De Jure Regni apud Scotos*. This appeared in print several years after its composition in 1579, exclusively in Latin, to avoid provoking Elizabeth, who did not want its arguments circulating in the vernacular. But Buchanan enjoyed cordial relations with English diplomats like Sir Thomas Randolph and Henry Killigrew and his work was appreciated in England, by Sir Philip Sidney among others.[24] Like Buchanan, who relied more on Roman and Stoic traditions than Calvinist theology, other Scots also drew on classical ideas to justify political activism.[25] Some fused concepts of the commonwealth with chivalric ideals of honor, duty, and valor, to emphasize the special responsibility of nobles to protect their country against tyrants.[26] David Hume of Godscroft's *History of the Houses of Douglas and Angus*, published only in 1648 but reflecting ideas circulating in Angus's circle since at least the 1580s, expressed this synthesis with particular clarity.[27] The fusion of humanist ideals of civic virtue and "patriotism" with medieval concepts of martial courage and honor was by no means unique to Scotland. Broadly similar patterns of thought developed among Huguenots during the French wars of religion, in the Dutch circle of William of Orange, and in the outlook of English figures like Sidney and Leicester.[28]

---

[23] The classic discussion of English puritan voluntarism is Patrick Collinson, *The Elizabethan Puritan Movement* (Berkeley: University of California Press, 1967).

[24] Ian D. McFarlane, *Buchanan* (London: Duckworth, 1981), 301, 387, 392; J. E. Phillips, "George Buchanan and the Sidney Circle," *Huntington Library Quarterly* 12 (1948): 23–55; *The Warrender Papers*, ed. Anni Cameron, 2 vols (Edinburgh: Scottish History Society, 1931–2), 1.146.

[25] Treatments of the subject include Williamson, *Scottish National Consciousness*. But cf. the qualifying arguments about Scottish traditions of loyalty to the crown in Roger Mason, *Kingship and the Commonweal: Political Thought in Renaissance and Reformation Scotland* (East Lothian: Tuckwell Press, 1998), esp. chapters 1 and 3.

[26] A. H. Williamson, "A Patriot Nobility? Calvinism, Kin-Ties and Civic Humanism," *Scottish Historical Review* 72 (1993): 1–21; Mason, *Kingship and Commonweal*, chapter 3, "Chivalry and Citizenship: Aspects of National Identity in Renaissance Scotland," 78–103.

[27] Hume was a client and protégé of Angus, whose book reproduces letters and recollects conversations dating from the 1580s. I wish to thank Arthur Williamson for calling my attention to this work.

[28] Arlette Jouanna, *Le devoir de révolte: La noblesse française et la gestation de l'État moderne* (Paris: Fayard, 1989); below, Chapter 4.

Although sometimes given a particular Scottish inflection, the ideas of Melville, Buchanan, Hume, and other Scots therefore corresponded to wider emphases within Calvinist and humanist political cultures of northwest Europe that were thoroughly familiar to well-educated English Protestants. But in England the rule of a Protestant queen inhibited the openness with which some ideas might be expressed. Even the Bond of Association made no mention of a right of resistance against an anointed queen, instead sanctioning lynch law against the heir to the throne as an act of loyalty to the current occupant. Scottish Protestants, by contrast, had defended their Reformation by deposing Mary in the 1560s and many felt acutely suspicious of James in the 1580s. They accordingly had fewer inhibitions about not only justifying but actually engaging in forceful resistance to royal authority.

This resistance soon became entangled with disputes over control of the Kirk and the role of bishops within it, drawing the English into an unacknowledged *de facto* alliance with Scottish presbyterians, even as Elizabeth and Whitgift struggled to stifle presbyterianism in England. This alignment had not existed prior to d'Aubigny's arrival and Morton's fall. Instead the pro-English regent had repeatedly clashed with leaders of the Kirk, over the appointment of his kinsman, John Douglas, as archbishop of St. Andrews in 1571, his attempt to increase crown revenue by reducing the number of ministerial stipends in 1574, and the installation of his chaplain, Patrick Adamson, as Douglas's successor at St. Andrews in 1578. These clashes fueled efforts by more active clergy, who were achieving a greater sense of solidarity as their numbers increased, to establish a more effective system for supervising preaching and moral discipline without relying on the crown or the bishops. Andrew Melville gave this movement a more coherent theological basis, but his presbyterian ideas won followers largely because they provided a solution to immediate practical problems. In 1578 the Kirk adopted its *Second Book of Discipline*, which called for an amalgamation of the local Kirk sessions that had existed since the 1560s into a national system of fifty presbyteries, or committees of elders and ministers, each with jurisdiction over several adjacent parishes. These would report to regional synods, whose work would be overseen in turn by periodic national assemblies.[29] The first thirteen presbyteries actually appeared only in 1581.[30] Until he lost power, Morton resisted these developments, partly because they threatened his control of ecclesiastical patronage but probably also to please Elizabeth, by preventing the Kirk from diverging from the model of the Church of England. In doing so he alienated the Kirk's

---

[29] For a concise discussion of these developments see Alan R. MacDonald, *The Jacobean Kirk, 1567-1625: Sovereignty, Polity and Liturgy* (Aldershot: Ashgate, 1998), 8-11.

[30] Ibid., 21; Julian Goodare, *The Government of Scotland 1560-1625* (Oxford: Oxford University Press, 2004), 194.

leaders, allowing his enemies to gain their backing by promising to support the suppression of episcopacy.[31]

According to John Spottiswood, James also came into conflict with presbyterian clergy at about the time of d'Aubigny's arrival, over agitation for changes in the Kirk that would have compromised his control. At this point the disputes did not pit Protestants against Catholics and suspected papists, so much as zealous reformers against a Protestant king, Protestant bishops, and a recently deposed Anglophile regent. Spottiswood nevertheless remarked that James's anger at the ministers encouraged several Catholics in academic posts, who had previously kept their views hidden, to come into the open. "In Dumfries, Mr. Ninian Daliel, schoolmaster, did read to his scholars the Roman catechism and in Paisely a number of papists assembling together did in derision sing a soul mass for the ministers, as if they and their religion had been utterly gone."[32] These signs of a Catholic revival provoked clerical protests. Fortuitously, d'Aubigny appeared on the scene as these disputes erupted.

Seizing an opportunity, Morton tried to exploit the suspicions aroused by d'Aubigny and his allies to regain Protestant support.[33] In April 1580 Elizabeth instructed her ambassador in Edinburgh, Robert Bowes, to attempt to detach the Protestant earls of Argyll and Montrose from d'Aubigny's faction and reconcile them to Morton.[34] Although d'Aubigny responded by signaling his readiness to convert to Protestantism and asked that a "French preacher" be sent from London to instruct him in the faith,[35] the ministers doubted his sincerity, noting that he supported "papists and practisers in this realm" and "dallied" in performing his promises to them.[36] In October one prominent clergyman, John Dury, preached a sermon inveighing against "papists (with great ruffs and side bellies) suffered in the presence of the King." James complained about the accusation but the following day another minister, James Lawson, supported Dury's charges.[37] Delegates from a synodal assembly then in session petitioned the king, complaining about d'Aubigny and asking for the removal of one of his French associates.[38] A few months later another Edinburgh clergyman, Walter Balcanqual, preached that "within four years popery had entered in the country, not only in the court but in the king's hall, and was maintained by a great champion, who is called Grace," meaning Lennox (as d'Aubigny had now become).[39] An Englishman reported that a general preaching campaign against the king's new favorite was being conducted during the same month in boroughs throughout Scotland,

---

[31] *The Diary of Mr. James Melville, 1556–1601* (Edinburgh, 1829), 59.   [32] Spottiswood, 308.
[33] So, at least, thought Cadenet: "il [Morton] a suscité audit seigneur d'Aubigné une si grande et forte querelle avec les ministres et les a si bien animés et tous les protestants d'Ecosse contre ledit sieur d'Aubigné qu'ils le veulent contraindre de faire profession de leur religion ou d'abandonner le pais, en quoi ledit sieur se trouve bien en peine et le petit prince qui l'aime" (TNA PRO31/3/28, fol. 84v).
[34] BL Cotton Mss. Caligula CVI, fol. 13v.   [35] Ibid., fol. 95v.
[36] Ibid., fol. 98v.   [37] Ibid., fol. 95.   [38] Ibid., fol. 98v.
[39] Calderwood, *History of the Church of Scotland* (1680), 119.

as pro- and anti-Lennox factions prepared to face off in an upcoming parliament. Letters denouncing Lennox and Arran were cast into the king's privy chamber, "whereat his Majesty is greatly moved."[40]

In January 1581 "the town of Edinburgh and many other offered liberally" to free Morton from prison, although he discouraged them by saying that he "refused to be delivered in any other sort than by the order of the laws. Mr. John Cragge in his sermon on the Sunday following did... inveigh against false accusations, whereupon James Stewart (as it is informed for the truth) threatened him with his dagger drawn."[41] In January and February Scottish ministers "continually in their sermons preached against the disorders of the court and confusion of the State." They proclaimed a general fast during the second week of March "to prevent the wrath of God."[42] But Lennox still enjoyed considerable support, including among Protestants, especially when facing down English pressure. Although Mary rejoiced at the news of Morton's execution, Mendoza realized that it was not a Catholic triumph but an act motivated "by private rancor" and Lennox's desire to consolidate his position.[43] It nevertheless reinforced the view of the English council and many Protestant Scots that Lennox acted as a tool of Guise and the Catholic cause. Walsingham complained in early September about "advertisements" that James had submitted "to his mother's direction" and that Catholics hoped "for a general alteration of religion in that realm."[44] Rumors circulated that Catholics would soon abduct James and convey him to France or Spain, to facilitate his conversion and marriage to a Catholic princess.[45] There was more than a grain of truth to them, since Philip II had approved such a plan.[46]

Shortly thereafter the Scottish council attempted to muzzle clerical criticism by commanding the ministers to silence. But some preachers remained defiant, "railing against the king, the nobles and all the council," among them Dury, who was imprisoned and threatened with execution.[47] Lennox allegedly assaulted some ministers and laid ambushes for others, attempting to have them killed, in futile efforts to silence criticism. James's council issued a proclamation forbidding people from attending "convocations and assemblies" on pain of treason. It seems to have had the desired effect, since a contemporary reported that whereas previously when ministers passed through the streets of Edinburgh to preach "the inhabitants would follow them in great heaps and numbers," after the proclamation the preachers had "no auditors but go up and down like masterless hounds, casting into the king's teeth the example of young kings of old times ruled by wicked counselors, and menace the punishment of Sodom and Gomorrah to be poured over the realm." Some nobles joined the opposition to Lennox. Lord

---

[40] BL Cotton Mss. Caligula CVI, fol. 187.   [41] BL Harleian Mss. 6999, fol. 4.
[42] BL Sloane Mss. 3199, fol. 80v.   [43] *CSPSp* 3.124.   [44] HMC Salisbury 2.81.
[45] BL Cotton Mss. Caligula CVI, fols 5, 10, and 11. According to Mendoza, Elizabeth took these reports seriously, *CSPSp* 3.37.
[46] Teulet, *Papiers d'état*, 3.252.   [47] *CSPSc* 6.51-2.

Lindsay became so incensed when he found the king conferring in French with one of Lennox's men that he pointed to the weapon hanging at his side, saying "this sword and buckler hath helped to drive the Frenchmen forth of Scotland, and I fear it must be imported to that use again," before storming off "in great fury."[48] These developments overlapped with the sharpening confessional polarization in England following the collapse of the Anjou match, as well as the earliest discussions between Mendoza, Henry Howard, Guise, and Mary Stuart's agents of plans to attack Elizabeth by promoting a Catholic revival in Scotland. This encouraged contemporaries to view disputes over the administration of the Kirk as opening moves in a wider contest that would determine the religious future of both British kingdoms.

In October 1581 James attempted to counter accusations that he favored popery with a speech proclaiming his allegiance to the reformed faith, denouncing the so-called Holy League of popish "bastard Christians" composed of "Frenchmen and Spaniards," and calling for the creation of a "counter-league" of "true Christian princes," beginning with an alliance between himself and Elizabeth.[49] He assured the English that Lennox had become a Protestant.[50] But many people continued to mistrust both James and Lennox: with reason, since at almost exactly the same moment Lennox and other Catholic nobles were secretly meeting with a priest sent with Mendoza's encouragement, while in January James also met with Catholic emissaries.[51] He and his supporters kept insisting that his presbyterian critics falsely maligned his religious beliefs so as to win popular applause and gain power. This claim resembled the accusations of courting "popularity" that Whitgift and other English conformists leveled against puritans.[52] But James's own secret conduct, which never remained entirely hidden, kept undercutting the message, not least with Elizabeth, who should otherwise have sympathized with it.

The appointment in early 1582 of a Lennox protégé, Robert Montgomery, as archbishop of Glasgow, allegedly in return for a promise to pay Lennox £500 Scots yearly from his episcopal revenues, provided another flashpoint. The presbytery of Glasgow attempted to block Montgomery's elevation and gained support from its newly erected counterpart in Edinburgh.[53] But Lennox continued backing Montgomery, causing "great suspicion and murmuration universally in Scotland ... [that] he intendeth alteration of religion by all the policy and device he can practice." On March 8, Montgomery entered an Edinburgh church accompanied by "a number of the guard and, the minister being in the pulpit, pulled him by the sleeve, saying come down sirrah." The minister refused and it appeared that

---

[48] Ibid.   [49] *CSPSc* 6.72.   [50] BL Lansdowne Mss. 31/31.
[51] *CSPSp* 3.169, 194–5, 292–3, 298; Teulet, *Relations Politiques*, 5.234; Teulet, *Papiers d'état*, 3.278–9 and 280.
[52] Peter Lake, "The Politics of Popularity and the Public Sphere: The 'Monarchical Republic' of Elizabeth I Defends Itself," in *The Politics of the Public Sphere in Early Modern England*, ed. Peter Lake and Steven Pincus (Manchester: Manchester University Press, 2007), 59–94.
[53] Calderwood, *History*, 116 (erection of the Edinburgh presbytery), 119 (Montgomery's appointment).

a brawl might break out, until Montgomery retreated. The Stirling presbytery then suspended Montgomery from the ministry.[54] On May 24, Dury preached another provocative sermon in Edinburgh, before an auditory that included several noblemen, in which he called Montgomery "an apostate and main sworn traitor to God and his Church... Even as the Scribes and Pharisees could find none so meet to betray him as one of his own scholars and disciples, even so this duke with the rest of his faction cannot find so meet an instrument to subvert the religion planted in Scotland as one of their own [i.e. the ministers'] number.' Dury went on to criticize the king for having recently accepted a present from "that bloody persecutor," the duke of Guise, warning: "if God did threaten the captivity and spoil of Jerusalem because their king Hezekiah did receive a letter from the king of Babylon, shall we think to be free committing the like, or rather worse." "I see that all that are nearestly known to be enemies to the Church are most nearest his [James's] person," he warned darkly, adding: "I know I shall be called to an account for these words here spoken, but let them do with this carcass of mine what they will for I know my soul is in the hands of the Lord and therefore I will speak and that to your condemnations." He concluded with a prayer that God either "convert or... confound the duke" of Lennox.[55]

A few weeks later, as the Glasgow presbytery prepared to excommunicate Montgomery, the town's provost and a party of citizens intervened, assaulting the presbytery's moderator and knocking out some of his teeth. This provoked a riot by students at the university that gave the archbishop's adversaries control of the city, allowing them to issue the sentence of excommunication. Montgomery's court supporters responded by having the archbishop proclaimed "a true Christian and good subject notwithstanding the pretended excommunication." But when Montgomery attempted to enter the town, escorted by Arran, his party was turned back. The inhabitants prepared to greet the bishop, "some with batons, some with stones and rotten eggs... Had he not been conveyed by the provost... he had hardly escaped."[56] A General Assembly at Perth drew up a list of complaints against the court's misgovernment and presented them to Arran, who "asked with a frowning countenance, who dare subscribe these treasonable articles," to which Andrew Melville replied: "we dare and will subscribe and render our lives in the cause."[57] According to Mauvissière, a Scottish synod agreed to promote a campaign of preaching against Lennox, "to make him hated of the people and to incite them to some sedition."[58] The earl of Angus stirred up the

---

[54] Ibid., 121.
[55] I have pieced this account of the sermon together from two sources, BL Cotton Mss. Caligula CVII, fol. 12v, BL Add Mss. 48027, fol. 130 and BL Sloane Mss. 3199, fol. 291.
[56] Calderwood, *History*, 128–9.   [57] Ibid., 128.
[58] "[Ils] résolurent dernièrement, en un synode fait entre eux, de prêcher tout ce qu'ils pourront pour le faire haïr aux peuples et les inciter à quelque sédition contre mon dit sieur de Lennox." Castlenau dispatch of July 6, 1582 in Teulet, *Relations Politiques*, 3.125–6.

clergy before the king's person and then fled to Berwick, where Elizabeth sent Lord Carey to debrief him.[59]

That summer events appeared to be moving toward a bloody climax. As Guise began preparations to invade Britain, Lennox wrote to Mary offering to lead an army to free her from captivity.[60] In consultation with Crichton, he had devised a plan to recruit several thousand troops in France to invade Scotland and then England, which even Mary thought overly bold.[61] Rumors circulated about the Association scheme, whose terms included a repudiation of the legitimacy of Mary's deposition and James's title to the crown. As an English observer pointed out, this would have voided the legality of all acts carried out in the king's name since 1567, opening all those who had supported his party to charges of treason.[62] Mary told Mendoza that she hoped to increase her influence over her son, convert him to Catholicism and persuade him to accept an alliance with Spain to assert their joint claim to the English throne.[63] In July, according to David Calderwood, Lennox and Arran prepared to strike back against the Edinburgh presbyterians by occupying the city with troops, while a special commission empowered to investigate and punish those responsible for agitating the populace against Montgomery did its work. The court party intended to "have hanged drowned, fined and punished," as the duke pleased.[64]

The English as yet had limited information about James's and Lennox's dealings with Jesuit emissaries, Mary, and the duke of Guise. But suspicions had been aroused and grew as Walsingham began to unravel the Throckmorton Plot, a conspiracy to invade Britain, assassinate Elizabeth, and place Mary on the throne. Although it took some time to sift the evidence, it was becoming apparent that Catholics hoped to convert James VI and then involve him in a coordinated attack by English and Scottish Catholics and an invading army.[65] These revelations

---

[59] Calderwood, *History*, 126.
[60] Teulet, *Relations Politiques*, 5.234, 235–6, 237. James was apparently kept in the dark about plans to invade England.
[61] Teulet, *Papiers d'état*, 3.278, 280–1, 286.
[62] BL Sloane Mss. 3199, fols 290v–291, Henry Wodrington to Walsingham, May 25, 1582: "It is given out that the Duke and Arran are about to procure the king to make resignment of his estate to the queen his mother and to receive it again from her, for as it is now they let him understand that he is but an usurper and no lawful king, and all his doings not valeable [sic], which is thought to be done upon great policy by the duke and Arran for the better comprehending of their purposes, which they are about (as it is said) for the infringing of all matters and orders set down by the ministry and barons in the time of his minority, and thereby to take the advantage against them as to have them within the compass of treason for their proceedings at that time in the same without sufficient warrant or commission."
[63] *CSPSp* 3.290.   [64] Calderwood, *History*, 129.
[65] For a masterful reconstruction of the plot's discovery and evaluation of how much the English learned from it, see John Bossy, *Under the Molehill: An Elizabethan Spy Story* (New Haven: Yale University Press, 2001). The "smoking gun"—the 1582 memorandum cited in note 19, which stated explicitly that James knew of the invasion scheme—fell into English hands only in September 1584, when the Dutch captured Crichton, who was carrying a copy. See TNA SP12/153/79 and 155/29 for English summaries.

intensified the animosity Elizabeth already felt toward the young king, at the very moment that tensions within Scotland neared their peak. Mauvissière reported in July that Elizabeth "hates him [James VI] more than she ever did the queen of Scotland his mother, and thinks that one day her ruin will come from that quarter."[66] This must have made her more receptive to the pleas of Angus, then in English exile, who wanted funding for an attempted noble coup.[67]

On August 23, before Lennox and Arran managed to execute their campaign of repression, a group of discontented nobles, led by the earls of Marr and Gowrie, kidnapped James as he returned from a hunting trip and took him under guard to Ruthven Castle. They also seized and detained Arran but permitted Lennox to retire to Edinburgh, on the understanding that he would soon leave the country. Instead of doing so he retreated to the fortified port of Dumbarton, where the Spanish sent him 5,000 escudos to hang on.[68] Although the kidnappers promptly issued a statement saying that they only wanted to rid Scotland of popish counselors and restore the influence of the ancient nobility and the Kirk, they began to browbeat James with thinly veiled threats of violence. One of the Ruthven group later stated—possibly under duress—that the kidnappers had agreed to "hazard the king's own life and person" if he did not agree to banish Lennox, while another Scot reported that James's captors informed him that "he should not be the longest liver" among them if he stuck by his favorite.[69] Mendoza believed that Huntingdon and Leicester were privy to the conspiracy and might be planning to poison James.[70] In December he reported that Elizabeth herself sent a message to Scotland about poisoning the king.[71] Whether or not these allegations had substance, James certainly had reason to fear for his safety.

Presbyterian clergy seized the opportunity to push for further ecclesiastical reforms. Dury, who had been banished from Edinburgh after denouncing Lennox from the pulpit, returned in triumph, processing past the duke's house escorted by "a great number of inhabitants singing psalms."[72] A series of articles issued by the Ruthven Raiders, as James's kidnappers became known, accused Lennox and Arran of attempting to reintroduce Catholicism.[73] James was coerced into accepting what amounted to a full presbyterian program, and the following spring a general assembly of the Kirk asked him to send an embassy to London to discuss the formation of a league of "Christian princes professing the true religion." In a gesture of solidarity with their puritan allies, they cheekily added that the Scottish

---

[66] "[Elizabeth] le [Jacques VI] hait plus qu'elle ne fit jamais la Reine d'Ecosse sa mère et estime un jour sa ruine de ce côté-la." Teulet, *Relations Politiques*, 3.128; cf. 124, 126.

[67] Teulet, *Papiers d'état*, 2.485.

[68] Teulet, *Relations Politiques*, 5.274. Five thousand escudos were roughly equivalent to £1,300 sterling.

[69] BL Cotton Mss. Caligula CVII, fols 41, 242.   [70] *CSPSp* 3.400.

[71] Ibid., 431.   [72] BL Cotton Mss. Caligula CVII, fol. 44.

[73] Calderwood, *History*, 130–2; BL Cotton Mss. Caligula CIX, fols 38r–39v; *Ane Declaratioun of... the Nobility* (1582).

embassy should urge Elizabeth to "disburden their brethren in England of the yoke of ceremonies laid upon them."[74] Elizabeth had effectively supported presbyterian ministers preaching defiance of royal authority, riotous crowds in Glasgow, Stirling, and Edinburgh and Scottish nobles prepared to use violence against their own king.

As these events played out, the English were also trying to decide what to do with their own Scottish royal prisoner. It was by now clear that Mary had involved herself in efforts to win her son for Catholicism and turn his kingdom into a base for plots against England. James's willingness to enter into the Association scheme advanced by his mother remained unclear. A "letter out of Scotland," undated but seemingly written around June or July of 1582, reported that he initially disliked the Association but pretended to go along with it to please his mother. Arran appeared to have misgivings but Lennox allegedly promoted it.[75] Mary's hopes for the plan reportedly made her determined "not to enter into any sort of agreement" with her English captors.[76] She denounced the Ruthven Raid as a treasonous conspiracy that threatened her son's life and complained that "puritans" wanted to subvert the power of queens in both realms.[77] But she also protested her innocence in plots against Elizabeth and desire for accommodation with her. In April 1583 she stated her willingness to renounce her claims to the English throne during Elizabeth's life, hinting that she might like to retire to France, or even to some quiet corner of England, leaving her son to rule in Edinburgh.[78]

This offer presented Elizabeth and her council with a difficult choice. An agreement to free Mary from prison in exchange for a recognition of Elizabeth's right to the English throne by both Stuart monarchs would potentially have solved numerous problems. Mary promised that she and her son would thereafter work to discourage Catholic plots. Liberating her also promised to improve relations with the French crown, whose cooperation might further insulate Scotland from the efforts of Guise and the Spanish to erect a militantly Catholic and Anglophobe party. Henry III dispatched an embassy to Edinburgh, with instructions to repair the ancient Franco-Scottish alliance and promote the Association scheme, but also to appease and settle divisions within the kingdom.[79] Although they did not welcome a revival of French influence in Scotland, at this stage the English government had reasonably good relations with Henry and wished to cultivate him as a counterweight to Philip II. On the other hand, the fact that the French delegation included "one of the chief devisers of the [Catholic] League in Picardy

---

[74] Calderwood, *History*, 138.
[75] BL Cotton Mss. Caligula BIV, fol. 284, unsigned and undated copy. Philip II also had misgivings because he feared that Mary's rehabilitation would increase French influence in Britain. See Teulet, *Papiers d'état*, 3.276.
[76] *CSPSp* 3.393, Mary to Mendoza, July 29, 1582.   [77] BL Cotton Mss. Caligula CVII, fol. 79.
[78] BL Cotton Mss. Caligula CIX, fols 81v, 82v.
[79] BL Harley Mss. 291, fol. 46r; cf. fols 48v–50v.

against the Protestants" aroused suspicion.[80] A National Assembly of the Kirk protested against its arrival as a "special grievance," while the ministers of Edinburgh "declaimed bitterly" against the French representatives, especially one who wore the white cross insignia of the Order of the Holy Spirit on his shoulder, which "they called the badge of Antichrist."[81] One of Henry's envoys took such alarm at a report that John Dury had urged the Edinburgh populace to pull him and his mass priests out of their house that he fortified it and began going about in armor.[82] "The present condition of this state is so tickle," Elizabeth's ambassador, Robert Bowes, reported "and deeply entangled with French practices and particularities among the nobility as hardly shall it continue to be saved an while from hasty and perilous change."[83]

Nevertheless, Lennox's death in exile in the spring of 1583 appeared to make accommodation easier, by removing the individual the English most mistrusted. This momentarily increased interest in a negotiated agreement with the Stuarts. Mauvissière believed in May that the two queens would shortly reach an accord; to hasten the process along he encouraged Mary to mend fences with Secretary Walsingham and to cultivate Leicester's nephew, Sir Philip Sidney.[84] "If things be tickle in Scotland it is good for her Majesty to take that good she may by this lady [Mary], who now pretendeth to seek her Majesty above all the world," the staunchly Protestant privy councilor, Sir Walter Mildmay, advised.[85] Mary's continuing detention in England arguably no longer served any real purpose. Her deteriorating health made her seem less dangerous and her son more so. Walsingham commented in a letter to Burghley that "I find the ill-affected are altogether inclined to that king [James], being now resolved that his mother cannot live long. They defend his proceedings, and wish no good fellowship between the two crowns."[86] An undated memorandum prepared for the council urged that so long as James seemed prepared to support his mother, killing her would prove counter-productive, by giving her followers a further motive for revenge without depriving them of a leader.[87] Mary had shown a pragmatic willingness to cooperate with Protestants while queen of Scotland and it seemed possible that she might abandon conspiracy if given sufficient incentives.[88] A plausible case therefore existed that allowing her to return home or retire to France might actually be safer than continuing her captivity. The Ruthven group strongly disagreed with this argument when they got wind of it,[89] and after considering the question the privy council also agreed that sending Mary back

---

[80] Calderwood, *History*, 138.   [81] Spottiswood, 325.
[82] BL Cotton Mss. Caligula CVII, fol. 193.   [83] Ibid., fol. 160.
[84] Teulet, *Papiers d'état*, 2.567.
[85] BL Cotton Mss. Caligula CVII, fols 88, 89 (letters of June 11 and 17).
[86] Hatton, 339.   [87] BL Cotton Mss. Caligula CVIII, fol. 192.
[88] The ambiguities in Mary's position are stressed in Julian Goodare's balanced article on her in *ODNB*.
[89] BL Cotton Mss. Caligula CIX, fol. 89v; cf. Questier, *Dynastic Politics*, 146–7.

to Scotland would entail unacceptable risks. But in reporting this decision to Bowes, Mildmay betrayed an almost wistful desire to find some way out of the conundrum. He urged Bowes to "think of such inconveniences as might ensue" if Mary returned, and try to "foresee how the same might be prevented, for if she could be well placed in that state without working any dangerous alteration she might be right well spared here."[90]

Negotiations eventually collapsed for several reasons, including revived concerns about James's intentions. So long as he remained under the control of the Ruthven Raiders the English had some assurance that he would not plot against them. Unfortunately, a strong aristocratic party hostile to the Anglophile group still existed, and early in 1583 reports of fresh Catholic plots to free the king surfaced. "I hold Scotland for lost unless God be merciful unto this poor island," Walsingham lamented in January: "God open her majesty's eyes to see her peril."[91] He feared that the only hope for Scotland's future depended on a tiny minority of deeply committed Protestants, who were much less numerous than those who outwardly conformed to the Kirk.[92] In an effort to reinforce its control, the English council agreed in March to distribute £10,000 in *douceurs* to James and various Scottish nobles.[93] But in May the Scots sent a new favorite of the king, Colonel William Stewart, on an embassy to England to ask for even more money for his palace guard and other expenses. Although warmly received by Leicester and Walsingham, Burghley and Elizabeth thought his demands exorbitant and he reportedly left England ill-satisfied.[94] According to Bowes, once he returned home he set about detaching James from his Anglophile entourage and strengthening the Marian party.[95]

The council had therefore once more failed to find a way of neutralizing the Stuart threat by any means short of killing both Mary and her son. Leicester may have favored this drastic solution. He warned the queen against trusting either monarch, describing them as rivals who "by practices have entered into the minds and hearts of all your hollow hearted subjects." He wanted an Act of Parliament barring them from the throne if they should undertake any further hostile acts.[96] According to Mendoza, Leicester had found a rival candidate for the succession in the young Arabella Stuart, whom he hoped to marry to his own son, a plan that would have repeated his father's maneuver of marrying Leicester's elder brother

---

[90] BL Cotton Mss. Caligula CVII, fol. 246v.
[91] TNA SP12/158/33. For reports of Catholic plots see SP12/168/30 and BL Cotton Mss. Caligula CVII, fols 136 and 137v, 205.
[92] BL Harley Mss. 291, fol. 83r, "The only hope we have resteth upon the well affected in religion in that realm, which number in respect to the rest that are worldly given is, I fear, but very small (a thing that falleth out ordinarily in all places where the gospel is professed) being found by experience that though the number of such the profess the religion be great, yet of such as be inwardly religious there are but few, of whom men may make a sound reckoning."
[93] Ibid., fol. 150; TNA SP52/31, fol. 48.
[94] Teulet, *Papiers d'état*, 2.573 and 575; Teulet, *Relations Politiques*, 5.210, *CSPSp* 3.471-2, 472-3.
[95] BL Cotton Mss. Caligula CVII, fols 260 and 261v.   [96] TNA SP12/161/46.

Guilford to Lady Jane Gray.⁹⁷ But Elizabeth rejected violent solutions, knowing that in addition to setting a precedent that might some day rebound against herself they would alienate Henry III, with whom she desperately wanted to maintain good relations.⁹⁸

Scottish politics therefore kept raising embarrassing questions about whether the defense of the Reformation and Elizabeth's own security justified the forcible compulsion, and perhaps even the murder, of sovereign rulers. Like their Scottish brethren, puritans believed that their queen and her bishops defended popish practices within her half-reformed Church. But few puritans seriously thought that Elizabeth and Whitgift wanted to restore the Roman allegiance. They therefore distinguished between opposition to specific ceremonies and ecclesiastical structures, and more generalized disobedience to the queen and her laws. Even John Field's presbyterian campaign remained targeted, non-violent, and limited in its goals. The Scots did not have that luxury because they had reasonable grounds to suspect that James and members of his entourage might try to restore Catholicism and were prepared to engage in bloody repression while doing so. Loyalty to their faith and their desire for self-preservation therefore came into direct conflict with their duty of allegiance. Even Scottish nobles who were not especially ardent supporters of the Reformation, but who had grudges against Lennox and Arran, had reasons to ally themselves with radical protests. By encouraging opposition to the Scottish crown, in the form of defiant sermons, crowd demonstrations, and noble coups, Elizabeth and her council tacitly violated principles on which her own authority rested. The view in the Scottish mirror displayed latent strains of radicalism, ruthlessness, and hypocrisy in the conduct of the English state that Elizabeth and her entourage very much wanted to keep hidden.

James's Escape and the Resumption of Conflict, 1583–1585

In the summer of 1583 rifts emerged among the Ruthven Raiders, who had not managed to eliminate an aristocratic group hostile to their coup.⁹⁹ In August, almost exactly a year after his capture, the king finally escaped. He wrote immediately to Guise, thanking him for his support and exhorting him to resume his project of invading England to rescue Mary. He also boasted of having freed the Jesuit William Holt, who had been captured in Scotland, "to the great displeasure

---

⁹⁷ *CSPSp* 3.452.
⁹⁸ Castlenau's correspondence shows him consistently trying to restrain Elizabeth throughout this period, while reassuring her about French intentions in Scotland (Teulet, *Relations Politiques*, vol. 3, passim).
⁹⁹ For a discussion of the anti-Ruthven group see Grant, "George Gordon, Sixth Earl of Huntly," 53–6.

of the English ambassador and many others."¹⁰⁰ Burghley soon received ominous reports of the importation of copes and chalices into Scotland in preparation for a restoration of the mass, along with plans in France to send military assistance.¹⁰¹ Guise had regarded the Ruthven coup and Lennox's subsequent death as serious setbacks that induced him to call off plans to mount an invasion of Britain.¹⁰² After hearing from James he sent an envoy to the pope suggesting that the time was ripe to attempt a landing of 4,000 Catholic troops in Scotland.¹⁰³ The Ruthven Raid contributed to a warming of relations between Guise and Philip II, who had previously reacted coolly to plans for invasions of Britain, worrying that if they succeeded they might turn both England and Scotland into a French satellite.¹⁰⁴ But James's captivity by an Anglophile faction seriously alarmed Philip and he instructed his ambassador in Paris to consult with Guise on the situation and assure him of Spanish support in any attempt to restore Lennox.¹⁰⁵ Spain gained a port opposite England by capturing Dunkirk, at almost the same moment that James escaped.¹⁰⁶

In this period Arran emerged as the dominant figure in Scottish politics. Even more than Lennox, he inspired widespread hatred and mistrust, as "a scorner of religion, presumptuous, ambitious, needy, and careless of the commonweal, and a despiser of the nobility and all honest men."¹⁰⁷ His wife, who had divorced the earl of March before marrying him, was equally detested. Although no one regarded them as Catholics, they were widely seen as indifferent to religion, ambitious, greedy, and eager to destroy noble families so as to profit from the spoliation of their estates. Arran launched a vendetta against the Ruthven Raiders, persuading James to banish several of them, including the earls of Angus, Glams, and Mar, as he plotted to destroy Gowrie, who had gained the king's favor.¹⁰⁸ At about this time James readily agreed when a French diplomat warned him against trusting

---

¹⁰⁰ Teulet, *Relations Politiques*, 5.305, 306.
¹⁰¹ Hatfield House Cecil Mss. 162, fols 22, 127v, 128v.
¹⁰² Teulet, *Papiers d'état*, 3.337–8. He had earlier said that he wanted to lead the invasion in person (ibid., 307–8).
¹⁰³ Teulet, *Relations Politiques*, 5.275, 281, 282, 284, 289–90, 308–9. The Catholic Lord Seton had traveled to France and Spain in July, while James was still captive, seeking military assistance to free him.
¹⁰⁴ Teulet, *Papiers d'état*, 3.276, 291, 292, 310.
¹⁰⁵ Ibid., 313–14. The prospect that Henry of Navarre would soon become heir to the French throne, since Henry III was childless and Anjou's health appeared to be failing also contributed to this rapprochement (ibid., 315).
¹⁰⁶ Teulet, *Papiers d'état*, 2.593. Compare Questier, *Dynastic Politics*, 149–53 for a basically similar assessment.
¹⁰⁷ Melville, *Memoirs*, 281. Cf. the slightly more nuanced but essentially similar assessment of the French diplomat Fontenay in a letter to Mary: "Et lui [Arran] et elle [sa femme] également ont l'esprit vif, pénétrant, fin, convoiteux de bien et grandeurs, hautain, hardi à entreprendre et capable de beaucoup d'affaires, bref, qui possède si avant le roi que la plupart du peuple et des seigneurs estime véritablement qu'il a été par eux ensorcelé. Tout ce que je crains en ceci et la haine qu'universellement tous les plus grands seigneurs et peuple même leur porte jusques au mourir" (HMC Salisbury 3.51).
¹⁰⁸ Melville, *Memoirs*, 300; Teulet, *Relations Politiques*, 5.306; William Davison, *Letters and Papers Relating to Patrick, Master of Gray* (Edinburgh, 1835), 1–3.

great nobles, adding that he had therefore decided to rely "on simple soldiers and gentlemen like Arran and Colonel Stewart, whom he could always humble when it seemed good to him."[109] Although shockingly at variance with conventional wisdom, this policy broadly resembled Henry III's efforts, in just this period, to diminish the influence of magnates like the dukes of Guise and Montmorency by relying on a group of *mignons* drawn from the lesser nobility, and Philip II's determination to keep great nobles like the duke of Alba and prince of Parma under control.[110]

But it predictably inspired violent resentment against Arran by many nobles, especially those recently ousted from power, but eventually including even figures like the Catholic earl of Huntly.[111] Evidence meanwhile continued to accumulate of Scottish involvement in schemes by Elizabeth's continental enemies. Sir Edward Stafford, the English ambassador in Paris, reported in February 1584 that the Catholic Lord Seton, who had helped shelter defeated English rebels as they fled north in 1569, had traveled to France to discuss plans with Guise and Mary's representative, John Leslie, the Catholic archbishop of Glasgow. The Spanish ambassador and papal nuncio to France were also brought into their conversations.[112] Early in the spring of 1584 Angus and several members of the Ruthven group gathered a few hundred horse with English help and advanced toward the strategic fortress of Stirling, hoping that other Scots would rally to them.[113] The earl of Gowrie told Bowes that they felt compelled to strike "before the French or Spaniard can be landed in Scotland. For verily he is persuaded that strangers are to be brought hither."[114] But broad support for the coup failed to materialize and many Scots rallied instead to the king. Colonel Stewart, the former commander of a regiment in the Dutch wars, levied 500 soldiers in Edinburgh to oppose the rebels, who gave up and fled to England, except for Gowrie, who was captured at Dundee.[115] Robert Parsons triumphantly celebrated the failure of this latest English plot in a letter full of admiration for the young king of Scots.[116] Shortly afterwards James asked Henry III to lend him the famous *Garde Ecossais* of the

---

[109] HMC Salisbury 3.57.

[110] For the situation in France see, esp., Nicolas le Roux, "Courtisans et favoris: l'entourage du prince et les mécanismes du pouvoir dans la France pendant des guerres de religion," *Histoire, Economie et Société* 17 (1998): 377–87 and Nicolas le Roux, *Le roi, la cour, l'état: de la Renaissance à l'absolutisme* (Paris: Champ Vallon, 2013), 63.

[111] Grant, "George Gordon, Sixth Earl of Huntly," 81–3.

[112] *A Collection of State Papers Relating to Affairs in the Reign of Queen Elizabeth*, ed. William Murdin (London, 1759), 392. Cf. Grant, "George Gordon, Sixth Earl of Huntly," 89–91.

[113] Castlenau was convinced that Elizabeth had assisted the coup attempt: Teulet, *Papiers d'état*, 2.656.

[114] BL Cotton Mss. Caligula CVII, fol. 380.

[115] Teulet, *Relations Politiques*, 5.281, 282; Hume, *History of Scotland*, 385; Spottiswood, 330; BL Cotton Mss. Caligula CVIII, fols 9 and 13, 19v. For Stewart's regiment, which numbered 2,250 men, see *Papers Illustrating the History of the Scots Brigade in the Service of the United Netherlands, 1571–1782*, Scottish History Society Volumes, Series 1, vol. 32 (Edinburgh, 1899).

[116] Knox, *Diaries*, 355.

French court for two years, as protection against Elizabeth and her friends.[117] Henry politely declined but two months later Philip II agreed to subsidize a Scottish royal guard.[118]

A memorandum probably written by a Scot for presentation to Walsingham at this time "set down for a maxim that the king [James VI] is enemy to her Majesty and her Estate, which needs no probation for it is so manifest; therefore I conclude that his felicity is her infelicity."[119] Although less inclined to blame James directly, William Davison, who had been sent to Edinburgh to report on the situation, reached an almost equally pessimistic conclusion: "neither her Majesty's person or estate at home or her cause abroad or religion in either country can be in surety if this course [in Scotland] be continued."[120] In August Arran launched a ruthless vendetta against the Ruthven group and other victims that further inflamed hatred against him, while disgusting Walsingham and Elizabeth.[121] The king and his associates, Davison reported, were proceeding "roundly to the cutting off of all such as of old they know or supposed to be the principal favorers of religion or of the amity with us, both of the nobility, gentlemen, ministers and principal burgesses of the boroughs and towns," to make themselves "safe at home" so that they might "with more facility go on to the execution of the rest."[122] They had erected a system of military control over Edinburgh. Arran had himself appointed Provost of the city, with fifty quarter masters under his command, "each having under him 500 or 600 men... who are all under pain of *lèse majesté* to attend with their furniture upon summons, each one his ward." His brother, William, "is lately come out of Sweden and will be Captain of Edinburgh Castle. He is accounted a brave man for execution."[123] Several of the town's "best and most religious burgesses" were expelled and commanded not to come within twelve miles of Edinburgh on pain of treason.[124]

Relations between Elizabeth and the two Stuart monarchs had therefore taken another turn for the worse. Both parties shared responsibility for the impasse. By supporting the Ruthven Raiders, the English had shown that they would not willingly allow James to rule his own kingdom independently, while Elizabeth's refusal to allow discussion of the identity of her successor prevented any possible arrangement through which James's future claims might have been recognized in exchange for an agreement that he would support Elizabeth while she lived. English Protestant fear of the Stuarts tended to have a self-fulfilling quality, by leading to policies that left James and Mary feeling that they had little choice but to seek support from the queen's adversaries. But James's duplicity in his dealings with Jesuits, Guise, and Philip II also gave the English ample cause for mistrust

---

[117] Teulet, *Relations Politiques*, 5.268–70.   [118] Ibid., 5.338.
[119] BL Cotton Mss. Caligula CVIII, fol. 32.   [120] Ibid., fol. 71v.
[121] *Papers Relating to the Master of Gray*, 1–3 and 7; *The State Papers and Letters of Sir Ralph Sadler*, ed. Arthur Clifford, vol. 2 (Edinburgh, 1809), 395 and 399.
[122] Ibid., fol. 44.   [123] HMC Salisbury 3.72.   [124] TNA SP52/35/7.

and resentment. The staunch Protestantism of the English ambassadors to Scotland, Robert Bowes and William Davison, and their handler, Secretary Walsingham, also played a role in fanning ill will.

Patrick Adamson's Appeal to the English Bishops

This climate of suspicion continued to foster English support for staunch Scottish Calvinists who wanted to eliminate episcopacy and defy their king's efforts to assert his supremacy over the Kirk. But at the same moment, the elevation of John Whitgift as archbishop of Canterbury in 1583 led to a renewed effort to suppress English puritanism by compelling clergymen to subscribe to articles upholding the validity of the ceremonies prescribed by the Book of Common Prayer, on pain of suspension from their livings and denial of their license to preach. Viewed solely from the perspective of ecclesiastical policies, James VI, Arran, and Scottish bishops like Patrick Adamson and Robert Montgomery looked more like natural allies of Elizabeth and her bishops, if not necessarily of Walsingham and Leicester, than ministers like John Dury or nobles like the Ruthven Raiders. In 1583 Archbishop Adamson of St. Andrews traveled to England, ostensibly to seek a health cure, but in reality, to attempt to persuade Whitgift and Elizabeth to embrace this perspective.

The former chaplain of the Regent Morton, Adamson had emerged as the most articulate spokesman among the relatively small group of Protestant clergy who continued to support James and his claims to exercise a Scottish royal supremacy in ecclesiastical affairs. Shortly after the Ruthven Raid he preached a sermon before the king in which he denounced his fellow clergy and the lords who had taken James captive. The Synod of Fife retaliated by ordering him to appear before it on charges of having consorted with witches.[125] Instead of obeying, Adamson left for England, carrying a set of articles laying out the theoretical basis for his opposition to presbyterianism, which he sent to Whitgift in hopes of persuading him to oppose further English support for James's radical opponents. Some of the articles were evidently intercepted by agents of Secretary Walsingham, who took a dim view of Adamson's efforts.[126] Although he promised to seek an opportunity to discuss matters with the queen, Whitgift remained too cautious to embrace an open alliance with the Scottish court's ecclesiastical allies.[127] But he seems to have been receptive to Adamson's arguments that James's clerical opponents resembled the English puritans Whitgift so disliked, who under "pretext of religion" dared to "blaspheme princes" and "animate subjects to bloodshed by order of law and

---

[125] William Scott, *An Apologetical Narration* (Edinburgh: Wodrow Society, 1846), 50.
[126] BL Add Mss. 32,092, fol. 75r. [127] Lambeth Palace Library Mss. 4701, fol. 13.

damn the order of God in his Church, namely in bishops."[128] Whitgift sent Adamson some articles of his own, arguing against puritan positions, along with a copy of a tract he had written opposing the views of the English presbyterian Thomas Cartwright.[129] Adamson promised to reciprocate with a copy of a tract he was currently finishing. The Scottish archbishop also allegedly met with the French and Spanish ambassadors in London, fanning suspicions of his involvement in popish plots.[130]

After learning of James's escape from the Ruthven Raiders, Adamson returned home, where he further antagonized Scottish presbyterians by taking his seat in the 1584 Scottish Parliament as an archbishop, and helping to orchestrate the campaign to pass a set of statutes soon named the Black Acts. These re-established the authority of bishops and prohibited the summoning of a general assembly of the Kirk without royal consent. He also spearheaded a Scottish subscription campaign, in which all ministers had to surrender their stipends to the crown, which they would receive back only after signing their names to a document affirming their support for James's authority over the Kirk.[131] About twenty refused and left for England, where several joined John Field's campaign in London to agitate for presbyterian reforms within the English Church. In Edinburgh James filled their pulpits with two ministers of his own household, John Craig and John Duncanson, along with Adamson.[132] For good measure Buchanan's *De Juri Regni apud Scotos* was banned and his *Rerum Scoticarum Historica* ordered expurgated.[133] "The King hath assumed to himself an absolute jurisdiction," Davison concluded disapprovingly.[134]

During these events, Adamson continued to correspond with Whitgift, assuring him that James's efforts to establish episcopacy in Scotland did not reflect any sympathy for popery but a commitment to God's word, "which his highness in his heart doth reverence to conform such a policy as may be an example to other commonwealths, as I did show your grace in particular conference at your main house of Lambeth."[135] His efforts to forge a common front with the English bishops quickly attracted hostile attention from both Scottish presbyterians and some members of the English political establishment. From Edinburgh, Davison sent home scathing reports of Adamson's efforts, "both publicly and privately to deface and persecute the ministers, as he hath done in supplanting the discipline." He accused the archbishop of sexual incontinency, repeated the earlier accusations of his consorting with witches and reported that Adamson had spread malicious stories about the earl of Leicester and promoted the association between James and Mary.[136] In London, the exiled Scottish minister, James Carmichael, had

---

[128] BL Add Mss. 32,092, fol. 78v.   [129] Ibid., fol. 76v.
[130] Ibid., fol. 42r; BL Harley Mss. 291, fols 162v–163.
[131] TNA SP52/36/31.   [132] Spottiswood, 334; TNA SP52/36/31.
[133] Pauline Croft, *King James* (Basingstoke: Palgrave Macmillan, 2003), 17–18.
[134] BL Cotton Mss. Caligula CVIII, fol. 62.   [135] BL Add Mss. 32,092, fol. 79v.
[136] TNA SP52/35, 8 and 18; 36/7 (dispatches of June 10 and 23 and August 2, 1584).

meanwhile begun a scholarly defense of the presbyterian cause, with the assistance of Thomas Randolph, Henry Killigrew, Robert Bowes, the ministers of the French Church, "and other good brethren." He presented a draft of his work to Walsingham who, after a two-hour conference, asked to borrow and review it, while offering to lend Carmichael the services of a scribe to copy out a revised draft.[137] Carmichael and several other Scottish ministers also had long meetings with Leicester and Sir Philip Sidney, in which they provided detailed accounts of Catholic efforts to turn James VI against Protestantism. At the invitation of local puritans, several preached from London pulpits. One, John Davidson, warned in the church of St. Olave's in the Old Jewry "of a great visitation and affliction approaching the Church of England and showed plainly that Scotland was the place where the furnace was kindled."[138]

Adamson had already protested to Whitgift in June against Elizabeth's decision to permit "such slanderous persons [as the Scottish ministers] under pretext of religion to abide in her country to infest the state of England with their seditious practices."[139] In August he wrote again, asking to have the Scots silenced. This time Elizabeth listened and banned the exiles from preaching in London, the first clear victory of the episcopal lobby against the council's presbyterian alliance. "Thus you see how kindly they are dealt with that have best deserved at our hands, which cannot but greatly wound and grieve the best affected," Walsingham grumbled.[140] Even before this date Whitgift may have made disparaging comments about Scottish clergy, since Robert Beale told the archbishop in May that he did not mind his insults, having heard that he had said worse things about "Calvin, Beza, Junius and the ministers of Scotland."[141] Beale taunted Whitgift by telling him how much Mary Stuart approved of his persecution of her puritan enemies and handling of the English Church, which in her view "lacketh nothing but the setting up of the mass again." He then took a gratuitous swipe at Adamson, "lately departed hence [England] with such an approbation of our rites as carrieth with it a condemnation of the form used there [in Scotland]."[142]

In 1585 Adamson anonymously published a defense of the Black Acts entitled *A Declaration of the Kings Majesties intentioun and meaning toward the late actis of parliament*, possibly the tract he had promised to send Whitgift. It undoubtedly did express James's views and may well have been written at his direction, although the king would later disclaim any responsibility for it.[143] After accusing the clergy of libeling James to "cover their seditious enterprises under pretext of religion," the *Declaration* went on to develop a case for royal authority in

---

[137] *The Miscellany of the Wodrow Society*, ed. David Laing, vol. 1 (Edinburgh, 1844), 413–14.
[138] Ibid., 425–6, 428–9.   [139] BL Harley Mss. 7704, fol. 3.
[140] BL Cotton Mss. Caligula CVIII, fol. 108v; TNA SP52/36/16.
[141] BL Lansdowne Mss. 42/82.   [142] BL Lansdowne Mss. 42/79, 82, 89.
[143] Below, p. 411.

ecclesiastical affairs.[144] Although Christ alone is truly head of the Church, "notwithstanding his Majesty surely understands by the scriptures that he is the chief and principal member, appointed by the law of God to see God glorified, vice punished and virtue maintained within his realm, and a sovereign judgment for a godly order and quietness in the commonwealth." It is "intolerable arrogance in any subject, called before his prince... to disclaim his authority," especially when questioned for preaching "factious sermons and stirring up of the people to rebellion." By claiming independent authority for the Kirk even in opposition to the crown, the presbyterians behaved in precisely the same manner as the pope and his agents.[145] According to a hostile Scottish source, these arguments were "greedily embraced by the English bishops," who caused Adamson's *Declaration* to be "reprinted with an odious preface" in London and inserted into Holinshed's *Chronicles* in 1587.[146] The views expressed in *The King's Declaration* certainly corresponded closely to Whitgift's own.[147]

But for the moment the effort to break English support for the presbyterians by appealing to English conformists stalled because of the obvious threat posed by James's friendly relations with Guise, Mary, and Philip II. Bowes, Davison, and Walsingham regarded the Arran regime as totally committed to the cause "of the king's mother with the manifest peril of religion" and Elizabeth's own safety.[148] Bowes thought "that the king is now greatly guided by the advice and direction of Guise,"[149] while Davison suspected Mary's hidden hand.[150] "Let her Majesty plainly see," he remarked, "that all these changes and alterations here, howsoever they be dignified have for their *summum finem* the offence and trouble of her person and state."[151] He wrote a long letter to Christopher Hatton, trying to persuade him of these views.[152] Walsingham agreed: "there is no hope of recovery of this young prince, if his power may agree to his will [he] will become a dangerous enemy."[153] Robert Beale, who had been delegated to deal with Mary Stuart, warned that by encouraging Adamson and silencing godly preachers in England Whitgift had, whether knowingly or not, become complicit in this sinister plan. In both kingdoms, papists now had more latitude to pursue their plots, while

---

[144] *A Declaratioun of the Kings Majestis intentioun and meaning toward the lat actis of Parliament* (Edinburgh, 1585), sig. Aii.

[145] Ibid., sigs Aiii and A iiii.   [146] Scott, *Apologetical Narration*, 52.

[147] Cf the words of his 1583 Paul's Cross sermon: "We give princes supremacy in ecclesiastical causes but not to execute ecclesiastical functions, as to preach, minister the sacraments, or consecrate bishops... Their office is to see God served, and honored, and obeyed by their subjects. They have both the tables committed unto them" (*The Works of John Whitgift*, 3 vols, ed. John Ayre, Parker Society Publications, 46–8 (Cambridge, 1851–3), 3.586).

[148] BL Cotton Mss. Caligula CVIII, fol. 44; cf. Bowes's comments, 45v, on the general fear spreading through all Scotland of a general persecution.

[149] BL Cotton Mss. Caligula CVII, fol. 293.   [150] TNA SP52/35/7.

[151] Ibid., fol. 72.   [152] BL Harley Mss. 291, fols 143r–144v.

[153] BL Cotton Mss. Caligula CVII, Walsingham to unnamed lord, September 15, 1583. James reciprocated this hostility, refusing to deal with Walsingham (Cotton Caligula Mss. CVIII, fol. 159).

the papists' strongest enemies "are put to silence, so as the wolf may enter and make havoc with the flock."[154]

Recent Scottish incursions into Ulster, which James was thought to have encouraged, magnified English alarm.[155] So did new rumors that he would soon convert to Catholicism and more reports of the arrival of Jesuits in Scotland. This background explains why, in the autumn of 1584, the Bond of Association targeted James as well as his mother, and why the English warned her that if conspiracies against Elizabeth did not stop they would "take some such course for our own safety as *both she and her son* shall have no cause to like of, being not ignorant of the practices that are entertained betwixt her son and the house of Guise tending to the trouble and disquiet of our state."[156] Despite their complaints about the Church of England, everyone knew whose side Scottish presbyterians would take if Guise landed an army in Britain. For the moment this consideration trumped all others.

Nevertheless, rifts had started to appear within the governing circle in London with respect to policies toward Scotland. According to the courtier James Melville, Walsingham so mistrusted and despised Arran that he had refused even to meet with him during a brief trip to Scotland in late 1583. But Burghley thought Walsingham's attitude too "precise" and instructed the resident ambassador, Davison, to initiate discussions with James's favorite.[157] A short time later, the queen's cousin, Lord Hunsdon, who commanded the Berwick garrison, was also encouraged to begin negotiating with Arran over a restoration of amity between the two kingdoms. Hunsdon concluded that Arran and James really did want an English alliance and that relying on presbyterian rebels was a mistake.[158] He complained when Angus and nearly a hundred of his armed followers took up residence in Newcastle after the failure of their attempt to seize Stirling in 1584. The Scots frightened the town's residents by strolling around at night with their pistols at the ready, he reported, and sent a steady stream of messengers back and forth across the border. Although they had come as friends, allowing them to become too intimately acquainted with the kingdom's frontier defenses seemed unwise.[159]

Hunsdon realized that Elizabeth and her council had given both Arran and James ample grounds for fear and resentment. He reported that the king had convinced himself that Morton's relatives, the powerful border family of the Douglases now led by Angus, wanted to kill him and Arran to avenge the regent's death.[160] James grew

---

[154] BL Lansdowne Mss. 42/82 (Beale to Whitgift, May 7, 1584).
[155] BL Cotton Mss. Caligula CVIII, fol. 98; cf. TNA SP63/111/72 and 112/49.
[156] BL Cotton Mss. Caligula CVIII, fol. 42, emphasis added. [157] Melville, *Memoirs*, 328.
[158] TNA SP52/35/58 and SP52/36/72. [159] BL Cotton Mss. Caligula CVIII, fol. 159 r–v.
[160] Ibid., fol. 110, Hunsdon to Walsingham, August 14, 1584. This was certainly a plausible fear in the case of Arran, who was in fact hacked to death while attempting to traverse Douglas territory a few years later.

especially alarmed over a report that the English had attempted to reconcile the Douglases to their former enemies, lords John and Claude Hamilton, who had been exiled from Scotland since 1579.[161] Early in 1585 several Scots were arrested and executed for alleged involvement in a Hamilton–Douglas plot to murder the king.[162] The English tried to soothe James's fears but Elizabeth had, in fact, tried to win over the Hamilton brothers and draw them into an alliance with Angus.[163] Since the Hamiltons possessed the best claim to inherit the Scottish throne if James and his mother died without heirs, it did not take much imagination to foresee what such an alliance might portend.

From Enmity to Fragile Alliance, 1584–1587

Maneuvering over Stuart claims to the English crown had therefore given rise to a vicious cycle of suspicion and hostility between the two British courts that kept increasing as each took aggressive measures to protect itself against the other. But despite their mutual grievances, both parties realized that they had an interest in backing away from an adversarial relationship. The growing threat from the Continent as Spain recovered its position in the Low Countries and Guise assembled a powerful Catholic coalition in France made friendlier relations with Scotland imperative for the English state, while the instability and violence of Scottish politics gave James and his circle strong reasons for wanting to curtail English support for their domestic enemies. As hated upstarts with no independent base of support, Arran and Colonel Stewart were especially exposed. Henry III's cold reception of their pleas for assistance against Elizabeth in the summer of 1584 may have heightened their sense of vulnerability. Arran admitted to Hunsdon that foreign princes had tried to enlist James in projects to destabilize England but claimed disingenuously that the king always rebuffed them, adding that if he had not done so "there had been no small company of French within Scotland ere now to disquiet her Majesty." He falsely denied that James had admitted Jesuits into Scotland, saying that "to his knowledge he never saw Jesuit in his life," but then added with more reason that even if they had entered Scotland their preaching would do less damage than exiled presbyterian ministers "will do in England if they preach such doctrine as they did in Scotland."[164]

James also protested his innocence, telling Bowes that he extended favor to Catholics like the earl of Huntly and lords suspected of French sympathy only to

---

[161] Ibid.
[162] David Moysie, *Memoires of the Affairs of Scotland*, ed. J. Dennistoun, Bannatyne Club Publications (Edinburgh, 1830), 52. Two of the accused confessed, while the others died professing their innocence.
[163] BL Cotton Mss. Caligula CVIII, fols 172v, 151, 169.
[164] BL Cotton Mss. Caligula CVIII, fols 110–11.

"declare himself indifferent to his nobility and subjects and not to be indirectly led away or governed by any private party or person, trusting thereby to reconcile his nobility in concord and to establish all in quietness."[165] The king's religious views at this date remain elusive. Some Catholics who interviewed him came away with the impression that he only awaited a good opportunity to declare his allegiance to Rome. On the other hand, he not only assured Protestants of his undying commitment to the reformed faith but told the French envoy Courcelles in 1586 "that although he had been brought up among a company of mutinous knave ministers whose doctrine he had never approved... he knew his religion to be the true religion." He repeated these sentiments a few years later to the earl of Huntly.[166] Since in both cases he was speaking privately to Catholics, he presumably had no reason to exaggerate his attachment to the reformed faith. A nuanced report by a French diplomat may provide insight into the king's actual views. It stated that while James stubbornly persisted "in his doctrine [en sa doctrine]," he nevertheless differed from Luther and Calvin on a number of points, denying predestination and affirming that "faith is dead without good works." He believed that people who had sufficient faith might achieve salvation in any church to which they happened to belong.[167] These attitudes would explain how he felt justified in maintaining good relations simultaneously with staunch Calvinists and Catholics like Huntly.

Despite their desire for better relations, the English remained deeply mistrustful of both James and Arran. In August they had their worst suspicions confirmed when Protestant pirates captured William Crichton and papers he carried that revealed the Scottish king's ongoing negotiations with Guise and other Catholics on the Continent.[168] Nevertheless Elizabeth badly needed to secure her northern frontier and therefore welcomed the arrival in London in December of the ambassador James had sent to conclude an alliance, Patrick Master of Gray. Gray had recently spent several years in France consorting with Mary's supporters, causing figures like Walsingham and Davison to regard him with suspicion, as a "gentleman... always noted in religion a professed papist, in affection French... that hath confessed himself to be inwardly acquainted with the whole course and proceedings and intents" of the Scottish queen and her Guise allies.[169] Mary thought him a friend who would advance her Association scheme and her efforts to persuade the English to release her from prison. But during his mission

---

[165] BL Cotton Mss. Caligula CVII, fol. 266.
[166] Extracts from the Despatches of M. Courcelles, French Ambassador at the Court of Scotland, MDLXXXVI-MDLXXXVII (Edinburgh, 1828), 8; Keith Brown, Bloodfeud in Scotland 1573-1625: Violence, Justice and Politics in an Early Modern Society (Edinburgh: John Donald, 1986), 164: "I love the religion they [the Scottish clergy] outwardly profess and hate their presumptuous and seditious behavior."
[167] Fontenay to Mary Stewart, August 1584 in HMC Salisbury 3.51.
[168] BL Add Mss. 32,092, fols 34v, 35.
[169] BL Cotton Mss. Caligula CVIII, fol. 122; the words are those of Secretary Davison.

Gray ignored Mary's pleas and instead worked with Walsingham to draft an alliance treaty, finally ratified in 1586.[170]

Gray's conduct cut the ground from under Mary's efforts to persuade the English that an accommodation with her offered their only chance of improved relations with Scotland. In October 1584 even Walsingham wanted to make "some trial" of Mary's offers, since he believed that without her "assent (who doth altogether direct the king) there will be no hold taken of Scotland."[171] But Gray made it clear that James was not as beholden to his mother as the English believed. Mary understandably felt betrayed by his conduct, which she blamed on "some evil ministers about her son."[172] It soon became apparent that James was now negotiating on his own behalf, rather than acting as a proxy for Mary and her Guise relatives. He repudiated the Association scheme and in late 1584 issued a proclamation banishing Jesuits and Catholic priests from his kingdom. It may also have been in this period that he wrote a paraphrase of the Revelation of John the Divine that endorsed the standard Protestant identification of the pope as Antichrist. Although it remained unpublished until 1616, Elizabeth seems to have received a manuscript copy, evidently intended to reassure her of James's detestation of popery.[173]

Relations began to improve as James acted the part of Elizabeth's Protestant ally, promising to punish Scottish Catholics who secretly attended mass, working out agreements with "the ministers for the orders of the Church," and engaging her ambassador in a long conversation about the current state of Europe in which "not so much as Sir Francis Drake's voyage was forgotten."[174] In England Gray made particular efforts to cultivate Sir Philip Sidney and the earl of Leicester, offering in February 1585 to raise Scottish troops for the army Leicester would eventually lead to the Netherlands.[175] He also entered into discussions with the exiled Scottish lords, who had by now left the North of England for London.[176] Although Walsingham and others on the English council still remained distrustful of Arran, they initially discouraged efforts to overthrow him from fear of antagonizing James, whose affection for his favorite remained undiminished.[177] But in July of 1585 followers of one of Arran's close allies, Lord Farnihurst, killed the earl of Bedford's son, Sir Francis Russell, after a quarrel broke out during a day of truce intended to settle disputes along the Anglo-Scottish border. No hard evidence

---

[170] G. R. Hewit, "Patrick Gray, sixth Lord Gray," in *ODNB*.
[171] *State Papers of Sadler*, ed. Clifford, 2.420–1.   [172] Ibid., 466–7.
[173] Jane Rickard, *Authorship and Authority: The Writings of James VI and I* (Manchester: Manchester University Press, 2007), 78; Daniel Fischlin, "'To Eate the Flesh of Kings': James VI and I, Apocalypse, Nation and Sovereignty," in *Royal Subjects: Essays on the Writings of James VI and I*, ed. Daniel Fischlin and Mark Fortier (Detroit: Wayne State University Press, 2002), 388–420.
[174] BL Cotton Mss. Caligula CVIII, fols 429v, 440.
[175] BL Cotton Mss. Caligula CIX, fols 170v, 222. A Frenchman reported in March 1586 that 6,000 Scots were to be levied for Leicester's army; if so they would almost have equaled the number of English soldiers Elizabeth had agreed to send. Teulet, *Papiers d'état*, 2.756.
[176] Hume, *History of Scotland*, 362.   [177] BL Add Mss. 32,657, fols 95r, 103r.

indicated that Arran was in any way responsible for the crime, which damaged his interests, but the opportunity to use the incident to weaken him appeared too tempting to pass up.[178] Elizabeth's council demanded that Arran stand trial in England, while several of Russell's kinsmen demanded revenge.[179] James ordered his favorite arrested but then released him, producing a new chill in Anglo-Scottish relations and momentary disillusionment with Gray at the English court. But Gray then collaborated with several of Elizabeth's councilors in urging that money be given to the exiled Scottish lords to allow them to attempt another coup. Elizabeth resisted until late September before finally agreeing.[180] The exiles raised 7,000 men and succeeded in seizing Stirling Castle and capturing Arran's brother and Captain William Stewart. As other prominent Scots, including the Chancellor, John Maitland, turned against Arran James capitulated to the pressure, banishing his favorite from court and grudgingly pardoning the exiles for their former offenses. The English thus appeared to have destroyed or co-opted all the leading figures at the Scottish court they had previously regarded as adversaries.

How Much Had Really Changed?

The seizure of Stirling seemed to mark a turning point not only in James's relations with Elizabeth but also in his governance of Scotland. He ended his reliance on favorites like Lennox and Arran, opened his court to the Scottish nobility, and gradually improved his relations with leading presbyterians. But the reasons for this reorientation and the degree to which it really did involve a major change in the king's objectives are less clear. Historians have often assumed that because the English alliance helped James stabilize Scotland, while improving his chances of succeeding Elizabeth, he embraced it unreservedly. Although he continued trying to pressure the queen into sending him more money and naming him as her successor, obliquely threatening to cause her trouble if she refused, he avoided doing anything that would inflict serious damage on their relationship. But this is a retrospective view. Strictly contemporary evidence suggests that for some time after the autumn of 1585, James's English alliance and reconciliation with Anglophile Scots still looked tenuous.

Although in January 1586 a Scottish parliament completed the rehabilitation of the Stirling lords and the Hamiltons, James resisted the pleas of Angus and the duke of Hamilton to banish Colonel Stewart and other soldiers associated with the Arran regime from his presence. In early February both Angus and Hamilton left the court, "malcontent."[181] Hamilton's younger brother, Claude, became openly

---

[178] Ibid., fol. 134r.   [179] Ibid., fols 138r, 142r.
[180] Ibid., fols 190r, 196r, 198r, 212r.   [181] TNA SP52/38, fol. 16.

Catholic and plotted with other Catholic peers to ruin Angus and the pro-English lords.[182] Maitland, who had now become the king's principal secretary and chief minister, remained supportive of the English alliance.[183] But Walsingham fretted over Elizabeth's penurious refusal to generously reward other Scottish friends, including the Master of Gray, and worried that the English party in Edinburgh would collapse as a result.[184] Rumors circulated in July of a plot to murder Angus, Gray, and Maitland, while in October Angus's enemies tried to discredit him by spreading reports that he wanted to kill the king.[185] The end of the year saw an upsurge in factional maneuvering among the nobility, with a resurgent Catholic party hoping to take power.[186]

The king's relations with the Kirk and its plebeian followers remained stormy. In the wake of the seizure of Stirling, students at the University of St. Andrews arrested Adamson and turned him over to the coup leaders.[187] He was quickly released and restored to the king's favor but his synod suspended him from preaching, and when he defied it by trying to give a sermon he was told that a crowd of students and citizens intended "to take him out of the pulpit and hang him."[188] A parliament that convened in January opened with a sermon by the king's household minister, John Craig, defending the clergy who had subscribed to Adamson's articles and urging the returning exiles to "crave pardon and grace" for their disobedience. James aggressively resisted presbyterian attempts to repeal the Black Acts, "playing *rex*, scorning and taunting all... triumphing over the ministers and calling them clowns, smacks, seditious knaves and so forth."[189] He rudely interrupted a sermon by Walter Balcanquhal on the parity of ministers, saying "he would prove that there should be bishops and spiritual magistrates."[190] In May an Edinburgh synod refused a royal demand that it endorse the pre-eminence of bishops as commanded by the Word of God, while grudgingly conceding "that they must tolerate it [episcopacy] in case it be forced upon them by the civil power."[191]

---

[182] TNA SP15/29, fol. 133. Claude would continue his efforts for several months (see, e.g., Teulet, *Relations Politiques*, 5.351).

[183] For Maitland's career see Maurice Lee Jr., *John Maitland of Thirlstane and the Foundations of Stewart Despotism in Scotland* (Princeton: Princeton University Press, 1959).

[184] BL Cotton Mss. Caligula CVIII, fol. 447v; *Correspondence of Robert Dudley Earl of Leicester*, ed. John Bruce (London, 1844), 275–6.

[185] TNA SP52/40 (report of Randolph's embassy); *Despatches of Courcelles*, 6.

[186] *Despatches of Courcelles*, 21; CSPSp 3.682, 683.   [187] BL Add Mss. 32,092, fol. 83v.

[188] James Gabriel Fyfe, ed., *Scottish Diaries and Memoirs, 1550-1746* (Stirling: E. Mackay, 1928), 105. In the sermon Adamson apparently attacked Melville and referred to inhabitants of St. Andrews as goats. See Mark C. Smith, "The Presbytery of St Andrews, 1586-1605: A Study and Annotated Edition of the Register of the Minutes of the Presbytery of St Andrews, vol. 1," unpublished University of St Andrews PhD 1985, 11.

[189] *Miscellany Wodrow*, ed. Laing, vol. 1, 438–9; cf. Calderwood, *History*, 193–5, 197.

[190] Calderwood, *History*, 197; BL Cotton Mss. Caligula CVIII, fol. 398.

[191] BL Add Mss. 32,092, fol. 89.

Efforts to rally noble support behind the presbyterian program proved unavailing.[192] "Men sought themselves and neglected God his cause and friends," one minister lamented in a letter to Carmichael, who had remained behind in London. "Wicked men, whom laws both of God and men would have justly punished are escaped, overseen and permitted to pass where they please. Some of the very wicked rejoice the king's ear." Masses were being celebrated, while priests and Jesuits continued to infiltrate the kingdom: "Satan is manifesting himself." But the writer refused to relinquish the fight. "Good men and professors of the truth are beginning to take their old courage... I trust the kingdom of Satan in this country is even at an end. Brother James, I beseech you and all other our brethren that are there, pray for us and haste yourselves home to fight the battle, for now the Lord craves of us to bear his standard. Comfort the brethren of England. Desire them not to be discouraged for our trial and their disappointed expectation."[193]

Another minister, James Gibson, preached a sermon comparing James to Jeroboam, a king of Israel who had set up idolatrous altars and forbidden his subjects to worship in Solomon's temple. "It was thought before that the two Hamiltons and Jezebel, one of their wives, were the cause of misgovernment both of church and commonwealth," he added, "but it now appeared it was [the king] himself, which unless he repented the plague of God was imminent."[194] Imprisoned and hauled before James to explain himself, Gibson refused to back down in a stormy interview:

K[ING]: Hath you been in England?
M[INISTER]: Yes, sir.
K: What chased you there? Or what moved you to go away?
M: Please you that which moved others, moved me.
K: What was that?
M: Persecution.
K: Persecution? Persecution? (doubling his words). What call you persecution? Can you define it?
M: I were not worthy the office I bear if I could not define it.
K: What is it then?
M: Shortly, sir, it is a troubling the saints of God for professing a good cause and namely for Christ's sake.
K: (Angrily and in great rage): Say ye that ye were persecuted for Christ's sake? Who were your persecutors?
M: Captain James Stewart [i.e. Arran].

---

[192] *Miscellany Wodrow*, ed. Laing, vol. 1, 438–9.   [193] LPL Mss. 3471, fol. 85.
[194] HMC *Report on the Manuscripts of the Earl of Ancaster* (London, 1907), 18, Sir Drue Drury to Walsingham, January 24, 1586.

As James proceeded with the interrogation, matters escalated:

M: And so having occasion to speak of our persecuted kirk, I said I thought it had been Captain James Stewart, Colonel Stewart, William Stewart and the Lady Jezebel that only had persecuted the same but I saw it was the king's self because he went forward in that cursed course they began.
K: What (in great anger), call you me a persecutor?
M: Yes sir, so long as you maintain those cursed acts against God and the liberties of the Church [the Black Acts] you are a persecutor.[195]

The case would drag on for several years, with James demanding that the Kirk repudiate and punish Gibson, while the general assembly delivered only a mild rebuke and temporary suspension.

This sparring between the king and outspoken clergy took place against a backdrop of widening religious war in northwest Europe, as Guise rallied militant Catholic forces in France to prevent Henry of Navarre from succeeding to the French throne, a Spanish army under the prince of Parma conquered most of Brabant and Flanders, and Elizabeth agreed to send an army to the Netherlands, which arrived at the end of 1585.[196] The English had more reason than ever to worry about the security of their northern border, and Philip II and Guise additional motives for trying to overthrow Protestant rule in Britain. Guise sent an agent to Scotland in September 1585, carrying a secret message for James, who sent his own envoy to France a short time later.[197] Jesuits were reported to "keep a great stir in the north part" of Scotland, "saying mass openly and leading great numbers of people to visit relics and chapels here and there," while nothing was done to stop them.[198] Henry III sent an embassy to Edinburgh early in the new year, headed by a man rumored to be a supporter of Guise, who had brought with him a store of gold to distribute as bribes.[199] Arran traveled secretly to Edinburgh to consult with him and the English grew seriously worried that the French initiative might succeed.[200] Ministers denounced the French representatives from Edinburgh pulpits, whereupon James tried to make amends by ordering the town's magistrates to feast them. The preachers responded by declaring a general fast on the day appointed for the feast, and preaching three sermons denouncing the magistrates and nobles who complied with the king's orders.[201] Henry of Navarre sent his own envoy to Edinburgh, appealing to James to maintain his solidarity with Elizabeth and other Protestants against the popish enemy.[202]

---

[195] BL Add Mss. 32,092, fols 86v and 87. The text identifies the minister as William Watson rather than Gibson (fol. 82) but I have assumed this was an error, since the reported circumstances and content of the exchange with James closely correspond to reports of Gibson's sermon.
[196] See below, pp. 271–7.   [197] TNA SP52/38/56 and 71; Teulet, *Papiers d'état*, 2.742.
[198] TNA SP52/38/56.
[199] BL Cotton Mss. Caligula CVIII, fols 404v and 441v; TNA SP52/39/4.
[200] BL Cotton Mss. Caligula CVIII, fol. 418v.   [201] Spottiswood, 324.
[202] Teulet, *Papiers d'état*, 2.705–6.

James tried to keep his options open by welcoming the French overtures even while continuing his English alliance. Although England's friends, including Angus and Maitland, now dominated the Scottish privy council, James's chamber remained full of Catholics and Catholic sympathizers, many of them clients of Huntly, the great magnate of the Scottish northeast.[203] In March 1586 Huntly and two other Catholic lords wrote to Philip II, on the advice of Guise and probably with James's knowledge, appealing for his aid to free the king from the English party and restore Catholicism in Scotland.[204] They also sent an envoy to Spain named Robert Bruce, who asked specifically for 6,000 troops and 150,000 crowns in aid, in return for which the Catholic lords promised to deliver two Scottish ports into Philip's hands. Guise warmly recommended the plan to Philip, who was interested but asked for time to consider and consult with Parma.[205] Before reaching a decision Philip learned of the Babington Plot to assassinate Elizabeth in preparation for the invasion of Sussex that Guise was preparing. Guise wanted Philip to support a second simultaneous landing in Scotland or the English borders. The Spanish king thought it a promising plan, on which he did not give up even after the Babington Plot collapsed.[206] Colonel Stewart, who retained James's confidence, traveled to the Continent in December, renewing appeals for Spanish help in "freeing" the king from his English captors. He claimed that James detested the presbyterian ministers and the lords who had seized Stirling and wanted to purge Scotland of both.[207] The king almost certainly encouraged Huntly's and Stewart's pursuit of European aid in hopes of pressuring Elizabeth to name him her successor, and as an insurance policy in case Guise or Philip did land an army in Britain.[208] He succeeded in keeping alive English fears that Philip might invade England through Scotland.[209] Mendoza and Guise strongly favored such a project and in early 1586 Parma began gathering a fleet to convey an army from Dunkirk to Leith.[210] Philip soon abandoned the plan, to concentrate instead on preparing the direct invasion of England that would come in 1588.[211] But the English remained unaware of this strategic reorientation, and continued to worry that the Spanish intended to attack through Scotland.

James's efforts to pressure Elizabeth won him no concessions, while his efforts at playing the English off against Guise and the French, and the English party in Scotland against Catholic nobles, cost him considerable trust and good will on all sides. His relations with his mother deteriorated badly over the summer because

---

[203] The most detailed study of Huntly's political activities is Grant, "George Gordon, Sixth Earl of Huntly," see 108–9 for the Scottish privy council.
[204] Ibid., 135. Teulet, *Papiers d'état*, 3.412–17 reproduces these letters, written in Latin.
[205] Teulet, *Papiers d'état*, 3.432, 469; Grant, "George Gordon, Sixth Earl of Huntly," 136–8.
[206] Teulet, *Papiers d'état*, 3.437 and 451.   [207] Teulet, *Relations Politiques*, 5.442–4.
[208] As some historians have concluded. See, e.g., Grant, "George Gordon, Sixth Earl of Huntly," 135.
[209] Below, p. 326.
[210] Teulet, *Papiers d'état*, 3.476, 479; Grant, "George Gordon, Sixth Earl of Huntly," 213–14.
[211] Teulet, *Relations Politiques*, 5.403, 431.

he refused to convert to Catholicism and accept her Association scheme.[212] Philip came to regard him as a confirmed heretic who did not deserve Spanish support. But the king's warm relations with Huntly and other Catholics continued to inflame the anger of Scottish clergy and English jealousy. Mary's trial and condemnation in October 1586, after Walsingham produced proof of her involvement in the Babington Plot, further polarized Scottish politics. A wave of sympathy for the fallen queen fueled a Catholic revival and calls for vengeance, should the English carry out the death sentence.[213] This put James in a delicate position. His relationship with his mother had deteriorated to a point at which he now saw her as an adversary, or at least so he told the English.[214] His alliance with Elizabeth had made Mary's execution more likely, as several contemporaries observed. He must have known that war with England would be suicidal unless he received substantial aid from a major European power. But to uphold his honor and reputation he needed to show support for his mother in her hour of need. As a small step he ordered the clergy to pray from their pulpits that God would soften Elizabeth's heart and spare Mary's life, only to meet with blunt refusals.[215] He retaliated by committing the ministers of Edinburgh to ward, effectively shutting down most preaching in the city. He then appointed a day of solemn prayers for his mother on February 3, 1587, and appointed Archbishop Adamson to preach a sermon in St. Giles's church, Edinburgh. The ministers arranged for a young preacher, John Couper, to occupy the pulpit instead, setting up another confrontation.[216]

James accompanied Adamson to the church and ordered Couper to vacate the pulpit. Couper refused and

> began to menace and threaten the king, protesting before the whole people that the very stones of the Church should in the day of judgment rise up against him and condemn him because he had resisted the servants of God being sent to deliver the glad tidings of the gospel. At which there was a wonderful cry in that church made chiefly by the women who did rise of their stools and cried to the king, 'O God, what is this?' At which sudden cry the king being amazed began to retire himself among his nobility to consult what was best to be done.[217]

---

[212] Teulet, *Papiers d'état*, 3.424–5. Several English and European statesmen thought in 1588 that the Armada's target would be Scotland rather than southern England. See below, p. 326.

[213] Grant, "George Gordon, Sixth Earl of Huntly," 147; *Despatches of Courcelles*, 21.

[214] *Despatches of Courcelles*, 6–7: James said "he had seen with his own eyes a letter before Fontenay's departure out of Scotland, written unto him, whereby she sent him word that if he would not conform himself to her will and follow her counsel and advice that he should content himself with the lordship of Darnley, which was all that appertained unto him by his father. Further that he had seen other letters of her own hand confirming her evil will towards him, besides that she had often times gone about to make a regent in Scotland and to put him besides the crown."

[215] Ibid., 33–4.   [216] Spottiswood, 354.

[217] LPL Mss. 4701, fol. 91r, a much fuller account of this incident than those provided by Spottiswood and Calderwood. Courcelles also briefly reported this incident, *Despatches of Courcelles*, 33–4.

The king's guard threatened Couper, who withdrew to a private house to continue his sermon, followed by many in the congregation. Adamson still needed protection to occupy the pulpit and preach on the Christian duty of charity even toward the wicked, especially in the case of princes. Midway through his sermon a commotion outside the church caused him to break off in panic, but he eventually managed to finish. As news of what had transpired spread, "the people did give out that they would stone him as he came from the church if they might come by him, which caused the bishop to wait hard by the king's heels all the way down to Holyrood."[218]

This humiliating episode may have helped convince James that he needed to placate the Kirk and its popular supporters. The following week he attended another public sermon, after which he rose to address the congregation. He complained of the "mischief" caused by those who sought to "defame him and steal the people's hearts from him, concluding with an apology for himself showing that ever since he had taken the government of the kingdom into his hands he had always sought the advancement of the religion now professed in Scotland and further that so long as life would last it would continue the same." This appeased many people, although "the preciser sort with some of the ministers... said the king did it but to win the peoples' hearts."[219]

James protested vociferously after hearing the news of his mother's execution, initially refusing to receive the ambassador Elizabeth sent to explain it, but he did not end his English alliance or remove its supporters from power. On the other hand, Huntly remained in favor and began attending the court more regularly. In August James appointed him acting chamberlain, consolidating the Catholic earl's control over the royal household.[220] The king's ultimate intentions and allegiances therefore remained deeply uncertain, arousing mistrust and hostility among both Catholic partisans and some English like Hunsdon, who warned Elizabeth and Burghley against trusting the Scottish king.[221] The growing certainty in 1588 that Spain was preparing to attack Britain finally forced James to commit himself, at least outwardly. Between February and July he cooperated with a general assembly on measures to combat Jesuits and other Catholics, sanctioning the formation of a "Band" that was in some ways a Scottish counterpart to the Bond of Association. It pledged Scottish Protestants "to convene and assemble ourselves publicly in arms" to resist "whatsoever foreign or intestine powers, papists and their partakers... shall arrive or arise within this island," and granted local bodies extraordinary powers to resist and imprison Catholic partisans. But it was also an emphatically

---

[218] LPL Mss. 4701, fol. 91r.   [219] Ibid., fols 91r–v.
[220] Grant, "George Gordon, Sixth Earl of Huntly," 203. The office of chamberlain belonged to the second duke of Lennox, son and heir of James's former favorite, who was under age.
[221] TNA SP59/25, fols 182, 186, and 196. Mary's partisans had distributed libels attacking James, as well as Elizabeth, the Scottish clergy, and other individuals held partly responsible for her death in the streets and pulpits of Edinburgh in March (BL Cotton Mss. Caligula CIX, fol. 227).

royalist document that described James as "a constant and inflexible professor" of the faith with "the selfsame friends and common enemies" as all British Protestants, and stipulated that any extraordinary measures were to be carried in his name and with his explicit authorization.[222] In May he led an armed force against the Catholic Lord Maxwell, who had raised a few soldiers with the intention of supporting the Spanish if they landed in Scotland. Maxwell fled and was arrested by Arran's brother, William Stewart, and detained by the king's orders, although the earl of Bothwell soon rescued him. The Scots captured a captain carrying Spanish gold destined for Catholic nobles, but Huntly managed to free him. On August 1, James issued a proclamation putting the provisions of the Band into effect by mobilizing militia forces against a possible Spanish landing.[223]

He also launched a rhetorical and literary campaign to consolidate his credentials as a godly prince. According to Calderwood, as rumors circulated concerning the Armada's preparations during the winter of 1587-8, the king began working on a new discourse on the Apocalypse. Characteristically, he kept it private until he knew the Armada had failed and then issued it from the press as *An fruitfull Mediatioun contening ane plane and facill exposition of... the Revelatioun*.[224] He followed this a year later with *Ane Meditatioun upon the first buke of the Chronicles*. Both tracts adopted the Calvinist practice of applying scriptural texts to contemporary politics; they were, in effect, closet sermons.[225] As Jane Rickard has pointed out, James thereby assumed a role analogous to that of a minister in the pulpit, as a privileged interpreter of God's word and vehicle for prophetic utterances. Prefaces by the presbyterian clergyman and former ally of the Ruthven raiders, Patrick Galloway, emphasized this parallel, hailing the king's words as evidence that he had become a "nursing father" to the godly.[226] James had managed to usurp a clerical prerogative with the Kirk's public approval, by using scriptural precedent to justify the special role of prophetic kings ruling over godly nations.

The *Fruitfull Meditatioun* unequivocally identified the pope with Antichrist, exhorting all Protestants to "concur with one another as warriors in one camp and citizens of one beleaguered city, for maintenance of the good cause God hath clad us with, and in defense of our liberties, native country and lives."[227] Although it displeased Elizabeth, who preferred that he remain single, James's marriage to Anna of Denmark in 1589 reinforced his standing as a nursing father to the godly, because Denmark was another Protestant kingdom that appeared willing to consider allying itself with Calvinist states against Spain. Reports spread that James hoped to forge an alliance not only with the Danes but other German

---

[222] Calderwood, *History*, 218-24.   [223] Ibid., 225-6.   [224] Edinburgh, 1588.
[225] Indeed, the full title of *An Fruitfull Meditatioun* describes it as being "*in forme of ane sermone.*"
[226] Rickard, *Authorship and Authority*, 72-6.
[227] *An Fruitfull Meditatioun* (1588), sigs Bii, Biii-Biv; reissued in a more Anglicized form in *The Workes of the Most High and Mighty Prince James* (1616), quotation at 80. I have been guided by the 1616 version in modernizing the language and orthography.

princes, "for the general support and maintenance of the common cause of religion," as an approving English diplomat commented.[228] In his *Meditatioun upon the first buke of the Chronicles* the king identified himself with David, who had called out the "elders," "captains," and "prophets" of Israel to battle against the Philistines. In the same way he claimed to have summoned the nobles, lairds, and captains of Scotland to resist Spanish aggression, after seeking "the special concurrence of God's ministers appointed to be spiritual rulers in his Church," the prophets of his own time.[229]

Although this last statement sounded impeccably Calvinist, in making it James tacitly reasserted his right to act as a kind of royal superintendent of the Kirk, in line with the claim of Adamson's 1585 *Declaration* that "his Majesty surely understands by the scriptures that he is the chief and principal member [of the Church], appointed by the law of God to see God glorified."[230] As Rickard points out, the rhetorical construction of James's meditations elides the distinction between his words, the pronouncements of King David and holy writ.[231] And although he wrote as king of Scotland, he explicitly referred to the struggles of the godly "in these *two* kingdoms," just as the Band had called upon Scots to combat papist enemies who should arise anywhere "*in this isle.*" To all intents and purposes this was an assertion of divine right British monarchy, articulated through a godly language that Scottish presbyterians and English puritans would find difficult to reject. But the king who issued these tracts continued to preside over a household filled with Catholics, while certainly tolerating and probably encouraging the secret contacts that Huntly and other favored courtiers maintained with Spain. Rumors of an impending political reversal that would bring Anglophobe Catholics to power in Edinburgh therefore persisted. The nominally Protestant but opportunist and turbulent earl of Bothwell added to the sense of instability by making it clear that he shared Huntly's desire to topple Maitland. At times he also joined Huntly and other nobles in advocating vengeance against England for having killed a Scottish queen.[232] As late as March 1589, the English ambassador reported that gentlemen and noblemen about the court continually pestered James with complaints against the English: "hath they not cut off your mother's head, have they not defaced your title to England, do they not keep from you your birthright...beside stirring up factions in your country." A knight in the service of the discontented earls boasted that he would soon witness "such an alteration in Scotland as was not this forty years," adding that his patrons "had twenty thousand pistols [Spanish coins] in hand and should have forty thousand more in fourteen days to serve their turns."[233]

---

[228] BL Egerton Mss. 2598, fol. 201.   [229] *Workes*, 84–5.   [230] *Declaratioun*, sig. Aiii.
[231] Rickard, *Authorship and Authority*, 69–70.   [232] TNA SP52/43/64.
[233] TNA SP52/43/26 and 43. For a continuation of the story into the 1590s see below, pp. 414–26.

James's "Alliance" with the Kirk in Scottish, English, and European Perspectives

But even without burning his bridges to Scottish and European Catholics, James made concerted efforts to cultivate a cooperative relationship with the Kirk and to present himself as a godly king. His reasons for doing so included his need to conciliate presbyterian clergy and nobles, as well as crowds in Edinburgh and other burghs, who had the ability to challenge his power. But he also almost certainly had additional motives. According to David Hume of Godscroft, after the seizure of Stirling in 1585 Angus had tried to persuade his followers that rather than continuing to threaten James with force, the best way to consolidate their victory was to appeal to him to rule as a Protestant monarch.[234] Despite his past errors, James remained "the most apparent instrument that is in Europe (and so of the world) of whom we can expect greatest good and comfort of the Church of God, as being the only king that hath been bred in the purity and sincerity of religion."[235] Moreover embracing this role would serve the king's future interests, since in England as well as Scotland the godly were now appreciably stronger than both Catholics and the bishops.[236] To secure his title to Elizabeth's throne after her death, James therefore had incentives to act as a champion of the gospel.

Although he never appears to have liked or trusted Angus, James's conduct suggests that he appreciated the merit of this argument. He must have noticed that since 1585 Leicester and his clients had significantly enhanced their military capabilities by their campaign in the Netherlands and preparations against the Armada, while English Catholics were being harassed and disarmed. At about this time intriguing hints begin to appear that he and Leicester had started to develop a collaborative relationship.[237] In 1585 Leicester paid two couriers for carrying messages to Scotland.[238] The Master of Gray claimed in November 1586 that "my Lord Leicester has sent at diverse times an offer of the propriety of the Low

---

[234] Hume, *History*, 412–27, esp. 425–6.   [235] Ibid., 426.

[236] Ibid., 426–7: "Such papists as are within the island [Britain] are of small force, and almost none of none yet in Scotland, and not so many in England as to counterpoise the Protestants. Bishops there stand by the State, not the State by them; men of mean birth, of no great riches, less following, attendance or friendship; easy to be threat to that course he pleaseth...Those that seek reformation are the strength of that country, and certainly the wisest in it, of greatest power by the people's favor, and credit in Parliament and everywhere...Gain these, gain that country."

[237] Lodge, *Illustrations* (1838) 2.332–3; Adams, "Protestant Cause," 85–8. Leicester seems to have been especially eager at this date to keep James allied with Elizabeth rather than Spain, and if possible to draw him into a Protestant League with England, the United Provinces, and Henry of Navarre. See, e.g., the minute of a letter from the Council to Leicester dated August 8, 1587 in TNA SP84/17, fol. 45v: "And concerning the advice your lordship doth very wisely deliver that the King of Scots might be wrought to be assured of her Majesty we do therein concur in opinion with your lordship and always have done and have not omitted from time to time to deliver faithfully our opinions to her Majesty in that matter, perceiving very well as your lordship noteth the practices used abroad to withdraw that king from her Majesty's amity."

[238] BL Add Mss. 78,178, fol. 36r. The messengers were identified as "Mr. Palmer" and "a Scot going into Scotland."

Countries"—an offer of sovereignty over the United Provinces—to James.[239] At about the same date Leicester told James's representative in London, Archibald Douglas, that if the king accepted the execution of his mother and remained steadfast in his Protestantism, he would assist him in succeeding Elizabeth on the throne.[240] The following May James instructed Douglas to thank Leicester for an unspecified "honest and friendly offer" that the king said he "willingly accepted." Douglas should also assure Leicester of the king's goodwill, and firm belief that the earl had played no role in his mother's death. James almost certainly knew that Leicester and Walsingham had pressed for Mary's execution but pretended otherwise.[241] In June, James told Douglas that he felt assured of the "good will" of both Leicester and Walsingham and blamed recent troubles in his relations with England on the queen and some of her other "near favorites."[242] Leicester and the king seem to have begun a correspondence at about this time, although Maitland and others at the Scottish court reportedly tried to hinder it.[243] Toward the end of the year, the earl believed that Parma was preparing to invade Scotland and that Philip II "is dealing with the king of Scots to set him on to his right against her Majesty and doth offer him men and money." This made it imperative, he argued, that Elizabeth take steps to keep James's friendship and alliance.[244]

Elizabeth refused to make concessions to James but Leicester and Walsingham may have been more willing to give him private assurances, to keep him from conspiring with Parma. Since they would have needed to keep their communications secret, probably from the queen and certainly from the public, we have no way of knowing exactly what undertakings they made. But in July 1588 James refused to believe a report that Leicester and Walsingham had worked against his interests at the English court.[245] On hearing the news of the earl's unexpected death in September he became seriously upset, telling Douglas that he had formed a "secure and perpetual friendship" with Leicester and regarded him as "the meetest and only man in England to serve his [James's] purpose." "All his [James's] resolutions thereby were altered and now he was to begin some other new course."[246] An arrangement with Leicester would almost certainly have required efforts to mend fences with English puritans and overcome the mistrust engendered by his previous dalliances with Guise and Jesuit missionaries, and his

---

[239] *State Papers*, ed. Murdin, 572, Gray to Archibald Douglas, November 10, 1586; cf. Adams, "Protestant Cause," 87.

[240] Adams, "Protestant Cause," 88.

[241] Scottish agents in London were reporting in December 1586 that although Burghley seemed flexible, Leicester and Walsingham wanted Mary killed, the opposite of what James later professed to believe. See *Warrender Papers*, ed. Cameron, 1.244 and 252.

[242] HMC Salisbury 3.261.   [243] Ibid., 261, 282, 301.

[244] *CSPF (Holland and Flanders)*, 21.3.424; HMC Salisbury 3.298.   [245] HMC Salisbury 3.334.

[246] Ibid., 354–61, R. to Archibald Douglas, September 16, 1588. The letter instructs Douglas to assess "who was like to succeed my Lord of Leicester in handling of the affairs of state ... and then ... to crave your opinion, such like as you thought metes that his Majesty should enter in dealing with in place of him." A couple of months earlier James had sent instructions to Douglas to reassure Leicester and Walsingham that he would refuse to believe reports that they opposed his interests in England (ibid., 332–41).

ongoing favor to Huntly and other Scots Catholics. Improving his relations with the Kirk and constructing himself rhetorically as a godly successor to King David and declared enemy of the Roman Antichrist served that purpose.

Within a wider European context, James's equivocal behavior invites comparison with that of other European rulers facing comparable levels of confessional polarization and violence, chief among them Henry III of France. Like James, Henry attempted to mediate between the warring religious parties, earning the scorn and distrust of fierce partisans on both sides as he did so. He also resembled James in trying to co-opt leadership of the stronger confessional camp. In the same period that James wrote his meditations on scripture and delivered harangues to auditors in Edinburgh's largest church, Henry erected both the chivalric order of the Holy Cross and a new penitential order within his court. He joined with his *mignons* to perform rituals of self-mortification, and proclaimed his determination to preserve the Catholic character of the French monarchy. His efforts failed to achieve the desired results because militant Catholicism had become too intense and politically powerful to be appeased by symbolic gestures. But his strenuous effort to make such gestures, even as he refused to break definitively with Henry of Navarre and the Huguenots, challenges comparison to James's publication of eschatological Protestant tracts while he remained good friends with Huntly. James's balancing act ultimately proved more successful than Henry's, partly because the Kirk lacked a noble champion of comparable stature to Guise, especially after Angus's premature death in August 1588. Its more astute leaders therefore saw advantages in working with the king and accepting his attempts to justify strong royal authority in broadly Calvinist language. Leicester and Walsingham evidently thought it expedient to overlook James's dalliances with British and European papists so as to co-opt him as a Protestant heir to Elizabeth.

James was therefore able to go on burnishing his credentials as a godly king while simultaneously favoring Catholic nobles and using them to maintain unofficial contacts with Spain. But his inconsistent, if not downright duplicitous, conduct remained difficult to sustain and his balancing act finally collapsed in 1596, as a later chapter will describe. By the time this happened, Leicester and Walsingham had died, the English godly had suffered a number of reverses, and the international situation had also been transformed, as England and the United Provinces allied Henry IV of France, who had converted to Rome in 1593, against Philip II. In this new situation James found it easier to adopt a more aggressive stance toward the Kirk's presbyterian leaders without losing English support. In the interim the Protestant state in England had confronted a number of additional challenges in Ireland, the Atlantic Ocean, and nearby parts of the European Continent, particularly the Low Counties. These required not only political management, espionage, and diplomacy but also aggressive military action. Before continuing our discussion of the challenge of the 1580s we need to examine the cultural attitudes and forms of social action that gave the English state its capacity to engage in commerce raiding, Irish colonization, and European war.

4
Entrepreneurial Violence and the Protestant State

Knight Errantry and Chivalric Policy

At the end of his narrative of Elizabeth's 1578 progress, Churchyard appended two poems celebrating recent voyages by Sir Humphrey Gilbert and Martin Frobisher. In a neo-chivalric idiom that anticipated Spenser and other writers of the following decade, he praised these adventurers for leaving the comforts of home to strike out in search of adventure, profit, and glory:

> I marveled how this knight could leave his lady here,
> His friends and pretty tender babes that he did hold so dear
> And take him to the seas where daily dangers are.
> Then weighed I how immortal fame was more than worldly care;
> And where great mind remains, the body's rest is small:
> For country's wealth, for private gain or glory seek we all.
> And such as marks this world, and notes the course of things,
> The weak and tickle stay of states, and great affairs of kings,
> Desires to be abroad for causes more than one.[1]

In seeking fame and wealth, Gilbert and Frobisher not only brought glory to themselves but also employment and moral improvement to the sailors who joined their expeditions:

> ...you would set men a-work,
> And call them to account in haste that close in corners lurk:
> And if they say they have no mind the lofty clouds to climb
> Yet would you wish they should see what on earth is found,
> And search the proof, and sail by art about the world so round.
> At home to tarry still but breeds gross blood and wit;
> Then better with the falcon fly than here on dunghill sit.[2]

---

[1] Nichols, *Elizabeth*, 2.228. [2] Ibid., 229.

Rather than consuming their lives in idleness and crime, these mariners have been swept up in a great adventure that benefits the entire state and commonwealth. The image Churchyard developed in describing the queen's progress, of a harmonious hierarchical society with its ancient rituals of deference, did not culminate in a celebration of domestic peace, as we might have expected, but in exhortations to revive the spirit of knight errantry through oceanic enterprise.

These verses formed part of a growing corpus of texts and pageants employing medieval romance traditions to glorify adventurous and bellicose forms of public service. For Elizabethans this chivalric imagery recalled not only the Middle Ages but also the robustly masculine rule of Henry VIII. "In the renowned reign of that noble prince," Churchyard commented in another tract:

> All chivalry was cherished, soldiers made [much] of and manhood so much esteemed that he was thought happy and most valiant that sought credit by the exercises of arms and discipline of war. Which did so animate the noble minds of men that in a manner he was counted nobody that had not been known to be at some valiant enterprise.[3]

Although historians now regard Henry's wars against France and Scotland as futile, many Elizabethans remembered them as glorious achievements. Almanacs and chronological tables recorded the capture of Boulogne in 1544 more often than any other event in his reign.[4] Some contemporaries contrasted the blunt force with which Henry had asserted his power to Elizabeth's timidity. "He might have lived in better season in the time of King Henry the eight, when princes were resolute to persist in honorable attempts," Walsingham remarked ruefully, in commenting on Sir John Perrot's Irish service: "but our age hath been given to other manner of proceeding."[5]

Historians have often depicted the romantic medievalism of Elizabeth's reign as a fantasy culture, in which, as Simon Thurley puts it, "Hercules, Abraham, King Arthur, Julius Caesar and King David all coexisted in a never-never land of chivalric values underpinned by heraldic display."[6] Some have associated

---

[3] Thomas Churchyard, *A Generall Rehearsall of Warre, called Churchyard's Choice* (London, 1579), sig. Ai.

[4] David Trim, "The Context of War and Violence in Sixteenth-Century English Society," *Journal of Early Modern History* 3 (1999): 233–55 at 247; Bernard Capp, *Astrology and the Popular Press: English Almanacs, 1500–1800* (London: Faber & Faber, 1979), 218.

[5] TNA SP63/121/50, Walsingham to John Long Archbishop of Armagh, December 1585.

[6] Simon Thurley, *Hampton Court: A Social and Architectural History* (New Haven: Yale University Press, 2003), 99–100. For a somewhat dated but still useful survey see Arthur Ferguson, *The Chivalric Tradition in Renaissance England* (Washington, DC: Folger Books, 1986); Arthur Ferguson, *The Indian Summer of English Chivalry* (Durham, NC: University of North Carolina Press, 1960); Frances Yates, "Elizabethan Chivalry: The Romance of the Accession Day Tilts," in *Astraea: The Imperial Theme in the Sixteenth Century* (London: Routledge, 1975), 88–111; and Roy Strong, "Fair England's Knights: The Accession Day Tournaments," in *The Cult of Elizabeth* (London: Thames and Hudson, 1977), 117–28.

neo-medievalism with the growth of xenophobic anti-Catholicism, especially during the great Armada War of 1588 to 1603. In this period—so the standard account goes—chivalric tropes of honor and prowess fused with militant Protestantism and incipient nationalism, to provide a bellicose cultural language for celebrating military exploits and encouraging enlistment in Elizabethan armies.[7] That language persisted into the seventeenth century in the entourage of Prince Henry and the writings of neo-Spenserian poets. But although useful as wartime propaganda, chivalric ideals and imagery had long since become outdated as a military revolution changed the nature of warfare. Elizabethan and early Jacobean medievalism amounted to what one scholar called a final "Indian summer of English chivalry."[8]

This picture undeniably contains elements of truth. The earl of Leicester, the court's leading advocate of military support for European Protestants until his death in 1588, lived in the great medieval castle of Kenilworth and entertained the queen there with a neo-Arthurian pageant.[9] His nephew, Sir Philip Sidney, participated actively in court jousts, while Leicester's stepson and political heir, Robert Devereux earl of Essex, was famously associated with neo-chivalric culture in the 1590s.[10] But while Arthurian and chivalric imagery unquestionably did provide a romantic vehicle for Protestant bellicosity, this was by no means the whole story. Donna Hamilton has identified currents of Catholic chivalric culture that also seem to have intensified in the late 1570s, among writers like Anthony Munday, who enjoyed the patronage of the Howard earls of Northampton and Arundel and other Catholic peers.[11] Munday's works included translations of Spanish romances, a reminder that chivalry was an international tradition that influenced Iberian conquistadors and French nobles as deeply as Elizabethans. We need a less insular approach to the subject that recognizes the many ways in which medieval chivalric and "modern" humanist culture not only coexisted but also combined into patterns that were simultaneously traditional and innovative.

---

[7] See, for example, Yates, "Elizabethan Chivalry"; Strong, *Cult of Elizabeth*, esp. 129–86; Roy Strong, *Henry, Prince of Wales and England's Lost Renaissance* (London: Thames and Hudson, 1986), 138–83; David Norbrook, *Poetry and Politics* (Oxford: Oxford University Press, 1984); Richard McCoy, "Old English Honour in an Evil Time: Aristocratic Principle in the 1620s," in *The Stuart Court and Europe: Essays in Politics and Political Culture*, ed. R. Malcolm Smuts (Cambridge: Cambridge University Press, 1996), 133–55; and William Hunt, "The Spectral Origins of the English Civil War," in *Reviving the English Revolution: Reflections and Elaborations on the Work of Christopher Hill*, ed. Geoff Eley and William Hunt (London: Verso, 1988), 305–32.

[8] Ferguson, *Indian Summer*.

[9] Richard Morris, "'I was never more in love with an olde howse nor never newe worke could be better bestowed': The Earl of Leicester's Remodelling of Kenilworth Castle for Queen Elizabeth I," *Antiquaries Journal* 89 (2009): 241–305.

[10] Rich McCoy, *The Rites of Knighthood: The Literature and Politics of Elizabethan Chivalry* (Berkeley: University of California Press, 1989).

[11] Donna Hamilton, *Anthony Munday and the Catholics, 1560–1633* (Aldershot: Ashgate, 2005), 11, 17, 73–112. Hamilton's view of Munday as a Catholic remains controversial but there can be no doubt about the Catholicism or church popery of his Howard patrons, and there is ample evidence that several prominent Catholic families felt a deep attachment to chivalric honor culture.

Literary scholars long ago recognized that to understand poets like Sidney and Spenser we need to pay close attention to the interplay between medieval, humanist, and Protestant elements in their work. But historians have until recently done less to explore how medieval chivalric values combined and interacted with newer currents of Renaissance thought.[12] Although Elizabethan medievalism involved playful, fantastic, and deliberately archaizing features, these qualities should not blind us to the serious role that chivalric concepts of courage, prowess, and adventure still played in the period's political culture.

The modern practice of treating military history, along with the histories of Atlantic exploration and Irish colonization, as specialized subfields, normally considered separately from mainstream political history has obscured that role. This segregation reflects the fact that in our world, war has become a state monopoly entrusted to highly trained professionals, who normally stand apart from civilian society and politics.[13] But although the professional military officer had already begun to emerge by the mid-Tudor period, military service of one kind or another still remained widely diffused within the upper ranks of society.[14] Like other Europeans, the English still regarded warfare as the natural vocation of peers and gentlemen. In both northern Europe and Italy, courtly literature in the fifteenth and early sixteenth century associated prowess and military skill with service to a prince.[15] Henry VIII's martial ambitions, followed by the wars of the mid-Tudor period, gave these ideals a practical relevance for three generations of English nobles and gentlemen seeking to advance themselves through crown service. Most peers and about half the gentlemen elected as knights of the shire in the reign saw military service under Henry VIII.[16] The campaigns of the 1540s

---

[12] Compare, for example, Mervyn James's view of chivalric honor culture as a disruptive and increasingly obsolescent code in "English Politics and the Concept of Honour, 1485–1642" and "At a Crossroads of the Political Culture: The Essex Revolt, 1601," in *Society, Politics and Culture: Studies in Early Modern England* (Cambridge: Cambridge University Press, 1986), 308–415 and 416–65 with Richard McCoy's more complex view in *Sir Philip Sidney: Rebellion in Arcadia* (New Brunswick: Rutgers University Press, 1979) and *The Rites of Knighthood*. Paul Hammer's more recent work—e.g. "Upstaging the Queen: The Earl of Essex, Francis Bacon and the Accession Day Celebration of 1595," in *The Politics of the Stuart Court Masque*, ed. David Bevington and Peter Holbrook (Cambridge: Cambridge University Press, 1998), 41–63—reinforces and extends McCoy's analysis.
[13] Although the increasing reliance on private contractors by the American government in its wars in the Middle East and on mercenaries employed by other states arguably suggests a worrying erosion of this consensus.
[14] Steven Gunn, *The English People at War in the Age of Henry VIII* (Oxford: Oxford University Press, 2020), 54–5.
[15] The Burgundian court, especially, had developed a neo-chivalric literature on noble virtue emphasizing service to the prince, described by Arjo Vanderjagt, "The Princely Culture of the Valois Dukes of Burgundy," in *Princes and Princely Culture 1450–1650*, ed. Martin Gosman, Alasdair MacDonald, and Arjo Vanderjagt (Leiden: Brill, 2003), 51–80. But French and English aristocratic culture had broadly similar emphases. The picture of honor culture developed at the start of Mervyn James, "English Politics and the Concept of Honour" derives largely from treatises in this tradition, as the footnotes show. Castiglione also stressed the importance of service in war in his famous *Book of the Courtier*.
[16] Gunn, *English People at War*, 53–4.

and 1550s remained living memories for older Elizabethans. Most of the great families of the Elizabethan court, including the Dudleys, Sidneys, Radcliffes, Russells, Herberts, and Howards, had played conspicuous roles in Tudor wars against France and Scotland, while several had risen primarily through military service. Tales of exploits during their campaigns must have passed from generation to generation as family folklore.[17] In a few cases competition and jealousy over military commands contributed to bitter rivalries, like the long-standing feud between the Dudleys and the senior Howard line, which dated back to Henry VIII's campaigns in Normandy in the 1540s.[18] Even during the relatively peaceful first half of Elizabeth's reign, campaigns in Scotland and Normandy in the 1560s, the Northern Rebellion of 1569, and the chronic problem of suppressing Irish rebellions kept a tradition of military service alive, which Churchyard celebrated it in his massive 1579 compendium, *The Generall Rehearsall of Warre*.[19]

Court culture remained saturated with chivalric rituals and imagery celebrating martial service to the crown. Although the tournament may have suffered a relative decline in the reigns of Edward VI and Mary, it revived under Elizabeth and flourished in the late 1570s.[20] John Casimir's visit to London in early 1579 led to a series of "great tiltings... barriers and other shows," which the young earl of Essex delayed his return to Cambridge to witness.[21] The Anjou courtship had an even greater impact. Even before Anjou's arrival the courtly love tradition had gained a new lease on life in England, when the earl of Oxford initiated a fashion for Petrarchan love sonnets devoted to the queen, which other courtiers promptly imitated. Leicester's Kenilworth Entertainment of 1577 employed Arthurian imagery to flatter and woo Elizabeth.[22] In the late 1570s Petrarchan conceits fused with chivalric concepts of courtly love to provide a language that expressed

---

[17] Too little attention has been paid to the process through which noble families—including those freshly ennobled—created dynastic legends. Three suggestive studies are W. J. Sessions, *Henry Howard, the Poet Earl of Surrey: A Life* (Oxford: Oxford University Press, 1999); *Patronage, Culture and Power: The Early Cecils 1558–1612*, ed. Pauline Croft (New Haven and London: Yale University Press, 2002); and Michael Brennan, *The Sidneys of Penshurst and the Monarchy, 1500–1700* (Aldershot: Ashgate, 2006). For a suggestive study of how a sense of dynastic tradition may have been inculcated in the young, see Sheila ffolliot, "The Italian 'Training' of Catherine de Medici: Portraits as Dynastic Narrative," in *Queens and the Transmission of Political Culture: The Case of Early Modern France*, ed. Melinda Gough and R. Malcolm Smuts, Special Issue of *The Court Historian* 10 (2005): 25–36.

[18] This point is effectively brought out with reference to the rivalry between the Howards and Dudleys in W. A. Sessions, *Henry Howard, the Poet Earl of Surrey: A Life* (Oxford: Oxford University Press, 1999), esp. chapters 11 and 12.

[19] David Trim, "Fighting 'Jacob's Wars'. The Employment of English and Welsh Mercenaries in the European Wars of Religion: France and the Netherlands, 1562–1610," unpublished University of London PhD thesis, 2001, traces this engagement in detail.

[20] Alan Young, *Tudor and Jacobean Tournaments* (London: George Philip, 1987) argues for a decline. The subject should perhaps be revisited.

[21] Folger Shakespeare Library Mss. La243, R. Broughton to R. Bagot, February 1, 1579.

[22] For Oxford and Petrarchanism see Steven May, *Elizabethan Courtier Poets: The Poems in their Contexts* (Columbia: University of Missouri Press, 1991), 52 and passim; a more general treatment of erotic themes in Tudor culture is Katherine Bates, *The Rhetoric of Courtship* (Cambridge: Cambridge University Press, 1992).

not only devotion to the queen but also the ambition of men as different as Casimir, Anjou, and Leicester to serve her by leading troops into battle. The public Accession Day Jousts, which seem to have begun about this time, expressed the same impulse.[23]

Catholic and church-papist peers participated as eagerly as Protestants in this chivalric cult. A broadsheet produced on behalf of Philip Howard earl of Arundel for a joust of 1581, of which a copy survives in the Folger Shakespeare Library, provides a glimpse into the romantic world of Elizabethan jousting. Callophisus, as Arundel styled himself, "proclaimed by the sound of trumpet and a herald," that he would defend against all comers the assertion that his mistress, "for beauty of her face and the grace of her person the most perfect creature that ever...the eye of man beheld," was so dazzling that "it was impossible for any other whosoever to abide the beams of his mistress's look."[24] For the tournament Arundel appeared with two ushers, four pages, and twenty richly liveried followers.[25] This was not mere histrionic display in an age when lords still raised armies by mobilizing their territorial followings. Spectators would have known that Arundel's jousting partners had the potential to become recruiting agents and captains of companies serving under his banner.[26]

The share of the peerage with direct military experience declined under Elizabeth to a low of 36 percent around 1600, before rising again in the early seventeenth century.[27] But even peers and gentlemen who did not serve directly in foreign wars made contributions by helping to guard the borders or acting as lord lieutenants, deputy lieutenants, and militia captains in their counties.[28] Participation in foreign wars also declined among the yeomanry and prosperous townsmen, who in the late Elizabethan period were permitted to pay substitutes to do their military service for them.[29] During the war with Spain and the Nine Years War in Ireland the crown had to fill its armies by conscripting mostly unwilling men, often landless laborers and sometimes vagabonds. But more prosperous tenants and tradesmen continued to serve in county and urban militias, and over the course of the reign thousands of soldiers enlisted voluntarily, either in

---

[23] Strong, "Fair England's Knights"; Yates, "Elizabethan Chivalry"; David Cressy, *Bonfires and Bells* (Berkeley: University of California Press, 1989), 50–7. The fact that Leicester and Anjou occupied somewhat analogous positions, as suitors for the queen's hand in marriage who also wanted her to finance their military ambitions, may have helped establish an equation between erotic courtship and military service, employing the language of the tournament and medieval courtly love traditions.
[24] Philip Howard earl of Arundel, *Callophisus* (1581).   [25] Nichols, *Elizabeth*, 2.315–16.
[26] Cf. Simon Adams, "A Puritan Crusade? The Composition of the Earl of Leicester's Expedition to the Netherlands, 1585–6," in *Leicester and the Court: Essays on Elizabethan Politics* (Manchester: Manchester University Press, 2002), 176–95.
[27] Roger Manning, *Swordsmen: The Martial Ethos of the Three Kingdoms* (Oxford: Oxford University Press, 2003), 28–9. Trim, "Fighting 'Jacob's Wars'," gives the somewhat lower figure of eighteen peers, or about a quarter of the total, as having significant military experience under Elizabeth.
[28] Gunn, *English People at War*, 71.
[29] Ibid., 103.

the queen's armies or in "mercenary" companies that went abroad to fight for the Huguenots or Dutch. The crown tacitly encouraged these volunteers, both to support co-religionist allies on the Continent without openly going to war on their behalf, and as a way of maintaining a supply of veteran soldiers and officers even while the realm remained at peace.[30] On one occasion, according to the Huguenot soldier Agrippa d'Aubigné, Elizabeth personally helped select the members of a volunteer company.[31]

Although little direct evidence survives as to why young men joined these companies, several motivations must have played a role. A significant minority of recruits were lesser gentlemen or younger sons, who would have shared the chivalric values of greater landowners, without having comparable opportunities in civilian life.[32] Others were household servants or tenants of captains, military patrons, or gentlemen in the ranks, inspired by personal loyalty. The idea that tenants had a duty to fight for their lords remained alive in the period, and in some districts, leases required tenants to provide military service.[33] The earl of Shrewsbury recruited a guard to keep watch over Mary Stuart from among his tenants, arming them at his own expense. Sir Ralph Sadler saw these men as much more reliable than a force recruited by other methods, and when it became necessary to replace them he suggested recruiting some of the *queen's* tenants, whom he thought would prove especially loyal.[34] Young men lacking opportunities in civilian life also enlisted as volunteers, attracted by the prospect of regular pay and adventure. Religious convictions undoubtedly inspired some soldiers, while an emphasis on valor and combativeness in popular culture must also have helped recruitment. Alexandra Shepard's study of court records in seventeenth-century Cambridge has uncovered a subculture among male adolescents of middling rank that emphasized the importance of defending personal honor by fisticuffs.[35] English society associated physical aggressiveness, courage, and even a degree of destructiveness with youthful masculinity. Oral traditions about English prowess in medieval and early Tudor wars probably also helped sustain an emphasis on valor and combativeness even among fairly humble strata of the male population. English troops earned a reputation for ferocity on European battlefields, suggesting that military values had penetrated well beyond the ranks of the gentry.[36]

Although rooted in a vernacular culture of medieval origins, this emphasis on physical combat, aggressive self-assertion, and personal loyalty was never entirely

---

[30] David Trim, "The 'Secret War' of Elizabeth: England and the Huguenots during the Early Wars of Religion, 1562–1577," *Proceedings of the Huguenot Society of Great Britain and Ireland* 27 (1999): 189–99; Trim, "Fighting 'Jacob's Wars'."
[31] Trim, "Fighting 'Jacob's Wars'," 107–8.   [32] Ibid., 255–9.
[33] Ibid., 255.   [34] BL Add. Mss. 33,594, fols 30, 80r, 157v.
[35] Alexandra Shepard, *Meanings of Manhood in Early Modern England* (Oxford: Oxford University Press, 2003), esp. chapters 4 and 5.
[36] For a suggestive analysis see Trim, "War and Violence."

static and archaic. Protestant concepts of holy warfare drawn from the Bible supplemented chivalric emphasis on courage and valor, while studies of ancient warfare and observations of contemporary military practices both reinforced and modified older medieval ideas. As warfare became more specialized in the sixteenth century, commanders of troops needed to master an increasing body of technical skills, requiring them to supplement physical prowess with up-to-date learning. As William Segar put it, "very rarely doth any man excel in arms that is utterly ignorant of good letters, for what man unlearned can conceive the ordering and disposing of men in marching, in camping and fighting without arithmetic? Or who can comprehend the ingenious fortifications or instruments apt for offence or defense of towns or passing of waters, unless he hath knowledge of geometry."[37] Although professional captains were recognized as the real experts in modern warfare, many peers and gentry felt the need to acquire some proficiency in the emerging science of war.

In a youthful treatise advocating the establishment of an academy for training young gentlemen, Sir Humphrey Gilbert referred to the fusion of modern knowledge with medieval warrior ideals as "chivalric policy and philosophy."[38] The curriculum he proposed began with instruction in Greek, Latin, and Hebrew, as well as rhetoric, logic, and practice in the "making of orations." It then moved on to the study of both civil and military "policy," and specific forms of specialized knowledge that would equip gentlemen to serve their country in both war and peace. These fields included mathematics and its application to the design of fortifications and use of artillery; cosmography, navigation, the drawing of maps and sea charts, along with methods of managing a ship; medicine and natural philosophy; the handling of weapons; modern languages; heraldry; basic instruction in divinity; and, almost as an afterthought, some grounding in both civil and common law.

Although this impossibly ambitious project never got off the ground, abundant evidence points to the seriousness with which Elizabethans sought to employ academic learning—sometimes of a very innovative kind—as an aid to warfare and maritime enterprises. Gilbert's friend Richard Grenville departed on a voyage in 1580 with his ship's cabin "so well furnished and stored with books, sea cards and other commodities as if he were at court."[39] The sea cards and probably some of the books in this floating library would likely have proven useful as aids to navigation, and Grenville may well have tried to add to the store of knowledge they contained as he explored previously uncharted waters. He conceived his voyage as an act not only of nautical but also intellectual exploration: an exercise in "chivalric policy."

---

[37] William Segar, *Honor Militarie and Civil* (1602), 200–1.
[38] *Queen Elizabeth's Academy*, ed. F. J. Furnival (London, 1869), 12.
[39] TNA SP63/74/58 Nicholas White to Walsingham, June 22, 1580.

Military Treatises

By the Elizabethan period a substantial body of literature had developed on the arts of war that included both translations of continental treatises and original works by English captains and amateur enthusiasts. Close examination of these tracts reveals several common themes, especially concerning the critical role of disciplined military force in upholding civil societies. The treatises consistently sought to justify military life as religious and honorable, in opposition to unnamed contemporaries who scorned soldiering as a "vile and damnable occupation." Writers usually attributed this negative attitude to "the vulgar multitude," whose "beastly" speeches "affirm...that the worst sort of men (and such as for the vileness of their conditions the earth is not able to sustain) are fit for the wars, and accordingly do call out the refuse of the people to be soldiers."[40] Parish officers charged with pressing soldiers came in for special abuse, for allegedly filling their quotas with the poorest and most dissolute conscripts available. "In England when service happeneth we disburden the prisons of thieves, we rob the taverns and alehouses of tosspots and ruffians, we scour both town and country of rogues and vagabonds," Barnaby Rich complained: "and is not a captain that is furnished with such company like to do great service and to keep them in good discipline?"[41] A few writers acknowledged that the problem lay not just with petty constables but people further up the social scale. "He that will rather spend a hundred pounds in building a banqueting house in his garden than a hundred shillings in a subsidy to aid the charges of his prince...is no lover of arms," Gates asserted.[42]

Recent work has qualified the once prevalent assumption that Elizabethan armies consisted overwhelmingly of a refuse population of vagrants and misfits, like those recruited by Shakespeare's Justice Shallow.[43] But it is clear that this pejorative image of common soldiers already existed in the period. Even Gates, an apologist for the military profession, admitted that some men went to war "more to spoil than to serve," engaging in "swearing, drunkenness, shameless fornication, dicing and thievery" before returning home "corrupted with all manner of evils" as "a venomous brood to their native country."[44] When it suited her purposes Elizabeth pretended to share this bias. She told Mendoza in 1578 that since the English soldiers who had gone to serve in Flanders "were people of small account, they would take good care not to return to her country, and they were not of sufficient importance for her to order them to do so."[45] Since she was trying to dissimulate her secret encouragement of these volunteers, we should take her

---

[40] Geffrey Gates, *The defence of the miltarie profession* (1579), 43 and 18.
[41] Barnaby Rich, *A Path-Way to military practice* (1589).   [42] Gates, *Militarie profession*, 46.
[43] Trim, "Fighting 'Jacob's Wars'," 38 and passim.
[44] Gates, *Militarie profession*, 43.   [45] *CSPSp* 2.600.

words with a large dose of salt. But she must have calculated that they would seem credible because they reflected a widespread prejudice.

The military theorists responded by arguing that when properly pursued, a soldier's vocation was not only honorable but godly. Gates conceded that gentlemen had a right to disapprove of debauched soldiers but insisted that they had a duty to demonstrate their respect for military virtue by practicing the use of arms themselves, seeking the company of men able to instruct them in warfare, honoring good soldiers and sponsoring public shows of military proficiency, especially when the queen visited their neighborhoods.[46] Rich agreed: "it is the soldiers that protecteth the prince in his seat, it is the soldier that defendeth the divine in his pulpit, it is the soldier that upholdeth the judge in his place of justice, it is the soldier, as Varo saith that resisteth the outward force of enemies, that represseth domestical seditions, and defendeth the liberty of the subject. If his service be then so beneficial to all, O what pity he is not better considered of."[47] Gentlemen should set examples through exercises that "prepareth the body to hardiness and the mind to courageousness."[48] Churchyard approvingly mentioned the Roman practice of awarding soldiers who distinguished themselves in battle with crowns of leaves, which entitled them to public deference even from members of the Senate.[49] This custom helped explain Rome's spectacular victories, he thought. By publishing an account of the careers of English captains who had served in Irish and European wars since the reign of Henry VIII, he hoped to win them similar recognition.[50]

Nearly all the Elizabethan military apologists described warfare as a religious vocation, sanctioned by both Old and New Testaments. In the time of Israel, Gates wrote, God's "sanctuary" could not be redeemed from Antichrist "till the Lord had provided his army and appointed his chieftains of courage, faith and military prudence, fit for the wars of Jacob." Lest anyone miss the intended application, he immediately added: "as were Frederick, John and Maurice the renowned princes in honor, chivalry and virtues, dukes of Saxony" who defended Luther's Reformation.[51] David Trim has shown how Gates developed a systematic analogy between "Jacob's wars"—meaning Israel's wars in the Old Testament—and the campaigns in which English volunteers fought to defend continental reformed churches, particularly in the Netherlands.[52] This implied a concept of Protestant nationhood transcending political borders. Churchyard similarly exhorted his readers to "look in the scriptures and search from the death of Abel, coming down orderly to the birth of Christ and see whether soldiers were made of

---

[46] Gates, *Militarie profession*, 44.   [47] Rich, *Path-Way*, sig. B2.
[48] Barnaby Rich, *Allarme to England* (1572), sig. Gi v.
[49] Churchyard, *Rehearsall of Warre* (1579), sig. Oiii r.
[50] Ibid., passim.   [51] Gates, *Militarie profession*, 42.
[52] David Trim, "Calvinist Internationalism and the English Officer Corps, 1562–1642," *History Compass* 4 (2006): 1024–48.

or no."⁵³ Rich provided a string of scriptural precedents to show "that wars have been acceptable before the majesty of God and sometimes more available [acceptable] than peace."⁵⁴ A prayer for the army the earl of Leicester led to the Netherlands in 1585 repeats this emphasis: "Grant that as Joshua overcame Amalech that sought to hinder the children of Israel... that our noble counselor, valiant soldier and faithful servant to her Majesty may prevail and vanquish thy enemies... thou hast made England a chosen shaft, and put him in thy quiver."⁵⁵

While accumulating scriptural precedents for holy wars, these writers simultaneously advanced a more pointed Augustinian argument that human depravity required the exercise of military violence. "When preaching, process, plea or persuasion cannot prevail in reforming the outrages and evils of the wicked," Gates wrote, "then must the sword of violence be put in execution by the hands of them that are able and skillful."⁵⁶ "The first foundation and use of arms," he thought, "was erected of necessity to restrain and repress the violent cruelty and beastly disorder of men and to establish social peace and justice."⁵⁷ Rich agreed: "Christ would not that the state of civil policy should be overthrown but rather established and confirmed, and therefore as he hath not wrested the sword out of the hand of a magistrate, so neither would he have a soldier to want his weapon."⁵⁸ Civic peace required "the soldier clad in armor," ever ready to repel "with dint of sword" threats to the commonwealth. "It is the sins of the people that draweth the soldier's sword, and when it pleaseth the almighty to punish by war all the things upon the earth are pressed to fight under his banner, yea even the ambitiousness of princes, to punish themselves, one by another."⁵⁹ Gates believed that in extreme cases armies must be prepared to exterminate a "disordered multitude... that peace and civil justice may possess and rule the land."⁶⁰ He also justified wars against tyrants, "for the Lord God in his justice hateth tyranny and destroyeth tyrants from the face of the earth."⁶¹ Gates conceded that God sometimes allowed military despotism to punish sinful peoples. This explained the Muslim conquests of the "bastard Christians" who had allowed the Church of Constantine to become "suffocated with heresies and ruinated with persecutions... wherein the Lord hath showed forth... his intolerable wrath." The churches of the West should take warning.⁶² Peace and prosperity may also lead to destruction since, "when the Lord meaneth to plague a wicked nation for sin and to translate them to the power

---

⁵³ Churchyard, *Rehearsall of Warre*, Mi v.   ⁵⁴ *Allarme* Aii v.
⁵⁵ *A most necessary and godly prayer for the preservation of the Earl of Leicester* (1585). The prayer continues in eschatological language: "And forasmuch (O Lord) as this discord abroad reacheth almost to the throat of our Church and commonweal and that our enemies, O Lord, especially those that have the mark of Antichrist seek to build like the moth in another man's possession and garment, and seek to swallow up thy people as a grave. Make O Lord (we pray thee) a hedge about us and thy house and let thy Church be like Solomon's bed, about which there was always a watch, and let the fruit of the English Church be meat unto others and the leaf thereof medicinal to thy afflicted and scattered people."
⁵⁶ Gates, *Militarie profession*, 10.   ⁵⁷ Ibid., 36.   ⁵⁸ *Alarme*, sig. Aiiii v.
⁵⁹ Barnaby Rich, *Faults, Faults, Nothing but Faults* (London, 1606), 48.
⁶⁰ Gates, *Militarie profession*, 10.   ⁶¹ Ibid., 27.   ⁶² Ibid., 17–13.

and scepter of another nation, then he filleth them with the fatness of the earth, and giveth them peace that they may wax idle in idleness, and become of dull wits, slow of courage, weak handed and feeble kneed that when the soldier cometh they may in all points be unfurnished of warlike prowess."[63]

Sometimes a secular emphasis on civic discipline and virtue replaced or supplemented the emphasis on godliness. "Christ would not that the state of civil policy should be overthrown but rather established and confirmed," Rich insisted: "and therefore as he hath not wrested the sword out of the hand of a magistrate, so neither would he have a soldier to want his weapon."[64] Anna Bryson has shown that the concept of civility or "civil conversation" percolated slowly into sixteenth-century England, largely through continental treatises on education and manners by writers like Erasmus and Stefano Guazzo.[65] Modern historians have sometimes associated the spread of this ideal with the decline of older violent habits, but Markku Peltonen has demonstrated that this is a mistake. The Italianate concept of civil manners developed in tandem with the code of the duel, an early modern innovation unknown to medieval society.[66] What distinguished civility from the older chivalric code was not a rejection of violence but a much stronger emphasis on concepts of civil ordering, associated with the Latin word *civilitas*. This concept referred both to the arts of government and to self-governance and "civil" behavior, which in turn depended on a highly developed sense of personal dignity that made people especially sensitive to insult. That sensitivity necessitated more elaborate codes of civil manners, to prevent needless offense. Duels flourished within this system as the ultimate means of exacting retribution against those who violated its rules. What changed as societies moved from a condition of barbarity to civility was therefore less the prevalence of violence than the manner in which men employed it. Instead of engaging in casual and sporadic brutality, they learned to fight only under specific circumstances and in highly structured ways.[67]

If on an individual level this meant fighting duels, the military treatises suggest that in wider contexts it required disciplined armies capable of reacting with lethal efficiency to the incivility of foreign tyrants and domestic rebels. Rich and Gates both contrasted soldiering with the law, as complementary professions needed to maintain justice, while insisting that soldiers ultimately deserved more credit than lawyers, because they provided the final line of defense against civic chaos.[68] An anonymous tract of 1579 dedicated to Francis Walsingham, revealingly entitled *Of Cyvile and Uncyvile Life*, described only three professions worthy of a gentleman:

---

[63] Ibid., 20–1.   [64] *Allarme*, sig. Aiiii v.
[65] Anna Bryson, *From Courtesy to Civility: Changing Codes of Conduct in Early Modern England* (Oxford: Clarendon Press, 1998).
[66] Markku Peltonen, *The Duel in Early Modern England: Civility, Politeness and Honour* (Cambridge: Cambridge University Press, 2003).
[67] Bryson, *Courtesy to Civility*, 49–51.   [68] Gates, *Militarie profession*, 10.

the common law, needed for domestic government in time of peace, the civil law, for use in diplomacy, and military affairs.

It followed from these arguments not only that "the soldier ought... to be a civil man, to fear God, to live orderly in his degree,"[69] but that an army should function as a model of civic discipline. "As the armed host is the extreme remedy to chastise and repress insolency," Gates wrote, "so should the regiment of war be free from the same and every vice in a soldier strongly bridled and extremely punished... For where corruption and liberty is suffered in a soldier, there is the confusion and shame of arms."[70] If armies consist of poor and dissolute men, "in the day of tumult the armed servant will be a commander of his unarmed master."[71] Rich also stressed that soldiers must be "honest, zealous in religion," while Leonard Digges observed that "of all other the ruffian that liveth idly and seeketh the wars only in hope of spoil is most unfit to make a soldier, yea by experience it is commonly seen that they are the only cause of mutinies, and one such is able to disorder and corrupt a whole band."[72] In addition to obeying the religious and moral codes that applied to all men in civil societies, soldiers needed to undertake extraordinary exertions. A captain must keep his men busy, Digges insisted, "making them sometimes to shoot for wagers with the harquebus, sometimes to wrestle, to run and leap in their armor, to march in array, to cast themselves in a ring, to retire in order, and marching suddenly to stand, and such like... both to delight and also make his soldiers perfect, and to far better spend their time than in foul lewd pastimes."[73] Troops must learn to march and maneuver in formation "to the sound of the drum... no less assuredly than men are taught to dance by the sound of musical instruments." Even intricate formations unsuited to battle can be useful in training, he insisted, since they teach bands of soldiers to move as one body. By mastering these movements raw recruits will become competent soldiers, he claimed, whereas even veterans of many wars who have not mastered the art of maneuvering in formation should be regarded as "untrained soldiers and raw bands."[74]

Although not everyone agreed with Digges in placing more emphasis on parade ground drills than combat experience, his advice reflected the evolution of military tactics in the period, partly under the influence of Greek and Roman models.[75] Without going into the same level of detail, other writers agreed on the importance of rigorous training. "There is nothing more rather to incite an enemy than where he findeth sloth and negligence," Rich commented: "more armies have been overthrown through want of skill than either from want of strength or courage."

---

[69] T. P., *The Knowledge and Conduct of War* (1578), fol. 19.   [70] Gates, *Militarie profession*, 37.
[71] *Allarme*, sig. Iiiii v; Gates, *Militarie profession*, 52.
[72] *An arithmeticall, militare treatise named Stratioticis* (London, 1579), 81.
[73] Ibid., 94.   [74] Ibid., 103.
[75] Geoffrey Parker, *The Military Revolution: Military Innovation and the Rise of the West, 1500–1800* (Cambridge: Cambridge University Press, 1988), 20–3.

An army of 10,000 men kept in good order will normally outperform one three times its size that lacks discipline.[76] The second earl of Essex made an even stronger argument. "An army may consist as well of too great as too small a number. For an army or body politic as well as a natural may be so huge *ut magnitudine laboret*. Such ponderous and unwieldy bodies are burdensome to themselves and cannot be kept in order and nothing can last that cannot be governed." A troop of 3,000 men able to maneuver as one will therefore be able "to fight with any army in the world," Essex claimed, and easily overmaster an untrained force many times its size.[77]

Even more than private soldiers, officers needed an exceptionally high level of moral integrity and set of specialized skills. An anonymous treatise argued that a general needed to display a "fatherly mind and regard" not only for the "general and public weal" of his army but "the state and necessities of private persons" who belonged to it.[78] A manuscript memorandum by a certain Captain Milford pointed out that in addition to overseeing the training and conduct of his troops, a general needed to manage the "emulation and confusion" that inevitably arose from rivalries among even "the best leaders and captains."[79] Several writers emphasized the importance of officers setting examples of virtue. "A general therefore must especially both love and fear God," Rich argued; "he must not be without learned preachers and ministers of God's word, which must instruct and teach the army."[80] A "grave and wise general," Digges insisted, "is able to change the nature and fortune of a whole nation." As evidence he pointed to the success of the prince of Orange in turning Flemings, a people known for "riches and delicate life" and reputedly lacking in valor, into soldiers that had on occasion "given the famous Spaniards the foil."[81] Along with virtue and courage, a general had to master requisite bodies of knowledge.[82] According to Rich he needed not only skill in directing troops in battle but experience with munitions and provisions, the administrative capacity to keep track of his men's wages, food, and weapons, and sufficient familiarity with the methods of "engineers, armorers, carpenters, smiths, masons and pioneers" to select and supervise them.[83] Even the hygienic arrangements of an encampment needed proper oversight by a designated provost.[84] Several writers insisted on the importance of mathematics, among them John Dee, Henry Savile, and Leonard Digges, who illustrated his point with a series of puzzles that might confront officers as they worked out the dimensions of a camp, calculated the amount of powder required by various artillery pieces, assigned rations or determined how many soldiers were needed for a particular formation. A grounding in military histories, especially of Roman warfare, was

---

[76] *Faults*, fol. 50v.　　[77] BL Add Mss. 74,287, fol. 160v.
[78] T. P., *Knowledge and Conduct of War*, sig. 10.
[79] SRO D593/s/4/12/20. The memorandum is undated but appears to be from the late 1580s.
[80] Rich, *Path-Way*, sig. Ei.　　[81] *Stratioticis*, 147.
[82] Ibid.　　[83] *Path-Way*, sig. E2v.　　[84] Ibid., sig. C3v.

also deemed essential. Digges sprinkled Roman examples through his treatise, while in the 1590s several works of classical translation focused attention on military problems. Henry Savile added an appendix on Roman warfare to his 1592 translation of Tacitus's *Histories* and *Agricola*,[85] while eight years later Sir Clement Edmondes published his *Observations upon the First Five Books of Caesar's Commentaries, setting forth the practice of the art military in the time of the Roman Empire*, a work that went through three editions in nine years. The period also saw the printing in translation of military manuals by Italian, French, and Spanish experts.[86]

Most writers insisted, however, that no amount of private study and drill compensated for lack of combat experience. "The host of an unskillful multitude in arms is before an army of experimented warriors as a flock of sheep before a troop of wolves," Gates commented,[87] while Rich scathingly dismissed amateur captains who thought a little private study equipped them to lead armies. If ordinary trades required an apprenticeship of seven years, he asked, why should anyone think it possible to master the art of war without long practice?[88] The most systematic treatises in English on the need for experienced captains and soldiers were written by the professional soldier Roger Williams. Although some people wrongly think that victory depends on numerical superiority, he argued, in truth "the wars consist altogether in good chiefs and experimented soldiers, and ever did since the world began to this hour." The citizens of Paris, Ghent, and Antwerp thought they could form adequate militias by drilling civilians and selecting officers well-read in military treatises, "but when they were tried with the fury of great executioners, their wars proved but May games."[89] Even when commanded by an accomplished general, an army lacking experienced captains will founder like "a navy in a tempest without masters or pilots."[90]

Military success will therefore normally fall to the country that has maintained an army in continuous action for the longest time, and Williams had no doubt that in his own age this was Spain. The Army of Flanders "hath been in action unbroken since Charles the fifth his troubles against the Germans," and now represented a pattern that others should imitate.[91] "A camp continually maintained in action," he explained, "is like an university continually in exercises; when famous scholars die as good or better step in their places. Especially in armies,

---

[85] Henry Savile, *The End of Nero and Beginning of Galba* (1592).
[86] Giorlamo Cataneo, *Most briefe tables to know briefly how many footmen... go to the making of a just battaile* (London, 1588); Raimond de Beccarie de Pavie, Baron de Fourquevaux, *Instructions for the warres, amply, learnedly and politiquely, discoursing the method of militarie discipline*, trans. Paul Ive (London, 1589); Luis Gutierrez de la Vega, *A compendious treatise entitled, De re militari* (London, 1582); Jacques Hurrault, *Politicke, moral and martial discourses* (London, 1595); François de la Noue, *The Politicke and militarie discourses of Lord de la Noue* (London, 1587); Niccolò Machiavelli, *The arte of warre* (London, 1588); Bernardino de Mendoza, *Theorique and practise of warre* (London, 1597); Francisco de Valdez, *The segieant maijor* (London, 1590).
[87] Gates, *Miltarie profession*, 45. [88] *Allarme*, sig. Iii.
[89] *The Works of Sir Roger Williams*, ed. John Evans (Oxford: Clarendon Press, 1972), 4.
[90] Ibid., 10–11. [91] Ibid., 14–15.

where there be every day new inventions, stratagems of wars, change of weapons, munition and all sort of engines newly invented and corrected daily," continuity will produce gradual cumulative improvements for which no adequate substitute exists.[92] Some modern discussions have argued that true military professionalism only developed with the establishment of standing armies and established procedures for promotion through merit.[93] Williams's analysis foreshadows this view, treating the Spanish army as a laboratory for the invention of superior military techniques, in which promotion depended more on experience and merit than inherited rank.

Although with different emphases, these treatises invariably depicted armies as social microcosms requiring an extraordinary level of organization and discipline. This concept appears even in some of the mediocre verse published to celebrate the English muster at Tilbury as the Armada sailed up the Channel:

> Each Captain had his colours brave,
> Set over his tent in wind to wave,
> With them their officers they have,
> To serve the Queen of England.
> The other Lodgings had their sign,
> For soldiers where to sup and dine,
> And for to sleep, with orders fine,
> In Tilsbury Camp in England.
> And victualing booths, there plenty were,
> Where they sold meat, bread, cheese and beer
> One should have been hanged for selling too dear
> In Tilsbury Camp in England.[94]

Everyone and everything in its designated place, and summary execution for those who broke victualing regulations: such was the ideal.

Conditions of Military Recruitment and Service

At least in theory. In practice the strong prescriptive emphasis on order and discipline was needed precisely because actual conditions of military service so

---

[92] Ibid., 27; cf. 33: "Although the ground of ancient discipline is the most worthiest and most famous, notwithstanding, by reason of fortifications, stratagems, engines, arming with munition, the discipline is greatly altered; the which we must follow and be directed as it is now: otherwise we shall repent it too late."

[93] See the editor's introduction to David Trim, ed., *The Chivalric Ethos and the Development of Military Professionalism* (Leiden: Brill, 2003), esp. 8–9.

[94] *A joyful song of the royall receiving of the Queenes most excellent Maiestie into her highnesse campe at Tilsburie* (London, 1589), n.p.

often threatened to undermine both qualities. Armies needed quality recruits and effective leaders in order to have any chance of maintaining their cohesion. Although the crown resorted to conscription to flesh out its armies for Ireland and for service on the Continent after 1586, many Elizabethan soldiers, including virtually all serving in Dutch and Huguenot armies, enlisted voluntarily.[95] Under Henry VIII the court nobility and gentlemen of the privy chamber provided the core elements of English campaigns by summoning their retainers, levying their tenants, and organizing recruitment around their estates.[96] Although with some erosion, this system essentially survived into Elizabeth's reign. Leicester acted as the court's premier military patron, assisted by his brother Ambrose Dudley earl of Warwick, the queen's master of ordnance, and other Protestant landowners.[97] Leicester maintained a private arsenal in Kenilworth Castle, while his extensive landholdings in the west midlands and parts of Wales gave him a large base of tenants, some of whom were required to serve him as soldiers by their leases. He raised 400 of his tenants for the army he led to the Netherlands in 1585. His network of clients among the gentry further extended his ability to raise significant bodies of troops, as became evident in the mobilization of his army.[98] Even before this date, Leicester's brother-in-law, Sir Henry Sidney, drew heavily on military clients of the Dudley family, including some that had served under Leicester's father in campaigns in France, to enlarge the queen's Irish army in the 1570s.[99] Other major Protestant peers with ties to the court, notably the earls of Rutland, Bedford, and Pembroke, also raised volunteer companies. Three hundred English soldiers who went to fight in Flanders in the early 1570s wore Pembroke's livery colors of blue and red, while two of the most distinguished captains, Sir Roger Williams and Thomas Morgan, seem to have begun their careers as soldiers Pembroke recruited in Wales.[100] The Irish soldier and crown servant Nicholas

---

[95] The fullest discussion is Trim, "Fighting 'Jacob's Wars'," esp. 226–35. For example, Trim calculates (227) that in 1585, 40 percent of the troops in the queen's army sent to the Netherlands but 90 percent of the slightly larger contingent of English serving under Dutch pay were volunteers; see also his table on 228.

[96] David Starkey, "Intimacy and Innovation: The Rise of the Privy Chamber, 1485–1547," in *The English Court from the Wars of the Roses to the Civil War*, ed. David Starkey et al. (London: Longman, 1987), 71–118 at 86–91. Cf. Gunn, *English People at War*, esp. 56–61.

[97] In addition to the sources listed below, Trim, "Fighting 'Jacob's Wars'," chapters 7 and 8 provides a systematic discussion.

[98] Below, pp. 299–300; Adams, "Puritan Crusade?" See also in the same volume (*Leicester and the Court*), "The Dudley Clientele, 1553–63," 151–75, "The Gentry of North Wales and the Earl of Leicester's Expedition to the Netherlands, 1585–6," 235–52, and "'Because I am of that Countrye & Mynde to Plant Myself there': Robert Dudley, Earl of Leicester and the West Midlands," 310–63.

[99] Nicholas Canny, *The Elizabethan Conquest of Ireland: A Pattern Established, 1567–76* (Hassocks: Harvester, 1976), 73–5.

[100] Trim, "Fighting 'Jacob's Wars'," 27–8, 107; Canny, *Elizabethan Conquest*, 114; *The History of Parliament: The House of Commons 1558–1603*, ed. P. W. Hasler (London: Boydell and Brewer, 1981) under Morgan, Thomas. For the importance of military retinues and military recruitment among tenants on noble estates see Trim, "Fighting 'Jacob's Wars'," 85–6 and 245–75.

Malby began his career serving under John Dudley earl of Warwick in a campaign in France.[101]

Although the sex of Elizabeth's privy chamber servants prevented them from recruiting and leading armies, in a few cases their male relatives did the job for them. Henry Champernowne, who fought actively in the Huguenot cause, was the nephew of the chief gentlewoman of the privy chamber in the 1560s, Katherine Ashley.[102] Sir John Norreys, the most distinguished English commander of the 1580s, was the grandson of a groom of the stool to Henry VIII, whose father, Lord Henry Norreys, had remained close to the court, forming a close relationship with John Dudley duke of Northumberland and subsequently with his son, Leicester. Lord Henry's wife, Marjorie, was another of Elizabeth's intimate female servants.[103] Regional and family connections were also important. Champernowne belonged to a group of interconnected gentry families in Devon and Cornwall, active in military ventures, Irish colonization, and privateering, whose other members included Gilbert and his half-brother, Sir Walter Ralegh. This gentry network collaborated with ship-owning families from the region's port towns, like the Winters and Hawkinses. As Trim has shown, some captains came from puritan families whose members included clergymen and civilian publicists, such as John Stubbs.[104]

The wars against France and Scotland that had provided opportunities for warlike noblemen and courtiers and their clients in the 1540s and 1550s ceased under Elizabeth, apart from brief campaigns in the first years of the reign. The loss of Calais in 1559 meant the disbandment of what had been the largest permanent English garrison. The apparatus of military recruitment and leadership that existed in the mid-Tudor period therefore grew less active. But it continued to supply volunteer companies for Dutch and Huguenot armies.[105] As Trim argues, it was "pyramidal" in the sense that the great military patrons like Leicester and Warwick relied on their gentlemen retainers and friends, who in turn enlisted their own servants and tenants.[106] Companies therefore tended to have a strong regional base, and to contain small clusters of men who had previous ties to each other as neighbors, friends, economic partners, or masters and servants in civilian life.

Apart from small garrisons in Carlisle and Berwick, Ireland provided the only significant outlet for military service under the crown. The queen's Irish army grew from just under 1,000 in the 1560s to 6,000 during the height of Desmond's rebellion, before falling back to around 2,000 thereafter.[107] Leicester used Irish

---

[101] Churchyard, *Rehearsall of Warre*, sigs Dii–iii.   [102] Trim, "Fighting 'Jacob's Wars'," 108.
[103] John S. Nolan, *Sir John Norreys and the Elizabethan Military World* (Exeter: Exeter University Press, 1997), 5–10.
[104] Trim, "Calvinist Internationalism" and "Fighting 'Jacob's Wars'," 303–8.
[105] Trim, "Fighting 'Jacob's Wars'," passim.   [106] Ibid., 259.
[107] For troop levels in Ireland see Ciaran Brady, "The Captains' Games: Army and Society in Elizabethan Ireland," in *A Military History of Ireland*, ed. Thomas Bartlett and Keith Jeffrey (Cambridge: Cambridge University Press, 1996), 136–59, at 144–6. Gunn, *English People at War*, 55 stresses the importance of Irish service to career soldiers after 1558.

patronage to keep several of his military clients in service while awaiting opportunities elsewhere, including Sir John and Edward Norreys, Sir William Stanley, and Sir William Pelham, all of whom would go on to play important roles in his campaign in the Low Countries in 1586. Unfortunately, Ireland provided few opportunities to experience the advances in weaponry, tactics, and siege operations that had transformed warfare on the Continent.

To remain active in continental warfare before 1585, captains needed to find a foreign paymaster, usually in the wars of the Low Countries or France. Trim has estimated the number of English troops fighting in the Netherlands in Dutch pay at between 2,000 and 3,000 in the early 1580s, rising to as many as 8,000 in 1586, in addition to the 6,400 foot and 1,000 horse in the queen's army.[108] Inevitably, the most active captains tended to become somewhat less dependent on their English patrons as they gained credit with foreign leaders, like Henry of Navarre and William of Orange.[109] Even among leading courtiers, loyalty to the queen sometimes ended up in competition with dedication to a European Protestant cause and the men who led it. Leicester cultivated John Casimir's friendship so assiduously in 1578 that he missed several council meetings, causing Elizabeth to rebuke him before his colleagues: "You have quite forgotten us all and business too, apparently, since we cannot get you here for the discussion of it."[110]

The queen's reliance on Anjou as her proxy in the Netherlands presented some delicate problems for Protestant captains and military patrons. Despite their misgivings about his relations with Elizabeth, Leicester and his clients very much wanted to participate in Anjou's campaign. Sir Philip Sidney worried that his letter opposing the Anjou match might ruin his ambition of pursuing a military career in the Netherlands, where the duke's influence was likely to remain paramount. He sought the advice of his friend, the Huguenot diplomat Hubert Languet, on how to appease Anjou, and enlisted the prince of Orange's services as a mediator.[111] For a few months in 1582, Norreys left his troops to join Anjou's court in the Netherlands, in an effort to extract money for his soldiers after the Dutch failed to pay them.[112] A few months later he found himself caught in the middle after Anjou's Catholic troops sacked Antwerp, thoroughly antagonizing the Dutch, although Elizabeth continued to support her French suitor.

Even when they achieved good relations with foreign commanders, English captains faced numerous difficulties in sustaining their careers through service on the Continent. A successful captain had to maintain a clientele of subordinate officers who knew how to recruit troops at the start of a campaign, train them for combat, and then lead them in the field. But those subordinates would remain

---

[108] Trim, "Fighting 'Jacob's Wars'," 321–8 and the table on 492–3.
[109] Ibid., 147–50.   [110] *CSPSp* 2.648.
[111] *The Correspondence of Philip Sidney and Hubert Languet*, ed. Steuart Pears (London, 1845), 188.
[112] Nolan, *Sir John Norreys*, 56.

loyal only so long as their patron continued to find them work. Almost invariably captains had to use their own money and credit to pay and arm their companies at the beginning of a campaign, on promise of eventual reimbursement from their paymaster. Since the Huguenots and the Dutch were chronically short of cash, it often took years to recoup an initial outlay, and even the current wages of troops in the field frequently fell into arrears. By 1582 Sir John Norreys was owed £50,000 for his service in the Netherlands during the previous two years, of which £11,000 had still not been paid a decade later, although in the interim he and his friends had raised a further £22,000 for the Portugal expedition of 1588–9.[113] Maintaining a military band required an ability to raise large sums of money on credit and then avoid bankruptcy when paymasters failed to honor their commitments. Unfortunately, the long Elizabethan peace diminished the activities of the great noble military patrons until Leicester began preparations for his Dutch campaign in 1585, and few captains possessed the deep financial resources and social connections that would have allowed them to easily raise very large sums of money and hold off creditors for years. Norreys, as the son of a baron with links to the privy chamber, was something of an exception, but other professionals like Roger Williams had risen from fairly humble circumstances. Even Norreys had nothing like the resources of Leicester and other earls such as Pembroke and Bedford.

Just how the captains managed is not entirely clear, although loans from sympathetic merchant communities, contributions from English parishes and the congregations of European exiles that had settled in the kingdom, along with profits from plunder must all have played a role.[114] Diplomats like Davison sometimes raised money on their own credit to supply the needs of English soldiers.[115] Smaller Dutch and English creditors, including retailers in garrison towns, extended credit to English captains and soldiers for food and other necessities, not always willingly. Since garrisons had to be fed and housed whether they were paid or not, shopkeepers had little choice but to accept IOUs in hopes of eventual payment when overdue wages finally arrived. A garrison whose wages remained unpaid for too long would quickly wear out its welcome with the townsmen who had to support it. The absence of steady employment and full pay threatened not only the captains' solvency but also their companies' morale and the infrastructure on which military effectiveness ultimately depended. John Cobham complained in 1582 that 4,000 of "our poor English soldiers" had deserted after their wages fell badly in arrears.[116] Three years later Morgan's regiment in the Dutch army grew so discontented that three of its captains

---

[113] Trim, "Fighting 'Jacob's Wars'," 205, 210–11, 216.
[114] Ibid., chapter 6 is the fullest discussion to date of how captains raised the money needed to create and sustain their companies. The evidence is patchy but the conclusion that wide credit networks involving merchants as well as landowners must have been involved is convincing.
[115] Ibid., 212–17; TNA SP84/4/32a. [116] Hatfield House Cecil Mss. 162, fol. 68.

mutinied and threatened to lead their soldiers back to England, causing the irascible commander to attack one with a knife.[117] As Elizabeth prepared to send a fresh army to the Netherlands in 1585. The English soldiers already there continued to suffer acute privations.[118] "We have had but one month's pay since our coming over," one soldier complained in January 1585: "we have rotten houses to cover ourselves... the poor soldiers are worn out of clothes, their limbs taken away with cold... they are almost starved."[119] In the same month, Morgan believed that some of his captains intended to desert to the enemy, "having gotten the Prince of Parma's passports," once they received their back pay.[120]

Captains coped with these privations through practices that were technically corrupt but virtually inevitable under the circumstances. They pocketed the "dead pays" of soldiers no longer in the ranks, requisitioned goods and services from civilians, sometimes but not always in return for tickets intended to ensure eventual repayment, and made profits buying arms and clothing on the market and selling them at a mark-up to their troops. Occasionally they sold military supplies and horses, which they pretended had been lost. A group of captains serving in the Netherlands in 1589 claimed that they needed to collect dead pays to provide discretionary funds for repairing or replacing lost and broken weapons and worn out clothing, buying medicine for sick and injured soldiers, and paying ransoms for men captured by the enemy. In addition, they topped up the wages of gentlemen serving as privates in their bands, whose superior bravery improved the performance of entire companies, but who would not serve for an ordinary soldier's meager pay.[121] Since the queen provided no money for any of these things and a soldier's wages barely sufficed to cover his food, clothing, and ammunition, some means had to be found to cover such expenses. Although corrupt captains who blatantly cheated both the queen and their own men certainly existed, even honest commanders had little choice but to employ creative methods to compensate for inadequate and chronically delayed payments.

Elizabeth's parsimony made these problems as common among her own troops in Ireland—and after 1585 on the Continent—as among those serving financially strapped European paymasters. Irish warfare went through boom-bust cycles, with English forces ballooning during major rebellions, only to shrink just as quickly the moment the queen felt able to curtail her expenses. When she reduced the number of horse soldiers allotted to Ireland from 500 to 200 in 1580, Lord Deputy Grey complained bitterly of the "disgrace" visited upon "well deserving poor gentlemen that have ventured their lives and worn out their bodies for

---

[117] TNA SP77/1/15. The mutinous captains claimed to have obtained Elizabeth's instructions for their return.
[118] TNA SP84/5/30, 31 and SP84/4/32a.   [119] TNA SP84/1/25.   [120] TNA SP84/1/12.
[121] BL Cotton Mss. Galba Dii, fols 52–3 (alternative numeration 56–7).

peccadalia," only to be unceremoniously cashiered.[122] Two years later her hasty reduction of the Irish military budget left bands of unpaid troops stranded in Dublin and other Irish ports, clamoring for relief. "Our soldiers go naked for lack of money and victuals are as scarce and I still bated and hated for these wants," Grey lamented.[123] In this case the queen's parsimony allowed the rebellion to regain strength, partly because some disbanded troops deserted to the enemy, requiring an expensive military build-up the following year, followed by another precipitous reduction. Delayed payment of wages and other privations also contributed to the desertion to the enemy of soldiers recruited in the Pale.[124]

Supplying an army in the field presented additional challenges, especially in districts stripped bare of food by English and rebel bands. The earl of Ormond had to break off an offensive against the chief rebel strongholds in Munster during the winter of 1579–80 because he lacked shot for his demi-cannons and pay and victuals for his soldiers, who were "worn with travail, sickly, un-appareled, un-moneyed" and poorly fed after returning from a previous campaign.[125] "I hear the queen mislikes that her service hath gone no faster forwards but she suffereth all things needful to be supplied to want," he complained to Walsingham:

> I would to God I could feed soldiers with the air and throw down castles with my breath and furnish naked men with a wish, and if these things might be done the service should on as fast as her highness would have it. This is the second time I have been suffered to want all these things, having the like charge that I have but there shall not be a third, for I protest I would be sooner committed as a prisoner by the heels than to be thus dealt with again.[126]

The few foodstuffs that did arrive were spoiled in transit.[127] Although Burghley tried to procure relief, Elizabeth adamantly refused to send more money or supplies until she received a full account of how previous aid had been spent.[128] In addition to lack of adequate food, soldiers suffered from long marches over difficult terrain while carrying heavy muskets, on which they often wore out their shoes.[129] The privations of Ormond's soldiers strained their loyalty, making them receptive to seditious rumors circulating in the province and "more disposed to embrace undutifullness than God's laws or the queen's."[130] One Irish official

---

[122] TNA SP63/78/30, Grey to Walsingham, November 12, 1580.
[123] TNA SP63/93/24, same to same, June 16, 1582.
[124] LPL Mss. 607, fol. 62r; cf. LPL Mss. 597, fol. 307.
[125] TNA SP63/70/64, Ormond to Burghley December 27, 1579. Sir William Pelham had told Ormond on December 6 that "there is not in all Ireland so many cannon shot as will maintain your necessary battery, neither is there provision for the mounting of those pieces which you desire" (LPL Mss. 597, fol. 139r).
[126] TNA SP63/71/3.   [127] TNA SP63/71/43.
[128] TNA SP63/72/5.   [129] LPL Mss. 614, fol. 268 r–v.
[130] TNA SP63/72/7, Warham Sentleger to Burghley, March 8, 1580.

blamed the victualing problem on corrupt English purveyors.[131] Whatever its source, it had a debilitating effect on Ormond's army that delayed the suppression of the Desmond rebellion.

The alternative to relying on inadequate supplies from England was for English companies to appropriate food and other goods from Irish civilians. In the 1570s Sir Henry Sidney had authorized a tax, called the cess, to support the queen's Irish army. In principle it was supposed to replace traditional exactions of food and shelter, known as coign and livery, that Irish peasants had to supply to their lords' military followers.[132] In practice the traditional exactions continued while English companies levied the cess. Although the privy council intended payments of cess to be negotiated in an orderly way with Irish lords and freeholders, collections were often made on an ad hoc basis as troops appropriated what they needed, or simply what they could get away with taking.[133] When these supplies proved insufficient, townsmen had to feed and house garrisons in return for tickets that in principle entitled them to repayments, deducted from soldiers' back wages. Since captains serving in Ireland were responsible both for collecting the cess, receiving and paying out their troops' wages, and settling accounts with Irish who had provided goods on credit, the system was wide open to abuse. In 1580 Sir William Pelham, at the time the chief officer of the crown in Ireland, reported that rather than support English garrisons inhabitants of Irish towns had deserted their homes and offered themselves "to the devotion of the enemy."[134] The inhabitants of Galway rioted against an English company, "marching up and down the streets with the sound of drum, with spiteful speeches of their conquest of the English soldiers, terming them and all the rest no better than English churls."[135] Eighteen years later, a report charged one garrison with marching through the countryside at the slow pace of three or four miles a day, "taking, yea rather extorting from the poor subjects not only meat and drink...but also all the officers in every band would violently urge their hosts every morning to give them three, four or five shillings apiece; to every soldier 12d or 2s; to every one of their women as much, to every boy 6d or 8d at least. If they had it not then they carried away for pawns garrans [horses], coverlets, mantles, sheets and other household stuff, and sold them at their pleasure."[136] Some soldiers apparently demanded wine or whiskey with their meals while billeted on poor householders.[137]

A disgusted captain complained that because of these exactions "the queen's army is in manner as great an enemy to the subjects of Ireland as are the rebels."[138] The majority of the cess fell on the Pale and relatively prosperous and settled districts around major towns where English garrisons were stationed, although

---

[131] Ibid.   [132] The standard account is Canny, *Elizabethan Conquest*.
[133] See BL Add Mss. 48,017, fol. 41, instructions to Sir Nicholas Malby on how to negotiate payments of the cess.
[134] LPL Mss. 597, fol. 297v.   [135] LPL Mss. 619, fol. 37r.   [136] TNA SP63/202.2/108.
[137] LPL Mss. 612, fol. 63.   [138] BL Add Mss. 34,313, Thomas Lea's "Book of Sundry Abuses."

forays into the Gaelic countryside also yielded large numbers of animals. An assize of 1596 conducted by Lord Deputy Russell heard many "grievous and lamentable complaints" from inhabitants of the "Pale and countries adjoining greatly impoverished through the extortion and intolerable hard dealings of the soldiers."[139] To make matters worse, marauding bands of Irish outlaws pretending to be soldiers "ranged up and down the country, spoiling and robbing the subjects."[140] According to an Exchequer memorandum, townsmen were also cheated of money by collusion between company captains and the Treasurer for Ireland, Sir Henry Wallop. When overdue money arrived from England the captains arranged to have their own arrears settled first, so that townsmen who came to Dublin in hopes of having their tickets redeemed were told that cash had run out and fobbed off with promises of payment "when the next money comes."[141]

These abuses furnished one means by which captains compensated for the crown's penury and delays. They were, in effect, shifting their cash-flow problems onto Irish civilians, and in some cases compensating for inadequate returns on their investments in setting out a company through robbery and extortion. Although captains were customarily allowed to profit from a limited number of dead pays, some were accused of allowing their companies to diminish by a third to a half, while remaining at full strength on paper, so as to increase their profits.[142] To prevent these abuses the crown relied on muster masters, who kept books containing the name of every soldier and a record of what he was owed. The muster books were supposed to be updated periodically by mustering each company and removing the names of men no longer in service. But captains found impostors to take the place of missing soldiers during a muster and bribed muster masters to return false reports. Many filled vacancies with Irish recruits willing to serve for lower wages, so that their companies came to consist largely of Gaelic soldiers. Several Irish servitors claimed in 1597 that two-thirds, three-fourths, or "the greater part" of the queen's army consisted of Irish soldiers, "who run away and revolt to the rebels daily and hourly."[143] The Irish council confessed in 1598 that the situation had become so confused that they found it impossible to discover how many of the 7,466 soldiers sent a few years before remained in service.[144] Ormond reported that from eighteen companies that should have numbered well over 2,000 men, he was barely able to draw together 600 to take the field, although the dispersal of troops in garrisons was partly responsible.[145]

---

[139] BL Add Mss. 4728, fol. 67v.
[140] *Calendar of the Carew Manuscripts Preserved at the Archepiscopal Library at Lambeth*, 4 vols. (London, 1867–73), 3.262.
[141] TNA E407/12.   [142] BL Add Mss. 34,313, fol. 101; TNA SP63/98/50.
[143] *CSPI* 6.421; TNA SP63/202.1/56; BL Add Mss. 46,369, fol. 39v.
[144] *CSPI* 7.98–9.   [145] TNA SP63/202.1/1.

Soldiers sometimes sold their arms, many of which ended up in the hands of the enemy after generating a healthy profit to merchants acting as middlemen.[146] "There is not a soldier found in any garrison with a good sword but some gray merchant or townsman will buy it from him," one of Robert Cecil's Irish correspondents reported in January 1600:

> the solider being poor and beggarly selleth his sword for 10 or 12s if it be excellent good. Such a sword is worth commonly among the rebels three or four pounds. A graven murreon bought of a poor soldier for a noble or 10s is likewise worth among the rebels three pounds. The poverty of the soldier is such that he will likewise sell one pound of powder for 12d. And the gray merchants or townsmen will collect by one pound, half a pound and quarter of a pound from the poor distressed soldier who sells it for very necessity and penury, unless he be prevented by a prudent captain. And one of these will in a short time make up a barrel or two of powder, selling each pound to the traitors for three shillings or ten groats, and so the enemy is served both with munition and the best arms in her Majesty's army besides all other helps they can do, by reason of their money.[147]

Especially in the 1590s, the poor quality of conscripts sent to Ireland, "who come so wretched as they be half dead when they first land," "already starved before their setting out," compounded other problems.[148] Many deserted even before they left England; others were reported "to die wretchedly and woefully in the streets and highways, far less regarded than any beasts." Some deserted to the enemy or took to living by robbery, saying they would rather "be hanged... than to stay to be starved."[149] According to Sir John Norreys, of 3,500 men sent to Ireland in the first half of 1596, all but 1,000 were "either dead, run away or converted into Irish" by the beginning of July.[150]

The Council repeatedly issued instructions and attempted to enforce rigorous procedures for keeping records and punishing offenders, only to find its intentions frustrated by intractable problems on the ground. When the government decided to embark 2,800 conscripts bound for Ulster from Chester, in 1600, it ordered their commander, Sir Henry Dowcra, to travel from Ireland to meet them, and dispatched a muster master with a list of "the names, surnames, furniture, armor and weapons of every soldier," as certified by the deputy lieutenants and muster commissioners of the counties where they had been raised. He was to check each soldier against this list, turning over any who answered to a false name

---

[146] BL Add Mss. 4745, fol. 10, instructions to Lord Mountjoy on preventing the practice.
[147] LPL Mss. 614, fol. 268v, John Dowdall to Cecil, January 2, 1600. Gray merchants were itinerate Irish peddlers.
[148] *CSPI* 6.379–81; BL Add Mss. 34,313, fol. 114.
[149] *CSPI* 6.255; BL Add Mss. 46,369, fol. 40.   [150] *CSPI* 5.21.

"to suffer rigor and extremity of law."¹⁵¹ Despite these precautions, the conductors responsible for getting the conscripts to Chester had taken bribes to discharge many of them along the route, substituting less desirable replacements. Soldiers who did reach the port immediately began to desert. Some were then replaced by deserters returning from other units already in Ireland, who hoped in this way to acquire the new uniforms and wages that fresh companies received.¹⁵² The Council railed against the "corrupt" captains it held responsible, ordered a few deserters executed as a warning to the others, and reprimanded the Lord Mayor of London for the "lewd and vagabond" men his officers had conscripted. But it then reluctantly approved filling the ranks with Irish "runaways," as the only method that would allow the expedition to go forward. It also suggested that the "idlers" who attached themselves to the London soldiers as they marched north, who were thought to have encouraged and aided desertions, might be spared the punishment they deserved, if they agreed to enlist in the new force.¹⁵³ Dowcra cannot have ended up with very motivated troops, although this did not stop the queen from complaining bitterly, after he finally got them to their destination of Loughfoile, about his failure to harass Tyrone's rear with greater energy.¹⁵⁴

After continuing problems with supplies and victuals again impeded offensive operations in 1597,¹⁵⁵ the crown at last made a concerted effort to create a more adequate system for sending and monitoring supplies to its Irish army. It negotiated contracts with merchants in England to send specified quantities of goods to depots in Irish ports, with a provision that they would be responsible for any losses or shortfalls not caused by shipwreck or enemy action. The London merchants John Jolles and William Cocken agreed to ship victuals for 4,000 men for 84 days to Dublin and Gallway for £5,950. Their cargoes were to be inspected in English ports as they were loaded and again by commissaries in Ireland to make certain that everything promised had actually arrived. The food would be turned over to the captains only after the completion of the final audit.¹⁵⁶ The quantities of provisions supplied in this way were truly substantial. In 1599 the commissary of Cork certified the receipt of 52,000 pounds of biscuit, 1,500 pounds of butter, 56 quarters and seven bushels of meal, 30,000 pounds of cheese, and 2,500 fish.¹⁵⁷ Although some problems persisted in getting supplies to companies distant from the main depots, the crown had at last begun to construct a more organized logistical system.¹⁵⁸

---

¹⁵¹ BL Add Mss. 4757, fols 28, 31, 71.   ¹⁵² Ibid., fol. 43v.   ¹⁵³ Ibid., fol. 78v.
¹⁵⁴ Ibid., fol. 140.   ¹⁵⁵ CSPI 6.287, 366, 379–80.
¹⁵⁶ TNA E407/12, contract between the crown and John Holles; BL Add Mss. 4757, 15v–16 instructions of the privy council to the commissary of Carickfergus to inspect Holles's cargo (Holles is called Jollis in the latter document).
¹⁵⁷ TNA E401/12, certificate of victuals received by Allen Astley, commissary for victuals at Cork.
¹⁵⁸ For lingering problems see, e.g., CSPI 8.29 and 36.

Comparable problems quickly hampered the effectiveness of the royal army sent to the Netherlands under Leicester's command at the end of 1585. Before embarking, Leicester drew up a set of regulations for his soldiers, reflecting the emphasis on strict morality, discipline, and religious observance of the military manuals. He appointed the mathematician Thomas Digges as his muster master and trench master general. Never a modest or self-effacing man, Digges was soon sending back to England a series of confident pronouncements on everything from alleged deficiencies in the Dutch army to the deplorable state of the fortifications of Ostend.[159] In November he drew up a series of orders for mustering the English army, which Leicester and the privy council approved.[160] On the appointed day each band was to assemble "in battle array" for inspection and the soldiers called out by name from a roll previously submitted by the captain. Any soldier answering to a wrong name would lose a month's pay, while smaller mulcts would be levied on those with deficient weapons. A set of detailed notes among Digges's papers concerning parade ground maneuvers, marching to the drum, the proper method of issuing commands, and the training of the shot suggest that in addition to counting soldiers he hoped to supervise and improve their drills and maneuvers. Among other things, the notes show that he had already grasped the tactical innovation that historians used to attribute to Maurice of Nassau, of drawing up musketeers in ranks to fire continuous volleys.[161]

On paper the system of discipline and military administration therefore looked impeccable. But it quickly broke down in the field. Large numbers of soldiers died or deserted over the winter and were variously replaced by fresh recruits from England or soldiers previously serving in Norreys's army under Dutch pay. According to a Dutch complaint, some captains retained "freebooters" from among the local population, "the which, albeit they neither watch nor ward yet will they very willingly pass musters thereby to enjoy the privileges of soldiers if haply they be taken prisoners by the enemy in robbing and picking abroad in the country."[162] Leicester diverted some money intended for his army to meet other

---

[159] TNA SP84/6/7a. [160] TNA SP84/5/58a; BL Add Mss. 48,084, fol. 295.
[161] BL Add Mss. 48,084, fols 302-3. "In teaching to give volleys the ancient and vulgar manner of discipline, which is that the whole volley shall be given of all the shot in one battalion or troop at an instant, as well of them behind as before, is utterly to be condemned, for either the hindermost must venture to shoot their fellows before through the heads or else will overshoot and so spend their shot unprofitably. Besides the volley being once given, the enemy comes on without impeachment or annoyance. But instead of this kind of volley at once, which only serves to make a great crack, let the first rank only give their volley, and if the battalion march then that rank that have given their volley to stand and the second to pass through and so to give their volley and so to stand, and the third to come up and consequently all the ranks. If the battalion stand then the first having given their volley shall fall back and the second come in their places and so the third and fourth, till the first rank become the last and the last rank first, and so the volley shall be continued and the enemy be never free from annoyance."
[162] BL Add Mss. 48,116, fols 102v-103.

urgent needs, making it impossible to pay companies in full. Since musters were traditionally conducted only as soldiers received their pay, shortages made it impossible for Wilkes to carry out his duties. Jealousies and bickering among English and Dutch commanders, Leicester's political quarrels with Dutch politicians, and Elizabeth's delays in delivering the money she had promised to fund the expedition further compounded these administrative problems. While Leicester managed to avoid a major breakdown in discipline and even scored a success in the autumn with the capture of Zutphen, his army suffered from chronic shortages of money. After his departure from the Netherlands in November 1586 matters grew even worse, until in February some English companies began living off the countryside in Holland, provoking threats by Dutch commanders to drive them out by force.[163]

We need to make allowances, in reviewing this litany of problems, for the likely exaggerations of officers seeking to impress the privy council with their needs, while remembering that chronic arrears in pay, occasional mutinies, and problems of desertion were endemic to all early modern armies, including those of Spain. Veteran commanders like Norreys expected newly recruited companies to lose as much as half of their members within six months through death and desertion, and took it for granted that they would have to compensate by finding new recruits, often in the country where they served. But it is clear that, even in nominally royal armies, companies were raised and maintained largely through private enterprise requiring risky financial investments. Many captains were no doubt motivated by religion, devotion to queen and country, and a sense of honor. But none wanted to go bankrupt and, in addition to their own finances, they needed to take care of soldiers under their command. Doing so required unsavory practices, ranging from the bribing of muster masters to plundering civilians.

Privateers and Pirates

Although privateering had some analogous features to land warfare and eventually attracted many of the same patrons, it had traditionally featured less prominently in the culture of the English landed elite, outside a few coastal regions. It had long been carried on but was more often financed by mercantile families in port towns than by courtiers and great lords. Privateers had done an especially brisk business in the 1540s, when Henry VIII tacitly permitted them to seize cargoes not only from the subjects of his enemy, the king of France, but his ally Charles V. One study has argued that the resulting boom in commerce raiding never really subsided, even after peace returned and the crown withdrew its letters

---

[163] Below, pp. 316–17.

of marque, becoming a festering grievance that contributed to the deterioration of Anglo-Spanish relations several decades later.[164] Piracy provided an alternative source of employment and income for seagoing communities in periods when legitimate commerce slackened. It became entrenched in some districts, despite efforts by the authorities to crack down. The English were victims as well as perpetrators. In 1576 Mauvissière commented on the "extreme displeasure" the queen and her council had conceived against the prince of Orange over Dutch piracy, while the following year he reported the seizure of sixteen French ships by the English authorities, in retaliation for English prizes that were sold at the Ile de Ré, just off La Rochelle, evidently by Huguenot corsairs.[165]

Despite these conflicts the seagoing communities of the Netherlands, France, and England had close ties, further cemented by the migration of Flemish and French refugees fleeing religious persecution to ports like London, Norwich, and Rye, where the French congregation counted 642 members in 1572.[166] These relations and the bond of a common religion made collaboration natural. Like expeditions of volunteer soldiers, collaboration with Dutch Sea Beggars and Huguenot corsairs received underhanded encouragement from the crown and more active support from privy councilors and Protestant landowners. English and French mariners began cooperating immediately after Elizabeth concluded an alliance with the Huguenots in 1562, turning the Norman port of Le Havre— which the English briefly occupied with Huguenot support—into their main base. Sir Arthur Champernowne, who had raised companies for Huguenot land campaigns, encouraged collaboration on the seas in his capacity as vice admiral of Devon and through his business connections with ship owners and captains, including John, Richard and William Hawkins.[167] The proximity of Devon ports like Exeter and Plymouth to Normandy and Brittany, with their active Protestant maritime communities, made this a natural alliance. The Channel Islands, with their francophone populations and Calvinist churches, probably also played a role.[168]

---

[164] James McDermott, *England and the Spanish Armada: The Necessary Quarrel* (New Haven: Yale University Press, 2005), esp. chapter 2.

[165] TNA PRO31/3/27, fols 75, 137.

[166] Hugues Daussy, *Les Huguenots et le Roi: Le combat politique de Philippe Duplessis-Mornay (1572-1600)* (Geneva: Droz, 2002), 87.

[167] Mickaël Augeron, "Coligny et les espagnols à travers la course (c. 1560-1572): une politique maritime au service de la cause protestante," in *Coligny, les protestants et la mer*, ed. Martine Acerra and Guy Matinière (Paris: Presses de l'Université de Paris-Sorbonne, 1997), 166; Harry Kelsey, *Sir John Hawkins: Queen Elizabeth's Slave Trader* (New Haven: Yale University Press, 2003), 43-5; N. A. M. Rodger, "Queen Elizabeth and the Myth of Sea-Power in English History," *Transactions of the Royal Historical Society*, 6th series, 14 (2004): 153-74 at 154.

[168] See Jean-Yves Carluer, "L'horizon maritime des protestants Bretons," in *D'Un Rivage à l'Autre: Villes et Protestantisme dans l'Aire Atlantique (XVIe-XVIIe siècles)*, ed. Guy Martinière, Didier Poton, and François Souty (Paris: Imprimerie Nationale, 1999), 101-12.

Although Elizabeth had to be careful about supporting Protestant corsairs too openly while she remained at peace with France and Spain, she recognized their utility. Privateers increased pressure on Spain during two trade disputes with England in 1563–4 and 1569–72, helping the English obtain better terms. In 1570 the Spanish ambassador in London reported that Huguenot, English, and Dutch pirates had formed a combined fleet of 45 ships that had free use of English ports, effectively chasing Spanish vessels from the Channel and North Sea.[169] Dutch Sea Beggars and French privateers based in Normandy and La Rochelle found safe havens in England, where émigré communities helped create networks for disposing of prizes.[170] Significant numbers of English mariners also joined Huguenot and Sea Beggar crews.[171] For their part, English ship captains took out letters of marque from William of Orange, Henry of Navarre, the prince of Condé, and the Portuguese pretender Dom Antonio, and resupplied themselves in the friendly ports of the Netherlands, Normandy, and La Rochelle.[172] This network of Protestant coastal towns significantly extended the range of privateers, providing bases that stretched from the North Sea to the Bay of Biscay, where ships could shelter from storms, sell cargoes, and replenish their stores.[173] Welsh and Irish ports also participated.[174]

Most English privateering vessels remained small. As late as 1589–91, by which time average tonnage had probably increased, a large majority were of less than 100 tons, with many below 50.[175] Kenneth Andrews has calculated the value of a ship of 50 tons at about £150, while the cost of equipping it with artillery, munitions, and sufficient supplies for a six-month voyage might cost another £174.[176] Individual merchants and partnerships among ship captains, sometimes assisted by local tradesmen and gentry, raised such sums with little difficulty. Crews commonly served without wages, in exchange for a third of the profits, while the cost of victuals and other supplies might also be reduced by giving suppliers a share of the prizes, restocking ships at sea from captured vessels, or

---

[169] Carlos Gomez-Centurion Jimenez, *Felipe II, La Empresa de Inglaterra y el Comercio Septentrional (1566–1609)* (Madrid: Editorial Naval, 1988), 43–5, 58–9.

[170] Ibid., 107–17.   [171] Trim, "Fighting 'Jacob's Wars'," 109–10.

[172] In addition to being the titular—and from the 1570s the actual—leader of the Huguenots, Navarre was admiral of Guyenne, with jurisdiction over the whole French Atlantic coast south of the Loire, including La Rochelle. He was therefore legally entitled to issue letters of marque and to establish tribunals to adjudicate disputes over prizes. See Alan James, *The Navy and Government in Early Modern France 1572–1661* (Woodbridge: Royal Historical Society, 2004), 15–16. For examples of English privateers acting under authorizations from Condé and Dom Antonio see TNA HC/141, fol. 175; *CSPSp* 2.210.

[173] For an example of an English crew disposing of a prize at La Rochelle see TNA HCA13/28, fol. 52v.

[174] For evidence suggesting that the Norreys brothers, Sir John and Thomas, were involved in privateering see TNA HC13/25, fols 192–3.

[175] Kenneth Andrews, *Elizabethan Privateering: English Privateering during the Spanish War 1585–1603* (Cambridge: Cambridge University Press, 1964), 32.

[176] Ibid., 49.

bartering prize goods for food in foreign ports.[177] These methods were in any case essential on long voyages, since privateers had limited storage capacity and sailed with large crews. One of Drake's voyages supplied itself on the outward voyage by capturing a Spanish fishing boat returning from Newfoundland. When this cargo ran out, the crew spent some time fishing off the coast of Africa, and then resupplied itself a third time on a Caribbean island, whose natives exchanged food for a few trinkets.[178] Privateers in desperate need of supplies did not scruple to victimize neutral ships. One had started to return to England because it had run out of beer, when it seized a French vessel carrying 32 tons of sack, which the English crew appropriated for their own use. A Baltic ship was stripped not only of its drink and victuals but powder, guns, and tackling, so that it had difficulty struggling into the nearest port.[179]

Privateering ventures therefore cost relatively little, except when carried out by especially large ships that did require substantial investments. A new Danish ship of 400 tons purchased for £1,200 in 1588 required an additional £400 worth of refitting, not counting the cost of guns, ammunition, and victuals, before it was considered strong enough to undertake a privateering voyage to the Caribbean.[180] But lesser vessels compensated by joining together in small fleets, either at the start of a voyage or though ad hoc agreements made at sea. This sometimes allowed them to overpower much larger prizes, especially because English ships frequently carried a heavier armament of iron cannon than foreign vessels of similar size. In 1589 two privateers of 30 and 80 tons named the *Conclude* and the *Moonlight* sailed from Plymouth to the Caribbean, where they encountered a group of somewhat larger London privateers off Santo Domingo. Almost immediately after the meeting eleven Spanish ships sailed into view, whereupon all the privateers gave chase. Most of the Spaniards managed to escape in an afternoon squall, but the tiny *Conclude*, the fastest sailor of the group, managed to stay on the tail of a Spanish vessel more than ten times its size that had separated from the rest of its fleet throughout the following night. To assist his partners, the *Conclude*'s captain placed a lantern on his mainmast, which the *Moonlight* and one of the London ships, the 150-ton *Harry and John*, managed to follow. Early the next morning all three English ships caught up to their prize, a 350-ton galleon with a crew of more than fifty and nine cannon. It put up a stiff fight for about ninety minutes before finally succumbing, mainly to the *Harry and John*, whose armament of twenty-two cannon proved decisive.

Great prizes meant huge windfall profits—in this case an estimated £20,000—while even the capture of a small ship might more than pay for a voyage if it had a

---

[177] Ibid., chapter 3.
[178] For concrete examples see the anonymous narrative, *A Summarie... of Sir Francis Drake's West Indian Voyage* (1589), 5, 10–11.
[179] TNA HCA13/28, fols 27r–28, 29, 377.   [180] TNA HCA13/28, fols 306–7v, 379–80.

valuable cargo, like the 280 chests of sugar and 270 quintals of Brazil wood carried by a small Portuguese vessel captured in 1589.[181] But most prizes consisted of cheap goods like grain or fish and some privateers failed to capture anything of value. To lessen the risk, privateering was frequently combined with legitimate trade, as armed merchant ships with legal cargoes picked off prizes when opportunities arose. The distinction between merchants, privateers, and pirates blurred, not only because merchantmen captured prizes but because Spanish cargoes were not always easy to distinguish from those belonging to neutral parties or English merchants, who continued to trade with Spain using Dutch and Hanseatic ships right through the Armada War. One privateering captain captured a Hamburg ship bound from Portugal, only to discover to his horror that its cargo belonged to a consortium of London merchants and rich widows, who promptly sued him for damages in the Admiralty court.[182] Crews of captured ships were sometimes tortured and probably killed to prevent them from revealing that the cargoes they carried belonged to neutral merchants. After capturing a Swedish ship bound for Spain, a privateer crew "consulted and said what shall we do with the merchant and these mariners, if we cast them not overboard we shall never make the goods good prize... and they threatened to carry them to La Rochelle." Another captain ripped up the papers showing that the cargo in the Spanish ship he had just captured belonged to Dutch merchants and threatened to take the captive crew to Barbary, presumably to be sold as slaves.[183] We know about these incidents only because the threats were not carried out. Crews of other captured vessels almost certainly had worse luck.

The crown attempted to prosecute pirates and provide redress through its courts to foreign merchants victimized by unscrupulous English sea captains. But it also forgave pirates if their talents seemed sufficiently useful. Sir John Perrot received orders to suppress any pirates he came across while guarding the coast of Ireland against Spanish incursions in 1579, except in the case of "one Courtney," who had recently attempted some "bold enterprise... upon the rebel's ships" and was therefore to be offered a pardon, so that "you may use his service in this exploit as you shall see cause."[184] In any case, it proved practically impossible to crack down effectively on local infrastructures for disposing of prizes, involving shopkeepers, small merchants, and gentry integrated into the local economies and power structures of coastal districts. Even legitimately seized cargoes had a way of disappearing quickly once they reached shore, before royal officials

---

[181] TNA HCA13/28, fol. 15v.

[182] For an example see TNA HCA13/28, fol. 116, the case of a Hamburg ship seized by English privateers, coming from Portugal with a cargo belonging to a consortium of two London merchants and two London widows. The ship itself had also once belonged to London's merchant fleet; one assumes the owners transferred it to Hamburg to get around Philip II's prohibition on trade with England.

[183] TNA HCA13/28 fols 160, 391.   [184] TNA SP12/131/74.

managed to inventory the cargoes and demand the shares rightfully belonging to the Lord Admiral.

Most captains must have known of small ports where they might dispose of dubious cargoes with few questions asked. One English ship sailing under Henry of Navarre's letters of reprisal seized a cargo of wine from a French vessel, which it quickly sold on the Isle of Wight to middlemen acting on behalf of London merchants.[185] Irish and Welsh ports also appear to have done a brisk business in disposing of illegal prizes.[186] In Wales some coastal communities seem to have expected any privateer that landed in their havens to share its booty. On two occasions around 1,590 privateers carrying seized cargoes of wine into different Welsh ports were immediately boarded by swarms of local people with empty bottles and cans, begging for free samples, followed by local magistrates expecting larger gratuities. In both cases the captains' refusal to gratify the Welsh led to their arrest along with their crews on charges of piracy, whereupon the locals helped themselves to the ships' cargoes. One vessel became the site of a week-long drunken party.[187] If all else failed a captain might dispose of illegally seized Spanish prizes at La Rochelle or someplace even further from the reach of the Admiralty courts. Mendoza claimed Spanish prize goods seized illegally by English ships were sent to La Rochelle with the connivance of Secretary Walsingham, before returning to England with falsified bills of lading.[188]

Before about 1580 nearly all English privateering took place in European waters. Although it inflicted some losses on Spanish commerce, its contribution to the kingdom's security remained limited. The real pioneers in the use of commerce raiding as a strategic weapon were the Dutch and Huguenots. In France, Admiral Coligny encouraged the seagoing communities of Normandy and La Rochelle, which had gravitated toward Protestantism from an early date, to develop a fleet of corsairs by capturing and re-outfitting Catholic ships.[189] He then taxed prizes they brought in at 20 percent.[190] English ship captains were drawn into this campaign by the admiral's brother, Odet de Coligny, who resided in London. Henry of Navarre, who as admiral of Guyenne possessed jurisdiction over La Rochelle and other French Atlantic ports south of the Loire, pursued a similar strategy, according to the duke of Guise earning as much as 800,000 écus (roughly £240,000 sterling) a year by issuing letters of marque and collecting levies on prizes.[191] These revenues played a significant role in financing Huguenot armies. The Sea Beggars, whose crews included Englishmen, reignited the Dutch revolt against Spain in 1572 by seizing coastal towns in Holland and Zealand. The Dutch then developed a system for taxing trade with the enemy by demanding fees

---

[185] TNA HCA13/28, fols 24v–25.   [186] Ibid., fols 155, 186v–7 for Welsh examples.
[187] Ibid., fols 94–5, 365–7. The ports were in Caernarvonshire and on the Isle of Anglesey.
[188] *CSPSp* 3.297.   [189] Augeron, "Coligny," 157.   [190] Ibid., passim.
[191] James, *Navy and Government*, 19. The hostile source is the duc de Guise.

for the safe-conduct of ships engaged in it, and using privateers to seize ships whose captains refused to pay.[192] Well before the great expansion of English privateering in the 1580s, French and Dutch leaders had learned to use privateers to fulfill the maxim that when money runs out "a brave chief will force his enemy's countries to maintain his actions."[193]

The French had also gotten a head start over the English in raids on Spanish shipping in the Caribbean and in New World colonization, with plantations in Brazil and Florida, the latter a specifically Huguenot venture wiped out by the Spanish in 1565.[194] When English ships did venture into American waters, they often benefited from Huguenot experience. One historian has suggested that Hawkins's participation in Huguenot privateering enterprises in the 1570s may have first awakened him to the possibilities of extending warfare into the Caribbean.[195] John Hawkins benefited from Huguenot experience in his early voyages to the Caribbean and sailed with Huguenots among his crew, as did Drake during his voyage around the world.[196] Frobisher's project for colonizing what is now eastern Canada reminded Mauvissière of an earlier proposal that "a certain Albaigne from La Rochelle once proposed to the late King Charles [IX]."[197] When Gilbert planned an expedition to American waters in 1578 he worried that he might encounter a French fleet under the Sieur de Roche in the New World. He asked Cadenet to help him work out a prior agreement that if this should happen the English and French would collaborate against Spanish forces and divide any spoils they acquired, instead of fighting each other.[198]

The French also preceded the English in creating a printed literature on American colonies and in appreciating the strategic significance of the Atlantic in military conflicts with Spain.[199] But much of this French literature quickly became available in English, while French ideas about Atlantic strategy also percolated into England through diplomatic and military contacts. The fullest

---

[192] Yvo van Loo, "Pour la liberté et la fortune: La course néerlandaise pendant la guerre de religion aux Pays-Bas 1568–1609," in *Coligny*, ed. Acerra and Matinière, 91–107.
[193] *Works of Williams*, ed. Evans, 7.
[194] N. A. M. Rodger, *The Safeguard of the Sea: A Naval History of Britain 660–1649* (New York: W. W. Norton, 1999), 239. Sebastien Cabot had sailed to Newfoundland under the patronage of Henry VII and English fishing boats may already have visited the New World in the late fifteenth century but the English lagged behind during the first two-thirds of the sixteenth century.
[195] Mickaël Augeron and Laurent Vidal, "Refuges ou réseaux? Les dynamiques protestants au xvie siècle," in *Villes et Protestantisme*, ed. Martinière et al., 30–61 at 45.
[196] Kelsey, *Hawkins*, 61, 2, 117–18; Frank Lestringant, "Le Drake Manuscrit de la Morgan Library: Un document exceptionnel en marge des 'nouveaux horizons' français au Nouveau Monde," in *L'Expérience Huguenote au Nouveau Monde (XVIe siècle)* (Geneva: Droz, 1996), 265–90.
[197] TNA PRO31/3/27, fol. 36.   [198] Ibid., fol. 210.
[199] The fullest treatment of Huguenot thought on the New World is to be found in the works of Frank Lestringant, esp. *Le Huguenot et le sauvage: l'Amérique et la controversé coloniale en France au temps des guerres de religion* (Geneva: Droz, 1999). For a concise review of the subject in English see Philip P. Boucher, "Revisioning the 'French Atlantic': or How to Think about the French Presence in the Atlantic, 1550–1625," in *The Atlantic World and Virginia, 1550–1624*, ed. Peter Mancall (Chapel Hill: University of North Carolina Press, 2007), 274–306.

account of the Florida colony, written in London by the Huguenot Jean Ribaut, quickly appeared in a printed English translation by Thomas Hackett in 1563.²⁰⁰ A few years later, Hackett translated a French tract on Brazil as *The New found World or Antarctike*, dedicating it to Sir Henry Sidney.²⁰¹ An Englishman with a strong interest in French colonial ventures in this period, the Cambridge educated humanist Richard Eden, entered the service of the Huguenot Jean de Ferières, Vidame de Chartres in 1562. He subsequently published a treatise advocating colonization.²⁰² The pioneering English literature on Atlantic voyages by Richard Hakluyt the younger built directly on this tradition. Hakluyt began working on his *Principle Navigations* (published 1589) while serving as chaplain to the English embassy in Paris, where he cultivated relations with writers and merchants who had knowledge of the New World.²⁰³ Many of the central themes in what we have come to associate with English Protestant or puritan literature on America— including the goal of capturing Spanish treasure fleets, the concept of New World settlements as refuges from religious persecution, and debates about treatment of Native Americans—originated with Huguenot writers of the 1560s and 1570s.

The Huguenot leader, Gaspard de Chatillon, Admiral Coligny, played a central role in developing strategies for weakening Spain through attacks in the Atlantic and New World. After his death in the St. Bartholomew's Day massacres of 1572 other Huguenots, including Philippe du Plessis Mornay, picked up his ideas and developed them further.²⁰⁴ Coligny and du Plessis Mornay had close relations with the Dutch and English, and a recent study has concluded that the latter's strategic thinking evolved thorough exchanges with "an international group of Protestants" that included Walsingham, Sir Philip Sidney, and possibly Drake.²⁰⁵ From an early date, Huguenot, Dutch, and English leaders canvassed possible joint operations against Spanish wealth in the Americas. In 1568 Elizabeth discussed with the prince of Condé a plan to send the Huguenot captain Jacques de Sores to the Indies with a large Anglo-French squadron, while in 1571 the Huguenots and Dutch considered assembling an expedition of forty ships to seize the Spanish silver fleet.²⁰⁶ Mendoza reported from London in June 1578 that "when [the Huguenot agent] Champigny was here it was agreed with the earl of Leicester,

---

²⁰⁰ Jean Ribaut, *The whole and true discoverye of Terra Florida* (London, 1563); André Thevet, *The New found worlde, or Antarctike* (London, 1568).
²⁰¹ Lestringant, *Huguenot et le sauvage*, 171.
²⁰² Andrew Fitzmaurice, *Humanism and America: An Intellectual History of English Colonisation 1500–1625* (Cambridge: Cambridge University Press, 2003), 33–4.
²⁰³ Peter Mancall, *Hakluyt's Promise: An Elizabethan's Obsession for an English America* (New Haven: Yale University Press, 2007).
²⁰⁴ *Coligny*, ed. Acerra and Matinière; Daussy, *Huguenots*, esp. 87–9, 282–3.
²⁰⁵ Daussy comments: "C'est un veritable 'internationale' protestante que Mornay est integer et l'idéologie politico-religieuse va s'imposer comme ligne directrice de toute son action politique jusqu'en 1584" (ibid., 88–9). Alternatively, Mornay may have known one or more Norman seamen who sailed with Drake, as Didier Poton has suggested.
²⁰⁶ Augeron and Vidal, "Refuges ou réseaux?," 46.

in his own chamber, the queen being present, that the way to be safe from Your Majesty [Philip II] and to injure your posterity was to make the Indian voyage and rob the flotillas... Orange continues to urge this course, he being of the same opinion."[207] A year later, Mendoza reported that "some pirates from here and from France have alerted me that they are treating to go seek the *flota* of the Indies."[208] Drake sought out Mauvissière in 1580 to discuss possibilities for Anglo-French collaboration in colonizing the New World.[209] Six years later, when Drake attempted to seize the Isthmus of Panama, across which Spanish silver was transported, Burghley remarked: "it is a matter that many years past I did project to the Prince of Orange's ministers to have attempted."[210]

The Expansion of English Oceanic Enterprise, 1577–1586

The imperial and oceanic ambitions that expanded so rapidly in England around 1580 were therefore in large part offshoots of earlier continental Protestant ideas and initiatives. But not entirely, since some awareness had long existed that England needed to expand its commerce and challenge the Iberian monopoly on trade with Africa, Asia, and the Americas, for strategic as well as economic reasons. The authorities needed to protect the cloth trade to avoid risking serious social unrest. In addition, the kingdom's security against invasion depended heavily on its merchant fleet, since large navies consisting of purpose-built warships had only begun to develop in this period.[211] Although both Spain and England accelerated shipbuilding programs in the 1570s, for some time neither possessed a large fleet. In 1588 the Royal Navy had only thirty-four ships, several of them quite small. Both the Armada and the fleet opposing it consisted primarily of merchant vessels hired or conscripted for the occasion.[212]

Ominously, at the start of Elizabeth's reign, England's relatively small commercial fleet had declined in size since the time of Henry VIII, because so much English trade had become concentrated in Antwerp, a short sail from London easily made by small vessels. As late as 1572 only fourteen English merchant ships exceeded 200 tons, compared to about eighty from the single Spanish port of

---

[207] *CSPSp* 2.591.
[208] *CDIHE Felipe II*, 389: "Algunos piratas de aqui y Francia me advirtieron que tartan de ir á aguardar la flota de Indias."
[209] TNA PRO31/3/28, fols 190v, 268v–269.   [210] *Leicester Correspondence*, 199.
[211] For a survey see Jan Glete, *Warfare at Sea, 1500–1650: Maritime Conflicts and the Transformation of Europe* (Abingdon: Routledge, 2000), chapter 4.
[212] Patrick Villiers, *Les corsairs du littoral: Dunkerque, Calais, Boulogne de Philippe II à Louis XIV (1568–1713)* (Villeneuve d'Ascq: Presses Universitaires du Septentrio, 2000), 101; Colin Martin and Geoffrey Parker, *The Spanish Armada* (New York and London: W. W. Norton, 1988), chapters 1 and 2. As Villiers points out, only twelve of the queen's ships were newly constructed and one of the larger vessels had actually been constructed at the direction of Philip, while he was king consort of England in the 1550s.

Seville, whose fleets had to cross the Atlantic, a few years later.²¹³ It was fortunate indeed that so many of the ports on the opposite sides of the North Sea and Channel, with their significant merchant fleets, had fallen into Protestant hands, and that the Dutch revolt ended Antwerp's role as the great entrepôt of northern trade. But a Spanish victory over the Dutch would cancel these benefits, leaving England vulnerable. The crown therefore had a vital interest in encouraging an expansion of the kingdom's merchant fleet by opening new opportunities for trade, especially in relatively distant markets that would stimulate shipbuilding. Under Edward VI, the privy council had encouraged a voyage to discover a northeast passage to Asia that had instead found a trade route to Russia through the White Sea. It led to the formation of England's first joint-stock venture, the Muscovy Company. Individual merchants purchased shares in this enterprise, generating a larger capital than any could have provided alone, while a governor and board of directors managed its affairs. These arrangements provided a model for later mercantile and colonial ventures, including the Levant, East India, and Virginia Companies. The leader of Edward VI's regime, John Dudley duke of Northumberland, and the secretary of state, William Cecil, both strongly supported the Muscovy venture.

A generation later, Cecil, along with Northumberland's sons, Leicester and Warwick, remained highly cognizant of the strategic importance of trade and sea power.²¹⁴ Cecil commented in 1585 "that there was nothing more needful for the King of Spain than to have more and better places on Flanders side than he yet hath for shipping, as well to send aid of men, money and victuals from Spain or from France by friendship as to keep ships of war to offend all passengers betwixt England and Zealand or Holland."²¹⁵ Keeping Dutch and Flemish ports in Protestant hands was always one of his chief priorities when dealing with the Netherlands.²¹⁶ Individuals whose associations with Cecil or the Dudley family extended back to the reign of Edward VI played significant roles in promoting sea power and voyages of discovery under Elizabeth. Richard Eden, whose ties to Huguenot maritime enterprise were mentioned earlier, had served as Cecil's secretary in the 1550s. Under Elizabeth he became the single most active English translator of Spanish books about the Americas. Two former clients of Northumberland, Edward Clinton earl of Lincoln and William Winter, served as the admiral and surveyor general of Elizabeth's navy in the 1570s.²¹⁷ Leicester and

---

²¹³ Gomez-Centurion Jimenez, *Felipe II*, 41; BL Cotton Mss. Vespasian CV, fols 91–8 (a survey of shipping in Iberian ports, 1579).
²¹⁴ Kenneth Andrews, *Trade, Plunder and Settlement: Maritime Enterprise and the Genesis of the British Empire, 1480–1630* (Cambridge: Cambridge University Press, 1984), 15.
²¹⁵ Burghley to Leicester, December 26, 1585 in *Leicester Correspondence*, 39.
²¹⁶ See, e.g., his comment about the desirability of taking Dunkirk and Newport, ibid., 359.
²¹⁷ R. Malcolm Smuts, "Pirates, Politicians and Urban Intellectuals," in *The Circulation of Culture in the Urban Atlantic World: From Early Modern to Modernism*, ed. Leonard van Morze (Basingstoke: Palgrave Macmillan, 2016), 73–99 esp. 93–4.

his brother, Warwick, remained active patrons of the Muscovy Company.[218] Leicester purchased his own privateering vessel in 1580 and seems to have kept a look out for promising seamen deserving his patronage.[219] Francis Walsingham also had close ties to the Muscovy Company through his first wife, Anna Carleill, the daughter of one of its leading shareholders. He involved himself in nearly all significant oceanic projects between the 1570s and his death in 1591.[220]

John Dee, who had tutored the future earl of Warwick, wrote a number of tracts dealing with navigation, Atlantic geography, and the importance of sea power in the 1570s, with the encouragement of Leicester, Hatton, and the queen herself. In one, published anonymously in 1577, Dee analyzed the economic benefits of sea power based on the model of the ancient Athenian Empire. "What would that noble, valiant and victorious Athenian Pericles say if now he were living and a subject of authority in this British kingdom?" he asked.[221] Surely he would advocate the creation of "a pretty naval royal of three score tall ships (or more) but in no case fewer," to dominate the seas around England and guarantee that Englishmen, rather than foreigners, reaped the profits from the resources those seas provided.[222] The resources included the herring fishery that "Guicciardini in his description of the Low Countries" described as a source of "490 thousand pounds sterling" in yearly profits to the Dutch.[223] Dee saw the navy as a strategic asset serving "the perpetual politic security and better preservation of this famous kingdom," and he again cited Pericles in arguing that "skillful sea soldiers" were generally superior to land soldiers and thus an ideal reservoir of military prowess.[224] The only way to convince the English to invest in a strong navy, he thought, was by showing them that they would reap material benefits by so doing. Once people began to experience the economic rewards that sea power will bring, he argued, "O lord what load would be laid on then among the godly, wise and able subjects to the better maintenance of a bigger navy and of new devised, more warlike ships? How many would contend with other virtuously to excel herein as zealous benefactors to the weal public?"[225]

The Londoner Michael Lok, whose family had connections to the Dudleys going back to Edward's reign, became deeply impressed, while serving as a merchant factor in Lisbon and Seville in the 1550s, with the rich cargoes from Asia and the Americas unloaded in those ports. He returned home fired with an

---

[218] He wrote to the earl of Shrewsbury in 1574 that if he "had £10,000 in my purse I would have adventured every penny," in the Muscovy Company (Lodge, *Illustrations*, 2.46). My thanks to Glyn Parry for information about Ambrose Dudley's connection to the company.
[219] *CSPSp* 3.2–3; cf. BL Cotton Mss. Otho EVIII fols 82–3 for letters to Leicester or his secretary vetting "the young Hawkins" and another navigator.
[220] Andrews, *Trade, Plunder and Settlement*, 15.
[221] [John Dee], *General and Rare Memorials* (London, 1577).
[222] Ibid., 3.   [223] Ibid., 26.   [224] Ibid., sigs Biii v and 6.
[225] Ibid., 18. For a study of Dee see Glyn Parry, *The Arch-Conjuror of England: John Dee* (New Haven: Yale University Press, 2011).

ambition to help English mariners break into these lucrative markets, and spent twenty-four years and £500 amassing a vast "collection of books, maps, charts and instruments" and a "ream" of notes relating to navigation and trade in American and Asian waters.[226] Significant lines of continuity therefore connected the earlier interest of Edward VI's council in Atlantic commerce to the patronage of privateers and voyages of discovery under Elizabeth. As in land warfare, the Dudley clientage network that Leicester had inherited from his father played an especially significant role, albeit with the support of other leading members of the privy council. The West Country network to which Ralegh and his half-brother Gilbert belonged also contributed. John Hawkins of Plymouth attempted to break into the Atlantic slave trade with a voyage to Africa and the Caribbean in 1565.[227] He lost several ships and men to the Spanish, but rather than discouraging him the setback inflamed his desire for revenge by plundering Spanish settlements in the Americas. He had developed a precocious interest in methods of navigation while still a student, which Walsingham actively encouraged.[228] Gilbert claimed to have sold land valued at 1,000 marks (£666) to finance a voyage of exploration.[229] He died at sea. His half-brother Ralegh also financed and on occasion participated personally in commerce raiding voyages to the Caribbean, while sponsoring the ill-fated Roanoke Colony. He employed Thomas Harriot, the most distinguished English mathematician of the period, to train his mariners in navigational arts.[230]

But while men like Hawkins and Gilbert might occasionally achieve impressive results, transatlantic voyages were always high-risk ventures that often failed.[231] Any sustained expansion of English commerce and sea power into the Western Atlantic and other distant waters would require not just a few intrepid sea captains but substantial investments in larger and more heavily armed ships and fleets, better knowledge of navigational methods and American geography, and a strategic vision encompassing both military and economic calculations. Several developments in the 1570s brought these ingredients together to initiate a new phase of English oceanic enterprise. In 1574 some friends in the Muscovy Company introduced Lok to an ambitious young ship captain and pirate named Martin Frobisher, whom he soon came to see as the man who would turn his dreams of expanding English commerce into reality. Lok adopted Frobisher as his protégé, and after sharing with him the fruits of his research invested £1,600 of his own money and £800 more raised through his connections to other London merchants

---

[226] TNA SP12/119/29; James McDermott, "Lok, Michael (c. 1532–1620)," *ODNB*; Smuts, "Pirates, Politicians and Urban Intellectuals," 87–9. My thanks to Glyn Parry for alerting me to the Loks' connection to the Dudleys.
[227] Kelsey, *Hawkins*. [228] TNA SP12/125/70 and 126/44.
[229] *The Voyages and Colonising Enterprises of Sir Humphrey Gilbert*, ed. David Quinn, vol. 2 (London: Hakluyt Society, 1940), 534.
[230] Smuts, "Pirates, Politicians and Intellectuals," 85–6.
[231] Hawkins's slaving voyage had resulted in losses of ships, men, and money and Gilbert died at sea in 1583.

in a new joint-stock Cathay Company, to provide the young captain with a fleet to search for a northwest passage to China.[232] Frobisher failed to find a route to Asia but returned from his voyage with ore that resembled gold. The prospect of opening a gold mine in Labrador, perhaps capable of rivaling Potosi as a source of treasure, aroused considerable excitement, attracting Walsingham's favorable notice and investments from both London merchants and members of the court.[233] Elizabeth sank £4,000 into the project, the earl of Oxford £,2520, while other privy councilors together pledged an additional £3,640.[234] Unfortunately the ore eventually turned out to be worthless, whereupon many of the wealthy investors reneged on their pledges, causing Lok to go bankrupt.[235] But the venture demonstrated the willingness of leading courtiers to invest very substantial sums in an Atlantic enterprise.

Fortunately, disappointment over Frobisher's ore was soon more than counterbalanced by the spectacular success of Sir Francis Drake's three-year voyage around the globe, completed in 1580, during which he plundered Spanish shipping in the virtually unguarded Pacific. The profits, officially calculated at just over £300,000, equivalent to more than a year's income for the crown, probably actually amounted to about twice that sum. Leicester and Walsingham wanted to invest the queen's share of the haul in support for the Dutch rebels and Huguenots.[236] In reaping huge windfall profits, Drake had exposed the weakness of Spain's empire in the Pacific. In an interview with the queen, who at the time was in the midst of negotiations to marry the duke of Anjou, he outlined a scheme for creating a joint Anglo-French overseas empire. New expeditions were quickly planned. Early in 1581, Mendoza warned Philip of preparations for one by Drake bound for the Indies and another, led by Gilbert, destined for Cuba.[237] A few days later he reported that Elizabeth had granted Drake £10,000 of the money from his earlier voyage. In April 1581 the Spanish diplomat discovered that "a meeting has taken place between Walsingham, Leicester, Drake, Hawkins, Winter, Frobisher and Bingham, all the latter being experienced mariners," in order to discuss "the Indian project."

> The queen frequently has him [Drake] in her cabinet and never goes out in public without speaking to him; often, indeed, walking with him in the garden. Drake told her the other day that if she ordered three of her ships, which he would choose, he would guarantee to place affairs on the route to the Indies in such a state that your majesty [Philip II] would gladly send her what they call here a 'blank-signet' for her to dictate her own conditions.[238]

---

[232] TNA SP12/119/29. See SP12/110, fol. 51 for the company's articles of incorporation.
[233] TNA SP12/122/3 and 125/34. [234] TNA SP12/149/42.
[235] Smuts, "Pirates, Politicians and Intellectuals" tells the story in greater detail.
[236] So, at least, Mendoza reported (*CSPSp* 3.74). [237] Ibid., 75–6. [238] Ibid., 80.

An estimate had, in fact, been drawn up for the cost of outfitting eight ships and six pinnaces "in warlike manner" for a voyage of four months under Drake's command.[239]

The arrival in England shortly thereafter of Dom Antonio and his entourage of Portuguese pilots and ship captains, whose number Richard Hakluyt estimated at between one hundred and six score, provided another large injection of expertise and strategic ideas.[240] Antonio soon began to send out his own privateers from English ports and in October Mendoza reported that "a multitude of Englishmen with ships" had asked Antonio's agent to grant them letters of marque. He feared that once they began operations these ship owners would "enormously increase their strength by dint of their plunder, much as boy's snowballs get bigger as they role," presumably by incorporating captured vessels into their fleets, as the Huguenots had been doing for several years. He accused Sir Francis "Knollys, a kinsman of the queen and Leicester" of being "the head of the pirates" and of thwarting all his efforts to stop them.[241] Apparently at Elizabeth's direction, discussions began in May between Drake and Antonio about a new expedition to the Azores.[242] Six ships from La Rochelle were drawn into the scheme and an effort was made to enlist the additional support of the French crown.[243]

A Portuguese pilot, Simon Fernandes, had accompanied Drake in his circumnavigation of the globe and later guided Ralegh's Roanoke colonists to their destination.[244] In 1584 John Hawkins suggested that the best way to weaken Spain was to encourage ships sailing with Dom Antonio's letters of marque to operate freely from ports in western England, in exchange for a payment of five or ten percent of the value of any prizes they took. He predicted that this would rapidly attract not only investments from the chief merchants of London and the West Country but the "Flushings" (Dutch), Huguenots, Scots, and inhabitants of the Portuguese Atlantic islands. "Our own people as gunners (whereof we have few) would be made expert and grow in number, our idle people would grow to be good men of war both by land and sea," while the fisheries and commerce of Spain would be crippled. Rather than an exclusively English enterprise, he proposed to advance privateering by a "party" of "Englishmen ... French, Flemings, Scots and such like" operating from English ports. Elizabeth chose not to implement the scheme but the fact that Hawkins proposed it shows that he and others continued to regard an assault on Spain's transatlantic commerce as a collaborative international enterprise.

---

[239] TNA SP12/148/43, document dated April 3. [240] TNA SP12/167/7.
[241] *CSPSp* 3.210. Mendoza may have meant Sir Francis Knollys, although Henry Knollys was more actively involved in privateering.
[242] TNA SP89/1, fol. 193. [243] TNA SP89/1/54; BL Lansdowne Mss. 31/81.
[244] Was the Portuguese pilot, Amador de Silva, who according to a Spanish complaint embarked with Drake and a fleet of five ships in 1581 a follower of Dom Antonio? (BL Lansdowne Mss., 30, fol. 10).

Leicester played an active role in fostering collaborations between English and foreign mariners, nautical experts, and senior members of the council. His cordial relations with Dutch and Huguenot leaders helped forge links between English mathematicians, scholars interested in trade and navigation, and European experts, including the cartographers Mercator and Ortelius. His eagerness to draw promising younger men into a network that included both experienced mariners and senior members of the council is revealed by the journal of a young clergyman named Richard Madox, who showed up unannounced at the earl's London residence, seeking employment on an ocean voyage. Leicester immediately invited him to dinner, where Madox found himself seated at a table with Drake and the director of the Muscovy Company, George Barnes. Over the next several days Madox dined with a bishop, had supper with Walsingham, and spent a night in the house of John Dee. He was introduced to Burghley and Lord Charles Howard, the future English commander against the Armada.[245] He obtained the job he wanted, as chaplain on a galleon belonging to Leicester about to depart for a voyage intended for the Moluccas in present-day Indonesia and China through the Straits of Magellan.[246]

The scale and organization of this same voyage demonstrates not only the resources that the earl and his friends had assembled but also an impressive degree of detailed planning. Fitting it out cost £6,400, of which Leicester contributed the largest share at £3,000, followed by Drake at £700, the earl of Oxford at £500, and Frobisher and the expedition's commander, Edward Fenton, at £300 each. The earls of Pembroke and Warwick, lords Howard and Hunsdon, Sir Christopher Hatton and Walsingham each invested £200.[247] Most of the investment therefore came from members of the council, although three sea captains also contributed. At the council's direction, the sheriff of London assisted in mustering the crew, while Barnes, who was a London alderman in addition to leading the Muscovy Company, helped oversee preparations.[248] According to Mendoza, the two largest of the four ships in the fleet carried substantial armaments of 70 and 30 cast-iron cannons.[249] They had crews of 120 and 84 men, while another 35 sailed on two smaller vessels. Although the great majority were sailors, including a half dozen already familiar with the Moluccas as veterans of Drake's expedition, four merchants, two ministers, the pilot Simon Fernandes, a surgeon, two jewelers, two apothecaries, and five musicians also accompanied the fleet.[250] The musicians were presumably included merely to entertain the crews, but the jewelers, who had

---

[245] Smuts, "Pirates, Politicians and Intellectuals," 84–5; *The Troublesome Voyage of Captain Edward Fenton, 1582–1583*, ed. E. G. R. Taylor, Hakluyt Society Publications second series 113 (Cambridge: Cambridge University Press, 1959), 150–1 and 155.
[246] BL Cotton Mss. Otho EVIII, fol. 132v.
[247] Ibid., fols 106v–107. The document does not specify which Lord Howard but it was probably Charles, the future earl of Nottingham.
[248] BL Cotton Mss. Otho EVIII, fol. 132.   [249] *Troublesome Voyage*, ed. Taylor, 37–8.
[250] BL Cotton Mss. Otho EVIII, fol. 151.

the expertise to evaluate any precious stones encountered during the voyage, and the apothecary, who must have possessed a detailed knowledge of medicinal plants, were no doubt recruited to gather useful knowledge. Two friars captured from a Portuguese ship, who had long resided in Brazil, were interrogated about harbors along the Brazilian coast, the names and sizes of Spanish settlements in the region, and the depth of the River Plate.[251] Someone drew up a list of commodities to be found along a stretch of the North American coast extending from 35 to 45 degrees latitude: fish, salt, dates, almonds, figs, raisins, oak and cedar timber, aromatic gums, pitch, tar, building stone, pearls and precious stones, lead, copper, silver, "colors for dies and paints," hides, wax and "potiary drugs." "And hereafter may be had from thence corn, wine, sweet oil, sugar and rice," with which a trade might be carried on "to the most part of all the West Indies."[252] Leicester and his partners intended the expedition not only to reap immediate profits but also to gather intelligence for use in future raids on Spanish settlements and the planning of English colonies and new commercial ventures.

The organizers drew up a book of orders for regulating the behavior of the crew and assuring regular religious services.[253] The emphasis on moral discipline, religion, and methodical organization found in treatises on land warfare carried over into ocean voyages. Unfortunately, these measures proved no more effective at sea than they often did on land. A small mutiny broke out even before the fleet cleared the Channel. The crew insisted on plundering a neutral ship, much to Madox's disgust: "After noon Captain War and Mr. Walker came to us and told how greedy they were, especially Mr. Bannester, who for all his creeping hypocrisy was the more ravenously set upon prey than any the most beggarly felon in the ship and those which at the shore did counterfeit most holiness were now furthest from reason, affirming that we could not do God better service than to spoil the Spaniard of both life and goods but indeed under color of religion all their shot is at the men's money."[254] Fenton, the expedition's leader, eventually found an excuse not to proceed to the Straits of Magellan and returned to England after engaging in trade and plunder off the coasts of Spain and Africa. John Hawkins's brother William, the captain of another ship in the fleet, concluded that "the Spaniard's friends or the Spaniards themselves" had sabotaged the voyage by bribing its commander, although Fenton's greed and ambition offers a more likely explanation.[255]

The Literature of Oceanic Enterprise

The careful planning and disappointing outcome of Fenton's voyage illustrates the tensions that had started to develop between the simple quest for maritime

[251] *Troublesome Voyage*, ed. Taylor, 231. [252] Ibid., fol. 167.
[253] BL Cotton Mss. Otho EVIII, fols 91v, 128v, 141.
[254] *Troublesome Voyage*, ed. Taylor, 166–7. [255] BL Cotton Mss. Otho EVIII, fol. 223.

plunder and more serious strategic and commercial ambitions. Most privateering voyages remained modest enterprises dedicated to seizing cargoes, but the largest oceanic ventures attracted major investments from wealthy London merchants, peers, members of the council, and the queen. They were variously intended to weaken Spain by striking at its oceanic supply lines, expand English commerce, and acquire bases in distant waters that would turn England into an Atlantic and American power. Even more than land warfare, long-distance maritime enterprises required a combination of raw physical courage and adventure, and specialized forms of knowledge and technical skill. They exemplified Gilbert's concept of "chivalric policy."

A growing literature on Atlantic exploration and combat reflected this complex orientation. It celebrated voyages and raids as chivalrous adventures but also argued that sea power and American colonization would spread Christianity, increase England's wealth, and provide employment to subjects who might otherwise turn to crime. This literature invariably treated the pursuit of economic gain as legitimate, so long as it did not conflict with Christian values or the public good. Although Churchyard defended Gilbert against the charge that he set out on his voyage merely from "greedy hope of gain," he had no hesitation in attributing his hero's exploits to a mix of altruistic and self-interested motives: "for country's wealth, for private gain or glory seek we all."[256] Far from being sinful, the desire for fame and money provided a spur to "show what wit and skill men have, and serve the Maker's thought."[257] In the same spirit, a sea captain named Bingham exhorted Gilbert's crew:

> Then launch ye noble youths into the main
> No lurking perils lie amid the way:
> Your travail shall return you treble gain,
> And make your names renowned another day.[258]

The advocates of sea power and overseas colonies wanted not only to challenge Spain but also to provide solutions to problems of overpopulation and underemployment, which had troubled Tudor theorists for more than a generation. Tackling those problems required not just the seizure of silver fleets and raiding of commerce but efforts to locate and exploit profitable commodities. The profit motive provided a spur to virtue, whose great enemy was not greed but indolence.

A similar emphasis on the compatibility of strategic objectives with private profit distinguishes Richard Hakluyt the younger's 1584 manuscript treatise, *A Discourse of Western Planting*, and the slightly earlier printed tract by the Catholic Sir George Peckham, *A true reporte of the late discoveries by Sir*

---

[256] Nichols, *Elizabeth*, 2.229, 228. [257] Ibid., 229.
[258] Preface to Sir George Peckham, *A true reporte, of the late discoueries by Sir Humfrey Gilbert* (London, 1583). Examples could be multiplied.

Humfrey Gilbert (1583). Both were written to attract support for Gilbert's scheme to establish a colony of English Catholics in the region of the present Carolinas. The project won the backing of Walsingham—to whom Peckham dedicated his treatise—and other Protestants on the council, an example of confessional differences taking a back seat to secular objectives. Since Peckham consulted Hakluyt it is not surprising that their tracts advance many of the same arguments, although with significant differences in emphasis. Both deny Spanish claims to have discovered America by invoking the story of the Welsh navigator Owen Gwyneth or Guyneth, who allegedly founded an American colony in 1170.[259] But whereas Peckham saw Spanish and Portuguese colonization as a positive example that the English should imitate, Hakluyt showed more concern with the role of New World treasure in strengthening Spanish power and threatening England.[260] Peckham simply wanted Englishmen to share in the wealth and opportunities of America, whereas Hakluyt outlined a strategic plan for challenging Spain's American monopoly.[261]

The two writers agreed in seeing America as a source of valuable commodities capable of generating wealth and employment back home. Hakluyt pointed out that the lands the English might hope to settle in America corresponded in latitude—and therefore presumably in climate—to the entire extent of the Old World from Barbary to Muscovy. America might therefore provide everything the English obtained in trade from Europe and North Africa, at lower cost and with less danger, since the open ocean was less infested with pirates than European waters.[262] He and Peckham both thought that by seeking to supplant the French, Dutch, and Spanish in the Newfoundland fisheries England would reap not only immediate profits but the benefits of an expanded shipbuilding industry and a larger supply of seamen; both also foresaw the rise of an American shipbuilding industry capable of exploiting an abundant supply of good timber.[263] Hakluyt argued that New World exploration might cure English piracy, citing as evidence the small number of Spanish and Portuguese pirates since the discovery of America, which he attributed to the legitimate opportunities that New World colonies provided.[264] He and Peckham also agreed in thinking that Native American populations would provide a large market for English cloth since, as

---

[259] Peckham, *True report*, sig. Div; Richard Hakluyt, *A Discourse of Western Planting*, ed. David B. Quinn and Alison M. Quinn (London: Hakluyt Society Publications, 1993), 88.

[260] This is the subject of an entire chapter by Hakluyt entitled: "That the mischief that the Indian Treasure wrought in time of Charles the late Emperor father to the Spanish King is to be had in consideration of the Queen's most excellent majesty, lest the continual coming of the like treasure from thence to his son work the unrevocable annoy of this realm, whereof already we have had very dangerous experience" (*Western Planting*, 36).

[261] Ibid., 35, 36 (mentioning Ribault's colony as an example for the English), 40, 43 and passim.

[262] Hakluyt, *Western Planting*, 16.

[263] Peckham, *True report*, sig. Ei v; Hakluyt, *Western Planting*, 67–70.

[264] Hakluyt, *Western Planting*, 28.

Peckham remarked, "it is well known that all savages... so soon as they shall begin but a little to taste of civility, will take marvelous delight in any garment."[265]

The work of supplying the ships, crews, colonists, and trade goods for exchange with Native Americans would employ countless men, women, and children in England; and if all else failed, some of the surplus population might be exported as colonists.[266] Hakluyt cited the example of bees who, "when they grow to be too many in their own hives at home are wont to be led out by their captains to swarm abroad and seek themselves a new dwelling place... let us learn wisdom of these small weak and unreasonable creatures." He suggested transporting criminals to America instead of hanging them. John Hawkins made a similar point, in verse prefaced to Peckham's book:

> The Romans, when the number of their people grew so great,
> As neither wars could waste, nor Rome suffice them for a seat,
> They led them forth by swarming troops to foreign lands a main
> And founded diverse colonies unto the Roman reign.
> Th'Athenians used the like device, the Argives thus have done
> And fierce Achilles Myrmidons when Troy was over run.
> But Rome nor Athens nor the rest were never pestered so,
> As England where no room remains, her dwellers to bestow,
> But shuffled in such pinching bonds that very breath do lack:
> And for the want of place they crawl one o're another's back.
> How nobly then shall they provide that for redress herein,
> With ready hand and open purse this action doth begin.
> Whence glory to the name of God and country's good shall spring,
> And unto all that further it, a private gain shall bring.[267]

Even factious clergy might be cured of their tendency to carp at church ceremonies, Hakluyt argued, if missionary work in the New World provided more constructive outlets for their energies.[268]

As David Armitage has shown, this emphasis on trade and industry reflects concepts of human interdependence derived from Aristotle's *Politics*, which Hakluyt had been studying.[269] Armitage contends that this distinguishes Hakluyt's secular and philosophical view of colonization from the religious justifications found in later writers like Samuel Purchas. But the argument holds only if we equate religion with strict Calvinism. The need to transform idle and

---

[265] Peckham, *True report*, sig. Eii; cf. Hakluyt, *Western Planting*, 28–31.
[266] Peckham, *True report*, sig. Eii v; Hakluyt, *Western Planting*, 31.
[267] "M. Iohn Hawkins, his opinion of this intended Voyage," in Peckham, *True report*, n.p.
[268] Hakluyt, *Western Planting*, 28, 11.
[269] David Armitage, *Ideological Origins of the British Empire* (Cambridge: Cambridge University Press), 70–5.

criminally prone segments of the population into productive workers was a major theme of Christian humanist literature going back to Thomas More's *Utopia*. Hakluyt and Peckham saw American plantation as, among other things, a means of redirecting human energy away from vicious pursuits toward activities beneficial both to individuals and the community, in moral and spiritual as well as material terms. In that sense we can see their program as a classic example of Erasmian reform, an effort to translate Christian charity into a disciplined rational program of action. This Christian emphasis becomes more explicit in the comments both writers make about the impact of plantation on Native Americans. They are absolutely clear that in addition to pursuing the economic benefits of plantation and trade, the English have a duty to bring the gospel and habits of civility to the New World. They acknowledge an obligation to treat Americans with respect, by learning their languages and wooing them "by friendly signs and courteous tokens," such as "looking glasses, bells, beads, bracelets, chains or collar...For such be the things, though to us of small value, yet accounted by them of high price and estimation."[270] After these initial trinkets, more substantial benefits will follow: Christianity; the "knowledge of how to till and dress grounds"; "mechanical occupations, arts and liberal sciences"; protection against the cruelty of "their tyrannical and blood sucking neighbors the Cannibals"; and the saving of children from the barbarous customs of blood sacrifice reputedly used in the New World.[271]

According to these writers, the process of moral and material reform should extend to American natives and even to the American landscape, which will be improved through English methods of cultivation. God will reward the English for carrying on this mission to Christianize and civilize the Americas through rich profits. "We forgot that godliness is great riches," Hakluyt wrote, "and that if we first seek the kingdom of God all other things will be given unto us, and that as the light accompanieth the sun and the heat the fire, so lasting riches do wait upon them that are zealous for the advancement of the kingdom of Christ and the enlargement of his glorious gospel; as it is said, I will honor them that honor me."[272] Churchyard had made much the same point in praising Frobisher: "He that lives idly at home and hopes that God will cast kingdoms in his lap may as well catch at the clouds in the air as come by any commodity of the earth. But to those that travail abroad, a double or treble part is allotted, as man might say that destiny makes her dole and giveth an alms to them that reacheth out their hands for it."[273] Peckham also believed that the religious and cultural gifts Englishmen intended to bring to the New World justified their expectation of material rewards. He quoted Saint Paul—"if we have sown unto you heavenly things, do

---

[270] Peckham, *True report*, sig. Ciii.   [271] Ibid., Fiii v.
[272] *Diverse Voyages Touching the Discovery of America* (London, 1582), 13–14.
[273] Thomas Churchyard, *Martyne Frobishers Voyage to Meta Incognita* (London, 1578), sigs. Ciii v–Ciiii.

you think it much that we should reap your carnal things?"—and adds that having been brought from "brutish ignorance to civility and knowledge" Americans will "understand how the tenth part of their land may be so manured and employed, as it may yield more commodities to the necessary use of man's life than the whole doth now... And in my private opinion, I do verily think that God did create land to the end that it should by culture and husbandry yield things necessary for man's life."[274]

Hakluyt connected these concepts of economic and moral improvement to a military strategy for challenging Spain's hold on the New World through alliances with American tribes. "The savages of Florida are the Spaniards' mortal enemies and will be ready to join with us against them," he wrote, "as they joined with Captain Gourgue of Gascoigne, who being but a private man and going thither at his own charges by their aid won and raised three small forts which the Spaniards about twenty years ago had planted in Florida after the slaughter of Jean Ribault." To the north of Nova Hispania the Chichimici, "big and strong men and valiant archers, which have continual wars with the Spaniards," would benefit from English armor, just as Irish rebels have profited from arms supplied by Spain.[275] Indeed the Spaniard's greatest fear is that Englishmen will colonize America and ally with its native inhabitants.[276] For Philip II's

> dominions and territories out of Spain lie far distant from Spain his chiefest force and far distant one from another, and are kept by great tyranny, and *quos metuunt oderunt*. And the people kept in subjection desire nothing more than freedom. And like as a little passage given to water it maketh his own way, so give but a small mean to such kept tyranny, they will make their own way to liberty, which way may easily be made. And entering into the consideration of the way how this Philip may be abased, I mean first to begin with the West Indies as there to lay a chief foundation for his overthrow and like as the foundation of the strongest hold undermined and removed, the mightiest and strongest walls fall flat to earth, so this prince spoiled or intercepted for a while of his treasure, occasion by lack of the same is given that all his territories in Europe out of Spain slide from him, and the Moors enter into Spain itself, and the people revolt in every foreign territory of his and cut the throats of the proud hateful Spaniards their governors.[277]

Philip governs the Americas by "opinion" rather than "might," convincing the natives that he has thousands of soldiers at his command when in reality he

---

[274] Peckham, *True report*, sig. Fiii. The Pauline quotation is identified as 2 Corinthians 9. The argument that the productivity of American lands will be increased tenfold by English methods of cultivation anticipates a strikingly similar argument in Locke's *Second Treatise of Government* by nearly a century.

[275] Hakluyt, *Western Planting*, 35.   [276] Ibid., 36.   [277] Ibid., 40.

controls only a few strongholds scattered through a vast country, in which Spaniards are greatly outnumbered. In much the same way did the Romans subdue the ancient Britons, who might easily have regained their liberty had they realized their superiority and attacked the Roman outposts. As Drake, Hawkins, and other English mariners know, not only Native Americans but also escaped African slaves hate their masters and already "maintain frontier wars against the Spaniard." It remains only for a few intrepid Englishmen to puncture Spain's aura of invincibility by furnishing modern weapons and effective leadership.[278] With the aid of the Chichimici and Cimarron—the escaped slaves of Central America—Philip can be deprived of his American silver, "the apple of his eye," whereupon "his old band of soldiers will soon be dissolved, his purposes defeated, his power and strength diminished, his tyranny utterly suppressed."[279] Drake tried unsuccessfully to carry out this project on the Isthmus of Panama in 1586. Although justified primarily by humanist arguments, it also corresponded to the chivalric code's emphasis on a knight's duty to rescue the weak and oppressed from tyranny.

What stands out is the striking degree to which strategic thinking about the Americas represented an extension of ideas about Europe and England, involving the need to combat problems related to poverty and overpopulation, and strategic threats not just to England's physical security but also to its commerce and economy. Protecting the home island required extending the struggle to the Atlantic's far shores because England's resources were considered insufficient to support her own people, much less to mount an effective defense against enemies enjoying the profits of a global empire. And since the crown lacked the resources to furnish the required number of ships and mariners entirely on its own, the queen's subjects needed to be enticed to contribute as well. Economic growth and social stability depended on entrepreneurial energy and, given the opposition that Spain would inevitably present, entrepreneurial violence. The struggle to safeguard England might be depicted in eschatological language, as the battle of a chosen people against infidels, or in more neutral Aristotelian and humanist terms that did not necessarily imply implacable hostility to Spain. The differences in emphasis were, of course, important. But godliness, civility, and material "improvement" were so closely related in the thought of the period that writers moved easily from fervently Protestant ideas to outwardly secular arguments. This allowed Calvinists to develop religiously neutral justifications for their attempts to harm Catholic enemies when it suited their purpose to do so. It also allowed Catholics to participate in projects that served English strategic interests, such as Gilbert's projected colony, with no sense that they had betrayed religious principles.

[278] Ibid., 43. [279] Ibid., 44.

War with Spain and the Reshaping of Oceanic Enterprise

Interest in maritime exploration peaked in the early 1580s, the period not only of Fenton's expedition but also several other efforts to initiate trade or plant colonies in America. In 1582 Gilbert embarked on the voyage to Virginia in which he lost his life. Walsingham's stepson and Barnes's nephew, Christopher Carleill, who helped raise money for Gilbert's voyage among Bristol merchants, set forth a colonizing scheme of his own the following year.[280] Sir Philip Sidney agreed in 1583 to purchase 3,000 acres of land in Peckham's projected colony. In 1584 Ralegh sent an expedition to Virginia to scout the coast in preparation for the settlement he planted at Roanoke in 1585. In these same years, French efforts to colonize the Americas faltered after Admiral Philippe Strozzi's crushing defeat in the Azores in 1582, and the resumption of religious civil war following Anjou's death in 1584. Although Huguenot privateers continued to raid the Caribbean, French colonial projects ceased. Since the fledgling Dutch republic remained precarious, England emerged by default as the kingdom best able to follow through on schemes for penetrating the Americas worked out in international Protestant circles over the previous several decades.

But toward the middle of the decade the pressure of growing military conflict with Spain began to alter the trajectory of English oceanic enterprises, away from colonial projects that required long-term investments, toward voyages that promised more immediate strategic gains, through the seizure of large amounts of Spanish treasure or direct attacks on Iberia itself. The lure of quick profits had, of course, been present from the start but several things magnified the importance of plunder after about 1584. Until then Elizabeth had refused to openly sanction the seizure of Iberian ships by issuing her own letters of marque. But in that year Philip II impounded all English vessels in Spanish ports and the queen retaliated by authorizing her merchants to capture Spanish prizes. Since Philip had also imposed a trade embargo, merchants involved in trade with Spain and Portugal had little choice but to turn to privateering to supply themselves with Spanish, American, and Asian goods. It soon became clear that seizing prizes on the high seas sometimes provided a cheaper way of obtaining them than legitimate commerce. Contemporaries commented that by the 1590s, products like Spanish oranges and Brazilian sugar were actually less expensive in London than in Spain, because captured cargoes had glutted the market.[281]

At least equally important, in the summer of 1585 Leicester and his clients began investing huge sums of money in the army he would take to the Netherlands that autumn. This not only precluded any further investments in ocean voyages for the foreseeable future. It also led the council to promote raids

---

[280] Andrews, *Trade, Plunder and Settlement*, 191 and 197; BL Lansdowne Mss. 37, fol. 72.
[281] Andrews, *Trade, Plunder and Settlement*, 250.

intended either to damage Spain's military resources or to yield large immediate profits that would help fund land war in the Low Countries. Drake departed in September with a fleet of twenty-three ships, including two furnished by the queen, with the intention of seizing as much plunder as he could off the coast of Spain and in the Caribbean. He then landed on the Isthmus of Panama and attempted to seize the shipments of silver from Potosi that had to cross it, with the aid of escaped Spanish slaves known as Cimarrons. The following July, Walsingham informed Leicester that the council would not decide how much further assistance to send to the Netherlands "until the success of his [Drake's] voyage be seen, whereupon, in very truth, dependeth the life and death of the cause."[282] Unfortunately, Drake failed to seize Panama or capture a large amount of silver. But after returning home he traveled to the Netherlands in October and attempted to persuade the States General to contribute ten substantial ships and five flyboats to a fleet intended to carry eight or ten thousand soldiers to assist Dom Antonio in recovering Portugal from Philip II. He confidently predicted that 20,000 Portuguese would rally to the cause once the invaders had landed.[283] The states declined to involve themselves directly, brushing Drake off with an offer to encourage individual towns to make voluntary contributions and a promise that any goods adventured with Dom Antonio's fleet would not have to pay duties.[284] Leicester failed again the following May to advance a similar project.[285]

The Dutch finally agreed to contribute sixty transports to an English attack on Iberia in 1589, ostensibly intended both to destroy the remnants of the Armada before it could be refitted and to seize ports. This offensive, jointly led by Drake and Sir John Norreys, carried 10,000 soldiers and was financed in large part by London merchants. It attracted a number of ship captains more interested in plunder than strategic objectives. Defying the queen's orders to destroy Spanish ships in the ports along Spain's northern coast, it instead attempted but failed to seize Lisbon. Several thousand men perished on the expedition, which achieved none of its major objectives. The English persisted in trying to capture a Spanish silver fleet for the remainder of the century but never succeeded, and none of the subsequent raids on the Caribbean conducted by Drake, Hawkins, Ralegh, and other captains came close to equaling the success of the voyage of 1577–80. The hope of financing war against Spain by seizures of Spanish wealth proved illusory. Although privateering expanded and flourished, generating substantial profits for some individuals, the crown reaped only limited returns.

Writing in the 1960s, Kenneth Andrews condemned the government's failure to mobilize English maritime resources more effectively behind a coordinated

---

[282] *Leicester Correspondence*, 341.
[283] Pieter Bor Christiaenszoon, *Oorsprong, Begin, en Vervolgh der Nederlansche Oorlogen* (Amsterdam, 1680–81), pt. 2, 753, 769, 770.
[284] Ibid., 772.   [285] BL Add Mss. 17677C, fol. 297r.

military strategy as "a disintegration of power, resulting from the conjunction of an antiquated system of government and the acquisitive drive of vigorous private interests."[286] This is misleading. The crown's ability to mobilize extensive resources to serve a coherent oceanic strategy had not disintegrated because it had never existed in the first place. Creating a state-controlled system for projecting power throughout the Atlantic would have required much greater resources than Elizabeth had available.[287] She was no more able to fund a large blue water navy commanded by officers answerable solely to the crown than she was to pay for a standing army with a robust system of logistical support and the expectation of always receiving adequate pay on time. In principle, the creation of a professional army and navy, adequately supported by tax revenues efficiently administered by royal officials, would have substantially improved England's military performance. Unfortunately, in the late sixteenth century this was not an achievable goal.

But even if it did not deliver a decisive blow against Spain in the Atlantic, the expansion of both the Royal Navy and privately financed English shipping did produce both short-term and longer-term gains. In conjunction with Huguenot and Dutch maritime activity, English privateering helped drive Iberian ships from the Channel, the North Sea, the Baltic, and parts of the Caribbean.[288] During the Armada War, English privateers probably captured over a thousand Spanish and Portuguese prizes, reportedly inflicting an estimated six million ducats of damage on the Iberian maritime economy that undoubtedly contributed to a decline in Spanish shipbuilding.[289] Trade between Iberia and northern Europe continued but it was increasingly carried by ships based in the ports of southern England, Holland, Zealand, western France, and the Baltic, rather than Spain and Portugal. Despite some intermittent embargoes, Philip II hesitated to enforce prohibitions on trade with the North that would have a devastating impact on parts of his kingdom and his own fleet, which depended on Baltic supplies of timber, hemp, and pitch.[290] Rather than dominating Atlantic commerce, as still seemed possible as late as the early 1580s, Philip's kingdoms lost control over important segments of their own trade.

In addition to its effects on commerce, privateering contributed to several long-term trends important to the evolution of English sea power. It further stimulated

---

[286] Andrews, *Elizabethan Privateering*, 238.
[287] As Andrews himself came to recognize in *Trade, Plunder and Settlement*.
[288] Kenneth Andrews, "The English in the Caribbean, 1560–1620," in *The Westward Enterprise*, ed. Kenneth Andrews, Nicholas Canny, and P. E. H. Hair (Liverpool: Liverpool University Press, 1978), 103–24.
[289] Andrews, *Trade, Plunder and Settlement*, 248–50.
[290] Following the Anglo-Dutch attack on Cadiz in 1596 Philip wanted to seize all Dutch ships in his ports to form a fleet to counter-attack. He desisted after local officials persuaded him that without the Dutch he would be unable to supply his fleet with food and other necessary materials. Gomez-Centurion Jimenez, *Felipe II*, 289–301.

a rapid expansion in the manufacture of iron guns already underway in the middle decades of the century that turned England into Europe's leading producer of small and medium-sized artillery pieces.[291] Indeed the English enjoyed a virtual monopoly of the manufacture of iron ordinance until Dutch entrepreneurs created a competitive industry in Sweden in the 1590s.[292] This meant that in England, unlike Spain, the cost of cannon declined to a level well within the reach of ordinary ship owners. For a time, the production of such pieces may have outstripped the supply of men capable of managing them properly, as the gunners of the Tower of London complained in a petition of 1581, calling for the erection of schools to train and certify gunners.[293] Although nothing came of this plan, a London Artillery Company chartered under Henry VIII did expand significantly in the 1580s, attracting the patronage of about three hundred merchants before the end of that decade. The supply of competent gunners must have increased, since ship owners continued to send out heavily armed ships.[294] The Royal Navy undoubtedly benefited from the growing number of men who had learned to handle artillery during privateering voyages, while the Ordnance Office was able to rely on private contractors to supply the crown's needs.[295]

The growing availability of iron guns and the demands of privateering encouraged changes in ship design and naval tactics, although these took some time to evolve.[296] Early sixteenth-century naval battles were essentially seaborne infantry campaigns, with soldiers boarding enemy ships and attempting to capture them in hand-to-hand combat, perhaps after a preliminary bombardment. This encouraged the use of big ships with large crews and high fore- and aft castles. As is well known, the English pioneered in developing smaller, more maneuverable and heavily armed warships, designed to stand off and bombard an enemy from a distance, although only about a dozen had been added to the royal fleet by 1588. But it was very difficult to sink a wooden ship with cannon fire, as the Armada showed by running the gauntlet of English artillery through the Channel with minimal losses. English commanders learned to use cannon fire more effectively during the course of the engagement and inflicted heavier damage in the battle off Gravelines, after fire ships had driven the Armada from Calais. But in doing so they exhausted their supplies of shot and powder, so that if the Armada had not retreated it might have succeeded in its mission of providing a shield for Parma's forces as they attempted to cross the North Sea. The new form of naval combat

---

[291] Rodger, *Safeguard*, 214.   [292] Glete, *Warfare at Sea*, 23.   [293] TNA SP12/147/91.
[294] G. A. Raikes, *The History of the Honourable Artillery Company of London*, vol. 1 (London, 1878), esp. 33–4.
[295] On this subject see Richard Winship Stewart, *The English Ordnance Office 1585-1625: A Case Study in Bureaucracy* (Woodbridge: Boydell Press, 1996). I wish to thank Lois Schwoerer for stimulating discussions of this topic.
[296] The following is indebted to Glete, *Warfare at Sea*, esp. chapter 2.

made possible by plentiful artillery required changes in tactics and logistics that the English had not yet mastered.[297]

In principle, a heavier load of guns should have allowed ships to increase their range by maintaining their fighting capacity with smaller crews that would consume stores of food more slowly. But even in American waters privateers continued to use boarding tactics and to carry large crews prepared to fight hand-to-hand, although artillery sometimes helped in softening up an opponent before boarding, intimidating ships into surrendering without a fight, and fending off Spanish counter-attacks. In 1593 a single English ship that had anchored in the port of the island of Santa Margarita, near Trinidad, beat off an attack by a galley brought up by the Captain General of the Province of Cartagena by using its artillery, killing the island's governor and many of his men. But when the English tried to plunder the island three months later they did so by landing four hundred soldiers, who were driven off by the local militia, expertly commanded by a veteran officer of the Army of Flanders, who had recently arrived on the island. Thereafter the English avoided attacking Santa Margarita until 1595, when Sir Walter Ralegh made another attempt that was again repulsed with the loss of forty Englishmen.[298] The seizure of permanent bases in the New World and raids on fortified coastal towns required complex amphibious operations, which rarely succeeded in this period. But privateers continued to seize soft targets, like canoes manned by African slaves sent out to dive for pearls, carrying off hostages and quantities of booty, and completely disrupting the Caribbean pearl fishery, the mainstay of the local economy. They employed a variety of weapons and tactics, ranging from quick opportunistic raids to attacks involving hundreds of men and attempts to form alliances with natives who disliked Spanish rule.[299]

Over time, as it became apparent that big heavily armed ships were more effective in seizing the most lucrative prizes, especially the huge Portuguese carracks involved in the Brazil and East Indies trades, the English began to build more of them.[300] Ship designs improved through experimentation and the sharing of information between royal dockyards and shipbuilders working for figures like Ralegh and Leicester.[301] In the 1580s some shipwrights may have begun, for the first time, to design ships on paper.[302] Methods of organizing and financing maritime expeditions also progressed, most obviously through joint-stock ventures like the Muscovy and Levant Companies but also through more informal consortiums of gentry, peers, and merchants. Innovations and strategic

---

[297] Colin and Parker, *Armada*, Part III.   [298] BL Add Mss. 36,316, fol. 169.
[299] Ibid., 54v–55, 73v, 96v, 175v and passim. This volume consists of transcripts (and some translations) of letters in the Archivo de los Indios in Seville relating to attacks on the pearl fisheries, the island of Trinidad, and the Orinoco region of Venezuela. Both the earl of Cumberland and Ralegh landed armed forces on Trinidad itself, where, using native guides as translators, they promised to help the indigenous inhabitants free themselves from Spanish rule (fols 134, 151v–152, 154).
[300] Andrews, *Elizabethan Privateering*, 231.   [301] Ibid., 228–31; Rodger, *Safeguard*, 218–20.
[302] Andrews, *Elizabethan Privateering*; Rodger, *Safeguard*, 219–20.

initiatives related to war with Spain played an especially important role in English penetration of Mediterranean commerce. The desire to exert pressure on Spain's vulnerable eastern flank encouraged efforts to establish links with the Ottoman Empire and local rulers in North Africa.[303] A secret agent named William Harborne was dispatched to Constantinople, where in 1579 he worked out an agreement with Sultan Murād III, who was interested in importing English lead and tin for his armaments industry. The Turkey Company, ancestor to the seventeenth-century Levant Company, was officially incorporated in London in 1581. Harborne remained at the Ottoman court until 1585, where he encouraged the sultan to resume offensive operations against Spain. Elizabeth possessed an advantage in negotiations with the Ottomans, since she could open direct contacts not only with the sultan but also the influential sultana Walide Saiye, wife of Murād II and mother of his successor, Mehmed III, something no male ruler was permitted to do. The two women exchanged gifts as Elizabeth attempted to persuade the sultana to promote policies calculated to harm Spanish interests.[304]

Large heavily armed ships built for privateering proved effective in penetrating the pirate-infested Mediterranean and establishing English trade networks with the Levant. Hawkins helped pioneer direct trade between England and Constantinople in the 1570s and Walsingham drafted a memorandum advocating the opening of commercial relations in 1578, which he hoped would encourage the construction of strong ships. In the Levant, as in American waters, English merchants learned to combine privateering and legitimate trade, by sending cargoes in heavily armed vessels capable of taking prizes when opportunities arose. In both cases they could usually rely on local authorities in disposing of their illegal cargoes, despite prohibitions by the king of Spain and the sultan, although in the Caribbean they sometimes needed to make a show of force, to "compel" the colonists to trade. Privateering formed one strand within a wider set of readjustments that allowed the English mercantile economy to grow significantly, despite the saturation of its traditional North European markets and disruptions caused by war. The total number of sailors employed in merchant trade and privateering is estimated to have increased from 16,000 to 50,000 between 1582 and 1603, signaling England's emergence as a major commercial power.[305] The benefits extended beyond the maritime community to shopkeepers who sold new products, cloth workers whose livelihoods depended on overseas

---

[303] See, for example, the anonymous tract of 1579, advocating an alliance with the king of Barbary in TNA SP12/132/17.

[304] On this see Lisa Jardine, "Gloriana Rules the Waves: Or the Advantage of Being Excommunicated (and a Woman)," in *Elizabeth I and the Expansion of England: A Conference Held at the National Maritime Museum Greenwich, 4-6 September 2003* published as *Transactions of the Royal Historical Society*, 6th series, 14 (2004): 210-22.

[305] Villiers, *Corsaires du littoral*, 41.

markets, and a government acutely worried that poverty and idleness might produce political instability.

Given his vastly greater financial resources and ability to draw on ships not only from Spain but also from Portugal, the kingdom of Naples, and his ally Genoa, Philip II would have had decisive long-term advantages in a naval contest fought solely between the English and Spanish crowns. Privateering helped even the odds. It not only magnified England's maritime power but also forced the Spanish crown to invest heavily in forts and convoys to protect American commerce, an Atlantic navy, and an infrastructure of ship yards and supply depots.[306] Privateers also significantly inflated the costs of the masts and naval stores that Spain imported from the Baltic and the victuals needed to send ships to sea. They thereby diverted resources that would otherwise have been available for the Army of Flanders or renewed assaults on England or Ireland. Although shipments from the Potosi mines recovered after a slump between 1589 and 1594, reaching new heights in the late 1590s, more of the profit was consumed convoying the treasure to Spain, while delays caused by fear of privateers disrupted Spanish war planning.[307] Even though the English never captured a silver fleet, the strategic gains were therefore far from insignificant.

Conclusions

The history of both land warfare and privateering during Elizabeth's reign provides a striking example of the three-way interaction between sovereign royal authority, voluntary private initiatives, and the stimulus of external challenges in driving the development of a more robust state. Since the crown lacked both the financial resources and the organizational capacity to mobilize the armies and fleets needed to defend the kingdom, it had no choice but to rely on entrepreneurial initiatives by its subjects. The involvement of major courtiers like Leicester, Burghley, Walsingham, and Ralegh as patrons of soldiers and maritime expeditions further blurred the boundary between "private" and "government" initiatives. When Elizabeth needed to raise an army, she relied not only on her authority as queen but also on the clientage networks of major courtiers and their clients, the professional captains. When she needed to assemble a large fleet, as in 1588, she conscripted merchant vessels to supplement the ships of her own navy. Ambitious voyages of exploration, like Frobisher's to Labrador in 1579, and offensive operations, like the attack on Portugal a decade later, were organized

---

[306] On which see David Goodman, *Spanish Naval Power: Reconstruction and Defeat, 1589–1665* (Cambridge: Cambridge University Press, 1997), Part I.
[307] Gómez-Centurion Jiménez, *Felipe II*, 241–55.

essentially as joint-stock enterprises in which the queen was sometimes the leading shareholder but others collectively contributed greater resources.

These "public–private" partnerships were motivated not only by allegiance to the sovereign but also by the profit motive and cultural values variously rooted in the chivalric code, Protestantism, and humanist concepts of service to the commonwealth. The resulting systems of belief kept evolving in response to challenges and opportunities presented by threats to the kingdom's security, especially from Spain. Those threats sustained a serious interest in the art of war on land and new forms of commercial and military enterprise at sea. The results included studies of ancient military tactics, innovations in mathematics, cartography, and navigational methods, and a significant improvement in English gunnery. Contemporary scholars and statesmen came to better understand and appreciate the interdependence of military strength, economic growth, and social discipline. Armies were described not just as instruments of conquest but as bodies of men that simultaneously exemplified and sustained the hierarchical organization of civil societies. Commercial expansion and colonization were seen as requiring armed protection but also as generating wealth and skills that supported military strength. Soldiers and sailors served civic, as well as strictly military functions.

5
Defending the State in Ireland

In addition to governing England, Elizabeth and her ministers oversaw a second, much more fragile, Irish state, whose problems placed heavy demands on English resources and periodically threatened to unsettle English politics.[1] Maintaining control of Ireland at an affordable cost presented a challenge that vexed England's leaders and stimulated literally hundreds of treatises on Irish political, social, and religious reform.[2] Ireland consequently provided a major, if often overlooked, stimulus to *English* political thought, of a kind that often assumed a more radical character than discussions of affairs in the home island. With its weak institutions, even weaker Church, and powerful lords possessing seigneurial armies, the Irish state relied more heavily on armed force than its English counterpart. When military theorists like Barnaby Rich and Stephen Gates discussed the need for disciplined soldiers to suppress savagery and rebellion, they often had Ireland in mind. But while Ireland's unsettled conditions vexed the crown's servants, some English believed that by forcibly uprooting Ireland's barbaric customs they might create a virtual *tabula rasa*, on which to construct ambitious schemes of improvement that would civilize the Irish while generating substantial profits.[3] Plantations, intended partly to encourage such reforms, attracted substantial investments and thousands of colonists. In short, Ireland provided ample scope for the side of Elizabethan culture examined in the last chapter, with its emphasis on adventure, innovation, and entrepreneurial violence, and its propensity to regard force as a necessary tool of godly civil governance. Irish history displays in stark relief the opportunistic and brutal underside of the Elizabethan ideal of a Protestant state or commonwealth.[4]

---

[1] For the emergence of the concept of Ireland as a state, starting around the late 1570s, see Mark Hutchinson, *Calvinism, Reform and the Absolutist State in Elizabethan Ireland* (London: Routledge, 2016).

[2] David Heffernan, *Debating Tudor Policy in Sixteenth-Century Ireland: 'Reform' Treatises and Political Discourse* (Manchester: Manchester University Press, 2018).

[3] The most famous example of this attitude is, of course, Edmund Spenser's *A View of the Present State of Ireland*, written in 1595-6 and first published, with modifications, in 1633. The influence of this tract and the views it expressed has been especially emphasized by Nicholas Canny, e.g. in *Making Ireland British* (Oxford: Oxford University Press, 2001), chapter 1. A useful perspective is provided by the essays in *Political Ideology in Ireland, 1541-1641*, ed. Hiram Morgan (Dublin: Four Courts Press, 1999).

[4] Cf. the slightly different argument in Hutchinson, *Calvinism, Reform and the Absolutist State* that Protestant officials abandoned the concept of Ireland as a commonwealth after concluding that the great majority of its population lacked the grace and confessional allegiances necessary for collective governance within a mixed polity. While I find this broadly persuasive, it needs emphasis that there was

Ireland's Complex Social and Cultural Landscape

The instability of sixteenth-century Ireland derived in part from the island's history as an incompletely conquered territory, in which pockets of English settlement had long existed in close proximity to indigenous inhabitants who had never fully accepted English rule, and who differed from their overlords in language and culture. Since the twelfth century English writers had stigmatized the Irish as a wild and savage people, a stereotype that remained very much alive in the Tudor period. The fact that the medieval colony had occupied most of the best arable land, pushing the native population into mountainous, wooded or boggy districts, reinforced the view of them as primitive, violent, and poor: a population that scratched out an existence by herding animals in environments scarcely modified by human labor. One Elizabethan claimed that "at this instance the Irishmen (except [in] the walled towns) are not Christians, civil or humane creatures but rather savage brute beasts," as shown by their custom of going about naked except for a cloak, the squalid lodgings—often little better than English pigsties—in which they allegedly slept in promiscuously mixed groups, and their supposed ability to subsist on shamrocks and field grass during times of famine.[5] "Forasmuch as the cohabiting and living of men together breedeth love and civility," William Lyon, bishop of Cork, commented, "the contrary of necessity bringeth hatred and barbarousness, and dispersed dwellings abroad, which is a maintenance of idleness and thieves." By living "scattered by bogs' and woods' sides, and [in] such remote places where idle men and thieves do lurk," the Irish had purportedly succumbed to these vices.[6] English observers misinterpreted Irish transhumance—the practice of moving herds of animals from summer to winter pastures—as nomadism, allowing comparisons to ancient peoples like the Scyths, from whom Edmund Spenser thought the island's inhabitants had descended. Protestant hostility to traditional Irish religion added another layer of prejudice. Ireland "is greatly darkened by the want of good preachers," one Englishman complained, leaving its people devoid of any sense of duty to God or their queen, so that they "wallow themselves (most brutishly) in all murder, theft, rebellion and

---

almost always a coercive and sometimes violent side to English commonwealth thought, which paired emphasis on public engagement by the virtuous and godly with a recognition that vicious and reprobate enemies of the common good had to be forcefully suppressed. An especially trenchant discussion of this point is Ethan Shagan, "The Two Republics: Conflicting Views of Participatory Local Government in Early Tudor England," in *The Monarchical Republic of Early Modern England: Essays in Response to Patrick Collinson*, ed. John McDiarmid (Aldershot: Ashgate, 2007), 19–36. The disjunction between the concept of a commonwealth and a more authoritarian or absolutist notion of a state is therefore not quite as stark as Hutchinson believes, although he is certainly correct in arguing that the prevalence of Catholicism in Ireland gave rise to a more autocratic style of government, associated with the emergence of a concept of an Irish state. The discussion in this chapter tries to show in more detail how certain strains of commonwealth thought fed into emphases on ruthless state control.

[5] TNA SP63/85/39.   [6] *CSPI* 6.19.

whoredom, whereof they make no sin."⁷ In all these ways Irish society appeared the very antithesis of civility.⁸

But as so often happens in societies characterized by sharp ethnic or racial distinctions, strong prejudices existed alongside a considerable amount of practical interaction and mutual accommodation. Intermarriage between English colonists and native Irish and the employment of Irish domestic servants in English households must have eroded cultural and linguistic divisions from the very earliest period of medieval colonization. Centuries of coexistence and the Gaelic revival of the late Middle Ages led to further exchanges and alliances. In many districts, prominent local families of mixed ancestry moved easily between English and Irish environments. Some new planters succeeded by learning to do the same thing. The ambitious English settler, Richard Boyle, got his start in Munster after marrying Joan Apsley, the daughter of an English captain and a mother from a well-connected Munster family of mixed Irish and Old English descent, with long ties to the earls of Desmond. As Boyle began to acquire lands confiscated from Desmond, his wife's maternal kin provided him with invaluable assistance.⁹ He would later go on to establish kinship alliances with far more prominent Irish and Old English families, including the earls of Kildare.¹⁰ Although a Protestant born in Kent, as he acquired a vast landed estate and the title of earl of Cork he made a sustained effort to integrate himself and his family into Ireland's indigenous elite.

Long before the sixteenth century, the heirs to the English lordships of the original colony had developed ties of kinship and social alliance to Irish lineages living in the vicinity of their estates, and sometimes further afield. Most had absorbed Irish customs like the patronage of bards and some, such as the Burkes of Clanricard, had become thoroughly Gaelicized.¹¹ At levels below the elite, Gaelic surnames show up in lists of residents of English towns and litigants in English courts.¹² In the Tudor period landholders in the Pale frequently took on

---

[7] TNA SP63/69/64. The writer is Geoffrey Fenton in 1579.

[8] Similar stereotypes existed of Highland Scots and other North European pastoralists. See Arthur Williamson, "Scots, Indians and Empire: The Politics of Civilization, 1519–1609," *Past and Present* 150 (1996): 46–87.

[9] David Edwards, "The Land-Grabber's Accomplices: Richard Boyle's Munster Affinity, 1588–1603," in *The Colonial World of Richard Boyle First Earl of Cork*, ed. David Edwards and Colin Rynne (Dublin: Four Courts Press, 2018), 166–88. The term Old English, apparently coined by Edmund Spenser, refers to descendants of the original medieval colonists and other English who had migrated to Ireland in the Middle Ages, as opposed to the New English, like Boyle, who had come to Ireland more recently.

[10] Patrick Little, "The Geraldine Ambitions of the First Earl of Cork," *Irish Historical Studies* 33 (2002): 151–68.

[11] S. J. Connolly, *Contested Island: Ireland 1460–1603* (Oxford: Oxford University Press, 2007), chapter 1.

[12] Ibid., 30–5 and 46; Vincent Carey, "Neither Good English nor Good Irish": Bi-lingualism and Identity Formation in Sixteenth Century Ireland," in *Political Ideology in Ireland*, ed. Morgan, 45–61; Brendan Kane, "Popular Politics and the Legitimacy of Power in Early Modern Ireland," in *Becoming and Belonging in Ireland AD c. 1200–1600: Essays in Identity and Cultural Practice*, ed. Eve Campbell, Elizabeth FitzPatrick, and Audrey Horning (Cork: Cork University Press, 2018), 328–43 at 334–5.

Irish tenants, who were willing to pay higher rents than Englishmen, with the result that the Irish language was heard even in the vicinity of Dublin.[13] One tract complained that "the maintaining of Irish harpers, rhymers, bards and such other their likes in the Pale" had corrupted its inhabitants' manners.[14] In the 1570s members of the O'Toole and O'Byrne septs, whose ancestors had long raided the Pale, migrated into a lowland district south of Dublin, adopted methods of arable farming and began trading peacefully with neighboring English towns, while shipping their grain surpluses as far north as Carickfergus. Sir Henry Sidney described them as living "loyally" under the queen's government, enjoying a "rich" and "plentiful" existence through the profits of commercial agriculture.[15] But they continued to speak Irish, rather than English, as their primary language, as, apparently, did many residents of English towns in other parts of Ireland. A visitor found it worthy of remark "that more English than Irish" was spoken in the old colonial settlement of Wexford.[16]

Although in many Gaelic regions the local economy remained predominantly pastoral, so that wealth was measured in cows rather than money or land, the Irish had long practiced arable farming and continued to do so, even in regions like Ulster.[17] They grew flax in considerable quantities to supply a linen industry, traded with European nations, and exploited the rich fisheries along the island's western and northern coasts by charging licensing fees and providing services to European fishing vessels.[18] Irish pastoralism was not invariably backward: in Munster, Boyle took over practices of commercial breeding of cattle from the O'Sullivan Bears and O'Driscolls.[19] The Irish had developed a more varied and sophisticated agrarian economy than many contemporary English accounts suggest.[20]

Over-emphasis on the distinction between English and native Irish culture can obscure a more variegated pattern of differences, rooted in geography and social stratification more than ancestry or language. Whether of English or Irish descent,

---

[13] Vincent Carey, *Surviving the Tudors* (Dublin: Four Courts Press, 2002), 25.

[14] Bernadette Cunningham, "Loss and Gain: Attitudes towards the English Language in Early Modern Ireland," in *Reshaping Ireland 1550-1700: Colonization and Its Consequences*, ed. Brian Mac Cuarta SJ (Dublin: Four Courts Press, 2011), 163-86; BL Add Mss. 46,369, fol. 42v.

[15] Christopher Maginn, *'Civilizing' Gaelic Leinster: The Extension of Tudor Rule in the O'Byrne and O'Toole Lordships* (Dublin: Four Courts Press, 2005), 183-6.

[16] LPL Mss. 597, fol. 597.

[17] K. W. Nicholls, *Gaelic and Gaelicized Ireland in the Middle Ages* (Dublin: Lilliput Press, 2003), 131-8. Nicholls thinks that frequent warfare in the sixteenth century may have led to a retreat of arable farming.

[18] Ibid., 143, 144-7; Colin Breen, *The Gaelic Lordship of the O'Sullivan Beare: A Landscape Cultural History* (Dublin: Four Courts Press, 2005), 113-17; Colin Breen, "The Maritime Cultural Landscape in Medieval Gaelic Ireland," in *Gaelic Ireland c. 1250-1650: Land, Lordship and Settlement*, ed. Patrick Duffy, David Edwards, and Elizabeth FitzPatrick (Dublin: Four Courts Press, 2001), 418-36.

[19] Audrey Horning, "Shapeshifters and Mimics: Exploring Elite Strategies in the Early Modern British Atlantic," in *World of Richard Boyle*, ed. Edwards and Rynne, 27-42 at 35.

[20] Breen, *Gaelic Lordship*, 107.

tenants on thickly settled lands near Dublin and other towns led a very different existence from inhabitants of isolated districts, like that dominated by a leader of the McWilliam Burkes named Richard Inyeren, "who dwelling in a remote place near the sea in the northwest, environed with woods, bogs and mountains, where (to any man's memory) no English governor hath been at any time, thought his country so strong as that no Englishman would ever attempt to enter the same." Inyeren therefore felt safe in taking advantage of an invitation to join the Desmond rebellion by recruiting followers from Mayo, Ulster, and the Scottish Isles to conduct a campaign of plunder through Galway and Roscommon.[21] Although most of Ireland had long been cleared of virgin woods, mountains, bogs, and scrub forest existed in many patches, especially along boundaries between lordships.[22] These topographical features, along with a scarcity of good roads and bridges, allowed local populations in many parts of the island to exist in relative isolation, without ready access to commercial markets or oversight by the Dublin government.

That in turn allowed time-honored practices of raiding to continue unchecked. Cattle raids replenished herds depleted by disease or other natural causes, displayed the prowess of men who engaged in them, and provided booty for lords like Inyeren to distribute among their followers. Raiding also served to weaken rivals and impede the penetration of English authority and English plantation in Irish regions. It was especially prevalent in districts protected by natural barriers, like Inyeren's territory in County Mayo, or Clanbrassil (*Clann Bhreasail*) in northern Armagh, described by an Englishman as "a very fast country of wood and bog inhabited with a sept called the Kellies, a very savage and barbarous people given altogether to spoil and robberies, greatly affected to the Scot, whom they often draw into these countries for the spoiling of the subject."[23] But the practice of stealing animals was sufficiently widespread that few parts of Ireland were entirely secure from it. In 1597 the English broke up an organized school for horse and cattle thieves in the vicinity of Cashell in Munster, but were unable to prevent its usher and several students from escaping arrest with the aid of local peasants.[24] A few years earlier a prominent official complained about predatory bands living

---

[21] TNA SP63/72/39, Nicholas Malby's discourse on his service in Connacht, April 1580. As the name suggests, the McWilliam Burkes were descendants of Anglo-Norman colonizers who had become Gaelicized. For background on Inyeren or an Iarran, whose territory lay in modern County Mayo, see Ciaran Brady, *The Chief Governors: The Rise and Fall of Reform Government in Tudor Ireland, 1536–1588* (Cambridge: Cambridge University Press, 1994), 282–3.

[22] An older view (expressed, for example by Nicholas Canny, *The Elizabethan Conquest of Ireland: A Pattern Established, 1567-76* [Hassocks: Harvester, 1976], 1) that as much as half of Ireland was covered by woods, bogs, and mountains has been challenged and superseded, but significant patches of woodland did exist. For a thorough assessment see Kenneth Nicholls, "Woodland Cover in Pre-Modern Ireland," in *Gaelic Ireland*, ed. Duffy et al., 181–206.

[23] LPL 611, fol. 281.

[24] *Calendar of the Carew Manuscripts Preserved at the Archepiscopal Library at Lambeth*, 4 vols. (London, 1867–73), 3.212.

"even within the sight of the smoke of Dublin," under the leadership of a certain "Pheage McHugh, who, like one absolute within himself, with his den of thieves, ruleth all things in his own country at his own will, refusing in person to come to the governor and spoiling his neighbors."[25]

Woods and bogs also sheltered masterless men, variously described in English sources as woodkern or Robin Hoods. In 1576 a leader named Rory Oge gathered together several hundred woodkern and led them in a campaign of plunder until Sir Henry Sidney managed to capture him.[26] Even small bands of woodkern threatened settled property holders. "Kern signifieth (as noblemen of deep judgment informed me) a shower of hell because they are taken for no better than rakehells or the devil's black guard," Richard Stanihurst commented.[27] When not fighting rebellions, English soldiers in the countryside often hunted woodkern, executing them under martial law commissions expressly granted for the purpose. "The Robin Hoods of Kilkenny and Tipperary have had the evil fortunes this last week in being killed and hanged," Francis Lovell happily reported to Walsingham in March 1585.[28] But during times of war both Irish lords and English captains recruited kern as foot soldiers, keepers of the herds of cattle that followed armies into the field as a mobile food-source, or porters to carry baggage on their backs when horses were unavailable.[29] This must sometimes have made it hard to distinguish vagrants from soldiers and camp followers serving Irish or English armies. To the English, the root problem appeared to be an over-abundance of idle men lacking gainful employment, a category that in their eyes included not only vagrants but many of the followers of Irish lords. The authorities tried to deal with it by demanding that lords supply them with lists of followers and then trying to hang any men found wandering the country who were not so enrolled.[30] But the challenge proved virtually insurmountable.

Crown servants repeatedly claimed that the island's more prosperous inhabitants, whether English or Irish, wanted protection against petty crime and predatory raids, and therefore welcomed rigorous English law enforcement. When he conducted criminal trials in Ulster, Chief Justice Robert Gardiner reported, he found "a most rare obedience, even among the best, yea most wild, yielding to and calling for justice, each with marvelous patience though to loss of life."[31] The problem with English law enforcement in the opinion of the Irish, he asserted, was not that it was too harsh but too lenient and inconsistent. The granting of pardons and protections to Irish rebels in return for their submission to the crown

---

[25] Ibid., 44.   [26] *Annals of the Four Masters*, Corpus of Electronic Texts edition, 1692.
[27] Richard Stanihurst, "The Description of Ireland," in Raphael Holinshed, *Chronicles*, vol. 2 (London, 1586), 45.
[28] TNA SP63/101/40 and 115/9; LPL Mss. 597, fol. 244v.
[29] *Campaign Journals of Sir William Russell*, ed. David Edwards (Dublin: Irish Manuscripts Commission, 2014), 69–70; *CSPI* 6.298.
[30] LPL Mss. 597, fols 190v and 191r and 619, fol. 32.   [31] *CSPI* 6.219.

alienated loyal subjects, because it allowed predators not only to profit from their thefts but to retaliate against loyal householders who had refused to assist them.[32] "Where the people are not defended by the prince's sword, nor cannot have right by the ordinary course of justice," Humphrey Gilbert commented, "they neither love nor serve but are enforced to depend on others."[33] Paucity of information about the views of ordinary residents of Ireland makes these statements hard to test. But they find some confirmation in the comment of the Irish chronicle *The Annals of the Four Masters* that when the first president of Munster, Sir John Perrot, left his post after hanging hundreds of criminals, his departure "was lamented by the poor, the widows, the feeble and the unwarlike."[34] Many middling property holders must have found themselves caught in the middle during times of rebellion and disorder. The notion that they would cooperate with the strongest party in their locality, while resenting half-measures that left them exposed to the hostile attentions of both sides, seems highly plausible.

Lordship in Ireland

Unfortunately, Ireland's difficult topography made centralized royal justice extraordinarily difficult to enforce. On a day-to-day basis, local lords and their armed followings usually provided a closer and more reliable source of protection than the distant government in Dublin, a fact that considerably impeded the crown's ability to retain loyalty. Even in the Pale, common law procedures were less regularly employed than in England, while the defense of other principal areas of English settlement had long since devolved to powerful lords whose manorial tenants owed them military service, arrangements broadly comparable to those existing in the English marches facing Wales and Scotland.[35] Like their English marcher counterparts, some Irish magnates grew into overmighty subjects. The greatest of them in the mid-fifteenth century, Richard duke of York, launched the campaign that placed his son, Edward, on the English throne from Ireland.[36] His lordship in County Meath, northwest of Dublin, subsequently disintegrated because his heirs, Edward IV and Richard III, had too many other worries to devote adequate attention to it. This left a power vacuum eventually filled by the expanding power of the Fitzgerald earls of Kildare. Although they never tried to

---

[32] BL Add Mss. 34,313, fol. 52; Add Mss. 48,017, fol. 201.   [33] BL Add Mss. 48,017, fol. 118v.
[34] *Annals of the Four Masters*, 1666.
[35] For a systematic and illuminating comparison see Steven Ellis, *Defending English Ground: War and Peace in Meath and Northumberland, 1460–1542* (Oxford: Oxford University Press, 2015).
[36] Richard of York was, of course, also a major landholder in England and in France until the English position there collapsed but Ireland offered him a retreat after his initial efforts to seize the royal court failed and the base from which he reconstituted his power.

seize the throne for themselves, the Kildare Fitzgeralds were heavily involved in the conspiracy to replace Henry VII with the impostor Perkin Warbeck, and by the 1530s their power and influence, especially in the Pale but also elsewhere in Ireland, appeared to Henry VIII to threaten his own authority. He therefore cut them down to size by sending an army to break the dynasty, in much the way that he and his successors also broke the great militarized lordships of the English North belonging to the Percies, Nevilles, and Dacres.

But in large parts of Ireland virtually autonomous militarized lordships survived. In eastern Munster the earl of Ormond enjoyed a palatine jurisdiction that gave him control of the administration of justice and the right to appoint sheriffs within his earldom, which centered on a rich agricultural basin in Kilkenny, containing a city and five towns along the main commercial route between Dublin and Cork.[37] In addition to the authority delegated to him by the crown, his power rested on his possession of manors comprising 90,000 acres spread over 78 parishes, along with 25 castles and alliances with lesser landowners.[38] By granting beneficial leases he attracted client families along the edge of his estate in north Kilkenny and neighboring Kildare, an upland region and frontier zone fought over by a number of Old English and Irish families.[39] This gave Ormond control of sizable military forces that the crown found indispensable during the Desmond rebellion and Nine Years War.

Gaelic and Gaelicized lordships normally lacked a comparable base of thickly populated manorial settlements. They operated instead through aristocratic lineage groups called *slioghts* or septs that exercised collective use-rights over large tracts of land in predominantly pastoral regions. In each generation the sept would select a leader from among the close male relatives of the previous head, a practice known as tanistry.[40] Although in theory a consensual process, it frequently led to violent conflicts. Successful candidates normally rewarded both allies within the kindred and defeated rivals with grants of territory within the lordship. The repetition of this process over multiple generations meant that major septs invariably had many subordinate branches, operating with various degrees of autonomy on their own lands. Weaker septs also frequently managed to retain lands as dependents of a major lordship. Known as *uirriagh* (literally sub-kings), the heads of these sub-lineages and minor septs owed allegiance to the main lord, along with rents usually paid in kind, military service, and other

---

[37] David Edwards, *The Ormond Lordship in the County of Kilkenny, 1515–1642: The Rise and Fall of Butler Feudal Power* (Dublin: Four Courts Press, 2003).
[38] Ibid., 14–16.   [39] Ibid., 17–26.
[40] Nicholls, *Gaelic and Gaelicized Ireland*, 23–31 is a concise description of Gaelic lordship; for tanistry see 29. As he points out, the cohort of eligible candidates, called the *derbfine*, technically consisted of all descendants of a former head of the lineage through four generations, including illegitimate offspring, although the list of viable candidates was invariably much smaller. A few septs, like the O'Sullivan Bear in the southwest, practiced primogeniture.

obligations, especially supplying the lord and his entourage with hospitality.[41] Additional lineages supplied the lord with galloglass warriors,[42] brehon jurists, who arbitrated disputes according to Irish legal custom, and poets who, in addition to composing encomiastic verse praising a lord and his ancestors, kept and constructed genealogies, acted as arbiters of honor, and, when angered, wrote rhymed curses believed capable of inflicting physical injury and even death.[43] Property belonging to the church also had hereditary custodians, called *erenaghs* or *coarbs*, whose families supplied priests and other ecclesiastics.[44]

Although often described in English sources as petty despotisms, in reality Irish lordships more closely resembled hierarchical coalitions of lineage groups exercising collective control over large tracts of land, the animals and other resources that the land supported, and a subordinate peasantry enjoying few rights. Relations within a lordship were shaped by a distinctive code of honor and customary expectations, sustained in part through the ritual life of a lord's principle residence.[45] This typically consisted of a towerhouse attached to a bawn or walled enclosure containing various service buildings and a large hall, a complex that functioned simultaneously as a defensible stronghold, a symbolic manifestation of power, a center of estate administration over adjacent demesne lands, and a seigneurial court that provided a setting for lavish hospitality, recitations of bardic poetry, and consultations between the lord and his dependents.[46] Lords also possessed additional towerhouses, sometimes located in the territories of their subordinates, that helped secure control of strategic sites. But *uiiriaghs*, galloglass, and brehons also had castles and military followings, and their loyalty could not always be taken for granted. Irish lordships depended on webs of obligations and loyalties between distant kin and other interested groups that were frequently

---

[41] Ibid., 26-7 and 34-40 describes the various forms of rent or tribute; Patrick Duffy, "Social and Spatial Order in the MacMahon Lordship of Aighialla in the Late Sixteenth Century," in *Gaelic Ireland*, ed. Duffy et al., 115-37, provides a detailed examination of the hierarchical division of land in one South Ulster lordship.

[42] See below, p. 238.

[43] Nicholls, *Gaelic and Gaelicized Ireland*, 50-7 (for brehons) and 93-5 (for poets).

[44] For a concise summary see Brian Mac Cuarta, *Catholic Revival in the North of Ireland, 1603-1641* (Dublin: Four Courts Press, 2007), 23-4. *Coarbs*, hereditary representatives of saints who were often keepers of relics or custodians of holy sites, had a higher status than *erenaghs*, who merely controlled church lands. Since rules of clerical celibacy were not strictly observed in Ireland before Tridentine reforms gradually took hold in the seventeenth century, ecclesiastical positions were sometimes passed from father to son. Although focused on an earlier period, Katharine Simms, *Gaelic Ulster in the Middle Ages: History, Culture and Society* (Dublin: Four Courts Press, 2020), part 2, is a highly illuminating discussion of all matters touched on in this paragraph.

[45] For a sensitive discussion of Irish honor culture see Brendan Kane, *The Politics and Culture of Honour in Britain and Ireland, 1541-1641* (Cambridge: Cambridge University Press, 2010).

[46] James Lyttleton, *The Jacobean Plantations in Seventeenth-Century Offaly: An Archaeology of a Changing World* (Dublin: Four Courts Press, 2013), chapter 5, esp. 63-107; Nicholls, *Gaelic and Gaelicized Ireland*, 142; Rolf Loeber, "An Architectural History of Gaelic Castles and Settlements, 1370-1600," in *Gaelic Ireland*, ed. Duffy et al., 271-314.

disrupted by internal rivalries and conflicts of interest. Maintaining them required considerable skill and effort, involving both force and negotiation.

Although Irish society had always been warlike, Katharine Simms has shown that it grew more militarized over the course of the Middle Ages, in ways that increased the arbitrary power of sept leaders over their dependents and a subject peasantry.[47] In addition to elite horsemen from among their own kindred and bands of lightly armed kern or peasants, lords acquired forces of galloglass, descended from Scottish Gaelic mercenaries, who fought in chain mail with heavy swords or axes. They also gained a customary right to compel their peasants to feed and shelter their soldiers, an obligation known as coign and livery. Well before the sixteenth century, surviving English lordships in Ireland had adopted these Gaelic practices, which enabled both Old English and Irish lords to muster seigneurial armies of considerable size. At the start of his rebellion Desmond reportedly commanded 160 cavalry, 800 galloglass and as many kern, in addition "to a number of loose persons that are run to him out of sundry countries in this province [Munster]." His elite followers brought him an additional 100 horse, 500 galloglass and 800 kern.[48]

Although pitched battles did occasionally occur, Irish warfare tended to involve skirmishing in wooded or boggy terrain and raids to steal or destroy food and livestock, rather than attempts to seize and hold territory.[49] For this reason, human casualties often remained limited in comparison to very large losses of animals and other property. Ormond claimed in 1565 that his conflict with the earl of Desmond had resulted in the theft or slaughter within his lordship of 13,000 cattle, 6,000 plough horses, 31,000 sheep, and 10,000 pigs, compared to the killing of 165 people.[50] Even in times of relative peace, lords sometimes sought to harness predatory energies and direct them outward, to plunder, harass, and weaken rivals, including those who shared a common political allegiance.[51] In addition to his running conflict with Desmond, which eventually merged into royal efforts to suppress that earl's rebellion, Ormond pursued at least two other campaigns of theft and harassment along the borders of his earldom against dependents of lords loyal to the crown. He had a running feud with Barnaby FitzPatrick, baron of Upper Ossory, whose lordship lay just to the north of Kilkenny, that led to "daily robberies" committed by followers of both

---

[47] Katharine Simms, *From Kings to Warlords: The Changing Political Structure of Gaelic Ireland in the Later Middle Ages* (Woodbridge: Boydell Press, 1987).

[48] TNA SP63/72/8.

[49] For an illuminating discussion see David Edwards, "The Escalation of Violence in Sixteenth-Century Ireland," in *Age of Atrocity: Violence and Political Conflict in Early Modern Ireland*, ed. David Edwards, Pádraig Lenihan, and Clodagh Tait (Dublin: Four Courts Press, 2007), 34–78, esp. 38–53.

[50] Anthony McCormack, *The Earldom of Desmond, 1463-1583: The Decline and Crisis of a Feudal Lordship* (Dublin: Four Courts Press, 2005), 107.

[51] As has often been pointed out, "the martial culture of Irish lordship meant that rulers had to demonstrate their ability to rule through the incursion and plundering of neighbouring lordships" (Lyttleton, *Jacobean Plantations*, 95).

aristocrats.[52] Although of Gaelic descent, Upper Ossory had, like Ormond, grown up at the English court, as a childhood companion of the future Edward VI, with whom he formed a close friendship. A convinced Protestant, he also enjoyed good relations with the earl of Leicester. He cooperated outwardly with the crown, promising to introduce reforms into his lordship, while taking care to avoid any substantive changes that might weaken his control.[53] But despite Ormond's efforts to suggest otherwise, he remained basically loyal.[54] In 1579 and 1580 the Irish lord Justice, William Pelham, tried to end the feud, by calling the two lords before him, compelling them to shake hands, making both enter into bonds to restore stolen animals, and trying to arrange further meetings to arbitrate their disagreements.[55] He failed not only to resolve the conflict but also to prevent its escalation, as Ormond's heir, viscount Montgarret, led a campaign of destruction into the FitzPatrick lordship. Pelham had to admit to Upper Ossory that he was simply too busy suppressing Desmond's rebellion to deal with Montgarret for the moment, and pleaded with him not to retaliate in kind.[56]

In 1580 Thomas Maisterson, the royal governor of Wexford, whose hinterland bordered Ormond's earldom to the southeast, complained bitterly about the depredations of a band of Irish with the charming name of Art Boys that had been raiding his territory. The Art Boys were followers of a senior branch of the once powerful MacMurrough sept, ancient kings of Leinster, whose territorial claims had formerly extended into Wexford. The crown had suppressed the MacMurrough lordship in 1557 to facilitate expanding English control and plantation, but the Art Boys evidently continued to resist their sept's displacement twenty years later.[57] Maisterson reported that they assembled "in warlike manner to the number of two hundred persons, eating and taking coign and livery and black rents... and in the English country wasting, burning and murdering at their pleasure." In all they conducted forty-nine separate raids over a three-year period starting in 1577, stealing or killing well over a thousand cattle and numerous horses and pigs, burning two settlements, and murdering several people. Maisterson responded by assembling his forces and killing or hanging fifty-nine Art Boys, and then carried two to Dublin for trial. Ormond thereupon wrote to the Irish privy council, demanding that it release Maisterson's prisoners and commit him to prison in their place. He appears to have been acting as the group's patron,

---

[52] LPL Mss. 597, fol. 22r.
[53] See David Edwards, "Collaboration without Anglicisation: The MacGiollapdraig Lordship and Tudor Reform," in *Gaelic Ireland*, ed. Duffy et al., 77–98.
[54] LPL Mss. 597, fol. 20, Upper Ossory to Leicester, June 7, 1581, complaining of his imprisonment on charges fabricated by Ormond.
[55] LPL Mss. 597, fols 22r and v, 37v, 40v and 41v, 180r.   [56] Ibid., fols 270v–271v.
[57] See Nicholls, *Gaelic and Gaelicized Ireland*, 203–4 for the background. The name must specifically have derived from that of one of the three sons of Murrough Ballach, king of Leinster in the early sixteenth century named Art Buidhe or Boy (d. 1517) and his son, Murtough Mac Art Boy, the penultimate McMurrough king of Leinster, who died in 1547.

probably in an effort to keep new English plantations and more direct English governance away from his lordship.[58] Maisterson had to appeal to Walsingham to protect him from the queen's cousin and the commander of her army in Munster.

Negotiation or Radical Reform? The Dilemmas of Irish Governance

These localized eruptions of violence and theft, involving an English governor and two lords raised at the English court, stand in ironic contrast to the happier situation in Ulster reported by Sir Henry Sidney in 1578. Here the powerful Irish lord Turlough O'Neill relied on the lord deputy's intervention to obtain justice for the killing of his son by followers of the rival O'Donnell sept, rather than starting a feud that might have plunged the whole province into conflict. Sidney praised O'Neill's restraint, while adding that neither he nor O'Donnell sought "to entertain Scots [as mercenaries] or seek their own revenges," but instead sued to him "for aid of English forces" and conformed to his orders. As a result, Ulster remained "quiet" and "a good neighbor to the Pale."[59] This was a prime example of the kind of pacification through English mediation that royal servants like Sidney hoped to impose on the entire island. It unfortunately proved impossible to achieve consistently, not because Irish lords were necessarily disloyal but because whether loyal or not they pursued their own interests, attempting whenever possible to draw the crown and its armed forces into their private quarrels, and acting unilaterally when the Dublin authorities failed to satisfy their demands.

Failure to respond adequately to predatory raiding damaged the authority of any lord in Ireland, including the queen of England. But Elizabeth's Irish army remained far too small to suppress disorder everywhere in a consistent way. That made it tempting, especially for a queen who hated spending money, to rely on Irish lords to police their own territories, while trying to persuade them to adopt more orderly English habits and promote crown initiatives like the appointment of sheriffs and the planting of small English colonies. This was essentially the strategy pursued by Anthony St Leger during long terms as head of the Dublin government under Henry VIII, Edward VI, and Mary. Central to it were agreements of "surrender and regrant" by which Irish lords renounced their rights under Irish custom in return for title to their lands under English common law,

---

[58] TNA SP63/73/66 I and II. Cf. the similar efforts of the McCarthy earl of Clancar to prevent the new Munster plantation from spreading too close to his territory in the far southwest by fomenting raids, described in Breen, *Gaelic Lordship*, 124–9.

[59] LPL Mss. 601, fol. 73v.

supplemented in some cases by a grant of nobility as an Irish earl or baron.[60] These arrangements required the replacement of tanistry by primogeniture and, at least in principle, a transition from customary Gaelic notions of collective possession of territory to more clearly defined individual freeholds and tenancies. Some lords welcomed the changes, which, in addition to securing their ability to pass their position down to their eldest sons, gave them tighter control over occupants of their lands and opportunities to expand their income by charging cash rents.[61]

But there were inevitably losers, including the younger sons and other close relatives of the lord who lost their right to compete to succeed him. In several cases this led to local wars that forced the crown to intervene, or even serial rebellions by aggrieved parties, in which local power struggles became entangled with wider issues.[62] Two sons of Ulick Burke first earl of Clanricard, whose claims to succeed their father the crown had denied, escaped from captivity in Dublin and raised a revolt in the earldom in 1576. As they did so they discarded their English dress, to suggest that they rebelled against English domination as well as to settle their own private grievances. Four years later when they rebelled again they embraced "the Pope's cause." Although they may have done so for purely opportunistic reasons, their behavior shows how private quarrels were becoming linked to ethnic and religious resentment of English rule.[63] When Clanricard's third son, William Burke, returned to the province "out of England" in 1580 he was welcomed by a mass celebrated in his honor, attended by a large number of people.[64] One wonders if a local clergyman had not arranged the event as a way of co-opting William for the Catholic cause.

Even under a system of delegated authority, the king or queen retained ultimate responsibility for keeping the peace and overseeing the administration of justice throughout Ireland, once the island had been formally defined as a kingdom in 1542. Deputy lieutenants, as the monarch's representatives, therefore had to mediate disputes among the Irish and intervene with force when mediation failed and conflict escalated to unacceptable levels. St Leger performed these functions with reasonable effectiveness but under his successors disputes within Ireland became entangled with factional competition at the English court and within the Dublin administration. In his conflict with Desmond, Ormond enjoyed the support of the earl of Sussex, the queen's deputy during the early years of her reign, whereas Sussex's successor, Sir Henry Sidney, who depended on Sussex's

---

[60] Heffernan, *Debating Tudor Policy*, 45, argues that these grants were always a *pis aller* from the perspective of English reformers and governors, necessitated by the refusal of Henry VIII and his successors to invest in more systematic campaigns of conquest.
[61] For an example see Bernadette Cunningham, *Clanricard and Thomond, 1540–1640: Provincial Politics and Society Transformed* (Dublin: Four Courts Press, 2012), esp. chapter 4.
[62] The standard account is Brady, *Chief Governors*.
[63] Cunningham, *Clanricard and Thomond*, 34.   [64] LPL Mss. 619, fol. 32.

rival Leicester, initially showed greater sympathy for Desmond. Throughout the period Ormond had both supporters and detractors at the court in London and among English officials and captains in Ireland, while in the early 1590s similar disagreements erupted over how to handle the earl of Tyrone. Competition and rivalry among Ireland's English rulers, along with the relatively short terms of most deputy lieutenants after the 1570s, impeded firm and consistent policies, making the task of managing Ireland's internal conflicts still more difficult.[65]

Quite apart from these practical problems, some crown servants chafed at conciliatory policies that in their view encouraged disobedience by abdicating the queen's responsibility to enforce justice rigorously in a savage island. They advocated a more thorough transformation of Irish society through measures to curb the excessive power of Irish lords, suppress "barbaric" customs, and promote a more civil pattern of life. We should not, however, oversimplify the distinction between policies of accommodation and forcible reform, since the choice between these approaches often depended more on specific circumstances than philosophical principles. "Moderates" like St Leger led brutal campaigns of reprisal against septs that openly defied their authority, while aggressive deputies like Sidney and Sir John Perrot employed negotiation as well as violence. Rather than choosing one method over the other, English officials had to decide when and how to employ each in turn to deal with specific challenges. But a variety of English views did develop about the nature and scale of the reforms required to rule Ireland, and the amount of force needed to achieve them.

As Brendan Bradshaw demonstrated in the 1970s, some reform schemes originated as early as the second decade of the sixteenth century among the Old English of the Pale. Although colored by humanist ideas, they also reflected the outlook of a community that had long supplied the Dublin government with lawyers, judges, and administrative officers, and whose members often trained at the Inns of Court in London. The reformers blamed recent Irish governors for failing to enforce the common law throughout the island. They attributed the declining use of the law to an expansion of barbaric Gaelic culture during the recent past, as well as the rapacity and tyranny of great English lords like the earls of Kildare, Desmond, and Ormond, who had become virtually independent of the crown.[66] Their proposed solutions included the curtailment of magnate power; an enlargement of the authority of the king's deputy; greater reliance on middling landowners, rather than magnates, in keeping order; the encouragement of trade and arable farming; and a revitalization and expansion of the machinery of crown government, not just in the Pale but throughout Ireland. Some reformers also

---

[65] Brendan Bradshaw, *The Irish Constitutional Revolution of the Sixteenth Century* (Cambridge: Cambridge University Press, 1979). Cf. Ciaran Brady, "From Policy to Power: The Evolution of Tudor Reform Strategies in Sixteenth-Century Ireland," in *Reshaping Ireland*, ed. Mac Cuarta, 21–42.
[66] Bradshaw, *Irish Constitutional Revolution*, 38–9.

wanted a renewal of colonization by new English plantations, and the construction of a network of castles and walled towns to dominate the countryside.[67] While hostile to native Irish custom, they had some sympathy for the Irish population, which they hoped to assimilate within a civil society or commonwealth loyal to the crown.[68]

Although Bradshaw does not stress the point, his research suggests that the common law may have seemed even more important to the descendants of English colonists in the Tudor Pale and Irish towns than it did to most people in England, because in Ireland people were unable to take its role for granted.[69] Even Dubliners lived within sight of districts in the Wicklow Mountains where very different legal customs applied, and felt vulnerable to Irish raids and the arbitrary power of lords like Kildare. The common law formed part of their identity as civil English inhabitants of Ireland, while affording them opportunities for employment in the judicial and administrative machinery of the Dublin government, and protection against seigneurial oppression. They accordingly viewed common law governance as a means of extending their power, influence, and way of life. The 1542 act establishing Ireland as a kingdom and extending the protections of the law to the native population represented a triumph for this vision, at least on the statute book. On the other hand, Mark Heffernan's more systematic recent analysis shows that the promotion of common law and other instruments of "civilizing" reform should not be over-emphasized. The main emphasis in the great majority of the early Tudor treatises was on the expansion of the English Pale through military conquests in Leinster.[70]

Rather than an alternative to forceful conquest, reform was often envisaged as its concomitant, since the extension of "civil" English governance required the crushing of rebellions and forceful methods of dealing with marauding septs and thieving woodkern. Some reformers envisaged a transitional period of military rule in less settled regions, to create conditions in which a civil government under the common law became practical. Something like this had taken place in Wales after its incorporation into England by statute in the 1540s. The Welsh precedent helped inspire the appointment of presidents backed by small military forces in Munster, Connacht, and eventually Ulster, who were charged with suppressing crime and rebellion and mediating local disputes, with the goal of slowly drawing smaller septs and landowners into dependence on the crown, rather than regional magnates. The project enjoyed some early success in Connacht and Munster in the 1570s.[71]

---

[67] Ibid., 44–8.   [68] Ibid., 48–55.   [69] Cf. Brady, "From Policy to Power," 27.
[70] Heffernan, *Debating Tudor Policy*, esp. 10–11, 26–7, and 45–8.
[71] Canny, *Elizabethan Conquest*, 106–14; Cunningham, *Clanricard and Thomond*; Heffernan, *Debating Tudor Policy*, 124–7.

But the queen's refusal to accept a large increase in the military budget for Ireland, along with the resistance of many lords to reductions of their own authority, impeded progress. Sussex and, more especially, Sidney attempted to deal with the problem by expanding and systematizing levies known as the cess, previously imposed on an ad hoc basis, in order to finance an expansion of the Irish army with Irish resources.[72] The experiment succeeded remarkably well in the present-day County Mayo in western Connacht, where the local president, Nicholas Malby, eventually secured the cooperation of the district's two dominant lords, the earls of Clanricard and Thomond. By cooperating with Malby in the collection and administration of the cess they managed to consolidate their own power, while he succeeded in enlarging the armed forces at his disposal from 350 to 1,000 men through the use of local resources.[73] But as discussed in the previous chapter, in many parts of Ireland coign and livery continued to be exacted, the effort to turn the cess into a regular tax faltered, and bands of soldiers used it as an excuse to extort food and lodging from Irish peasants.[74]

To inhabitants of the Pale, the new tax looked like another arbitrary abuse of power that violated the subject's common law rights. Organized opposition surfaced as early as 1561 at the Inns of Court, when twenty-five students born in Ireland signed a petition against the cess. Another petition circulated in the Pale in 1574, two years before Sidney's arrival in Ireland. Several preachers, along with merchants and landowners, joined the agitation. In 1576 two Pale lawyers, Henry Burnell and Richard Netterville, traveled to London to present their case against the cess to the queen. Their arguments offended her and they ended up in the Tower, but opposition continued into the 1580s, spearheaded by lawyers who styled themselves "commonwealthmen."[75] The belief in the common law as an instrument of reform had come into collision with the program of an impatient deputy lieutenant, who believed reform demanded a more drastic military program funded by a tax imposed by prerogative authority, which he felt entitled to use as the queen's representative.

---

[72] Canny, *Elizabethan Conquest* is the classic treatment of Sidney's program. For the vague origins of the cess and its initial expansion by Sussex see Brady, *Chief Governors*, 87–9. Brady, "From Policy to Power," 30–5, sees a significant shift of emphasis, from earlier reforming attempts to eliminate coign and livery and the armed force it supported to Sidney's attempt to standardize and absorb coign and livery, rechristened as cess, within a new system of English military control. Heffernan, *Debating Tudor Policy*, 124–46 argues that Canny exaggerated the importance of Sidney's deputyship in what was, in reality, a more gradual process. For Sidney's own views see *A Viceroy's Vindication: Sir Henry Sidney's Memoir of Service in Ireland, 1556–1578*, ed. Ciaran Brady (Cork: Cork University Press, 2002), 30–6.
[73] Cunningham, *Clanricard and Thomond*, chapters 1–3.   [74] Above, pp. 194–5.
[75] Nessa Malone, "Henry Burnell and Richard Malone: Lawyers in Civic Life in the English Pale, 1562–1615," in *Religion and Politics in Urban Ireland, c. 1500–c. 1750: Essays in Honour of Colm Lennon*, ed. Salvador Ryan and Clodagh Tait (Dublin: Four Courts Press, 2016), 89–107; Brady, *Chief Governors*, 238. Heffernan, *Debating Tudor Policy*, 147–51 again argues for the gradual growth of opposition to perceived arbitrary acts of governing authority and the burdens of the military expansion of crown authority, rather than a more narrowly focused reaction to Sidney.

As this happened, the eruption of Desmond's rebellion, followed by that of Baltinglass within the Pale itself in 1580, further hardened the views of English officials sympathetic to Sidney. They grew more convinced than ever that Ireland required drastic reforms carried out by force and that anyone who impeded such measures was effectively an enemy of the queen and the state. Sir Nicholas Malby, who had been brought to Ireland by Sidney, advised that "the only mean to preserve the realm to her majesty is to settle sufficient forces in every province by which the evil disposed men [may] be kept from mischiefs and forced to obey."[76] This argument served the interests of Malby and other captains, who stood to gain from an expanded English military presence. But it also reflected the conviction repeatedly expressed in military treatises that disciplined bands of soldiers provided the last bulwark against anarchy in societies where law, morality, and religion failed to restrain perverse human behavior. Stereotypes of Irish savagery and bestiality made it easier to justify large-scale killing. Some proponents of severity came close to advocating genocide. Sir Henry Wallop told Walsingham that "there is no way to daunt this people but by the edge of the sword and to plant better in their places."[77] "The first means to reduce Ireland into subjection must be to extirpate this generation of vipers out of Leinster...viz. the Cavanaghs, the O'Byrnes, the O'Tooles, O'Murres and O'Connors," he stated on another occasion.[78] An anonymous manuscript treatise by an embittered Munster planter, attributed by Hiram Morgan to Edmund Spenser, variously compared the Irish to Amalekites—a tribe that earned God's condemnation by assaulting the Jews on their flight from Egypt—moors whose blackness can never be cleansed, and noxious plants. "Out with your mowers, give them scythes in their hands: let them make smooth work. Cut down all before them, for all that are left are weeds."[79]

Despite such language it is not clear that these writers regarded Irish incorrigibility as an inherent racial trait, rather than something caused by environmental conditions, religious hatred, and ethnic antagonisms. In another passage, the

---

[76] TNA SP63/74/50.   [77] TNA SP63/85/27.
[78] TNA SP63/84/4, Wallop to Burghley, August 6, 1581.
[79] BL Add Mss. 34,313, fols 110v ("Weeds they are O Queen, the natural plants of their own soil; the earth of Ireland is their natural mother, a stepdame to us. You can never so cherish us, what care for ever you take about our planting, unless you seek to supplant them") and 118r; 111v ("They are that very Amalekites that God hath often given (as he doth now) into the hands of England. They have always been thorns in the sides of us, because we have neglected the charge that God hath given us. What his sentence was against Amkaecke in the time of Isarel, the same is his sentence now against the Irish, his enemies, in the time of the gospel"); and 108r ("They are black moors O Queen; wash them as long as you will, you shall never alter their hue. Your mercy will not change their manners; your benefits, be they never so abundantly showered (?) upon them will never wash away the corruption of their nature, nor the blessings of God, did they in number pass the stars in heaven or the sands in the seas"). For the attribution to Spenser see Hiram Morgan, "'Tempt not God too long, O Queen': Elizabeth and the Irish Crisis of the 1590s," in *Elizabeth I and Ireland*, ed. Brednan Kane and Valerie McGowen-Doyle (Cambridge: Cambridge University Press, 2014), 209–38. A printed edition of this tract edited by Wiley Maley appeared in *Analecta Hibernica* 36 (1995): 3–77.

Munster planter blamed Ireland's misery on the mistakes and injustices of English officials, including the queen: "Our sins set up Irish government, plucked down the English; our sins blinded the eyes of understanding in our chief rulers. Instead of justice they set up injustice; instead of the pillar of peace they set up the flag of disturbance."[80] He blamed differences in faith, manners, and customs for intensifying Irish animosity toward their rulers:

> The contrarieties in religion, the diversity in language have been the hatchers of this deadly hatred in the hearts of the people; they have sat brooding upon them until they have brought out this mortal hate against us, against our laws, against our customs. Wiser they are in their generations than we or our rulers were. They see what force uniformity of speech hath to procure love and friendship, to continue a society and fellowship; they have therefore proclaimed it in their camp death to speak English, death to wear English apparel.[81]

Rather than rooting out the Irish people the English needed to eradicate Ireland's language, manners, and popish superstition, for "every conqueror brings ever three things with him to establish his conquest: religion, the law and the language of his country: without the which he can never have any firm footing ... but that an age or twain will wear him out."[82] These comments parallel the descriptions of the Norman Conquest penned a few years later by Samuel Daniel and Sir John Hayward, as an event that began with the harsh rule of the sword but soon led to the transformation of English society through the imposition of Norman customs.[83]

Although Spenser attributed the Irish penchant for violence partly to their descent from the Scythians, he also blamed Irish education "in their own kind of military discipline," the influence of bardic poetry—which nevertheless contained passages "of sweet wit and good invention"—and the tendency of a pastoral economy to encourage idleness, incivility, and warlike habits.[84] He advocated a reformation by the sword but stipulated that it should entail the "cutting off of ... evils ... and not of the people which are evil, for evil people by good ordinance and government may be made good, but the evil that is of itself evil will never become good."[85] But reform did require draconian methods because barbaric customs and resistance to English control were so deeply rooted. As Sir Philip Sidney put it, merciful policies appealed to gentle natures but

---

[80] BL Add. Mss. 34,313, fols 91r, 96r, 103r, 103v (popery as the root of rebellion); 85v–86, 87v and 100 (mistakes in English governance, the last two passages explicitly blaming Elizabeth); 92 (quotation). Cf. Wallop's comments in Ciaran Brady NA SP63/102/85, where his complaints are directed against Irish Catholicism and attachment to Spain.

[81] BL Add. Mss. 34,313, 115r.   [82] Ibid., 114v–115.   [83] Above, pp. 15–16.

[84] Edmund Spenser, *A View of the Present State of Ireland*, ed. L. W. Renwick (Oxford: Oxford University Press, 1970), 4.

[85] Ibid., 94–5.

truly the general nature of all countries not fully conquered is plainly against it. For until by time they find the sweetness of due subjection, it is impossible that any gentle means should put out the fresh remembrance of lost liberty. And that the Irishman is that way as obstinate as any nation, with whom no other passion can prevail but fear, beside their [hi]story, which plainly paints it out, their manner of life wherein they choose rather all filthiness than any law and their own consciences who best know their own natures, give sufficient proof of it. For under the sun there is not a nation which live more tyrannously than they do one over the other.[86]

Sir John Perrot agreed: "It is far from me to desire any extirpation but rather that all might be saved that were good for the country to be saved. Yet this I say, till your majesty's sword hath meekened all, I think it neither honor nor safety to grant mercy to any."[87]

A view of Ireland as a place where the basest human instincts had been allowed to run amok gave rise to the belief that recent English arrivals were prone to degenerate in an Irish environment, and the conviction that descendants of most of the original English colonists had long since done so. It helps account for the way in which Spenser and other writers associated Irish savagery with the undeveloped state of Ireland's landscape, as if the island's woods, bogs, and thickets corresponded to the condition of its inhabitants' souls. The failure to exploit Ireland's natural commodities and improve the landscape appeared symptomatic of a savage society, in which people preferred to live idly by herding cows and robbing each other, instead of seeking profit through productive labor. Better methods of tillage and new industries would therefore lead not only to material profit but also beneficial changes in habits and behavior. Perrot proposed establishing shipbuilding and iron industries, with the threefold purpose of strengthening the navy, generating gainful employment, and thinning the woods that sheltered rebels.[88] He insisted that even Ireland's notorious bogs might yield employment and profit if thoroughly searched. "A reformation will breed a competent wealth and competent wealth retain the men in a liking obedience, where desperate poverty and beggary runs head long into rebellion."[89] Pelham also wanted to convert Irish timber into English ships, while cracking down on piracy and smuggling, so that the river valleys of Munster would become a source of profit to the crown and the Irish themselves, instead of a seed bed of rebellion.[90] In the early 1580s Sir Henry Sidney sought to establish an Irish cloth industry, "for the suppression of idleness and profit of the people with gain by custom for the

---

[86] *Miscellaneous Prose of Sir Philip Sidney*, ed. Katherine Duncan-Jones and Jan Van Dorsten (Oxford: Oxford University Press, 1973), 11.
[87] BL Add Mss. 48,017, fol. 64.
[88] BL Add Mss. 48,017, fol. 70v, Perrot's proposals for reforming Ireland, 1581.
[89] Ibid., fols 70v, 71r.   [90] Ibid., fol. 85.

queen"; to further the project he resettled forty Protestant families fleeing religious persecution in the Low Countries in a decayed Irish town, which they promptly re-edified.[91]

Not all New English officials in Ireland shared a belief in the need for drastic reforms imposed by the sword. Heffernan has shown that the majority of reform treatises written between 1579 and 1603, by men born in England as well as Ireland, blamed the island's problems primarily on abuses by royal officials and soldiers rather than on Irish savagery.[92] Emphasis on forceful compulsion and systematic social and economic reform was especially characteristic of a particular group of officials with close ties to Leicester, Sidney, and Walsingham.[93] Although he supported schemes of economic development, Burghley felt uncomfortable with the violence used to suppress the Desmond rebellion, writing that "it is no marvel that the [Irish] people have rebellious hearts, for the Flemings had not such cause to rebel by the oppressions of the Spaniards as it is reported the Irish people have." He told one acquaintance that if the deputy lieutenant who suppressed the revolt, Arthur Lord Grey, had lived under Henry VIII he would have been decapitated for alienating the hearts of the crown's Irish subjects.[94] The Old English judge, Nicholas White, similarly warned that a "violent and warlike form of government will but exhaust her majesty's treasure, waste her realm, depopulate her pale, weaken her English nobility that have been and may be made the surety of this state."[95]

But despite such misgivings, with which the queen had considerable sympathy, harsher methods often prevailed, in part because they appealed to many crown servants of military background tasked with upholding royal authority on the ground. Thomas Churchyard's approving description of the methods employed by Sir Humphrey Gilbert exemplifies this attitude. When confronting Irish rebels Gilbert would first offer them the queen's mercy, "which if they once refused, although it were with never so mild an answer or that they did but so much as throw a stone at the messenger, were he but a horse boy, he [Gilbert] would never after by any means receive them to grace but would subdue them by the sword." He "killed man, woman and child and spoiled, wasted and burned the ground... leaving nothing of the enemy's in safety, which he could profitably waste or consume." Gilbert justified these methods both on practical grounds—since women and boys furnished food for Irish soldiers, killing them helped starve enemies into submission—and because it was dishonorable for a prince's representative to spare rebels. The queen's wounded dignity required ferocious retribution. After a victory,

---

[91] Ibid., fol. 147r.   [92] Heffernan, *Debating Tudor Policy*, 175–89.   [93] Ibid., 177–85.
[94] TNA SP63/93/17, Wallop to Burghley, paraphrasing the latter's attitude.
[95] TNA SP63/87/55, White to Burghley, December 23, 1581.

his manner was that the heads of all those (of what sort they were) which were killed in the day should be cut from their bodies and brought to the place where he encamped at night and should there be laid on the ground, by each side of the way leading to his own tent, so that none could come into his tent for any cause but commonly he must pass through a lane of heads, which he used *ad terrorem*, the dead feeling nothing the more pains thereby, and yet did it bring great terror to the people when they saw the heads of their dead fathers, brothers, children, kinfolk and friends lie on the ground before their faces as they came to speak with the said colonel.

Churchyard conceded that this "course of government may be thought by some too cruel" but justified it on the grounds that the Irish committed similar atrocities, and because it worked. Gilbert so terrified his opponents that "they made sundry songs and rhymes of him (and his black curtal horse), imagining himself to have been an enchanter that no man could hurt, riding on a devil." "Through the terror which the people conceived of him, it made short wars. For he reformed the whole country of Munster and brought it into a universal peace and subjection within six weeks."[96]

To a degree, captains like Gilbert adopted methods, including scorched-earth campaigns and the taking of heads as battle trophies, used by the Irish themselves.[97] English commanders felt they had little choice but to wage war in the Irish manner, by seizing animals and food stocks and burning settlements, because their enemies conducted hit-and-run campaigns and retreated into wild terrain when pursued. The only way to defeat them was therefore to strip the countryside on which they depended bare of resources.[98] Ruthless tactics also seemed necessary because the enemy so often outnumbered English forces. Superior weaponry and discipline usually, although not always, allowed English armies to prevail in set battles.[99] But prolonged guerrilla campaigns in difficult terrain wasted armies, which suffered more losses from disease than encounters with the enemy. This prospect, together with urgent demands from London to conserve treasure by crushing rebellions quickly, inspired efforts to break Irish resistance through terror. Gilbert's construction of head hedges took place during a campaign against Irish forces that outnumbered his own troops by about four-to-one, which might easily have defeated him in a war of attrition if he had not terrified them into surrendering.[100] In addition, *ad terrorem* methods struck some theorists

---

[96] Thomas Churchyard, *A General Rehearsall of Warre* (London, 1579), sigs Qiv–Ri.
[97] *The Annals of the Four Masters* provides numerous examples, dating back to legends of prehistoric battles and extending to the sixteenth century.
[98] TNA SP63/74/5.I.   [99] Maginn, *Leinster*, 160–5.
[100] Rory Rapple, "Sir Humphrey Gilbert," in *ODNB*; cf. Rapple's comments about the exemplary character of violence in Irish campaigns in Rory Rapple, *Martial Power and Elizabethan Political Culture: Military Men in England and Ireland, 1558–1594* (Cambridge: Cambridge University Press, 2009), 237–8.

as especially effective against uncivil enemies, "for the hearts of rebels trembleth where the prince's power is presented and the wits and purposes of a savage people goes a wool gathering, when the civil soldier is certainly grounded in manly determination."[101]

Whereas Irish raids tended to have a sporadic quality, English captains resorted to systematic killing on an expanded scale. After winning battles they routinely put captives to the sword. Grey boasted of executing almost 1,500 Irish of note during his three years in Ireland, "not accounting those of the meaner sort, nor yet executions by law and killing of churls, which were innumerable."[102] While establishing a garrison to protect the frontiers of the Pale in 1581, he made a sweep through the adjoining territory, slaying "diverse in those woods," burning villages, and destroying food supplies.[103] Spenser allegorized his patron's exploits through the partnership of Artegall—representing Lord Grey, as well as the quality of Justice—with the Iron Man Tallus, who mows down offenders with his terrible flail. Derricke had earlier celebrated Sir Henry Sidney's methods in similar terms: "He mauls them down. / He strikes them in the chase."[104] Non-combatants, including children, were not spared. When Malby finally took Richard Inyeren's remote castle in April 1580 he slaughtered everyone he found within it, "men, women and children." Other castles in the district then promptly surrendered.[105] Pelham summarily executed fifty people he found within a castle he took in the same month, including sixteen Spaniards, shortly after he and Ormond completed a campaign through rebel territory in which they slaughtered "people where so ever we found them."[106] At about the same date Pelham's forces completed a sweep through bogs and woods in the Shannon valley in which they burned "many towns and habitations" and put to the sword an estimated 400 people.[107] "Albeit it were to be wished that the common people should not with their blood bear the burden of the earl's [Desmond's] offense," Pelham wrote, "yet for as much as they are all united as it were one man to shake your majesty's government, and to adhere to a new master, the example of terror must light upon some, for the reducing of a great number."[108] According to *The Annals of the Four Masters* the victims included "blind and feeble men, women, boys, girls, sick persons, idiots and old people."[109]

Harsh as they were, none of these methods broke definitively with the goal of turning Ireland into a civil commonwealth, where the rule of law, productive labor, and economic improvement would advance the pubic good, as responsible householders cooperated in governing their communities. But the emphasis had unquestionably tilted markedly toward the use of coercive force and terror. Mark Hutchinson has convincingly shown that a change in vocabulary, involving the growing frequency of references to the Irish administration as a *state* rather than a

---

[101] Churchyard, *General Rehearsal*, sig. Riii v.   [102] Connolly, *Contested Island*, 178.
[103] TNA SP63/83/45.   [104] *Image of Ireland*, sig. Eiii.   [105] TNA SP63/72/39.
[106] TNA SP63/72/28.   [107] LPL Mss. 597, fol. 483.   [108] Ibid.   [109] 1731.

commonwealth or mixed polity, accompanied this recourse to brutal force. In some cases, the choice of words seems to have been highly self-conscious. The secretary of the Irish council after 1580, Geoffrey Fenton, had earlier translated Guicciardini's *History of Italy*, the major work of an author credited by some modern scholars with inventing the concept of reason of state. His colleague, the clerk of the council Lodowick Briskett, also had a deep familiarity with Italian humanist political thought.[110] Hutchinson thinks that the influence of Bodin's *Six livres de la république*, published in 1576, with its development of a unitary concept of sovereignty, was probably also influential. Where earlier reformers had written of an Irish commonwealth to emphasize the role of the Old English elite in promoting constructive change, New English officials now spoke of a state based on the crown's prerogative powers as deployed by lord deputies and military officers.

The Religious Dimension

Frustration with the slow pace of progress in transforming Ireland into an obedient and "civil" kingdom contributed to this greater emphasis on authoritarian commands and coercion. But so, even more, did a growing recognition that the Reformation had failed to take root on the island, so that the vast majority of the population remained Catholic, and therefore of suspect loyalty. The way in which the Desmond and Baltinglass rebellions both presented themselves as Catholic uprisings aroused fears that religion was starting to inspire a level of unified opposition to English rule that had never existed in the past, and that might well imperil English control if the queen's forces did not react quickly and decisively. Malby warned Lord Burghley in 1580 that "wherever before these times the country people devised small occasions to rebel as for private quarreling it is now converted to a matter of religion, by which it is become so general a cause."[111] Captain Gregory Fenton predicted that if the queen did not quickly subdue Desmond and Baltinglass she would face "a twenty years war in Ireland."[112] Deputy Lieutenant Grey agreed: the "seed" of popery had had become too "plentiful in this land. Your Majesty must be careful therefore to root it out, otherwise would heaps of care, mass of treasure, continual war never account to sway this government."[113] Crown officials worried that the revolt would spread into Ulster and that a much larger invading force sponsored by Spain or the papacy might come to its aid.[114] If the Irish received more foreign assistance,

---

[110] Hutchinson, *Calvinism, Reform and the Absolutist State*, 86–92.   [111] TNA SP63/75/82.
[112] TNA SP63/96/29, Fenton to Burghley, October 14, 1582.   [113] TNA SP63/79/25.
[114] For persistent rumors of Spanish fleets and armies preparing to embark for Ireland during the Munster rebellion see TNA SP63/73/27; 74/12 and 63; 75/12; 77/51; 90/15. Reports of contacts between Turlough O'Neill and Munster malcontents persisted even after the suppression of Desmond's rising. See, e.g. SP63/111/43.

Sir George Carew predicted, "it will be hard for any Englishmen to dwell in this land, for there is no wars among themselves but all upon us, nothing so hateful as the name and habit of an Englishman."[115]

These alarmist pronouncements mirrored the arguments Nicholas Sander deployed to build support for Desmond's revolt, which in turn reflected the hopes of the community of English exiles in Rome described in a previous chapter.[116] Sander not only urged Irish lords to rebel for religious reasons; he also spread reports of an imminent Spanish invasion of Ireland or England, to encourage confidence and pressure wavering lords to join in resisting English rule. "Touching the controversy of inheritance which is said to be between your brother and you," he wrote to Ulick Burke, one of the discontented sons of the loyalist second earl of Clanricard, "where may you hope to have that better decided than in his holiness's camp?" But a prompt commitment was essential. "The time yet is such that you may deserve thanks and rewards, but when our aid is come, which daily we look for, when the Scottish and English nobility are in arms, as we doubt not they will be shortly, and when strangers begin to invade England itself, as diverse of the self English nobility labor and procure; afterwards (I say) it shall be small thanks before God and man to be of our company."[117] Sander and Desmond had even begun reallocating the lands of the crown and its supporters in Munster, in the expectation that a papal nuncio would soon arrive to confirm their acts.[118] The "cause of religion," Pelham lamented in November 1579, had procured sympathizers for the rebels even in the Old English towns, who believed reports "that a wonderful navy is prepared in Italy under the conduction of Romans, Neopolitans and Spaniards to come to the relief of the papists here."[119] "Every man of Munster is persuaded of foreign aid," he lamented in February 1580, an expectation that led several "gentlemen and freeholders of Limerick that have until now depended on her Majesty" to slight their castles and desert to the rebels.[120] The president of Munster, George Carew, concurred: "I dare assure your lordship there is no corporation, nor almost any kern in Munster that doth not look for a navy of Spaniards to arrive shortly."[121]

Until recently most authorities on the subject, including Nicholas Canny and Ciaran Brady, have discounted the role of Catholicism in Desmond's revolt, believing that Counter-Reformation ideology had not grown strong enough by 1580 to motivate more than a few people to take arms against the crown. But Henry Jeffries has vigorously contested this conclusion.[122] Efforts to spread

---

[115] TNA SP63/78/50. [116] Above, pp. 47–60, 87, and 97–8. [117] LPL Mss. 597, fol. 84v.
[118] Ibid., fol. 127r. [119] Ibid., fol. 115v. [120] Ibid., fol. 244.
[121] Ibid., fol. 219. For further evidence that Irish resistance was encouraged by rumors of imminent Spanish or continental assistance, often spread by Sander and other priests, see TNA SP63/72/23, 35, 39, SP63/71/43 and SP63/72/7, 28 and 55.
[122] *The Irish Church and the Tudor Reformations* (Dublin: Four Courts Press, 2010); Henry Jeffries, "Tudor Reformations in Cork," in *Religion and Politics in Urban Ireland*, ed. Ryan and Tait, 51–69;

Protestantism in Ireland had mainly failed, he argues, because of an extreme paucity of dedicated preachers, caused partly by the absence of schools for training them but also, apparently, by the fact that very few young Irish men wanted to become Protestant ministers. Even counties like Meath that had a number of reasonably endowed parishes therefore had few preaching ministers.[123] Although government pressure had some initial success in compelling attendance at prayer book services, very few converts were gained, except possibly in the town of Galway. Catholicism, by contrast, showed considerable signs of vigor. In the Pale the deprived Marian bishop of Meath, William Walsh, may have set up an underground network of priests to keep the faith alive. Many elite families began sending their sons to Catholic schools on the Continent.[124] Dominican and Franciscan friars helped sustain a vigorous Catholic community that the bishops of the official church did little or nothing to suppress. Friars turned Waterford into a center of Counter-Reformation activity and operated openly even in Galway. Protestants, on the other hand, "were forced to maintain a low profile for fear of their fellow citizens." When Sidney visited Galway, he was met by the nominally Protestant bishop and clergy in full Catholic vestments singing a *Te deum* in Latin.[125] Even where Protestantism had made inroads it remained far weaker than the rival faith.

Jeffries argues that attempts to impose conformity by Sidney and the Irish High Commission through stiff fines, which peaked just before the outbreak of widespread revolt, stirred significant resentment that added to the sense of grievance already felt over issues like the cess. "Religion, and a virulent anti-English sentiment, gave cohesion to the more mundane motivations of the rebels, while helping to sustain them over several difficult years when simple self-interest would have been far better served by submission to the crown."[126] Hopes of Spanish or papal assistance promised by Sander simultaneously made the prospect of overthrowing English rule appear more realistic.[127] Many lords who refrained from joining the rebellion but also did little to suppress it may have been waiting to see whether a large foreign army really would invade. Had it done so they would probably have joined in opposing the English and re-establishing Catholic worship. Jeffries believes that the earl of Kildare belonged to this cohort. His wife was accused of sheltering Catholics, including Sander.[128] New English officials had more justification than some historians have allowed for believing that most of the

---

Henry Jeffries, "Tudor Reformations Compared: The Irish Pale and Lancaster," in *Frontiers, States and Identity in Early Modern Ireland and Beyond: Essays in Honour of Steven G. Ellis*, ed. Christopher Maginn and Gerald Power (Dublin: Four Courts Press, 2016), 71–92.

[123] Jeffries, *Tudor Reformations*, 168–73.
[124] Jeffries, "Tudor Reformations Compared," 85–8.
[125] Jeffries, *Tudor Reformations*, 156–68, 174, 196–9.   [126] Ibid., 208.
[127] Ibid., 211–14.   [128] E.g. TNA SP63/80/61.

Pale elite were at least indirectly involved in activities connected to the Baltinglass rebellion.[129]

These arguments broadly parallel those of revisionist historians who argue that English Catholicism remained more vital and politically potent well into Elizabeth's reign than historians used to suppose. They raise similar issues, including that of working out relationships between different varieties of Catholic or Crypto-Catholic belief. No one argues that by 1580 the Counter-Reformation had yet made much of an impression outside Irish towns and a few country districts where friars were particularly active. But it is probably significant that, unlike Gaelic areas of Scotland, Ireland had experienced a revival of Franciscan missionary activity in the late Middle Ages that continued through the sixteenth century.[130] Even in some remote, Irish-speaking areas the late medieval Church had laid foundations on which to build a later campaign of proselytization. The weakness of any Protestant challenge to traditional Catholic beliefs and practices, such as attachment to saints, relics, and pilgrimage sites, may have mattered even more. Lancashire, often seen by historians as the most Catholic county in England, at least had a vigorous center of Protestant and puritan belief in Manchester, whereas Galway, probably the most Protestant town in Ireland around 1580, nevertheless seems to have had a predominantly Catholic population. Unlike Galway, Manchester lacked a cohort of preaching friars to challenge its Protestant ministers. The failure of the Reformation to win many converts in the Pale and the towns, where much of the population was bilingual, hampered the ability of the official Church to find clergy capable of preaching in Irish.[131] As late as 1596 the Protestant bishop of Cork reported that not a single minister fluent in Irish existed in the whole of Munster.[132] Gaelic-speaking regions of Scotland that had gone over to the Reformation might have remedied this deficiency, if the resistance of the English authorities to any sort of Scottish penetration into Ireland had not prevented this from happening. Although the earl of Ormond and a few other Irish lords conformed to the official Church, none of them promoted efforts to convert Irish-speaking populations within their lordships to Protestantism with nearly the vigor of the Scottish earl of Argyll.

In Ireland, even more than in England, the main task of Catholic missionaries was not to convert Protestants, who were very thin on the ground, so much as to transform passive Catholics and conventional Christians into committed Catholics prepared to make a stand for their creed. This did not necessarily

---

[129] Jeffries, *Tudor Reformations*, 218; cf. Grey's statement in TNA SP63/95/32: "Upon my return [to Dublin] the discovery of the Pale conspiracy broke out, which was of that sort as not one of account therein but either was himself or had of his nearest blood touched it."

[130] Tadhag Ó hAnnracháin, *Catholic Europe 1592-1648: Centre and Peripheries* (Oxford: Oxford University Press, 2015), 48-9.

[131] Ibid., 46.   [132] *CSPI* 6.14.

require any deep change in beliefs or behavior, aside from matters like occasional attendance at Prayer Book services. Primarily it involved getting people to perceive their own identity and that of their community as connected to the Catholic Church and its ancient traditions, in opposition to novel heresies. The fact that in Ireland strong support for the Reformation came mainly from a cohort of soldiers, government servants, and colonists newly arrived from England, whom many Irish had ample reason to dislike for causes unconnected to religion, must have made this easier to accomplish. State efforts to promote the Reformation almost entirely through punitive fines for non-attendance at church, sporadic punishment of Catholic clergy, and vandalism of Catholic shrines probably provoked a backlash, making it easy to equate Catholic belief with defiance of the bullying behavior of unpopular outsiders, with no respect for the traditions and property of local communities.

Like seminary priests in England, friars arriving in Ireland after training on the Continent created networks that linked Catholic partisans together, making it easier to coordinate activities in different districts. They gave their flocks a sense of participation in resistance to heretical English authority that extended not only beyond their locality but also beyond Ireland. Fitzmaurice's tiny invasion of Munster in 1579 mattered as a symbolic gesture of papal and foreign support even though it brought only paltry military assistance. Walsingham initially dismissed the threat after hearing that "Fitzmaurice's forces are very small, being not above two or three hundred men and half a dozen baggage boats, whereby there is little to be feared from him."[133] But the future Chancellor of Ireland, Edward Waterhouse, who was closer to the scene, thought "this rebellion of James Fitzmorris and the rest is the most perilous that ever was before in Ireland" because of its potential to trigger wider defections from the queen's allegiance.[134] Burghley also grew alarmed, fearing that the possession of a coastal haven, even by a very small force, would allow the rebels to receive assistance from France or Spain. "This small entrance of Fitzmorris will be a gate for any of those two princes to offend her Majesty in Ireland in recompense of former offences offered unto them," in addition to giving "comfort to all lewd and discontented people of Ireland; whereof I think three parts of four, or rather nine parts of ten, are for matter of religion evil satisfied with the English government."[135] Before long, Walsingham admitted that his initial assessment had been wrong.

Catholic missionary activity not only reinforced Irish resistance to the more unpopular features of New English rule, it also began to connect pockets of discontent in different parts of the island to each other and to potential foreign allies. Whether Desmond and many of the sept leaders who joined his revolt felt any deep commitment to the Catholic cause is open to doubt, but also in some

---

[133] TNA SP63/68/8. [134] TNA SP63/68/2. [135] Hatton, 121–2.

ways beside the point. Even if they took arms primarily from a sense of personal grievance or in hopes of acquiring plunder, Catholic activists furnished not only ideological justifications for their actions but practical help in appealing to other Irish and lobbying for foreign assistance. The fragmented nature of power in Ireland made the potential role of Catholicism as a unifying creed all the more important. Although the English had always had to contend with outbreaks of disorder, these normally remained localized and the crown usually found allies from among the Irish enemies of whatever sept they needed to fight. Although this remained the case during the Desmond rebellion, English officials worried that Catholic solidarity would eventually alter the dynamic. As Malby put it, whereas "before these times the country people devised small occasions to rebel as for private quarreling it is now converted to a matter of religion, by which it is become so general a cause."[136] Contact with foreign powers, as well as the experience of fighting the English, simultaneously began to spread greater awareness of modern arms and battle tactics. "Whereas in time past they had no weapons but darts and galloglasses," Andrew Trollope remarked in 1581, the Irish had lately begun to furnish themselves "with all kind of munition," and were growing "as well practiced therein as Englishmen."[137] Desertions and sales of arms by English soldiers, as well as Irish contacts with pirates and Spanish and Portuguese fishing vessels that brought "powder, calivers, sculls, targets, swords and other munition" for purposes of trade, contributed to a gradual modernization of Irish armies.[138]

At least in the short-to-medium term, English fears and Irish hopes that a general Catholic revolt assisted by foreign arms would sweep across the island proved overblown. Spain failed to send significant assistance, Ormond and other Irish assisted in suppressing Desmond's rebellion, and most of the Pale held aloof from Baltinglass's revolt. Ulster also remained quiet. Even so, rebellions between 1579 and 1583 cost more than £200,000 to suppress. This expense, and a realization that the situation might easily have grown far worse if the Spanish had sent more aid to the rebels, was used to justify a campaign to starve Desmond's followers into submission. Warham St Leger estimated that a famine deliberately caused by the English army killed 30,000 people.[139] While that figure is impossible to verify, large parts of the province were depopulated. To a degree the ruthless suppression of the revolt fit a wider pattern of growing Protestant alarm and reaction in Britan as well as Ireland, as Catholic resistance became more assertive and better organized. The starving of Munster roughly coincided in time with an increase in executions of seminary priests and imprisonment for recusancy in England and the Ruthven Raid in Scotland. But for several reasons repressive measures were exceptionally ruthless and bloody in Ireland. Anti-Catholicism reinforced and extended views of the Irish as a savage people deserving harsh

---

[136] TNA SP63/75/82.   [137] TNA SP63/85/39.   [138] BL Add Mss. 48,017.
[139] TNA SP63/91/41, Sentleger to Perrot, April 23, 1582; McCormack, *Earldom of Desmond*, 194.

discipline by adding the additional claim that their idolatry and criminal behavior provoked God's wrath. The terrible suffering inflicted on Munster was attributed not just to English military actions but also to divine retribution. Justice John Meade positively welcomed the famine, "justly lighted upon this nation for their long continuance in offending and transgressing of God's laws and commandments and now their unnatural rebellion."[140] Although war and hunger "have left not the tenth man alive," so that the survivors "are not sufficient to manure the hundredth part of the land," this merely demonstrated the "two edged sword" of divine justice.[141] In punishing the Irish, God had cleared the land for English improvements: "cities, towns, castles and habitations, the readiest means both of reformation and advancement of her majesty's profit," as Sir John Perrot put it.[142] English Protestants described the extermination of perhaps tens of thousands of Irish as a harsh but necessary and ultimately beneficial prelude to a redemptive reformation.

From a more secular perspective, the plantation of lands vacated by the famine and confiscations of the estates of Desmond and his followers promised to generate rents and payments that would help the queen recover her costs in suppressing the rebellion. Grey had already begun drawing up valuations of lands he intended to confiscate in the spring of 1581.[143] Two and a half years later Fenton reported that "the late accident in Munster" had created a windfall of vacant tenancies,[144] while in late 1584 Wallop remained hard at work surveying the fertile fields of Limerick and Connacht, the less hospitable terrain of County Kerry—whose bogs and hills might nevertheless maintain herds of cattle, he thought—and the country west of Cashell, which war and famine had depopulated. "God grant her majesty may take such a course as she may re-people it again with a better race of and kind of people than the former were," he piously concluded.[145]

In England, ties of kinship and friendship between Catholic and Protestant neighbors—and in some cases Catholic landowners and Protestants on the privy council—inhibited harsh repression. But Ireland's governing institutions had fallen increasingly into the hands of Englishmen with few ties even to elite families in the Pale, much less to the bulk of the Irish population. Whereas in the 1550s men born in Ireland occupied three-fourths of the administrative and legal posts within the government centered in Dublin, by 1580 the proportion had declined to one-half.[146] As the personnel of the state grew increasingly distinct from and suspicious of the people they governed, violent measures came to seem more acceptable. The Irish authorities also had less reason to worry that draconian

---

[140] TNA SP63/89/23.   [141] TNA SP63/192/103.   [142] TNA SP63/111/70.
[143] TNA SP63/82/48, Grey to Walsingham, April 24, 1581.   [144] TNA SP63/106/4.
[145] TNA SP63/112/10 Wallop to Walsingham, October 16, 1584.
[146] Valerie McGowan-Doyle, "Elizabeth I, the Old English, and the Rhetoric of Counsel," in *Elizabeth I and Ireland*, ed. Kane and McGowan-Doyle, 178–9.

methods would disrupt the normal operation of local governance, because civil rule under crown-appointed magistrates scarcely existed in much of the island. Despite the restraining influence exercised by some remaining Old English officials and the instinctive caution of Burghley and the queen, the harsh methods and authoritarian attitudes already developing before the eruption of Desmond's rebellion solidified after its suppression.

By impeding efficient communication, Ireland's challenging terrain simultaneously made it more difficult to restrain the behavior of English captains of the ground. The fact that in the countryside most Irish did not live in nucleated villages, and that their main source of wealth consisted of animals that could be easily moved and hidden, presented challenges to captains trying to impose their authority. Faced with resistance from people prepared to retreat into woods or bogs and ambush their forces, captains continued to retaliate with punitive raids and by carrying out summary executions, often under martial law.[147] The crown also experimented with martial law commissions intended to deal with problems of vagrancy in England but few if any executions resulted and in most places the commissions were quickly discontinued.[148] Irish captains employed martial law with many fewer inhibitions, allegedly using it not only to deal with suspected criminals but also to extort money from the poor by threatening them with hanging if they did not pay.[149]

Some of the methods employed by English garrisons resembled those used by Irish sept leaders in policing their territories and waging wars against each other. These included the grisly practice of taking the heads of enemies. Rewards were given to Irish who presented heads purportedly taken from criminals or rebels. An Irishman named Feagh Hugh, who wanted to prove his loyalty in 1586, did so by sending six heads to the deputy lieutenant, Perrot. Eleven years later Feagh's own head was taken by another lord deputy, Thomas Lord Burgh.[150] Justice Gardener claimed that the authorities gave "head silver to such as bring heads, never examining or knowing whose heads, neither the best or worst, so no safety for any man to travel, a strange course in a Christian estate."[151] The practice intensified after the outbreak of the Nine Years War in 1594. William Russell received thirty-five heads sent in by one captain in January 1596, another thirteen from the sheriff of Carlow the following April, and twenty-eight from the earl of Ormond in May.[152] Captains conducted forays in which they captured large numbers of animals, burned houses and stores of grain, and killed people indiscriminately.

---

[147] The widespread use of martial law has been especially emphasized by David Edwards, "Ideology and Experience: Spenser's *View* and Martial Law in Ireland," in *Political Ideology in Ireland*, ed. Morgan, 127–57 and in his "Escalation of Violence."
[148] For a discussion see R. Malcolm Smuts, "Organized Violence in the Elizabethan Monarchical Republic," *History* 99 (2014): 418–43 at 428–31.
[149] TNA SP63/202.1/73.   [150] CSPI 6.287.   [151] TNA SP63/150/4.
[152] *Campaign Journals*, ed. Edmonds, 270, 276, and 278.

As Rory Rapple has shown, they generally asserted their right to do so on the basis of the queen's prerogative, which they regarded as superior to the law even in England.[153] But what they really wanted was to appropriate the prerogative for their own use.

At times the captains claimed to act as benefactors of the common Irish against the "tyranny" of their lords. Malby's successor as president of Connacht, Sir Richard Bingham, asserted in 1586 that his violent conflict with the Burkes of County Mayo stemmed from his efforts to restrain "the lords and great men from their accustomed cuttings and extortions upon their tenants." His protection had allowed some of those tenants to achieve unprecedented prosperity, he boasted. "The lords and gentlemen wonderfully repined at it...some would cast out a word and say that this new governor would shortly make the churl their master."[154] The peasants themselves termed him "captain of the churls," he claimed. But Bingham's credentials as benefactor of the common Irish are undercut by his boast that in fighting the Burkes he had killed not only 1,500 or 1,600 adults but as many "boys, women and children," not counting additional victims dispatched "by my brother George and the gentlemen of the country," who left the beaches and rivers clogged with corpses.[155] The fact that he and other captains, including Malby, employed native protégés to help collect their rents and enforce their authority, while billeting soldiers who were often of Irish parentage on civilians, must have further blurred the distinction between English rule and the most oppressive practices of Irish lords.[156]

As Justice Gardiner pointed out, whenever an Irish lord offended a captain like Bingham, "all the country must be spoiled by taking prey of some two or three thousand cows, whereby all inhabitants become thieves of other countries," since having lost their own animals they had to steal those of their neighbors to survive.[157] He believed that arbitrary and capricious uses of martial law discredited English justice. The Irish would gladly have turned criminals over to the English for trial, were it not for the fact that they saw "no difference of offence, no ordinary proceeding, no decorum observed either in prosecution or execution, but a butcher like spoiling of Christian blood." They therefore "do utterly...desist from apprehending the greatest as smallest offenders."[158] Because higher authorities in Dublin failed to hold men like Bingham accountable, the Irish hesitated to report abuses for fear of retaliation.[159] The heads of neighboring septs—which in Bingham's case included the O'Donnells and O'Neills of Ulster—saw his

---

[153] Rapple, *Martial Power*, 168–97.   [154] *CSPI* 3.199, 225.
[155] Ibid., 183.   [156] Rapple, *Martial Power*, 221–4.
[157] TNA SP63/150/4, Gardener to Walsingham, January 4, 1590.
[158] TNA SP63/150/4I, draft proclamation of April 1590. On this whole subject see Ciaran Brady, "The Captains' Games: Army and Society in Elizabethan Ireland," in *A Military History of Ireland*, ed. Thomas Bartlett and Keith Jeffrey (Cambridge: Cambridge University Press, 1996), 136–59.
[159] For an example see TNA SP63/150/23 v and vi.

aggressiveness as a threat to their ability to protect their own lands and people. They needed to fight back to maintain their credibility as leaders, although doing so inevitably risked involving them in conflicts with the Irish state.[160]

The Civil Irish as Enemies of the State

In addition to justifying even more brutal treatment of the native Irish, fear of Catholicism intensified suspicion of the "civil" inhabitants of the Pale and Irish towns, who under other circumstances might have provided the Dublin government with a pool of administrative talent and natural allies. To be sure, this suspicion was never entirely a matter of religion. It involved elements of factional competition, arguments over secular issues like the cess, and the long-standing belief that English people in Ireland tended to degenerate through contact with Gaelic culture. But a perception that even ostensibly loyal Old English had become hostile to the Protestant state for religious reasons reinforced and extended these other forms of mistrust. Even some conforming Protestants, of whom the earl of Ormond is the most conspicuous example, came under suspicion because they had Catholic friends and clients and were well-integrated within an overwhelmingly Catholic society. Reformers had long regarded magnates like Ormond as obstacles to good government, not without reason. "We that are born here know it to be true ... as long as our noblemen live the state shall never want secret enemies ever ready upon the least occasion to raise wars and rebellion," the Palesman Edward White advised Walsingham in 1579.[161] Ormond also had personal enemies: Sidney considered him "my professed foe," who "with clamor but oftener with whispering did backbite me" with false accusations.[162] Rather than assuaging these complaints, Ormond's conspicuous role in the campaign against his rival, Desmond, amplified them in some quarters because it allowed him to shield his clients. Ralegh commented in March 1581 that after two years under Ormond's command as lord general, Munster contained "at this instant a thousand traitors more than there were at the first day."[163] Although more appreciative of Ormond's services during the Desmond revolt, Pelham also wanted the earl's palatine authority eliminated and replaced by "a severe kind of English government."[164] Some crown servants believed that if the tide ever turned against English rule Ormond would happily go over to the enemy, as did Bernardino de Mendoza, who reported being told "by Englishmen that he [Ormond] has sent word to them that

---

[160] Hiram Morgan, *Tyrone's Rebellion: The Outbreak of the Nine Years War in Tudor Ireland* (Woodbridge: Boydell Press, 1999), 57–65.
[161] TNA SP63/68/22.   [162] BL Add Mss. 48,017, fol. 148v.
[163] *Letters of Sir Walter Ralegh*, ed. Agnus Latham and Joyce Youings (Exeter: Exeter University Press, 1999), 6.
[164] BL Add Mss. 48,017.

if they make any movement or foreigners arrive in Ireland they may be certain that he will rise with the rest."¹⁶⁵ In 1600 Mountjoy thought that although Ormond wanted to remain loyal, "I have great reason to be confident that, despairing in the force of England to protect him, he had already opened his heart to some other foundation to make good his estate."¹⁶⁶

Ormond's personal relationship with the queen and the support of other English, both in Ireland and at the court, allowed him to survive these accusations. But they demonstrate the paradox that the very qualities that made him such a valuable supporter of the state—his command of armed force, substantial power base, and alliances with both Old English and Irish lineages—simultaneously invited distrust. Given the prevalence of Catholicism and extent of discontent with English rule in Ireland, any effective lord would inevitably have ties to Catholics of suspect loyalty. This made it difficult for the English to have confidence in their ostensible allies, a problem that arose again in the early 1590s in disagreements about the real intentions of the earl of Tyrone. Similar doubts surrounded the inhabitants of the Pale and Irish towns, especially after the Baltinglass rebellion. As in England, recusancy and circumstantial evidence of an individual's connections to known traitors often appeared to nervous Protestant officials as signs of hidden disloyalty. Lord Justice Henry Wallop complained in 1583 of "the danger of this state, amongst whom there is hardly one sound man to be found that is not in religion either an apparent papist or a known hypocrite," as shown by the absence of the Pale elite from religious services and the disparaging comments they made about Protestant ministers when among their friends. Religious disaffection led them to spread rumors about the return of fugitive rebels and armies being levied in Spain to free Ireland from English rule, he asserted.¹⁶⁷

Fragmentary evidence that leaders of the commonwealthmen had become implicated in treason provided Sidney and his supporters with opportunities to strike back hard. The Nugents, a prominent family of landowners and lawyers based along the Pale's western border, became a particular target.¹⁶⁸ Christopher Nugent fifth baron Delvin was an Old English landowner who sympathized with many Gaelic traditions. He patronized an Irish bard and presented the queen with a primer on the Irish language while studying at Cambridge in the 1560s, telling her that by promoting its study she would facilitate reform. His eighteen children married into both Old English and Irish families, creating a network tying the Nugents to the Kildare Fitzgeralds, other Pale gentry, and several midland septs. A nephew, Nicholas Nugent, embarked on a promising legal career, training at

---

¹⁶⁵ *CSPSp* 3.19.   ¹⁶⁶ *CSPI* 10.138.   ¹⁶⁷ TNA SP63/102/58.
¹⁶⁸ The following three paragraphs derive from Fionnán Tuite, "Family Feud in Early Modern Meath," in *Community in Early Modern Ireland*, ed. Robert Armstrong and Tadhg Ó hAnnracháin (Dublin: Four Courts Press, 2006), 69–90 and the articles on Christopher and Nicholas Nugent by Colm Lemon and William Nugent by Helen Coburn Walshe in *ODNB*.

Lincoln's Inn before serving on several commissions charged with establishing assizes in Munster and the Irish midlands during the 1570s. The Nugents had a long tradition of serving the Dublin government as lawyers and administrators and believed firmly in extending Dublin's control beyond the Pale.

Their belief in the common law and the protections it provided for the liberties of the subject led them to take a leading role in the opposition to the cess, earning Nicolas Nugent two spells of imprisonment, in 1577 and 1578. After Sidney's recall, however, he won a major victory through his appointed as chief justice of the Irish court of common pleas. His elevation increased the animus of Sidney's allies, especially an Irish Protestant lawyer, Robert Dillon, who wanted the post for himself. Another relative, William Nugent, had meanwhile become at least peripherally involved in discussions among dissident recusant gentry that preceded the outbreak of the Baltinglass rebellion. Although the Nugents never openly supported Baltinglass, Delvin compromised himself enough to allow the authorities to arrest him. He spent eighteen months imprisoned in Ireland before being sent to England for further interrogations that ultimately cleared his name. But his brother, William, had joined forces with the Ulster rebel Turlough O'Neill. William's treason gave Dillon the excuse he needed to bring new charges against Nicholas Nugent. Despite the flimsiness of the evidence, the newly appointed Lord Deputy Grey pressured the jury to return a guilty verdict. The chief justice's hanging in 1581 shocked the Pale community.

Like Lord Paget, Nicholas Nugent had fallen victim to a personal vendetta by a local enemy with support in high places, and an assumption of guilt-by-association. His demise was intended to strike a blow not only against his own family and its local influence but also the independence of the Old English legal community in Dublin and its ability to oppose the unfettered use of prerogative authority by the queen's New English officials. It formed part of an ongoing contest between those officials and an overwhelmingly Catholic Old English elite whose members had always considered themselves the prime upholders of law and civility in Ireland. The further spread of Catholic resistance in the Pale and other areas of Old English settlement intensified this conflict. Fears of an organized rebellion and collusion between Irish Catholics and foreign powers did have some foundation. One observer thought that "students returning from foreign universities" had contributed significantly to the spread of rebellion in the early 1580s.[169] After escaping to the Continent, William Nugent was sent to Rome in 1584 by the duke of Guise, and then "in the company of certain Scottish lairds and servants of the king of Scots into Scotland," where he met with James's confidant, Patrick Master of Gray.[170] He subsequently returned to Ireland "with some pretended bishops" appointed by the pope, with "intentions to seduce the

---

[169] TNA SP63/90/14, John Usher to Walsingham, March 8, 1582.
[170] TNA SP63/107/46 and 113/12.

people to new stirs, abusing them with hope and promises of foreign aid."[171] His travels and contacts further illustrate the formation of networks linking Catholics in the Pale to the queen's enemies in Scotland and on the European Continent that the English state had ample reason to regard with suspicion.[172]

But the authorities failed to prevent growing numbers of Catholic clergy trained on the Continent from arriving in Ireland. These included not only friars and seminary priests but also Catholic bishops so that, as the Protestant Bishop William Lyon of Cork complained in 1596, "there is never a bishopric in Ireland but it hath two bishops, one from her majesty and the other from the Pope."[173] In Ulster the Catholic bishop of Derry and papal legate, Redmond O'Gallagher, traveled about the country in pomp. The Protestant archbishop of Cashel, Meiler McGrath, regarded the bard-turned-Jesuit Desmond Creagh, Catholic bishop of Cork and Cloyne, as perhaps the most dangerous man in all Ireland.[174] Catholic schools and networks of priests were established in Dublin and some other towns.[175] Lyon reported that Cork and the territory around it was full of priests and friars supported by the town's aldermen and merchants, who celebrated mass and baptized children in private houses, "and when I am out of town they walk openly and commonly in the streets, accompanied with the aldermen and officers of the city, and conveyed forth of the town when they go to say their masses in the country."[176] These clerical activities continued to build self-conscious recusant communities, like the "great nest...of massmongers" Perrot uncovered in 1584 that included gentlemen and gentlewomen "of good sort," merchants and lawyers.[177]

The loyalty of Old English towns, and especially their most well-educated and well-connected residents, therefore grew increasingly suspect. "The sting of the rebellion, which in times past remained among the Irishry," Sir Richard Whyte informed Burghley in May 1590, "is transferred and moved into the hearts of the civil gentlemen, aldermen, burgesses and rich merchants of Ireland, papistry being the original cause and ground." "The commons would be soon reformed," he thought, if the Old English elite had not fomented resistance. "At Cork...Sir Warham St Leger knight and Andrew Skidmore assaulted me upon the north bridge for religion with a great train following them; they arrogantly barking condemned the religion established...Skidmore comparing her Majesty's godly proceeding to the vile sects of Anabaptists and Family of Love." The Catholics of Limerick received encouragement from "some men of countenance in Dublin," while the aging Bishop, who had renounced the Reformation during Mary's reign,

---

[171] TNA SP63/107/42G.
[172] Colm Lennon, "Taking Sides: The Emergence of Irish Catholic Ideology," in *Taking Sides? Cultural and Confessional Mentalités in Early Modern Ireland: Essays in Honour of Karl S. Bottigheimer* (Dublin: Four Court Press, 2003), 197–206.
[173] *CSPI* 6.19. [174] Jeffries, *Tudor Reformations*, 251–3.
[175] Ibid., 256–7. [176] *CSPI* 6.6. [177] TNA SP63/112/45.

did nothing to promote reform. "A number of the gentlemen of England there dwelling are papists, fortifying their countrymen." In Waterford Irish soldiers among the local garrison "seemeth to overrule the rest of the English soldiers," dissuading them from preventing attendance at mass.[178] Recusancy had increased alarmingly at Dublin, according to a report by Lord Deputy Fitzwilliam and Chancellor Loftus.[179] "Most of the Pale gentry do glory" to be accounted Catholics, Fitzwilliam reported, "being persuaded by such as have prepared their minds for the Spanish invasion that the gentlemen and inhabitants of the realm generally, and especially those so affected, shall not be touched by the invaders," whose only goal is "to establish the Romish religion and to root out the English and that the native shall be in better case than now they be."[180] He saw the Nugents, whom he believed had established secret communications with Philip's general in the Low Countries, Parma, as ringleaders, but recommended imprisoning an additional twenty leading gentlemen of the Pale in the Tower of London as a precaution.[181] By the late 1590s priests had reportedly begun to threaten to excommunicate any Irish, in the towns as well as the countryside, who did *not* assist rebel forces. Some gentlemen in the Pale, who feared becoming involved in treason, sent emissaries to Rome to request papal dispensations permitting them to remain obedient to the queen's government.[182]

English rule therefore seemed threatened less by the alleged savagery of the Irish than by the stubborn popery of the Old English, who possessed the capacity for organized action of a civil people, along with a thorough familiarity with common law procedures and arguments. Trade from Irish ports facilitated contact with the queen's European enemies, while shared antipathy to the English forged connections between Old English and native Irish. Brendan Kane has argued that by the end of the sixteenth century, cooperation between Catholic lawyers, Counter-Reformation priests, and bards had begun to generate a more broadly based Irish political consciousness, with the potential to challenge both the English state and the Gaelic elite.[183] The Old English knew how to play upon the queen's dislike of harsh policies to win her sympathy and impede policies they disliked, while their continuing, albeit diminishing presence within the administrative apparatus of the Dublin government and their role as local magistrates allowed them to infiltrate and undermine the state from within. This increased the determination of alarmed Protestant officials to transfer control over the Irish courts and administration to the safe hands of the New English Protestants, while restricting the ability of Catholic lawyers to plead cases in Irish courts. Efforts to marginalize the Old English elite contributed further to Old English alienation.

---

[178] TNA SP63/152/15.   [179] TNA SP63/150/74.   [180] TNA SP63/152/3.
[181] Jeffries, *Tudor Reformations*, 237–8.   [182] *Calendar of Carew Manuscripts*, 3.385–6 and 454.
[183] Kane, "Popular Politics."

Confessional polarization therefore not only deepened other patterns of division but also impeded the sort of reforms that might otherwise have gradually integrated the native Irish within a polity framed by English laws and institutions. As Mark Hutchinson has shown, it gave rise to a concept of the Irish government as a state under the control of English-born *arrivistes* that had a basically adversarial relationship with the Catholic population over which it ruled, and which therefore adopted an "absolutist" view of its own powers.[184] From here it was but a short step to the arguments of people like Edmund Spenser and Richard Becon that only a merciless policy of military conquest, followed by "a thorough and absolute mutation and change of ancient laws, customs and manners of the people, and finally the commonwealth itself, into a better form of government," would cure the island's problems.[185] Ireland was to become a prime example of a state founded by conquest that imposed not only a new order of government but a completely different culture, religion, and pattern of social organization on the conquered.

As Hutchinson also remarks, the forward Protestants who embraced this approach continued to regard England as a mixed polity, in which Parliament and responsible subjects had a right and duty to participate in public affairs, and where the rule of law needed to be scrupulously respected. The disjunction becomes even sharper if we recall that in Scotland the English council and its diplomatic representatives tacitly encouraged active and forcible resistance to James VI. Sir Philip Sidney, who defended his father's imposition of the cess and other uses of prerogative power in Ireland, simultaneously befriended the earl of Angus, who helped lead two coup attempts against James VI. The seeming inconsistency is explained by the fact that in Scotland the main threat to Protestant rule appeared to come from the royal court, while the defense of the Reformation depended on an alliance between a segment of the nobility, the clergy, and the grass-roots organization of the Kirk, especially in the towns. That made angry crowd demonstrations against bishops, incendiary sermons, and noble coups appear justifiable and even necessary. But in Ireland, where the most effective clergy, the population of the towns, and majority of the peerage were all Catholic, the state needed to minimize political participation while imposing its will by armed force. Sidney and others who shared his outlook alternately embraced both resistance theory and its opposite, support for an absolute royal prerogative supported by armed violence, as their overriding commitment to continued Protestant rule dictated.

---

[184] Hutchinson, *Calvinism, Reform and the Absolutist State*, esp. 62–80.
[185] Richard Becon, *Solon his Follie, or, A Politique Discourse Touching the Reformation of the Common-weales Conquered, Declined and Corrupted*, ed. Clare Carrol and Vincent Carey (Binghamton, NY: Medieval and Renaissance Texts and Studies, 1996), 39.

In pursuing their prescriptions for forcible reform, Irish officials sometimes had to circumvent the queen's reluctance to sanction the ruthless use of her powers. At times they received support from members of the council. In 1591 Elizabeth told the president of Munster, Sir George Carew, in an interview at the English court that she thought Lord Deputy Fitzwilliam "too forward in dealing with matters of religion, which might cause some stir." When Carew replied that Irish recusants had grown so "insolent" that the government needed to react he received Burghley's support, who urged that "if the bridle were left at liberty it might well prove more perilous, with which opinion she seemed to be well resolved."[186] Sir John Perrot's reported outburst—"she shall not curb me, she shall not rule me ...base, coward piss-kitchen woman"—is the most notorious example of impatience with the queen's mildness, which Sidney and other deputies shared.[187] Paradoxically, one of the principal constraints on the expansion of arbitrary prerogative governance in Ireland therefore came from the queen herself and some members of her council, who objected not on grounds of principle so much as because of their distaste for ruthless measures and fear of provoking resistance. "What would you have her [Elizabeth] do?" Robert Cecil demanded of the advocates of forcible Irish reform in 1599. "Should she make a conquest of all Ireland again? Then must she root out all the race of that people and plant it anew, for so long as any of them were left living they would never live in any other fashion. Would it have been easy for the queen to set the king of France in his kingdom, to protect all the Low Countries, to encounter the king of Spain and all his forces, and to spend men and treasure in conquering Ireland?"[188]

This hesitancy about pushing matters to extremes led to something of an impasse, in which the Irish state ruled with enough arbitrary force to cause widespread alienation but without the wholehearted backing from London required to enforce full compliance with its orders. The stalemate gave further impetus to the dynamic that many New English officials in Ireland had long warned against, in which the wrong kinds of civil influences—preaching by Counter-Reformation friars and priests, trade with Catholic Europe, and greater contact with the commonwealthmen of the Pale—threatened to turn the "wild" Irish into more formidable adversaries. Pressure by the state and its military agents made it increasingly difficult for sept leaders to maintain their positions without looking beyond their own territories and updating their methods of resistance. So long as they remained embedded in traditional local worlds, and dependent on strategies of resisting outside interference through cattle raids and local insurrections, they would always find themselves disadvantaged when fighting a centralized state with a modern army. In the long run their only hope of

---

[186] LPL Mss. 618, fol. 58 (so marked in the manuscript but followed by fol. 55 and identified as fol. 55 in the Calendar).
[187] Hutchinson, *Calvinism, Reform and the Absolutist State*, 79.   [188] *CSPD* 5.352.

preserving their independence lay in constructing broader alliances with other septs, Old English communities, and foreign powers, and learning to fight on a wider scale with more modern methods.

Hugh O'Neill became such a formidable enemy to the Irish state precisely because the English education he had received in his youth allowed him to transition easily between his native Ulster, the Pale, and the English court, which he visited on three occasions in 1567, 1587, and 1590. Although a practicing Catholic, he conformed to the established Church when in Dublin or London, fostering an impression of flexibility and moderation in religious matters. But he also knew how to function as an effective and ruthless leader of his Ulster lineage.[189] "A shrewd and dissembling politician and a clever manipulator of men," he came out on top in a vicious contest for leadership of the O'Neills, primarily because he procured English assistance by acting as the crown's loyal agent in Ulster. He then forged alliances with rival Ulster septs, especially through an arranged dynastic marriage with the O'Neills' ancient enemies, the O'Donnells.[190] By serving as the crown's ally against Desmond and disruptive septs in the North, he grew familiar with English tactics and was able to use government money to train his Irish followers in their use. But he adapted English methods by substituting light calivers for heavier muskets and shortening the pikes his troops carried, to increase their mobility and flexibility while skirmishing in woods, bogs, and mountain passes.[191] His ties to Catholic clergy in Ulster opened channels of communication with Irish exiles in Madrid, who in turn connected him to the Spanish government. While avoiding open involvement in the exiles' plots to enlist military support for an Irish rebellion, he kept himself apprised of their efforts and developed discrete contacts with Spanish agents.[192]

Like Ormond, O'Neill knew how to encourage smaller septs to wage proxy wars that served his interests, while allowing him to preserve an appearance of loyalty to the state. A recent study describes his behavior as a policy of "strategic deception" that drew English forces away from his territory and pressured Elizabeth into making concessions, while he built up his strength.[193] Knowing that he could count on the queen's reluctance to precipitate widespread rebellion, not least because of the treasure its suppression would require, he skillfully played for time. Meanwhile, he expanded arable farming and started a small armaments industry in his territory, fostered trade with Irish towns and Glasgow, and constructed a network of storage depots and system of convoys to

---

[189] Morgan, *Tyrone's Rebellion*, 97.   [190] Ibid., 140 for quotation.
[191] James O'Neill, "'Their Skill and Practice Therein Far Exceeding their Wonted Usage': The Irish Military Revolution, 1593–1603," in *Becoming and Belonging in Ireland*, ed. Campbell et al., 293–312.
[192] Morgan, *Tyrone's Rebellion*, 140–3. Cf. Lambeth Mss. 618, fol. 268v for an argument by an English captain that calivers were more appropriate to Irish warfare than muskets.
[193] James O'Neill, "Death in the Lakelands: Tyrone's Proxy War, 1593–4," *History Ireland* 23 (2015): 14–17.

keep his troops fed.¹⁹⁴ He also built a network of secret supporters in Connacht, Leinster, the Pale, and Dublin itself.¹⁹⁵ A Dublin alderman, Nicholas Weston, reportedly lodged O'Neill in his house and once helped him leave the city quickly at three in the morning to avoid unwelcome attention by the authorities. Weston acted as a go-between in procuring six tons of lead, ostensibly to roof a castle at Dungannon but in fact to forge bullets.¹⁹⁶ James VI and the earl of Huntly also gave O'Neill secret encouragement.¹⁹⁷

These preparations eventually enabled O'Neill and his ally, Hugh O'Donnell, to destabilize English rule over much of Ireland through a series of local rebellions and raids, starting in the mid-1590s, and ultimately to erect an alternative structure of command and obedience over most of the island. For the most part they relied on methods of rewarding allies and punishing or assassinating those who refused to cooperate. They collected tribute or black rents from settlements their forces did not directly occupy, another traditional Irish practice. They left towns under English control because taking them would have entailed time-consuming siege operations and keeping them the diversion of soldiers from their field armies to act as garrisons. But the fact that O'Donnell and O'Neill were able to march through the Pale and into Munster without encountering serious opposition suggests that townsmen were either secretly supportive or sufficiently intimidated to keep within their walls.¹⁹⁸ Merchants within the towns sold arms and other goods to rebel forces. When the president and council of Munster pressured the mayors of Cork, Waterford, and Limerick to crack down on this trade, the magistrates retorted that merchants would stand "upon their charters to free them from any danger" of penalties, "inferring that martial law cannot touch any of them for selling the same [supplies] within the corporation, otherwise than by a penal or pecuniary course."¹⁹⁹ The liberties and privileges enshrined in town charters and local custom obstructed government efforts to ban trade with the enemy, a problem Leicester also encountered in the Netherlands. While O'Neill and O'Donnell waged armed rebellion, the townsmen initiated an increasingly organized campaign of peaceful legal resistance to government demands. Carew remarked in December 1600 that Munster towns had lately begun electing lawyers as their magistrates, while simultaneously sending agents to the court in London to lobby for an enlargement of their chartered privileges.²⁰⁰

In the later stages of the war, several towns began refusing to receive English troops that had grown undisciplined after their wages fell badly into arrears, as

---

[194] Morgan, *Tyrone's Rebellion*, 14; James O'Neill, *The Nine Years War, 1593-1603* (Dublin: Four Courts Press, 2017), 108-16.
[195] *CSPI* 6.38 and 7.10-11 and 61. [196] HMC Salisbury, 6.529-30.
[197] The English knew this but had difficulty proving it, as shown by numerous references in *CSPI*. See also Enrique García Hernan, *The Battle of Kinsale* (Madrid: Ministerio de Defensa, 2013), 80.
[198] O'Neill, *Nine Years War* but cf. Ruth Canning, *The Old English in Early Modern Ireland: The Palesmen and the Nine Years' War, 1594-1603* (Woodbridge: Boydell, 2019).
[199] *CSPI* 10.183.   [200] *Calendar Carew Manuscripts*, 3.492-3.

Dutch towns would also do during the winter of 1587.[201] Priests and Jesuits encouraged this resistance, threatening in Limerick to excommunicate any residents who assisted the queen's soldiers.[202] Limerick appears to have become a particular hotbed of resistance. A riot erupted there after a quarrel between an alderman and an officer in the queen's army who was a brother of Lord Burke, in which armed citizens, reportedly 500 strong, beat soldiers in the street while crying "kill, kill, down with them, there shall not escape a man alive." This precipitated a further dispute between Limerick's mayor and the garrison commander about whether an army officer could be tried in a civilian court. "The mayor in the hearing of my Lord Burke, Captain Clare, Captain Brook and others said that nobody had any jurisdiction in the city but himself, which Justice Gold did reprove." The townsmen murdered the constable of the local castle, cutting off his head and turning into a football. "They brag likewise that they have executed a lord justice and buried many Englishmen in their cellars."[203] In October 1599 Limerick prevented two English companies from coming within its walls, claiming "that they will obey no directions for placing of soldiers but such as the mayor shall be pleased with, and affirming that by charter they are to be commanded not by any but by him." The old soldier Warham St Leger recommended bringing the townsmen "to conformity" by erecting "a small citadel," the same remedy that Alba used to overcome resistance in Antwerp.[204] There is some evidence of wider organization behind these protests. Carew complained to the English privy council in 1600 that the agents sent to London by Irish towns and some private gentlemen deliberately multiplied "suits and causes" in English courts intended to obstruct government action in Ireland.[205] St Leger reported that some of Tyrone's adherents openly boasted in Cork "that there was a thousand gentlemen that had sworn never to submit themselves, till there might be a general freedom of religion."[206] Some of these gentlemen almost certainly had legal training.

One official had complained in 1596 that Catholics in Munster customarily prayed after meals for the good health and safe return of the late earl of Desmond's son, who was imprisoned in the Tower of London. Two years later rebel forces swept away the Munster plantation while the towns offered little resistance, and installed James Fitzthomas Fitzgerald as the new earl of Desmond. Elizabeth reacted by sending 20,000 men under the earl of Essex to recover Ireland. But the rebels managed to stall Essex's campaign in Munster, while inflicting significant casualties on his forces.[207] After Essex returned to England, the Irish *Annals of the Four Masters* reported that he had left Ireland "without peace or tranquility, without lord justice, governor or president," while Ulster remained "a still pool, a

---

[201] O'Neill, *Nine Years War*. [202] TNA SP63/207.2/7.
[203] Ibid. [204] *CSPI* 8.200. [205] *CSPI* 9.130. [206] *CSPI* 8.200.
[207] For an Irish account of the skirmish that stopped Essex's army see *The Annals of the Four Masters*, 2117.

gentle spring, a reposing wave, without fear of battle or incursion, while every other territory [in Ireland] was in awe of them."[208] O'Neill and O'Donnell had, in effect, constructed a state that for the moment controlled much more of Ireland than the crown. The English were fortunate that the assurances a Spanish ship captain gave O'Neill and O'Donnell in 1596 that Philip II was already raising to troops to assist them proved misleading, and that the expedition that did land at Kinsale in 1600 had been scaled back from 10,000 to fewer than 3,500 men, due to shortages of money and losses at sea. This made it too small to undertake an offensive on its own or risk marching north to join the main rebel army in Ulster. Instead O'Neill and O'Donnell decided to march across the length of Ireland to Kinsale, where they lost a conventional pitched battle with an English army under the new lord lieutenant, Charles Blount Baron Montjoy. This proved to be a turning point, although it took a further scorched-earth campaign and deliberately induced famine through Ulster to finish the rebellion. The English state in Ireland survived. But it had been a close call and if the Spanish had had better luck in their efforts to land a formidable army of their own in Ireland the outcome might well have been entirely different.

[208] Ibid., 2139 and 2143.

6
The Earl of Leicester, the Protestant Cause, and the Failure of English State Building in the Netherlands

In the late spring and early summer of 1584, as Arran consolidated his power in Edinburgh, the trials of Francis Throckmorton and his accomplices proceeded in London, and officials in Ireland fretted over Catholic disaffection, two deaths on the Continent further magnified the sense of crisis besetting England's Protestant state. On June 10, Anjou succumbed to tuberculosis. Despite his failures as a political and military leader, he had remained the queen's proxy in the Netherlands, and his disappearance brought her closer to the point at which she would have to decide whether to intervene openly to support the Dutch or abandon them to their fate. By making Henry of Navarre heir to French throne, after the childless Henri III, Anjou's death also plunged France into all-out civil war. Guise resurrected the Catholic League, an alliance of nobles, clergy, and town magistrates pledged to prevent the accession of a heretic king and cleanse France of heresy.[1] In September he concluded the Treaty of Joinville with Philip II, in which Spain agreed to subsidize the League's armies. James VI privately agreed to cooperate with this alliance.[2] Burghley worried that the Scottish king would soon marry a daughter of Philip II or the Guise House of Lorraine, consolidating the Stuarts' alliance with European dynasties hostile to Elizabeth and Protestantism.[3]

On July 10, an assassin sent by the prince of Parma murdered William of Orange. This event magnified fears for Elizabeth's safety. The Portuguese pretender Dom Antonio and the English ambassador in Paris, Edward Lord Stafford, both passed along rumors of fresh conspiracies against the queen's life. "There is no doubt she is the chief mark they shoot at," Stafford commented: "and seeing there were men cunning enough to enchant a man . . . to kill the Prince of Orange in the middle of Holland, and a knave found desperate enough to do it, we must think hereafter that anything may be done."[4] In addition, Orange's death deprived the Dutch of their most effective leader, at the beginning of a summer campaign in

---

[1] The League had first emerged on the national scale in 1576, although local leagues in various provinces had preceded it as far back as the 1560s.

[2] Arlette Jouana, *La France du xvie siècle 1483–1598* (Paris: Presses Universitaires de France, 2nd ed., 1997), 579 asserts that James agreed to cooperate with the alliance, without giving a source.

[3] HMC Salisbury, 3.68.   [4] Stafford to Walsingham, July 17, 1584, HMC Salisbury, 3.44–7.

which Parma captured Brussels and Ghent and invested Antwerp, the last major Protestant stronghold remaining in the South. The fall of the rich provinces of Brabant and Flanders deprived the Dutch state of nearly half its revenues, raising fears that the whole Revolt would soon collapse. In October Burghley began drafting memoranda for the Council's deliberations over whether to enter the Dutch war openly.[5] The following June Elizabeth rejected an invitation to assume sovereignty over the rebel provinces in place of Philip II but agreed to assist them with 2,000 volunteer soldiers, later increased to 4,000, under the command of Sir John Norreys. Sadly, this stopgap measure failed to save Antwerp, which capitulated on August 17. Three days later Elizabeth finally consented, in the Treaty of Nonsuch, to send an English army of 6,400 foot and 1,000 cavalry in her own pay to the Netherlands, at a cost of £126,000, equivalent to roughly half her income, for the next year.

In January 1586 that army's commander, the earl of Leicester, violated Elizabeth's express instructions by accepting an appointment as governor general of the Netherlands, with nominally absolute powers. His action infuriated the queen and soon embroiled him in contentious disputes with Dutch politicians, which escalated after Leicester returned to England in December without surrendering his office, and then reached a climax following his return to the Low Countries in the summer of 1587. By the end of that year he had resigned his governorship and abandoned his campaign, leaving the Anglo-Dutch alliance in tatters. With few exceptions, historians of both England and the Netherlands have passed over this episode fairly quickly.[6] In English historiography it has seemed chiefly significant as the event that triggered the Armada War, while Dutch historians have traditionally treated Leicester's governorship as the last in a series of ham-fisted efforts by foreigners to rule the Netherlands, before the triumphant emergence of a successful republic in full control of its own affairs in the 1590s.[7] Both perspectives rely on hindsight, in ways that make it more difficult to understand the motivations and calculations of English and Dutch leaders in the period.[8] This chapter seeks to recover a better sense of strictly contemporary perspectives on the war in the Netherlands between late summer 1585 and spring 1588, while explaining why Leicester and his supporters believed that his assumption of supreme political authority offered the only remaining hope of defeating

---

[5] Ibid., 67–72; cf. the similar memoranda and additional documents related to this discussion in BL Cotton Mss. Caligula CIX fols 86–9.

[6] The major exceptions are F. G. Oosterhoff, *Leicester and the Netherlands 1586–1587* (Utrecht: HES Publishers, 1988) and Roy Strong and J. A. van Dorsten, *Leicester's Triumph* (Oxford: Oxford University Press, 1964).

[7] For example, Jan den Tex, *Oldenbarnevelt*, trans. R. B. Powell, 2 vols (Cambridge: Cambridge University Press, 1973).

[8] Those events included the assassination of the duke of Guise on the orders of Henry III, shortly after the Armada's defeat, the assassination of Henry himself by a Catholic partisan in 1589, and Philip's decision to intervene in the civil wars of France with the Army of Flanders.

Parma and saving European Protestantism; why and how the earl's attempt to remodel the Dutch state failed; and why that failure did not have the fatal consequences that many contemporaries expected.

Perspectives on the Crisis of the Mid-1580s

Although by 1585 the English council had grown increasingly worried about Philip II's hostility, it did not foresee that within three years he would launch a seaborne invasion of their country. Preparing the coasts against possible attack was only one of the many precautionary measures taken in response to the deteriorating situation in Europe.[9] The victories of Philip's armies not only improved Spain's military situation but promised to enhance Spanish economic power. Parma had regained cities that until recently formed the industrial and commercial heartland of the Low Counties, the most economically dynamic region of northern Europe. In comparison to Antwerp, Amsterdam remained a port of distinctly secondary importance, whose prosperity depended on trade in bulk commodities like grain, timber, and fish. After the loss of the great cities of the South, the United Provinces looked like a "shrinking, floundering state with its traditional bulk carrying trade temporarily contracting, burdened with military costs beyond its means, and surrounded to the south, east and northeast by Spanish forces."[10] It seemed a bad risk, whether for merchants fleeing Antwerp and other southern cities—who mostly preferred to settle in North Germany, Italy, or England rather than the northern Netherlands—or the English crown. Elizabeth worried that if she became more involved in the Low Countries her treasury would have to assume most of the expenses of the war, as Dutch resources collapsed.[11] Her anxiety on this score provided one of the strongest arguments against intervention.

But the consequences of leaving the Dutch to their fate seemed even more ominous. If Parma completed his conquest, Philip II would regain control of Netherlandish ports that between them possessed the largest mercantile fleet in Europe, giving him the power to strangle English commerce.[12] His recent seizure of English ships in Spanish ports and embargo on English trade left little doubt that he would exploit this advantage to the hilt. The resulting disruptions would deplete customs revenues, the largest source of Elizabeth's income, while

---
[9] BL Cotton Mss. Caligula CIX, fol. 66.
[10] Jonathan Israel, *Dutch Primacy in World Trade* (Oxford: Oxford University Press, 1989), 17.
[11] HMC Salisbury, 3.69–70; TNA SP84/1/44 (Minute of Davison's instructions, going to the Netherlands, February 18, 1585).
[12] In the words of a remembrance for Davison: "What with Spain for the west and these countries [the Netherlands] for the east, England shall traffic no further any of these ways than he [Philip] shall give leave but that every voyage shall ask the charge of a whole navy to pass withal" (TNA SP84/6/85).

spreading unemployment in coastal towns and clothing districts that might well lead to serious unrest. Spanish successes in the Low Countries would simultaneously encourage James VI to continue his dalliances with Spain and the French League, and English and Irish Catholics to hatch new plots. The threat from Spain eventually overcame the traditional English reluctance to allow any expansion of French influence in the Low Countries, persuading the queen and her council to hope that Henry III would rescue them by spearheading opposition to Parma and the League.[13] Elizabeth presented him with the Garter in early 1585 in a charm offensive. But Henry soon made it clear that he had no intention of becoming embroiled in a war with Spain and the English worried that he might soon capitulate to Guise's pressure and join the League's campaign against the Huguenots. If this happened, and if Philip also broke the back of Dutch resistance, England would almost certainly become the next target. James VI's recent conduct suggested that he might well join the attack, while the Throckmorton Plot had shown that some English Catholics were prepared to murder their queen. Philip II would undoubtedly find many opportunities to destabilize England's Protestant state, even without having to launch a full-scale invasion. England's ruling circle needed to decide whether to undertake an expensive campaign to save the shaky Dutch state from defeat, while hoping that Henry III would continue to resist League pressure, or to resign themselves to the probable collapse of Dutch and possibly also Huguenot resistance, while falling back on a strategy of home defense. The council divided over the issue, although Burghley, Leicester, and Walsingham favored supporting the Dutch and Hatton seems to have gone along with their consensus.[14]

The debate over entering the war in the Netherlands was bound up with the larger issue of how aggressively England should respond to the growing unity and assertiveness of militant Catholic forces under Spanish leadership embodied in the Treaty of Joinville. In addition to the finest army in Europe, Philip II possessed a superb diplomatic network and the resources of a global empire, giving him multiple ways of assisting his allies.[15] The papacy and missionary orders reinvigorated by the Counter-Reformation provided a complementary source of organized transnational support for the Catholic cause. Protestant forces lacked

---

[13] Walsingham wrote to Burghley in January 1585 that the queen remained "loath that the French king should have any absolute interest in the Low Countries not at present possessed by the Spaniards in respect of some future peril that might grow thereby to this crown" but then argued forcefully that the immediate peril of a Spanish victory outweighed worries about long-term dangers (TNA SP12/176/5).

[14] Sir James Croft was almost certainly opposed to intervention, while Whitgift was probably skeptical (see below, pp. 336 and 346-7). The views of religiously conservative Elizabethan councilors and courtiers likely to sympathize with Spain are poorly documented and so hard to reconstruct, in contrast to the copious surviving letters of Burghley, Walsingham, and to some degree Leicester. See Neil Younger, "How Protestant was the Elizabethan Regime?" *English Historical Review* 133 (2018): 1060-90.

[15] A valuable although somewhat controversial discussion is Geoffrey Parker, *The Grand Strategy of Philip II* (New Haven: Yale University Press, 1998).

comparable leaders and resources. The Dutch and to a degree the Huguenots had managed to construct their own states, capable of levying taxation and raising armies; but those states were essentially coalitions of Protestant nobles, towns, and a few rural districts. As such they had built-in fissiparous tendencies, since their individual leaders and local units tended to give top priority to their own immediate interests. Their financial resources were, in any case, never remotely comparable to those of the Spanish crown, and since they were not yet recognized as free states by most of Europe they sometimes found it difficult to conduct diplomacy. In France the stature of Henry of Navarre, as a titular king and probable heir to the French crown, helped mitigate these disadvantages. But especially after the murder of William the Silent, the United Provinces lacked a similar head.

A real danger existed that by concentrating his resources, Philip would succeed in crushing Protestant resistance sequentially, first in the Low Countries and subsequently in France and Britain, while defenders of the reformed faith remained too divided to mount a coordinated defense. Traditionally the king of France provided the main counterweight to Habsburg ambitions, but Henry III's Catholicism and caution about challenging the League removed him from that role. Elizabeth remained the only obvious alternative but she also hesitated. She did not want to provoke Philip II into an attack on her kingdom, resisted pouring her treasure into the sink-hole of European campaigns, and also had scruples about assisting rebels against other sovereigns. The forward Protestants on her council—especially Leicester, Walsingham, and Burghley—worked to overcome her reluctance by arguing that she had no realistic choice, since Philip had become her determined enemy. She needed to strike at him while she still had European allies. Having recently moved to contain domestic threats of Catholic rebellion through the Bond of Association and the revival of the lieutenancy, in 1585 they advanced three initiatives to counter the Spanish threat beyond England's borders.

One was the large expedition led by Drake, funded partly by the crown and partly by private investors, discussed in Chapter 4. It had been planned for several years, initially as a trading voyage to the Molucca Islands in the Indian Ocean, then as a more aggressive challenge to Philip's control of the Portuguese Empire in Asia on behalf of Dom Antonio, and finally as an attempt to strike at Spain's vital Atlantic supply lines, especially the shipments of silver that helped pay for Parma's army.[16] But down to the summer of 1585 Elizabeth had refused to turn Drake loose. The second measure involved support for the earl of Angus and his followers to stage the coup discussed in Chapter 3, in a bid to force James to

---

[16] Simon Adams, "The Outbreak of the Elizabethan Naval War against the Spanish Empire: The Embargo of May 1585 and Sir Francis Drake's West Indian Voyage," in *England, Spain and the Grand Armada 1585–1604: Essays from the Anglo-Spanish Conference, London and Madrid 1988*, ed. M. J. Rodriguez-Salgado and Simon Adams (Edinburgh: John Donald, 1991).

purge his court and solidify his new English alliance. The queen's dislike of "violent courses" again proved an obstacle, leading Walsingham to complain at one point that Elizabeth's refusal to act more boldly in Scotland might provoke "God's judgment toward us" in England.[17] Thirdly, the councilors urged Elizabeth to send a substantial army and commit to spending a very large sum of money— Walsingham wanted £400,000 over two years—in the Netherlands.[18] In late summer they finally prevailed on all three fronts. Angus departed for Scotland within days of the signing of the Treaty of Nonsuch. Roughly three weeks later, on September 14, Drake set sail with a fleet of two dozen ships, led by a 600-ton galleon from the Royal Navy. These virtually simultaneous actions look like complementary components of a coordinated plan to go over onto the offensive by eliminating James VI's tacit alliance with Guise and Philip II, severing Spain's vital Atlantic supply lines and reinvigorating Dutch resistance.

But if Elizabeth had conceded for the moment, she had not entirely overcome her misgivings. The die was now cast in Scotland, where Angus's success vindicated the councilors' policy, at least for the moment, and after several agonizing delays due to contrary winds, Drake managed to sail far enough away to make his recall impossible. But the army for the Netherlands—by far the most important of the three initiatives—would take months to assemble and Elizabeth continued to experience eruptions of doubt about whether she had made the right decision. In October Walsingham lamented to Burghley that she had told several courtiers of "the great mislike she hath of her own resolves taken in this cause of the Low Countries." If her loose talk reached either the Dutch or the Spanish, he warned, it would do real damage.[19] Even apart from these misgivings, Elizabeth did not see her aid to the United Provinces as support for a sovereign foreign state fighting to maintain its independence, because she had never recognized the Dutch claim to have renounced their allegiance to Philip II. In her eyes, the inhabitants of the northern Netherlands remained his subjects, who had a right to secure their traditional liberties and freedom of religion against Philip's tyranny but not to cancel his hereditary right to rule over them. Although Philip regarded the dispatch of an English army to the Netherlands as tantamount to a declaration of war, and several modern historians have agreed with him, Elizabeth did not see things this way. She wanted only to convince Philip to make significant concessions by stalling Parma's conquests and making the cost to Spain of a complete military victory prohibitive. As one of Burghley's notes put it, the objective was "first to show strength, then to offer peace upon conditions."[20] The Dutch, on the other hand, regarded even discussions of a negotiated peace as dangerous and

---

[17] TNA SP52/35/13.   [18] TNA SP12/176/54.   [19] TNA SP12/183/56.
[20] TNA SP12/184/50 rough notes of Burghley's goals for 1586, dated November 25, 1585. Cf. Adams, "Protestant Cause," 42–3.

abhorrent, since it might raise false hopes among the populace that would weaken the war effort.

The Treaty of Nonsuch therefore masked significant disagreements not only between the two allies but also within the ruling group at Whitehall that would bedevil Anglo-Dutch relations over the next two years, beginning with the question of the allies' ultimate goal in fighting Spain. Shortly before the treaty's ratification, an English gentleman in the Netherlands predicted that Elizabeth would betray her allies by reaching an accord with Philip that secured her own interests at their expense.[21] Despite English denials, similar rumors continued to circulate over the next two years, with Spanish encouragement. According to the queen's ambassador in the Netherlands, William Davison, Parma began spreading false reports of secret Anglo-Spanish talks to undermine confidence in the alliance almost from the moment of its inception.[22] In January 1586, shortly after the arrival of the queen's army in the Low Countries, a report arrived from Antwerp, "very credibly that the English house there was in preparing (by order of the prince of Parma) for the earl of Leicester, who was not come to make any war but under that color to prepare the minds of the States and others in Holland and Zeeland to yield them to a peace."[23] Even before this, in August, Parma outfitted a house in Brussels, claiming it was "for an ambassador coming out of England" to ratify a secret peace that he said Elizabeth had concluded with Spain.[24]

The fact that the Dutch had ceded control of two cautionary towns along the coast to their allies and that English garrisons soon occupied several other strongholds increased worries about secretive negotiations. If Elizabeth had wanted to sacrifice the Netherlands in order to secure an accord with Philip, she might have done so by turning over these strategically important places to the enemy. But the main reason rumors of secret talks between the English and Spanish persisted was that they were true in substance, if not always in detail. Elizabeth and Burghley initiated back-channel communications with Parma in August, within weeks of the ratification of the Treaty of Nonsuch, and appointed a commission to negotiate with the Spanish general in March 1586.[25] Leicester and Walsingham, who disapproved of these negotiations, tried to soothe Dutch suspicions by dissimulating their knowledge of the queen's secret diplomacy, only to have their attempts at deception unmasked, initially by leaks of information from the Spanish Netherlands and London, but eventually by Elizabeth's open avowal of her intentions.[26]

---

[21] TNA SP84/3/5.   [22] TNA SP84/3/96.
[23] BL Add Mss. 48,014, fol. 152r.   [24] TNA SP84/9/72.
[25] Adams, "Protestant Cause," 43; TNA SP84/6/121; BL Cotton Mss. Titus BVI, fol. 93v; TNA SP77/1/54 and passim.
[26] TNA SP12/183/56, Walsingham to Burghley, October 1585; SP84/7/32, Leicester to Burghley, March 17, 1586; SP84/7/83, Leicester to Burghley, April 7, 1587; SP84/8/71, Leicester to queen, June 6, 1586. In this case the queen wanted to keep her negotiations a secret but reports from Antwerp had correctly identified one of the merchants she was using as a go-between with Parma.

The Problem of Sovereignty in the United Provinces

English mistrust of the Netherlanders' ability to manage their own affairs provided another source of friction. This lack of confidence stemmed not only from the string of defeats the Dutch had suffered over the previous two years and their chronic shortage of money, but also from disapproving incomprehension of the seemingly dysfunctional federated structure of the United Provinces. The Dutch state appeared to lack not only a personal sovereign but *any* source of central authority, requiring it to reach all decisions through intricate negotiations before implementing them through further negotiations rather than authoritative commands.[27] It presented in microcosm the problems of localism and private interest that threatened to impede resistance to Spain across Europe. During the negotiations with England the States General had granted temporary executive authority to a council of state. But the States then forgot to renew the council's authority after its term expired, until Elizabeth crossly demanded that they do so.[28] Provincial bodies, especially the states of Holland, regularly attempted to interfere in executive decisions, including petty matters like the granting of military commissions.[29] Even small local corporations obstructed important actions, as during the siege of Antwerp, when the city's butcher's guild blocked a decision to breach a dike and flood the surrounding countryside to prevent Parma from investing the city, because the butchers did not want pastures on which they fattened their animals inundated.[30] Dutch politics reminded Robert Beale of Thucydides' description of squabbling Greek city states: "For albeit these provinces be termed united, yet shall a man find little good will and safe friendship between them," as "the Prince of Orange was wont to make grievous complaint."[31]

Although the Dutch system had some advantages, they remained largely invisible to the English. Decentralized rule forced merchant oligarchies from different towns to collaborate with each other. Although the process was often

---

[27] Cf. Robert Devereux 2nd earl of Essex's slightly later description in *An Apologie of the Earle of Essex* (London, 2nd ed., 1603), n.p.: "The [Dutch] state hath not (as the state of *Rome* had, and the state of *Venice* hath) one place that as the head doth command and direct all the parts of the body, but is compounded of equal parts. *Zealand* is as absolute as *Holland*, *Friesland* as either of them, yea not only the least province, but the least town holds itself to have a kind of Sovereignty, and will have as free a voice as the greatest."

[28] TNA SP84/3/80.

[29] For a full discussion see J. W. Koopmans, *De Staten van Holland en de Opstand: De Ontwikkeling hun functies en organisatie in de periode 1544–1588*, Hollandse Historische Reeks 13 ('s-Gravenhage: Stichting Hollandse Historische Reeks, 1990), esp. chapters 5 and 6.

[30] James Tracy, *The Founding of the Dutch Republic: War, Finance, and Politics in Holland, 1572–1588* (Oxford: Oxford University Press, 2008), 219; Erik Swart, "'The Field of Finance': War and Taxation in Holland, Flanders and Brabant, 1572–1585," *Sixteenth Century Journal* 42 (2011): 1051–71.

[31] BL Add Mss. 48,014, fols 572–4. Although writing in 1587, Beale claimed that the analogy had first occurred to him "about ten years before"; his subsequent observations of Dutch politics had merely left him "more and more confirmed in my former opinion" (fol. 572r).

cumbersome, it occasionally led to productive partnerships.[32] In Holland, town corporations found it easier to raise loans than the provincial government because their members knew the lenders personally and therefore inspired greater trust. But this meant that local authorities had first call on revenues as they came in, so that many of the "payments" made to the central treasury amounted to paper transactions, in which anticipated proceeds of local taxes were written off against the wages of a garrison, the settlement of accounts with victualers who had extended credit to unpaid soldiers, or the payment of interest on previous loans. Prosperous towns distant from the front lines took care of their own financial interests, while garrisons facing the enemy went unpaid. To prevent interference in its affairs, Holland's government refused to reveal its accounts even to the States General and council of state.[33] This system mystified English observers, who complained of the great "multitude of officers," "partiality of the provinces or towns restraining their contributions to their own use," and "general corruption of the States, which have sought to enrich themselves by the common purse beyond all measure."[34] Leicester's muster master, Thomas Digges, believed that fully three-quarters of the taxes paid by the common people were diverted into the coffers of venal oligarchs and officials.[35]

The scarcity of great nobles in the still-independent northern provinces and the resulting predominance of mercantile town elites compounded these problems in English eyes. After the death of William the Silent the Dutch lacked any leader of high noble rank, apart from William's younger son Maurice, who had not yet reached his eighteenth birthday when the Treaty of Nonsuch was signed. The English had preferred dealing with William because his title as *prince* of Orange gave him the standing to conclude treaties and wage war on his own authority, even though Orange was a small territory distant from the Netherlands that he no longer controlled. His death removed even this fig leaf of legitimacy. Elizabeth and her council had to deal with a government dominated by merchants and lawyers from towns that did not even possess the great patrician dynasties and international financial institutions of urban republics like Genoa, Venice, and Antwerp. Some English felt squeamish about even negotiating with the Dutch. "They are not all ambassadors that are sent to any prince or people to deal with them in matter of state," one of Hatton's correspondents wrote in May 1584. Although rebels might send "deputies" to negotiate with their own prince, he argued, "no prince or state" had the right to accredit ambassadors "unless he be absolute and

---

[32] For a discussion of state formation in the Republic, focused almost entirely on the seventeenth century, see Julia Adams, *The Familial State: Ruling Families and Merchant Capitalism in Early Modern Europe* (Ithaca: Cornell University Press, 2005).
[33] On this subject see Tracy, *Founding of the Dutch Republic*, esp. chapter 11.
[34] TNA SP103/33, a document relating to the treaty negotiations, July(?) 1585.
[35] Ibid., 245–6; Thomas Digges, "Advertisements of these Low Countries," TNA SP84/7/23a; cf. Tracy, *Founding of the Dutch Republic*, 245–6.

sovereign of himself... Subjects cannot constitute or send ambassadors... without peril of treason."[36] If Elizabeth ever entertained such scruples she soon overcame them. But she privately complained that it was no wonder that the Dutch kept making exorbitant demands on her purse, "seeing the government of those countries resteth in the hands of merchants and advocates, the one regarding profits, the other standing upon vantage of quarrels and terms of advantage."[37] Although he avoided social sneers, Burghley also saw Dutch oligarchs as unreliable partners, especially when it came to money: "whatever the country itself offers it cannot be relied upon to pay, as experience has taught."[38]

With the collapse of resistance in the South, the center of the Revolt had moved back toward its earlier heartland, the provinces of Holland and Zeeland. But in 1585 Holland had its own leadership vacuum, having recently lost its military governor or stadtholder, William of Orange, and dismissed its chief civilian officer, the Advocate Paul Buys. The province filled the hiatus in 1586 with the appointment of two men who would preside over the affairs of the United Provinces for the next generation, Maurice of Nassau and Johan van Oldenbarnevelt.[39] They were probably elevated, as Leicester suspected and as several modern historians have also thought, in an effort to block English interference in Holland's affairs. But Maurice's youth and the fact that Oldenbarnevelt had only very recently risen from the secondary post of pensioner of Rotterdam meant that neither had much of a reputation. Leicester and most other English politicians would consistently underestimate them.[40]

It was not simply the English who harbored doubts about the effectiveness of the Dutch state; many Netherlanders did as well.[41] The capitulation of Antwerp, barely a week after the signing of the Treaty of Nonsuch, had a particularly devastating effect. In addition to regaining the last and greatest of the major rebel strongholds in the South, Parma's siege had turned the city's absentee mayor, Philip van Marnix, lord of St Aldegonde, into a proponent of negotiated surrender.[42] An early supporter of William of Orange, lifelong member of the Dutch Reformed Church and former Anglophile, Marnix felt deeply shaken by the privations inflicted on the city during the siege. He lost all confidence in the Dutch capacity for continued resistance. "We are in every respect weaker than our enemies," he wrote. "Their authority is well grounded and stable, resting on the title of the great and puissant king, whereas our authority is not only floating on the waves of the populace, it is also almost completely ineffective... I do not know

---

[36] Hatton, 374.   [37] TNA SP84/4/100, Walsingham to Davison, reporting the queen's views.
[38] HMC Salisbury, 3.69.   [39] Den Tex, *Oldenbarnevelt*, 1.41, 47.
[40] As late as March 1588 Robert Cecil scathingly dismissed "Count Maurice, in whom there is neither outward appearance of any noble mind nor inward virtue. In my life I never saw a worse behavior, except it were one that lately came from school," TNA SP77/2/98.
[41] BL Add Mss. 33,594, fol. 62r.
[42] For a collection of essays on Marnix see *Philips van Marnix van Sint Aldegonde* (Antwerp: Uitgeverij Pandora, 1998).

whether we have a commander at all, or whether some shadow of authority remains with the governors, whether the soldiers and men-at-arms have preserved some notion of obedience."[43] His record as a former champion of the Revolt made his defeatism all the more devastating.[44] "If her majesty means to have Holland and Zeeland her highness must resolve presently," Roger Williams warned shortly before Antwerp's surrender, because "Aldegonde hath promised the enemy to bring them to compound. Here are arrived already his ministers, which know all his dealings about Antwerp... The people say in general they will accept a peace unless Her Majesty doth sustain them presently."[45]

Unlike the duke of Alba, whose brutality had stiffened Dutch resistance, Parma had the good sense to offer generous terms to towns that surrendered, sometimes including a grace period for Protestants in which they might decide whether to become Catholics or sell their property and emigrate.[46] He prevented his soldiers from pillaging. This made it easier for people to regard the restoration of Spanish rule—or in the case of firm Calvinists, emigration to England or Germany—as preferable to the privations of a long siege, especially when the ultimate outcome seemed inevitable.[47] Divisions among Dutch leaders, chronic arrears in the payment of troops, heavy taxation, and accusations that corrupt officials were embezzling state funds added to public discontent. Fearing a complete collapse of morale, English and Dutch leaders both wanted to create the impression that their new alliance would have a transformative effect. Netherlands politicians and Englishmen stationed in the country both began clamoring for Leicester's arrival, hailing him as a savior around whom the discouraged forces of resistance might coalesce. "Certainly we lack good men," one Netherlander wrote, "but much more we lack a leader of great authority, under whom those who presently command can voluntarily range themselves in good order."[48]

This felt need for "a leader of great authority" stemmed in large measure from a structural problem. Centralized executive power in the Low Countries had always run in the name of the counts of Holland, the dukes of Burgundy, or their Habsburg successors, rather than provincial institutions. Although the States

---

[43] Quoted in Peter Arnade, *Beggars, Iconoclasts and Civic Patriots: The Political Culture of the Dutch Revolt* (Ithaca: Cornell University Press, 2008), 329.

[44] For a Dutch reaction see, for example, TNA SP84/4/101, Villiers to Walsingham, October 23/November 2, 1585.

[45] TNA SP84/3/23.

[46] Violet Soen, "Reconquista and Reconciliation in the Dutch Revolt: The Campaign of Governor-General Alexander Farnese (1578–1592)," *The Journal of Early Modern History* 16 (2012): 1–22 is a careful analysis.

[47] Both English and Dutch observers repeatedly warned in late summer and autumn of 1585 of the dangers of capitulation to Parma and the damage done by his propaganda and Marnix's writings. See, e.g., TNA SP84/3/23 and 29/4/67 and 101.

[48] TNA SP84/2/65, Gerard Prouninck to Davison, August 10, 1585: "certainement bons hommes nous manquent, mais beaucoup plus un chef de grande autorité, sous qui à ceux qui présentement commandent se rangent volontiers en bonne correspondance."

General had the authority to legislate and grant taxes, it had not traditionally supervised the carrying out of its decisions. During the Revolt it began to exercise executive functions by entrusting them to committees, as did the provincial states of Holland. But neither body was suited to making quick decisions, since every important measure required debate, a majority vote, and in some cases consultation with constituents. The disappearance of William the Silent, whose charisma and military leadership had given him considerable moral authority, made matters worse. The absence of an unambiguous locus of sovereignty not only complicated Dutch relations with other powers but also impeded internal management, especially with respect to the conduct of war. Many people both within and outside the United Provinces believed the best solution was to replace Philip II with an alternative sovereign from a major European dynasty. Granting sovereignty to a foreign prince did not particularly trouble the Dutch because they had lived with such an arrangement since the death of the last duke of Burgundy, Charles the Bold, in 1477, and in the case of Holland even longer, since the Burgundian dukes did not reside in the North. A foreign sovereign who delegated authority to local men, while respecting local liberties and institutions and protecting the provinces from aggression, seemed the ideal solution. Anjou had conspicuously failed to satisfy in this role but after his death the Dutch offered their sovereignty first to Henry III and then to Elizabeth. While both rulers had their partisans within the United Provinces, many Protestants hoped that Elizabeth would be more supportive of their cause. If she sent a governor to rule in her name who strongly backed resistance to Spain, they might hope for substantial improvement.

But Elizabeth refused the offer of sovereignty precisely because she did not want to challenge Philip's position too directly or make an irrevocable commitment to a Dutch state that seemed in danger of imminent collapse. She therefore equivocated by styling herself the protector, rather than the sovereign, of the United Provinces and signing a contract pledging support for one year only. Her lack of confidence in her allies meant, however, that she wanted considerable control over how they ran their affairs. She demanded and obtained the right to name two Englishmen to the Dutch council of state and extracted a promise that the States General would consult the general of her army on all important decisions, while cooperating with him in taking order "for the reestablishment of public authority and for restitution and maintenance of the discipline of war," which had failed "by reason of the equality of governors and confusion of council" under the existing system. She made the Dutch promise that controversies "between the provinces or any towns shall be referred to her majesty or her highness's general governor to take order therein with the council of state."[49] Leicester received instructions "to

---

[49] BL Add Mss. 48,116, fol. 99, articles of agreement between Elizabeth and the United Provinces, 20 and 26.

use all good means to redress the confused government of those countries" and to admonish the Dutch that unless they followed his advice "her Majesty would think her favor unworthily bestowed upon them."[50]

Elizabeth therefore wanted Leicester, as her representative, to exercise many of the functions that would have fallen to a governor appointed by a sovereign ruler. But she insisted that his supervision operate informally and behind-the-scenes, so it would not look like an attempt to establish English rule over the United Provinces, or inhibit her from cutting her losses if the situation continued to deteriorate. Simon Adams has provided evidence that she almost certainly revised his instructions so as to curtail Leicester's freedom of action during the months before his departure in December.[51] Although the Dutch would have preferred a more formal and public commitment, they agreed to accept Elizabeth's terms in return for military assistance. This left the question of the English role in reforming the government of the United Provinces unresolved. Virtually everyone, including most Dutch politicians, agreed on the need for reform and the importance of more authoritative leadership. It was also clear that bringing about required changes would prove contentious and difficult. Walsingham wrote to Davison in December, bemoaning "the great confusion" that Leicester would encounter in the Netherlands and the difficulty in curing it because of the "sundry practices held in those parts to breed division." He urged Davison to consult "with some of the best affected patriots there about some plot" to remove "the great abuses reigning there, as also the establishing of some settled government," especially over state revenues.[52] But while Elizabeth had given Leicester a mandate to reform abuses, she had denied him any formal authority to do so. Under the terms worked out at Nonsuch, the United Provinces would remain a formally acephalous confederation, even if the Dutch themselves wanted an authoritative head.

Assembling and Paying for Leicester's Expedition

For the moment, issues of Dutch reform seemed less pressing in England than the task of assembling and financing military forces. Leicester had serious doubts about whether Elizabeth would adequately support his army. He told Burghley that he hoped that she would "take this matter...to heart, as a cause that doth concern her life and estate," but added that "if her Majesty be not persuaded and fully resolved that the cause is of other importance than as it were to make a show and become only a scarecrow, it were better never to have entered in it."[53] As he began to assemble his army, Elizabeth sent him an order to stay his preparations,

---

[50] *Leicester Correspondence*, 12; TNA SP 84/5/80. [51] Adams, "Protestant Cause," 52–3.
[52] TNA SP84/5/50. [53] Leicester to Burghley, August 28, 1585, HMC Salisbury 3.108.

although the Dutch representatives in London "were ready to kneel to me for to make haste."⁵⁴ "I . . . am heartily sorry to see the matter of the Low Countries in my opinion even lost and only for lack of timely hearkening," he grumbled in early November.⁵⁵ Walsingham also complained of the queen's prevarications: "When we give advice to use some way of prevention then are we thought authors of unnecessary charges and when we lay open the apparent dangers then are we held as men possessed with vain fears."⁵⁶

Despite Leicester's misgivings he pressed on, sending out "above 200 letters to my servants and sundry my friends, to prepare themselves . . . with all the speed they could possibly, to serve her Majesty, under me, in the Low Countries." Edmund Carey raised 300 men in Suffolk, while Sir John Tracy and Sir Thomas Shirley supplied 500 soldiers each. In all, some fifteen gentlemen recruited 3,350 volunteers.⁵⁷ Most of the cavalry and at least half the foot Leicester led to the Netherlands were supplied by a network of locally influential landowners. As Simon Adams puts it, his army amounted to a large entourage composed of many smaller entourages belonging to individual gentlemen and peers.⁵⁸ The earl supplemented these English levies with Irish troops supplied by his clients there, although he asked Walsingham to press the queen to allow him to conscript an additional "600 or 1000 of your idle Irish men . . . for that they be hard and will abide more pains than our men."⁵⁹ He and his allies also provided much of the money required to outfit the army. Leicester mortgaged his lands to raise a loan of £25,000 from London aldermen and by his own account eventually invested more than £35,000 in the expedition by January 1587.⁶⁰ Davison extended his personal credit to pay Norreys's troops when the Dutch failed to do so.⁶¹ Walsingham later claimed that his son-in-law, Sir Philip Sidney, spent 30,000 crowns or £7,250 on service in the Netherlands, while Burghley asserted that his son Thomas Cecil bestowed £5,000 on his government of the cautionary town of Brill.⁶² Sir William Pelham spent £800 supplying his company. Although impossible to tally exactly, private contributions must have amounted to a sizable fraction of the cost of the English expedition. Elizabeth's refusal to lend Leicester even more money, despite his offer of land as security, touched off another series of bitter complaints.

---

⁵⁴ *Leicester Correspondence*, 5–6. The Dutch were, in fact, pleading with Leicester to hasten his arrival. See, e.g., BL Add Mss. 17,677B, fol. 317r.
⁵⁵ TNA SP12/182/1, Leicester to Walsingham, November 1, 1585.   ⁵⁶ BL Add Mss. 32,657.
⁵⁷ BL Add Mss. 48,084, fol. 99, list of captains who levied voluntary companies. See also Simon Adams, "A Puritan Crusade? The Composition of the Earl of Leicester's Expedition to the Netherlands, 1585–6," in *Leicester and the Court: Essays on Elizabethan Politics* (Manchester: Manchester University Press, 2002), 176–95. David Trim, "Fighting 'Jacob's Wars'. The Employment of English and Welsh Mercenaries in the European Wars of Religion: France and the Netherlands, 1562–1610," unpublished University of London PhD thesis, 2001, 163–7 and 492–3 provides further detail, especially concerning troops recruited by Norreys and others to serve under Dutch pay.
⁵⁸ Adams, "A Puritan Crusade?," 186.   ⁵⁹ *Leicester Correspondence*, 26.
⁶⁰ TNA SP12/183/16; AMAE CPH2, fol. 44.   ⁶¹ TNA SP84/1/432a.
⁶² BL Add Mss. 17,677 C.

"I see her Majesty will make trial of me...but resolved I am that no worldly respect shall draw me back from my faithful discharge of my duty toward her, though she shall show to hate me."[63] "If the Queen fail yet must I trust in the Lord and on him I see I am wholly to depend," he confided to Walsingham: "I can say no more but pray to God that her majesty never send general again as I am sent. And yet I will do what I can for her and my country."[64] "If it be the will of God to plague us that go yet let us not be negligent."[65]

By her usual standards Elizabeth had nevertheless spent liberally on military preparations over the summer. Although the States General had agreed to pay Norreys's 4,000 volunteers, in August the queen agreed to furnish 50,000 guilders or about £5,000 to arm and equip them and to lend the Dutch money to cover their wages for three months.[66] Norreys in fact received £5,000 and his captains an additional £1,620 in June. The exchequer then disbursed a total of £26,248 to transport the companies to the Low Countries and pay their wages between August and December, on the expectation that the Dutch would eventually reimburse £16,950 of this sum.[67] The English treasury ultimately spent £41,521 covering expenses for which they held the Dutch responsible, although the United Provinces later disputed English claims and failed to reimburse most of the money.[68] The disagreement became entangled with an accord reached in late summer that Norreys's men would be transferred to Leicester's army under the queen's pay. Just how many did so and at what date, and whether some of the queen's money had gone to pay additional volunteers raised by Leicester in expectation that the Dutch would pay their wages, remained unclear.[69] Already in October 1585 Elizabeth was becoming angry over what she regarded as her allies' failure to honor their commitments, which she attributed to "contempt" rather than "want or necessity."[70]

---

[63] TNA SP84/5/96, Leicester to Walsingham, December 7, 1585.
[64] TNA SP84/5/89, Leicester to Walsingham, December 5, 1585.
[65] TNA SP84/5/88, Leicester to Walsingham, December 3, 1585.
[66] BL Add Mss. 17,677B, fols 153v and 162r.   [67] TNA AO1 292/1097.
[68] BL Add Mss. 48,116, fol. 112; Add Mss. 17,677B 302v–306r and 322 (Exchanges between the Dutch deputies in London and Davison in the Netherlands relating to payments of Norreys). The Dutch denied responsibility for paying all but 1000 of Norreys's men, while acknowledging a certain obscurity (*duisterheyt*) in the terms of the treaty.
[69] BL Add Mss. 78,172, fols 48r and 48v; Add Mss. 48,116, fol. 112; TNA AO1 292/1097. Trim, "'Fighting Jacob's Wars'," 164–9, concludes that most of Norreys's troops were absorbed into Leicester's army in the autumn of 1585 but that further recruitment eventually brought over 8,000 English soldiers serving under Dutch pay, in addition to Leicester's army. Matters were further confused by high levels of mortality and the lack of regular musters discussed in Chapter 5, which made it difficult to distinguish new levies that increased the size of the two armies from those that merely replaced soldiers who had disappeared from the ranks, and to determine how many soldiers required payment at any point in time.
[70] TNA SP84/4/100, Walsingham to Davis, October 23, 1585; BL Add Mss. 17,677B, fol. 323 (Elizabeth's complaint to the Dutch delegates over their manner of dealing).

In any case, she had already spent £33,000 on Norreys's army before even beginning to raise Leicester's.[71] Norreys then continued to siphon off money intended for the main English army for the remainder of 1585. In December he received an additional £7,000 in back wages owed his troops, from both the earl's war treasury and a loan raised on Davison's credit.[72] The costs of assembling and paying Leicester's army came on top of these other expenses, beginning with two disbursements to the earl in July and a third in August, totaling £47,000, and a further payment of £20,000 to the English treasurer in the Netherlands, James Huddleston, also in August, along with £10,000 to repay a loan from the Merchant Adventurers Company staple in Middleburg, Zeeland. Thomas Cecil and Sir Philip Sidney also received £2,000 each in fines collected from recusants to help them assemble companies of cavalry.[73] By the time Leicester and his army arrived in the Low Countries, in December 1585, Elizabeth had therefore already spent at least £114,000, nearly as much as she had promised to supply in twelve months in the Treaty of Nonsuch.[74] The private expenditures of Leicester and his allies probably added another £40,000 or £50,000, and possibly more.

The Establishment of Leicester's Governorship

Leicester landed at the cautionary town of Flushing (Vlissingen) on December 10, where his nephew, Sir Philip Sidney, had already assumed command as the town's governor. In addition to his army, he had brought along sixteen musicians, seventeen actors, and a royal herald to give an impression of princely magnificence.[75] The same

---

[71] TNA AO1 292/1097 records, in addition to the payment of £5,000 and £1,620 to Norreys and his captains in June and £1,798 for coat and conduct money and ship transport to Flanders, various other payments for wages and captains' entertainment totaling £18,616. Total disbursements for Norreys's army for the first four months beginning August 12, 1585, and thus not including the payments in June, are given as £22,278, although a few other additional recorded expenses brought the total to £26,248.

[72] TNA AO1 292/1096 and 1097; BL Add Mss. 78,172, fol. 47, which states that Norreys's men were given a month's pay, amounting to £7,000 "or thereabouts" and that in order to pay this sum the English treasurer in the Netherlands, James Huddleston, had employed £3,500 borrowed by Davison and £4,325 10s from Leicester's funds.

[73] TNA AO1/292/1096 and E351/2029. The warrants for Leicester's payments are dated July 10 and 28 and August 28, while that for Huddleston's money and the repayment of the Merchant Adventurers October 3. It is not clear whether Leicester's payments were a loan or a gift from the crown. The forces are described as "100 lances with armor" for each man. Cecil and Sidney would go on to command the garrisons within the cautionary towns of Brill and Flushing (Vlissingen). Oosterhoff (*Leicester*, 85) states that the initial payment to Huddleston, intended to cover two months' wages for Leicester's army, was only £20,000 but this overlooks the substantial sums apparently paid directly to the earl himself and to other people earlier in the summer.

[74] That is £33,000 for Norreys's army, £47,000 for Leicester, £20,000 for Huddleston, £10,000 for the Merchant Adventurers, and £4,000 for Cecil and Sidney. It is clear that narratives that only include money sent to the English treasurers of war, Huddleston and his successor Sherley, have substantially understated the amount of money Elizabeth disbursed.

[75] Sally-Beth MacLean, "The Politics of Patronage: Dramatic Records in Sir Robert Dudley's Household Books," *Shakespeare Quarterly* 44.2 (1993): 175–82; Strong and van Dorsten, *Leicester's Triumph*, 85.

evening he received a visit from Maurice of Nassau and a welcoming delegation sent by the council of state, which urged him to set about "the redressing of the government, greatly declined, as they confess, for want of authority."[76] For the next three weeks he made a triumphant progress through Zeeland and Holland, slowed by mists and bad weather, and even more by the lavish entertainments provided along his route. These conformed to an ancient Netherlandish tradition of welcoming sovereigns and the governors they appointed to rule in their name with celebratory entries into major towns.[77] Rotterdam and Delft, one Englishman reported, gave Leicester an even grander welcome than they had put on for Charles V, "the people so joyful and thronging to see his lordship as it was wonder."[78] The earl inspected an Anglo-Dutch fleet of 300 sail at Steenbergen on the Rhine,[79] then celebrated Christmas at Delft, which he glowingly described to Walsingham as "another London almost for beauty and fairness." He praised the companies of soldiers mustered to greet him—"a marvelous fair sight and as tall able personages as ever I saw"—and the enthusiasm of the crowds that lined his route, shouting "God save Queen Elizabeth, as if she had been in Cheapside… The states dare not but be Queen Elizabeth's, for, by the living God, if there should fall but the least unkindness through their default the people would kill them, for these towns will take no direction but from the queen of England, I assure you."[80] From Delft he proceeded to The Hague, which honored him with more "solemn shows in the streets" and fireworks, and then on to Harlem and finally Amsterdam, where a procession of boats and artillery salutes greeted him, with "pretty devices of fish swimming on the river hard by his landing place and… several shows… as he went toward his lodging."[81]

During his progress Leicester dined repeatedly with Maurice and other Dutch leaders, who offered abundant advice and information about pressing military and political problems.[82] So did other Englishmen. The captains who had taken charge of the cautionary towns around the beginning of October complained that they needed reinforcements, to deter both Spanish attacks and betrayals by disloyal inhabitants.[83] Thomas Wilford and Digges inspected the defenses of Ostend, the southernmost port still in Dutch hands, and found them badly in need of strengthening.[84] Norreys complained about the privations suffered by his troops due to the failure of the Dutch to pay their promised wages. Leicester faced considerable pressure to divert funds intended for his army to cover other emergencies: it was becoming clear that even the substantial investments made by the queen and the earl and his followers had not come close to covering all the

---

[76] TNA SP84/5/112, Leicester to council, December 14, 1585; BL Add Mss. 48,014, fol. 149.
[77] Arnade, *Beggars, Iconoclasts and Civic Patriots*.
[78] TNA SP84/5/149, Edward Burnham to Walsingham, December, 27, 1585.
[79] BL Add Mss. 48,014, fol. 149v.
[80] *Leicester Correspondence*, 31 (Leicester to Walsingham, December 26, 1585).
[81] BL Add Mss. 48,014, fols 149v, 154.   [82] Ibid., fols 149–54.
[83] See, e.g., TNA SP84/3, 33 and 94, SP84/4/22, 31 and 79, SP84/5/2.
[84] TNA SP84/5/114, Wilford to Walsingham, December 14, 1585.

necessities of the Dutch war. But Elizabeth immediately dug in her heels at the suggestion that she increase her assistance. "The note sent by your lordship of the wants of Ostend was not best welcome to her Majesty," Walsingham informed Leicester: "we begin already to grow so weary of the charge of the war and fear so much the long continuance thereof as it was half doubted lest some over hasty course would have been taken for some dangerous and dishonorable peace."[85] By early January Walsingham had begun withholding information from Elizabeth about shortages of money in the Netherlands, for fear that it would strengthen a court lobby that wanted to scuttle the Anglo-Dutch alliance.[86]

Numerous Dutch leaders urged Leicester to assume greater authority. Some may have hoped either to turn him into a figurehead or to enlist his support against local rivals, but many genuinely believed that the country needed him to take charge of its affairs.[87] Not all their arguments have come down to us but one public oration by a southern refugee who would become one of the earl's staunchest supporters, Gerard van Prouninck, has survived. It painted a dismal picture of "a policy without justice, soldiers without discipline and countries without government," in which humble people paid "insupportable" taxes to little effect because of inefficiency and corruption. One province maneuvered against another, as magistrates turned their attention to trade rather than government. There were "almost as many leaders as provinces, not to say towns: each province...reserving to itself the levying, cashiering, reviewing, mustering and paying of as many garrisons as it thinks good." Prouninck hailed Leicester as a man sent by God to restore the country to its pristine vigor by reforming these abuses.[88] An anonymous memorandum in French, presumably from a Dutch source, urged the earl to appoint governors in towns including Delft, Rotterdam, and Harlem to keep a watchful eye over the municipal councils. It warned of enemy sympathizers and self-interested men who would try to manipulate him.[89] In private conversations Leicester heard about the resentment against the States General of "captains, governors and soldiers in all places...desperate for pay" and the "universal hate and mislike" that the common people felt for their own leaders.[90]

On New Year's Day a delegation of dignitaries offered to name Leicester governor general of the United Provinces, with absolute authority over military and civil affairs, command over all local governors and military officers, and

---

[85] TNA SP84/5/135. [86] TNA SP84/6/11, Walsingham to Leicester, January 11, 1586.
[87] Den Tex, *Oldenbarnevelt*, 1.53–5 for a discussion.
[88] TNA SP84/5/160, the oration of monsieur Deventer to Leicester, December 1585. Since Prouninck was often called Van Deventer (Tracy, *Founding of the Dutch Republic*, 218), I have assumed he was the orator. The occasion for this oration is not specified but it may well have been the "solemn speech in French" presented to Leicester on behalf of the councils of Holland and the States General on December 28 (BL Add Mss. 48,014, fol. 149v). If so, its scathing indictment of the Dutch system is all the more remarkable.
[89] TNA SP84/5/169. [90] *Leicester Correspondence*, 81.

control of ordinary taxes.[91] He initially asked that the offer be delivered in writing and requested time to consider, but after further entreaties he accepted and began exercising his authority even before taking his oath of office on February 4.[92] Although not quite a sovereign, Leicester had effectively been appointed the sovereign's designated representative, on the model of previous governor generals under Charles V.[93] But the identity of the sovereign who had selected him, and who might therefore send him binding instructions or remove him from office, remained unclear, since not only the States General but representatives of individual provinces had urged him to take the office, and he remained Elizabeth's subject, the "general governor" of her army and her chief representative in the country.[94] This ambiguity would lead to repeated disputes, beginning barely ten days after he assumed office, when he refused to receive a set of instructions relating to Dutch taxation, "as tending to the prejudice of the treaty and likewise the delation of the government bestowed upon him."[95] The confusion was compounded by the fact that the Dutch had granted Leicester absolute power—the Latin articles of appointment read *"summum imperium et authoritatem habet, absolutam seu supremam"*—and then somewhat contradictorily tried to specify things he was not allowed to do.[96] Since his appointment was meant to address a vacuum of authority, no one apparently felt the need to spell out exactly how it had happened or whether any institution had the right to regulate his actions.

Despite these ambiguities, Leicester's office gave him the standing to issue authoritative commands and promote systematic reforms, even in the face of opposition. Understanding just what this entailed requires a brief excursus into Dutch history. The Revolt against Spain had reinforced the strong emphasis on local liberties and privileges long characteristic of Netherlands political culture, giving rise to what one historian has described as a form of "civic republicanism," imbued with an ethos "of corporatism, urban rights and checks on sovereign authority," whose "most enduring and symbolically resonant figure" was the *poorter* or town citizen.[97] The destruction of hated Spanish citadels by crowds of citizens armed with picks and shovels became a resonant symbol of the fight for

---

[91] TNA SP84/6/2. For an account of the circumstances surrounding Leicester's appointment see Oosterhof, *Leicester and the Netherlands*, 63–8.

[92] *Leicester Correspondence*, 58; TNA SP84/6/35; Bor, *Oorsprong*, pt 2, 690.

[93] There had never been a Spanish viceroy in the Low Countries because these provinces had never been a kingdom, but the governor general had enjoyed similar authority. The closest English parallel would be a lord deputy of Ireland.

[94] For the concurrence of the individual provinces see Bor, *Oorsprong*, pt 2, 685.

[95] BL Add Mss. 48,116, fol. 111v.

[96] BL Add Mss. 48,084, fol. 334v. In addition to the grant of *"summum imperium et authoritate absolutam et supremam in rebus multifarious,"* he was granted "as full and absolute authority in matters of policy and justice as any Governor general had in the time of the Emperor Charles V *salvis iuribus et privilegiis* and likewise power to establish a Council of estate according to the treaty." The things he was expressly prohibited from doing included negotiating with the enemy over peace (Bor, *Oorsprong*, pt 2, 689).

[97] Arnade, *Beggars, Iconoclasts and Civic Patriots*, 7.

liberty. Religion had reinforced this defiant independence. But even at a local level the concrete meanings of liberty, citizenship, and religion remained ambiguous. They appeared to imply a notion of popular sovereignty, or at least a polity in which power was widely diffused. But many Dutch leaders resisted this idea. Thomas Wilkes paraphrased them as denying that the Netherlands was governed "by the common people, as some are persuaded." Instead "the species of that commonweal is not popular or democratic but aristocratic or *paucorum potentia*, and consisteth in every city or town, called by the name of *vroestschap*, who are the chiefest and most wealthy burghers." These local oligarchs served for life and filled vacancies in their ranks by recruiting new members, much like the closed vestries of some English parishes. Many had first come into office under the Habsburgs and not a few had politically checkered pasts or suspect religious views. An anonymous correspondent warned Leicester that of the twenty-four magistrates who ruled Deventer, only six were reliable Protestants; "all the rest be either papists and never knew the true religion or else they have forsaken it and have been spectators of the Spanish cruelty over their own burgers."[98] Strong supporters of the Revolt and the Reformed Church had little confidence in these local oligarchs. But since town magistrates selected representatives to the States General from their own ranks, supervised the collection of taxes, appointed local militia captains, and administered trade it was virtually impossible to implement any policies without their support.[99]

On the other hand, more broadly-based town militias and guilds and urban crowds also played roles in civic life, so that oligarchic control was never absolute.[100] Factional struggles were common. High literacy rates in this urbanized region further contributed to Dutch fractiousness, giving rise to numerous pamphlets, ballads, satiric images, and politically charged sermons, as well as published edicts and remonstrances issued by various town and provincial authorities, advocating or protesting specific measures. These were often printed for broad circulation.[101] Military forces and their commanders also occasionally intervened in local politics. A few supporters of the Revolt, like the author of a tract entitled *Le Vray Patriot aux Bons Patriots*—probably the reformed minister Petrus Beutterich—gloried in this diffusion of authority and urged the Dutch to adopt a "Swiss" system of government, in other words a loose association of

---

[98] *Brieven over het Leysterische Tijdvak uit de Papieren van Jean Hotman*, ed. R. Boersma and G. Busken Huet, Bijdragen en Mededeelingen van het Historisch Genootschap 34 (Amsterdam: Johannes Müller, 1913), 59.

[99] Thomas Wilkes to Elizabeth, July 12/22, 1587, in *Correspondentie van Robert Dudley, Graf van Leycester, en andere documenten betreffende zijn Gouvernemente Generaal*, ed. Hajo Brugmans, 3 vols (Utrecht: Keminken Zoon, 1931), 2.398.

[100] Although guilds were less important in Holland than in the southern provinces.

[101] The frequency with which these quasi-official documents were printed, often in the context of contentious disputes, can be appreciated from Bor, *Oorsprong*, which reproduces many of them.

self-governing localities.¹⁰² But few people had much confidence in the ability of a Swiss style confederation to hold off Parma's army. Some source of unifying authority seemed urgently necessary; the question was how to create it without subverting cherished traditions of local independence.¹⁰³

The Revolt had begun to engender a sense of common identity, expressed through symbolic imagery of resistance to Spain, and the resonant term "patriot," used twice in Beutterich's title. Patriots gave their loyalty not to a prince but to a *patria* or fatherland and its liberties.¹⁰⁴ English sources from the period frequently refer to Dutch patriots but never apply the word to other Englishmen, since it seemed inappropriate to the subjects of a monarch.¹⁰⁵ But what exactly did loyalty to the *patria* mean in a region that traditionally lacked any clear sense of territorial or linguistic identity above the level of individual provinces and towns, and where many of the soldiers fighting against Spain were in any case Germans, Scots, English, or French, rather than native Netherlanders?¹⁰⁶ Most so-called patriots were Protestants, although a few Catholic publicists tried to appropriate the title and we occasionally find references to "Catholic patriots." The need to unify "all good patriots" to fight the Spanish seemed clear to everyone, including Elizabeth, who instructed Davison to do exactly that as he returned to the Netherlands to prepare the ground for Leicester's arrival.¹⁰⁷

But it remained unclear whether a good patriot owed primary allegiance to his own province, to a wider Netherlandish cause that might embrace refugees from the conquered southern provinces, or even to the general defense of civil and religious liberty throughout Europe. The ambiguity had practical consequences, when the interests of Holland came into conflict with the desire of southern

---

¹⁰² Arnade, *Beggars, Iconoclasts and Civic Patriots*, 310; Martin van Gelderen, *The Political Thought of the Dutch Revolt, 1555-1590* (Cambridge: Cambridge University Press, 1992), 187-91.

¹⁰³ Gelderen, *Political Thought*, 171-4.

¹⁰⁴ For a discussion of the word, which had featured earlier in discourses by Italian humanists as well as French and German publicists, see Alastair Duke, "In Defence of the Common Fatherland: Patriotism and Liberty in the Low Countries, 1555-1576," in *Networks, Regions and Nations: Shaping Identities in the Low Countries, 1300-1560*, ed. Robert Stein and Judith Pollmann (Leiden: Brill, 2010), 217-39. For the earlier German background see Robert von Friedburg, "'Lands' and 'Fatherlands': Changes in the Plurality of Allegiances in the Sixteenth-Century Holy Roman Empire," in the same volume, 263-82.

¹⁰⁵ For examples see John Strype, *Annals of the Reformation* (London, 1728), 3.118 (official instructions to William Davison on his embassy to the Netherlands); *Correspondentie*, ed. Brugmans, 3.264 (Elizabeth to Lord Buckhurst, May 7/17, 1587), ibid., 350 (Leicester to Burghley, December 1, 1587).

¹⁰⁶ This topic will be greatly illuminated by a forthcoming book by Arthur Williamson, *Scotland and the Rise of Social Thought*, chapter 2, "The Patriot Cause and the Advent of '*un Evangelisme civil*'." See also his "The Rise and Decline of the British 'Patriot': Civic Britain c. 1545-1645," *International Review of Scottish Studies* 36 (2011): 7-32 and "Patterns of British Identity: 'Britain' and its Rivals in the Sixteenth and Seventeenth Centuries," in *The New British History: Founding a Nation State*, ed. Glenn Burgess (London: I. B. Tauris, 1999), 138-73 at 140-3. I wish to thank Arthur Williamson for sharing with me his work on this subject in advance of publication and for stimulating discussions. Cf. Arnade, *Beggars, Iconoclasts and Civic Patriots*, 272-4.

¹⁰⁷ Strype, *Annals of Reformation*, vol. 3, Appendix, 118.

refugees in Leicester's entourage to direct resources to the recovery of their homelands.[108] Some Holland politicians denied that a native of Brabant like Prouninck could be considered a patriot, entitled to hold political office, in another province. On the other hand, some patriots were prepared to challenge Holland magistrates and even the authority of the States General. When Utrecht celebrated Leicester's appointment as governor general by ringing bells, some townsmen said that "they rang their states out of government."[109] The earl appeared ready to step into William the Silent's role as the leader and symbol of a Dutch patriotism that transcended narrow provincial loyalties. Although he had no estate in the country, he was a reputed friend of Dutch liberty and a great nobleman with a resplendent following that would eventually include four other English peers, a son of the earl of Bedford, two sons of the Portuguese pretender, Dom Antonio, and numerous knights and esquires. He had arrived as Elizabeth's representative and general of an army that the people hoped would save them from Spanish tyranny, and as governor general he possessed a formal authority that Orange had never enjoyed. This combination of qualities initially gave him some credibility as the new leader of patriot resistance to Spain.

In the weeks following his installation Leicester participated in another series of lavish entries in Harlem, Amsterdam, and Amersfoort, celebrating Elizabeth's role as protectress of the Netherlands and his own as the man who would defend them in her name. Harlem constructed an effigy of the queen as the personification of Justice, treading Envy and Tyranny underfoot as she extended her helping hand to the Dutch provinces, and another pyramidal image of the Dudley family tree with verses hailing Leicester as "Prince of Peace." Amsterdam's pageants included an image of Elizabeth supporting Moses as he prayed for divine aid against the Philistines, and one of Leicester as Joshua leading the Israelites into battle.[110] The earl established a resplendent household, costing £1,000 a month, in the ancient cathedral town of Utrecht, which he made his capital.[111] It functioned virtually as a vice regal court and was described as a court by contemporaries. Leicester's celebration of the Feast of St. George in late April was especially magnificent.[112] He rode in a great cavalcade to the cathedral, preceded by

---

[108] Cf. Oosterhoff, *Leicester*, 79–82.

[109] TNA SP84/6/37. James Huddleston reported in February 1586 that "it is a wonder to hear how reproachfully they [Dutch citizens] will speak against such as we call the States and how glad they are they might no longer have government" because of Leicester's appointment.

[110] Strong and van Dorsten, *Leicester's Triumph*, 65–6.

[111] *Leicester Correspondence*, 166. For a list of the household's officers see BL Cotton Mss. Galba C viii, fol. 107. They included four secretaries, a clerk controller, three gentlemen ushers, a master of the tents, a chaplain, two physicians and two surgeons, four trumpeters, assorted cooks, bakers, and pastry makers, two keepers of greyhounds and other dogs, four grooms of the chamber and three of the body, nine bargemen, seven men employed as armorers or tent keepers, twenty-six grooms of the stable, and forty-four musketeers.

[112] Raphael Holinshed, *The first and second volumes of Chronicles* (London, 1587), 1437–8. There is an online edition at http:www.msns.ox.ac.uk/Holinshed/texts.php?text1=1587_9135.

trumpeters in scarlet robes trimmed with silver lace, carrying bannerols of his arms. Next came forty gentlemen and officers, "richly adorned in cloth of gold, silver and silks of all colors"; a company of knights and barons escorting the council of state; the young earl of Essex, accompanied by the bishop of Cologne and a son of Dom Antonio, styled "prince of Portugal"; officers of the earl's household carrying white staves; and two gentlemen ushers escorting the Portcullis herald, "in a rich coat of arms of England." Eight ranks of Utrecht burgers, "wearing scarfs knit like roses white and red upon their arms" in token of their allegiance to England, lined the streets.

Upon reaching the cathedral, Leicester donned the robes of the Order of the Garter before entering the building, accompanied by a guard "of fifty halberds in scarlet cloaks." Within he found a throne and canopy or "state" adorned with Elizabeth's arms standing to the right of the altar, to which he bowed before seating himself to hear a sermon. He then returned to "his court...a fair and large house belonging in times past to the Knights of Rhodes, in which was a very great hall hung with tapestry, at the upper end whereof was a most sumptuous cloth and chair of estate for the queen's majesty, with her arms and style thereon, and before it a table covered with all things so requisite as if in person she had been there." Standing before the state, he knighted a Dutch gentleman, Martin Skink, and presented him with a gold chain valued at 1,000 crowns. Trumpets then announced the arrival of a dinner provided for the household and numerous Dutch dignitaries, "most abundant and prince-like served on the knee."[113] A few days later Leicester knighted John Norreys "in the presence chamber at Utrecht": he had reproduced the ceremonial layout of an English palace.[114] At some point he had a great seal made, showing his arms on either side.[115] This apparatus of magnificence and symbolic authority, rarely seen in the Netherlands since the departure of Habsburg governors general, strongly suggested that Elizabeth had become the country's sovereign and the new focus of popular allegiance, despite her refusal to accept the role.

By assuming the position of a *de facto* viceroy, Leicester had made opposition to his authority almost inevitable, since the provinces of the Netherlands had a long record of strenuous resistance to efforts by previous governor generals and resident sovereigns to exercise their authority. Even William the Silent had constantly found himself at loggerheads with other Dutch politicians, especially in Holland. Leicester had taken on the task of overcoming local opposition because the pleas of many of the country's leaders, as well as the advice of

---

[113] Ibid.; Thomas Digges, *A true Report of the Service in the Lowe countries* (London, 1587), n.p. [9].
[114] TNA SP84/7/103, Leicester to Burghley, April 17, 1586, reporting the herald's death; Leicester wanted him replaced and "someone of mean degree" sent along as an assistant; "they shall do service and increase their skill with the knowledge of the armories of the countries." BL Add Mss. 48,014, fol. 155v.
[115] TNA SP84/15 fol. 160v.

English colleagues and his own observations had convinced him that "if I had not accepted this place of government as I did and when I did, this whole state had been gone and wholly lost."[116] Believing himself to have the support of the country's chief patriots, he threw himself into his new duties, consulting with Dutch leaders, rearranging garrisons and seeking to cover the most egregious arrears in army pay, even when it meant diverting money intended for his soldiers or borrowing on his own credit.[117] He sought to enhance Dutch naval preparations and wrote enthusiastically to Burghley about the maritime strength of the Netherlands and the benefits England would reap from the alliance if Philip II should try to attack England by sea.[118] Preoccupied with preparations for the summer's military campaign, he began planning to hire German mercenaries and started recruiting more English volunteers, before he had secured a source of money with which to pay them.

Signs of dissension quickly arose. Davison complained of "diverse bad instruments," in other words men opposed to the English alliance, who tried to arouse the jealousies of Maurice of Nassau and another prominent general in the Dutch army, the German Count Hohenlohe, "under the pretext of the particular prejudice which might rebound to the one and the other" from Leicester's authority.[119] Both generals would eventually clash with Leicester. The earl's refusal to submit to instructions from the States General, as inconsistent with his "absolute" authority, aroused concerns that his ignorance of Dutch customs would lead him to govern in an arbitrary manner.[120] But in this early period the Dutch generally proved cooperative and Leicester believed he was making progress. "I think there was never seen in so short a time so great an alteration as is now to that when I arrived first. All men begin now to join well together and very earnestly and will contribute willingly for to further the matters of these wars... We are dressing of an army to take the field."[121]

Elizabeth Reacts

During the first few months of his governorship the most serious damage inflicted on Leicester's authority came not from Dutch opponents but Elizabeth. She had

---

[116] TNA SP84/7/31, Leicester to Burghley, March 17, 1586. Other Englishmen in the Netherlands agreed. See, e.g., SP84/7/43, Gilpin to Walsingham, March 21 and SP84/7/14, William Knollys to Walsingham, March 7, 1586.

[117] *Leicester Correspondence*, 58 and 81; TNA SP84/6/35 and 37; BL Cotton Mss. Titus BVI, fol. 93v and Add Mss. 48,084, fol. 338v. The States General asked Leicester to pay for new levies of troops by using his own credit: BL Add Mss. 48,116, fol. 117.

[118] Bor, *Oorsprongk*, pt 2, 691; TNA SP84/6/60.

[119] TNA SP84/3/96, Davison to Walsingham, September 25, 1585.

[120] Emanuel van Meteren, *Historie der Nederlandscher ende haerder naburen oorlogen ende geschieden* (Graven-Hague, 1614), fol. 239r.

[121] TNA SP84/6/138, Leicester to Burghley, February 28, 1586.

expressly commanded him not to accept formal leadership of the Dutch state and saw his disobedience as a personal betrayal. She feared that Philip II would consider his appointment evidence of a collusive arrangement, by which she had rejected sovereignty over the Low Countries with one hand, while reaching out to grab it under the table with the other.[122] She regarded the appearance of her duplicity that this impression created, along with the violation of her will by her subject and creature, as stains on her honor.[123] Davison, who undertook the thankless task of traveling to London to justify Leicester's actions, had trouble even obtaining an audience. After Walsingham finally gained him access to the queen he spent two fruitless days trying to talk her out of her decision to send a courtier, Sir Thomas Heneage, to the Netherlands with peremptory orders that Leicester resign his office immediately and that the Dutch rescind his appointment. With Burghley's assistance Davison at least managed to have a clause inserted into Heneage's instructions, allowing him to delay the delivery of the queen's message "if he found it might hurt the common service."[124] This gave Heneage an excuse to avoid telling the Dutch of Elizabeth's demands until she finally relented and rescinded them in June. But he was unable to entirely conceal her displeasure with Leicester, even though he recognized that revealing it would undermine the earl and imperil the reforms he was attempting to carry out.[125] "I fear I will not restore the much repaired wreck of these far decayed noble countries," he complained to Burghley: "a loose, disordered and unkind estates needs no shaking but propping... I do not yet find how I shall possibly satisfy her Majesty in her desire and not do exceeding hurt."[126] Sidney concluded that Heneage "hath with as much honesty in my opinion done as much hurt as any man this twelvemonth have done with naughtiness."[127]

Burghley described his own efforts to assuage Elizabeth's anger as "more cumbersome and more severe to me and others that hath sundry times dealt therein... than any whatsoever since I was a councilor."[128] During one heated

---

[122] TNA SP84/6/53, draft of Burghley to Leicester, January 26 and 110, draft of Elizabeth to the estates of Holland, February 1586.

[123] TNA SP84/7/77, Elizabeth to Heneage, April 1, 1586.

[124] TNA SP84/6/121, Davison to Leicester, February 1586. A draft of the clause in question read: "But withal we think meet that before you enter into any dealing with the States you do carefully inform yourself by all good means how the execution of this purpose for the revocation of the Earl's authority will be taken and what alteration the same is likely to work in the hearts of the people, to the end that if you shall see by conference with them of best judgment there that the execution thereof is likely to breed by the practice of such as are ill affected to this state such an alienation in them as may haply work a revolt unto the Spaniard, you may in that case forbear to deal with them and advise us first of the causes and reasons that move you to think so" (SP84/6/110).

[125] TNA SP84/7/26.

[126] TNA SP84/7/86, Heneage to Burghley, April 7, 1586; cf. his similar complaints in SP84/8/24 and 44.

[127] TNA SP84/7/37, Sidney to Burghley, March 18, 1586. For another discussion of this episode see Strong and van Dorsten, *Leicester's Triumph*, 22–3.

[128] *Leicester Correspondence*, 268.

argument he asked her to relieve him of his offices if she would not relent.[129] His task was evidently rendered even more difficult, as a Spanish report stated and as Walsingham suspected, by individuals near the queen who deliberately fed her rage, along with reports from the Netherlands that fueled her anxieties over the mounting costs of the war.[130] Someone told Elizabeth in early February that Leicester's wife, a woman she cordially detested, would soon join him in the Netherlands with "a train of ladies and gentlewomen and such rich coaches, litters and side saddles as her Majesty had none such." The queen replied "with great oaths [that] she would have no more courts under her obedience than her own," and threatened again to recall Leicester immediately before her councilors managed to calm her down.[131]

Elizabeth's opposition undercut Leicester's governorship in several ways. It weakened the earl's standing among Dutch politicians as he attempted to consolidate his authority and raise money for his summer campaign. Her refusal to allow her deputy to assume command revived fears that she wished to evade responsibility for the defense of the Netherlands and might soon withdraw her aid. Leicester complained, probably justifiably, that letters sent over by English Catholics and other detractors, exaggerating Elizabeth's displeasure and predicting his imminent ruin and the withdrawal of his forces, alarmed the Dutch. "Never man so villainously handled by letters out of England as I have been, which not only advertised her Majesty's great dislike of me before this my coming over hither but that I was odious in England and as long as I tarried here bade them look for no help out of England... That I was but here for a time till a peace were concluded between her Majesty and the Prince of Parma."[132] Fears that Elizabeth would abandon the Netherlands led some former supporters of the English alliance, notably the diplomat Paul Buys, to look for another protector, such as the king of Denmark. This may have helped poison Buys's relationship with Leicester, as the earl later claimed, although the two also disagreed about other matters.[133] Elizabeth's anger led her briefly to assume direct control over

---

[129] Ibid., 197.
[130] *CSPSp* 3.588, unsigned letter to Philip II, June 30, 1586; *Leicester Correspondence*, 239–40.
[131] *Leicester Correspondence*, 112.
[132] TNA SP84/7/83. Cf. Leicester to Burghley SP84/7/32: "Your papists in England hath sent over word to some in this company that they ever hoped for is come to pass that my Lord of Leicester shall be called away and in greatest indignation with her Majesty...I myself have seen a letter that her Majesty is [illegible] with a secret peace."
[133] TNA SP84/8/106 and 107, Leicester to queen, June 20, 1586. Leicester saw Buys's project to make the king of Denmark the Netherlands' sovereign as a serious threat not only to his own position but also to English interests, since between them the Dutch and Danish fleets would be able to control the North Sea. Historians have attributed Buys's increasingly bitter quarrel with Leicester to other disagreements over issues like trade with the enemy. Leicester wrote to his secretary, Jean Hotman, in October 1586 that he "could not imagine" why Buys had become so hostile but that the estrangement had started shortly after his appointment as governor general (AMAE CPH2, fol. 100: "Et che e stata la causa dell sua mutatione verso di me io non posso imaginare. Ma io son certo che dopo poci giorni ch'io haveva ricevuto la mia autoritá dagli Stati non ha mostrato haver nessuna cura di me, quanto stranieri io fussi a

English policy in the Netherlands, circumventing not only Leicester but also Walsingham and Burghley, whom she regarded as his collaborators. When Leicester complained bitterly in April about the lack of communication from his colleagues in London, Walsingham plaintively replied "that her majesty retaining the whole direction of the causes of the country [the Netherlands] to herself and such advice as she receiveth underhand, they [members of the Privy Council] know not what to write or advise."[134] For several weeks England had no coherent policy in the Low Countries because Elizabeth was at cross purposes with her general in the field, the leading members of her Council, and even her personal envoy, Heneage.

Although it lasted less than five months, from February until early June 1586, the queen's fury over Leicester's appointment inflicted long-term damage. Even after she forgave him she remained sufficiently mistrustful to send other envoys— first Thomas Wilkes and later Lord Buckhurst—to consult independently with Dutch leaders and report back to her. Leicester felt deeply shaken by the queen's disapproval, which intensified his worries that she had sent him on a thankless errand that would end in his ruin. "For my faithful, true and loving heart to her majesty and my country," he complained, "I have utterly undone myself; for favor I have disgrace; and for reward utter spoil and ruin."[135] He told Elizabeth in May that he lived "trembling continually with the fear" of her fresh disapproval.[136] His anxiety increased his paranoia about secret enemies who sought to poison the queen's mind against him and tepid friends who failed to defend him adequately, making him acutely suspicious of any Englishmen in the Low Countries who did not appear totally loyal to himself. He upbraided his own secretary, Jean Hotman, for writing to the queen without his permission.[137] The earl's fear of betrayal by his colleagues and determination to punish them for real or imagined assaults on his credit with the queen turned minor misunderstandings into bitter quarrels, rendering it virtually impossible for other Englishmen to mediate disputes between him and Dutch leaders or to offer constructive criticism and advice.[138] The cohort of English diplomats, administrators, and captains in the Low

---

quel tempo non solamente a li costumi di qusto paese, ma anzi a tutte le persone et città di esso: cosi lasciandomi passar comme un huomo travagliando in oscurità, et non contento con quello, ma lui principalemente ha cercato di alterar il buono animo de li Stati verso di me").

[134] *Leicester Correspondence*, 226, 237.   [135] Ibid., 102.   [136] TNA SP84/8/50.

[137] AMAE CPH2, fol. 65, Leicester to Hotman, February 20, 1587: "I marvel not a little what should move you to write to her Majesty without my knowledge, being my servant and left there only for my affairs, and so doth her Majesty also. I pray you let me know the cause of it."

[138] Many earlier discussions, such as Den Tex, *Oldenbarnevelt*, 1.72–3, have depicted Wilkes and Buckhurst as strong critics of Leicester. It is difficult to be certain exactly how critical Wilkes's initial detailed report really was, since it appears not to have survived (Oosterhoff, *Leicester*, 126). But his subsequent correspondence, like that of Buckhurst, indicates a balanced attitude, broadly supportive of Leicester's goals and authority, while critical of some of his methods. Both men saw the earl's conflicts with Dutch leaders as destructive but neither placed the blame entirely on Leicester. Oosterhof, *Leicester*, 124–7 provides a more balanced assessment of Wilkes's position.

Countries divided into a group of the earl's partisans and others he regarded as adversaries, even though in many cases they had considerable sympathy for his position. This fissure suggested to the Dutch that he did not have the united support even of his own countrymen, tempting some of them to try to undermine him further by sending complaints to London. Leicester's knowledge that they were doing so hardened his animosity toward his Dutch critics and prompted him to look for ways of discrediting them.[139]

Walsingham and Davison both thought that Elizabeth's anger at Leicester had revived her "sparing humor," causing her to withhold further installments of the money promised for his army. Whether for this or other reasons the money was certainly slow in coming.[140] Having spent the initial installment of £20,000 by February, Leicester had to wait until April for an additional £24,000 to arrive and thereafter received no more money until August, when he was sent £45,000, followed by another £30,000 in October. He compounded the problem by failing to take advantage of an authorization by the States General to raise an immediate loan in the cities of Holland, while they negotiated over his request for a further increase in taxation of 400,000 gulden or £40,000.[141] He may not have understood the Dutch system of funding military operations through loans while tax receipts slowly trickled in, or he may have found the task of dickering with town oligarchs distasteful. He did raise £10,000 from the Merchant Adventurers on his own credit but this failed even to cover the back wages of his own army, while leaving nothing for other military expenses.[142]

Lack of money at the start of the campaigning season slowed Leicester's preparations, threatening to provoke mutinies and leaving him at a numerical disadvantage against Parma.[143] A Dutch memorandum reported that he went into the field "very weak" (*zeer zwaak*).[144] In the end Elizabeth supplied £119,000 in the calendar year October 1585 to October 1586, just short of the £126,180 she had promised, while an "extraordinary contribution" by the Dutch netted 340,414

---

[139] See AMAE CPH2, fol. 308v, Warmond de Stöchelel to Leicester, February 15, 1587, reporting that after the betrayal of Deventer and Zutphen by captains Leicester had appointed, his enemies "ont écrit et fait écrire lettres à S. M. et de son excellence, pleins de reproches et mécontentement, tachant de mettre son excellence en disgrâce et mauvais prédicament [sic] avec sa dite majesté."

[140] TNA SP84/6/121, Davison to Leicester, February 1586; BL Cotton Mss. Titus BVI, fols 65r, 93v.

[141] Tracy, *Founding of the Dutch Republic*, 229, 275–6; NA 13.01.14/184A. For the Dutch extraordinary contribution see NA 13.01.14/187 and Bor, *Oorsprong*, pt 2, 691. The subsidy, finally agreed to in August, amounted to 400,000 Dutch pounds, equivalent to roughly £40,000 sterling.

[142] Leicester complained to Burghley in March that he had had to pay his horse soldiers by borrowing money, TNA SP84/7/32.

[143] Oosterhoff, *Leicester*, 85–7; *Leicester Correspondence*, 339, Leicester to Walsingham, July 8, 1586: "Mr. Secretary I tell you if our people shall be no better relieved, by the Lord, I look for the foulest mutiny that ever was made, both of our men and these country soldiers."

[144] NA 13.01.14.184A. Van Meteren, *Historie*, fol. 250v described Leicester's force in the spring as "a small army of 3000 foot and 1200 horse," although other troops commanded by Hohenlohe and Norreys were also in the field.

gulden or nearly £35,000.¹⁴⁵ Even so, the costs of Leicester's army were never adequately covered. Because cash shortages prevented Digges from conducting musters, Leicester had no precise idea of how many soldiers he had left in service after the ravages of winter had taken their toll on his army. Money was wasted by paying the full wages of companies whose numbers had declined, in some cases, to barely half their original strength.

These problems were especially serious because Leicester had decided to disobey another of his instructions by launching an offensive campaign, rather than conducting the purely defensive war the queen wanted.¹⁴⁶ In principle this made good military sense since, as Norreys and other experienced commanders pointed out, a purely defensive strategy would have ceded the initiative to Parma, allowing him to concentrate his forces against individual cities, while most Dutch and English troops remained tied down in garrisons far from the front lines.¹⁴⁷ But offensive operations required a substantial field army, including expensive units of heavy cavalry, whereas ordinary Dutch revenues did not even cover the full costs of existing garrisons, which could not be reduced until their arrears had been paid without risking mutinies.¹⁴⁸ Leicester's offensive therefore entailed a significant further increase in expenditures from taxation and loans. The Dutch later claimed to have spent 300,000 florins (£30,000) in the summer and a further 800,000 in the autumn "in arming, victualling and other imprests made to the English, Scottish and Irish soldiers," an amount virtually identical to Elizabeth's own contribution of £119,000 in the same period.¹⁴⁹

By late spring, English soldiers in the Netherlands included not only those in Leicester's and Norreys's original armies but additional contingents of "voluntaries" more recently recruited.¹⁵⁰ Elizabeth briefly tried to prevent these new English recruits from going to the Netherlands in May, much to Walsingham's disgust, before relenting.¹⁵¹ The earl peppered Burleigh, Ralegh, and others back in England with requests to raise soldiers and pioneers (laborers for siege operations), while complaining of the "marred and spoiled" recruits they sent, whose behavior showed the folly of the "cockney kind of bringing up at this day of young men."¹⁵²

---

[145] Although if we add the money spent during the summer and autumn of 1585 her expenditures greatly exceeded £126,180. For the extraordinary contribution see NA 13.01.14.187. Total Dutch expenditures for 1586 are given by this document as 1,863,734 gulden.

[146] The clause in his instructions read: "We therefore do think it very meet and so do require you that you rather bend your course to make a defensive than offensive war and that you seek by all the means you may to avoid the hazard of a battle or any other fight or attempt with disadvantage" (BL Add Mss. 48,084, fols 42v-44). For Leicester's explanation of why he disobeyed this clause see *Leicester Correspondence*, 72.

[147] For Leicester's own explanation of his rationale for going on the offensive see BL Add Mss. 48,116, fol. 76r-v.

[148] BL Add Mss. 48,084, fols 335 ff.   [149] BL Add Mss. 48,014, fol. 380.

[150] See the table of these companies in Trim, "'Fighting Jacob's Wars'," 492-3.

[151] *Leicester Correspondence*, 272-3.

[152] *Leicester Correspondence*, 228; ibid., 86 reports Leicester's effort to enlist Ralegh's aid in recruiting 1,000 Cornish miners for use as pioneers during siege operations.

Many of these new soldiers replaced troops who had died or deserted during the winter but it is clear that Leicester tried to expand the size of his army well beyond the level that Elizabeth had agreed to support. Clients like Sir Thomas Sherley, Sir Thomas Conway, William Stanley, and Lord Audley received recruitment quotas of as many as 1,000 men each, with the goal of raising 5,000 additional English and Irish soldiers.[153] The Master of Gray also recruited actively for Leicester in Scotland, pressing his friends to raise volunteers. "I shall make all the expedition I can to haste men over to you," he wrote in September: "Your excellency shall, God willing, have all the number he [you] craved and seven companies more within a month, wind serving."[154] But although Gray apparently received £2,000 from England to cover his initial expenses, Walsingham and Leicester tried to discourage him from sending too many soldiers, fearing they would be unable to pay the Scots' wages.[155] About 1,000 fresh Scottish soldiers eventually did arrive in the Low Countries, "for the service of the Queen of England."[156]

The high rate of mortality among Leicester's original troops during the winter, the absence of musters, and the confused state of his own finances and those of the United Provinces make it impossible to know precisely how large his army had actually become and what proportion of the soldiers' wages remained unpaid. Elizabeth later told a Dutch diplomat that in 1586 she had sent "fifteen, sixteen, indeed seventeen or eighteen thousands" of English soldiers, more than double the number promised in the Treaty of Nonsuch.[157] Whatever the exact figure, Leicester undoubtedly presided over a significant build-up, gambling that it would allow him to reverse Parma's advances and that he would somehow find the money to pay for it. In February the States General agreed in principle to cover the costs by raising additional revenues, but the excise taxes on salt, soap, beer, and other commodities proposed for this purpose encountered stiff opposition. The deputies of Holland tried to shift the burden onto the shoulders of English merchants by raising an alternative tax on imported wool cloth.[158] Although

---

[153] TNA SP84/6/58; BL Add Mss. 48,084, fol. 336v.
[154] *Correspondence inédite de Robert Dudley, comte de Leicester et de François et Jean Hotman*, ed. P. J. Blok (Harlem: Soosjes, 1911), 143.
[155] TNA SP84/6/30 and SP84/9/18 mention a warrant to pay Grey £2,000, although it is not clear if the money was actually disbursed. *Leicester Correspondence*, 275 and SP84/9/81 for attempts to discourage Grey from over-recruiting.
[156] TNA SP52/41 fol. 11, M. Courcelles to M. D'Aisneval, August 30, 1586, stating that 900 to 1,000 soldiers have been sent under four named captains, while "the rest" are awaiting embarkation. A list of allied forces before Zutphen in September of 1586 records the presence of 947 Scots, of whom 478 were sick or hurt (*CSPF* 21.2.167).
[157] BL Add Mss. 17,677C, fol. 176: "Je vous ais envoyé cette anné quinze, seize, voir dix-sept ou dix-huit milles homes." Trim, "'Fighting Jacob's Wars'," 329–30, estimates that in 1586 there were probably about 8,000 English soldiers serving in Dutch pay in addition to the 7,400 in the queen's army. If this is right then Elizabeth's claim that she had sent between 15,000 and 18,000 soldiers to the Low Countries is fairly conservative, since replacements for troops who had died after arriving in the Low Countries also need to be included.
[158] Bor, *Oorsprong*, pt 2, 691.

additional revenues were eventually raised they were slow in coming in and never proved nearly sufficient. Leicester tried to assure that his own army, rather than garrisons and other local contingents, had first call on Dutch revenues by erecting a council of finances under the control of his Dutch clients. This provoked fierce complaints within the Netherlands, especially in the summer, when Leicester deprived Dutch garrisons of their wages so as to fund his English levies.[159]

But the earl's colleagues on the English council supported him. "In that opinion we do firmly yet remain," Burghley wrote in June, on behalf of Walsingham and Hatton as well as himself, "that without earnest perseverance by your lordship's means in that action [the summer campaign], having sufficiency of men both for defense of your towns and to be also strong in the field, the cause will fall, the enemy will rise and we here must stagger."[160] Leicester claimed that the Dutch were also initially enthusiastic.[161] But the queen not only adamantly refused to increase her promised aid but suggested that, in compensation for her agreement to allow Leicester to keep his office as governor general, he should try to reduce it.[162] Since she had not approved his offensive campaign she felt no responsibility to finance it; if the States General wanted his military build-up "they were to bear the charge themselves."[163] She questioned the wisdom of adding to the tax burden of the Netherlands' population, however, instructing Wilkes to interrogate the Dutch about the kinds of exactions they had imposed and the reasons "the vulgar people are seduced to grudge" against their payment.[164] She had meanwhile dispatched a high level delegation to Ostend to initiate peace talks with Parma. Although she did not immediately inform the Dutch of this, they had their suspicions.[165] Heneage tried to reassure them that Elizabeth would not make peace without "their privity," only to receive an official rebuke from Elizabeth for doing so.[166] By reviving Dutch suspicions that she was dealing with the enemy behind their backs, while making it clear that she disliked Leicester's ambitious strategy and had no intention of funding it, she further undermined his credibility.

Leicester managed to take the field in May and scored a minor victory by capturing the settlement of Doesburg. But thanks partly to shortages of money he failed to move quickly enough to prevent Parma from capturing two more towns, Graves and Venlo, in early June. The garrisons of both surrendered quickly,

---

[159] Ibid., 721, 747; Van Meteren, *Historie*, 249v. [160] TNA SP84/8/97.
[161] *Leicester Correspondence*, 136 for the initial Dutch enthusiasm.
[162] TNA SP84/8/97, Burghley to Leicester, June 17, 1586: "Your lordship must so deal earnestly with the States as you must be furnished indeed with sufficient money"; TNA SP84/8/110, memorial for Mr. Atey going to the Netherlands, June 20, 1586: "You shall signify to his lordship that her Majesty doth not only look that he shall not exceed the charges of £126,190 per annum but also is in good hope (now she is content to yield to a toleration of the authority conferred upon him by the States General) that through his good care and diligence some part of the said sum of £126,190 will be abated."
[163] BL Add Mss. 48,084, fol. 334.
[164] BL Add Mss. 48,014, fols 263, 264, 265 (Thomas Wilkes's instructions on going to the Netherlands, July 1586).
[165] BL Cotton Mss. Titus BVI fol. 83v; TNA SP84/8/71. [166] TNA SP84/7/112.

despite adequate supplies and strong fortifications, arousing suspicions of disloyalty and inducing Leicester to order the commander at Graves summarily executed for dereliction of duty. But he and Elizabeth inevitably received some of the blame.[167] Shortly afterwards an English memorandum reported that "the people" had begun "to murmur" that under English leadership their taxes had increased while "their most strong and important towns" continued to fall to the enemy. Elizabeth's popularity had "diminished" since she seemed "unwilling to address a royal army for their defense, to remedy these injuries."[168]

Leicester and the Dutch Politicians

As these events transpired, ominous signs began to surface of serious friction between Leicester and major Dutch leaders. In early March, the day after the appointment of Oldenbarnevelt as advocate, the states of Holland complained that Leicester and the council of state kept sending them propositions and letters written in languages other than Dutch, a practice they regarded as prejudicial to the "privileges, customs, state and justice" of their province and its inhabitants.[169] Several weeks later a memorandum reported popular murmurs against the English and stated that "the Count Maurice hath not been these three months with his lordship: he is utterly discontented and... repineth secretly that her Majesty should have anything to do in the government of the country; it is to be feared his hidden malice will do much mischief." Hohenlohe resigned his commission as Leicester's lieutenant general and formed an alliance with Maurice, leading the earl "to suspect that he is either inclined to the Spanish faction or so alienated... as he cannot safely repose any trust in him."[170] Hohenlohe and Maurice reconciled with Leicester in July but the earl continued to quarrel with other Dutch officials, venting his frustrations in letters to colleagues in London. "Though they be country dullards and drunkards," he informed Burghley, the Dutch "have shrewd and subtle heads as ever I found anywhere." "There is no more such people to deal withal," especially the "rich and politic fellows, they hunt after their own wealth and surety."[171] By early August, another Englishman reported, mistrust between Leicester and some local dignitaries had reached a point at which neither would agree to meet in a place under the control of the other, for fear of violence.[172]

All modern accounts agree in attributing these clashes to a struggle for power pitting Leicester and his partisans against politicians based mainly in the province

---

[167] TNA SP84/8/39, Lord North to Burleigh, May 23, 1586 on Leicester's direction of "the making of trenches" by his soldiers.
[168] TNA SP84/8/106, paper dated June 20, 1586.   [169] Bor, *Oorsprong*, pt 2, 702.
[170] Ibid.   [171] TNA SP84/9/40, 57, Leicester to Burghley, July 10 and 20, 1586.
[172] TNA SP84/9/75, Thomas Doyley to Burghley, August 8, 1586.

of Holland.¹⁷³ Although essentially correct, this view needs to be fleshed out and qualified through reference to specific sources of dissension. In the initial stages of Leicester's governorship even Holland proved unusually cooperative, taking the unprecedented step of giving him first call on the province's revenues for his summer campaign. Although it was virtually inevitable that Leicester would have difficulties with politicians in Holland and elsewhere, the depth of the rift that soon opened requires explanation. The earl's inability to speak Dutch and very limited sympathy for the Netherlands' fractious political system undoubtedly played a role. The product of an aristocratic upbringing and courtly environment, in the most centralized monarchy in Europe, he had little understanding of, or patience with, the prolonged processes of negotiation and compromise that Dutch politics required. Like many Englishmen, he tended to divide the Dutch into well-defined categories of "true patriots" willing to make unlimited sacrifices, traitors wanting to help Spain, and self-interested men who claimed to support the cause of liberty while feathering their own nests. He assumed that his critics belonged to the last two groups. At least to a degree he shared Digges's view that venality and inefficiency wasted most of the proceeds of Dutch taxation, so that a reform of the fiscal system would substantially increase available revenues without laying additional burdens on the population. Infighting among Dutch politicians and the influence of several exiles from the South within his entourage who disliked the Holland regents, notably Prouninck and the secretary of the council of state, Daniele de Borchgrave, reinforced these prejudices. Leicester never relied solely on other Englishmen: his circle of advisors and partisans always included Netherlanders, whose mistrust of the States General and Holland politicians matched or exceeded his own.¹⁷⁴ The heavy investments that he and several of his followers devoted to his campaign made him even more impatient with natives whom he perceived as unwilling to make financial sacrifices for the common cause.

Leicester's religious partisanship also colored his view of Dutch politics, leading him to regard strong Calvinists as natural allies and people of other religions as suspect. He demonstrated his support for international Calvinist solidarity by publicly taking communion in the French Church in Amsterdam and lobbying the estates of Zeeland to assist Huguenot craftsmen attempting to resettle in Middleburg.¹⁷⁵ His chaplains, John Newstub and Humphrey Fenn—both

---

[173] For different variants of this interpretation see Tracy, *Founding of the Dutch Republic*, chapter 12; Jonathan Israel, *The Dutch Republic: Its Rise, Greatness, and Fall 1477–1806* (Oxford: Clarendon Press, 1995) 220 and the Dutch works therein cited; Oosterhoff, *Leicester*; and, for a particularly full account, very unsympathetic to Leicester, den Tex, *Oldenbarnevelt*, 1.41–120.

[174] Cf. the complaint of Leicester's secretary, Jean Hotman, in January 1587 about Leicester's partisans in Utrecht who love him "with all their hearts" but "do many things very rashly," separating themselves from other Dutch and intriguing against each other (*Brieven over het Leysterische Tijdvak*, 121).

[175] BL Add Mss. 48,014, fol. 154; *Correspondentie*, ed. Brugmans, 1.96–7.

appointed with the approval of London's puritan conference—were firm Calvinists, while he may also have consulted regularly with the famous presbyterian Thomas Cartwright, who had taken up residence in the Netherlands. His army probably employed an order of service modeled after that of the exiled English Church of Geneva in Mary's reign rather than the Book of Common Prayer.[176] In June he encouraged a synod that prescribed a fully Calvinist system of church government and attempted to establish clerical censorship of the press.[177] When the queen admonished him over reports that he discriminated against Catholic patriots he replied by arguing that there really were no such people. Dutch papists differed little from English papists: they might pretend loyalty "but they both love the Pope above all and no longer hide it than severe laws keep them under." In all towns where papists reside they have secret correspondence with Parma; the only "assured towns" in the country were those that had expelled all Catholics before he arrived.[178] These views, which were shared by his follower Lord North,[179] corresponded to the earl's disapproval of Elizabeth's admission of Catholics to her court, which he believed put her life at risk, since "there is no right papist in England that wisheth Queen Elizabeth to live long."[180]

Leicester regarded lukewarm Protestants as unreliable because they were too ready to cooperate with papists, and therefore wanted to exclude them from power. He later complained bitterly to Walsingham about the policy of sending emissaries to deal with Parma who "were not too hot but temperate in religion," adding: "I pray you take example by my lord Buckhurst's dealing here, for he presuming greatly the peace should proceed would deal with no Protestants here, whom he thought zealous, but with the most notorious papists of the whole land he conferred daily...and yet was he thought a man far onward in zeal to religion."[181] Leicester attributed complaints about his support for the Dutch synod and Dutch Calvinists to Englishmen who hoped to destroy his credit and undermine the Protestant cause. His enemies back home had effectively allied with "all the papists, Anabaptists and Spanish hearted" inhabitants of the Low Countries.[182] He stigmatized opponents as irreligious men of weak moral character: "as for P. B. [Paul Buys] he is of no religion but those he favors are papists and there is not in all these countries a more notorious drunkard."[183] His views won Leicester support among devoted adherents of the Dutch Reformed Church. The Calvinist

---

[176] Adams, "Protestant Cause," 66–8.
[177] An English translation of the Synod's resolutions is in BL Add Mss. 48,014, fols 193 ff; the article on press censorship is at 196v.
[178] TNA SP84/8/120.
[179] TNA SP84/8/121, North to Burghley, attributing the fall of Venlo and Grave to machinations by papists within the gates.
[180] TNA SP84/9/106, Leicester to Burghley, August 29, 1586.
[181] *Correspondentie*, ed. Brugmans, 3.132, Leicester to Walsingham, September 16/26, 1587.
[182] BL Add Mss. 48,116, fol. 69.   [183] TNA SP84/9/81, Leicester to Burghley, August 10, 1586.

clergy "are for your excellency because they know your godly proceedings and your good will," the earl's secretary, Jean Hotman, reported during the earl's absence from the Netherlands in early 1587, "the ministers have been with me sundry times and are about some work that shall be for your excellency's credit."[184] But the earl's religious partisanship antagonized many Dutch politicians, including former supporters of William of Orange, who favored a pragmatic policy of religious toleration because they realized that committed Calvinists were a minority in most of the Netherlands.

Disagreements over military strategy further contributed to Leicester's political difficulties. Some embittered exiles from the South believed that Holland's leaders cared little about the security of provinces distant from their own and even took satisfaction in the fall of cities like Antwerp, whose trade they hoped to capture. Although this was unjust, the leaders of Holland and its ally, Zeeland, did see the defense of their own provinces as their top priority. While not opposed in principle to a campaign to recover the South, they did not want to over-extend scarce military resources in ways that might imperil their own security. The English, on the other hand, had a greater strategic interest in the ports of Zeeland and Flanders than in the northern Netherlands, since those ports lay closer to England and had traditionally handled most of the kingdom's overseas trade. Burghley had briefly considered confining England's intervention to the defense of these towns, allowing the Dutch to take care of the rest of the Netherlands.[185] Like Leicester, he hoped ultimately to extend an offensive along the southern coast all the way to Newport and Dunkirk on the French frontier, thinking these havens "to be of greater account than Bruges or Ghent for England."[186]

So long as offensive operations in the southern or eastern Netherlands were carried out with sufficient vigor to reverse the momentum of Parma's gains, these divergent priorities would remain submerged. But if Leicester seemed intent on a reckless strategy, whose failure might imperil the northern heartland of the Revolt, objections would mount. Hohenlohe claimed to have resigned his commission as lieutenant general under Leicester for precisely this reason. He believed that Leicester lacked sufficient cavalry forces to defeat Parma in the South or East, so that his determination to mount an offensive in one of these areas would only lead to more humiliating defeats and a further collapse of Dutch morale. Any commander involved in a failed campaign would suffer a loss of reputation. Having received blame for earlier military reversals, he had no desire to risk his good name serving an inexperienced superior whose plans would likely end in disaster. He preferred instead to fight in Holland and Zeeland, where Parma's cavalry advantage could be neutralized by cutting dikes and flooding the country. Here he

---

[184] *Brieven over het Leysterische Tijdvak*, 168–9. [185] BL Add Mss. 48,084, fol. 29v.
[186] TNA SP84/9/81, Burghley to Leicester, August 10, 1586.

hoped to make small gains that would boost morale, even if it became a matter of winning a village while losing a city.[187]

Although Hohenlohe eventually overcame his misgivings, perhaps because Leicester managed to recruit additional cavalry, other professional soldiers also feared that the governor general wanted to achieve too much with too few resources. An English soldier protested in August: "We are now going to the field (God prosper us for his mercy) but our wants are so many as I fear we shall hardly hold out a month."[188] He worried about what might happen if the large army Leicester had assembled disintegrated from lack of pay. The following month a Dutch remonstrance complained that Leicester had enlarged the army to the point at which receipts from taxation could not sustain it. The resulting arrears in pay spread confusion and anger among the troops, ruining military discipline.[189] Even Sidney hinted at his dissatisfaction when his uncle's campaign drained resources away from his own garrison in Flushing. "To complain of my Lord Leicester, you know I may not but this is the case. If once the soldiers fall to a thorough mutiny this town is lost in all likelihood. I did never think our nation had been so apt to go to the enemy as I find them."[190] Leicester may have decided to gamble on a decisive offensive because he thought Elizabeth would tire of a long war of attrition and the Dutch would prove too weak for Parma without her help. He therefore needed to reverse Parma's advances quickly. Whatever the rationale, his determination strained Dutch resources to the breaking point. He finally achieved limited successes in the autumn when his army captured Zutphen and Deventer, diverting Parma from an offensive further west. But these gains came at a seemingly unsustainable price. In January 1587 the Dutch calculated the total cost of the previous year's campaign at £560,000.[191]

The size and quality of the following Leicester had brought to the Netherlands— the "giant retinue composed of a number of smaller retinues"[192]—further complicated his relations with Dutch and some English commanders. Several of his followers had little or no previous military experience, while others had fought in Ireland or during previous European campaigns. But whether experienced or not they believed that their social position, along with the money and personal influence they had invested in assembling their companies, entitled them to positions of authority. To satisfy his English clientele Leicester had to find suitable commands for them, even when it meant stepping on the toes of Dutch officers or professional English soldiers long in service. When he failed to do so quickly enough, they sometimes complained to their friends at court. Lord North grumbled to Burghley

---

[187] BL Add Mss. 48,014, fols 473-4, "Cause e ragioni perche il signor Conte de Hohenlo desidera non carase piu alt anche in Hollanda e Zelanda."
[188] TNA SP84/9/95, Batholomew Clerk to Burghley, August 16, 1586.
[189] BL Add Mss. 48,014, fol. 407v.
[190] TNA SP84/9/90, Sir Philip Sidney to Walsingham, August 14, 1586.
[191] CSPF 21.2.314.   [192] Adams, "A Puritan Crusade?," 186.

when he did not immediately receive a post befitting an English peer after arriving in the Netherlands in January. Within a month Leicester gratified him, whereupon North became one of the earl's most enthusiastic supporters: "my good lord these beginnings and good proceedings... giveth such courage to us all as every man is willing to hazard his life and venture what he is all." In July Leicester appointed North "governor of Harlingen, the strongest town of all Friesland and because it were too small a government the strong castle of Staveron was annexed to his commandment."[193] Leicester's nephew, Sidney, commanded the garrison at Flushing and his stepson, Essex, "was made General of the horsemen with £400 per annum."[194] The outward magnificence of some of the new English companies antagonized veterans who resented being eclipsed by these new arrivals. After watching the arrival of Sir William Pelham's company in July, an Englishman reported that many thought "it strange that he should be allowed such a rich guard and the Count Honhenlohe being lieutenant general next to his Excellency had none. Also others said they would have no marshal until they were in camp."[195] By favoring his English clients and their troops, Leicester antagonized veterans of other nationalities and some civilians. He was accused of spending Dutch revenues in England on fresh recruits while Dutch companies went unpaid; of trusting only his own countrymen; and of imposing English commanders on companies of other nationalities.[196] These grievances eroded the spirit of cooperation that had led the Dutch themselves to assign native regiments to English officers at the outset of Leicester's campaign. After his arrival as governor of the cautionary town of Flushing, the states of Zeeland had appointed Sir Philip Sidney commander of a mainly Flemish and Walloon regiment of 2,824 soldiers in Dutch pay, but when Leicester placed additional Dutch troops under Sidney's command in the autumn of 1586 he provoked a storm of protests about forcing men to serve under "foreign" officers.[197] After Sidney's death his Flemish regiment was assigned to a Dutch colonel rather than the new governor of Flushing, Sir William Russell, who bitterly resented the perceived slight. Leicester's deteriorating relations with Holland politicians was therefore matched by a growing rift between his English military following and other units serving in the Dutch army. In August 1587 a French newsletter reported "a grand following at the court [Leicester's residence] of English lords and gentleman, attending to seek employment, but few or none other."[198]

---

[193] TNA SP84/6/58, as Lord North did to Burghley: "I live here without credit and to my intolerable charge of £26 a week, desiring nothing but that I may be entertained as a nobleman"; SP84/6/136, same to same, February 28; SP84/9/26, Thomas Doyley to Burghley, July 16, 1586. Doyley added the editorial comment: "you may see how his Excellency doth establish his kindred and favorites in the strongest parts of the country."
[194] BL Cotton Mss. Titus BVI, fol. 66v.   [195] TNA SP84/9/26.
[196] Van Meteren, *Historie*, fols 251v, 265r, and 268v.
[197] Trim, "'Fighting Jacob's Wars'," 362–3; Van Meteren, *Historie*, fol. 282r.
[198] TNA SP84/17 fol. 150, newsletter of August 21: "Il y a une grande suite à la court tant de seigneurs que de gentilhommes anglais mais peu ou nul autres, attendant d'être employer."

Leicester's clients clashed not only with Dutch and other European officers but also with Englishmen already serving in the Netherlands, especially Sir John Norreys and his clients. As the most distinguished English veteran captain serving in the Netherlands and supreme commander of the queen's troops there before Leicester's arrival, Norreys expected to play a central role in the forthcoming campaign. But his record of success and the esteem it had brought him inspired envy. Since he had his own military clients and financial interests to look after, conflicts over patronage and money with old rivals and newly arrived members of Leicester's entourage were probably inevitable. Even before the earl's arrival, Norreys clashed with Davison over the appointment of a garrison commander in the town of Ramekins. Hohenlohe, who had an old quarrel with Norreys, may have deliberately fomented the dispute by suggesting that Davison ask Roger Williams, rather than Norreys, to recommend a man for the post. By following this advice Davison provoked a furious reaction from Norreys's brother, Edward, who denounced Williams's choice and suggested a rival candidate. Davison saw this as a challenge to his own authority, stood his ground and won the argument, although not before both sides had appealed to the privy council.[199] Davison subsequently complained that Norreys promoted unfit men to other commands.[200] Shortly after arriving in the Netherlands, Digges accused the English treasurer-at-war, Thomas Huddleston, of diverting money intended for Leicester's army to gratify Norreys.

By April 1586 Walsingham had become sufficiently disturbed by reports of factional quarrels within the English army to recommend removing Norreys from the Low Countries. He suspected that some of Leicester's enemies at the English court had encouraged Norreys, whose mother was a lady of the queen's bedchamber, to challenge Leicester's control. "The chief experience and nurture that he hath received in the war hath been in those countries where neither discipline military nor religion carry any sway, and therefore it hath taught him nothing else but a kind of licentious and corrupt government."[201] Some English companies, including one belonging to Norreys, had grown mutinous over arrears in pay and Walsingham evidently held the veteran general partly responsible.[202] A month later, an Englishman reported that Leicester had begun violating Norreys's commission by appointing officers over his companies.[203] Digges accused Norreys not

---

[199] TNA SP84/5/31 and 42 (Minute of Davison to Burghley, November 11, 1585, complaining of Norreys; Edward Norreys to Walsingham, November 15, presenting his side of the story).

[200] TNA SP84/5/31, Davison to Burghley, November 11, 1585.

[201] *Leicester Correspondence*, 222, Walsingham to Leicester, April 11, 1586.

[202] Ibid., "So have I just cause, weighing the late mutiny happed at Utrecht by a band pertaining unto Colonel Norreys, to think the removing of the one [Norreys] as necessary as the placing of the other [Sir William Pelham, whom Leicester was endeavoring to bring from Ireland]. I see some reason to doubt that the ground of the said colonel's carriage of himself towards your lordship grew by practice from hence."

[203] TNA SP84/8/41, D. Doyly to "my lord" (Burghley?), May 24, 1586.

only of diverting money intended for the queen's army but pocketing it instead of paying his soldiers.[204] Another Leicester client, Sir George Digby, tried "to have drawn a regiment out of Sir John Norreys's [army] and told him [Norreys] before a number at Utrecht that he doubted not but to do her Majesty as good service as he." Digby also attempted to command one of Norreys's officers by "alleging that he [Digby] was a colonel and a counselor at war but Captain Wilson answered he would take his direction of Sir John Norreys and none other under his Excellency."[205] Leicester excluded Norreys from an active role in the planning and execution of the summer campaign in Flanders.[206]

Edward Norreys accused Leicester of telling junior officers that his brother had blocked their promotion, encouraging them to slander him and threaten to hang him.[207] Sir John complained to Burghley that Leicester's open hostility had so diminished his standing that he found himself "braved by the worst and simplest in the company."[208] Hohenlohe happily cooperated in belittling his old rival, pointedly excluding Norreys and his captains when he invited other English officers to join him in a raid on Spanish territory in late summer. Sidney nevertheless brought Edward Norreys along on the expedition, with disastrous results. During a drinking party among English and Dutch officers Edward quarreled with Leicester's favored client, Pelham. Hohenlohe watched the argument escalate before picking up the cover of a large bowl and hurling it in Norreys's face, cutting him to the bone. Norreys's friends subsequently advised him to leave quickly before Hohenlohe attempted to have him assassinated. A witness surmised that the German commander acted as he did to curry favor with English enemies of the Norreys clan.[209] Norreys later challenged

---

[204] This dispute dragged on for months, leaving a paper trail through the State Papers. See TNA SP84/17 fol. 81 for a summary of Digges's accusations and Norreys's replies.
[205] Both quotations are from TNA SP84/8/41, D. Doyly to Burghley, May 24, 1586.
[206] TNA SP84/9/32, Norreys to Burghley, July 18, 1586.
[207] TNA SP84/10/36.   [208] TNA SP84/9/96.
[209] TNA SP84/9/76 provides a very detailed account. The altercation began when Pelham toasted Norreys's parents with a large glass of wine. Custom demanded that Norreys respond by draining the contents of the glass but he demurred, requesting Pelham instead to use a smaller glass, "saying it would be no pleasure in his lordship to see him drunk." Being pressed he emptied the glass and then proposed a toast to the countess of Essex, Leicester's wife. Hohenlohe had meanwhile pretended to misunderstand Pelham, asking "who was Horse [instead of Norreys] and that he used not to pledge horses." Essex explained two or three times but Hohenlohe still professed to be baffled. As the toasting continued Norreys declined to drink, provoking an argument with Pelham, who chose to interpret his abstemiousness as an insult. Hohenlohe listened in silence for a time and then hurled the cover. Norreys's friends persuaded him to leave the next day. The anonymous reporter of the incident concluded: "certainly Count Hollock [Hohenlohe] saw how the stream went and thought to have done a pleasure to the company in killing him [Norreys]." The day after Norreys's departure "the said company met at the Count Hollock's house and were all in so good terms that not one of the company had either falling band or ruff left about his neck untorn away and yet there was no blood drawn." One suspects that heavy consumption of alcohol did nothing to smooth relations between Hohenlohe and English officers.

Hohenlohe to a duel, causing additional disruption in relations between officers in the rival camps.[210]

But Norreys still had allies at court. The queen, who appreciated his ability and experience, ordered Leicester to reconcile with him in July, and instructed Wilkes to patch up the quarrel.[211] She also wanted Leicester to improve his strained relations with Maurice and Hohenlohe.[212] Leicester nevertheless remained hostile to Norreys, who had begun sending critical reports of his leadership back to London.[213] Although the earl retained the loyalty of other veteran English officers, notably Sir Roger Williams, as well as some professional Dutch soldiers like Diederick Sonoy, the commander of forces in North Holland, his vendetta against Norreys and prickly relations with Maurice and Hohenlohe fractured the professional military establishment in the Low Countries. The situation worsened appreciably toward the end of the year when Leicester again antagonized Hohenlohe, by failing to visit and consult with him before he departed for England in November.[214]

As he quarreled with professional soldiers, Leicester also collided with civilian politicians over taxation, his council of finances, and his attempts in the summer to reform the Dutch currency and regulate the minting of coins.[215] But the most contentious dispute involved trade with the enemy. The heavily urbanized Netherlands had long depended on shipments of Baltic grain, handled mainly by merchants in the northern provinces. Cutting off this supply would have exacerbated serious food shortages that already existed in the South, hampering Parma's ability to supply his army.[216] But a complete ban would also damage the commercial economies of Amsterdam and other northern ports and therefore Holland's revenues, on which the solvency of the Dutch state depended. The Holland regents had attempted to deal with the problem by developing a system for licensing and taxing trade with the enemy, but privateers based in Zeeland and inhabitants of several inland provinces exposed to Spanish attacks, as well as the

---

[210] For the text of the challenge and Hohenlohe's reply, in which he disingenuously claimed never to have had any intention of insulting Norreys's honor, see AMAE CPH2, fol. 161; unfortunately no date is given.

[211] TNA SP84/9/38, Elizabeth to Leicester, July 19, 1586.

[212] AMAE CPH2, fol. 88, Elizabeth to Leicester, undated but apparently summer 1586, instructing him: "First that Count Maurice and Count Hollocke find themselves trusted of you, esteemed of me, and to be carefully regarded if ever peace should happen, and of that assure them on my word, that yet never deceived any. And for Norreys and other captains that voluntarily without commandment have many years ventured their lives and won our nation honor and themselves fame, be not discouraged by any means, neither by new come men nor by old trained soldiers elsewhere."

[213] E.g. TNA SP84/9/32, SP84/9/96.

[214] At least this was the reason Hohenlohe gave for the breach; see TNA SP84/13/98. At the time Hohenlohe was recovering from a wound in a house in Delft; Leicester passed nearby but did not make a detour to pay his respects.

[215] Bor, *Oorsprong*, pt 2, 691; NA 13.01.14/184A, fol. 163; TNA SP84/8/106 and 120; Bor, *Orsprong*, pt 2, 721, 745, 747.

[216] As the English knew. See, e.g., the report on Parma's problems in SP77/1/46.

towns of Dordrecht and Utrecht, wanted stronger measures. In 1585 the States General proposed a total ban.[217] Although this would have violated too many powerful interests to be enforceable, at least over any prolonged period, it had become clear that regulations on trade with the enemy needed to be tightened. Elizabeth and Leicester objected to Holland's trade with the Spanish provinces as early as the autumn of 1585.[218]

Both English and Dutch members of Leicester's entourage, who saw Holland merchants as self-interested men who cared only about their own profits, hardened this view.[219] It was a matter, as one English official put it, of promoting the general cause rather than a few "greedy appetites" of people willing to "endamage and overthrow the state of a country" for the sake of private gain.[220] These counselors persuaded the earl to impose a stringent ban through his own authority and then to hang a few merchants who violated his new orders.[221] Leicester issued instructions to punish not only merchants but inn holders and others who assisted their illicit trade.[222] The Dutch historian Jan den Tex believed he enacted a prohibition that he knew wealthy merchants would violate, so that the council of state might convict them on capital charges and extort huge payments in return for pardons. In this way Leicester hoped to fund his offensive against Parma at the expense of people he regarded as war profiteers.[223] This supposition is almost certainly correct. The English official Thomas Wilford had suggested making examples of Dutch merchants who traded with the enemy by hanging a few back in January, while the head of Leicester's finance council, Jacques Ringault, would later claim that Holland politicians had launched a vendetta against him because he advised raising two or three million florins by "execution" of the plakkard against trade with the enemy.[224] At Ringault's urging, Leicester toyed with a scheme to examine the accounts of provincial officials going back to the summer of 1584 and fining them for failing to enforce previous prohibitions.[225] He seems to have approved of squeezing merchants and punishing them if they resisted. After his final return to England he was reported to have retaliated

---

[217] Oosterhoff, *Leicester*, 57–61 gives a balanced account. For Zeeland's attitude see *Correspondentie*, ed. Brugmans, 1.23–4.
[218] BL Add Mss. 17,677B, fols 260v, 319, 327v.
[219] See, for example, the memorandum, probably by William Herle, reproduced in *CSPF* 21.2.300: "The ambition of Amsterdam would destroy Emden and all other places, yea our traffic of England, and reduce it within their jurisdiction, to exercise their avarice over strangers and naturals, having to this end abandoned Antwerp and Brabant and Flanders. What will they then do to strangers? [In the margin: they are neither true in the towns nor valiant in the field and so their treachery bewrays]. The policy of Holland is to plunge her majesty into wars with the whole world, and so being made hateful to compel her to aid them, and so undutifully to exclude her, and so they have mocked the world." The term often used to describe the merchants was *lorendraaijers*, i.e. interlopers or illicit traders.
[220] SP84/7/43, Edward Gilpin to Walsingham, March 21, 1586.
[221] For Leicester's plakkard authorizing the death penalty for trading with the enemy see Bor, *Oorsprong*, pt 2, 704.
[222] Nationaal Archief Mss. 1.01.01.10/13.   [223] Den Tex, *Oldenbarnevelt*, 1.59–63.
[224] TNA SP84/6/55; *CSPF* 21.2.175.   [225] Oosterhoff, *Leicester*, 93–5.

against the English Merchant Adventurers Company, for declining to lend him more money during his Dutch campaign, by urging the queen to dissolve their corporation.[226]

To prevent Parma from obtaining supplies through neutral ports such as Calais, Leicester extended the embargo to cover northern France as far as Normandy.[227] According to the contemporary historian Emanuels van Meteren, Ringault wanted not only to starve the enemy but to erect an Anglo-Dutch lordship over the North Sea that would allow Leicester to compel all merchants trading within it to purchase licenses from him in order to do so. The resulting revenue stream would then fund the earl's military operations.[228] But although initially supportive of a wider embargo, the English council backed down when confronted with howls of outrage from the Hanse towns, Denmark, and Henry III, and ordered Leicester to desist.[229] That left the prohibition on trade with the enemy in force solely within the United Provinces, compounding the damage to Dutch merchants. The virtually universal opposition of the Holland mercantile community and its powerful political allies soon made Leicester's restrictions impossible to enforce.

By the time the earl's long-awaited military offensive began in earnest in August, his relations with the leadership of Holland and the States General had broken down almost completely. But he retained considerable support in Utrecht, where the previous April a group of militia captains styling themselves Tribunes of the People had overthrown the town's pro-Holland regents, expelling sixty leading citizens. When his Utrecht allies attempted to rally popular support elsewhere in the Netherlands against Holland's leaders and the States General they escalated the conflict. A few of Leicester's English followers advised him that the best way of dealing with his Dutch opponents was "to master them with superior forces and when any of them may be taken with any manifest fault to proceed against them with severity."[230] In reaction Oldenbarnevelt and his supporters set out to undermine Leicester and destroy Ringault. On September 10, complaining bitterly "of the States backwardness," Leicester asked Elizabeth's permission to return to England. Although it took her some time to agree she eventually did, and two months later he left the Netherlands.[231] But he retained some popular support. His secretary, Jean Hotman, reported that news of his impending departure dismayed people throughout the United Provinces, causing them to cry out against the States General for antagonizing the man they regarded as their savior.[232] Leicester

---

[226] Bodleian Library (Oxford) North Mss. a.2, fol. 92v.
[227] TNA SP84/7/50 provides the French text of Leicester's prohibition on neutral trade with the Spanish Netherlands.
[228] Van Meteren, *Historie*, 249v.
[229] Ibid.; Strype, *Annals of Reformation*, 3.120; TNA SP84/6/28; Oosterhoff, *Leicester*, 89–95.
[230] BL Add Mss. 48,014, fol. 265, unattributed paper entitled "A brief of the perils and remedies," July 1586.
[231] BL Cotton Mss. Titus CVI, fol. 66.   [232] AMAE CPH2, fol. 104.

and his allies would henceforth continue, through sermons, printed tracts, and visual imagery, to condemn his Dutch opponents as men whose churlish ingratitude threatened to destroy the English alliance on which the safety of the Netherlands depended. In response they depicted him as a leader who had fallen under the sway of a corrupt clique of self-serving men, whose misguided actions imperiled Dutch liberties.[233]

Leicester's opponents probably believed they had finally gotten rid of him, since from their perspective his departure made no sense except on the assumption that he had given up on the Netherlands. But while it is clear that he had grown disillusioned and had no wish to return, he also had other considerations. Despite his office as governor general, his position still depended above all on Elizabeth's continuing favor. He knew that his absence from her side made it easier for his enemies at the English court to poison her mind against him and that criticism of his conduct of affairs in the Low Countries made their task easier.[234] He needed to return to London to renew his personal bond with the queen and convince her to accept his version of what had transpired during his stay in the Netherlands, rather than the reports of his detractors. He also knew that the following winter would bring a final effort by his colleagues on the council to have Mary Stuart executed.[235] He wanted to aid their efforts.

Power Struggles, the Buckhurst Embassy, and the Renewed Problem of Sovereignty

Leicester's departure emboldened his Dutch adversaries and discouraged his supporters, who found themselves more exposed to attack.[236] Ringault was swiftly driven from office and imprisoned, escaping execution only because Wilkes connived at his escape to Spanish territory. Leicester's absence might have mattered less if he had left behind a unified command under a capable and forceful subordinate. Unfortunately, the death of Sir Philip Sidney from wounds suffered

---

[233] For a description of opposing medallions conveying these two messages see Van Meteren, *Historie*, 253v. Printed material feeding the controversy included official protests critical of Leicester issued by the States General and states of Holland, and a response defending him while denouncing the ingratitude of these representative bodies issued by the magistrates of Utrecht (ibid., 278r).

[234] Cf. the shrewd assessment of Lord Henry Howard in BL Cotton Titus Mss. CVI, fol. 68v: "No man could be greater in the favor of his sovereign or more strongly fortified by friends about the person of the queen, the greater part having been planted and settled by himself than my lord of Leicester, and yet after he was once enameled with that title of Excellency in the Netherlands and grown powerful by her favor in his heart, there passed scant any month wherein she did not exercise his patience with some bitter sullen [illegible] and letters written by her own hand to make him weary of his place. And yet upon his first approach to her own presence both the sickness of the sea and of her indignation, which indeed is most truly called *morbus regius*... did vanish instantly."

[235] See his letter to Walsingham urging him on to demand justice against Mary of October 10, 1586, *Leicester Correspondence*, 431.

[236] *Brieven over het Leysterische Tijdvak*, 146.

in a skirmish at Zutphen and the fatal illness of Sir William Pelham, Leicester's preferred choice to take control of the army, deepened the leadership vacuum. Leicester ordered Norreys, who had wanted to leave the Netherlands, to stay behind and take overall command of English forces but then granted other officers independent commissions after they refused to serve under him.[237] The divided command hampered military operations.[238] Even more unfortunately, the earl appointed his Irish client Sir William Stanley as commander at Deventer, despite repeated warnings about Stanley's erratic and dictatorial behavior from Wilkes, Norreys, and the Dutch.[239] In January Stanley betrayed the city to the enemy and joined the Spanish army, along with his Irish Catholic troops.

In addition to wiping out the most important gains of Leicester's summer campaign, this act of treason did immense damage to English credibility. "Immediately after the loss of the said town," Wilkes later recalled,

> there grew a wonderful alteration in the hearts and affections of the people against the English. They uttered lewd and irreverent speeches of his excellency and the whole nation and we, finding that there were some secret consultations had by the States and Count Hohenlohe to advise how we might be all removed out of the countries – as had happened in the time of monseigneur the French King's brother – letters were written by Sir John Norreys remaining at Utrecht and by myself from the Hague to the [English] governors of Flushing, Brill, Ostend and Begues to look carefully to their several charges.[240]

The surrender of Deventer amplified rumors circulating since at least September that Elizabeth had reached a secret accord with Parma to return the Dutch provinces to Spain.[241] A German visitor reported hearing loose talk that the queen had planned Stanley's betrayal, as part of a conspiracy to restore Spanish sovereignty.[242] Oldenbarnevelt vented his fury at a meeting of the council of state, "crying out in spite and fury in a loud voice" against misgovernment by a secretive "cabinet council," beholden to a governor who now resided in England.[243] Leicester's ally, Prouninck, tried to counter the damage by spreading reports that Oldenbarnevelt had taken Spanish bribes.[244] Each side accused the other of

---

[237] Oosterhoff, *Leicester*, 136–7.
[238] E.g. AMAE CPH2, 233v–4, explaining that Norreys was unable to carry out a planned operation because cavalry refused to serve under one of his officers.
[239] TNA SP84/11/28; *CSPF* 21.2.66.   [240] *Correspondentie*, ed. Brugmans, 2.447.
[241] BL Add Mss. 48,083, fol. 192; TNA SP84/18/108; *CSPF* 21.3.370, 92.
[242] TNA SP84/13/27 and AMAE CPH2, fol. 308r–v.
[243] AMAE CPH2, fol. 261: "Etait aussi demandé en quoi était si mal gouverné et qui en étaient les causes, sur quoi ledit Barnevelt comme passionné de dépit et colère, criant à haut voix, disait, que c'était le conseil du cabinet, où que plusieurs choses se firent, que personne n'en sceut que ce dudit cabinet; comme naguères apparut par la retroacte que y était fait par aucuns particuliers, sans le sceu des conseillers..."
[244] Den Tex, *Oldenbarnevelt*, 2.90.

treason. Hotman reported being "hunted at Delft from house to house and then besieged in my lodging four or five hours together," and feared assassination at the hands of Leicester's adversaries.[245]

Leicester's expansion of the army over the summer to a level that Dutch resources could not sustain made a reduction in forces inevitable, and his departure from the country rendered it easier for Maurice, Hohenlohe, and Oldenbarnevelt to disband companies most loyal to him, while protecting those under their own control.[246] The betrayal of Deventer simultaneously raised suspicions about the loyalty of other English commanders, giving Leicester's adversaries an excuse to demand that all captains take new oaths of loyalty to Maurice and the States General. Sonoy in North Holland and a few other officers who resisted these demands out of loyalty to Leicester were threatened with attack by troops commanded by Hohenlohe or Maurice. Sir William Russell prepared to defend the cautionary town of Flushing against any efforts by Maurice or Hohenlohe to seize it.[247] Many of Leicester's captains had meanwhile returned home, leaving their companies leaderless and reinforcing the impression that the English had deserted their posts.[248] Some left behind unpaid debts to Dutch tradesmen who had been feeding and supplying their troops.[249] Continued shortages of money, exacerbated by the determination of Maurice and Hohenlohe to satisfy their own companies while squeezing those loyal to Leicester, worsened the suffering of English soldiers, who began to mutiny and desert in large numbers.[250] Some tried to make ends meet by selling their weapons, further scandalizing the Dutch.[251]

Gray's Scottish troops also suffered.[252] He had pleaded with Walsingham back in September that his cavalry, in particular, should be well taken care of, "for it standeth me on my credit, they all most being of good calling and houses and only for my pleasure drawing arms." Reports of the poor treatment of humbler foot soldiers, he warned, had reached Scotland, causing volunteers to desert their companies.[253] Gray blamed Elizabeth rather than the Dutch for the mistreatment of his recruits, complaining bitterly: "I have employed for the queen's service in the Low countries so many of my friends and servants as would do for me, which

---

[245] *Brieven over het Leysterische Tijdvak*, 139, 146.
[246] Ibid., 85; NA 1.01.10.10/4, fol. 45; Den Tex, *Oldenbarnevelt*, 1.64; *Correspondentie*, ed. Brugmans, 1.299, 308, 310; BL Egerton Mss. 1694, fols 64 and 95; Add Mss. 48,084, fol. 353. For a summary see Oosterhoff, *Leicester*, chapter 8.
[247] TNA SP84/13/96.
[248] *Correspondentie*, ed. Brugmans, 2.51–2; AMAE CPH2, 233v, States General to Leicester, January 14, 1587: "Monsieur le chevalier Norreys nous a déclaré que tous les capitaines des compagnies étant en garnisons sont présentement en Angleterre, aussi qu'il n'y a pas des capitaines de la cavalerie anglaise par deçà, qui est cause par trop dangereuse…"
[249] BL Add Mss. 48,084, fol. 285.
[250] BL Egerton Mss. 1694, fol. 84; TNA SP84/6/51, fol. 126v; *Correspondentie*, ed. Brugmans, 2.8.
[251] BL Add Mss. 17,677 C, fol. 142r.   [252] Above, pp. 299–300.
[253] *Correspondence de Leicester*, ed. Blok, 145.

is now turned into a debauchery." "Seeing England minds to make a pair of old boots of [my] men, I shall serve them [the English] then in their own humor."[254] Shortages of money in the Netherlands deprived the English of an important ally in Scotland, who had played a central role in constructing James's alliance with Elizabeth. They also allowed Hohenlohe to co-opt some of Gray's companies for use as counterweights to English garrisons.[255] Norreys thought that Holland politicians wanted to appoint a new governor general and break the English alliance, but Elizabeth's prevarications prevented him from reacting decisively. "If her Majesty's mind were known to us, it would be no hard matter to turn all their devices upside down; but not being acquainted with her purpose it maybe we should run a wrong course in striving with the Hollanders." He therefore advised Wilkes, who was now the English council's chief man of business in the Low Countries, to "hold good correspondence" with all parties, "till we hear from England."[256] Unfortunately clear instructions did not arrive for more than another two months because, Walsingham later explained, he and his colleagues "could not draw Her Majesty to any resolution." The queen's fury with her councilors over the unauthorized dispatch of Mary Stuart's death warrant in early February, which had still not entirely abated by April, "maketh us very circumspect and careful not to proceed in anything but wherein we receive direction."[257] As had happened a year earlier, wrangles between Elizabeth and her inner circle effectively paralyzed policy toward the Netherlands for several critical months.

Even before he betrayed Zutphen, the States General had received complaints against Stanley for running what amounted to an extortion racket to pay his company in the absence of money from England, causing the council of state to request his removal.[258] After the betrayal of Deventer, Dutch towns began refusing to admit English garrisons, depriving soldiers of food and shelter. Norreys told Wilkes that he would invade Holland unless alternative quarters and enough food to keep his troops from starving were found.[259] In January English companies began plundering Holland's countryside, provoking lethal peasant resistance.[260] Several commanded by Norreys again invaded Holland on the last day in February, provoking more peasant resistance, while threatening The Hague. The states of Holland instructed Hohenlohe to use his cavalry to drive the English out, as he and Maurice stationed their own troops to block the English advance. Wilkes

---

[254] HMC Cecil, 3.190-9, Gray to Archibald Douglas, November 6, 1586; SP52/41, fol. 61, same to same, November 16, 1586: "Bot seeing Ingland myndis to mak a pair of auld bouttis of men I shall serve them in their heurmur."
[255] BL Egerton Mss. 1694, fol. 62, Wilkes to Leicester, December 6, 1586.
[256] TNA SP84/13/6.   [257] TNA SP84/14, fol. 73.
[258] TNA SP105/91, fol. 23, SP84/11/38, BL Add Mss. 17,677 C, fols 69r, 95r-v; TNA SP84/11/38; *Brieven over het Leystersiche Tijdvak*, 130.
[259] BL Egerton Mss. 1694, fols 81, 106; SP84/13/14; NA 3.01.14/2005, fol. 74.
[260] Bor, *Oorsprong*, pt 2, 887.

finally defused the tense stand-off by borrowing seven or eight hundred pounds on his own credit, to relieve the soldiers' suffering.[261]

Since the English still had some support in the Netherlands, the conflict between Leicester and his adversaries threatened to erupt into violent conflict. In March Wilkes reported popular stirs and small-scale armed resistance to Hohenlohe in several places.[262] He wrote to Leicester's clerical allies, urging them to stir popular opposition to the campaign against the earl waged by the States General.[263] Russell passed on a rumor that Utrecht and Dordrecht had begun to levy new forces to support Leicester, while the provinces of Holland and Zeeland did the same on behalf of the States General.[264] A letter sent from London by one of Henry of Navarre's agents claimed that the English parliament that met that winter had offered pay for an army of 20,000 men to help the Low Countries, but that the "good and laudable" design had been overturned when a letter arrived in London from Holland's leaders, complaining of Leicester's misgovernment.[265] Copies of this report were widely distributed. Gilpin, the only important member of the English diplomatic delegation who did speak fluent Dutch, described the country as thoroughly divided between supporters and opponents of the States General, with a significant faction wanting to return to Spanish rule. "In sum here is jealousy, discontentment, dislikings, division and emulation from the highest to the lowest... and no superiority duly known or respected."[266] With a new campaigning season fast approaching the prospects looked ominous.

Wilkes struggled to uphold Leicester's authority and interests, earning Hotman's praise but not Leicester's forgiveness, who remained so hostile that Wilkes began to fear for his safety.[267] Both he and Hotman urged Leicester's speedy return, arguing that his appearance would quell opposition. But Leicester had no desire to plunge back into the quagmire of Dutch politics.[268] Instead the queen sent another member of her council, Thomas Sackville Lord Buckhurst, with instructions to investigate conditions in the Netherlands, admonish the

---

[261] Ibid., 904-6.
[262] TNA SP105/91, fol. 40r-v.; *CSPF* 21.2.424; BL Add Mss. 48,078, fol. 130: "The people have now grown into so great a mislike of the doings of the States that they begin not only to murmur thereat publicly but in some places have put themselves into arms, as namely within these two days at Horne in North Holland... The inhabitants of Horne, Enchusen and Medeublyke have openly protested that they will live and die with the Queen's Majesty and that whosoever shall attempt to sever her from them they will cut their throats. The like garboil was begun at Amsterdam, where the like protestation is made by the people. These beginnings are feared will grow to some dangerous events not to be prevented but with the power of a governor" (dispatch of March 26, 1587).
[263] BL Add Mss. 48,014, fols 422v-3.   [264] TNA SP84/13/54.
[265] TNA SP84/13/13, copy of a French "letter from the English court" distributed in the Netherlands, March 10, 1587; Oosterhoff, *Leicester*, 164.
[266] TNA SP84/13/121, Gilpin to Walsingham, March 1587.
[267] *Brieven over het Leysterische Tijdvak*, 89-90, 122, and 147; Brigham Young University Library vault Mss. 457 (Robert Beale collection of letters), fol. 33v.
[268] TNA SP105/91, fol. 44; SP84/14 fol. 77; BL Add Mss. 48,014, fol. 423; *Brieven over het Leysterische Tijdvak*, 229-30.

Dutch about their "contempt" for Leicester's authority, and threaten that if they did not mend their ways she would withdraw her aid. He was also to inform them of her negotiations with Parma and demand that the States General appoint a delegation to join in with them, a directive certain to exacerbate Dutch mistrust of English intentions. After consulting with Wilkes and Norreys and meeting Dutch leaders, Buckhurst concluded that he first needed to mediate among the contending factions and personalities. He estimated that the Dutch had spent a staggering £432,473 the previous year and the Queen another £150,000. The costs for the next summer would be similar, but since the Dutch had already anticipated future revenues their contribution would necessarily decline. The queen must therefore do more; otherwise, Buckhurst and Wilkes predicted, the Dutch "will fall into greater confusion than they were before," leading to the loss of all territory except Holland and Zeeland.[269] Some money needed to arrive quickly, along with 2,000 fresh soldiers to replenish losses in the English army, since Parma had already begun to move.[270] Buckhurst negotiated an agreement that the States General would find the additional revenues required if Elizabeth agreed to lend them £50,000 and continue her support at the same level as in 1586.

Recognizing the importance of effective military leadership, Buckhurst also urged the appointment of professional officers rather than "court captains... with gold lace and gay garments."[271] He concluded that Norreys must remain in his post, since his skill and experience were irreplaceable, and that Hohenlohe needed to be conciliated, since he had too much support among both Dutch politicians and a segment of the army to be sidelined.[272] Buckhurst therefore set about trying to heal Hohenlohe's feud with Norreys and his brother, while reconciling all three to Leicester. He succeeded in negotiating an agreement that Hohenlohe would exercise supreme command in actions west of the Meuse River, while Norreys would do so in Guelders, Friesland and Overijssel.[273] Both commanders, along with other Dutch politicians, professed themselves ready to serve Leicester, should he return to the Netherlands. "I have reduced all matters of difference and unkindness to love and unity," Buckhust wrote to Walsingham in mid-April, adding that Maurice, the States General and even Paul Buys had agreed to seek the governor general's friendship.[274] Norreys had meanwhile conducted a survey of the queen's army, which showed that despite modest reductions in strength most units had held up better than expected over the winter, largely because gaps created by death and desertion had been filled by soldiers released from English companies formerly serving in the Dutch army that

[269] BL Add Mss. 48,078, fol. 111; SP105/91, fol. 43v.
[270] TNA SP84/14, fol. 59, Norreys to Walsingham, April 11, 1587; BL Add Mss. 48,078, fol. 107, Buckhurst to Elizabeth, April 19.
[271] BL Add Mss. 48,078, fol. 113.
[272] BL Add Mss. 48,078, fol. 112; *Correpondentie*, ed. Brugmans, 2.494–5.
[273] BL Add Mss. 48,078, fol. 95.   [274] BL Add Mss. 48,078, fol. 112.

had been dissolved.²⁷⁵ Norreys hoped for a vigorous campaign, which he believed would turn the tide against Parma, and set out with 2,000 soldiers to intercept enemy troop movements in early May.²⁷⁶ Buckhurst wrote to London, urging that support for Norreys in a quick and vigorous early offensive would save money in the long run.²⁷⁷

Hohenlohe, Maurice, and Oldenbarnevelt hoped that Leicester would remain in England, giving them *de facto* control in cooperation with Norreys, whose ability they respected. But Buckhurst did not share that objective. Like most Englishmen in the Netherlands since 1585, he saw Dutch politics as hopelessly fractious and dysfunctional and believed that a reassertion of Leicester's personal authority provided the only viable solution. "All things here by reason of my lord of Leicester's absence remain without order as a ship that wants his master to steer him," he informed the queen, while in a letter to Walsingham he argued that the United Provinces needed "one head who may only and absolutely command and guide," to prevent the country's endemic "civil dissensions" from bringing "utter ruin and confusion."²⁷⁸ To Leicester he wrote in April: "*veni, veni, veni,* you cannot come soon enough and you may easily come too late."²⁷⁹ While urging the importance of a "mild manner of proceeding and receiving those that will seek and sue for your [Leicester's] favor," he and Wilkes soon recognized that Maurice and Hohenlohe were insincere in their professed willingness to serve under the governor general. They advised that Leicester should therefore arrive with as many English soldiers as possible, to overawe opposition.²⁸⁰ In any case England needed to act, since uncertainty about whether Leicester would return had itself become a cause of hesitation and confusion, "their state now being governed neither by her majesty's authority nor by their own."²⁸¹

In short, Buckhurst wanted a reassertion of English authority carried out with sufficient tact and finesse to avoid needless antagonism, backed with enough money and force to overcome internal opposition and inflict losses on Parma. Unfortunately, he had reckoned neither with Elizabeth's determination to limit her investment in the Netherlands nor with Leicester's implacable refusal to forgive Norreys and the Holland politicians. And since Leicester now had the queen's ear, her views on Dutch politics increasingly reflected his own. Her contempt for Dutch leaders and political culture comes through vividly in a draft of Buckhurst's instructions. "Their nice and curious standing upon terms of liberty may well be thought to proceed of vain and unnecessary jealousy,"

---

²⁷⁵ BL Add Mss. 48,084, fol. 123; cf. fols 119, 125. While Roger Williams's company had shrunk to 50 men, most still had 125 to 130, compared to their theoretical full complement of 150 soldiers.
²⁷⁶ BL Add Mss. 48,078, fols 74v–75.   ²⁷⁷ Ibid., fol. 76.
²⁷⁸ Ibid., fols 121, 93; cf. Wilkes's similar assessment in BYU vault Mss. 457, fol. 33v.
²⁷⁹ Ibid., fol. 109v.   ²⁸⁰ Ibid., fols 88, 133; for Wilkes see BYU Mss. 457, fol. 35v.
²⁸¹ BL Add Mss. 48,078, fol. 65v, Buckhurst to Elizabeth, May 10; cf. fol. 94: "no man knowing certainly either what course to take or whereunto to trust, men are unwilling as yet to discover themselves, whereby even those that should deal and give direction are loath to meddle."

while the secretive "indirect practices" meant to undermine Leicester proceeded "from a few turbulent spirits amongst them, who desire to keep things there (in respect of their ambition and particular profit) in confusion as men that love to fish in troubled waters."[282] In April she reacted to unconfirmed rumors that Hohenlohe had begun his own negotiations with Parma by directing Buckhurst to work with Wilkes and Norreys to draw him into a conference where he would be arrested and tried for treason. Norreys was also to attempt to replace Hohenlohe's garrisons in frontier towns.[283] These instructions appalled Buckhurst and Wilkes, who realized that attempting to carry them out would turn Dutch affairs upside down on the basis of unsubstantiated information that was probably false.[284] Although it is not clear whether Hohenlohe ever learned of Elizabeth's plan, her orders make it easier to understand why he told associates that he feared Leicester would try to have him assassinated.[285]

The rancorous disputes between Leicester's partisans and adversaries raised once again the problematic issue of sovereignty within the United Provinces. Already in January the States General had issued a declaration of the duty of each of its members to oversee and protect "religion, conservation of privileges, policy and justice" even against acts by "the sovereign, his lieutenant or particular provinces and towns."[286] For this reason, the states must remain in session, except for brief intermissions, throughout the war. Even after the return of peace its members would retain the right to reassemble if they believed that religion, privileges, or liberties were endangered in any province.[287] By contrast, some of Leicester's most ardent supporters, such as Ringault, had for some time been urging him to assume "the sovereignty" by using armed force to suppress "any public privilege whereby the prince may be bridled." "The means to attain thereto is to deal with the captains and other principal men in the towns and not with the magistrates. The states in every town are not above three or four persons with the pensionary, who being taken for a while and committed if they should resist, all the rest would be commanded easily."[288] This prescription reflected Ringault's view that Dutch magistrates and the delegates to provincial estates and the States

---

[282] BL Add Mss. 48,084, fols 57, 74.

[283] TNA SP84/14/76, Elizabeth to Buckhurst, April 15, 1587: "You should confer with our servants Colonel Norreys and Wilkes what course were mete to be taken therein, which as we perceive may be best performed by seizing of the person of Hohenlohe, wherein, before the execution thereof an especial care would be had that he might be drawn under color of conference with you about matters of great importance contained in certain letters sent from us unto you in great diligence... wherein you may take order for his restraint, being first well furnished with sufficient matter to charge him withal, which we wish to be done in the presence of such principal persons of that country as are held for good patriots and have credit with the people." She goes on to instruct Buckhurst to confer with Norreys about how to prevent Hohenlohe's garrisons in frontier towns from defecting to the enemy when news of his restraint arrived.

[284] *CSPF* 22.3.35 and 41; BL Add Mss. 48,078, fol. 99.

[285] BL Add Mss. 47,078, fol. 88; SP84/14, fol. 93.   [286] AMAE CPH2, fol. 194.

[287] Ibid., fol. 195.   [288] TNA SP84/9/94.

General selected by them were not true representatives of the people, but men who sought to monopolize power to serve their private interests. Some of Leicester's English followers had similarly begun referring sarcastically to the States General and the states of Holland as "the men calling themselves the State." The opponents of English authority over the Netherlands, Wilkes asserted in February 1587, "though they be of the greatest, are not many; the towns and people for the most part remain devoted to your majesty."[289]

The coup in Utrecht of April 1586 that installed a magistracy sympathetic to Leicester was justified as an act by "the people," carried out by the town's militia. In late winter and early spring 1587 Leicester's partisans in other towns started to look for popular support against the states of Holland, the States General, and Maurice and Hohenlohe. In North Holland the governor general's loyal ally, Diederik Sonoy, and forces commanded by Maurice and Hohenlohe, both tried to occupy the province's chief towns, in opposition to each other. In Hoorn a citizen's uprising overturned a decision by the town government to admit a company of Holland loyalists.[290] In Enkhuizen and Medembljk, Wilkes reported, the inhabitants "have openly protested that they will live and die with the queen... The like garboil was begun at Amsterdam, where the same protestation is begun by the people. These beginnings are feared will grow into some dangerous events."[291] Gorcum and Dordrecht had defied an order by the states of Holland, whose publication Russell had also prevented in Brill.[292] Even in Leicester's absence, the contest between his allies and adversaries had started to devolve into a series of local insurrections and military coups. Gilpin warned that if the conflict continued much longer it might provide an opening for a faction that wanted to restore Spanish rule.[293]

When the states of Holland asserted their own sovereignty over the province and used it to alter military commissions, Wilkes felt compelled to respond.[294] In March he issued a detailed memorandum arguing, on grounds borrowed without acknowledgement from Jean Bodin that the provincial states could not claim sovereignty because its members were chosen by and answerable to the towns from which they came, whereas a sovereign can by definition have no earthly superior. Wilkes admitted that Leicester, as governor general, was only a "*dispoitarius* or guardian of sovereignty," appointed by "the towns and provinces" of the Netherlands acting on behalf of the true sovereign, the people. But as such Leicester held an authority that only the people themselves, and not the States General or the states of Holland, had the right to revoke or control. In trying to limit that authority the members of the states "either do not understand what you

---

[289] *Correspondentie*, ed. Brugmans, 2.99.
[290] Tracy, *Founding of the Dutch Republic*, 284; cf. Wilkes's report on this incident in *CSPF* 21.2.424.
[291] TNA SP105/91, fol. 40r.   [292] BL Add Mss. 48,014, fol. 422v.   [293] TNA SP84/13/121.
[294] E.g. NA 3.01/14/2005, fol. 73v.

have been doing... or else you are guilty of the crime of disobedience."[295] The states of Holland commissioned a response from a young lawyer and protégé of Oldenbarnevelt, François Vranck. He argued that sovereignty in Holland did not reside in the people as a whole but in the province's most distinguished residents, the nobles and town magistrates, on whose behalf the Holland states exercised authority.[296] For 800 years this elite had exercised power jointly with the counts of Holland and their successors, in a system of consensual governance that Leicester's conduct now threatened. Although essentially a myth, this view of Holland's ancient political order was later reiterated by Hugo Grotius and continued to provide the theoretical basis for the position of a states' party until the late seventeenth century. It resembled in many ways what we have come to regard as a concept of an ancient constitution. But Vranck remained vague about the precise mechanisms through which agreement between the prince and sovereign community was to be achieved and maintained, and the legitimate remedies available if it broke down. Unlike modern constitutional thinkers, he never spelled out procedures through which a sovereign group of people might delegate their authority for specified periods and with well-defined limiting conditions, to individuals and institutions empowered to act in their name. In the absence of such a concept of how a theoretically unlimited and indivisible power can be limited and distributed in its practical operation, the location of sovereignty within a decentralized state like the United Provinces remained inherently problematical. The issue arose again in the conflict between Maurice and Oldenbarnevelt in the late 1610s and subsequent contests between states partisans and supporters of the House of Orange later in the seventeenth century. In every case, as in 1587, armed force determined the outcome.

Leicester's Return and Final Defeat: June-October 1587

The immediate practical danger, as Wilkes, Buckhurst, and Gilpin all foresaw, was that the standoff between Leicester's partisans and adversaries would paralyze the United Provinces from within in the face of Parma's renewed onslaught. They all wanted Leicester to return with fresh English reinforcements, but they also tried to

---

[295] An English version of Wilkes's statement is printed in *Texts Concerning the Revolt of the Netherlands*, ed. E. H. Kossman and Albert Fredrik Mellink (Cambridge: Cambridge University Press, 1974), 273; for the Dutch text see Bor, *Oorsprong*, pt 2, 921. For a brief discussion of the controversy see Tracy, *Founding of the Dutch Republic*, 291–5. For Wilkes's report of the controversy to Leicester see BL Add Mss. 48,014, fol. 423. For an analysis of the intellectual context of the dispute, with references to relevant secondary literature, see S. Groenveld, "Verlatinge en de erkeening van een nieuwe staat," in *Facetten van de Tachtigjarige Oorlog: Twalf Artikelen over de eriode 1559-1652* (Hilversum: Verloren, 2018), 183–205, esp. 184-94.

[296] Tracy, *Founding of the Dutch Republic*, 293. The estates "do not mean to speak of themselves, but of their principals, that is the town corporations and the college of nobles."

mediate his quarrels with Maurice, Hohenlohe, and the states of Holland. Unfortunately, Leicester interpreted their efforts to heal old disputes as a conspiracy to unite his English and Dutch enemies against him.[297] Elizabeth, who now shared her favorite's low view of Holland's leadership, rebuked Buckhurst for not taking a harder line. He had attempted to wash wounds with water rather than vinegar, she complained, although he should have realized "that festering wounds had more need of corrosives than lenitives." His "slight and mild kind of dealing with a people so ingrate and devoid of consideration as the states" would "increase their contempt."[298] She peremptorily rejected the £50,000 loan he had negotiated, scolding him for suggesting it when he knew of her shortage of treasure. It soon became clear that Norreys would have to resign his command, despite Dutch pleas that he be allowed to stay and the efforts of Walsingham and others to placate Leicester's hostility toward his former client.[299] In June the queen ordered him to return to his post in Munster, ostensibly to prepare the province against a possible Spanish incursion.[300]

Elizabeth delayed her decision about whether to send Leicester back to the Netherlands for months. He had mixed feelings about the matter, wishing to support his Dutch followers, but dreading the prospect of more wrangles with his adversaries.[301] If he did go, he told Walsingham, he wanted the matter resolved quickly and hoped Elizabeth would finally determine "to spend her money in that measure which may do good to the cause."[302] He attempted to pressure her to do this by refusing to return to the Netherlands unless she supplied him with the troops and money he believed he needed to succeed. But she reacted angrily to the pressure, telling Walsingham to summon the earl to court and saying that he "will go with those forces that she thinketh fit."[303] A decision to send him back was finally reached in early June. To prepare the ground Leicester instructed his Dutch servant, Junius, to rally support by spreading reports lauding his and Elizabeth's determination to fight Spain and blaming his political adversaries for undermining their efforts. He also wanted Junius to explain away the English negotiations with Parma, which Buckhurst had revealed to the States General, and which the Dutch also knew about from the reports of their own agent in London, Joachim Ortel.[304] Leicester wanted his friends to receive assurances that the talks had been very tentative and insignificant, although Buckhurst had maliciously exaggerated

---

[297] BL Add Mss. 48,127, fol. 7. Leicester stated "that my Lord [Buckhurst] at his arrival seemed to be my great friend and in every place till he came to The Hague showed it so openly. And then was the Count Hollock [Hohenlohe] and Sir John Norreys open enemies one going guarded each for other, within eight days he brought them to be great friends and cast all the dislikes towards me."
[298] TNA SP84/14, fol. 184, Elizabeth to Buckhurst, May 3, 1587.
[299] TNA SP84/14/119; SP84/15/19; *CSPF* 21.3.125; *Correspondentie*, ed. Brugmans, 2.132.
[300] *Correspondentie*, ed. Brugmans, 334.
[301] TNA SP84/14, fol. 172, Leicester to Sonoy, May 1, 1587.
[302] TNA SP84/14/247; *CSPF* 21.3.70.   [303] BL Harley Mss. 6994, fol. 70r.
[304] Bor, *Oorsprong*, pt 2, 906.

their importance. He must have known this was untrue, since his instructions included a directive to persuade the Dutch "to hearken and incline to a peace." But the strong Calvinists who provided his main base of support especially disliked talk of peace.[305]

Dutch leaders complained to Buckhurst that "the earl, by diverse letters and bruits of his followers, hath given out to the people that the only cause why her Majesty hath not better holpen them hath been for that the states wrote" a letter of complaint against him. This referred to a list of grievances sent to the queen in February. Leicester spread the story reported by Navarre's representative that an army of 20,000 authorized by Parliament to aid the Netherlands was withheld because of Elizabeth's anger over the insults offered to his reputation.[306] "This is a most dangerous course," Buckhurst warned, "for if the earl come with a mind to revenge the cause will come to subversion."[307] But when Leicester learned that Junius had been arrested in Delft on orders of the States General, he responded: "I must suffer this to my shame or revenge it to their utter danger, for I know I can with a word make them all smart for it."[308] For its part, the States General reacted to the news of Leicester's imminent return by passing a resolution that executive authority should henceforth rest with the council of state and that all orders previously enacted by the governor general's sole authority alone should be canceled.[309]

Leicester's arrival in Flushing on June 28 with 4,500 fresh English troops touched off a joyous reception by local citizens, crying "that the enemies will be compelled to depart for her Majesty's lieutenant was now returned."[310] For the next several weeks Parma's siege of Sluis, along the southern coastal border of Dutch territory, consumed all his energies. His political adversaries gave him almost no support. Hohenlohe's refusal to dispatch more than a token force, which he excused by the demands of his own campaign in Brabant, touched off another rancorous public quarrel. Hohenlohe stated in a printed tract that although he would serve Elizabeth to the uttermost of his ability if she assumed sovereignty over the Low Countries, he felt it beneath his dignity to take orders from a mere earl.[311] After Maurice and the fleet of Zeeland failed to come to his aid, Leicester decided he lacked sufficient forces to attack Parma's besieging army.

---

[305] BL Cotton Mss. Galba DII, fol. 25 and TNA SP84/15/71, Leicester to Junius, June 10, 1587; SP84/15, fol. 125, draft of Leicester's instructions; Bor, *Oorsprong*, pt 2, 689 for the text of the prohibition.
[306] Above, p. 317.
[307] CSPF 21.3.117; a similar letter is in *Correspondentie*, ed. Brugmans, 2.356.
[308] TMA SP84/16/12. [309] BYU vault Mss. 457, fol. 138.
[310] TNA SP84/15, fol. 170, Richard Lloyd to Walsingham, June 28, 1587. The cry in Dutch was recorded by an English witness as "*viant mult aweight track*," which is obviously garbled but corresponds phonetically to "vijand moeten wegtrekken" (= the enemy must depart) if we divide the words differently and allow for the silent "n" at the end of moeten and wegtrekken.
[311] Bor, *Oorsprong*, pt 3, 14; *Verantwoordinge vanden welgeboren heer Philips grave van Hohenloe* (1587), sig. A3.

After a long heroic resistance by its garrison, including English troops under Williams, the town surrendered on August 5.

Leicester blamed "the young imp [Maurice] and his vice admiral [of the Zeeland fleet]" for the defeat, which reinforced his view that to have any chance of defeating the Spanish he first needed to vanquish his opponents within the United Provinces.[312] Elizabeth was now also "persuaded fully that it is necessary for your lordship not only to continue in that government but to have it more amply established and perfected... especially with money and men." In the period following the loss of Sluis, Leicester and his supporters made some desultory attempts to seize power by force in the major towns.[313] He may have planned to kidnap Maurice and Oldenbarnevelt and convey them to England, as the latter claimed.[314] But his adversaries had secured military control of the wealthiest parts of Holland, Zeeland, and Friesland in May, as a precaution against just such a contingency, and they rather quickly defeated the governor general's efforts.[315] An attempt to seize Leiden was prevented through the arrest of several of Leicester's local agents and the execution of three.[316] His allies retained their ascendancy in Utrecht, despite increasing internal squabbles and attempts to bring the town to heal by military pressure.[317] In early September Leicester had a lengthy remonstrance justifying his conduct printed in Dutch and French and distributed throughout the United Provinces.[318] But his ability to command in most of the Netherlands, especially in the provinces that provided the bulk of the Dutch state's revenue, had effectively collapsed. He reacted by sending a stream of complaints about Dutch duplicity and disloyalty back to London. Dutch leaders conduct war "more for their own profit and rule than any care of their country or love to their commonwealth," he told the queen. To Walsingham he wrote that the States General "are men that hinder with hatred all things that appertain to her Majesty and disgrace all men... that do love and affect her," with the aim of establishing "a popular government."[319]

None of this prevented Leicester from continuing to warn against the pitfalls of negotiation with Spain or complaining about anyone who encouraged Elizabeth to limit funds for his army.[320] "I see our enemies have dealt more like politic men than we have; I mean you there," he scolded Walsingham, since Philip II continued to support his army's offensive, while the English council starved him of

---

[312] TNA SP84/16, fol. 189; Den Tex, *Oldenbarnevelt*, 1.112.   [313] Oosterhoff, *Leicester*, 180–2.
[314] Den Tex, *Oldenbarnevelt*, 1.117–20; Bor, *Oorsprong*, pt 3, 51.
[315] See SP105/91, fol. 48v for Wilkes's report on measures to circumscribe Leicester's territorial authority before his arrival.
[316] *CSPF* 21.3.391.
[317] For reports of Meur's attempts on Utrecht see BL Cotton Mss. Galba DII, fol. 9 and TNA SP84/15/9, and 17, fols 119v, 150, and 163. Statements of loyalty to Leicester by the town's magistrates can be found in BL Add Mss. 48,083, fol. 48 and 18,014, fol. 334v.
[318] Bor, *Oorspong*, pt. 3, 30, 39.   [319] *Correspondentie*, ed. Brugmans, 3.220.
[320] Ibid., 3.132.

resources, so that he found it difficult to sustain even defensive operations.[321] There was reason to suspect Parma intended to invade England through Scotland, he warned.[322] But if only Elizabeth would lead, he protested, the Dutch people would support her against their own politicians in a vigorous war.[323] She refused to listen, preferring to pursue her negotiations with Parma and insist that the Dutch join them, whether they wanted to or not. The loss of Sluis, the erosion of Leicester's authority, and the mounting costs of war had convinced her that the United Provinces lacked the leadership and resources needed to defeat the Spanish, leaving negotiation as the only viable option.[324] In her eagerness for a settlement she gave credence to optimistic reports from one of her envoys to Parma, the former Spanish pensioner Sir James Croft, despite the exasperated skepticism of other members of her Council. "I am unfit to be the executor of these sudden directions, especially where the effects are so heavy and dangerous," Burleigh moaned to Walsingham in July, when Elizabeth directed him to order a cease-fire in the Netherlands without first consulting Leicester: "but lords and ladies command and servants obey."[325]

Although the hoped-for truce never took effect, reports of the queen's negotiations continued to reach the Netherlands, further sapping Leicester's remaining credit. For different reasons, Oldenbarnevelt and Parma both spread them.[326] Oldenbarnevelt used the copy of Leicester's official instructions and other leaks of information supplied from London by Ortel to spread fears that Leicester and Elizabeth wanted to establish arbitrary control over the United Provinces and deliver them to Spain.[327] He claimed that Leicester and Elizabeth planned to seize Dutch towns and turn them over to the Spanish in return for a peace settlement protecting England.[328] Although Leicester did his best to counter these reports, Elizabeth's determination to force the Dutch to the negotiating table undercut his efforts.[329] By October, one Englishman reported, many former supporters of Leicester had grown so alienated by the queen's pursuit of peace that they became partisans of Maurice and Hohenlohe.[330] Sir William Russell feared that the local population might try to overwhelm his garrison at Flushing, in the belief that Elizabeth intended to surrender the town to Parma.[331] Leicester correctly suspected that Parma and Guise wished to use negotiations to lull the English and Dutch into a false sense of security as they planned fresh attacks, and he feared the outcome if England did not continue to wage a vigorous offensive while peace talks continued. But he had grown so disillusioned that he now believed that "except her Majesty for her part and these people [the Dutch] for theirs be fully

[321] Ibid., 3.287.   [322] Ibid., 3.348.   [323] Ibid., 3.288, 193.
[324] See, e.g., BL Add Mss. 48,084, fol. 62v, instructions for John Harbert esq.
[325] TNA SP12/202/56.   [326] Den Tex, *Oldenbarnevelt*, 1.114–1.
[327] Add Mss. 48,127, fol. 38; *CSPF* 21.3.384; TNA SP84/16/78; *Correspondentie*, ed. Brugmans, 3.96–7.
[328] BL Harley Mss. 6994, fol. 94r.   [329] TNA SP84/17, fol. 215.
[330] TNA SP84/18/108, Richard Lloyd to Walsingham, October 15, 1587.
[331] TNA SP84/18, fol. 322, Russell to Walsingham, October 20.

resolved to spend freely for the maintenance of their war, any peace will be far better for them." "For my own part," he added, "I am even heartily weary of my generalship... there is no likelihood of any worthy wars to be made under these men."[332] In November he admitted defeat: "Your Majesty, I hope, will consider that I cannot do now as I might the last year; they of this country have found means to draw all their soldiers in Holland and Zeeland from my commandment, besides all your English new forces and the old in the State's pay be all discharged, so that I have no bands to dispose."[333] Elizabeth commanded him to return home, blaming Dutch perversity for the failure of his government.[334]

As he left the Netherlands Leicester resigned his office as governor general. By this time, he had convinced himself that the public opposition to a peace mediated by England displayed by Dutch leaders masked their secret "determination to fetch the King of Spain again" by their own means. Malevolent politicians had made an instrument of "the imp Maurice," promoting his reputation among the common people as "a noble patriot" and "the image of his noble father," so that under the pretense of preparing for war they might "take the very highway to bring in the enemy."[335] Unfortunately, the earl's departure did not immediately resolve Anglo-Dutch conflicts. News of his resignation was not widely divulged until the following April, leaving both his supporters and adversaries under the impression that he might return and attempt once again to assert his authority. He left behind the remnants of his army and officers, such as Russell, who were among his most committed supporters. They continued to see Maurice and Hohenlohe as adversaries and remained as determined as ever to build an English party in the Netherlands. In North Holland, Sonoy also remained loyal to Leicester and Elizabeth and adamantly resisted the efforts of Maurice and Hohenlohe to bring him under control, even when they started massing troops around his main garrison at Medemblik. The tattered remnants of English power continued to provide an alternative source of authority around which disaffected Netherlanders attempted to rally. Prouninck remained unwilling to reconcile with the Dutch authorities as late as June 1588.[336] Over the winter, unpaid garrisons on the island of Walcheren, close to the cautionary town of Flushing, mutinied against the Dutch state and offered to place themselves and the places where they were stationed under the sovereignty of the English crown. Russell encouraged them. Elizabeth, true to form, welcomed their support but declined to accept sovereignty over any Dutch territory or to pay their wages, despite Walsingham's pleas that she do so.[337] The affair dragged on into May 1588 without a clear resolution.[338]

---

[332] *Correspondentie*, ed. Brugmans, 3.130. [333] Ibid., 288. [334] TNA SP84/19/40.
[335] *Correspondentie*, ed. Brugmans, 3.350. [336] TNA SP84/24/3.
[337] TNA SP84/23, fol. 58, Walsingham to Willoughby, April 10, 1588.
[338] It left an extensive paper trail in the English State Papers: *CSPF* 21.4.56, 65, 68, 94, 112, 232, 251, 269, 276–7, 290, 361, 358 383, 394, 395, 400, 410, 500; TNA SP12/22, fols 54, 70; SP84/21, fol. 261; SP84/22, fols 40, 118, 125v; SP84/23, fols 40, 130, 324, and 383.

Elizabeth once again failed for several months to provide clear instructions to her servants in the Netherlands, leaving them uncertain about what course to pursue. She also did not send enough money to pay her remaining troops. Leicester's successor as general of the English army, Lord Willoughby, found himself in much the same situation Norreys had faced the previous winter, struggling to control his unpaid troops, while bickering with hostile Dutch politicians and some of Leicester's aristocratic officers, and pleading for clear instructions from London that almost never arrived. He complained repeatedly, pleading to be relieved of his duties unless the queen paid his soldiers and told him what she wanted done. "I wish some more excellent person had dispossessed me of [my command]," he sarcastically told Walsingham, "that could make men live without money, meat or contentment." He repeated the comment in slightly different words to Burghley, suggesting he be replaced by someone who knew how to make a soldiers live without food for five or six weeks.[339] The Dutch had accepted his commission to command the queen's soldiers only on condition that he take an oath of loyalty to the States General and even then limited his term to two months.[340] He nevertheless thought it both possible and desirable to rebuild English authority, since he had little confidence in Dutch leadership. "The encumbrances of this state goeth *a malo in pejus*," he wrote to Burghley in January. "They embrace their liberty as apes their young. To that end is Count Hollock [Hohenlohe] and Maurice set on the stage, and to entertain the common people her Majesty and my late lord general are not forgotten." He feared that Hohenlohe would defect to the Spaniards.[341] As for Maurice, he was but a "cypher," driven by "childish ambition," encouraged by "the covetous and furious counsel of the proud Hollanders" as well as "our slackness and coldness to entertain those friends that willingly would give their lives to preserve our safeties... The provident and wisest sort weighing what a slender ground the appetite of a young man is, unfurnished of sinews of war, to manage so great a cause, for a good space after my lord general's departure gave him afar off the looking on, to see him play his single part on the stage; but as the skittish horse is assured of that he feared by little and little, perceiving the harmlessness thereof, so they, finding no safety of neutrality... and no overturning nor barricade to stop his rash wild chariot, followed."[342] But with proper managing "there is no doubt but he might be catched and kept in a fish-pool, while in his imagination he may judge it a sea."[343]

In early March, Willoughby finally did receive clear instructions to cooperate with Maurice in negotiating an end to the stand-off between Sonoy and the army of the States General around Medemblik. He saw those instructions as a capitulation that would lead to the ruin of England's friends in the Netherlands, and

---

[339] TNA SP84/20, fol. 34; *CSPF* 21.4.7. [340] TNA SP84/20, fols 10, 34.
[341] *CSPF* 21.4.21. [342] Ibid., 105. [343] Ibid., 13.

tried to stand his ground in tense negotiations with delegates from the states of Holland over Sonoy's position.[344] But he eventually complied and by April he was employing "his best wits to the compounding of controversy" and "appeasing mutinies."[345] His cooperation with the Dutch and the belated publication of Leicester's resignation brought about a "sudden alteration" and "great friendship between the Count Maurice and my lord Willoughby." Elizabeth wrote on the 29th, thanking both commanders for their efforts to calm dissension.[346] Willoughby's new conciliatory stance provoked a quarrel with Russell, who thought him too ready "to yield unto the States and thereby to be much withdrawn from the good course which might best further her Majesty's service."[347] But it finally soothed relations between the English crown and the men who controlled the United Provinces. When the English requested the assistance of Dutch mariners in case the Spanish should attempt to invade their island, Oldenbarnevelt readily agreed.[348] Having won the political struggle, he could afford to be cooperative, particularly in a matter that so directly affected both countries' interests.

Final Assessments

Leicester's attempt to build a strong centralized state in the northern Netherlands had finally petered out. Instead of unifying the Dutch and cementing their alliance with England, his efforts had intensified disputes that threatened to erupt into armed clashes between English forces serving in the Netherlands and other units of the Dutch army. He so alienated Holland's leading politicians that they probably concluded in the summer of 1587 that the loss of Sluis to Parma was preferable to a victory that would have enhanced his standing. The earl's complaints reinforced Elizabeth's lack of confidence in the government of the United Provinces and her desire for a settlement with Spain that would permit her to cut her losses and leave the Dutch to their own devices. As the campaigning season of 1588 approached many English observers in the Netherlands predicted catastrophic losses.

Leicester must unquestionably bear major responsibility for this debacle. His attempt to squeeze Holland merchants by imposing an unenforceable total ban on trade with the enemy was a serious error of political judgment that turned an inherently difficult relationship with the province's leaders into one of implacable hostility. The trust he placed in Sir William Stanley, despite many warnings not to do so, was another disastrous lapse. Traits of personality also damaged his

---

[344] Ibid., 157; TNA SP84/22/51B.   [345] *CSPF* 21.4.304.   [346] Ibid., 306, 335.
[347] TNA SP84/23, fol. 362, Russell to Walsingham, May 29, 1588.
[348] *CSPF* 21.4.326; Den Tex, *Oldenbarnevelt*, 1.134–7.

leadership. Given the nature of Dutch politics, his position as governor general required a thick skin, considerable tact, and a willingness to forgive small slights in the interest of building consensus over large issues. Instead he was haughty, quick to suspect disloyalty, and relentless in pursuing anyone he perceived as an adversary. Even Davison had to endure his recriminations, as he struggled to appease the queen's fury over the earl's elevation as governor general.[349] Walsingham sprang to his hurt colleague's defense: "Poor Mr. Davison doth take it very grievously that your lordship should conceive so hardly of him as you do... the conceit of your lordship's disfavor hath greatly dejected him."[350] Wilkes confided his fears of Leicester's vindictiveness to Walsingham with a freedom that suggests he felt confident the secretary would agree that Leicester was a man whose "nature is not so facile to forget as ready to revenge."[351] When the earl learned in July 1587 that Parma had offered Roger Williams a command in the Spanish army, he immediately assumed that Williams would commit treason and warned several other officers to beware of him. Williams, who had rejected Parma's invitation—to serve against the Turks in the Mediterranean rather than the English and Dutch—was left "wonderfully perplexed that for his faithful service he should reap his utter undoing and to be accounted a traitor to his prince. He wisheth he were at home upon condition he should never bear arms here, for he knoweth the condition of Themistocles [Leicester] to be such as he will leave no means unsought to overthrow his credit."[352] Leicester rapidly calmed down and restored Williams to favor upon learning the truth. But his hasty overreaction suggests why people found him such a difficult man to serve, why he made so many enemies so quickly, and why his disagreements with Dutch leaders nearly always produced a permanent breach that no amount of later mediation was able to heal.

The earl's suspicious and vindictive temperament made him vulnerable to people who tried to promote their own agendas by feeding his mistrust of others. Walsingham blamed Leicester's secretary, Sir Arthur Atye, for incensing him against Wilkes. In July 1587 an Englishman reported that Lord North had not only further inflamed the governor general's animosity to Maurice, Hohenlohe, and the States General but had also "been the cause that he hath of late fallen out with his best soldiers and men of war, even so far as Sir William Russell... [who] mindeth to give over his place of general of the horse... which if he do, Lord North is likely to succeed him."[353] Leicester's willingness to believe damaging accusations against colleagues and his penchant for dividing the world into loyal allies and malignant enemies compounded his already difficult political challenges. These traits made it very hard for Dutch politicians to oppose or obstruct

---

[349] *Leicester Correspondence*, 165.   [350] Ibid., 206.
[351] *Correspondentie*, ed. Brugmans, 2.202.
[352] CSPF 21.3.236, Francis Nedham to Walsingham, August 12, 1587.   [353] Ibid.

any of his individual policies without alienating him completely. In a state as dependent on negotiation and consensus-building as the United Provinces in the 1580s, this was a disastrous problem.

But Leicester does not bear sole responsibility. Elizabeth's penchant for second-guessing his actions and attempting to manage Dutch affairs from London also caused serious damage. So did her refusal to face up to the real costs of the Dutch war, her myopic pursuit of a negotiated settlement with Parma, and her stubborn determination to bring her Dutch allies, kicking and screaming, to the conference table. If she had consistently supported Leicester and supplied him adequately with men and money, he might have succeeded in overcoming opposition and establishing control in the Netherlands, despite his political blunders. Her decision in the summer of 1587 to support his absolute authority, while limiting his military resources and insisting that he bring the Dutch into peace negotiations they bitterly opposed, was particularly unrealistic. Even the most astute and tactful statesman would have failed in these circumstances. Elizabeth's bouts of indecision, emotional volatility, and eruptions of anger at the leaders of her own council contributed materially to Leicester's difficulties. Although his suspicious nature magnified his paranoia, his insecurity about the effects of malicious reports by his enemies and false friends at court and critical reports from the Netherlands was by no means irrational. He did have enemies, even if not always the ones he imagined, and his hold over Elizabeth's affections and respect was badly shaken in the spring of 1586. His decision to abandon his supreme office in the Netherlands during the winter of 1586–7, in order to return to the English court and repair his personal relationship with the queen was not a mistake in judgment, however much it damaged his credibility with the Dutch. He had no realistic option other than to give top priority to his standing with her. If he could not do this without abandoning his foreign post, the fault lay with Elizabeth rather than himself.

Leicester's role as leader of a great affinity of landowners and professional soldiers also constrained him. He might have done a better job of managing conflicts between Sir John Norreys and pushy aristocrats like Digby, Pelham, and Russell, but tensions of this kind were inevitable, given the make-up of the army and officer corps he brought with him. Favoring professional soldiers over socially prominent amateurs might have improved military performance in the short run, but at the cost of jeopardizing his ability to muster support from aristocratic friends and allies, not only during his Dutch campaign but in the future. He was never in a position to make military decisions on the basis of military criteria alone. Finally, we need to remember early modern prejudices favoring hierarchy, noble birth, and authoritative decision-making by a single leader advised by a select council, in preference to a dispersal of power among decentralized institutions largely under the control of merchants and lawyers. We have become so accustomed in the twenty-first century to seeing republican governments, constitutional monarchies, and federal states work efficiently that it takes some effort to appreciate the outlook of a period with very different experiences. Although the closed aristocratic republic of Venice had acquired a reputation for stability, other famous republics like Florence, Sienna, and Lucca had fairly recently been absorbed into new princely states, after internal divisions rendered them vulnerable. This makes the mistrust of Dutch institutions and politicians displayed not only by Leicester but also by Elizabeth, Burghley, and others readily understandable. But the deficit in trust—the English belief that to preserve the Netherlands they first needed to save the Dutch from themselves through a strong dose of externally imposed discipline—made political conflict inevitable. Elizabeth's desire to have matters both ways by imposing English control while refusing to take formal responsibility only made matters worse. So did Leicester's need to justify his acceptance of the governor generalship by persuading Elizabeth that the Dutch state would collapse without his guidance.

It needs emphasis that this lack of confidence in Dutch institutions and leaders was not simply an English prejudice. Many Netherlanders shared the belief that their country needed a strong leader to overcome the local particularism and private interests that obstructed efficient decision making. Leicester always had Dutch supporters, some of whom felt even more strongly than he did that Holland merchants and their political allies were selfish men driven by greed rather than patriotism, and that the fragmented nature of authority in the United Provinces made unified resistance to Spain impossible. It is not clear whether Leicester ever read Machiavelli's *The Prince*, although he might easily have done so, since he had a command of Italian. But more than any place else in Europe, the northern Netherlands in the mid-1580s fit the situation Machiavelli described in that treatise, in which "a new state" had to be built on the ruins of a collapsed political order, to provide its people with the *virtu* and military capacity needed to defend themselves from foreign domination. Already in 1579 one Dutch tract, probably by Leicester's later ally Prouninck, argued that the problems afflicting the Netherlands could only be "surmounted by the virtuousness of a new prince," a prescription strikingly similar to Machiavelli's.[354] Whether or not Leicester had read Machiavelli, the similarity between the circumstances he found in the Netherlands and those analyzed in *The Prince* helps explain his determination to present an appearance of strength and magnificence, his reliance on Calvinist religion to unite and motivate supporters of the state, and his willingness to employ ruthless methods. Like Machiavelli and other early modern theorists, he believed not only that liberty required active public virtue, but that establishing an ethos of virtue required strong leadership by a prince willing to override private interests and claims of privilege that obstructed the common good. He believed

---

[354] Gelderen, *Political Thought*, 171–2. The tract was Emanuel-Erneste, *A Dialogue of Two Persons on the State of the Netherlands*.

that God had called him to play that role in the United Provinces, and that the preservation not only of Dutch liberty but European Protestantism depended on his success, a view shared by other Protestant statesmen like du Plessis Mornay.[355] As in Ireland, although for different reasons, the salvation of the common weale therefore seemed to require an absolutist state under a surrogate king. Delegated royal authority in unstable environments had to operate with more ruthless efficiency than the queen's direct authority in England.

Unfortunately, this view too often induced Leicester and his partisans to dismiss Dutch leaders who resisted his decisions as factious obstructionists, rather than difficult partners with whom he needed to negotiate mutually acceptable compromises. Those leaders naturally resented his suspicions and rigidity and responded in kind with smear campaigns against the earl and his associates that broadened into attacks on the English nation after Stanley's betrayal of Deventer. These slurs infuriated not only Leicester but Elizabeth too, who saw them as evidence of the ingratitude of Dutch burgers who took her money and then insulted not only the man she had sent to rescue them from Spanish tyranny but also her soldiers and her own honor. Digges's claims that the Dutch had cheated her out of tens of thousands of pounds added fuel to the fire. She even blamed Stanley's betrayal of Deventer on the Dutch, for not paying his garrison its wages. Men like Buckhurst, Norreys, and Wilkes, who wanted to establish a more cooperative Anglo-Dutch relationship, always faced an uphill task, particularly when they had to ask her to spend more money.

Matters began to improve in the spring of 1588 not just because of Leicester's departure—although that certainly helped—but due to almost accidental causes. Willoughby's letters make it clear that he began to cooperate with Maurice and Hohenlohe over matters like the mutiny on Weckerlin and Sonoy's defiance in North Holland, not because he wanted to but because Elizabeth had ordered him to do so. Her orders did not stem from any new-found confidence in the Dutch, but her determination to limit her commitments and financial investment. Now that Leicester's government had collapsed she wanted to let Maurice, Hohenlohe, and Oldenbarnevelt sink or swim on their own, with limited English help. Somewhat to Willoughby's surprise the new cooperative relationship worked remarkably well. It soon became clear that the withdrawal of English authority had not produced the disintegration of the Dutch polity that Leicester and others had predicted.

Even so, the real test would not come until summer, when Parma renewed his assault. Willoughby remained pessimistic. In June he described the military

---

[355] *Correspondence de Leicester*, ed. Blok, 169–70: "Vous avez en même temps délivré la Flandre, secouru la France, assuré l'Angleterre; le moindre des trois est digne d'un triomphe. Et qui veut bien faire l'un ne le peut faire qu'il ne face en quelque sort tous les trois. Monseigneur, pensez en somme que Dieu nous élève pour relever son église."

position of the Dutch and English as "very weak." Whereas Parma had grown strong enough to besiege two cities simultaneously the Dutch were scarcely able to relieve one, even with the help of his forces, which had declined badly over the winter. He regarded himself as "a general that hath neither men, means, authority or credit to offend or defend withal."[356] It was clear that while negotiating with Elizabeth's commissioners Parma had engaged in a major build-up of military supplies along the coast of the Spanish Netherlands, which the Dutch and English had not matched. The chances that Ostend and other places in Dutch hands would hold out long once the Spanish general launched his assault seemed very slim. What Willoughby and most other English leaders had still not fully grasped was that Parma was preparing not only a new attack on the south flank of the United Provinces but an invasion of England. To be sure, there had been warnings and plenty of suspicions. "It is most certain that the duke of Parma's provisions for the sea go forward," Leicester had written back in November: "They be not all for these places. It is more than time her Majesty had a strong navy abroad."[357] But Spanish intentions remained unclear.

Philip II's decision to launch a massive but badly planned invasion of England set in train a series of events that, over the next two years, transformed the strategic situation in northern Europe. It relieved the military pressure on the Dutch, giving them time to consolidate administrative and military reforms already underway.[358] The assassination of Guise by Henry III's bodyguard in 1588 ended any immediate prospects of a Franco-Spanish alliance. Instead the French king's own murder the following year made Henry of Navarre the titular heir to the French throne and deepened a civil war in which Philip decided to intervene directly. This further diverted Spanish resources from the Low Countries, allowing the Dutch army, under Maurice's unexpectedly capable leadership, not only to halt Spanish advances but to recover lost territory. The fledgling Dutch state survived and began to prosper thanks largely to the overreach of its enemy.

This outcome seemingly vindicated Leicester's opponents—Maurice, Oldenbarnevelt, and the Holland oligarchs—while casting further discredit on his experiment in English rule. But although certainly not a success, we should not regard his campaigns in the Netherlands as unmitigated failures. The victories of English forces at Zutphen and Deventer in 1586 momentarily halted Parma's offensive, and if Leicester failed to save Sluis the following summer, he did delay the town's capitulation, preventing the Spanish from rapidly redeploying against another target. The earl's ambitious military build-up in 1586 helped spur the

---

[356] *CSPF* 21.4.463, 501.   [357] *CSPF* v. 21.3.428.

[358] A particularly devastating account of the flaws in planning and execution of the Armada campaign is Manuel Fernández Álvarez, *Felipe II y su tiempo* (Madrid: Espasa, 1998), 541–76. Parker's *Grand Strategy* is more temperate in its criticisms but also highlights the flaws in Spanish preparations.

Dutch to tap new sources of revenue, while also providing a much-needed boost to morale after the defeats of the previous year. His contentious efforts to establish a centralized treasury contributed to an eventual reform of financial administration. The need to combat Leicester also gave his Dutch opponents a greater incentive to work together. Revealingly, Hohenlohe's standing began to decline rapidly as the threat of English interference receded in early 1588. Already in February he tried to ingratiate himself with the English by complaining about Maurice and the states of Holland, while in April Sir Henry Killigrew reported that he had "fallen into great discredit with the states and I am secretly informed they will be rid of him."[359] The partnership of Maurice, Oldenbarnevelt, and the states of Holland lasted much longer, but it too eventually collapsed. Some thirty years later Maurice destroyed the power of his old ally and brought him to the scaffold.

Leicester had helped buy time, in which a new generation of Dutch leaders emerged, important administrative reforms were initiated and new configurations in Dutch politics began to take form. Even more important, English intervention in the Netherlands, along with Drake's attacks on Spain and its American outposts, provoked Philip II into sending the Armada, which in turn forced Elizabeth into an open war in alliance with the United Provinces and eventually with Henry of Navarre. The international front led by sovereign monarchs that Leicester, Walsingham, and Burghley had so badly wanted to create in the mid-1580s finally came about. The Spanish king's efforts to claim the thrones of both France and England for his daughter then prompted a reaction even among many French and English Catholics against Habsburg ambitions to establish a "universal monarchy." Instead of a collection of basically separate Calvinist revolts in France and the Low Countries, led by nobles and town corporations, the fight against Spain turned into something more closely resembling a conventional war between rival dynastic states.

Within the English court, Spanish aggression discredited the position of men like Sir James Croft and probably John Whitgift, who wanted to avoid involvement in European wars of religion. Serious disagreements that had threatened to erupt over Leicester's expedition dissipated. The earl's death in September 1588, barely a month after the Armada's defeat, further smoothed the waters by removing him and his grudges from the scene. This eased the rehabilitation of Buckhurst, Norreys, and others who had incurred his enmity. But it also underlined the fact that the cohort of leaders that had governed England since the early 1570s, and in some cases since 1558, were now nearing the end of their lives. A generational transition within the fairly near future had become inevitable, although its timing and ultimate outcome remained uncertain. That uncertainty created new sources of conflict and rivalry, as younger men jockeyed for position.

---

[359] CSPF 21.4.142, 327.

The future of the Church also appeared uncertain. Mary Stuart's execution in 1587 had made it less likely that Elizabeth's death would trigger a Catholic restoration. But if the continuance of some kind of Protestant rule looked more secure than it had a few years before, the question of just what kind of Protestantism would prevail remained unsettled. The puritan godly had launched a vigorous campaign for fundamental reform in the 1587 Parliament, which had support in high places. The queen blocked their effort but she was now an aging woman. How long she would continue to live and what might happen under her as yet undetermined successor remained deeply uncertain.

The year of the Armada—and more especially the period 1587-9—therefore emerges as something of a watershed for reasons that go well beyond the obvious significance of Spain's defeat. Many of the problems central to the crisis of the mid-1580s were at least provisionally resolved, while other issues started to emerge. As several historians have claimed, the last fifteen years of Elizabeth's reign had distinctly different characteristics from those of the preceding two decades.[360] But we need to beware of exaggerating and oversimplifying this transition. If the political and religious dynamic changed in important ways, there remained considerable elements of continuity with the recent past. The next two chapters attempt to take a fresh look at the years between the Armada and Elizabeth's death. The first will focus narrowly on cultural and political changes within the English court and the second on intra-Protestant conflicts within both British kingdoms.

---

[360] See esp. *The Reign of Elizabeth: Court and Culture in the Last Decade*, ed. John Guy (Cambridge: Cambridge University Press, 1995) and the critique of its thesis by Alexandra Gajda, "Political Culture in the 1590s: The 'Second Reign of Elizabeth'," *History Compass* 8 (2010): 88-100.

7
War, Virtue, and the State
Political Culture and the Essex Circle

At the beginning of his famous *Apology*, Robert Devereux second earl of Essex described himself as a "faithful subject" and "zealous patriot."[1] Faithful subjects were ubiquitous in Elizabethan England, but Essex may have been the first Englishman to style himself a patriot. The word had previously always designated foreigners, especially Dutch fighting against Spain.[2] The earl's phrasing therefore suggested, in ways that would probably have struck some contemporaries as provocative, a dual allegiance to both queen and country, the latter conceived not as a kingdom but a *patria*, possessing liberties and interests that might not always coincide with its ruler's will. This may sound like a classic expression of monarchical republicanism, balancing loyalty to the sovereign against dedication to an English commonwealth, in ways that perhaps foreshadowed the earl's 1601 revolt. But although his detractors accused Essex of pursuing "commonwealth courses," he himself seems never to have used the word, and his own writings show minimal interest in the common law, the privy council, and the fashioning of parliamentary legislation, except to provide money for war and to secure the title of James VI as Elizabeth's successor.[3] He never described himself as an active citizen, cooperating with other citizens in deliberative processes to advance the common good. Instead he referred to his service to his "country," or less commonly to "the public," in ways suggesting that he regarded both as relatively

---

[1] *An Apologie of the Earl of Essex* (London, 2nd ed., 1603), sig. Ai. The difficult question of how far members of the earl's entourage, rather than the earl himself, contributed to the tract's composition will not be discussed here; in any case it was intended to present his viewpoint. For a discussion of the early manuscript circulation and unauthorized publication of the first edition of the *Apologie* see Hugh Gazzard, "'Idle Papers': *An Apology of the Earl of Essex*," in *Essex: The Cultural Impact of an Elizabethan Courtier*, ed. Annaliese Connolly and Lisa Hopkins (Manchester: Manchester University Press, 2013), 179–200. The construction of a "textual voice" for Essex by members of his entourage is discussed by Andrew Gordon, "Essex's Last Campaign: The Fall of the Earl of Essex and Manuscript Circulation," in the same volume, 153–67.

[2] The 1601 printed edition of the *Apologie* is the first to use the word among the books entered in EEBO TCP. In a letter to Hubert Languet in 1574 Sir Philip Sidney commented, "I would rather be charged with lack of wisdom than of patriotism," but since he made this remark in the context of a discussion of Dutch affairs it is not entirely clear whether his patriotism meant loyalty to England or partisan attachment to the Dutch cause. See *The Correspondence of Philip Sidney and Hubert Languet*, ed. Steuart Pears (London, 1845), 67.

[3] See, for example, Alexandra Gajda, *The Earl of Essex and Late Elizabethan Political Culture* (Oxford: Oxford University Press, 2013), 52, 164. My thanks to Alex Gajda for calling these accusations to my attention.

passive entities needing the help of men like himself. Alternatively, when he did want to stress the need for collective effort, he referred to the "state,"[4] a term he employed with considerable frequency, including fifty-three times in the *Apology*'s forty-eight printed quarto pages.[5]

This vocabulary merits closer scrutiny. What did Essex and his circle mean by the state, and how did they connect this concept to their views on war and peace, public duty and patriotism, the royal court and its politics, and service to the queen? Although historians used to dismiss Essex as a feckless lightweight elevated beyond his abilities by Elizabeth's favor, this view has shifted in the last twenty years, thanks especially to the scholarship of Paul Hammer and Alexandra Gajda.[6] They have made a persuasive case for regarding Essex as not only an important political figure but a significant patron of innovative thought. This chapter attempts to build on their analyses in two ways: first by teasing out connections between the earl's view of his own political role and his concept of an English state, and second by comparing his outlook to that of earlier Elizabethans who shared his strong interests in European war and politics. In this way I also hope to place the 1590s in a fresh perspective. Most recent scholarship has treated this decade in relative isolation, stressing the ways in which its politics and political culture differed from those of the central Elizabethan period. I want to refine and qualify this view by identifying elements of continuity as well as change, and showing how

---

[4] Ibid., 166.

[5] My count, using the edition cited in note 1, which includes both singular and plural uses as well as a handful of cognate terms like statesman and estate. The figure of 48 pages comes from this edition; a previous edition had run to 37 pages plus prefatory material.

[6] Paul Hammer, *The Polarisation of Elizabethan Politics: The Political Career of Robert Devereux, 2nd Earl of Essex, 1585–1597* (Cambridge: Cambridge University Press, 1997); "Base Rogues and Gentlemen of Quality: The Earl of Essex's Irish Knights and Royal Displeasure in 1599," in *Elizabeth I and Ireland*, ed. Brendan Kane and Valerie McGowan-Doyle (Cambridge: Cambridge University Press, 2014), 184–208; "The Earl of Essex and English Expeditionary Forces," in *The Oxford Handbook of John Donne*, ed. Jeanne Shami, Dennis Flynn, and Thomas M. Hester (Oxford: Oxford University Press, 2011), 435–46; "Shakespeare's *Richard II*: The Play of 7 February 1601, and the Essex Rising," *Shakespeare Quarterly* 59.1 (2008): 1–35; "How to Become an Elizabethan Statesman: Lord Henry Howard, the Earl of Essex and the Politics of Friendship," *English Manuscript Studies* 13 (2007): 1–34; "The Smiling Crocodile: The Earl of Essex and late-Elizabethan Popularity," in *The Politics of the Public Sphere in Late Elizabethan England*, ed. Peter Lake and Steven Pincus (Manchester: Manchester University Press, 2007), 95–115; "Upstaging the Queen: The Earl of Essex, Francis Bacon and the Accession Day Celebrations of 1596," in *The Politics of the Stuart Court Masque*, ed. David Bevington and Peter Holbrook (Cambridge: Cambridge University Press, 1998), 41–66; "Myth-Making: Politics, Propaganda and the Capture of Cadiz in 1596," *Historical Journal* 40 (1997): 621–42; "New Light on the Cadiz Expedition of 1596," *Historical Research* 70 (1997): 182–202; "Essex and Europe: Evidence from Confidential Instructions by the Earl of Essex, 1595–6," *English Historical Review* 111 (1996): 357–81; "Patronage at Court, Faction and the Earl of Essex," in *The Reign of Elizabeth: Court and Culture in the Last Decade*, ed. John Guy (Cambridge: Cambridge University Press, 1995), 65–86; "The Uses of Scholarship: The Secretariat of Robert Devereux, Second Earl of Essex, c. 1585–1601," *English Historical Review* 109 (1994): 26–51; Gajda, *Essex and Political Culture*; "The Earl of Essex and Politic History," in *Essex: The Cultural Impact*, ed. Connolly and Hopkins, 237–59; "Political Culture in the 1590s: The 'Second Reign of Elizabeth'," *History Compass* 8 (2010): 88–100; "Debating War and Peace in Late Elizabethan England," *Historical Journal* 52.4 (2009): 851–78; "The State of Christendom: History, Political Thought and the Essex Circle," *Historical Research* 81 (2008): 423–46.

older ideas, values, and patterns of political competition were not so much supplanted as reshaped and reconfigured toward the close of the reign.

Public Service, the Meanings of Virtue, and Applied Knowledge

Gajda has commented on the importance in the period of "schema that defined political causation in terms of the morality of political actors, the virtues and vices of rulers and elites," while both she and Hammer have stressed Essex's obsessive determination to display his own virtue.[7] This was not, in itself, unusual. Norman Jones has demonstrated the importance of concepts of virtue to Burghley's political outlook.[8] Sir Philip Sidney offers an even closer parallel, not least because, unlike Burghley but like Essex, he especially wanted to display virtue in ways involving personal risk, such as European warfare and long ocean voyages.[9] Sidney's penchant for risk-taking earned a rebuke from his Huguenot friend and correspondent, Hubert Languet, who urged him to concentrate on statesmanship rather than rash acts courage. "That is the misfortune, or rather the stupidity of our age: that most of those born in high places believe it is more glorious to usurp the job of a soldier than of a leader, and prefer to become famous more through boldness than through intelligence. And so among our nations you hardly can find a mature and experienced leader, which is due to our rashness. Only the Spaniards do not suffer from this kind of stupidity, which is why they have leaders highly experienced in warfare."[10] Languet warned prophetically that Sidney's attraction to danger might one day deprive his country of his talents. A few years later Sir Christopher Hatton admonished Essex in similar terms, shortly after the earl's younger brother, Walter Devereux, died fighting in Normandy. "My good lord, let me be bold to warn of a matter your friends here greatly fear, namely that the late accident of your noble brother, who hath lately spent his life in his prince's and country's service, draw you not through grief or passion to hazard yourself over venturously."[11]

Contemporaries would have perceived the conflict between venturous boldness and prudent restraint partly as a function of age, rashness being a special quality of young men. But it also corresponded to different forms of public service and, to a degree, ideas of social rank. Essex and Sidney belonged to a cohort of Elizabethan peers and gentry who regarded war as the natural vocation of gentlemen and

---

[7] Hammer, *Polarisation of Politics*, 19–20; Gajda, *Essex and Political Culture*, 178, 227, and 239.
[8] Norman Jones, *Governing by Virtue: Lord Burghley and the Management of Elizabethan England* (Oxford: Oxford University Press, 2015).
[9] Cf. Blair Worden, *The Sound of Virtue: Philip Sidney's* Arcadia *and Elizabethan Politics* (New Haven: Yale University Press, 1997).
[10] *The Correspondence of Sir Philip Sidney*, ed. Roger Kuin, 2 vols (Oxford: Oxford University Press, 2012), 2.813.
[11] Hatton, 494–5.

aspired to lead armies, while playing roles not just in English but also in European affairs. These preoccupations differed from that of a man like Burghley, who managed the queen's finances and helped the council oversee county magistrates, although the contrast should not be overstated. Burghley, who had briefly served on a campaign against the Scots in his youth, recognized England's need for swordsmen, while Essex knew that armies required funding and logistical support. Their main preoccupations were therefore essentially complementary. Nevertheless, they served the queen and the public in different ways that required different virtues and aptitudes. Unlike Burghley or Henry VIII's great minister, Thomas Cromwell, neither Essex nor Sidney showed much interest in the drafting of statutes, detailed financial administration, or "commonwealth" reforms to address problems like poor relief or the regulation of economic activities.[12] Their main concerns lay elsewhere, in military science, diplomacy, and the projection of English power beyond the kingdom's borders, on the European Continent or in Ireland and the Atlantic.

This orientation affected not only the specific meanings they attached to the concept of virtue but also their approach to learning and intellectual pursuits. Virtually all members of the Elizabethan elite received a youthful humanist education in rhetoric, classical languages, and literature that emphasized the importance of applying learning to practical tasks. But in adulthood more specific individual interests tended to inflect this generic training, in ways that gave rise to specialized kinds of expertise. Essex's intellectual formation reflected the fusion of chivalric ideals of adventure and courage with humanist learning and Protestantism explored in Chapter 4, exhibited in Elizabethan military treatises and by the careers of men like Sidney, Sir Humphrey Gilbert, and the earl's own father, who died of a fever contracted while attempting to plant a military colony in Ulster. In this he also followed in the footsteps of his stepfather, Leicester, whose position as the court's chief military leader and patron he attempted to fill.

Within this cohort of Elizabethan swordsmen and adventurers, Essex showed less interest in oceanic exploration and colonial projects than Gilbert, Ralegh, and his own father. His main preoccupations were warfare, especially on land, and the gathering and analysis of European intelligence.[13] This contrast reflects a shift in emphasis brought about by England's deeper engagement in continental warfare and politics after 1585. Although Essex himself never undertook a grand tour of Europe under the supervision of a humanist tutor, several members of his entourage, notably Robert Sidney and Sir Henry Neville, had done so in the 1580s, and in the winter of 1595–6 he probably wrote or helped to write several

---

[12] Although here again others associated Essex with care for the poor and promotion of their welfare. See Gajda, *Essex and Political Culture*, 167–8.
[13] For examples of Essex's direct interest in the process of gathering intelligence see *Memoirs of the Reign of Queen Elizabeth from the Year 1581 till her Death*, ed. Thomas Birch, 2 vols (London, 1754), 2.429 and 444.

letters advising the earl of Rutland about his planned European travels.[14] These letters stressed the need to compare the features of different polities through direct observation. Essex retained the services of Anthony Bacon, who had spent thirteen years on the Continent as one of Walsingham's agents, to construct an intelligence network for him.[15] Bacon and probably others in Essex's entourage produced a lengthy strategic discussion of European politics, entitled *The State of Christendom*.[16]

In addition to gathering and analyzing detailed information about other European countries, Essex and his circle stressed the importance of insights gained through reading ancient texts, particularly works by historians like Livy and Tacitus, for an understanding of political causation. Although already foreshadowed in early sixteenth-century humanist culture, this method became especially favored as part of the training of young men for careers of service to the crown from around the mid-1570s. In that period Sir Henry Sidney retained the services of the Oxford scholar Gabriel Harvey to guide his sons, Philip and Robert, through a reading of Livy intended to illuminate issues relating to Ireland.[17] Languet advised Philip Sidney to read Cicero's letters, not only "for the beauty of the style" but the way in which they revealed "the causes which overthrew the Roman Republic."[18] Philip told his brother Robert that the principal points to note in studying history, in addition to "the examples of virtue or vice, with their good and evil successes," were "the establishment or ruins of great estates with their causes."[19] Robert's grand tour and that of his friend, Neville, was overseen by the future translator of Tacitus, Sir Henry Savile. It is not entirely clear how far Essex's own education, which took place initially at Cambridge and later under the supervision of his guardian, Lord Burghley, gave comparable weight to the critical application of historical knowledge.[20] But the earl would later surround himself by men who had undergone such training, and at some point early in his career as a court favorite he developed a particularly strong interest in Tacitus.[21]

On the European Continent, historically informed analysis of political causation was increasingly discussed under the rubrics of political prudence or reason

---

[14] The authorship is disputed among modern scholars but the letters were linked by contemporaries to Essex. See Paul Hammer, "Letters of Travel Advice from the Earl of Essex to the Earl of Rutland, Some Comments," *Philological Quarterly* 74 (1995): 317–25 and Brian Vickers, "The Authenticity of Bacon's Earliest Writings," *Philological Quarterly* 94 (1997): 248–96. No one disputes that, at the very least, the letters came from Essex's immediate circle.

[15] Chris Laoutaris, "'Toucht with Bolt of Treason': The Earl of Essex and Lady Penelope Rich," in *Essex: The Cultural Impact*, ed. Connolly and Hopkins, 201–36 at 210.

[16] Gajda, "State of Christendom."

[17] Anthony Grafton and Lisa Jardine, "Studied for Action: How Gabriel Harvey Read his Livy," *Past and Present* 129 (1990): 30–78.

[18] *Sidney-Languet Correspondence*, ed. Pears, 22.

[19] *Correspondence of Sir Philip Sidney*, ed. Kuin, 1007.

[20] The best brief account of his early careers is Hammer, *Polarisation of Politics*, Part I.

[21] Gajda, *Essex and Political Culture*, chapter 6 and below, p. 369, pp. 370–1, and p. 374.

of state. Although England lagged in producing a theoretical literature on these concepts, we have seen that the word state began to appear with some frequency in practical discussions of politics from at least the 1570s, especially with reference to Ireland, Scotland, and European societies like the Netherlands. This suggests that, at least in England, a concept of the state initially developed primarily among working politicians rather than scholars, especially in the context of discussions of unsettled political conditions in neighboring countries. But it must have been clear that reading and analysis of classical texts and modern histories might illuminate the operation of states, and in the comments just quoted about the utility of writers like Cicero, Livy, and Tacitus we can see this starting to happen. By the 1590s more systematic published treatises prominently employing the term state started to appear. *The State of Christendom*, probably written in 1594,[22] Richard Becon's *Solon His Folly*, also of 1594, and Edmund Spenser's *A View of the Present State of Ireland*, written in 1596, possibly for Essex, are conspicuous examples.[23] In 1586 Essex watched his stepfather's efforts to rebuild "the state" in the United Provinces from close quarters, and a few years later in England he associated with men who had both a practical and a more academic interest in the study and analysis of states. His own fondness for the word must derive from this background.

Essex's early close association with Leicester and his expedition to the Netherlands also shaped his outlook and career trajectory in other ways. While serving as the commander of his stepfather's cavalry he developed a deep comradery and admiration for Sir Philip Sidney, a somewhat older colleague who seemed to embody the virtues he most valued. After Sidney's death, Essex inherited his sword and married his widow, Walsingham's daughter Frances, thereby renewing the dynastic pact between Leicester and the secretary. Essex also inherited the role Sidney had previously occupied, as the young man groomed to become Leicester's political heir. Had Sidney survived he would almost certainly have acted as partner and mentor to the young earl, as both sought to advance themselves at court under Leicester's auspices. Sidney's premature death,

---

[22] Henry Wotton [attributed], *The State of Christendom or, A most exact and curious discovery of many secret passages and hidden mysteries of the times* (London, 1657), 132. The fullest discussion of this tract, which suggests that it may have been written by Anthony Bacon, is Gajda, "State of Christendom." For its date see 106, referring to an event of 1569 as "some twenty-four years ago," 248, saying that Henry IV "is become a Catholic but remains excommunicate," a situation that obtained between July 1593 and September 17, 1595; 144, referring to the alleged plot of Robert Lopez to poison Elizabeth, first exposed in February 1594, and 257, where the Archduke Ernestus, who died in February 1595, is described as still alive. A date between February and March 25, 1594 (still 1593 for Elizabethans, who began the new year on the latter date) would be consistent with all these references, although the possibility cannot be ruled out that the work was completed slightly later with references in the text dating from an earlier stage of writing left unrevised. Gajda's article dates the work from 1594–5 (424) and discusses the possible connection to Bacon on 425–6.

[23] For Essex's relation to Spenser's tract see Chris Butler and Willy Maley, "'Bringing Rebellion Broached on his Sword': Essex and Ireland," in *Essex: The Cultural Impact*, ed. Connolly and Hopkins, 133–52.

followed within less than eighteen months by Leicester's own demise, meant that Essex instead found himself obliged to fill the void left by his stepfather's disappearance sooner than anyone had anticipated. Walsingham's death in 1590 removed another mentor. Although Burghley and Hatton continued to provide Essex with guidance, he was not the main protégé of either man. Instead he soon came to rely on the advice of men of his own generation, along with a few older hands who were essentially outsiders to the Elizabethan court, notably Lord Henry Howard and the Spaniard Antonio Perez.

The Court and Its Politics

Men like Essex, whose primary interests lay in European war and politics, normally paid relatively little attention to institutions of domestic governance. But the royal court was a conspicuous exception. In a personal monarchy, even service beyond the realm required the queen's support and approval. Professional soldiers like Sir John Norreys, Atlantic adventurers like Gilbert, and Irish servitors like Sir Henry Sidney went to considerable lengths to cultivate their connections to the court, while Sir Francis Drake, who was not a gentleman by birth, found himself drawn into the court's orbit after his spectacularly successful voyage around the world. Since he aspired to play a major role in shaping crown policies, Essex had to cultivate an especially close relationship with the queen, as his stepfather had done before him. That required mastering not only the arts of war and methods of intelligence gathering but also the courtly skills needed to excel in tournaments and charm the queen through conversation and gestures of devotion, such as love poems addressed to her. He also had to cultivate good relations with other courtiers of both sexes who might advance his interests.

Although fundamentally important, relations between the queen and courtiers belonging to her inner circle were not always happy. Her penchant for procrastination and indecision, notorious aversion to spending money, and eruptions of anger even toward intimate confidants caused significant frustration and pain within her inner circle. Although the composition of her council looks remarkably stable in retrospect, several of its leading members suffered spells of insecurity. Elizabeth imprisoned both Ralegh and Leicester for displeasing her and banished even Burghley from her presence after Mary Stuart's execution, berating him as "a traitor, false dissembler and wicked wretch" as she did so.[24] Maintaining her favor became especially difficult when a courtier had to leave her side for a prolonged period, since absence made it impossible to monitor the queen's moods and intervene quickly if something displeased her. Courtiers appointed

[24] TNA SP12/202/1.

to command armies sent to Europe or Ireland were especially vulnerable because their assignments required them to spend substantial sums of money and take initiatives without receiving the queen's prior approval. Since Elizabeth hated loosening her purse strings and resented any loss of control over the execution of her policies, she tended to react sharply whenever her generals failed to achieve quick results at minimal costs, or made independent decisions in the field.

Elizabeth's subordinates regularly responded with injured protests about her ingratitude for their best efforts. "Her Majesty I see will make trial of me, how I love her and what will discourage me from her silence," Leicester wrote during his Dutch campaign, "but resolved I am that no worldly respect shall draw me back from my faithful discharge of my duty toward her, though she shall show to hate me, as it goeth very near."[25] "Three times her Majesty hath sent me her deputy into Ireland," Sir Henry Sidney complained, "and in every of the three times I sustained a great and a violent rebellion, every one of which I subdued and (with honorable peace) left the country in quiet. I returned from each of those three deputations three thousand pounds worse than I went."[26] Walsingham lamented to Hatton the queen's churlish treatment of loyal servants: "Surely, Sir, it standeth not with her Majesty's safety to deal so unkindly with those that serve her faithfully. There is a difference between serving with a cheerful and a languishing mind."[27] Essex's father, the first earl, had special cause for bitterness, since the withdrawal of Elizabeth's support for his Ulster project after he had mortgaged his lands to pay for it left him deeply encumbered by debt. As Hammer points out, Essex had little choice but to pursue a career at court because Elizabeth's favor and largesse offered the only means of salvaging his estate from a disaster for which she was arguably to blame. While still a young man he must have heard multiple tales of the queen's penurious and ungrateful treatment of loyal servants from his stepfather, captains in the Netherlands, and members of his own family. Some of this resentment probably spilled over into criticism of leading members of her council like Burghley, who was accused by some contemporaries of trying to consolidate his own dominance by holding back virtuous and independent men.[28] Essex must have known about the serious rift, inspiring bitter recriminations, that developed between Burghley and Leicester in the winter of 1587.[29]

---

[25] TNA SP84/5/96.
[26] *A Viceroy's Vindication: Sir Henry Sidney's Memoir of Service in Ireland, 1556–1578*, ed. Ciaran Brady (Cork: Cork University Press, 2002), 44.
[27] Hatton, 76.
[28] For example by Edmund Spenser in *The Ruins of Time*, ll. 449–53:

> O grief of griefs. O gall to all good hearts,
> To see that virtue should despised be
> Of him that first was raised for virtuous parts,
> And now broad spreading like an aged tree,
> Lets none shoot up that nigh him planted be

[29] TNA SP12/198/19 is a bitter letter of complaint by Leicester to Burghley, accusing him of betraying their friendship.

The earl's later, oft-quoted complaints about Elizabeth and members of her court therefore broadly conformed to a well-established pattern. His recriminations were more frequent and even more bitter than those of Leicester and other previous favorites but not fundamentally dissimilar in their expressions of frustration, hurt, and paranoia. What requires explanation is why, in Essex's case, these fairly commonplace resentments eventually produced a rupture within the court and council without parallel since at least the 1560s. Most recent accounts have attributed this outcome to the rise of factional divisions that had not existed in the mid-Elizabethan period. Although it contains some truth, this interpretation requires closer scrutiny.

Historians used to regard court faction as a characteristic feature of the entire Elizabethan period, until Simon Adams successfully challenged this view in a series of seminal essays in the 1980s.[30] His work produced a new consensus that factions had ceased to exist in Elizabethan politics between about 1570 and the late 1590s, as relations among Elizabeth's council remained collegial and cooperative.[31] Patrick Collinson reflected this view in his influential discussions of the Elizabethan monarchical republic, by describing the main conflicts within the regime as contests between the queen and a unified council, over differences relating to issues including the succession, Mary Stuart, and foreign policy.[32] Most scholars came to regard the privy council in this period as a cohesive body dominated by strong Protestants who worked harmoniously together, especially Burghley, Leicester, and Walsingham.[33]

But while Adams's core argument remains convincing, some conclusions drawn from it are more questionable. In debunking received ideas about court faction he especially targeted two more specific assumptions: the view that Leicester and Burghley headed the court's main factions, and that their rivalry gave rise to competing patronage networks. This last claim stemmed in part from efforts to read back into the late sixteenth century Sir Lewis Namier's analysis of

---

[30] Simon Adams, "Faction, Clientage and Party: English Politics, 1550–1603," *History Today* 33 (1982): 33–9; "Eliza Enthroned? The Court and its Politics," in *The Reign of Elizabeth I*, ed. Christopher Haigh (Basingstoke: Macmillan, 1984), 55–77; and, especially, "Favourites and Factions at the Elizabethan Court," in *Princes, Patronage and the Nobility: The Court at the Beginning of the Modern Age, c. 1450–1650*, ed. Ronald G. Asch and Adolf M. Birke (Oxford: Oxford University Press, 1991), 265–87. These have been conveniently gathered together and reprinted as chapters 1–3 of Simon Adams, *Leicester and the Court: Essays on Elizabethan Politics* (Manchester: Manchester University Press, 2002).

[31] A view that Adams endorsed in "The Patronage of the Crown in Elizabethan Politics: The 1590s in Perspective," in *The Reign of Elizabeth*, ed. Guy, 20–45, reprinted as chapter 4 of Adams, *Leicester and the Court*, 68–94. Gajda, "Political Culture in the 1590s" is another examination of the topic.

[32] Patrick Collinson, "De Republica Anglorum: Or, History with the Politics Put Back" and "The Monarchical Republic of Queen Elizabeth I," in *Elizabethan Essays* (London: Hambledon Press, 1994), 1–30 and 31–58; Patrick Collinson, "The Elizabethan Exclusion Crisis," *Proceedings of the British Academy* 84 (1993): 51–92.

[33] This view has, however, been challenged by Neil Younger, "How Protestant was the Elizabethan Regime?" *English Historical Review* 133 (2018): 1060–92.

factional competition in Hanoverian Britain. Adams showed that, unlike leading politicians in the age of Sir Robert Walpole, Leicester and Burghley did not maintain opposing networks of clients but instead usually backed the same men. A Namierite description of factional politics therefore would not work for the mid-Elizabethan period. We can readily accept this finding, along with Adams's further argument that privy councilors generally worked together to conduct the queen's business, without concluding that their relationships were therefore entirely devoid of tension and disagreement. This becomes especially true if we broaden the focus beyond Leicester and Burghley to include people like the earl of Sussex and Sir Christopher Hatton—who according to Cathryn Enis did support a rival patronage network to Leicester's in Warwickshire[34]—along with members of the court who did not belong to the privy council but did enjoy regular access to the queen, like ladies of the privy chamber and their relatives. Patchy documentation makes it difficult to assess the precise views and influence of most of these people.[35] But we cannot assume that unrecorded conversations in the privacy of Elizabeth's privy apartments had no impact on the queen's decisions, or that an outward appearance of harmony among leading members of the council did not sometimes mask hidden tensions.

In some circumstances the very absence of organized factions espousing clear party lines probably increased the anxiety of major courtiers worried about losing royal favor, by making the attitudes of their colleagues less predictable. Leicester's predicament in 1586–7 illustrates the point. Although he had the initial support of Burghley, Walsingham, and apparently Hatton for his expedition to the Netherlands, we have seen that from the beginning other courtiers tried to persuade Elizabeth to abandon the whole project. Leicester tried to pressure Whitgift into declaring his support, evidently with limited success, while the queen's ambassador to France, Edward Stafford, was another skeptic. In a letter to Burleigh, whom he evidently regarded as receptive to his views, Stafford accused Leicester and Walsingham of trying to manipulate Elizabeth by filtering the information she received about Dutch affairs.[36] Stafford had a back-channel to the queen through his mother, Dorothy, Elizabeth's mistress of the robes and one of her most intimate servants, who may well have expressed similar accusations in the privacy of the privy chamber. Although Hatton supported intervention for strategic reasons, he did not see the contest in the Low Countries in the way Leicester and Walsingham did, as a religious crusade. Given his intense dislike of

---

[34] Cathryn Enis, "The Dudleys, Sir Christopher Hatton and the Justices of Elizabethan Warwickshire," *Midland History* 39 (2004): 1–35. See also Glyn Parry, "Catholicism and Tyranny in Shakespeare's Warwickshire," in *The Oxford Handbook of the Age of Shakespeare*, ed. R. Malcolm Smuts (Oxford: Oxford University Press, 2016), 121–38. The importance of Hatton and Sussex is also stressed by Younger, "How Protestant was the Elizabethan Regime?"
[35] For a discussion see Younger, "How Protestant was the Elizabethan Regime?"
[36] TNA SP78/16/72.

puritanism, he must have disapproved of Leicester's patronage of men like Thomas Cartwright, and his alliance with strong Dutch Calvinists. By early 1587 at the latest even Burghley had begun to worry about the expense of the Dutch campaign and the risk that it would draw England into a full-scale war with Spain. In late February Leicester told the Dutch representatives in London that he and he and Burghley had exchanged "great and very heavy words" of disagreement over policy towards the Netherlands in a meeting of the privy council in the queen's presence.[37]

The range of opinions that existed within the court meant that Elizabeth was never entirely isolated even in periods when her principal councilors closed ranks in support of a policy she disliked, as in the fracas over Leicester's governor generalship during the spring and summer of 1586. This diversity not only made it more difficult for those councilors to pressure her into changing her mind; it also created conditions in which rumors of hidden intrigues and impending changes within the court more easily arose. The rumors did not have to be true to cause anxiety and jealousy. Firm evidence exists of reports that Burghley and the queen had turned against Leicester and planned to ruin him, which circulated during his absence in the Netherlands. A couple of Mary Stuart's supporters, as well as Parma and his agents seem to have believed them.[38] Leicester learned of these rumors and was evidently encouraged by some associates to take them seriously. "There hath been many that have sought to do evil offices between my Lord Treasurer [Burghley] and me, and my Lord Chancellor [Hatton] and me," he commented in April 1587: "but for my own part I will esteem them as they are, for they are bad people."[39]

We have seen that Leicester believed that Catholics within the court sought to destroy him; that his relations even with close allies like Davison at times grew tetchy; and that he came to believe that his junior colleague on the council, Lord Buckhurst, and more marginal figures like Wilkes and Norreys had betrayed him. In a number of respects his behavior during and immediately after his Dutch campaign strikingly anticipates that of his stepson, Essex, following his appointment as lord deputy of Ireland some eleven years later. Both favorites complained bitterly that they and the soldiers under their command had not received adequate support from London and blamed both the queen and their colleagues on the

---

[37] Bor, *Orsprong*, pt 2, 929: Leicester told the envoys "datter in de laste vergaderinge des Raeds selfs in presentie van haare Majesteit tusschen hem en den Tresorier groote en zeer heftig woorden waren geweest, voornementelik belangende de rekeninge van ontfang en uptgifte...." The letter of recrimination from Leicester to Burghley cited in note 29 indicates that the rift derived in large measure from the earl's perception that Burghley had fed, rather than trying to restrain, Elizabeth's resentment of the cost of his campaign, while encouraging her to lend an ear to accusations by his Dutch adversaries that he had misappropriated money.
[38] *CSPSc* 8.248 and 266, Monsieur de l'Aubespine and Thomas Morgan to Mary, March 16 and 21, 1586.
[39] HMC Salisbury, 3.251.

council for this neglect. Both saw themselves as targets of a whispering campaign within the court. Leicester worried that Burghley would sabotage his efforts, just as Essex came to believe that Robert Cecil had become his secret enemy.[40] Each favorite tried to recover his position by deserting his foreign post in order to return to Elizabeth's side and renew his personal bond with her. They then launched similar counter-attacks on their perceived adversaries by targeting relatively secondary figures: Buckhurst, Wilkes, and Norreys in the one case, and Lord Cobham and Sir Walter Ralegh in the other. They sought proof that the queen and council still trusted them by demanding the sacrifice of men they insisted on treating as adversaries, despite the protests of the intended victims and efforts by other courtiers to bring about a restoration of better relations. Because this confrontational behavior caused unavoidable rifts within the court's inner circle, it carried serious risks, for Leicester no less than Essex. Walsingham reported in January 1588 that Leicester's friends were trying to persuade him that his relentless attacks on Buckhurst would ultimately cost him the queen's favor.[41]

The parallels between the two situations are striking enough to suggest that Essex may have consciously followed his stepfather's example. But the effects of Leicester's vendetta remained contained, inflicting little lasting damage on the council's cohesion and even failing, in the long run, to derail Buckhurst's career, whereas Essex's attack on Cobham and Raleigh escalated into a deeper factional conflict that culminated in his 1601 rebellion. Several things explain the different outcomes. By the late 1580s Leicester, Burghley, and the queen had worked together for more than twenty years, establishing resilient relationships that had already weathered several periods of strain, whereas in 1599 Essex and Robert Cecil were both still young men, with only a few years' experience at the center of government. Leicester obtained the queen's prior approval before returning to London, whereas Essex returned from Ireland without her authorization or knowledge, surprising her by bursting unannounced into her presence. His brazen conduct severely strained his bond with Elizabeth, which was never as deep to begin with as Leicester's, leading to his imprisonment and trial in Star Chamber.

But it may also be significant that in the late 1580s events conspired to defuse issues that might otherwise have accentuated emerging disagreements within the court and council, whereas this did not happen a decade later. Leicester's abandonment of his ambitions in the Netherlands in late 1587 made any reservations his colleagues felt about his role there less salient. The Armada then

---

[40] Burghley wrote to Leicester about "many tales brought to me" of the latter's "misliking" of his "doubtfulness or coldness" in supporting the expedition to the Low Countries. Both men seem eventually to have agreed to blame the friction on malicious third parties who sought to sow dissension between them. See John Strype, *Annals of the Reformation* (London, 1728), 3.347 and HMC Salisbury, 3.251.

[41] TNA SP12/208/1.

scuppered efforts by councilors like Croft to negotiate an agreement with Spain. Disagreements between fervent supporters of international Protestant causes and pragmatic, Catholic and Crypto-Catholic politicians who wanted to stay out of Europe's religious wars lost much of their edge. The urgent need to defend the realm against a threatened invasion instead drove the council—and the political nation beyond the court—to close ranks. Barely a month later, Leicester's unexpected death removed him and his grudges from the scene. We can only speculate about what might have happened under other circumstances: for example, if Philip had held off on his invasion of England while trying to exploit rifts between the English and the Dutch and within the English court through Parma's negotiations, or if Elizabeth, rather than Leicester, had died in September 1588. It seems hard to believe that leading members of the council had not discussed among themselves how to settle the succession, but no firm evidence survives of whether they had reached consensus. Even if they had privately agreed to unite in support of James VI or some other claimant, disagreements over foreign policy and the Church at the start of a new reign would probably have caused serious friction, between Leicester and Walsingham on one side and Whitgift, Hatton, and figures like Croft on the other.[42] Elizabeth's longevity, the outbreak of open war with Spain, and Leicester's death prevented this from happening.

By contrast, events in the late 1590s magnified latent disagreements between Essex and other leading members of the council rather than assuaging them. The peace negotiations occasioned by Henry IV's decision to withdraw from the war with Spain reopened issues that had lain dormant since 1588. Essex regarded negotiations as a trap that threatened to lead to English abandonment of the Dutch and a resultant collapse of the United Provinces.[43] As Gajda has persuasively argued, he also gave credence to rumors that the Cecils were plotting to divert the succession to Philip II's daughter, the Archduchess Isabella. Essex was wrong about this, as well as about the Cecils' true attitude toward peace with Spain, which differed less from his own views than he realized.[44] But his beliefs concerning their intentions reinforced grievances rooted in more personal frustrations. The relationship he had cultivated with James VI, who shared his paranoid suspicions of the Cecils' intentions, simultaneously gave his rivals on the council reason to fear that he might soon be in a position to take revenge against them. The contrast between the council's apparent cohesion in the late 1580s and its bitter division a decade later owed more than a little to contingent circumstances that muted divisions in the earlier period, while exacerbating them in the later one.

---

[42] It should be remembered that Whitgift, Hatton, and Hatton's chaplain, Richard Bancroft, launched a vigorous attack on puritanism immediately after the Armada's defeat. It is hard to imagine that campaign proceeding without vigorous opposition at the start of a new reign, especially if Leicester had remained alive.
[43] Gajda, "Debating War and Peace." [44] Gajda, *Essex and Political Culture*, 100–7.

The Diminished Role of Religion and the Virtue of Noble Races

Another disparity between the two periods involved the issues at stake in disagreements within the court and council. Leicester interpreted opposition to his conduct in the Netherlands in religious terms, accusing his detractors of Catholicism or insufficient zeal for the faith. While this was unfair to Wilkes and Norreys, who were both firm Protestants, Leicester's sympathy for puritans and firm commitment to godly causes did set him apart from councilors like Hatton, Croft, Whitgift, and probably Buckhurst, as well as the queen herself. Although possibly exaggerated, his fear that secret Catholics and tepid Protestants wanted to sabotage his support for the Dutch was never irrational. Essex placed less emphasis on confessional differences, defining his conflicts with his adversaries instead as a contest pitting virtue against envy and detraction.

This diminished emphasis on godly religion initially appears surprising since, as Hammer and others have stressed, Essex carried on the work of Leicester and Walsingham in championing war against Spain. He inherited Leicester's military following and aspired to his stepfather's role as the court's leading expert on military affairs and advocate of intervention in European wars. In the seventeenth century he enjoyed a posthumous reputation as an exemplary Protestant hero, alongside Sir Philip Sidney and James I's warlike son, Prince Henry. His heir, the third earl, who would command Parliament's army at the start of the Civil War, and the sons of his sister Penelope, Robert and Henry Rich earls of Warwick and Holland, carried on the family tradition, engaging in military service against Spain and supporting the revolt against Charles I in 1641. But the second earl redefined the anti-Spanish cause in ways that downplayed its confessional dimensions.[45] Although he continued to see his own role in providentialist terms—"I know God hath a great work to work by me; I thank God I see my way smooth and certain"[46]—he took little interest in the wave of apocalyptic speculation that developed after the defeat of the Armada. Unlike Leicester he did not assume that all Catholics supported Spain or that convinced Calvinists provided the indispensable core of resistance to Spanish aggression.[47] He saw the key issue not as Catholic belief but Habsburg and papal tyranny: "The Spanish are champions of the Church of Rome vowing to compel all to worship the beast...We impeach his usurpation...for the defense of liberty of all Christendom."[48]

Essex had no compunctions about treating Henry IV as an ally after his conversion to Rome, because Henry extended toleration to Huguenots and continued to fight Spain. Like several others in his circle, but unlike Leicester and Burghley, the earl disapproved of attempts to force consciences even by Protestants. *The State of Christendom* asserted unequivocally that "papists and

---

[45] As Gajda rightly comments, ibid., 23. [46] *Memoirs of Queen Elizabeth*, ed. Birch, 2.484.
[47] Gajda, *Essex and Political Culture*, 23, 67–9, 85, 109–26. [48] BL Add Mss. 74,287, fol. 158v.

Protestants may live in peace together," citing as evidence the situation in Poland and several Swiss cities where "the papists and Protestants eat together, lie in bed one with another, marry together and that which is most strange in one church you shall have a mass and a sermon, and at one table upon fish days fish and flesh."[49] Essex did not hesitate to include English Catholics like Anthony Standen, or foreign Catholics like the former Spanish secretary of State, Antonio Perez, among his followers.[50] He protected and patronized both puritans and the former Jesuit, Thomas Wright, and enjoyed consistently friendly relations with Whitgift, showing his willingness to befriend people who differed widely in their personal beliefs.[51] Although Perez teased him about his Protestant piety, Essex at times proved surprisingly receptive to Catholic devotional practices, in ways that anticipate later Laudian attitudes.[52] He wrote a poem of prayer to the Virgin Mary:

> Ah thou fair Queen of mercy and pity
> Whose womb did once the world's Creator carry
> Be thou attentive to my painful ditty,
> Further my suits dear gracious Blessed Mary
>   If thou begin the Choir of holy saints
>   Will all be helping to refer my plaints.[53]

He sympathized with Perez's expressed desire to retreat into a monastery after the death of his wife: "Happy you in your ecclesiastical character who, while you see courtiers, soldiers and all of us secular men involved in misery, have retired to a sanctuary, where neither fortune nor death itself can reach you...St Antonio pray for us."[54] Sidney, who disdained monasticism and retirement, would presumably have been appalled.

This diminished emphasis on confessional allegiances led to a correspondingly greater stress on virtue. Although virtue and godliness had always been closely linked ideals, the confessional polarization of the mid-1580s and the circumstances surrounding English intervention in the wars of the Low Countries put a premium on religious commitment.[55] In Essex's circle in the 1590s the pendulum began to swing back in the opposite direction. The earl and his circle not only talked continually about the role of virtue in politics; they also gave additional layers of meaning to the concept. They explicitly regarded virtue as a special characteristic of noble lineages or "races," the common term for bloodlines in

---

[49] *The State of Christendom*, 132.
[50] Gajda, *Essex and Political Culture*, 103–25; Hammer, *Polarisation of Politics*, 174–5; Gustav Ungerer, *A Spaniard in Elizabethan England: The Correspondence of Antonio Perez's Exile*, 2 vols (London: Tamesis, 1974).
[51] Gajda, *Essex and Political Culture*, 120–2, 127–40. [52] Hammer, *Polarisation of Politics*, 79.
[53] Steven May, *Elizabethan Courtier Poets: The Poems and their Contexts* (Columbia: University of Missouri Press, 1991), 255.
[54] *Memoirs of Queen Elizabeth*, ed. Birch, 2.368. [55] Below, p. 390.

the period.⁵⁶ Although Gajda is right in saying that a "vocabulary of virtue and corruption ... sprang more naturally to Essex's mouth and pen than the language of ancient lineage,"⁵⁷ he nevertheless saw an intrinsic connection between the two. That linkage first appeared very early in his career, in the funeral sermon preached by Richard Davies for his father in 1577, which was distributed among the family's "well willers and special friends" in the young earl's name.⁵⁸ Davies assured Essex that his father's "virtues, as temperance, courtesy, affability, liberality and constancy be peculiar to your house, descending by nature and grafted as it were in your principles, so that to degenerate into the loathsome contraries of these ... shall be harder for you and more impossible for the contrariety of your nature."⁵⁹ The claim that men of noble birth had an innate propensity to virtue, especially in public service and war, reflected a widespread European belief that gave rise to a substantial body of theoretical literature on the Continent, with which Essex and his circle were probably familiar.⁶⁰ Several members of his circle, including Fulke Greville and Lord Henry Howard, embraced the fundamental premise of this literature that nobles differed from commoners in much the way that superior breeds of dogs and horses differed from mongrels and plough animals.⁶¹ In their view the preeminent power and influence wielded by men of high birth derived less from social convention than natural causes and, ultimately, the will of God. "In holy histories the succession of nobility is recorded," Essex argued: "God himself chose not only a nation but also a line from which Christ should be born and therefore he liketh the calling of nobility."⁶²

These views reflected much older prejudices dating back to medieval reactions against "new men" promoted by royal favor that the history plays of Marlowe and Shakespeare represented as a major source of conflict in the reigns of kings like Edward II, Richard II, and Henry VIII.⁶³ Such views implied that the displacement of the ancient nobility from positions of leadership would lead to a loss of virtue in

---

⁵⁶ For a general discussion of such attitudes in early modern culture see Brendan Kane and R. Malcolm Smuts, "The Politics of Race in England, Scotland and Ireland," in *Age of Shakespeare*, ed. Smuts, 346–63.

⁵⁷ Gajda, *Essex and Political Culture*, 178.

⁵⁸ Folger Shakespeare Library Mss. La239, Richard Broughton to R. Bagot: "I have sent herewith to my cousin Th[omas] Newport certain pretty[?] book of the funeral sermon preached at my Lord's death as memorial by the young earl of his father's well willers and special friends. The like he hath bestowed on sundry noblemen and ladies, which are accepted as jewels of great importance."

⁵⁹ Richard Davies, *A Funeral Sermon ... at the burial of Walter Earle of Essex* (London, 1577), n.p.

⁶⁰ Arlette Jouanna, *L'idée de race en France au XVIème siècle et au début du XVIIème siècle: 1498–1614* (Paris: Champion, 1976).

⁶¹ *The Works in Verse and Prose Complete of the Right Honourable Fulke Greville, Lord Brooke*, ed. A. B. Grossart, 4 vols (Blackburn, 1870), 4.7–8: "It is ordinary among men to observe the races of horses and other breeds of cattle. But few consider that as diverse humours mixed in men's bodies make different complexions, so every family hath as it were diverse predominant qualities in it, which as they are tempered together in marriage, give a certain tincture to all the decent."

⁶² Yale University Beineke Library Mss. 370, fol. 5.

⁶³ Steven Gunn, *Henry VII's New Men and the Making of Modern England* (Oxford: Oxford University Press, 2016).

the state or body politic, through the spread of forms of corruption that came naturally to men of "base" parentage. As we saw in Chapter 1, Catholics and Protestants alike, in England as well as other countries, incorporated these assumptions in polemical attacks that identified false religion with tainted bloodlines. In England this pattern of thought had been especially characteristic of tracts like the *Treatise of Treasons* and *Leicester's Commonwealth*, produced by writers associated with Mary Stuart and old Catholic aristocratic families like the Howards.[64] As the Protestant stepson and political heir of Leicester, Essex cannot have shared the blanket condemnation of the Dudleys and other leading families of Elizabeth's court. But he did absorb the generic prejudice against upstart courtiers embedded in the Catholic polemics, and it is tempting to speculate that the influence of his supporter and advisor, Lord Henry Howard, encouraged this attitude. In a manuscript treatise written for Essex, around the time of the earl's appointment as earl marshal, the official responsible for upholding inherited honor, Lord Henry Howard claimed that by granting coats of arms to men of base descent, Elizabethan heralds had corrupted the state and society. He especially disliked the elevation of clergymen and their offspring into the ranks of the gentry. The promiscuous breeding of married clergymen, he asserted, "clogs the state with an offspring of unprofitable drones daintily and idly brought up, which having wastefully consumed and unthriftily misspent the revenues, leases and commodities" of ecclesiastical livings seek to support themselves through other kinds of venality. "Like caterpillars in a pleasant orchard, towards the latter end of summer, when all the fruits are bloated and the sun grows faint, [they] are transformed into butterflies" by the purchase of coats of arms. This not only brought "honor into more base contempt," by creating "confusion in our English policy" but encouraged the degradation of noble bloodlines through marriages to newly promoted inferiors.[65] "There is a kind of leprosy, or at least of dross and contagious corruption in base descents," which creates "a bar which neither can education alter, nor instruction...qualify."[66] The assertiveness of base families newly equipped with heraldic shields, by "encroaching on elder houses out of ambition and pride," will "breed faction in provinces, corruption in families and raise that bank on which they desire to build anarchy."[67]

Howard's references to clogging "the state," "confusion in our English policy," "breeding of faction," and promotion of "anarchy" indicate one way in which concepts of natural virtue shaded into views about the state. Although Essex would not have associated this picture of social and moral decay with the rise of Protestantism, he did share the view that many of Elizabeth's intimates, including

---

[64] Above, pp. 66–8; Peter Lake, *Bad Queen Bess? Libels, Secret Histories, and the Politics of Publicity in the Reign of Elizabeth I* (Oxford: Oxford University Press, 2016), esp. chapters 3, 5, and 6; Adams, "Favourites and Factions at the Elizabethan Court."

[65] Folger Shakespeare Library Vb5, fol. 66.   [66] Ibid., fols 23, 24.   [67] Ibid., fols 42–3.

Burghley and his son Robert Cecil, were his natural inferiors in birth as well as virtue. His rivalry with the Cecils for some time remained muted because they agreed with him about the need to lend military support to the Dutch and Henry IV. But a sense of competition for future leadership of the court, and divergences in outlook over specific issues, nevertheless injected an undertone of jealousy into the relationship. Essex felt both wounded and affronted, for example, by Cecil's almost contemptuous dismissal of the death of his younger brother in Normandy, during "an unnecessary light skirmish," involving "no great service but even mere bravery."[68] The Cecils saw warfare as a disagreeable, if sometimes necessary, activity and valued qualities like valor and courage only insofar as they achieved results. "Mere bravery" exercised without foresight counted for little or nothing in their eyes. By contrast, Essex saw valor as a noble virtue vital to the health of the body politic that the queen and state had a duty to nurture and reward. He would have agreed with Lord Burgh, who wrote to him in 1595 that a "virtuous man unexercised is like the plants in winter, whose sap is retired to the root; and being called to practice, is beautified as they be when their fruits make appearance. There is nothing that hurteth states more than security."[69] Like Burgh, Essex would have regarded an excessive desire for security and an exaggerated reliance on related qualities like prudence as qualities of "base" natures.

Assumptions about the connection between virtue and noble blood did not lead Essex to regard all men with titles as allies and all commoners as foes. He knew that sloth, luxury, and other vices might corrupt a "noble" nature and he acknowledged the need to supplement martial valor with prudence, experience, and intellectual attainments. He specifically criticized the English nobility for paying inadequate attention to learning. But his racialized concept of virtue unquestionably did reinforce his belief in his own duty to serve his country in war and his right to enjoy the queen's support in doing so.[70] He shared the belief of some French theorists, described by one historian as "positive racism," that commoners who had no natural propensity toward virtue might nevertheless act in noble ways if inspired by the leadership of their natural superiors.[71] In time of war, he argued, men of noble nature would exert themselves to defend their country, whereas "without question the common and baser sort are not capable of these noble considerations, which would incite and inflame their courages but what [when]

---

[68] *Letters from Sir Robert Cecil to Sir Christopher Hatton, 1590–1591*, ed. Paul Hammer, Camden Society Publications series 5, vol. 22 (1999), 197–267 at 252.

[69] HMC Salisbury, 5.406.

[70] As shown by a number of his remarks. For example, when asked by Sir Robert Sidney if he included the Lord Admiral Thomas Howard among the "atheists and caterpillars" he considered his enemies at court, Essex replied negatively: "I mean men of more base conditions, though in more greater favor with her majesty, who have laid secret plots and damnable devices to bereave me of my life. Judge you, good brother, whether it came with grief or no to a man descended as I am... to be shut up so long together and to have been trampled underfoot by such base upstarts." Folger Shakespeare Library Mss. V.a 164, fols 6v–7.

[71] Jouanna, *L'idée de race*, 319.

they see before their eyes" examples set by men of distinguished lineage.⁷² By setting the right example men like himself might lead commoners to sacrifice for the common good. For this reason, Essex's sense of his inborn superiority also demanded that he adopt a popular manner. Barnaby Rich recalled a few years after the earl's death: "I myself [when] a boy have seen him in the French wars to communicate in sport and sometimes in serious matters with men of mean condition and place, *their fortunes and parentage* valued; to be delighted and exercise in laboring with mattock in trenches, fosses and in other works among his battles; to be busied in setting of watches, in making of barricadoes at his quarter, and in often walking the round."⁷³ Shakespeare's *Henry V*, a play that Peter Lake has convincingly interpreted as an endorsement of Essex's belief in the need to regenerate England through foreign war,⁷⁴ depicts its hero king acting in very much the same way, circulating *incognito* among his soldiers on the eve of the Battle of Agincourt so he may learn what they are thinking, and then proclaiming that by fighting bravely common soldiers will, in effect, become gentlemen. "For he that this day sheds his blood with me / Shall be my brother, be he ne'er so vile / This day shall gentle his condition."⁷⁵

Essex and His Friends

This conviction that virtues innate to noble bloodlines were essential to the state's health dovetailed into Essex's beliefs about the importance of friendship. His concept of friendship derived from both the chivalric ideal of comradeship in arms and classical sources. The most famous Latin discourse on the subject, Cicero's *De Amicitia*, celebrated bonds between men united by admiration for each other's virtues, who join forces to serve the public and defend its liberties. Robert Sidney exemplified this ethos in telling Essex that "if you can with your care do anything for me, you shall do it for one that will bring an unremovable affection to the good of the queen's service, and a constantness in loving and honoring you. But for me hinder not the public course. I shall be exceeding glad if I see any worthy man preferred, and shall think myself thereby benefited."⁷⁶ In the early 1590s Essex gathered a cohort of friends who shared his commitment to active policies, while possessing talents and wells of personal experience capable of informing his decisions. We catch a glimpse of him conferring with friends in a letter of Anthony Standen from December 1593. "The earl yesterday after council called for his coach and put Sir Roger [Williams] and me within, and carried us to

---

⁷² BL Add Mss 74287, fol. 161.   ⁷³ *Four bookes of offices* (1606), 180.
⁷⁴ Peter Lake, *How Shakespeare Put Politics on the Stage: Power and Succession in the History Plays* (New Haven: Yale University Press, 2016), chapter 15.
⁷⁵ *Henry V*, IV.iii.61–3.   ⁷⁶ HMC Salisbury, 5.442.

Gorhambury, four miles hence, whither he went to talk with Antonio Perez, and so we accompanied him back to the court this morning. He is gone to dine at Sion with Sir Thomas Sherley."[77] Since Williams was a veteran captain, Perez an experienced Spanish statesman, and Standen and Sherley both aspiring court politicians who had traveled on the Continent, Essex would undoubtedly have discussed European politics with them as he traveled in his coach and sat down to dinner. He also recruited talented young academics, including Oxford's Regius Professor of Greek, Henry Cuffe, into his circle. Working and conferring together, Essex and his friends gathered pertinent information—the European network intelligence constructed by Anthony Bacon playing a key role—and digested it into policy prescriptions. As Neil Younger has shown, the earl also turned the recruitment of soldiers for his Cadiz expedition in 1596 into an exercise in friendship. Instead of turning to the lord lieutenants and their deputies to levy soldiers and pay for their equipment from county rates, as was becoming the normal practice, he issued commissions to several associates and wrote letters to other gentlemen asking for their help, and assuring them that by giving it they would earn his affection.[78]

Since it was common in the period to describe patron–client relations as a form of friendship, Essex's devotion to his friends differed more in degree than kind from normal Elizabethan practice. Men like Perez, Standen, and Anthony Bacon served him in much the way that other men of business had long assisted Burghley, Leicester, and Walsingham. As Younger points out, Essex's use of "friends" to recruit and arm volunteer soldiers was actually more typical of normal European practice than the Council's reliance on conscripts assembled by deputy lieutenants and paid by county rates. It also resembled Leicester's methods in 1585.[79] But for several reasons Essex's circle of friends stood somewhat apart from already established networks. As a young man of great ambition striving to rise within a court dominated by much older figures, he needed to build his own entourage rather than integrating himself into the clientage network of a more senior courtier. Unfortunately, he started out from a relatively weak position. Unlike the Dudleys, who had played a leading role in national affairs since the 1540s, the Devereux had never counted for much outside a few neighborhoods in Staffordshire and Wales. They were not major patrons of humanist scholars and they lacked significant ties to great Protestant dynasties like the Herberts, Russells, and Hastings. Whereas Leicester's family connections had given him numerous advantages from the outset of his career at court,[80] Essex had few natural

---

[77] LPL Mss. 649, fol. 426.
[78] Neil Younger, "The Practice and Politics of Troop-Raising: Robert Devereux, Second Earl of Essex, and the Elizabethan Regime," *English Historical Review* 127 (2012): 566–91.
[79] Above, pp. 299–300; Simon Adams, "A Puritan Crusade? The Composition of the Earl of Leicester's Expedition to the Netherlands, 1585–86," in *Leicester and the Court*, 176–95.
[80] Simon Adams, "The Dudley Clientele, 1553–63," in *Leicester and the Court*, 151–75.

followers. The entourage he eventually constructed included only a handful of figures, like the Bacon brothers, from established Elizabethan court families. Aside from Lord Howard, Perez, and a small number of veteran captains like Roger Williams, it consisted mostly of young men with strong intellectual and credentials but limited practical experience.[81] Howard's Catholic connections and suspicions of his past participation in treasonous plots, Perez's identity as a Spanish exile, and the open Catholicism of other Essex followers like Standen aroused mistrust.

Howard regarded the youthfulness of Essex's friends as an advantage because they provided a pool of talent on which the government might draw as older men retired or died. He advised Essex "to hold ever in your protection and care a seminary of forward minds and spirits to be recommended to places of importance and of special trust when occasion doth serve and, in the meantime, draw them into such peculiar actions of merit to the state as, being settled in gracious opinion *pendente spe*, they may be found more capable of benefit and honor *accidente opportunitatae*."[82] Essex's support for his young virtuous friends was therefore another service to "the state." But Elizabeth resisted Essex's efforts to push his untested friends forward, for example rejecting his effort to advance Francis Bacon to the office of attorney general because she thought him too young, and perhaps also because he had tactlessly opposed a grant of supply in Parliament. Essex blamed her refusal to advance his clients on the jealousy of other courtiers, who were afraid to attack him directly and therefore undermined his friends instead. He warned Standen in 1593 to take care "that your affection to me breed not too much jealousy in the other parties or offense against you," and suggested he try to overcome the obstacle by cultivating Burghley's support in addition to his own.[83] But over time, as Gajda has suggested, the belief that his court rivals were sabotaging his friends started to become self-fulfilling. By aggressively promoting his own young followers, instead of working collegially with other privy councilors to advance men enjoying more general backing, he ended up producing a sharper distinction between his own patronage network and those of more senior courtiers and councilors.[84] As this happened the earl and his circle glossed their conflicts with "other parties" as a contest between their own youthful, masculine, and noble virtues and less desirable qualities like timidity, luxury, envy, and procrastination that they associated with the rule of a woman, aging politicians like Burghley, and "base natures." Howard described Essex's rise at court as a miraculous infusion of youthful vitality into "a council of the state waxing old with the time itself, which dulleth and abateth oftentimes the most pregnant wits." The young favorite's appearance on the scene served "to quicken spirits and to give encouragement to others that should follow him. Nature having

---

[81] Hammer, "Uses of Scholarship."   [82] Hammer, "How to Become a Statesman," 17–18.
[83] LPL Mss. 649, fol. 332.   [84] *Essex and Elizabethan Political Culture*, 142.

infused this spark wanted only a fresh gust of wind to kindle it."[85] Francis Davison, son of the disgraced secretary of state William Davison, described Essex's rivalry with the hunchbacked Robert Cecil as a vastly unequal competition between a hero and a deformed dwarf: "If my lord break their necks, as nature hath broke their backs, they may comfort their fall with the nobleness of the author; and his arch enemy (i.e. made like an arch) may glory in himself that *Aeneae magni dextra cadit.* But what glory shall it be to him that hath so notably beaten the greatest monarch of the world at his door to cut off such a viper's tail; or being a Hercules, to beat a pigmy?"[86] The assertiveness of Essex and his friends not only gave rise to a pattern of factional competition that had not existed in England for some time; it also gave that competition something of an ideological edge.

The Emotional Economy of the State

This view of the court as an arena where vices contended with virtues connected to another characteristic feature of Essex's thought, his belief in the importance of emotional forces in political life. Linda Pollock has called attention to the emphasis that early modern people placed on affect or emotion in the operation of social relationships.[87] Essex shared this trait and tended to see affairs of state as driven by various passions. He described his service to the queen as an expression of erotic love and his favors to his friends as the outgrowth of masculine affection. He explained his care for English captains and common soldiers by proclaiming that "I love them for my country's sake."[88] As his command in Ireland began to fail in July of 1599, he begged Elizabeth, in emotionally charged language, to love her soldiers even if she rejected him as their commander: "Cherish them, I humbly beseech you upon the knees of my heart; for they must sweat and bleed for you when a crew of those which now more delight you will prove but unprofitable servants."[89] Love and friendship also shaped his attitude toward international affairs, as in his devotion to Henry IV or his statement to his secretary, Edward Reynoldes, that "I have loved the duke [of Bouillon] more than all strangers of Christendom, almost more than all mine own country."[90] His bond with Henry aroused Elizabeth's jealousy as early as 1591, when she berated him for giving "ear to the king's persuasions," rather than obeying her commands. He replied in emotionally charged language, saying he felt "much grieved your Majesty thinks my duty, my faith and my humble affection so small as I should compare you with

---

[85] Hammer, "How to Become a Statesman," 15.
[86] *Memoirs of Queen Elizabeth*, ed. Birch, 2.185, Francis to William Davison, October 16, 1596.
[87] Linda Pollock, "The Affective Life in Shakespearean England," in *Age of Shakespeare*, ed. Smuts, 437-57.
[88] *Apologie*, sig. B3r.   [89] *Memoirs of Queen Elizabeth*, ed. Birch, 2.424.   [90] Ibid., 483.

a stranger."[91] Rather than interpreting Elizabeth's rebuke as evidence of her determination to maintain control of the English army and assure that it served her interests rather than Henry's, he treated it as a personal affront that unjustly called into question his passionate devotion to her. The fact that he had recently "lost his dearest and only brother, spent a great part of his substance, ventured his own life and many of his friends in seeking to do your Majesty service" compounded her callousness.[92] "No unkindness from you," he complained, "though it break my heart, can diminish my affection but I will end my life complaining of your injustice and approving mine own constancy."[93] Although Leicester had also complained that Elizabeth reciprocated his love with hate, Essex's correspondence elaborated on this charge in much more detail, effectively accusing the queen not just of indifference but emotional abuse.

Considered in isolation, Essex's laments about Elizabeth's unkindness might be explained away as a literary affectation shaped by the vogue for Petrarchan conceits in court culture.[94] But his preoccupation with the emotional wellsprings of political behavior extended well beyond his discussions of his relations with the queen and his companions in arms. He conceived of virtues like courage, honor, and public service less as abstract principles than emotional drives, in conflict with baser impulses, such as addiction to luxury and indolence. Individuals participated in affairs of state by exercising virtuous or vicious passions, whose quality determined the role they played. A passage from his *Apologie*, describing his youthful participation in the Lisbon expedition of 1589, illustrates this attitude with particular clarity. "When I was but nineteen years old," he writes, "I saw the state of England not only disposed to great actions but engaged in them." Having "little grace and few friends" at court, he found himself "upbraided ... with more retiredness than was fit for my years." The rebuke led him to engage in a fight to defend a "poor distressed exiled king," the Portuguese pretender, Dom Antonio, against an "insolent cruel and usurping nation," by seeking "to deliver the oppressed out of the hands of the oppressor." This was no mere personal crusade. "All the brave hearts of this kingdom boiled" with a desire to teach the king of Spain "both to know himself and to value us." Essex pictures both his own conduct and that of "the state of England" as determined less by government policy than a set of chivalrous passions: shame over inaction, indignation at the sight of oppression, compassion for the weak, determination to put a tyrant in his place, and excitement at the opportunity to join in "great actions." Those passions motivate a fight for justice that he pictures as both intensely personal and ultimately transnational in scope, extending to a defense of European liberty against the Spanish tyrant.[95]

---

[91] BL Add Mss. 74,286, fol. 19, italics added.   [92] Ibid., fol. 25.
[93] BL Add Mss. 74,286, fol. 22, Essex to Elizabeth, November 14, 1591.
[94] May, *Elizabethan Courtier Poets*.
[95] This also explains his sense of solidarity with foreign comrades in arms, like Henry of Navarre or the duke of Bouillion.

This habit of viewing national and international politics as driven by emotionally charged moral instincts connected to Essex's keen sense of honor, a quality he regarded as a passion natural to men of noble birth. In addition to an acute concern for reputation, honor involved a proud sense of independence and drive toward self-assertion, often in competition with others. Essex's circle saw competitive emulation as yet another emotional force invigorating the state. In the words of Fulke Greville:

> ... never any state
> Could rise or stand without this thirst for glory.
> For else, what governor would spend his days
> In envious travail for the public good?
> Who would in books search after dead men's ways?
> Or in the war what soldier lose his blood?
>   Liv'd not this Fame in clouds, kept as a crown;
>   Both for the sword, the scepter and the gown.[96]

The belief that "honor that is gained and broken upon another hath the quickest reflection," as Francis Bacon put it, so that "a man ought to contend to excel any competitors to his honor," injected a volatile element into Essex's relations with other swordsmen, contributing to the bitter quarrel that destroyed his relationship with Sir Frances Vere.[97] But despite its sometimes unfortunate effects, he and his circle regarded the passion for honor as an essential bulwark against injustice. "You know we are bound by nature to defend ourselves against our equals, much less our inferiors," Sir Robert Sidney admonished the earl of Southampton, "and you cannot but know, or at least conjecture that if we should yield ourselves we willingly put ourselves in the wolves' mouths."[98] The indignant refusal of noblemen to submit to abuse and indignity tamed the "wolves."

By no means everyone in the period shared this view. Some contemporaries associated honor instead with obedience to the prince and the law, civil restraint, and self-control.[99] But the association of noble honor with assertiveness and fierce

---

[96] *Works of Greville*, ed. Grossart, 2.69–70.
[97] Bacon, *Works*, 6.505 ("Of Honor and Reputation").
[98] Folger Shakespeare Library Mss. V.a 164, fols 144v–145r.
[99] This subject has given rise to a growing body of historical literature. The classic discussion of this competitive and violent honor code is Mervyn James, "English Politics and the Concept of Honour, 1485–1642," *Past and Present* Supplement no. 3 (1978), reprinted in Mervyn James, *Society, Politics and Culture: Studies in Early Modern England* (Cambridge: Cambridge University Press, 1987), 308–415. More recent work, especially by Linda Pollock, Richard Cust, and Courtney Erin Thomas has qualified and to a degree undercut James's analysis. The ideas he describes were, however, prevalent within Essex's circle, especially among his military followers. See in particular Linda Pollock, "Honor, Gender and Reconciliation in Elite Culture, 1570–1700," *Journal of British Studies* 46.1 (2007): 3–29; Richard Cust, "Catholicism, Antiquarianism and Gentry Honour: The Writings of Sir Thomas Shirley," *Midland History* 23 (1998): 40–70; Richard Cust, "Honour and Politics in Early Stuart England: The

independence characterized the outlook not only of Essex and members of his circle but many aristocratic swordsmen throughout Europe. In France it gave rise to a belief that nobles possessed not only a right but a duty to rebel in defense of their own liberties and those of their dependents.[100] Much the same attitude led William the Silent to conclude that he had a duty, as a great nobleman of Brabant, to lead patriot resistance to Philip II.[101] Essayists, poets, and playwrights, including Shakespeare, recognized this fiercely assertive credo as an important, if frequently dangerous element in political life. Samuel Daniel described "emulation" as "the strongest pulse that beats in high minds," but immediately added that it "is oftentimes a wind but of the worst effect" in propelling a man to cross "all the world." John Chapman exemplified the anarchic propensities of honor values in his portrayal of the French nobleman, Bussy d'Ambois:

> When I am wrong'd and that law fails to right me,
> Let me be king myself (as man was made)
> And do a justice that exceeds the law.[102]

Contemporaries recognized that this fierce self-assertion and rejection of perceived injustice often had destructive consequences. But they also connected it to noble leadership of Dutch and Huguenot revolts and other forms of resistance to tyranny.

Essex's obsession with honor, reputation, and the emotions they aroused shaped his view of relations between governments as well as individuals. "All states do stand as much by reputation as by strength, especially where their dominions are divided far, and where a few give the law to great multitudes."[103] Like noblemen, kingdoms and republics need to uphold their reputations by avoiding any appearance of weakness. They must also take care to preserve their allies' reputations. Thus Essex complained in 1591 that if Elizabeth followed through with her intention to withdraw her army from France, she would not only "utterly overthrow my poor reputation," but also cause "this king [Henry IV]" to lose "his state."[104] Five years later, as the Spanish laid siege to Calais, he admonished her again: "Wars being made as much by reputation as by force, heed is to be taken how we suffer an enemy to grow great without seeking to impeach or

---

Case of Beaumont vs. Hastings," *Past and Present* 149 (1995): 57–94; and Courtney Erin Thomas, *If I Lose Mine Honour I Lose Myself: Honour among the Early Modern English Elite* (Toronto: University of Toronto Press, 2017), esp. the introduction and chapter 1. This last work concedes that the concept of honor described by James did exist in the period but argues that it was held by a subset within the English elite, partly under the influence of French ideas of military honor, rather than being characteristic of English society as a whole.

[100] Arlette Jouanna, *Le devoir de révolte: La noblesse française et la gestation de l'État moderne, 1559–1661* (Paris: Fayard, 1989).
[101] *The apologie or defence of the most noble Prince William... Prince of Orange* (Delft, 1581).
[102] John Chapman, *Bussy d'Ambois*, II.i.197–201.   [103] *Apologie*, sig. Ci, v.
[104] BL Add Mss. 74,268, fol. 25.

diminish him: that they are not so soon overcome that lose a battle, as they that by not following their actions do confess a yielding."[105] He sent the Council an even more pointed warning: "I assure your lordships it is time for her Majesty to draw her sword, for by doing nothing and the enemy's being so undertaking strikes a terror into the people of these parts and I fear me as much in other quarters of the realm."[106] Failure to save Calais will not only hurt France but demoralize Elizabeth's own people by raising doubts about her ability to defend them and inducing the debilitating passion of "terror." Unfortunately, Essex believed, the base fear and self-love of some of the queen's associates led them to oppose his call to action. He warned Elizabeth against "two sorts of persuaders: the one amazed with the enemy's good success and possessed with a general fear would wish your majesty to do nothing: the other... of a self-loving humor [who] would have your majesty lose all your royal sea and land forces to serve their turns."[107]

Rather than evaluating military options by prudent calculations of risks and potential gains, Essex therefore reduced them to a contest of opposing emotional reactions that would extend from the royal court to the nation at large and ultimately into the international arena. Just as common soldiers would fight bravely if inspired by the example of a valorous leader, populations that had previously submitted to Spanish tyranny through fear would find the courage to rise against their oppressors if Englishmen led the way. But if the timidity of fearful and self-interested "persuaders" deterred English action, the terror inspired by Spain's reputation would spread, undermining the fight against tyranny even in places like France and the Netherlands, where it was currently being waged. Philip would never agree to peace with England because he knew that his subjects would perceive such an act as a sign of weakness: "Now let the Indies, Low Countries, Naples, Milan see that Spain that hath so long tyrannized over them is glad after so many overthrows, disgraces, losses to make peace with England upon equal terms, and they will come to know that the Spanish are *hombros commo losotros* and that it hath been baseness in them all this while, *servitutem suam*."[108] Essex wanted to occupy Cadiz after the English took the city in 1596 because he believed that doing so would not only divert Philip's forces but dishonor and discredit him by exposing his inability to defend his own kingdom. On the other hand, he felt relatively indifferent to Irish wars until the very late 1590s because he believed they offered few opportunities to gain reputation.[109] Most Europeans cared little about Ireland and had a low regard for Irish soldiers, so victories on the island would count for nothing in their eyes. The main theaters of European war in

---

[105] *Memoirs of Queen Elizabeth*, ed. Birch, 2.19.   [106] TNA SP12/257/10.
[107] *Memoirs of Queen Elizabeth*, ed. Birch, 2.19.   [108] *Apologie*, sig. Ci v.
[109] Ralegh took a very different view. See HMC Salisbury, 4.357, Ralegh to Robert Cecil, May 10, 1593: "We are so busied and dandled in these French wars, which are endless, as we forget the defence next the heart. Her Majesty hath good cause to remember that a million hath been spent in Ireland not many years since."

France and the Low Countries provided much better opportunities to win honor and diminish Spain's reputation, a matter of critical strategic importance because of its effect on the emotional reactions, and therefore behaviors, of countless people throughout Europe and the Americas.

Even in dealings between allies, Essex believed in the importance of projecting confidence and strength by displaying the right emotional responses. In 1595 he secretly advised Henry IV that Elizabeth had sent him an ambassador to discover whether he was "discontented with England and negotiating with Spain." If Henry expressed satisfaction with Elizabeth's conduct, Essex warned, she would continue haggling over details while doing little to assist him. He must instead react coldly to the embassy, complaining that the English were behaving as if they hoped to make a separate peace with Spain, or else had become corrupted by Spanish bribes, "so as to give us jealousy." He should try to cause the queen's ambassador to "send us thundering letters," warning that the French were ready to break their alliance with England unless they received more aid.[110] "For what impels men but appetite and terror," he wrote to his friend Perez about Elizabeth's relations with Henry. "We know how obstinately to deny those who humbly ask."[111] "Appetite and terror," rather than dispassionate calculations of strategic advantage, ultimately determined the conduct of states.

In the final analysis the strength of every state depended on preserving the human passions that sustained its particular order of command and obedience. Timid and self-interested statesmen, like most of the leaders of Elizabeth's court, will prove weak and unreliable allies unless goaded into vigorous action by fear and self-love.[112] Even allies sometimes need to be managed by threats. Tyrannical states, especially large tyrannical empires, must rely on terror to rule their subjects, whereas free states depend on their subjects' love of liberty, dedication to the public good, and confidence in their ability to defend themselves. Contingent circumstances and misguided decisions that undercut the passions on which a state depends will imperil its existence. A passage in Essex's *Apologie*, describing the likely effects that peace with Spain will have on the Dutch, illustrates this view with particular force. The Spanish will never agree to a peace in the Low Countries, he writes, without a formal acknowledgment of their sovereignty over the entire Netherlands. If Spain wins this concession "the authority of the general estates and the present form of the government of the United Provinces shall be broken and dissolved," leaving no effective check on "the prince's absoluteness except his own will," even if other clauses in the treaty guarantee Dutch liberties. The Spanish will feel no obligation to honor agreements made with "heretics" and "rebels." Since the Dutch know this, "province shall strive with

---

[110] *Memoirs of Queen Elizabeth*, ed. Birch, 2.353–4.   [111] Ibid., 296.
[112] In the letter to Perez just cited, Essex described the English as "usurers" among whom "all things are to be sold."

province and man with man who shall be most obsequious, and show themselves most servile, all care of defense neglected." The magistrates who led the fight for independence will flee the country to avoid retribution, causing "the state of the Low Countries" and the Dutch army to dissolve. Spain will insist on the reintroduction of Catholicism, creating a "plurality of religions," a crime "against the policy of all states because where there is not unity in the Church there can be no order in the state."

The passage elides different meanings of the word state, as a legislature ("the general estates"), a condition ("the state of the Low Countries"), and a government ("the policy of all states"). But the logic is clear: the concession of Spanish sovereignty and toleration for Catholicism will unravel the whole nexus of religious, moral, and emotional structures that have made resistance to Spanish tyranny possible.[113] The patriotic passion that has propelled resistance to Spain will give way to "obsequious servility," internal bickering, and fear, while the unity forged by the war for independence will dissolve as provinces compete with each other to please their tyrannical sovereign. Essex goes on to argue that the decentralized structure of power in the United Provinces aggravates this threat. The "authority of the governors of the state," lodged in the States General, commands no "absolute and necessary but [only] a limited and voluntary obedience." The Dutch lack not only a personal sovereign but *any* locus of supreme power. Their state "hath not, as the state of Rome had and the state of Venice hath one place that as the head doth command and direct all parts of the body, but is compounded of equal parts." Every province guards its own rights, while even petty towns claim "to have a kind of sovereignty" over their own affairs. Rather than meeting to "resolve and conclude" the central organs of government must therefore "sound and feel the disposition of every province," knowing that even resolutions adopted by majority vote will prove unenforceable if a minority opposes them vigorously. Unlike Leicester and many other Englishmen, Essex did not condemn this system as dysfunctional. The absence of a clear locus of sovereignty did not, in his view, make the United Provinces any less "a state." But he does make the obvious point that a state of this kind can only defend itself so long as it retains broad public support and confidence, which in turn depends on conditions in which patriotic passion and other public virtues are rewarded rather than punished.[114] Anything that weakens those conditions, whether an ill-judged peace treaty or the withdrawal of English assistance, risks creating a cycle in which fear, self-love, and obsequiousness destroy the will to resist aggression and tyranny, on which the survival of a free state depends.

---

[113] *Apologie*, sig. C2r–v.   [114] Ibid., sig. C4v.

The Queen and the State

England was a very different kind of state, in which authority flowed from the monarch. But just what this meant remained open to different interpretations. Although Elizabeth did not speak of states nearly as often of Essex, it is clear that she regarded the state in England very much as an extension of her own volition. She expected her ministers to counsel her about policy decisions but remained determined that they should always act as her servants, directed by her commands, and when they behaved in ways that called into question her full control of English policy she reacted fiercely. Robert Cecil reflected this view when he advised Essex, after his first serious quarrel with Elizabeth in 1591, that he should seek to recover favor by making "her majesty's absolute will his perfectest reason."[115] Some members of Essex's entourage agreed, warning him to accommodate the queen's humors and avoid "wrestlings" with her over policy issues.[116] In a personal monarchy, the success of individual courtiers and the smooth functioning of the state depended on unquestioning obedience to the prince. But Essex and some other members of his circle disagreed. Submitting tamely to Elizabeth's every wish not only affronted his sense of honor but seemed a dereliction of duty. While not denying that all authority flowed from the queen, they nevertheless insisted that her servants had a responsibility to resist her wayward impulses and wrong-headed decisions. As *The State of Christendom* put it:

> Wise and discreet officers unto princes will not presently obey their hasty, furious and unadvised commandments but give them time to allay and pacify, and to consider with themselves what they have commanded, and what mischiefs and inconveniences may follow of their commandments. And the prince that hath such [officers] may think himself happy; and when of a servant to his passions he returneth happily to himself that is to be a right prince, then he will thank them for their good counsel.[117]

A royal will driven by "hasty, furious and unadvised" passions can never be regarded as "perfectest reason," and royal servants therefore have a duty to resist it. By doing so they perform one of the key offices Cicero ascribed to a friend, by providing guidance that assists the processes of detachment, self-criticism, and careful deliberation necessary for rational virtue.[118]

To a degree this attitude reflected commonplace ideas about the responsibility of courtiers to guide princes to act virtuously, if necessary through artful

---

[115] *Letters from Cecil to Hatton*, ed. Hammer, 260.
[116] Hammer, "How to Become a Statesman," 10–12.
[117] Second numeration, 10.
[118] Cf. Gajda, *Essex and Political Culture*, 159–65.

dissimulation, as Castiglione had famously advised.[119] Leicester, Walsingham, and Burghley also tried to steer Elizabeth to support policies they favored and complained about her indecision and eruptions of temper when she rebelled against their advice. But as a royal favorite Essex's influence depended to an extraordinary degree on the queen's emotional attachment to him, while his youth made his displays of independence especially provocative. The effects of this disparity in age and experience, which naturally made Elizabeth skeptical of Essex's criticisms of her decisions, was probably reinforced by growing emphasis on the absolute, divinely sanctioned and inspired quality of royal authority, influenced by new currents of European political thought, especially in France.[120] Although Robert Cecil also sometimes disagreed with the queen, he learned to do so with extreme tact and deference, as revealed by a letter he wrote in 1600 to the Irish official Sir George Carew about their shared displeasure over Elizabeth's decision to send one of the former earl of Desmond's relations back to Ireland as the new earl:

> I pray you therefore write to me in this sort, that you will not presume to say to your sovereign what may be the reason of this manner of sending him, because her Majesty will have it so, to whose divine and piercing judgment you will subscribe; but you cannot be so dull as not to be bold to say to me that you cannot discover yet the mystery of this proceeding.[121]

This kind of obsequious indirection affronted Essex's sense of his dignity as a nobleman and duty to offer frank advice. But even more than Leicester, he needed the unequivocal backing of the council to have any hope of getting away with defying the queen's wishes, and even when he enjoyed such backing his disagreements with her tended to provoke especially sharp reactions. But Essex's conviction that ordinary people needed to be led by the positive example of their natural superiors made it seem imperative that he resist Elizabeth forthrightly when he believed her behavior threatened to harm the public good. The nexus of personal and emotional bonds that in his view allowed the state of England to defend itself and its allies depended on her exercising the right kind of leadership, without allowing errors of judgment and defects of character—such as feminine caution and indecisiveness, penuriousness and jealousy—to get in the way. A "faithful subject" and "zealous patriot" had no choice but to strive against destructive royal vices.

---

[119] The classic exposition of this idea was Book III of Baldassare Castiglione, *The Book of the Courtier*.
[120] For which see esp. Arlette Jouanna, *Le pouvoir absolu: Naissance de l'imaginaire politique de la royauté* (Paris: Gallimard, 2013).
[121] Cecil to Sir George Carew, September 29, 1600, *Calendar of the Carew Manuscripts Preserved at the Archepiscopal Library at Lambeth*, 4 vols. (London, 1867–73), 3.452.

These views dovetailed into Essex's further conviction that the state's capacity for waging war depended less on material resources than the moral condition of its people. In his *Apologie* he responded to arguments that England could not support the cost of continuing war by asking:

> Was Rome so brave a state as the very ladies to supply the common treasure to maintain the wars spoiled themselves of their jewels and ornaments? And is England so base a state that the men in it will not bestow some of their superfluous expenses to keep themselves from conquest and slavery... There will ever be found some *Valreii* that so the state may stand and flourish, [who] care not though they leave not wherewithal to bury themselves, though other bury their money not caring what case they leave the state.[122]

"The state" here becomes identified with the nation's moral condition, especially its willingness to sacrifice ease, luxury, and private wealth to support a war to maintain liberty. A "brave" and free state may take the form of a monarchy, a republic, or even a loose confederation of independent towns and provinces, but in every case its survival will depend on the public virtue of its people. A queen who fails to nurture virtue therefore undermines the state.

When faced with desertions by his troops in Ireland, Essex blamed Elizabeth for sapping the martial spirit of her army. "The state and minds of your people are strangely altered," he told her, "when your army, which never yet abandoned the body of any principle commander being dead, doth now run away from their chief commander being alone and in fight; and that your people had rather be hanged for cowardice than killed or hurt in service."[123] The crown might conscript as many soldiers as it wanted but unless the men levied obeyed orders and displayed some fighting spirit it would do little good. Military success depended on a chain of emotionally charged personal bonds, descending from the queen as sovereign through himself as her loving servant and general,[124] to his friends among the captains, and finally the tenants and neighbors of those friends who had signed on to fight. By denying him both the material and moral support he needed and thus punishing his subordinates and their troops, Elizabeth imperiled these ties. Like Leicester in 1586, and almost certainly with even more reason, he blamed his predicament on enemies within the court who wanted to ruin him, even at the cost of jeopardizing continuing English control of Ireland. But unlike Leicester, he

---

[122] *Apologie*, sig. D3 r–v; italics added.
[123] *Life and Letters of Robert Devereux second Earl of Essex*, ed. Walter Bouchier Devereux, 2 vols (London, 1853), 2.59.
[124] Essex repeatedly insisted that he served Elizabeth not only through duty but love, which he also often described as unrequited. See, e.g. ibid., fol. 110: "When I did hope I sold my liberty to be servant to my love but since your Majesty hath driven me to despair." The inescapable implication is that a man driven to despair may lose his will to act, depriving not only the queen but his country of his services.

openly accused Elizabeth of knowingly enabling these covert enemies. "Why do I talk of victory or success?" he wrote her:

> Is it not known that from England I receive nothing but discomforts and wounds? Is it not spoken in the army that your Majesty's favor is diverted from me; and that already you do bode ill both to me and it? Is it not believed by the rebels that those whom you favour most do more hate me out of faction than them out of duty and conscience? Is it not lamented of your majesty's faithfullest subjects both there and here that a Cobham or a Ralegh (I will forbear others for their places sake) should have such credit and favor with your Majesty, when they wish the ill success of your Majesty's most important action, the decay of your greatest strength and the destruction of your faithfullest servants?[125]

By undermining devotion and courage, while rewarding factious jealousies and selfishness, Elizabeth's behavior corrupted and endangered the state.

In passages like this, Essex came perilously close to equating his own honor and reputation with the valor and moral health of England. He talked and behaved as if he and his friends alone possessed the virtue necessary to preserve the country from the forces of decay that the queen's weakness and the self-seeking machinations of her entourage had unleashed. Elizabeth recognized this insinuation and reacted sharply. She sarcastically dismissed Essex's claims for the superior qualities of the young men he appointed to lead her army. "It doth sound hardly in the ears of the world that in a time when there is a question to save a kingdom, and in a country where experience giveth so great advantage to all enterprises, regiments should be committed to young gentlemen that rather desire to do well than know how to perform it, a matter wherein we must note that you have made both us and our council so great strangers as to this day (but by reports) we know not who they be that spend our treasure and carry places of note in our army."[126] Essex's claim that the morale of her army depended on the appointment of his friend, the earl of Southampton, as commander of its cavalry, infuriated her. "For the matter of Southampton, it is strange to us that his continuance or displacing should work so great an alteration either in yourself (valuing our commandments as you ought) or in the disposition of our army," especially since everyone knew that she had expressly prohibited Essex from employing him. By doing so anyway he had affronted *her* honor, not least by calling into question the willingness of her people to serve her and their country without the additional motive of loyalty to himself. His valuing of his "own pleasing" and "own glory" above his duty as a subject was an affront no monarch would stomach.[127] By converting arguments over policy into a contest pitting his own elevated sense of virtue and honor against

---

[125] *Memoirs of Queen Elizabeth*, ed. Birch, 2.417–18.   [126] LPL Mss. 601, fol. 180v.
[127] LPL 601, fol. 181r–v.

Elizabeth's judgment and right to command her subjects, Essex had picked a fight he had no chance of winning.

Politic History, Tacitus and Essex

Several scholars have argued that the earl's highly critical view of the queen and her court derived in large measure from readings of classical historians, above all Tacitus.[128] This is an outwardly plausible claim because Tacitus's narratives of early imperial history do describe the erosion of old republican virtues amidst the climate of sycophancy, fear, and palace intrigue that developed under Augustus and his successors. But it raises two basic questions that turn out to be difficult to answer: how and when did Essex and his entourage first acquire a strong interest in Tacitus, and how much difference did the Roman historian ultimately make to their thinking? Gajda suggested that Tacitus's account of Roman imperial politics provided Essex with a "template" for interpreting his own experiences, while Richard Tuck has gone further by arguing that the late sixteenth-century fashion for Tacitus reflected the rise of a disenchanted "new humanism" that broke decisively with the ethical and constitutional emphases of a more idealistic "old humanism," whose favorite author was Cicero.[129] These arguments raise tricky issues about how far reading habits and the influence of individual authors caused changes in outlook, rather than reflecting and perhaps reinforcing attitudes that already existed. The fact that we have gotten this far in our analysis without finding it necessary to mention Tacitus may suggest that his influence was less decisive than some historians have supposed.

But even if reading Tacitus did not directly cause Essex and his circle to become suspicious of Elizabeth and her entourage, it is certainly possible that his bleak narratives of Roman imperial politics helped them refine and amplify critical attitudes toward the queen and her court that they had already developed for other reasons. We might expect as much, given the fashion for "applying" ancient

---

[128] For the growing literature on this subject see, esp., J. H. M. Salmon, "Seneca and Tacitus in Jacobean England," in *The Mental World of the Jacobean Court*, ed. Linda Peck (Cambridge: Cambridge University Press, 1991), 169–88; David Womersley, "Sir Henry Savile's Translation of Tacitus and the Political Interpretation of Elizabethan Texts," *Review of English Studies* 42 (1991): 313–42; Malcolm Smuts, "Court-Centred Politics and the Uses of Roman Historians," in *Culture and Politics in Early Stuart England*, ed. Kevin Sharpe and Peter Lake (Basingstoke: Macmillan, 1994), 21–44; Gajda, *Essex and Political Culture*, 226–33; Paulina Kewes, "Henry Savile's Tacitus and the Politics of Roman History in Late Elizabethan England," *Huntington Library Quarterly* 74 (2011): 515–51; J. H. Waszink, "Henry Savile's Tacitus and the English Role on the Continent: Leicester, Hotman, Lipsius," *History of European Ideas* 42.3 (2016): 303–19; R. Malcolm Smuts, "Varieties of Tacitism," *Huntington Library Quarterly* 83 (2020): 441–66; Alexandra Gajda, "Tacitus and Political Thought in Early Modern Europe, c. 1530-1640," in *The Cambridge Companion to Tacitus*, ed. A. J. Woodman (Cambridge: Cambridge University Press, 2010), 253–68.

[129] Gajda, *Essex and Political Culture*, esp. chapter 6; Richard Tuck, *Philosophy and Government, 1572-1651* (Cambridge: Cambridge University Press, 1991).

histories to analyses of political causation within his circle and in the period more generally. Some evidence exists that an interest in Tacitus had already developed among humanists who accompanied Leicester to the Netherlands, where it would have found nourishment through contact with the Roman historian's most distinguished European editor, Justus Lipsius, who held a professorship at Leiden University. Leicester heard Lipsius lecture on Tacitus during a ceremonial visit to the university in 1586 and Lipsius started to prepare a book about Roman triumphs for him.[130] The earl's secretary, Jean Hotman, had already corresponded with Lipsius before this date. Lipsius had also discussed technical issues related to Tacitus with another member of Leicester's entourage, Thomas Savile, the younger brother of Henry Savile, the translator of the first English edition of a Tacitean history that appeared in 1591.[131] Lipsius had sufficiently warm relations with Sir Philip Sidney to feel comfortable criticizing Leicester's conduct in a letter to him.[132] Some years earlier Sidney had recommended Tacitus, among several other Roman historians, to his brother Robert, who at the time was traveling on the Continent under Henry Savile's guidance. Since Savile had made notes on Tacitus a few years before this date, it seems likely that he would have discussed the Roman historian with his pupils. In early 1585 William Davison procured a French translation of Tacitus.[133] An Italian humanist, Giovanni Mareia Manelli, independently dedicated an Italian translation of Tacitus's *Agricola* to Robert Sidney in 1585, which John Wolfe published in London.

Although no direct evidence has come to light of attempts by members of Leicester's circle to use Tacitus as a guide to politics, it would not be in the least surprising if they did so, in conversations among themselves and perhaps through exchanges with Lipsius, who initially supported Leicester's mission. If this did happen, Essex, as a member of Leicester's entourage with an interest in scholarship, would probably have become aware of the fact.[134] But in the absence of hard evidence we can only speculate. Lord Henry Howard also demonstrated a precociously early interest in Tacitus, quoting the Roman historian repeatedly in his *Defensative against the poyson of proposed prophecies* (1583) and in a manuscript treatise defending the virtue of female statesmen presented to both the queen and Essex in 1590.[135] But although all this evidence suggests how Essex *might* have acquired an interest in Tacitus as early as the late 1580s, none of it proves definitively that he had done so.

Savile's 1591 translation of Tacitus's *Histories* and *Agricola*, which included an appendix on Roman warfare, a short narrative of Nero's fall that Savile himself

---

[130] *Correspondence of Sidney*, ed. Kuin, 1218.
[131] Waszink, "Savile's Tacitus"; G. H. M. Posthumus Meyjes, *Jean Hotman's English Connection* (Amsterdam: Koninklijke Nederlandse Akademie van Wettenschappen, 1990).
[132] *Sidney Correspondence*, ed. Kuin, 1307. [133] TNA SP84/1/30 and 68.
[134] For the earl's scholarly interests see Hammer, *Polarisation of Politics*, 24–9.
[135] The treatise on female rule is in BL Add Mss. 24,562.

had written, and extensive notes explicating the text, has long been associated with Essex, partly on the strength of a claim by Ben Jonson in 1618 that the earl supplied it with a preface, entitled "A. B. to the Reader." But the reliability of Jonson's assertion is open to question, and J. H. Waszink and Mordechai Feingold have recently disputed whether Essex had anything to do with Savile's edition.[136] Feingold argues, on the basis of a manuscript copy of Savile's translation in the Cecil archives at Hatfield House that Burghley was the actual patron. The evidence on these points again appears too exiguous to permit firm conclusions.[137] Since manuscripts circulated freely in the period and Burghley is known to have taken an interest in texts relating to political questions, the copy at Hatfield House proves little, particularly since a second copy of unknown provenance survives in the Folger Shakespeare Library. Essex would later claim in his *Apologie* to have had a long association with Savile, although he did not say when it began.[138] A bond by Essex to Elizabeth for 10,000 marks, witnessed by Savile and others and dated August 7, 1590, proves that some kind of relationship had already developed by that date but does not establish how close the two had become.[139] We also have no firm evidence of when or why Savile began to compile his edition. It would obviously have required substantial effort to complete, but whether this involved a concentrated burst of activity over several months in 1590–1, or a more leisurely process of preparation extending well back into the 1580s, we have no way of ascertaining.[140] We also do not know whether Savile first conceived the project in its entirety as a work for the press, or initially produced a piece of it that he later expanded into the full edition, either on his own initiative or with the encouragement of a court patron.

It nevertheless appears safe to conclude that Savile completed and probably started to circulate his translation within the same general environment in which Essex began his career as a royal favorite. Savile was not only a scholar but a pedagogue who tutored several young men destined for careers in court service between the 1580s and the early seventeenth century. By 1591 he had direct connections to the court and the queen, with whom he discussed Greek and Roman texts. His edition of Tacitus amounted, self-evidently, to an effort at applied scholarship in the humanist manner, intended to elucidate contemporary problems through study of the past in ways that Essex would certainly have found interesting. Even if Burghley or Elizabeth had acted as Savile's primary patron,

---

[136] Waszink, "Savile's Tacitus"; Mordechai Feingold, "Scholarship and Politics: Henry Savile's Tacitus and the Essex Connection," *Review of English Studies* 67 (2016): 855–74.
[137] I have discussed the problem in "Varieties of Tacitism."
[138] *Apologie*, sig. A1v. I wish to thank Alexandra Gajda for calling my attention to this passage.
[139] TNA SP12/223/30. Thanks to Paul Hammer for calling this document to my attention and supplying me with a copy.
[140] I wish to thank Alexandra Gajda, Paul Hammer, Paulina Kewes, and Mordechai Feingold for useful discussions of the issues covered in the preceding two paragraphs.

they might well have shared his translation with Essex, with whom both had good relations at the time, although again we cannot be sure.

What is clear is that Savile's work addressed a number of issues that had considerable topical relevance within the English court around 1591. One, indicated by the appendix on military lore and several notes on Tacitus's descriptions of battles, was Roman warfare. Maurice of Nassau employed the study of Roman tactics and military technology to guide his innovations in the Dutch army in this period and, as Hammer has shown, Essex belonged to a circle of military officers intent on promoting similar innovations in England.[141] Tacitus would continue to be regarded as an excellent source of information about Roman warfare throughout the 1590s, for example by Sir Clement Edmondes.[142] As A. B.'s preface and Savile's own narrative of Nero's fall both stressed, the text also furnished a case study of the topic Sidney had recommended as of special interest to his brother Robert, "the ruins of great estates with their causes."[143] A. B. described Tacitus's *Histories* as a narrative revealing "all the miseries of a torn and declining state," while Savile described Nero as "a prince in life contemptible and hateful in government, having thereby disarmed himself of the love and fear of his subjects," who found himself bereft of support once a serious rebellion against his rule gained traction.[144] The story of Nero's fall and the civil war over the succession to the imperial throne that followed, recounted in *The Histories*, might have reminded some contemporaries of the collapse of Spanish power in the Netherlands. But the most obvious comparison was to France, where Henry III had been widely reviled by both Huguenots and ultra-Catholics as "a Prince in life contemptible and hateful in government," before his assassination in 1589. Like the three emperors whose rise and fall Tacitus narrates, Henry IV was attempting in 1591 to re-establish a monarchical state that had suffered a calamitous collapse. In the early part of that year the English council debated whether to send an army to help him, which it eventually dispatched under Essex's command. As Paulina Kewes points out, Savile used modern titles and place names, such as France instead of Gaul, to call attention to the topical relevance of his text.[145]

In describing Nero's overthrow Savile stressed the role of a young man named Julius Vindex, who did not initially occupy a prominent post in the Empire, although he was the son of a Senator and a descendant of ancient kings of "France." Having determined to liberate his country from Nero's tyranny or lose his life in the attempt, Vindex acted with such boldness that he drew a more senior

---

[141] Hammer, *Polarisation of Politics*, 234–7. The military emphasis perhaps makes it more likely that Essex was among the principal intended readers of Savile's work, although other young swordsmen, including Savile's former pupil Sir Robert Sidney, would have shared his interest in war.
[142] See my "Varieties of Tacitism" for a discussion.
[143] *Correspondence of Sidney*, ed. Kuin, 1007.
[144] Henry Savile, *The Ende of Nero and Beginning of Galba* (London, 1591), 11.
[145] Kewes, "Savile's Tacitus," 534.

commander, Galba, into his project, whereupon Nero's power collapsed. Vindex then lost his life while incautiously approaching a city held by a recently reconciled enemy, either by accident or secret treachery, as Savile pointedly comments. Savile summed up by describing Vindex as a man "more virtuous than fortunate, who having no army provided, no legion, no soldier in charge, whiles others looked on, first entered the lists, challenging a prince upholden with thirty legions, rooted in fourteen years' continuance of reign, not upon private despair to set in combustion the state, not to revenge disgrace or dishonor... but to redeem his country from tyranny and bondage." Warszink argues that Savile intended Vindex's story as a warning against incautious military adventures but this is not convincing, since contemporaries usually regarded men who died fighting for worthy causes as heroes rather than failures.[146] It does seem likely, however, that Savile intended a double-edged message, endorsing decisive action, while warning against reckless self-endangerment and naïve trust in former enemies. This would have fit Essex's situation, as a young aspiring military leader who, in the opinion of older members of the court sometimes behaved recklessly.

Significantly, Savile chose to translate *The Histories*, covering a period of civil war, and *The Agricola*, describing the Roman conquest of Britain, rather than Tacitus's *Annals*, which dealt with the establishment of imperial despotism during the peaceful reigns of Augustus and Tiberius. This would have made his translation relevant to the religious wars of the Continent and English efforts to establish firm control over Ireland. Several of his notes do nevertheless underline and comment upon brief passages in Tacitus's text concerning stratagems used by members of the imperial court to discredit and destroy men of virtue. Those notes especially highlight how the jealousy and envy that weak rulers feel toward virtuous subjects provide opportunities for clever courtiers to arouse the ruler's resentment and mistrust, often with lethal consequences. Whether or not Savile prepared his edition with Essex in mind, it would have appealed to the earl's interest in Roman warfare and belief in active virtue. It also anticipated, and may have helped to shape, his later animus against the "persuaders" and backbiters whom he blamed for turning Elizabeth against him. This does not mean that Savile saw Elizabeth as a weak ruler prone to vindictive jealousy. More likely, he intended his notes as warnings of pitfalls that existed in all royal courts, a message that even the queen may not have found objectionable.[147] But the way in which a few of Savile's notes anticipate Essex's later polemical attacks on his court "detractors" is nevertheless suggestive.

---

[146] On this see James, "English Politics and the Concept of Honour," 315–16. William of Orange and Sir Philip Sidney are both examples of heroes widely lauded after their violent deaths.

[147] Gajda points out that "Elizabeth encouraged her courtiers to imagine themselves engaged in this state of perpetual internal rivalry: 'Look to thyself, good Essex, and be wise to help thyself without giving thy enemies advantage'" (*Essex and Political Culture*, 150).

After about 1593 evidence for an interest in both Tacitus and Machiavelli among the earl's circle of friends and confidants—notably Anthony and Francis Bacon, Antonio Perez, and Henry Cuffe—becomes stronger. Several passages in *The State of Christendom* appear to echo Machiavelli, in discussing the utility of religion as a political tool, the role of colonies in establishing despotic power, the widespread practice among princes of breaking leagues with other states for the sake of political advantage, and the military prowess of free peoples like the Swiss and the Dutch, who rely on citizen armies.[148] At some point during 1593 or 1594 Anthony Bacon's Edinburgh correspondent Thomas Moresin promised to send him "a commentary on Tacitus made by a Scot of Plaisance [a street on the outskirts of Edinburgh], in the form that Machiavelli made on Titus Livy, comparing events of today with those of the past, a book worthy of being viewed... because it contains all that is fitting for war or peace, policy or pleasure."[149] This suggests not only an interest in Tacitus on Bacon's part but an inclination to read him in a Machiavellian manner. By 1598, when Richard Greenway dedicated his translation of Tacitus's *Annals* to Essex, the earl's strong admiration for the Roman historian was widely recognized.

But even if, as seems likely, reading Tacitus sharpened Essex's awareness of the role of dissimulation and backbiting in court politics, this did not amount to a fundamental shift in his outlook. The belief that conspicuous virtue will attract envy was a Renaissance commonplace in which Essex already believed and, as Lake has correctly argued, claims that Machiavellian courtiers conspired to exclude virtuous nobles from positions of power had been repeatedly recycled by earlier English and European polemics, targeting Leicester and Burghley among others.[150] English chronicle histories provided stories of conflicts between warlike nobles and courtiers of low birth during the reigns of monarchs like Edward II and Richard II, which Marlowe and Shakespeare brought onto the stage. Tacitus's accounts of how sycophants and informers exploited a prince's envy and jealousy therefore meshed with attitudes already prevalent within late Elizabethan culture. His contribution lay not in any of these themes so much as the subtle psychological insight he displayed in exploring them, which went beyond anything found in the chronicles or polemical tracts like *Leicester's Commonwealth*. A few of Savile's notes in his 1591 edition call attention to Tactus's snippets of psychological analysis, which soon provided a model for

---

[148] See 50, 66, 98, and 103–4.

[149] LPL Mss. 649, fol. 498: "Je vous prepare deslivres pour la semaine à venir et un encoure que monsieur Selin n'a ni vu ni lu, un commentaire sur Tacite fait par un Scoti de Plaisance à la forme que Machiavelli fit sur Titus Livie, comparaient les faits d'aujourd'hui à ceux du passé, livre digne d'être vu principalement de notre temps si point d'autres qui se fait car il contient tout ce qu'est beau pour guerre ou paix, polic or plaisir." Plaisance is a street on the edges of Edinburgh. I have not been able to trace the identity of this tract, which may or may not have been delivered to Bacon (see ibid., fol. 501).

[150] Lake, *Bad Queen Bess?*

some English writers interested in politics.[151] John Hayward's *First Part of the Life and Raigne of King Henrie IIII* (1599), which the author dedicated to Essex, drew heavily on Savile's edition to expand the account of Richard II's conflict with Henry Bolingbroke found in Holinshed, by furnishing much fuller treatments of Richard's relations with unworthy favorites and Bolingbroke's calculations in launching his invasion of England.[152] Hayward also tried, rather clumsily, to imitate Tacitus's method of sprinkling pointed aphorisms throughout his narrative, indicating how various episodes demonstrated universal features of political life.

We should not exaggerate the novelty of this kind of borrowing. Earlier humanists had also drawn upon ancient historians to illustrate political maxims—Machiavelli's *Discourses* and *The Prince* provide famous examples—while English playwrights like Marlowe, Jonson, and above all Shakespeare were developing rounded psychological portraits of protagonists in historical conflicts. Rather than evidence of a radically "new humanism," the fashion for Tacitus and "politic" histories modeled after him developed out of an older humanist culture that had long employed ancient texts to illuminate modern political life, and that was now doing so in ever more complex and sophisticated ways.[153] But the attraction of Essex and his circle to Tacitus does point to a special preoccupation with the arts of political disguise and the importance of royal envy as central features of court politics during the reigns of weak rulers. Although these were by no means exclusively Tacitean themes, his writings gave them special prominence and explored them with exceptional subtlety. *Leicester's Commonwealth* had earlier discussed at length how Leicester deceived the queen, in part by preying on her fear of Catholic plots, but it did not develop a nuanced portrait of Elizabeth as a timorous woman, whose fears and jealousies made her an easy victim for such manipulation. Tactitus's histories, along with texts by other ancient writers like Suetonius and Plutarch, contributed to a sharper awareness of ways in which a ruler's insecurities and character flaws can generate pernicious patterns of political behavior.

Tacitus also differed from the English chroniclers and many other Roman historians such as Livy, in the way he embedded his stories of political infighting within an overarching narrative of how the old Republic and the values that had sustained it gave way to a corrupt system of one-man rule. There is evidence that English readers recognized this fact. In translating the opening pages of *Annals*,

---

[151] Smuts, "Court-Centred Politics," 28–9.
[152] Lisa Richardson, "Plagiarism and Imitation in Renaissance Historiography," in *Plagiarism in Early Modern England*, ed. Paulina Kewes (Basingstoke: Palgrave Macmillan, 2003), 106–18; R. Malcolm Smuts, "The Political Thought of Sir John Hayward," in *Doubtful and Dangerous: The Question of the Succession in Late Elizabethan England*, ed. Susan Doran and Paulina Kewes (Manchester: Manchester University Press, 2014), 276–94, esp. 278–84.
[153] I have developed this point at greater length in Smuts, "Varieties of Taciticism."

which succinctly summarize this alteration, Greneway repeatedly juxtaposed the English words *state* and *commonwealth* to translate different Latin terms in ways that heightened the effect of Tacitus's narration. Some of these translations were natural, for example in renderings of *res publica* as *commonwealth* or *civitatis statu* as "state of the city." But others are more arbitrary, as when *veteris populi Romani* is translated as "the ancient Commonwealth" or *novis ex rebus* as "the present estate." By consistently using *commonwealth* when referring to republican institutions and traditions, and *state* to describe the system of power founded by Augustus, Greneway set up a verbal contrast that did not exist in the original Latin text, amplifying Tacitus's message that an old system of government based on the collective pursuit of the common good gave way to a new order dominated by a single man and his debauched heirs.[154]

This reading of early imperial Roman history set up a chain of associations between the character flaws of weak or depraved rulers like Tiberius, Nero, and perhaps Elizabeth, vicious competition for power at the political center, and a broader decline in the moral fiber and military prowess of a society that results in a loss of liberty. Essex and his followers added a further inflection by equating ancient virtue with military valor and the vigorous pursuit of war, and moral decay with excessive fondness for peace. A number of other classical sources in addition to Tacitean texts, many of them newly translated into English in the period, fleshed out the picture of the Roman transition.[155] These included Lucan's *Pharasalia*, partially translated by Christopher Marlowe (published 1600); Thomas North's edition of Plutarch's *Lives of the Noble Grecians and Romans* (1579), which provided the main source for Shakespeare's *Julius Caesar* and *Anthony and Cleopatra*; the tragedies and moral essays of Seneca, which had long been available but now came into wider use;[156] the histories of Suetonius and Dio Cassius, which although untranslated remained available in Latin;[157] and the satiric poets Juvenal, Martial, and Horace, who were widely imitated in the late 1590s. Poets and playwrights, including Marlowe, Jonson, Daniel, and Shakespeare, assimilated these materials and applied them to an understanding of politics in the past in ways intended to have implications for the present.[158] The Essex circle's attraction to Tacitus appears symptomatic of a larger trend toward the use of a widening array of classical sources, especially from the early imperial

---

[154] The quotations are drawn from *The Annales of Cornelius Tacitus*, trans. and ed. Richard Greneway (London, 1598), 1–2, compared with the online edition of the same chapters of the original Latin text at http://www.perseus.tufts.edu/hopper/text?doc=Perseus%3Atext%3A1999.02.0077%3Abook%3D1%3Achapter%3D4, accessed January 4, 2016.

[155] Paulina Kewes, "Roman History, Essex, and Late Elizabethan Political Culture," in *Age of Shakespeare*, ed. Smuts, 250–68.

[156] Curtis Perry, "Seneca and English Political Culture," in *Age of Shakespeare*, ed. Smuts, 306–21.

[157] Hammer, "How to Become a Statesman," points out that Dio Cassius is the single most frequently cited author in Howard's notes about Essex. Suetonius was first translated in 1606.

[158] Lake, *Shakespeare*, chapter 5.

period, to illuminate Rome's political history in ways that suggested very critical views of recent trends in England.

But contrary to Tuck's claims, this development did not involve the replacement of an older ethical vision of politics modeled after Cicero by a new amoral Tacitean outlook. If anything, Essex and his circle placed even greater weight on the importance of virtue than earlier Elizabethans, like Leicester, whose correspondence shows less obsession with the topic. By the late 1590s the earl and his followers had developed an especially keen preoccupation with the *subversion* of virtue, at both the individual and societal level, through the influence of weak rulers, manipulative self-seeking courtiers, and corrosive cultural and economic trends like the growth of luxury in times of peace. Earlier Protestant figures like Sir Philip Sidney, as well as Catholic polemics had to a degree anticipated this attitude. But Sidney had advanced his critique of the Elizabethan court in general and oblique ways, in a novel that remained unpublished during his lifetime, while the Catholic polemics associated moral corruption specifically with heresy and religious hypocrisy. By the late 1590s a preoccupation with the spreading forces of corruption had begun to lose its confessional edge, while simultaneously becoming more open and widespread.

Disagreements over the Conduct of War and Essex's Revolt

Readings of Tacitus and other Roman writers therefore may have sharpened, but did not fundamentally cause the growing estrangement of Essex and his circle from the queen and the dominant figures on her council. The frustration of the earl's personal ambitions and those of his followers, along with policy disagreements, especially over the conduct of war, proved more decisive. Those disagreements intensified after 1595, as Essex supported military aid to Henry IV and a plan by Sir Francis Drake to attack Panama, while the queen and Burghley held back. The council's decision to launch an amphibious assault on the Spanish port of Cadiz, which Essex planned and then led collaboratively with the lord admiral, Charles Howard, and Sir Walter Ralegh, momentarily relieved tensions in 1596. But Essex quarreled with Howard and Ralegh when they rejected his plan to leave an English garrison in possession of Cadiz, and rather than being showered with honors after his return, as he believed he deserved, the queen disparaged his leadership. The fact that in their eagerness to sack the town the expedition's leaders had allowed the Spanish to destroy cargoes worth almost £3,500,000, equivalent to more than ten years of Elizabeth's income, infuriated her.[159]

---

[159] R. B. Wernham, *The Return of the Armadas: The Last Years of the Elizabethan War against Spain 1595–1603* (Oxford: Clarendon Press, 1994), 102.

Rather than enhancing his position at court, Essex's great triumph at Cadiz damaged it.

Essex saw the constraints that Elizabeth and the council placed on his conduct and that of other like-minded swordsmen as a serious impediment to the effective conduct of war. But the queen had valid reasons for worrying about the political, as well as military consequences of over-straining her kingdom's resources. When confronted with arguments about the crushing financial burdens war had inflicted on the crown and English society, the earl had a twofold response. He argued that qualities of valor and discipline, combined with bold strategic initiatives, would prove more decisive to the outcome of the war than financial resources, and that England was in any case capable of raising at least an additional £250,000 per annum by sacrificing superfluous luxuries. The queen, Burleigh, and Robert Cecil had much less faith in both the ability of valorous captains to win the war on the cheap, and the willingness of the English elite to give up its luxuries to fund armies.

Beneath the moralizing rhetoric about English valor there accordingly lurked substantive disagreements over strategy and taxation. Essex plausibly argued that in a prolonged war fought in multiple theaters, the vast dominions and superior resources of the Spanish Empire would ultimately prevail. England needed to nullify the enemy's advantages through vigorous offensive operations that would quickly cripple Spain's strength.[160] To that end he proposed creating a small but highly disciplined strike force, which he insisted would easily outfight less disciplined armies of far larger size,[161] and then using it to attack the weak points in Spain's defenses, especially coastal towns of the Iberian Peninsula, defended only by untested local militias, consisting "for the most part of artificers and clowns who know nothing of the wars and little use of the arms they carry."[162] By seizing one or two Spanish ports Elizabeth would leave "as it were a thorn sticking" in the king of Spain's foot, while simultaneously "making all the enemies of Spain in Christendom to depend upon her" as "head of the party" because "she only might be said to make the wars with Spain...to purpose."[163] By proposing to leave a garrison at Cadiz he attempted to implement this plan.

On their face, Essex's arguments had some merit, since Spain would have advantages in a long war of attrition, and the formation of a relatively small but

---

[160] See, e.g., his argument in Folger Shakespeare Library Mss. V.b 214, fol. 103: "For we have as the Athenians had, with the ancient usurping Philip, *Praelium facile, bellum difficile*; therefore it is our disadvantage to draw the war into length."

[161] "An army may consist as well of too great a number as of too small. For an army or politic body as well as a natural may be so huge *ut magnitudine laboret*. Such ponderous unwieldy bodies are burdensome to themselves and cannot be kept in order and nothing can last that cannot be governed. An army of 3000 is able...to undertake any actions or to fight with any army in the world...where so ever such an army of disciplined men shall invade the defendants are in despair if he only trust to numbers" (BL Add Mss. 74,287, fol. 160v).

[162] Folger Shakespeare Library Mss. V.b 214, fols 162, 161.   [163] Ibid., fols 104v–105.

highly trained and disciplined army might well have improved military outcomes, while reducing corruption and inefficiency. Maurice of Nassau achieved good results by improving discipline in the Dutch army, and the British state would later enhance its international standing by developing more professional armies during the Civil War and under William III. Essex was also justified in claiming that England might in principle have mobilized considerably greater resources for war. The burden of taxation and the resources of the crown had both declined during Elizabeth's reign, in absolute terms and in proportion to national wealth. Although economic statistics for the period are imprecise, calculations by modern historians suggest that in real terms the crown's ordinary income may have decreased to as little as 40 percent of the level reached at the death of Henry VII, while as a percentage of GNP the *peak* year of Elizabethan wartime expenditure in 1601 may have just equaled the normal *peacetime* level of the 1550s.[164]

But it is much less clear that the political nation, dominated as it was by a landed elite that had benefited disproportionately from these trends, was prepared to remedy the situation. Taxation had not only declined; it had also become more regressive as wealthy estates were under-assessed and the burden shifted onto middling landowners and artisans, through local rates to pay for things like the coat and conduct money used to equip conscript troops.[165] Unfortunately, the inflation and food shortages of the 1590s hit the middling strata of society especially hard. Essex's claim that England might pay for war by curtailing expenditure on "superfluities" shows that he recognized the basic problem of under-taxation of the wealthy. But this does not mean that he had a politically viable solution for it. Suggestively, *The State of Christendom* surveyed medieval precedents for wartime taxes and spoke ominously of "the interest that princes have in their subjects' goods and the power that is given unto kings in the Old Testament over the lands and possession of as many as live under their obedience."[166] These remarks, which anticipate the most authoritarian arguments of later clerical defenders of the Forced Loan, occur in the midst of an argument that Elizabethan recusants should be grateful that the queen had not taken more of their money. But they might equally have justified higher and more arbitrary taxation of loyal Protestant subjects.

Far more cautious than Essex about the political risks of higher taxation, Elizabeth and Burghley struggled to keep military expenditures under control. While the queen recognized the need to strike at Spain's naval preparations, she

---

[164] For a concise review of these figures with citations to the relevant specialized studies see Conrad Russell, *King James VI and I and his English Parliaments: The Trevelyan Lectures Delivered at the University of Cambridge, 1995*, ed. Richard Cust and Andrew Thrush (Oxford: Oxford University Press, 2011), 6–7.
[165] This was especially true in London, for which see Ian Archer, "The Burden of Taxation in Sixteenth-Century London," *Historical Journal* 44 (2001): 599–607.
[166] *The State of Christendom*, 183–4, 189.

wanted to do so in ways that minimized her own costs and risks, while replenishing her treasury by seizing Spanish wealth. She bitterly resented the fact that after most expeditions the lion's share of the profits went to soldiers and sailors who embezzled the loot, before she received her own share. Although they never fully spelled out the reasoning behind their aversion to much higher wartime taxation, it is surely significant that Elizabeth and Burghley had both lived through an earlier period of military adventurism in the 1540s and 1550s that ruined crown finances, while touching off a disastrous cycle of inflation through debasement of the coinage that contributed to serious social unrest. A string of bad harvests and an abortive rising by the rural poor in Oxfordshire in 1596 must have triggered their memories of the Western Rebellion and Kett's Rebellion nearly a half-century earlier. Increasingly alarming reports were also arriving from Ireland as the rebellion of Tyrone and Tyrconnell gained momentum.

The queen's refusal to put matters to the test means that we will never know for certain how much more taxation the political nation would have tolerated. But it seems unlikely that Essex's proposal for an additional £250,000 per annum to fund offensive operations was politically viable. He also underestimated the intrinsic difficulties of long-distance offensive campaigns under early modern conditions: the problem identified by *The State of Christendom* that "plagues, pestilence, famine, tediousness of the way, want of water, tempests by sea and sudden sickness have always and will continuously weaken the forces" of any expedition "sent far from home by any prince whatsoever."[167] The spectacular success at Cadiz in 1596 punctuated a long string of frustrations and defeats, beginning with the Portugal expedition of 1589, which cost the lives of between 6,000 and 10,000 English and Dutch soldiers and sailors, and extending through Essex's unsuccessful Islands Voyage of 1597 and the final expedition to the Caribbean of Drake and Hawkins, on which both commanders died. The Spanish also suffered a series of setbacks as Atlantic storms and logistical problems defeated new armadas launched against England and Ireland. But the longer the war continued, the greater the odds grew that the weather and other contingent circumstances would some day favor Spain.

None of this prevented Essex and his partisans from seeing the fiscal restraint and the desire for peace of Elizabeth and the Cecils as evidence of strategic blindness and moral weakness. Anthony Bacon complained in the winter after the Cadiz expedition of the court's drowsy leaders, "lulled asleep in a most dangerous security," when they had the chance to "break the neck of Spanish tyranny" once and for all by following up on the previous summer's victory.[168] But unfortunately, Essex had begun to quarrel not only with the queen and his fellow-commanders at Cadiz, Ralegh and Howard, but also with Sir John Norreys and Sir

---

[167] Ibid., 71.   [168] *Memoirs of Queen Elizabeth*, ed. Birch, 2.273.

Francis Vere, arguably the two most distinguished English generals of the period. Whereas in the early 1590s he had served as the chief court advocate for a loose coalition of veteran commanders seeking to reform and improve the kingdoms' armies, after 1596 English military experts divided between his remaining friends and new adversaries.[169] The largest contingent of English troops on the Continent served under Vere, who was now anything but an ally.[170] Essex and his circle had therefore grown estranged not just from older and more cautious members of the council but also from several professional soldiers who should have been his natural allies when a new dispute about whether to enter into peace negotiations with Spain erupted in 1598.

The earl attributed his isolation and lack of reward to envy.[171] "I felt that my fortune had bred me envy," he declared in his *Apologie*, "and that envy procured me strong and dangerous opposition, and this opposition would not be overcarried but by her Majesty's great favour, and...greatness of...merit...by my service in the wars."[172] He concluded that his envious foes were winning the battle because they had the queen to their side. "I live in a place where I am hourly conspired against and practiced upon," he complained in December 1596: "What they cannot make the world believe that they persuade themselves unto; and what they cannot make probable to the queen that give they out to the world. They have almost all the house to serve them for instruments. Yea the very oracles, I mean those that are counted to be plain and sincere, do...speak the largest language and strongest faction."[173] Several of his associates, including Henry Cuffe, Antonio Perez, and Francis Davison encouraged his conviction that envious rivals, preying upon Elizabeth's fears and jealousies, had sabotaged his ambitions while betraying the state and *patria*.

Frustrated at the court, Essex attempted to present his case to a wider public. While returning from Cadiz he wrote a long description of the sack of the Spanish port, magnifying his own role, which he then attempted to have published under a false name.[174] Although the council got wind of this plan and thwarted it, he and his circle resorted to the circulation of manuscript texts as an alternative means of publicity. Two years later Essex almost certainly helped secretly arrange for the widespread scribal publication of his *Apologie*. Forty-nine manuscript copies are known to have survived, and although a few of these date from the early seventeenth century, many others produced in the earl's lifetime have undoubtedly been lost. The latest scholar of the subject concludes that as many as a hundred or more copies may have been produced, including a few translated into French and Dutch

---

[169] Hammer, *Polarisation of Politics*, 235–6.
[170] David Trim, "War, Soldiers, and High Politics under Elizabeth I," in *Age of Shakespeare*, ed. Smuts, 82–102 at 95–101.
[171] Gajda, *Essex and Political Culture*, 141–3.   [172] Sig. A3v.
[173] *Life and Letters of Essex*, ed. Devereux, 1.409; cf. Gajda, *Essex and Political Culture*, 146–7.
[174] Hammer, *Polarisation of Politics*, 252.

that circulated on the Continent.[175] Although only one of several tracts debating the merits of peace with Spain, *The Apologie* was by far the most widely disseminated. As Hammer remarks, the earl's use of scribally produced texts amounted to an appeal "over the heads of the queen and council to the wider literate population."[176] The tactic flowed naturally from his views about the crucial importance of vigorous noble leadership to the moral quality of the common people. Since Elizabeth and her council were conspicuously failing to set the proper example, it fell to him to do so in their place.

Once started, the publicity Essex launched proved impossible to control. It eventually rebounded to further discredit him in the eyes of his royal mistress and the council. In May 1600, while under house arrest after his unauthorized return from Ireland, he was seriously embarrassed by the appearance of a printed edition of his *Apologie*, evidently produced by two journeyman printers with no connection to him, who hoped to capitalize on a growing market for topical material.[177] He was again embarrassed by the sale of an engraved equestrian portrait of him in armor, in a pose traditionally associated with kings and emperors. A number of sympathetic preachers who prayed for him from London pulpits and at Paul's Cross further angered the queen.[178] In early 1601 sermons preached in his London house attracted large crowds, leading the earl's friends to fear he might be imprisoned in response.[179] There were also dark mutterings against the queen's government. Robert Cecil complained during the earl's trial in Star Chamber after his return from Ireland, about "false and wicked libels" spread around London "against her Majesty's late proceedings" and "faithful councilors."[180] In Norfolk a few months later a false report of the queen's death inspired "some of the common people [to] say that this kingdom should be governed according to the government now used in the Low Countries."[181] According to Camden some preachers publicly affirmed that "the superior magistrates of the realm had power to restrain kings."[182]

The earl's public appeals were especially provocative in light of very recent challenges to royal authority in France by the duke of Guise and the Catholic League, and an accompanying flood of libels and polemics that sought to sway what some writers already called "public opinion" (*l'opinion publique*).[183] Contemporaries noted the parallels.[184] The circulation of materials friendly to

---

[175] Gazzard, "'Idle papers'," 186–90; Hammer, "Smiling Crocodile."
[176] Hammer, *Polarisation of Politics*, 253–4.   [177] Ibid., 179–80.
[178] TNA SP12/273/59 and 274/1; *CSPD 1598–1601*, 365; HMC *Report on the Manuscripts of Lord DeLisle and Dudley, Preserved at Penshurst Place*, 6 vols (London: HM Stationery Office, 1925–66), 2.427; LPL Mss. 3470, fols 216, 218.
[179] *Memoirs of Queen Elizabeth*, ed. Birch, 2.473.   [180] BL Harl. Mss. 6854, fol. 269.
[181] LPL Mss. 3470, fol. 212.
[182] *The history of the most renowned and victorious princess Elizabeth* (London, 1688), 607.
[183] Nicolas le Roux, *Le roi, la cour, L'état: de la Renaissance à l'absolutisme* (Seyssel: Champ Vallon, 2013), 223 and chapter 12.
[184] Gajda, *Essex and Political Culture*, 195.

Essex and hostile to the court reinforced the determination of the queen and some members of her council to discipline Essex. But he refused to bow to royal displeasure, which he interpreted as further proof of his enemy's machinations. This conviction then became self-fulfilling, as Ralegh and eventually Robert Cecil concluded that Essex wanted to destroy them and might soon have an opportunity because of his close relationship with the queen's probable heir, James VI. Hammer argues that they therefore decided to strike first by deliberately provoking his revolt, in February 1601, by spreading reports that they intended to have him tried for treason.[185] His attempted coup collapsed within a few hours, leading to his execution and that of his protégé, Henry Cuffe, and the imprisonment of several other followers.

Essex's Legacies

Essex's memory and the nexus of values and critical attitudes toward the court and monarch that had taken shape around him left a complex legacy to the next two reigns.[186] As John Adamson has pointed out, nearly all the leaders of the opposition to Charles I in the House of Lords in 1641 were sons of Essex, his sister Penelope, or their close relatives.[187] Like him they were prepared to use physical force, in the shape of both armies and crowds in London streets, to constrain a wayward monarch and purge his court of figures they regarded as public enemies. But despite this family connection, the relationship between Essex's example and later parliamentary resistance to the Stuarts should not be oversimplified. One of Essex's followers, Charles Danvers, confessed shortly after the revolt that if it had succeeded "there would be about Michaelmas a parliament called; and that [Essex] himself and his friends would make a good party in the house and propound some things for the good of the state."[188] Danvers did not explain what those "things" would involve but they almost certainly would have included a ratification of James VI's claim to the succession, some sort of condemnation of Essex's enemies, and, possibly, financial support for war either through traditional subsidies or a new tax on "superfluous" luxuries.

The earl's circle had therefore in some ways anticipated the later attempt in the 1640s to use parliament as an instrument to reform the state by imposing conditions on its royal head. But little evidence exists in the earl's own writings

---

[185] Hammer, "Shakespeare's *Richard II*."
[186] Richard McCoy, "Old English Honour in an Evil Time: Aristocratic Principle in the 1620s," in *The Stuart Court and Europe: Essays in Politics and Political Culture*, ed. R. Malcolm Smuts (Cambridge: Cambridge University Press, 1996), 135–55.
[187] John Adamson, *The Noble Revolt: The Overthrow of Charles I* (London: Weidenfeld & Nicolson, 2007), esp. the genealogical tables on xii–xiii.
[188] *Memoirs of Queen Elizabeth*, ed. Birch, 2.473; cf. Gajda, *Essex and Political Culture*, 53.

of any extensive parliamentary program. Although a few of his followers, notably Sir Francis Bacon, did later promote legislated reforms, this was never a central preoccupation of Essex himself or of most of his followers. Despite his admiration for the United Provinces and republican Rome, he does not seem to have taken a particular interest in republican institutions or classical concepts of citizenship. He did not seek to create an English republic or a system of institutional checks on the crown, but to purge the court and restore "the old English valor" through the traditional baronial method of armed revolt.

Some historians have accordingly portrayed the 1601 rising as an anachronism, the last pathetic gasp in a dying tradition of neo-feudal rebellion. But this is less clear if we see it from an international perspective. Essex's attempt to seize Elizabeth by a quick armed strike resembles the 1560 Huguenot Conspiracy of Amboise, the Ruthven Raid, and the seizure of Stirling by the earl of Angus and his followers in 1586. The earl's attempt to rally the London populace to his cause paralleled the seizure of Paris by Guise and his allies in 1588. The attempt at Amboise failed, the Ruthven Raid succeeded for less than a year, and Guise died by assassination at the hands of the king's bodyguard. But despite the lack of long-term success, armed coups remained a frequent feature of early modern politics. French nobles continued to use armed revolts in efforts to extort concessions from the crown down to the 1620s. The Scottish parallels lend a note of irony to the near certainty that James VI knew of and approved Essex's plans to seize Whitehall in 1601. James may have relished the prospect that his chief noble ally in England would soon do to Elizabeth what her Scottish noble allies had twice done to him a few years earlier. Essex's revolt looks hopelessly outdated only if viewed from a narrowly insular perspective. Nevertheless, the revolt's dismal failure must have reinforced the view most contemporaries already held that efforts to deal with an inadequate monarch by armed coercion would only make matters worse.[189] In that way it probably made a negative contribution to later patterns of resistance, by showing the need for alternative, institutional methods of imposing conditions on a monarch and displacing hated courtiers.

In other respects, the legacy of Essex's career continued shaping political attitudes in more straightforward ways.[190] The most direct was through a pattern of thought associating the preservation of English virtue with the vigorous pursuit of war, while blaming the decline of virtue on a combination of weak royal leadership, corruption at court and the corrosive influence of ease and luxury during times of peace. So-called "patriot lords," including Essex's former friend the earl of Southampton, espoused these views in the Parliament of 1621.[191]

---

[189] Gajda, "Political Culture in the 1590s."
[190] Maureen King, "The Essex Myth in Jacobean England," in *The Accession of James I: Historical and Cultural Consequences*, ed. Glenn Burgess, Rowland Wymer, and J. Lawrence (Basingstoke: Palgrave Macmillan, 2006), 177–86 reviews the earl's posthumous reputation.
[191] McCoy, "Old English Honour."

The same presumptions colored attacks on the duke of Buckingham a few years later, although this is a more ambiguous case since he and Charles simultaneously attempted to replicate Essex's role in rallying the country in a war against Spain and calling upon it to make sacrifices in the cause. Like Essex, Buckingham saw himself and was seen by Charles I as a victim of envy. Both sides in the contest between the duke and his enemies attempted to draw on themes Essex had once advanced.

The earl's professed contempt for "soft loving men [who] love ease, pleasure and profit," in contrast to heroic "men of action" who served their country in arms, found numerous echoes in James's reign.[192] "Our minds are effeminate," the Irish soldier, Barnaby Rich, complained, "our martial exercises and disciplines of war are turned into womanish pleasures and delights, our gallants think it better [to] spend their lands and livings in a whore's lap than their lives in a martial field for the honor of their country."[193] Francis Bacon agreed: "the arts which flourish in times while virtue is in growth are military; and while virtue is in state, are liberal; and while virtue is in declination, are voluptuary; so I doubt that this age of the world is somewhat upon the descent of the wheel." Bacon also blamed the Jacobean peace for an increase in litigation. "Times of peace, drawing for the most part with them abundance of wealth and fineness of cunning, do draw also in further consequence multitude of suits and controversies and abuses of laws by evasions and devices."[194] Thomas Scott, in his notorious pamphlet, *Vox Populi*, portrayed the Spanish ambassador Gondomar bragging about how, under James's rule, English "bodies by long disuse of arms were disabled and their minds effeminated by peace and luxury, far from what they were in 88 when they were daily fleshed in our blood and made hearty by customary conquests."[195]

The myth that England had failed to defeat Spain only because a weak queen and her courtiers had constrained the kingdom's swordsmen also survived well into the seventeenth century. In a tract written for Prince Henry, Essex's former rival, Ralegh, asserted that Elizabeth "did all by halves," thwarting commanders who would otherwise have reduced Philip II to a "king of figs and oranges" by seizing the wealth of his overseas empire.[196] Even more than Essex, Ralegh had confidence in England's ability to vanquish Spain because of his inflated belief in the superiority of his country's valor. "If therefore it be demanded whether the Macedonian or the Roman were the best warrior, I will answer: The Englishman." History demonstrated that the English had repeatedly vanquished enemies

---

[192] *Apologie*, sig. B3.
[193] Barnaby Rich, *The Irish Hubub, or, the English Hue and Cry* (London, 1619), 8.
[194] Bacon, *Works*, 7.314–15.
[195] Thomas Scott, *Vox Populi. Or Newes from Spain translated according to the Spanish copies* (London, 1620), 11.
[196] BL Cotton Mss. Vitellius CXVIa, fol. 338; Malcolm Smuts, "Prince Henry and his World," in *The Lost Prince: The Life and Death of Henry Stuart*, ed. Catharine MacLeod (London: National Portrait Gallery, 2012), 19–31 at 26.

"far superior to us in numbers and all needful provisions, yea as well trained as we, or commonly better," and there was no reason to doubt that they could do so again if given the chance.[197]

Even some men relatively unaffected by chivalric nostalgia, who should have known better, endorsed such views. "The principle point of greatness of any state is to have a race of military men," Francis Bacon asserted: "neither is money the sinews of war (as it is trivially said), where the sinews of men's arms, in base and effeminate people, are failing."[198] This dubious belief furnished a ready excuse for thinking England might fight Spain without increasing taxation. "There was never any war, wherein the more valiant people had to deal with the more wealthy, but that the war, if it were well conducted, did nourish and pay itself."[199] This facile assumption, nurtured by exaggerated memories of profitable privateering and Elizabethan dreams of seizing Spain's treasure fleets, long obscured the real issue of how far the English propertied elite would sacrifice its own material interests to finance more robust military initiatives.

It needs emphasis that arguments for renewed war usually overlooked the enormous sacrifices that the Elizabethan conflict with Spain had demanded. David Trim has estimated that, at least on paper, the crown mobilized over 80,000 men for continental war between 1585 and 1603. As a proportion of the population this compares to English mobilization during the First World War. Although Trim's figure may include some fictitious dead-pays, probably more than 70,000 soldiers actually went to France, the Low Countries, and a few other European theaters.[200] Over 42,000 more, most of them conscripts, went to Ireland. Charles Carlton has estimated death rates at over 37 percent for soldiers in continental campaigns and 50 percent in Ireland, figures considerably exceeding those for World War I. He thinks that probably another 74,000 served at sea, in the navy or aboard privateers, of whom approximately a third died.[201] If accurate these estimates suggest that nearly a quarter of the adult male population (23.7 percent) engaged in some kind of military service beyond England's borders, experiencing horrific death rates as they did so. Given the nature of the sources, such calculations can be no more than educated guesses, but they point to the terrible human cost of Elizabeth's wars. In financial terms the crown spent about £4,500,000 on war between 1585 and 1605, roughly £300,000 a year on average, slightly more than its total ordinary income.[202] Ralegh's claim that Elizabeth fought her wars by half-measures is believable only if we conclude either that

---

[197] Sir Walter Ralegh, *History of the World*, ed. George Patrides (London: Macmillan, 1971), 327.
[198] "Of the True Greatness of Kingdoms and Estates," in Bacon, *Works*, 6.444-52 at 446.
[199] "Of the True Greatness of the Kingdom of Britain," in Bacon, *Works*, 7.47-64 at 55-6.
[200] David Trim, "Fighting 'Jacob's Wars': The Employment of English and Welsh Mercenaries in the European Wars of Religion in France and the Netherlands, 1562-1610," University of London PhD thesis, 2002, 340, 515, cited in Charles Carlton, *This Seat of Mars: War and the British Isles, 1485-1746* (New Haven: Yale University Press, 2011), 53.
[201] Carlton, *Seat of Mars*, 53-5.   [202] Ibid., 56.

she was capable of drastically increasing her revenues, or that her government's military strategy was so fundamentally misguided that it squandered huge resources for small gains, when an alternative approach would have won the war at less cost. Neither view seems credible. The cult of English valor promoted by Essex and other Elizabethan swordsmen encouraged a destructive tendency to underestimate the true financial and human costs of military conflict.

8
The Battle over Erastian Episcopacy in Two British Kingdoms, 1588–1603

In July 1588, upon hearing that the Armada had entered the Channel, Philip Howard earl of Arundel caused a priest to celebrate a mass for the taking away of schism in the Tower of London, where they were both imprisoned.[1] The futility of this gesture by the titular head of England's leading Catholic noble family reflects the condition into which militant opposition to Protestant rule had declined.[2] Although we can never know for certain how many Catholics might have rallied to the Army of Flanders if it had landed in England, they did nothing effective to impede the crown's defensive preparations. The predictions of exiles like Persons and Allen that the great majority of the population would actively assist a Catholic liberator had proved hollow. The response might well have been different had the Armada tried to land in Ireland or Scotland, where Lord Maxwell did prepare to assist the Spanish. But even a successful landing in either of those kingdoms would have left the invading army distant from the heartland of the English state, facing major logistical difficulties as it tried to advance. The fact that the Armada made no attempt to link up with the earl of Huntly as it retreated past his lands in northeast Scotland, or to disembark forces in Ireland showed that, at least for the moment, Spain had given up on schemes to destabilize the Elizabethan state by supporting religious insurrections along its periphery. Mary Stuart's execution and James VI's continuing fidelity to his English alliance and Protestantism had simultaneously diminished the odds of a Catholic succeeding Elizabeth on the throne.

Barring a new and more successful armada, Protestant rule therefore appeared more secure than in the recent past. But the *kind* of Protestantism that the state would promote remained in doubt. Every English monarch since Henry VIII had fundamentally redefined the character of the English Church and there was no good reason to assume that the same thing would not happen after Elizabeth died. For thirty years she had stubbornly defended the Erastian episcopal church settlement of 1559, which many Protestants had always regarded as an interim

[1] BL Add Mss. 48,029, fols 78–89; *A Complete Collection of State Trials*, ed. Sollom Emlyn, 2 vols (2nd ed., 1730), 1.158.
[2] As son and heir to the late duke of Norfolk, Arundel headed the senior branch of the Howard dynasty, which of course included several junior branches whose heads would be awarded with titles as earls of Nottingham, Northampton, and Suffolk under Elizabeth and James.

compromise that further reforms would supersede. In the parliaments of 1584–5 and 1586–7 the Commons debated fundamental changes in the Church, and on the latter occasion the queen had to intervene to prevent legislation from passing. Behind this campaign lay a network of puritan conferences that had sprouted across much of East Anglia and the midlands, starting in about 1584, as an underground presbyterian system. Delegates from the individual conferences met periodically in London or Cambridge for "general assemblies," the Scottish term for national synods. The conference movement drafted and debated a "Book of Discipline," probably between 1585 and 1587, to serve as a blueprint for an English presbyterian church that would have closely resembled other reformed churches across Europe, from Hungary to Scotland.[3] Several members of the privy council, especially Leicester and Walsingham, had considerable sympathy for this initiative. In Scotland James VI began to bend to pressure to back away from his staunch support for episcopacy. As the queen's most likely, if never quite inevitable successor, his ecclesiastical policies had considerable relevance to the future of the English Church.

Modern historians have told the story of the puritan classis movement and its defeat in the 1590s almost entirely as an English event, more or less unconnected to the ecclesiastical politics of Scotland and happenings elsewhere in Europe.[4] This insular focus derives partly from hindsight. We now know that the Elizabethan settlement not only survived James's succession but became a model for highly contentious changes that he and Charles I eventually tried to impose in Scotland. Since James had earlier tried to bring the Kirk into closer alignment with the Church of England in 1584, it seemed natural to assume that his ecclesiastical policies remained consistent, so that presbyterianism was always destined to remain an opposition movement in both British kingdoms. But in the early 1590s James's policies *did* appear to shift in the direction of greater sympathy for the Kirk and English puritanism. Although an anti-puritan conformist position had simultaneously triumphed in England, its victory remained fragile because it depended on the support of an aging monarch. The contest over the

---

[3] Patrick Collinson, *The Elizabethan Puritan Movement* (Berkeley: University of California Press, 1967), parts 6 and 7; *Conferences and Combination Lectures in the Elizabethan Church, 1582–1590*, ed. Patrick Collinson, John Craig, and Brett Usher (Woodbridge: Boydell Press, 2003).

[4] See, in particular, Partick Collinson, *Richard Bancroft and Elizabethan Anti-Puritanism* (Cambridge: Cambridge University Press, 2013); Partick Collinson, "Ecclesiastical Vitriol: Religious Satire in the 1590s and the Invention of Puritanism," in *The Reign of Elizabeth I: Court and Culture in the Last Decade*, ed. John Guy (Cambridge: Cambridge University Press, 1995), 150–70; and Peter Lake, *Anglicans and Puritans? Presbyterianism and English Conformist Thought from Whitgift to Hooker* (London: Unwin Hyman, 1988). Collinson did sometimes note connections between English puritans and Scottish presbyterians in earlier work (e.g. *Elizabethan Puritan Movement*, 275–7 and elsewhere), but ignored Scotland in his book on Bancroft. Lake's often insightful work on the succession problem was produced after *Anglicans and Puritans*. For some Scottish dimensions of religious politics in the 1590s see Paul McGinnis and Arthur Williamson, "Radical Menace, Reforming Hope: Scotland and English Religious Politics, 1586–1596," *Renaissance and Reformation/Renaissance et Réforme* 36 (2013): 101–26.

future of the Church was bound up with the problem of the succession, and therefore with events not only within England but beyond its borders.

The Bill and Book Campaign of 1587, Leicester, and the Dutch Connection

In addition to events in Scotland, disputes over the structure of the Church took place against a backdrop of European confessional wars. The puritan conference movement reached its culmination at roughly the same moment that Leicester led his army to the Low Countries. For devout contemporaries the two events appeared connected, since the purification of worship within England and support for a holy war in the Low Countries were both enjoined by God's will. Since Elizabeth refused to reform her Church and hesitated to give Leicester's campaign adequate backing, godly Englishmen felt impelled to take their own initiatives to promote each goal, in the confidence that God would support them even if the queen did not. Sir Philip Sidney confided to his father-in-law, Walsingham, that he believed Leicester's campaign would succeed *despite* Elizabeth's failure to support it adequately. "If her Majesty were the fountain I would fear, considering what I clearly find that we should wax dry. But she is but a means whom God useth and I know not whether I am deceived but I am faithfully persuaded that if she should withdraw herself other springs would rise to help this action. For methinks I see the great work indeed in hand, against the abuses of the world, wherein it is no greater fault to have confidence in man's power than it is hastily to despair of God's work."[5] If winning the war depended on divine help, it made sense to believe that the promotion of preaching and religious discipline at home would contribute to victory by encouraging God's assistance, whereas tolerance of abuses within the Church might have the opposite effect.

We have noticed how, in his capacity as governor general, Leicester convened a national synod in the Netherlands in the autumn of 1586 that drew up a uniform presbyterian order of worship for the Dutch Reformed Church.[6] A few months later, in the winter of 1587, an English House of Commons tried to implement similar reforms through what historians have called the Bill and Book campaign. The same assembly urged Elizabeth to reconsider her refusal to assume sovereignty over the Netherlands and offered a hefty grant of supply if she would do so. The connections between the Bill and Book initiative and English involvement in the United Provinces seem to have extended beyond the fact that both drew support from much the same cohort of people. Patrick Collinson pointed out

---

[5] *The Correspondence of Sir Philip Sidney*, ed. Roger Kuin, 2 vols (Oxford: Oxford University Press, 2012), 2.1212–13.
[6] P. 304.

long ago that the book of the Bill and Book—a Calvinist order of service meant to replace *The Book of Common Prayer*—derived from a document drawn up for the English Church associated with the Merchant Adventurers Company staple in Middleburg, Zealand, and printed in that city by a certain Richard Schilders. Schilders had close connections to a community of puritan ex-patriates living in the Low Countries, including the presbyterian divine Thomas Cartwright.[7] Collinson apparently failed to notice that the title page of the service book bore the inscriptions, "*cum privelegio*" and "printer unto his Excellency," the title by which Leicester was generally known in the Netherlands. This suggests that Leicester may have sponsored its publication, perhaps because he intended to use it in his army. The earl summoned Cartwright home from the Netherlands in 1587, appointing him to direct a hospital he had endowed in the town of Warwick, with a stipend of £50 per annum.

Schilders went on to print at least two further texts related to the Bill and Book campaign: Dudley Fenner's *A defence of the godlie ministers, against the slanders of D. Bridges*, and a lengthy *Humble Petition of the Communaltie* to the queen. This second tract, which historians have previously overlooked, stands in a line of puritan petitions dating back to John Field's *Admonition to Parliament* in 1572, which Cyndia Clegg sees as contributions to campaigns of printed material coinciding with parliamentary sessions, calling for reforms of the Church. These were directed, she thinks, both to MPs and a wider readership.[8] The most immediate predecessor of the *Petition of the Communaltie*, entitled *A Lamentable Complaint of the Commonality, by way of supplication to the high court of parliament, for a learned ministry*, was printed by Robert Waldegrave during the parliamentary session of 1584–5. It departed from earlier doctrinal arguments for presbyterianism by focusing on the practical need for a learned ministry rather than arguments about the form of the primitive Church. It condemned the bishops not for exercising a supremacy contrary to God's word but for failing to provide an adequate supply of preaching, thereby condemning "a huge army of people in this land spiritually slain by Satan" through lack of instruction in the faith.[9] Parliament needed to remedy the failure by reforming the governance of the Church along presbyterian lines.[10] This text and several other puritan critiques of the Church printed by Waldegrave so angered the authorities that they shut down his press, which explains why the 1587 petition had to be printed in the Low Countries.

---

[7] Collinson, *Elizabethan Puritan Movement*, 308.

[8] Cyndia Clegg, "Print in the Time of Parliaments, 1560–1601," in *Tudor Books and Readers: Materiality and the Construction of Meaning*, ed. John King (Cambridge: Cambridge University Press, 2010), 138–59. Clegg's generally thorough discussion misses the "petition" printed by Schilders.

[9] *A Lamentable Complaint of the Commonality, by way of supplication to the high court of parliament, for a learned ministry* (London, 1585), 60.

[10] Ibid., 41.

That petition continued to emphasize the need for more preaching, while escalating attacks not only on the bishops but also on the queen herself for failing to provide it. Its arguments also closely resemble those of another printed tract of 1587, written by the radical puritan John Penry, in the form of a petition to the queen and Parliament that demanded more preaching in his native Wales.[11] According to *The Petition of the Communaltie*, the dearth of preaching not only made it easier for papists to foment disloyalty and treason but, more importantly, consigned millions of English souls to hell by denying them the means to receive saving grace.[12] At the same time, "hundreds of worthy men are shut up and enclosed in the two universities of Oxford and Cambridge" and "many worthy preachers" restrained for refusing to "approve the relics of Antichrist" remaining within the Church. Since the bishops had not remedied this abuse in twenty-nine years, no one should trust them to do so in the future.[13] The queen must "hear the voice of Christ your well beloved, that saith open unto me dear sister... unto whom, we pray you, make no unkind excuse."[14] If she failed to respond, the petition broadly hinted, God might withdraw his protection from her. Without advocating disobedience, it implied that unless Elizabeth permitted fundamental ecclesiastical reform she might fall victim to the next assassination plot or some similar calamity. God had his mysterious plan for England and its inadequate Church, and Elizabeth was not necessarily part of it.

While no one had the temerity to utter such a blunt statement on the floor of the Commons, one MP, Job Throckmorton, came close. Suggestively, he sat for the Dudley pocket borough of Warwick and seems to have owed his election to the support of nearby puritan gentry, and probably to Leicester himself.[15] "If I were to give her Majesty advice upon my allegiance," he proclaimed, "I would humbly desire her after so many deliverances she would beware she sleep not upon them in peril of her life."[16] He exhorted his colleagues to pray God to "waken Her Majesty's heart before the day of her account that she speed such things as are amiss, especially her ignorant and unlearned ministry."[17]

---

[11] John Penry, *A Treatise Containing the Aequity of an Humble Supplication which Is to be Exhibited Unto Hir Gracious Majesty and this High Court of Parliament in behalfe of the Countrey of Wales* (Oxford, 1587).

[12] *The Humble Petition of the Communaltie* (Middleburg, 1587). At this point in the text the signature numbers cease for several pages; the quotation occurs three leaves after A4.

[13] Ibid., sigs B3v–B4 (as designated in the text).

[14] Ibid., n.p. but eight pages after B4. Cf. *Humble Petition*, sigs B2v–B3: "Now is the Lord Jesus become an earnest petitioner, in the person of this poor people, unto your highness [Elizabeth]: cause not his countenance to fall down, neither send him empty away, seeing he hath never sent you empty in all the petitions you have made to him."

[15] See the articles on Throckmorton by Patrick Collinson in *ODNB* and in *The History of Parliament: The House of Commons 1558–1603*, ed. P. W. Hasler (London: Boydell and Brewer, 1981). I want to thank Cathryn Enis for communications concerning Leicester's likely role in procuring Throckmorton's election.

[16] *PPEI* 2.313–14. [17] Ibid., 319.

Throckmorton's refusal to defer to Elizabeth's direction of the Church corresponded to his caustic attitude toward other European monarchs. He accused Philip II not only of tyranny but also licentiousness and incest, Henry III of conspiring with Spain, and James VI of duplicity: "Whither then shall we cast our eye? Northwards towards the young imp of Scotland? Alas it is a cold coast (ye know) and he that should set up his rest upon so young and wavering a head should find cold comfort too, I tell you."[18] Instead of relying on kings, God had made it clear that England must ally with the Dutch, in a pact not between two crowns but two peoples, united in defense of the true Church and resistance to tyranny.[19] The offer of sovereignty made to Elizabeth was divinely inspired, a "blessing" that previous English kings "would willingly have redeemed at any price," which had now "by the good providence of God fallen into our laps."[20] Rejecting that gift invited God's anger, although this was, of course, precisely what Elizabeth had already done.[21] "Is there any man amongst us so dim sighted that doth not here plainly behold the very finger of God directing us (as it were) by diameter to the Low Countries, as who should say, 'there only is the means of your safety, there only is the passage laid open unto you'."[22]

Throckmorton went on to criticize the English court for its complacency. "It is wondered at above that simple men of the country should be so forward and it doth amate [dismay] us in the country that wise men of the court should be so backward. If it be more than need in us to fear everything, it is less than due for them to sit down with *omnia bene* and fear nothing. Is it a fault in a private man to be busy and can it be excused in a councilor to be sleepy?"[23] Similar views circulated beyond Parliament. A correspondent told Burghley that news of the fall of Antwerp in August 1585 had unleashed a torrent of abuse against him, with men "exclaiming openly and everywhere that you and your temporizing sought to starve all men, to call in the enemy of Spain even to Billingsgate... That England was become *regnum Cecilianum*, your building infinite to kings' palaces."[24] While necessarily more discreet in their public comments, Leicester, Walsingham, and other members of their circle shared this impatience with courtiers and monarchs. Walsingham privately warned James VI that kings who violated the rule of justice were often deposed, giving Edward II as an example.[25]

---

[18] Ibid., 277, 280, and 285.   [19] Ibid., 284–5.   [20] Ibid., 283.
[21] Ibid., 284: "Thus and thus it seemeth to me that the Lord doth, as it were, sound in our ears concerning this cause we have in hand [intervention in the Netherlands], being indeed a cause of that importance to us ward as in the rejecting or refusal thereof I can see nothing but a fearful beholding of some lamentable distress in time to come. I know the Lord in his infinite power can work without means, as he can feed the body without bread; but yet willfully to reject the means when it is offered, what is it else but to tempt the Lord and provoke his wrath?"
[22] Ibid., 285.   [23] Ibid., 312.
[24] TNA SP12/181/32, William[?] Herle to Burghley, August 13, 1585.
[25] BL Add. Mss. 12,520, fol. 53v.

But other members of the council, who desperately wanted to preserve good relations with France and Scotland in the wake of Mary Stuart's execution, disliked Throckmorton's attacks on Henry III and James VI, and when the Scottish ambassador complained, Burghley promised to throw the offending MP in the Tower.[26] Sir Christopher Hatton then rebuked Throckmorton in the Commons. "The reverence to princes is due by God... Hard and intolerable to use ill speeches of the king of France, continuing in league and friendship with us... Matter nearer than this glanced at and also touched against the king of Scotland, a prince young, of good religion, a friend and in league with her Majesty... A prince representing *figuram dei hominis*."[27] Hatton also denounced the Bill and Book, claiming the measure would subvert not only royal supremacy over the Church but lay property rights in the form of impropriated tithes.[28]

Although Hatton had supported Leicester's expedition to the Netherlands, Whitgift appears to have demurred when asked to do so, while raising principled objections to aiding rebels against the king of Spain.[29] Attitudes toward church reform, deference to kings, and involvement in European religious wars therefore tended to correlate with each other. These linkages were forged in a climate of deep uncertainty about the future, caused by the unsettled state of European affairs and the possibility that Elizabeth might die at any moment, whether through assassination or natural causes. People like Penry, Throckmorton, and the unnamed authors of the *Complaint of the Communaltie*—and to a degree also Sidney, Walsingham, and Leicester—felt that uncertainty as a call to action to promote God's will on multiple fronts. Their sense that they acted as instruments of a divine plan gave them the courage to defy worldly authority and the tenacity to keep fighting even after multiple setbacks. By contrast, figures like Whitgift and Hatton saw the clouded future as a threat to stable structures of hierarchical authority they wanted to preserve, not only against Spanish aggression and Catholic plots but also radical Protestant reforms. To do that effectively they needed not only to defeat specific measures like the Bill and Book, but to strike at the root of the problem by breaking up the presbyterians' organized networks and depriving them of the support they received from a large and influential cohort of gentry, peers, and members of the privy council. Until they succeeded in this last task, any momentary victory they achieved in their defense of the Church would remain vulnerable to sudden reversal by contingent events over which they had no control. The debate over presbyterian reform was embedded in wider contexts and related to concerns that superficially appeared to have little to do with the structure of the Church.

---

[26] "Job Throckmorton," in *History of Parliament*, ed. Hasler.   [27] Ibid., 389–90.
[28] Ibid., 336.
[29] John Strype, *The Life and Acts of John Whitgift*, 3 vols (Oxford, 1822), 2.228–9, 231.

Puritans, Popularity, and the State

But during the eighteen months following the conclusion of the 1587 session, several developments complicated efforts to draw the connections between religious reform in England, support for robust intervention in the Netherlands, and skepticism about European monarchs that Throckmorton's speeches exemplify. Leicester's "puritan crusade" in the Low Countries petered out in frustration. Burghley concluded that his colleague's effort to take control of the United Provinces was a mistake that had drawn Elizabeth "more deeply into the malice of the Spanish king and the contempt of other princes her neighbors," without yielding any positive results.[30] He also regretted Drake's raids on the Indies as a further provocation that had not significantly weakened Philip II, and dreaded a retaliatory attack not just from Spain but an alliance of Spain, France, and Scotland.[31] For this reason he even had second thoughts about Mary Stuart's execution and English support for Scottish "factions" bent on "curbing the king" and procuring her death.[32] Others on the council, including Hatton, Whitgift, and Sir James Croft, almost certainly shared these misgivings.

But instead of undergoing simultaneous attacks by France, Spain, and Scotland, in the summer of 1588 England survived the Armada, while Henry III remained neutral and James VI a nominal ally. The unsuccessful invasion compelled Elizabeth and her more cautious councilors to abandon negotiations with Parma and accept the need to fight Spain openly. This in turn revived the Dutch alliance. The storms that struck the Spanish fleet as it sailed home were widely interpreted as signs that providence continued to favor to Elizabeth and her realm: God had not abandoned her after all. Through Philip's actions more than her own, she had solidified her reputation as the principal European champion of the Protestant cause and resistance to Spanish tyranny. Preachers and lay Protestants rallied to her support, making criticism of her conduct more difficult.

In December 1588, the murder of the duke of Guise and his brother on Henry III's orders ended worries that the French crown would join forces with the Catholic League and Spain. The French king's assassination by a Catholic fanatic the following August then made Henry of Navarre heir to the French throne. He joined the alliance between Elizabeth and the Dutch and maintained it for five years after his conversion to Rome in 1593, as Philip II intervened in the French civil war and attempted to claim the crown of France, as well as that of England,

---

[30] TNA SP12/203/62, memorandum by Burghley of September 1587.

[31] Ibid. (fol. 121r). He had feared this possibility at least as early as the previous February, telling the Dutch agents in London that Elizabeth could not increase her aid to them because she had to prepare to withstand "the kings of Spain, France and Scotland that all had conspired together against her Majesty" (BL Add Mss. 17,677C, fols 193–194v).

[32] TNA SP12/203/62: "Another cause of the never ceasing conspiracies against the realm of England is the factions maintained in Scotland for the curbing of the king present and the death of the Scottish queen."

for his own daughter. This antagonized many Catholics in both countries, who rallied to support their kingdoms' independence from foreign domination. The fight against Philip and his militant allies no longer depended so exclusively on beleaguered coalitions of Calvinist nobles and local Protestants movements. It instead united the Protestant queen of England with the Catholic king of France and the Dutch Republic, in opposition to the threat of a Habsburg "universal monarchy" over western Europe. These new conditions encouraged more unquestioning support for legitimate royal authority, making it easier to portray disparaging remarks about monarchs as acts of disloyalty that would only weaken united resistance to the foreign enemy.

The death of Leicester in September 1588 had meanwhile removed the puritans' single most powerful and determined advocate on the privy council. In the aftermath of the Armada, Whitgift and Hatton intensified their counter-offensive against presbyterianism and puritan non-conformity. A sermon at the outdoor pulpit of Paul's Cross in London by Hatton's chaplain, Richard Bancroft, in January 1589, foreshadowed the new offensive, which soon came to involve more rigorous prosecutions, in common law courts as well as before ecclesiastical commissioners, of Protestant non-conformity and critics of the established Church.[33] One contemporary claimed that Whitgift, Hatton, and Judge Anderson "labored the queen" to use the courts to enforce subscription to ecclesiastical articles, over the objections of the lord chief justice, presumably of the King's Bench, who said that "the matter is dangerous because the number of precisians is great and they the best subjects. And so Judge Anderson went away with a flea in his ear." An attempt was made to "daunt" Whitgift by gathering the signatures of numerous gentlemen on a petition to the privy council protesting his crackdown, but its chief instigators was imprisoned.[34] Prosecutions commenced, some under statutes originally passed to restrain Catholics that were now repurposed for use against puritans.

But instead of moderating their tactics in this new climate, one cohort of puritans escalated the rhetorical contest. In 1588 Schilders produced a second edition of the *Petition of the Communaltie*, enlarged through the addition of a clerical petition to convocation that had been suppressed by the bishops, and one additional document. Waldegrave had meanwhile acquired another press, which he set up in a secret location. With it he printed several more tracts by Penry, including two presented as further petitions to Parliament lamenting the lack of preaching in Wales, the sins of ignorant ministers and abuses by the High Commission, along with a series of satirical tracts under the pseudonym of Martin

---

[33] See, esp., Collinson, *Elizabethan Puritan Movement*, part 8; Patrick Collinson, *Richard Bancroft and Elizabethan Anti-Puritanism* (Cambridge: Cambridge University Press, 2013), chapters 2–4 and 6.

[34] LPL Mss. 3740, fol. 120, Bancroft's summary of "the effect of a certain letter written by Mr. Bradley now in prison."

Marprelate.³⁵ These attacked the bishops with ribald humor, while retailing scandalous stories about their personal behavior.³⁶ Martin's racy colloquial style and love of scurrilous gossip mimicked vernacular forms of slander used in village quarrels, with the goal of stripping bishops of their dignity and turning them into objects of ridicule.³⁷ Although the authorities suspected Penry, modern scholarship has identified Job Throckmorton as the principal author. When the government's agents finally began to close in on his press, Waldegrave fled to Edinburgh, where James VI appointed him royal printer. Penry followed, assisted by money from Throckmorton, and continued to produce tracts against the bishops that Waldegrave printed.³⁸ These continued to depict the issue of church reform as an apocalyptic test of England's relationship with God: "the lord meaneth certainly either to establish certainly the scepter of his son Christ Jesus in a glorious manner among us, or to make England an example of his vengeance for the rejecting of it."³⁹ The print campaign for puritan reform continued under the protection of the prince Throckmorton had recently described as a duplicitous "young imp," but who now began to look more like an ally of the godly.

Efforts to suppress presbyterian agitation and Protestant non-conformity raised fundamental questions about the religious foundations of the English state, epitomized by an exchange between the puritan John Udall and his judges at the Surrey assizes in 1591. Udall, who was being tried for publishing a seditious book, demanded to know "how is it possible that a preacher of the same religion

---

³⁵ John Penry, *An exhortation unto the governors and people of her Majesties countrie of Wales, to labour earnestly to have the preaching of the Gospell planted among them* (London, 1588); *A defence of that which hath been written in the questions of the ignorant ministerie, and the communicating with them* (London, 1588); *Th'appellation of John Penri, unto the highe court of Parliament from the bad and injurious dealing of th'Archb. of Canterb. & other his colleagues of the high commission* (London, 1589); *A viewe of some part of such publick wants and disorders as are in the service of God, within her Majesties countrie of Wales together with an humble petition, unto this high Court of Parliament for their speedy redress* (London, 1589). One Martinist tract, *Hay any work for the cooper*, mocked the authorities for failing to find Waldegrave's press by suggesting they should "put every man to his oath / and find means that Schilders of Middleborough shall be sworn too / so that if any refuse to swear / then he may be thought to be the printer" (Clegg, "Print in the Time of Parliaments," 148).

³⁶ Joseph Black, ed., *The Martin Marprelate Tracts: A Modernized and Annotated Edition* (Cambridge: Cambridge University Press, 2008); Joseph Black, "The Rhetoric of Reaction: The Martin Marprelate Tracts (1588–89), Anti-Martinism and the Uses of Print in Early Modern England," *Sixteenth Century Journal* 28 (1997): 707–25; Collinson, *Bancroft*, chapter 5 and works cited therein.

³⁷ Patrick Collinson, "Ecclesiastical Vitriol: Religious Satire in the 1590s and the Invention of Puritanism," in *Reign of Elizabeth*, ed. Guy, 150–70.

³⁸ *A brief discovery of the untruths and slanders (against the government of Christ) contained in a sermon, preached the 8 of Februarie 1588 by D. Bancroft* (Edinburgh, 1589); *An humble motion with submission unto the right Honorable LL of her Majesties Privie Counsell Wherein is to be considered, how necessarie it were for the good of this lande, and the Queenes Majesties safety, that ecclesiastical government were reformed* (Edinburgh, 1590); *A treatise wherein is manifestly proved, that reformation and those that sincerely favor the same, are unjustly charged to be enemies unto her Majesties, and the state* (Edinburgh, 1590). For further details see the *ODNB* articles on Waldegrave by A. J. Mann and on Penry by Claire Cross.

³⁹ *An humble motion*, sig. 2v.

which her Majesty professeth and maintaineth, who is known continually to pray unto God for her Highness's prosperity and happiness, both of soul and body; how is it possible, I say that such a one should be maliciously affected towards her?" The statute under which he stood accused was intended for use against papists and therefore did not apply to men like him.[40] One of his judges retorted that the statute did apply because Udall's book had maliciously defamed the bishops for "exercising their government which the queen hath appointed them and so it is by consequence against the queen." "It is plain in your book," he went on, "that you wrote not only against them [the bishops] but you wrote against the State, when you say that it is easier to live in England a papist, an Anabaptist or the Family of Love and what not ... What is this but a plain slandering of the State?"[41]

Efforts to define puritan dissent as a crime against the state drew upon two earlier strands of conformist argument. Ever since the 1570s, Whitgift had accused puritans of "popularity," the crime of appealing to the common people against authority.[42] Puritans were in some ways even more dangerous than Jesuits, he and other conformists argued, because their pretense of loyalty to Elizabeth and Protestantism made their attacks on royal and episcopal authority all the more insidious. Catholics and church papists had long argued along similar lines that puritans and Jesuits were equally disloyal, since both dissented from the ecclesiastical order established by law. They should therefore receive equal treatment. But many Protestants found this view implausible, since Catholic extremists had organized three conspiracies against the queen's life between 1582 and 1587, whereas puritans had simply tried to modify the Church through the legal and traditional method of parliamentary legislation.[43] Moreover, puritanism enjoyed the support of peers and gentlemen whose birth, wealth, and standing in their localities far exceeded that of Whitgift and his fellow bishops, who were essentially "new men," of modest origins, elevated solely by the queen's favor.[44] This made the accusation that puritans wanted to destroy property and social distinctions outwardly implausible. To make that charge stick the conformists had

---

[40] *State Trials*, ed. Emlyn, 1.166. [41] Ibid., 167.

[42] Peter Lake, "Puritanism, (Monarchical) Republicanism and Monarchy: or John Whitgift, Antipuritanism and the 'Invention' of Popularity," *Journal of Medieval and Early Modern Studies* 40.3 (2010): 463–95 and "A Tale of Two Episcopal Surveys: The Strange Fates of Edmund Grindal and Cuthbert Mayne Revisited," *Transactions of the Royal Historical Society* 6.18 (2008): 129–63; Collinson, *Bancroft*.

[43] Cf. the comment by Sir Francis Knollys in 1591 (BL Lansdown Mss. 66/52): "I do marvel how her Majesty can be persuaded that she is in as much danger of such as are called puritans as she is of papists, and yet her Majesty cannot be ignorant that the puritans are not able to change the government of the clergy but only by petition at her Majesty's hands, and yet her Majesty cannot do it but she must call a parliament first and no action can pass thereof unless her Majesty will give her royal assent thereunto."

[44] Cédrique Michon, *La crosse et le scepter: les prélats d'état sous François Ier et Henri VIII* (Paris: Tallandier, 2008), demonstrates that whereas in France leading bishops usually came from noble families, often of very high rank, in England they were almost invariably of yeoman, artisanal, or minor gentry background. This remained true under Elizabeth and partly explains the disdain in which bishops were often held by the lay elite.

to mischaracterize puritans by depicting them as younger, less educated, and more detached from elite support than was actually the case—as Whitgift famously liked to do by berating his clerical adversaries as "mere boys"—while simultaneously equating disobedience to their own commands with sedition against the queen. Ultimately at stake was the status of *delegated* royal authority, when it came into conflict with the moral and religious authority of godly preachers backed not so much by a rabble multitude as by pillars of local communities, and privy councilors like Leicester. In this respect the bishops' position resembled that of deputy lieutenants and other crown officials in Ireland, or indeed in English shires under the revitalized militia system. Like these other officials, the bishops were open to charges of abusing the authority granted them in a tyrannical fashion, in ways that violated common law while damaging the queen's true interests. A few conformist clergy countered by advancing arguments for *jure divino* episcopacy that allowed them to stigmatize presbyterians as rebels against God as well as their prince. Hatton's chaplain, Richard Bancroft, appeared to hint at this position in his 1589 Paul's Cross sermon, without explicitly endorsing it. But by staking out this claim, the bishops' defenders opened themselves to the further charge that they denied the authority of parliament and the queen over the Church, by resurrecting Catholic claims for the independence of the ecclesiastical order. Sir Francis Knollys vigorously pressed this point in several letters to Burghley.[45]

The scandal mongering and populist idiom of the Marprelate tracts nevertheless did lend some color to depictions of puritans as popular and seditious, particularly in light of the role that satiric libels had recently played in undermining respect for royal authority in France, contributing to a climate in which crowds whipped up by fiery sermons took control of Paris, and a Catholic monk murdered the king, thinking it a holy act.[46] Although English puritans had never gone nearly that far, it did not seem entirely implausible that Marprelate's scurrility and charges that the bishops had murdered millions of souls might eventually push England in the same direction. In 1591 proponents of this argument enjoyed a major boost, when an apparently illiterate and mentally unbalanced son of a Northamptonshire saddle-maker named Martin Hacket proclaimed himself a prophet with knowledge of God's secret will. He embraced the cause of presbyterian ministers imprisoned by the authorities and predicted the deaths of several privy councilors if these "martyrs" were not released. Two of Hacket's followers, Henry Arthington and Edmund Coppinger, then mounted a cart in Cheapside from which they proclaimed him the new Messiah. This blasphemy quickly led to Hacket's trial and execution for treason and a book by Bancroft's friend Richard Cosin. It presented Hacket's story as one of a dangerous

---

[45] HMC Salisbury 3.412; BL Lansdown Mss. 61/54 and 64/69.
[46] Nicolas le Roux, *Le roi, la cour, l'état: de la Renaissance à l'absolutisme* (Paris: Champ Vallon, 2013), 223–37.

conspiracy to murder the queen and most of the privy council, and incite an uprising similar to the great German peasant rebellion of the 1520s.[47] Cosin also documented Hacket's contacts with various puritans, making them appear guilty by association. Here at last, or so it seemed to some, was a presbyterian popular conspiracy worthy to stand alongside the popish plots of Throckmorton, Parry, and Babington.

Collinson has described the Hacket affair as a key turning point that allowed a group within the Elizabethan establishment, led by Hatton, Whitgift, and Bancroft, to introduce authoritarian methods of religious suppression against the opposition of Burghley, whom Collinson sees as struggling to moderate the conformist reaction.[48] But although there is clear evidence that Burghley disapproved of Whitgift's "inquisitorial" practices against some puritan ministers, the claim that he tried to prevent Hatton and Whitgift from exploiting the blasphemous utterances of Hacket's followers lacks foundation. A letter from Robert Cecil to Hatton shows that Burghley was actually *more* determined than Whitgift to portray Hacket not as a madman but a fanatic whose wild pronouncements pointed to a dangerous conspiracy:

> I am commanded by my lord my father to let your lordship understand that, in his perusal of the book which my lord [of] Canterbury sent your lordship, which likewise was delivered me by your lordship to show my lord here, he doth find that in this book is not aptly conveyed what were fit to be published. For where by Athington's confession the supposed madness of that monster Hacket was laid open and proved but only a dissembled frenzy, this pamphlet in the end doth note him to be a mad distracted person, which were not convenient by any writing authorized to be spread abroad and therefore in my lord father's judgment it doth not meet with that which it should do.[49]

The letter goes on to convey Burghley's advice that the whole affair be more thoroughly investigated, with instructions "to the archbishop of Canterbury to use his pleasure therein." A few months earlier Burghley had written a note to himself of tasks to accomplish: "first to have care that all papists and recusants, which by their wealth and credit may seem dangers, be restrained and punished according to the laws... Of this nature also is the care to be taken to suppress all the turbulent precisians who do violently seek to change the external government of the Church."[50]

---

[47] Collinson, *Bancroft*, 138–47; Richard Cosin, *Conspiracy for Pretended Reformation* (London, 1592), 34–6, 81, 85 and passim.

[48] Collinson, *Bancroft*, 115–16 and passim.

[49] Burghley to Christopher Hatton, August 6, 1591, printed in *Letters from Sir Robert Cecil to Sir Christopher Hatton, 1590–1591*, ed. Paul Hammer, Camden Society Publications, series 5, vol. 22 (1999), 226–7.

[50] TNA SP12/231/103; the note was written in April 1590.

By 1591, Elizabeth's leading councilors agreed on the need to suppress both "dangerous Catholics" and "turbulent precisians." While they still sometimes differed over which individuals to include in these two categories, they were united in their determination to suppress people of whatever stripe who appeared to threaten the existing ecclesiastical order, and in their willingness to bend or break the law in doing so. Burghley does not seem to have objected to the execution of Hackett and his associates, the imprisonment of recusants without trial on orders of the Council, or a conciliar order of 1596 authorizing the use of torture during interrogations of Oxfordshire enclosure rioters and a group of gypsies apprehended in Northamptonshire.[51] Although he complained about Whitgift's "Romish inquisition" when the High Commission used *ex officio* oaths against ministers Burghley regarded as good Protestants and loyal subjects, it is stretching the evidence to see him as a man with principled objections to harsh authoritarian methods in defense of the state.[52] Wartime conditions intensified worries on the council about challenges to the queen's authority, which made the excesses of Martin Marprelate and other puritan attacks on the bishops seem especially unacceptable. That made it easier for Hatton, Whitgift, and Bancroft to harry outspoken puritans, while throwing supporters of the godly onto the defensive. The drive for presbyterian reforms collapsed under this pressure. In 1593 the conformists succeeded in passing new legislation, against strenuous opposition in the Commons, making it easier to prosecute puritans.

The Scottish Mirror (Again)

But in Scotland, where presbyterianism had always been stronger and episcopal authority weaker than in England, religious politics followed a different course. As in the mid-1580s, Scotland offered a mirror that reflected while also distorting English religious controversies, giving them a different appearance. In one respect James VI followed a course of action diametrically opposite to the policies pursued by the English council. While the English authorities cracked down simultaneously on Catholic recusancy and puritan non-conformity, James continued to shelter and favor Catholic nobles within his court, while compensating, as we have seen, by displaying his support and sympathy for godly Protestantism and appearing to agree to presbyterian reforms. His seemingly equivocal behavior reflected the relative weakness of the Scottish crown and bishops, and the strength of both Catholic and presbyterian aristocratic factions. It also stemmed from his desire to cultivate godly support for his future bid to succeed Elizabeth, without antagonizing English Catholics or European powers.

---

[51] APC 26.322–3, 325, 373.   [52] BL Lansdowne Mss. 42/47.

But by declining to enforce a consistent religious settlement, James allowed a dynamic to continue in which each confessional extreme fed off its opposite. The contacts that Huntly and other Catholic peers maintained with Spain and France, probably in some cases with the king's knowledge and encouragement, kept alive fears of popish plots to exterminate Scottish Protestantism that increased support for an increasingly vociferous and well-organized presbyterian Kirk. Because great Scottish nobles still possessed seigneurial armies, they at times appeared to threaten not just the faith but the also the physical safety of Protestants, who needed to organize their own militias in response. Presbyterians therefore continued to believe that they needed not only to purify the Kirk but to defend it against violent attack, and that when the king failed to help they had to take matters into their own hands. But because James wanted the support of the Kirk he compensated for his protection of Catholic nobles by making concessions to its demands and cooperating with its defensive measures. The weakness of Scotland's legal institutions in comparison to those of England and the uncodified state of Scottish law simultaneously magnified the importance of theological arguments in political life. As the English crown used common law courts to prosecute Protestant non-conformity, puritans sought to defend themselves through legal, rather than purely religious arguments. In some districts they were also able to rely on sympathetic secular magistrates to impose moral discipline through restraints on sins like Sabbath-breaking, drunkenness, and fornication, obviating the need for an open system of Calvinist church discipline. But in Scotland both local campaigns of moral reformation and contests over relations between the crown and the Kirk at the national level were conducted mainly on religious grounds.

For all these reasons, religious politics in Scotland remained even more contentious, as well as less constrained by fear and respect of royal authority, than in England. Scottish clergy felt entitled to criticize the moral and spiritual delinquencies of their king, his wife, and his courtiers with a directness rarely displayed by English puritans. The main source of contention remained James's favorable treatment of Huntly and other Catholics. In the summer of 1588 the Kirk strongly objected when the king arranged a marriage between Huntly and Henrietta Stewart, daughter to the first duke of Lennox and sister to the second, who had become the new royal favorite.[53] The Edinburgh presbytery refused to solemnize the marriage and prohibited others from doing so unless Huntly first subscribed to a Protestant confession of faith. Archbishop Adamson, acting on royal instructions, celebrated the marriage anyway, whereupon a general assembly of the Kirk suspended him from the ministry. Adamson complained to the king, pointing out that he was being punished for obeying a royal command. But although highly provoked, James did not want a public quarrel with the Kirk at a moment when he

---

[53] This was the son of James's previous favorite Esmé Stuart, who had died in exile in 1584.

awaited the imminent arrival of his new bride, Anna of Denmark. He therefore dissimulated his anger.⁵⁴ He also knew that his favor to Huntly and other Catholics antagonized not only Scottish presbyterians but also the English government and its ambassador to Scotland, Robert Bowes.⁵⁵

He also began to soften his resistance to presbyterian demands for changes in the Kirk, at almost exactly the moment that Hatton, Whitgift, and Bancroft intensified their attack on English presbyterianism and began to show more interest in forming an alliance between anti-presbyterian forces along the lines that Adamson had proposed back in 1583.

Bancroft's Paul's Cross sermon of 1589 signaled this desire for solidarity. Preached on the biblical text, "believe not every spirit but try the spirits whether they be of God, for many false prophets are gone out into the world,"⁵⁶ it identified false prophets with Anabaptists, Familists, and puritans, whom Bancroft lumped together as a sectarian fringe seeking to model the government of modern churches after Mosaic rules which "the Jews did imitate in their particular synagogues."⁵⁷ He related this "Jewish" ecclesiology to leveling attacks on property, abuses of scripture by "prattling old women," "babbling sophisters," and an international presbyterian movement that had already subverted legitimate authority elsewhere in Europe and now threatened to do the same in England. Scotland provided his central example and the 1584 *Declaration* issued in James's name, which Bancroft accepted as the king's work, his detailed material.⁵⁸ The sermon approvingly rehearsed the story of the passage of the Black Acts and insisted that James had not since altered his position.⁵⁹ Wherever presbyterianism triumphed, Bancroft proclaimed, it led to rebellion and the publication of treatises, like the *Vindicae contra tyrannus* and Buchanan's *De jure regnum apud Scotos*, which taught that "the people of themselves may set up God's service and abrogate superstition [and that] it is lawful for the people by force of arms to resist the Prince, if he hinder the building of the Church."⁶⁰

While noticing Bancroft's equation of puritanism with European and Scottish presbyterianism, historians have generally assumed that his real targets remained

---

⁵⁴ Calderwood, 226; Spottiswoode, 376–7.
⁵⁵ Cf. the anonymous report to Walsingham of January 1, 1588, TNA SP52/42, fol. 87 after John Pont upbraided James to his face: "Although his Majesty be not angry with this great reproof there is many that are good Protestants that is very angry with the ministers that they should mel with his Majesty with such sharp reproofs in open audience, he being so well inclined to religion as he is."
⁵⁶ Richard Bancroft, *A Sermon at Paul's Cross* (London, 1588), sig. Bi.   ⁵⁷ Ibid., 8.
⁵⁸ Ibid., 72: "I have thought good to make this matter more plain unto you by a very manifest example, authorized in a declaration published by the King of Scots." A reasonably detailed paraphrase of Adamson's treatise immediately followed.
⁵⁹ Ibid., 75: "It may here be said (for they dare say what they list) that now the king is of another mind and that this declaration was made when he had conceived some displeasure against them. For the king he is not altered. His crown and their sovereignty will not agree together."
⁶⁰ Ibid., 78–9.

the English conference movement and Martin Marprelate.⁶¹ This is convincing up to a point. Bancroft realized that by pointing out the fact that in the rest of Europe presbyterian church polities had developed either in urban republics like Geneva or in close association with insurrectionary movements, as in France, the Netherlands, and Scotland, he might suggest that English presbyterians were actually republicans in disguise. This strengthened his argument that attacks on the bishops amounted to the opening gambit in a campaign to undermine hierarchical structures of secular government and expropriate private property, to enrich a self-appointed godly clique. But we will miss the full point of Bancroft's polemic if we treat it as no more than a rhetorical maneuver in a debate over English ecclesiology. Even on a purely rhetorical level the thrust of his argument implied a rejection not just of presbyterianism but the support for foreign Protestant rebellions that the English crown had provided for nearly thirty years. Bancroft spelled this out five years later in his *Daungerous positions and proceedings published and practiced within this island of Brytaine*.⁶² This began with a brief review of recent Scottish history in which Bancroft disapproved of every major victory that Anglophile Scottish Protestants had achieved over their Catholic and royalist adversaries, from the 1559 rebellion of the Lords of the Congregation down to the seizure of Stirling of 1585. Knox, Buchanan, and the Protestant nobles that Walsingham and Leicester had supported became the villains of Bancroft's account, while Mary of Guise, Mary Stuart, and the earl of Arran all received at least qualified sympathy. Naturally Bancroft also disapproved of the bonds that had developed between exiled Scottish clergy and leaders of the English puritan movement, and the eagerness with which English presbyterians awaited news from Scotland following Arran's ouster.⁶³ He stressed the way in which Scottish exiles had returned home in 1586 to cause "new stirs" over religion, while ignoring the fact that they had received an English subsidy to do so. Although he tactfully omitted any reference to the roles of Walsingham, Leicester, and Burghley in the events he described, it did not take much imagination to see that he had effectively repudiated their entire Scottish policy.

Not content simply to score rhetorical points by referring to readily available information, Bancroft constructed his own Scottish intelligence network, relying initially on the young diplomat and future secretary of state, Robert Naunton, and subsequently on an English stationer in Edinburgh named Robert Norton, after Naunton had to leave Scotland.⁶⁴ In December 1589 Bancroft dispatched nearly two dozen detailed queries about the Scottish campaign against episcopacy, the

---

⁶¹ Collinson noticed relationships between English and Scottish ecclesiastical contests at several points in *Elizabethan Puritan Movement* but virtually ignored Scotland and never mentioned Adamson in *Bancroft*.
⁶² London, 1593. ⁶³ Bancroft, *Dangerous Positions*, 5–6.
⁶⁴ Gordon Donaldson, "The Attitude of Whitgift and Bancroft to the Scottish Church," *Transactions of the Royal Historical Society*, series 4, vol. 14 (1942): 95–115, at 108.

structure and operation of the presbyteries, clerical interference in secular affairs, and the degree to which the Kirk's disciplinary methods conflicted with Scottish law.[65] He also wanted more information about the seizure of Stirling in 1585 than he had been able to cull from Holinshed's chronicle.[66] By the summer of 1590 and probably for some time before, he was communicating with Adamson through an intermediary named John Tawle. Adamson discussed with Bancroft his desire to publish in England books he had recently finished, and put him in touch with an Englishman living in Scotland named Patrick Blair, who had written a manuscript history of the Kirk highly critical of the presbyterians. This text was almost certainly forwarded to Bancroft.[67] Blair's work contained detailed accounts of sermons slandering the king and a caustic summary of the grass roots operation of Scottish discipline:

> They have in most parishes a presbytery that is a minister and a certain number of elders and deacons of such persons as pleaseth the minister to appoint but most commonly of the basest sort or of his friends, because he may the more easily overrule them and [make them to] be at his commandment. Their meetings commonly is in their vestry or church if they have any, for a number of their parish churches are altogether ruinous and decayed and few or none of them well repaired or kept except in cities or towns, for so long as bishops governed by ecclesiastical laws the offenders were commanded to repair them, for the overthrow of the one hath been the decay of the other.[68]

Blair confirmed Bancroft's suspicion that Scottish ministers taught that the people had the authority to "set up God's service and abrogate superstition" without higher authority. They agreed with "your Martinists that the gospel is not truly preached in England... that God hath forsaken you," and looked "for some change of estate" in both kingdoms, anticipating that this would require the overthrow of England's entire legal system, including assizes and quarter sessions.[69]

Although much of this information was grossly exaggerated, Bancroft and his Scottish sources had fastened on aspects of presbyterianism that did genuinely challenge pre-existing patterns of social and political authority. Presbyterian ecclesiology rested on the doctrine of the two kingdoms: the claim that the Church, consisting only of the elect, had received authority from God to govern itself independently of any secular jurisdiction. Christ alone was king of his

---

[65] BL Egerton Mss., fols 244^{r-v} provides the text of 23 "questions to be resolved."
[66] Ibid., fol. 242.
[67] LPL Mss. 3471, fol. 57: Adamson "desireth effectually to be in some place where the books he hath now already penned may be printed, wherein the proceedings and resolutions of these malcontents is specified, *quasi ad unguem*"; LPL Mss. 3471, fols 31–50.
[68] Ibid., fol. 46. [69] Ibid., fols 37r, 48r, 50r.

Church, which he governed through his ministers and elders, to whom worldly kings were subject in all spiritual matters.[70] Andrew Melville famously expressed this claim by plucking James's sleeve, calling him "God's silly vassal" and telling him there were two kingdoms in Scotland, his own and God's, "whose subject king James VI is, and of whose kingdom he is nor a head, nor a lord but a member."[71] Although the king had control of secular politics, preaching, doctrine, and discipline fell under the Church's jurisdiction and the ministers fiercely resisted any transgression of this boundary. But while they denied that the king or any secular court had the right to punish words spoken in the pulpit, they emphatically did *not* believe that the doctrine of the two kingdoms prevented the clergy from commenting on secular politics. In Scotland the concept of "doctrine" encompassed not only abstract theology and scriptural interpretation but the application of God's word to human behavior.[72] The ministers had a duty to rebuke anyone, including the king, who failed to follow God's commandments and properly serve the Church. They also felt entitled to exhort the laity to combat sin in all its forms, whether that meant cracking down on drunkenness, fornication, and petty violence in the localities, chastising nobles for their feuds, or mobilizing to fight popery by arms as well as words. The context of Andrew Melville's famous rebuke to James was not an argument over ecclesiastical policy but a conference at which ministers remonstrated with the king over rumors that he intended to pardon Huntly and another Catholic earl, Errol, for their treasonous dealings with Spain. It ended with Melville telling James that when he was in his "swaddling clouts Christ reigned freely in this land, in despite of all his enemies," through "his officers and ministers," who looked after the kingdom's interests and James's own "welfare" until he was old enough to do so for himself. Having benefited from this benign supervision since infancy, the king had no right to complain when ministers tried to warn him about his mistakes in government. According to Calderwood this harangue actually calmed James down, causing him to dismiss the ministers "pleasantly," and with reassurances.[73]

The published sermons of Robert Bruce, many originally delivered at James's court, further illustrate this presbyterian mindset and its socio-political

---

[70] Calderwood, 102–3: (quoting from the *Book of Policy* of 1580): "It is proper to kings, princes and magistrates to be called lords and dominators over their subjects whom they govern civilly, but it is proper to Christ only to be called lord and master in the spiritual government of the kirk, and all others that bear office therein ought not to usurp dominion therein, nor be called lords, but only ministers, disciples and servants. For it is Christ's proper office to command and rule his kirk universally, and every particular kirk, through the ministry of men. Notwithstanding, as the ministers and others of the ecclesiastical estate are subject to the magistrate civil, so ought the person of the magistrate be subject to the kirk spiritually, and in ecclesiastical government. And the exercise of both these jurisdictions cannot stand in one person ordinary."

[71] Ibid., 330.

[72] Julian Goodare, "The Scottish Presbyterian Movement of 1596," *Canadian Journal of History* 45 (2010): 21–43 at 41.

[73] Calderwood, 330.

implications. Bruce regarded the successes of the Scottish Reformation as evidence of God's special favor, which entailed an extraordinary obligation to fulfill divine commandments.[74] Scots instead indulged in every manner of iniquity. "The great men in this country are become companions to thieves and pirates, oppressors and manifest blasphemers against God and man. You see murder, oppression and bloodshed is the only thing they shoot and mark at. As to the simple sort of people they are altogether godless."[75] This ingratitude presaged terrible punishments unless "every man according to his calling put to his hand to reform, according to the bounds and power that is committed to him." The heaviest obligations fell on the nobles and, even more, the king.[76] Bruce acknowledged James's personal righteousness but warned that as "supreme magistrate" he needed to "make an end of this confusion" before "this confusion shall make an end of him."[77] The clergy had an obligation to act as "trumpets of the Lord," warning all Scots, but particularly the king, of the imminence of God's wrath without mincing words. "We may not sound mercy when the Lord biddeth us sound judgment...the sins of the land craveth that all pulpits sound judgment."[78]

By this logic any train of events might be interpreted as a sign of the need for further reform. Every success of the Kirk revealed God's favor, which brought with it an obligation to redouble efforts to serve his will, while every failure and threat to a godly society, whether a Catholic plot or the persistence of blood feuds and other sins, demonstrated national ingratitude that threatened to provoke divine vengeance. The general assembly of 1592 cited a run of bad weather among the reasons why it had declared a national fast of repentance and prayer.[79] Since every order of society and every Scot had displeased God by his or her actions, everyone had to submit to clerical chastisement, not only in general terms but through pointed personal rebukes. This included kings, who were immediately suspect because, as Bruce put it, "since the evangel began [kings] hath ever conspired to explode Christ out of the number of kings and so to root out his kingdom that he should not bear rule in earth."[80] In 1592 Bruce demanded that James humble himself on his knees for not taking sterner action against Huntly.[81] In the same year Walter Balcanquhal accused the king and nobility of Scotland of failing in their duty to suppress feuds, threatening them with the fate of the regent Morton, i.e. public execution.[82] Two years later a third minister, Robert Pont, again publicly censured James for countenancing evil men.[83] The irreverent attitude

---

[74] Robert Bruce, *Sermons* (Edinburgh, 1617), 274.   [75] Ibid., 182.
[76] Robert Bruce, *Sermons Preached in the Kirk at Edinburgh* (Edinburgh, 1591), sig. D8v.
[77] Calderwood, 283.   [78] Bruce, *Sermons*, sig. D8v.
[79] *The Causes of this general fast to begin the first Sabbath of August nixt, 1595* (Edinburgh, 1595), n.p.
[80] Bruce, *Sermons*, sig. T8^v.   [81] James Kirk, "Bruce, Robert (1554–1631)," *ODNB*.
[82] Keith Brown, *Bloodfeud in Scotland 1573–1625: Violence, Justice and Politics in an Early Modern Society* (Edinburgh: John Donald, 1986), 189–90.
[83] James Kirk, "Pont, Robert (1524–1606)," *ODNB*.

toward monarchs that Throckmorton had displayed in the Commons in 1587 remained alive and well among the Scottish clergy.

This hectoring from the pulpit without regard to rank, along with the humiliating public penances imposed by kirk sessions, struck Bancroft and his allies as an especially odious feature of presbyterianism. His dossier of damning evidence about the Kirk contained numerous complaints on this score. "In all their sermons," one of his informants wrote, "they depend much of one point, which they call application, wherein they do apply every man's peculiar faults to some offenders mentioned in scripture... being nothing scrupulous to name the parties offending as thou lord, thou burgess, thou mistress... which public detection breedeth such an inward grudge as the best arguments they can make against the persons detected cannot subdue their concealed hatred."[84] Another informant thought it particularly objectionable that a person accused from the pulpit "hath no court to appeal unto for remedy but must even abide the bitter malice of his minister and the sentence of these ignorant elders and deacons."[85] Presbyterianism amounted to a form of tyranny that, for all its pretended disdain for popery, actually erected a pope in every parish, answerable to no one but himself.[86] Although for polemical reasons Bancroft did his best to associate presbyterianism with democracy and republicanism, what he really found most objectionable were campaigns by self-selected godly oligarchies intent on imposing their own vision of religious, moral, and political reform, without the permission of bishops or princes. He realized that the godly had infiltrated institutions of English secular government, at every level from the privy council and House of Commons down to local magistracies. But although he might freely target clerical radicals like Udall and Cartwright, he knew better than to portray peers and privy councilors who sheltered puritans as popular subversives. His Scottish evidence provided a route around this difficulty. By showing how the Kirk had slandered and brow-beaten a Protestant king, and by documenting its efforts to impose its discipline on all ranks of Scottish society, he sought to demonstrate where puritan principles would lead if ever allowed to develop unchecked, without directly impugning the motives of people like Lord Burleigh and the earls of Pembroke and Bedford.

But in adopting this line of attack he initially failed to reckon with the evolving attitudes of his Scottish royal protagonist. In Bancroft, Adamson had at last found the staunch English ally he had long sought, but at a time when his own influence had begun to collapse. As the king sought to mend fences with the Kirk, his close association with the archbishop of St Andrews became an embarrassment, which Bancroft's polemics only exacerbated. The Kirk's leaders immediately suspected

---

[84] LPL Mss. 3471, fol. 57r–v, John Tawle to Bancroft, August 25, 1590.
[85] Ibid., fol. 46r; the writer is Patrick Blair.
[86] Ibid., fol. 43v; Bancroft, *Sermon at Paul's Cross*, 76.

Adamson of assisting Bancroft, whose attacks they interpreted as part of an English episcopal assault on the godly in both kingdoms. In 1590 they launched a multi-pronged counter-offensive. In January James Melville opened a general assembly in Edinburgh with a sermon denouncing "the belly god bishops of England" and "the old serpent," Adamson, the traitor within the gates who had assisted them.[87] Bruce wrote to Walsingham, denouncing Bancroft as an instrument of the devil, demanding that he be publicly reprimanded and hinting that if he were not the Scottish clergy would reconsider their support for England. Elizabeth must understand that Scottish presbyterians had much more to offer her than an obscure English cleric. Bruce also asked Walsingham to do his best to prevent the English bishops from extending "their power to the imprisoning and torture of Christ's members, for we hear daily to our great grief of such things."[88] The Kirk simultaneously launched a devastating attack on Adamson. The general assembly stripped him of his revenues, encouraging the king to transfer them to the duke of Lennox, and denied him the use of his episcopal palace. In St Andrews he was subjected to manuscript libels and denunciations from the pulpit. Someone turned a scandalous story that he had tried to poison James into a ballad, "printed and publicly sold at London."[89] In January 1591, the Scots intercepted a letter from Bancroft to Adamson, inviting him to England and promising Whitgift's patronage. This redoubled their hostility.[90] Impoverished, in failing health and thoroughly humiliated, Adamson had to make a public recantation in which he exonerated James from any role in producing the *Declaration*, blaming it instead on Arran and John Maitland of Thirlestane.[91] Before his death in 1592 he suffered the final humiliation of having to beg charity from Andrew Melville.

James not only abandoned his former ally but tried to please the Kirk by writing a letter to Elizabeth, at the urging of Robert Bruce, on behalf of John Udall. A short time later Waldegrave produced two tracts by Penry refuting Bancroft's sermon and advocating presbyterian reforms in England.[92] James then added his own voice to the chorus defending the Kirk and attacking English ecclesiology, telling a general assembly that he

> praised God that he was born in such a time as in the time of the light of the Gospel; to such a place as to be king of such a kirk, the sincerest kirk in the world. The kirk of Geneva, said he, keepeth Pasch and Yule, what have they from them? They have no institution. As for our neighbor kirk of England their service is an evil said mass in English; they want nothing of the mass but the liftings. I charge you my good people, ministers, doctors, elders, nobles, gentlemen and barons to

---

[87] Calderwood, 286.   [88] BL Add Mss. 48,117, fols 189–90v.
[89] LPL Mss. 3471, fols 61v, 64v.   [90] Calderwood, 259.   [91] Ibid., 259–62.
[92] *A briefe discovery of the untruths and slanders* (1590) and *An humble motion with submission to the right Honorable LL of Hir Majesties Privie Counsell* (1590).

stand to your purity and to exhort the people to do the same and I, forsooth, so long as I brook my life and crown shall maintain the same.[93]

By spring 1590 the escalating rhetorical conflict threatened to become a significant irritant in Anglo-Scottish relations. Elizabeth instructed Bowes to protest against James's patronage of Waldegrave and demand Penry's expulsion from Scotland. James excused his appointment of Waldegrave by saying that Scotland lacked competent printers but agreed to issue a proclamation banishing Penry.[94] He apparently did nothing to enforce it, however, and in June Whitgift received information that Penry continued to frequent Waldegrave's printing house and that another reply to Bancroft by someone named "Baal, Bell or Beale" was in preparation.[95] This may have been a revised version of Robert Beale's criticism of Whitgift's anti-puritan campaign, on which he had been working in 1584.[96]

In the event Waldegrave printed nothing in this period by Beale or any other author with a similar name. But he did issue a further attack on Bancroft by the Scottish minister John Davidson, who presented it to Maitland with a request that he procure the king's official approval. This embarrassed James, who passed his copy of the treatise to Bowes, who in turn dispatched it to Burghley.[97] On July 6, Elizabeth wrote to James, warning "that there is risen both in your realm and mine a sect of perilous consequence, such as would have no kings but a presbytery and take our place while they enjoy our privilege, with a shade of God's word, which none is judged to follow right without by their censure they be so deemed. Yea look well unto them, when they have made in our peoples' hearts a doubt of religion and that we err if they say so, what perilous issue this may make."[98] She went on to demand that he silence ministers who "presume to make occasions in their pulpits for the persecuted in England for the Gospel. Suppose you, my dear brother, that I may tolerate such scandals of my sincere government?"

Faced with this pressure James suppressed Davison's book and ordered his clergy to suspend the public prayers they had been making, on the orders of the general assembly, for "the afflicted brethren of England" who suffered "for the confession of the purity of religion."[99] He also agreed to start a search for Penry, who had recently published yet another presbyterian treatise, and to require Waldegrave to cease printing books insulting to the Church of England.[100] Bowes complained that his role in procuring these orders caused several Scottish ministers who had been his confidential friends to stop speaking to him, damaging his ability to fulfill his duties.[101] But James also counter-attacked by lodging a

---

[93] Calderwood, 286. [94] TNA SP52/45/43. [95] LPL 3471, fol. 55.
[96] BL Lansdowne Mss. 42/79.
[97] TNA SP52/46/48; John Davidson, *D. Bancroft's rashness in rayling against the Church of Scotland noted in an answere to a letter of a worthy person of England* (Edinburgh, 1590).
[98] TNA SP52/46/5. [99] Calderwood, 254; TNA SP52/45, fol. 361; 46, fols 223–4.
[100] TNA SP52/46/64 and 73. [101] TNA SP52/46/58, 64.

formal complaint against Bancroft, for falsely claiming that he had written Adamson's *Declaration*. Burghley responded by talking to Bancroft, who wrote a rather grudging letter of apology and explanation, saying that he had been mistaken about the *Declaration* and had never intended to offend the Scottish ministers.[102]

James's "Alliance" with the Kirk

As an organized presbyterian movement collapsed in England, Scottish presbyterians therefore seemed to have consolidated their position with royal support. The marked alteration in James's attitude since 1584 calls for closer examination, since Bancroft was undoubtedly right in arguing that the Kirk challenged his authority. This makes it tempting to dismiss the king's alliance with the presbyterians, between about 1588 and 1596 when he reversed course yet again, as a tactical maneuver, abandoned once it had served its purposes. But even if this is partly correct, we still need to explain why James found it expedient to conciliate the Kirk for several years and why his efforts to do so finally collapsed.

Although his penchant for dissimulation and telling people what he knew they wanted to hear make his actual religious beliefs difficult to pin down, fairly strong evidence suggests that James had become a convinced Protestant, albeit one who continued to resent "mutinous knave ministers." In addition, he recognized that the Kirk had become a powerful force in Scottish society, whose support or opposition might well determine the success or failure of his efforts to restore royal authority. He also wanted to win the support of the English godly, in case he needed it in a future contest over the succession, which meant overcoming the suspicions aroused by his earlier dalliances with popish agents and his continuing warm relations with Catholic nobles. As we have noticed, he attempted to solidify his credentials as a godly king not only through actions but words. As early as 1586 he welcomed the prospect of war against the united forces of popery, as a special favor God had bestowed on "his elect," to separate them from "hypocrites" and the "company of the wicked." In "these latter days, wherein God doth permit the devil most to reign," he asserted, Christians had to be especially wary of false brethren. The opportunity for a great trial of strength against a confederation "of all the bastard Christians (I mean the papists)" made it easier to separate the sheep from the goats.[103] His *An fruitfull Mediatioun contening ane plane and facill exposition of... the Revelatioun* (Edinburgh, 1588)[104] and *Meditatioun upon the first buke of the Chronicles* elaborated on this message, by identifying the pope

---

[102] TNA SP52/46/58, Bowes to Burghley, October 24, 1590 with marginal note in Burghley's hand, "I have spoken with Mr. Bancroft"; LPA Mss. 3471, fol. 29, copy of Bancroft's letter.
[103] BL Cotton Caligula CIX, fol. 276v.   [104] Edinburgh, 1588; above pp. 167–8.

with Antichrist and proclaiming his leadership of true Christians throughout the entire Isle of Britain.[105]

Shortly after the publication of these tracts, James married Anna of Denmark, sister to the Lutheran Danish king, Christian IV. In 1590 he sent Colonel William Stewart and other diplomats to German Protestant princes—including the Elector Palatine and dukes of Saxony and Mecklenburg—to ask them to offer their services as mediators between Elizabeth and Philip II, but also to join in an alliance with England, France, and James's own kingdom if Philip refused to make peace. This initiative, which closely imitated a similar Danish effort a few years earlier, appeared to open the prospect of a grand alliance of Calvinist and Lutheran princes and republics against Spain and the papacy.[106] James probably knew that it had little chance of success, but by signaling his readiness to join in such a project he laid the foundations for a reformulation of Protestant apocalyptic thought, focused on the role of godly monarchs in resisting popish tyranny.[107] John Napier's *Plaine discovery of the whole Revelation of St John*, published by Waldegrave in 1593, developed this theme in considerable detail. It identified Elizabeth's victory over the Armada and Henry of Navarre's accession to the French throne as events heralding the beginning of the final war against the kingdom of Antichrist foretold in St John's prophecy. Napier predicted that the contest would climax in the early seventeenth century, as more and more European monarchs rallied to the anti-papal cause. The baptism of James's son, Prince Henry, in 1594, inspired more celebrations of Stuart dynasticism with apocalyptic overtones. A pageant purportedly devised by the king himself featured a ship with a sail bearing the arms of Scotland and Denmark. The Latin baptismal sermon "discoursed of the genealogies, alliances, leagues and unities contracted between the king of Scots... and every one of the princes sending to this baptism their ambassadors." Most of those princes were Protestant. Andrew Melville commemorated the event with a Latin poem, *Principus scoti britannorum natalia* that hailed Henry as a prince destined by birth to unite England and Scotland and then lead a great alliance of Protestant monarchies against Spain and Rome:

> What will confederated Danish forces not achieve
> Under the Dane supported by Scoto-Britannic soldiers
> Unafraid to die for their country?

---

[105] *An Fruitfull Meditatioun* (Edinburgh, 1588), sigs Bii, Biii–Biv, reissued in a more Anglicized form in *The Workes of the Most High and Mighty Prince James* (London, 1616), quotation at page 80. I have been guided by the 1616 version in modernizing the language and orthography.

[106] TNA SP52/45/59. James had also pressed the Danes to enter into an alliance with Henry of Navarre and Elizabeth, in "defense of religion and the common cause" (TNA SP52/45/43).

[107] Still valuable on this topic is Arthur Williamson, *Scottish National Consciousness in the Age of James VI: The Apocalypse, the Union and the Shaping of Scotland's Public Culture* (Edinburgh: John Donald, 1979), 20–39 and 86–96.

> Already prey to the winds, to the waves and to the British,
> Are you not due a new contest against British arms,
> O proud crown of the winged Hesperia![108]

The poem was published by Waldegrave and in a separate edition from a Dutch press, which circulated on the Continent. The militantly Protestant apocalyptic imagery that developed around Henry as Prince of Wales in England had its roots in this earlier dynastic propaganda.[109]

James could safely promote such imagery because no one expected an impoverished king of Scotland to play a major role in a great European war. Offering to join in grand alliances gave him a chance to portray himself and his heir as prospective leaders in the battle against Antichrist at some vague point in the future, while others—Elizabeth, Henry of Navarre, and the Dutch—assumed all the immediate costs and risks. But on a rhetorical plane he recast his personal and dynastic authority within frameworks of scriptural interpretation and apocalyptic hope calculated to appeal to militant Protestants, not least by foreshadowing a future role for the united kingdoms of England and Scotland in defeating Spain and the papacy, once he had inherited Elizabeth's throne.

In addition to improving his standing with the godly in England, better relations with the Kirk gave James solid advantages in regaining control over his own kingdom, as the head of his council, John Maitland of Thirlestane, recognized.[110] In the absence of a developed system of royal administration in the provinces the support of the Kirk, with its organized local sessions and national network of elders and ministers, potentially offered invaluable assistance in gathering information, restraining criminality and abuses of noble power, and mobilizing popular support for the crown. According to one of Bancroft's informants, shortly before the summer of 1590 James created a secret council of three presbyterian ministers, Patrick Galloway, Robert Bruce, and David Lindsay.[111] Whether or not this council actually existed, Galloway was soon thereafter appointed one of the king's household ministers, while Bruce and Lindsay also received royal favor. Working cooperatively with leaders of the Kirk made it easier to avoid contentious fights over his ecclesiastical authority. Throughout the period

---

[108] Paul McGinnis and Arthur Williamson, trans. and eds, *George Buchanan: The Political Poetry* (Edinburgh: Scottish History Society, 1995), 280. Melville's entire poem is here translated under the title *On the birth of the Scoto-Britannic Prince*. For the dual publication in Edinburgh and The Hague see TNA SP52/54, fol. 34. Elizabeth lodged a formal protest at Melville's presumption in assuming that Henry would succeed to her throne. Bowes reported that one of Melville's associates at St Andrews had caused many copies of the poem to be dispersed in England.

[109] Peter McCullough, *Sermons at Court: Politics and Religion in Elizabethan and Jacobean Preaching* (Cambridge: Cambridge University Press, 1998).

[110] Maurice Lee, *John Maitland of Thirlstane and the Foundations of Stewart Despotism in Scotland* (Princeton: Princeton University Press, 1959) remains valuable on Maitland's role.

[111] LPL Mss. 3471, fol. 57v, John Tawle to Bancroft, August 25, 1590; the letter states that the council was "of late erected."

James retained the right to summon and dismiss national assemblies and to share in the appointment of commissioners charged with overseeing the local operation of the Kirk, without dispute. The clause in the Black Acts affirming his ecclesiastical supremacy was never repealed and the office of bishop never explicitly abolished, even after the Golden Acts of 1592 transferred episcopal revenues to the crown. By refraining from appointing new bishops, while raising no objections as the system of presbyteries expanded, until by 1593 forty-eight were in operation, covering most of the country, James created an impression that he had agreed to the establishment of a presbyterian system without actually doing so.[112] Despite lingering tensions that periodically flared into angry quarrels, a partnership between Kirk and crown gradually developed.

The efforts of James and his chancellor, Maitland of Thirlestane, to work with the Kirk stemmed partly from the awareness of both men of their vulnerability to noble dissidence. They did not feel entirely safe even within the royal court, where some magnates were prepared to threaten the king and his chief servants with violence. Despite his continuing favor to Huntly after the discovery in January 1589 of the earl's correspondence with Spain, an English diplomat reported that James feared for his life. He instructed Maitland to raise a horse guard of 100 in case Huntly should attempt to storm Holyroodhouse and appealed to the citizens of Edinburgh for additional support in case of need, knowing that he "dare not deal in such sort as is to be required till he have raised a new strength about him."[113] Although the feared assault did not materialize, Huntly and his associates continued to conspire. The Protestant earl of Bothwell, "an able and undertaking man, as they here term such," frightened James even more.[114] Although in opposing confessional camps, Huntly and Bothwell both disliked Maitland, whom they tried to discredit by "casting abroad" libels, while claiming "to advance the credit of the ancient nobility."

Dissident nobles not only enjoyed access to the court; some also commanded larger military forces than those of the king. Approximately 1,000 Spanish soldiers and sailors shipwrecked along Scotland's coasts in 1588, unable to return home because the English and Dutch had cut the sea routes between Britain and Spain, found shelter in the military retinues of Catholic nobles. The English worried that these professionals would improve the quality of the lords' private armies and that Parma might try to smuggle over additional reinforcements.[115] In April, Huntly and Bothwell attempted to surprise the king and Maitland at Holyroodhouse, failing only because James had departed unexpectedly, while the chancellor

---

[112] Alan MacDonald, *The Jacobean Kirk, 1567–1625: Sovereignty, Polity and Liturgy* (Aldershot: Ashgate, 1998), 30–40.
[113] TNA SP52/43/23, 25, 29, 32, dispatches of Thomas Fouller and William Asheby.
[114] BL Egerton Mss. 2598.
[115] Michael Yellowlees, *So Strange a Monster as a Jesuite: The Society of Jesus in Sixteenth Century Scotland* (Colonsay: House of Lochar, 2003), 116; Spottiswood, 374; TNA SP52/43/25.

decided to lodge in Edinburgh on the night of the attack.[116] This outrage finally prodded James into action. He gathered loyal forces and led them in person, first against Bothwell and then Huntly and his ally the earl of Errol, whose forces dissolved at the approach of the royal force. The two Catholic nobles surrendered just outside Aberdeen, in what became known as the Brig o' Dee.

This quieted matters for a time but James eventually released Huntly and Errol, while Bothwell escaped captivity. All three nobles resumed their plotting. Although some contemporaries blamed James's leniency, the root problem was that he simply lacked the resources needed to suppress rebellions and govern his kingdom without his nobles' assistance. Although the king's forces "daily increase," an English diplomat reported at the height of the campaign against Huntly and Errol, "the poverty of Scotland will not keep them together; if his ability were to pay four or five hundred shot and two hundred horse but three months he would root out the pillars of popery in this country and so bridle his discontented nobility as they should not be able to make arms against him."[117] But since he did not have enough money to keep an army in the field for more than a few weeks, James was incapable of breaking the power of nobles with strong regional power bases, "linked by blood and alliance one with another."[118] Even loyal forces hesitated to pursue an offensive too vigorously, for fear of starting a feud.[119] Elizabeth might have given James the resources to sustain a prolonged campaign against the Catholic earls but she turned a deaf ear to the pleas of her diplomats in Scotland to do so. Lacking the ability to follow through after his victory at Brig o' Dee with a systematic campaign to reduce the North to obedience, James probably felt he had little choice but to forgive Huntly and restore him to favor. In any case, destroying the power of Catholic nobles would have left him even more vulnerable to coercion by the Kirk and its noble allies, including the turbulent Bothwell.

Barely a year later James returned from his voyage to fetch Anna of Denmark from Norway and announced his intention to reduce the number of superfluous servants in his household. This projected reform, which struck at the interests of several nobles who had placed their clients on the royal payroll, provoked new attempts to topple Maitland, who was blamed for promoting it. To protect himself and his chancellor, in April 1590 James created a new court guard of 100 horse and 100 foot. But since he lacked the money to pay them and Elizabeth again refused to help, the new guard lasted barely a month, and in July Huntly and Errol again threatened to seize Maitland and hang him.[120] The next spring James tried once more to create a guard to protect himself and apprehend "notorious offenders, which presently presume to range in the country without fear." Again, lack of money defeated his good intentions.[121] In 1593 he sent an

---

[116] TNA SP52/43/49.   [117] TNA SP52/43/59.   [118] TNA SP52/43/69.
[119] TNA SP52/43/64.   [120] TNA SP52/45/28, 33, 43, 51; 46/9.   [121] TNA SP52/47/58.

ambassador to England to ask the queen to finance a small standing force to pursue "rebels, papists and [the] Spanish faction." Elizabeth once more refused to listen.[122]

In these circumstances the Kirk offered an alternative means of mobilizing local militia forces that would unquestionably support James against Catholic peers, if not necessarily against Protestants like Bothwell. An erosion of strong noble support for presbyterians after the death of Angus in 1588, together with the fact that as much as a third of the nobility remained Catholic, gave the Kirk an incentive to cooperate with the crown.[123] Hatred of Maitland among the nobility now threatened to provide Catholics like Errol and Huntly with broader support, in much the way that hatred of Arran had previously widened the appeal of presbyterian opposition. Bowes reported in the spring of 1590 that "noblemen and others associated at the road of Stirling" were ready to join with the "confederates of the Brig o' Dee" in a "party to provide the king may govern with his nobility... not by private persons hated."[124] To resist this pressure James had to rely on the ministers to rally the remaining Protestant members of the high nobility, such as Hamilton, Mar, and Argyll, and lesser Protestant lords, lairds, and burgesses, who in many cases served the Kirk as elders and representatives to national assemblies. He was in no position to resist Bothwell, Huntly, and Errol at the same time unless he had the Kirk on his side.

The King, the Kirk, and the Catholic Earls

But if he became too reliant on armed support provided by the Kirk and its remaining noble allies, James would lose his freedom of action. To rebuild his personal authority, he needed to remain independent of rival confessional and noble factions, so that all of them would have an incentive to seek his good will. This dynamic goes a long way toward explaining his repeated indulgence toward Huntly and Errol, although other considerations probably also played a role. James seems to have liked Huntly, with whom he had a personal relationship extending back to the early 1580s, and who possessed the handsome appearance and personal charisma that James always found attractive. The influence of Huntly's numerous friends at court, beginning with his very able wife, Henrietta countess of Lennox, also should not be discounted. By the early 1590s James had developed a deep and justified fear of Bothwell, a border lord who was prepared alternately to ally with Huntly or to pose as a champion of the Kirk, as his personal

---

[122] TNA SP52/50/52.
[123] Keith Brown, *Noble Society in Scotland: Wealth, Family and Culture from Reformation to Revolution* (Edinburgh: Edinburgh University Press, 2000), 20, 23.
[124] TNA SP52/45/46.

interests dictated. Isolating Bothwell became one of his chief priorities, providing another reason to maintain good relations with Huntly and Errol.

James did not believe he faced a serious Catholic threat, except in the increasingly unlikely event of a Spanish invasion of his kingdom. He told Bowes that although "Jesuits and instruments...for their own reliefs and reputations endeavor...to allure the king of Spain" to support conspiratorial plots, he thought few men of any sense would be drawn into them so long as they knew that he remained a firm Protestant and that the "best part of the realm [were] determined to withstand such enterprises."[125] Although the Jesuits might think they had the support of a sizable noble faction, he knew that most of the men on their list of friends were either too sensible to risk rebellion or too incompetent to pose a serious danger. James professed to believe that a good king should extend favor and justice to all subjects, regardless of factional alignments, a view probably reinforced by memories of how Arran had created a large and embittered group of enemies by his vindictive pursuit of rivals and habit of enriching himself with the spoils of their estates. Pacifying Scotland required him to reconcile feuding nobles, rather than taking sides in private and religious quarrels. He almost certainly also regarded his relationship with Huntly as an insurance policy in case Spain ever gained the upper hand in its war with England. In an uncertain environment, he wanted to keep his options open.

Finally, he knew that Scottish traditions of blood feud and kinship solidarity meant that harsh punishment of any great noble risked being perceived as an attack on an entire network of kindred and allies, who might continue to seek vengeance for years to come. As he melodramatically put it in discussing Huntly's case in 1596, "one of the two courses was needful to be followed with him and the rest that were in his condition that is either to utterly exterminate them, their race and posterity or...upon their humble acknowledgement...receive them in favor."[126] Attempting to exterminate a family like the Gordons, with its approximately 150 junior branches and numerous connections to highland clans, would rapidly turn into a very bloody and dangerous business. Since an extended feud had broken out in the North between Huntly and a number of other families, eventually including the Campbells, James would have had allies in any effort to break the Gordons' power. But the chief beneficiary might well have been Bothwell, who had attempted to create an alliance of nobles sharing the Stewart surname during James's absence in Scandinavia in 1589.[127] Since James believed that Bothwell wanted either to kill him or shut him up in a castle and rule in his name, he would have regarded this as a catastrophic outcome.[128]

But although the king had solid reasons for treating Huntly and his allies with indulgence, these failed to satisfy the Kirk. Conflict over his indulgence toward

---

[125] TNA SP52/49/35.   [126] Spottiswood, 417.
[127] See Brown, *Bloodfeud in Scotland*, 145–61.   [128] TNA SP52/49/10.

Catholic nobles continued to disturb James's relations with the presbyterians throughout the early 1590s, inspiring criticism of his conduct from the pulpit and efforts to pressure him to take stronger measures. While he often tolerated court sermons that criticized his laxity toward Catholics, he continued to resent the Kirk's refusal to punish what he regarded as slanderous and seditious attacks.[129] In 1592 a proposal to give the Kirk representation in Scottish parliaments was derailed by "a bitter storm risen betwixt the king and the ministers," after the general assembly watered down an act that would have inhibited defamatory sermons against James and his council.[130] One observer reported that the king became so angry that he "is wholly bent to break the Kirk, if he can."[131] In 1595 he again became enraged when told that David Black, a minister at St Andrews, had preached a sermon calling his mother a whore and murderer. Other clergy managed to appease James after getting Black to promise "to be more circumspect in his words" thereafter, a promise he did not long keep.[132] The Edinburgh minister Walter Balcanquhal also provoked the king that year by announcing from his Edinburgh pulpit that the former earl of Arran had returned to court for a secret conference about his restoration to power.[133]

The most vexing conflicts between James and presbyterian ministers usually involved Huntly and his allies.[134] To a population familiar with stories of Alba's atrocities in the Netherlands and the St. Bartholomew's Day massacres in France, whose older members still remembered the Scottish civil war of the 1570s, these peers looked extremely menacing. According to Calderwood a panic broke out in Edinburgh on a January night in 1590 over rumors that papists intended to surprise the town. The temporary residence of several Catholic nobles in Edinburgh and the "sight of many uncouth faces" who had accompanied them "augmented the fear," as did "a report that some Spaniards were to be sent by the duke of Parma to Leith."[135] Nine months later Bowes received information "that sundry sorts of the nobility of this realm and in great number have determined to winter in this town of Edinburgh," especially "papists and Spanish factioners," who were trying "to draw hither speedily such as favor their plots." The town's

---

[129] For example James Hudson reported in 1591 that a preacher "about the king"—probably Patrick Galloway—repeatedly spoke out against the faction of the Brig o' Dee, seconding his own complaints about James's reluctance to prosecute them with rigor (CSPSc 10.600), while a year later Bowes reported that "sundry preachers in their sermons before the king have exhorted him to hear and take the counsel of the ancient and religious earls, lords and barons and of the true and honest burgesses... This advice is listened to" (TNA SP52/48/8).

[130] Spottiswood, 393; TNA SP52/48/44.   [131] HMC Salisbury, 4.205.

[132] TNA SP52/56/88.   [133] Ibid.

[134] MacDonald, *Jacobean Kirk*, 48–54. For a generally sympathetic but well-researched account of Huntly and his relationship with James see Ruth Grant, "Friendship, Politics and Religion: George Gordon, Sixth Earl of Huntly and James VI, 1581–1595," in *James VI and Noble Power in Scotland, 1578–1603*, ed. Miles Kerr-Peterson and Steven Reid (London: Routledge, 2017), 57–80 and Ruth Grant, "George Gordon, Sixth Earl of Huntly and the Politics of the Counter-Reformation in Scotland, 1581–1595," Edinburgh University PhD thesis, 2010.

[135] Calderwood, 245.

ministers had been warned "to regard themselves and their lives."[136] In October 1592 more rumors circulated of a plan by papists "to attempt some sudden massacre and uproar to change the religion and state and to possess the person of the king."[137] The rumors coincided with a dispute within the town provoked by a ban on trade with Spain, favored by the ministers but bitterly opposed by some merchants and craftsmen, which had led to the strewing of libels about the streets and threats that "some using to trade with Spain" would "party the favorers of Spain."[138]

But Edinburgh's fear of Catholic violence stemmed even more from other recent events. Toward the end of the previous year Bothwell had attempted a coup, with the assistance of his ally the earl of Moray. James outlawed both earls and granted Huntly—who had a bitter feud with Moray—a commission to hunt them down. In February Huntly and his men surprised Moray and brutally killed him. Many people saw Moray's murder as a Catholic plot and suspected the king of complicity in it, a view encouraged by some ministers as well as Bothwell, who seized on the chance to pose as a guardian of Protestantism. Keith Brown plausibly sees the Golden Acts adopted by Parliament in 1592 as the price James had to pay to appease anger over his perceived acquiescence in Moray's murder.[139] Not content with this victory, the ministers coordinated a national program of action against the Catholic threat. In July, Bowes learned that several ministers intended to press the king to renew the Band of 1588, empowering "well-affected noblemen, barons, boroughs and ministers" to pursue and arrest Catholics in their localities.[140] The presbytery of Edinburgh wrote to other presbyteries, seeking to gather voluntary contributions to support military action against Huntly and Errol, without waiting for James's permission.[141] On August 6, the provost of Edinburgh and a delegation of ministers waited on the king and presented him with a petition to banish Jesuits from Scotland and punish Huntly. James exploded at this attempt to pressure him but two weeks later he reissued the Band and subsequently tried to reassure the ministers of his good intentions.[142]

The Kirk's leaders remained unconvinced. A general assembly that convened in November launched a remarkable set of initiatives. It began by instructing ministers to "acquaint themselves" with the histories of the Council of Trent and Catholic plots and atrocities in other countries, so as "to inform their congregations" of what was at stake. It then proceeded to set up a standing committee of eight ministers—including two of the king's household clergy, Patrick Galloway and John Duncanson, and his confidant Robert Bruce—to meet at least weekly

---

[136] TNA SP52/46/48. [137] TNA SP52/49/35, 121. [138] TNA SP52/49/39.
[139] Brown, *Bloodfeud*, 160. On the passage of these acts see also Alan MacDonald, "The Parliament of 1592: A Crisis Averted," in *Parliament and Politics in Scotland, 1567–1707*, ed. Keith Brown and Alastair J. Mann (Edinburgh: Edinburgh University Press, 2005), 57–81.
[140] TNA SP52/48/71. [141] MacDonald, *Jacobean Kirk*, 51.
[142] TNA SP52/49/3, 12 and 18.

and confer "upon such advertisement as shall be made to them from diverse parts of the country" about Catholic activities. The committee appointed James Carmichael as its permanent agent in Edinburgh until the next general assembly, with instructions to gather information about popish practices from "merchants and passengers coming from other countries" and ministers throughout Scotland, who should inform him of any suspicious goings on in their own districts. If Carmichael sensed that a dangerous situation had started to develop he was to notify the committee of ministers, which had the authority to summon a wider meeting of "the brethren" for consultation. In addition to keeping a record of all the information he received, Carmichael should "write the memoirs of the Kirk's proceedings and dealings with the prince, council and estates of the realm... since the reformation of religion, to be a monument." The assembly instructed all the presbyteries to transmit any relevant documents in their possession to Walter Balcanquhal for inclusion in this collection. It then appointed Robert Bruce to keep a common purse of contributions to meet any "necessary expenses" and inform "the brethren" if a need for more money arose.

Lastly, the assembly sent a delegation to meet with James and demand that he appoint a commission composed "of the best affected noblemen, barons, gentlemen and magistrates within the boroughs," to execute existing laws against priests and Jesuits. It wanted him to summon noblemen well-affected to the Reformation to reside in Edinburgh over the following winter "and longer till the conspiracies, plots and attempts of the enemies of religion within this country be disappointed and repressed," and demanded that he confer regularly with his secret council.[143] These measures amounted to a national program of political action, comparable to the Huguenot state within a state in France and John Field's puritan network in England. Carmichael played a role similar to those of Field and Philippe du Plessis Mornay, as a collector of information, compiler of documents and author of occasional pamphlets. But in Scotland, with its fairly rudimentary printing industry, the pulpit rather than the press provided the main vehicle for disseminating news and controversial arguments. By establishing set channels of communication between Edinburgh and local presbyteries, the Kirk provided a kind of bush telegraph through which events anywhere in Scotland could be quickly reported and interpreted to congregations throughout the kingdom. This allowed for the efficient transmission of resolutions taken at the political center to the localities, potentially providing an infrastructure for mobilization in a new civil war, should that become necessary.

Throughout the controversy Bothwell waited menacingly in the wings, hoping for an opportunity to intervene, ostensibly as a supporter of the Kirk but with the objective of seizing power for himself.[144] The court had become another bed of

---

[143] Calderwood, 272–4. The secret council was the Scottish counterpart to the English privy council.
[144] TNA SP52/49/4.

intrigue, with the gentlemen of James's chamber maneuvering against each other.[145] Toward the end of the year Elizabeth sent a stinging letter adding her voice to the chorus rebuking James for inaction: "if you mean therefore to reign, I exhort you to show you worthy of the place, which can never be surely settled without a steady course held to make you loved and feared." She scolded him for "cherishing sundry for open crimes," leading his subjects to rely on private vengeance rather than royal justice, and warned that if he continued to treat plots against himself as toys he would earn "such contempt I dread to think and dare not name."[146] Barely a month later, on January 1, 1593, additional seemingly treasonable correspondence of Huntly, Errol, and other Catholic nobles with the king of Spain came to light.[147] Eight days later a group of ministers and barons met in Robert Bruce's gallery to draft a set of articles for the disciplining of popish conspirators.[148] The duke of Lennox, earl of Mar, and other courtiers sympathetic to the Kirk tried to dissuade the ministers from presenting this document to the king, knowing that it would infuriate him. But after considering matters the clerical delegation proceeded to the court, accompanied by the magistrates of Edinburgh and about a thousand citizens. James made the petitioners wait for about an hour—was he trying to control his temper?—before admitting Bruce and David Lindsay and telling them that he disliked their irregular meeting but "excused them because of their zeal."

Shortly thereafter he summoned Huntly and Errol to Edinburgh to answer for their offenses. The Catholic earls played into the hands of their enemies by defying this order. James proclaimed them traitors on February 5, gathered military forces and advanced on Aberdeen, where he appointed a commission to govern the North that included many of Huntly's enemies.[149] But he never apprehended the Catholic peers and after a parliament in July failed to pass an act confiscating their estates John Davidson preached another angry sermon, praying that God "would compel the King by his sanctified plagues" to secure "the welfare of his kirk."[150] The synod of Fife declared a public fast of repentance for collective sins that included "the king's slowness in repressing papists and planting of true religion."[151] But when Huntly, Errol, and another of their associates, the earl of Angus, suddenly appeared before the king in October and begged his clemency James again treated them leniently. After receiving another clerical petition calling for strict justice he told Huntly that he hated the ministers' "presumptuous and seditious behavior."[152] In February 1594 a minister in Perth, John Ross, preached a sermon calling James "a reprobate, a traitor and a rebel to God." The local synod

---

[145] Ibid. [146] HMC Salisbury 4.227–8.
[147] These documents became known as the Spanish blanks because they included blank pages with the earls' signatures on the bottom, on which Philip was allegedly supposed to write down the details of the aid they would provide if and when his forces invaded Scotland.
[148] Calderwood, 277. [149] Brown, *Bloodfeud*, 162. [150] Calderwood, 287.
[151] Ibid., 289. [152] Brown, *Bloodfeud*, 104.

reprimanded Ross but declined to suspend him from the ministry.[153] James's alliance with the Kirk seemed to have reached its breaking point.

But the intransigence of Huntly and Errol postponed the day of reckoning. Early in 1594 they rejected the generous terms James offered and their estates were declared forfeit. In early March they began gathering forces in the North. A cargo of Spanish money, intercepted and impounded in Aberdeen, was released to the rebels when they threatened retribution against the town. On March 15, James issued a commission of fire and sword against Huntly to three of the earl's enemies, Atholl, Lord Forbes, and the eighteen-year-old earl of Argyll. The latter, who had begun to reassert Campbell power and challenge Gordon control in parts of the Highlands, levied at least 6,000 men, while the Catholic earls hastily raised a smaller but more professional and better equipped force. This routed Argyll's lightly armed highlanders in a fierce battle at Glenlivet. A Spanish witness described priests brandishing crucifixes and exhorting Huntly's and Errol's troops before the battle, as they advanced under banners displaying images of Christ, the Virgin Mary, John the Evangelist, and a cross with Constantine's motto, *In hoc signo vinces*.[154] Despite their victory Huntly and Errol remained on the defensive, as James led another army north. Although they again evaded capture by retreating into Sutherland, they soon abandoned the struggle and departed into exile. Bothwell, who had reversed course by allying with Huntly and Errol, also departed Scotland after being excommunicated. These new circumstances momentarily restored cooperation between James and the Kirk in 1595.[155]

But the king still refused to execute the sentence of forfeiture against Huntly's and Errol's estates, which remained in the hands of their wives, or to expel the earls' supporters from his court. Both the Kirk and the English therefore remained unsatisfied. The outbreak of rebellion in Ulster raised the further alarming possibility that Huntly's highlanders might link up with Tyrone's forces. In December Robert Cecil received intelligence from a priest and double agent named John Cecil that "an archbishop of Ireland" had lately arrived at the Spanish court to request Philip's help in bringing such an alliance about and assisting it with Spanish troops. This would create a diversion, Cecil reported, while Spain attempted to seize the Isle of Jersey as a base in the Channel.[156] Alarm increased when reports reached Britain that Philip was preparing a fleet larger than the Armada. Although most likely intended for use against England or Ireland, the possibility that Scotland somehow figured in Madrid's plans could not be ruled out.

These events provided part of the context for the climactic confrontation between James and the Kirk that developed over the spring, summer, and autumn.

---

[153] MacDonald, *Jacobean Kirk*, 55.
[154] TNA SP31/3/29; BN Mss. Français 15972, fol. 55v, relation of Don Balthasar to Cardinal Gaeton.
[155] MacDonald, *Jacobean Kirk*, 59.   [156] TNA SP12/255/22.

In March James asked a general assembly of the Kirk for a voluntary contribution to meet the costs of preparing to repel a Spanish invasion, only to be told by Andrew Melville that he should start by appropriating the property of Huntly and Errol.[157] On the same day the assembly asked the king to authorize Kirk sessions to choose captains to muster and train householders and select commanders in "diverse shires to convene in arms at all occasions" against "foreign and intestine" enemies.[158] It wanted to create a militia under its own control. The assembly extended the political machinery created in 1592 by delegating ministers "resident about the court" or others "to be appointed out of diverse parts of the country" to form a standing body to oversee the Kirk's interests at the political center.[159] James's appointment of a commission charged with reforming court expenditures, consisting of eight officers soon nicknamed the Octavians, contributed to suspicions of his intentions because two of the eight were reputed Catholics.[160] Burghley thought the Octavians "evil disposed" and "hollow papists" and urged Bowes "by secret conference with some of the ministers" to uncover the truth about them and "devise some remedy."[161] The English had learned from John Cecil that a Scot named John Ogilby had visited the papal court, claiming to act as James's representative. After assuring the pope of James's secret sympathy for Catholicism, Ogilby asked for money to help suppress heretics and return Scotland to the Roman fold.[162] Robert Cecil transmitted this information to Bowes, who probably shared it with his presbyterian friends. Although James denied any knowledge of Ogilby's mission, suspicions had been aroused.[163] An agent named Balthazar de Lil had visited the Scottish court some time earlier to discuss with James and Huntly a plan to aid "Scottish Catholics against the heretics" with money supplied by the pope and other Catholic princes.[164] He reported that James initially agreed to join the Catholic initiative but subsequently betrayed it.[165] The king was likely playing some sort of double game, although the

---

[157] Calderwood, 313.
[158] Ibid.; *Acts and Proceedings of the General Assembly of the Kirk of Scotland*, part 3, vol. 1 (Edinburgh, 1845), 859, 860.
[159] Calderwood, 323.
[160] Julian Goodare, "The Octavians," in *James VI and Noble Power*, ed. Kerr-Peterson and Reid, 176–93.
[161] TNA SP52/59/4.   [162] TNA SP52/59/5.   [163] TNA SP52/59/19.
[164] BN Mss. Français 15972, fol. 62r.
[165] Ibid., fol. 36r–v is a French translation of a Spanish account of this incident. "Pour faire découvrir tous les catholiques [d'Ecosse] le conseil de la reine [d'Angleterre] s'avisa d'une ruse, de faire que le roi [Jacques ?] écrive de sa propre main au comte de Stanley pour faire assembler en la ville de St John tous les catholiques d'Ecosse, promettant que s'ils se jugeaient assez fort pour résister aux hérétiques qu'il se joindrait avec eux à chassait de son royaume tous les ministres qu'il parlera en sa lettre … séditeux … Les catholiques s'assemblèrent à la ville de St John le jour de St Simon et St Jude. Les ministres les trouvent aussi armés de pistolets plus que bibles, mais non sceu de gens de guerre ils furent au palais du roi du Lithe les armés, éloignés l'une de l'autre de huit lieus." Renewing his communications with the Catholics, James demanded that they furnish money for a war but a Jesuit who went to Rome to obtain the money was arrested after his return to Scotland before he could meet with one of Huntly's kinsmen. Catholics freed him and appealed again to James to honor his promise to assist them but English

extent of his involvement in Huntly's schemes and any counter-schemes devised by the English and Anglophile Scots remains obscure, no doubt because he took precautions to cover his tracks.

In August rumors that turned out to be true began circulating that Huntly had returned secretly to Scotland, as his wife and other friends at court negotiated his submission on easy terms. James summoned a convention of nobles regarded as well-disposed to Huntly to meet in September and advise him on the terms he should offer the Catholic earls. Several ministers immediately objected to this plan.[166] The king tried to calm matters by meeting privately with Robert Bruce and explaining why he thought it prudent to restore the exiled nobles to favor, provided they agreed to acknowledge their fault and "embrace the true religion." According to Spottiswood, Bruce disparaged the king's arguments, saying "that Huntly could not be pardoned, being so hated as he was." James asked him to think the matter over and return in two days. Bruce did as asked, but then delivered an ultimatum: "I see, Sir that your resolution is to take Huntly in favor, which if you do I will oppose and you shall choose whether you shall lose Huntly or me, for both of us you cannot keep." Spottiswood claimed that this "saucy reply" destroyed Bruce's relationship with the king.[167] James tried to win over the two other members of his clerical council, David Lindsay and Patrick Galloway, along with James Nicholson and James Melville. They also rebuffed him, saying that even if the Catholic earls sincerely repented and were received back into the bosom of the Kirk, James remained obligated, in the interest of justice, to execute them and confiscate their estates.[168]

In early September Bowes reported intense lobbying on both sides, with Queen Anna interceding for Huntly, while several ministers and their supporters pressed James to expel him once more from Scotland and seize his lands.[169] The Kirk's standing committee sprang into action, writing to all the presbyteries about the unauthorized return of the exiled earls and the likelihood that they would receive full pardons. Ministers "were desired to inform their flocks" of the situation and "both in public doctrine and private conference to stir up the country people to apprehend the danger and to be in readiness to resist the same so far as lawfully they might." The Kirk's committee in Edinburgh appointed a day of public humiliation on December 1, and asked that a number of additional commissioners be selected "out of all quarters of the country" and sent to the capital to confer about "the most expedient" response.[170] It also directed that Sir Alexander Seaton, the highest judicial official in Scotland and a suspected Catholic, be summoned before the synod of Fife on charges of "keeping intelligence with Huntly."

---

pensioners on James's council got wind of their communication and procured 50,000 *angelots* from England to bribe James to banish Catholics from Scotland. James thereupon raised 10,000 soldiers under the command of the earl of Arcadia (Argyll?) to invade Huntly's lands.

[166] TNA SP52/59/25 and 28. [167] Spottiswood, 416–18. [168] Ibid., 418–19.
[169] TNA SP52/39, fol. 34v. [170] Spottiswood, 417–18.

Ministers began to "inveigh and protest" against the exiled earls and their supporters from the pulpit, spurred on "by daily informations given them of the practices against religion and this discipline established, and also much pressed by religious barons, burghs and others."[171] Although in their sermons the ministers conceded that the exiles should be pardoned if they sincerely acknowledged "their errors in religion" and other offenses, they also spread fresh reports that Huntly and his associates had formed new plots with Spain and wanted to delay matters until they could bring these to fruition.[172]

In the midst of these contentions another controversy erupted in St Andrews over David Black, the minister previously admonished for calling the king's mother a whore and murderer. In late October he preached a sermon in which, according to several witnesses, he insulted Queen Anna, called the nobility "godless dissemblers and enemies to the Church," termed the king's council a group of "cormorants," asserted that "all kings were devils and come of devils," proclaimed that "the religion of England was but a show of religion," and accused Elizabeth of atheism.[173] Sensing an opportunity to win English support, James sent a report of Black's sermon to Bowes through his English bedchamber servant, Roger Aston, asking that it be forwarded to London.[174] When informed of the matter Elizabeth demanded a full investigation and due punishment of Black if he had indeed defamed her. James thereupon summoned Black to answer before his council.

Denying that he had spoken any of the offensive speeches attributed to him, Black first asked to have his case transferred to a court in England, but subsequently demanded instead that it be heard by his own presbytery, since words "uttered in the pulpit must be judged by the Church" rather than a secular tribunal.[175] Andrew Melville traveled with him to Edinburgh to support this plea and persuaded the Kirk's commissioners to do so as well on November 17.[176] The next day a formal declinature was drawn up, in which Black denied the council's right to try him because a minister in the pulpit was an "ambassador" of "the Lord Jesus," whose duty to God prevented him from submitting to "any civil law of man."[177] The commissioners circulated this document among the presbyteries, urging ministers to subscribe to it and promote Black's cause in their sermons and prayers.[178] One supporter claimed that 400 of the approximately 500 ministers in Scotland complied.[179] Even if exaggerated, this suggests widespread sympathy for Black. James saw the circulation of the declinature as an act of

---

[171] TNA SP52/59/40, 41, 46. [172] TNA SP52/59/60.
[173] Among the many reports of Black's sermons see Spottiswood, 423 and the account of David Moysie in *Scottish Diaries and Memoirs, 1550-1746*, ed. James Gabriel Fyfe (Stirling: E. Mackay, 1928), 77-8.
[174] TNA SP52/59/63 and 66. [175] Ibid. [176] Calderwood, 336.
[177] Ibid., 337. A declinature was a formal plea in Scots law disputing a court's jurisdiction over a case.
[178] Calderwood, 339; Spottiswood, 422.
[179] Goodare, "Presbyterian Movement," 26-7. Calderwood reported 300-400 subscriptions.

mutiny and incitement to rebellion. He issued a proclamation accusing "certain of the ministry" of contriving plots against his authority and seeking to "make insurrection."[180] Even before Black's challenge, the king had warned a delegation from the Kirk that "there could be no agreement so long as the marches of the two jurisdictions were not distinguished," meaning his crown and the Kirk.[181] The case brought to a head a longstanding dispute over whether the king and his council had the right to punish seditious words spoken in the pulpit.

From Negotiation to Confrontation and Rupture

But since neither party in the dispute wanted a complete rupture they both tried to find a way out of the impasse. James offered to forgive Black and dismiss the case if the minister would simply clarify what he had said in his sermon "on his conscience" and satisfy Bowes that he had not impugned Elizabeth's honor.[182] After some witnesses against Black retracted their testimony the whole affair seemed ready to blow over, rendering the dispute over the council's jurisdiction moot.[183] But Black refused to make any concessions on the principle at stake, telling James that if he did so "it might move your Majesty to attempt further in the spiritual government of the Church of God to the provocation of his high displeasure against your Majesty."[184] James, for his part, thought it beneath his dignity to come as "a complainer" to a presbytery.[185] A few days later a meeting was arranged between the king and a delegation of ministers to try to find a way for both sides to save face. James again offered that if the clergy "would pass from the declinature," or at least concede that it applied only to the case at hand and was not a general statement of principle, he would drop the matter and pardon Black. The clergy thereupon drew up another declaration, saying they had no intention of harming the king's authority in civil or criminal matters that did not involve conflicts with the word of God or the duty of ministers in spiritual matters. But this really conceded nothing and failed to satisfy James.[186]

Further behind-the-scenes negotiations followed, apparently generating contests between hard-liners and moderates in both camps. James's English bedchamber servant, Roger Aston, told Robert Cecil that "the wisest of the ministers" wanted to compromise but were blocked by those "more precise than wise." He added that some courtiers also "blew the coal," so "that [which] was done at night was altered tomorrow," as James vacillated between conflicting counsels.[187] Spottiswood also believed that sensible ministers were overruled by more

---

[180] Spottiswood, 422. [181] Ibid., 418.
[182] TNA SP52/59/92, Roger Aston to Robert Cecil, November 22, 1596. [183] TNA SP52/59/76.
[184] LPL Mss. 3471, fol. 79, "David Black's declaration to the king and council, 22 November 1596."
[185] Spottiswood, 425. [186] Calderwood, 340. [187] TNA SP52/59/92.

hot-headed colleagues who ran headlong into a confrontation with the king, while Calderwood makes it clear that the presbyterians thought that members of James's entourage deliberately aggravated the quarrel.[188] Unfortunately the sources do not provide much detail about who the moderates and hard-liners were, but this picture seems entirely plausible. We would certainly expect courtiers sympathetic to the Kirk to have tried to head off a damaging confrontation, while Catholic and Crypto-Catholic supporters of Huntly and Errol would have wanted to see a complete breakdown in the king's relations with their hated presbyterian adversaries. It is equally credible that some ministers were more cautious than others about pushing James too far.

Unfortunately, Black's declinature had raised an issue over which neither party felt able to compromise, since the one that did would suffer permanent damage in the contest over James's efforts to control the Kirk. As each side struggled to avoid defeat the conflict acquired a momentum that overwhelmed all efforts to resolve it. On November 24, James summoned the moderator of the previous general assembly, James Nicholson, and demanded that he produce a copy of the letter sent to the presbyteries with Black's declinature. Upon reading this document James declared it "evil... seditious and treasonable," leading Nicholson to correctly conclude that the king would soon order the Kirk's commissioners to leave Edinburgh. This further attack on the Kirk's independence provoked the commissioners to resolve that since they met by "the warrant of Christ and his Kirk" they must resist any royal command to disperse. They also voted to summon a general assembly to Edinburgh on January 2 without obtaining the king's approval, thereby challenging the power to convene general assemblies that James had previously exercised without question.[189] Three days later James again summoned Black before his council, "by sound of trumpet at the market cross" in Edinburgh, and issued a proclamation forbidding the ministers' supporters from assembling to accompany him. He had another proclamation drafted, restraining conventions of ministers and lay elders. He initially intended to delay its publication but changed his mind and issued it that same afternoon. He then sent private letters to the Kirk's commissioners, ordering them to leave Edinburgh.[190] The commissioners voted to defy this order "so long as conveniently they might" and ordered a preaching campaign in the town to defend their position. They also tried to blackmail the Octavians by threatening to blame them for their quarrel with the king and seek their punishment if the Kirk prevailed.[191] James's fury over these fresh rebukes precipitated a quarrel with Galloway, who suffered a temporary suspension from his duties as a minister of the royal household. The king had now broken with two of the three members of his

---

[188] Spottiswood, 422; Calderwood, 364.   [189] Calderwood, 340.
[190] Ibid., 341 (the private letters), TNA SP52/59/70, 76 (the proclamation).
[191] Spottiswood, 422; Calderwood, 339, 341–2.

presbyterian council.[192] On November 30, the ministers drew up a formal protest against James's recent proclamations, terming them "the dreg of Antichristianism," and resolved to draft a new and stronger declinature for Black.[193]

Another attempt at compromise began in early December but broke down within three days after the ministers refused to make any concessions that might appear to acknowledge the legitimacy of Black's trial before the council. A royal letter intended to appease them, read before the Edinburgh presbytery on the seventh, was judged "no ways sufficient."[194] On the ninth the presbyterian leaders again defied the king by issuing a statement that as "office-bearers of the kingdom of Christ they durst not for fear of committing spiritual high treason" refrain from "fighting against" his proceedings with all spiritual weapons at their disposal. Three days later they followed up with a day of fasting, during which "the doctrine sounded powerfully."[195] Events then moved swiftly toward a climax. On the thirteenth James threatened to cut off the ministers' stipends. The next day he again ordered the commissioners to leave Edinburgh.[196] This time most of them did so, but only after coordinating plans with the town's ministers to continue resisting the king. Rumors had meanwhile circulated that James, the Octavians, or possibly Huntly planned a violent attack on the ministers and their supporters, causing several Edinburgh burgesses to organize a defense force. On the sixteenth James ordered those burgesses, twenty-four in number, to leave town within twelve hours upon pain of horning (outlawry). Bowes heard a report he thought credible that the council had selected eighty additional burgesses for expulsion in the next few days.[197]

As these events transpired fears of impending violent conflict gripped the Scottish capital. "The king is determined to peril both life and crown," Aston wrote to an English acquaintance: "the ministers are determined to give their lives before they go back... I never thought the king in peril till now. No man dare deal with him in this matter."[198] He attributed the crisis to unnamed "secret instruments" who sabotaged every attempt at accommodation. Another Edinburgh resident blamed Huntly and his agents at the court. He too thought matters would end violently: "the people shall open themselves against the king or the king shall run to his own destruction."[199] No surviving evidence appears to corroborate reports that courtiers sympathetic to Huntly fanned the conflict.

---

[192] TNA SP52/59, 70. [193] Calderwood, 343, 345–6.
[194] Ibid., 350–3; Spottiswood, 424–6. [195] Calderwood, 356, 58. [196] Ibid., 358.
[197] TNA SP52/59/87.
[198] *Memoirs of the Reign of Queen Elizabeth from the Year 1581 till her Death*, ed. Thomas Birch, 2 vols. (London, 1754), 2.231; a fuller text of this letter (without identifying the author) is in Lambeth Palace Library Mss. 3471, fol. 81.
[199] *Memoirs of Elizabeth*, ed. Birch, 2.130. Bowes also reported "that there is no man with the king but all papists and atheists" and that the ministers were resolved "to suffer persecution," in vindication of the liberty of the kirk, "even till death" (ibid., 251).

But Aston, as a royal bedchamber servant, was probably in a position to know the inside story. In any case, many people believed the rumors.

On the morning of the seventeenth Walter Balcanquhal preached a sermon giving his view of the causes of the "troubles." According to Spottiswood and two other near contemporary accounts, he blamed people about the king for the crisis and exhorted his auditors to "stand fast in defense of religion" and "to take the cause of God upon them and defend the Church from persecution."[200] At the end of the sermon he invited the noblemen and burgesses in his audience to reconvene in the Little Church—the east end of St Giles's, Edinburgh's principal church—that afternoon. Julian Goodare estimates that between 400 and 500 people attended this meeting, including at least thirteen nobles and lairds and two Highland chiefs.[201] They would have brought with them many retainers who knew how to handle weapons, which lay close at hand in Edinburgh houses and lodgings. One source speaks of "a great concourse of diverse...knights and gentlemen, together with the provost, bailiffs and chief inhabitants of Edinburgh."[202] Calderwood states that Bruce opened the meeting by laying out "the danger wherein the Kirk was by the returning of the popish lords and the favor showed them," and asking those present to hold up their hands "and swear to defend the present state of religion against all opposers whatever."[203] The gathering then resolved to send a delegation consisting of lords Lindsay and Forbes, the lairds of Bargenie and Blairquhan, two Edinburgh burgesses, and Bruce to present a petition to the king, who was in the nearby Tollbooth presiding over a judicial case. As the delegates departed, Michael Cranstoun began reading the biblical story of Haman and Mordecai, in which a timely distribution of arms to the intended victims thwarted a plan to slaughter all Jews living in the Persian Empire.

When presented with the meeting's petition James angrily dismissed it, demanding to know "who were they that durst convene against his proclamation?" To this Lindsey allegedly replied that "they durst do more than so and that they would not suffer religion to be overthrown."[204] The king withdrew to another room, where his attendants bolted the door, in effect challenging the petitioners to assault him with brute force. Instead of doing so they returned to the Little Church to consider their next move. The sources differ about exactly what happened next. Calderwood claimed that "some of the cubicular courtiers" who detested the Octavians for trying to cut off their pensions and perquisites provoked a riot by raising cries of "fie, save yourselves" and "armor, armor," as if the town were

---

[200] Spottiswood, 427; TNA SP52/59/92, Aston to Robert Cecil, December 22, 1596; LPL Mss. 3471, anonymous information from Edinburgh dated December 26, 1596. Calderwood, 364, gives a somewhat different and milder account of the contents of Balcanquhal's sermon. The best modern treatments are Goodare, "Presbyterian Movement" and "The Attempted Scottish Coup of 1596," in *Sixteenth-Century Scotland: Essays in Honour of Michael Lynch*, ed. Julian Goodare and Alasdair MacDonald (Leiden: Brill, 2008), 311–36.
[201] Goodare, "Attempted Coup," 436.   [202] BL Cotton Mss. Caligula Di, fol. 153.
[203] Calderwood, 364–5.   [204] TNA SP52/59/87; Spottiswood, 427.

under attack. This provoked an uproar, as crowds rushed to the Little Church and the Tollbooth to save both the ministers and the king from what they thought was an armed Catholic assault. Eventually the Provost of Edinburgh managed to calm the crowds and restore normalcy.[205]

Goodare, who has written the most thorough modern accounts of the incident, sees this story as an attempt to exonerate the presbyterian leadership from responsibility for what was actually an attempted coup. But although several other contemporary or nearly contemporary sources fail to mention the malicious efforts of third parties to provoke a riot, one does say that courtiers took advantage of the quarrel between the king and Kirk by attempting "quietly and underhand to stir the ministers and inhabitants of Edinburgh" against the Octavians.[206] These stories about courtiers trying to provoke a confrontation almost certainly derive from rumors circulating at the time, although how much truth they contained may now be undiscoverable. The preponderance of contemporary evidence supports Goodare's argument that those gathered in the Little Church poured into the streets on the instructions of their leaders, rather than because of anonymous warnings of an impending attack. Spottiswood claimed that Lord Lindsay took the lead, crying "let us stay together that are here and promise to take one part and advertise our friends and the favorers of religion to come unto us, for it shall be either theirs or ours." Another early anonymous account describes Robert Bruce exhorting the meeting "to hold up their hands to live and die together," whereupon the gathering began to chant, "arm, arm."[207]

But even if Lindsay and Bruce did act in the way that Spottiswood and the anonymous narrative state, it would not prove that they sought to carry out a premeditated coup. Another plausible interpretation is that in the over-heated atmosphere created by the escalating stand-off between James and the Kirk a new crowd demonstration erupted, probably encouraged by presbyterian leaders who wanted to intensify pressure on the king, although possibly in reaction to false rumors of an imminent Catholic attack. This would explain why, according to Spottiswood, a section of the crowd led by one of the deacons of Edinburgh's craft gilds protected the royal party in the Tollbooth, why the Provost of Edinburgh, who generally supported the presbyterian cause, helped calm the riot, and why, according to both Bowes and Spottiswood, several ministers did *not* join the crowd in the streets but instead tried to calm the disturbance and expressed disapproval of what had happened.[208] Rather than a coup carefully planned in

---

[205] Calderwood, 364–5.
[206] BL Cotton Mss. Caligula Di, fol. 153; another copy is BL Harl. Mss. 4674, fol. 51.
[207] LPL Mss. 3471, fol. 83.
[208] Spottiswood, 428; TNA SP52/59/91. Spottiswood says the ministers remained in the Little Church and expressed their disapproval after the crowd had disbursed, an action that might be construed as an attempt to exonerate themselves after the fact. But it was by no means already clear that the presbyterians had lost by early evening on the 17th. Bowes stated on the 21st that the ministers

advance, the Tumult, as it was thereafter known, looks like a disorganized and confused event, whose leaders conspicuously failed to press their advantage at the crucial moment. Backed into a corner by James's assault on their political organization and his defiance of the veiled threat of force represented by the Little Church meeting, some presbyterian leaders may have decided to escalate by leading an armed crowd to the Tollbooth, hoping this would terrify the king into finally backing down. When the tactic failed they faced a stark choice between battering down a bolted door and dragging their sovereign out by the ears, or quietly dispersing and pretending that the whole affair had been caused by a false alarm. Revealingly, they chose the latter option. Before long, the Provost or chief magistrate of Edinburgh, who until that point had been in bed recovering from an illness, stepped in to restore calm, evidently with no objections from the presbyterian leaders.

But it must quickly have become clear that with these events the presbyterians had passed a point of no return. Whether planned or not, the Tumult certainly looked like a coup attempt. For some time the king and his council had remained besieged by armed crowds crying "bring out Haman"—the evil Persian counselor who advocated the massacre of the Jews—and "the sword of Gideon"—a reference to a peasant leader who on God's command destroyed a pagan altar, miraculously defeated and killed two enemy kings with an army of only three hundred men, and then refused to be crowned as king, saying that God alone ruled his people.[209] Bowes reported that evening that "the papists triumph," thinking their enemies had overreached. James spent the night in Holyroodhouse—too afraid to sleep according to one account—then departed early the next morning, leaving behind a proclamation declaring the events of the previous day a "treasonable uproar moved by certain factious persons of the ministry of Edinburgh."[210] He ordered all who were not permanent residents to leave the town within six hours on pain of treason, suspended the operation of the law courts, and ordered the members of the Session—the high court of Scotland—to prepare to leave Edinburgh and travel to whatever alternative place he named.[211]

For presbyterians not yet ready to capitulate the only way forward now lay in greater armed resistance. At this point some partisans of the Kirk undoubtedly did begin planning a coup, as Goodare has shown. On the nineteenth Bruce attempted to stiffen nerves with a sermon on the 51st Psalm, with its message of repentance

---

had tried to appease the crowd. This might again reflect an attempt to disguise their role after the fact but there seems to be no clear evidence that the ministers had actively planned or encouraged the armed demonstration in the streets. It seems entirely plausible that they quickly realized that events had spun out of control in ways likely to damage their cause, although Bruce, at least, also appears to have realized that they now had no choice but to push forward by mobilizing more force, since anything less would leave them exposed to James's retribution.

[209] Spottiswood, 428; BL Cotton Mss. Caligula Di, fol. 153.   [210] Spottiswood, 429–30.
[211] Calderwood, 366.

and concluding hope that God would "rebuild the walls of Jerusalem" in return for his people's contrition:

> The removal of your ministers is at hand. Our life shall be extremely sought but ye shall see with your eyes that God shall guard us and be our buckler and defense. The hypocrisy of many and iniquity of some shall clearly appear. The trial shall go through all men, through king and queen to council and nobility; from, sessions to barons, from barons to burgesses, yea to every craftsman. Sorry I am that I should see such weakness in many of you that ye dare not utter one word for God's glory and the good cause. It is not we that are party in this cause. No, the quarrel is betwixt a greater prince and them.[212]

But to have any chance of success the presbyterians needed the support not only of Edinburgh craftsmen and merchants but lairds and noblemen. Bowes reported that already on the seventeenth the presbyterians had decided to form a "band... for the defense of religion whereunto the religious noblemen, barons, burgesses and ministers shall be moved to subscribe."[213] Nobles who had participated in the tumult—Lindsey, Huntly's northern enemy Lord Forbes, and the head of the MacLeans—provided an initial nucleus. But the movement needed to recruit a more powerful leader. The presbyterians therefore sent letters to Lord John Hamilton, who according to Bowes had remonstrated with the king about his lax treatment of Huntly, and the earl of Argyll. Hamilton drew back at the invitation to lead an armed rebellion and passed on the letter he had received to the king. Argyll assembled some followers and moved toward Edinburgh but happened to encounter James before arriving. He then felt he had no choice but to join the king's entourage.

These responses effectively sealed the fate of militant presbyterianism. On December 23, Bruce and Balcanquhal fled over the English border into Yorkshire and the two other Edinburgh ministers hid themselves in Fife, after James ordered the burgh's officers to arrest them.[214] In the remaining days of December the king ordered the confiscation of the estates of Lindsey and Forbes. An Act of Council directed all clergy to subscribe to a "band" or oath acknowledging the king's authority to act as "sovereign judge" of seditious words spoken in the pulpit. Refusers were threatened with the loss of their stipends.[215] A proclamation issued on the twenty-seventh commanded magistrates, barons, and "gentlemen of power" to "interrupt ministers uttering false and treasonable speeches, tending to sedition from pulpits."[216] In January this was strengthened

---

[212] Ibid.   [213] TNA SP52/59/87.
[214] Goodare, "Attempted Coup," 430; HMC, *Mar and Kellie Manuscripts* (London, 1904), 46; TNA SP52/59/92; Calderwood, 367; Spottiswood, 430–1.
[215] Calderwood, 367; TNA SP52/59/93, 60/24 (giving the text of the band).
[216] Calderwood, 369.

into an order to arrest preachers who spoke against the king, as ministers filling the vacant pulpits in Edinburgh had evidently continued to do.[217] James rejected a petition for mercy from Edinburgh's civic corporation and imprisoned the dignitaries who presented it to him. He charged all the town's officers and 1,200 of its burgesses—probably between a quarter and a third of the adult male population—with sedition, and threatened to withdraw his court and the law courts from the burgh, steps that would have ruined its economy.[218] Some nobles about the court reportedly spoke of razing the town and erecting a pillar on its site as "a monument of the insolency committed and the just punishment thereof."[219]

On January 4, the king re-entered his thoroughly cowed and humiliated capital, as the armed retinues of three loyal noblemen lined its streets and guarded its gates. But he was not yet done. On March 5, the burgh's magistrates appeared for a public trial before the king at Perth. Because one magistrate absented himself, James declared the burgh and its burgesses guilty of rebellion and confiscated the rents that supported the civic corporation. The sentence precipitated the mass resignation of Edinburgh's magistrates. Finally, on the twenty-first, the king allowed Edinburgh's provost, bailiffs, council, and deacons to approach him and once again beg forgiveness on their knees. After rebuking them a final time he agreed to pardon the burgh in return for a fine of 20,000 marks and other concessions, including the confiscation of the houses of the ministers, who did not receive their pardons and permission to return home for almost another month.[220] By the end of April the storm had finally passed. James may then have decided not to challenge the stories put out by presbyterian ministers and others, who sought to explain away the Tumult as an almost accidental event, "stirred up by some rash and base persons," rather than "complotted and practiced by the noblemen, barons, burgesses and ministers," since this made it easier to pardon the offenders and take them back into his service after they submitted to his demands.[221]

The king's indulgence came at a price. Over the next few years James reasserted his control over the summoning of general assemblies and demanded that ministers accept his right to act as "their sovereign judge" in all cases involving subscription, while promising to avoid meddling in "the civil and politic of the country."[222] These measures encountered stiff resistance. But clergy who had been united in December soon began quarreling among themselves, much to the king's

---

[217] TNA SP52/60/14. "The ministers cease not to take liberty in their sermons to inveigh against these present proceedings, in regard they think thereby the religion and person of the king shall be endangered or else that the Spanish course shall be advanced."
[218] TNA SP52/59/91, 60/8; Calderwood, 369.
[219] Spottiswood, 443, confirmed by TNA SP52/60/14, Bowes to Burghley, January 13, 1597.
[220] TNA SP52/60/58.
[221] TNA SP52/60/29, Bowes to Burghley, February 1, 1597, summarizing the conclusions reached by an examination of the causes of the Tumult.
[222] TNA SP52/60/14; BL Add Mss. 48,117, fol. 10.

delight, impeding efforts to sustain a united resistance.[223] Unlike in 1584, the English declined to shelter ministers fleeing James's "persecution." An appeal for shelter to the earl of Essex was politely but firmly rebuffed.[224] Following instructions, the English ambassador Robert Bowes urged his presbyterian friends to behave with moderation. The Kirk also failed to receive the active aristocratic support it had enjoyed a decade earlier. As the Scottish ambassador to England, Archibald Douglas, put it, "the present state of the realm is such that never a nobleman will countenance the ministry, such excepted as have private quarrels to debate."[225] Royal control over clerical pensions provided another tool for breaking down resistance, throwing defenders of the Kirk's privileges and pretentions onto the defensive as James pressed his advantage. In 1598 he reintroduced the representation of the Kirk by its bishops in a Scottish parliament. Although he still disclaimed any intention "to bring in papistical or Anglican bishops," he had taken the first step toward the restoration of Scottish episcopacy.[226]

It helped that James agreed to pardon Huntly, Errol, and a third Catholic exile, Angus, only on condition that they submit to the Kirk. He wrote Huntly a stern letter telling him that if he refused this condition he must "make for another land . . . where you may freely use your own conscience, your wife and bairns shall in that case enjoy your living but for yourself look never to be a Scottishman again."[227] Huntly complied and, although his conformity proved short-lived and insincere, he retired to his estates and stopped conspiring with Spain. This helped undercut the rumors that had been spreading in the immediate aftermath of the Tumult that Jesuits and Spanish agents planned to exploit the Kirk's discomfiture to restore Catholicism.[228] The English had also become significantly less worried about Huntly and the threat of Spanish incursions into Scotland, even before the Tumult. In a letter to Bowes of August 1596, Cecil essentially endorsed James's decision to pardon Huntly, writing that "to my poor understanding . . . it seemeth very disputable whether he [Huntly] may not do more harm out of the realm [Scotland] ill affected than in the realm reduced and confirmed."[229] Cecil proposed that Bowes arrange for Elizabeth to act as a mediator on Huntly's behalf, to gain some influence over him. The suggestion appalled Bowes, who warned that "well affected" Scots, "heartily devoted to her Majesty, will be extremely wounded with the discovery" that Elizabeth wanted to help their great enemy.[230] But Cecil's

---

[223] BL Add Mss. 48,117, fol. 166: "At this assembly [at Perth in March 1597] Mr. Andrew Melville and Mr. John Johnson of St Andrews were commanded away, Mr. Robert Bruce was at words both with Mr. Peter Galloway and Mr. Robert Rollock, and sundry cross words was amongst many of them. Whereat the king took pleasure and blew the bellows openly to increase the fire."
[224] HMC Salisbury, 10.97.
[225] TNA SP52/60/78, memorandum on the affairs of Scotland, May 1597.
[226] Calderwood, 418. For a survey of developments in these years see, esp., MacDonald, *Jacobean Kirk*, 74–102.
[227] Spottiswood, 438. [228] For these rumors see TNA SP52/60/14.
[229] TNA SP52/59, fol. 135. [230] TNA SP52/59/37.

pragmatism suggests yet another reason why Calvinist solidarity no longer seemed as important to the defense of Britain against popery as it had a few years before.

The Scottish Political Theology of James VI, c. 1597–1603

By reasserting his control of the Kirk and taking the first cautious steps toward restoring Scottish episcopacy, James had unquestionably moved closer to the position of Whitgift, Bancroft, and their conformist allies in England. It had become significantly less likely that he would support major changes to the Church of England, if and when he succeeded Elizabeth. His outlook nevertheless remained the product of a Scottish political and intellectual environment that differed from that of England in significant ways, as close examination of his two famous political treatises written in this period, *Basilikon Doron* and *The Trew Law of Free Monarchies*, demonstrates.[231] Despite his dislike for "knave ministers" and reaction against his former tutor, George Buchanan, his thought patterns remained rooted in the blend of humanist ethical teachings and Calvinist religiosity drummed into him during childhood and adolescence. Rather than rejecting that legacy he reshaped it to provide a philosophical and theological justification for personal monarchy. Buchanan wrote that "kings at first were institute for maintaining of equity."[232] In *Basilikon Doron*—composed as a book of advice for Prince Henry—James not only repeated this idea but extended it by arguing that by enforcing equity and justice kings acted as God's agents on earth.[233] He then gave the argument a further pious twist by stating that although a prince should certainly study the ethical teachings of Greek and Roman literature, he must above all know the scriptures, "which contain more moral precepts than all the philosophers." The account of good and evil rulers in *Kings* and *Chronicles*, which had already inspired one of his published meditations, were particularly relevant. To the study of the Bible a good king will "join...the careful hearing of the doctrine with attendance and reverence"; in other words he will diligently listen to sermons.[234] Unlike some English conformists, who had begun to criticize what they regarded as puritan over-emphasis on preaching, James never lost his appetite for it.[235] On the other hand, he had nothing much to say about the set prayers and liturgical ceremonies that English conformists increasingly

---

[231] For the background on how these treatises were written, published, and subsequently (mis) interpreted see Jenny Wormald, "James VI and I, *Basilikon Doron* and *The Trew Law of Free Monarchies*: The Scottish Context and the English Translation," in *The Mental World of the Jacobean Court*, ed. Linda Levy Peck (Cambridge: Cambridge University Press, 1991), 36–54.
[232] George Buchanan, *De Jure Regnum apud Scotos* (London, 1680), 24.
[233] McIlwain, 18, 1–17.   [234] Ibid., 12–13.
[235] McCullough, *Sermons at Court*, chapter 3; James VI and I, *A meditation upon the Lord's prayer written by the Kings Majesties* (London, 1619); *A meditation upon the 27, 28, 29 verses of the XXVII chapter of St. Matthew* (London, 1620).

emphasized. He had once cited David's dancing before the Ark as proof that religious ceremonies were warranted by scripture, and he had erected a Chapel Royal within his household staffed mainly by choristers and musicians, like that of England. But at this stage he showed no concern for the promotion of ceremonial decorum, which held little appeal in Scotland, even for a man like Patrick Adamson, who criticized the burden of "ceremonies and injunctions" imposed on the English Church.[236]

Buchanan had argued that monarchical power degenerated when kings began to rule by "lust... instead of laws," conniving "at many things out of favor, hatred or self-interest."[237] James again echoed and expanded his tutor's view, writing that a good king will acknowledge that he is made for his people and subject his appetites and affections to their needs, whereas a tyrant will think his people exist to serve his pleasure and attempt to rule them by promoting faction and dissension. He buttressed these assertions with citations to classical authorities—Aristotle, Xenophon, Plato, Cicero, and Tacitus—much as Buchanan might have done, and warned that a tyrant's misdeeds will arm his subjects to become his executioner.[238] He then went on to state that a king must strive to bridle not only his own lusts but the disordered appetites and self-interested behavior of his subjects. He must, for example, make sure that his parliaments are not abused "for private men's particulars."[239] This advice also applied to religion: "beware ye wrest not the word [of God] to your own appetite," he warns Henry, "making it like a bell to sound as ye please to interpret."[240] "Learn wisely to distinguish betwixt points of salvation and indifferent things, betwixt substance and ceremonies; and betwixt the express commandment and will of God in his word, and the invention or ordinance of men... For in anything that is expressly commanded or prohibited in the book of God ye cannot be over precise... But as for all other things not contained in scripture, spare not to use or alter them as the necessity of the time shall require."

In referring to "indifferent things" James invoked a concept long used by English conformists to justify the state's authority to regulate religious ceremonies and ecclesiastical institutions, and that he himself would later invoke in imposing English-style ceremonies on the Kirk after 1617. But in 1597 he quickly dropped the subject without elaborating on how "the necessity of the time" might require

---

[236] BL Harley Mss. 291, fol. 134r. In criticizing ministers who had fled to England, Adamson contrasted the religious cultures of the two courts and realms: "Albeit his majesty loveth and maintaineth the gospel she is a rare auditory of the preaching and except in Lent and few solemn days hears no sermons. His highness the privy exercise used in his house every day after dinner and supper by any learned minister expounding the chapter, observeth solemnly the sermons every Sunday twice with his whole nobility and council, and sicklik [similarly] on every Wednesday and Friday in the year. Her majesty hath continued the reformation of King Edward, wherein the Kirk is burdened with sundry ceremonies and injunctions[?], whereto their clergy is asticktit, wherewith his highness hath not burdened his realm." He went on to point out that Bullinger had criticized the English Prayer Book.

[237] Buchanan, *Jure*, 24–5.   [238] McIlwain, 18–19.   [239] Ibid., 19.   [240] Ibid., 21.

changes in the Kirk's liturgy or administrative structure. He again came close to English conformist thought, including anti-Martinist satires by writers like Nashe, in identifying pride, ambition, and avarice as the besetting vices of churchmen, ever since the days of the apostles.[241] But his prescriptions for restraining clerical pride again differ from the emphasis on set liturgical forms favored by English conformist divines. He stressed instead the need to listen critically to sermons. When ministers "speak to you anything that is well warranted by the word, reverence and obey them as heralds of the most high God," he urged: "but, if passing that bounds they urge you to embrace any of their fantasies in the place of God's word... acknowledge them for no other than vain men."[242] He takes it for granted that religion centers around preaching and hearing, rather than ceremonies and set prayers.

James next moved on to develop another idea that he shared with Buchanan, namely that a good king must act as a physician to the body politic by purging vices rooted in passion, selfishness, and pride, especially among the privileged and powerful.[243] He gives a concise account of the characteristic vices of the three estates of Scottish society and the measures needed to bring them to order. The tumultuous origins of the Scottish Reformation have encouraged the clergy—or some "fiery spirited men" among them—to desire "a democratic form of government," which they hope to rule "by leading people by the nose." To that end they have promoted the doctrine of ministerial parity, "the mother of confusion." "As a preservative against their poison" he urges a policy of repressing "proud puritans," while encouraging godly, learned and modest men, settling "good pastors," reforming and maintaining the universities, and keeping a vigilant eye over the purity of doctrine.[244] Make certain that ministers in the pulpit do not stray from the explication of biblical texts into political questions, he advises, and do not allow the clergy to gather in assemblies and conventions without royal permission.[245] These passages reflected the king's recent experiences and his determination to bring the Kirk under his control. But he says nothing about the need for episcopal authority or prohibitions against people "gadding to sermons" beyond their own parish church, another preoccupation of English conformists.

The royal duty to restrain and punish pride extends beyond the ecclesiastical sphere. James describes the Scottish nobility as prone to "a feckless arrogant conceit of their greatness and power," which leads them to oppress the common people, maintain their followers' criminal behavior and engage in feuds, "to bang it out bravely, he and all his kin against him and all his." The remedy is to enforce the laws against feuding and other abuses, while encouraging men wronged by

---

[241] McIlwain, 23.   [242] Ibid., 17.
[243] Buchanan, *Jure*, 15. A ruler who "as a physician" seeks to quiet disturbances, must "so take care of all the members [of society] that the weaker may not languish for want of nutrition, nor the stronger become luxuriant too much."
[244] McIlwain, 23–4.   [245] Ibid., 39.

great lords to sue for royal justice in person, instead of acting through noble mediators, "for intercession to saints is papistry."[246] Here he advocated a direct and personal style of kingship, unmediated by courts of law and other intermediary authorities. James acknowledged that bringing the nobility under the law will be difficult, since hereditable sheriffs and regalities have effectively taken the administration of justice out of the king's hands. He recommends abating these seigneurial forms of justice as much as possible in order to reform the administration of law after the pattern of England. But this will take time and in the interim the best solution is to discipline lords who misuse their powers. Turning to the third estate, James stated that Scottish merchants "think the whole commonwealth ordained for making them up" and engage in sharp practice to enrich themselves at the expense of the people, while Scottish craftsmen are also guilty of dishonesty and shoddy workmanship. Encouraging the trade of foreign merchants and immigration of foreign craftsmen will alleviate these problems, as recent English experience demonstrated.[247]

James continued to emphasize the personal nature of kingship in stating that a prince should attend his own council and occasionally preside over trials, so as to exhibit his direct involvement in supervising government and enforcing justice.[248] Kings must be prepared to wage war and Henry should prepare himself by training his body through physical exercise and his mind by reading military treatises, especially Caesar's *Commentaries*, the best practical discussion of war and politics written in antiquity. But wars should only be undertaken in cases of necessity and after due preparation, especially in gathering the necessary money. A king should begin his reign by administering justice with severity but thereafter he should use clemency in moderation, taking care that the laws remain "rules of virtuous and social living" rather than "snares to trap your good subjects."[249] In addition to governing his subjects wisely he must carefully regulate his own behavior and that of his entourage, since a king "is as one set upon a stage" who can never be too precise. He should accordingly avoid vices like drunkenness, gluttony, and effeminacy that breed contempt, "the mother of rebellion and disorder." Remember that subjects will follow the example of their prince and live in a manner that inspires virtue, he warns.

Outwardly much of this advice appears to center on secular concerns rather than religion. But the way in which James kept connecting a king's political functions to both his personal morality and his reception of biblical texts and sermons recalls the Calvinist concept of discipline. That concept connected soteriology—the operation of saving grace within an individual soul—to social morality and ultimately to eschatology, by treating participation in a collective battle against sin as the necessary consequence of saving faith. In receiving God's

---

[246] Ibid., 25.   [247] Ibid., 26-7.   [248] Ibid., 39.   [249] Ibid., 38.

grace, the elect are drawn into the epic struggle between the forces of God and Satan that will culminate in the Apocalypse. For a king, with his responsibility to punish wrongdoing and promote the welfare of his subjects, discipline took on additional layers of meaning. The royal "office," James insisted, "is mixed betwixt the ecclesiastical and civil estate," rather than "mere *laicus*," contrary to what papists, Anabaptists, and many puritans taught.[250] For kingcraft properly involved the continual forging of connections between religion, individual morality, and the regulation of social behavior. A good king had to understand and apply God's word and fulfill God's intentions by reforming abuses and, if "the necessity of the times" required, leading his people in wars against Antichristian armies, in imitation of ancient Jewish rulers like David. In this way he becomes the multi-purpose instrument of God's will on earth and, as a result, God's surrogate and image.

This understanding of kingship continued to inform James's thought and conduct well after his departure for London. He only gradually relinquished the interest in apocalyptic thought and the identification of the papacy with Antichrist displayed in his early work on *The Revelation of John the Divine*. He explicitly described the unification of England and Scotland under his rule as an event ordained by providence that he and his subjects had a sacred duty to promote.[251] After the failure of the Gunpowder Plot he tried to impress upon a Venetian ambassador "the fact that he was under divine providence and protection, proving it by many other accidents from which he had been miraculously preserved. He especially desires that everyone should hold this belief."[252] His concern with supernatural causation had already surfaced in *Daemonologie*, published two years before *Basilikon Doron*, in which he equated the denial of witchcraft with atheism and stated that he regarded his supervision of witchcraft trials as one of his most important royal duties.[253] "The king by his own especial travail hath drawn Sampson the great witch to confess plainly her wicked estate and doings and to discover sundry things," Robert Bowes reported in December 1591.[254] Although James expressed skepticism about prophetic dreams and portents in his published writings, he would later tell John Harington that his mother's death was known in Scotland before it happened by visions of a head dancing in the air. Supernatural visions intrigued him, although he was apparently uncertain what opinion to hold about their authenticity.

Notably absent from James's view of a good king's role in advancing God's will on earth is any developed discussion of institutional structures and ancient laws. He ignores the question, much-debated among divines in the 1590s, of whether

---

[250] Ibid., 45.   [251] Below, p. 451.   [252] *CSPV* 10.327.
[253] *Daemonologie* (Edinburgh, 1597), 54–5.
[254] TNA SP52/46/69. For the significance of witchcraft in Scottish culture see Williamson, *Scottish National Consciousness*, chapter 2.

the primitive Church had a presbyterian or episcopal structure. Although he does advise Henry to "study well your own [i.e. your kingdom's own] laws" and to "spy" on his judges, he devotes fewer words to the subject of Scottish law than he does to a prince's recreations.[255] He shows no interest in concepts of tradition and ancient custom central to the thought of Richard Hooker and, a few years later, the "common law mind" of jurists like Sir Edward Coke. Instead he describes laws as instruments created by edicts of ancient kings to assist them in carrying out their responsibilities: "The kings therefore in Scotland were before any estates or ranks of men within the same, before any parliaments were holden or laws made: and by them was the land distributed (which at first was wholly theirs), states erected and discerned and forms of government devised and established."[256] A good king will normally obey the law, both to set an example to his subjects and because settled laws are helpful in securing civic peace. But he may also set them aside if the public good requires him to do so in particular cases.[257] There is very little sense in *Basilikon Doron* that a king needs to operate within a well-developed structure of institutional procedures and customary rules that give monarchy a permanent, impersonal existence that transcends the acts of individual rulers.

This relative indifference to institutional forms dovetails into another distinction between James's thought and that of many English conformist divines in the 1590s. Lake has shown that English conformists sought to undercut puritan emphasis on discipline by distinguishing between the invisible Church, consisting solely of true believers, and the visible Church that comprised all members of a formally Christian society. In their view, outward forms of worship and ecclesiastical organization pertained only to the visible Church, which provided no more than a framework of formal worship within which God worked to gather and direct the invisible community of the faithful through the operation of his spirit.[258] The visible institutionalized Church therefore had a very limited role to play in the eschatological unfolding of the kingdom of heaven, although it was central to the maintenance of social order and stability. Its clergy must certainly preach against sin and church courts must levy fines and impose penances for offenses like fornication, but conformist divines did not generally see their Church as engaged in an aggressive effort to transform society. They also played down the contest with Rome and its apocalyptic associations. These attitudes led some churchmen, including Bancroft, toward quietism.[259] A few even came to regard fundamental political questions, like whether subjects ever had the right to resist their rulers, as matters that depended on the laws and customs of individual countries, rather than invariant religious rules.[260]

Lake argues that Richard Hooker departed from these patterns of thought by developing an alternative view of the role of the institutional church in "edifying"

---

[255] McIlwain, 39, cf. 48. [256] Ibid., 62. [257] Ibid., 63.
[258] Lake, *Anglicans and Puritans?* [259] Ibid., 139. [260] Ibid., 133.

or building a Christian society through the effect of its rituals in instilling attitudes of piety and reverence, which deepened faith while simultaneously helping to maintain social order. But even Hooker saw edification as a gradual process, taking place largely on a subliminal level, unlike the round of sermons and public penances involved in presbyterian discipline, which James never seriously tried to suppress. James did not attempt to restrict the moral discipline of kirk sessions, which he generally approved as conducive to his goal of promoting civility and combating practices like the feud, although he did step in when he believed that the Kirk's efforts to discipline individuals threatened to cause serious political problems. Rather than eliminating Calvinist discipline he tried to harness and regulate it as a flexible tool of royal governance.[261]

The scant attention paid to rituals, traditions, and institutional forms in *Basilikon Doron* reflects not only the austerity of the Kirk but the relative informality of Scottish governance. The Scottish context may also explain a series of comments, scattered through the text, concerning the importance of family relationships, bloodlines and purity of blood as constituents of the social and political order. For although an emphasis on lineage and family was also found in England and throughout early modern Europe, kinship loyalty and alliances played an exceptionally important role in Scotland. Like many thinkers of the period James regarded the nobility not only as a social elite but an intrinsically superior "race."[262] A king must exercise discretion in dealing with his nobility, he advised, to prevent them from damaging the commonwealth by feuds and oppression or stacking the royal court with their dependents, problems with which he had ample experience. Certain offices, especially those involving finance, are best given to mean men, who are much easier to discipline when they commit frauds.[263] Nevertheless, because "virtue followeth oftenest noble blood,"[264] a king should delight "to be served by men of the noblest blood that may be had." Even the youths and boys recruited to serve as companions to royal children should come from families "that are come of a good and virtuous kind, *in fide parentum*, as baptism is used: for though *anima non venit ex traduce* but is immediately created by God and infused from above, yet it is most certain that virtue or vice will oftentimes, with the heritage, be transferred from the parents to the posterity, and run on a blood (as the proverb is), the sickness of the mind becoming as kindly in some races as these sicknesses of the body that infect the seed."[265]

A prince must have an especially keen sense of obligation to his own bloodline, defending the honor of his parents and ancestors, for "how can they love you that hated them whom-of ye are come?"[266] James asserted that he always found that his

---

[261] McIlwain, 3.
[262] On this subject see Brendan Kane and R. Malcolm Smuts, "The Politics of Race in England, Scotland and Ireland," in *The Oxford Handbook of the Age of Shakespeare*, ed. R. Malcolm Smuts (Oxford: Oxford University Press, 2016), 346–63.
[263] McIlwain, 32.   [264] Ibid., 25.   [265] Ibid., 30–1.   [266] Ibid., 20.

mother's supporters served him loyally, while her enemies, although nominally his own partisans during the civil wars, frequently betrayed him. The commitment to parents extended to an obligation toward old family servants "and their posterity," who should continue to receive favor. But enmity was also inherited and James urged Henry to maintain "your constant hatred of them that I hated."[267] These comments came close to contradicting his advice, elsewhere in *Basilikon Doron* that a king must "be of no surname or kin but equal to all honest men," and that in punishing offenses he must begin "at his elbow" with his own ordinary companions. We can sense him striving, not always successfully, to reconcile his duty to administer impartial justice with his acute awareness of the degree to which Scottish politics depended on family alliances and his very Scottish sense of kin loyalty.

His preoccupation with lineage and family honor becomes even more pronounced in his comments about his son's future marriage. Henry must select a mate "of a whole and clean race, not subject to hereditary sickness either of the soul or of the body: for if a man will be careful to breed horses and dogs of good kinds, how much more careful should he be for the breed of his own loins."[268] Naturally she must also be "honest" (chaste) to assure the legitimacy of her offspring. But James also insisted less conventionally that a prince must avoid polluting his body through fornication before marriage and adultery afterward. Although the world counts fornication a light sin, God unequivocally forbids it. In an extraordinary passage he writes that God punished his grandfather's adulteries by the premature deaths of two sons, the "double curse" of an infant female heir, and a bastard son, James earl of Moray, who would later betray that heir by driving her from the throne. "And what good her posterity hath gotten since of some of that unlawful generation Bothwell his treacherous attempts can witness."[269] James V's sexual transgressions had, in short, cursed his legitimate offspring with an illegitimate line that evidently bore one of those inheritable "diseases of the soul," involving a congenital propensity toward treason, to which *Basilikon Doron* had earlier referred. Here again James connected seemingly secular concepts of lineage and family loyalty to providentialist religion.

He went on to urge Henry to prevent his wife from meddling in political affairs, to raise his children properly and to leave all of his kingdoms to his eldest son, rather than attempting to divide them. Should he fail to produce children he must respect the rights of the next legitimate heir, "for kingdoms are ever at God's disposition and in that case we are but life-renters." His preoccupation with pure bloodlines merged with his belief in hereditary divine right as a sacred institution.

---

[267] Ibid., 31.   [268] Ibid., 36.

[269] Ibid., 34–5: "Have the king my grandfather's example before your eyes, who by his adultery bred the wrack of his lawful daughter and heir in begetting that bastard who unnaturally rebelled and procured the ruin of his own sovereign and sister. And what good her posterity hath gotten since of some of that unlawful generation, Bothwell his treacherous attempts can bear witness."

Behind these arguments we can sense the pressure of difficult and painful experiences: his complex relationship with his mother and her tarnished moral reputation; his efforts to settle noble feuds; his often-strained relations with Anna of Denmark;[270] and his anxieties about whether the English would recognize his right as hereditary heir to their monarchy. Although *Basilikon Doron* outlines a theory of divine right kingship, we will miss its full significance by approaching this tract as an abstract work of political philosophy, without recognizing that it also reflected James's long effort to come to terms with his role as king in a turbulent environment, and the intensely personal nature of his efforts to free himself from the bullying influence of Buchanan and presbyterian clergy and the fraught circumstances of his youth. Although he was in some senses an Erastian and cautious episcopalian, James's thought remained fundamentally different in any number of respects from that of English divines like Whitgift, Bancroft, and Hooker. At the time of his succession to the English throne, the degree to which he would prove their reliable ally remained unclear.

James and the English Conformists

But as Peter McCullough has shown, when the time came Whitgift and Bancroft rapidly moved to co-opt him by arranging a series of sermons along his route south and at Whitehall, presenting the case for preserving the Church in its existing form and warning against the dangers of innovation.[271] Something of a test came barely three months after his arrival in London, as he prepared to undergo the elaborate medieval liturgical ritual of an English coronation, involving rites that many in his Scottish entourage regarded as popish and superstitious, and about which he himself had doubts. Thomas Bilson, bishop of Winchester, a veteran defender of conformist positions, preached a sermon on this occasion that suggested ways in which James's concept of divine right monarchy might be synthesized with an English conformist emphasis on ceremonial symbolism. Bilson's insight was to recognize that the divine right of kings might be justified not only by stories of Old Testament kings but the New Testament imagery used to describe Jesus of Nazareth as the Messiah, or king of the last days. Scripture described Jesus's messianic status through multiple metaphoric allusions to the ritual paraphernalia of ancient monarchy, including the ceremony of anointing, which had given Christianity its very name, after the Greek word *christos*,

---

[270] In 1592 Henry Wotton heard a rumor in Italy that Anna had conspired with a Scottish earl—almost certainly Bothwell—to have James murdered, "compelling the king to run away." Three years later Patrick Galloway won James's gratitude by preaching a persuasive sermon on "the duties of man and wife" that evidently had a salutary effect on the queen. *Life and Letters of Sir Henry Wotton*, ed. Logan Pearsall Smith, 2 vols (Oxford: Clarendon Press, 1907), 1.284–5; TNA SP52/56/88.
[271] McCullough, *Sermons at Court*, 101–6.

meaning anointed with oil. Bilson began his sermon with the observation, which James had also made in *Basilikon Doron* that Psalm 82 refers to kings as gods. Princes obviously are not gods by nature, Bilson observed, so scripture must mean "that they are gods by office, ruling, judging and punishing in God's stead and so deserving God's name here on earth": very much the position James had taken.[272] The sermon then elaborated. God not only lends his name to kings but uses their

> names and signs to show the unity and sovereignty of his kingdom and to sever it from all other kinds of government, for Christ is never called in scripture a consul, a senator or a tribune of the people but the name on his garment and on his thigh, as St John saith [Revelations 19] is king of kings and lord of lords, that is a most mighty king and lord. Insomuch as when Christ is described in the scriptures as a king all the ornaments and emblems of a kingdom are namely recited and personally referred to him... Thy throne O God, endureth forever saith the scripture of Christ [Psalm 45], as the apostle expoundeth it the scepter of thy kingdom is a scepter of righteousness [Hebrews 1]. Wherefore God, even thy God, hath anointed thee with the oil of gladness above thy partners [Revelations 19]. On his head, saith St John, are many crowns and out of his mouth (as working his will by his word) goeth a sharp sword, wherewith he will smite the heathen. To princes then as partakers with Christ in the power, honor and justice of his kingdom here on earth are allowed of God a sword in sign of power, a crown in sign of glory, a scepter for a token of direction, a throne for a seat of judgment and inunction [anointing] as a pledge of outward protection and inward infusion of grace.[273]

These signs have spiritual meanings when applied to Christ and an earthly significance when applied to kings, but the two symbolic systems remain parallel and conjoined, so that every political function of a king corresponds to a religious mystery. Even in this world kings receive not only formal power from God but active spiritual assistance, "wherewith they are guided in doing their office." Just as God inspired his prophets to reveal the Truth, he endows kings "with a principal spirit" "to keep his people in peace and piety."[274] The ritual of anointing, which James had just undergone, symbolizes this inward infusion of supernatural grace, demonstrating a king's "resemblance with the Son of God."[275]

Although he warned that kings are not to be obeyed when their commands conflict with God's,[276] Bilson's sermon was for the most part unequivocally absolutist. After finishing his discussion of sacred signs, he went on to argue that kings have an unqualified right to dispose of their subjects' lives and property

---

[272] Thomas Bilson, *A sermon preached at Westminster* (London, 1603), n.p.   [273] Ibid.
[274] Ibid.   [275] Ibid., sig. B1r.
[276] McCullough, *Sermons at Court*, 104; Bilson, *Sermon*, sig. B6r.

as they see fit.[277] But this unlimited power does not merely exist to keep order in a fallen world; it also plays a role alongside faith in reconciling human souls with God, through the contemplation of aspects of royal power and authority that correspond to divine attributes. Bilson describes how this process works in ways strikingly parallel to Hooker's views on the role of liturgical ceremonies in instilling pious dispositions. He had found a way of seamlessly connecting edifying Christian worship, as described by Hooker, with the ceremonies of a royal court, and both these ceremonial systems with the practical operation of royal power. This made it possible to view the magnificence of a royal court as similar and complementary to worship within a church. Although of course he could not say so explicitly, Bilson came close to describing kingship as a kind of sacrament, a sign through which God incorporated believers within the body of his Church while imparting a deeper faith within their souls.

These ideas implied a view of monarchy as central to the sacred historical drama of human redemption, and thus a kind of royalist eschatology. The natural order of the creation, disrupted by the fall of Adam, will be gradually restored through the authority of kings who wield God's scepter on earth. Subjects will participate in that process through their obedience, which subjugates their fallen nature to a higher power and regulates their conduct toward others. Bilson did not develop these ideas in his relatively short sermon but he laid foundations on which the Laudian Church would later build. In the short term, however, his suggestive parallels between monarchy and Christianity did not immediately transform the political thought of either most English divines or King James. They remained only one among many available ways of understanding the religious significance of monarchy. The Scottish king and his new English (and Irish) subjects still needed time to adjust to each other, as they digested the implications of the dynastic union of Britain under a single crown, opportunities for consolidating royal control of Ireland following the successful conclusion of the Nine Years War, and a gradually receding tide of religious war across Europe.

---

[277] Bilson, *Sermon*, sig. C1r.

9
King James's Peace, the Laws of the Realms, and the Forging of a United Kingdom?

The English Invention of *Rex Pacificus* and Its European Context

On April 7, 1603 King James first entered his new kingdom at Berwick and inspected the garrison and artillery that had previously stood guard against Scots like himself. "Among which warlike train...his Majesty was very pleasant and gracious. So to show how much he loved and respected the art military he made a shot himself out of a cannon, so fair and with such sign of experience that the most expert gunners there beheld it not without admiration."[1] Knowing that people regarded leadership in war as a key responsibility of kings, he behaved as he had advised Prince Henry to do in *Basilikon Doron*: "Be in your own person warlike, diligent and painful, using the advice of such as are skillfulest in the craft...Be homely with your soldiers as your companions, for winning their hearts, and extremely liberal."[2] But as he traveled south, James encountered orators who praised him not as a warrior but as a bringer of peace. A panegyric by Samuel Daniel, read to the king as he passed through Rutland, hailed him as a ruler whose "princely wisdom hath allur'd / A state to peace, left to thee turbulent" during his Scottish reign, and who would now work a similar change in England:

> Thus mighty rivers quietly do glide,
> And do not, by their rage, their powers profess,
> But by their mighty workings, when in pride
> Small *Torrents* roar more loud and work much less:
> Peace, greatness best becomes: calm power doth guide
> With a far more imperious stateliness
> Then all the swords of violence can do,
> And easier gains those ends she tends unto.[3]

---

[1] Nichols, *James I*, 1.65–6. [2] McIlwain, 29.
[3] Samuel Daniel, *A Panegyrike congratulatory to the Kings Majestie* (London, 1603), n.p. (stanza 32).

At Stamford Hill, Sir Richard Martin of the Middle Temple delivered an oration on behalf of the sheriffs of London and Middlesex that looked forward to the expansion of commerce that, he predicted, an end to war with Spain would soon bring. "The ports and havens of these kingdoms, which have long been barred, shall now open the mouths of their rivers to the gentle and just traffic of all nations, washing away our reproach of universal pirates and sea wolves."[4]

By the end of May, James had taken the hint and altered his demeanor. The Venetian ambassador reported that when he first entered the Tower of London, he did so "without a sword at his side, on purpose, and now declares that as he came to his kingdom in peace he will preserve it in peace for himself and his subjects."[5]

James's self-proclaimed attachment to peace has colored his reputation ever since, particularly with respect to his conduct after the outbreak of the Thirty Years War in 1618.[6] But in 1603 that conflict lay far in the future and James's embrace of peace had different meanings, related not only to war with Spain but also to the preservation of England's domestic peace and relations between the three kingdoms now dynastically joined under his rule. The speed with which fear of civil war dissipated in 1603 has made it easier for historians to ignore the huge relief that many English people felt over James's non-violent succession. But contemporary evidence leaves no doubt about the matter. "I dare assure you the contentment of the people is unspeakable, seeing all things proceed so quietly, whereas they expected in the interim their houses should have been spoiled and sacked," Thomas Lord Burghley reported to his brother, Robert Cecil, from the North.[7] Enthusiastic crowds turned out to greet James as he traveled south, lending credibility to panegyrists' descriptions of the people's unified support for their new king. As he approached Robert Cecil's mansion of Theobalds teamsters "ran from their carts, leaving their team of horses to their own unreasonable directions." Multitudes of people arrived not only from London but also from "Kent, Surrey, Essex and Middlesex, besides many other counties."[8] In London French diplomats reported that on the eve of Elizabeth's death the council closed the ports and rounded up about a thousand vagabonds, ostensibly to provide soldiers for the Dutch but actually to "get rid of this dangerous canaille during a time of change."[9] Armed citizens began patrolling the streets. But after James's proclamation passed without incident the citizens returned to their private affairs, amidst artillery salutes and celebratory fireworks. "Thus day chases away night and new joy causes pain to be forgotten."[10] Lady Anne Clifford and her

---

[4] Nichols, *James I*, 1.131.   [5] *CSPV* 10.67.
[6] By far the fullest treatment is W. B. Patterson, *King James VI and I and the Reunion of Christendom* (Cambridge: Cambridge University Press, 1997).
[7] HMC Salisbury, 15.11.   [8] Ibid., 136.   [9] TNA, PRO33/3/35, fol. 274.
[10] TNA PRO33/3/35, fol. 16: "Hier soudain que la proclamation fut fait, le peuple qui était en armes aussi tôt se retira, chacun à son métier et a ses affaires et le canon de la Tour fut céchargé et les feux de joies firent le soir en réjouissance; ainsi le jour chasse la nuit et la nouvelle joie fait oublier la douleur" (Beaumont to Villeroy, April 5, 1603).

mother accepted an invitation to move in with the countess of Warwick, "for fear of some commotions," thinking themselves safer in a large aristocratic household than in their rented lodgings in Clerkenwell if trouble broke out. But the king's "peaceable" proclamation soon reassured them and "within two or three days we returned to Clerkenwell again."[11]

Some anticipated that the new king would seek revenge against statesmen he blamed for his mother's execution, while perhaps rewarding her Catholic friends. The Venetian ambassador wrote in late April that "Elizabeth's portrait is being hidden everywhere and Mary Stuart's shown instead with declaration that she suffered for no other cause than for her religion."[12] But James insisted that he had come not to pursue old quarrels but to heal them. He kept Robert Cecil in office but also released several of Essex's former followers from prison.[13] Daniel praised his forbearance:

> A king of England now most graciously
> Remits the injuries that have been done
> To king of Scots, and makes his clemency
> To check them [the English ministers] more than his correction.[14]

The king's best efforts could not prevent courtiers from jockeying for position and resenting the Scots he had brought south with him, or the efforts of both Catholics and puritans to win concessions. Inevitably, some people were left disappointed and embittered. They included the earl of Northumberland, who had hoped to prosper as a spokesman for the ancient nobility but soon grew discontented, along with Sir Walter Ralegh, Lord Cobham, and a few other political insiders who became entangled in the Bye and Main Plots, uncovered in the autumn.[15] England's peace and stability under its new king continued to look vulnerable.[16] Nevertheless, the regnal transition had occurred without major disruption or violence.

This relative smoothness ultimately owed less to the king's own wishes than to wider European events that prevented a concerted challenge to his succession, while giving Spain reasons to end its long conflict with England.[17] After decades of fighting, the great wars of the late sixteenth century had devolved into a stalemate that prevented all the main protagonists from achieving their full goals, while imposing enormous burdens upon each of them. Serious enough in themselves,

---

[11] *The Diaries of Lady Anne Clifford*, ed. D. J. H. Clifford (Phoenix Mill: Sutton, 1990), 21.
[12] Ibid., 10.   [13] *CSPV* 10.33.   [14] Nichols, *James I*, 1.126.
[15] For Northumberland see *Memoire de Maximilien de Béthune, Duke de Sully*, 5 vols (London, 1778), 5.16.
[16] As shown especially by Susan Doran, "1603: A Jagged Succession," *Historical Research* 93 (2020): 443–65. I wish to thank Sue Doran for allowing me to read this piece in advance of its publication.
[17] Paul C. Allen, *Philip III and the Pax Hispanica, 1598-1621: The Failure of Grand Strategy* (New Haven: Yale University Press, 2000), traces much of the background.

the costs of war exacerbated strains caused by population growth pressing against available resources, a deterioration in the West European climate during the 1590s, and outbreaks of plague. France suffered severely, inducing Henry IV to abandon his Dutch and English allies by making a separate peace with Spain in 1598. Castile's population began to decline as Spain's agricultural and commercial economy contracted and plague struck the Iberian Peninsula. Ireland experienced even more devastating famines caused by a combination of harvest failure and English efforts to starve Ulster into submission, while a devaluation of the Irish currency had a devastating effect on trade.[18] Although England suffered less severely, economic historians have calculated that in the late 1590s the purchasing power of wages reached their lowest level since the mid-fourteenth century, while wartime taxation eroded the prosperity of middling levels of society, and conscription sent tens of thousands of unwilling young men to untimely deaths.

A combination of economic crises, state bankruptcies, and military failures led to a widespread if never universally shared view, in France and Spain as well as Britain that continued war had become unsustainable and needed to end, so that governments might concentrate instead on retrenchment and internal reform. Between the Franco-Spanish peace of 1598 and 1609, when the Spanish and Dutch finally agreed to a truce, all the major conflicts were at least provisionally settled.[19] Even the papacy sought to reduce warfare in northern Europe, to enable Spain and other Catholic powers to concentrate on threats from the Ottoman Empire in the Balkan Peninsula and Mediterranean.[20] Rather than a personal quirk, James's embrace of peace was broadly consistent with the dominant attitude among his generation of princes and statesmen.[21]

Like the Bourbons in France, the Stuarts were a new royal dynasty in England. Henri de Bourbon had ended a French civil war of religion, while James Stuart had arguably prevented one. Although France experienced a more severe the confessional and dynastic crisis, in both kingdoms the triumph of the hereditary principle had secured civil peace. Supporters of both dynasties claimed that God had placed them on the throne and that subjects therefore had not just a legal but a religious duty to submit and obey, including with respect to the king's authority over the public exercise of religion. Subjects who did not share their ruler's faith might try to practice their religion in private, or in France in places where royal authority permitted Protestant worship, but active disobedience amounted not

---

[18] The latest survey is James O'Neill, *The Nine Years War, 1593–1603* (Dublin: Four Courts Press, 2017).
[19] For a systematic discussion of this transition in Spain see Bernardo José Garcia Garcia, *La Pax Hispanica: Política Exterior del Duque de Lerma* (Leuven: Leuven University Press, 1996).
[20] Christian Schneider, "A Kingdom for a Catholic: Pope Clement VIII, King James VI/I and the English Succession (1592–1605)," *International History Review* 37 (2015): 119–41.
[21] This generational inclination to support peace has been stressed by Luc Duerloo, *Dynasty and Piety: Archduke Albert (1598–1621) and Habsburg Political Culture in an Age of Religious Wars* (Farnham: Ashgate, 2012).

only to sedition but sacrilege, since it challenged God's decision in giving the king his crown. Not only followers of the dominant religion but also some English Catholics and French Protestants accepted this reasoning because it gave them an excuse to seek peaceful accommodation with the dominant confession, rather than continuing to jeopardize lives and property in futile efforts to challenge it.

It needs emphasis, however, that the principle of hereditary succession had never commanded unequivocal support in either France or England in the sixteenth century, and the degree to which contemporaries had subsequently embraced it from deep conviction, rather than because doing so proved convenient under existing circumstances, remains questionable. Publicists for both Henry IV and James VI and I sought to bolster their claims by citing not only their hereditary right but supposed miracles that had smoothed their ascent. Henry's victories over numerically superior League armies provided the main support for such claims in France, endowing him with a special charisma.[22] James lacked a comparable military record but his apologists pointed to his escape from the Gowrie Plot in Scotland and later the Gunpowder Plot in England as miracles proving that he enjoyed God's special protection. The anniversaries of both escapes became public holidays, commemorated by sermons on the evils of rebellion emphasizing how the king's escape from danger saved his subjects from civil broils.[23] In both kingdoms stress on the hereditary principle led to a somewhat diminished emphasis on coronations, since a hereditary king possessed full authority without the need for ritual anointing and other ceremonies.

Engendering Peace: Royal Biology and the Refashioning of States

The principle of divine right applied not only to individual kings but also to their bloodlines, a position that elevated the importance of the ruler's children and the wife who bore them, giving rise to veritable cults of royal procreation in

---

[22] Arlette Jouanna, *Le pouvoir absolu: Naissance de l'imaginaire politique de la royauté* (Paris: Gallimard, 2013), chapter 13 and 298: "L'aspiration qui portait à sacraliser la personne royale ne pouvait se concrétiser qu'à condition de rencontrer un monarque capable d'incarner la transcendance dont elle voulait l'investir. La charisme remarquable d'Henri IV lui offrit cette opportunité. Un charisme, il est vrai, tout autant construit qu'inné. Des 1585, l'entourage de l'héritier légitime commença à diffuser systématiquement des images et des textes à sa louange, puis redoubla d'efforts après son avènement; la diffusion précoce de la légende du bon roi Henri accrédita l'idée qu'il était le seul à pouvoir rassembler les Français."

[23] In July 1603 James instructed Whitgift to order commemorations of the Gowrie Plot in English parishes and in December 1604 John Chamberlain reported that "the tragedy of Gowrie with all the action and actors hath been twice represented by the king's players, with exceeding concourse of all sorts of people," Nichols, *James I*, 1.470. For a systematic discussion of commemorations of both the Gowrie and Gunpowder plots see Anne James, *Poets, Players, and Preachers: Remembering the Gunpowder Plot in Seventeenth-Century England* (Toronto: University of Toronto Press, 2016), esp. chapters 1–2.

both kingdoms as a biological process that secured civic peace and political legitimacy.[24] In France the birth of the *dauphin*, Louis XIII, was celebrated through elaborate ceremonies, while in the years following Henry IV's death poets and artists developed a complex system of imagery around Marie de Médicis as the mother, guardian, and protector of the heir to the throne.[25] Although Britain escaped the experience of a female regency, the Stuart court also placed enormous emphasis on the king's role as husband and father. This had already begun to happen in Scotland, through events like the festivities welcoming Queen Anna on her arrival in Edinburgh in 1589 and the christening of Prince Henry in 1594. It continued in England, starting with Anna's spectacular arrival in London, after she traveled south separately from James with a large entourage, and subsequently in numerous court ceremonies and entertainments.

James saw the operation of the hereditary principle not only as a source of legitimacy, but a means through which God governed the affairs of kingdoms and peoples. The marriages, births, and deaths that determined which dynasties died out and which succeeded to multiple crowns were not random accidents but elements in a divine plan to unite warring factions and nations in peace. As he explained to his first English parliament, his "descent lineally out of the loins of Henry VII... reunited and confirmed in me the union" between the houses of York and Lancaster affected by Henry's marriage to Elizabeth of York. That dynastic union provided the "groundlayer" of England's peace in the sixteenth century and eventually opened the way to the "union of two ancient and famous kingdoms" in a "peace... annexed to my person" whose benefits are "made in my blood."[26] This sort of historical process had also unfolded elsewhere in Europe, as a multitude of petty kingdoms and seigneuries were, "in process of time, by ordinance of God, joined into great monarchies." James went on to claim that "it is manifest that God, by his almighty providence, hath pre-ordained" the union of Britain by giving the English and Scots "a common language, religion and similitude in manners" before uniting them under his crown, "in the end and fullness of time." "What God hath conjoined then, let no man separate. I am the husband and the whole isle is my lawful wife; I am the head and it is my body."

These claims implied a rather different concept of sacred kingship from that foreshadowed in Bishop Bilson's coronation sermon, with its focus on parallels

---

[24] James, *Poets, Players, and Preachers*, 31.
[25] See, esp., Jean-François Dubost, *Marie de Médicis: La reine dévoilée* (Paris: Payot, 2009); Jean-François Dubost, "Rubens et l'invention d'une image politique: la France personifiée, XVIe–XVIIe siècle," in *The Age of Rubens: Diplomacy, Dynastic Politics and the Visual Arts in Early Seventeenth-Century Europe*, ed. Luc Duerloo and R. Malcolm Smuts (Turnhout: Brepols, 2016), 65–110; Nicola Courtright, "The Representation of the French-Spanish Alliance in the Medici Cycle: 'Concorde perpetuelle'," in *The Age of Rubens*, ed. Duerloo and Smuts, 39–63, esp. 46–9; Nicola Courtright, "A New Place for Queens in Early Modern France," in *The Politics of Space: European Courts ca. 1500–1750*, ed. Marcello Fantoni, George Gorse, and R. Malcolm Smuts (Rome: Bulzoni, 2009), 267–92.
[26] *Journal of the House of Commons*, vol 1 (London, 1803) 143.

between the ritualized installation of a new ruler and the messianic imagery of the New Testament.[27] Bilson's sermon depicted a timeless homology between kingship and Christianity, encoded in ceremonial forms, whereas James's concept of a royal peace "made in my blood" and achieved "in the end and fullness of time" embedded kingship within history, giving royal successions not only a political but a prophetic and eschatological significance. While not strictly incompatible—the Messiah was, after all, an eschatological figure—the two views reflect divergent patterns of thought whose integration would require some effort. At the start of James's English reign, Bilson's concept of sacred monarchy seems to have been fairly unusual, whereas James's view that the dynastic union of the two British kingdoms fulfilled a providential design had roots in earlier discourses, dating back through the propaganda campaign of Protector Somerset during England's war with Scotland in the 1540s to even earlier tracts.[28] Probably for that reason, it evoked more responses.

Although in different ways, two early celebrations of the new reign—Daniel's 1603 "Panegyric" and a pageant at Temple Bar devised by Ben Jonson for the king's formal entry into London in March 1604—reveal English poets seeking to come to terms with a view of the Stuart succession as a major historical turning point ordained by God to unify Britain. Daniel does this by describing a transformation of "the state" brought about by the operation of different forms of love that have intertwined and reinforced each other through a complex chain of historical causation. He begins by asserting that divine love has cleared all obstacles to the flowering of the people's love for their new king:

> Our love we see concurs with God's great love,
> Who only made thy way, thy passage plain,
> Level'd the world for thee, did all remove,
> That might the shew but of a let retain:
> Unbat'd the North, humbled the South, did move
> The hearts of all, thy right to entertain,
> Held other states embroiled, whose envy might
> Have fostered factions to impugn thy right.[29]

He then connects this outpouring of devotion to a much longer work of preparation through royal marital diplomacy. The critical moment had come exactly a

---

[27] Above, pp. 443–5.
[28] Arthur Williamson, *Scottish National Consciousness in the Age of James VI: The Apocalypse, the Union and the Shaping of Scotland's Public Culture* (Edinburgh: John Donald, 1979), 97–107; Roger Mason, *Kingship and the Commonweal: Political Thought in Renaissance and Reformation Scotland* (East Linton: Tuckwell Press, 1998), chapters 2 and 9.
[29] Nichols, *James I*, 1.123.

century before, with the marriage in 1503 of Henry VII's daughter, Margaret Tudor, to James IV of Scotland:

> Thus hath the hundredth year brought back again
> The sacred blood lent to adorn the North,
> And here return'd it with greater gain,
> And greater glory than we sent it forth:
> Thus doth the all-working Providence retain,
> And keep for the great effects the seed of worth,
> And so doth point the stops of time thereby
> In periods of uncertain certainty.

Anticipating James's own outlook, Daniel's verse pictures civic peace as the fruit of reproductive biology, the planting of "seed" and circulation of "sacred blood." Henry VII's mother, Margaret of Richmond, set the process in motion by arranging the marriage of her granddaughter and namesake. The two Margarets, "from whence th'Almighty worker did transfer / This branch of peace...didst both conceive, beget, / And bring forth happiness to this great state" by allowing the younger Margaret's womb to become the vehicle through which union was achieved. She thereby consolidated the work performed by her grandmother, in giving birth to Henry VII, and her mother, Elizabeth of York, whose marriage to Henry united the dynastic claims of York and Lancaster, restoring peace to an English "state" left "disjointed" and "unruly" by the Wars of the Roses.[30]

But dynastic unions restore "states" only when legitimate kings command willing obedience. "God makes thee king of our estates," Daniel tells King James, "but we / Do make thee king of our affections." This free gift rendered the English "a people tractable, obsequious, / Apt to be fashioned to any form of honor, t'any way / Of high attempts thy virtues shall assay," while foiling the viperous efforts of those who seek "to embroil the State" in discord.[31] Like the earl of Essex, whose patronage he had once enjoyed, Daniel pictured the state as a body politic whose vitality derives from emotionally charged bonds between the prince and his subjects more than laws, institutions, or coercive force. The "continued current of love" connecting the new king to his people has caused "the pulse of England" to beat stronger, generating "a comfortable heat" that diffuses itself through "the whole complexion of the commonwealth,"[32] while equipping the king with a "calm power [that] doth guide / With a far more imperious stateliness, / Than all the swords of violence can do."[33] James therefore does not need to use compulsion in reforming the state:

---

[30] Ibid., 129–30 (quotations), 128. [31] Ibid., 122, 23. [32] Ibid., 124–5.
[33] Ibid., 127.

> Such power hath thy example and respect
> As that without a Sword, without debate,
> Without a noise (or feeling in effect)
> Thou wilt dispose, change, form, accommodate
> Thy kingdom, people, rule, and all effect,
> Without the least convulsion of the state,
> That this great passage and mutation will
> Not seem a change, but only of our ill.

Without altering "the foundation thy ancestors have laid of this Estate" or grieving "the Land with innovation" he will bring about a fundamental "mutation" for the better, through a process described in ways strikingly reminiscent of an idealized portrait of a happy marriage, in which the wife willingly submits to her husband's guidance with a quickened pulse and "comfortable heat" that alters her complexion.

Daniel never spells out just what this transformation will entail but he does go on to praise the king's purported virtues in language that effectively offers advice about how he should rule. James will prevent individuals from engrossing his favor, root out bribes and corruption, shun flatterers and detractors, and preserve ancient laws and institutions.[34] He will discourage greed while fostering "improvement," to generate widespread prosperity rather than excessive profits for a few, tame his subjects' litigiousness and halt the acts "of sacrilege, exaction and of waste" that have marred the recent past.[35] The good example of his own chastity and frugality and the moral order of his court will restore "ancient modesty," routing the "humor of luxuriousness" and addiction to "foreign sins" that have corrupted England's gentry and nobility.[36] Like Essex and many other contemporaries, Daniel emphasizes the importance of the monarch's moral example and leadership. He also echoes his former patron's condemnations of luxury and self-serving behavior. But he omits any references to chivalric virtues like valor. Rather than directing their energies outward to defend British and European liberties against a foreign tyrant, the king and state in Daniel's poem purge inward corruption.

While retaining references to God's providential assistance, Daniel avoids any mention of apocalyptic battles between the forces of Christ and Antichrist. God's mysterious guidance of human history is pictured as healing divisions rather than sharpening them. This benevolent process will forge a new British state in which English and Scottish identities are subsumed:

> Shake hands with Union, O though mighty State!
> Now thou art all Great Britain and no more;
> No Scot, no English now, nor no debate:

---

[34] Ibid., 125–6.   [35] Ibid., 127–8.   [36] Ibid., 131.

> No borders but the ocean and the shore;
> No wall of Adrian serves to separate
> Our mutual love, nor our obedience;
> Being subjects all to one Imperial Prince.[37]

Rather than a conquest brought about by "swords of power, by blood, by fire," the new state will be grounded in mutual "love," like the royal marriages that have literally engendered it.

Whereas Daniel situated James's accession within a long perspective of medieval English and British history, Jonson's pageant at Temple Bar during James's entry into London on March 15, 1604 looked even further back to the advent of the ancient Augustan *Pax Romana*.[38] In doing so it underlined not only similarities but differences between Roman and British history, in ways intended to shield the new dynasty from associations with the vices and tyranny of early imperial Rome. The pageant featured an arch representing the temple of Janus Quadrifrontus—Janus of the four faces—a variant on the two-faced Roman god associated with thresholds, the month of January, and the beginning of the New Year. By identifying Janus Quadrifrontus as the god of the four seasons, Jonson associates him with the transition from winter to spring around the time of the royal entry. The doors of the Roman Temple of Janus famously stood open during wars but closed at the conclusion of peace. Jonson referenced this tradition by stipulating that the doors of his structure should close at the king's approach, signaling James's role as peacemaker. But he made it clear that his was a British, rather than a Roman temple by prominently displaying the king's arms on its front. Below those arms a statue of "Irene or Peace," accompanied by "Plutus or Wealth," triumphed over a groveling image of Mars. Other figures personified victories by Quiet over Tumult, Liberty over Servitude, Safety over Danger, and Felicity over Unhappiness. Two Latin inscriptions quoted passages from Virgil, alluding to the return of the Golden Age and proclaiming that "there is no safety in war" and that "all pray for peace."[39]

A confused Roman priest or flamen appeared, awakened from his long sleep by the noise of the entry, and prepared to celebrate the rites of the obscure goddess Anna Perenna, whom he identified as "Mars his guest," with a feast day on the Ides of "Mars his month." But a figure representing the Genius of London told the flamen to forgo his "dead rites" and instead honor the approach of "he / Who

---

[37] Ibid., 133.
[38] For a modern critical edition of this and other pageants during James's entry see Thomas Dekker, Stephen Harrison, Ben Jonson, and Thomas Middleton, "The Whole Royal and Magnificent Entertainment of King James through the City of London, 15 March 1604, with the Arches of Triumph," ed. R. Malcolm Smuts in *Thomas Middleton: The Collected Works*, general eds Gary Taylor and John Lavagnino (Oxford: Clarendon Press, 2007), 219–79; Jonson's pageant is at 264–75.
[39] Ibid., 264–9.

brings with him a greater Anne than she, / Whose strong and potent virtues have defaced / Stern Mars his statues, and upon them placed / His and the world's blessed blessings." This referred, of course, to James's consort, Anna of Denmark, who rode in a chariot a short distance behind him in the procession. The Genius went on to praise the triumph of "Sweet Peace" and virtuous rule that signals the return of a "better ore"—the gold of the Golden Age:

> Now innocence shall cease to be the spoil
> Of ravening greatness, or to steep the soil
> Of raised peasantry with tears and blood.
> No more shall rich men, for their little good,
> Suspect to be made guilty, or vile spies
> Enjoy the lust of their so murd'ring eyes.
> Men shall put off their iron minds and hearts,
> The time forget his old malicious arts.[40]

Jonson, who had recently converted to Catholicism, associated spies, false accusations, and "malicious arts" with the tyranny of Henry VIII and excesses of the Reformation, as he would soon make clear in a "Panegyre" written to celebrate James's opening of his first English parliament.[41] But his imagery also recalled Tacitus's descriptions of the early empire, on which Jonson drew at about this time to construct his *Tragedy of Sejanus*. Although characteristic of both Tudor and Roman imperial government, he implied, these abuses will cease in the new reign.

The date of the procession on the anniversary of Julius Caesar's assassination would have suggested a contrast between the civil wars that his murder ignited, and the peaceful process through which the Stuarts took possession of their new capital city. Augustus needed the assistance of Mars to establish his power but James did not, and the rites performed in the British Temple of Janus therefore lacked the martial dimensions of Roman religion. On the other hand, Jonson freely appropriated the imagery of a renewed golden age of peace, prosperity, and moral reformation that Virgil and other poets had woven around Augustus's reign. Two Latin inscriptions on the arch conveyed this parallel.[42] The first, attributed to "the Senate and People of London," hailed James as "Emperor of the Britons" and a "new Augustus," along with Anna, "the associate of his most blessed wedding chamber" and Prince Henry, who like the sun "has lately cleared the funereal and most intemperate air." The second proclaimed the closing of the gates of the Temple of Janus in words reminiscent of a famous prophecy in the

---

[40] Ibid., 271 (ll. 2469–76).
[41] Malcolm Smuts, "Court-Centred Politics and the Uses of Roman Historians," in *Culture and Politics in Early Stuart England*, ed. Kevin Sharpe and Peter Lake (Basingstoke: Macmillan, 1994), 31–2.
[42] "The Whole Royal and Magnificent Entertainment," ed. Smuts, 272–3.

Aeneid (1.284-97), predicting the rise of the Julian dynasty and establishment of world peace under its auspices.[43] Both inscriptions underlined the arrival not just of a new king but a royal family that would live on after James's death, securing peace to future generations. Jonson no doubt intended to contrast this prospect with the story of murderous infighting among Augustus's successors: the poisonings of Germanicus and Caligula, Nero's murder of his own mother, and the civil wars that followed Nero's deposition. The absence of strict hereditary succession in the Roman state led to vicious intrigues and warfare. But happily Stuart Britain is not like that. The harmonious relations between the king, the queen, and their eldest son presaged future political harmony.

Since Jonson soon emerged as James's favorite English poet, while Daniel became the chief poet and writer of masques in Queen Anna's household at the start of the reign, both succeeded in attracting favorable notice. Each recognized that he needed to celebrate not just the start of a new reign but a dynastic transition that reshaped Britain. But the two poets approached this task within alternative English medieval and Roman frameworks that point to different historical reference points available to contemporaries as they tried to decode the meaning of current political events. Suggestively, Daniel used his native materials to stress continuities with the Tudor and pre-Tudor English past and warn against disruptive innovation, whereas Jonson's pageant compares the Stuart succession to events that fundamentally altered the ancient Roman state. Arguably this contrast foreshadowed disputes over legal and institutional reforms that would soon arise, pitting figures like Francis Bacon and the civil lawyer Sir John Hayward, who both cited Roman precedent to justify innovation, against people who insisted on the need to preserve immemorial English laws against any sort of change. But as tends to be the case with panegyrics, neither text offered much concrete detail about the kinds of alterations that the new king might bring about. They could afford to be vague because, during the first several months of his English reign, James's intentions still remained fairly nebulous.

The Union of the Crowns, the Concept of Conquest, and the Common Law Mind

This began to change in early 1604, with the meeting of the Hampton Court Conference in January to settle controversies in the Church, followed by the start of an English parliament in late March. Both events, but especially the latter, provided the first important clues as to how the king wanted to translate his stated commitment to peace and union into practical courses of action. As historians

---

[43] Ibid., 273, ll. 2525-37 and notes.

have remarked, "multiple kingdoms," created by the amalgamation of territories with different laws, institutions, and traditions under a single dynasty were common in early modern Europe. But once formed, such states often experienced significant tensions and did not always endure. In Scandinavia the multiple kingdom of Denmark and Sweden had broken apart in the early sixteenth century. Philip II had to confront not only the revolt of his Dutch provinces but the need to subdue Portugal and a Catalan rebellion in 1593. France provided an even better example of a kingdom that had almost disintegrated through a combination of confessional wars, institutional conflicts, and provincial particularism. During the 1580s and 1590s *parlements* in Paris and other cities defied crown authority, several provincial towns tried to assert their independence and exert control of their hinterlands, while rebellious nobles led armed resistance to the crown in both Catholic and Huguenot provinces.[44] Some observers, including the Englishman Sir George Carew, wondered whether France would survive as a unified kingdom or dissolve into a welter of petty states like the Holy Roman Empire.[45] Henry IV had to restore unity through a combination of military campaigns, negotiated settlements with rebellious nobles and towns, and propaganda elevating his role as savior of the nation.[46]

James faced the somewhat different challenge of having to forge bonds between English and Scottish kingdoms that had never been united before, while simultaneously consolidating royal control over Ireland after the defeat of Tyrone's forces. In doing so he needed to deal with social, cultural, and religious differences not only between his three kingdoms but within each of them. He knew that English puritan grievances against the bishops evoked considerable sympathy in Scotland, providing a potential basis for unified religious dissent in both kingdoms. He had to unite his kingdoms in ways that strengthened, rather than weakened, his ability to command obedience. His success or failure at this task might well determine whether the dynastic union survived in the long run. It would certainly have considerable bearing on his ability to deal with any renewed foreign threats, since internal fissures within Britain and Ireland inevitably weakened the crown's ability to fight foreign wars.

---

[44] Among many studies see, in particular, Jean Marie Constant, *La Ligue* (Paris: Fayard, 1996), esp. chapter 7 on provincial towns and Nicolas Le Roux, *Le roi, la cour, l'état: de la Renaissance à l'absolutisme* (Paris: Champ Vallon, 2013), parts 2 and 3.

[45] Carew saw the political dismemberment of France as advantageous to Britain and thought it might be "easily accomplished," since "many potent families within the [French] realm" as well as Spain would join in the project. See *An historical view of the negotiations between the courts of England, France and Brussels, from the year 1592 to 1617*, ed. Thomas Birch (London, 1749), 528.

[46] Ronald Asch, *Sacral Kingship between Disenchantment and Re-enchantment: The French and English Monarchies 1587-1688* (New York: Berghahn, 2014), 31 comments on the civic processions that combined Catholic piety with emphasis on the king's role in securing national peace and unity. Dubost, "Rubens et l'invention d'une image politique," 72-82 offers an especially well-documented account of some of the visual representations of Henry as savior of the nation.

Among the several individuals in both England and Scotland who drew up memoranda dealing with the problems of British union, the one best connected to the royal court was probably the king's solicitor general, Francis Bacon.[47] He would, in any case, soon emerge as the leading spokesman in the House of Commons for a government project to integrate the laws and institutions of England and Scotland. Bacon argued on historical grounds that unions of kingdoms followed two "several kinds of policy," one involving the retention of "ancient forms still severed, and only conjoined in sovereignty; the other to superinduce a new form agreeable and convenient to the entire estate." In other words, the choice lay between preserving distinct national laws and institutions under a common ruler, or creating a unitary state with a single legal and institutional structure. He correctly noted that the first policy was more common and easier to accomplish in the short run. Both the Habsburgs and the kings of France had followed it. But Bacon regarded the second as far preferable. Historical evidence showed that allowing institutional differences to persist under a single sovereign made "the addition of further empire and territory... rather matter of burden than matter of strength," by keeping "alive the seeds of revolts and rebellions for many ages, as we may see in a fresh and notable example of the kingdom of Aragon" during the Catalonian revolt.[48] On the other hand, the durability of an extended state ruled through uniform laws and institutions was proved by the record of ancient Rome, "the best state in the world," which Bacon adopted as his model.[49] He specifically urged reforms in four areas: "union in name, union in language, union in laws and union in employments."[50] Using a chemical analogy, he asserted that if this were achieved, "time and nature" would gradually fuse the English and Scots into a single people through a process of "perfect fermentation and incorporation."

We should note the conspicuous absence here of any reference to union in religion, arguably the single most important problem facing the new British state and an item very much on James's agenda.[51] The obvious reason was that including religion in proposals drawn up for presentation to the English and Scottish parliaments would have opened the 1559 Elizabethan settlement to debate and revision, while simultaneously fanning long-standing Scottish fears that James intended to remodel the Kirk along English lines. It would also have

---

[47] Brian Levack, *The Formation of the British State* (Oxford: Oxford University Press, 1987), 43–4; *The Jacobean Union: Six Tracts of 1604*, ed. Bruce Galloway and Brian Levack, Scottish History Society, 4th series, 64 (Edinburgh: C. Constable, 1985); *The British Union: A Critical Edition and Translation of David Hume of Godscroft's* De unione Insulae Britannicae, ed. Paul McGinnis and Arthur Williamson (Aldershot: Ashgate, 2002).

[48] Bacon, *Works*, 10.96. Bacon's former associate Antonio Perez had been a leading protagonist in the Aragonese rebellion and may have influenced his thinking on the subject.

[49] Ibid., 94–5.   [50] Ibid.

[51] As he revealed in telling Parliament on April 13, 1604 that at his death he above all hoped to leave "One worship of God, 2. One kingdom entirely governed and 3. One uniformity in laws" (*Journal of the House of Commons*, 1.170–1).

invited an alliance between English puritans and Scottish presbyterians in opposition to the English and Scottish bishops. Since James and his council wished to avoid these outcomes, they left problems of religious diversity off the legislative docket, intending to deal with them by other methods that we will later examine.

Among the four items Bacon did mention, a union of language seemed to be occurring naturally as a result of growing commercial, religious, and intellectual exchanges and through the influence of print in fostering a common vernacular. But Bacon's other three points of union required action. The union of names appears to have reflected the James's own agenda, as the Venetian ambassador noticed as early as April 1603, when the new monarch had proceeded no further south than Berwick.[52] The king also wanted to promote a greater "union in employments," a free interchange of English and Scots in service to a unified crown. But he prudently backed away from actively pursuing this goal after two early appointments of Scots to English offices aroused strong protests.[53] It is not entirely clear, on the other hand, where the impetus behind a proposal to unite the two kingdoms' laws originated. Although it conformed to James's general agenda, eight years previously Bacon had urged Elizabeth to promote "a general amendment of the state of your laws and to reduce them to more brevity and certainty."[54] He and others with similar views may have seized upon the union project as an excuse to advance legal reforms they had long envisaged.

Legal uniformity was highly uncharacteristic of nearly all European monarchies of the period, which almost always tolerated a diversity of local laws within their dominions. England was a conspicuous exception in possessing a single common law administered through a centralized system of royal courts.[55] This makes it seem likely that the drive to enact a new reformed code of British law primarily reflected the priorities of English lawyers and statesmen like Bacon more than the king himself, although James happily supported the initiative. The English civil lawyer John Hayward, who shared Bacon's view that the common law would benefit from judicious pruning and codification, also agreed with him that the union of Britain under a single crown required the institution of a single British legal code. "What so ever appearances are used to make two states seem one," he wrote, "if they have not one community of laws they remain notwithstanding, and upon small occasion will show themselves disjointed, even in the noblest and strongest limbs of government."[56] Hayward also shared Bacon's belief that an "entire alteration of government" was sometimes needed to preserve a state. He

---

[52] *CSPV* 10.5.   [53] Levack, *Formation*, 60–1.
[54] Bacon, *Works*, 7.315–16 (Dedicatory Epistle to Maxims).
[55] Scotland had a single law, although one that was badly in need of codification, but lacked a strong system of judicial institutions under the control of the crown for enforcing it.
[56] John Hayward, *A Treatise of Union of the Two Realmes of England and Scotland* (London, 1604), 9.

gave Augustan Rome as an example.[57] Ancient Rome provided another anomalous example of a large state ruled by a single system of law.

But the Augustan model cannot have reassured English subjects who regarded the early empire as a tyranny, described on the first page of Richard Greneway's translation of Tacitus as a "new government," forged through the subversion of an "ancient commonwealth" by "flatterers," "fear," and the reduction of the Senate, magistrates, and nobility to dependence on a single prince.[58] The proposal to modify the common law in the interest of greater unity with Scotland quickly met with complaints that doing so risked undermining settled patterns of English governance. The antiquarian Henry Spelman agreed with Bacon and Hayward that "differences in laws, manners and language" perpetuated divisions between nations, but he regarded English and Scottish laws as too dissimilar to permit their unification. He argued that "to change laws is no sudden action but a work of time and of many ages," pointing out that although Henry II had introduced English law into Ireland four centuries earlier the Irish still persisted in rebelling "to restore their ancient country usages."[59] Sir Henry Savile also warned against excessive haste: "Betwixt nations where hath been ancient enmity, a straight union at the first will be harshly taken on both sides." Trying to unify the two kingdoms' laws would bring "an infinity of inconveniences."[60] Speaking in Parliament, Sir Edwin Sandys said he could find no examples of kingdoms united by dynastic marriage that had adopted a uniform set of "laws, customs, privileges and titles of honor." The Low Countries provided a notable example of provinces that had retained their distinct laws even while accepting a common sovereign, and the outcome of Philip II's efforts to tamper with those laws was notorious.[61] The Commons objected to changing their kingdom's name, on the grounds that doing so would invalidate the laws, a position with which the judges agreed.

Several motives fueled this opposition, which ultimately scuttled the crown's legislative initiatives. In addition to national pride and xenophobic prejudice, contemporaries associated radical changes in the law with acts of conquest that obliterated the customs and liberties of a defeated people. They worried that agreeing to revise the common law would allow a conquest by stealth, by granting James discretionary powers that his predecessors had never possessed, *as if* he had gained England by force, rather than as the legitimate heir to an ancient crown. A surge of interest in the Norman Conquest during the late Elizabethan and early Jacobean period, including considerable debate about whether it had brought about fundamental changes in English laws and customs, reflected these

---

[57] Ibid., 9, 12–13.
[58] *The Annales of Cornelius Tacitus. The Description of Germany*, trans. Richard Greneway (London, 1598), 1.
[59] BL Sloan Mss. 3521, fol. 16r–v.   [60] LPL Mss. 251, fol. 166.   [61] TNA SP14/7/63.

anxieties.[62] One writer asserted in 1602 that English monarchs had the right to demand "tribute and subsidy...as a remembrance of a conquest," without parliamentary consent.[63] If that could be said about a conquest more than 500 years in the past, the need to avoid treating James's succession as in any way a new conquest seemed obvious.

King James and the Lawyers: A Conflict over Absolutism?

As Glenn Burgess has argued, suspicions of James as a foreign, Scottish king therefore stiffened resistance to the union project, while enhancing belief in the importance of the common law as a bulwark against arbitrary power.[64] The new king's arrival crystallized the formation of what J. G. A. Pocock famously described as "the common law mind": an obsession with medieval precedents as reflective of allegedly immemorial English customs that defined the fundamental character of the nation, while preserving a proper balance between the king's authority and his subjects' liberties.[65] But while attractive and correct as far as it goes, this picture needs qualification and fleshing out through attention to trends in late Elizabethan and wider European politics that also raised anxieties about the growth of lawless arbitrary power. Attempts to place limits on royal power by invoking ancient customs were by no means peculiar to England. Appeals to a largely mythical past appeared in the writings of George Buchanan in Scotland, French *malcontent* and Huguenot tracts during the 1570s and 1580s, and in the Netherlands, in opposition to Spanish tyranny and Leicester's attempts to exert his "absolute" authority.[66] Late Elizabethan and early Stuart lawyers rarely invoked these foreign tracts, probably because doing so would have risked undercutting their case for a distinctively English system of law and custom. But they were certainly aware of European concepts of ancient custom developed by writers like du Plessis Mornay and François Hotman. The "insularity" of common law

---

[62] Rei Kanemura, "Historical Perspectives on the Anglo-Scottish Union Debate: Re-reading the Norman Conquest in the 1610s," *History of European Ideas* 40 (2014): 155–76. Despite the title, this article discusses tracts from as early as 1599.

[63] William Fulbeck, *Pandectes* (London, 1602), fol. 69v.

[64] Glenn Burgess, "Pocock's History of Political Thought, the Ancient Constitution, and Early Stuart England," in *The Political Imagination in History: Essays Concerning J. G. A. Pocock*, ed. D. N. DeLuna (Baltimore: Owlworks, 2006), 175–208.

[65] John Pocock, *The Ancient Constitution and the Feudal Law: A Study of English Historical Thought in the Seventeenth Century. A Reissue with a Retrospect* (Cambridge: Cambridge University Press, 1987). Subsequent discussions include Glenn Burgess, *The Politics of the Ancient Constitution: An Introduction to English Political Thought 1603–1642* (University Park: Pennsylvania State University Press, 1992) and *Absolute Monarchy and the Stuart Constitution* (New Haven: Yale University Press, 1996), and J. P. Sommerville, *Politics and Ideology in England, 1603–1640* (Harlow: Longman, 1986).

[66] These arguments have often been described by modern historians as examples of early modern constitutional thought, although that term was rarely, if ever, employed at the time, except with more restrictive meanings similar to those outlined in the introduction to this book.

thought, which Pocock strongly emphasized, did not stem from ignorance so much as a conscious effort to prevent the contamination of English law by foreign ideas.

Contemporaries also knew that kings elsewhere in Europe, especially in Spain and France, had lately expanded both their actual power and their claims to absolute authority. This awareness reinforced worries that similar things might happen in their own country. But we need to be careful about equating early Stuart kingship too readily with continental absolutism, or indeed of adopting a simplistic model of absolutism as a wholly uniform phenomenon. A recent revisionist study of French absolutism by Arlette Jouanna provides a useful point of comparison that can help identify both similarities and important differences between early Stuart and early Bourbon concepts of monarchy. Jouanna disputes the conventional claim that a fully developed doctrine of royal absolutism already existed in France before the wars of religion. Although French kings of the early sixteenth century did possess an acknowledged authority to act outside the law during times of emergency, she sees this doctrine as qualified by a belief in the "sovereignty of reason," conceived within a scholastic framework as submission to an underlying system of natural law embodying universal principles of justice that also reflected the will of God.[67] The ruler's power to rule as an "absolute king" (*un roi absolu*), in the literal sense of the Latin route *absolutus*, meaning loosed or absolved from constraints, was regarded as a necessary evil, for use only in rare circumstances, when strict legality might endanger the public. For the same reason, the right of French kings to legislate by decree remained limited by the need for laws to conform to "reason." If the judges of a *parlement* considered a decree unreasonable they might refuse to register and enforce it, compelling the king to reconsider. If he still insisted on enacting the decree it would possess "coactive" or coercive force, but not moral legitimacy in the eyes of his subjects. This would hinder the decree's effectiveness. A king who consistently abused his absolute authority by acting against the dictates of reason would undermine belief in his own legitimacy and so diminish, rather than enhance, his power.

Jouanna shows that this outlook began to unravel as the wars of religion shattered the possibility of consensus about the meaning of natural and divine justice. Civil war also created an environment in which emergencies requiring extraordinary acts of power became far more frequent, giving kings greater opportunities to employ their absolute authority. She argues that in these circumstances, recourse to antiquarian myths of fundamental laws provided an alternative means of justifying constraints on the ruler, and thus an indirect way of restoring the sovereignty of reason. Such arguments also seemed for a time to offer

---

[67] Jouanna, *Le pouvoir absolu*. See chapter 8 for a discussion of legal antiquarianism and myths of an original constitution in France. See also her *Le prince absolu: Apogée et déclin de l'imaginaire monarchique* (Paris: Gallimard, 2014).

Protestants and their *malcontent* allies a strategy for limiting the king and his entourage, through recourse to institutions like the *parlements* and estates general. Huguenots hoped to use these institutions to make edicts of religious toleration permanent and binding, rather than revocable at the king's pleasure. But the strategy backfired as it became clear, during a meeting in 1585, that far from guaranteeing tolerance, the estates general would insist on more rigorous persecution.

Efforts to justify institutional limitations on royal authority had meanwhile produced an intellectual reaction that included Jean Bodin's highly influential *Six Livres de la République*, a book that attracted widespread interest in England as well as France. In addition to his famous definition of sovereignty as the supreme power within a polity, against which no appeal existed, Bodin argued that laws derived their authority purely from the sovereign's will, rather than from their conformity to transcendent principles of justice. He qualified this assertion by arguing that sovereigns nevertheless remained bound by the laws of God and nature, because a ruler who acts contrary to universal norms may stir such revulsion that his power collapses. Jouanna argues that there are good reasons for thinking that Bodin believed this had actually happened to Henry III. Bodin was therefore not an absolutist in the sense of someone who thought that no constraints of any kind limited what a king might do. But his equation of legal legitimacy with the sovereign's will was an important step in the direction of later seventeenth-century concepts of absolute power.[68]

In the late 1580s and 1590s, the Catholic League attempted to subordinate royal authority to religion, by demanding that the king join in efforts to eradicate heresy and arguing for the right to depose him and elect an alternative ruler if he failed to do so. But these efforts lost credibility as they perpetuated civil war and appeared to serve Spanish interests. In reaction, support grew for a view of Henry IV as not only the legitimate king but a charismatic leader uniquely inspired by God, whose personal authority provided the sole possible basis for national unity and reconstruction. Bodin's argument that law derived from the sovereign's will fused with this cult of heroic kingship, to produce an essentially new concept of absolutism that treated the king's will as the soul of the French state, which must operate without constraint to defend the kingdom against internal and external enemies.[69] Although the king still ruled according to a mysterious "reason of state," he alone had the authority to decide what this meant and normal moral principles did not necessarily limit him.

In Britain few people appear to have made the full transition Jouanna describes. James was not among them. Although in *Basilikon Doron* and *The True Law of*

---

[68] Although Bodin seems to have granted magistrates some discretion in refusing to enforce edicts they regarded as contrary to natural or divine law.

[69] Jouanna, *Pouvoir absolu*, chapter 13.

Free Monarchies he claimed to rule by divine appointment as an "absolute king," he nevertheless stressed the "reciproque duties" of princes and subjects. As we have seen, in describing a king's duties he began by stressing the importance of moral norms derived not only from reason and moral philosophy but, above all, from scripture. He had, in effect, modified the concept of the "sovereignty of reason" to bring it into line with a Calvinist emphasis on the Bible and God's mysterious will. Other aspects of his record support this conclusion. His favorite literary genre, to which he returned repeatedly between the late 1580s and his death in 1625, was a "meditation" on a scriptural passage that turned into an essay on a topical political theme. In 1604 he demanded that the English Parliament enact a more complete union with Scotland, not because it was his will but because it was God's will. But James also believed that in most circumstances God's will, natural law, and human reason were entirely congruent. In *Basilikon Doron* he freely acknowledged the existence of the sort of prudential checks on misrule Bodin and earlier thinkers had stressed. Although rebellion was always sinful, he wrote, flagrant abuses of power might nevertheless provoke subjects beyond endurance, and God sometimes permitted rebels to overthrow a tyrant in retribution for his misdeeds.

Even though he believed he possessed a residual "absolute" authority to rule outside the law, James therefore freely acknowledged that in almost all circumstances it would be both unjust and unwise for him to do so. Since respect for the law allowed royal authority to operate smoothly and protected kings as well as subjects, his own interests dictated that he set an example by submitting to the laws of his kingdoms. He did complain about overly "nice" judicial interpretations that in his view distorted the law, as well as confusion about the law's meaning generated by a rising tide of litigation and the proliferating number of recent statutes and judicial decisions. But most of his subjects agreed with him about these perceived abuses and the need for some kind of reform to correct them.[70] James claimed at times that he had the authority to correct abuses in the operation of the law in accordance with his rational understanding of justice but he never tried to alter or dispense with the law through his arbitrary will.

Views resembling French absolutist theories did, nevertheless, occasionally surface in England, starting well before 1603. Robert Cecil's admonition to the earl of Essex in 1591 that he should make "her majesty's absolute will his perfectest reason" is arguably an early example.[71] A sermon published in 1604 insisted that "the right rules of religion give no remedy to subjects against the highest authority but in the necessity of either suffering or obeying." Bilson's claim that God infused

---

[70] David Chan Smith, *Sir Edward Coke and the Reformation of the Laws: Religion, Politics and Jurisprudence, 1578–1616* (Cambridge: Cambridge University Press, 2014), 31–53 discusses this topic in detail.
[71] Above, p. 365.

a special wisdom into the minds of kings, giving them insights that other men lacked, paralleled one of the central arguments used to support French absolutist doctrines. Other clergy also supported this idea. Kings not only rule by "the ordinance of God" but "the spirit of God [is] doubled and his graces multiplied upon them, beyond the common sort of men."[72] "There is *diviniation in labiis regis*, divination in the lips of a king...so they do often foresee, forespeak and foretell things to come," another preacher insisted.[73] Because of this superior wisdom, subjects must refrain from judging the actions of kings and submit unconditionally to their decisions. In the Commons in 1601 one MP stated that he wondered "'that the House will stand upon the granting of a subsidy or the time of payment, when all we have is her majesty's and she may lawfully at her pleasure take it from us, yea she hath as much right to all out lands and goods as to any revenue of her crown,' at which all the house hemmed and laughed."[74] Two years later an English poet celebrating James's succession asserted: "Our king is his [God's] anointed / And what we have, we farm it but as his."[75] Bodin's concept of sovereignty as an uncontrollable supreme power had become familiar in England well before James's accession. "The estate of your highness is a monarchy, that is to say a sovereignty and absolute power and authority," Thomas Digges told Elizabeth.[76] We have seen that Wilkes invoked the same concept to justify Leicester's claims to "absolute" power over the United Provinces.[77] None of these claims were newly imported into England by James VI and I. They point to tensions developing within English political culture that his succession may have accentuated but cannot, by itself, have caused.

Sweeping assertions about the unbounded scope of royal authority prompted reflections on how sovereignty might be limited. Robert Sidney second earl of Leicester (1595–1677) compiled notes on the subject, deriving "partly out of a paper of my father," Sir Philip Sidney's younger brother, Robert, in his commonplace book. "The prerogative of the king is...that power which belongeth to the sovereignty...In a kingdom it is in the king himself, but more or less as the monarchy is more or less absolute...This power ought to be limited."[78] William Camden agreed. "Methinks now he that in every country should take upon him the describing of the prerogative under which he lives," he wrote, "should not take upon him an unreasonable piece of work, though a difficult. For what is it in the name of a king that imports so much it cannot be limited...If the prerogative be not to be limited how is it that some kings are more absolute than others? Because they are called gods will they think themselves so in all points of power over

---

[72] Richard Edes, *Six learned and godly sermons* (London, 1604), fols 75v, 66v.
[73] John Howson, *A sermon preached at St. Maries in Oxford* (London, 1602), sig. D1v.
[74] *PPEI* 3.338.
[75] Henry Petoe, *England's Caesar* (London, 1603) quoted in Nichols, *James I*, 1.237.
[76] Folger Shakespeare Mss. Vb214, fol. 79v, undated tract perhaps c. 1590.
[77] Above, pp. 321–2.   [78] Library of Congress microfilm 041/Camb.793A, fol. 711.

their subjects?"⁷⁹ Bodin would have found the notion that a king may be "more or less" sovereign absurd, since for him sovereignty was by nature undivided, unqualified, and unlimited. Leicester and Camden simply refused to accept Bodin's argument because they found the conclusion to which it led unacceptable.

This issue had practical, as well as theoretical, ramifications. Although England escaped the French experience of prolonged civil war, in more attenuated ways it nevertheless experienced the pressures that reshaped French political thought and culture. Elizabeth and her council had responded to the emergencies of the 1580s and 1590s and the challenge of both Catholic and puritan dissent through measures that circumvented common law procedures. The council imprisoned Catholics and some puritans without trial, eliciting a protest from the judges in 1592, and imposed restrictions on them after their release that had no explicit legal basis. It employed ecclesiastical commissions, with their power to administer *ex officio* oaths, and the prerogative court of Star Chamber to prevent both Protestant and papist non-conformists from taking advantage of common law rules against self-incrimination. In a few cases it allowed the use of torture, which also violated common law. Since High Commission and Star Chamber had their own rules and procedures, they were not completely arbitrary. But the Elizabethan council certainly acted on the assumption that it had available alternative institutional and legal methods to the common law for dealing with threats to the state.

Most of these alternative procedures derived from the queen's prerogative power to act outside the law in defense of the public interest, the functional equivalent of the French king's emergency *pouvoir absolu*. Elizabeth used her prerogative not only to deal with specific crises but also to create new institutional structures, notably the lieutenancy. As a military institution, the lieutenancy operated under different and more arbitrary rules than JPs and common law courts. If an invasion or major rebellion had taken place, those powers would have expanded to include authority to execute people under martial law. Even in normal times, the actions of deputy lieutenants occasionally provoked local resistance, appeals to the law, and conflicts between the council's authority and that of the courts.⁸⁰ In January 1588 the judges granted an attachment to two suitors against the Suffolk deputy lieutenants, Sir Robert Wingfield and Sir Arthur Heveningham, who had imprisoned them on the authority of their lord lieutenant, Sir Christopher Hatton. The council responded by telling the judges that the services of Wingfield and Heningham were urgently required and instructing them to annul the attachment.⁸¹ On several occasions the council experimented,

---

⁷⁹ "William Camden's Discourse Concerning the Prerogative of the Crown," ed. F. S. Fussner, *Proceedings of the American Philosophical Society* 101 (1957): 204–15 at 209.
⁸⁰ Neil Younger, *War and Politics in the Elizabethan Counties* (Manchester: Manchester University Press, 2012), 124–31; A. Hassell-Smith, *County and Court: Government and Politics in Norfolk, 1558–1603* (Oxford: Oxford University Press, 1974), 124–31.
⁸¹ *APC* 14.332.

in a rather desultory fashion, with commissions of martial law and the appointment of provost marshals equipped with arbitrary powers of arrest, to deal with wandering vagrants and disbanded soldiers.[82] In a youthful tract, dated by James Spedding to 1587, Francis Bacon argued that although the common law does restrain what an English prince can do, nevertheless "we see daily in experience that whatsoever can be procured under the great seal of England is taken *quasi sanctum*; and although it be merely against the laws, customs and statutes of this realm, yet it is defended in such sort that some have been called rebellious for not allowing such void and unlawful grants."[83] He went on to describe the charter establishing the London house of correction of Bridewell as an example of such an illegal abuse, claiming that it violated Magna Carta by granting provost marshals authority to imprison vagrants and loose women without trial. In London the actions of provost marshals and their subordinates provoked local protests and an apprentice riot in 1595, which the Lord Mayor wanted to suppress and punish through martial law.[84]

In England as in France, the perceived threat of religious and civic disorders had therefore expanded opportunities for more aggressive use of the ruler's arbitrary emergency powers, including by inferior officers who abused their authority in ways that provoked complaints from both ordinary subjects and higher authorities. In 1592 the judges of King's Bench and Common Pleas and barons of the Exchequer joined in a petition to Hatton, asking him to intercede with the queen to prevent the imprisonment of subjects contrary to law "by commandment of any noblemen or councilor" for a variety of reasons, including preventing them from pursuing actions in common law courts. They also protested the continuing imprisonment of people whose release the courts had ordered.[85] Because England never experienced a true collapse of civic peace, except in a few districts for limited periods of time, the use of arbitrary power remained limited. But the absence of civil war also made the expansion of arbitrary power seem less necessary. "As...absolute administration in time of war when all is in arms, and when the laws hold their peace because they cannot be heard, is most necessary," Sir Thomas Smith wrote in 1583, "so in time of peace, the same is very dangerous, as well to him that doth use it, and much more to the people upon whom it is used."[86] As the fears generated by war with Spain ebbed toward the turn of the century, the attitude expressed by Smith gained traction.

---

[82] Lindsay Boynton, "The Tudor Provost Marshal," *English Historical Review* 77 (1962): 437–55; R. Malcolm Smuts, "Organized Violence in the Elizabethan Monarchical Republic," *History* 99 (2014): 418–43 at 429–33; BL Lansdowne Mss. 60/86 and 62/26; Folger Shakespeare Library Mss. L.a. 821; TNA SP12/228/22 and 23 and 231/24.
[83] Bacon, *Works*, 7.511–12.   [84] BL Lansdowne Mss. 71/17 and 78/64.
[85] BL Lansdowne 68/87; Smith, *Edward Coke*, 69.
[86] Thomas Smith, *De Republica Anglorum* (London, 1583), 7.

The fact that extra-legal powers were delegated to officers who sometimes exploited them for private gain raised additional issues, concerning the perversion of royal authority by dishonest crown servants. The judges' petition to Hatton included complaints about pursuivants accused of arresting serjeants as they went about the routine business of serving writs and extorting money by imprisoning people on spurious charges.[87] Even justices of the peace came under attack in the Elizabeth's last parliament, although some MPs rose to defend them. "Who almost are not grieved at the luxuriant authority of justices of the peace?" one speaker demanded: "for magistrates be men and men have always attending them two ministers, *libido et iracundia*. Men of this nature do subjugate the freeborn subject." "A justice of the peace is a living creature that for half a dozen chickens will dispense with a whole dozen penal statutes," another complained.[88] In 1596 a student at the Inns of Court challenged the queen's right to conscript soldiers for foreign service as contrary to law. The council threw him in the Fleet Prison without trial until he recanted.[89] The well-known attack on monopolies in Elizabeth's last parliament provides another example of the reaction that had set in against perceived abuses of government power. It quickly led to complaints, not only in parliament but public spaces, about misuse of the prerogative. "The parliament matters are ordinary talk in the streets," Robert Cecil complained: "I have heard myself, being in my coach, these words spoken aloud: 'God prosper those that further the overthrow of these monopolies. God send the prerogative touch not our liberty.'"[90] "To what purpose is it do anything by act of parliament when the queen will undo the same by her prerogative?" one MP complained.[91] Growing resistance to expansive uses of the prerogative evidently led Lord Buckhurst to commission a treatise in its defense in 1598, from the antiquarian John Dodderidge.[92]

Suggestively, the early Stuart "oracle of the common law," Sir Edward Coke, had been involved as a young man in suits involving complaints against Sir William Heydon, and Sir Arthur Heveningham, the two deputy lieutenants involved in the 1588 dispute just mentioned.[93] He had also acted as attorney for the Catholic exile, Thomas Lord Paget and the puritan minister William Fleming,

---

[87] BL Lansdowne Mss. 68/87.   [88] *PPEI* 3.424, 416.   [89] *APC* 26.3–4.
[90] *PPEI* 3.398.
[91] Shakespeare Folger Library Mss. Vb215, n.p., speech of Mr. Francis Moore, November 20, 1601.
[92] BL Add Mss. 5220, fol. 4r: "Considering your lordship's [Buckhurst's] commandment...I have resolved to the uttermost of my ability to undergo the imposed charge, that is to write in the maintenance of the ancient prerogative royal of her majesty drawn out of the laws, constitutions and records of the realm against but the unadvised writing of the ignorant stranger and the undutiful surmise of the seditious subject." Despite his recourse to "the laws, constitutions and records of the realm," Dodderidge went on to argue (fol. 4v) that the prerogative originally derived from "the law of nature."
[93] Allen D. Boyer, *Sir Edward Coke and the Elizabethan* Age (Stanford: Stanford University Press 2003), 69–78.

after they ran afoul of the Elizabethan state.[94] As Elizabeth's attorney general he prosecuted numerous cases in Star Chamber and other courts against court officers, JPs, militia officials, and royal purveyors accused of abusing their delegated powers.[95] Long before he first articulated a theory of the common law as a body of immemorial custom that protected the liberties of English subjects, he had engaged in legal pleadings to protect individuals from high-handed acts by royal officials. The late Elizabethan reaction against abuses by the crown and its officers carried over into the new reign. The king's purveyors, who had the authority to compel the sale of agricultural provisions at below-market rates and to borrow carts for the service of the royal household became a particular target. Resistance to them reached such a pitch by April 1604 that people openly disobeyed warrants for the taking of post horses signed by the king's own hand.[96] A bill to restrain purveyance was introduced into the Commons on the same day it began debating the proposed union of the laws.

Even before the arrival of a Scottish king, resistance to European currents of absolutist thought and reactions against the expansion of arbitrary government power in wartime had therefore started to produce a backlash. But anxiety about James, as a foreign king unfamiliar with English ways, together with specific objections to his union project, undoubtedly added momentum to this trend. The reaction did not directly challenge James's view of his office, since in principle he also believed in the rule of law. In 1610 he told an English parliament "that though he did derive his title from the loins of his ancestors, yet the law did set the crown upon his head and he is king by the common laws of the land," adding "that he had no power to make laws himself, or to exact any subsidies *de jure* without the consent of his three estates."[97] But in Scotland he had grown accustomed to greater flexibility in administering the law than the more formal English system normally allowed. In *The True Law of Free Monarchies* he qualified his statement that a good king will follow the law by adding "that the health of the commonwealth [must] be his chief law" and that "general laws, made publicly in parliament, may upon known respects to the king by his authority be mitigated and suspended, upon causes only known to him."[98] Although he grew more cautious about such claims in England, he continued to see himself as head of a legal system with multiple branches that included not only the common law but church courts administering canon law, the prerogative courts of Wales, the North and Star Chamber, the civil law Admiralty courts, and eventually a revived court of honor under the Earl Marshal.[99] When these jurisdictions clashed, he believed he had the

---

[94] Ibid., 50–1 and 65–6.   [95] Smith, *Edward Coke*, 77–82.   [96] HMC Salisbury, 16.50.
[97] *Parliamentary debates in 1610*, ed. Samuel Rawson Gardiner, Camden Society Publications, OS 81 (1862), 24.
[98] McIlwain, 63.
[99] Richard Cust, *Charles I and the Aristocracy, 1625–1642* (Cambridge: Cambridge University Press, 2013), chapter 1.

right to settle their disputes according to his own sense of reason and equity.[100] His theological view of kings, as instruments chosen by God to promote justice and fulfill the ends of divine providence, implied as much.

That view unsettled some common lawyers and others who worried that allowing a foreign-born king too much discretion to reform even recognized problems in the operation of the law would lead to dangerous consequences. In response to James's invocation of his own reason and common sense they began to develop an alternative concept of natural law and reason, as embodied in ancient legal custom, through which universal principles of justice had allegedly been adapted to English circumstances through centuries of usage.[101] The earliest systematic development of this view of custom in England did not come from the pen of a common lawyer but that of a theologian, Richard Hooker, who developed it while defending the existing practices of the English Church against puritan calls for further reformation. His formulation made crystal clear the perceived connection between custom, nature, and God's will: "The general and perpetual voice of men is as the sentence of God himself. For that which all men at all times learned, Nature herself must needs have taught; and God being the author of Nature, her voice is but his instrument."[102]

Although Hooker had died by the time James inherited the English thrown, his one-time student and patron, Edwin Sandys, emerged as a leading opponent to the unification of English and Scottish law in English parliaments. Sir Edward Coke adapted Hooker's concept to defend the customary maxims and ancient precedents of the common law as a system of "artificial reason," grounded in many centuries of use. The law, which required years of study to master, represented the wisdom of the ages. The proper solution to abuses in the operation of the legal system lay in the law itself, if properly understood by jurists trained in its ancient maxims, procedures, and applications.

The theoretical dispute between James and Coke therefore turned on the question of how the concept of natural reason and justice that both saw as the basis of law should be understood and applied to a set of specific issues having to do with delegations of royal authority and the rules and procedures through which that authority operated in governing England. It was in some respects a narrow dispute, since Coke readily conceded that England was a monarchy in which the king enjoyed extensive powers, including the right to dispense with law in certain emergencies, while James agreed that he had a duty to uphold his kingdoms' ancient laws in virtually all circumstances. The debate over the union of the laws nevertheless brought subtly divergent attitudes about the relationships between

---

[100] Paul Christianson, "Royal and Parliamentary Voices on the Ancient Constitution," in *The Mental World of the Jacobean Court*, ed. Linda Peck (Cambridge: Cambridge University Press, 1991), 71–95.
[101] Burgess, *Politics of the Ancient Constitution*, 37–58.
[102] *Of the Lawes of Ecclesiastical Politie. Eight Books* (London, 1598), 62 (1.8).

reason, law, and the role of the king into head-on collision. If civic peace and harmony depended above all on a shared personal allegiance to the king, and if it was God's evident intention to bring the two British nations into a close and perpetual union, then it followed that English and Scots needed to adjust their legal systems to facilitate those goals. But if the law had an independent existence rooted in centuries of custom, allowing any king—or indeed any parliament—to tamper with it risked profoundly destabilizing consequences.

The logic of this last position seems to have driven some opponents of the Union to adopt a much more uncompromising view of the common law's immemorial origins and consistency over time than had been common only a few years before. Elizabethan commentators routinely admitted that their country's laws had always undergone continual adaptation in response to changing circumstances. "Never in all points one commonwealth doth agree with another," Sir Thomas Smith had written in *De Republica Anglorum*: "no, nor any long time one commonwealth with itself. For all changeth continually to more or less, and still to diverse and diverse orders, as the diversity of the times do present occasion, and the mutability of men's wits doth invent and assay new ways to reform and amend that which they do find at fault."[103] A few years later Thomas Wilson commented that old laws were constantly falling into disuse and new statutes passed, so that "the laws of England alter like the moon."[104] "As the alteration in a natural body doth require sometimes some change of medicines, so doth the alteration in a politic body of a commonwealth require sometimes some change of laws," Justice Yelverton told Parliament in 1598.[105] This view easily elided into a conclusion that kings had often been responsible for legal innovation, and perhaps even for the original creation of the law itself. As Bacon put it:

> King Alfred first divided the land into shires and provincial law days. William the Conqueror brought in the Exchequer, and kept the Chancery and Common Pleas at his court. Henry III settled the Common Pleas at Westminster. Edward III erected the Admiralty and Duchy; Edward IV the councils of Star Chamber and the Marches. Henry VIII set up the Court of Requests, of Wards and Liveries and the Council at York. And although some of these were since approved by statute law, yet the author and life giver of them all was the prerogative of our kings.[106]

From Bacon's perspective, James simply followed in the footsteps of his English predecessors in seeking to reform and harmonize the laws of his two kingdoms.

---

[103] *De Republica Anglorum*, 22.
[104] Thomas Wilson, *The State of England, Anno Dom. 1600*, ed. J. F. Fisher, Royal Historical Society Camden, fifth series, 52 (1936), 37.
[105] *PPEI* 3.200.   [106] Bacon, *Works*, 10.373.

Recent work on Coke suggests that even in the Elizabethan period he had an unusually well-developed reverence for the legal reasoning of medieval judges and advocates, which led him to an exceptionally conservative view of the common law.[107] If the law sometimes appeared confused and contradictory, he believed, the fault lay in the sparsity of accurate records of what past judges had actually said rather than any inherent defects and inconsistencies. His chief motive in producing his first Elizabethan *Reports* was to set matters straight by demonstrating that if correctly understood the decisions of the judges in previous cases displayed far greater coherence and consistency than many ill-informed lawyers and other people believed. Although probably a minority view in the 1590s that still remained open to dispute in James's reign, Coke's arguments addressed a felt need to lend greater consistency, coherence, and certainty to the law. Legislated reforms provided one possible solution to that problem. The monumental efforts that went into the compilation of Coke's eleven published volumes of *Reports* between 1600 and 1615 offered another.

Coke effectively sought to elevate technical proficiency in the law—the sort of deep knowledge of the correct forms of pleas, medieval reports, year books, and precedents that he himself had acquired—into a science capable of controlling acts of the king and perhaps even the king-in-parliament. James felt compelled to reject this position for much the same reason he rejected the claims of presbyterian clergy to enjoy a privileged right to interpret and apply scripture. From his point of view, the problem resided not in the law itself but factious lawyers, who used precedents and procedural quibbles to obstruct his pursuit of constructive reform and foment resistance to his authority by spuriously claiming to defend the subjects' liberties, in very much the way that Scottish clergy had stirred resistance by claiming a privileged right to interpret God's will. Others had long shared his prejudice against the legal profession. In 1602 Archbishop Matthew Hutton complained to Elizabeth about "lawyers, who being grown to an exceeding great number by reason of the long peace, have fined their wits to the very quintessence of reason (as they think) to make *quidlibet ex quolibet, ex ante non eus, ex non ante eus*, and so by reason overthrow both right and reason."[108] Bacon stated the case with particular clarity during a dispute in 1607 over the jurisdiction of the court of the Welsh Marches:

> Monarchies in name do often degenerate into aristocracies or rather oligarchies in nature by two insensible degrees. The first is when prerogatives are made envious or subject to the construction of laws; the second when law as an oracle is

---

[107] Boynton, *Sir Edward Coke*.
[108] HMC Salisbury 12.112. Cf. James's alleged comment reported by Dudley Carleton: "he plainly told the lawyers he would leave hunting of hares and hunt them in their quirks and subtleties, with which the subject had long been abused." *The Court and Times of James I*, ed. Thomas Birch, 2 vols (London, 1848), 2.99.

fixed to place. For by the one the king is made accountable and brought under law; and by the other the law is over-ruled by the judge; and by both all tenures of favor, privy council, nobility and personal dependencies (mysteries that keep up states in the person of the prince) are quite abolished, and magistracy enabled to stand by itself.[109]

Over-emphasis on law subverted monarchy by favoring impersonal structures of authority, rather than "personal dependencies" deriving from a king's decisions about whom to favor, which undergirded the royal state.

Fortunately, James had no need to engage in a protracted battle over these theoretical issues, since in most respects English common law served his purposes very well. He knew that as a practical matter he would have to delegate power to inferior magistrates to carry out his primary duty as a king, "to maintain concord, wealth and civility among" his subjects.[110] The common law did this not only through its maxims and precedents but even more through a system of legal administration under the direction of royally appointed judges and county magistrates. As Thomas Wilson put it, the English system provided that no magistrate should have "more authority than the meanest but as he deriveth it from the prince by commission, and thereby none able to make a head but where the prince's name goeth, nor daring to resist the prince's commandment."[111] One anonymous treatise likened the king's position in this system to that of a spider sitting in the middle of a web, whose "many instruments and substitutes" allow him to feel "the least motion tending to the disturbance of the peace and tranquility of his state" in any part of his kingdom even while remaining at rest at its center.[112] Far from trying to tamper with this structure, James introduced it into Scotland, by establishing justices of the peace and local constables in 1610, and encouraging hereditary sheriffs to sell their jurisdictional powers back to the crown.[113] He boasted of this achievement in an address to a Scottish parliament in 1617, saying that although some Scots scorned the justices and constables he had established and some lords obstructed their work, "he would have both one and the other to know that it was a place of no small honor to be a minister of the king's justice in the service of the commonwealth," and that any who opposed their work "should be accounted with him enemies to his crown."[114]

Rather than a major clash between royal absolutism and the law, James's reign saw a series of skirmishes over more limited legal issues, which the king often won. Although he eventually had to concede defeat in his effort to unify English and Scottish law, the judges upheld his goal of extending full legal rights in England to

---

[109] Bacon, *Works*, 10.371. [110] McIlwain, 55. [111] *State of England*, 41.
[112] BL Lansdowne Mss. 798, fol. 114.
[113] Julian Goodare, *The Government of Scotland 1560–1625* (Oxford: Oxford University Press, 2004), 189–90 and 203.
[114] Spottiswood, 530.

his Scottish subjects in Calvin's Case (1608). In Bates's Case (1606) they affirmed his right to collect the "New Impositions" on foreign trade recently devised by Robert Cecil. With the support of Bacon and Lord Chancellor Egerton, James easily beat back Coke's attempt to further centralize justice in Westminster by weakening the authority of the council of Wales. In the latter years of his reign he overrode the objections of some common lawyers to resurrect the court of the Earl Marshal. His decision not to tamper with the Elizabethan settlement gave him the considerable advantage of being able to deal with ecclesiastical disputes by defending a "Church established by law." In most respects, the defeat of his and Bacon's efforts to harmonize the laws of his two British kingdoms did little to hamper his effectiveness in ruling England.

The most important exception involved the way in which legal objections to new forms of taxation not approved by a parliament constrained his ability to increase his revenues and alleviate his chronic indebtedness. This was as much a political as a legal problem, however, rooted in the natural resistance of propertied men to higher taxation, compounded by resentment of James's generosity to Scottish courtiers and disapproval of his failure to bring costs under control. The belief of some lawyers that Cecil's New Impositions were illegal contributed to James's difficulties with parliaments in 1610 and 1614, but did not prevent him from collecting the tax. In theory he might have solved his financial problems through reforms enacted in a parliament, as Salisbury attempted with the Great Contract of 1610. Alternatively, medieval precedents existed to create a plausible, if not incontrovertible legal justification for various additional sources of revenue, if James had wanted to press the issue. But he knew that doing this would cause a political storm that he felt it wiser to avoid. James's indebtedness nevertheless fed anxieties that at some point he or one of his successors would override Parliament's control over taxation by pleading financial and military necessity. The question of how far English kings had the right to tax without parliamentary consent if they felt compelled by urgent need simmered beneath the surface throughout the reign, periodically erupting into the open.

Behind the tensions between law and royal authority lurked the old question of how a king might free himself from legal constraints when a public emergency demanded that he do so, without thereby sanctioning abusive arbitrary power. And behind that issue lay the more concrete threat that a renewal of religious war might place unbearable strains on the kingdom's fiscal and institutional arrangements. England under James I was a stable, peaceful kingdom and seemed likely to remain so indefinitely, provided it did not have to deal with a serious threat of foreign invasion, a major new rebellion in Ireland, or some comparable emergency. But Elizabeth's war with Spain had failed to produce a permanent system for financing the kingdom's military defenses, and the reaction against some of the wartime measures adopted during her reign created further obstacles to doing so in the future. Suspicions of James's intentions as a foreign king and resentment of his bounty to favored courtiers and mismanagement further compounded the problem. As by far the richest, most populous, and most stable of James's kingdoms, England needed to provide the bulk of the crown's resources. English resistance to higher taxation therefore made the avoidance not only of foreign war but serious unrest in the two other Stuart kingdoms necessary. To minimize the chances for such unrest in the long term, James and his ministers believed they needed to extend royal authority over regions that had never been strictly governed in the past, while simultaneously dealing with problems of Catholic and presbyterian resistance. Their lack of resources meant that they had limited margins for error and so needed to tread carefully.

Law and Society across Britain and Ireland: The Problem of Diversity

Most discussions of the attempted union of James's kingdoms have focused on efforts to pass legislation bringing the laws and institutions of England and Scotland into alignment, which had failed by late 1606. This approach makes some sense for England, where the common law, administered by royal judges and royally appointed magistrates, had become embedded in the social fabric of local communities.[115] But in Scotland, the greater part of Ireland, and even a few remote English districts along the Scottish border, royally administered law operated much more sporadically. In these regions the absence of strong centralized royal justice had allowed alternative methods of keeping order and waging disputes to persist and develop. Even if it had succeeded, the drive to legislate outward legal uniformity would have done little, by itself, to establish an effective and unified system of royal governance. For this to happen stronger institutional structures and habits of obedience needed to be built from the ground up, in places where they had either collapsed or never previously existed. James had begun extending royal authority in Scotland before 1603, while in Ireland the defeat of Tyrone and Tyrconnell presented unprecedented opportunities to expand and consolidate crown control over the whole island. But in both places the king and his servants faced choices between trying to impose laws and institutions based on the English model of centralized justice or adopting alternative methods more in keeping with local traditions and social practices. The failure to achieve greater institutional uniformity through legislation may actually have allowed them more flexibility in experimenting with alternative strategies for extending royal control.

To understand the challenges facing the king and his servants, we need to view the problem of union not from the perspective of formal legal and institutional

[115] Cynthia Herrup, *The Common Peace: Participation and the Criminal Law in Seventeenth-Century England* (Cambridge: Cambridge University Press, 1987).

structures defined by statute, but the ways in which laws and other forms of authority operated on the ground. A provocative article by R. A. Houston provides a good starting point.[116] It argues that the English system defined rights and responsibilities through a hierarchy of spatially defined jurisdictions, whereas Scottish, Irish, and Welsh legal codes placed more emphasis on membership in social groups. Houston follows Steve Hindle in identifying the parish as the basic local unit in the English system, as had become the case in some districts.[117] This oversimplifies, however, since other local institutions, particularly manors, in other places remained still more important. Even in the early seventeenth century, far more litigation took place in manorial courts and other local tribunals than in the central common law courts.[118] But Houston's basic point that the English had grown accustomed to conducting their legal and political affairs within spatially defined jurisdictions, ascending from face-to-face village communities through hundreds and counties to the kingdom as a whole, remains convincing. Whether dealing with petty crime, the distribution of poor relief, or the maintenance of roads and bridges, they worked through parish or manorial structures and dealt with communal problems through unpaid local officers selected from within the community, and what amounted to committees of neighbors charged with specific functions, such as parish vestries and juries of presentment. Social bonds and values contributed strongly to the operation of this system. But the key social group, for purposes of the law and governance, was the neighborhood, rather than more dispersed bodies of kin.

The whole system ultimately rested on the even smaller units of individual tenures.[119] Concepts of different kinds of tenure, each carrying precisely defined rights and obligations, were fundamental to the common law. In giving an individual and his household rights over a piece of land, a tenure simultaneously prescribed his relationship to a landlord and a manorial community, whose customs and institutions determined how he might use his land and where any disputes with his neighbors would be settled. Freehold tenures gave their holders additional rights and responsibilities, including protection by the king's courts, membership in the county court, the privilege of voting in elections for members of parliament and royal coroners, and the duty to serve on juries of both trial and presentment. Even after the protection of royal courts was extended to

---

[116] R. A. Houston, 'People, Space and Law in Late Medieval and Early Modern Britain and Ireland', *Past and Present* 230.1 (2016): 47–89.

[117] Steve Hindle, *The State and Social Change in Early Modern England* (Basingstoke: Palgrave Macmillan, 2000).

[118] Tim Streatton, "The People and the Law," in *A Social History of England 1500–1700*, ed. Keith Wrightson (Cambridge: Cambridge University Press, 2017), 199–220 at 201; Brodie Waddell, "Governing England through the Manor Courts, 1500–1850," *Historical Journal* 55 (2012): 279–315. Houston does recognize the importance of manorial courts, "People, Space and Law," 64–5.

[119] Here I differ from Houston, although I believe my modification of his argument basically strengthens it.

copyholders in the late Middle Ages, freeholders continued to occupy a privileged position.[120] A mystique developed around them, leading English authors from at least as early as the fifteenth century to attribute the greater liberty, prosperity, and valor of England, in comparison to Scotland, France, and other societies, to the prevalence of freeholders. A freehold provided an individual with both the material and legal basis for his role in a largely self-governing local community. London and other boroughs substituted an alternative criterion of membership in a gild, conferring the right to engage in retail trade, along with participation in the guild's regulation of its craft and the right to vote in city elections and hold civic office. The paradigm in both cases was one of a society of householders, rendered self-sufficient through their possession of freehold land or the "freedom" of a town, who were individually responsible for governing their own families and servants, and collectively responsible for maintaining good order in their community.[121] The parish was formally incorporated within this system at the Reformation, with the special duty of organizing poor relief. County magistrates, appointed by the crown but usually drawn from among a county's wealthiest landholding families, supervised the parish and manorial institutions, while acting as go-betweens in dealings with the privy council.

Cultural values, such as an emphasis on the virtue of neighborliness and the importance of reputation or credit within the community, reinforced this system.[122] In the early modern period the paradigm was complemented by a frequent bias favoring commercial towns and nucleated arable villages with well-defined social hierarchies, over districts with more dispersed settlements, especially upland zones and regions like the fens of East Anglia and Lincolnshire, where the existence of large tracts of unfarmed common land

---

[120] Copyholders were able to defend their tenurial rights by suing in a royal court and they participated in manorial institutions but they were not legally entitled to serve on juries in crown courts (see, e.g., Richard Brownlow, *Reports of diverse choice cases in law* (London, 1651), 194 for the statement that jurors can be challenged for not possessing a freehold). John Cowell, *The Interpreter: or Booke containing the signification of words* (London, 1607) asserts, on the basis of a passage from the fourth *Reports* of Sir Edward Coke that in manorial courts baron freeholders acted as judges, while copyholders had to submit to the judgment of their lord or his steward (Cowell, n.p., *sub* courts baron).

[121] This also explains the common law adage that "an Englishman's home is his castle," within which he enjoyed certain immunities, and the doctrine that a wife had no independent existence in the eyes of the law apart from her husband. Although Houston stresses the role of local officers, the importance of juries of presentment and other bodies such as parish vestries that functioned as committees responsible for fining delinquents or reporting them to higher authorities also needs stress. The cooperation of neighboring householders in policing their own communal affairs and cracking down on those who failed to do their civic duty was fundamental. For good discussions see Linda Pollock, "'Little Commonwealths I: The Family and Household Relationships" and Malcolm Gaskill, "Little Commonwealths II: Communities," in *A Social History of England*, ed. Wrightson, 60–83 and 84–104.

[122] Keith Wrightson, "The Decline of Neighbourliness Revisited," in *Local Identities in Late Medieval and Early Modern England*, ed. Daniel Woolf and Norman Jones (Basingstoke: Palgrave Macmillan, 2007); Craig Muldrew, *The Economy of Obligation: Credit and Social Relations in Early Modern England* (Basingstoke: Palgrave Macmillan, 1998); Andy Wood, *Faith, Hope and Charity: English Neighbourhoods, 1500–1640* (Cambridge: Cambridge University Press, 2020).

permitted a looser fit between economic subsistence and tenurial arrangements.[123] That bias encouraged the crown to back schemes of fen drainage, ostensibly to "improve" both the land and its inhabitants by converting commonly owned marshes into privately held arable fields, and undisciplined fen dwellers into a more regimented workforce.[124] Even stronger prejudices existed with respect to the pastoral economies prevalent in most of Gaelic Ireland, especially transhumance, misunderstood as nomadism. The seemingly free and random movements of pastoralists and lack of sustained labor on fixed plots allegedly encouraged idleness and thievery. In both Ireland and their own country, English writers associated the "improvement" of land through more intensive arable farming with the spread of law and civility. By increasing taxable wealth, improvement also benefited the king's finances, giving royal officials an added reason to promote it.

In much of England economic pressures had already begun to undermine the role of freehold and secure copyhold tenants by the early seventeenth century, as smallholdings were amalgamated into larger leasehold farms.[125] By the eighteenth century and in many districts well before then, small and middling tenants enjoying secure control of their land had been largely supplanted by substantial farmers, whose social and economic position owed more to the quantity of land they held than the tenure by which they held it. But legal and political entitlements appear to have lagged behind economic trends, although how completely and for just how long remains somewhat unclear.[126] Some crown officials, particularly in Ireland, continued to see the prevalence of free tenants enjoying secure possession of their holdings as fundamental to

---

[123] Margaret Spufford, *Contrasting Communities: English Villagers in the Sixteenth and Seventeenth Centuries* (Cambridge: Cambridge University Press, 1974) is a classic study of these differences.

[124] Eric Ash, *The Draining of the Fens: Projectors, Popular Politics, and State Building in Early Modern England* (Baltimore: Johns Hopkins University Press, 2017). Cf. David Underdown's comments on perceptions of differences between predominantly arable districts with nucleated villages and woodland dairying districts with more dispersed settlement patterns in *Revel, Riot, and Rebellion* (Oxford: Clarendon Press, 1995), 5. Interestingly, Sir John Fortescue, writing in the fifteenth century, had a different and almost opposite bias, extolling animal husbandry in enclosed pastures as conducive to spirituality and intellectual development, while denigrating arable farmers, whose "moiling in the ground...engendereth rudeness of wit and mind" (Sir John Fortescue, *De laudibus legem Angliae* (London, 1616), 66–7).

[125] Craig Muldrew, "The Middling Sort: An Emerging Cultural Identity," in *Social History of England*, ed. Wrightson, 290–309 at 299–300 states that by the early seventeenth century the majority of land in most of southern England was already held by large farmers in units of 75 acres or more that would have required wage laborers to work.

[126] My thanks to Steve Hindle and Andy Woods for advice on this issue although, of course, they should not be held responsible for my conclusions. An interesting indication of uncertainty on this point is a statute of 13 Elizabeth I (1575), which stipulates "that no farmer or farmers for term of years...not having estate in freehold" should be entitled to serve as a sewer commissioner. Although it affirms the principle that only freeholders can serve, the need for such a statute suggests that exceptions were probably already being made. See *The Reading of the famous and learned Robert Callis...upon the statute of 23 H. 8* (London, 1647), 196–7.

England's free and civil society, and therefore also to their efforts to introduce English civility into Gaelic regions.[127]

Houston remarks that, in contrast to England, in both the Scottish Highlands and Ireland "Gaelic lordship was about men more than land, lords measuring their power by their ability to retain tenants and followers," so that "practical law enforcement over much of Britain and Ireland was based on social relationships, which were only incidentally linked with space."[128] The prevalence of seigneurial control over the courts and mechanisms of law enforcement in most of Scotland and much of Ireland contributed to this contrast. Although Scotland resembled England in having a uniform national law, in nearly all localities the crown had granted the hereditary right to hold courts and judge criminals to individual nobles or lairds.[129] This allowed nobles and some middling landowners to use their authority to protect followers, harass enemies, and extend control not only over their own tenants but other inhabitants within the territories they administered. In the Highlands and border regions some nobles "presided over extensive criminal networks involving protection, blackmail, terrorization, raiding and murder."[130] The boundary between public justice administered in the king's name and private self-help and vengeance therefore blurred. People did not expect the law to be impartial and impersonal, because its operation was so fully bound up with local structures of friendship, alliance, and subordination.[131] In Ireland the palatine jurisdictions of Old English lords like the earl of Ormond, the delegation of authority to Gaelic lords, and commissions of martial law granted to English captains had similar effects.[132]

In addition to lordship, alliances based on actual or presumed ties of patrilineal kinship, defined by a common name, played a central role not only in Gaelic regions of Ireland and the Highlands but also in Lowland Scotland and districts along the Anglo-Scottish border.[133] Kinship solidarity operated in complicated ways, with significant regional variations. Clans and septs sometimes absorbed

---

[127] See below for Ireland. For Scotland see, for example, the discourse on "The State of the Scottish Commonwealth" (c. 1580) in *CSPSc* 5.564–5, which blames the political instability of the kingdom on the exorbitant power of the nobility and paucity of freeholders, which is alleged to render the peasantry dependent on their lords and thus ready to follow them into battle even against the crown.

[128] "People, Space and Law," 69.

[129] Goodare, *Government of Scotland*, 70–1. Lairds were untitled landowners, comparable in most respects to English gentry.

[130] Keith Brown, *Bloodfeud in Scotland 1573–1625: Violence, Justice and Politics in an Early Modern Society* (Edinburgh: John Donald, 1986), 20. For Tyrone see TNA SP63/223/2.

[131] Jenny Wormald, "Bloodfeud, Kindred and Government in Early Modern Scotland," *Past and Present* 87 (1980): 54–97 at 96.

[132] David Edwards, *The Ormond Lordship in the County of Kilkenny, 1515–1642: The Rise and Fall of Butler Feudal Power* (Dublin: Four Courts Press, 2003). For the earl of Tyrone's sponsorship of local criminality, exposed by local testimony after his flight from Ireland, see TNA SP63/223/2.

[133] Brown, *Bloodfeud*, 18–19; Keith Brown, "Honour, Honours and Nobility in Scotland between the Reformation and the National Covenant," *Scottish Historical Review* 91 (2012): 42–74 at 47–8; Keith Brown, *Noble Society in Scotland: Wealth, Family and Culture from Reformation to Revolution* (Edinburgh: Edinburgh University Press, 2000), 4–7. Scottish historians normally use the term clan,

unrelated individuals as members[134] and formed alliances or clientage relations with each other, commonly cemented through marriage alliances or the practice of fostering, by which the son of one chief was raised in the household of another. The Highland Clan Chattan consisted not of a single lineage but a coalition of twelve smaller kindreds. But despite the variants, social positions rooted in kinship played pivotal roles in both Scottish and Irish society.[135] What also distinguished large parts of Ireland, Scotland, and the Borders from most of England was the prevalence of clusters—dozens or even scores of families, with hundreds or even thousands of members—that shared a surname, lived in more or less contiguous areas, and recognized a sense of obligation to each other and to a common head. This had a number of consequences, beginning with a blurring of distinctions between ownership of land and control over the people who lived on it. In Gaelic regions land commonly belonged not to individuals but to the clan or sept, or alternatively to its head, who in some cases had the right to redistribute holdings among its members. Even in the Scottish Lowlands and Irish Pale, the scarcity of freeholds and secure copyholds meant that few tenants had any legal protection against arbitrary eviction by their landlords. Although highly despotic in theory, in practice, a lord's power was often tempered by his customary obligations to other members of his kindred—and sometimes to allied kindreds—as well as the practical need to avoid antagonizing subordinates. Land was managed through contractual arrangements involving payments of rent or tribute in return for use rights, known in Scotland as "tacks," which might be spelled out in written documents, but which often rested on a verbal agreement or a traditional arrangement that could be several generations old.[136] Although expectations about mutual rights and responsibilities existed, they were not enforceable at law.

Writing about Ireland, K. W. Nicholls has plausibly attributed these practices to conditions in a sparsely settled country with a predominantly pastoral economy, in which land had little value in itself without the animals needed to make use of it, and the manpower required to protect those animals from raids. Once established, the pattern persisted even where population levels grew and arable farming

---

derived from a Gaelic word meaning "the children," in referring to these groups, whereas most Irish historians refer to septs. For a brief discussion, which argues that the two terms are essentially interchangeable, see K. W. Nicholls, *Gaelic and Gaelicized Ireland in the Middle Ages* (Dublin: Lilliput Press, 2003), 8–11. There appear to have been local differences in how clans or septs operated, not only between Scotland and Ireland but also between regions within both kingdoms but these have not been systematically explained. For the Borders see below, pp. 489–94.

[134] Irish marriage practices made this virtually inevitable, since illegitimate children of a sept leader were counted as full members of the sept and women had the right to declare the paternity of their children. Hugh O'Neill earl of Tyrone was the grandson of a blacksmith's wife who claimed that the O'Neill had sired his father. See Nicholls, *Gaelicized Ireland*, 83–90.

[135] Ibid., 44–6, 52–3, 91–93, 100–1 takes note of several of these.

[136] Ibid., 8–14 and 41–3; Rabb Houston, "Custom in Context: Medieval and Early Modern Scotland and England," *Past and Present* 211 (2011): 35–76. In Scotland such relationships were more likely to be codified in written bonds of manrent but since these were difficult to enforce much continued to depend on customary expectations and the application of force when agreements broke down.

became more important. The militarization of Gaelic society in the Middle Ages also played an important role by placing a premium on a leader's ability to retain and maintain fighting men.[137] This tended to ge..te hierarchical relationships of clientage and dependence between individuals a..oups possessing different degrees of military strength, while depressing the sta..Peasants who had only rudimentary weapons.[138] Broadly similar trends presu..operated in Scotland, which supplied Irish chiefs with galloglass warriors an..hank" mercenaries. Clan chiefs did not use the Irish term coign and livery ...supported their military followers in similar ways.

The different legal treatment of fiefs and titles held from ... and Ireland added further complications. In Scotland feudal ... in Scotland nized by the courts did not always correspond to actual patte...nd recog- When they did not, discrepancies were resolved by additional pay...pancy. or rent and the creation of new bonds of subordination, through...ibute nominally held land from the titular owner.[139] Written bonds that p...an the late Middle Ages and sixteenth-century often codified these arr... A few great nobles, notably the earls of Huntly and Argyll, formed relat... large numbers of clans, affording a kind of hegemony over extensive ... Although Irish lords did not employ bonds of manrent, the Butler ea... Ormond and Fitzgerald earls of Kildare and Desmond developed less formal apparently similar alliances with septs living within their lordships. Surrender a regrant agreements negotiated by the Tudors led to situations in which lands hel... in theory as feudal grants were occupied by Irish groups living under their traditional customs. Both countries had therefore produced hybrid systems mingling Gaelic custom with feudal concepts of tenure. As Nicholls points out, the common law had trouble in dealing with this hybridity because its tenurial rules had developed in very different English circumstances, where distinctions between proprietary title and customary rights of usage were less important. Scottish lawyers developed more flexible concepts of tenure that left them better able to accommodate Gaelic customs.[140]

The importance of groups, rather than individuals, in Scottish and Irish society also affected treatments of crime. In England all serious crimes, such as major thefts, assaults, and murders, were treated as felonies, offenses against the king punishable by death. By contrast, Scottish and Irish Brehon law treated many thefts and acts of violence as incidents in conflicts between groups requiring

---

[137] Katharine Simms, *From Kings to Warlords: The Changing Political Structure of Gaelic Ireland in the Later Middle Ages* (Woodbridge: Boydell Press, 1987).

[138] K. W. Nicholls, *Land, Law and Society in Sixteenth Century Ireland*, the O'Donnell Lecture, 1976 (Cork: University College, 1976), 19–20.

[139] Allan Macinnes, *Clanship, Commerce and the House of Stuart, 1603–1788* (East Linton: Tuckwell Press, 1996), 5–13 provides a clear summary.

[140] Nicholls, *Land, Law and Society*, 20.

settlement through arbitration and payments of compensation.[141] Scottish traditions of the feud treated an attack on one member of a lineage as an act of aggression against the entire "blood," justifying retaliation not only against the perpetrator but also his kin. An overlord would also feel compelled to retaliate if he believed that an assault on someone enjoying his protection had violated his honor. Scottish courts, especially the Court of Sessions in Edinburgh, worked out procedures for appointing panels of arbitrators to settle the resulting disputes, and guidelines for determining appropriate levels of compensation. They codified settlements of feuds in written instruments that the crown would then attempt to enforce.[142] Rather than simply punishing crimes, royal justice in Scotland therefore provided mechanisms for mediating disputes between kindreds. Although the common law courts of Ireland never developed comparable procedures, native Brehon law operated through broadly similar principles and procedures.[143] Ancient codified schedules of compensatory payments for wrongs dating as far back as the seventh century had become obsolete, but Brehon lawyers continued to arbitrate disputes in accordance with Irish custom.[144] Edmund Campion described their methods in the 1560s. They "consider of wrongs offered and received among their neighbors, be it murder, felony or trespass; all is redeemed by compensation (except the grudge of parties seek revenge)... The Breighoon (so they call this kind of lawyer) sitteth him down on a bank, the lords and gentlemen at variance around him, and they proceed."[145] This sounds very much like a less formal variation of the Scottish practice.

Naturally compensation applied only in cases of individuals possessing the means to provide it, whether through their own resources or the aid of a patron.

---

[141] Houston remarks, "The very idea of public offence or felony seems to have been subordinated to that of individual injury or tort in Scotland (delict), Wales (*cam* or *anghyfraith*) and Ireland – perhaps also in the north of England – until at least the sixteenth century." He then adds, "none of the societies of north and west Britain and Ireland conceived liability to pay criminal compensation in exclusively individual terms, but as a burden of reparation to be shared among kindred or affiliation" ("People, Space and the Law," 73).

[142] Wormald, "Bloodfeud, Kindred and Government," is a classic discussion that should now be qualified by Brown, *Bloodfeud in Scotland*. Additional information on the structure and operation of Scottish clans is provided by the opening chapters of Macinnes, *Clanship*. Nicholls, *Gaelic and Gaelicized Ireland*, is a succinct and accessible survey of the broad features of Irish society down to the early seventeenth century.

[143] Neil McLeod, "Assault and Attempted Murder in Brehon Law," *Irish Jurist* n.s. 33 (1998): 351-91; Neil McLeod, "Property and Honour Price in Brehon Law Glosses," *Irish Jurist* n.s. 31 (1996): 280-95. The level of compensation was determined by both the status of the victim and the nature of the offense. For example, an assault with a blunt instrument causing a bruise was less serious than one with an edged instrument that shed blood.

[144] Cf. Nicholls, *Land, Law and Society*, p. 6: "The Irish brehons, who settled disputes, were arbitrators not judges and their decisions awards, not judgements; that is to say they were based on the principle of arriving at a reasonable compromise between conflicting interests rather than on that of enforcing a known legal rule." But it is also clear that finely calibrated rules did evolve in Ireland at a very early date, setting amounts of compensation reflecting both the status or "blood price" of the victim and the seriousness of the crime against him.

[145] *Two Histories of Ireland, The one written by Edmond Campion, the other by Meredith Hammer* (Dublin, 1633), 19.

Common criminals in both Scotland and Ireland were subject to arbitrary justice usually carried out by lords, although commissions of martial law allowed English captains to mete out the same sort of peremptory justice. If a powerful lord or clan refused to offer compensation, or committed an offense so outrageous that no compensation seemed adequate to atone for it, all of its followers might find themselves targeted by retaliatory justice. In such cases the Scottish crown issued commissions of "fire and sword," authorizing a nobleman to wreak indiscriminate havoc on the offenders and their territory. In extreme cases it would outlaw an entire lineage. In the early seventeenth century, James VI declared it a capital crime to bear the surname of the Highland clan of the MacGregors because of their lawless behavior, or the Lowland noble lineage of the Ruthvens, after their leaders tried to assassinate him.[146] Although the English crown never officially adopted similar measures, in practice English captains in Ireland repeatedly waged campaigns of indiscriminate violence against septs that had offended them. Rather than simply targeting individual offenders, law enforcement in Scotland and Ireland often amounted to localized warfare, with many collateral victims caught in the cross-fire.

Kingship, Law, and Lordship

To have replaced this system with a firm structure of government by royal magistrates in the English manner would have required major changes in patterns of landholding and land use, cultural values, and forms of social solidarity and allegiance. This is precisely what some English reformers in Ireland, such as Richard Beacon and Edmond Spenser, proposed. But in the late sixteenth century both Elizabeth and James VI usually preferred the less drastic method of accepting the importance of lordship and kinship, and negotiating agreements with local lords or clan chiefs to suppress violence among their own followers and cooperate in bringing about incremental change. Both resorted to full-scale military campaigns only when this milder approach broke down. For several reasons James usually had more success in avoiding outright conflict than his English cousin. As a resident king he was able to build relationships with his nobles over many years, sustained through their attendance at his court. These relationships did not always guarantee absolute loyalty: even the king's prime favorite, Lennox, may have cooperated with the earl of Bothwell in an attempted coup in 1591.[147] But

---

[146] In neither case was the threat carried out systematically, although several Ruthvens had to leave the country and the MacGregors suffered under a series of punitive raids sanctioned by the crown but mostly carried out by nobles like Huntly and Argyll.

[147] Adrienne McLaughlin, "Rise of a Courtier: The Second Duke of Lennox and Strategies of Noble Power under James VI," in *James VI and Noble Power in Scotland, 1578–1603*, ed. Miles Kerr-Peterson and Steven J. Reid (London: Routledge, 2017), 148.

James's long familiarity with his nobles must have given him a better ability to differentiate between those he might safely forgive and rehabilitate and the few, like Bothwell, who had become so dangerous that they needed to be destroyed or driven into permanent exile. By contrast Elizabeth did not know most of the great lords of Ireland, with the conspicuous exception of Ormond, and her lord deputies nearly always served for relatively brief periods and lacked kinship ties with the Irish elite that might have helped them build local clientage networks.

James had gradually extended his control over Scotland by repeatedly intervening, on an ad hoc basis, to settle private disputes and conduct campaigns against lawlessness in particular regions. The king's advocate, an official roughly equivalent to the English attorney general, also began to play a more active role in initiating prosecutions.[148] James personally led seven punitive raids against criminal gangs along the English border between 1594 and 1599, and several times summoned individuals involved in feuds to appear before him and his council, where he pressured them into settling their disputes. On a few occasions he compelled entire kindreds to sign written bands or acts of surety to abide by specified conditions.[149] But he also delegated responsibility to great nobles to enforce law and order in his name. In certain regions, notably the border counties, his bedchamber entourage connected him to important landowning families below the level of the nobility that assisted him in managing local affairs.[150]

James's governance of Scotland therefore provides a classic example of Bacon's concept of a system run through "tenures of favor, privy council, nobility and personal dependencies," rather than an impersonal structure of law and "magistracy enabled to stand by itself."[151] Instead of supplanting existing structures of solidarity within Scottish society, James sought to infiltrate and redirect them. By the time he departed for London, these methods had gained enough traction to continue operating without his immediate presence. His council in Edinburgh made his authority felt through numerous ad hoc interventions in private and local affairs. Its registers between 1604 and 1607 show it outlawing individuals for unpaid debts, interfering in the efforts of kirk sessions to discipline people for adultery and Catholicism, ordering the captain of the king's guard to sequester a house that threatened to become the subject of a violent quarrel between rival heirs, intervening in a factional dispute in the borough of Dundee, disciplining a lord for failing to control his followers, ordering individuals involved in feuds to become friends, setting up commissions to investigate abuses in the Western Isles, and repeatedly dealing with ministers who refused to accept the king's right to

---

[148] Goodare, *Government of Scotland*, 164–5.
[149] Anna Groundwater, "'He Made them Friends in his Cabinet': James VI's Suppression of the Scott-Ker Feud," in *James VI and Noble Power*, ed. Kerr-Peterson and Reid (London: Routledge, 2017), 98–116.
[150] Ibid.   [151] Above, pp. 473–4.

appoint moderators of their assemblies.¹⁵² Although the English privy council also intervened in private and local disputes, it usually relied on county magistrates, lord lieutenants, or bishops as intermediaries when doing so, whereas the Scottish council often acted more directly.

But despite their differences, the contrast between reliance on institutional structures and the more informal methods of personal negotiation favored in Scotland can be overstated. The two systems shared enough common elements to make James's experiences in governing Scotland relevant to his role as king of England and Ireland. Although English lords did not possess independent hereditary jurisdictions, their influence over county magistrates and jurors gave them considerable influence over the law's operation. They were often consulted about the appointment of magistrates in counties where their lands were concentrated. Their cooperation certainly helped make the wheels of local government turn efficiently. In England no less than Scotland, it behooved a king to cultivate good relations with his nobles and to work through informal social networks between his court and the localities, as James attempted to do. He also sought to conciliate and reconcile rival groupings or factions among his nobles. He expanded the privy council, which had become a restricted body in Elizabeth's last years, rehabilitated the Howards, including the Crypto-Catholic Lord Henry, retained the services of Robert Cecil, but also rehabilitated and attempted to befriend surviving followers of the late earl of Essex. Just as he had promoted marriages between the Gordons and Lennox Stuarts in Scotland, he arranged matches between Cecils, Devereux, and Howards in England. He tried to use his court as an instrument for unifying his kingdoms, by turning it into a social center and marriage market for the nobility of all three of them. Members of several prominent Irish lineages and a handful of titled Scots contracted marriages with English heiresses through the court, so that by the 1620s the earls of Ormond, Kildare, and Argyll all had English wives. James turned the household of Prince Henry into an academy for noblemen's sons, cementing their ties to his heir.¹⁵³ Although Henry's premature death meant that the experiment did not bear fruit, had the prince survived he would have benefited from long friendship with leading English nobles, analogous to the relationships his father had formed with the earls of Huntly, Lennox, and Bothwell during his youth. The wives of a number of prominent peers found prestigious posts in Queen Anna's household.

---

¹⁵² *Register of the Privy Council of Scotland*, vol. 7, *1604–1607*, ed. D. Masson (Edinburgh: H. M. General Register House, 1906), 6, 8, 16, 19–20, 37, 59, 178, 225, 317–18, 395–6 (disciplining Catholics and adulterers), 13, 82, 93, 104, 109, 112, 260–1, 299–300 and passim (refractory ministers), 19 (punishing a lord for not controlling his followers), 24–5 (seizing a house in a property dispute), 58, 234 (enforced reconciliations to end feuds), 59–60, 68 (enquiries into conditions in the Isles), and 94–7, 303 (dispute in Dundee).

¹⁵³ Tim Wilks, "Poets, Patronage and the Prince's Court," in *The Oxford Handbook of the Age of Shakespeare*, ed. R. Malcolm Smuts (Oxford: Oxford University Press, 2016), 159–78.

In short, James carried over into his English reign a style of kingship he had developed in Scotland that relied on his management of personal relationships, more than institutional channels, to exert political control. Through his notoriously open-handed distribution of bounty, including not only material rewards but honors, he attempted to extend this method. He dubbed 934 knights during his first nine months on the English throne, more than double the number Elizabeth dubbed in forty-five years. The peerage of all three kingdoms expanded markedly after a period of stability in the late sixteenth century, roughly doubling in size in both England and Scotland and trebling in Ireland. While this "inflation of honors" provoked an outcry, it also erected a number of new titled families that James tried, with mixed success, to turn into a service aristocracy. By granting Scots a near monopoly of posts in his bedchamber, he compelled English courtiers to seek their assistance in efforts to procure his bounty. The English complained bitterly about this arrangement but had no choice but to make the best of it.[154] The distribution of royal largesse thereby served as a means of promoting a certain kind of friendship and unity between his kingdoms. In the latter half of his English reign his favorites, Robert Ker earl of Somerset and George Villiers duke of Buckingham, became patronage-brokers on a massive scale, in Ireland as well as England in Buckingham's case. Although this again provoked strong protests, it provides yet another illustration of James's attempt to rule through "tenures of favor, privy council, nobility and personal dependencies," as he had in Scotland.

But he also attempted, simultaneously, to impose some English-style institutional forms on Scotland. Even before 1603 legal and institutional structures had been slowly gaining in importance in the operation of Scottish kingship, through the expanding role of the central Court of Session in Edinburgh and lawyers associated with it in arbitrating disputes, the updating and codification of Scottish law through new statutes, a marked increase in the number of public officials, and the work of the king's council in supervising local authorities and settling disputes.[155] In 1610 James introduced justices of the peace and constables into Scotland and established a Scottish High Commission.[156] Despite the failure of the union project of 1604, we can therefore detect signs of a partial and gradual but significant convergence of methods used to govern his kingdoms that drew upon both English and Scottish models. James seems to have cared less about the formal structures through which his authority worked than the results achieved. When laws and institutional channels served his goals he happily employed them; when they appeared to fall short he adopted more informal, alternative methods. The next chapter will furnish repeated examples of both approaches.

---

[154] Neil Cuddy, "The Revival of the Entourage: The Bedchamber of James I, 1603–1625," in *The English Court from the Wars of the Roses to the Civil War*, ed. David Starkey et al. (London: Longman, 1987), 173–225.
[155] Goodare, *Government of Scotland*, esp. 55–6, 71–3, 81–5, 121–44, 161–5, 177, and 219.
[156] Ibid., 154, 204.

But the king's flexibility and pragmatism did not mean that his methods always worked. On balance, they achieved mixed results, advancing the unification of all Britain and Ireland under a single crown in some ways, while falling short in others. He was largely, although never entirely successful in dealing with old problems of disorder and rebellion in the more unsettled regions of his dominions, but his attempts to master problems stemming from religious diversity and conflict proved less effective. It is to these topics that we must now turn.

10
The Stuart State and Its Peripheries

James believed he had a sacred duty to promote peace and justice throughout his dominions, since that is what God created kings to do. In addition to forging bonds of unity between his kingdoms, this meant promoting the spread of civil manners within each of them. Like many contemporaries, he saw most English, Lowland Scots, and residents of the Pale and towns of Ireland as civil people, while regarding the inhabitants of the Scottish Isles and Highlands and much of Ireland as more barbaric. The differences between civil and uncivil regions within each kingdom seemed to him in many ways more significant than those between civil English, Scots, and Irish. But he also knew that even in civil regions, dangerous and uncivil attitudes and behaviors persisted. Lowlanders as well as Highlanders had their feuds and English gentlemen engaged in the bloody and savage crime of dueling. More serious still were forms of religious demagoguery capable of inciting the kind of violence he had escaped in Edinburgh in 1596. By perverting Christianity to foment conflict, Jesuits and extreme puritans undermined civility even in other wise civil societies.

Religious disorder became even more dangerous when it linked up with the chronic disorderliness that existed in the darker corners of his realms. That is what had made Tyrone's rebellion so dangerous to Elizabeth's crown and Bothwell's hypocritical embrace of presbyterian causes such a threat in Scotland. In both cases, James believed, religion served as a cover for the self-serving behavior of violent lords based in turbulent regions, as they sought to acquire a national following. Securing Stuart rule presented two distinct but fundamentally related challenges. The king and his ministers needed to impose firm government over the more barbaric parts of his kingdoms, so they would no longer serve as a reservoir of manpower for armed rebellions and an inviting target for the hostile attentions of foreign states. But the crown simultaneously needed to prevent the wrong kinds of religion from forging connections between uncivil populations and defiance of royal authority closer to the political center.

Frontier Zones: The Borders and Irish Sea

The turbulent territories that James wanted to bring under control included not only Gaelic regions of Scotland and Ireland but upland districts along the Anglo-Scottish border. In the Middle Ages the Borders had been home to powerful lords who at times rebelled against their own kings, notably the Black Douglasses of Scotland and the Percy and Neville earls of Northumberland and Westmoreland. Henry VIII had diminished the power of the great northern English lords, which collapsed almost completely after the 1569 rebellion. But border magnates, including Archibald Douglas earl of Angus and James Stewart earl of Bothwell, continued to plague James VI well into the 1590s, even as he and Arran also drew support from other powerful border landowners. The turbulence of Scottish politics between 1582 and 1585 spilled over into violent conflict in the shires along Scotland's English frontier, linked to some cross-border raiding.[1]

Despite this disorder, by the late sixteenth century the lowland zone along the eastern border, near the English garrison in Berwick, had grown stable and peaceful. But in more sparsely settled upland districts further west the reduction of magnate power created a vacuum in which raiding by organized bands flourished.[2] Known locally as surnames because they usually shared a common patronym, the largest and most powerful of these bands had scores of branches and hundreds of members, ranging from wealthy lairds or gentry down to poor farmers. The wealthier members of a surname would grant beneficial leases—known in Scotland as kindly tenures—to their poorer kin, cementing solidarity.[3] The Grahams, an extended family descended from an early sixteenth-century century founder that flourished on crown lands in Cumberland confiscated from the rebel Lord Dacre in 1569, were a prime example.[4] About a third of the tenants living on lands held by propertied Grahams also bore the name Graham, contributing to a pool of manpower from which armed and mounted raiding parties, numbering as many as 500, were quickly assembled.[5] Like Irish septs, the Grahams also controlled territory through the possession of more than a dozen fortified stone structures.[6] Although inhabited by English speakers, northern Cumberland was a region where the common law had little relevance and kinship solidarity provided the main organizational principal of social relationships. Like highland clans further north, surnames on each side of the border forged alliances with each other, sometimes cemented by marriage, while engaging in deadly feuds.[7]

---

[1] Jenna M. Schultz, *National Identity and the Anglo-Scottish Borderlands, 1552-1652* (Woodbridge: Boydell Press, 2019), 246-52.
[2] Maureen M. Meikle, *A British Frontier? Lairds and Gentlemen in the Eastern Borders, 1540-1603* (East Linton: Tuckwell Press, 2004).
[3] Anna Groundwater, *The Scottish Middle March, 1573-1625* (Woodbridge: Boydell Press, 2010), 17, 60-3.
[4] Sheldon J. Watts with Susan J. Watts, *From Border to Middle Shire: Northumberland 1586-1625* (Leicester: Leicester University Press, 1975), chapter 6; R. T. Spence, "The Pacification of the Cumberland Borders, 1593-1628," *Northern History* 13 (1977): 59-160 at 61-2.
[5] Spence, "Pacification of the Borders".   [6] Schultz, *National Identity*, 94.
[7] Jarad M. R. Sizer, "The Good of this Service Consists of Absolute Secrecy: The Earl of Dunbar, Scotland and the Border (1603-1611)," *Canadian Journal of History/Annales canadienne d'histoire* 36 (2001): 229-57 at 243; Anna Groundwater, "'He Made them Friends in his Cabinet': James VI's

In 1593 Lord Maxwell and 700 of his followers were slaughtered during an especially lethal encounter, the Battle of Dyrfe Sands, with his Scottish enemies, the Johnstones, and their allies.[8]

The crowns of both England and Scotland delegated authority over the border regions to wardens of corresponding East, Middle, and West marches, who had their own courts and special legal powers, which in England included the right to inflict capital punishment for the crime of march treason, involving offenses like selling arms to Scots without a license or helping raiders escape across the frontier.[9] The failure of the wardens to put a stop to cross-border raiding provided a constant irritant to relations between James VI and Elizabeth. The queen blamed criminality in the region partly on a long-standing feud between the warden of the Scottish Middle March, Sir Walter Scott of Buccleuch, and his enemy Robert Ker of Cessford. In 1596 Scott of Buccleuch enraged the queen by leading a daring raid that freed one of his followers, Kinmont Willie Armstrong, from imprisonment in the royal castle of Carlisle. Elizabeth saw this as an insult to her honor and demanded satisfaction. Not wishing to antagonize the English council, James had already begun to crack down on border crime by compelling the region's lairds to enter into general bands to maintain peace and order. In 1597 he ordered both Scott and Cessford to surrender themselves to English custody and give satisfaction for their offenses. After their release he summoned them to Edinburgh and, in a meeting in his own cabinet, pressured them into ending their feud and becoming friends, in much the way that Sir William Pelham had once tried to end the quarrel between Ormond and Upper Ossory.[10] James's intervention proved more effective than Pelham's, inducing Buccleuch and Cessford to redirect their energies into suppressing crime rather than fighting each other. The extensive networks of local dependents possessed by both men made their efforts effective and the king rewarded both with seats on the Scottish privy council, titles of nobility, as Lord of Buccleuchh and Lord Roxburgh, and grants of land and money.[11]

But elsewhere along the border, especially on the English side, the absence of personal attention by the monarch allowed raiding and feuding to continue unabated. Although they lived on a royal manor, the Grahams and their region had no meaningful ties to the far-away court in London. A shortage of substantial resident gentry in northern Cumberland made it impossible for the crown to find suitable local candidates as sheriffs and justices of the peace, forcing it to rely

---

Suppression of the Scott-Ker Feud," in *James VI and Noble Power in Scotland, 1578–1603*, ed. Miles Kerr-Peterson and Steven J. Reid (London: Routledge, 2017), 98–116; Schultz, *National Identity*, 108–9, 117–26.

[8] Schultz, *National Identity*, 120–1.
[9] Watts and Watts, *From Border to Middle Shire*, 32–6; Schultz, *National Identity*, 21–88.
[10] For the details see Groundwater, "'He Made them Friends'"; for Pelham, above, p. 239.
[11] Ibid., 113, 114. See also Anna Groundwater, "From Whitehall to Jedburgh: Patronage Networks and the Government of the Scottish Borders, 1603 to 1625," *Historical Journal* 53 (2010): 871–93, esp. 883–4.

on lesser gentlemen and absentees.¹² Normal methods of English government therefore proved ineffective. After the retirement of the forceful but notoriously corrupt warden, Sir John Foster, in 1590, the crown turned administration of the district over to men who lived outside it, under the supervision of the fairly distant Council of the North in York. The Grahams and a few other surnames demonstrated the ineffectiveness of these arrangements a few days after James passed into his new kingdom, declaring as he did so that he intended to abolish the frontier and its march laws and convert the whole region into the "middle shires" of a united Britain. They asserted that the laws of England were suspended until the new king reached Westminster and went on a ten-day rampage known as the Busy Week. Pillaging as far south as Penrith, they allegedly killed six men, held fourteen prisoners for ransom, stole 5,000 animals, and inflicted £6,750 in damage, before soldiers sent from Berwick managed to stop them.¹³

After reaching London, James initially attempted to pacify his middle shires by methods similar to those he had already used to settle the Scottish border districts. He delegated responsibility to two large local landowners with ties to his court: his old companion, the treasurer of Scotland George Home, whom he raised to the Scottish peerage as earl of Dunbar and appointed to the English privy council, and another English privy councilor, George Clifford earl of Cumberland. Although Cumberland's estate lay some miles south of the border in Westmoreland, he had ties to gentry further north, and the king tried to strengthen his regional power base by granting him the former Dacre estate on which the Grahams resided. He also appointed Cumberland warden of the west and middle marches, keeper of Carlisle Castle, and Lord Lieutenant of Cumberland, Westmoreland, and Northumberland. The fact that Cumberland's deputy, Richard Musgrave, belonged to an important border surname reinforced his influence. Dunbar also received extensive grants of royal land in Northumberland as well as the Scottish border shires and began to construct a large mansion in Berwick.

In an undated memorandum probably composed in 1604, Cumberland argued that common law methods were unsuited to conditions along the border, where people were "even from their cradles bred up and brought up in thefts, spoils and blood," and loyalties of kinship and neighborhood inhibited jurors from convicting delinquents. "Therefore can it not be hoped for that the same form of government used in all other parts of the realm is or can be holden meet and sufficient for that country," until a thorough reformation of manners was achieved through "fear of severe punishment."¹⁴ He appeared ready to adopt the methods of summary judgment used to deal with common criminals in Scotland and by English captains in Ireland. But despite an energetic start, the display of ferocity soon abated. Although Musgrave arrested 160 reivers following the Busy Week

---

[12] Meikle, *British Frontier?*, 90–5; Watts and Watts, *Border to Middle Shire*, 57–66.
[13] Spence, "Pacification," 91–2.   [14] TNA SP14/6/43.

and Cumberland indicted a further 600 in July 1603, only seven men were actually hanged.[15] Instead of draconian punishment Cumberland soon settled on a policy of negotiating the removal of the Grahams by sending them as colonists to Ireland or conscripts for English forces serving in the Netherlands. Fortunately, the Graham's long lease on their lands had recently expired. This, together with the threat of harsh punishment and the fact that local gentry had been demanding stronger action against them since 1598, gave Cumberland the leverage he needed to force the surname's leaders to agree to the forced removal of most of their followers.[16] Although the Grahams proved poor soldiers and colonists, their deportation did reduce crime.[17]

In 1605, the year of Cumberland's death, James appointed two five-man commissions of *oyer et terminer*, one on each side of the border, both supported by a force of twenty-five horsemen. Two years later he replaced them with another commission dominated by Dunbar, who received an appointment as Lord Lieutenant of Cumberland, Westmoreland, and Northumberland, making him the region's most powerful magnate, following the forfeiture of the estates of the earl of Northumberland after his implication in the Gunpowder Plot.[18] As a privy councilor and confidant of the king, who regularly traveled between the court and Scotland, traversing the middle shires as he did so, Dunbar was a prime example of James's style of personal kingship, carried out through reliance on a trusted agent. But despite his unified command and James's desire to prosecute criminals throughout the region in a uniform way, significant differences between English and Scottish border counties persisted.[19] On the Scottish side crime continued to be dealt with mostly through the hereditary jurisdictions of local landowners, supplemented by the efforts of Dunbar and his deputy, Sir William Cranstoun, who displayed considerably greater zeal than Cumberland and Musgrave in hunting down and executing malefactors. An order of the Scottish council in 1606 approved Cranstoun's practice of "quickly dispatching a great number of notable and notorious thieves and villains by outing them to present death without proceeding to trial of jury or assize," on the grounds that the "prolix forms accustomed in the civil parts of the kingdom" could not be safely used in a region with so many desperate outlaws and so few peace-keepers.[20] But English borderers stubbornly insisted on trying criminals by common law and generally treated them more leniently.

Perhaps partly for this reason, sporadic raiding and other crimes continued to plague districts as far south as Carlisle. Some thieves escaped capture by fleeing to

---

[15] Spence, "Pacification," 98–9.   [16] Ibid., 86–8.   [17] Ibid., 110–13.
[18] Watts and Watts, *Border to Middle Shire*, 138–43.
[19] These differences are especially emphasized by Schultz, *National Identity*.
[20] *The Register of the Privy Council of Scotland*, series 1, vol. 7, ed. David Masson (H. M. General Register House,1906), 7.286.

Ireland, while twenty-three of the deported Grahams had come back by 1618.[21] Nevertheless, conditions did gradually improve. Northern Cumberland slowly grew more civil and the local economy began to prosper as crime abated. The trend benefited the district's gentry, making it easier for the crown to find suitable resident JPs.[22] Even a few Grahams prospered by adapting to the new order. In a nice irony, when Cumberland's indebted heirs sold his border estate in the early 1620s it was purchased by Sir Richard Graham, the son of a notorious reiver and brother of a participant in the Busy Week, who had gone south to London, probably on foot, and entered the service of the duke of Buckingham, with whom he developed a close relationship. Through Buckingham he attracted the attention and favor of both James and Charles, accompanying the prince to Spain in 1623 and winning an appointment as one of his gentlemen of the horse. He seems to have used this post to retain several other Grahams and kinsmen in the royal stables. Through royal favor and Buckingham's largesse he also acquired the wealth to purchase the Cumberland estate. He went on to lead a campaign to restore the fabric of ruined churches in the district, while serving as an MP for Carlisle in 1626 and 1628, a JP, and an active member of a commission charged with suppressing crime in the region.[23]

Contrary to James's wishes, the outcome of attempts to settle the border region therefore effectively reinscribed the different character of English and Scottish governance on the two sides of the former frontier. Northern Cumberland came to resemble more closely the rest of England, as the Graham's kin-based alliance collapsed and governance under resident magistrates grew more effective, while in the Scottish shires the dominant local families maintained their hereditary control over local courts of justice, as they cooperated with Dunbar and Cranstoun. But since James accepted these contrasts because his principal goal of imposing order on the region was being achieved. Administrative uniformity mattered less than practical results.

To the north and west of the Anglo-Scottish border, a second maritime frontier separated Ulster from the Scottish Isles and western Highlands, comprising a region "where the sovereignties of Scotland, England and Ireland had long met and comingled in the Irish sea world."[24] The clans of the Scottish Isles had for centuries furnished mercenaries known as redshanks to warring septs in Ulster.[25] A branch of one Scottish clan, the MacDonnells, had for some time been

---

[21] TNA SP14/97/60 I, report of a commission of 1618 under Lord William Howard and SP14/97/62.
[22] Spence, "Pacification," 145–6.
[23] Ibid., 148; Schultz, *National Identity*, 78–9; R. T. Spence, "The First Sir Richard Graham of Norton Conyers and Netherby, 1583–1653," *Northern History* 16 (1980): 102–29.
[24] Martin MacGregor, "Civilising Gaelic Scotland: The Scottish Isles and the Stewart Empire," in *The Plantation of Ulster: Ideology and Practice*, ed. Éamonn Ó Ciardha and Micheál Ó Siochrú (Manchester: Manchester University Press, 2012), 33–54 at 33.
[25] Ross Crawford, "Noble Power in the West Highlands and Isles: James VI and the End of the Mercenary Trade with Ireland, 1594–96," in *James VI and Noble Power*, ed. Kerr-Peterson and Reid, 117–35, esp. 117–19.

attempting to expand into eastern Ulster under its leader, Sorley Boy. The English and Scottish crowns both had trouble exercising direct control within this zone and therefore preferred to delegate power to local magnates, the Campbell earls of Argyll in Scotland and Hugh O'Neill earl of Tyrone in Ulster. But in the 1590s internal disputes within the Campbell network weakened the young earl of Argyll, while Tyrone launched his great rebellion.

When the MacDonnells and their allies began recruiting a force of 3,000 redshanks to aid Tyrone, Elizabeth wrote to both James and Argyll asking them to stop the levy. Proclaiming his inability to control the inhabitants of the Isles, James delegated the task to Argyll, who in turn passed the responsibility on to one of his followers, Lachlann Mòr MacLean of Duart. A committed Protestant, who had distinguished himself fighting against the earl of Huntly's forces at Glenlivet, MacLean also had a personal grudge against Tyrone, who had murdered one of his cousins. He set about wooing clans in the Isles away from the MacDonnells and managed to ambush and capture 700 redshanks on their way to Ireland. The English navy then trapped another MacDonnell contingent on an island off the Irish coast. Although some of the redshanks did reach Ireland and a few more crossed the frontier in subsequent years, they proved of minimal use to Tyrone. Elizabeth rewarded MacLean by sending him £150 and James also briefly favored him. But the king soon came to distrust MacLean and expressed relief upon hearing the news of his death in a battle against the MacDonnells in 1598. According to the English ambassador, George Nicholson, three considerations explained his displeasure: MacLean's excessive eagerness to pursue Huntly after the battle of Glenlivet; his rumored efforts to involve Argyll in the attempted presbyterian coup following the Tumult; and his willingness to offer his services to Elizabeth, which called his loyalty to the king into question.[26] While momentarily curtailing the redshank problem, MacLean's independence had underlined James's lack of control over his kingdom's western fringe.

He had trouble controlling the Isles because, apart from Argyll, he had few ties to its local rulers, just as Elizabeth's Irish state had few ties to Tyrone's *uiiriaghs* and independent septs in parts of Ulster not under his control. The union of the crowns and Tyrone's capitulation created opportunities to tackle these problems. But through what methods? James continued to deal with both Ulster and western Scotland by delegating responsibility either to old lords whose loyalty he hoped to win, or colonial entrepreneurs seeking to erect what amounted to new lordships, in the expectation that the lords would in return promote civility and allegiance to the crown. He also toyed with uses of violent coercion to deal with especially intractable populations. He had conceived a real animus toward the inhabitants of the Scottish Isles, whom he viewed as "utterly barbarous." In *Basilikon Doron* he

---

[26] This paragraph relies heavily on Crawford, "Noble Power."

advocated "planting colonies among them of answerable inlands subjects that within short time may civilize the best inclined among them." But the island's natives quickly wiped out the colony he tried to plant on Lewis in 1598, increasing his frustration and inducing him to condone harsher methods. In 1608 he asked lord deputy Chichester to gather four or five hundred troops to join an English amphibious force he planned to dispatch, "to perform some service upon the isles of Scotland for the better settling of civility among them" by breeding "terror into the hearts of the rude people."[27]

But James soon found he lacked the resources to subdue Scotland's western frontier and so again delegated the task to Argyll, who was already hereditary sheriff and lieutenant of the Isles as well as the region's most powerful magnate. In 1603 the king brokered a pact between Argyll and Huntly, until this point bitter enemies, and divided authority over the Highlands between them. They combined forces to harry the MacGregors in the North but otherwise kept to their separate spheres. Argyll expanded Campbell power with the king's blessing at the expense of rival clans, especially the MacDonnells, whose hold over the Kintyre peninsula he broke between 1614 and 1617. His growing hegemony was, however, contested by the energetic bishop of the Isles, Andrew Knox, who proposed bringing the region under control through different methods. Knox devised an agreement with the local clan chiefs known as the Statutes of Iona, ratified in 1609. Under its terms, they agreed to send their sons to be educated in the Lowlands, provided for the settlement of Protestant ministers in their territories, and promised to eliminate Gaelic bards. They also promised to compel the "idle" mercenary soldiers traditionally supported by the hospitality of clan leaders to find employment as farmers or laborers, or else depart the region. Knox argued that these measures would increase the profits of the chiefs by freeing them from the need to maintain superfluous followers, while augmenting agricultural productivity, thereby enabling higher rent payments to the crown. He proposed, in short, to tame the Isles through a distinctively Scottish scheme of "improvement," involving preaching, the exposure of clan leaders to the civil culture of Edinburgh, the elimination of traditional military followings, and the development of a profit-oriented economy. But the eruption of a new local war persuaded James to abandon Knox's project and revert to his original solution of allowing the Campbells and another local clan, the MacKenzies, to pacify the Isles by force.

Old and New Lordships in the Integration of the Kingdoms

As in the Borders, James therefore cared more about end results than the means used to achieve them. After failed experiments with a colonial project, a punitive

[27] TNA SP63/223/1.

expedition carried out by the English navy, and a negotiated settlement worked out by one of his bishops, he fell back on the traditional expedient of delegating responsibility to a local magnate. A man of European horizons, the seventh earl of Argyll married an Englishwoman, converted to Catholicism and spent some years on the Continent before retiring to a townhouse in London, whereupon control over his lordship passed to his son, the future Covenanter leader. The Campbells had already introduced written leases on their mainland estates in the sixteenth century and extended the practice to parts of the Isles in the seventeenth. They promoted the building of mills and attempted to reclaim abandoned lands.[28] The MacKenzies were also outward looking and entrepreneurial. After carrying out "a swift and ruthless military conquest" of the Isle of Lewis, they imported English craftsmen to establish a local iron industry and brought in a consortium from Zeeland to establish a fishery.[29] The clan's head, Colin MacKenzie, strengthened his connection to the Edinburgh administration by marrying a daughter of the lord chancellor, the earl of Dunfermline, in 1614, and was rewarded with the title earl of Seaforth in 1623. The redshank bands, who now lacked opportunities in Ireland, soon disappeared. As in Cumberland, an initial attack on disorder by armed force set the stage for schemes of economic improvement, in which the crown played only a very indirect role.

Somewhat similar changes took place elsewhere in the Highlands, as James sanctioned the predatory feuding of a few favored clans by issuing them commissions of fire and sword and titles to disputed lands, while stigmatizing others, like the McLeods of Lewis and the MacGregors, as bandits and barbarians deserving expulsion or eradication.[30] While strengthening the position of favored lineages that often had connections to the Lowlands and the royal court, this policy facilitated the gradual elimination of the system of enforced hospitality that supported the military retinues of clan leaders. As in the Isles, it encouraged a shift toward forms of estate management that increased profits, which had the further effect of connecting formerly isolated regions to national and international markets. The substitution of cash rents for customary payments in kind, along with the mounting debts of Highland lords, as they acquired a taste for luxuries like fine clothing and brandy that they had difficulty affording, added impetus to the trend.[31] Although these changes did not eliminate seigneurial power they did affect its operation.

---

[28] Allan Macinnes, *Clanship, Commerce and the House of Stuart* (East Linton: Tuckwell Press, 1996), 69–70.
[29] John Callow, "Archibald Campbell seventh earl of Argyll (1575/6–1638)," in *ODNB*; MacGregor, "Civilising Gaelic Scotland."
[30] Robert A. Dodgshon, *From Chiefs to Landlords: Social and Economic Change in the Western Highlands and Islands, c. 1493–1820* (Edinburgh: Edinburgh University Press, 1998), 89.
[31] Dodgshon's book, cited in the previous note, systematically examines these changes.

Across the Irish Sea the eastern coast of Ulster was meanwhile being settled and developed by an indebted Rutland gentleman, Sir Edward Cromwell, and three Scots: Hugh Montgomery, Sir James Hamilton, and Sorley Boy's younger son, Randall MacDonnell.[32] The Nine Years War had left the region depopulated and impoverished, compelling some indigenous lords to sell their lands to clear debts. This created opportunities for newcomers prepared to invest in plantations of English and Scottish settlers. James encouraged the process with large grants of land on generous terms, including clauses reducing the power of royal officials to interfere within the new estates.[33] The Irish lord deputy, Sir Arthur Chichester, who had his own ambitions to settle in Ulster, resisted these grants, but some of the grantees, particularly MacDonnell, had ties to the royal court that allowed them to overcome Chichester's objections.[34] Along with title to his estate, James granted MacDonnell the authority to erect a jail, arrest malefactors and regulate alehouses.[35] He and other planters expanded the jurisdiction of their manor courts to deal with most legal issues, so that although assizes did take place in east Ulster their business remained light. Some landlords prevented the king's sheriffs and sub-sheriffs from delivering writs and performing other duties without their permission. MacDonnell allegedly stocked a sub-sheriff for challenging his authority over his tenants. Landlords also resisted interference by the Church of Ireland, helping their tenants avoid payment of tithes. MacDonnell sheltered Catholic priests, promoted Catholic evangelism in the Scottish Isles, and welcomed Scottish Catholics fleeing persecution. Hamilton established presbyterianism on his lands.[36] Between them, they turned eastern Ulster into "a permissive frontier, where religious allegiance, unacceptable to the authorities in the metropolitan area, could be more freely practiced."[37]

MacDonnell refurbished forts, established fairs, and constructed towns that formed "a network of settlements across his estates, centers of trade and small-scale industrial activity."[38] This Catholic Gael and former Tyrone ally thus became another agent of commercial improvement that helped spread "civility." Rewarded in the 1620 with the title of earl of Antrim, he divided his time between Ireland and the royal court during the reign of Charles I, and in 1640 received royal backing to recruit a mainly Catholic army to strike the presbyterian earl of Argyll's forces from the rear.[39] The planting of eastern Ulster had therefore

[32] Raymond Gillespie, *Colonial Ulster: The Settlement of East Ulster* (Cork: Cork University Press, 1985).
[33] Ibid., 47–9.
[34] Ibid., 87–8; Colin Breen, "Randall MacDonnell and Early Seventeenth-Century Settlement in Northeast Ulster," in *The Plantation of Ulster*, ed. Ó Ciardha and Ó Siochrú, 149–51.
[35] Gillespie, *Colonial Ulster*, 106.
[36] Ibid., 88–94; Brian Mac Cuarta, "The Catholic Church in the Ulster Plantation 1609–1642," in *The Plantation of Ulster*, ed. Ó Ciardha and Ó Siochrú, 131.
[37] Mac Cuarta, "Catholic Church in Ulster," 131–2.   [38] Breen, "Randall MacDonnell," 151.
[39] Jane Ohlmeyer, *Civil War and Restoration in the Three Kingdoms: The Career of Randal MacDonnell, Marquis of Antrim* (Cambridge: Cambridge University Press, 1993).

resulted in arrangements more similar to those in many parts of Scotland, where lords exercised extensive legal authority over their territories, than to the English system of government through crown-appointed magistrates. Settlers came mainly from western Scotland, with a smattering from the Borders and a few from other parts of Scotland and England.[40] They included a handful of outlaws fleeing persecution, MacDonnell tenants displaced by the Campbells, and other Scots squeezed off the land by population growth or the conversion of kindly tenures into farms let at market rates.[41] The migration of these settlers anticipated and eventually overlapped with the better-known British plantation of central Ulster after 1608. As in central Ulster, some Irish tenants were allowed to remain on their ancestral lands.

But whether dealing with natives or settlers, landlords resisted granting freeholds or long leases, and some moved their tenants around on their estates, perpetuating the fluidity of traditional Irish tenurial customs. Leases were now enrolled in manor courts as contractual obligations rather than informal arrangements sanctioned by custom, in a concession to the literate ways of a civil society, but their essential character changed little.[42] Although the region's poverty slowed the pace of development, improvements were made and the rental value of estates climbed steeply in the 1610s and 1620s, before declining in the next decade.[43] East Ulster probably had somewhat more than 3,000 new inhabitants by 1614 and perhaps 4,500 planters by 1630, many of whom probably spoke a Gaelic dialect as their native language.[44] The overall picture therefore includes considerable elements of continuity with the past, along with changes carried out almost entirely through private initiative.

Further west in the heartland of Ulster, the crown initially restored most of the powers of the earls of Tyrone and Tyrconnell in exchange for assurances of future loyalty and a few other concessions. But when the earls fled Ireland in 1607, fearing that their continued secret communications with Spain were about to be exposed, they opened the region to the largest new British plantation.[45] As with previous plantation schemes dating back to the mid-Tudor period, the crown attempted to plant a colony of loyal Protestants, prepared to defend the province against future rebellions and to turn wastelands into productive agricultural districts, while founding towns to act as centers of trade and manufacturing.[46] An Irish committee of the English privy council commissioned maps and surveys. It decided to assign about a fifth of the available land to "deserving" Irish and another fifth to English servitors in Ireland, while dividing nearly all the

---

[40] Gillespie, *Colonial Ulster*, 32–3.   [41] Ibid., 35–42.   [42] Ibid., 60.   [43] Ibid., 136–7.
[44] Ibid., 51–6.
[45] J. McCavitt, "The Flight of the Earls, 1607," *Irish Historical Studies* 29 (1994): 159–73.
[46] Phil Withington, "Plantation and Civil Society," in *The Plantation of Ulster*, ed. Ó Ciardha and Ó Siochrú, 55–77.

remainder evenly between English and Scottish undertakers.[47] While allowing the remaining Irish landowners to keep Irish tenants, the crown initially required British undertakers to settle English and Scottish tenants on their estates, with fixed quotas of freeholders and leaseholders. It assigned the district around the decayed settlement of Derry, which had its origin as an English garrison during the Nine Years War, to the London livery companies, which had to be pressured into accepting the project and finding the £60,000 needed for its implementation.[48] The government intended to make the largest and wealthiest city in Britain responsible for developing two Ulster towns, Derry (or Londonderry) and Coleraine.

Although the plantation did attract about 12,000 British settlers by the early 1620s, in many respects it fell short of expectations.[49] Most settlers remained clustered around Derry and Coleraine, leaving large parts of Ulster occupied almost entirely by Irish. The requirement for British undertakers to settle English or Scots on their lands soon required modification. We find a broadly similar picture in the rest of Ireland, especially in the earlier years of James's reign, with several Gaelic and Old English lordships persisting alongside newly erected structures of seigneurial power by English *parvenus*, along with a patchwork of new plantations. Investigations into defective titles to land held by Irish proprietors and confiscations following minor Gaelic uprisings cleared lands for new settlements. After the death of the tenth earl in 1614, the earldom of Ormond was sequestered and lesser landowners in Kilkenny threatened with enquiries into their titles. The authorities appropriated about a third of the land in County Kilkenny and transported opponents of further plantation in Wexford to Virginia.[50] In 1617 the state seized the territory of the O'Brennans and, over the next few years, parceled it out to English newcomers.[51] Captains of disbanded companies found employment as commanders of the wards and garrisons erected by Chichester, while soldiers and former soldiers collected taxes and performed other routine administrative duties.[52]

Nicholas Canny has persuasively argued that the eventual success or failure of the resulting settlements depended primarily on the presence or absence of urban centers. Where towns had previously existed or were newly established they

---

[47] Editors' "Introduction," 8–9, and Raymond Gillespie, "Success and Failure in the Ulster Plantation," in *The Plantation of Ulster*, ed. Ó Ciardha and Ó Siochrú, 98–118 at 106–7. The editors state that undertakers were allotted 30 percent of the land, while Gillespie claims that English and Scottish undertakers were assigned 18 percent each.

[48] Ian Archer, "The City of London and the Ulster Plantation," in *The Plantation of Ulster*, ed. Ó Ciardha and Ó Siochrú, 78–97. For the decayed condition of Derry on the eve of plantation see *CSPI JI*, 1.451–2.

[49] Nicholas Canny, *Making Ireland British* (Oxford: Oxford University Press, 2001), 211.

[50] Ibid., 282.

[51] David Edwards, *The Ormond Lordship in County Kilkenny: The Rise and Fall of Butler Feudal Power, 1515–1642* (Dublin: Four Courts Press, 2003), 273–8.

[52] Canny, *Making Ireland British*, 303–5.

provided a pool of investment capital for colonizing settlement, as merchants and tradesmen bought and improved land in adjoining districts, either as investments managed by professional agents or as a way of turning themselves into country gentry or yeomen. As in Scotland, heavy debts contracted by indigenous landowners in an increasingly monetized economy fed a lively land market. This pattern was found not only in parts of Ulster adjacent to new or newly developed towns like Derry, Stewartstown, Strabane, Dungannon, and Lurgan but also on the estates of the earl of Cork, the Irish Protestant earl of Thomond, and the Old English Catholic earl of Clanricard, all three of whom recruited skilled Protestant immigrants to towns on or near their lands. As in the Scottish Isles and Highlands, some enterprising nobles promoted and benefited from economic and commercial development, while other lords failed to adapt and fell victim to heavy debts or the crown's hostile attentions. On the other hand, several plantations by politically well-connected investors collapsed because they did not attract enough tenants and investors.[53] Plantations created pockets of New English and Scottish settlement in a few districts but still left Ireland's natives in control of most of the island.

The conventional view that Tyrone's defeat in 1603 and flight four years later marked the end of the old Irish social and political order therefore needs qualification.[54] At least in the short run, what took place was less a wholesale replacement of Irish lordship than a more complex process of adaptation, in which both Gaelic and Old Irish dynasties and English and Scottish newcomers all participated. Although outcomes depended on a host of particular circumstances, the success or failure of a lord or a group of smaller proprietors in taking advantage of commercial opportunities usually proved crucial. But commercial enterprise did not necessarily spell the end of traditional Irish patterns of land-use, kin-based alliances, strong seigneurial control over local populations, or Gaelic customs like patronage of bards. Whether of Irish, Old English, or New English extraction, successful lords in Ireland increasingly tended to combine practices of commercial improvement with more traditional ways of maintaining power through kinship alliances and brute force, supplemented in some cases with grants of authority obtained through connections to the royal court.

The earldom of Ormond, discussed in an earlier chapter, provides one illustration. Despite the developed commercial economy of its core territories around Kilkenny, David Edwards concludes that "the power of the Ormond dynasty was essentially local and personalised," dependent on marriage alliances, favorable leasing arrangements, and negotiated agreements between the earl and a large collection of allies.[55] The tenth earl had extended his territory with crown grants, secured through his personal relationship with the queen, in much the way that the earl of Huntly benefited from his relationship with James VI.[56] The erosion of

---

[53] Ibid., 327–34.   [54] Edwards, *Ormond Lordship*, 263–82.
[55] Ibid., 74; see above, p. 236.   [56] Ibid., 98–100.

these ties to the court contributed significantly to the Butler dynasty's decline in the seventeenth century. Although he lacked close personal ties to the queen, Hugh O'Neill had also benefited both from Elizabeth's favor and a degree of agricultural and commercial development in his territory, which allowed him to generate a cash income from the export of agricultural products.[57] To a degree he therefore acted as an "improving" lord, even while remaining a traditional sept leader. Richard Boyle earl of Cork provides a third example of this eclectic pattern. In some ways the quintessential New English entrepreneurial planter, who gradually amassed a commercially oriented estate of more than 100,000 acres across six counties in Munster, along with additional lands in Connacht and Leinster,[58] he nevertheless relied heavily on the cultivation of kinship alliances to establish himself in Ireland.[59] By settling former soldiers on his lands he provided himself with military muscle.[60] He patronized Irish bards and musicians, had his children learn Irish, and took a strong interest in Irish culture and genealogy. In 1629 he purchased the wardship of the earl of Kildare, whom he married to his daughter. He then redeemed leases on Kildare lands and refurbished the main Kildare seat at Maynooth. He had earlier married another daughter into the English Digby family, which had a residual claim to the Kildare title if the main line died out. In this way he sought to assure an alliance between his heirs and both major branches of the Kildare Fitzgeralds, once the greatest Old English dynasty in Ireland.[61] Ormond, O'Neill, and Boyle differed from each other in any number of ways, but all had learned to adapt to a world where commercial enterprise and relations with the royal court had become essential to survival, but in which local Irish customs and kin networks still remained crucial.

Noble prestige and power not only survived but prospered in Jacobean Ireland, incorporating as it did so New English *parvenus* alongside ancient Irish and Old English lineages, as Jane Ohlmeyer has emphasized.[62] The Irish peerage expanded from twenty to seventy members over the course of the reign. James attempted to use the nobility to assist the Dublin administration in governing the island, appointing over 50 peers as regional governors or administrators, if we include old servitors with newly acquired titles. As in Scotland, the crown played favorites, undermining septs and sept leaders it considered disloyal, while strengthening the power of other lineages, such as the O'Brien earls of Thomond and MacWilliam

[57] Hiram Morgan, *Tyrone's Rebellion: The Outbreak of the Nine Years War in Ireland* (Woodbridge: Boydell Press, 1999), 14; James O'Neill, *The Nine Years War, 1593–1603* (Dublin: Four Courts Press, 2017), 109–16.
[58] David Heffernan, "Reconstructing the Estate of Richard Boyle, First Earl of Cork," *History Ireland* 23 (2015): 18–20.
[59] Discussed above, p. 231.
[60] For the kinship connections see above, p. 231 and Michael MacCarthy-Morrogh, *The Munster Plantation: English Migration to Southern Ireland 1583–1641* (Oxford: Clarendon Press, 1986), 147–51.
[61] Ibid., 159–62.
[62] Jane Ohlmeyer, *Making Ireland English: The Irish Aristocracy in the Seventeenth Century* (Oxford: Oxford University Press, 2012).

Burke lords of Clanricard, with grants of regional office and other benefits. In some cases, the king sanctioned the right of a dominant sept leader to collect tribute from smaller septs in his territory, although these payments were euphemistically called rents and defined as a form of legal tenancy rather than customary Gaelic tribute.[63] James succeeded in drawing several Irish nobles into the orbit of his court in London. Ohlmeyer comments that he attempted, with partial success, to promote a "cultural transformation of the titled nobility from a noble elite that drew its status primarily from blood, lineage and standing within a community to one determined by royal status and a title held from the king." But this was necessarily a protracted and uneven process. Since about a third of Irish peers eventually married wives from English landed families, while within Ireland marriages between Protestants and Catholics, as well as Old English, Irish, and New English noble families also became relatively common, old ethnic and religious divisions were being eroded at the top of society.[64] Some individual lords were broken, but lordship remained deeply embedded in the foundations of the new political order as an intermediate layer of power and agent of socio-economic change.

Crown Officials, the Old English, and the Contested Role of the Common Law in Ireland

Nevertheless, James's willingness to delegate control to Irish lords remained in tension with the desire of some New English officials to impose more direct state control in imitation of English methods of governance. This impulse had diverse and, to a degree, even contradictory roots. It harked back to justifications for the original English medieval occupation of Ireland as a civilizing mission, and even more to the reform proposals of early Tudor humanists in the Pale described in a previous chapter. But as we have seen, the status of the law had already become contested in the Elizabethan period, as lord deputies like Sidney quarreled with Old English lawyers over the cess and other issues. The rise of a servitor interest of former soldiers and state servants who had settled in Ireland and looked to the Dublin government to provide them with estates or salaried positions added another layer to this old dispute. In the early seventeenth century, the servitors' viewpoint was well-represented at the heart of the Dublin administration by two old soldiers who served as successive lord deputies: Sir Arthur Chichester (1605–15) and Oliver St John viscount Grandison (1616–22). Chichester and

---

[63] Mary O'Dowd, "Land and Lordship in Sixteenth- and Early Seventeenth-Century Ireland," in *Economy and Society in Scotland and Ireland, 1500–1939*, ed. Rosalind Mitchison and Peter Roebuck (Edinburgh: John Donald, 1988), 18.

[64] Ohlmeyer, *Making Ireland English*, esp. 64 (quotation), 184–7, 214, 219–23.

the energetic Irish solicitor general, Sir John Davys, who had arrived from England in 1603, saw the common law as a tool for strengthening prerogative rule and imposing Anglicizing reforms on Irish society. Ireland "is not to be ruled by grammar rules nor moral philosophy nor by the examples of the Romans and Grecians," Davys told Robert Cecil, "but by that policy and those laws which have made England one of the best commonwealths in Christendom."[65] He saw the law as an authoritative instrument, through which the state might compel conformity to the official church, extend its control over the entire island, and transform the rude Irish into a civil people.

This view clashed with that of the Old English commonwealthmen, whose determination to defend their liberties through the law remained as strong as ever. Irish common law differed in detail from English law because English statutes did not apply to Ireland, whereas those passed by Irish parliaments did. The Old English also regarded local privileges, enshrined in custom or documents like town charters, as part of their common law heritage. But the basic maxims and procedures of the law were very similar in both kingdoms and the continuing attendance of Old English gentlemen at the Inns of Court in London kept Irish lawyers abreast of recent developments in English legal culture.[66] Lawyers in the Pale and some Irish towns possessed all the intellectual equipment and social confidence needed to mount a defense of their community's interests by fashioning a "rhetoric of counsel" rooted in common law principles.[67] They continued to dispatch representatives to the English court armed with petitions voicing their grievances, who cited precedents and law maxims, while claiming to be loyal subjects informing the king of abuses that risked provoking new rebellions.[68]

In Ireland the common law therefore served simultaneously as the instrument of an aggressive New English state and a language of complaint and resistance against that state's proceedings. This resistance offers parallels to the efforts of English lawyers like Coke to restrain the growth of prerogative powers exercised by officials like deputy lieutenants and royal purveyors.[69] But since the Pale and Irish towns suffered from much higher levels of taxation, abuses by lawless soldiers, and bullying attempts to impose religious conformity, lawyers in Ireland had many more grievances to protest against. Their complaints tended to have an even sharper edge than those of English lawyers and provoked

---

[65] TNA SP63/217, fol. 11, Davys to Cecil, February 24, 1605.
[66] For a summary see Jon G. Crawford, *A Star Chamber Court in Ireland: The Court of Castle Chamber, 1571–1641* (Dublin: Four Courts Press, 2005), 27–31.
[67] Valerie McGowan-Doyle, "Elizabeth I, the Old English, and the Rhetoric of Counsel," in *Elizabeth I and Ireland*, ed. Brendan Kane and Valerie McGowan-Doyle (Cambridge: Cambridge University Press, 2014), 178–9.
[68] For an example see BL Add Mss. 4757, fol. 63, a letter of 1600 from the privy council to the lord deputy and council of Ireland, directing them to give a sympathetic hearing to Lord Hoath and Sir Patrick Barnewall, who were returning after laying their complaints before the English government.
[69] Above, pp. 467–70.

reactions from Irish officials similar to James's exasperated comments about jurists like Coke. Lord Deputy Montjoy described one lawyer as "the veriest kindle-fire and rebellious-spirited man that ever I did hear speak."[70]

We have noticed how in 1600 towns in Munster began electing lawyers to municipal office, many of whom had friendly relations with Jesuits and Catholic priests.[71] Shortly after Elizabeth's death and Tyrone's surrender, a wave of Catholic protests led by clergymen and lawyers erupted across Munster. The magistrates of Cork and a crowd in Waterford resisted the proclamation of James I, in the former case citing the town corporation's jurisdictional privileges in justification.[72] In Waterford "Dr. White made a public sermon that now they might thank God that every man might fully enjoy the fruit of his vineyard and sit under his own olive, whereas before all things were extorted from them by the rapine of the soldiers...for Queen Jezabel is dead."[73] Friars in both towns, "assisted by some disorderly people and not resisted by the magistrates," took possession of churches and openly celebrated the mass.[74] Waterford commemorated Good Friday with a procession of flagellants proceeded by a cross, which spectators were compelled to reverence. The protest soon spread to Kilkenny, Wexford, and parts of Leinster. Richard Boyle reported that the towns' actions inspired efforts in neighboring rural parishes "to stand for the liberty of their consciences."[75] Mountjoy claimed to have credible information that the towns had "made a combination for perseverance and joining together to make good what they have done for the public profession of their religion and that some of them are so bold as to speak of the title of the Infanta."[76] When challenged by the Dublin authorities, the sovereign of Wexford and mayor of Waterford both pleaded that Catholicism had enjoyed *de facto* toleration in their towns for some time and that the people expected James to accord them the same favor, especially since, the sovereign of Wexford added, "his Majesty is thought by the common judgment of all men here few excepted to be Catholic."[77] The magistrates stressed their citizens' ancient allegiance to the crown, as descendants of the original Anglo-Norman conquerors, but protested against religious coercion, especially during the transition between two reigns.[78] In Kilkenny the people "thought it not against the law to profess their religion publicly till the king's coronation and his pleasure to restrain them should be signified by some public edict."[79]

According to Mountjoy, townsmen in Cork imprisoned crown officers, while its mayor and recorder attended a sermon by a friar "who openly preached that the king's majesty is not a lawful king until the pope hath confirmed him."[80] The inhabitants strengthened their bargaining position by making off with the doors

---

[70] Crawford, *Star Chamber in Ireland*, 282.
[71] Above, p. 268; Crawford, *Star Chamber in Ireland*, 285.   [72] LPL 619, fols 167–9.
[73] Ibid., fol. 619.   [74] TNA SP63/215/33, Mountjoy to Robert Cecil, April 19, 1603.
[75] TNA SP63/215/36.   [76] TNA SP63/215/40.   [77] TNA SP63/215/40 II and III.
[78] TNA SP63/215/52.   [79] TNA SP63/215/52.   [80] TNA SP63/215/47.

and ammunition magazine of the nearby fort of Halebowling, denying provisions to its garrison and appropriating two cannon, which they set on their walls.[81] They imprisoned the chief victualer of Munster and disarmed other English within the town.[82] When Mountjoy dispatched a force under Sir Charles Wilmot to bring Cork to heal, the townsmen resisted, shooting the cannon at his forces and sending out letters "to all the noblemen and chieftains of the countries to rise in arms."[83] The conflict soon devolved into

> open war of all sides, the townsmen barricading up their gates, breaking down the top of the south gate, and by the help of an Englishman at arms mounted a demi-culverin upon it, shot both with great and small shot both at the bishop's court (where the commissioners then lay) and at Standon Castle... Neither were our men idle with them but got into the highest towers and steeples thereabouts, which looked into the town, and would now and then with their small shots fetch off a man and lay him dead... Neither did the townsmen spare (having the king's store of arms and munitions in their hands) to furnish all that wanted with powder, shot, muskets, calivers, pikes or anything else they wanted, also to make barricades in the streets for the safety of their men, with planks, deals or anything else the store afforded.[84]

The inhabitants excused their behavior by claiming they feared that Wilmot's ethnically Irish soldiers would sack the town and "dispose the townsmen's wives and goods at their pleasures."[85] As civil English inhabitants of Ireland they had the right to defend themselves against barbarous natives, including those who served in the king's army.

Mountjoy wanted to punish this defiance but complained that "the town is strong enough but against artillery and all the king's artillery and munitions almost of Ireland is in that town."[86] On May 10, more than six weeks after the mutiny began, he finally assembled enough troops and artillery pieces to compel its submission. The citizens tacitly protested by entertaining him with "a dumb show of plough irons and having on both sides of the street from the port to his lordship's lodging, intimating how by that the soldiers by their extortions and rapines had wasted the country, making all those ploughs to be idle which should have sustained their country."[87] Two days later Mountjoy presided over a trial in which a schoolmaster who had maintained the Spanish Infanta's right to inherit the crown and a tradesman were condemned to death.[88] He allowed the town's mayor and magistrates to escape serious punishment but sharply upbraided them, inducing the recorder to fall on his knees and plea for mercy.[89] Waterford also

---

[81] TNA SP63/215/36 and 48.   [82] LPL 619, fol. 169v.   [83] TNA SP63/215/55.
[84] LPL 619, fol. 171r.   [85] TNA SP63/215/55; *CSPI JI* 1.55–6.   [86] TNA SP63/215/48.
[87] LPL 619, fol. 172v.   [88] Ibid., fol. 173r–v.   [89] Ibid.

manned its walls after a local Jesuit persuaded its citizens to take an oath "that they should be true to the pope and maintain the Roman religion with their goods and their lives."[90] When Mountjoy arrived with a body of troops, a delegation demanded that he not enter the town with more soldiers than the mayor would permit, citing a charter issued by King John as justification for their right to do so.[91]

This resistance fanned the resentment of English captains and officials who knew that merchants in towns including Limerick, Waterford, and Cork had sold arms and other supplies to Tyrone's forces, and that nominally loyal districts of the Pale and Munster had failed to resist raids by rebel Irish forces.[92] Although the authorities in Dublin and other towns of the Pale did not attempt to seize churches and erect the mass by physical force in the manner of Cork, Waterford, and Kilkenny, they did engage in non-violent demonstrations demanding religious toleration. Here, even more than in Munster, priests and lawyers cooperated in fomenting and organizing protests that drew together religious and secular grievances. In June the bishops of Dublin and Meath wrote to the king, arguing that the current agitation for toleration stemmed from the long-standing disaffection of most of the Pale's inhabitants to the existing state, nourished by priests, Jesuits, and lawyers. Without ever erupting into open rebellion this discontent had produced tacit collusion with Tyrone's forces and efforts to sabotage the government's war efforts, in which "certain solicitors" had played a prominent role. Possessing "some superficial skill in the laws of the realms," they "would still apply themselves by misinterpretations, by strained restrictions and by casting doubts of many inconveniences and dangers that might follow the admitting of any new precedent to cross and overthrow whatsoever proceeded from the State." In addition to a few violent outrages, this malevolent attitude had now moved some of "the more wily and therefore more dangerous" leaders of the Old English community to draw "themselves into diverse public assemblies and consultations," where "certain selected solicitors and suitors" were chosen to travel to the court in London and petition James for liberty of conscience.[93] The lord deputy and council of Ireland soon seconded this complaint. Catholic "insolence" had "its original proceeding from the Jesuits, friars and massing priests who instill the poison into the hearts of the people" but was also "strongly supported and born up by some lawyers practices at the bar and some offices of the King's Majesty in his several courts," encouraging "all the chief leading men to countenance the contempt of the gospel."[94]

In addition to religious grievances, the populations of the Pale and Munster suffered from high taxes, the effects of harvest failures and a debasement of the

---

[90] TNA SP63/215/47.   [91] Ibid.
[92] For trade see above, p. 268, and the persuasive argument in O'Neill, *Nine Years War*. But cf. the qualifications of Ruth Canning, *The Old English in Early Modern Ireland: The Palesmen and the Nine Years' War, 1594–1603* (Woodbridge: Boydell, 2019).
[93] TNA SP63/215/68.   [94] TNA SP63/215/77.

Irish currency that had driven up prices and seriously disrupted trade. Material hardships must have created fertile ground for priests and friars seeking to blame Ireland's problems on heresy and heretical New English captains and officials. The restoration of ancient churches and holy sites to Catholic use and the defense of local autonomy and customary legal rights became complementary ways of protesting the perceived assault on the Pale community and its traditions by an oppressive state. But from the perspective of men like Chichester and Davys, the protests revealed a pervasive disloyalty that might well lead to renewed rebellion if not severely suppressed. Even in times of peace, they contended, Catholic resistance compounded the difficulty of rooting out entrenched forms of corruption that drained crown resources while obstructing effective governance. Chichester compared Ireland to "Pharaoh's lean oxen" that consumed "the fat of his Majesty's other kingdoms and is ever lean itself." He thought the only remedy lay in a general reformation imposed by the strong hand of a powerful governor, prepared to use as much force as necessary to ensure obedience to the king's laws and "good orders."[95] This emphasis on fundamental reform imposed by force echoed the advice of previous lord deputies going back to Sidney, and of New English writers like Richard Becon and Edmund Spenser.[96]

But unlike Spenser, who believed the common law unsuited to Ireland, Chichester and Davys wanted to use it as their primary instrument of reform. Davys shared Coke's view that the common law antedated the Norman Conquest, as a system so exquisitely "framed and fitted to the nature and disposition" of the English people that it was "co-natural to the nation."[97] He attributed England's failure to subdue Ireland after the medieval conquest to the fact that Henry II and his successors never imposed English law throughout the island. Because the native Irish lived for centuries beyond the law's protection, "so as every Englishman might oppress, spoil and kill them without controlment," they remained "outlaws and enemies to the crown of England."[98] Irish custom perpetuated "barbarism" by giving the "chieftains of every country" the right to redistribute lands in each generation, while rendering the succession of chiefs unstable through the practice of tanistry. Irish tenants had no incentive "to build

---

[95] *CSPI JI* 1.149, Chichester to Cecil, March 22, 1604.

[96] Nicholas Canny, *The Elizabethan Conquest of Ireland: A Pattern Established, 1567-76* (Hassocks: Harvester, 1976); Canny, *Making Ireland British*, chapter 1; Richard Becon, *Solon his Follie, or, A Politique Discourse Touching the Reformation of the Common-weales Conquered, Declined and Corrupted*, ed. Clare Carrol and Vincent Carey (Binghamton, NY: Medieval and Renaissance Texts and Studies, 1996); Edmund Spenser, *A view of the state of Ireland, written dialogue-wise betweene Eudoxus and Irenaeus, in the year 1596* (Dublin, 1633); David Edwards, "Ideology and Experience: Spenser's *View* and Martial Law in Ireland," in *Political Ideology in Ireland, 1541-1641*, ed. Hiram Morgan (Dublin: Four Courts Press, 1999), 127-57.

[97] Sir John Davys, *Le primer report des cases & matters en ley* (Dublin, 1615), sig. 2v; Sir John Davys, *A discoverie of the state of Ireland with the true causes why that kingdom was never entirely subdued* (1613), 127.

[98] Davys, *Discoverie*, 116-17.

and to plant and to improve their lands," since they had no guarantee that their posterity would inherit them. The chieftains' total power over the land allowed them to force the peasantry to serve in rebellions against the crown, as had happened in past centuries in England, when "such tenants at will did enable the earl of Warwick in the time of Henry VI and the great lords in the time of the Barons' Wars to raise a great multitude of men." In England the crown had solved the problem by extending the protection of its courts to manorial tenants against oppression by their landlords. "At this day if any of your great lords of England should have a mind to stand upon their guard, well may they have some of their household servants or retainers and some few light brained factions gentlemen to follow them," but tenants who enjoy long leases or copyholds protected by the law will not risk "the undoing of themselves, their wives and children for...the best landlord that is in England."[99] The failure to establish similar legal protections in Ireland perpetuated the tyrannical and violent rule of overmighty subjects.

Having failed to break the power of indigenous chieftains, Davys argued, medieval kings delegated the task of keeping the native Irish at bay to English lords, whose descendants married Irish wives, settled Irish tenants on their lands, and subjected their remaining English tenants to the same tyrannical practices that Irish lords had always employed. In saying this he implicitly criticized not just past practice but the reliance on private undertakers that continued to characterize James's approach to the pacification of provinces like Ulster. The English colonists "became degenerate and mere Irish in their language, in their apparel, in their arms and manner of fight and all other customs."[100] Even in the late queen's reign, lord deputies "who went about to reform the civil affairs of Ireland," such as "the earl of Sussex, Sir Henry Sidney and Sir John Perrot," behaved like ancient kings of Israel who "did not cut down the groves and high places but suffered the people still to burn incense and commit idolatry." In other words, they allowed "the people to worship their barbarous lords and to remain weakly ignorant of their duties to God and the king."[101]

The solution to these problems, Davys insisted, lay in eliminating any particular jurisdictions and seigniorial powers that might interfere with direct government by the crown and its officers, disarming the Irish commoners who furnished lords with their private armies, and erecting a uniform system of common law administration.[102] These measures would finally complete the civilizing English conquest of Ireland, left in abeyance since the twelfth century, while achieving "a perfect union between the [English and Irish] nations." "For the conquest is never perfect till the war be at an end; and the war is not at an end till there be peace and unity; and there can never be unity and concord in any kingdom, but where there is but one king, one allegiance and one law."[103] Davys therefore agreed

---

[99] TNA SP63/215, fol. 13, Davys to Cecil, April 19, 1604. [100] Davys, *Discoverie*, 29–30.
[101] Ibid., 258–9. [102] TNA SP63/216, fol. 13. [103] Davys, *Discoverie*, 120.

with Bacon in thinking that a full and durable union required uniform laws and institutions. But he also shared the belief of men like Becon and Spenser that Ireland required exceptionally strong measures to impose that uniformity. "The people of this island," he observed to Cecil, "if they suffer injustice either in deed or but in their own opinion, resort presently to the sword, to right themselves, being impatient of the delays that are found in the ordinary process of law."[104] The state had to compel them to relinquish this impatient propensity to violent self-help and engage instead in litigation in the king's courts.

Davys regarded the holding of regular assizes in all parts of Ireland as the single most important means of accomplishing this goal. He made extravagant claims for the civilizing effects of assizes, claiming they had "reclaimed the Irish from their wildness, caused them to cut off their gibbs and long hair, to convert their mantles into cloaks [and] to conform themselves to the manner of England in all their behavior and outward forms. And because they find a great disadvantage in moving their suits by an interpreter, they do for the most part send their children to schools especially to learn the English language, so as we may hope that the next generation will in tongue and heart and every way become English."[105] More than simply a procedure for holding criminal trials, he regarded an assize as a potent tool for uprooting barbarism and inculcating English civility.

Although exaggerated, these views had some substance. As they penetrated into more remote regions, assizes established points of contact between the Irish state and local communities, where in some cases people had rarely, if ever, encountered government officials.[106] This had once also been true in England, before the establishment of regular communication between JPs and the privy council, and the more frequent resort of landowners to the royal court diminished the importance of reports brought back by judges from their circuits. An English assize remained an important social occasion and an opportunity for ritualized displays of crown authority and judicial harangues. But its business had largely become routine, carried out collaboratively by royal judges, county magistrates familiar with the relevant legal rules and procedures, and jurors who also generally knew how the law worked. By contrast, in parts of Ireland assizes had been rare or non-existent before the seventeenth century, county magistracies were being established for the first time, and local people asked to resolve disputes and report criminal behavior through unfamiliar legal procedures rather than in accordance with Irish customs. An assize therefore had an educative as well as a judicial function. As Davys put it, in England "the government is so well established that

---

[104] TNA SP63/215, fol. 114. [105] Davys, *Discoverie*, 271.
[106] See, e.g., the comments of Chief Baron Humphrey Winche to Salisbury in 1608 (TNA SP63/223/33): "the employment of fit men in circuits are a great service for the well establishment of justice in expelling barbarism from the mean sort of people, restraining oppression in the mightier, instructing of justices and sheriffs in their manner of government, reproving the negligent and cherishing the diligent."

things do themselves in a manner, but here a disorderly people is to be drawn to obedience by the wisdom and discretion of the magistrate."[107]

By demonstrating the state's determination to enforce its will through regular processes, in places where government interventions had previously been sporadic, inconsistent, and capricious, an assize invited the native population to enter into collaborative relationships with the king's judges. Especially in its early modern form, the common law functioned as a participatory system that depended on jurors of trial and presentment, witnesses and private suits and prosecutions in order to operate. The success or failure of efforts to reform Ireland would depend in no small measure on whether Irish people proved willing to perform these functions, instead of continuing to rely on traditional forms of mediation by brehons and self-help. In 1606 Davys commented that in Waterford and Wexford, which had long lived under the common law, assizes went smoothly, although even here he was encouraged that more than twenty land disputes among Irish speaking inhabitants were brought before the judges for resolution. "We were glad to see them relinquish the trial of the sword and judgment of their barbarous brehons and so willingly descend to the trial of the common law." "But in the County of Wicklow, containing all the wild and mountainous country of the Birnes and Tooles (which was never reduced into shire ground until the last year but the inhabitants thereof, even at the elbow of the state, were suffered to live like outlaws)... the very appearance" of the inhabitants before the king's judges signified meaningful progress.[108] It showed, Davys claimed, the readiness of "rude" people to free themselves from the "barbarous customs" and tyranny under which they had always lived, in exchange for the "extraordinary liberty and protection" afforded by English justice. The fact that the chief inhabitants attended "in English apparel, which they had never before worn" struck him as another sign of their "inclination to civility" that augured well for the future.[109] In County Clare, where assizes had taken place sporadically in the late sixteenth century, people dressed in Irish garb appeared before the judges but in some cases "spoke good English and understood the course of our proceedings well."[110]

Although we should take these reports with a dose of salt, many Irish do seem to have welcomed the assistance of royal judges in settling property disputes and providing redress against thefts, cattle raids, and other crimes. In parts of the Wicklow Mountains, assizes filled a vacuum created by the destruction of local septs that had previously kept order; in other places, including Ulster, they offered an alternative to the rule of old lords like Hugh O'Neill and new ones like Randall MacDonnell. To be credible in this role the judges had to show that the state possessed sufficient power to enforce court decisions. This was not always easy.

---

[107] TNA SP63/216, fol. 9.   [108] TNA SP63/219/132.   [109] Ibid.
[110] TNA SP63/218, fol. 53.

Davys commented in 1604 that Chichester had sent soldiers to apprehend a band of about eighty or a hundred kern under the command of a certain Edward McBrian that had spoiled parts of Carlow and Wexford: "but they will as soon take them as a hare with a tabor, for they have already scattered themselves, and are fled into the Butler's country and into Munster; but the soldiers shall be no sooner retired than they will return with a greater number." "The insolency of those mountain kerns," he continued, "has ever bred in the Irishry a scorn and contempt of the English government; for they think it an easy matter to make a head... when they perceive that, under the eye or nose of the state, a rabble of rude churls do continually affront and condemn the public justice."[111] Chichester had to deal with another outbreak of disorder in Down and Antrim by a band of about sixty to eighty men under a Scottish Gael named Gillespie McAlexander. He subdued them through a punitive expedition on which he hanged about forty offenders, in cooperation with "the earl of Tyrone [who] hath done the like with those upon his borders, not sparing his own nephew."[112] When Chichester accompanied a judicial commission to the region in 1606, he took along an escort of about 150 foot and fifty or sixty horsemen to show he meant business.[113]

But even if it did not by itself eliminate banditry, an assize often helped identify not only the bandits but local landowners who had not done enough to stop them. "If Donald Spanaigh would but deserve his pardon that he hath of the king," Davys wrote about the situation in Wexford, "or if the sons of Feagh McHugh would do a service for their several pardons... the gentlemen that are honest subjects of that country declared that they could bring in their [outlaw's] heads or their bodies at their pleasure."[114] In addition to trying crimes, assizes initiated processes of negotiation and pressure to persuade Irish lords and gentry to cooperate in the suppression of cattle raiding and spoiling, in much the way that James had pressured Sir Water Scott of Buccleugh and Robert Ker to crack down on reiving. If this method failed to work, the state might unleash harsh military justice. To settle the North, Chichester advocated the appointment of provost marshals to cut off "kern straggling here and there to do mischief."[115] He wanted a general muster followed by the confiscation of private arms and a statute making the possession of guns or pikes a capital offense. "The king of Spain holds this course with nations that are more civil and less mutinous than this."[116] Once the propensity toward violence had been broken, he expected the Irish to avail themselves of common law remedies. After accompanying another Wexford assize in 1606, he triumphantly reported receiving "at least 300" petitions and twenty suits over titles of land, "the mere Irish being parties in most of these trials."[117]

---

[111] TNA SP63/216/15.   [112] TNA SP63/216/15 and 26.
[113] *Collectanea de rebus Hibernicus*, ed. Charles Vallency, vol. 1 (Dublin, 1786), 143.   [114] Ibid.
[115] TNA SP63/218 fols 57, 65.   [116] *CSPI JI* 1.146.   [117] TNA SP63/219, fol. 132.

In addition to asserting state authority, assizes allowed Irish officials to gather detailed information by questioning local people.[118] They therefore served administrative and intelligence-gathering purposes, in addition to their judicial functions. On his way to Ulster in 1606, Chichester paused in an open field outside the settlement of Mellifont where, after receiving petitions, he interrogated inhabitants about landownership in the region and impaneled a jury to report on conditions in the church, including the patrons and incumbents of each parish, the condition of the fabric of church buildings, and the value of each living.[119] In Fermanagh in County Tyrone, Davys compiled a list of some 200 freeholders worth 40s or more, again on the basis of local testimony. He then summoned the more prominent freeholders and "told them he came of purpose to understand the estate of every particular man in that country, to the end to establish and settle the same according to His Majesty's directions out of England."[120] In ways like this, assizes furnished state officials with a level of specific knowledge they could obtain only by venturing far into the countryside and receiving testimony on oath. Chichester took advantage of his travels on judicial circuits to inspect fortifications and identify places of strategic importance that required state attention. In 1605 he allotted 300 acres to endow a fort near Dungannon, and identified a largely uninhabited district infested with outlaws located along the usual route between Derry and the Pale. He recommended settling an English servitor with twenty foot soldiers and six horsemen—perhaps a certain Captain Leigh who was already living nearby, he suggested—to secure the district, and identified a number of other places near transportation routes requiring similar action.[121] Circuits were also used to establish local officials, including sheriffs, JPs, coroners, and constables, and to instruct them in the proper performance of their duties.[122] These appointments sometimes encountered opposition, as in Ulster, where Tyrone and several new planters resisted the appointment of magistrates they felt unable to control.[123] Efforts to redefine customary Irish concepts of land use into the fixed categories of freehold, copyhold, and leasehold recognized by the common law proved equally contentious.[124] But the ability of Chichester or royal judges to intervene directly in the localities by holding assizes and interrogating local people provided the state with some leverage against obstruction.

For in many cases the judges encountered not only resistance but support and cooperation. Tyrone claimed that virtually the entire county of Tyrone consisted of his own demesne, and that he had the right to compel its inhabitants to remain on his lands and under his control. Davys found these assertions contrary to both

---

[118] John McCavitt, *Sir Arthur Chichester, Lord Deputy of Ireland, 1605–1616* (Belfast: Institute of Irish Studies, Queen's University of Belfast, 1998), 104.
[119] Ibid., 153–4. [120] Ibid., 169. [121] TNA SP63/219, fols 157v–158.
[122] TNA SP63/215, fols 13, 217, 157v. [123] E.g. TNA SP63/215 fol. 114.
[124] K. W. Nicholls, *Land, Law and Society in Sixteenth Century Ireland*, the O'Donnell Lecture, 1976 (Cork: University College, 1976), 20.

common law and "reason of state or policy," since they would make the earl's dependents think "they had no other king but Tyrone because their lives and their goods depended on his will."[125] Fortunately, Tyrone's claims were also contested by other Ulster landowners, including members of his own O'Neill kindred, who in 1605 petitioned the crown to uphold their claim to hold their lands in freehold. A similar situation arose in the territory of the young earl of Tyrconnell.[126] These disputes placed Chichester and Davys in the strong position of referees and mediators. They persuaded Tyrconnell to acquiesce in the erection of a number of freeholds in Donegal. Tyrone temporarily outmaneuvered them by agreeing to grant freeholds to several of his close relatives but not to men likely to challenge his power.[127] But the following year the crown issued a new commission authorized to investigate titles to land and revoke all claims based on Irish customs of tanistry and gavelkind, the dominant forms of inheritance in most Gaelic areas.[128] Armed with this weapon Davys conducted another tour of the North and found to his own satisfaction "that the chief lords of every country had only a chiefry or seignory consisting of certain rents or duties and withal some special demesnes, and that the tenants or inferior inhabitants were not tenants at will, as the lords pretended, but freeholders." The "cutting and usurpations" exacted by lords like Tyrone were therefore "a mere usurpation...taken *de facto* and not *de jure*" by armed force.[129] Assizes and commissions provided instruments for weakening Tyrone's control over his own lordship by strengthening the position of lesser landowners within it.

After the flight of Tyrone and Tyrconnell, Chichester and Davys conducted further assizes in Tyrone and Donegal, in which they again enlisted the help of Irish freeholders in convicting the earls of treason and dismantling what remained of their affinity. In Donegal they impaneled a jury, headed by the second largest landowner in the county after Tyrconnell himself and consisting of thirteen Irish and ten English landowners, so "that there might be no exception of partiality." Proceedings were conducted in both English and Irish and "a great deal of evidence" presented to convince "the people" of the earl's treason. The jury readily condemned Tyrone and Tyrconnell but initially hesitated to find the earls' followers guilty, for lack of sufficient evidence. Davys eventually persuaded them "that an indictment was but an accusation and no conviction and that such as did adhere to a known traitor might well and justly be accused to be partakers." With the use of "a little rhetoric" he thereby obtained a bill of indictment subscribed with the names of all twenty-three jurors. In Tyrone the sheriff returned a jury of nineteen men, the majority of whom were again Irish, with Sir Henry Oge O'Neill,

---

[125] TNA SP63/216/15.   [126] TNA SP63/217/63.
[127] Hans Pawlisch, *Sir John Davies and the Conquest of Ireland: A Study in Legal Imperialism* (Cambridge: Cambridge University Press, 1983), 68.
[128] Ibid., 69.   [129] TNA SP63/219/132.

"the best man now left" in the county, acting as foreman. This jury was charged with deciding whether Tyrone had assumed the Irish title of the O'Neill since James's accession. It found that he had done so on the basis of the jurors' "own private knowledge." When presented with a list of men Tyrone was accused of having murdered the jury added additional names to it, saying that he had hanged them by martial law, although his victims were of sufficient rank that he had no authority to do so. "The next day as we were passing homewards, some of the country people followed us and informed us of more murders committed by the earl," along with "base thefts of cows and plough horses... and that he [Tyrone] relieved and maintained many notorious thieves."[130] The earls' local enemies and victims evidently welcomed the opportunity to assist the authorities in uncovering his crimes.

But despite these successes, the extension of common law rule appears to have had a limited impact on underlying structures of landholding and social relationships. The large, self-sufficient body of Irish free tenants, liberated from dependence on their landlords that Davys and other reformers dreamed of creating, never really materialized. Even in areas of new plantation, Irish tenants-at-will remained the norm. They usually now held their tenancies by contracts rather than Irish custom but they remained at the mercy of their landlords.[131] It had simply proved more profitable and convenient for landowners to rely on tenants-at-will, including Irish willing to pay higher rents and work the land under more disadvantageous conditions than English settlers.[132] In one part of Donegal, for example, eight Scottish planters were each originally allotted 1,000 acres, on condition that they clear their lands of Irish inhabitants and establish two freeholders on every allotment. But they soon sold their interest to a bedchamber servant of the king named John Murray, the future earl of Annandale, whose agent failed to evict Irish tenants and created no freeholders.[133] Although freeholders were established on other allotments in Donegal, the original intention of establishing a network of nucleated villages inhabited by Scottish and English colonists was only partly fulfilled, and Irish subtenants remained common.[134] Even in the heart of the Pale, landlords took on Irish tenants-at-will prepared to pay higher rents.[135] Although the topic has not received sufficient study, freeholders seem to have remained thin

---

[130] TNA SP63/223/2.   [131] Gillespie, "Success and Failure," 107–9.
[132] Robert J. Hunter, "Plantation in Donegal," in *Donegal History and Society: Interdisciplinary Essays on the History of an Irish County*, ed. William Nolan, Liam Ronayne, and Mairead Dunlevy (Dublin: Geography Publications, 1995), 283–324, esp. 293–4; David Heffernan, "Theory and Practice in the Munster Plantation: The Estates of Richard Boyle, First Earl of Cork, 1602–1643," in *The Colonial World of Richard Boyle First Earl of Cork*, ed. David Edwards and Colin Rynne (Dublin: Four Courts Press, 2018), 43–63 at 50–1; Vincent Carey, *Surviving the Tudors* (Dublin: Four Courts Press, 2002), 25; Canny, *Making Ireland British*, 211; Raymond Gillespie, "Gaelic Catholicism and the Ulster Plantation," in *Religion and Politics in Urban Ireland, c. 1500–c. 1750: Essays in Honour of Colm Lennon*, ed. Salvador Ryan and Clodagh Tait (Dublin: Four Courts Press, 2016), esp. 132–3.
[133] Hunter, "Plantation in Donegal," 293–4.   [134] Ibid., 304–9.
[135] Carey, *Surviving the Tudors*, 25.

on the ground in most of Ireland. In the parliamentary election of 1641, County Cork managed to muster 314 freehold voters but County Tyrone had only 62 and Armagh 57. Although some freeholders no doubt stayed away from the polls, these figures suggest that Irish counties normally had many fewer freeholders than those in England.[136] In 1635 an attempt to hold an assize in Coleraine failed for lack "of a sufficient number of freeholders... to do the service."[137] And since many Irish freeholds had been created by redefining the status of land once held under Irish custom by minor septs and other lineage groups, they did not necessarily supplant traditions of kinship loyalty. When he held criminal trials in County Monaghan, Davys found himself impeded by the fact that "three or four names only, as McMahon, McKenna, McCabe and O'Connolly" were so prevalent that it proved impossible to impanel juries that did not include kinsmen of accused criminals. "And therefore it is probable the malefactors were acquitted for favor." In addition, "the poor people seemed very unwilling to be sworn of juries, alleging that if they condemned any man his friends in revenge would rob or burn or kill them for it; and that the like mischief had happened to diverse jurors since the last sessions." The judges had to fine and imprison jurors who failed to convict prisoners against whom there was abundant evidence in order to overcome these obstacles.[138] Even as common law rule was extended across the whole of Ireland, it failed to bring about the revolution in tenurial systems, social arrangements, and cultural attitudes that reformers like Davys envisaged. Local governance remained more oligarchic and autocratic than in most of England. Although some relatively privileged Irish benefited from the new order, considerable numbers of people were forced off their ancestral lands or compelled to farm them as under-tenants of new settlers. Some joined the bands of woodkern that continued to raid plantation settlements and suffer from the state's military sweeps.[139]

Law, State Power, and Religious Resistance in Ireland

The fact that efforts to extend common law governance over the whole of Ireland encountered little organized resistance, especially after the flight of Tyrone and Tyrconnell, nevertheless represented an apparent victory for the Dublin administration. The one major limitation to that victory involved the state's failure to enforce even nominal conformity to the official Church or to impede the

---

[136] Brid McGrath, "Electoral Law in Ireland Before 1641," in *Law and Revolution in Ireland*, ed. Coleman Dennehy (Dublin: Four Courts Press, 2018), 265–88.
[137] Marsh's Library (Dublin) Ms. Z3.1.6, number 5. I owe this reference to Brid McGrath, whom I also want to thank for sending me the paper cited in the previous note in advance of publication and for an enlightening conversation on the subject of Irish freeholders.
[138] *Collectanea de rebus Hibernicus*, 1.152–3.
[139] David Edwards, "Out of the Blue? Provincial Unrest in Ireland before 1641," in *Religion and Politics in Urban Ireland*, ed. Ryan and Tait, 95–114 at 102; for Leinster see *CSPI JI* 2.250.

continued spread of Catholic defiance. English officials in Ireland, like members of the privy council in London, disagreed about how serious a problem this was. Mountjoy, who remained influential in the formulation of Irish policy after his return to England in 1604, disapproved of compulsion because he thought that "all religions do grow under persecution."[140] But others, including Chichester, thought the Irish would never become loyal subjects so long as they differed in religion from their king and the English officials he appointed to rule under him. The stirs in Munster at the start of the reign seemed to show that so long as Catholic clergy enjoyed almost unfettered freedom to encourage resistance, royal control would remain fragile and contested. He acknowledged the impossibility of converting the population by compulsion alone. "Men's consciences must be won and persuaded by time, conference and instructions" and "the education of the youth" rather than violence.[141] But for persuasion to work the Irish needed exposure to sermons and religious instruction, which remained impossible so long as, under the goading of their priests, they refused to attend Protestant services.

The problem appeared to require a three-pronged solution, involving the provision of better preaching and religious services in the official Church, the suppression or banishment of Catholic priests, and the targeting of recusancy, particularly among the elite, whose example was thought to have a preponderant effect on the behavior of ordinary Irish. Significant obstacles stood in the way of all three objectives. A shortage of human and material resources hampered the Church of Ireland. Few of its parish clergy possessed the education needed for effective preaching, especially in Irish, while many of its bishops were complacent and complicit in abusive practices. The bishops certainly knew about abuses, Davys sarcastically remarked, because "some of them are privy and party to them," but they would act like "country churchwardens" by delivering reports of *omnia bene* "when the verdict should be *omnia pessime*":

> If the business is to be really performed, let visitors be sent out of England, such as never heard a cow speak and understand not that language that they may examine the abuses of the Court of Faculties, of the demoniacal contracts, of the dilapidations and disherison of churches; that they may find the true value of the benefices and who takes the profits and to what uses; to deprive these serving men and unlettered kern that are now incumbents, and to place some of the poor scholars of the college that are learned and zealous Protestants; to bring others out of that part of Scotland that borders upon the North of Ireland...[who] can preach in the Irish tongue; to transplant others out of England and to place them within the English Pale.[142]

---

[140] Crawford, *Star Chamber in Ireland*, 281.   [141] TNA SP63/219/147.
[142] TNA SP63/216/4.

But attracting talented churchmen to Ireland required money to pay adequate salaries. Unfortunately, as Davys also remarked, the large number of impropriated benefices in Ireland, many controlled by Catholics, made it impossible to do this with Irish resources. Tithes went into the pockets of laymen, who appointed "poor unlettered clerks" at very low stipends to serve rural parishes or, even worse, endowed Catholic priests sheltered by lay patrons. "Nay (that which is most incredible, but I heard it of one that hath a place of special credit in this kingdom) the agent or nuncio of the Pope that lieth lurking here in this land hath £40 or £50 a year out of the profits of a parsonage that lieth within the Pale."[143] Attempts to recover tithes and other Church revenues met with systematic resistance that priests encouraged.[144] When the official Church did manage to collect tithes and fees it aroused fierce resentment, especially from poor Irish, who had no interest in its services and for whom the payment of even modest sums amounted to a significant burden.[145] But James's financial problems precluded any attempt to solve the problem by large infusions of English money.

The inadequacy of the official Church meant that efforts to supplant Catholicism needed to rely primarily on pressure and compulsion. Especially in the North, which had suffered disproportionately during the final stages of the Nine Years War, the authorities did make some progress in the first decade of James's reign in pressuring *erenaghs* and traditional priests into outward conformity. But true conversions were extremely rare.[146] The fact that Catholicism remained entrenched not only among the general population but within the ranks of the Dublin administration, including some of the judges and officers of its courts, made rigorous measures difficult to implement. The chief justice of Munster, William Saxey, thought that religious disloyalty sapped the state's authority from within:

> The due administration of justice doth require the immediate ministers thereof to be religious and faithful to the State wherein they serve, which in the government of that kingdom falleth to the contrary, for so long as recusants and detected traitors are daily countenanced and cherished in the bosom of the State, and (as Catiline in the heat of his rebellion had a place in the senate-house) made partakers of their counsels, whereby they get fit opportunity to betray the same, there is small hope of the amendment of the state of that kingdom.[147]

---

[143] Ibid. See also Rory Masterson, "The Dissolution of the Monasteries and the Parishes of the Western Liberty of Meath in the Seventeenth Century," in *Religion in Urban Ireland*, ed. Ryan and Tait, 134–55.

[144] *CSPI JI* 1.179.

[145] Brian Mac Cuarta, *Catholic Revival in the North of Ireland, 1603-1641* (Dublin: Four Courts Press, 2007), 56–60.

[146] Ibid., 50–6.

[147] *CSPI JI* 1.219, Saxey to Cranbourne (Cecil) 1604. *Erenaghs* were hereditary keepers of ecclesiastical property who often doubled as priests.

In February 1605 Davys complained that "for want of a competent number of judges to supply the three circuits" of Ulster, the commission included "the recorders of Dublin and Drogheda, notorious recusants, and one of them (we hear) a lay brother of the Jesuits." To make matters worse, state servants who were not Catholic were often corrupt or indolent. Davys therefore wanted to import more Protestants trained in the law to act as judges, sheriffs, and magistrates. He complained to Cecil in 1604 that the Irish courts of King's Bench and Common Pleas had only two judges each "and the second judges are but weak," and urged sending some of the "superfluous sergeants" in England to serve in Ireland as circuit judges.

To succeed fully the reform of the Irish state's personnel needed to extend beyond the Dublin administration to the magistracies of towns, the ranks of country landowners from which sheriffs and JPs were selected, and even the middling freeholders who served as jurors and under sheriffs.[148] Davys also wanted to deprive lay patrons of benefices of their rights of presentation if they installed Catholics or ignorant men as parish clergy.[149] He faced the conundrum that the English system he sought to impose delegated so much authority to amateur magistrates and middling freeholders that it required a substantial population of propertied men loyal to the crown in order to work. In nearly all of Ireland that population did not exist, due to both the devastation caused by the Nine Years War and the fact that even in relatively prosperous districts many of those most expert in English law and administration remained actively hostile to the government's religious policies. The fact that Irish statute provided for a fine of only a shilling for refusal to attend church compounded the problem of forcing propertied Irish to attend Protestant services. Acts passed at the start of Elizabeth's reign did grant the Irish council authority to extend an Oath of Supremacy to individual office holders and dismiss those who refused to take it.[150] This allowed the government to purge a number of Catholic officials from town corporations and imprison the newly elected mayor of Dublin, after he captiously argued that the legislation no longer applied because it referred to the queen's authority over the Church rather than the king's.[151] The Irish council also demanded that judges and attorneys pleading before Irish courts take the Oath, making it more difficult for Catholics to engage in litigation. But these measures were inadequate to deal with solid majority support for Catholicism throughout Ireland.

As Hans Pawlisch has demonstrated, Davys went about overcoming this difficulty by crafting legal arguments to expand the king's prerogative powers to fill gaps in existing law. When necessary he obtained judicial resolutions—

---

[148] As Chichester remarked to Salisbury: *CSPI JI* 1.325–6 and 328. Mac Cuarta, *Catholic Revival*, 60–2, remarks on the difficulty of enforcing religious conformity locally while most under sheriffs remained Catholics.
[149] Mac Cuarta, *Catholic Revival*, 143.   [150] Ibid., 106–10 for the following paragraph.
[151] Ibid., 212–13.

collective opinions of the Irish judges arising not from a specific case but an issue referred to them for resolution—that amounted to "judge made law."[152] In 1603 the lord president of Munster, Sir Henry Brouncker, began expelling priests on his own authority, and shortly thereafter the bishops of Dublin and Meath, supported by the lord deputy and Irish council, wrote to James asking his help in banishing Catholic clergy. The king responded with a proclamation applying to Ireland the provisions of an English statute of 1584, banishing Jesuits and priests trained on the Continent, which the Irish council attempted to enforce.[153] It also sent out letters called mandates to prominent recusants, ordering them to attend Protestant services on specified dates. Writing to Cecil, Davys claimed that the same tactic had been used successfully in England under Edward VI, "when more than half the kingdom...were papists" and again under Mary and Elizabeth.[154] In Dublin the mayor, seven aldermen and nearly four hundred others capitulated to the mandates, while several merchants who remained obdurate were summoned before the Court of Castle Chamber, the Irish Star Chamber, and sentenced to fines of between £50 and £200.[155] Because the fines were for contempt of the council's authority, rather than non-attendance at church, they could be much higher than the shilling payments provided by the Irish Act of Uniformity. The lord deputy and council reported with satisfaction in December 1605 that resistance had crumbled and Dublin churches "are now better frequented than they have been at any time these dozen years."[156] But in Munster the mayor and aldermen in all towns except Waterford defied the mandates and were removed from office and heavily fined.[157]

In the Pale the mandates provoked a petition signed by 219 prominent residents and five Irish peers, who appealed over Chichester's head to the English council, claiming that "all the learned in the laws" in Ireland regarded the lord deputy's proceedings as so illegal and "preposterous" that they risked laying "the foundation of some future rebellion."[158] Chichester identified three Old English lawyers, Henry Burnell, Richard Netterville, and Sir Patrick Barnewall, as ringleaders of this protest. He placed Burnell and Netterville, both old men who had helped stir opposition to Sidney over purveyance in 1577, under house arrest, while Barnewall and two peers were jailed and heavily fined by Castle Chamber. When finally released Barnewall traveled to the court in England to plead his case. Priests spread reports that he would "receive grace rather than reproof" and

---

[152] Pawlisch, *Sir John Davies*, 69.
[153] For the text of the proclamation see TNA SP63/217, fol. 49.
[154] TNA SP63/217 fol. 94. For the mandates policy see McCavitt, *Chichester*, 116–18.
[155] TNA SP63/217/78.   [156] TNA SP63/217/95.
[157] Pawlisch, *Sir John Davies*, 109. A more critical view of the mandates policy is Crawford, *Star Chamber in Ireland*, 288–307.
[158] TNA SP63/217/96, Barnewall to Salisbury, December 16, 1605. For a modern account of Chichester's use of Castle Chamber and Barnewell's role in opposing it see Crawford, *Star Chamber in Ireland*, 290–9.

obtain a "toleration of the Romish religion and great alteration in this kingdom's government."[159]

The English council reacted by asking Davys to comment on the argument that the mandates policy violated the law because it had no basis in Irish statutes. He responded by citing medieval precedents, including the English statute of *praemunire*, to contend that kings of England had always possessed prerogative powers over the Church entitling them to issue mandates and punish offenders, and therefore needed no statutory authority to do so. Although this argument settled doubts about the legality of the policy,[160] the council worried about provoking forcible resistance and in January 1606 ordered Chichester to act with greater restraint.[161] But it allowed him to make examples of notorious recusants and he continued the pressure.[162] In November 1606 Davys accompanied a judicial circuit that cracked down on recusancy in the counties of Wexford and Waterford. The sovereign of the town of New Ross, who had led a noisy procession of 200 Catholics into the town's church while its minister was trying to preach his Easter sermon to a tiny congregation, was bound over with some others to answer for his offense in Castle Chamber. In the town of Wexford, a grand jury was bullied into indicting recusants by threats that they would be prosecuted in Castle Chamber if they refused. In Waterford the principal Catholic aldermen were fined £40 or £50 each by the authority of the President and Council of Munster, who also levied the statutory fine of a shilling for every Sunday of absence from church on humbler recusants. Despite the paltry sums involved these small fines raised £240, suggesting that there were about 4,800 of them. "This being done we impaneled a special jury and charged them to inquire of the number of the benefices with cure of souls in that county, of the reparation and decay of the several churches of the incumbents, of the patrons and of their yearly value." It was ordered to report within twelve months.[163] The following March a special commission of *oyer et terminer* was issued to levy the shilling fines for refusal to attend church on the population of Drogheda. Davys summoned recusants to answer individually, "by the poll to plead for the indictment" and claimed to have brought 200 to conformity.[164] The government employed informers, commissioners armed with authority to invade gentry houses, and provost martials to search for priests, a few of whom it then executed by martial law. Some priests temporarily abandoned their cures under the pressure.[165] Poor tenants also deserted their lands to avoid having to pay recusancy fines.

---

[159] Pawlisch, *Sir John Davies*, 110–13; Nessa Malone, "Henry Burnell and Richard Netterville: Lawyers in Civic Life in the English Pale, 1562–1615," in *Religion and Politics in Urban Ireland*, ed. Ryan and Tait, 89–107; Crawford, *Star Chamber in Ireland*, 291–2.
[160] Pawlisch, *Sir John Davies*, 110–14.   [161] McCavitt, *Chichester*, 118.   [162] Ibid., 118–21.
[163] TNA SP63/219/132.   [164] TNA SP63/221/35.
[165] Mac Cuarta, *Catholic Revival*, 169–74.

But although Davys, Chichester, and Brouncker believed these measures had started to meet with success in breaking down recusancy and producing conversions to Protestantism, organized opposition continued.[166] The state's bark proved worse than its bite, with many of the heavy fines imposed by Castle Chamber remaining uncollected, apparently leading numerous Irish to conclude that *de facto* toleration still existed.[167] Although thirteen of Dublin's twenty-four aldermen were imprisoned in 1607 and fined a total of £1,145, the London privy council soon ordered their release and lowered the financial penalty after vigorous protests orchestrated in part by the head of Dublin's Jesuit mission, Christopher Hollywood.[168] In Munster subordinate officials used the threat of fines for recusancy to extort bribes, further discrediting the state and multiplying the number of complaints.[169] The towns, Chichester complained, "in general do study noting more than how to oppose our proceedings in matters of religion," while priests run "from place to place," gathering signatures to petitions in an effort "to terrify us with the multitude of their factious combination."[170] The lord deputy deposed five successive mayors of Waterford in an effort to impose conformity and launched a preaching campaign by twenty-two ministers. But this failed to break Catholic resistance.[171]

Barnewall, who appeared to be having some success in persuading the council in London to restrain Chichester, became a popular hero. A convocation of Catholic priests agreed to levy a collection for his support and quickly gathered £32, with hopes of many additional contributions. The same assembly sent agents to the king of France and the Archduke Albert in Brussels, asking them to urge James to grant religious toleration in Ireland.[172] The belief that Barnewall had gained concessions stiffened public defiance.[173] In November 1607 Chichester passed on a report "that most of the principle men of the cities, towns and countries in the province of Munster have subscribed to an instrument of combination" to uphold the Catholic religion.[174] Nearly all the mayors and officers of the province's towns refused to take the Oath of Supremacy,[175] and the Irish council reported that "in many places" people were resorting to mass in greater numbers than ever, while "multitudes" of priests gathered in "general councils and conventicles." If the authorities tried to arrest a seditious priest, "both men and women will not stick to rescue the party." The few Irish who did attend Protestant worship were "everywhere derided, scorned and oppressed by the multitude," causing people who had conformed to withdraw themselves again.[176] Chichester's

---

[166] For claims of success see TNA SP63/219/134 and 147.
[167] TNA SP63/221/87 and 222/112. In the latter document Chichester reported that only about £80 had been collected of £7.000 in fines imposed.
[168] Crawford, *Star Chamber in Ireland*, 299.   [169] TNA SP63/222/112.
[170] TNA SP63/218/1.   [171] McCavitt, *Chichester*, 121.   [172] TNA SP63/221/24.
[173] TNA SP63/221/8 and 222/15.   [174] TNA SP63/222/153.
[175] TNA SP63/221/190, Earl of Thomond to the Council, March 21, 1607.
[176] TNA SP63/217/18 and 222/159.

efforts to enforce the proclamation banning Jesuits and missionary priests from Ireland collapsed in the face of universal resistance. Having requested, but failed to receive, authority to execute Jesuits, seminarians, and "hedge priests" by martial law, he found that "every town, hamlet and house is to them a sanctuary."[177] Even the lord president of Munster, Richard Burke earl of Clanricard, protected and encouraged Catholic missionaries.[178]

The Irish council complained that priests coming from the Continent "do land in every port and creek of the realm (a dozen or more together sometimes), " so that Catholics "vaunt that they have more priests here than his majesty hath soldiers."[179] The number of priests and friars trained on the Continent increased significantly after 1603, supplying many gentry households with chaplains and gradually spreading more rigorous Tridentine forms of Catholicism.[180] Material support for European seminaries training Irish clergy came from sympathetic peers and gentry as well as Irish commoners. Gray merchants who carried goods from the towns into the countryside arranged for cattle donated by smallholders to be driven to port towns, slaughtered and processed, to supply the Franciscan college in Louvain with salted beef.[181] Franciscans played an especially active role in evangelizing Ulster, especially after 1610, provoking resistance from traditional, locally trained priests whose influence and lax attitudes toward matters like clerical celibacy they challenged.[182]

Chichester failed not only to drive Jesuits and friars from Ireland but to prevent the Catholic Church from setting up a parallel structure of ecclesiastical authority competing with that of the official Church. "There is not a bishop's see but is supplied double," he wrote in 1609, "one being placed by the king and another by the Pope." Priests and friars preached and celebrated mass openly, under the protection of civic authorities or local landowners. In Kilkenny, the thirty priests active in 1604 had increased to fifty a decade later.[183] Chichester, Brouncker, and Thomond warned the privy council in 1607, shortly before the flight of Tyrone and Tyrconnell that Catholics were plotting a new rebellion, alleging that some Irish priests had known in advance of the Gunpowder Plot and were now seeking to encourage sedition by spreading rumors that the Spanish planned a new invasion of Ireland.[184] The "priests make the people believe there will shortly [be] some trouble in England and that O'Sullivan Beare and John McThomas of Desmond are kept in Spain and other Munster men and to be in readiness to be shipped for Ireland upon the first occasion." Some priests had even begun

---

[177] TNA SP63/214/17, Chichester to Devonshire, February 26, 1606.
[178] Bernadette Cunningham, "Nuns and their Networks in Early Modern Galway," in *Religion and Politics in Urban Ireland*, ed. Ryan and Tait, 156–72.
[179] TNA SP63/222/159, Irish to English council, October 27, 1607.
[180] Mac Cuarta, *Catholic Revival*, 151–7.   [181] Ibid., 90–1.   [182] Ibid., 72–82, 84.
[183] Edwards, *Ormond Lordship*, 263–6.   [184] TNA SP63/221/12, 15 and 92; 223/14.

organizing collections of victuals to supply an invading army.[185] Rumors of this kind often seem to have originated from among the extensive Irish diaspora on the Continent, whose members remained in contact with kinsmen and friends back home.[186] It was said, no doubt with a bit of exaggeration that "in Munster there are few men of quality but hath his particular kinsman or ally pensioned with the king of Spain, which from time to time doth give them occurrences from those parts."[187] English officials complained of priests "casting abroad libels and spreading a thousand false rumors and reports."[188] An especially active Franciscan Provincial on the Continent named Father Florence spread reports that Philip III was prepared to aid an Irish rebellion with 10,000 infantry and 200 horse, and sought to enlist the support of Irish soldiers in the Spanish army in the Low Countries.[189] Secular grievances and protests led by lawyers continued to blend with and reinforce Catholic opposition. The earl of Thomond reported that in Connacht and Thomond "diverse gentlemen" had set out to undo the composition negotiated to set levels of taxation in the previous reign, "under color to bring the old Irish customs afoot."[190] The archbishop of Dublin complained that Irish who had trained at the Inns of Court returned home "armed to pervert others" as "ringleaders of this people in their recusancy." In the Pale the countess of Kildare patronized Jesuits, the Nugents protected priests on their estates, and Lord Delvin protected a friary, while in the northeast the two newly erected Scottish Catholic lords, Randall MacDonnell and George Hamilton, supported Franciscans and Jesuits. They turned the diocese of Derry into a center of Catholic activism where meetings of as many as eighty clergy convened annually in Strabane, to exchange political information, including rumored invasions by the Army of Flanders' Irish regiment, and discuss the further evangelization of the North.[191]

Early in James's reign the English government had encouraged the recruitment of unemployed Irish soldiers to fight in foreign armies, in hopes that this would help rid the island of trouble-makers.[192] Chichester thought this a mistake, worrying that some of the soldiers would eventually return as "firebrands of new rebellion here,"[193] and in time Salisbury came to share his concern. An Irish lobby in Madrid, supported by Spanish clergy, did attempt to persuade Philip III to assist armed Irish resistance to Stuart rule.[194] The earl of Tyrone and the new earl of Tyrconnell had renewed their contacts with Spain, while also

---

[185] *CSPI JI* 2.451, Chichester to Devonshire, April 23, 1606.
[186] On the diaspora see Óscar Reio Morales, *Ireland and the Spanish Empire, 1500–1825* (Dublin: Four Courts Press, 2010).
[187] TNA SP63/218/4, Illegible to ?, January 16, 1606.
[188] TNA SP63/222/153, Chichester to Salisbury, October 9, 1607.
[189] TNA SP63/222/105 and 128.   [190] TNA SP63/222/125.
[191] Mac Cuarta, *Catholic Revival*, 105 and 180–5.
[192] *CSPI JI* 1.298; Gráinee Henry, *The Irish Military Community in Spanish Flanders, 1586-1621* (Dublin: Irish Academic Press, 1882p, esp. 32–6.
[193] TNA SP63/223/21.   [194] Morales, *Ireland and the Spanish Empire*, 50–3.

communicating with Catholic priests and leaders in the Pale, Munster, and other parts of Ireland, laying contingency plans for future revolts. Both won pensions of 4,000 ducats a year from Madrid in return for a promise to renew their rebellion if and when the Spanish crown asked them to do so. John McCavitt has shown that fears that their secret plans were becoming known to the English government and that the crown might therefore imprison or execute them played a key role in precipitating the earls' flight into exile in the autumn of 1607.[195] In the short run their departure increased the alarm of James and his council, not least because it coincided with preliminary reports of an impending truce between Spain and the Dutch that would potentially have freed Spanish forces to intervene in Ireland.[196] Fortunately for the British crown, it eventually became clear that the Spanish government did not want to risk a new war by aiding Irish rebels, while the Ulster lords now lacked the capacity to mount the sort of insurrection they had waged in the mid-1590s without foreign support. But alarm over the possibility of a new, large-scale Irish revolt induced the privy council to order Chichester to relax pressure on Catholics. The lord deputy kept these instructions secret, for fear of encouraging a new campaign for formal religious toleration, but he knew he had to comply.[197]

Prosecutions of recusants momentarily revived in 1611, in part through the influence of Andrew Knox, after his appointment to the Irish bishopric of Raphoe.[198] Nobles, lawyers, and municipal officials were again targeted, grand jurors repeatedly fined for failing to return indictments of recusants, and the octogenarian Catholic Bishop O'Devany of Down and Connor and Tyrone's former chaplain, Patrick O'Lourghan, hanged.[199] In 1612 Chichester granted charters to forty English settlements, many quite small, entitling them to elect MPs to the Irish parliament he planned to call the next year. He intended in this way to pack the Commons with Protestants who would pass stiffer penal legislation. Davys had meanwhile succeeded in eroding the chartered privileges of Irish corporations, including their control over local customs revenues, by initiating *quo warranto* proceedings.[200] This campaign—which anticipated the later efforts of Charles II and James II to purge Whigs from English boroughs and pack an English parliament in 1688—met with furious opposition. A new delegation that again included Barnewell went to London to protest, supported by a "benevolence" gathered by "collectors appointed in every barony" of the Pale.[201] James initially treated them courteously but eventually grew exasperated and

---

[195] John McCavitt, "The Flight of the Earls, 1607," *Irish Historical Studies* 29 (1994): 159–73.
[196] Below, p. 566; Morales, *Ireland and the Spanish Empire*, 48–50.   [197] TNA SP63/222/112.
[198] McCarthy-Morrogh, *Munster Plantation*, 173–5.
[199] Ibid., 175–6; Crawford, *Star Chamber in Ireland*, 301–2.
[200] Pawlisch, *Sir John Davies*, 39, 129, 133.
[201] *Desiderate Curiosa: or a Collection of Divers Scarce and Curious Pieces Relating Chiefly to Matters of English Histgory*, 2 vols, ed. Francis Peck (London, 1779) 1.160 and 209–10.

threw several of the delegates in prison.²⁰² He felt torn between a desire to support Chichester and crush Catholic resistance, and apprehension that by doing so he might provoke a new rebellion.

In June 1613 the ambassador of the Habsburg Archdukes Albert and Isabella reported that the king talked of compelling religious conformity in Ireland by armed force. But since he lacked money and feared provoking Catholics into taking "extreme measures" and seeking help from foreign princes, it seemed unlikely that he would follow through.²⁰³ When the Irish Parliament convened with its newly minted Protestant majority, Catholics boycotted it.²⁰⁴ In November Spain's ambassador, the Conde de Gondomar, reported that Archbishop Abbot and the English Chancellor, Thomas Egerton, pressed for a crackdown on Irish Catholics during a meeting of the privy council, against the opposition of the Howard earls of Northampton and Suffolk, who urged "softness and mildness" (*suavidad y blandura*).²⁰⁵ By the start of the new year, this softer policy had prevailed, probably helped along by reports from James's ambassador in Brussels that Irish exiles in the Spanish Netherlands were actively planning a fresh revolt and soliciting Habsburg assistance.²⁰⁶ In January the king sent his former ambassador to Spain, Sir Charles Cornwallis, to Dublin with instructions to "compose the controversies and alterations," and negotiate an agreement permitting the private practice of Catholicism, in return for assurances that the mass would not be celebrated in public.²⁰⁷ Before departing, Cornwallis consulted with Gondomar, promising to provide "a great service for God" and the king of Spain.²⁰⁸ Although still sensitive about Irish reports that he had granted religious toleration, James did not want a violent confrontation and so decided to try to calm the waters. The planned penal legislation was dropped and Chichester's campaign to suppress recusancy met with another setback.

The Catholic Church in Ireland thereafter continued to grow in strength and remained defiant in the face of Protestant authority. By 1621 a single continental seminary in Bordeaux had supplied twenty-eight priests to Waterford, and many more to other Irish towns.²⁰⁹ In some districts Protestant ministers hid themselves in woods and mountainous areas to escape harassment by priests and scores of lay Catholics.²¹⁰ In Ballintobber (County Mayo) in 1619 "an assembly of between

---

²⁰² MacCarthy-Morrogh, *Munster Plantation*, 193–4.
²⁰³ HHStA Belgien PC46, fols 166v–67.
²⁰⁴ MacCarthy-Morrogh, *Munster Plantation*, 173–7; Edwards *Ormond Lordship*, 267–76; Crawford, *Star Chamber in Ireland*, 301–7.
²⁰⁵ *CDIHE, Gondomar*, 3.65–6; cf. HHStA Belgien PC47, fol. 201 for more on Abbot's arguments.
²⁰⁶ TNA SP77/10, fols 332, 337v, 358v, William Trumbull dispatches of September 13, October 6, and November 25, 1613 relaying reports of Irish plots from Brussels.
²⁰⁷ Or so, at least, the Archbishops' ambassador reported: HHStA Belgien PC47, fol. 27v.
²⁰⁸ *CDIHE, Gondomar*, 1.65–6: "Hame venido a ver el Cornuales muy confidentemente y dichome que ha de hazer alli [in Ireland] un gran servicio a Dios y a Vuestra Magestad."
²⁰⁹ *CSPI JI*, 4.318–19; the manuscript list of these priests extends over four pages.
²¹⁰ Ibid., 21.

three and four score fathers and their priests" gathered, "armed with swords, daggers and pistols, each of them having besides two serving men, and all armed like their masters."[211] In Ulster the Catholic Church strengthened its position, despite the presence of Protestant plantations. Although local diocesan life had almost completely collapsed during the Nine Years War, by the 1620s three-quarters of Ulster parishes had resident Catholic priests, many trained on the Continent or in schools within Ireland. Franciscan friars preached open air sermons on the estates of Catholic gentry, attracting people from miles around as they spread a message that Ulster's tribulations, including famine during the war period and the establishment of British plantations, were punishments for sin. They stigmatized Protestantism as a source of spiritual pollution that brought material suffering to the Irish people, encouraging some Irish to view violence against Protestant settlers as acts of purification.[212] In parts of Ulster, Protestant ministers feared to go abroad in public without an armed escort.[213] In Wexford "popish priests and other ill-disposed neighbors" stirred opposition to a new plantation. A certain "Morris McEdmond Cavanaugh, a bastard of that ever-rebellious race of the Cavanaughs, with a crew of wicked rogues gathered out of the bordering parts entered into the plantation, surprised Sir John Carrol and Mr. Marwood's houses, murdered their servants, burned their towns and committed many outrages."[214]

Although the state had eliminated the old threat posed by Irish warlords, it therefore faced newer forms of organized resistance, spearheaded by networks of priests, lawyers, and large landowners that connected more peripheral districts to the Pale, Old English towns, and European centers of the Counter-Reformation. Drogheda grew into an especially active center that eventually housed at least seven religious communities and a number of lay confraternities, while serving as a nodal point for communications between the Continent, the Pale, and Ulster.[215] Several thousand veteran Irish soldiers serving in the Army of Flanders added to the danger. For the moment resistance remained non-violent, aside from occasional local flare-ups, which meant that it did not immediately imperil the state's ability to function and spread its control over more secular matters, like the suppression of crime and adjudication of property disputes. Ireland slowly grew less violent, more "civil," and more integrated through the effects of government initiatives and the gradual expansion of a market economy. But the lingering grievances of many sectors of the population and the crown's utter failure to deal effectively with religious disaffection, either by an effective program of Protestant evangelization or a policy of tolerance and accommodation, rendered these achievements fragile. Although the bulk of the population remained quiescent

---

[211] Ibid., 493.
[212] Mac Cuarta, "Catholic Church in Ulster," esp. 134; Mac Cuarta, *Catholic Revival*, esp. 85–90.
[213] *CSPI JI*, 5.23. [214] Ibid., 5.304. [215] Mac Cuarta, *Catholic Revival*, 212–18.

under Stuart rule, the extent of its loyalty and support for the new political order remained highly questionable. Ireland's stability therefore depended to a perilous degree on the state's coercive instruments, including an army that had diminished from 17,000 troops at the height of the Nine Years War to about 2,000 soldiers. Despite its small size, this force suffered periodic interruptions to its pay and supplies caused by James's chronic shortages of money, impairing its ability to function. In 1621 Lord Deputy St John complained of "the weak and wretched state of this army, which is now two years unpaid, and is reduced to extreme misery," with soldiers "so starved, so poor, so ragged that if there should be occasion to draw them from their garrisons they should find many of them to have not so much as a pair of shoes to put upon their feet."[216] Although still more than adequate to deal with bands of a few dozen woodkern, the army's performance in any serious emergency was very much open to doubt. And if it once lost control it was by no means clear where James would find the money to re-establish English rule.

The evident vulnerability of English control over Ireland made both the government and the Irish themselves highly sensitive to any fluctuations in the Stuart crown's relations with Spain. In the early 1620s, anticipation of a Spanish match for Prince Charles encouraged new Catholic hopes and assertiveness, reportedly leading towns across Ireland to elect recusant sovereigns and mayors, "so that his majesty's sword in all those quarters is become recusant." Collections were gathered to erect a number of new friaries and churches in anticipation that pressure from Spain would soon compel the crown to grant religious toleration.[217] The collapse of the match dashed these hopes but also led to a new effort led by the earl of Westmeath and Sir William Talbot to organize a general contribution of money in the Pale to support a Catholic delegation to the court in London. Although it soon collapsed, for several weeks Lord Deputy Falkland feared that this initiative would provide a cover for secret preparations for a popish insurrection.[218] As England drifted toward open war with Spain, fresh rumors spread of Spanish invasions and Irish revolts. Falkland reported receiving "daily advertisements from every corner of this kingdom" of "some sudden commotion and general massacre of the English, who are almost afraid to continue their habitation in the country."[219] These rumors proved overblown and Ireland remained quiet during Charles I's war with Spain between 1625 and 1629. But the climate of uncertainty and insecurity encouraged Catholic hopes and resistance. It also helped in bringing a more definitive end to the crown's efforts at enforcing religious conformity. From the late 1610s *de facto* toleration of public, as well as

---

[216] *CSPI JI*, 5.337.   [217] Ibid., 5.458.   [218] Ibid., 5.440.
[219] Ibid., 5.485. For other reports and rumors see ibid., 504 and BL Add Mss. 17,677 K, fol. 353, a report by a Dutch envoy of rumors arriving in London, including a report from Brussels by Sir William Trumbull that 1,500 old soldiers from the Irish regiment in Flanders had embarked for their homeland.

private, Catholic worship prevailed, allowing for the consolidation of the position of strength the Roman Church had already begun to attain before then. Although pacified for the moment, the Irish periphery of the British state still looked highly vulnerable, especially if Britain ever had to fight another prolonged war with a major Catholic power.

Presbyterian Resistance in Scotland

Although less serious than in Ireland, religious dissension also continued to trouble the other two Stuart kingdoms. In the late twentieth century James gained a reputation among many historians of England for shrewdness and moderation in handling religious issues. They credited him with broadening the English Church by appointing bishops who held a fairly wide range of theological views, while generally favoring Calvinists, who promoted measures like the expansion of preaching that puritans favored. Historians argued that this approach dampened ecclesiastical controversies, especially in the period between the appointment of the Calvinist George Abbott as English primate in 1611 and the renewed intensification of religious controversy triggered by the outbreak of the Thirty Years War and consternation over the king's negotiations for a Spanish alliance from around 1618.[220] In conformity with this view, some scholars blamed the ineffective harrying of Catholics in Ireland on officials like Chichester rather than the king, and the revival of serious religious tensions in Scotland almost exclusively on Charles I and Archbishop Laud.

This interpretation stands in need of significant qualifications. Although often flexible and effective in dealing with individual nobles and moderate clergy, James showed less skill and patience when confronted with petitioning campaigns and protests expressed through representative bodies like parliaments and Scottish general assemblies. He tended to regard the leaders of such movements as demagogues deserving exemplary punishment, rather than leaders with whom he had to reach agreement. He did sometimes back down when convinced that refusing to do so risked seriously damaging consequences, as in his sporadic attempts to restrain Chichester and Davys from putting too much pressure on Irish recusants. But even in these cases his compromises were usually accompanied by expressions of sharp anger and the imprisonment of protesters like Barnewell. When he believed he had the upper hand James often bullied people who opposed his will, and when this tactic failed he preferred to prevent meetings

---

[220] See, in particular, Patrick Collinson, *The Religion of the Protestants: The Church in Engl Society, 1559–1625* (Oxford: Oxford University Press, rev. ed. 1984); Kenneth Fincham, *Prelate Pastor: The Episcopate of James I* (Oxford: Oxford University Press, 1990); Nicholas Tyacke, *A Calvinists: The Rise of English Arminianism c. 1590–1640* (Oxford: Clarendon Press, 1990).

that seemed intent on defying his orders from assembling. His well-known difficulties with English parliaments have parallels in the tumultuous Irish session of 1613–14, after which he never again summoned a parliament in Ireland, and repeated clashes with Scottish general assemblies, which he tried to manipulate and browbeat. Even in England, the relative religious harmony of the 1610s had already started to collapse by the early 1620s, while in Scotland he picked a fight by trying to impose ceremonial innovations on the Kirk against fierce opposition in 1617. Although it had not yet come close to provoking rebellion, Protestant anger mounted in both British kingdoms, costing James considerable good-will.

Although they intensified toward the end of James's reign, religious controversies had never entirely abated in Scotland after 1596. During the six years following the Tumult, the king managed to win concessions from majorities in national assemblies, leaving only a hardened minority of ministers in obdurate opposition as he extended his control over the Kirk.[221] His appointment of three new bishops in 1600, the first elevated in more than a decade, passed without major incident. Shortly before his departure for London he reconciled with Robert Bruce, with whom he had again quarreled in 1600 after Bruce refused to endorse his account of the Gowrie conspiracy in a public sermon.[222] But new tensions flared when, a few months after his arrival in England, James ordered presbyteries in northeastern Scotland to suspend their rigorous pursuit of Catholics and excommunication of Huntly for recusancy, possibly in an effort to facilitate his negotiations for a peace with Spain.[223] The union project set off alarm bells among presbyterians worried that James intended to remodel the Kirk along English lines, giving rise to what one historian has called "an organized campaign of national resistance."[224] James Melville reacted to a report of the Hampton Court conference by urging the presbytery of Edinburgh and the Synod of Fife to pray for "our persecuted brethren in England," who were about to suffer for their ⟨vin⟩dication "to the cause of the sincerity of the gospel and liberty of Christ's ⟨king⟩dom common with us."[225] James ordered Melville's imprisonment, along ⟨with⟩ that of his uncle, Andrew Melville, but the Scottish council failed to carry ⟨hi⟩s instructions, probably from fear of provoking a fierce reaction.[226] The ⟨a⟩mbassador in London passed on a report in January 1605 that the ministers ⟨ha⟩d "are more animated than ever against the bishops and the puritans of ⟨the⟩y have recently presented a very arrogant and hardy petition in which ⟨show⟩ed much anger and discontent against the king."[227] The Synod of

⟨Mac⟩nald, *The Jacobean Kirk, 1567–1625: Sovereignty, Polity and Liturgy* (Aldershot:

MacDonald, *Jacobean Kirk*, 101.   [223] MacDonald, *Jacobean Kirk*, 101–3.

Calderwood, 477–8 and 489.

⟨Jacobea⟩n *Kirk*, 106; *Register of the Privy Council of Scotland*, ed. Mason, 82.

⟨⟩0, fols 102v and 132.

Lothian accused two bishops, John Spottiswood and John Law, of trying to overthrow the Kirk.[228]

In 1605 Spottiswood urged the king to call off a planned meeting of the general assembly in Aberdeen for fear that it would present a collective protest against his ecclesiastical policies. James did so, but nine of Scotland's fifty presbyteries nevertheless elected delegates to the suspended assembly and eighteen ministers actually convened. They were reported to have received encouragement from "some principally in the State," apparently including Scotland's chancellor, Alexander Seton, earl of Dunfermline.[229] When the ministers disobeyed a royal order to disband, James insisted on trying them for sedition. Most submitted and received pardons but six remained obdurate and were imprisoned. The king issued a proclamation threatening to punish with death anyone who criticized the punishment of these ministers in a sermon or private conversation, or who heard such criticism without reporting it to the authorities.[230] But this failed to prevent a rash of angry sermons, charging James with the intention of suppressing general assemblies and introducing English rites into Scotland.[231] Several presbyteries and the Synod of Fife began planning a national day of fasting in support of the "six martyrs."[232] Their imprisonment had revived the old quarrel, dating back to the Tumult and ultimately to the Black Acts of 1584, over whether the king's council had jurisdiction over seditious words spoken in the pulpit and other conduct that the Kirk interpreted as relating to spiritual affairs.[233]

By this date James had already given bishops a majority on the commission he appointed to oversee the Kirk, but the extent of their authority remained unclear and hotly disputed. In July 1606, forty-three ministers signed a declaration condemning episcopacy as contrary to the ordinance of God and an institution that "the experience of previous ages hath testified to be the ground of great idleness, palpable ignorance, unsufferable pride, pitiless tyranny and shameless ambition."[234] Undeterred, James pressed ahead with efforts to force the Kirk's governing bodies to submit to his authority through a mixture of cajolery, intimidation, and political management. He summoned eight leading presbyterian clergymen to London, ostensibly for consultations, but in reality to neutralize their opposition to his policies. The ministers had to listen to sermons on the virtues of episcopacy and the duty of obedience to kings by English bishops. Two, James and Andrew Melville, were imprisoned in the Tower, while the six ministers incarcerated in the previous year were now banished from Scotland.[235] Even one

---

[228] MacDonald, *Jacobean Kirk*, 105.
[229] Spottiswood, 487. For the identity of those who gave high-level encouragement to the ministers see ibid., 495–6 and *Ambassades de Monsieur de la Boderie en Angleterre... Depuis les Années 1606 Jusqu'en 1611*, ed. P. Burdin (Paris, 1750), 1.120–1.
[230] Calderwood, 517.   [231] Spottiswood, 487–9.
[232] MacDonald, *Jacobean Kirk*, 105–13; *Register of the Privy Council of Scotland*, ed. Mason, 7.82, 93.
[233] Calderwood, 512–13.   [234] Calderwood, 527–8.   [235] MacDonald, *Jacobean Kirk*, 125.

of James's new bishops protested against the harshness of these measures, asserting before the Scottish council that the Melvilles "were more strictly kept than Jesuits and murderers," and demanding their immediate release or transfer to more comfortable confinement.[236] The minister of Canongate proclaimed from the pulpit "that every good Christian should prepare himself, for the day of persecution was nearer than they were aware of, that the persecution of the primitive church began with their barks, next with stripes and whips, and last to their lives." He too was imprisoned for meddling in "affairs of estate."[237]

James pressed on by nominating ministers to attend a convention that he and his ecclesiastical commission would later style a general assembly, in a transparent attempt to circumvent the traditional right of presbyteries to choose their own delegates.[238] His principal agent in dealing with Scotland, Dunbar, then pressured this meeting to pass a resolution imposing "constant" or perpetual moderators nominated by the king on all presbyteries and synods. Many of those so chosen were bishops.[239] James intended to install bishops and other men he thought he could trust at the head of the Kirk's representative bodies, as a first step toward bringing these under full royal and episcopal control. "For all the next year there was no matter that troubled the [Scottish] council" so much as the enforcement of this act, which the synods of Fife and Perth and several presbyteries elsewhere in Scotland refused to obey.[240] The Scottish council dispatched "commissioners" to cajole and pressure presbyteries and synods to accept the appointed moderators, and in several cases ordered ministers to stand trial for refusing to comply with the king's wishes.[241] At Perth a synod began with a four-hour sermon exhorting "the brethren in no wise to give obedience" to the king's commissioners, before proceeding to elect a moderator "by their auld custom." An effort by one of the king's commissioners, David Lord Scone, to stop the meeting initiated a shoving match, in the course of which Scone overturned a table on a minister as he attempted to lead a prayer. Scone then ordered all the synod's members arrested on charges of treason, before locking the church doors to prevent any further assembly. His actions almost caused a riot by residents of Perth who rushed to the ministers' support. In the end the synod managed to resume its meeting in the churchyard before a gathering of "people weeping and cursing the instruments of

---

[236] *Register of the Privy Council of Scotland*, ed. Masson, 7.105: "The bishop of Ross in council declared that the said Mr. John Forbes and Mr. John Welsh were hardly kept and more straightly used nor either Jesuits or murderers and therefore desired they might be either put to liberty or transported to some more gentle ward."
[237] Ibid., 121.   [238] MacDonald, *Jacobean Kirk*, 126; Calderwood, 550.
[239] Calderwood, 550; William Scott, *An Apologetical Narration* (Edinburgh: Wodrow Society, 1846), 178–9.
[240] Spottiswood, 503.
[241] *Register of the Privy Council of Scotland*, ed. Masson, 7.343, 312, 406, 407.

that disturbance."²⁴² The synod of Fife also defied the king's instructions and was prohibited by the council from conducting further business until it gave satisfaction.²⁴³ James appointed "a meeting of the commissioners of the Kirk" to act in its place during its suspension.²⁴⁴ In the town of Duns a group of ministers attempted to act as a synod without the king's authority and were summoned to answer before the Scottish council "under pain of rebellion."²⁴⁵ Two commissioners who failed to report back to the council on the results of their mission were "denounced as rebels."²⁴⁶ Disputes over excommunications and other sanctions against Scottish Catholics continued to excite controversy, although on these matters James sometimes submitted to the Kirk's demands.²⁴⁷

During and immediately after these disputes bishops assumed a more prominent role in carrying out the crown's ecclesiastical policies.²⁴⁸ According to the staunch presbyterian David Calderwood, they also attempted to create an episcopal party in the next general assembly, while intimidating their opponents by modifying ministers' stipends and visiting presbyteries.²⁴⁹ Calderwood believed that the bishops' supporters spread reports that "the earl of Dunbar with some English doctors and a great number of old and new-made earls, barons and knights were coming down to overthrow the discipline and government of the Kirk at one blow at the next general assembly."²⁵⁰ By doing so they hoped to foster a belief that unless the Kirk bowed to the king's demands he would impose even more drastic changes. In 1610 James finally proceeded to a full-scale restoration of episcopacy and in January of that year he established a Scottish High Commission.²⁵¹ He then sent a letter to the bishops, formally instructing them to take on the general administration of the Kirk. According to Spottiswood, they resisted doing so "without the knowledge and approbation of the ministers." The king therefore summoned a general assembly for Glasgow to give its assent. Spottiswood presided, while Dunbar and two Scottish officials kept a close eye over the proceedings. After several days of debate, the assembly adopted articles stating that henceforth archbishops or bishops should preside over synods and that bishops should have the authority to conduct visitations of their dioceses and perform various other ecclesiastical functions.²⁵² Having obtained this victory, James prorogued the general assembly indefinitely.

---

²⁴² Ibid., 347–8 and 385–8; Calderwood, 567. I have attempted here to synthesize the two accounts by Calderwood and the Scottish council, which differ in detail but do not contradict each other. The council's narrative mentions the four-hour sermon and states that at one point the minister who delivered it shoved Scone away, while Scone's subsequent actions are recorded by Calderwood.
²⁴³ *Register of the Privy Council of Scotland*, ed. Masson, 7.427, 440.   ²⁴⁴ Ibid., 369.
²⁴⁵ Ibid., 453.   ²⁴⁶ Ibid., 413.
²⁴⁷ MacDonald, *Jacobean Kirk*, 141; *Ambassades de Boderie*, 1.15, 23 and 349; HHStA Belgien PC44, n.p., Hoboque dispatch of September 30, 1608.
²⁴⁸ MacDonald, *Jacobean Kirk*, 143.   ²⁴⁹ Calderwood, 584.   ²⁵⁰ Calderwood, 585.
²⁵¹ MacDonald, *Jacobean Kirk*, 130–45.   ²⁵² Spottiswood, 512.

Despite these measures—or perhaps because through them James had finally gained the upper hand—religious dissension subsided for several years. The bishops' willingness to continue pressuring Scottish Catholics and the absence of further provocative changes produced a relative calm. But from 1616 controversy began to heat up again over what turned out to be justified fears that James intended to impose changes in forms of worship. The installation of an organ and altar in the royal chapel at Holyrood, in preparation for a royal visit to Scotland, and a plan to install wooden statues of the apostles there, provoked objections from Scots who regarded these changes as popish. Several bishops wrote to the king, advising him to desist from setting up the statues.[253] He reluctantly agreed but expressed anger at the Scots' objections.[254] In August a national assembly presided over by the king's commissioner, the earl of Montrose, recommended that a uniform liturgy be drawn up for the Kirk. When James received this proposal he demanded the insertion of an additional article requiring that henceforth Scots should receive communion while kneeling rather than seated, as had been the custom since the Reformation. Articles requiring this change, along with confirmation by bishops and the celebration of Christmas, Easter, and three other holy days, were drawn up and forwarded to Scotland.[255] Knowing that they would encounter stiff resistance, Spottiswood urged the king to delay his attempt to have them ratified. James agreed to do so but only until his arrival in Scotland.[256]

The bishops next urged the king to delay his visit for a year to give them more time to prepare the ground. This time James refused. After pressuring the City of London, the tax farmers, and Dutch merchants to lend him £100,000 to finance it, he set out on his great progress in the spring.[257] Realizing that many Scots anticipated that he would try to alter the Kirk to bring it more closely into line with the Church of England, he issued a proclamation denying that he had any such intention.[258] But it soon became clear that this claim was disingenuous. In May in the Chapel Royal at Stirling he participated in a Prayer Book service, complete with choristers, an organ, and clergy wearing copes. A month later several bishops and nobles received communion kneeling in his presence at Holyroodhouse.[259] He summoned a Scottish parliament and pressed it to enact a statute affirming his right, after receiving the advice of the bishops, to make changes in "matters of external policy" concerning the Kirk. The bishops

---

[253] Ibid., 158.   [254] Spottiswood, 530; Scott, *Apologetical Narration*, 246.
[255] Spottiswood, 528.   [256] Ibid., 529.
[257] Ibid., 530; *The Letters of John Chamberlain*, 2 vols, ed. Norman Egbert McClure (Philadelphia: American Philosophical Society, 1939), 2.42: "this loan of £100,000 which he [James] borrowed of the city, though it be not yet raised, but yet must be done *nolens volens*, and they call in very mean men to help to bear the burden. Sir Noel Caron hath made offer of £20,000 from the strangers of the Netherlands, £60,000 there is made underhand of jewels, and the farmers are engaged for £50,000. Other provisions there be and yet it is feared all will scant serve."
[258] Spottiswood, 529.
[259] Calderwood, 674; cf. Alan R. MacDonald, "James VI and I, the Church of Scotland and British Ecclesiastical Convergence," *Historical Journal* 48 (2005): 885–903, esp. 896.

themselves voiced muted objections to this demand, arguing that "in the making of ecclesiastical laws the advice and consent of the presbyters was also required." James vigorously disagreed but ultimately accepted a compromise wording entitling him to make changes with the advice of the bishops "and a competent number of the ministers."[260] Despite the amendment, the statute reinforced belief that James intended to force through changes in the Kirk's liturgy. One minister preached a sermon in Edinburgh denouncing English ecclesiastical ceremonies "and praying God to save Scotland from the same," while several others subscribed to a formal protest against changes in forms of worship.[261] The protests incensed the king and some of the English clergy in his entourage. But in November a thinly attended general assembly, most of whose members appear to have been hand-picked by the bishops, refused to ratify the articles.

James returned to England furious at his defeat, which he blamed not only on presbyterians but also his bishops, for failing to support him more vigorously. He reportedly vowed "to let the Kirk of Scotland know what it is to have to do with an old king or to abuse his lenity."[262] He renewed his push to secure ratification of the articles at a general assembly in Perth in July 1618, which he subjected to intense pressure, including a display of royal horsemen around the chamber in which it sat and threats that ministers who voted the wrong way would suffer deprivation and banishment.[263] This finally achieved his desired result, although between forty-one and forty-seven members of the assembly, probably including a majority of the parish ministers present, voted again to reject the proposed changes.[264] Resistance continued, with large numbers of parishioners refusing to kneel at the altar and abandoning churches whose ministers required them to do so.[265] Tracts denouncing the Five Articles of Perth, as they became known, and in some cases also the institution of episcopacy, were printed in the Netherlands and smuggled into Scotland. James applied pressure on the Dutch authorities to prevent their publication, while the Scottish council tried, with limited success, to shut down booksellers who distributed them.[266] But this merely encouraged the scribal publication and circulation of additional writings against his policies.[267]

Edinburgh sermons by Spottiswood and another clerical supporter of the king, William Struther, denouncing opposition to the Articles and threatening harsh punishment for it, had little effect. James tried to quell opposition by ordering the

---

[260] Spottiswood, 531.   [261] Ibid.   [262] Scott, *Apologetical Narration*, 253.
[263] Calderwood, 714.   [264] MacDonald, *Jacobean Kirk*, 158–63.
[265] Resistance to the Article has been examined in a series of works by Laura Stewart. See her "'Brothers in Treuth': Propaganda, Public Opinion and the Perth Articles Debate in Scotland," in *James VI and I: Ideas, Authority and Government*, ed. Ralph Houlbrooke (Aldershot: Ashgate, 2006), 151–68; "The Political Repercussions of the Five Articles of Perth: A Reassessment of James VI and I's Religious Policies in Scotland," *Sixteenth Century Journal* 38 (2007): 1013–36; *Urban Politics and British Civil Wars: Edinburgh 1617–1663* (Leiden: Brill, 2006), 8–13; and *Rethinking the Scottish Revolution* (Oxford: Oxford University Press, 2016), esp. 38–43.
[266] Calderwood, *History*, 732.   [267] Stewart, "'Brothers in Treuth'."

imprisonment of a number of Edinburgh citizens for assisting and supporting the ministers in their resistance.[268] Over the course of several years more than thirty ministers were warded, suspended, or deposed for failing to enforce the Articles. Although these measures eventually forced Edinburgh's ministers into compliance, resistance continued beyond the capital and among the laity within it, as thousands of people absented themselves from churches where kneeling at the altar was enforced.[269] On Easter Sunday in 1620 Calderwood claimed that out of a congregation of 1,600 people only "about twenty" agreed to take communion kneeling, most of them paupers brought out of a hospital. The following Christmas "a hundred booth doors" of Edinburgh shopkeepers stood open, in defiance of the article requiring observance of the holiday.[270] As it became harder to find churches where communion could be received without kneeling, some citizens began resorting to private conventicles. James ordered a crackdown that the Scottish council failed to carry out rigorously.[271] The resistance may have deterred the king from pressing ahead with plans to implement more systematic liturgical changes by imposing a Prayer Book modeled after that of England.[272] That project was left for Charles I and Archbishop Laud, but James had already conceived it by 1619.

In 1621 a Scottish parliament ratified the Articles after again coming under intense pressure. But opposition remained stiff and "the parliamentary campaign had enabled the opposition to rediscover the political voice that had made religious dissent so potent in Scotland during the 1580s and 1590s."[273] "It was the Five Articles of Perth that created the sophisticated, well-organised and popular movement that by the 1630s was capable of challenging the government," one historian has concluded.[274] Significantly, the furor over kneeling at communion overlapped in time with James's highly controversial pursuit of a Spanish match for Prince Charles, the eruption of the Thirty Years War in Germany, and the conquest of the lands of the king's son-in-law, Frederick V Elector Palatine, by Spanish and Bavarian armies. Public opposition to the match and expressions of support for Protestants on the Continent were more limited in Scotland than in England, perhaps because the local ecclesiastical dispute took precedence. But many Scottish Protestants, who had always felt strong solidarity with their co-religionists in other countries, knew about the king's diplomatic approach to Spain and the collapse of the Protestant cause in Central Europe. In December 1620 the kirk in Edinburgh urged a day of fasting in sympathy for the churches of Germany.[275] In 1622 "advertisements sent from England of the enlargement of

---

[268] Calderwood, 718–19, 722, and 754.
[269] MacDonald, *Jacobean Kirk*, 164; Stewart, "Political Repercussions of the Five Articles," 1024.
[270] Calderwood, 758.   [271] Stewart, "Political Repercussions of the Five Articles," 1024–5.
[272] MacDonald, "James VI and I and British Ecclesiastical Convergence," 897, shows that James was contemplating doing this as early as 1619.
[273] Stewart, "Political Repercussions of the Five Articles," 1027.   [274] Stewart, *Urban Politics*, 9.
[275] Calderwood, 753, 758.

certain priests and papists" from prison, together with a royal command that Scottish clergy refrain from preaching about predestination or meddling with affairs of state, sparked rumors that James intended both to grant a general toleration of Catholicism and to restrain "the spirit of God" by muzzling preachers.[276] While emphasizing somewhat different issues, the godly in both British kingdoms had grown increasingly suspicious of their king's intentions. According to David Calderwood, news of Prince Charles's journey to Spain in early 1623 caused a general alarm, leading even "the formalists" in Scotland to grow "ashamed of the liberal commendations they had given in former times of the king" and to regret their earlier conformity to his popish articles.[277] To a degree unparalleled since the 1580s, Scots had begun to doubt whether they could rely on the Stuarts to protect their faith.

Conclusions

It is striking that in both Scotland and Ireland James and his agents reacted to religious disaffection by targeting individuals with heavy fines or imprisonment, usually imposed by the Scottish council and High Commission, or the Irish council and its judicial arm, the Court of Castle Chamber. In Ireland in 1613 and repeatedly in Scotland, James's servants also attempted to pack parliaments or general assemblies and to intimidate members of those bodies into doing the king's will. One historian has suggested that unsuccessful efforts to browbeat the Irish Parliament of 1613 provided a precedent for the more successful intimidation of the Perth general assembly of 1618.[278] These actions have faint echoes in the desultory and strikingly unsuccessful attempt of court undertakers to manage the English Parliament of 1614 and the imprisonment of a handful of English MPs after the session of 1621. They also anticipate the famous uses of Star Chamber by Charles I and Archbishop Laud to repress puritan dissent by punishing publicists like William Bastwick, Andrew Burton, and William Prynne, as well as methods used during the Tory Reaction of the 1680s to crush Whig dissent. In each case the remedies failed to address the underlying problem, which involved not just a few seditious individuals but intense dislike of royal ecclesiastical policies among large segments of the population. Lacking the kind of enforcement machinery necessary for sustained, widespread, and effective religious compulsion, the Stuarts compensated by bullying public assemblies and making examples of a few people regarded as ringleaders of opposition. These tactics achieved a few temporary successes, especially in Scotland, but only at the cost of creating martyrs, deepening public resentment, and in several cases provoking organized resistance.

---

[276] Spottiswood, 543. [277] Calderwood, 801. [278] MacDonald, *Jacobean Kirk*, 162.

Francis Bacon had warned in 1604 that if James's kingdoms failed to unify comprehensively their conjunction under a single crown would in the long run prove a source of weakness rather than strength. Twenty years later his ominous prediction looked more relevant than ever, even though the state's principal vulnerabilities derived less from the legal and institutional diversity that Bacon had wanted to eradicate than the stubborn persistence of religious differences. Ecclesiastical disputes had not yet triggered a major rebellion or a functional breakdown in the machinery of royal governance. but they had graphically demonstrated the limits of James VI and I's ability to achieve absolute obedience, whether voluntarily or by force. Active religious dissension vitiated other significant achievements. By using a variety of methods, the king and his agents had made considerable progress in extending some form of royal control over remote regions of his dominions. Former frontier districts in places as diverse as Cumbria, Ulster, and the Scottish Isles had grown more peaceful and "civil"; seigneurial armies and private warfare had been largely eliminated in Ireland and significantly curtailed in Scotland; and although only limited progress had been made toward bringing the laws and institutional structures of England and Scotland into closer alignment, the authority of sheriffs and commissions of the peace had been introduced into Scotland and had grown substantially in Ireland. These were far from negligible accomplishments.

But whenever the king tried to demand more than routine compliance with orders that many of his subjects regarded as incompatible with their own interests and religious beliefs, he met with obstruction and resistance. Whether it came to obtaining legislation to unify the laws of England and Scotland, money to clear his debts, or outward compliance with a uniform set of ecclesiastical institutions and ceremonies, his subjects stubbornly resisted his wishes. He presided over a state strong enough to go on functioning indefinitely so long as only minimal demands were placed upon it, but one that lacked ability either to project British power beyond its borders, or to respond in a robust fashion to any new internal emergency. Even in the absence of a major crisis, this situation left James in an awkward position, especially with respect to international power politics. As Elizabeth's successor and the greatest Protestant king in Europe, foreign states and his own subjects expected him to play an active and effective role in the Continent's affairs. But he found his ability to do so constrained, not only by his own professed dedication to peace but, even more, by his poverty and vulnerability to domestic disturbances, especially in Ireland but to an extent also in his two other kingdoms. To remain secure, he had to avoid entanglement in a foreign war, but to uphold his honor as Europe's greatest Protestant king he needed to avoid the appearance that his fear of being attacked limited his willingness to oppose Catholic aggression. The following two chapters explore his efforts to cope with this challenge and the reasons why, by the end of his life, his efforts to do so had largely failed.

11
Peace Without
The European Policies of James VI and I until 1617

James VI and I's policies toward Europe remain an understudied and frequently oversimplified subject, commonly viewed through the distorting lenses of seventeenth-century polemic and later historiographical biases. The fixation of early Stuart historians on domestic politics relatable to the origins of the Civil War partly explains this situation, but so does the state of the evidence. There is simply too much of it: nearly 200 volumes of diplomatic state papers for James's reign, about fifty more of correspondence preserved by his ambassador in Brussels, Sir William Trumbull, now in the British Library, and numerous other relevant British collections. And this is only half the story, since equally voluminous materials exist in European archives. Rather than trying to conquer this mountain of source materials, historians have too often preferred to recycle generalizations derived from older studies, going back to S. L. Gardiner's Victorian narrative.[1] Although a few episodes, such as the negotiation of the 1604 Treaty of London ending war with Spain, have received reasonably close analysis, we still lack a comprehensive published study of British foreign policy based on primary sources covering the entire first quarter of the seventeenth century.[2]

Accounts of James's European policies have also tended to read his reign backwards, by interpreting his pursuit of a dynastic alliance with Spain between 1617 and 1623, and reluctance to enter the Thirty Years War as symptomatic of a consistent preference for peace with the Habsburgs from 1603 onwards. Focusing on the period after the eruption of a new religious war in Central Europe reinforces emphasis on confessional conflict as the defining feature of European politics, encouraging a view that James faced a straightforward choice of alliances "between Spain or the Netherlands," as the title of an influential article by Simon

---

[1] Samuel R. Gardiner, *The History of England from the Accession of James I to the Outbreak of the Civil War, 1603–1642*, 10 vols (London: Longman, 1887–91).

[2] The last and best attempt at such a study remains unpublished: Adams, "Protestant Cause." Adams summarized some of his conclusions in essays cited below in this chapter. See also W. B. Patterson, *King James VI and I and the Reunion of Christendom* (Cambridge: Cambridge University Press, 1997), a valuable and deeply researched study but one that in my view takes James's claims to act as a peace-maker and mediator too much at face value.

Adams put it.³ Since this foreign policy choice maps fairly neatly onto domestic disputes between godly puritans, who felt a sense of solidarity with European Calvinists, and so-called Arminians, who did not, it fits into accounts of growing dissension over religion that culminated in the Civil War, and therefore into a political narrative focused primarily on domestic politics.

The disparaging view of James prevalent until fairly recently among historians of England added another layer to this interpretation by making it easier to depict his attraction to Spain as a symptom of naivety, weakness, and self-indulgence. Already foreshadowed in some contemporary pamphlets opposing the Spanish match, this assessment of the king was more fully developed by German confessional historians in the nineteenth century, who in turn influenced Gardiner's classic narrative and subsequent British historiography.⁴ Maurice Lee's book on James's relations with Henry IV of France, for example, characterized him as "lazy, extravagant, conceited, imbued with an inflated sense of his power... unwilling to learn or to distinguish good advice from bad," and hence prone to damaging errors.⁵ James has often been portrayed as addicted to grandiose pronouncements on subjects like the divine right of kings and virtues of peace, but deficient in practical political skills. In his dealings with Europe his belief in the ideal of peace and commitment to principles of royal legitimacy allegedly deterred him from acting effectively in the face of Habsburg aggression. C. V. Wedgwood's influential history of the Thirty Years War, published in 1938, implicitly compared his refusal to fight Spain to Neville Chamberlain's appeasement of Hitler.⁶ In the 1970s some historians described his pursuit of a Spanish alliance as proof of irresponsibility and "senile incompetence," by contrast to the purportedly healthier instinct of the British public to resist the triumph of "reactionary Catholicism."⁷ Simon Adams's impressive thesis, completed in 1973, adopted a more temperate and balanced view, acknowledging that James's dislike of expensive foreign wars did not differ markedly from Elizabeth's attitude. But Adams still argued that "Elizabeth was willing to exploit existing situations while James attempted to elevate political decisions to matters

---

³ Simon Adams, "Spain or the Netherlands: The Dilemmas of Early Stuart Foreign Policy," in *Before the English Civil War: Essays on Early Stuart Politics and Government*, ed. Howard Tomlinson (Basingstoke: Macmillan, 1988), 79–101. The detailed analysis in this essay focuses mainly on the period after 1618, extending into the reign of Charles I.
⁴ Peter Wilson, *The Thirty Years War: Europe's Tragedy* (Cambridge, MA: Belknap Press, 2009), 7.
⁵ Maurice Lee Jr., *James I and Henry IV: An Essay in English Foreign Policy 1603–1610* (Urbana: University of Illinois Press, 1970), 5.
⁶ For the historiographical influences see Wilson, *Thirty Years War*, 7 and 49.
⁷ For example, Frances Yates, *The Rosicrucian Enlightenment* (St Albans: Paladin, 1972), esp. 50–1 and Roy Strong, *Henry Prince of Wales and England's Lost Renaissance* (London: Thames and Hudson, 1986), esp. 15. Yates employs the adjective "reactionary," in describing European Catholicism and claims that James's refusal to resist it sabotaged his relations with Parliament and the English public.

of principle."[8] More recently a few historians have presented James's commitment to peace in a favorable light. W. B. Patterson published a sympathetic book on the king's pursuit of religious reconciliation, while Peter Wilson has claimed that "James was in fact one of the few entirely sensible European monarchs" of his generation because he "much preferred peace to war."[9] But these scholars continue to depict him as committed to high-minded principles more than hard-headed calculations of political advantage: "complacent, pompous and escapist," but "sincerely" committed to peace.[10]

This view, it must be acknowledged, finds some apparent support in James's own rhetorical self-construction as *Rex Pacificus*, and the contemporary reactions it elicited. James's panegyrists praised him as a British Solomon, presiding over an age of peace and plenty, anticipating Peter Paul Rubens's spectacular posthumous tribute on the ceiling of the Whitehall Banqueting House.[11] His critics, both in Britain and Europe, characterized him as overly scrupulous, weak, and timid. Sir John Eliot hailed his death for ending "the fearful security and degenerate vices of a long-corrupted peace."[12] But while statements like this tell us a good deal about how people viewed James during and immediately after his lifetime, we should be wary of taking them at face-value. It will be argued here that although not entirely wrong, the conventional view of James's principled aversion to religious war stands in need of serious qualification. On one basic level he undeniably does deserve his reputation as a pacific king, since he ruled for twenty-one years free from significant armed conflicts, sandwiched between Elizabeth's great war with Spain and the disastrous foreign conflicts that Charles I initiated immediately after his succession in 1625. But merely pointing this out begs the question of how far the absence of war stemmed from

---

[8] Simon Adams, "The Road to La Rochelle: English Foreign Policy and the Huguenots, 1610–1629," *Proceedings of the Huguenot Society of London* 22 (1975): 414–29 at 415. Adams presents a longer and more complex view of James's outlook, stressing his commitment to principles of royal legitimacy, in "The Protestant Cause," esp. 154–6. He prefaces his discussion with the statement that before 1603, "in his candidacy for the English throne James VI of Scotland had pursued a careful policy of appearing all things to all men." The implication, never fully explored, is that something transformed James from an opportunistic equivocator into a principled upholder of legitimist principles and ideology after he reached London. For reasons that will gradually become clear, I remain skeptical that this transformation ever took place, although I readily concede that James was sometimes *perceived* as a rigid and naïve upholder of legitimist principles by many contemporaries.

[9] Patterson, *James VI and I and the Reunion of Christendom*, 247.   [10] Ibid., 286.

[11] Gregory Martin, *Rubens in London* (London: Harvey Miller, 2011). I have attempted to examine and qualify James's reputation as a peace-maker in three previous articles: Malcolm Smuts, "Concepts of War and Peace in Stuart Court Culture," in *Frieden und Krieg in der Früheb Neuzeit: Die europäische Staatenordnung und die aussereuropäische Welt*, ed. Ronald Asch, Wulf Eckart Voss and Martin Wrede (Munich: Wilhelm Fink Verlag, 2001), 215–38; "The Making of *Rex Pacificus*: James VI and I and the Problem of Peace in an Age of Religious War," in *Royal Subjects: Essays on the Writings of James VI and I*, ed. Daniel Fischlin and Mark Fortier (Detroit: Wayne State University Press, 2002), 371–87; and "International Politics and Jacobean Statecraft," in *The Oxford Handbook of John Donne*, ed. Jeanne Shami, Dennis Flynn, and M. Thomas Hester (Oxford: Oxford University Press, 2011), 589–99.

[12] *Proceedings in Parliament 1625*, ed. Maija Jansson and William Bidwell (New Haven: Yale University Press, 1987), 491.

James's philosophical convictions, rather than a combination of self-interested political calculations and external circumstances. Elizabeth had entered into open war with Spain reluctantly, and in 1598 she and Burghley initiated peace negotiations with Spain that Robert Cecil continued to pursue intermittently over the next several years, until they finally succeeded in the second year of James's English reign. In 1625 Charles and Buckingham embarked on a more bellicose course than James had wanted to pursue. But within four years, military defeats, along with domestic political and financial pressures, led to a renewed withdrawal from European conflicts. The important question is not whether James preferred peace to war—he unquestionably did—but how he managed to avoid having to fight a war, and why his efforts at doing so started to break down toward the end of his reign. What tactics and strategies did he employ in dealing with foreign states and why did they apparently succeed better in the period before about 1618 than thereafter?

In addressing this question, we need to recognize that although religion always remained important in European politics during the period, the precise ways in which it did so varied considerably with changing circumstances. Some events, like the Treaty of Joinville between Philip II and the French Catholic League in 1584, and the outbreak of a new religious war in Central Europe in 1618, sharpened patterns of confessional polarization. But Henry IV's conversion to Rome even while he continued to fight Spain had the opposite effect, opening the door to cross-confessional alliances rooted in shared secular interests. Viewing James's options as a straightforward choice between "Spain and the Netherlands" obscures the importance of France and other Catholic states like Venice and Savoy that were at times eager to join with Protestant powers in opposition to Spain or the papacy. It also overlooks the anxiety that British statesmen felt about bitter conflicts among Protestants in the Netherlands and elsewhere that threatened to undercut confessional solidarity. The early seventeenth century witnessed not only continuing Protestant–Catholic rivalry and simmering conflict but significant intra-confessional disputes within both major camps: between Gallicans and Jesuits, Lutherans and Calvinists, and different factions within both Lutheran and Calvinist churches. Confessional loyalties interacted in complicated ways with secular interests and personal rivalries to produce complex and shifting political alignments.

Even the role of the Habsburgs as champions of Catholicism should not be oversimplified, since significant disagreements over policy existed between different branches of the dynasty and within the Spanish court.[13] The whole subject of relations between the British crown and the rest of Europe needs re-examination, with an eye to adding nuance and complexity to a subject too often discussed in

---

[13] Many of these are traced in Luc Duerloo, *Dynasty and Piety: Archduke Albert (1598-1621) and Habsburg Political Culture in an Age of Religious Wars* (Farnham: Ashgate, 2012).

overly stark terms.[14] The following two chapters claim to provide no more than a preliminary effort to tackle this huge subject. But I hope to show that even a partial examination of the primary sources, together with attention to recent studies of European politics, leads to a much more complicated and ambiguous picture of James's objectives, successes, and failures in foreign policy.

Military Exhaustion, Strategic Calculations, and the Pursuit of Peace: The European Context

We have noted that James inherited the English throne at a time when the great religious wars of late sixteenth-century Europe had devolved into a ruinously expensive stalemate, from which many statesmen in both confessional camps wanted to withdraw.[15] But in doing so they needed to protect their own interests and reputations. In 1598 Anglo-Spanish peace negotiations collapsed partly because the Spaniards still hoped that a direct attack on Elizabeth's dominions might win them substantially better terms. Between 1596 and 1600 they sent out three invasion fleets. The first two were driven back by storms with heavy losses, although the second managed to reach the entrance to the Channel and nearly intercepted Essex's fleet as it straggled back from the Islands Voyage, with its ships battered and crews and stores depleted. If a change in the weather had not forced the Spaniards to withdraw they might have inflicted catastrophic losses on England's sea defenses. The third expedition began as a plan to attack England with 20,000 soldiers conveyed by 111 ships. Acute financial problems soon forced the Spanish council to scale back the enterprise into an alternative scheme for a diversionary assault on Ireland by 6,000 or 7,000 soldiers. Additional financial difficulties and losses at sea eventually reduced this force to less than 3,500 men by the time it landed at Kinsale in southwestern Ireland, in October 1601. Too small to oppose Montjoy's army, which moved quickly to deal with the threat, the Spanish force remained bottled up on the Kinsale Peninsula.[16] When the earls of Tyrone and Tyrconnell marched south to rescue their allies, Montjoy defeated them in the decisive battle of the war, whereupon the Spaniards surrendered. The debacle helped convince Philip III—who had succeeded his father in 1598—and his chief minister, the duke of Lerma, of the futility of further conflict, particularly in light of immense debts that had forced the Spanish crown to declare bankruptcy

---

[14] Continental studies that I have found especially useful include Ruben Gonzáles Cuerva, *Baltasar de Zúñiga: Unar encrucijada de la Monarquía Hispana (1561–1622)* (Madrid: Ediciones Polifeno, 2012); Jean-François Dubost, *Marie de Médicis: La reine dévoilée* (Paris: Biographie Payot, 2009); Duerloo, *Dynasty and Piety*; Bernardo José Garcia Garcia, *La Pax Hispanica: Política Exterior del Duque de Lerma* (Leuven: Leuven University Press, 1996); and Wilson, *Thirty Years War*.
[15] Above, pp. 448–9.   [16] Garcia Garcia, *Pax Hispanica*, 31–41.

in 1598, and harvest failures and plagues that were ravaging Castile.¹⁷ The replacement of Elizabeth by James, who had never been at war with Spain, made an end to hostilities easier. A number of contentious issues involving trade, religious policies, and English aid to the Dutch still needed to be worked out, but by the summer of 1604 a treaty that both sides felt able to ratify had finally been drafted.¹⁸

The ending of war with Spain therefore owed at least as much to the attitude of Spanish statesmen as to James's desire for peace, which should not be exaggerated. For him, as for other contemporary princes and their ministers, a preference for peace did not require the renunciation of the use of force under all circumstances. States and dynasties still had interests to protect and they continued to mistrust each other, which made armies, navies, and limited wars necessary. The challenge lay in preventing limited conflicts from escalating into general wars with unpredictable and potentially ruinous consequences. If James's embrace of peace sometimes appeared more absolute than that of other contemporary princes and their leading ministers, this had as much to do with Britain's relatively marginal position in most continental conflicts as any underlying ideology. Lerma and the Archduke Albert both wanted to end their war with the Dutch but felt compelled to keep fighting until they obtained terms that would not look like a humiliating defeat. By contrast, although James had an interest in preventing the collapse of the United Provinces, so long as a rough military stalemate continued in the Low Countries he had less at stake. Crises in the Rhineland and conflicts involving the duchy of Savoy directly threatened the security of France's eastern frontier and the vital Spanish Road linking Habsburg Milan to the Low Countries. France and Spain therefore had little choice but to become involved. James had an indirect interest in these disputes, since they affected the interests of small Protestant states with which he had allied, but they did not immediately imperil his own security. The relative poverty of the British crown, in comparison to those of Spain and France, provided another compelling reason to shun military adventures. While all governments of the period struggled to avoid insolvency, the revenues of the two great continental monarchies far exceeded those of Britain, giving them greater potential to generate surpluses through financial reforms, as Sully demonstrated in France. Like the Dutch but unlike Britain, both also had

---

¹⁷ Ibid., 31–74 traces the transition from active war to pursuit of peace by the Spanish crown. The same author's "Peace with England: From Convenience to Necessity," in *Material and Symbolic Circulation between Spain and England, 1554–1604*, ed. Anne J. Cruz (Aldershot: Ashgate, 2008), 135–49, provides a more concise summary in English.

¹⁸ The most thorough study of peace negotiations between England and Spain in 1604 is Robert Cross, "To Counterbalance the World: England, Spain and Peace in the Early Seventeenth Century," unpublished Princeton PhD thesis, 2012. For a different view see Pauline Croft, "*Rex Pacificus*, Robert Cecil and the 1604 Peace with Spain," in *The Accession of James I: Historical and Cultural Consequences*, ed. Glenn Burgess and Rowland Wymer (Basingstoke: Palgrave Macmillan, 2006), 140–54.

permanent land forces they could redeploy to meet sudden emergencies. James had greater difficulties in raising armies than the French, Spanish, or Dutch statesmen, and usually fewer incentives to use them. Although he did nevertheless occasionally resort to force, his reluctance to become embroiled in conflict with major European powers requires little explanation. High minded pronouncements about his love of peace provided a convenient excuse for prudent and self-interested caution.[19]

A King of Artifices Who Dissimulates

James also differed from most contemporary rulers in his remarkable volubility and fondness for theological and philosophical argument, which he expressed through printed tracts as well as apparently spontaneous utterances before courtiers, diplomats, and anyone else within earshot. His penchant for discussing "all matters freely at his [dinner] table," especially "scholastic disputes" about religion, led one French diplomat to anticipate several modern historians by describing him as a foolishly loquacious king whose preoccupation with pedantic arguments blinded him to political realities.[20] But James's record in Scotland, where he had mustered rhetorical and theological arguments with considerable skill and flexibility, should make us question this view. Although he certainly took ideas seriously, he had learned early in life to wield intellectual arguments as political tools, not only to persuade others but sometimes to mislead them about his true intentions. Some foreign ambassadors recognized this characteristic. The great Spanish diplomat, Diego Sarmiento de Acuña count of Gondomar, commented on the need for caution in negotiations with James because of his "art of listening to and graciously admitting (as it seems) contrary arguments and his subtle way of speaking equivocal words that he can interpret in his own fashion and according

---

[19] See, e.g., James's initial rejection of a proposed league with France and the Netherlands during an interview with the Dutch ambassador Noel de Caron in *Johan van Oldenbarnevelt Bescheiden Betreffende zijn Staatkundig Beleid en zijn Familie, tweed deel, 1602–1613*, ed. A. J. Veenendaal, Rijks Geschiedkundige Publicatien 108 ('s-Gravenhage: Martinus Nijhoff, 1962), 252: "In effect the reply was that the king in no way can or should break his peace with the king of Spain [and] that this proposed league stood directly against the treaty made with Spain and might force the king into a war with Spain." This sounds like a principled stand but its effect was to shun a treaty that might have threatened to drag the British crown into a war that it lacked the resources to fight effectively.

[20] The quotations are from a description by the French ambassador Christophe de Harlay in 1603, BN Mss. Français 1503, fols 273v–274. Harlay went on to attribute James's apparent coolness toward the Dutch to his excessive scrupulosity with respect to abstract ideas of peace and legitimacy "... ce prince selon son instinct naturel qui le porte aveuglement à la paix et à la superstition qu'il a en son conscience à la cause de messieurs des Etats qui l'empêche de sainement considérer combien il est intéressé à leur conservation."

to his interests."²¹ A few years later a French ambassador, the Marquis de Tillières, gave a blunter assessment of "this king of artifices who dissimulates above all the rest of the world."²²

James's fondness for artifice and dissimulation can make it difficult to disentangle his actual beliefs from statements intended to mislead others by telling them what he knew they wanted to hear. His handling of negotiations with France, the United Provinces, and Spain at the outset of his English reign illustrates the point. In an unpublished thesis Cynthia Fry has shown that while ruling Scotland James presented himself as a godly king who sought confessional alliances with the Netherlands, Denmark, and other Protestant states, as he simultaneously cultivated good relations with Spain and the papacy.²³ This equivocal policy continued right up to the moment of Elizabeth's death. In February 1603 he warned Henry IV that Robert Cecil wanted to make peace between England and Spain and suggested that the French should counter by proposing a grand offensive alliance between England, France, Scotland, and other Protestant states. Henry did not take the suggestion very seriously, especially after Elizabeth indicated that she did not want an offensive alliance with Scotland, so nothing came of the proposal. In the same period a pro-Spanish group within the Scottish court discussed a possible marriage of James's heir, Prince Henry, to a Spanish infanta, and when the Habsburg rulers of the southern Netherlands sent an envoy to Edinburgh, barely a week before Elizabeth's death, James welcomed him warmly and promised to allow the recruitment of Scots for the Army of Flanders. He told the envoy privately that he disliked the Hollanders and their cause, and that if he became king of England he would make peace with Spain.²⁴ A report of this conversation reached Archduke Albert almost simultaneously with news of Elizabeth's death, inducing optimism that English support for the Dutch would soon end.²⁵

James's equivocations became harder to sustain once he succeeded to the English crown since, along with Elizabeth's throne, he inherited her war with

---

²¹ *CDIHE Gondomar* 1.339: "su arte en oír y admitir gratamente (el parecer) lo que se le dice en contra y la sutileza que tiene en decir palabras equívocos, que él pueda sin prendarse interpretar a su modo y como le conviniere, y lo que procura penetrar lo que quiere decir quien le habla y el ánimo y fin con que se lo dice, esto me ha obligado a ir siempre con cuidado."

²² BN Mss. Français 15,989, fol. 61: "ce roi qui est artificieux et dissimule par-dessus tout le reste du monde."

²³ Cynthia Fry, "Diplomacy and Deception: King James VI of Scotland's Foreign Relations with Europe (1585–1603)," unpublished University of St Andrews PhD thesis, 2014.

²⁴ BN Mss. Français 15,972, fols 115 and 122; *Correspondance de la cour d'Espagne sur les affaires des Pays-Bas au XVIIe siècle*, eds Henri Lonchay and Joseph Cuvelier (Brussels: Libraire Kiessling, 1923), 123, 139–40, and 141; Fry, "Diplomacy and Deception," 131. The agent, Nicolas Scorza, arrived in Scotland on March 24 new style or March 14 old style and received an audience with James on March 30, n.s. (March 20, o.s.). A French letter reporting Scorza's reception by James is dated April 2, 1603, n. s. (March 24, o.s.), the day Elizabeth died. Scorza was still in Scotland when word of the queen's death arrived.

²⁵ *Correspondance de la cour d'Espagne*, 144.

Spain, her treaty with the Dutch, control of the cautionary towns of Brill and Flushing, and claims to more than a million pounds in debt that the United Provinces and the French owed to England, which he was hardly in a position to write off. His succession also came at a crucial point in the Eighty Years War, as the Dutch and Spanish both neared exhaustion but struggled to make gains that would tip the balance in any final settlement. The prolonged Spanish siege of Ostend was especially important in this respect. Although Henry IV had broken his formal alliance with England and the United Provinces by making peace with Spain in 1598, he continued to provide financial assistance to the Dutch and his irritation with Spain had lately increased. Although not yet ready to embark on a new war he had begun to consider eventually doing so. But since Elizabeth had entertained peace feelers from the Habsburg archdukes, England's ongoing commitment to war with Spain appeared in doubt.

James's succession added another major source of unpredictability to this already fluid situation. As he slowly made his way to London in April 1603 all Europe watched, with a mixture of hope and anxiety, to see what he would do. Henry IV demanded detailed reports from his ambassador in London, Christophe de Harlay, and his representative to Scotland, the Baron du Tours, who joined James's procession south.[26] Although hopeful that England would continue its war with Spain, Henry worried that false rumors spread by Spanish agents and disgruntled Huguenots about his own efforts to prevent James's succession might poison their relationship. Since the English ambassador in Paris, Thomas Parry, evidently believed these reports, the French king had reason for concern.[27] The Dutch badly wanted increased English and French support to relieve Ostend but feared that James might instead withdraw his assistance and prevent them from recruiting English soldiers, who comprised about a fifth of their army.[28] On April 8 their agent in London, Noel de Caron, reported that the English council had informed him that it now lacked authority to instruct JPs in the provinces to help Dutch recruiting.[29] Within weeks the States General dispatched a high-level embassy to England that included Count Henry of Nassau and Johan van Oldenbarnevelt.[30] But the Habsburg archdukes also wasted no time in dispatching an embassy of congratulations that met James even before he arrived in London.[31] The king's warm response to this embassy increased French and Dutch anxiety, which grew even more acute in May, when on three separate occasions James expressed disapproval of the Dutch rebellion and sympathy for the Habsburg's claims of sovereignty over the Netherlands during conversations at his dinner

---

[26] *Recueil des lettres missives d'Henry IV*, vol. 6, ed. M. Berger de Xivrey (Paris: Imprimerie Impériale, 1853), 161.
[27] Ibid., 62; TNA SP78/49, fol. 11.   [28] TNA SP84/64, fol. 13.
[29] BL Add Mss. 17,677G, fol. 40; cf. fols 150v and 152r.
[30] TNA SP84/64, fol. 9.   [31] HMC Salisbury, 15.55.

table.³² He declared that "he would not oblige himself to the causes of his predecessor" and blamed Henry IV for supporting Dutch rebels, saying that this induced the Spanish to promote plots to destabilize France.³³ He talked of his desire to arbitrate the dispute between the United Provinces and the archdukes. Reports of his unsympathetic attitude soon reached the Netherlands, reportedly bringing the inhabitants of the cautionary town of Flushing "within an ace of cutting the English garrison to pieces."³⁴

On their face James's public comments do appear to reflect his principled aversion to rebellions against legitimate kings. But there is another possible explanation. Elizabeth had been dead for less than two months when he made them and although so far everything had gone fairly smoothly, he had not yet consolidated his hold over his new kingdoms. Rumors circulated about plots to install Arabella Stuart in his place and the machinations of his wife, who was widely perceived as a pro-Spanish Catholic who disliked James and hated his Scottish courtiers.³⁵ Would she conspire with English malcontents to cause trouble? The Bye and Main Plots would soon unfold, while the rebellions of Munster towns had already started.³⁶ James had every reason to deter the Spanish from conspiring with Catholics and malcontents to undermine him. Making general pronouncements at his dinner table provided an easy way of doing this, by suggesting that the Habsburgs had everything to gain by cooperating with him, while avoiding concrete commitments.

In fact, he had already signaled a more flexible position in private conversations with the English diplomat Thomas Lake, who had traveled north to meet him. Lake noted that James had given soothing words to the archduke's ambassador but reported that the king also wanted the Dutch to send commissioners to London to discuss their relationship with him. When Lake urged him to continue supporting the United Provinces James appeared receptive, saying "on behalf of the States that he would not abandon them."³⁷ In early May he assured the Elector Palatine that he would vigorously support the "common cause" of religion in Europe.³⁸ His expressions of sympathy for the Habsburg's position nevertheless alarmed both Henry IV and the Dutch. Henry sent "his most inward and

---

³² BL King's Mss. 123, fols 123, 144, and 160. The source of the information is the French ambassador.
³³ TNA SP78/49, fol. 71v; *CSPV* 10.40–1.   ³⁴ *CSPV* 10.50.
³⁵ For two such views of Anna of Denmark in May of 1603 see P. Laffleur Kermaingant, *L'Ambassade de France en Angleterre sous Henri IV. Mission de Christophe de Harlay, Comte de Beaumont (1602–1605)*, 2 vols (Paris: Bibliothèque de l'école des chartes, 1895), 2.112 and BN Mss. Français 3502, fol. 37.
³⁶ Above, pp. 505–7.   ³⁷ HMC Salisbury 15.30.
³⁸ TNA SP78/49, fol. 96v: "comme nous nous estimons très heureux de la grâce que Dieu nous a faite de nous de nous fait naitre et vivre en la connaissance et profession de la vrai et pure religion, aussi nous vous prions de croire et vouse assurer que là où le besoin le requerra, nous serons toujours de même affectionné et dispose à nous employer sincèrement de notre part pour le bien et advancement de cette cause commune."

confidant servant," the Huguenot marquis de Rosny (better known today by his later title, Sully), as an extraordinary ambassador charged with urging "a joint union betwixt these two crowns for the protection of the Low Countries."[39] Rosny arrived in June to a hero's welcome from London crowds.[40] For a brief period, the chief ministers of the Netherlands, France, and Britain were all in London, engaged in face-to-face negotiations over the future of their relationship.

Although James remained non-committal during his first audience with the Dutch delegates on May 25, he seems to have reassured Oldenbarnevelt during a private interview shortly thereafter.[41] On June 13 he went a step further, signaling his desire for an accord with France in a conversation with Harlay. James denounced at length Spanish perfidiousness, expressed his mistrust of their professions of friendship, and stated that he needed to maintain his guard against them even if he managed to conclude a peace treaty.[42] He subsequently told Oldenbarnevelt, who in turn told Rosny, that he had experienced a change of heart about the Netherlands. At first, he said, he "did not much worry about their safety, being carried away with the beautiful name of peace that resounded in the mouths of the English councilors." "But after deeper consideration" of the courses necessary to obtain a secure and durable peace, "and [of] the condition in which England would stand if the king of France or the king of Spain achieved peaceful possession of all seventeen provinces of the Netherlands, he seemed to awake as if from a profound sleep," and realized that he needed to listen to the proposals of Henry's ambassadors.[43] At his first audience with Rosny, James repeated his denunciations of Spanish ambition and deceit, adding for good measure the insulting comment that the "present king of Spain lacked the vigor of body and spirit to make as much progress as his predecessors" in achieving his nefarious designs.[44] Since the audience was a semi-public occasion, a number of people heard this anti-Spanish diatribe, including members of the Dutch delegation.[45]

In a subsequent interview later in the month James added that he hoped for a firm friendship with Henry IV to resist "the pernicious and ambitious designs of those who aspire to the [Universal] Monarchy over Christendom, who have continually troubled [Europe] by wars and seditions": in other words, the Habsburgs.[46] Rosny optimistically reported that the king and "almost everyone here" had relinquished the vain hope of "amity with everyone."[47] In his memoirs, written between 1611 and 1617, the French statesman recollected that in one

---

[39] Ibid., fol. 4, Thomas Parry to Robert Cecil, April 4, 1603; *Recueil des lettres missives*, 6.82.
[40] BL King's Mss. 123, fols 241v–242; Add Mss. 17,677 G, fol. 78r.   [41] TNA SP84/64, fol. 21.
[42] BL King's Mss. 123, fol. 212.   [43] Ibid., fols 231v–232.   [44] Ibid., fol. 245v.
[45] *Memoirs of Maximilien de Bethune, Duke of Sully*, 6 vols, trans. Charlotte Lennox (London, 1778), 5.10–11. The report of the audience in the *Memoirs* is confirmed by Rosny's contemporary dispatch, cited in the previous note.
[46] BL King's Mss. 123, fols 231v–232 and 245v. James had also twice expressed his mistrust of Spain to Harlay, ibid., fols 212, 310.
[47] Ibid., fol. 254.

meeting James blamed Robert Cecil for his initial friendliness toward Spain, upbraiding him for his bad advice before several other English councilors and commanding him to prepare papers for an alliance with the French and Dutch. Rosny came away from the interview impressed by James's solid judgment but worried that Cecil would seek "to render ineffectual" his master's good intentions.[48] He had undoubtedly misread the situation. Although Cecil did want peace with Spain, he also favored continued British support for the United Provinces, and within a year the French would revise their assumptions to a point at which both Harlay and Henry IV sought to enlist Cecil's aid in managing the king.[49] But for several months Rosny's assessment convinced the French monarch, who told both his own ambassador to Venice and the Landgrave of Hesse later in the summer that he had complete confidence in James's friendship and alliance, but mistrusted Cecil.[50]

As his memoirs make clear, Rosny believed that he had influenced the young king of England through personal charm and persuasive arguments. But it seems more likely that by appearing to submit to Rosny's charm and agreeing with his analysis of the European situation, James subtly misled the French statesman and his master.[51] He not only gained the trust of Rosny and Henry but predisposed them to blame any future limitations of British cooperation with France on Cecil rather than himself. Suspicion of Cecil gave the French incentives to offer James better terms, for fear that his principal minister might otherwise sabotage any accord. A secret agreement, the Treaty of Hampton Court, was hammered out before Rosny's departure in early July and formalized later in the month. Under its terms James agreed to allow the Dutch to levy an additional regiment of 2,000 Scots commanded by Lord Buccleuch. The French would pay the full costs but would be allowed to deduct a third of their disbursements from the debts they owed the English crown. The two kings also agreed that if either were attacked by Spain the other would come to his aid with an army of at least 6,000 men.[52] In August James declined to formally authorize Buccleuch's recruitment, but he quietly allowed it to proceed.[53] He thereby strengthened the Dutch military position at no additional cost to his own treasury, while leaving himself free to

---

[48] *Memoirs of Sully*, 3.130, 134.
[49] BN Mss. Français 3506 fol. 13r, dispatch of March 30, 1604 and *Mission de Harlay*, ed. Kermaingant, 2.256-7, Henry IV to Harlay, July 29, 1604: "Continuer à bien ménager et bien entretenir le maitre par le serviteur à notre dévotion et amitié."
[50] *Recueil des lettres et missives*, 6.128, 139, 143, and 192.
[51] Cf. the very similar conclusion about this episode in Cross, "To Counterbalance the World," 136-47. Cross's astute discussion of James's methods of political management, which reached me after this chapter was virtually completed, strikes me as entirely convincing and essentially complementary to the arguments I have presented. While differing in some details our accounts seem to point in the same direction.
[52] See Oldenbarnevelt's description of the negotiation of this agreement in *Oldenbarnevelt Bescheiden*, ed. Veenendaal, 478-81 and AMAE, CPA 25, fol. 31v.
[53] BN Mss. Français 3502, fol. 303v; TNA SP84/64, fol. 43.

tell the Habsburgs that he had done nothing harmful to their interests. Buccleuch's men, he protested, were volunteers serving under Dutch pay rather than soldiers of the British crown. Since he could not stop his warlike subjects from enlisting in foreign armies, the Habsburgs had no right to blame him for the soldiers' departure to the Netherlands, especially since Albert had plenty of Irishmen in his own army. James also managed to convince Albert and Isabella that he had more sympathy for their position than the members of his council, encouraging them to negotiate directly through him.[54]

Although the French soon realized that they could not prevent peace negotiations between Spain and England, Rosny's mission encouraged them to believe that James would continue to cooperate in supporting the Dutch and containing Habsburg ambitions.[55] They hoped that in time this cooperation would grow into a full military alliance. James worked assiduously to encourage this impression. In late September Henry told Harlay that James promised to inform him and seek his advice before concluding any agreement with Spain. Henry thought that if the English obtained the right concessions a peace treaty might actually weaken Spain's position.[56] He therefore did not wish to interfere in James's dealings with Madrid.[57] Harlay reported that the English seemed determined not only to maintain their alliance with France and support for the Dutch but to "favor and foment war against the Spanish." In an effort to further probe James's intentions, Henry dispatched an expert huntsman named monsieur de Vitry to England, on the correct assumption that James, as an avid hunter, would form an intimate bond with him.[58] After about a month spent in the king's company, Vitry returned to Paris with a detailed report of James's respect and affection for his brother of France.[59] In early November Henry told the Landgrave of Hesse: "That which contents me the most is that the king of England has assured me again by his ambassador that he will make no contract with Spain prejudicial to our alliance or the estates of the Low Countries; that being the case the Spaniards will be unable to do any mischief."[60] Although the Dutch remained more worried, James gave

---

[54] See the instructions of the Baron de Hoboque on his appointment as the archduke's agent in England in HHStA Belgien 44 (unfoliated), dated March 3, 1605. Hoboque was told on all occasions to address himself principally to the king, either by word of mouth or in writing, "because we have more confidence in him and his affections than in those of his council" but he was also to cultivate the earl of Northampton, the Lord Treasurer Devonshire, and Cecil, especially the latter as "he who can do the most and in whom you must show great confidence and persuade him, if you can that we have commanded you to hold a tight [forte étroite] correspondence with him, advancing our principal affairs through his favor and authority."

[55] *Recueil des lettres et missives*, 6.143.

[56] English, rather than British seems the right term in this context, since Scotland had never been at war with Spain and was not involved in the treaty negotiations.

[57] *Recueil des lettres et missives*, 6.168.   [58] TNA SP78/49, fol. 247.

[59] *Recueil des lettres et missives* 6.160, BN Mss. Français 3503 fols 27, 53, 62.

[60] *Archives ou correspondence inédite de la maison Orange-Nassau*, ed. G. Groen van Prinsterer, series 2, vol. 2 (Utrecht: Kemink et Fils, 1858), 229–30; *Recueil des lettres et missives*, 6.172.

strong reassurances to Caron in October.⁶¹ Even in late July of 1604, as the English prepared to ratify their new peace treaty with Spain, Henry reiterated his belief "that the king of England, my good brother, will honor his word to me," by not abandoning the Dutch. A month later he expressed his opinion that the treaty's terms were so favorable to England that they had diminished Spain's reputation.⁶²

Gradually, however, French doubts about the new king of England began to set in. They noticed that English diplomats sent to other European states were saying things that appeared to contradict James's promises to them.⁶³ Henry felt disparaged when James delayed sending an extraordinary ambassador to Paris to reciprocate Rosny's mission and by perceived slights over ceremonial precedence at the English court.⁶⁴ He worried about the pernicious influence of Queen Anna, the effect that Spanish bribes and deceptions might have on the English council, and false tales meant to discredit him, told by discontented Huguenots to their English friends.⁶⁵ James's debts and poverty, already evident to the French by the end of 1603, raised concerns that he might make damaging concessions to Spain simply to save money.⁶⁶ Finally, Henry feared that over time the traditional English hatred for France would reassert itself, leading to an Anglo-Spanish alliance. To counteract this danger, he encouraged Harlay to cultivate friendship with Scots both in London and Scotland, to preserve the auld alliance in case of future need.⁶⁷ Harlay noted with satisfaction the open animosity between English and Scots around the court and the rancorous disputes in Parliament over the union project. Henry's disillusionment reached something of a climax toward the end of 1604, after Cecil categorically refused to contribute monetarily to the Dutch war effort for the coming year and James declared that he no longer felt bound by the agreement he had negotiated with Rosny, which he claimed was valid for only a year.⁶⁸ "I conclude," the French king declared in disgust, "that we must distrust his intentions, his inconsideration and natural weakness and, to the contrary, hope for more from his inconstancy, timidity and bad conduct than from his prudence, and the sincerity of his affection."⁶⁹

As this comment suggests, the French attributed the disparity between James's words and conduct more to his weak character than deliberate attempts at deception. Although Harlay did comment at one point on the king's "duplicity and dissimulation,"⁷⁰ he and other French statesmen normally depicted James as a

---

⁶¹ BN Mss. Français 3503, fol. 81v; TNA SP84/64, fol. 69r.
⁶² BN Mss. Français 3503, fols 282, 283. The treaty was signed on August 18/28.
⁶³ BN Mss. Français 3503, fol. 108.   ⁶⁴ TNA SP78/50, fol. 103v.
⁶⁵ *Mission de Harlay*, ed. Kermaingant, 2.158, 173–4, 214; TNA SP78/50, fol. 105v.
⁶⁶ *Recueil des lettres et missives*, 175.
⁶⁷ *Mission de Harlay*, ed. Kermaingant, 2.188. The duke of Lennox ranked high among the recipients of French attention, although Harlay had a low opinion of his abilities: "il est un gentilhomme d'honneur est vraiment français mais d'esprit fort simple."
⁶⁸ The French strongly disagreed. See BN Mss. Français 3509, fol. 1v.
⁶⁹ *Mission de Harlay*, ed. Kermaingant, 2.283 (Henry IV to Harlay, December 5, 1604).
⁷⁰ BN Mss. Français 3504, fols 131v–132.

man with "an innocent soul" hobbled by natural timidity, lack of ambition, weakness, and a lazy inattention to the business of government, which made him dangerously susceptible to manipulation by others.[71] They thought that his excessive legalistic scrupulosity and hatred of war, deriving from a "base and weak heart," led him to avoid conflict even by "imprudent, shameful and bad" methods.[72] This assessment reflected the French conviction that the Habsburgs—including the Belgian and Austrian branches of the dynasty—posed a grave threat to all other European states because of their ambition to achieve a universal monarchy. The king of Britain therefore had a clear interest in allying with France and the United Provinces to thwart Habsburg ambitions. Since James appeared to share this view, the only possible explanation for his failure to act were the malign influence of members of his entourage and his cowardice, laziness, and temperamental inability to take consistent action. Well-intentioned but inexperienced and feckless, he was simply not up to the task of ruling Britain properly.

This picture resembles that drawn by Maurice Lee and other twentieth-century historians.[73] But while it is possible to read the evidence this way, a more plausible explanation is that James had attempted, with considerable success, to encourage the Dutch to continue occupying Spain's military forces while their own taxpayers and France paid the bills, leaving him free to terminate Elizabeth's expensive war without risking his own security. As David Trim has shown, the number of Britons serving in the forces of the United Provinces actually increased after 1603 and the Anglo-Spanish peace treaty of the following year, as James quietly assisted Dutch efforts to recruit English and Scottish volunteers.[74] Doing so cost him nothing, while having the additional benefit of maintaining several thousand veteran British troops who would remain available in case of future need. Although neither principled nor generous, his conduct served his interests, at least in the short term. Limited efforts to help the Dutch and French seemed logically at odds with his efforts to achieve better relations with Spain but arguably contributed to that objective, since so long as the Spanish monarchy remained bogged down in the Netherlands and threatened by France it had ample reason to seek his friendship, whereas an end to the Dutch war and Franco-Spanish rivalry might have emboldened Spain to challenge Stuart interests more directly. James therefore had good reasons for encouraging France, the United Provinces, and other states to pursue their conflicts with the Habsburgs, provided that doing so

---

[71] E.g. *Mission de Harlay*, ed. Kermaingant, 2.165 (Henry IV to Harlay, December 7, 1603): "ledit roi d'Angleterre possède une âme si innocente et équitable" that he is easily misled; BN Mss. Français 3504, fols 21v, 82v–83; 3505, fols 90v–91, 110r.

[72] BN Mss. Français 3509, fol. 92v.   [73] Lee, *James I and Henry IV*.

[74] David Trim, "Calvinist Internationalism and the Shaping of Jacobean Foreign Policy," in *Prince Henry Revived: Image and Exemplarity in Early Modern England*, ed. Timothy Wilkes (London: Paul Holberton, 2008), 238–58 at 245; David Trim, "Fighting 'Jacob's Wars': The Employment of English and Welsh Mercenaries in the European Wars of Religion: France and the Netherlands, 1562–1610," unpublished University of London PhD thesis, 2002, 337–9, 343 fig. 7, and 514 fig. 18.

cost him little and did not unduly compromise his "amity" with Philip III. By alternately proclaiming his support for the "common cause" of Protestantism, his opposition to Habsburg universal monarchy, and his commitment to ideals of peace, he constructed high-minded justifications for what amounted to self-serving opportunism.

But this course of action diminished the good will and respect of allied statesmen, including Oldenbarnevelt, Henry IV, and Sully, who resented his unwillingness to take risks and spend money in the common cause. Henry eventually grew weary of subsidizing the United Provinces without British help and refused to increase his contributions, while Oldenbarnevelt concluded that without more international assistance continued war would place an unsustainable burden on Dutch taxpayers. The Spanish also faced acute financial difficulties, especially after a hurricane in November 1605 sank four galleons carrying American silver and disrupted shipments of New World treasure to Spain for two full years. In December 1606 the council of state decided to halve expenditures on war in the Low Countries, whereas Albert and Spinola, whose troops had begun to mutiny for lack of pay, believed they needed more Spanish money to go on fighting.[75] In the spring of 1607 Albert and Oldenbarnevelt negotiated a temporary armistice of ten months, on terms favorable to the United Provinces. Although James's professed desire to promote the peace of Europe prevented him from objecting in principle to this truce, he complained vigorously that the Dutch had not consulted him in negotiating it. The archduke's agent Hoboque, the French and Venetian ambassadors in London, and the French foreign minister, Nicolas de Neufville seigneur de Villeroy, all concluded that he was displeased "because," as the Venetian commented, "the continuance of the war protected him from the Spanish." The flight of the earls of Tyrone and Tyrconnell from Ireland in the autumn of 1607 increased British worries about a truce that promised to free the Army of Flanders for action elsewhere in Europe.[76] Henry Wotton commented that news of the truce "hath put us almost here [in London] into a cold sweat."[77] If a peace was to be concluded James at least wanted to help mediate it, to protect his interests and demonstrate his credit with all parties involved.[78]

---

[75] Patrick Williams, *The Great Favourite: The Duke of Lerma and the Court and Government of Philip III of Spain, 1598–1621* (Manchester: Manchester University Press, 2006), 128–36.

[76] In March 1608 the French ambassador reported that Salisbury was lamenting the "extreme" necessity of the British crown, due to the need to reinforce the army in Ireland; the ambassador thought that this made the British government extremely fearful of Spain (*Ambassades de Monsieur de la Boderie en Angleterre... Depuis les Années 1606 Jusqu'en 1611*, ed. P. Burdin, 5 vols (Paris, 1750), 3.160). Hoboque's dispatches in the period also contain frequent references to worries about Ireland and suspicions that the Habsburgs or the pope might be secretly fomenting Irish rebellion (HHStA PC44 (unfoliated), e.g. letters of October 2 and 17, and December 5 and 31, 1607, March 26, April 23, May 14, and June 20, 1608 and May 6, 1609).

[77] BL Stowe Mss. 169, fol. 21.

[78] *CSPV* 10.492; *Ambassades de la Boderie*, ed. Burdin, 2.144; *Oldenbarnevelt Bescheiden*, ed. Veenendaal, 158; HHStA Belgien PC21, fol. 5v (a reported conversation in January 1609, in which

Fortunately, Philip III refused to conclude peace on the terms Albert had provisionally granted, leading to two years of further negotiations. This allowed James to dispatch two envoys, Robert Spencer and Sir James Winwood, to consult with the Dutch and French, who had also sent an emissary, as haggling over the terms of a peace treaty or longer truce proceeded. Spencer and Winwood received instructions to support the conclusion of a truce in public, while privately encouraging the Dutch to continue the war if they thought that doing so would win them better terms.[79] The pair were told to stress that the cessation of war would lead to an excessive reduction of the Dutch army and the taxes needed to support it, while allowing divisions between and within individual provinces to erupt into debilitating civil quarrels. Since both eventualities threatened to endanger the survival of the United Provinces should a new war break out, its leaders were to be exhorted to do everything possible to preserve unity, while maintaining reasonable levels of taxation and a strong army, including their regiments of English and Scottish volunteers.[80] Although James's professed dedication to peace prevented him from openly opposing an agreement to end the war, these instructions strongly suggested that he tried to encourage resistance within the United Provinces to accommodation with Spain.

He also anticipated that Henry IV would attempt to draw him into a pact to guarantee the truce by offering military support to the Dutch should Spain violate its terms. He was reluctant to take this step, since he knew that the Habsburgs would view it as a hostile act and feared being entangled in an expensive war. The archdukes' ambassador, the baron of Hoboque, reported that James also mistrusted Henry IV, suspecting him of secretly colluding with Spain to undermine Protestant interests in the Netherlands.[81] James therefore instructed Spencer and Winwood to remain coy about any proposals for a triple alliance between France, Britain, and the United Provinces, and he initially rejected proposals to join one.[82] In the end he concluded defensive alliance with the United Provinces after it became clear that the Dutch would otherwise become even more dependent on France. When the Spanish complained, he had his excuses ready. Through his ambassador in Madrid, Sir Charles Cornwallis, he asserted that he had acted partly

---

Villeroy told the archduke's agent, Pequius, that he believed the English wanted the truce negotiations to fail and had never been sincere supporters of peace in the Low Countries) and Belgien 44 (unfoliated) Hoboque dispatches of May 2 and 8, June 27, and August 1, 1607.

[79] *Memorials of Affairs of State in the Reigns of Queen Elizabeth and King James I*, ed. E. Sawyer, 3 vols (London, 1725), 2.334.

[80] Ibid., 330, 332, 333: "...you shall do well to recommend it to them above all things that the union of all the members of their own body be renewed. That they suffer not all payments to cease amongst the people but continue a yearly contribution for entertainment of the soldiers. That a certain number of English companies and Scottish may be appointed to remain in those services; that an honorable regard be had of Count Maurice, the better to keep him in devotion which way so ever they shall take."

[81] HHStA Belgien PC44 (unfoliated), dispatch of October 27, 1608.

[82] *Memorials of Affairs of State*, ed. Sawyer, 334 and 372; *Oldenbarnevelt Bescheiden*, ed. Veenendaal, 252.

at the behest of France but "principally from consideration of the present state of affairs," in which the Dutch would refuse to agree to a truce unless other powers guaranteed its terms. Since Spain wanted to end the fighting, he had actually helped Philip achieve his goals by forming a defensive league with Spain's adversaries. While his own interests would have been better served by a continuation of war, his overriding concern for "the general state of Christendom" led him to accept obligations "that permitted the achievement of peace." He deserved Spain's gratitude for his altruism.[83] To drive the point home, Salisbury "took occasion to speak with Sir Noel Caron and to desire him to acquaint the States (or such as he holds correspondency withal) with the strangeness of the expostulations of Spain and the archdukes [against the Anglo-Dutch treaty], to the end that in their conferences with the other commissioners they would take notice of it as a matter which did breed in them no little cause of jealousy." Salisbury did not expect this protest to satisfy the Spanish but he did think it would "at least to stop their mouths."[84]

James's Polemical Contest with Jesuits and the Pope

James's use of professions of dedication to peace to cover more self-interested motives should not, however, lead us to conclude that intellectual beliefs played no role in his conduct. Some ideas did matter deeply to him, not least because he believed they would have practical consequences. His early experience in Scotland had given him a healthy respect for the power of religious beliefs to ignite civil conflict, and the ways in which opportunists like Bothwell exploited religion for factious ends. Three months after his arrival in London, James told Harlay that he had little hope of seeing Europe at peace because of "the diversity of opinion on religion that is spread through all nations and the interest of the popes in making use of it by means of war to better establish their grandeur," along with the use of religion as a pretext by princes motivated by "interest or ambition."[85] Although presbyterians had caused James's most serious difficulties in Scotland, in a European context Catholic extremists appeared to pose the primary threat. Above all he claimed to detest Jesuits, whom he described as "puritan papists" and "the worst and most seditious fellows in the world... slaves and spies... the authors and instruments of all the great disturbances."[86] He told Rosny that "he hated the Jesuits no less than he did Spain," considering them "his personal enemies."[87]

---

[83] Ibid., 401. [84] *Memorials of Affairs of State*, ed. Sawyer, 403–4.
[85] BL King's Mss. 123, fol. 327. [86] McIlwain, 176; *Memoirs of Sully*, 3.142; CSPV 10.361.
[87] *Memoirs of Sully*, 3.142.

He knew that not only Protestants but many Catholics shared these views, including Gallican office holders in France, where the *parlements* of Paris, Dijon, Rouen, and Rennes had banished Jesuits from their jurisdictions following an assassination attempt against Henry IV in 1594, which they unfairly blamed on ideas spread by Jesuit preaching. One leading Gallican, Antoine Arnauld, depicted the Society of Jesus as an order that thrived on chaos and civil war, whose preaching and plotting "lay behind every League success and every failed uprising against the French monarchy and its officials" in recent years, along with plots to assassinate Edward VI of England and both Henry III and Henry IV of France.[88] Since Rosny was a Huguenot and Harlay the son of a leading Gallican opponent of the Jesuits, the first president of the *parlement* of Paris, Archille de Harlay, James probably felt he was preaching to the choir in echoing these views to Henry's ambassadors. He had less confidence in Henry himself, who lifted the ban on Jesuits in September 1603.[89]

For several centuries, James asserted, papal power had grown through the "laziness, negligence, ambition and division of Christian princes," to a point at which popes "were able to dominate them, impeding their freedom to rule, authorizing their subjects to rise against them and usurping a kind of absolute empire over crowns."[90] Although somewhat more contentious than his attacks on Jesuits, these views would also have met with measured sympathy from French royalists, who remembered the pope's excommunication not only of Henry IV before his conversion but of the Catholic Henry III, and the role of radical Catholic preaching in the civil wars of the late sixteenth century. In a further effort to appeal to Harlay's Gallican sentiments, James boasted of his own religious moderation, saying

> that he was not at all a heretic, that is one who refuses to recognize the truth, nor any more a puritan or separated from the Church; that he esteemed the hierarchy necessary and as a result that he would always acknowledge the Pope as the first bishop and as such president and moderator of councils, but not as chief or superior. As for ceremonies and other indifferent things that have been introduced in the Church either by the excessive zeal of the people or the ambition

---

[88] Eric Nelson, *The Jesuits and the Monarchy: Catholic Reform and Political Authority in France (1590–1615)* (Aldershot: Ashgate, 2005), 2, 31–2.

[89] In addition to Nelson, *Jesuits*, see the excellent discussion of Gallican attitudes in Jotham Parsons, *The Church in the Republic: Gallicanism and Political Ideology in Renaissance France* (Washington, DC: Catholic University of America Press, 2004).

[90] BL Kings Mss. 123r–v, fol. 324: "Il [James] me mit bien avant en discourir du droit et de la puissance des papes selon son opinion et sa condition qui l'obligent l'une par créance et l'autre par raison d'état à y être contraire, et me commença à dire que depuis plusieurs siècles elle s'était tellement accrue et fortifiée par la lâcheté, négligence, ambition et division des princes chrétiens qu'aujourd'hui par son moyen les papes les dominaient en toute et non seulement leur empêcheraient la liberté de régner, autorisant et émouvant leur sujets contre eux, mais usurpaient une sorte d'empire entièrement absolu sur les couronnes."

and avarice of ecclesiastics that he would always agree that a part should be kept and another removed, according to the good or evil that one foresees will result. As for differences of faith, he would submit them to the decree of a general council legitimately assembled in a neutral place.[91]

He probably knew that the hope of reconciling western Christendom through an impartial general council was illusory for the foreseeable future.[92] But he was aware that Catholic, as well as Protestant, irenicists shared this aspiration and that many Gallicans believed in the supremacy of church councils over the pope. He accordingly sought to redefine the main religious conflict in Europe, as a battle not between Protestants and Catholics but of papal absolutists and their firebrand Jesuit agents against defenders of the liberty of national churches, the freedom of secular states to govern without clerical interference, and the settlement of religious differences through reasoned argument and compromise rather than violence.

In doing so he provided not just a practical but an ideological justification for cross-confessional alliances, by invoking a black legend of Jesuit intrigue that had developed in close association with a black legend of Spain in the late sixteenth century. He no doubt did this partly for effect, hoping to win the sympathy of moderate Catholics who disliked Spain in places like France and Venice. But James, like many of his Protestant subjects, harbored a real and not entirely unjustified fear of Jesuit intrigues and militant Catholicism. He knew that the Jesuits had established continental seminaries for the training of English, Scottish, and Irish priests, whose graduates continued to infiltrate his kingdoms. He seems to have harbored a particular grudge against Robert Parsons, whose *A Conference about the Next Succession* had skillfully challenged his title to the English succession a few years earlier. Some of James's Protestant servants fed his worries about Jesuit plots. In 1610 his ambassador in Brussels, William Trumbull, reported that several Jesuits had "lately gone into England" because of "an assured hope which they have of affecting some treason upon the sacred person of his Majesty or

---

[91] Ibid., fol. 326: "Qu'il n'était point hérétique, c'est-à-dire refusant de reconnaître la vérité. Qu'il n'était plus puritain ni moins séparée de l'église. Qu'il y estimait la hiérarchie nécessaire, par conséquent qu'il avouerait toujours le Pape pour le premier évêque en icelle président et modérateur au concile, mais non chef ni supérieur. Que quant aux cérémonies et autres choses indifférent qui avait été introduite en l'église, ou par trop de zèle des peuples, ou par l'ambition et avarice des ecclésiastiques, qu'il consentirait toujours qu'une partie fut ôtée et l'autre gardée selon le bien ou le mal que l'on jugerait en devoir réussir. Et quant aux points controversés de la foi qu'il en remettrait la décision au décret d'un concile générale assemblée en lieu neutre."

[92] Patterson, *James VI and I*, takes the king's support of reconciliation through a general council at face-value, which seems to me a mistake. On the other hand, James's belief in the legitimate role of councils or synods in settling contested points of doctrine, often at the direction of kings or secular rulers but with final decisions left to the clergy, seems to have been genuine. The role of Convocation within England, of national assemblies summoned by the king in Scotland, and of the Synod of Dort in the Netherlands are all examples.

nursing some unexpected rebellions in his dominions."[93] Four years later Archbishop Abbott asked William Trumbull if he had "any inkling of great sums of money to the value of £50,000 at least in stock, which the Jesuits have in England, which I have secretly hunted after for the space of these three years but was never yet able to fall upon the right track thereof. Give me notice of any probable circumstances which may tend this way."[94] The 1610 plot and secret Jesuit treasury were figments of the writers' imaginations but such fictions, which were very difficult to disprove, contributed to paranoia.

In some contexts, denunciations of Jesuits served as a proxy for worries about strains of militant Catholic belief that had flourished during Philip II's wars against England and France and the rebellions of the French Catholic League. In addition to violent opposition to Protestantism, League apologists had argued that religion justified the deposition of heretical kings, that the pope might absolve subjects of their allegiance to Catholic as well as Protestant rulers, and that regicide was justifiable as a remedy against tyranny and heresy. The papacy and the Habsburgs had both backed away from these doctrines in the early seventeenth century. The archdukes instructed Hoboque that when English Catholics complained to him he should exhort them to patience and obedience and that if they revealed any projects damaging to the king's person or authority he should express disapproval.[95] But James and his ministers, who did not know for certain that Catholic governments had adopted this stance, remained suspicious that the archdukes and king of Spain secretly permitted British and Irish exiles living in their territories to plot against the Stuart crown. Moreover, so long as the papacy refused to explicitly repudiate doctrinal justifications for regicide and rebellion, some individual Catholics would undoubtedly continue to embrace such ideas and act upon them. Anxieties on this score diminished James's trust not only of the Habsburgs but other Catholic rulers too, including Henry IV. The French king's efforts to consolidate his authority by conciliating his former ultra-Catholic opponents, in some cases by granting them important local or national offices, appeared to pose a risk that the militant ideas that had once fueled the League would eventually capture the French state from within. If this happened, it might well lead to an alliance between the Continent's two great Catholic monarchies and a new crusade to eradicate Protestantism.

Doctrinal arguments that justified rebellions, royal assassinations, and papal bulls deposing kings and absolving subjects of their allegiance therefore looked highly dangerous. Even if the current pope and Catholic rulers showed little inclination to act on such ideas, they remained part of Rome's ideological arsenal,

---

[93] TNA SP77/9 part 2, fol. 160r.
[94] Abbot to Trumbull, August 31, 1614, Trumbull Mss., 1.16 (Library of Congress microfilm 041/Camb/194/1).
[95] HHStA Belgien PC44 (unfoliated) Hoboque's instructions, March 3, 1605.

lying ready-to-hand in case a new crusade against the reformed faith should ever commence. James also enjoyed theological disputes and prided himself on his abilities as a controversialist. Few things gave him more pleasure than besting an adversary in a doctrinal debate. In 1606, the Venetian ambassador reported that during a discussion of papal pretensions the king "expressed himself in most vigorous language to his own so obvious satisfaction that the lords of the council, who were present – though somewhat apart – declared that they had never seen him more content and delighted."[96] This makes it unsurprising that he not only attempted to encourage British and European theologians to enter the lists against "Jesuit" theories of papal authority but eventually did so himself. Some contemporaries, in Britain as well as on the Continent, saw this as behavior unbecoming a king, since it inevitably led to his being drawn into vitriolic controversies laced with undignified *ad hominem* attacks.[97] James initially shared this view, saying he "thought it not comely for one of my place to put my name to books containing scholastic disputations, whose calling is to set forth decrees in the imperative mode," especially in dealing with adversaries of relatively low birth.[98] But he would eventually change his mind, asserting that "I am persuaded that one of the ends for which God elevated me to the throne was that by speaking from a higher place in defense of God's honor, which is vilified in his lieutenants, I will be more readily heard."[99]

Previous studies have examined James's writings against papal authority in secular affairs chiefly from the perspective of the history of political ideas.[100] But while advancing theoretical arguments, his tracts also addressed specific political and diplomatic contexts and need to be considered in this light.[101] His earliest published denunciations of Catholic arguments for the pope's authority to depose princes came in the immediate aftermath of the Gunpowder Plot on November 5, 1605. His speech to Parliament celebrating his own and his people's delivery from this conspiracy was published in Latin as well as English, to make it available to a

---

[96] *CSPV* 10.360.
[97] See, for example, *Ambassades de la Boderie*, ed. Burdin, 4.248, 301–2, 310, 340, 374–5.
[98] *A Premonition to All Most Mightie Monarches, Kings, Free Princes and States of Christendom* (London, 1609), 4–5.
[99] *Déclaration du Serenissime Roy Jaques I Roy de la Grand' Bretaigne France et Irlande, Defenseur de la Foy. Pour le Droit des Rois et independance de leurs Couronnes, Contre le Harangue de l'Illustrissime Cardinal du Perron* (London, 1615), 2: "Car je suis persuadé que c'est une des fins pour lesquelles Dieu m'a élevé sur le trône, afin que parlant d'un lieu plus haut pour la défense de l'honneur de Dieu qui est vilipendé en ses lieutenants, je sois plus aisément entendu."
[100] See, esp. Bernard Bourdin, *La genèse théologico-politique de l'État modern: la controverse de Jacques 1er d'Angleterre avec le cardinal Bellarmin* (Paris: Presses Universitaires de France, 2004).
[101] I have made this argument at greater length in R. Malcolm Smuts, "Theological Polemics and James I's Diplomacy, 1603–1617," in *Ideologies of Diplomacy: Rhetoric, Ritual and Representation in Early Modern England*, ed. Jane Yeang Chui Wong, special issue of *The Journal of Medieval and Early Modern Studies* 50 (2020): 515–39. For another study that makes some attempt to do this see Michael Questier, *Dynastic Politics and the British Reformations, 1558–1630* (Oxford: Oxford University Press, 2019), 317–20, 331–2.

European audience. Although the pope and all major European monarchs expressed strong disapproval of the plot, James went out of his way to attribute it, not merely to the personal frustrations of a handful of embittered men, but to ideas promoted by the Roman Church. "The wretch" who led the conspiracy confessed "that there was no cause moving him or them but merely and only religion." "No other sect of heretics," the king proclaimed, "not excepting Turk, Jew or Pagan, no not even those of Calicute who adore the devil did ever maintain by the grounds of their religion that it was lawful or rather meritorious (as the Romish Catholics call it) to murder princes or people for quarrel of religion."[102] Because of these beliefs, although "honest men, seduced with some errors of popery, may yet remain good and faithful subjects... none of those that know and believe the whole ground and school conclusions of their doctrine can ever prove either good Christians or faithful subjects."[103] The English government attempted to prove through a highly tendentious use of available evidence that Jesuits not only encouraged but helped plan the conspiracy.[104] It tried and executed one Jesuit, Henry Garnet, for failing to reveal his prior knowledge of the plot, obtained in the confessional. William Camden then produced an extensive Latin summary of the evidence against Garnet.[105] Robert Cecil contributed another pamphlet, again issued in Latin as well as English, commenting on an alleged Catholic threat against his own life. In it he quoted an oration by Pope Sixtus V praising the assassination of Henry III of France, to refute Catholic claims that popes had never condoned regicide.[106] In addition to using the plot to dramatize the horrors of rebellion and disloyalty within Britain, the government attempted to exploit it internationally to associate doctrines the papacy refused to repudiate with a fanatical conspiracy that all responsible European rulers, including the pope himself, had condemned.

The Oath of Allegiance passed by Parliament in the wake of the plot was carefully drafted to distinguish purely spiritual issues from papal claims to authority in secular matters. It avoided saying anything about the pope's spiritual jurisdiction, including even his right to excommunicate kings for heresy or other religious offenses. In this respect it differed from the Tudor Oath of Supremacy, which had required subjects to recognize the monarch's supreme authority over

---

[102] *His Majesties speech in this last session of Parliament* (London, 1605), sigs B3v, C2r–v. The Latin edition is *Regis oratio, habita in postremo regni ordinum convent, Westmonasterii* (London, 1605).
[103] *His Majesties speech*, sig, C2v.
[104] The government's efforts to shape narratives of the plot and incriminate Jesuits in it are explored systematically by Anne James, *Poets, Players, and Preachers: Remembering the Gunpowder Plot in Seventeenth-Century England* (Toronto: University of Toronto Press, 2016), chapters 1–2.
[105] William Camden, *Actio in Henricum Garnetum Societatis Jesuiticae in Anglia superiorem, et caeteros qui proditione ongè immanissima sereniss. Britanniae Magnae Regem, et Regni Angliae ordines pulvere fulminali èmedio tollere coniurâeunt* (London, 1607).
[106] Robert Cecil earl of Salisbury, *An Answere to certaine scandalous papers scattered abroad under colour of a Cathlicke admonition* (London, 1606), sig. C2; the Latin edition was entitled *Responsio ad labellum quondam famosam, Catholicae admonitionis praetextu in vulgus spartim*.

the English Church. The new oath merely obliged them to swear that they regarded James and his heirs are rightful rulers of Britain to whom they owed unqualified obedience in temporal matters, and that they would continue to do so, despite any future papal sentence of excommunication or deposition. In addition, they had to state that they "abhorred, detested and abjured," as "impious and heretical" the "damnable doctrine" that excommunicated princes might be lawfully deposed or murdered.[107] A number of British Catholics, including the Archpriest George Blackwell, to whom the papacy had granted supreme authority over English Catholic clergy, agreed to take this oath. But Paul V issued two letters forbidding Catholics from doing so in September 1606 and August 1607, and the prominent Jesuit theologian Cardinal Robert Bellarmine wrote an open letter to Blackwell, criticizing his willingness to swear to it. A tract printed under the name of Robert Persons also denounced the Oath.[108]

This opposition infuriated James. According to Bishop James Montague, editor of the 1616 edition of the king's collected *Works*, the king initially commissioned a response from the bishop of Winchester, Thomas Bilson, and began drawing up notes for his use. But as he did so James's passion for scholastic argument got the better of him and "his pen ran out so fast that within six days" he had finished a draft of the tract soon published as *Tripli nodex, triplex cuneus. Or An Apologie for the Oath of Allegiance*, in English, French, and Latin editions. Although not listed as the author, James's copy had his arms prominently displayed facing the title page, and several foreign ambassadors who received copies were told it was the king's work.[109] It soon drew sharp replies from Persons and Bellarmine, the latter issued under the name of the cardinal's chaplain, Matthew Torti. The king again initially ordered two of his bishops to refute them but before long returned to his study at Royston, dispatching "frequent couriers to London to the bishops and other doctors, for passages of scripture and other information," to produce an expanded edition of his earlier tract and a second book that never actually appeared.[110] The Venetian ambassador reported in December 1612 that he remained "in almost absolute retirement in the company of one man, a dean, very learned," writing a reply to Persons, while a few weeks later the French ambassador, Boderie, also noted that he had shut himself up with a chaplain and one other minister.[111] Evidently the king continued to work on his rebuttal of Parsons until around the beginning of March, when Salisbury and the earl of

---

[107] For a text of the Oath see J. R. Tanner, *Constitutional Documents of the Reign of James I, 1603–1625* (Cambridge: Cambridge University Press, 1930), 90–1.

[108] *A treatise tending to mitigation towardes Catholike-subjects in England* (St. Omer, 1607).

[109] Boderie received his copy on February 14, 1608, *Ambassades de la Boderie*, ed. Burdin, 3.103.

[110] *CSPV* 11.127; *Ambassades de la Boderie*, ed. Burdin, 4.73, 193, 219.

[111] *CSPV* 11.360; *Ambassades de Boderie*, ed. Burdin, 3.5. Persons's tract was entitled *The judgment of a Catholike English-man, living in banishment for his religion Written to his private friend in England. Concerning a late booke set forth and entitled, Tripli Nodex, Tripli Cuneus* (St. Omer, 1608).

Northampton finally persuaded him to desist.[112] But he did produce a new edition of *Tripli Nodex*, this time openly acknowledging his authorship and adding a lengthy *Premonition to all the kings, free princes and states of Christendom*, exhorting them to reject the papacy's pernicious doctrines and destructive efforts to meddle in secular affairs. He then took considerable pains to arrange for his book's translation into French and Latin, employing the translator of Tacitus, Sir Henry Savile, several other English scholars, and "Bartly the French poet." "There is a little congregation of learned men that assembles every day before the king to revise and correct the translations," Boderie reported in May.[113] *The Premonition* reiterated James's claims about his own orthodoxy and religious moderation and once again blamed the Jesuits for the Gunpowder Plot, before concluding with a long discussion of reasons for thinking that the Antichrist foretold in the Apocalypse of St. John should be identified with the papacy. Although he described this view as merely his own "conjecture," James said he would not recant it until the pope "renounced any further meddling with princes."[114]

He next commissioned richly bound copies of his book for presentation to rulers throughout Europe and enlisted special envoys to carry them to courts at which he lacked a resident ambassador.[115] Paul V launched a counter-offensive to persuade Catholic princes to refuse to accept the volume. He succeeded with most Catholic rulers, including the king of Spain and the archdukes in Brussels, but Henry IV did receive his copy, turning it over to a committee of Catholic theologians for examination. They returned a guardedly favorable verdict, saying that although the book "contained errors" it was "full of wisdom and modesty as well as good intentions and conceptions, all tending to defend and conserve his royal and sovereign authority, rather than offending anyone." Surprisingly, in light of James's speculations about the identity of the Antichrist, they even commended him for speaking of the papacy "with honor and reverence."[116] These contrasting responses reflected the differing attitudes of the French and Spanish monarchies toward militant Catholicism and the religious origins of royal power. Having long presented themselves as champions of the Roman Church, the Spanish saw no reason to annoy the pope simply to please a heretic king. Concepts of the divine right of kings and liturgical ceremonies implying the sacred character of royal authority, such as anointing with oil during coronations, had never developed in Spain to nearly the same extent as in both France and England. The most prominent defenders of the pope's authority to depose kings for tyranny or heresy were Spanish, Portuguese, and Italian Jesuits, whose views derived from

---

[112] *Ambassades de Boderie*, ed. Burdin, 4.164.
[113] BL Stowe Mss. 171, fol. 36 reproduced in *The Court and Times of James I*, 2 vols, ed. Thomas Birch (London, 1848), 1.196; TNA SP14/44/98; *Ambassades de la Boderie*, ed. Burdin, 4.323.
[114] *Premonition*, 105–6.   [115] *Ambassades de la Boderie*, ed. Burdin, 4.344, 371, and 374–5.
[116] Ibid., 378–9: "plein de modestie et de sagesse, comme de bonne intentions et conceptions, toute tendantes à defender son autorité royale et souveaine, plus qu'a offenser personne."

scholastic concepts of the limits of legitimate political authority still accepted in Spain but not by French royalists or James I.

By contrast, in addition to holding views about the divine right of kings similar to those of James himself, Henry IV needed to mediate between ultramontane Catholics, Gallicans, and Huguenots within his own kingdom, while justifying his alliances with Protestant states. He and his ministers therefore sought to dampen controversies over contentious claims about papal authority, on which any position they took would alienate constituencies they needed to mollify. Through their ambassador in Rome they pointed out to the pope that tracts likely to provoke the ire of the king of Britain, through personal attacks or defenses of doctrines he detested, risked unleashing retaliatory measures against British Catholics, who were effectively at James's mercy.[117] Boderie simultaneously tried to persuade James and his ministers that the king's personal entry into the polemical fray would only make matters worse. Salisbury said he agreed but that James refused to listen to his advice on such matters.[118]

In addition to his own writings and tracts by supportive English bishops like Lancelot Andrewes, the king attempted to recruit foreign writers and office holders to his cause. These allies included leading Huguenots like Pierre du Moulin and Henry IV's former publicist, Philippe du Plessis Mornay, who in 1611 dedicated to James his *Le progress du mystère de l'iniquité*, tracing "how the several abuses of popery have crept into the Church."[119] But the recruits also included moderate Catholics. In 1610, when James's ambassador in Paris, William Becher, learned that a new book by Bellarmine was about to appear, he met privately with Gallican members of the *parlement* of Paris and successfully urged them to condemn it. Although Henry IV stepped in to prevent the *parlement* from acting, several of its members assured Becher that if the king was "not in town" they would have seized the opportunity to censor Bellarmine.[120] James wrote personally to Henry protesting his decision to block the *parlement*.

But James refrained from backing these aggressive rhetorical attacks on the papacy with forceful measures "in the imperative mode." The discrepancy between his bold words and restrained actions appeared with particular clarity in his response to a quarrel over clerical privileges between Venice and the papacy that broke out in 1606, leading to the imposition of an interdict on the republic.[121] For a time Venice and the papacy appeared ready to go to war. Spain backed the pope, France attempted to mediate, while James and his ambassador, Sir Henry Wotton, initially expressed strong support for Venice. The pope's actions, James proclaimed, amounted to no less "than the laying of the axe unto the root and the

---

[117] Ibid., 4.46, 89–90. [118] Ibid., 39.
[119] BL Stowe Mss. 172, fols 43 (quotation) and 163. [120] TNA SP79/56, fol. 2r–v.
[121] For a survey of this episode see William Bouwsma, *Venice and the Defense of Republican Liberty: Renaissance Values in the Age of the Counter Reformation* (Berkeley: University of California Press, 1968).

hewing down of the glorious tree of sovereignty, the care whereof must always be precious to all princes and states... He will never be found cold or backward in such an action as this."[122] Wotton received instructions to "use all the speeches you can to animate them [the Venetians] upon the confidence of his Majesty's resolution."[123] The ambassador proceeded to suggest to the Doge that Venice seek an alliance with German Protestant princes, offering his good offices to negotiate it if James and the Venetian government approved.[124] The Venetian ambassador in London reported in July that the king and his ministers were "anxiously watching" the progression of the dispute "and every rumor of an accommodation disturbs them greatly." "I gather they would like to see war break out in Italy and would gladly join the Republic and France," he concluded.[125] During a visit to England by his brother-in-law, the king of Denmark, James "took care to work him up" about Venice's quarrel with the papacy, "to such a heat that should matters come to an extreme pitch we will not have to pipe for long to that sovereign, for he will dance of his own accord without the need of our music."[126]

Wotton anticipated that the dispute would lead to a schism between Rome and the Venetian church, which he hoped would serve as a means to introduce Protestantism into Italy, a view shared by other European Protestants, such as du Plessis Mornay and the Palatine agent, Christoph von Dhona.[127] "I have upon the inclination of things that way begun to take order for an Italian preacher from Geneva, whatsoever it cost me."[128] Wotton was accused of having his own household chaplains preach in Italian rather than English.[129] When the Venetian government banned Jesuits from its territory he warmly applauded, taking advantage of the occasion to justify the English trial and execution of Henry Garnet in a speech before the Venetian College.[130] Convinced that Jesuits were plotting to undermine Venetian resistance and assassinate the Republic's leading controversialist, Paulo Sarpi, Wotton set spies on them in Rome.[131] James approved of his doing so.[132] The ambassador supplied the king and Salisbury with all manner of controversial material relating to the dispute, ranging from theological tracts to verbal and visual satires, including a caricature of the Antichrist.[133] James took delight in the satires and expressed his concern for the welfare of Sarpi and other Venetian theologians.[134]

---

[122] TNA SP99/3, fol. 153v.   [123] Ibid., fol. 154v.   [124] *CSPV* 10.455–6.
[125] *CSPV* 10.370, 388.   [126] Ibid., 424.
[127] TNA SP99/3, fols 55, 80. For European Protestant reactions see Adams, "Protestant Cause," 161–2.
[128] TNA SP99/3, fol. 7r.   [129] *CSPV* 11.16.   [130] TNA SP99/3, fol. 77v.
[131] Ibid., fols 19v, 88r, 156; *Life and Letters of Sir Henry Wotton*, ed. Logan Pearsall Smith, 2 vols (Oxford: Clarendon Press, 1907), 1.366; *CSPV* 10.362 and 11.9, 44, 75.
[132] TNA SP99/3, fol. 135.
[133] *Life and Letters*, 1.366, 377, 431 and 437, 444; TNA SP99/3, fols 76, 80r, 86v, 203.
[134] *Life and Letters*, 1.412; *CSPV* 10.499.

But when the Venetians asked him to follow through on his and Wotton's promises to assist them himself and recruit additional allies in Germany and Denmark, James demurred. "For his Majesty's more particularly engaging himself or dealing with his confederates in Denmark and Germany, his Majesty held that somewhat an untimely motion," Salisbury instructed Wotton, "and very improper to be undertaken by him, seeing as yet the Pope hath not proceeded to open action of hostility." Wotton should not encourage the Venetians to expect military assistance.[135] In a further letter Salisbury stated that he always doubted the Venetians and the pope would go to war; he thought the Serene Republic wanted to draw Britain into its quarrel only to obtain better terms.[136] One of Henry IV's ministers of state cynically but accurately remarked that James's words were more "full of animosity against the Pope than of any desire or will to incur risks. Although his ambassador gave large assurances to the Republic of the prompt disposition of his master to lend them aid and assistance in the present quarrel with his Holiness, we do not think that English arms will pass the Alps."[137] Fortunately the French managed to mediate a settlement, making Protestant support for Venice unnecessary.

James's inaction dismayed Sarpi,[138] just as his reluctance to lend more robust aid to the United Provinces had provoked the displeasure of French and Dutch statesmen. But although the contrast between his polemical aggression and physical restraint gave James a reputation for empty verbosity, his conduct is not difficult to understand. Although a new war against Spain or the papacy might have proved popular among puritans and sea captains eager to resume privateering, he had no reason to believe that his subjects would grant him the considerable sums needed to fight effectively. He had more than enough trouble dealing with problems in Ireland, without undertaking new commitments. In March 1608 Boderie overheard Salisbury complaining that "their necessity is extreme and that this last loan [extracted from the City of London] is almost entirely eaten up, since they were constrained to send most of it to Ireland." For this reason, Boderie added, "they will do what they can to maintain themselves with the Spaniards, not from the love they bear them, least of all on the part of the king, but the fear they have of them."[139] It is tempting to conclude that James pursued his quarrel with the pope because he knew that, unlike Spain, the Vatican had no physical means of attacking his kingdoms, allowing him to engage in rhetorical

---

[135] TNA SP99/3, fols 187v–188.   [136] TNA SP99/3, fol. 220r–v.
[137] *Ambassades de la Boderie*, ed. Burdin, 2.68: "Les paroles avec lesquelles le roi de la Grande Bretagne a envoyé ce bref à l'ambassadeur de Venise sont plus remplis d'animosité contre le pape que d'aucun désir ni volonté de vouloir suivre et encourir le hasard d'icelles. Car encore que son ambassadeur ait donné des grandes assurances à la république de la prompte disposition de son maître pour son secours et assistance en la présente occasion du différend qui est entre sa Sainteté et elle, si est que nous n'avons pas opinion que les armes anglaises passent des Alpes de ce côté-là."
[138] Bouwsma, *Venice*, 526–7.   [139] *Ambassade de la Boderie*, ed. Burdin, 160.

fusillades that reaffirmed his commitment to Protestant and anti-papal causes without cost and at minimal risk.

Conflict in the Rhineland and the Murder of Henry IV

Despite his relative poverty, James knew that he could not withdraw entirely from European affairs without gravely damaging his honor and reputation as Europe's leading Protestant prince, and potentially allowing serious dangers to his kingdoms to develop. He therefore tried to do just enough to maintain his credibility, while seeking to act only in conjunction with other powerful states, above all France. The principal theater of joint action in the years following the resolution of the Venetian interdict crisis and the suspension of hostilities in the Netherlands was western Germany, where a succession dispute in the territories of Jülich, Cleves, and Mark threatened to produce a new war. The old, Catholic, ruler had died without heirs on March 25, 1609, shortly before the formal ratification of the Twelve Years Truce between Spain and the Dutch on April 9.[140] Although a number of princes had some sort of claim to succeed him, the two strongest contestants were both Lutherans, the duke of Pfalz-Neuburg and the marquess of Brandenburg. The territories were strategically located, with Cleves straddling the Rhine at the point where it entered the Netherlands, at the northern end of the Spanish Road linking Milan to the Low Countries, while further south Jülich controlled access to the routes between the Rhine and the Meuse around the city of Cologne. The succession of a Protestant prince likely to sympathize with the Dutch therefore threatened to significantly damage Spain's strategic position. James's ambassador in the Habsburg Netherlands, Thomas Edmondes, reported that immediately upon receiving news of the old duke's death, Albert and Isabella dispatched a courier "with great diligence into Spain, express charge being given him (as is said) to be there in nine days."[141] Emperor Rudolph II moved to sequestrate the territories and submit a decision about the rightful heir to an imperial court, whereupon Brandenburg and Pfalz-Neuburg agreed to unite in opposition to his decision and submit their own rival claims to arbitration by impartial princes. They gathered a few troops and occupied the territories, with the exception of the town of Jülich, which had been seized by the emperor's cousin, Archduke Leopold.

For the moment the Protestant claimants—henceforth known as the "princes possessors"—had the upper hand, but the real question was whether the dispute

---

[140] For a succinct summary of the crisis in which this paragraph draws see Wilson, *Thirty Years War*, 230–8. A longer analysis from a Dutch perspective is S. Groenveld, "De Nederlanden en de Guliks-Kleefse erfopvolging, ca. 1592–1614," in *Facetten van de Tachtigjarige Oorlog: Twalf Artikelen over de eriode 1559–1652* (Hilversum: Verloren, 2018), 206–38.

[141] TNA SP77/9 part 2, fol. 22.

would draw in outside powers. Within the Empire, Brandenburg and Pfalz-Neuburg might hope for support from the Protestant Union formed under the leadership of the Calvinist Elector Palatine Frederick IV and his minister, Christian Anhalt, in May 1608, but potential opposition from Catholic bishoprics and principalities, several of which had concluded their own rival league under the leadership of Bavaria in the summer of 1609.[142] Rudolph's habitual hesitation, along with a quarrel between his brothers Mathias and Albert, each of whom hoped to succeed to the imperial title after his death, weakened the imperial position.[143] The potential intervention by Spain and its Army of Flanders posed a greater threat. Edmondes reported from Brussels in early July that "whatsoever show may be made they [the Spanish] have neither the will nor the means to return to the renewing of the war, so far are they unfurnished of all manner of provisions needful for the putting of an army into the field, which to supply will require very great sums of money."[144] But the Protestant powers and France remained nervous.

It seemed imperative for the Dutch, French, British, and German Protestants to demonstrate a united determination to counter any Spanish moves with their own military forces. Somewhat tentative discussions of joint action began over the summer, with all parties hoping to maneuver the others into assuming a larger share of the burden. Henry IV privately threatened to counter any Spanish invasion in July but held back on a public commitment because he preferred to let James take the lead. The leaders of the Evangelical or Protestant Union in Germany attempted to draw James and his brother-in-law, Christian IV of Denmark, into their confessional alliance.[145] But while professing his willingness to help, James refused to commit himself until other princes had first done so.[146] Through Salisbury, he protested that he was unable to make as large a contribution as Henry because Britain lay much further from the disputed territories. He also tried to make his cooperation with France conditional on the repayment of old French debts to the English crown, a demand Henry evaded by suggesting that the Dutch, who owed him money, should reimburse James on his behalf. The dispute became entangled in additional disagreements over the size of the debt and the question of whether the Treaty of Hampton Court remained in force, as the French insisted, or had lapsed in 1604, as James and Salisbury claimed.[147] Henry's ambassador in London, Boderie, had been warning since 1608 that James's need for money threatened to make Henry's willingness to acknowledge

---

[142] Wilson, *Thirty Years War*, 225–6.
[143] Ibid., 106–15; Duerloo, *Dynasty and Piety*, chapter 6.
[144] TNA SP77/9 part 2, fol. 63v.   [145] Adams, "Protestant Cause," 165–6.
[146] TNA SP77/9 part 2, fols 55v, 63; Bibliothèque nationale Cinq cents de Colbert Mss. 426, fol. 9v; *Memorials of Affairs of State*, ed. Sawyer, 2.86.
[147] Jan den Tex, *Oldenbarnevelt*, trans. R. B. Powell, 2 vols (Cambridge: Cambridge University Press, 1973),1.480.

and repay his debts the touchstone (*pierre de touche*) of Anglo-French relations.[148] Without a demonstration of good will on this point, Henry should not expect meaningful British support, he warned. But Henry remained recalcitrant because of his irritation over James's refusal to bear his fair share of the costs of subsidizing the Dutch after 1603 and his lack of confidence that James would spend money repaid to him supporting common objectives.[149]

Eventually a shared interest in deterring Habsburg efforts to install themselves or their proxies in strategic territories along the Rhine overcame these difficulties. In August 1609 James expressed confidence that a joint show of determination would prevent Spain from interfering and offered to do what he could for the common cause.[150] He sent the senior diplomat Ralph Winwood on a mission to the Netherlands and the princes of the Protestant Union, promising support if they acted in concert. After fears mounted that Spain or the emperor would intervene after all, France, Britain, and the Netherlands finally agreed early in the new year to join forces to evict Leopold and defend Jülich-Cleves.[151] James's contribution would comprise 4,000 English soldiers already serving in the Dutch army, whom he agreed to pay while they remained in Germany. The Protestant Union undertook to muster 10,000 men and the Dutch and French 23,000 between them.[152] James's allies had again agreed to shoulder most of the burden, but he had at least consented to spend some of his own money in their support.

He took this step in the knowledge that Henry IV had begun a major mobilization, as if in preparation for a full-scale war. The French king had also contracted a dynastic alliance with the duke of Savoy, who appeared ready to attack the Spanish duchy of Milan. These developments protected James's position, by making it less likely that the Habsburgs would risk escalating the crisis and assuring him that even if they did so and war resulted, Britain would remain part of a powerful European coalition. As Winwood pointed out, failing to act in these circumstances risked damaging James's honor by revealing his unwillingness to support a cause "not only of state but of religion," and effectively ceding the protection of European Protestantism to the Catholic king of France.[153] The French ambassador in London observed that the British played an active role in negotiating an alliance to support the Protestant claimants and contributed a few troops to their defense "principally to make it appear to the whole world that they

---

[148] *Ambassadede la Boderie*, ed. Burdin, 4.306, 321–2.
[149] Ibid., 4.330–1 and 5.66, Henry to la Boderie, February 22, 1610: "... car à vous dire la vérité, je me défie assez de la constance et fermeté de leur foi, principalement s'il faut que je rompe avec Espagne. C'est pourquoi je fais grand difficulté en ce cas de m'obliger de payer leurs dites dettes, ayant opinion que mon argent me sera plus nécessaire ailleurs, qu'il m'apportera d'utilité et de profit, le donnant aux anglais."
[150] TNA PRO31/3/41, de Vertau dispatch of August 12, 1609.
[151] *Memorials of Affairs of State*, ed. Sawyer, 3.97; TNA SP77, pt 2, fol. 97v.
[152] *Memorials of Affairs of State*, ed. Sawyer, 3.113; Wilson, *Thirty Years War*, 256.
[153] *Memorials of Affairs of State*, ed. Sawyer, 3.81.

are parties to this cause and that they want to run the same lance in it as" Henry IV.[154]

But on May 14, 1610 Henry fell victim to a Catholic assassin, François Ravaillac. Worried about domestic disturbances during the long minority of his eight-year-old heir, Louis XIII, the French government began acting more cautiously. When pressed by James's new ambassador in France, Thomas Edmondes, about sending the promised military forces to Cleves and Jülich, the French foreign minister, Villeroy, replied "that their resolutions are daily subject to change by reason of the present state of their affairs" and that many "do not think it fit to engage this state in a foreign war in the time when there is cause to apprehend the falling out of troubles within the kingdom."[155] The promised French troops did eventually arrive, although only after the crisis was on the verge of resolution. France's caution seemed likely to encourage Spanish ambitions. The death of the effective leader of the Protestant Union, the Elector Palatine Frederick IV on September 19, threatened to further weaken the coalition arrayed against the House of Austria.

These events put pressure on James to fill the void by asserting his own leadership, and he soon entered into negotiations for a defensive alliance with the Protestant Union that would eventually be cemented by the marriage of his daughter, Elizabeth, to the new Elector Palatine, Frederick V.[156] James tried to expand this league to include the Dutch—who joined in 1613—along with France, Sweden, and Denmark, who ultimately declined to do so.[157] The archdukes' ambassador in London, Batta Boisschot, reported that James spent considerable energy promoting this alliance because it fed his vanity by making it appear that he had become the leader of Protestants in Germany and throughout Europe.[158] Boisschot believed, probably correctly, that the king and his allies hoped one day to procure the election of a Protestant emperor.[159] But since, apart from the United Provinces, none of the members of this Protestant league seemed capable of raising a formidable army, going to war on its behalf would have exposed Britain to substantial risks. The failure of Salisbury's scheme for a Great Contract in the 1610 Parliament underlined this point.[160] It not only virtually guaranteed that the British crown would remain too poor to support a major war but

---

[154] TNA PRO31/3/41, dispatch of February 14, 1610: "pour faire paraître à tout le monde qu'ils sont partie en cette cause et qu'ils y veulent courent une même lance avec sa majesté."
[155] TNA SP78/56 fol. 146v; BL Stowe Mss. 171, fol. 227 is another copy.
[156] BL Stowe Mss. 171, fols 191, 273, and 337; *Memorials of Affairs of State*, ed. Sawyer, 3.222; *Oldenbarnevelt Bescheiden*, ed. Veenendaal, 506; Adams, "Protestant Cause," 165–6. Adams points out that the court of the Palatinate, the leader of the German Protestants, initiated proposals for a dynastic alliance with Britain at the suggestion of Henry Wotton, as the best means of drawing James into the Evangelical Union.
[157] HHStA Belgien PC46, fols 78v, 131r, 167r, 171v.   [158] HHStA Belgien PC47, fol. 257.
[159] HHStA Belgien 46, fols 376, 379. See below, pp. 616–18, for James's efforts a few years later to deny the Habsburgs the imperial crown.
[160] The Great Contract was a project to increase royal income by trading the abolition of obsolete but vexatious feudal exactions for more efficient and modern taxes.

demonstrated the discord between James and his English subjects before all of Europe, weakening his credibility. In 1614 he declined an invitation to enter into an offensive, as well as a defensive, alliance with the Protestant Union, and when a second dispute broke out over Jülich and Cleves in that year he resisted pleas to lend robust assistance to his ally, the marquess of Brandenburg.[161] The seeming paralysis of France induced James to act cautiously. But by further weakening constraints on Spain and its allies, his caution risked emboldening them to act more aggressively.

Even more worrying than that prospect, Henry IV's violent death aroused fears of a revival in France of the pro-Spanish Catholic militancy that the League had championed only a few years before. The fallen king's preparations for war against the Habsburgs had already provoked a strong Catholic reaction before his death. Parisian animosity toward the Huguenots, fanned by inflammatory sermons, appeared so threatening in July that Sully and the duke of Bouillon both barricaded themselves in their urban residences for protection.[162] Sully's fall from power the following year and the revelation that the French regent, Marie de Médicis, had begun negotiations to marry her son, Louis XIII, to the eldest daughter of Philip III and her own daughter, Elizabeth, to the future Philip IV, further increased British anxieties. The most thorough modern study of Marie de Médicis concludes that she promoted the marriages to deter Spain from trying to destabilize France during her son's minority, without any intention of breaking her husband's alliances with Protestant states.[163] But Protestant statesmen in London were understandably suspicious and seriously alarmed. They viewed a Habsburg-Bourbon dynastic alliance as "the rudest blow that this state could receive," the archdukes' ambassador to Britain, de Groote, reported.[164]

Political Intrigue and Polemic in France, 1610–1619

Preventing the consummation of that alliance, or failing that its effects in amplifying Spanish and Jesuit influence over the French crown, became a major preoccupation of James and his ministers for a full decade, drawing them into internal French politics. The weakness of the regency government and a resurgence of noble factionalism in the wake of Henry's murder afforded opportunities to meddle. In July 1610 a servant of the English ambassador in Paris reported that

---

[161] HHStA Belgien PC47, fols 37, 142.
[162] Nicolas le Roux, "A Time of Frenzy: Dreams of Union and Aristocratic Turmoil (1610–1615)," in *Dynastic Marriages 1612–1615: A Celebration of the Habsburg and Bourbon Unions*, ed. Margaret McGowan (Farnham: Ashgate, 2013), 19–38 at 24–5.
[163] Dubost, *Marie de Médicis*, 398–400.
[164] "Le plus rude coup que cet état pourrair recevoi," HHStA Belgien PC45 (unfoliated), dispatch of November 29, 1611.

the factions which had begun to swell between our great men [in France] are grown to such an exasperation as that they are almost broken out into open sedition and banding. There having been such alarms taken these three or four nights by those of the weaker side, as that the duke of Bouillon and the prince of Condé, with some other of their chief associates, did sit up with all their household in arms almost all those nights long, whereupon rumors of a tumult hath so generally and so strongly spread itself over all the town as that a man can see nothing almost in the street but carrying and providing of arms.[165]

Condé had recently returned from exile in the Habsburg Netherlands, where he had fled with his teenage wife to save her from Henry IV's amorous attentions. Although a young man of limited abilities, his status as a leading prince of the blood, who would soon become third in line for the crown after Louis XIII and his brother, Gaston d'Orléans, made him the natural leader of disaffected nobles and the center of a potential reversionary interest.

His ally, the Huguenot duke of Bouillon, was being courted by the regent, who wanted to send him as her extraordinary ambassador to London to reassure James that she would stand by her late husband's Protestant alliances. Bouillon refused the appointment "unless he may see clearly into their intentions here [in Paris]" and receive authority to offer James "more real satisfaction than ceremonial professions."[166] An experienced veteran of previous civil wars and political intrigues dating back to the 1570s, Bouillon had allied himself with Elizabeth and befriended the second earl of Essex.[167] Although he had strained relations with other Huguenot nobles like Sully and the duke of Rohan, his political connections extended well beyond France. His second marriage to a daughter of William the Silent linked him to the House of Orange and he had acted as guardian for Frederik V of the Palatinate, whose marriage to Princess Elizabeth he helped negotiate. His sovereignty over the fortified town of Sedan, along the French frontier with the Habsburg Netherlands, reinforced his international standing, while the academy he founded there made him an influential figure in Huguenot and European Calvinist intellectual culture. One of the first favors he received from James was the release of the Scottish Presbyterian Andrew Melville from imprisonment in the Tower of London, to take up a post at Sedan, where

---

[165] Trumbull Mss., 4, fol. 94, Beaulieu to Trumbull, July 14, 1610 (Library of Congress microfilms 041/Camb/195/1), printed in *Memorials of Affairs of State*, ed. Sawyer, 191.

[166] HMC Salisbury, 22.222, Edmondes to Salisbury, undated 1610.

[167] The most recent study is Romain Marchand, *Henry de la Tour (1555–1623): affirmation politique, service du roi et révolte* (Paris: Garnier, 2020). See also J. Marsollier, *Histoire de Henry de la Tour d'Auvergne, duc de Builllon* (Paris, 1719); Auguste Langel, "Le duc de Bouillon d'après des documents inédits," *Révue des deux mondes* 18 (1876): 897–920; Étienne Charavay, "Le Maréchal de Bouillon à la cour d'Angleterre," *Revue des documents historiques* 1 (1874): 54–9; and Adams, "Protestant Cause," 120–1, 126–7, 204–10.

Melville finished his life fighting against Arminian tendencies in the French Reformed Church.[168]

Bouillon sought to strengthen his party by pursuing an alliance with the house of Guise, which, despite its former role in leading the Catholic League, now appeared ready to make common cause with Huguenots against the dominant group within the regency government.[169] In a conversation with the English ambassador William Becher just after Henry's assassination, Guise proclaimed "that they had lost their king who could command them, that every man in this new world abounded in his own senses and that it was now for the king of England to undertake the affairs of Christendom and to show them what they had to do."[170] He wrote to James, assuring him that despite his personal Catholicism he believed "it was necessary for the state of the kingdom to suffer the party of the religion [the Huguenots] peaceably to enjoy their privileges and repose, and he would always be ready to preserve them from oppression." He suggested that they set up "some private means of correspondence" to communicate about French affairs.[171] James responded warmly to these overtures, instructing Edmondes and Lord Wotton, the extraordinary ambassador he had sent to condole Henry's death, to treat Guise and his family with special courtesy and confidence.[172] Guise reciprocated by sending an agent to London in December 1612.[173] In addition to the political advantages this alliance seemed to offer, James was acutely aware of the family connection through his grandmother, Mary of Guise.

The outward ideological complexion of this factional contest was deceptive, since most of the protagonists wanted primarily to promote their own interests. Guise would soon become a supporter of the regent after she satisfied his grievances, effectively ending his cooperation with his Stuart cousin. But religious issues and jealousy of Spain did shape public sentiment in France in ways that discontented nobles sought to exploit. Pamphlets broadcast Condé's claim that the dynastic marriage arranged by the regent would subordinate France to Spain, giving rise to an image of Marie de Médicis as a supporter of Spanish and ultra-Catholic policies that persisted in historical literature down to the late twentieth century. This perception was widely held at the time, especially among royal office holders.[174] Opposition to Henry's Protestant alliances by Catholic clergy and rumors of impending Catholic insurrections in parts of France in reaction to his military preparations fueled a backlash blaming the king's murder on radical preaching, religious fanaticism, and the Jesuits.[175] "It is a delightful theme now

---

[168] James Kirk, "Melville, Andrew (1545–1622)," *ODNB*.
[169] TNA SP78/56, fol. 196, dispatch of June 27; cf. BL Stowe Mss. 171, fols 268v–69.
[170] SP78/56, fols 111v–112.
[171] TNA SP78/56, fol. 184r, Edmondes to Salisbury, June 21, 1610.
[172] Ibid., fols 107 and 242r–v.   [173] HHStA Belgien PC46, fol. 377r.
[174] Dubost, *Marie de Médicis*, 402–3; Dubost argues forcefully that this image was inaccurate.
[175] On which Becher commented in January: TNA SP78/56, fols 4r–v.

in these pulpits to declaim against the whole society of these Jesuits," one Englishman wrote shortly after Henry's murder, "which some preachers have done openly within these two or three days, as against the wicked *forgerons* of all villainies."[176] Edmondes reported that members of the *parlement* of Paris "find that the damnable maxims, which have been insinuated these twenty years by seditious books and preachings, in derogation of the sacredness of the persons and authority of princes have been the chief occasion of this mischief."[177] When a new book by Bellarmine, written against a tract defending the Oath of Allegiance by the Scottish Catholic William Barclay, appeared the *parlement* of Paris condemned its arguments and decreed that possession of a copy would be punished as treason.[178] The pope's nuncio strenuously pressed the regent to quash this decision, while James instructed Edmondes to urge her to maintain it as a matter "concerning the estate of all sovereign princes."[179] James's quarrel with the pope had become mixed up with French politics.

He now faced a decision about how fully and openly to support noble opposition to the regent's government. Edmondes wrote to Salisbury, advising involvement. Inaction might well allow "the Pope's and the king of Spain's authority" within the French court to increase to an extent "that may prove very dangerous to their neighbors," whereas a decisive demonstration by James "with his other allies" would likely "keep matters from growing to any extremity."[180] James evidently agreed. In a conversation with Caron, he said he would threaten Marie de Médicis that he "had so good a part and correspondence with the nobles and princes and all those of the religion, her subjects, and also with the house of Guise, his near relations that he could well stop her progress."[181] His efforts to coordinate with French nobles opposed to the regent's plans for a Spanish dynastic alliance received a further boost in late April 1612 when Bouillon, who had finally agreed to serve as her ambassador, arrived in London.[182] James brushed aside the duke's assurances about Marie des Médicis' continuing fidelity to France's Protestant allies with the wry comment that "it was the fashion of princes, when they deceive their neighbors, first to deceive their own ambassadors."[183] But Bouillon also carried a proposal for a marriage between Prince Henry and one of Marie's daughters, which he presented as a means to strengthen opponents of the

---

[176] Beaulieu to Trumbull, May 23, 1610 in *Memorials of Affairs of State*, ed. Sawyer, 174.
[177] TNA SP87/56, fol. 136.   [178] Ibid., fol. 357v.
[179] TNA SP14/58/69, Thomas Lake to Salisbury, December 10, 1610.
[180] BL Stowe Mss. 172, fol. 181.
[181] *Oldenbarnevelt Bescheiden*, ed. Veenendaal, 495: "want hij haer oock wel wilde ontbieden dat hij soo goeden ende correspondentie met de prince ende heeren ende alle die van de religie, haer suiecten hadde, oock mede met die van 't huys Guise, sijne soo near verwanten, dat hij haer progress wel soude kunnen stoppen."
[182] The embassy lasted from April 26 to May 19.
[183] *An Historical View of the Negotiations between the Courts of England, France and Brussels, from the Year 1582 to 1617*, ed. Thomas Birch (London, 1749), 359. James asked Edmondes to remind Bouillon of this comment.

Franco-Spanish marriages and derail the project.¹⁸⁴ Although James ultimately rejected the marriage alliance, he and Prince Henry listened carefully to Bouillon's analysis of French politics in several long private audiences, from which even members of the privy council were excluded.¹⁸⁵ Bouillon also urged the need to block Habsburg ambitions in Germany by marrying Princess Elizabeth to Frederick V. The duke had recently visited Heidelberg to discuss this match with the elector's mother and worked assiduously to bring it about. He kept up his contacts with the British court after returning to France, through correspondence and discussions with Edmondes in Paris.¹⁸⁶

James has sometimes been described as trying to mediate French disputes in ways that ended up assisting the regent's efforts to promote alliance with Spain.¹⁸⁷ But if read carefully, the evidence points to a more duplicitous policy of fomenting opposition, while pretending to act as an honest broker and friend of civic peace. Since James had no desire to involve himself *directly* in a French civil war by sending an army to support the crown's rebels, as Elizabeth had done in the 1590s and Charles I would do in 1626, he had to act indirectly through Condé, Bouillon, and other dissident nobles, who were not always the most reliable of partners. He had few scruples about encouraging their opposition to policies he saw as detrimental to French, as well as British, interests, although he did at times advise them to avoid measures he thought imprudent. The princes of the blood "cannot but see themselves made fools and shadows by the ministers, especially in their alliance with Spain," he wrote to Edmondes in August 1612: "It is the proper office of princes of the blood in their king's minority to take care, *ne quid detrimenti respublica capiat.*"¹⁸⁸ He accordingly tried to patch up quarrels among the nobles to produce a common front, for example by promoting friendship between Bouillon and his Huguenot rival the duke of Rohan, and continuing to press his Guise cousins to join the opposition to "the cabal betwixt France and Spain."¹⁸⁹ In 1612 he encouraged an effort by Bouillon and other nobles to topple Villeroy, whom he blamed for promoting the Spanish alliance. James stated melodramatically that he received notice of this attempted purge on St. Bartholomew's Day, which reminded him that "we have great cause to fear that that bloody saint will

---

¹⁸⁴ Ibid., 352.   ¹⁸⁵ BL Stowe Mss. 172, fol. 284.
¹⁸⁶ E.g. *Historical Relations*, ed. Birch, 356; TNA SP78/60 fol. 101.
¹⁸⁷ Adams, "Road to La Rochelle," 419–20. This pioneering analysis recognized the importance of Bouillon in influencing James's policies and facilitating his correspondence with Condé. It also correctly pointed to James's support for the attempt to remove the French minister Villeroy, discussed below. But I disagree with Adams's reading of the evidence of James's policies toward France after about 1613, which seems to me to place too much emphasis on the reputed influence of Gondomar, and the king's professions of his desire to mediate French conflicts in the interest of peace, which I read as a cover for more insidious maneuvers. Adams was correct in thinking that James was unwilling to provide open assistance to militant Huguenots led by the duke of Rohan, but given the weaknesses and internal divisions of the Huguenots this can be defended as a prudent policy.
¹⁸⁸ *Historical Relations*, ed. Birch, 358–9.
¹⁸⁹ TNA PRO31.3.48 fol. 31; *Historical Relations*, ed. Birch, 359.

once again bestir himself in France if it be not timorously prevented."¹⁹⁰ Villeroy's past as a supporter of the League added to James's suspicions. "I have not seen the king so bent nor so violently set upon the success of any act as this," his new favorite, Robert Ker (later earl of Somerset) wrote to Edmondes about the effort to topple the French foreign minister.¹⁹¹

Although Villeroy survived the attack, disputes over the regent's dynastic alliance with Spain continued to roil French politics, while the outbreak of a conflict in north Italy over the succession to the duchy of Mantua, pitting the duke of Savoy against the Spanish crown, added another divisive issue. Condé, Bouillon, and James all advocated French intervention in support of Savoy, against the views of Villeroy.¹⁹² In February 1614 Condé issued a manifesto calling for the summoning of the French estates general to debate the Spanish marriages, and joined Bouillon in withdrawing from the court and threatening an armed demonstration to compel the regent to accept the demand. As they did so, the prince and duke again entered into friendly correspondence with James.¹⁹³ He initially counseled moderation, urging the princes to remain focused on the public cause rather than their private grievances and counseling them to avoid rebellion if at all possible. He hoped that the mere display of unified opposition would suffice to force a change in French policy and feared provoking a Catholic reaction.¹⁹⁴ But after the princes nevertheless revolted James backed their action, in part to avoid demoralizing his allies by appearing to support the regent against them.¹⁹⁵ By the summer he was urging Condé to press the case for "that right in managing the affairs which properly belongs to him in right of his place" as the leading prince of the blood.¹⁹⁶ After the regent agreed to summon the estates, James instructed Edmondes to press Condé to object to the assembly's appointed meeting place in Paris, a strongly Catholic city with close ties to the regency government, and to continue his opposition to "the former absolute government" of Marie's ministers. The ambassador should take care, however, to work through Bouillon or another intermediary, "to keep yourself from appearing in it" and disguise James's

---

¹⁹⁰ *Historical Relations*, ed. Birch, 358.   ¹⁹¹ Ibid., 61.
¹⁹² BL Stowe Mss. 174, fols 53r, 76r, 150r, 197r.
¹⁹³ TNA SP78/62 fols 37–51; HHstA Belgien PC47, fols 142v, 171v, 172r, 250v.
¹⁹⁴ Bl Stowe Mss 174, fols 232r, 235v–236, 237v, 242, 244r, 248v, 275v; for the fear of Catholic reaction see fols 1 and 341r.
¹⁹⁵ Ibid., fol. 306v. A Scottish minister who had migrated to France, David Hume, reported that the regent's supporter, President Janin, had told the princes that James had written to her disapproving of the princes' actions and offering "all manner of support" against them (ibid., 312r); James felt it necessary to refute this claim by showing his continued confidence in Bouillon and Condé.
¹⁹⁶ Michael Hayden, *France and the Estates General of 1614* (Cambridge: Cambridge University Press, 1975), 63 and 73.

involvement.¹⁹⁷ Marie was not fooled, concluding as early as May that James wanted to stir up Huguenot support for Bouillon "and the other malcontents."¹⁹⁸

Condé's effort to use the estates general to weaken the regent failed, because Marie's ministers orchestrated a successful campaign to secure the selection of delegates sympathetic to her.¹⁹⁹ Disappointed at this outcome, James voiced his displeasure over recent events in France to Caron in April 1615.²⁰⁰ But he continued to meddle, especially in support of an article placed at the head of the *cahier* or list of grievances of the representatives of the third estate, representing the common people. The article affirmed that French kings ruled by divine right and cannot be deposed by any earthly power, and called for an oath affirming these principles to be given to all office holders and teachers within the kingdom. It further demanded that the French clergy be required to refute any efforts to challenge the sacred and inviolable nature of royal authority. This proposal followed an *arrêt* (decree) of the *parlement* of Paris on June 26, condemning a newly published book by the Spanish Jesuit Francisco de Suarez, written at the command of the pope, against James's *Apologie for the Oath of Allegiance*. The *parlement* summoned several French Jesuit leaders and ordered them not to permit preaching in support of Suarez's doctrines. The third estate and *parlement* had effectively endorsed James's position in his quarrel with the papacy, including his view that controversialists like Suarez should be held responsible for Henry IV's murder.²⁰¹

The French Jesuit Order distanced itself from Suarez and Bellarmine by agreeing to accept the sanctity and inviolability of royal power in France, and emerged largely unscathed from the dispute.²⁰² But the pope and his nuncio in Paris fought back vigorously, and pressured the regent to annul both the *parlement*'s *arrêt* and the third estate's article. Within the estates general the representatives of the clergy, led by Cardinal Davy du Perron, attacked the article, as an attempt by laymen to violate the Church's control of religious doctrine, and a measure

---

¹⁹⁷ BL Stowe Mss. 175, fol. 58.

¹⁹⁸ HHStA Belgien PC47, fol. 256, Boisschot dispatch of May 29, 1614, reporting a conversation with the French ambassador in London.

¹⁹⁹ Dubost, *Marie de Médicis*, 431–6. The fullest treatment is Hayden, *Estates General of 1614*. For the pamphlet controversy see Roger Chartier and Denis Richet, *Représentation et vouloir politiques: Autour des États généraux de 1614* (Paris: École des hautes études en sciences sociales, 1982).

²⁰⁰ BL Add Mss. 17,677 I, fol. 59: "dat ick bevondt dat sijne mat in de saecken van Vranckryck niet wel edificert en was."

²⁰¹ The classic article on these episodes is Pierre Blet, "L'article du Tiers aux États Généraux de 1614," *Revue d'histoire moderne et contemporain* 2 (1951): 81–106 but this should now be supplemented by Eric Nelson, "Defining the Fundamental Laws of France: The Proposed First Article of the Third Estate at the French Estates General of 1614," *English Historical Review* 115 (2000): 1216–30 and Nelson, *Jesuits*, chapter 5. Nelson shows that a previously unknown preliminary draft of the third estate's article was sent to England by Edmondes, suggesting that someone wanted to keep the British government informed about the matter. See also Hayden, *Estates General*, chapter 8, esp. 143–4 and Dubost, *Marie de Médicis*, 440–1.

²⁰² Nelson, *Jesuits*, chapter 5.

promoted by Huguenots and the English. It had the tail of a fish, du Perron asserted, implying it had swum across the Channel. He succeeded in winning over the second estate representing the nobility and some delegates to the third, effectively killing the article. In an attempted compromise, at the end of the session the French crown ordered the article removed from the third estate's published *cahier*, with a blank space left in its place. Since everyone knew what had been intended this was not effective censorship, but it did comply outwardly with papal demands for the article's suppression.

The controversy quickly spilled beyond the estates general, giving rise to a lively exchange of pamphlets in which James joined by issuing a lengthy *Declaration du Serenissime Roy Jacques I Roi de la Grand' Bretaigne, France et Irlande... Pour le Droit des Rois et independance ce leurs Couronnes, Contre le Harangue de l'Illustrissime Cardinal du Perron*. Although published in London it was written in French and contained an erudite review of the history of resistance to papal demands by French kings since the Middle Ages; it was probably written by Pierre du Moulin, who was visiting England at the time of its composition.[203] James also instructed Edmondes to deliver a remonstrance to Marie de Médicis, complaining that her suspension of the *parlement*'s condemnation of Suarez "did cause much discontent in the minds of your subjects" and denouncing Perron's oration as a speech that subjected the French crown "to the tutelage of Rome," while spreading "reproaches and injurious invectives" against himself. This also soon appeared in print, in both English and French editions.

Throughout the period Condé continued to support the *parlement* and the third estate, incorporating their demands for the condemnation of doctrines upheld by figures like Suarez and Bellarmine alongside his opposition to the dynastic alliance with Spain, in the lists of grievances through which he justified his revolts. In June of 1615 he sent a personal emissary to England, who received a private audience with the king.[204] Over the summer, as Louis XIII and his sister slowly traveled to the Spanish frontier to conclude their marriages, Condé and Bouillon prepared a fresh revolt and appealed once more for British support. Although initially cautious, James and Edmondes remained in close contact with the dissident nobles. Their involvement had by now become too obvious to disguise. The French ambassador in London complained that James was "meddling in our affairs more than he should."[205] In a testy exchange he told the king that Edmondes's house in Paris had become "the ordinary resort of all the malcontents and ill affected persons of the State and that all his discourses were

---

[203] Patterson, *James VI and I*, 185–6; Boisschot also believed that Moulin had written James's book, HHStA Belgien PC48, fols 384v–385. Having struck up a correspondence with James several years before, du Moulin traveled to London at the express invitation of the king's Huguenot physician, Théodore du Mayerne, whom James had sent on a private mission to France (Patterson, *James VI and I*, 158–60; HHStA Belgien PC48, fol. 189r).
[204] TNA PRO31/3/48 fol. 26.   [205] TNA PRO31/3/48, fol. 112.

mutinous."²⁰⁶ James replied that "these were calumnies of the Jesuits and Jesuited persons," who sought to attack his own reputation by slandering his servant. He "protested the sincerity of his affection for the crown of France," whereupon the ambassador cut him off by "demanding to know what he meant by the crown of France, whether the king or the kingdom...his Majesty answered the king."²⁰⁷ Two days later James offered to mediate the dispute between Condé's party and the French crown. He claimed to be motivated by three main considerations: his belief that the Huguenots would face the danger of extermination "if the marriages with Spain shall be accomplished"; his dedication to "the welfare of Christendom, which cannot but run a great hazard if Spain shall be incorporated with France"; and his "care" for Louis XIII, "who being yet but in his minority should not be entangled in civil war by the misgovernment of them who aim at their own private ends for the maintenance of their greatness, to the dishonor of his crown and the disservice of the state."²⁰⁸ A few months later he stated that the "duty which God and nature doth bind him to bear to the maintenance of all absolute monarchs" compelled him to intervene in the affairs of a young king, "who by reason of the weakness of his years hath need of some support, both of faithful counsel and trusty friends."²⁰⁹ He wanted to treat Louis XIII in much the way that Elizabeth's council had treated him thirty years before, as an adolescent monarch incapable of recognizing his own true interests, who needed to be forced to purge his court and alter his policies by a noble rebellion backed by a foreign state.

Edmondes concluded that the dissident nobles would likely prevail if, but only if, they received substantial Huguenot support.²¹⁰ In late summer the Huguenots sent envoys to London for discussions with James. Condé also sent an emissary, the marquis de Bonivet.²¹¹ Although James declined to provide the open armed support the French rebels requested, he encouraged them in other ways, and rumors circulated in September that Condé had recruited English and Scottish volunteer soldiers.²¹² When the Huguenots convened a national assembly at Grenoble, James sent a Venetian Protestant who had entered his service, Giovanni Francesco Biondi, to address it. In another effort to dissimulate his meddling, he did not give Biondi letters of accreditation but instead sent him first to Bouillon, who was asked to manage his approach to the assembly. Biondi exhorted the Huguenots to seek peace but quickly added that if the French crown continued to violate its agreements with them, while trying "to incorporate France in Spain...which will be not only the ruin of this state but of Religion and

---

²⁰⁶ *Historical Relations*, ed. Birch, 387.   ²⁰⁷ BL Stowe Mss. 175, fol. 345r–v.
²⁰⁸ BL Stowe Mss. 175, fol. 347.   ²⁰⁹ BL Stowe Mss. 176, fol. 9.
²¹⁰ TNA SP78/63, fol. 317.   ²¹¹ HHStA Belgien PC48, fol. 412.
²¹² Ibid., fols 414v–15, 434r, 461v. Anna of Denmark, who disapproved of the French malcontents, told Boisschot that Bonivet had requested 12,000 soldiers but had not been given any.

all Christianity," James would "employ all his forces for the defense and propagation of religion and the maintenance of the liberty of Europe."[213]

While appearing superficially to discourage rebellion, this message simultaneously pointed to the need for collective action to foil a Spanish design that threatened Protestantism not only in France but throughout Europe and hinted at James's willingness to lend armed support to such an effort, although in sufficiently general terms to avoid committing him.[214] Until this point the Huguenots had not supported Condé but in 1615 several of their leaders, including the duke of Rohan, did so. Bouillon's eighteenth-century biographer, J. Marsollier, saw Biondi's intervention as decisive in bringing about this outcome.[215] With nearly 200 garrisoned *places de sûretés* throughout France, the Huguenots had considerable military resources. Although their intervention failed to stop the Spanish marriages, which finally took place in the autumn, it did prolong the revolt into 1616, at a cost to the crown equivalent to nearly a year's income.[216] This resulted in a settlement advantageous to Condé, installing him as the head of the royal council and granting him the right to counter-sign its *arrêts*, allowing him to limit the crown's actions. Edmondes played an active role behind-the-scenes in the negotiations of this settlement. James tried to intervene more directly, complaining that the agreed terms did not sufficiently uphold Huguenot interests or reaffirm the third estate's controversial article, but was advised to desist by his French allies.[217]

Over the following summer several ministers who had held office since the 1580s, including Villeroy, fell from power. Condé failed to take full advantage of the fluid situation by absenting himself from Paris for several months, but after he

---

[213] TNA SP78/64, fol. 63: "... dieu l'ayant fait protecteur de la religion, sa majesté n'avoir obligation que surpasse celle qu'il a à l'avancement du service et de la gloire de dieu, sur quoi ayant reconnu que vous avez rendu à la majesté de votre roi ce que doivent bons sujets à leur prince, et que nonobstant cela les édits de pacification soit en quelques sortes violées, et enfin que les lois de l'état soit ébranlées, qu'on taché d'incorpore la France en l'Espagne et de s'opposer aux arrêts du parlement, qui serait non seulement la ruine de cette état mais aussi de la Religion et de toute la Chrétienté, en tel cas sa majesté reconnait l'obligation qu'il a à dieu et à sa propre conscience d'employer toutes ses forces à la défense et propagation de la religion et au maintien de la liberté de l'Europe."

[214] For a different interpretation see Adams, "Road to La Rochelle," 430.

[215] Marsollier, *Bouillon*, 68–9: "Les esprits commencent à s'échauffé et les anciennes défiances à se réveiller, lorsque Jean-François Biondy vénitien arriva à l'assemblée de la part du roi d'Angleterre pour l'assurer de la protection de sa majesté britannique et de l'intérêt qu'elle prévoit à tout ce qui pouvait affermir le repos du parti et favoriser le progrès de leur religion. Le duc de Bouillon avait ménagé cet envoi, afin que l'on ne pût pas douter, Biondy déclara à l'assemblée que le roi d'Angleterre l'avait envoyé d'abord directement au duc de Bouillon pour prendre avec lui les mesures qui conviendrait aux avantages du parti; qu'ils lui avaient communiqué ses lettres de créances, et qu'il ne s'était rendu à l'assemblée qu'après avoir conféré avec lui et pris ses avis sur toutes choses."

[216] Edmondes attributed Condé's inability to stop the marriages by military means partly to Huguenot inaction, caused by the long deliberations at Grenoble during the summer. Since the exchange of brides took place at the border between France and Spain, rebel armies in southwestern France might potentially have prevented or delayed it by blocking the route south from Paris, although this would have required a confrontation with loyal military forces accompanying the king and his sister. In the event the rebels lacked sufficient strength to make the attempt.

[217] BL Stowe Mss. 176, fols 9, 10.

returned in July the regent agreed to grant the princes full access to diplomatic correspondence and Condé authority over the crown's finances.[218] A few of the prince's followers began to question in private the legitimacy of Henry IV's marriage to Marie de Médicis, and therefore Louis's title to the throne.[219] Delighted with this outcome, James sent his Scottish favorite, James Hay Lord Doncaster, as extraordinary ambassador to Paris, where he cultivated Condé and allegedly toasted him as a future king of France.[220] But on September 1 (new style) the regent and her supporters had Condé arrested on charges that he planned to kidnap the king, in a coup widely interpreted at the time as a triumph not only for the queen mother and her Italian favorite, Concino Concini marquis d'Ancre, but the Spanish party in France.[221] James sent a stinging protest, which Marie curtly rejected. Even the Dutch ambassador in Paris complained about Edmondes's continued machinations following Condé's arrest.[222] The prince's allies, including Bouillon, began preparations for yet another uprising that would sweep through France over the winter.

Arminianism, Vorstius, and Dutch Politics

As these events transpired in France, James became involved in another complex tangle of religious and political controversies within the United Provinces. Although the issues were very different, British mistrust of French intentions in the Netherlands and disagreements about Dutch policy toward France provided connecting threads. Even as he collaborated uneasily with Henry IV to support the Dutch against Spain, James remained jealous of French influence in the United Provinces and suspicious that Henry wanted to turn them into a satellite of France and have himself named their sovereign.[223] Caron lamented to Oldenbarnevelt that the mutual mistrust of the two kings made each wary of entering into a close alliance with the other, even in support of common objectives.[224] James's suspicion of France increased after Henry's death, as he began to fear that a French

---

[218] TNA SP78/66/1 (Condé's delays in returning to Paris), 16 (the regent's concessions to Condé and the princes).
[219] Dubost, *Marie de Médicis*, 496–504.
[220] Caroline Bitsch, *Vie et carrière d'Henri II de Bourbon, Prince de Condé (1588–1646)* (Paris: Honoré Champion, 2008), 170–80. It is possible that the story of Hay's toasting Condé as a future king was a malicious rumor, spread to discredit both the prince and his English backers.
[221] See, for example, William Trumbull's comments in TNA SP77/12, fols 184r and 203v and Edmondes's report (SP78/66/33) that the Spanish ambassador and papal nuncio had spent the night preceding Condé's arrest in the Louvre until one in the morning, and subsequently consulted regularly "with those which do now manage the affairs."
[222] BL Stowe Mss. 176, fol. 34; *Oldenbarnevelt Bescheiden*, ed. Veenendaal, 3.217, 218, and 242.
[223] With reason. See Den Tex, *Oldenbarnevelt*, 2.364.
[224] *Oldenbarnevelt Bescheiden*, ed. Veenendaal, 652, dispatch of October 19, 1607: "Waneer dese twee coningen dus in jalousie tusschen den anderen blijven dat se d'een d'anderen (in gevalle van diergelijck accident) niet en durven oft wilen beloven desselve handvastige, soe is eer apparent door

Catholic government tied to Spain through dynastic alliances would seek to undermine Dutch Protestantism and political unity. These worries dovetailed into concerns that he and other English statesmen had long felt about the impact peace would have on the Dutch state. Echoing views that had long existed within the Netherlands, the English tended to see the Dutch federation as a ramshackle structure held together by the external pressures of war that would likely disintegrate once armed conflict ceased.[225] The need to obtain consent for "levies of money" and other "matters of consequence," not only from the States General but individual provinces, one experienced diplomat commented, guaranteed that "their resolutions are slow and heavy," while turning "almost every common man" into a statesman, so that "the points of government from the highest to the lowest may be learned in a passage boat going from one town to another as well as in the assembly of the states general."[226]

It seemed doubtful that the Dutch would maintain the very high levels of taxation needed to support their army and navy once fighting had ceased. But a strong army appeared necessary, not only to defend against possible renewed Spanish attacks but also to maintain internal cohesion. As Sir Edward Conway put it in a letter to Prince Henry's secretary, Adam Newton: "These provinces to stand must have unity; and to keep that they must have full contribution from the particulars [i.e. towns and provinces] and the general that so they may pay their army, in which only consists their real authority. Their army cassed once, upon every offence and jealousy they will fly in a thousand pieces and must of course, for besides the unruliness of a multitude they have not a formed and grounded government."[227] But Oldenbarnevelt, who feared that resistance to high taxation would destabilize the United Provinces, sought to lighten the burden by reducing the army's size, against the strong objections of its commander, Maurice of Nassau.[228] The British government wanted the army kept at strength, but its

---

dese ligue [a defensive alliance with the United Provinces] meer misverstanden (door deselve jalousien) te rijsen dan eenich ander goet, soedat ic in effecte wil jugeren dat wij in't eynde van hier niet anders dan formaliteyten end sullen crijgen."

[225] See, e.g., Clement Edmondes, "Politia of the United Provinces," BL Add Mss. 48,163, fol. 36v: "it were not possible without an enemy abroad or an army at home to keep these provinces thus united. Every province, yea every town would be a sovereign commonwealth and take notice of no command but their own reason."

[226] Ibid., 33v. These views correspond closely to the earlier comments of the second earl of Essex about the Dutch state without a center and the belief of Leicester and his entourage that to survive the United Provinces needed a more centralized government under the direction of a single sovereign head (above, pp. 289–91 and pp. 363–4).

[227] *The Life of Henry Prince of Wales, Eldest Son of James I*, ed. Thomas Birch (London, 1760), 374–5. I have found little support in the sources for the view that James and other English statesmen had an ideological aversion to republics *as such*. To the contrary, the king expressed warm feelings toward Venice and claimed to be a supporter of the United Provinces. But many English certainly did have practical reservations concerning the efficiency and cohesion of Dutch institutions.

[228] Jonathan Israel, *The Dutch Republic: Its Rise, Greatness and Fall* (Oxford: Oxford University Press, 1995), 400; Den Tex, *Oldenbarnevelt*, 2.361 and 390.

demands that the Dutch begin repaying their war debt in regular installments made this even more difficult.

In addition to these secular issues, James took seriously his role as Europe's leading Protestant king and his royal title of Defender of the Faith. Ignoring the fact that it had originated in a papal grant, he interpreted that title as a mandate to protect all reformed churches, not just those of Britain, from heresy and schism. This attitude also reflected his belief, modeled partly on the example of the first Christian Emperor Constantine that princes had a duty to supervise the Church and prevent fractious disputes among its clergy from rending Christian unity. Because Europe had divided after the fall of the Roman Empire into different kingdoms and polities, each with its own territorial church, rulers needed to cooperate in exercising this oversight. But James felt entitled to take the lead in mobilizing other rulers of his own religion to do the job. Early in his English reign he tried to enlist the Elector Palatine to help him mediate a dispute between Huguenot theologians, and subsequently to iron out differences among Protestant churches in other territories.[229] He later enlisted Bouillon's aid in mediating a quarrel between the two Huguenot theologians, du Moulin and Tilenus, which he feared would divide the reformed church in France as Catholic pressure upon it mounted.[230] Aware of how easily religious controversies could spread across frontiers, disrupting political harmony as they did so, he wanted to nip problems in the bud.

The United Provinces presented a particular challenge since its religious disputes threatened to add a further disruptive element to an already fractious political culture, and because close commercial and religious ties between the Netherlands and Britain made it easy for theological controversies to spread from one country to the other.[231] Although the Dutch Reformed Church had never commanded the allegiance of more than a fairly small minority of the population, it saw itself as the guardian of the country's religion and champion of resistance to Spanish tyranny. It sought to define and enforce orthodoxy, while suppressing rival religions, above all Catholicism. Although to varying degrees, the majority of the regents who controlled the secular government of Dutch towns and provinces held more tolerant views. Some towns, including Amsterdam, were relatively supportive of the official Church and its Calvinist theology, while others were more "libertine."[232] In many places, ties of kinship and patronage reinforced divisions between supporters of the Church and advocates of greater toleration, giving rise to competing factions or parties.[233]

---

[229] TNA SP81/9, fols 45 and 129.   [230] BL Stowe Mss. 174, fols 12r, 214, 396r.
[231] For Dutch interest in puritan theology see Philip Benedict, *Christ's Churches Purely Reformed: A Social History of Calvinism* (New Haven: Yale University Press, 2002), 521–5.
[232] Israel, *Dutch Republic*, 382.   [233] Ibid., 392.

During the first decade of the seventeenth century a dispute within the University of Leiden, between a recently appointed professor of theology, Jacob Hermanszoon or Arminius, and several of his colleagues, led by Franciscus Gomarus, exacerbated these rifts. Gomarus sought to uphold the doctrine of double predestination—the view that all people have been destined by divine decree to heaven or hell, with no power to alter their fate—which many Calvinists had come to regard as a touchstone of orthodoxy, even though it actually derived from the teachings of Calvin's successor in Geneva, Theodore Beza, rather than Calvin himself.[234] Arminius and his successor at Leiden, Johannes Uitenbogaert, sought to modify this doctrine to allow a larger role for human free will.[235] They also wanted to alter the confession of faith of the Dutch Church to permit a wider range of opinions to exist within it. In July 1610 Uitenbogaert and his supporters issued a remonstrance calling upon the States General to alter the Church's confession of faith, which provoked an opposing counter-remonstrance by the Gomarist faction. The two sides thereby acquired the names of Remonstrants and Contra-Remonstrants. Oldenbarnevelt, who had procured Uitenbogaert's appointment, supported the Remonstrants, apparently less from theological conviction than from a dislike of clerical dogmatism.[236] He wanted to dampen controversy by compelling the two sides to coexist without undue acrimony within a Church open to different doctrinal positions. Having failed to persuade a synod to accede to this design, he sought to impose it by subjecting the Church to the control of the states of Holland.[237] But rather than quelling controversy his efforts inflamed it. The dispute spread beyond university and clerical circles, leading to serious disturbances in Alkmaar (1608) and Utrecht (1610), requiring the restoration of order by armed force.[238]

The Dutch and British churches had long enjoyed close ties, as indicated by the fact that Arminius first articulated his views about free will and predestination while critiquing a book by the English puritan William Perkins.[239] In 1607 a professor at the University of Franeker in Holland, Sibrandus Lubbertus, wrote to Andrew Melville complaining about Arminius. After Melville's arrest Franeker's letter ended up in the hands of Archbishop Bancroft, who was shocked at the views it attributed to the Arminians.[240] In November 1609 James instructed his newly-appointed ambassador to the Netherlands, Ralph Winwood, to press the Dutch to make sure "that religion should be taught and preached in purity and

---

[234] See Benedict, *Christ's Churches*, 297–313.
[235] Carl Bangs, *Arminius: A Study in the Dutch Reformation* (Nashville: Abingdon Press, 1971) surveys Arminius's life and doctrinal beliefs.
[236] Den Tex, *Oldenbarnevelt* 2.423–34.   [237] Israel, *Dutch Republic*, 422–3.
[238] Ibid., 423–4.   [239] Benedict, *Christ's Churches*, 305.
[240] Eric Platt, *Britain and the Bestandtwisten: The Causes, Course and Consequences of British Involvement in the Dutch Religious and Political Disputes of the Early Seventeenth Century* (Göttingen: Vandenhoeck & Ruprecht, 2015), 32–3. Platt's book is the most thorough and scholarly treatment of James's relations with the United Provinces during the Twelve Years Truce.

sincerity, without any mixture or adulteration, in all your provinces."²⁴¹ A few months later he warned a Dutch trade delegation about the need to restrain theological disputes in their country.²⁴² According to several Dutch delegates, who probably had Remonstrant sympathies, the king said that since it was impossible to be certain about predestination, controversy over the matter ought to be suppressed. Oldenbarnevelt cited their report as evidence that James supported his own position. But whether intentionally or not, he had almost certainly misconstrued the king's views. James would probably have preferred to see the Dutch Church adopt a position similar to the one he maintained in Britain, in which Calvinist teachings on predestination remained dominant, while clergy holding other opinions were tolerated so long as they conducted themselves discreetly.²⁴³ But he disapproved of the tolerance the Dutch had long afforded to public expressions of heterodox religious beliefs.

Nevertheless, he might have maintained a position of constructive neutrality had Oldenbarnevelt not made the serious blunder, which he later came to regret, of approving the appointment of the German theologian Conradus Vorstius to a professorship at Leiden in 1610. Although regarded as an orthodox, if tolerant, Calvinist at the time of his appointment, it soon became clear that Vorstius had heterodox views not only about predestination but the Trinity that even many Arminians found unacceptable. Lubbertus and the Englishman Matthew Slade, the rector of the Amsterdam Academy, quickly called the appointment to the attention of Archbishop Abbot, who in turn alerted the king, presenting him with a copy of Vorstius's *Tractatus theologicus de Deo*.²⁴⁴ James read it immediately and, horrified by its contents, drew up a list of errors he believed the book contained. He then instructed Winwood to tell the States General that he had previously warned them about allowing "seditious and heretical preachers," by which he meant followers of Arminius, "to creep into their state," and that he had now examined Vorstius's treatise and found it to contain "monstrous blasphemy and horrible atheism." "As a Christian prince and defender of the faith," he demanded that the Dutch authorities annul Vorstius's appointment and punish

---

²⁴¹ BL Add Mss. 17,677 G, "Propositions" for Winwood, November 14, 1609: "La troisième [sujet d'importance] est le soin de la religion, qu'elle soit enseigner et prêcher en pureté et sincérité par toutes vos provinces sans mélange et mixture."
²⁴² Platt, *Bestandtwisten*, 31–2.
²⁴³ Although controversial and perhaps somewhat overstated in certain respects, the central argument of Nicholas Tyacke, *Anti-Calvinists: The Rise of English Arminianism, c. 1590–1640* (Oxford: Oxford University Press, 1990) has held up to scrutiny. Amidst the vast literature on the early Stuart Church see also Kenneth Fincham, *Prelate as Pastor: The Episcopate of James I* (Oxford: Clarendon Press, 1990) and Anthony Milton, *Catholic and Reformed: The Roman and Protestant Churches in English Protestant Thought, 1600–1640* (Cambridge: Cambridge University Press, 1995).
²⁴⁴ Frederick Shriver, "James I and the Vorstius Affair," *English Historical Review* 85 (1970): 49–74 at 52.

him for his "damnable positions," and warned that he would be "infinitely displeased" if they did not.²⁴⁵

Winwood proceeded to encourage Vorstius's Dutch adversaries, while lobbying Prince Maurice and Oldenbarnevelt's son-in-law, Adriaan van der Mijle, to accede to James's demands.²⁴⁶ On the king's instructions Salisbury also pressed Caron to work for Vorstius's dismissal.²⁴⁷ But Oldenbarnevelt saw James's demands as a violation of the university's jurisdiction over its own affairs and the sovereignty of the states of Holland, and staunchly resisted. James stepped up the pressure by sending a letter written in his own hand, again demanding "the removing of this blasphemous monster." He included a list "of the most special atheistical points" he had found in the *Tractatus theologicus*. If the Dutch failed to comply, he threatened, "our first labor shall be to publish to the world their defection from the faith and the true Church of Christ."²⁴⁸ When the Dutch authorities instead arranged for a public hearing at which Vorstius had the chance to defend himself, Winwood accused them of slighting James's honor and warned that their behavior would cool British friendship toward their state.²⁴⁹

James had meanwhile ordered two of his bishops to begin preparing refutations of Vorstius's opinions.²⁵⁰ His letter denouncing Vorstius, along with Winwood's speech to the States General, were translated into Dutch and printed.²⁵¹ Vorstius responded with two pamphlets, one in Dutch and the other in Latin, answering the king's charges in language the English found indecorous. Winwood thought Vorstius's local "patrons and protectors" had encouraged him to do so.²⁵² The scholar Hugo Grotius, who had ties to Oldenbarnevelt, also wrote an *apologia* for Vorstius, which further offended James.²⁵³ Vorstius's supporters argued that "puritans" in the Netherlands and England had misled the king about his and Arminius's views and that James's attitude would change once he had been rightly informed. Some recalled the abuses of Leicester's government, which they blamed on puritan clergy who had "debauched" him. Overly "precise" ministers had undermined civil government in the 1580s, they argued, leading to the loss of Flanders and Brabant to the Spaniards; Contra-Remonstrants and their puritan allies now threatened to cause similar calamities. Oldenbarnevelt and Caron both shared this opinion.²⁵⁴

Winwood, by contrast, had begun to view Arminius and Vorstius as agents of a Spanish and French plot to undermine Dutch Protestantism from within. Noting

---

²⁴⁵ TNA SP84/68, fol. 117.
²⁴⁶ Ibid., fol. 135v. He did not press Oldenbarnevelt vigorously on the subject because the Dutch statesmen was ill and Winwood did not wish to upset him.
²⁴⁷ Ibid., fol. 122; *Oldenbarnevelt Bescheiden*, ed. Veenendaal, 485–6.
²⁴⁸ TNA SP84/68, fol. 147r.   ²⁴⁹ Ibid., fols 155v, 192v.
²⁵⁰ *Oldenbarnevelt Bescheiden*, ed. Veenendaal, 403.
²⁵¹ TNA SP84/68, fol. 173r.   ²⁵² Ibid., fol. 192.
²⁵³ HHStA, Belgien PC46, fol. 352v, Boisschot dispatch of December 6, 1613.
²⁵⁴ Ibid., fol. 176v; *Oldenbarnevelt Bescheiden*, ed. Veenendaal, 403, 490–1.

that a French ambassador had recently arrived in the Netherlands, carrying a proposal for a permanent peace with Spain on condition that Catholicism should be publicly tolerated, he commented:

> Now we think, if our judgments do not fail us that we have discovered the *pot aux roses*: what the reasons are that the new broached opinions of Arminius are so much countenanced by our greatest men, and solely received in many of the principal towns of Holland; that the ministers of the religion are disgraced and deprived of their charges; that Vorstius is thus peremptorily maintained not only against all reason of state but against common sense, only to make way *sensim sine sensu* that this overture might be, if not at the first aboard received with applause, yet quietly be hearkened to and not rejected.[255]

Oldenbarnevelt was, he claimed, trying to work with Lerma to turn the truce into a permanent peace and wanted greater religious toleration because he thought it would make an agreement easier to obtain. As a Catholic kingdom the French felt obligated to support demands for toleration of their faith in the Netherlands. Winwood's suspicions contained a kernel of truth, since Oldenbarnevelt did want a permanent peace and the French supported toleration of Catholicism, but his dark picture of a secret conspiracy to destroy Dutch independence by spreading heresy and disunity was grossly unfair. Early in the new year, an equally unfounded report spread through Remonstrant circles that James would soon send letters demanding the banishment of all Arminians from United Provinces.[256]

Caron had meanwhile been laboring to produce a face-saving compromise through negotiations with Salisbury and Abbot.[257] He failed to prevent James from publishing a book against Vorstius and sending a hundred copies to Winwood for distribution in the Netherlands in February 1612.[258] This further escalated a pamphlet controversy over Vorstius's case. But Salisbury and Abbot worked out an agreement by which Vorstius's appointment would be suspended rather than annulled, with a provision that he should be prohibited from residing in Leiden until his case had been resolved, with the advice of the reformed churches of France, Switzerland, Germany, and Britain.[259] Although this did not entirely satisfy James, he agreed to accept the compromise to avoid further damaging his relations with the Netherlands and possibly delaying the execution

---

[255] TNA SP84/68, fol. 194r–v.

[256] *Oldenbarnevelt Bescheiden*, ed. Veenendaal, 15–16. This rumor was reported to Caron by Oldenbarnevelt himself. For an account of the role of print in the controversies over Arminianism, Oldenbarnevelt, and relations with Spain see Andrew Pettegree and Arthur der Weduwen, *The Bookshop of the World: Making and Trading Books in the Dutch Golden Age* (New Haven: Yale University Press, 2020), 51–70.

[257] Platt, *Bestandtwisten*, 57–8.   [258] TNA SP84/68, fols 236v, 244.

[259] *Oldenbarnevelt Bescheiden*, ed. Veenendaal, 510–11.

of an agreement he had just worked out with Oldenbarnevelt over the repayment of Dutch debts to the English crown.[260]

Vorstius spent the next seven years in Gouda awaiting a settlement of his case, as the contest between Remonstrants and Contra-Remonstrants continued, with both sides seeking to win James's support and that of leading figures within the Church of England. Winwood remained a firm ally of the Contra-Remonstrants, while Caron, as a loyal servant of Oldenbarnevelt, tried to soften James's hostility toward Arminians. In 1613 he persuaded the king to sign a letter addressed to the States General that had actually been written by Uitenbogaert and revised by Oldenbarnevelt, urging that body to quell religious controversies. Oldenbarnevelt exploited the document, which he had printed for public consumption, to argue that James agreed with his policy of using state authority to restrain clerical quarrels.[261] He would continue to cite the letter as evidence that the king shared his views except when misled by "puritans" for the next several years. But James soon concluded that his letter was being misused to suggest, wrongly, that he had changed his views about Arminianism. He upbraided Caron about the matter.[262] In 1613 Grotius traveled to England as part of a delegation sent to discuss disputes over trade with the East Indies, with secret instructions from Oldenbarnevelt to seek support in England for the Remonstrants. He had some success in winning over Isaac Casaubon and bishops John Overall and Lancelot Andrewes. But he failed to impress Abbot or to alter James's views during two interviews.[263]

The Vorstius affair inflicted lasting damage on Oldenbarnevelt's relations with James and Winwood, who had already lost confidence in the Dutch leader by the end of 1611.[264] This friction complicated efforts to resolve disputes over the repayment of Dutch debts, trade with the East Indies, and other issues. In October 1611, at the height of the dispute over Vorstius, James threatened that if Oldenbarnevelt continued to delay the repayment of money owed to the English crown, he would begin impounding Dutch ships in English ports.[265] Three months later Winwood received complaints from English merchants that the

---

[260] Shriver, "Vorstius Affair," 464-70. See TNA SP84/68 fol. 264 for James's expression of displeasure. Toward the outset of the controversy, in December 1611, Salisbury had mildly rebuked Winwood for having issued a sharply worded protest concerning the failure of the Dutch to bow to James's demand for Vorstius's immediate dismissal and punishment. In doing so, however, Salisbury made it clear that James supported the substance of Winwood's position, even while objecting to some of the language in which it had been expressed and Winwood's timing, which threatened to disrupt delicate negotiations over the repayment of Dutch debts. Salisbury's letter and another one sent to Winwood by one of his correspondents near the court hint of discussions in which James's initial support for Winwood's sharp line was tempered by the arguments of members of his entourage who thought the theological dispute insufficiently important to risk a serious rupture in British-Dutch relations. There is no suggestion that James disapproved in principle of Winwood's staunch opposition to Vorstius or Arminianism. See *Memorials of Affairs of State*, ed. Sawyer, 3.316-20.

[261] Platt, *Bestandtwisten*, 72-5.   [262] *Oldenbarnevelt Bescheiden*, ed. Veenendaal, 548.
[263] Platt, *Bestandtwisten*, 81-5.
[264] TNA SP84/68 fol. 182v; *Oldenbarnevelt Bescheiden*, ed. Veenendaal, 563.
[265] TNA SP84/68, fol. 164v.

Dutch East India Company (VOC) was trying to exclude them from trade with Asia. He rightly felt pessimistic about obtaining redress, since the VOC "is a body by themselves, powerful and mighty in this state, and will not acknowledge the authority of the states general more than shall be for their private profit."[266] The Dutch argued that since the VOC had spent considerable sums forcing its way into the East Indies against the opposition of the Portuguese and Spanish, it should not have to allow English merchants to share in its trade unless they paid for the privilege. The English responded that the Dutch should grant them free access from gratitude for previous help in the fight against Spain. Despite the conclusion of compromise agreements, the issue continued to ruffle Anglo-Dutch relations for years to come. Other conflicts erupted over James's efforts to assert his sovereignty over the Narrow Seas around England by requiring Dutch fishermen to purchase licenses to ply their trade, disputes over whaling in the North Atlantic, and as a result of the Cockayne Project, an attempt to require that English cloths imported to the Continent be dyed and finished in England, rather than in the Netherlands, as had been the practice. The Dutch acted vigorously to protect their cloth-finishing industry, by prohibiting the importation of English dyed cloths, and starting to develop their own cloth weaving industry, ultimately forcing the English to back down, to James's considerable annoyance. He complained to the archduke's ambassador in 1614 that the Dutch had "now grown so much that they have more sea power than was anciently possessed by all states conjoined, so they deprive other nations including his of trade in all places, and now they are proceeding to introduce cloth manufacturing into Holland, speaking as if he much resented these things."[267]

Additional friction arose over policies toward France. Oldenbarnevelt had a well-deserved reputation as a Francophile, an attitude deriving from his correct perception that France had done far more than Britain to support the Dutch cause after 1603, and his belief that the French would likely prove a more reliable ally in the future. This orientation, along with his well-known desire to achieve a permanent peace with Spain, aroused suspicion among British statesmen and groups within the Netherlands fiercely hostile to Catholicism and Spain, including many Contra-Remonstrant clergymen. During three civil wars between Condé's supporters and the regency, Oldenbarnevelt consistently supported the latter. In 1615 he rebuffed James's demand that he join in protesting against the marriage alliance with Spain. He took this line because he did not trust Condé and Bouillon but did have confidence in Villeroy, with whom he had worked closely for many

---

[266] Ibid., fol. 231v.

[267] HHStA Belgien PC47 (dispatch of October 9, 1614): Having been aided by Elizabeth for reasons of state, the Dutch "avian cruscado agoar tanto que se yvan haziendos muchos poderosos por mar y mas de lo antiguamente avian todos estados juntos, y que quitavan a otros naciones y esta suy el trato in todas partes, y que agora yvan introduziendo en Holanda a la manufactura de anas, hablendo como sentido dello."

years. He felt confident that French support for the United Provinces would continue because the two countries shared so many strategic interests. He also needed to preserve the French subsidy his government received and prevent the withdrawal of French troops serving in the Dutch army.[268] But his reluctance to challenge Marie de Médicis and her pursuit of a Spanish alliance offended not only James but also a substantial segment of the Dutch public. Those who wanted to cooperate with Britain in opposing the Franco-Spanish alliance included François van Aerssen, who had served as the Dutch ambassador in Paris until Oldenbarnevelt dismissed him, following a rancorous quarrel, in late 1613. Aerssen came to believe that Oldenbarnevelt's policies would eventually lead to the subjugation of the United Provinces under Albert and Isabella. But his successor in Paris, Gideon van Boetzelaer, followed Oldenbarnevelt's policies and resolutely refused to cooperate with Edmondes's meddling in French politics.[269]

As its confidence in Oldenbarnevelt declined, the British government began cultivating Maurice of Nassau. This represented a significant shift, since Maurice had previously held such a low opinion of James that in 1609 he felt obliged to apologize for "inconsiderate and insolent speeches" implying that the king of Britain lacked the courage to stand up to Spain.[270] In 1611 James instructed Winwood to attempt to enlist Maurice's support against Oldenbarnevelt over Vorstius and the issue of the French marriages.[271] In June of that year Edward Conway visited Maurice and told him that Prince Henry had nominated him to the Order of the Garter, adding that "the prince did especially favor and affect his person" and often enquired after his affairs.[272] When James bestowed the Garter on Maurice, the States General objected that he was attempting to exert undue influence over their Stadtholder.[273] The French also complained that by honoring Maurice James sought to increase his leverage in Dutch politics.[274] This may well have been correct. According to Boisschot, in early 1612 Salisbury dispatched a secret agent to the United Provinces with instructions to try to strengthen Maurice's position, with the goal of eventually installing him—or alternatively the Elector Palatine—as sovereign of the United Provinces.[275]

Conflicts within the United Provinces and James's involvement in them continued to escalate in 1616, when Winwood returned home to become secretary of state and Sir Dudley Carleton replaced him as ambassador. James instructed Carleton at the start of his embassy that if arguments over theology should flare up again in the Netherlands, "you shall not forget that you are minister of that master, whom God hath made the sole protector of his religion." Carleton must

---

[268] Den Tex, *Oldenbarnevelt*, 2.497–500.   [269] Ibid., 481–7.
[270] *Memorials of Affairs of State*, ed. Sawyer, 2.12, 454.   [271] Den Tex, *Oldenbarnevelt*, 2.532–3.
[272] BL Harleian Mss. 7002, fols 105, 113.
[273] Platt, *Bestandtwisten*, 67; TNA SP84/68 fol. 275r.   [274] TNA PRO31/3/44, fol. 153.
[275] HHStA Belgien PC46, fols 114v, 141 (dispatches of May 4 and June 26, 1612).

therefore assist all "true professors of the gospel" while expressing the king's condemnation of "erroneous doctrines."[276] A few months later, in April, the Remonstrant government of Holland expelled the Contra-Remonstrant preacher Henricus Roseaus from his ministry in The Hague. Roseaus's followers, said to number six or seven hundred, began traveling every Sunday to the nearby village of Rijswijk to participate in Calvinist services.[277] Although Carleton admitted that Roseaus deserved censure "for his personal glancing at some chief men of this state," he thought his punishment too harsh, especially in comparison to Holland's lenient treatment of Vorstius. The following month Carleton noted almost daily conflicts between "the states of these provinces and their preachers, with whom the people do most concur; as likewise writings and answers betwixt the two factions," which caused "no small scandal." The polemical exchanges included a recent book by Vorstius, critical of James.[278]

Popular support for the Contra-Remonstrants had begun to unsettle the authority of Remonstrant magistrates in several Dutch towns. Pamphlets relating to the controversy proliferated, numbering 175 in 1617 and over 300 the following year.[279] In January 1617 Carleton wrote that the clerical factions led by Uitenbogaert and Roseaus were becoming aligned with the political followings of Oldenbarnevelt and Maurice, and that the provinces and towns had also begun choosing sides, although several provinces, including Holland, remained internally divided. Each party accused the other of seeking to change the system of government, with the Remonstrants claiming that Maurice had revived the designs of the earl of Leicester, while the Contra-Remonstrants charged Oldenbarnevelt with seeking "the bringing in of popery."[280] Carleton's own sympathies were by this time unequivocal: "the original cause of this disorder is easily discovered to be Arminianism; there will be faction in the state and schism in the church if it be not speedily, even at the present assembly, prevented." Although he felt unsure whether Oldenbarnevelt really wanted to establish Catholicism, he thought it noteworthy "that in those places where popery is most frequent, as Utrecht for a province and Rotterdam for a town, the Remonstrants were absolute and generally the papists hold with the faction. Some conjecture (and this is his Excellency's [Maurice's] opinion) that all this is done by monsieur Barnevelt in preparation of the time when the renewing of the truce or the bringing of it to a peace shall be brought into treaty, wherein it being likely the king of Spain will insist upon...toleration of the popish religion," and the way will have been prepared for suppressing the "Protestant party."[281] Carleton thought it especially worrying that the governors of most frontier

---

[276] Platt, *Bestandtwisten*, 6. [277] Ibid., 14. [278] Ibid., 23.
[279] Israel, *Dutch Republic*, 439. [280] Platt, *Bestandwisten*, 89. [281] Ibid., 88 and 89.

towns were Remonstrants, since if challenged from below by the other party they might call for Spanish assistance.[282]

A dispute about predestination therefore appeared to have acquired not only political but strategic importance, threatening to undermine Dutch resistance to Spanish and Catholic pressure at a time when the growing rapport between Spain and France made Protestant unity and resolution all the more crucial. In early 1617, Carleton promised Maurice and the Contra-Remonstrants James's support.[283] In part to counter the effects of the king's 1613 letter, which the Remonstrants were still using to claim that he supported their position, Maurice suggested to Carleton that James write a new epistle clarifying his views. When James responded with a document expressing support for Maurice, the stadtholder asked for its suppression because he feared that it would increase suspicions of his dependence on Britain and ambitions for self-aggrandizement. He instead helped draft an alternative text urging the Dutch Church to return to its reformed roots and calling for a national synod if no other means could be found to settle the present controversy. James agreed to sign a letter to this effect, which was promptly translated into French and Dutch, printed and widely circulated, despite Remonstrant efforts to have it suppressed. Carleton claimed that he felt compelled to arrange for its publication after someone else began distributing a false copy, "which runs through the whole country and works many visible good effects." This new letter earned James undeserved credit for having initiated the proposal for a national synod to settle the dispute in the Dutch Church, which had actually originated with the Contra-Remonstrants and Maurice. In late July, after visiting Sedan, the Elector Palatine also attempted to intervene in support of the Contra-Remonstrants, although Maurice again urged restraint from fear of causing a backlash.[284]

By this time the conflict had escalated to a point at which civil war appeared likely and many observers anticipated that Maurice would soon attempt a coup. Instead he moved gradually and methodically to consolidate his position. Five of the seven provinces already leaned toward the Contra-Remonstrants and even within Holland, the main bastion of Remonstrant strength, some regents had begun to waver in their loyalty to Oldenbarnevelt. As their position weakened Oldenbarnevelt and his supporters pushed a so-called Sharp Resolution through the states of Holland, establishing civilian militias called *waardgelders* under Remonstrant control in several towns, and declaring that military forces owed their allegiance to the provincial states rather than the States General. When the States General resolved to suppress the *waardgelders*, by a vote of five provinces to two, Oldenbarnevelt remained defiant, claiming that Holland was a fully sovereign

---

[282] Ibid., 97.   [283] Ibid., 100.
[284] Ibid., 105–12; Den Tex, *Oldenbarnevelt*, 2.580–81; *Letters from and to Sir Dudley Carleton, during his Embassy in Holland* (London, 1775), 121, 155, 166.

province whose decisions could not be overruled. This allowed Maurice and his partisans to charge their opponents with treason and provided grounds for using the Dutch army to suppress the *waardgelders* and purge the town governments that had established them, in the spring and summer of 1618.[285]

Throughout these events James and Carleton remained publicly committed to the Contra-Remonstrants. In the autumn of 1617 Carleton delivered a speech before the States General blaming the Remonstrants for the divisions in the Netherlands, which the Contra-Remonstrants then translated and printed. This was answered by a Remonstrant tract entitled *The Balance* that Carleton and James condemned as a libel. Carleton persuaded the States General, by a vote of four to three, to have it suppressed and to order that its author be tracked down and punished. Holland's refusal to implement this decision contributed to a growing dispute over the locus of sovereignty within the United Provinces.[286] Oldenbarnevelt attempted to win British support for his position by arguing that the main issue was not predestination but the authority of the state to regulate the Church. He succeeded in persuading the junior English secretary of state, Thomas Lake, who was aligned with a group on the privy council sympathetic to Spain, as well as bishops Andrewes and Overall. But he failed to win over James and the two bishops muted their sympathy to avoid antagonizing the king. Facing British hostility, Oldenbarnevelt turned for support to the French, who tried unsuccessfully to save him, seeming to confirm the view of his enemies that he was working with a Catholic foreign government against the orthodoxy and patriotism of the Dutch Church and the United Provinces' Protestant allies. He was arrested in late August, tried and executed for treason. The national synod for which James had called convened in Dordrecht—or Dort as the English called it—and included British representatives. Predictably, it condemned Arminianism.

Conclusions: James's Motives and Calculations

Close examination of James's conduct of relations with France and the Netherlands down to 1618 shows that the traditional image of him, as a king motivated chiefly by a principled devotion to peace, religious irenicism, and royal legitimacy, and who therefore wanted to promote a détente between Protestant Europe and Spain, stands in need of serious revision. Had this been the case he should logically have welcomed Oldenbarnevelt's efforts to achieve a permanent peace in the Netherlands, while showing more sympathy to the flexible and tolerant outlook of the Remonstrants rather than their Calvinist adversaries. He

---

[285] Israel, *Dutch Republic*, 441–9.
[286] Platt, *Bestandtwisten*, 113–19; *Letters to and from Carleton*, 206, 243. Carleton wrongly attributed the tract to Grotius, ibid., 228–9, 238.

should also have been less hostile to Villeroy, a moderate and pragmatic statesman dedicated to peace, and less inclined to encourage Bouillon and Condé. His actual behavior points to a more complicated and devious set of calculations. He unquestionably wanted to avoid having to fight a war himself, and for that reason remained cautious about taking too active a role in support of Protestant and antipapal causes on the Continent. His dislike of bloodshed and abhorrence of religious fanaticism no doubt contributed to this stance, but so did more self-interested and pragmatic calculations. Fully aware of his own relative poverty and the vulnerability of his kingdoms—especially Ireland—to foreign attack, he also recognized that in a general European war of religion between Calvinists and Catholics the former would likely find themselves at a serious disadvantage. If they ever united in a religious league, the combined strength of France, Spain, and other Catholic states would prove more than a match for Britain, the United Provinces, and a handful of German principalities. A prudent defense of the Protestant cause therefore required keeping the Catholic states divided and enlisting some of them in cross-confessional leagues of state. His financial problems reinforced these strategic calculations. His lack of money not only increased his aversion to expensive military ventures but led him to prioritize the repayment of debts owed to the English crown in his dealings with France and the Netherlands, even when doing so got in the way of other objectives.

James also had other priorities that normally mattered more to him than most European conflicts. These included both purely selfish motives, like his desire to enjoy his hunting without distraction, and internal British problems. Even when money became available he therefore usually preferred to spend it on other things than expensive military adventures. In 1617, for example, he reportedly gave away £60,000 of the £100,000 he had just borrowed from the City of London to other Scots, almost certainly in efforts to bribe them into supporting the religious articles he wanted to impose on the Kirk.[287] Even peripheral engagement in a European war would have forced James to go hat-in-hand to his parliaments seeking grants of money, while exhausting resources he needed for other purposes, thereby weakening his authority over his own subjects and his ability to force through measures like the Five Articles of Perth. All these considerations gave him ample incentives to avoid major conflicts with Spain and other European powers. But since he never entirely trusted the Spanish—or for that matter the French—he wanted to keep these powers hostile to each other and preoccupied with problems elsewhere in Europe. While trying to convince Spain of his amity and good intentions, he therefore continued to encourage the Dutch to maintain a strong army and the Princes of the Union in Germany to preserve their alliance. He also did everything in his power to prevent France from drawing closer to Spain.

---

[287] *CSPD JI* 2.465; above pp. 534–5.

Put crudely, James wanted to conserve his resources while inducing others to do his fighting for him, or at least to remain prepared to fight his potential adversaries so that he would not have to do so. But honor prevented him from acknowledging this attitude too openly. He therefore used diplomacy and royal rhetoric as safe and inexpensive ways of maintaining a more dignified profile on the European stage. His published attacks on the papacy and its Jesuit apologists buttressed his claims to act as "defender of the faith," just as his rhetorical support for Venice during the Interdict Controversy showed his commitment to the defense of "free states" against papal bullying. But when his alliances and rhetorical sallies threatened to draw him into dangerous and expensive conflicts, he invoked his dedication to the peace of Europe and his "amity" with Spain as excuses for inaction. This does not mean that we should entirely dismiss his dedication to peace and opposition to papal interference in secular affairs as insincere. He genuinely abhorred needless bloodshed, especially when justified in the name of religion, along with clerical meddling in politics. His appeals to other princes to resist papal bullying reflected real conviction, as did his protests that he abhorred not only Jesuit but "puritan" excesses. But even if his pronouncements on such subjects were sincere on some levels, they also frequently helped him construct rhetorical smokescreens to disguise his pursuit of his own interests.

The potential weakness in James's approach lay in his reliance on other states to preserve a balance of power in Europe. For his first six years on the English throne the war in the Low Countries and Henry IV's hostility towards Spain served him very effectively. But the truce between Spain and the United Provinces, followed by Henry IV's assassination and the prospect of a Franco-Spanish dynastic alliance threatened to produce a far more dangerous European environment. If Oldenbarnevelt succeeded in achieving a permanent peace with Spain and substantial reduction in the Dutch army, while France abandoned its opposition to Spanish ambitions, he might find his kingdoms isolated and exposed to attack or subversion by a newly emboldened Spain, or worse yet a Franco-Spanish alliance. James not only appreciated this danger but exaggerated it. His acute fear of militant Catholicism and Jesuit intrigues led him to overreact to apparent signs of a Jesuit and Hispanophile revival in France, while his genuine horror over Vorstius's views and worries that clerical squabbles would weaken the United Provinces from within magnified his distrust of Dutch Remonstrants and Oldenbarnevelt. He therefore entered into political intrigues and maneuvers against the leading ministers of both France and the Dutch Republic, in partnership with dissident nobles in the one case and Maurice of Nassau in the other. He succeeded briefly in the Netherlands, although Maurice's death and other irritants to British–Dutch relations would undo his victory within a few years. In France his meddling backfired by sowing mistrust of his intentions, without achieving any lasting positive results. In both France and the Netherlands, he misinterpreted policies motivated primarily by pragmatic calculations as evidence of sinister machinations by Catholic adversaries. His mistake stemmed, not from indifference to the Protestant cause in Europe but from his belief in a certain set of Protestant fears and assumptions.

James justified his meddling as necessary to defeat a nefarious Franco-Spanish cabal orchestrated by the pope and the Jesuits in France, and his duty to defend Protestant orthodoxy and the future independence of the United Provinces against efforts by France, Spain, and Dutch heretics to sow religious and political disunity. He even claimed to be defending the absolute authority of Louis XIII, by encouraging princes of the blood to rebel against policies carried out in that king's name by his mother and her ministers. Since in James's view those policies threatened to destroy the independence of the king of France, his brotherly concern for his fellow monarch compelled him to act. James always remained committed to lofty theoretical principles like the divine right of legitimate absolute kings. But he applied those principles to concrete historical circumstances with considerable flexibility and creativity. He continued doing this for the remainder of his life, as he sought to protect not only his own interests but those of his children and dynasty. Unfortunately, as he did so events in Europe began to limit his room for maneuver, while exposing the underlying weakness of his position, as the next chapter will show.

12
Dynastic Politics, Confessional Polarization, and the Challenge of New Religious Wars

Marital Diplomacy and Strategic Opportunism

In the seventeenth century arranged marriages between the children of ruling families were important diplomatic instruments. Although they rarely succeeded in producing durable alliances, the hope that they might do so led statesmen to treat them very seriously. As James's two eldest offspring, Henry and Elizabeth, approached maturity around 1610, the challenge of finding them suitable partners began to play a more prominent role in his relations with other states.[1] Some historians have argued that he approached the task with a straightforward agenda. By marrying each of his children to a leading member of one of Europe's two confessional blocs he hoped to increase his influence over both of them, and thus his ability to act as a mediator and peace-maker. He therefore sought to balance Elizabeth's engagement to the Calvinist Elector Palatine by arranging Henry's marriage to a Catholic princess, with daughters of the late king of France and the dukes of Tuscany and Savoy as the leading candidates. After Henry's unexpected death in November 1612 scuttled these plans, James began to search for a Catholic bride for Prince Charles and, after briefly considering a French match, decided instead to negotiate a dynastic alliance with Spain.

This interpretation implicitly rests on the very questionable assumption that Europe's Catholic dynasties were sufficiently united that a dynastic alliance with any one of them would confer influence over all the others. In reality this was far from the case. A Stuart alliance with Spain's traditional rival, France, or another Catholic state hostile to the Habsburgs would have done little to increase James's influence in Madrid. Although religion always played a role, marital diplomacy involved more complex calculations than a simple choice between a Protestant or Catholic partner, including considerations of prestige and James's need for a large dowry to help pay off his debts. In addition, he wanted to take precautions against the alarming prospect that a dynastic alliance between France and Spain might

---

[1] For another recent discussion see Nadine Akkerman, *Elizabeth Stuart, Queen of Hearts* (Oxford: Oxford University Press, 2021), chapters 3 and 4; citations of this book are to the Kindle edition.

unite the two great Catholic monarchies against him and his Protestant allies. According to the archdukes' ambassador Hoboque, British alarm over a potential Bourbon–Habsburg alliance erupted as early as 1609, after reports arrived in London that Henry IV wanted to strengthen his ties with Spain and contemplated doing so by marrying his heir to Philip III's eldest daughter.[2] James and his council reacted with a counter-proposal to Madrid, for a marriage between the Infanta and Prince Henry. This conjuncture may help explain why, in October, James declined to provide immediate aid to the Protestant claimants to Jülich and Cleves, and why reports circulated that he intended to treat Catholic recusants more leniently and professed not to be terribly upset by Bellarmine's latest reply to his book on the Oath of Allegiance.[3] So long as France and Spain appeared ready to settle their differences, he needed to appease them by signaling his own religious moderation and flexibility. But when, instead of allying with Spain, Henry mobilized for war over Jülich and Cleves, James reversed course agreed to send British troops to the Rhineland.

The resumption of negotiations for a Bourbon–Habsburg alliance by the regency government of Marie de Médicis prompted a more complex British reaction. Although James entertained proposals of marriages for both his children with members of the Spanish royal family, it soon became clear that irreconcilable disagreements over religion would prevent them from taking place. Elizabeth's union with the Elector Palatine Frederick V served the opposite purpose of strengthening James's ties with his Calvinist allies. Together with the defensive alliance he concluded with the Protestant Union, it complemented his efforts to encourage the Dutch to maintain the strength of their army, assuring that Britain would retain some continental allies if the French and Spanish grew hostile. Negotiations over Henry's marriage with Tuscany, France, and Savoy involved more complex calculations. Interest in a Tuscan match seems to have faded by 1611. As we have seen, Bouillon promoted Henry's marriage to a daughter of France as a means of strengthening the position of French nobles opposed to a Franco-Spanish alliance. Henry himself appeared to favor the French match for this reason in a letter to his father two months before his death: although the bride herself was Catholic, the marriage seemed likely to further Protestant and anti-Spanish interests.[4]

---

[2] HHStA Belgien PC44 [unfoliated], dispatch of August 18.
[3] Michael Questier, *Dynastic Politics and the British Reformations, 1558–1630* (Oxford: Oxford University Press, 2019), 324.
[4] *The Life of Henry Prince of Wales, Eldest Son of James I*, ed. Thomas Birch (London, 1760), 235: "Betwixt France and Savoy, if your majesty look to the greatness of the dowry then it is likely you will make choice of Savoy... But if you, laying aside the little bit of disgrace in being served after another [a reference to the reservation of the eldest daughter of Henry IV and Marie des Médicis for the Habsburgs] will respect rather which of these two will give the greatest contentment and satisfaction to the general body of Protestants abroad then I am of opinion that you will sooner incline to France than to Savoy."

A match with Savoy initially appeared more likely to improve relations with Spain because of Duke Charles Emmanuel's firm Catholicism and dynastic ties to the Habsburgs, and the fact that he had allied himself with Spain early in the century. He was even rumored to have ambitions to conquer Calvinist Geneva, which lay just outside his territory.[5] But the Savoyard ambassador who arrived in London in March 1611, carrying offers of marriages for both Henry and Elizabeth, assured the British court that his master had no such intentions. He had instead mobilized his army because he feared the intentions of the Spanish in their territory of Milan.[6] Over the next two years Duke Charles Emmanuel sought alliances with states hostile to the Habsburgs, as he looked for ways of expanding his North Italian territory at the expense of Milan and other Spanish satellites. In 1613 James's ambassador in Madrid reported "such an enmity and heart burning between them [the Spanish and Savoyards]...as is thought irreconcilable."[7] Because it took some time for British statesmen to believe that Charles Emmanuel really had changed from an ally to an enemy of Spain, support for his proposals within the British court initially came chiefly from Catholics and crypto-Catholics, while Salisbury and other Protestants remained opposed.[8] But it was obviously in the interests of Protestant states to encourage Savoy's conflicts with Spain, and since the Savoyards also offered a very large dowry and made minimal demands for religious concessions, interest in an alliance with them soon increased.[9] By the summer of 1612 many observers believed that James would marry his heir to a daughter of Savoy. The Spanish voiced displeasure at this prospect.[10]

Some Protestants nevertheless remained opposed because they did not regard Catholic Savoy as a reliable ally. A memorandum attributed to Sir Walter Ralegh opposed the Savoy match for this reason.[11] Even the prince's death did not entirely subdue the disapproval that negotiations over his marriage to a French or Savoyard princess had aroused. Boisschot reported that an unnamed bishop openly upbraided James before members of his council for wanting to marry his son to a Catholic. This and his remissness in failing to punish recusants rigorously,

---

[5] See, e.g., BL Stowe Mss. 171, fol. 51 and Trumbull Mss. vol. 4, fol. 98 (LC microfilms 041/Camb195/1).
[6] TNA SP92/1/62 and PRO31/3/41, fol. 11.
[7] TNA SP94/19, fol. 29r. He later reported, fol. 362r, that the Spanish "think they hate not the person of any living prince more" than Charles Emmanuel. For a modern study see Stéphane Gal, *Charles Emmanuel de Savoie: La politique du précipice* (Paris: Payot, 2012).
[8] TNA PRO31/3/41, fol. 13; HHStA Belgien PC45 [unfoliated], de Groote dispatch of July 7, 1611.
[9] Akkerman, *Elizabeth Stuart*, 51 reaches a similar conclusion.
[10] E.g. HHStA Belgien PC46, fol. 169v (Boisschot dispatch of July 6, 1612); HMC *Report on the Manuscripts of the Marquess of Downshire*, vol. 4 (London, 1924), 4 (Digby to Trumbull, January 4, 1613).
[11] BL Cotton Mss. Vitellius CXVI, fols 334–5; cf. TNA PRO31/3/41, fol. 14. Around the beginning of November 1612 the French ambassador heard a report that Abbot had objected to a Catholic marriage for Henry, suggesting a marriage to the daughter of the Landgrave of Hesse as an alternative (TNA PRO31/3/45, fols 253–4).

the bishop asserted, had aroused God's anger and led to the prince's death as divine punishment.[12] Rumors began to circulate that a secret correspondence with Maurice of Orange had turned Henry against the Savoy match and that he planned to accompany his sister to the Palatinate to avoid having to consummate it.[13] Members of Henry's entourage appear to have spread these reports and other tales of serious friction between the prince and his father.[14] There were even sinister rumors that Henry had been poisoned to prevent him from challenging James's authority.[15] It remains unclear how much substance the rumors had. Although Henry's surviving correspondence shows no trace of a serious rift with his father or his father's councilors, it remains possible that he felt dissatisfied but kept his discontent hidden from all but a select circle of associates, and that if written evidence of his rift with his father ever existed it was destroyed shortly before his death.[16] In 1618 James told Gondomar that he had learned of his son's intention to marry Frederick V's sister shortly after his death from the elector himself. But although possibly true the story is impossible to verify and the king may have told it for effect.[17] What is clear is that Henry's memory soon became associated with an upsurge in support for renewed war with Spain, on which Boisschot and other ambassadors commented. They attributed the Hispanophobia to exaggerated reports of Spanish designs to attack England, along with the desire of some segments of the mercantile community to resume privateering.[18]

Strict opposition to any Catholic marriages for James's children therefore did exist among some Protestants, whereas several Catholics and Crypto-Catholics, including Queen Anna and several members of the Howard family, promoted Stuart marriages with Spain and other Catholic dynasties in the hope that they would eventually lead to greater religious toleration and perhaps Britain's eventual return to Rome. But between these camps more pragmatic statesmen, including the king and Salisbury, sought to use marital diplomacy to construct cross-confessional leagues that united Britain to both Calvinist and Catholic powers. Far from favoring Spain, such coalitions were intended as a check on Habsburg ambitions and an insurance policy against potential British isolation. James's handling of marriage diplomacy around 1610 reflected the broader goals of his European policies: finding sources of money to alleviate his financial problems,

---

[12] HHStA Belgien 46, fol. 351.
[13] Catriona Murray, *Imaging Stuart Family Politics: Dynastic Crisis and Continuity* (London: Routledge, 2017), 76.
[14] Ibid., 75–86 and 146–57 provides an excellent discussion.
[15] HHStA Belgien PC48, fols 505r, 510v, and 108v.
[16] In one letter Henry professed his willingness "to be in love" with any princess his father selected as his bride (*Life of Henry Prince of Wales*, ed. Birch, 335).
[17] *CDIHE Gondomar* 1.347. The context was a conversation in which James was trying to impress upon the Spanish ambassador his own determination to achieve a Catholic marriage for his heir, against the resistance of many in his court. The story of Henry's intended elopement with a Calvinist princess would have reinforced that message.
[18] See, e.g., HHStA Belgien 47, fols 291, 297, and 313 and Belgien 48, fol. 11v.

strengthening his alliances with other Protestants, and simultaneously attracting Catholic allies, so as to avoid any contingency in which he might have to fight a new war of religion on unfavorable terms.

Diplomacy and Proxy Conflicts in Central Europe

Following his eldest son's death and daughter's marriage, the king continued to encourage continental states to resist Habsburg expansion. French caution made this first goal more difficult to achieve, but several smaller powers, including the United Provinces and Venice, the members of the Protestant Union and Savoy appeared ready to cooperate. Among them Savoy proved most willing to challenge Spain openly. Charles Emmanuel continued to seek a Stuart alliance, sending a new proposal for a marriage between one of his daughters and Prince Charles shortly after Henry's death, although it failed to gain much traction.[19] He also requested and received James's cautious diplomatic support as early as 1613 that later expanded into underhand material aid.[20] In November 1614 Edmondes "earnestly moved" Marie de Médicis, on James's behalf, to refrain from pressuring Savoy to disband its army, as the Spanish wanted. Savoy's forces, he argued, were "a means to retain the king of Spain's army there [in Italy]," preventing it from giving "further offence to Christendom, either in Germany or the Low Countries."[21] James remained coy about furnishing direct and open military assistance but did promise not to impede any of his subjects who volunteered to fight for Savoy.[22] He also encouraged an alliance between Charles Emmanuel and Maurice of Nassau.[23] In January 1615 he instructed Edmondes to encourage the French duke of Mayenne to raise an army in France to assist Savoy, by telling him that James "doth firmly resolve to embark himself in that cause."[24] A month later he told Caron that he had resolved to assist Savoy with £50,000 sterling, and in April he authorized Edmondes to subsidize Mayenne's efforts to levy soldiers, even though he insisted on doing so through secret channels, to disguise his action from the Spanish.[25]

---

[19] HHStA Belgien PC46, fol. 166.
[20] The diplomatic support seems to have begun as early as 1613 (BL Stowe Mss. 174, fols 53v, 76r).
[21] TNA SP78/62, fol. 144.   [22] HHStA Belgien PC47, fol. 212r.   [23] Ibid., fol. 357v.
[24] BL Stowe Mss. 175, fol. 215.
[25] BL Add Mss. 17,677 I, fol. 25r; Stowe Mss. 175, fol. 312: "Therefore if the duke of Mayne so so [sic, be so] scrupulous as he pretendeth, or if it be so dangerous for him to touch the moneys of foreign princes, some other medium amongst you must be found, into whose hands the moneys must be delivered, and accordingly to be disposed of as the necessity of the service shall require. But the agent of Savoy is a person most improper, for I can never consent that the king of Spain, whilst we are in amity with him, shall have this advantage, ever justly to say that the king our master hath delivered or caused to be delivered moneys into the hands of a servant of that prince with whom he is in actual enmity."

Around the same date he assured Caron that he had already spent £25,000 subsidizing Savoy's campaign.[26] In August he invited Venice to ally with Britain and the Protestant Union, in the belief that this would indirectly strengthen Savoy's position by posing an additional threat to Spanish interests in Italy.[27] He then promoted Charles Emmanuel's efforts to conclude an alliance with the Protestant Union.[28] He may also have encouraged the duke of Savoy's friendly contacts with the Huguenots and Condé in late 1615 and early 1616.[29] Biondi passed through Turin and obtained a long private audience with Charles Emmanuel in October 1615, on his return journey from France.[30] After learning in February 1615 that Philip III and the Spanish governor of Milan had discussed an attack on Asti, James launched a diplomatic offensive to persuade the Dutch, France, Venice, and the republics of Bern and Geneva to join him in assisting Charles Emmanuel's defense of the town.[31] Unfortunately, the Dutch declined to help because of their current preoccupation with the second crisis in Cleves-Jülich, the Venetians also refused from fear of Spanish retaliation, and Swiss assistance was slow to arrive. Boisschot reported talk in London of sending 8,000 men to Savoy's assistance, but correctly predicted that the expedition would never materialize.[32] Nevertheless, some English volunteer soldiers evidently did go to Savoy, since Carleton reported that they had led Charles Emmanuel's army "in their caps and feathers, [with] a jacobus piece [an English coin] for a jewel ... they have done as much honor as comes to have their names in a gazette and to be sung about Lombardy in ballads."[33] He added that "English pirates" also assisted Savoy by setting up "a platform for their artillery in the most eminent place of the town [of Asti], fittest to annoy the enemy, which is called the English battery."[34] But without more substantial foreign help Charles Emmanuel lacked the resources to defeat Spanish forces in Milan and in August he reluctantly sued for peace.[35] He felt abandoned by his former ally, France, which had failed to support his campaign.[36] His resentment led him to assist Condé and the Huguenots as they tried to prevent the completion of the Bourbon–Habsburg marriage alliance. He also again requested James's help in allowing him to join the German Protestant

---

[26] BL Add Mss. 17,677 I, fol. 59.   [27] Ibid., fol. 341v.   [28] TNA SP92/3 fol. 8v.
[29] NA SP92/4, fols 39v and 82r. Charles Emmanuel resented the lack of support he believed he had received from the regency government in France and so sympathized with Condé and Bouillon, who had advocated stronger support for him (ibid., fol. 3; BL Stowe Mss. 174, fol. 53).
[30] TNA SP92/4, fol. 3.
[31] BL Add Mss. 17,677 I, Caron to Estates General, February 17, 1615, reporting a conversation with James on the subject.
[32] HHStA Belgien PC48, fol. 82v.
[33] *Dudley Carleton to John Chamberlain 1603-1624: Jacobean Letters*, ed. Maurice Lee (New Brunswick: Rutgers University Press, 1972), 178.
[34] Ibid., 184.
[35] See Dudley Carleton's analysis of why the duke of Savoy had been forced to make peace, BL Stowe Mss. 175, fol. 335.
[36] For Charles Emmanuel's feeling of abandonment and betrayal by France see BL Add Mss. 18,639, Wake to Edmondes, December 29, 1615.

Union without becoming a Protestant.[37] Even without a dynastic alliance, he had become an eager partner of the king of Britain and other Protestant states.

Indeed, at times rather too eager. Although James valued his alliance with Savoy and the opportunities it afforded to tie down Spanish forces in Italy, he did not want to enter into an Italian war. Charles Emmanuel's reckless ambition risked igniting a conflict that Savoy had little chance of winning, with potentially catastrophic consequences. In late 1614 James reacted with alarm to a rumor that Philip III intended to depose Charles Emmanuel by force.[38] The following year the British ambassador in Turin, Isaac Wake, commented on the difficulty of restraining the duke.[39] Carleton described Charles Emmanuel as a man whose "courage is such that he is no ways apprehensive of danger, framing still in his conceits rather conquests than perils, and he hath often a speech of the late French king in his remembrance that he recovered his kingdom *sans hommes et sans argent.*"[40] Starting wars without the men and money needed to win them invited disaster. While remaining supportive, James therefore sought to restrain his ally from provoking Spain into a full-scale punitive assault on his territories. As he did so, he tried to take credit with the Spanish for mediating their conflicts in North Italy, even as he encouraged other states to assist Savoy and quietly furnished support himself. After learning in August 1617 that the Dutch had sent military aid, he told Caron that he had done so as well and that he would not abandon Charles Emmanuel.[41] He also intervened in a local war between Venice and the Archduke Ferdinand of Styria, the future Holy Roman emperor, promoting an alliance between Venice and the United Provinces that led to the dispatch of a Dutch fleet carrying 6,000 men to the Adriatic, to counter the naval assistance that Ferdinand hoped to receive from the Spanish viceroy of Naples He permitted a levy of English soldiers for Venice.[42] When he renewed his alliance with the

---

[37] BL Add Mss. 18,639, fols 38v–39, 55, and 118v (Isaac Wake dispatches from Turin of September 3/13 and 17/27 and November 3/13, 1615).

[38] HHStA Belgien PC47, fol. 350v, Boisschot dispatch of 6 November 1614: James had heard that the Spanish ambassador in Venice had informed the Republic that "la intencion de su magestad [Philip III] era de privar al ducque de Savoia de sus estados por reboleoso y inquieto y establecer su hijo en la possession dellos."

[39] For Wake's role in Savoy see Vivienne Larminie, "The Jacobean Diplomatic Fraternity and the Protestant Cause: Sir Isaac Wake and the View from Savoy," *English Historical Review* 121 (2006): 1300–26.

[40] TNA SP92/3, fol. 110: "The duke's courage is such that he is no ways apprehensive of danger, framing still in his conceits rather conquests than perils, and he hath often a speech of the late French king in his remembrance that he recovered his kingdom *sans hommes et sans argent.*" It does not require principled pacifism to realize that it is not prudent to encourage an ally to start a war without worrying whether he has men and money to fight it.

[41] BL Add Mss. 17,677 I, fol. 206.

[42] For a brief discussion of this topic from the perspective of Spanish statesmen see Ruben Gonzáles Cuerva, *Baltasar de Zúñiga: Una encrucijada de la Monarquía Hispana (1561-1622)* (Madrid: Ediciones Polifeno, 2012), 379–83. According to Cuerva, James subsidized Savoy with £15,000 in 1615 but began to back away from the duke's adventurism in 1617. The archdukes' ambassador in London, Batta van Male, reported in April 1617 that an ambassador from Savoy had left the English court unhappy over the king's lack of support, but two months later he reported that James had

Protestant Union in 1618 he proposed adding Venice and Savoy as members. Archbishop Abbot confided to the Venetian ambassador that James had assured him that "there will be no mention of the reformed religion in order not to give offense to anyone" in the treaty ratifying the alliance.[43] When Bohemian Protestants rebelled to prevent the election of the Archduke Ferdinand as their king, Savoy lent them military assistance, the only Catholic state to do so.

Far from supporting Spanish interests and trying to preserve peace, James and his diplomats had therefore encouraged and helped subsidize a series of small conflicts that challenged Spain and its ally, Austria, in North Italy. But he also took care to prevent these conflicts from escalating into a larger war. His policy in the second crisis in Jülich and Cleves followed the same pattern. That crisis broke out after one of the two original Lutheran heirs, the duke of Neuburg, formed a dynastic alliance with the Catholic duke of Bavaria, converted to Rome, and sought to enlist Catholic support in claiming the whole territory. His rival, the marquess of Brandenburg, had meanwhile converted to Calvinism and joined the Protestant Union. James said he feared the dispute would ignite a general war between Catholic and Protestant princes in the Empire, which he very much wanted to prevent.[44] Although he continued to lend diplomatic support to Brandenburg, he rebuffed an informal effort by his son-in-law to convert the Protestant Union into an offensive, as well as a defensive, alliance and refused the marquess's request for British military assistance.[45] The Dutch acted more boldly, sending Maurice of Nassau with their army to seize Jülich. Although James insisted that he disapproved of this act, Boisschot strongly believed that he had secretly encouraged it.[46] Whatever the truth, James continued resisting pressure to involve himself directly as a co-belligerent.[47] When Spinola responded to Maurice's intervention by seizing the Protestant city of Wesel James strenuously objected but did nothing concrete to help his allies.

Fortunately, the Spanish also wanted to avoid a major war and so issued a joint invitation to the kings of France and Britain to mediate a settlement. James jumped at the opportunity and became a guarantor of the Treaty of Xanten, by which both the Dutch and the Habsburgs agreed to withdraw from the disputed territories. When the Dutch dragged their feet about complying with the treaty's terms because they suspected that the Spanish had no intention to evacuate Wesel, James grew seriously annoyed and issued several sharply worded protests.[48] In this instance he therefore did act, at least to all outward appearances, as a mediator

---

dispatched a ship laden with munitions to assist Charles Emmanuel (HHStA Belgien PC 49, fols 81v and 102). The policy seems to have remained one of furnishing limited, underhand assistance without committing Britain to a significant military effort. For the soldiers see HHStA Belgien PC49, fol. 92.

[43] *CSPV* 15.444.   [44] HHStA Belgien 47, fol. 5r (Boisschot dispatch of March 26).
[45] Ibid., fol. 37.   [46] Ibid., fol. 315v.   [47] Ibid., fols 57r, 248r and PC48, fol. 82r.
[48] BL Add Mss. 17,677 I, fols 98 (James upbraids Caron over the Dutch refusal to evacuate Jülich, December 7, 1615), 172–177v and 180–183r (Carleton's two memoranda on the subject presented to the States General in December 1616 and January 1617).

committed to a settlement that avoided war on terms apparently favorable to Spain. But his stance reflected his fear of the consequences of military escalation more than any principled commitment to peace.

The Origins of the Spanish Match

The king meanwhile continued to pursue negotiations over the marriage of his remaining son, with an eye both to securing a large dowry and strengthening his leverage in European affairs. For a time, the leading candidate for Charles's hand was Christine de Bourbon, second daughter of Henry IV and Marie de Médicis. James instructed Edmondes, then serving as his ambassador in Paris, to initiate formal negotiations for the match on May 1, 1613.[49] Boisschot, who carefully reported on the progress of negotiations, believed that they almost reached fruition in 1614, before news of Condé's rebellion and a withdrawal of backing for the match by its erstwhile promoter, Bouillon, gave the British pause.[50] He claimed that support for a French marriage alliance came almost entirely from Scottish courtiers, led by the duke of Lennox, whereas all the English councilors were opposed, with some preferring an alternative Spanish alliance.[51] This was probably a fairly accurate assessment, although support for a Spanish alliance would presumably have come primarily from the Howard earls of Nottingham, Arundel, Northampton and Suffolk and their allies, rather than strong Protestants like Abbot and the earl of Pembroke. Christian IV of Denmark favored the French match, as apparently did James until at least March of 1615.[52] Thereafter enthusiasm for it cooled, although negotiations continued through the following summer.[53]

Proposals for a Spanish marriage alliance had meanwhile started to gain traction. They were not entirely new, since discussions for marriages between James's children and members of the Spanish ruling family had taken place periodically since even before his accession to the English throne.[54] Early modern governments floated marriage proposals for any number of reasons, not only as

---

[49] BL Stowe Mss. 174, fol. 37r.
[50] HHStA Belgien PC47, fols. 53r, 88, 92, 203v. For his earlier reports see PC46, fols 196r and 265v. For Bouillon's change of attitude see BL Stowe Mss. 174, fol. 307v; cf. 330r. Bouillon and Condé argued that the regent's ministers were deceiving James and using the match to buy time while they consolidated their Spanish alliance.
[51] Belgien PC 47, fol. 88.
[52] TNA SP75/5 fol. 102; HHStA Belgien PC47, fol. 97; BL Stowe Mss. 175, fol. 276v.
[53] HHStA Belgien PC49, fol. 92r; SP78/65, fol. 15v (Edmondes rebuked for moving too hastily to conclude the marriage treaty in January 1616); ibid., fol. 225 (Edmondes and James Hay authorized to treat and conclude the marriage alliance); SP78/66/17 (Hay and Edmondes protest James's decision to repudiate articles already agreed to and begin negotiations anew, July 31, o.s., 1616); SP78/66/21 (Hay and Edmondes instructed to continue negotiating, August 21, o.s.). Condé's arrest took place the following day.
[54] Robert Cross, "To Counterbalance the World: England, Spain and Peace in the Early Seventeenth Century," unpublished Princeton PhD thesis, 2012, traces these proposals. See also *El Hecho de los*

sincerely intended offers but gestures of good will, devices for probing the intentions of another state, and attempts to foment jealousy among third parties. But offers always needed to be treated seriously, to avoid offending the honor of the king making them, even when no one believed they had any chance of success. In addition to securing greater cooperation from the British in European affairs, the Spanish hoped that through a marriage alliance they might secure toleration for Catholics within Britain and perhaps the conversion of the heir to the throne. As Robert Cross points out, during his Scottish reign James appeared willing to allow one of his children to be raised at the Spanish court, implying that he "considered... or at the very least... wanted the right people to think that he was considering" allowing the conversion of Henry or Elizabeth to Catholicism.[55] As late as 1609 he reportedly offered to send Prince Charles to complete his education in Spain.[56] But once he had become king of all Britain, such a step would have provoked fierce opposition in both England and Scotland. For this reason, many informed observers, including the earl of Salisbury, the English ambassador to Spain, John Digby, and the French foreign minister Villeroy, all discounted the chances that negotiations concerning a Spanish match for either Henry or Elizabeth would lead anywhere.[57] The "point of religion" remained an apparently insurmountable stumbling block, although the two sides kept discussing how to surmount it.

As the British court's interest in a French match peaked and then declined around 1614, negotiations with Spain started to benefit from the work of two highly capable ambassadors: Diego Sarmiento de Acuña, later Count Gondomar and John Digby, the future earl of Bristol. Historians have often noted Gondomar's rapport with James and effectiveness in representing Spain, but Digby's less well-known achievements also deserve notice. Two years after his appointment as James's ambassador in Madrid in spring 1611, he managed to bribe one of the clerks charged with transcribing documents for secret discussions by the Spanish council.[58] He thereby obtained copies of Gondomar's dispatches, lists of English courtiers receiving Spanish pensions, and other sensitive material.[59] While some of his revelations angered the British government, in the long run his

---

Tratados del Matrimonio pretendido por el Principe de Gales con la serenissima Infante de Espana Maria/Narrative of the Spanish Marriage Treaty, ed. and trans. S. R. Gardiner, Camden Society Publications OS 101 (1869).

[55] Robert Cross, "'The onely soveraigne medicine": Religious Politics and Political Culture in the British-Spanish Match, 1596–1625," in *Stuart Marriage Diplomacy: Dynastic Politics in their European Context, 1604–1630*, ed. Valentina Caldari and Sara J. Wolfson (Woodbridge: Boydell Press, 2018), 67–78 at 68–9.

[56] HHStA Belgien PC44 [unfoliated], Hoboque to de Groote, August 18, 1609.

[57] BL Harleian Mss. 7002, fol. 178v; TNA PRO31/3/45, fols 27, 174, 199 and SP94/19 fols 15r, 25v, 389r; BN Mss. Français 3502, fol. 111v; *Memorials of Affairs of State in the Reigns of Queen Elizabeth and King James I*, ed. E. Sawyer, 3 vols (London, 1725), 3.291; cf. *Narrative of the Marriage Treaty*, ed. Gardiner, 106–7 and 108.

[58] TNA SP94/19, fol. 329.   [59] Ibid., fol. 371v.

supply of inside information probably helped to reassure his superiors in London that Spanish intentions were less aggressive than some of them had feared.[60] Digby's intelligence confirmed that Spain had too many financial problems and difficulties elsewhere in Europe to want conflict with Britain, especially involving "slight and uncertain enterprises of uncertain success."[61] In early 1614, for example, he revealed that the Spanish had resisted the pleas of an exiled Irish bishop to assist Catholics in Ireland, despite Gondomar's reports of English persecution.[62] Digby did not regard the Spanish as entirely benign—given a good opportunity, he predicted, they might still attack Britain—but he felt confident that for the foreseeable future they would act with restraint while seeking opportunities for cooperation.

Boisschot believed that discussions over a Spanish match had already made progress by early summer in 1614, although at this date they remained tentative.[63] The following March rumors swept through the court that James had begun serious negotiations, after a report from Digby that Spain's principal minister, the duke of Lerma, favored the project and said that Spain would not demand Charles's immediate conversion as a precondition.[64] Draft articles for a marriage treaty soon followed.[65] Digby had therefore already begun negotiations over a Spanish match for Charles in Madrid by the time Gondomar launched his own initiative early in 1616, by asking the English antiquarian Sir Robert Cotton to serve as an intermediary with James's favorite, Robert Ker earl of Somerset, in presenting a proposal to James.[66] Somerset's close relations with the earls of Suffolk and Arundel made it likely that he would favor a Spanish match and he decided to pursue the idea energetically, allegedly without fully informing the king.[67] Whether or not this was the case, discussions continued after Somerset's fall. Rumors of their progress soon began to alarm some of Britain's continental allies.[68] While the offer of a very large dowry made a Spanish marriage alliance attractive, the deterioration of James's relations with France was probably even more decisive. Condé's arrest and the disgruntled return of the king's extraordinary ambassador, James Hay viscount Doncaster, in November 1616 added momentum to a reorientation in British policy, away from France and toward

[60] HHStA Belgien PC47, fol. 171r.
[61] E.g. TNA SP94/10, fol. 173 (dispatch of December 3, 1613). [62] Ibid., fol. 247.
[63] HHStA Belgien PC47, fol. 26r.
[64] BL Stowe Mss. 175, fol. 261v (Trumbull to Edmondes, March 5/15); HHStA Belgien PC 48, fol. 122r (Boisschot dispatch of March 13).
[65] HHStA Belgien PC48, fol. 247r (Boisschot dispatch of May 8).
[66] HMC *Report on the Manuscripts of the Duke of Buccleuch and Queensberry*, vol. 1 (London, 1899), 163.
[67] For a succinct account of the Howard earls' political role see Alastair Bellany, "The Rise of the Howards at Court," in *The Oxford Handbook of John Donne*, ed. Jeanne Shami, Dennis Flynn, and M. Thomas Hester (Oxford: Oxford University Press, 2011), 537–53. For the assertion that Overbury had proceeded without James's "privity" and "clean in a contrary manner" to the king's intentions see Digby to James I, April 2, 1616, in TNA SP94/22, fol. 28v. How far this was actually the case, rather than something James wanted to make the world believe, is a very good question.
[68] BL Stowe Mss. 176, fol. 20v (Edmondes to Winwood, May 1616).

Spain.[69] "The French business has here given such distaste," Caron reported in November "that people no longer speak of that marriage but I have ascertained that people propose, and it is sufficiently resolved that ... the lord Digby ... will be sent [back] to Spain to treat for a marriage."[70]

It is important to note that these events transpired well before the eruption of a crisis in Bohemia in spring 1618 and its escalation into what became the Thirty Years War. In the historical literature the story of the Spanish match has always been closely linked to James's efforts to settle the dispute within the Empire through negotiation, and subsequently to obtain the restoration of the Palatinate after its conquest by Catholic armies. This has reinforced the assumption that he sought a Spanish alliance chiefly to strengthen his position as a peace-maker in European confessional conflicts. Most older accounts also presented the outbreak of religious war within the Holy Roman Empire as a virtual inevitability by the mid-1610s, requiring only a spark to set it off. But not all contemporaries shared this view and recent work has vigorously challenged it.[71] The outbreak of a major war in Central Europe and loss of the Palatinate were unforeseen events that overtook negotiations for a match between Prince Charles and the Infanta Maria in mid-course. Since they had not yet happened, they had nothing to do with the original motivations of either party to the proposed alliance.

Although religious and political tensions existed in many parts of Europe, before the Bohemian revolt and for several months after it, most statesmen in both Spain and Britain remained more preoccupied with disputes in Italy, the Rhine Valley, and France than with Central Europe. We have seen that in all these regions James continued to foment trouble for the Habsburgs and Bourbons with one hand, even while seeking an alliance with Spain and offering his services as a mediator. He did this to keep his options open and extract maximum advantage from "existing situations." No one knew whether his negotiations for a Spanish dynastic alliance would succeed. By October 1617 Digby had concluded that Philip III genuinely wanted a dynastic alliance "if the point of religion can be accommodated," but he remained unsure whether this would be possible. He therefore preferred to keep his discussions with Lerma secret, to avoid mutual embarrassment should they reach an impasse.[72] Complete confidentiality proved impossible because Gondomar simultaneously tried to push the match forward in

---

[69] Questier, *Dynastic Politics*, 371–2 reaches a similar conclusion.

[70] BL Add Mss. 17,677 I, dispatch of November 2, 1616: "De zaeken van Frankerijk hebbe alhier sulk een mismaek geven dat men niet meer van het huwelijk en spreekt, maar ick weet dat men preposeert, jae genoeg geresolvert is, dat den heer vice kammerlijk Digby die lest ambassadeur in Spagne naer Spagne sal worden gesonden omme te tracteren op he huwelijk van Spagnien."

[71] Geoff Mortimer, *The Origins of the Thirty Years War and the Revolt of Bohemia, 1618* (Basingstoke: Palgrave Macmillan, 2015) reviews the old historiographical consensus that war had become inevitable in chapter 1 before proceeding to question this view. Peter Wilson, *The Thirty Years War: Europe's Tragedy* (Cambridge, MA: Belknap Press, 2009), also disputes that the Empire was becoming irremediably destabilized by confessional conflict before 1618.

[72] TNA SP94/22, fol. 196.

London, in discussions with the king and his new favorite, Buckingham, in ways that caused rumors to spread. Louis XIII's bride, Anne of Austria, also boasted of the progress of negotiations for the marriage of her younger sister to Prince Charles at the French court.[73] But attempts to maintain secrecy by confining discussion to a small group of diplomats and ministers deepened uncertainty, even among people close to the centers of power in the two kingdoms, about where matters stood. Many remained skeptical that the proposed match would ever reach fruition.[74] James had a second representative in Spain, Francis Cottington, who expressed doubts that the Spanish were serious in January 1617, while ten months later the earl of Pembroke, a senior member of the privy council, scoffed at the suggestion that the match would succeed.[75]

Significant divisions of opinion within both the British and Spanish councils added to the uncertainty, as did James's notorious penchant for dissimulation and opportunism. As late as the beginning of 1619, Gondomar believed that James was keeping his options open: if the Habsburg's position collapsed in Germany he would abandon the match and throw in his lot with his Protestant allies and kinsmen, along with Savoy and Venice, to exploit Spain's vulnerabilities.[76] James not only pursued seemingly contradictory policies; to a considerable extent he did this through rival cohorts of ministers and diplomats who disagreed sharply with each other about the best course to follow.[77] Cottington and Digby reported to the Howard protégé, Secretary Thomas Lake, whom the archduke's ambassador, Batta Van Male, described as Spain's only true friend on the privy council,[78] whereas the strongly Protestant and anti-Habsburg ambassadors assigned to France, the Netherlands, Savoy, and Venice—Carleton, Doncaster, Edmondes, Wotton, and Isaac Wake—corresponded with the equally Protestant Secretary Winwood until his death in 1617, and subsequently with Sir Robert Naunton, who also sympathized with their views. Digby complained in October 1617 that several members of the council had spread reports that he and Lake were the only senior figures in

---

[73] TNA SP78/66/17, Edmondes and Hay to Winwood, July 31, 1616.
[74] Carleton to Trumbull, October 4/14, 1617, Trumbull Mss. vol. 15 (Library of Congress microfilm 041/Camb200/2/120); TNA SP78/67, fol. 132v.
[75] TNA SP94/22, fol. 106v; *CDIHE Gondomar* 1.135–6.
[76] *CDIHE Gondomar* 2.133: "es cierto que si en este equilibrio y balanza el imperio cae, y aun sólo con que se embarace, como se va haciendo de la parte hereje, no parece que puede haber duda de que el rey de Inglaterra se le arrimará, soltando el casamiento que trata con España y su amistad, y siguiendo en todo el otro partido que él terna por mayor y más seguro y más conforme a su religión y voluntad y su sangre, pues los hijos del conde Palatino son su nietos y sus sucesores, y Holanda y Venecia y Saboya desean y fomentan esto por cuantos medios puedan."
[77] As previously noted by Simon Adams and Michael Questier. See Adams, "Protestant Cause," 250; Questier, *Dynastic Politics*, 384. It is worth recalling that in the 1590s James had cultivated his English alliance through his chancellor, Maitland, and probably sanctioned the apocalyptic militantly Protestant rhetoric of Andrew Melville's poem celebrating Prince Henry's baptism, even while he tolerated and probably tacitly encouraged the dealings of Huntly and other Catholic aristocrats with Spain. He was no stranger to a strategy of keeping his options open by pursuing contradictory policies through different groups of agents and intermediaries.
[78] HHStA Belgien PC49, 133v, dispatch of June 5, 1618.

the government well-disposed to the Spanish match and that both would soon "have leisure enough to repent it." He urged Lake to keep details of the negotiation secret even from members of the council.[79] He also confided to the archduke's ambassador in May that public hostility to his role in negotiating the match made him afraid for his life to appear in the streets of London.[80]

This infighting and backbiting produced a contentious and seemingly unstable atmosphere at court, in some ways reminiscent of the late 1590s, especially as a series of scandals brought down several high-level figures—Somerset, the earl of Suffolk and his protégé Lake, Naunton and Lord Chancellor Bacon—between 1616 and 1621. Divisions on the council and uncertainty about James's ultimate intentions invited situations in which diplomats would overstep their instructions, in part because they had not received clear guidance from London and so had to improvise when pressed by foreign governments to clarify the British government's position. James may at times have wanted this to happen: we should remember his comment to Bouillon that when princes wish to deceive their neighbors they begin by deceiving their own ambassadors. Although he did not lie to his ambassadors he did sometimes fail to provide them with prompt and accurate information about his precise intentions, even when they demanded it. Although inattention and poor communications may have contributed to the problem, it is tempting to suspect that deliberate dissimulation also played a role.

Even if negotiations for the match had succeeded, they would not necessarily have required a complete reversal of Britain's European alliances. Dynastic marriages in the period almost never achieved such unequivocal results and often failed to resolve basic conflicts of interest.[81] The Spanish would undoubtedly require some concessions, including the curtailment of British support for the United Provinces. But the most difficult issues involved British *domestic* politics, namely Spanish demands for much more indulgent treatment of English, Scottish, and Irish Catholics and other religious concessions for the infanta and her household. James saw the Spanish alliance as a not unwelcome opportunity to pivot from harassing Catholics to suppressing puritan and presbyterian dissent with greater rigor. He told Gondomar as much in January 1618, although adding that without Spain's assured friendship he would be crazy (*loco*) to take such a step.[82] Digby promised the Spanish that James "would ruin the puritans" if the

---

[79] SP94/22, fol. 194.
[80] HHStA PC49, fol. 98: "Me ha contado Don Juan Digby vicecamraro d'este rey que le es tanta la rabia y envidia que tienen con el, porque va en España para tratar el dicho casamiento, que apenas puede andar seguro por estas calles de Londres, y me afirmo que notavia cosa tanto como que le harian matar antes de su partida."
[81] A series of marriages between the royal families of Spain and France in the sixteenth and early seventeenth centuries failed not only to resolve Franco-Spanish rivalries but to prevent wars between the two kingdoms. Charles I's marriage to Henrietta Maria in 1625 did little to prevent, and in some ways actually contributed to the outbreak of war between Britain and France by 1627.
[82] *CDIHE Gondomar*, 1.207.

match reached fruition.[83] We should probably see his insistence on imposing the Five Articles of Perth as, in part, an early trial of this policy. The king also released seventy-four imprisoned priests as a special favor to Gondomar to show his good will, and excluded the staunchly Protestant Secretary Winwood and Archbishop Abbot from the committee of the privy council charged with overseeing negotiations for the match.[84] But the harassment of Catholics in all three of his kingdoms continued, causing Van Male to become increasingly disillusioned and skeptical that the alliance would ever reach fruition in early 1618, even as Digby and Gondomar remained more optimistic.[85]

James's motives were undoubtedly complex. He wanted an alliance with Europe's greatest dynasty for reasons of prestige, in addition to its potential strategic advantages and the large dowry the Spanish were offering. But even if the match never took place, he calculated that negotiations over it would serve other purposes. Fear of a Spanish alliance might help persuade puritan landowners, merchants, and clergy to furnish him with money, so as to lessen his need for Spain's bounty.[86] He also wished to put pressure on France and the Dutch, in the latter case over disputes involving the cloth trade, conflicts in the East Indies, and his efforts to collect licensing fees from foreign vessels fishing in the "narrow seas" around Britain.[87] If the match succeeded, he hoped that it would facilitate his efforts to manage disputes between the Habsburgs and several of his allies, including Savoy and the Palatinate. His thinking on this topic may have been shaped by his experience of the role that marriages between noble families had long played in settling Scottish blood feuds. In both Edinburgh and London, he had arranged matches between noble dynasties with a history of mutual antagonism in efforts to ameliorate their rivalries. These unions did not usually remove all personal and political disagreements but they did buffer the effects of aristocratic rivalries. For example, the marriage James had arranged between the duke of Lennox's sister and the earl of Huntly did not prevent the earl from continuing to dabble in treasonous plots with Spain, while his brother-in-law remained loyal to the Kirk and the king. But when Huntly fled into exile and the crown confiscated his lands, James appointed Lennox to administer them and Lady Huntly remained behind at court lobbying for her husband's rehabilitation. This must have

---

[83] *Narrative of the Marriage Treaty*, ed. Gardiner, 101.

[84] HHStA Belgien PC49, fol. 44, dispatch of March 18, 1617 (the exclusion of Abbot and Winwood); BL Add Mss. 17,677 I, fol. 311v, *CSPD JI*, 2.543.

[85] HHStA Belgien PC49, fols 66r, 117v, 302–3; cf. *CDIHE Gondomar* 1.207, suggesting that James's professed willingness to ease persecution should be put to the test rather than dismissed out-of-hand.

[86] Digby advised James to call a parliament in 1617, saying that he felt confident that it would grant the king supply if it believed the match with Spain was otherwise likely to move forward (TNA SP94/22 fol. 197). In Suffolk an effort was made in December 1617 to canvass JPs and other prominent gentlemen to determine whether they would be willing "to raise a liberal contribution to the king to prevent the marriage with Spain": *CSPD JI*, 2.505. The French ambassador believed that James was using the match negotiations in an effort to obtain money from the clergy (TNA PRO31/3/52).

[87] For these disputes see, esp., BL Add Mss. 17,677 I, passim.

reassured the earl that James did not intend to ruin him, lessening the risk that his exile would provoke an all-out war between the Gordons' clients and enemies.

James probably envisaged a Stuart–Habsburg marriage alliance working in a similar way. It would not always avoid conflict but it would provide channels of communication and other mechanisms to prevent small disputes from escalating into bitter, winner-take-all contests that risked igniting wars that neither Britain nor Spain wanted to fight. Even without a dynastic alliance, the two kingdoms had already begun cooperating in this way in the second Jülich Cleves crisis and North Italy. It helped that Lerma, no less than James, wanted to contain disputes in both theaters before they forced him to take measures that would have ruined his efforts to restore Spain's finances, while diminishing the supply of money and patronage available for other purposes, including satisfying his large clientage network. Lerma also wanted to redirect Spain's military efforts, away from northern Europe toward confrontation with the Muslim enemy in the Mediterranean, an objective with which James sympathized.[88] A case therefore existed that closer cooperation between Spain and Britain might serve not only the interests of both crowns but also those of their respective allies. In 1617 Charles Emmanuel provoked another local war in which he suffered a crushing defeat at the hands of the Spanish governor of Milan, Pedro Álvarez de Toledo, marquis of Villafranca. Afraid of seeing his ally ruined if Villafranca pressed his advantage, James offered to mediate a peace. Fortunately, Lerma wanted to avoid a wider Italian war that might draw in the French, and so not only welcomed James's mediation but offered Charles Emmanuel fairly generous terms. Villafranca, who wanted to exploit his victories to the hilt, dragged his feet in honoring the treaty that Lerma had concluded, causing James to protest loudly and demand that Spain honor its promises.[89] But in doing so he was effectively supporting Spain's chief minister against an insubordinate military governor.

For this sort of relationship to work, the two protagonists did not have to resolve all their differences or even refrain from limited proxy conflicts with each other. But they did need not only to act with restraint but to control allies and subordinates, like Charles Emmanuel and Villafranca, whose aggressive acts

---

[88] On Lerma see esp. Bernardo José Garcia Garcia, *La Pax Hispanica: Política Exterior del Duque de Lerma* (Leuven: Leuven University Press, 1996); Antonio Feros, *Kingship and Favoritism in the Spain of Philip III 1598–1621* (Cambridge: Cambridge University Press, 2000) and Patrick Williams, *The Great Favourite: The Duke of Lerma and the Court and Government of Philip III of Spain, 1598–1621* (Manchester: Manchester University Press, 2006). Cuerva, *Zuñiga*, points out that the winding down of war in the Low Countries was accompanied by the expulsion of the Moriscos from Spain and stepped up campaigns against Barbary pirates, as well as a commitment to support the Catholic League in the Empire (270–4) and that in 1617 Lerma wanted to disengage from conflicts in Italy and Germany so as to redirect resources to a planned attack on the North African stronghold of Argel (380). Rather than the straightforward pursuit of a *pax hispanica*, he argues, this amounted to a redirection of Spanish attention and military resources to the South and East. James would have had every reason to applaud this reorientation.

[89] Garcia Garcia, *Pax Hispanica*, 96–7.

might otherwise lead to an unmanageable crisis. Effective cooperation would remain difficult because Spain and Britain had many divergent interests and remained wary and mistrustful of each other. English councilors like Abbot, who saw Spain as an implacable foe bent on world domination, had their counterparts in Madrid, who thought that English heretics would never cease trying to destroy Spain and the Catholic religion. James and Lerma had nevertheless begun to see each other as prudent statesmen, united by a common desire to prevent a major war. Unfortunately, after about 1615 Lerma's hold on power gradually declined. He remained at the center of Spanish affairs but with a steadily diminishing ability to control other ministers and officials, until his final retirement in October 1618. His son, the duke of Uceda, replaced him as Philip's leading minister, but Uceda's lack of sustained attention to foreign affairs created something of a decision-making vacuum at the Spanish court. Philip III's unexpected death in March 1621 precipitated another reshuffle, with the Count Duke of Olivares emerging as the new royal favorite, while his uncle, Baltasar Zúñiga, became the prime director of Spanish foreign policy until his own death in October 1622. For virtually the entire period of negotiations over the Spanish match, leadership of the Spanish government therefore remained in flux. This made it easier for officials like Villafranca and his counterpart in Naples, the duke of Oñate, to take initiatives without the approval of the council of state, in the knowledge that some ministers in Madrid shared their ambition to restore Spain's military reputation through aggressive action.[90] Diplomats like Gondomar and Spain's ambassador in Vienna, the duke of Osuna, were also less firmly controlled than would likely have been the case if a single cohesive ministerial team had retained a firm hold on power. The instability and infighting at the heart of the Spanish court—which in some ways resembled the factional rifts among James's ministers—made it even more difficult for those negotiating a dynastic alliance to discern the intentions and motives of the other side.

France, Bohemia, and Confessional Polarization, 1617–1620

This might have mattered less if events in other parts of Europe had not begun to produce sharper patterns of confessional polarization that made conflict more difficult to contain. Although it would culminate with the outbreak of the Thirty Years War, the trend began not in Germany but in France, where Condé's arrest initiated a turn toward more ruthless and absolutist crown policies under the aegis of Marie de Médicis's hated Italian favorite, Concini, assisted by three of her younger protégés: Claude Barbin, Claude Mangot, and Armand-Jean du Plessis,

---

[90] Cuerva, *Zúñiga*, is especially effective in tracing these shifts in power and influence and documenting the slippage in tight control that sometimes resulted.

the bishop of Luçon and future Cardinal Richelieu.[91] The British perceived these ministers, especially the bishop of Luçon, as strongly anti-Huguenot and pro-Spanish.[92] Edmondes reported that the papal "nuncio and the Spanish ambassador have now a hand in the swaying of all the principal councils of the court" and that the latter regularly engaged in secretive nighttime discussions with Concini and the regent in her apartments.[93] He warned that the duke of Epernon was attempting to start a new war of religion by attacking the approaches to La Rochelle.[94] James complained that "France governs itself now by the Pope, the king of Spain and the marquess of Ancre [Concini]."[95]

The new regime faced widespread public disaffection and a new noble revolt broke out in January 1617. Determined to vanquish this opposition, the queen mother and her ministers talked openly of calling in Spanish military assistance, a prospect that the Huguenots and the British had long dreaded.[96] As early as October 1615 Digby reported that the Spanish council had ordered Spinola to ready his forces for a possible incursion into France to deal with Condé's rebellion. In the following year James attempted, at Bouillon's request, to pressure Archduke Albert to pledge that Spinola would refrain from attacking Sedan by warning that "both for honor and reason of state" Britain would need to react if he did.[97] Albert gave a seemingly reassuring but evasive answer. As the spring of 1617 approached, Bouillon again feared that Sedan would become a target of the Army of Flanders and appealed to his foreign Protestant friends for support. He publicly announced that he was doing so by publishing an open letter to Louis XIII justifying his conduct, an act described by a French newsbook, the *Mercure françois*, as "the harbinger of a great trouble."[98] Carleton reported in December that his correspondents in France shared "a general opinion" that the kingdom was headed for "a war of religion" and that the French crown had begun purchasing arms in preparation. The Huguenots wished to do so as well but the Dutch authorities prevented them. The Huguenots therefore asked Carleton to purchase arms for them, ostensibly for shipment to England, and he requested and received permission to do so.[99] A few weeks later Carleton reported that Bouillon was employing

---

[91] Jean-François Dubost, *Marie de Médicis: La reine dévoilée* (Paris: Biographie Payot, 2009), 510–20.
[92] TNA SP78/66/52 and 56.   [93] BL Stowe Mss. 176, fol. 38v; TNA SP78/66/33 and 47.
[94] SP78/55, fol. 56.
[95] HHStA Belgien PC49, fol. 44v, Van Male dispatch of March 18, 1617, reporting a conversation with the French extraordinary ambassador, the baron de Tours, about the king's attitude.
[96] Dubost, *Marie de Médicis*, 521–2. Adams, "Protestant Cause," 267–8, comments that James's refusal to give open military support to the Huguenots in 1615 probably prevented a full-scale war in which Spinola would have intervened in support of the regent, while the Dutch and Elector Palatine were prepared to counter him with their own troops if James had agreed to join with them.
[97] TNA SP94/21 fol. 178v; SP77/12, fol. 1r–v.   [98] *Le mercure françois 1617*, 10.
[99] *Letters from and to Sir Dudley Carleton, Knt., during his embassy in Holland, from January 1615/16 to December 1620* (London, 2nd ed., 1775), 81 and 83; BL Stowe Mss. 176, fol. 72.

"his friends' credit and purses" to buy arms in the United Provinces, while preparing to raise 2,000 horse.[100]

The Huguenots and rebellious princes enjoyed considerable support among the Protestant population in the Netherlands and the regiments of French Protestant soldiers serving in the Dutch army. Several officers of those regiments had returned home to fight for Condé in the civil war of 1615, despite Oldenbarnevelt's efforts to prevent them from doing so. The following year the Dutch government felt obliged to disavow the actions of a captain of one of its warships, who on his own authority had come to the aid of La Rochelle against a threatened attack by forces under Epernon, shortly after Condé's arrest.[101] The French government not only demanded that the Dutch honor their alliance by denying any form of assistance to the rebels but that the 4,000 French troops serving in the Dutch army and 5,000 additional soldiers should be sent to France to help suppress the nobles' revolt. Louis threatened that if the Dutch and British abandoned him he would have no choice but to call in "the forces of Spain...to secure himself."[102] In January Concini went a step further, demanding that the United Provinces honor its treaty obligations by lending France five warships to help suppress rebellion, as well as transport for 3,000 newly recruited soldiers.[103]

James countered by asking the Dutch to join him in mediating the conflict, in the hope that he might protect Bouillon and the Huguenots by forestalling Spanish intervention. But although Maurice seemed receptive to the idea, and was even rumored to be considering going in person to aid the rebellious nobles, Oldenbarnevelt resisted. "Though he be sensible of the present misgovernment in that state and of the consequence thereof, yet it appears by many arguments that he for his particular is resolved to run a course with the queen regent," Carleton concluded.[104] Dutch politicians claimed to fear that offending Marie de Médicis would "make France conjoin itself with Spain and the Pope to their utter ruin," although "the truth," Carleton believed, was that they still hoped to collect a promised French subsidy that had fallen into arrears: *"qui beneficium accipit, libertatem vendit."*[105] James continued to apply pressure, instructing Carleton in April to tell Oldenbarnevelt that because of their bonds of alliance he expected the Dutch to "advise, consult and resolve together" with him on French affairs and warning that if they did not he would "provide for his own particular" with no regard to their interests.[106] But Oldenbarnevelt, Carleton wrote, continued to support the French government's demands.[107]

It is clear that James and his council believed that Spinola might attack Sedan and then use the Army of Flanders to crush the Huguenots.[108] In response the

---

[100] *Letters from and to Carleton*, 90.   [101] Ibid., 35, 62, 64–5.   [102] Ibid., 49, 67, and 85.
[103] Ibid., 92.   [104] Ibid., 50, 93, and 98.   [105] Ibid., 109.   [106] Ibid., 125.
[107] BL Stowe Mss. 176, fol. 81.
[108] TNA SP78/67, fols 1v, 26r, 44v, 59, 128, 131, 132v, 170; *CSPV* 15.2.

king conferred with the Elector Palatine, who had written to him in January urging support for Bouillon, about levying a Protestant counter-force.[109] Frederick predicted that the violent suppression of the French princes would not only imperil the Huguenots' survival but advance other designs of Spain and Rome "to the irreparable prejudice of all Christianity."[110] He feared that a new civil war in France would spread to the Empire, which had become even more polarized along confessional lines by the latest crisis in Jülich and Cleves. Protestants needed to look to their own defense but he feared that any military preparations would arouse jealousies and further undermine the "the general peace of Germany."[111] James tried to deter the French by warning their ambassador in London that since Britain was "full of warlike people that wanted employment, he could not hinder them from coming into France if the wars should go forwards."[112]

A French pamphlet of 1617 claimed that after the Dutch and several German princes turned down Bouillon's pleas for assistance, Frederick V interceded to help him raise 6,000 English volunteers, who attempted unsuccessfully to land in France in March.[113] I have found no corroborating evidence that this force ever existed and it may well have been invented by a French royalist writer seeking to discredit Bouillon. But some Englishmen evidently did volunteer to assist the Huguenots and James employed the threat of this happening in efforts to extract concessions from the French government. In March 1617 it looked as if a new war of religion that would involve British, Dutch, German, and Spanish soldiers would soon erupt in France.[114] The fear of France and Spain joining in a great Catholic alliance threatened to become self-fulfilling, by inspiring a rebellion supported by foreign Protestant states that in turn gave the queen mother and her ministers every incentive to appeal for Spanish assistance.

Fortunately, another coup in April, engineered by Louis's favorite the duke of Luynes, averted the danger. It resulted in Concini's murder and ended Marie de Médicis's government, sending her into internal exile. James welcomed this turn of events enthusiastically. Edmondes began urging the French to support a scheme to transfer the imperial title from the Habsburgs to the duke of Bavaria after the death of the current Emperor Mathias, who was not expected to live much longer. He claimed that the plan originated with the Catholic bishop and elector of Cologne, who had paid an unexpected visit to his close relative, Maximilian duke of Bavaria, to complain that the Habsburgs wanted to turn the Empire

---

[109] TNA SP81/15 fol. 1. [110] Ibid., fol. 20.
[111] Ibid., fol. 30: "il eut été impossible de faire aucune levée de guerre en ces quartiers sans mettre tous les autres états de l'Empire en la jalousie et émotion, ce qui eut altéré le repos public de la Germanie."
[112] TNA SP78/67, fol. 41.
[113] *La déscente des anglais...* (1617), esp. 7–8. A copy of this pamphlet exists at the Folger Shakespeare Library.
[114] Cf. Questier, *Dynastic Politics*, 377.

into a hereditary monarchy under their dynasty. To block their ambition, he urged the duke to stand as a rival candidate at the next imperial election and began canvassing support for him.[115] After learning of this initiative, the Elector Palatine and Edmondes traveled to Sedan in August 1617 to consult with Bouillon and the Dutch ambassador to France, and the Elector and Bouillon agreed to lend their support.[116] The participation of a Catholic elector made the scheme appear plausible, since Protestants controlled three of the seven votes in the electoral college. A few years earlier when Maximilian of Bavaria had spearheaded the formation of a Catholic league of German states to counter the Protestant Union, he had carefully excluded the Habsburgs from a leadership role in his alliance. Some Protestants regarded him as less "Jesuited" than the Habsburg candidate, Ferdinand of Styria.[117] Frederick, Bouillon, and Edmondes evidently hoped that Maximilian's ambition and concern for the peace of Germany would induce him to cooperate with them in depriving the Habsburgs of the imperial crown and restraining the "Jesuited" militants who threatened to unleash a new religious war. In a sense their efforts amounted to a further extension of James's strategy of preserving a balance of power in Central Europe by promoting cooperation between Protestants and middling Catholic powers like Savoy and Venice.

But from the perspective of Vienna or Madrid the challenge to Habsburg control looked like an extremely hostile and provocative act. James assured the Spanish that he had rebuked Edmondes for attending the meeting in Sedan and claimed to have instructed his ambassador to Heidelburg, Sir Albert Morton, to urge Frederick to cooperate fully with the emperor in matters relating the upcoming election.[118] But I have found no evidence in Edmonde's own correspondence that he ever received a rebuke, and it is clear that he continued lobbying the French court to support Maximilian's candidacy. Luynes seemed receptive, he reported, but James's old nemesis, Villeroy, who had since recovered his post as secretary of state, was staunchly opposed.[119] In March 1618 James himself advised Frederick to try to delay the election of a king of the Romans, the title traditionally give to the presumptive successor to the imperial throne.[120] He was again playing a double game, seeking to reassure the Habsburgs of his support while he looked for

---

[115] TNA SP78/67 fols 185r, 196, 206v–207; BL Stowe Mss. 176, fols 120v–121.
[116] As Gondomar, reported. See *CDIHE Gondomar*, 1.89 and 95.
[117] See TNA SP81/16, fol. 98v for the view that Maximilian was less Jesuited.
[118] Adams, "Protetant Cause," 275, correctly points out that James assured Gondomar that he had reprimanded Edmondes but erroneously cites *CDIHE Gondomar* 1.89, 95, and 150–1 as the source. The first two passages merely report that Edmondes had gone to Sedan for discussions, while the third does not mention him. The correct source is *Letters and other Documents Illustrating the Relations between England and Germany at the Commencement of the Thirty Years War*, 2 vols,, ed. Samuel Rawson Gardiner, Camden Society Publications, OS 90 and 98 (1865 and 1868), 1.30, a *consulta* of January 1619, shortly after James had agreed to mediate the crisis in Bohemia. For James's assurances about Morton's mission see *CDIHE Gondomar*, 150, 165, and 168.
[119] BL Stowe Mss. 176, fols 132v, 185r, 196.   [120] TNA SP81/15 fol. 119.

opportunities to weaken their position, acting largely through agents like Edmondes whose actions he might disavow if they became embarrassing.

As these maneuvers played out, the Luynes regime launched an offensive to subdue Huguenot strongholds, provoking James to complain that "it is a terrible government in France at this moment that wants to destroy the edicts of pacification."[121] The French also largely withdrew support from their former allies, Savoy and Venice.[122] The British ambassador in Turin, Isaac Wake, suspected a Franco-Spanish plot to destroy the liberty of Italy. James's efforts to prevent the French state from softening its resistance to Spain and hardening its attitude toward the Huguenots had, to all appearances, utterly failed. For this he had himself largely to blame, since Huguenot support for the rebellions of Condé and Bouillon that he had encouraged convinced French ministers that they needed to reduce the many Protestant *places de sûreté* to secure their state against future revolts.[123] Until they completed this task, they also needed to avoid conflict with the Habsburgs, since the French crown lacked the means to fight internal and external wars at the same time. The Luynes regime had already embarked on the project that would culminate in 1628, with Richelieu's reduction of the last remaining Huguenot stronghold of La Rochelle.

We now know that Louis's campaigns against Huguenot *places de sûreté* did not lead to the revocation of the Edict of Nantes and efforts to destroy French Protestantism by force, and that his *détente* with Spain would not last. Calculations of reason of state, more than militant religious ideology, would guide French policy for most of the next two decades. But many contemporary Protestants, both within and outside France, interpreted attacks on Huguenot strongholds as evidence of Catholic fanaticism fueled by Spanish, papal, and Jesuit agents, which threatened not only the survival of French Protestantism but the balance of power throughout Europe. They also drew parallels to the aggressive Catholicism of Ferdinand of Styria, which they blamed on Jesuit persuasion. Protestant states, along with those such as Savoy and Venice that valued their independence from papal and Spanish domination, felt under urgent pressure to unite before it was too late. Just as Calvinists had once looked to Elizabeth for salvation during the last period in which France appeared to have abandoned its role as a counterweight to Spain in the mid-1580s, they now turned to James I, as the only European prince with the standing and resources necessary to spearhead resistance against Spanish tyranny. For reasons of prestige he showed himself more willing than Elizabeth to promote a grand European alliance under his nominal leadership. But he remained, if anything, even more reluctant than she had been to shoulder the risks and burdens that went with such a position. As a Venetian diplomat commented about the king's efforts to draw Venice and Savoy

---

[121] TNA PRO31/3/52, fol. 253.   [122] *CSPV* 15.132.
[123] Dubost, *Marie de Médicis*, 611–14.

into an alliance with the Protestant Union, Britain and the United Provinces: "I fear from appearances that they [the British] will resolve upon nothing, and by offering a league as they have so often done, wish to bind others without binding themselves... The king will desire to serve as an ornament and be the chief of a great union in Europe but will have no other trouble beyond listening to the circumstances and accidents thereof."[124]

Although James's equivocations and opportunism had served him reasonably well so long as Henry IV's Protestant alliances and Lerma's caution preserved the peace of Europe, these traits proved less effective in the more polarized and volatile environment that began to develop around 1617, and that became even less stable with the eruption of a new crisis in the Empire the following year. His policies in this period were not as unambiguously pacific and pro-Spanish as some accounts have suggested. But he continued trying to keep his options open by pursuing seemingly contradictory courses of action, even as changing circumstances rendered that strategy increasingly untenable. By trying to act simultaneously as a peace-maker and the leader of the Protestant cause in Europe, he undermined his credibility in both roles.

By early 1618 the atmosphere within the Empire had grown tense with rumors of impending conflict. In January van Male reported hearing that the Elector Palatine and marquess of Brandenburg had requested James's support for "some enterprise of war" in Germany using soldiers returned from France.[125] Three months later Morton wrote of fears that the wars of Italy would be "transferred over the Alps into Germany," adding: "we live here as if all the soldiers now on foot or horseback were levied only for our guard."[126] A new crisis erupted in this already unstable environment in May, when disaffected members of the Protestant estates of Bohemia threw several representatives of their recently elected Habsburg king, Ferdinand of Styria, from a window in the tower of Prague castle. Although the victims survived, Ferdinand would find this act of defiance difficult to forgive, even if he wanted to do so. A civil war soon broke out that spilled over into the neighboring province of Moravia and parts of Austria, where Lutheran nobles had their own grievances against Ferdinand's rule.[127] The fact that the king of Bohemia possessed a vote in the electoral college raised the stakes, since if Protestants succeeded in deposing Frederick and replacing him with a Calvinist or a figure like Charles Emmanuel of Savoy, they would be able to deprive the Habsburgs of the imperial crown even without the support of German Catholic electors. It might even be possible to choose a Protestant emperor, something the Spanish had long suspected James and Frederick V of scheming to do.[128]

---

[124] *CSPV* 15.132.   [125] HHStA Belgien PC49, fol. 133r–v.   [126] TNA SP81/15, fol. 121v.
[127] Wilson, *Thirty Years War*, chapter 9 provides a clear narrative.
[128] TNA SP93/19, fol. 323r, reporting that James predicted Frederick would become emperor "in respect of the crown of Bohemia because they pretend it to be elective."

Nevertheless, most of the major powers initially saw the rebellion as a distraction and hoped to settle matters quickly. Bohemia was relatively remote not only from Britain but also from the main areas of Spanish concern in the Mediterranean, northern Italy, western Germany, and the Low Countries. Digby reported that the Spanish wanted a peaceful resolution because they were short of money and wary of being drawn into an expensive campaign in a region of limited strategic importance to themselves.[129] The members of the Protestant Union also initially refrained from assisting the Bohemians openly because they did not want to spark a wider war. Venice remained detached.[130] Even Ferdinand was too preoccupied with the upcoming imperial election to pay adequate attention to the revolt.[131] Bohemian uprisings were nothing new: previous ones had occurred in 1609 and 1611, extracting significant concessions for the kingdom's Protestant majority. From the distant perspective of London, it must have looked as if this crisis would probably end in much the same way as the previous disputes over Cleves and Jülich, in a brokered compromise after some military maneuvering and a few indecisive engagements.

When in November the Spanish invited James to act as a mediator, primarily to deter him from assisting the Bohemian rebels, he readily accepted. He then issued a circular letter to Frederick and other German princes, couched in ambiguous language. It proclaimed the king's desire to promote "the peace of the world" before stating that if it were determined that the Bohemians had taken up arms in defense of their just rights and privileges he would favor them, but if they intended to wage war against the Empire "they must be restrained and exhorted to quiet." It then added that James knew that as the authority of the Emperor Matthias waned, "Ferdinand, with the evil aid of the Jesuits, goes seeking to annihilate the reformed religion." He therefore requested that Frederick keep him informed of all "contingencies."[132] This implied that he had considerable sympathy for the rebel cause, but left an escape hatch, should the crisis escalate, by voicing his disapproval of a general war in the Empire.

James appointed the firmly Protestant Lord Doncaster to carry out his efforts at mediation, who arrived in Germany in June 1619, to find both sides preparing for a wider war.[133] Ferdinand seemed disinclined to heed pleas for compromise, probably, Doncaster believed, because Spain or Rome egged him on.[134] Doncaster therefore sympathized with Frederick's claim that "the Protestant party" was never "since their first establishment neither in so much danger nor in such apprehension." He thought the ecclesiastical princes intended to start a

---

[129] TNA SP94/23, fols. 48, 57v, 58; cf. Cottington's similar report in *Relations*, ed. Gardiner, 1.3.
[130] TNA SP84/86, fol. 163; *CSPV* 15.204.   [131] Wilson, *Thirty Years War*, 281.
[132] *CSPV* 15.359.
[133] For Doncaster's mission see Malcolm Smuts, "International Politics and Jacobean Statecraft," in *Oxford Handbook of John Donne*, ed. et al., 589–99.
[134] BL Add Mss. 36,444, fol. 101; *Relations*, ed. Gardiner, 1.164.

"war of religion" with Spain's assistance.[135] The Union was preparing an army under Frederick's command, intending to send it to the Upper Palatinate, near the Bohemian frontier, for employment "according as occasion shall offer."[136] Doncaster wrote to Buckingham, urging him to use his influence to persuade the king to send assistance "of men or money or, if that was refused, a special emissary to speak "*à cheval* to Ferdinand."[137] He also urgently requested further instructions about how he should conduct himself if Ferdinand remained "obstinate."[138]

The Princes of the Union had meanwhile written on their own to James, demanding that he honor his alliance with them by sending aid. He responded in early July with another evasive letter, exhorting them to do everything in their power to counter the mounting threats to German Protestantism by "the common enemy," but protesting that since they had not yet been directly attacked their appeals for assistance were premature. His position as a mediator in any case prevented him from taking sides, although he wished to assure them that if, through his mediation, the Bohemians accepted a reasonable settlement that Ferdinand refused to implement he would not abandon his co-religionists. More ominously, he added that if the princes were themselves attacked he would honor his obligations by sending troops to assist them, but that they would need to lend him the money to pay his soldiers, since he had none available for the purpose.[139]

Despite this thinly veiled warning, Frederick and his allies pressed ahead with military preparations, as the fighting in Bohemia continued. The rebels escalated the conflict by passing a resolution in August 1619, rejecting Ferdinand as their king and initiating a search for his replacement. They argued in justification that Bohemia was an elective monarchy legally entitled to depose its rulers. This was a questionable but defensible claim, since the Bohemian estates traditionally enjoyed the right to ratify the succession of a new king, although the crown had normally descended through primogeniture and had belonged to the Habsburgs for several generations. Anticipating the Bohemians' move in advance, Doncaster predicted that it would put an end to all mediation and that his mission therefore had no chance of success. He prepared to leave Germany in late August, "thoroughly discontented" with Ferdinand and the Spanish ambassador to the imperial court, Oñate, whom he blamed for escalating the conflict.[140] From Madrid, Cottington reported that although the Spanish still hoped for a mediated

---

[135] TNA SP84/86, fol. 62.   [136] TNA SP81/16, fols 52, 56v.
[137] Ibid., fol. 56; *Relations*, ed. Gardiner, 1.120 is a printed copy.   [138] TNA SP81/16, fols 64–5.
[139] Ibid., fol. 101; *Relations*, ed. Gardiner, 1.150–1 (printed copy): "s'il advenait que, l'entremise de notre dit ambassadeur ayant fait condescendre les Bohémiens à l'acceptation des conditions justes, c'est assavoir que soient raisonnables et sur pour eux, le roi Ferdinand refusant de se mettre à même raison de son côté, en ce cas nous sommes résolus et promettons de ne point abandonner ceux de notre profession, mais d'agir à bon escient pour les secourir et défendre."
[140] Wilson, *Thirty Years War*, 282–3; TNA SP81/16, fols. 164v, 170, 335v; BL Add Mss. 36,444, fol. 110; *Relations*, ed. Gardiner, vol. 2, Camden Society OS 98 (1868), 1.

settlement they were pressing ahead with warlike preparations "in all parts" to assist Ferdinand if negotiations failed.[141]

In two conversations with Caron in September, James expressed sympathy for the Bohemian cause but declined to commit himself to specific actions. He reported with apparent approval that the Bohemians stood "strong and fast" by their resolutions and had put "XXV [25,000?]" men in the field, and that his son-in-law was coming to their aid with another "XV [15,000?]." He expressed pleasure that the Dutch had sent the Bohemians aid and said he wanted to show his own "great inclination" not only for his son-in-law but the "common welfare of Germany and religion." But he resisted taking precipitous steps since, unlike the Dutch, he did not have an army ready for deployment and because winter was drawing near, making him confident that he had time to sort out the facts and determine the best means of helping his "children" and allies. "I am also a king and must remain fast and true in my words and actions," he added. He wanted a fuller explanation of why the Bohemians felt entitled to depose Ferdinand and elect Frederick in his place, so that he might help them in a manner consistent with his honor and reputation. But he approved of the United Provinces sending assistance.[142] True to form, he encouraged the Dutch to aid the rebellion while keeping his own options open, invoking his honor and commitment to legality as excuses for inaction.

The rebels hoped to elect as their new king the Lutheran duke of Saxony, the Transylvanian prince Bethlen Gábor, or even the duke of Savoy, who had agreed to help Frederick raise cavalry in northern Italy, at the suggestion of the English ambassador in Turin.[143] When all three candidates declined the honor, the Bohemian estates offered the crown instead to Frederick V. He immediately wrote to James urgently asking his advice, but then accepted the offer before receiving a reply. Historians have generally regarded this as a rash decision by a prince "who found it hard to distinguish between the possible and the probable."[144] But Doncaster had advised Frederick to accept the crown *without* consulting James, so that the king might tell Ferdinand and the Spanish that he had no part in the decision. Rather than seeking a specific endorsement, Doncaster suggested, the elector should rely on James's "wisdom and magnanimity," along with his paternal "love" to motivate him to "extend his hands to the sustaining of that cause into which" Frederick's "zeal" and "desire to be an instrument of God's glory had embarked him."[145] Although James's ambassador exceeded his

---

[141] TNA SP94/23, fol. 226.
[142] BL Add Mss. 17,677 I, fols. 442v and 446r–447v. The first conversation occurred in James's coach as he traveled to Bagshot with Prince Charles, Buckingham, and Caron.
[143] Wilson, *Thirty Years War*, 283–4; *Relations*, ed. Gardiner, 1.168. James approved this scheme, ibid., 2.4.
[144] Wilson, *Thirty Years War*, 284.   [145] *Relations*, ed. Gardiner, 2.48.

instructions in giving this advice, Frederick had some excuse for believing he had been given private encouragement to expect his father-in-law's support.

But when James heard of Frederick's decision he publicly and angrily disavowed it. Historians have generally taken him at his word, concluding that his respect for royal legitimacy, aversion to war, and desire for the Spanish match determined his attitude. While this view probably contains some truth, the king's actual motives were almost certainly more nuanced. The French ambassador in London reported hearing speculation, which he felt inclined to believe, that James was playing a double game as he waited to see if Frederick's adventure succeeded. If it did he would abandon the Spanish match and embrace the Protestant triumph in Germany, whereas if Frederick failed he would continue his role as a mediator.[146] As we have seen, Gondomar shared this view.[147] He believed that James disapproved of Frederick's act less on grounds of principle than because he doubted his son-in-law's ability to defend his new royal title against the forces that Ferdinand and Spain would raise against him. James also mistrusted Bohemian Protestants, regarding them as fickle and prone to quarrels with each other. By embracing their cause so unequivocally, Frederick had bought trouble. The king's public expression of principled scruples about Frederick's action therefore almost certainly masked more practical reservations. His defensive alliance with the Protestant Union had also boxed him in. It obligated him to defend his allies against an aggressor but not if they started a war without just cause. Raising questions about the legitimacy of the Bohemian revolt gave him an excuse, should he need it, to desert his German allies. It also preserved his claim to act as an impartial mediator, free to bargain away Frederick's claim to the Bohemian crown in return for concessions on other issues.

But since neither Frederick nor Ferdinand seemed prepared to compromise, James's efforts at mediation soon became irrelevant, as both parties gathered soldiers, sought allies, and tried to deliver a decisive blow. The rapid and complete collapse of Frederick's position after the Battle of White Mountain outside Prague in November 1620 has fostered an impression that his cause was doomed from the outset. But this was far from self-evident before the event, particularly in the previous year. Although the Bohemian rebels were weak and divided and the Protestant Union suffered from hesitations and internal disagreements, Ferdinand's position looked even more precarious. He had limited resources and faced revolts not only in Bohemia but also in his hereditary lands of Inner Austria, where Protestants held a majority among both the nobility and the people. In the summer of 1619 the intervention of the Hungarian Calvinist Bethlen Gábor, at the head of an army of 35,000 men, momentarily gave the Bohemian coalition the upper hand, allowing them to drive imperial forces from

---

[146] TNA PRO31/3/53, fol. 35.   [147] Above, p. 609.

their own territory and lay siege to Vienna.[148] These successes increased the widespread excitement that Frederick's elevation had already aroused among English Protestants, generating unwelcome pressure on James to join the great Protestant offensive. The French ambassador, the comte de Tillières, reported that "the puritans of this country make great celebration of this election... They say that Bohemia will not be the end of this affair but that the empire will follow." His Tuscan counterpart, Amerigo Salvetti, commented on the "prayers for their new king of Bohemia" in London churches, which James soon prohibited, and the constant talk "of this populace, with demonstrations of passionate affection," which the king also tried to restrain.[149] Londoners anxiously awaited news of Frederick's coronation and Gábor's progress, Salvetti reported, except for Catholics, who bemoaned the state of Germany. Although James prohibited his subjects from lighting bonfires in honor of his son-in-law's coronation, London's churches celebrated by tolling their bells.[150] "They think that milord the elector already has the imperial crown on his head," Tillières observed in December. Developments in Bohemia increased pressure on English Catholics, "because this people want to make it an affair of religion and want almost by force to compel this prince to do the same."[151]

Many courtiers and members of the council shared this enthusiasm. Caron reported in September 1619 that most great nobles at the court favored aiding Frederick, including Buckingham, the earl of Pembroke and even the normally pro-Spanish earl of Arundel.[152] In January Prince Charles "showed himself wonderfully affectionate" to the Bohemian cause and wished his father would act on its behalf. The prince's Scottish secretary, Thomas Murray, wrote to Doncaster that "I hope that God will work that in the public cause of Germany and Bohemia, which great princes do neglect."[153] James had to adjourn a meeting of the privy council to prevent it from advising him to assist the new king of Bohemia, causing resentment among its senior members.[154] "The greater part of these lords of the council and all the Scots run violently more than ever as Bohemian partisans and press his Majesty to give aid and assistance to his son-in-law," Salvetti reported in early December 1619.[155] About the same time Tillières wrote that Archbishop Abbot, Sir Henry Wotton, and Sir Thomas Edmondes, "all three great puritans," had rejoiced at Frederick's election while guests of a Frenchman residing in London. They hoped the new king of Bohemia would "batter the horns of the Pope and that the time had come to sacrifice the beast of the Apocalypse and ruin

---

[148] Wilson, *Thirty Years War*, 289–91.
[149] TNA PRO31/3/53, fol. 39v; BL Add Mss. 27,962 A, fols 217r, 220v.
[150] Ibid., fols 229r, 234v–235, 237v.   [151] TNA PRO32/3/53, fols. 61v, 62.
[152] BL Add Mss. 17,677 I, fol. 448v.
[153] *The Court and Times of James I*, 2 vols, ed. Thomas Birch (London, 1848), 2.182.
[154] Ibid., 188, 191; BL Add Mss. 17,677 I, fols 14v–15.
[155] BL Add Mss. 27,962 A, fols 241v–242.

Babylon." When their host objected that such talk would unite the Catholic princes of Europe, including the king of France, behind the emperor, Wotton angrily replied: "he wouldn't dare do anything and if he did we have two hundred thousand swords in France that will not neglect our service as soon as their king stirs."[156] Frederick's successes stoked Protestant war fever in London.

The magnitude of Ferdinand's predicament increased pressure on Spain and other Catholic states to come to his rescue, although it was by no means a foregone conclusion that they would do so. For a decade Lerma had resisted deep involvement in the affairs of the Empire and he continued to oppose intervention in Bohemia until his departure from the Spanish court. By contrast Zúñiga, who had previously served as Spain's ambassador to the emperor, argued forcefully that Spain had no choice but to intervene. Otherwise he predicted a domino effect, by which the Bohemian revolt would lead to a systematic assault on the Austrian Habsburgs by Protestants, Catholic adversaries like Savoy, and Gábor's patrons, the Ottomans. Without support, the dynasty's position in the Empire would collapse and the Spanish monarchy would soon come under attack as well. These arguments ultimately prevailed, probably helped by Philip III's sense of dynastic loyalty.[157] Ferdinand's discomfiture had meanwhile induced him to offer highly advantageous terms to Maximilian of Bavaria, if he would revive the Catholic League, which had dissolved in 1617, and employ it in the current dispute. The emperor promised to reward Maximilian with Frederick's electoral title and any lands belonging to Frederick or his allies that his army conquered. He might also retain possession of Catholic territories his forces occupied until the expenses of his campaign had been fully repaid. In addition, Maximilian secured a promise from Spain that Spinola would invade the Lower Palatinate along the Rhine, to prevent Frederick from using his army to attack Bavaria from the west as the Bavarian army moved eastward toward Bohemia. These agreements guaranteed that the conflict would spread beyond Bohemia and Austria, quite likely ending only with the complete victory of one or the other side.[158]

As the 1620 campaigning season approached, most interested parties, apart from the main protagonists, continued to act cautiously because they did not want a major war and feared the consequences of joining the losing side. Carleton noted in November 1619 that although the Catholic princes of Germany were arming they still claimed to do so only for their own defense. If "the new king of Bohemia [is] strengthened by himself and supported by his friends," he predicted, the Catholics "will, in all appearance, sit still." But if Frederick's cause once started to falter "they will then strive who shall show himself first for the House of

---

[156] TNA PRO31/3/35, fol. 59: "il fut interrompu par le dit chevalier Wotton qui commença en colère à dire il ne l'oserait faire et s'il l'avait entrepris, nous avons deux cent mille épées en France, qui ne dégaineront pour notre service dès que le roi branlera."
[157] Cuerva, *Zúñiga*, 390–5. [158] Wilson, *Thirty Years War*, 294–9.

Austria."¹⁵⁹ Although Frederick's allies in the Protestant Union made some preparations, a Dutch observer believed that unless they received assurances of British assistance they would begin to withdraw their support for the Bohemians.¹⁶⁰ No one seemed certain what James would do if his diplomatic balancing act collapsed, forcing him to choose between inaction or open support for Frederick and his allies. Even the earl of Pembroke misjudged the situation. Although "I believe the king will be very unwilling to be engaged in a war if by any means with his honor he may avoid it," he confided to Carleton, "yet I am confident when the necessity of the cause of religion, his son's preservation and his own honor calls upon him that he will perform whatsoever doth belong to the defender of the faith, a kind father-in-law and one careful of the preservation of that honor which I must confess by a kind of misfortune hath long laid under a kind of suspense."¹⁶¹

James continued trying to avoid an unequivocal stand by resorting to half-measures. Despite his protests about the dubious nature of Frederick's claim to the Bohemian throne, he tried to help his son-in-law through the sort of indirect methods that he had previously employed to assist the Dutch and that Elizabeth had used to aid continental Protestants before 1585. He authorized a levy of voluntary soldiers for the Protestant Union and thanked the Dutch when they promised to assist Frederick.¹⁶² Sir Andrew Gray attempted to recruit 1,500 Scots and 1,000 English to join the fight.¹⁶³ His recruiters publicly insulted Gondomar by beating a drum before his London residence, but their the call to arms yielded disappointing results.¹⁶⁴ "Our drums beat daily about the streets for the raising of men for this new service, but I hear of no great confluence," John Chamberlain wrote to Carleton in late June: "Our 4000 men are fallen to 2000 . . . and yet for this number here is such sharking and sharing and such a deal of discontent that I can scant promise myself any hope of success."¹⁶⁵ The paltry results led Gondomar to quip that he "must needs confess we are a very brave nation that dare adventure with 2,000 to encounter 10,000" enemies.¹⁶⁶ James permitted Sir John Seton to lead the Scottish regiment he commanded in the Dutch army, consisting of 1,200 veterans, to Bohemia. Although British forces arrived too late to participate in the battle at White Mountain, Seton's troops did hold out in Bohemia until 1622.¹⁶⁷ The veteran general Sir Horace Vere departed with another 2,250 British troops to defend the Rhineland Palatinate against Spinola. Like Leicester and Essex in the

---

¹⁵⁹ *Letters from and to Carleton*, 422–3.   ¹⁶⁰ TNA SP84/92, fol. 129v.
¹⁶¹ TNA SP14/110/81, Pembroke to Carleton, November 24, 1619.
¹⁶² TNA SP81/17, fol. 25; SP84/92, fol. 69v.   ¹⁶³ BL Add Mss. 17,677 K, fol. 34.
¹⁶⁴ BL Add Mss. 27,962 A, fol. 276v.
¹⁶⁵ *The Letters of John Chamberlain*, 2 vols, ed. Norman Egbert McLure (Philadelphia: American Philosophical Society, 1939), 2.307.
¹⁶⁶ Ibid., 310.
¹⁶⁷ Steve Murdoch and Alexia Grosjean, *Alexander Leslie and the Scottish Generals of the Thirty Years' War, 1618–1648* (London: Pickering & Chatto, 2014), 41–3.

previous century, he managed to attract a number of men of high rank to serve under him.[168] In all, a recent study has concluded that Britain contributed between 6,000 and 7,000 men to the Palatinate's defense, about a quarter of the troops engaged in the operation.[169] Salvetti reported efforts by the London clergy to encourage donations of money to support the cause. But an appeal in June for contributions from the provinces encountered resistance as an irregular measure sanctioned by neither the king nor a parliament.[170] In October Chamberlain reported on "the many projects propounded" to raise money, including efforts to pressure the wealthy into making substantial voluntary contributions.[171]

These measures failed for much the reason that Elizabeth's efforts to aid European Protestants without going to war had previously broken down: private volunteer companies and voluntary contributions never produced sufficiently impressive results to counter the military resources that Spain and other Catholic states poured into the contest. As it became clear that this would be the case, James's refusal to commit himself to war discouraged other Protestant states. During the summer of 1620 the military balance shifted to favor Ferdinand and his allies, who began an offensive that moved from Austria into Bohemia, while Spinola simultaneously overran much of the Lower Palatinate with 19,000 men. James protested loudly, saying that although he would not take sides in the dispute over Bohemia he was bound in honor to defend the patrimony of his daughter and son-in-law. But the Spanish ignored his threat, correctly assuming that he would not follow through.[172] The decisive defeat of Frederick's forces at White Mountain outside of Prague on November 8, 1620 led to the collapse of his position not only in Bohemia but elsewhere, as Bavarian troops overran the Upper Palatinate, while the Spanish remained in occupation of most of the Lower Palatinate, apart from a few fortified cities that still held out. The prominent role of Maximilian's army in these victories and the fact that it had seized not only portions of Frederick's patrimony but also lands belonging to Ferdinand that had gone over to the revolt, greatly increased Bavarian leverage. Ferdinand would find it extremely difficult to back away from his promises to sanction the wholesale dispossession of the Elector Palatine.

This catastrophe backed James into a corner that was partly of his own making. If he had consistently and forcefully sought to restrain his allies throughout the crisis, he might have dissuaded Frederick from taking the enormous risk of accepting the Bohemian crown, while increasing his credibility in Madrid and

---

[168] TNA SP14/116/1, Rowland Woodward to Francis Windebanke, July 2, 1620: "The captains are all or the most part lords and the companies will be filled with gentlemen."
[169] BL Add Mss. 36,444, fol. 136; Wilson, *Thirty Years War*, 322, Table I; Adam Marks, "Recognizing Friends from Foes: Stuart Politics, English Military Networks and Alliances with Denmark and the Palatinate," in *Stuart Marriage Diplomacy*, ed. Caldari and Wolfson, 173-85 at 181.
[170] BL Add Mss. 27962A, fols 282v, 292, 300v-301.
[171] *Chamberlain Letters*, ed. McLure, 2.320.
[172] BL Add Mss. 36,444, fol. 220; TNA PRO30/53/3, fols 115, 132.

Vienna as a constructive mediator. Instead, whether deliberately or by design, he left his son-in-law guessing about his attitude toward the Bohemian crisis until after the die had been cast. His support for maneuvers to block Ferdinand's election as emperor in 1618, Doncaster's obvious sympathy for the Protestant Union, and the support Frederick received from British volunteer soldiers undermined the king's claims to act as a neutral party, especially in the eyes of the imperial court and its resident Spanish ambassador, Oñate.[173] On the other hand, if James had given Frederick more open and substantial military support, other Protestant states would likely have done so as well, possibly averting the disaster of White Mountain. Of course, none of this is certain: even decisive leadership might not have restrained the rush to war in Central Europe or averted a Protestant defeat. But by failing to make entirely credible attempts either to prevent the war or to win it, James ended up looking disingenuous, irresolute, and ineffectual, diminishing his credit in both Catholic and Protestant camps.

He now had to face a choice similar to Elizabeth's in 1585, between abandoning his Protestant allies when their very survival appeared imperiled, or sending a large royal army to their rescue, at enormous cost and at the risk of provoking a retaliatory attack on his own kingdoms. The dilemma divided opinion within the court, but as in 1585 there was strong and vocal support for military action, if not in Bohemia then at least in defense of Frederick's hereditary lands. Even Cottington and Digby, who had alternated as James's ambassadors to Spain, shared this view.[174] Tillières thought that enthusiasm for the Spanish match had cooled after Spinola's invasion of the Palatinate: James complained "that the Spanish are fraudsters," while Charles, at the instigation of "puritans" in his entourage, asked his father to break off negotiations for his marriage.[175] The king nevertheless continued to prevaricate, much to the frustration of his allies. From The Hague, Carleton reported being "daily assailed with interrogatories" about James's intentions. The Dutch thought the salvation of what remained of the Palatinate depended on his resolution and wanted assurances that he would join with them before they committed their own army to its defense.[176] James rejected their plan for a diversionary attack on Flanders as dishonorable, since it would have meant a direct breach of his amity with Spain, but he told Caron in December that he had resolved to send an army of 20,000 men to the Palatinate itself.[177]

---

[173] For Oñate's criticism of Doncaster's bias see his letter to Olivares of February 28, 1621, reproduced in Biblioteca Digital Hispánica (bne.es), bdh-rd.ben.es/viewer.vm?id=0000141358&page-1, accessed May 12, 2022.

[174] BL Add Mss. 36,444, fol. 126; TNA PRO30/53/2, fol. 11. Cottington commented shortly after the catastrophe of White Mountain that the Spanish would try to keep James neutral, "which for my own part I conceive will be a thing very difficult for him and almost impossible to abandon his children in time of such extremity."

[175] BL Add Mss. 27962S, fol. 229v; TNA PRO31/3/53, fol. 60.

[176] *Letters from and to Carleton*, 431.

[177] BL Add Mss. 17,677 K, fols 77v–78, 85, 87 and Add Mss. 36,444, fol. 220.

In March 1621 the king's brother-in-law, Christian IV of Denmark, also urged action. "By God this business has gone too far to think it can be reduced with words only," he told James's ambassador: We "do find that of necessity one of these two things we must do, either to go with the emperor and let Marquis Spinola do what he please in the Palatinate and to those of the Union and their neighbors what he likes best (which will be grievous and dangerous to us) or else we must of necessity join our strength and forces, with the Majesty of Great Britain, the princes of the Union and the estates of the Low Countries, which we think is our safest and best course."[178] Together with his allies he promised to raise 30,000 men. James talked of adding 10,000 British troops as his contribution, while in June Caron reported that the earls of Southampton, Oxford, Essex and Lord Willoughby had begun recruiting volunteer soldiers in London and Westminster, which they intended to lead to Zeeland.[179] The king had meanwhile appointed a war council of veteran officers that recommended sending "a royal army" of 25,000 foot and 5,000 horse to Germany with twenty pieces of artillery, at an estimated initial cost of £258,740, plus £76,064 a month for as long as the campaign lasted.

James summoned a parliament that convened on May 4, 1621 in hopes of increasing his bargaining leverage by securing a grant of money to make his threats to go to war more credible. But since he still did not want a breach with Spain he had to perform a delicate balancing act that quickly ran into trouble. Although the Commons initially refrained from demanding an end to negotiations for the Spanish match, it petitioned for stronger legislation against Catholic recusants. Knowing that Spain would strongly resent any such measures James demurred, causing anger that probably encouraged the Commons to begin investigations into abuses of monopolies at court, potentially threatening the royal favorite, Buckingham.[180] Although James wanted to distinguish between the Emperor Ferdinand, with whom he said he might be willing to go to war, and the king of Spain, many in the Commons saw the House of Austria as a unified entity directed from Madrid. They favored a war of diversion involving the use of British sea power against Spain in the Atlantic and perhaps an attack on the coast of Flanders, in preference to a land war in Germany. The Dutch also favored this strategy, while Gondomar feared it.[181] "Although the king of England is poor," he warned his superiors, "his realm is very rich and full of treasure and has in London

---

[178] TNA SP75/5, fol. 235v.
[179] BL Stowe Mss. 176, fol. 179v (a memorandum on the proposed British–Danish alliance drawn up for the duke of Bouillon) and Add Mss. 17,677 K, fol. 149, Caron dispatch of June 29.
[180] Questier, *Dynastic Politics*, 398.
[181] On support for an oceanic war see Simon Adams, "Spain or the Netherlands: The Dilemmas of Early Stuart Foreign Policy," in *Before the English Civil War, Essays on Early Stuart Politics and Government*, ed. Howard Tomlinson (Basingstoke: Macmillan, 1988), 80–3 and Thomas Cogswell, *The Blessed Revolution: English Politics and the Coming of War, 1621–1624* (Cambridge: Cambridge University Press, 1989).

alone more than two hundred men who in eight days can put to sea an armada of ships and men, and most desire to do so."[182] But the blue water diversionary strategy rested on premises that made much less sense in 1621 than they would have three years earlier. Its proponents assumed that since the Austrian Habsburgs and their allies were too poor and weak to wage war without Spanish help, Spain might easily control them. While that might have been true in 1619, the decisive result of White Mountain, the wealth subsequently confiscated from Bohemian and German Protestants, and the rise of the Bavarian army, which now numbered 30,000 soldiers, had transformed the situation.

As is well known, during a second session in November the Commons, after receiving a misleading signal from Buckingham's client George Goring, petitioned James to break off negotiations for the Spanish match. This infuriated the king, who ended the parliament, sacrificing any hope of receiving further supply for the planned campaign to liberate the Palatinate. In the end none of the forceful measures James promised his allies reached fruition. That effectively sealed the Palatinate's fate, as Maximilian's army seized the few remaining parts of the elector's hereditary lands not already occupied by hostile forces. James's empty threats and broken promises made him appear not only weak but dishonest, cowardly, disloyal to his own kin, and indifferent to the fate of his co-religionists. In early 1621 the king had complained to Frederick that his ambassador, Baron Dohna, injured his honor by spreading reports that he had failed to live up to assurances made at the beginning of the troubles in Bohemia.[183] But since it was public knowledge that Dohna's charges were essentially true, his recriminations simply stated out loud what many people already believed.

Louis XIII's campaigns against the Huguenots compounded the damage by inflicting another calamity on the Protestant cause that James did nothing to prevent. A French diplomat debarking at Dover in June 1621 found 200 Huguenot refugees in the town, "complaining marvelously of the persecutions they had undergone." Six months later an Englishman commented that there were "few tides" that did not bring more Huguenot refugees to the Kentish port. Although the "better able" moved on to London many remained behind, "so that their numbers are growing somewhat great, and there being this day come over certain ministers with about fifty persons of the church of Dieppe, they desire me that on certain days they may have use of our church," a request that was soon granted.[184] A survey undertaken in October determined that Dover then sheltered 270 Huguenot exiles, including two clergymen and several merchants.[185] Bouillon and the deputies of La Rochelle both sent envoys to London, while du Moulin considered moving his family to England to escape the calamity in his own country. Huguenots enjoyed substantial support in Britain. "The ministers no

[182] *CDIHE Gondomar* 2.102–3.
[183] LPL Mss. 667, fol. 27.
[184] TNA SP14/121/70 and 122/8.
[185] TNA SP14/123/70.

longer preach the Word," the French ambassador reported in July 1621: "their text is France and the misery suffered by their brethren beyond the sea, over which they excite the people not only against France and French Catholics but even against their own king."[186] According to Salvetti, Scots were especially active in lobbying James to aid the Huguenots with arms.[187] The king responded by sending an envoy to La Rochelle, authorizing another voluntary collection of money in English churches that eventually netted £10,000, and instructing his ambassador in France to try to mediate a settlement.[188] But none of this stopped the French civil war. Corsairs based in La Rochelle began disposing of prizes in English ports, eliciting French protests that resulted in a royal order to stop the sale of seized cargoes.[189] Local authorities in Plymouth and other southwestern ports nevertheless appear to have assisted the maritime forces of La Rochelle under the duke of Soubise, by helping them obtain supplies and recruit English volunteers.[190] James also seems to have furnished the duke with ships.[191] As the French crown prepared a fleet to attack Soubise, an admiralty official in the southwest demanded instructions about what to do if the Huguenot fleet attempted to put in at Plymouth.[192]

The fact that the French crown and the Habsburgs had launched virtually simultaneous attacks on Protestants, just as the truce between Spain and the United Provinces neared its expiration date, created a sense of impending war and crisis on a scale unprecedented since 1603. It also made it very difficult for the British crown to support the Protestant cause in one part of Europe without appearing to sacrifice it in another, unless it was prepared to take on both of Europe's great Catholic monarchies simultaneously. This problem would bedevil royal policy for the remainder of the decade. Negotiations for Anglo-French cooperation in checking the Habsburgs broke down in 1623 over James's refusal to promise that he would not aid Huguenot rebels. His strained relations with France presented yet another disincentive to break with Spain.

Fortunately, he still had some leverage in negotiations with Madrid, because Spain had decided to renew its war with the United Provinces. The experience of the 1590s had taught the Spanish that they lacked the resources to fight the English and Dutch simultaneously, making it imperative that James at least remain neutral as fighting resumed in the Netherlands. Spain had not been a

---

[186] BN Mss. Français 15,989 fols 74, 88, 101, 105v, 122v; BL Egerton Mss. fol. 94.
[187] BL Add Mss. 27962B, fols 52v, 53v–54.
[188] BL Add Mss. 27,962 B, fols. 102r, 136v; Trumbull Mss. 7, fol. 60 (LC microfilm 041/Camb/195/2).
[189] TNA SP14/122/24 and 124/39.   [190] BN Mss. Français 15,989, fols. 277, 307, 327.
[191] BL Stowe Mss. 176, fol. 244, Edmondes(?) to duke of Bouillon: "Vous aurez pu savoir le malheur arrivé à monsieur de Soubise pendant qu'il attendait le vent à Plymouth, (où il est encore par la perte qu'il y a fait de quatre de ses vaisseaux fournis d'hommes et de provisions, qui sont péris dans le port par la violence d'une tempête extraordinaire) P S[?] À quoi supplie sa Majesté lui a fait fournir deux ou trois bons vaisseaux de cet rivière, outre les deux qu'elle lui avait auparavant bailler des siens qui sont chacun de 6 à 700 tonneau."
[192] TNA SP14/128/21.

party to Ferdinand's compact with Maximilian and Spanish statesmen saw no reason to compromise their own strategic interests to serve Bavarian ambitions. Once Ferdinand's position had been secured, Zúñiga wanted to disengage from the war in the Empire. He hoped to secure a treaty allowing for Spanish evacuation of the Palatinate in return for Frederick's submission to Ferdinand, and in order to propitiate James he also tried to prevent the emperor from transferring the Palatinate's electoral title to Maximilian. The Spanish were therefore not being entirely disingenuous in telling James that they wanted to satisfy his demands for a restitution of his son-in-law and that they disapproved of Maximilian's action in invading the Lower Palatinate and seizing Frederick's capital of Heidelberg in September 1622.[193] But Maximilian now held most of the Palatinate and Ferdinand remained dependent on his Bavarian ally. Pope Gregory XV also favored the transfer of the electoral title as a way of strengthening the Catholic position in the Empire. His ambassador told Ferdinand that failing to take this step would imperil his soul. Frederick's refusal to listen to James's advice and give up the fight—he joined the army of the German mercenary general Mansfeld in 1622 and continued to style himself king of Bohemia—also impeded a settlement.[194] It is therefore hardly surprising that Ferdinand resisted Spanish pressure by formally transferring Frederick's lands and electoral title to Maximilian at the Diet of Ratisbone in February 1623, another stinging defeat for James's diplomacy.

Although the Spanish government might have been prepared to make concessions to keep Britain from allying with the Dutch, it lacked the ability to impose its priorities on Ferdinand and Maximilian, whose armies were now driving events on the ground. In the face of Bavarian and imperial intransigence, the restoration of the Palatinate would have required at least a credible threat of Spain turning its forces against its own Catholic allies. Although the Spanish actually promised Digby that, if necessary, they would take this step, it was never a realistic prospect.[195] But to forestall British action detrimental to their own interests, Philip's ministers decided to spin out negotiations over both the Palatinate and the proposed marriage alliance for as long as possible.[196] They blamed Ferdinand and Maximilian for delays in restoring Frederick's lands and electoral title, insisting that they were working to resolve the problem.[197] They put the onus

---

[193] Trumbull Mss. 23, fols 131 and 133, Digby to Trumbull, September 18 and October 8, 1622 (LC microfilms 041/Camb/203/2).

[194] For the content of this paragraph see, esp., Cuerva, *Zúñiga*, 504–14.

[195] BL Add Mss. 48,166, fols 95, 100v, 103; TNA SP94/25, fol. 166. James told Caron in May 1621 that "the king of Spain has promised me by his letters written in his own hand," that if Frederick was persuaded to abandon his claims to Bohemia, Spain would restore the Palatinate and all his honors, and that if Philip IV cheated him in this matter he would break off negotiations for an alliance and go to war (BL Add Mss. 17,677 K, fols 132–3).

[196] Porfirio Sanz Camañes, *Diplomacia Hispano-Inglesa en el siglo xvii* (Cuenca: Ediciones de la Universidad de Castilla-La Mancha, 2002), 45–6, 56.

[197] TNA SP94/25, fols 1, 7v, 141v, 166; Trumbull Mss. 23 (Library of Congress microfilm 041/Camb194/2), fols 129, 130, 131, 133.

for delaying Charles's marriage to the infanta on the pope, expressing displeasure over his "unreasonable" demands for a complete toleration of British Catholics in return for the required dispensation. For the most part they succeeded in convincing the British ambassadors in Madrid, Digby and Sir Walter Aston, of their sincerity, although Digby briefly became disillusioned and advised breaking off negotiations in late 1621, telling Prince Charles that it would be better if he "should take to wife some Protestant princess" even at the cost of sacrificing a large dowry.[198] But Digby again grew more optimistic the following year, after receiving further Spanish assurances of good will, while in December Aston wrote that "we do understand the Match absolutely concluded here [Madrid]."[199] Gondomar's influence at the British court reached unprecedented heights. Tillières wrote in early 1621 that James and Buckingham "showed themselves more and more Spanish." Gondomar was no longer "simply an ambassador but one of the first councilors of state of the kingdom, being day and night at Whitehall where the most secret deliberations are not only communicated to him but they receive his counsels and follow them fairly precisely."[200]

By this time James had little choice but to trust Spanish professions of good will, since the only alternative was to start a war that he knew he lacked the resources to fight. But many of his subjects, including outspoken clergy, high ranking members of the court, and several of his leading diplomats, had long since concluded that the Spanish were deluding him. In late summer 1618 a minister preached a sermon against the match before a large auditory at Paul's Cross in London, attacking it, along with the pope and king of Spain, so vehemently that even "the very heretics were scandalized," or so Van Male claimed.[201] Carleton remarked to Trumbull in July 1620 that the Habsburgs "would continue our master in the way which he likes so well of negotiation, whilst they in the meantime provide for action."[202] A few months later he complained that despite "the secret designs and inward thoughts of our enemies tending to the utter ruin and destruction of our best friends, we will rather credit their [enemy] professions to the contrary and willingly give way to their known artifices."[203] "There is none so blind as him that will not see" another English diplomat, Simon Digby, wrote about the king in the same period.[204] Charles's chaplain, George Hakewill, preached a series of sermons denouncing the match and corruption within the royal court and then compiled a

---

[198] BN Mss. Français 15,989, fol. 168; Trumbull Mss. 7, fol. 32 and 23, fol. 152 (Library of Congress microfilms Camb/195/2 and Camb/203/2); BL Add Mss. 27962B, fol. 94.
[199] Trumbull Mss. 23, fols 136, 167 (Library of Congress microfilms Camb/203/2).
[200] BN Mss. Français 15,989, fols. 21v, 39v: "Gondomar qui n'est pas seulement ambassadeur main un des premiers conseillers de ce royaume, étant de jour et nuit au palais de Oulitalle où les conseils les plus secrets lui sont non seulement communiquer main on reçoit les siens et les suit on assez précisément."
[201] HHStA Belgien 49, fol. 207r, dispatch of September14, 1618.
[202] Trumbull Mss. 13, fol. 53 (Library of Congress microfilm 041/Camb200/3).
[203] Ibid., fol. 83.   [204] Trumbull Mss. 23, fol. 42 (Library of Congress microfilm Camb/203/2).

book against popish idolatry, ostensibly based on James's *Basilikon Doron*, which he presented to the prince.²⁰⁵ According to one contemporary report, James spotted his son reading the book, sent for Hakewill

> and asked him what he meant to abuse his authority and meaning, telling him that [in *Basilikon Doron*] he meant not the idolatry of the papists but the heathen. And after this in the presence of diverse bishops the king disputed with Hakewill before them, still observing the countenance of the bishops until one of them who is not named demanded of Hakewill how he could prove that the papists were idolaters, to whom Hakewill answered that he little expected that any bishop in England should ask such a question ... Why then, quoth Hakewill, look to your own canons, in such and such a canon and there you shall find it expressly defined wherein the papists do commit most detestable idolatry. With this both the king and the bishop were silent.²⁰⁶

Hakewill's temerity cost him his chaplaincy.

Other ecclesiastics, including Bishop Joseph Hall, also got themselves into trouble for speaking out against the match in sermons at court or in prominent London pulpits.²⁰⁷ In December 1621 James instructed the bishop of London to prohibit clergy from attacking the match from the pulpit.²⁰⁸ "The puritans are half-enraged by this order," one of Gondomar's correspondents commented, "saying publicly that the king is popish."²⁰⁹ The minister of St Martin's-in-the-Fields, John Everard, was imprisoned for defying it.²¹⁰ The earl of Oxford was also incarcerated, reportedly for saying that James "was but the king of Spain's vice regent and that his prerogative would absorb all the liberty of the kingdom."²¹¹ A letter attributed to Archbishop Abbot, criticizing James for helping "to set up the most damnable and heretical doctrine of the Church of Rome, the Whore of Babylon," circulated in manuscript. One copy found its way into the papers of Charles's Scottish secretary, Thomas Murray, another critic of the match who lost his post in a purge of Charles's entourage in 1621.²¹²

---

²⁰⁵ Peter McCullough, *Sermons at Court: Politics and Religion in Elizabethan and Jacobean Preaching* (Cambridge: Cambridge University Press, 1998), 194–204.

²⁰⁶ Folger Shakespeare Library Mss. X.d502/10. A different version of the story, in which Charles took Hakewell's book to his father, ignoring the warning of his secretary Thomas Murray not to do so, is in *CSPD* 10.284. My thanks to Jamie Reid Baxter for calling this to my attention.

²⁰⁷ Folger Shakespeare Library Mss. X.d502/10; BL Add Mss. 27962B, fols. 147r, 150r; BN Mss. Français 15,989, fol. 359v; Trumbull Mss. 7, fol. 102 (Library of Congress microfilm Camb/195/2); TNA SP14/110/71.

²⁰⁸ BL Add Mss. 27962B, fol. 110v.

²⁰⁹ TNA SP94/25, fol. 137, Vaumage to Gondomar, July 19, 1622: "les puritains sont demi enragés, disant publiquement que le roi est papiste."

²¹⁰ He would later recount this incident in John Everard, *Some Gospel Treasures Opened* (London, 1653), "Epistle to the Reader."

²¹¹ Trumbull Mss. 7, fol. 54 (Library of Congress microfilm Camb/195/2); cf. TNA SP14/122/21.

²¹² LPL Mss. 943, fol. 79.

The king's resentment of criticism had a dampening effect on the speech of courtiers and crown servants. A friend warned Trumbull not to include anything in his dispatches that seemed to question the wisdom of James's policies, since it was now regarded as "a kind of treason to make any ill interpretation [of] his Majesty's deep and judicious courses."[213] But the government proved incapable of stifling dissenting voices beyond the court. Sir Simonds D'Ewes, then a student at the Inns of Court, wrote in his diary "that daily more and more libels were dispersed, in which did plainly appear the misery of a discontented and most daring people."[214] Gondomar received death-threats in 1620 and his embassy suffered an attack by a London crowd the following year.[215] The appearance in July 1622 of a Latin tract supporting the marriage, entitled *Rosa Hispanica-Anglia*, greatly pleased the king, who ordered it translated into English but it was a rare exception amidst the torrent of criticism.[216]

As negotiations dragged on James—and to an even greater degree, Charles and Buckingham—grew increasingly impatient. The prince had long felt greater sympathy for Frederick's cause than his father: Caron had found him "wonderfully well-affected" (*wonderbaer geaffectioneert*) to the "Bohemian business" in January 1620 and still eager to help his brother-in-law maintain his title in November.[217] The fall of Heidelberg provoked Charles to talk of leading an army to Germany. In an effort to clarify Spanish intentions the council first tried sending a Catholic groom of the prince's bedchamber, Endymion Porter, to Spain. Porter had served as a teenager in the household of the duke of Olivares's father, developing a friendship with the man who was now Philip IV's favorite and chief minister. It was hoped that he would therefore be able to probe Spanish intentions more effectively and speed matters along. But although Porter received more assurances of Spanish good will, he could extract no concrete agreements. A few months later, in March, Charles and Buckingham resolved to travel to Spain in disguise. Although historians have continued to speculate over the thinking behind this project, the most plausible explanation is that they wanted to assess the intentions of Philip IV and Olivares for themselves through face-to-face negotiations, instead of relying on the reports of Digby, Aston, and Gondomar. They probably hoped that Charles would succeed in flushing out Spanish intentions by demanding direct access to the infanta, something the Spanish would

---

[213] Trumbull Mss. 7, fol. 101 (Library of Congress microfilm Camb/195/2).
[214] *The Diary of Sir Simonds D'Ewes, Journal d'un étudiant Londien sous le gègne de Jacques Ier*, ed. Elisabeth Bouchier (Paris: Didier, 1974), 135.
[215] BL Add Mss. 27962A, fol. 352v and B, fol. 7v; TNA SP14/98/18.
[216] BL Add Mss. 27962B, fol. 170v. For a brief discussion of the iconography of this tract see Erin Griffey, "The Materials of Marital Diplomacy: Henrietta Maria's Trousseau," in *The Age of Rubens: Diplomacy, Dynastic Politics and the Visual Arts in Early Seventeenth-Century Europe*, ed. Luc Duerloo and R. Malcolm Smuts (Turnhout: Brepols, 2016), 197–212 at 199–200.
[217] BL Add Mss. 17,677 K, fols 15r and 68, dispatches of January 14 and November 14.

have considered highly improper unless they genuinely regarded him as her fiancé.

But for everyone beyond his inner circle, the prince's journey added another layer of confusion and anxiety, spawning rumors that he would soon convert to Catholicism and fears that the Spanish might hold him hostage. "All the world wonders greatly at [this voyage]," Caron remarked, "and makes very strange constructions about it, none of them good."[218] In the short run Charles's presence in Madrid appeared to further diminish Britain's ability to resist Spanish pressure for more concessions. Even James felt frustrated and humiliated by the situation. Tillières predicted that Spanish prevarications would exacerbate jealousies, ultimately embroiling Britain and Spain in deeper conflict. Although English Catholics would pay a price for this, France would profit.[219] Two months later he reported that James had made a speech to the privy council saying that he had "lost honor, love and reputation" in seeking "the marriage with Spain" and found "himself at present despised [*méprisé*] by foreigners and shamed in his own kingdom."[220] In writing to Charles and Buckingham he began by praising their actions but soon changed his tone, calling them inept [*malhabille*] and saying that now that the Spanish had Charles they "might salt him and eat him, since he [James] did not lack an heir and would send for his grandson from Holland," referring to the son of Frederick and Elizabeth.[221]

In Madrid, Buckingham and Charles were becoming even more disillusioned, although Charles dissimulated his unhappiness.[222] They finally slipped away in October, determined to break off the match—which the Spanish at that point regarded as concluded—and prepare for war in what contemporaries called "a Blessed Revolution."[223] According to Caron, Charles paused at five in the morning while traveling from his landing place in Portsmouth, to send an express message to Archbishop Abbot, directing him to inform the lord mayor and aldermen of London of the prince's imminent arrival. He also asked Abbot to meet him as he approached the capital, with the result that Charles arrived at Buckingham's residence of York House in the archbishop's barge.[224] Given

---

[218] BL Add Mss. 17,677 K, fol. 244r: "Al de werelt is hier daerinne zeer verwonderd, ende maeken daerop wel vreemd construction, maer niemant eenig goed."

[219] BN Mss. Français 15,989, fol. 515r-v.   [220] Ibid., fol. 537.   [221] Ibid., fols 534v-535.

[222] A persuasive analysis is Brennan Pursell, "The End of the Spanish Match," *Historical Journal* 45 (2002): 699-726.

[223] The standard treatment is Cogswell, *Blessed Revolution*. Others include Roger Lockyer, *Buckingham: The Life and Career of George Villiers, First Duke of Buckingham* (London: Longman, 1981), chapters 5 and 6; Brendan Pursell, *The Winter King: Frederick V of the Palatinate and the Coming of the Thirty Years' War* (Aldershot: Ashgate, 2003), chapter 7; Glyn Redworth, *The Prince and the Infanta: The Cultural Politics of the Spanish Match* (New Haven: Yale University Press, 2003); and S. R. Gardiner, *Prince Charles and the Spanish Marriage, 1617-1623*, 2 vols. (London: Hurst and Blackett, 1869). Adams, "Protestant Cause," chapters 9 and 10 is a pioneering analysis that remains valuable.

[224] BL Add Mss. 17,677 K, fol. 315.

Abbot's reputation as an opponent of alliance with Spain and supporter of harsh treatment of English Catholics, this sent a very clear message.

As Thomas Cogswell and others have described in detail, Charles and Buckingham attempted over the next two years to build a "patriot coalition" in support of war with Spain, as they pushed James to initiate a conflict he still did not want.[225] Two of Buckingham's clients—viscount Doncaster, soon promoted in the peerage as earl of Carlisle, and Henry Rich, who received the title earl of Holland—went to Paris to negotiate a match between Charles and the French Princess Henriette Marie, in the expectation that this would lead to a military alliance. Preparations began to outfit a fleet to serve Frederick V by raiding Spanish commerce but soon stalled because James did not want them to go forward.[226] An infantry force was recruited to serve under the command of the mercenary general Count Mansfeld but remained stuck in England so long as the king lived. His death on March 27, 1625 finally removed the last impediment to war.

Peace and the Corruption of Religion and Virtue

Although controversy over the Spanish match and war in Europe centered partly on reactions to immediate events, it also intensified long-standing arguments that the Jacobean peace had produced a decline in religion and national virtue, for which the royal court was at least partly responsible. In many ways the origins of this perception stretched back even before James's accession, to at least the 1590s and the critiques of the Elizabethan court produced by Essex's circle. But the evident futility of James's European policies in the early 1620s, as Protestant fortunes collapsed on the Continent, breathed fresh life into old complaints about corrupt courts and weak monarchs, while adding new dimensions of criticism.

Contemporaries widely believed that societies had a natural tendency to degenerate during times of peace.[227] This view was connected to a cyclical theory of the rise and fall of states and empires that achieved greatness through vigorous military exertion, only to decline after security and prosperity sapped their

---

[225] See above, n. 223.

[226] BL Add Mss. 17,677 K, fols 348 and 352. Caron reported in May 1624 that preparations were proceeding "sleepily [slappelijk]."

[227] E.g. Barnabie Rich, *Faults, Faults, Nothing but Faults* (London, 1606), 53: As "peace breedeth plenty," Rich asserted, "so it armeth cape à pée all sorts of sins, and as war hath his associates, sword, fire, famine and murder, so peace hath his co-partners, pride, pleasure, idleness, lust, sensuality, drunkenness, gluttony, voluptuousness and so many enormities besides, as were but curiosity in me to hunt after. Peace draweth the very corruption of manners after it and there is nothing that brings so sweet and easy a subjection to vice as the season and idleness of peace."

peoples' capacity for sacrifice and public virtue. As Francis Bacon put it, "the arts which flourish in times while virtue is in growth are military; and while virtue is in state, are liberal; and while virtue is in declination are voluptuary: so I doubt that this age of the world is somewhat upon the descent of the wheel."[228] From here it was a short step to the sort of condemnation of James's reign that Thomas Scott's notorious pamphlet against the Spanish match, *Vox Populi*, attributed to Gondomar: "Their [English] bodies by long disuse of arms were disabled, and their minds effeminate by peace and luxury, far from what they were in [15]88, when they were daily fleshed in our [Spanish] blood and made hearty by customary conquests."[229]

This association of peace with effeminate luxury easily dovetailed into criticism of extravagance and venality at the royal court. In 1609 "a preacher, one Dr. Smith, head of a house in Cambridge...baited the great courtiers...for bribery and corruption and so schooled the king himself for being led by other men rather than by his own judgment and that so particularly and plainly that I know not how he hath escaped baiting himself."[230] Because courtiers had to spend very substantial sums of money on clothes, lodging, and other luxuries as they pursued their ambitions, they readily appeared as self-indulgent, venal people, incapable of dispassionate and honest service. "In courts...appetite directs," John Holles earl of Clare stated, "which as an antagonist to reason walks in all things obliquely, shunning the right line as a bat the daylight."[231] Because courtiers had to depend "upon another's will" to satisfy their appetites and ambitions, they had little capacity for independent action.[232] The fact that Gondomar was known to have distributed Spanish pensions among James's leading servants reinforced the perception of a court dangerously susceptible to corruption by foreigners. This lent credibility to Scott's claim in *Vox Populi* that although the English people generally hated the idea of a match with Spain, it drew support from Roman Catholics and "the begging and beggarly courtiers that they might have [money] to furnish their wants."[233]

Some contemporaries believed that the growth of the court had led to a rise in absentee landlordism by gentlemen lured to its vicinity, and an excessive concentration of riches in the hands of a small elite concentrated in London. Bacon argued that the concentration of wealth diminished a kingdom's ability to finance wars:

---

[228] Bacon, *Works*, 6.253 (*Advancement of Learning*, 2.x.13).
[229] Thomas Scott, *Vox Populi. Or Newes from Spain translated according to the Spanish copies* (London, 1620), 11.
[230] *Carleton to Chamberlain*, ed. Lee, 110.
[231] *Letters of John Clare Earl of Holles*, ed. P. R. Seddon, 2 vols. (Nottingham: Thoroton Society, 1983), 2.285.
[232] Ibid., 2.450.   [233] *Vox Populi*, sig. B2r.

Nothing is more certain than that those states are least able to aid and defray great charges for war or other public disbursements whose wealth resteth chiefly in the hands of the nobility and gentleman. For what by reason of their magnificence and waste in expense, and what by reason of their desire to advance and make great their own families and again... because they are fewest, small is the help, as to levies and charges that can be levied or expected from them towards the occasions of a state. Contrary it is of such states whose wealth lies in the hands of merchants, burghers, tradesmen, freeholders, farmers in the country and the like, whereof we have a most evident and present example before our eyes in our neighbors of the Low Countries.[234]

If, as the second earl of Essex had argued, a willingness to sacrifice superfluous luxuries to support war proved a country's virtue, then the accumulation of wealth and luxury among a small court elite during times of peace demonstrated the opposite.

Such reasoning made it possible to blame the wealth and extravagance of the court and the king's generosity in rewarding his Scottish friends and favorites like Buckingham for the crown's inability to mount effective military campaigns. As George Wither put it, early in Charles I's reign:

> Hence comes it that rents and royalties
> Of kings and princes, which did well suffice
> In former times to keep in comely port
> An honor'd and hospitable court
> (Yea and an army if occasion were)
> Can hardly now the charge of household bear.
> For they must either in their large expense,
> Come short of that profuse magnificence
> Among the vassals: or else waste away
> The price of many lordships to defray
> The cost of one vain supper.[235]

Wither exaggerated, since the cost of military expeditions far exceeded that of even the most lavish court banquets. But James did spend nearly £100,000 on his daughter's wedding in 1613, while expenditures by major courtiers on banqueting, building, and clothing reached levels that created an appearance of massive waste. Rubens would comment in the late 1620s that English courtiers invariably spent beyond their means, so that all were heavily in debt. The highly visible luxury of the court fed perceptions of James's reign as an age of voluptuous luxury and

---

[234] Bacon, *Works*, 6.60.
[235] *Britain's Remembrancer, containing a narration of the plague lately past* (London, 1628), 366–7.

social inequity, in which common tenants were squeezed as the warlike virtues of the old English nobility and gentry decayed. As Drayton summed up: "The pride in court doth make the country lean, / The abject rich hold ancient honor mean."[236]

The decay of honor and undervaluing of virtues that honor should properly reward was another fault commonly laid at the court's doorstep. "I can serve you, not after the manner of these mountebanks of our time, our greatest courtiers, but really according to the plain dealing of our ancestors, who overthrew their enemies at Agincourt and Flodden," John Holles wrote to a friend in November 1616.[237] Courtiers were mountebanks of honor because they relied on ostentatious display rather than real merit to win recognition. Some had acquired titles they did not deserve, so that they outranked men whose birth and actual worth far exceeded their own. The English found the bestowal of such honors on Scots and their sale by favorites like Somerset and Buckingham, who had themselves been catapulted to the top of the social hierarchy by a royal whim, especially galling. In March 1621 Tillières reported that the ceremonial precedence over English earls awarded to a number of recently created Scottish viscounts had given rise to a protest drawn up in private assemblies at the houses of the earls of Salisbury and Dorset, demanding that the Scots' titles be annulled and that in the future James should be "more reserved in giving such things, which greatly alienate the hearts of his subjects and cause them to lose the desire to do well because the rewards of virtue are distributed by money or favor." Buckingham, who had been responsible for the new creations, reacted by accusing Salisbury and Dorset of opposing the royal prerogative and himself, saying he had hitherto regarded them as friends but now saw his mistake.[238] Although for the moment the dispute remained detached from arguments over foreign policy, the perception that James had abused his right to confer titles of nobility in order to reward political subservience damaged his credibility, making it easier to question his judgment in other matters.

Jacobean complaints about the debasement of honor again echoed the charges that Essex and his followers had leveled against Elizabeth for listening to "base" courtiers rather than noble men of action. But while Elizabeth had been parsimonious in distributing the knighthoods and titles of nobility, James notoriously was not.[239] The inflation and venality of honor during his reign contributed to a perception that the king and his entourage presided over the systematic corruption of moral values that had once made the English a valorous people. This became an explicit issue in the Parliament of 1621, when several peers, including Essex's son, the third earl, and his friend Southampton introduced a "Petition of

---

[236] "The Owle," in *The Works of Michael Drayton*, ed. William Hebel, vol. 2 (Oxford: Shakespeare Head Press, 1941), 512.
[237] *Letters of Holles*, ed. Seddon, 2.146.   [238] BN Mss. Français 15,989 fol. 38.
[239] Lawrence Stone, *The Crisis of the Aristocracy* (Oxford: Clarendon Press, 1965), chapter 3.

the Nobility of England," complaining about the sale of honors and indiscriminate creation of new titles of nobility.[240] Although aimed most directly at Buckingham, it implicitly questioned James's conduct and reportedly infuriated him.[241] Salvetti reported in March that the king felt it necessary to address the Lords in an effort to quell by his presence "the torrent of violent spirits in both houses that begin to show signs of attacking not only the marquis of Buckingham but a good part, if not all of the royal prerogative."[242]

In many respects, criticism of James around 1620 therefore showed marked continuities with the analysis developed by Essex's circle two decades earlier, involving depictions of England as a state debilitated by a weak monarch, surrounded by corrupt and sycophantic courtiers, who allowed conditions to develop in which private wealth and luxury mattered more than public virtue. But there were also new elements in the picture, including increased emphasis on parliaments as agents of reform and national rejuvenation, and a corresponding belief that conflicts between kings and parliaments, often fomented by courtiers, impeded the body politic's capacity to recover its health. Whereas Essex had seen his conflict with his enemies in essentially personal terms, by the 1620s political controversy had acquired a more pronounced institutional dimension. This reflected a belief that since selfish private interests had taken over the court, distorting the king's judgment with bad advice, the state required rescue by disinterested representatives of the people.

The perceived role of parliaments as advocates of reform encouraged a belief that courtiers would try to sabotage them by misleading the king into thinking that their protests against misgovernment were attacks on the crown. In some ways this idea also had deep roots. The notion that Machiavellian courtiers had set out to delude the monarch and corrupt the whole system of royal governance had a long pedigree, stretching back to the early Elizabethan period and beyond.[243] But unlike in the Elizabethan period, these evil counselors were now pictured as trying to overthrow not only virtuous rule but the institution of parliament itself, along with common law protections that secured the subject's property from arbitrary seizure. James and some members of his council developed an equally sinister interpretation of the court's parliamentary critics, as a band of factious demagogues, "persons desirous to be remarkable and valued and esteemed above all others for their zeal, wisdom, learning, judgment and experience [who] have

---

[240] Richard McCoy, "Old English Honour in an Evil Time: Aristocratic Principle in the 1620s," in *The Stuart Court and Europe: Essays in Politics and Political Culture*, ed. R. Malcolm Smuts (Cambridge: Cambridge University Press, 1996), 133–55, esp. 144–6. See also Neil Cuddy, "The Conflicting Loyalties of a 'Vulger Counselor': The Third Earl of Southampton, 1597–1624," in *Public Duty and Private Conscience in Seventeenth-Century England: Essays Presented to Gerald Aylmer*, ed. John Morrill, Paul Slack, and Daniel Woolf (Oxford: Oxford University Press, 1993), 122–50.
[241] McCoy, "Old English Honour," 141.   [242] BL Add Mss. 27962A, fol. 422r.
[243] Peter Lake, *Bad Queen Bess? Libels, Secret Histories, and the Politics of Publicity in the Reign of Elizabeth I* (Oxford: Oxford University Press, 2016).

presumed to use in the lower house publicly very audacious and contemptuous speeches against the king's royal prerogative and power and his most gracious and happy government."[244] The two opposing interpretations fed on each other, since public awareness that the king and some of those close to him had come to mistrust parliaments increased anxiety that the crown would try to free itself from parliamentary interference.

James's cultivation of better relations with Spain added another, even more ominous layer of suspicion and fear. After the dissolution of the Addled Parliament the king was reported to have sent John Digby to tell Gondomar "how troubled and disgusted he was at the parliament and its evil proceedings; that the king needed to choose a side to which he might betake himself; that he wished to know" if Philip III "would be his firm and true friend." Gondomar naturally encouraged the king to think he could rely on Spain if he broke with the parliament and turned against "the puritans."[245] Whether this exchange actually took place as recorded, it appeared plausible because everyone knew that James's worries over money and difficulties with parliaments had increased his incentive to seek a large Spanish dowry, and that many of his courtiers enjoyed Spanish pensions. The idea that the king and some of those on his council, whose sympathy for Catholicism was also widely known or suspected, might betray the country and its church to the enemy therefore seemed to make sense. "Neither the king nor the late queen [were] ever in that danger by open violence or secret conspiracy as now by private whisperings," Sir William Walter asserted after a report that the bishop of Lincoln had slandered the House of Commons in 1614. "These men that should ring in his Majesty's ears the holy oracles of God did whisper nothing but sedition."[246] Archbishop Abbot told William Trumbull that "there want not some who studiously keep off parliament; it is more commodious for them to want them [parliaments] than to have them." He associated this attitude with the crown's "extreme want of money," and even more with a moral confusion within the political nation that left the kingdom vulnerable to the insidious influence of its principal foreign enemy. "The minds of our people are distracted at home and the adversary insulteth over us and scorneth us abroad, besides the secret machinations which they practice upon us, and we lie asleep as Jonas did in the storm… We are enchanted by the false, fraudulent, siren-like songs of Spain."[247] The perceived venality and moral decadence of the court,

---

[244] Louis Knafla, *Law and Politics in Jacobean England: The Tracts of Lord Ellesmere* (Cambridge: Cambridge University Press, 1977), 257; cf. Noah Millstone, "The Politic History of Early Stuart Parliaments," in *Writing the History of Parliament in Tudor and Early Stuart England*, ed. Paul Cavill and Alexandra Gajda (Manchester: Manchester University Press, 2018), 172–93.

[245] *Narrative of the Marriage Treaty*, ed. Gardiner, 286–7.

[246] *Proceedings in Parliament 1614*, ed. Maija Jansson (Philadelphia: American Philosophical Society, 1988), 343, 351.

[247] Trumbull Mss. 1, fol. 16 (Library of Congress microfilm Camb/194/1), Abbot to Trumbull, August 31, 1614.

threats to the Protestant cause in Europe, dismay over the king's strained relations with parliaments, and a belief that the common law was in danger of subversion all came together in a picture of impending doom.

A parallel evolution is evident in the handling of specific charges of corruption and malfeasance by royal servants. In themselves such charges were by no means novel. They regularly featured in the charges that rival crown servants lodged against each other in the late sixteenth century: the Elizabethan state papers for Ireland and the correspondence of people like Thomas Digges are full of them. But for most of the Elizabethan period such complaints rarely reached parliament or figured prominently in public discourse. This began to change toward the end of the queen's reign, with the heated controversies between Essex's supporters and adversaries and the debate over monopolies in the 1601 Parliament. Complaints about extortion by crown purveyors then erupted in the first parliament of James's reign. But not until 1621 did charges of bribery and corruption in a parliament bring down a major government official, Lord Chancellor Bacon. The examination of abuses of monopoly in 1621 also brought about the revival of the fifteenth-century procedure of impeachment, through which the Commons investigated wrongdoing and drew up charges for presentation to the Lords. Once re-established, impeachment became a weapon used by Prince Charles and Buckingham to attack Lionel Cranfield and the earl of Bristol in 1624, and then by Buckingham's enemies to attack him in 1626 and 1628. Parliament's vaguely defined duty to give the king sound advice while combating corruption in his entourage had gained definition through a procedural mechanism that rapidly became a weapon of political combat between rival court factions. Disputes among privy councilors with opposing views on policies toward European conflicts spilled onto the floor of the House of Commons, through *ad hominem* attacks on individuals accused of corrupting the moral fiber of the state.

The inescapable religious implications of both the Spanish match and the war with Spain that followed its collapse added to this pattern. A Spanish dynastic alliance appeared to threaten England's religion and liberties not only by making the infanta queen consort and the mother of future heirs to the throne, but because many of its strongest supporters on the council were Crypto-Catholics, or at least people with Catholic relatives. Buckingham had a Catholic mother, while Bristol's papist kin included a Gunpowder Plot conspirator. The growing influence of such people and simultaneous loss of favor by strong Protestants like Sir Robert Naunton and George Abbot in the early 1620s looked ominous to people worried about the subversion of reformed religion.[248] The predictably

---

[248] For Naunton's fall, caused by an indiscreet discussion with a French gentleman about a possible alternative to the Spanish match, see BN Mss. Français 15,989, fol. 23v; Trumbull Mss. 7, fol. 21 (Library of Congress microfilm Camb/195/2). Abbot remained archbishop of Canterbury but lost influence.

vociferous opposition to the match by men regarded as puritans induced James to shift his support to anti-puritan churchmen like bishops Andrewes, Overall, and Richard Neile, who were far less critical of his policies.[249] Revealingly, these figures were soon labeled Arminians, a label associated not only with heterodox views about predestination but an alleged previous conspiracy to weaken Dutch religion, so as to facilitate a peace with Spain on terms that would jeopardize the survival of the United Provinces. Calling people like Andrewes and Neile Arminians implied that they would now do something similar in Britain. Although it is not clear how quickly this view spread beyond fairly narrow circles among the godly, it eventually gained considerable traction, most notably in the Parliament of 1629 and ultimately the Grand Remonstrance of 1641.[250]

While some contemporaries reacted to James's European policies by focusing fairly narrowly on questions of Britain's strategic interest, others saw his refusal to beak with Spain as symptomatic of much more fundamental problems of moral, political, and religious corruption. At the time of the Blessed Revolution, people who agreed in wanting an end to the Spanish match and to initiate a new war with Spain might nevertheless differ in how they explained the attraction of James and a section of his court to a Spanish alliance. A comparison of the two most famous pieces of anti-Spanish publicity of the period, Thomas Scott's *Vox Populi* (1620) and Thomas Middleton's *A Game at Chess* (1624) may further clarify the issues at stake. The two works resemble each other in numerous ways. Scott's pamphlet amounts almost to a closet drama, presenting a report on England to a fictitious meeting of the Spanish council of state, while Middleton's is an actual play that enjoyed an enormously successful run on the London stage. Both highlight the duplicitous role of Gondomar in deluding James and subverting the British state, while depicting Jesuits, English Catholics, and Englishmen who secretly help Spain without becoming openly Catholic as his assistants. But they ultimately depict the story of the Spanish match in very different ways. Middleton treats it essentially as a factional contest within the court allegorized as a chess game, whereas Scott develops a picture of pervasive deformities within the English body politic extending well beyond the court that Gondomar successfully exploited but did not ultimately cause.

The main action in *Game at Chess* turns on acts of deception and intended seduction by the black knight (Gondomar) and his allies, and their unmasking by the white knight (Prince Charles) and white duke (Buckingham). By contrast Scott begins by having his fictitious Gondomar boast that English Catholics have long since transferred their allegiance from their own prince to the king of Spain. They

---

[249] For Neile and his followers see Nicholas Tyacke, *Anti-Calvinists: The Rise of English Arminianism, c. 1590-1640* (Oxford: Oxford University Press, 1987), chapter 5.
[250] Conrad Russell, *Parliaments and English Politics, 1621-1629* (Oxford: Oxford University Press, 1979), chapter 7.

have fallen under the influence of the Jesuits, the secret agents of Spain's "invisible kingdom," consisting of "unknown subjects in all dominions, who will show themselves and their faiths by their works of disobedience when so ever we shall have occasion to use that Jesuitical virtue of theirs."[251] If she becomes queen of England the infanta will have no need to create a fifth column of Spanish sympathizers, since that column already exists. She will simply have to serve as its figurehead and facilitator, by helping Catholics and Spanish sympathizers further infiltrate the court and royal administration. This will be easy, Scott's Gondomar claims, because in England all offices in the state and Church are already "for money exposed to sale," and Catholics are eager "to contribute largely of their estate to the Spanish collector," to provide a slush fund with which to purchase them.[252] In reply to an objection that English people who have not succumbed to Jesuit influences will resist a Spanish take-over in the way that they did in 1588, Gondomar replies that this will not pose a serious problem because "their bodies by long disuse of arms were disabled and their minds by peace and luxury effeminated."[253] He then boasts that he has turned James against parliament by exploiting dissension in the last session, which he managed to blame on puritans, although it was actually fomented by Catholics.[254] In any case parliament will never truly represent the people of England because the freeholders that choose members vote "to please their landlords and renew their leases," and therefore elect members selected by "great persons," rather than men who truly represent the interests of the community.[255] And if a session should nevertheless begin to investigate abuses "there are so many about him [the king] who blow this coal fearing for their own stakes, if a parliament should inquire into their actions that they use all their art and industry to withstand such counsels, persuading the king he may rule by his absolute prerogative."[256]

Nothing in Middleton's play contradicts the idea that by unmasking Spanish deception Charles and Buckingham have resolved the problems caused by James's misguided diplomacy and set the nation on the right path. On the other hand, Scott's pamphlet suggests that even if Gondomar and the Spanish match were to vanish, comparable threats to religion and English independence will continue to arise so long as the root causes of the kingdom's vulnerability continue to exist. The contrast points to the challenge Charles and Buckingham faced as they returned from Spain, intent on reversing James's policies and leading Britain into Europe's wars. They initially received heroes' welcomes from a populace that gave every outward appearance of wanting to follow their lead. They succeeded in putting together a coalition of pro-war peers and politically active gentry that held together over the next seventeen months, as they pushed ahead with military preparations and diplomatic initiatives to create a great European alliance

[251] Scott, *Vox Populi*, sig. A4v. [252] Ibid., B2r. [253] Ibid., B2v.
[254] Ibid., B3r. [255] Ibid., B3v. [256] Ibid.

against Spain. James fought a rear-guard effort to impede the outbreak of hostilities, until his death, shortly after the conclusion of a dynastic alliance with France. But starting a war proved much easier than winning it, and as frustrations accumulated mistrust of Buckingham and of Charles revived. Whether he realized it or not, in going to war with Spain Charles had set himself the formidable task of confronting the structural weaknesses of the British crowns and the legacy of mistrust and jealousy of the court that had built up over more than a generation. It is not in the least surprising that by doing that he provoked a serious political crisis that exposed various forms of dysfunction within the British state, in ways that intensified and solidified long-existent sources of division.

13
The Problem of Religious War and the Structure of Politics at the Accession of Charles I

Thirteen years after James's death the state in Scotland started to unravel amidst massive resistance to Charles I's effort to impose a Prayer Book on the Kirk. This led to a wider crisis with pronounced religious dimensions that over the next three years destabilized England and then Ireland, culminating in a collapse of royal control that plunged all three kingdoms into civil wars. This book was never intended as a direct contribution to the enormous and enormously contentious controversy over the causes of this upheaval.[1] But a few concluding comments seem appropriate concerning ways in which the developments we have examined structured the political environment in which Charles's reign unfolded. That reign saw two significant crises, near its beginning in the late 1620s and again after 1638, separated by several years of apparent peace and stability. Each crisis, along with the relative calm between them demand analysis.

Young Kings, Religious Wars, and the Rule of Favorites

Charles I inherited the throne at age twenty-five, determined to overcome the jealousies and divisions that he blamed for weakening Britain during his father's reign, and to reassert the reputation of his crown throughout Europe. In this he

---

[1] For general studies of Charles and his reign see, among many other books and articles too numerous to list, David Cressy, *Charles I and the People of England* (Oxford: Oxford University Press, 2015); Richard Cust, *Charles I: A Political Life* (London: Longman, 2005); Kevin Sharpe, *The Personal Rule of Charles I* (New Haven: Yale University Press, 1992). For the outbreak of the civil wars see John Adamson, *The Noble Revolt: The Overthrow of Charles I* (London: Weidenfeld & Nicolson, 2007); Michael Braddick, *God's Fury, England's Fire: A New History of the English Civil War* (London: Penguin, 2008), chapters 1–7; David Cressy, *England on Edge: Crisis and Revolution 1640–1642* (Oxford: Oxford University Press, 2006); Athony Fletcher, *The Outbreak of the English Civil War* (Caulfield: Anthony Arnold, 1981); Conrad Russell, *The Fall of the British Monarchies 1637–1642* (Oxford: Clarendon Press, 1991); Mark Charles Fissel, *The Bishops' Wars: Charles I's Campaigns against Scotland 1638–1640* (Cambridge: Cambridge University Press, 1994); Allan Macinnes, *Charles I and the Making of the Covenanting Movement 1625–1641* (Edinburgh: John Donald, 1991); Laura Stewart, *Rethinking the Scottish Revolution: Covenanted Scotland, 1637–1651* (Oxford: Oxford University Press, 2016); and David Stevenson, *The Scottish Revolution, 1637–1644: The Triumph of the Covenanters* (Edinburgh: John Arnold, 2nd ed., 2003).

broadly resembled his contemporaries, Louis XIII and Philip IV, who a few years earlier had also set out to revive the reputations of their monarchies after a period of perceived weakness and decline. Charles's succession contributed to a generational shift already underway, through which cautious older statesmen gave place to ambitious younger leaders, more prepared to take risks and confront head-on internal problems that hampered their ability to fight wars.

But to have any chance of reinvigorating his realm, a young king first needed to assert control of his own court and council, against the open or concealed resistance of older and more experienced political hands, who had their own ideas about how policy should be conducted, and their own priorities and agendas. While taking advice from more experienced ministers, he had to avoid losing his freedom of action by submitting too readily to their counsels. Louis, Philip, and Charles all responded to this challenge by relying on slightly older trusted confidants to act as the chief executors of their decisions. Although Buckingham never achieved a complete monopoly of Charles's favor, he dominated the new reign, just as Luynes dominated the French court between 1617 and 1622 and Olivares the Spanish court after 1623. In each case the new king and his favorite broke with the policies of the recent past to strike out with bold initiatives, and in all three kingdoms the transition proved highly contentious.[2]

Although widely resented among contemporaries and criticized by later historians, Charles's reliance on Buckingham in some ways therefore typified a wider pattern that might almost be described as a structural feature of European politics in the period.[3] The reasons for the king's partnership with his favorite are not difficult to understand. Lacking his father's long experience in maneuvering between rival factions and playing court politicians off against each other, Charles also disapproved of the dissimulation, evasions, and procrastination that James's way of governing required. He wanted to lead through actions rather than words and artifices, reaching decisions quickly and carrying them out boldly, as vigorous young princes were supposed to do. That was easier to accomplish by concentrating power in the hands of a single trusted supreme minister. Charles rightly perceived that attacks on Buckingham usually implied criticism of his own decisions, and that if he bowed to pressure to remove his favorite he risked opening the floodgates to further efforts to cajole and bully him into doing the bidding of other men. Rather than an absolute king he might then become a figurehead or "doge of Venice," something he wanted at all costs to prevent.

---

[2] Cust, *Charles I*, 78 makes the important point that Charles denied Buckingham an appointment as groom of the stole that would have given him nearly complete control over access to the bedchamber. Other court figures who continued to enjoy significant influence included the earls of Pembroke and Lennox.

[3] *The World of the Favourite*, eds J. H. Elliott and L. W. D. Brockliss (New Haven: Yale University Press, 1999).

But as also happened in France and Spain, the new king's reliance on his favorite intensified bitter factional conflicts already underway before his accession. The factional battles were even more venomous and ruthless in the two continental monarchies, especially France, than in Britain. Luynes and Louis established their control by having the previously dominant minister, Concini, murdered, his wife executed on trumped-up charges of sorcery, and the queen mother banished into exile. She and her chief counselor, the future Cardinal Richelieu, then fought their way back into power by leading two revolts. Charles's and Buckingham's assaults on James's Hispanophile ministers, Lionel Cranfield, John Digby earl of Bristol, and Thomas Howard earl of Arundel, appear almost civil by comparison. But the resulting disputes nevertheless generated considerable rancor that spilled over into Parliament and libels that circulated in the streets of London. In the Lords in 1626 Buckingham and Bristol accused each other of treason, with Bristol hinting darkly that the duke had murdered James I, a rumor that Spanish agents assiduously tried to spread.[4] Two prominent court nobles who had opposed the Spanish match and supported the Blessed Revolution, the earls of Pembroke and Lennox, also turned against the duke, as did the queen and her French household, acting on instructions from Paris. "They talk publicly of throwing him [Buckingham] in the river and saving the state by his death," Henrietta Maria's almoner wrote to his uncle, Cardinal Richelieu, in June.[5] After the Commons opened impeachment proceedings, Arundel told the French ambassador that if the king tried to save his favorite by dissolving the parliament he would be compelled within two months to "reassemble it or to see not only his affairs ruined but his house overturned."[6] Although the prediction did not come true, the fact that a senior nobleman who had served for years on the privy council made it shows just how acrimonious court politics had become.

Viewed solely within the context of English history, especially constitutional history, these recriminations look like extraordinary harbingers of fundamental conflict. But within a wider European perspective they again appear much less unusual. Deadly hatred of seemingly all-powerful courtiers, and conspiracies aimed at getting rid of them were normal features of European politics in the early seventeenth century, as indeed under personal monarchies in other periods, including ancient Rome and the Middle Ages. That is why Buckingham's enemies were able to tap into a long tradition of complaints about overmighty evil counselors, stretching back through medieval figures like Edward II's favorite, Hugh de Spenser to the infamous villain in Tacitus's *Annals*, Sejanus.

---

[4] *Proceedings in Parliament 1626*, ed. William Bidwell and Maija Jansson, 3 vols (New Haven: Yale University Press, 1992), 1.328; Alastair Bellany and Thomas Cogswell, *The Murder of King James I* (New Haven: Yale University Press, 2015).
[5] TNA PRO31/3/63, fol. 102.   [6] TNA PRO31/3/63.

But although intense conflicts over the role of royal favorites erupted in many early modern states, they played out in different ways, shaped by specific institutional structures and political traditions. Attacks on French favorites, such as Richelieu, took the form of palace conspiracies and noble revolts that continued a history of aristocratic dissidence stretching back to the wars of religion and beyond.[7] By contrast, assaults on Buckingham culminated in a parliamentary impeachment in 1626, which some members of the Commons tried to revive two years later. The difference reflected both the persistence in France but not England of seigneurial armies and semi-independent fortified towns, and the more aggressive role that early Stuart parliaments had gradually assumed in investigating malfeasance by royal ministers since 1621, along with the willingness of leading politicians, including Charles and Buckingham, to employ such proceedings to attack their rivals.[8] The heated controversy that raged around Buckingham was both typical in some ways of structural tensions that existed within systems of personal monarchy elsewhere in Europe, and a unique outgrowth of conditions peculiar to England in the 1620s.

Court Faction, Royal Leadership, and the Problems of Foreign Wars

In addition to the role of parliament, those conditions included issues relating to war with Spain and eventually also France. Initially many Britons saw the Spanish war as a resumption of the Elizabethan wars of the late sixteenth century. As such it carried considerable emotional and ideological freight. "It is wished to do all that is possible to renovate the ancient valor of this nation by taking up arms," Salvetti reported in June 1625, "and to induce neighbors to embark with it in the same action."[9] A fight with the old enemy would not only restore the ancient prowess of the English and Scots but enable them to construct and lead a grand European alliance against Habsburg aggression, as James had conspicuously failed to do. Although a seasoned French statesmen dismissed these aspirations as the sort of "vanities and sentiments" to which young kings and statesmen were prone, they appealed widely to a population accustomed to glorified images of Elizabethan

---

[7] Arlette Jouanna, *Le devoir de révolte: La noblesse française et la gestation de l'État moderne* (Paris: Fayard, 1989); Jean-Marie Constant, *Les conjurateurs: Le premier libéralisme sous Richelieu* (Paris: Hachette, 1987).

[8] TNA E403/2759, fol. 219r records a payment in January 1641 to Sir John Borough and his clerks by an order of May 1625 "for copies concerning attainders and other business to be used in this present parliament for his Majesty's especial service." Although the date of the payment at a critical time in the conflict between Charles and the Long Parliament raises suspicions, the entry clearly states the copying was carried out in 1625, suggesting that at the outset of his reign Charles wanted to gather ammunition for use against former ministers he wanted to bring down through parliamentary impeachments.

[9] Historical Manuscripts Commission, *Eleventh Report of the Commission on Historical Manuscripts* (London, 1887), appendix 4, part 1, 22.

martial heroism.[10] The belief that displays of English valor would enable the construction of a grand European coalition harked back, not so much to the cautious approach to war of Elizabeth and Burghley, as to the outlook of the second earl of Essex and other Elizabethan swordsmen like Sir Walter Ralegh. Charles and Buckingham shared Essex's belief in the importance of honor, reputation, and a strategy of leading by example through bold acts, as their rhetoric shows. "This being my first action," the new king proclaimed in his opening speech to Parliament in 1625, "all the eyes of Christendom will be upon me; and as I do in this, so it will get me credit and repute abroad and honor at home."[11] The lord keeper seconded his plea: "His majesty puts his fame, his reputation (which is all he hath as a king) upon us, not in desperation... but with greatest confidence."[12] The Parliament and the nation that elected it were being put to the test in precisely the way Essex had once urged, by a king who challenged his people to sacrifice for the common cause, just as he had sacrificed by contracting sizable debts to fund his fleets and armies. This implied that any refusal to grant adequate supply would amount to a betrayal of the king, the cause on which he had embarked, the honor of the crown and kingdom, and the Protestant religion. "Should it be said that by the forsaking of his subjects he has been forced to abandon religion, to seek for a dishonorable peace," pleaded Secretary John Coke.[13] "If we now grow cold," Viscount Conway warned, "the princes of Germany will divide, the king of France come in a party to the Catholic league, the king of Denmark make his peace with the emperor."[14] Similar arguments had once been used to dissuade Elizabeth from making peace, and to persuade James to take up the cause of the Bohemian rebels and Frederick IV. They were now redeployed to convince MPs of the need for new taxes.

In addition to obtaining supply, the king needed to mobilize and channel voluntary contributions to the war effort. Despite the long Jacobean peace, Britain did not entirely lack experienced soldiers and officers because significant numbers of English, Scots, and Irish had enlisted in continental armies. Although finally forced to surrender by a numerically superior enemy, Horace Vere's volunteer force had performed well in its defense of the Lower Palatinate only a few years before. The noble military retinues that had once formed the backbone of Tudor armies had disappeared by the 1620s, but the number of English peers with at least some military experience actually grew after 1603, approaching half of the total by 1605.[15] The Irish and Scottish nobilities were also highly

---

[10] AMAE, CPA34, Villeauxclercs to d'Effiat, April 22, 1625: "je dis vanités et sentiments, l'ambition fournissant les uns et le sang donnant les autres."
[11] *Proceedings in Parliament 1625*, ed. Maija Jansson and William B. Bidwell (New Haven: Yale University Press, 1987), 192.
[12] Ibid., 191.   [13] Ibid., 351, speech of Secretary John Coke in favor of supply, July 8, 1625.
[14] Ibid., 387.
[15] Roger Manning, *Swordsmen: The Martial Ethos in the Three Kingdoms* (Oxford: Oxford University Press, 2003), 17–19.

militarized.[16] Tenant loyalty and aristocratic influence remained sufficiently robust in all three kingdoms to make the support of militarized peers potentially significant in the crown's efforts to recruit motivated soldiers. In addition, a considerable segment of the mercantile community in London and other ports, along with a small number of peers and gentry, wanted to resume privateering.[17] The earl of Warwick assembled his own fleet of seven ships.

Like so much else at the start of Charles's reign, the task of harnessing these private resources behind the crown's war effort fell to Buckingham, who assumed the role of the court's chief military leader and patron of military men. In addition to directing the war and diplomatic relations with Britain's allies, he held the post of Lord Admiral, giving him a degree of control over military initiatives on both land and sea that not even Leicester or Essex had ever enjoyed. But unlike Leicester and even more than Essex, Buckingham lacked the advantage of an inherited family network of powerful allies and talented clients to support him in this role. He attempted to compensate by arranging the marriages of several close relatives into established noble families, and by using his control of royal patronage to build a clientage network. He made some progress: his loyal clients and allies included the earl of Dorset, who had married his sister; Warwick's younger brother the earl of Holland; a son of Viscount Manchester, Walter Montague; the Scottish peer and veteran diplomat, Carlisle; and for a time, several other peers. The third earl of Essex served as vice admiral of the fleet that attacked Cadiz in 1625, although the expedition's failure left him "badly satisfied with the voyage and its commander."[18] But Buckingham's ability to command the support of other British nobles remained tenuous due to wide resentment of his near monopoly of royal favor, the largesse showered upon him by the crown, and his promotion to the head of the peerage as England's only duke. The patriot coalition that he and Charles had constructed after their return from Spain remained fragile and disintegrated during the first year of the new reign. Rallying broad opposition to James's unpopular pursuit of a Spanish alliance proved far easier than building a durable and widely based coalition committed to supporting the considerable sacrifices that a major war entailed, and weathering the setbacks and disappointments that would inevitably occur once serious fighting commenced.

This was the more unfortunate because, even with a large amount of voluntary support from his subjects, Charles's objectives were going to be very difficult to achieve. Unlike Elizabeth, he had embarked not on a defensive war to defend his own kingdoms but an offensive one to restore the Palatinate. Britain lacked the resources to accomplish this task alone. The army of 14,000 men the crown had

---

[16] Ibid., 20–32.
[17] For the privateering interests of London merchants see Robert Brenner, *Merchants and Revolution: Political Conflict and London's Overseas Traders, 1550–1653* (London: Verso, 2003).
[18] AMAE CPA33, fol. 314, Blainville dispatch of December 20, 1625.

raised in 1624 and that Charles sent to the Continent the following year under the command of Count Mansfeld was considerably smaller not only than the armies of France and Spain but also of Bavaria. If deployed skillfully, in conjunction with larger forces supplied by British allies like France and Denmark, it might still have made a useful contribution. But without adequate coordination and sensible strategic planning it stood little chance of success. The alternative strategy advocated by some MPs, of fighting a diversionary war at sea, largely through privateering enterprises, was somewhat more realistic, since England's maritime resources remained formidable.[19] But to be truly effective, a blue water campaign would need to challenge Spanish power in the New World, where Spain possessed an infrastructure of fortified ports and local militias that Britain lacked. Plans for overcoming these disadvantages by seizing strategically located ports, choking Spanish trade routes, and forcing Spanish viceroys to redirect commerce toward England exist among the papers of the earl of Northumberland, Charles's lord admiral in the late 1630s.[20] They almost certainly reflect strategic thinking already underway a decade earlier. But implementing such schemes would have required large investments over a fairly lengthy period, and even if successful they would not have restored the Palatinate without an additional land campaign. A blue water strategy may have had its merits but by itself it did not offer a quick and affordable way of achieving Charles's goals.

Instead of concentrating their resources and energies on limited but achievable objectives, in 1624 Charles and Buckingham devised an enormously ambitious, multi-pronged strategy, which they attempted to carry out after James's death in March 1625. They first assembled a grand alliance that included the United Provinces and Denmark, whose king was promised a hefty subsidy to lead his army into the Empire, along with France. They prepared an army under Mansfeld to recover the Palatinate with the assistance of French cavalry, which they expected their ally to supply, and the help of the Danish army as it invaded from the North. Simultaneously, they tried to enlist Dutch help in an attempt to blockade the Spanish coast. In the autumn of 1625 they launched an amphibious assault on Cadiz, a port of little immediate strategic importance but considerable symbolic value because of its association with the great English triumph of 1596.[21] While unquestionably bold and comprehensive, this grand offensive depended to

---

[19] Cf. the motion of Sir Dudley Digges in the 1626 Parliament "for a war at sea, for defense and offense, by voluntary joint stock of adventures out of all counties of England to be encouraged by a settled course in Parliament, and by privileges to be granted to them without much prejudice to his Majesty's settled revenue." *Proceedings in Parliament 1626*, ed. Bidwell and Jansson, 2.279.

[20] The plans of the 1630s include the well-known efforts of the Providence Island Company, for which see Karen Kupperman, *Providence Island 1630–1641: The Other Puritan Colony* (Cambridge: Cambridge University Press, 1995). A number of additional schemes exist among the papers of Charles's Lord Admiral in the late 1630s, Algernon Percy earl of Northumberland. See Library of Congress microfilms 041 ALN 6, reproducing Alnwick Castle Mss. 14, fols 33v, 78r-v, 132–5.

[21] For the blockade project see AMAE CPA33, fol. 176v.

a perilous degree on the willingness of both English parliaments and Charles's European allies to follow his lead, and the expectation that a few initial successes would rally further support. It also required Britain to act as the leader of the Protestant cause throughout Europe, while simultaneously maintaining a cross-confessional French alliance.

Bold initiatives based on overly optimistic assumptions carry a very high risk of failure. By late summer, setbacks had started to accumulate, including the shambolic failure of Mansfeld's expedition, due in part to the French refusal to furnish the support that the British believed had been promised, and serious resistance to additional demands for supply in the Commons in August of 1625. The king and duke responded by minimizing difficulties and pressing on with their plans, since any other course would have required abandoning their stance of courage and resolution. After Parliament rejected a further grant of taxation, Charles told the French ambassador that "when his parliament grants him nothing he will not desert the league and that he had other resources." The ambassador wryly commented to his superiors that these resources were "so secret that one cannot discover them."[22] As the alliance with France started to fail in the autumn, Buckingham pretended not to care, boasting "of the greatness of English forces, the departure of the fleet [for Cadiz] and the strong understandings that he has with the Hollanders and the kings of Denmark and Sweden." He claimed that these strengths would soon compel the French to "have recourse to him."[23] In other words, he proposed to rely on a purely confessional Protestant league. Unfortunately, the Dutch remained cautions, plausibly fearing that the English would once again leave them to bear a disproportionate share of the costs of war, friction between the two Scandinavian monarchies kept Sweden on the sidelines, and Charles's financial problems prevented him from delivering his promised financial support to the king of Denmark.[24] In January 1626, after the further failure of the attack on Cadiz, Charles recalled 130 veteran sergeants from English companies serving the Dutch to "teach our train-bands all over England the use of arms, saying that he hoped by the grace of God's blessing and their industry England, within one half year, would be stronger by 100,000 men."[25]

The problems brought on by war stemmed *not only* from a lack of adequate revenues and inexperience in directing military campaigns, but the discrepancy between Britain's actual capabilities and a set of values and expectations rooted in experiences of the previous generation. Charles finally put to the test the claims of

---

[22] AMAE, CPA36, fol. 29: "Il dit hier à Tillières quand son parlement ne lui accorderait rien il ne se départirait point de la ligue, et qu'il a d'autres ressources. Elles son si secrete que l'on n'en peut rien découvrir."

[23] BN Dupuy Mss. 403, fol. 140.

[24] For Dutch skepticism, which had already begun to build before late 1625, see Adams, "Protestant Cause," 373–4.

[25] *The Court and Times of Charles I*, ed. Thomas Birch, 2 vols. (London, 1848), 1.74.

Essex, Ralegh, and some admirers of Prince Henry that Spanish power would quickly collapse under the onslaught of English valor, if only the crown gave free rein to the kingdom's swordsmen. He also relied on vague assurances repeatedly given by supporters of war that if he once broke unequivocally with Spain, parliaments would grant him the support he needed. Within a year of his succession it looked very much as if England had failed these tests. But precisely because of the way in which advocates of war with Spain, from the late Elizabethan period down to Charles himself, had presented it as a measure of the nation's virtue, religion, and honor, the lessons of that failure were too painful for many people to acknowledge. Rather than admit that English valor had proved inadequate and that the British crown lacked the ability to fight a major war without much higher levels of taxation, people preferred to look for scapegoats. And the scapegoating was again shaped by prejudices and assumptions rooted in the past. A society conditioned to believe in divine providence and collective punishment for sin readily found religious explanations for its defeats. Sir Robert Phelips proclaimed in Parliament in 1625 that the many "assaults upon the liberties of the people" within recent years "argue God to be our enemy, and that we must first make our peace with him or else in vain shall we send out armadas and maintain armies abroad."[26] Sir Nathaniel Rich agreed: "The Israelites could not prosper so long as the execrable thing was among them. We have as little hope of success as long as popish idolatry is so common."[27] If English fleets and armies returned home in defeat, lenient treatment of recusants was to blame.

These accusations pointed to a latent ambiguity in the rationale for war with Spain that soon turned into an additional political weakness. Charles presented the war as one fought to defeat Habsburg ambitions to establish a universal monarchy, a position that again harked back to Essex's arguments in the 1590s. It had the potential to incorporate the Protestant cause of resistance to Spanish and papal tyranny, while leaving room for cross-confessional leagues, especially the dynastic alliance with France. But in practical political terms this required promoting the war as a Protestant crusade to some domestic British audiences, while simultaneously working out delicate religious compromises with Catholic allies. The efforts of Charles and Buckingham to square this circle were further complicated by the fact that until James's death in March 1625 they needed the French alliance, since without it the old king would never have agreed to break with Spain or to jettison Hispanophile courtiers like Bristol and Arundel who had become the duke's enemies. For that reason, Buckingham's clients, Carlisle and Holland, found it impossible either to resist determined French demands or to obtain ironclad guarantees of support against the Spanish that the French did not wish to grant. They agreed to include secret clauses in the marriage treaty

---

[26] *Proceedings in Parliament 1625*, ed. Jansson and Bidwell, 397.   [27] Ibid., 414.

promising toleration for British Catholics and to lend the French a warship, ostensibly for use against the Spanish, that Richelieu actually wanted to employ against Huguenot corsairs based in La Rochelle. They also accepted nebulous verbal promises that the French would do what was necessary and appropriate to support their allies once war with Spain had commenced, that failed to commit Louis XIII and Richelieu to any specific actions. They avoided the contentious issue, of central importance to the French state, of how far and under what conditions the British crown would continue to support forceful Huguenot resistance to any further erosion of the liberties and privileges granted by the Edict of Nantes. Although Charles and Buckingham felt mounting frustration, impatience, and irritation with the French as the marriage negotiations reached completion, they dissimulated their displeasure by blaming relatively minor officials and preserving an appearance of excellent relations with Louis XIII and Richelieu.[28]

Beneath the surface, a number of latent tensions and unresolved questions therefore threatened to undercut the Stuart–Bourbon dynastic alliance from the beginning. Some of these quickly erupted into open view. The marriage treaty gave Henriette Marie the right to celebrate mass in her own household and to maintain a number of Capuchin monks, who regarded it as their duty to convert British heretics to Rome. Even more than these clergy, accurate suspicions about the treaty's secret articles promising toleration for English Catholics provoked complaints. "What the Spanish articles were we know," Phelips complained: "Whether those with France be any better is doubted. There are visible articles and invisible. Those we may see but these will be kept from us."[29] By late summer of 1625 Buckingham had grown sufficiently worried about the political costs of the French marriage to attempt to defuse the issue by privately telling MPs that he was prepared "to chase the French" attendants of the queen from England "and renew persecution of Catholics."[30] As during negotiations for the Anjou match nearly half a century earlier, a French dynastic alliance intended to bolster England's strategic position in a conflict with Spain aroused mistrust and anxiety because many Protestants saw it as a cover for secret designs to spread of popery within England.

Nevertheless, we should probably not exaggerate the significance of the queen's Catholicism in undercutting support for the king's policies. Most of the recorded complaints and anecdotes about the provocative behavior of her priests and

---

[28] I have discussed the marriage negotiations at greater length in R. Malcolm Smuts, "Religion, European Politics and Henrietta Maria's Circle, 1625–41," in *Henrietta Maria: Piety, Politics and Patronage*, ed. Erin Griffey (Aldershot: Ashgate, 2008), 13–38 and "The French Match and Court Politics," in *Stuart Marriage Diplomacy: Dynastic Politics in their European Context, 1604–1630*, ed. Sara J. Wolfson and Valentina Caldari (Woodbridge: Boydell Press, 2018), 13–28.

[29] *Proceedings in Parliament 1625*, ed. Jansson and Bidwell, 396.

[30] BN Dupuy Mss. 403, fol. 22; Smuts, "Religion, European Politics and Henrietta Maria's Circle," 16.

monks seem to have originated, not with puritans in Parliament or London, but Buckingham and figures close to him, or Charles himself. Rather than widespread public hostility, those complaints primarily reflect the determination of the king and the duke to prevent the queen's religion from becoming a political liability, by demonstrating their staunch opposition to the strident Catholicism of her clerical entourage, along with their efforts to wrest control of her household from her French servants. Since they did not speak English, Henrietta Maria's Capuchins had a limited ability to win converts. They posed much less of a threat to reformed British Protestantism than native Catholics and nominal Protestants who wanted to introduce "popish" practices within the national church, while stigmatizing orthodox Calvinists as puritans. Growing evidence of Charles's sympathy for such people did much more to undercut confidence in his leadership than the religion of his wife.[31] The growing influence of so-called "Arminian" clergy within the English Church seemed to some to presage a betrayal of the kingdom and its faith, just as Dutch Arminianism had allegedly underpinned a conspiracy to betray the United Provinces before 1618.

In early 1626 several Protestant peers tried to pressure Buckingham into breaking with the Arminians in a conference at his London residence of York House. His refusal to do so helped inspire the attempt to impeach him in the parliament that convened a short time later, in which strongly Protestant MPs made common cause with pro-Spanish peers like Arundel and the queen's friends in attacking their common foe. Having become the chief scapegoat for all that had gone wrong during Charles's first year on the throne, Buckingham was accused not only of mismanagement but treason. He had allegedly subverted virtue by selling titles of honor for money and promoting unworthy men, enriched himself at the expense of the crown and its subjects, and prevented honest counsel from reaching the king's ears. His popish mother and other Catholic associates raised suspicions that he had deliberately betrayed the Protestant cause. A Commons subcommittee blamed the spread of popery in the North on the appointment to positions of authority of three Buckingham clients said to be "popishly" affected, and concluded: "the committee conceives the duke to be the causing cause of the increase of popery there."[32] Charles's dissolution of the 1626 Parliament to save his favorite from impeachment and almost certain conviction in the Lords deprived the crown of a grant of supply it desperately needed to fund its war.

---

[31] A book by a Church of England clergyman named Richard Montague, arguing that theological and liturgical differences between the English Church and the Church of Rome were much smaller than most people believed, became a flashpoint of controversy. In 1626 the Commons accused Montague of giving "encouragement to popery, to withdraw subjects from the true religion established to the Romish superstitions and consequently to be reconciled to the See of Rome... by cunning and subtle ways," and raising "great factions and divisions in this commonwealth by casting the odious and scandalous name of puritans" on people who belonged to the Church of England (Folger Shakespeare Library Mss. Vb291, fol. 68).

[32] *Proceedings in Parliament 1626*, ed. Bidwell and Jansson, 2.357-8.

The grand alliance Charles and Buckingham had constructed then failed spectacularly, as Christian IV of Denmark suffered a crushing defeat at the Battle of Lutter, while the alliance with France collapsed in mutual hostility that soon led to war. From one perspective, this second armed conflict amounted to a resumption and escalation of James's earlier efforts to meddle in French affairs by encouraging noble and Huguenot revolts. Buckingham sent an agent, Watt Montague, to France on a mission to encourage noble rebellions and seek support from the dukes of Lorraine and Savoy in a campaign to topple Richelieu. The British crown simultaneously encouraged La Rochelle to rebel by promising military assistance, a step James had always avoided. The king and duke hoped to galvanize a general uprising by Richelieu's many enemies that would persuade Louis XIII to jettison his chief minister and reorient his policies, much as James had once sought to overthrow first Villeroy and then Concini. But their level of military involvement in French politics far exceeded anything James had contemplated.

The war with France that led to Buckingham's ill-fated expedition to the Ile de Rhé also amounted to a desperate attempt to re-establish Britain's military reputation, and consequently its heft in European politics, while simultaneously recovering support for the duke among English puritans by achieving a great victory for the Protestant cause in Europe. It unquestionably entailed considerable risks that many contemporaries thought irrational. As one French diplomat remarked, Buckingham seemed a man "whose conduct follows many rules that go beyond that which other men call prudence." But that was in part because a prudent approach of limiting losses while seeking to achieve small gains would never have won over his many enemies. To have any chance of doing that he needed a spectacular success, which he could never achieve without risking equally spectacular failure. Like Essex in the previous generation, he associated excess prudence with irresolution and cowardice, traits more disgraceful to a man of honor and destructive to the reputation of a great state than failure in a noble cause.[33] In the event he nearly managed to starve the main French fort on the Ile de Rhé into submission before the French managed to relieve it. But in the end, he lost his gamble in an even more humiliating defeat than the previous failures of Mansfeld and at Cadiz, thereby solidifying his position as the main scapegoat for all that had gone wrong since March 1625.

Since Parliament had withheld its grant of supply, Charles needed to support Buckingham's campaign by an unprecedentedly aggressive use of his prerogative powers. He levied the Forced Loan, in effect an arbitrary tax since he had no intention of repaying the money, enforcing its collection by the arrest without trial of several prominent loan refusers. He conscripted soldiers, including some Irish

---

[33] BN Dupuy Mss. 403, fol. 204.

Catholics, and billeted them on English householders in several southern ports, while declaring martial law in the affected areas to assure that military discipline was maintained.[34] Deputy lieutenants found themselves caught in the middle as the crown ordered them to enforce these highly unpopular measures. For some time, fears had existed that a king might someday invoke pleas of necessity and reason of state to justify violating his subjects' liberties and property rights in ways contrary to the law. In 1626-7 that appeared to have happened. The temporary occupation of a few English towns by bands of conscript soldiers led people to worry that still more arbitrary measures would follow. John Holles earl of Clare lamented to Bishop John Williams: "Besides these new regiments of disorderly soldiers that have ravaged the west countries, and now Sussex, a new praetorian regiment is to be raised and quartered hereabouts, to meet with such occasions as offer."[35]

A New Crisis Seen through Old Ideological Lenses

The political conflicts and maneuvers swirling around Buckingham had thus acquired ideological dimensions, accentuated by recent acts committed under the pressures of war but also rooted in English experiences since the late 1590s. To these we should add anxieties more reminiscent of Scottish politics in the 1580s, about whether a Stuart king, his courtiers and the bishops they appointed could be trusted to safeguard British Protestantism. Charles, Buckingham, and their supporters reacted to the breakdown in political harmony in ways equally indebted to established patterns of thought. Like Essex and his circle, the duke's friends blamed criticism of his actions on envy, the proverbial enemy of virtuous men. A masque Buckingham presented to the king and queen just before his departure for the coast of France in 1627 showed him pursued by "Envy, with diverse open-mouthed dogs' heads, representing the peoples' barking; next came Fame, then Truth, etc."[36] The duke also resembled Essex in presenting his relationship with the king as grounded in "love" and "friendship." Unlike Elizabeth, Charles loyally and steadfastly reciprocated this affection. After learning of the defeat on the Ile de Rhé, he assured his favorite "that no distance of place nor length of time can make me slacken, much less diminish my love to you."[37] He shielded Buckingham, not only because he believed that by doing so he protected

---

[34] Richard Cust, *The Forced Loan and English Politics, 1626-1628* (Oxford: Oxford University Press, 1987) is the definitive study of the Forced Loan. Roger Lockyer, *Buckingham: The Life and Political Career of George Villiers, First Duke of Buckingham 1592-1628* (London: Longman, 1981), chapter 9 remains useful on the planning and execution of the expedition to the Ile de Rhé.

[35] *Letters of John Clare Earl of Holles*, ed. P. R. Seddon, 2 vols (Nottingham: Thoroton Society, 1983), 2.338.

[36] *Court and Times of Charles I*, ed. Birch, 1.226.   [37] BL Harleian Mss. 6988, fol. 37.

his own authority, but because that was how a virtuous friend ought to behave. Submitting to Parliament's pressure would have meant betraying the trust and affection on which loyal service depended, and allowing the sordid motives of the duke's adversaries to corrode the moral fiber of his state. In addition to envy, the king and his supporters blamed the political impasse on demagogues and puritans, in ways that again followed lines of argument about the dangers of "popularity" and puritan extremism that had existed since the days of archbishops Whitgift and Adamson. A paper privately given the king in 1626 warned "that this great opposition against the duke was stirred up and maintained by such as seek the destruction of this free monarchy. Because they find it not yet ripe to attempt against the king himself, they endeavor it through the sides of the duke."[38] Clerics like William Laud and Richard Montague exploited the long-standing association between puritans and demagogic enemies of monarchy to undermine Charles's confidence in even moderate Calvinists like Archbishop Abbot.

The strains of war had therefore produced, not just a functional breakdown in the machinery of the state but a process of ideological polarization, caused by the ways in which contingent events injected fresh energy into old arguments, rooted in differing responses to past experiences of religious and political conflict, and established discourses about relationships between royal leadership, national virtue, and success in war. The combination of financial stress, wartime pressure, and ideological dissonance placed enormous pressure on the whole "order of command and obedience" through which the state functioned. The resulting crisis culminated in 1629, as the Commons tried to blackmail Charles into withdrawing his support for Arminian clergy and several of his ministers by refusing to grant him the customs revenues that every king had enjoyed since the fourteenth century, and encouraging merchants to refuse to pay them.[39] If it had remained effective for more than a few months this tax-strike would have bankrupted the crown during a war with both France and Spain, calling into question Charles's ability to defend his kingdoms.

Fortunately for Charles, two conditions provided him with an escape hatch. First, the crisis remained essentially confined to England, despite tensions caused by different issues in the other two kingdoms. In Ireland Charles attempted to appease the Catholic majority with a number of concessions known as "the Graces," which helped preserve quiet. Crown officials remained very worried about what might happen if either Spain or France tried to invade the island,

---

[38] John Rushworth, *Historical Collections of Private Passages of State*, 8 vols (London, 1721), 1.356.
[39] The customs, known as tonnage and poundage, were customarily granted in the first parliament of each reign. The 1625 Parliament granted them for only a year because it hoped to formulate language to prevent any future new impositions similar to those Cecil had devised at the start of James's reign but lacked the time to do so properly. The failure of the 1626 Parliament and the time consumed drafting the Petition of Right had prevented a renewal of the grant but the crown had gone on collecting customs duties anyway, since it could not afford to dispense with them.

but the dreaded incursion never came and Ireland remained at peace. In Scotland the king provoked considerable resentment at the start of his reign by claiming that he had the right to revoke royal grants of land and pensions dating back as far as 1566 and perhaps even earlier, thereby threatening the economic and political interests of the kingdom's aristocracy.[40] He also continued trying to enforce the Five Articles of Perth, angering the many Scots who regarded kneeling at the altar as popish. But although his actions led to sullen resistance and strained his subjects' good will, they had not yet ignited a general defiance of royal authority. Charles was therefore able to concentrate on the challenge posed by his English Parliament without having to worry unduly about Scottish or Irish rebellions.

Second, Britain's wars with Spain and France were ones of choice rather than necessity, and therefore relatively easy to terminate. Although still reluctant to abandon the contest, Charles eventually bowed to necessity by concluding treaties with both France and Spain. Once the strike against paying customs collapsed, as it soon did, he was free to dispense with parliaments, since he no longer urgently needed grants of supply. Over the next several years his ministers introduced Ship Money, Forest Fines, and other revenue measures that reduced, without ever entirely eliminating, his deficits. Under these conditions stability quickly returned. By convincing Charles that he needed to rule for the indefinite future without summoning a parliament, the crisis of the 1620s had altered conditions at the political center. But the operation of state authority in the localities—as well as in Scotland and Ireland—went on much as before. In England provincial gentry continued to serve the crown as unpaid magistrates and local populations continued to obey them, even when it came to paying Ship Money.[41] This shows how strong habits of submission to lawful authority remained, despite the turbulence of the war years. Since the major European powers remained too preoccupied fighting each other to have any desire to start a new conflict with Britain, royal authority looked reasonably secure. If war had exposed the latent weaknesses of the British state, the return of peace appeared to demonstrate its underlying resilience.

The Problem of Religious Disharmony, the Militarization of Politics, and the Collapse of the State

If Charles had remained content to live with this situation indefinitely he would probably have died in his bed after a fairly quiet reign. Instead he stumbled into a second, even more severe crisis triggered by his attempt in 1637 to impose a new

---

[40] See Macinnes, *Charles I and the Covenanting Movement*, chapter 3.
[41] The council made the county sheriffs responsible for collecting Ship Money and paying any deficits from their own purses, thus giving them ample incentive to enforce payment.

Prayer Book, resembling that of England but not identical to it, on the Scottish Kirk. In doing so he resumed a project that his father had briefly begun but then postponed in the late 1610s that was essentially a logical extension of the Five Articles of Perth. Although James never went as far as his son in trying to impose unwelcome ceremonial changes on Scottish worship, he had already started down the same road. The determination of both kings to force the Scots to adopt liturgical rituals they disliked calls for explanation. James's earlier efforts to impose constant moderators on synods and general assemblies and bishops had served a political purpose, by consolidating his control over the machinery of Kirk governance and making it easier to deal with ministers who tried to interfere in affairs of state. Ceremonial changes lacked such obvious political implications but aroused more widespread resistance because they affected the laity as well as the clergy. Far from consolidating James's political victory over presbyterianism, his effort to impose "popish" ceremonies jeopardized it, by giving dissatisfied presbyterians a fresh cause that enjoyed extensive lay support. The 1637 Prayer Book intensified this resistance to a point at which the king's ability to command his Scottish subjects collapsed.

Since James always insisted that ceremonies were "matters of indifference," the Stuarts' willingness to incur such high political costs by imposing them requires explanation. They appear to have had several motives. Sharing the widespread belief that religious diversity impeded social and political unity, they regarded the stubborn singularity of Scottish worship as an obstacle to the integration of the two British kingdoms. But the problem might more easily have been ameliorated by compromises that removed the most objectionable facets of the English liturgy before insisting that Scots conform to what remained. Although such a step would have encountered stiff resistance from some English clergy, many Protestants in the southern kingdom would have welcomed it. Moreover, the argument that religious diversity weakened unity and political authority applied even more strongly to Catholic Ireland than to Scotland. But although Charles and his Irish viceroy in the 1630s, Sir Thomas Wentworth, probably did anticipate that the crown would one day need to suppress Irish Catholicism, they were sensible enough to postpone that project indefinitely, from fear of provoking a rebellion that might tempt foreign powers to intervene.[42] Although religious changes in Scotland had met with strong local resistance this had always been overcome in the recent past. Scotland had not experienced a general rebellion since the 1560s, and no European state had an obvious reason to involve itself in a dispute over the

---

[42] See Anthony Milton, "Thomas Wentworth and the Political Thought of the Personal Rule," Nicholas Canny, "The Attempted Anglicanisation of Ireland in the Seventeenth Century: An Exemplar of 'British History'," and John McCaferty, "'God Bless your Free Church of Ireland': Wentworth, Laud, Bramhall and the Irish Convocation of 1634," all in *The Political World of Thomas Wentworth Earl of Stafford 1621–1641*, ed. J. F. Merritt (Cambridge: Cambridge University Press, 1996), 133–56, 157–86, and 187–208.

Kirk's liturgy. This background may have induced Charles to believe, wrongly as it turned out, that he might assert his authority over his northern kingdom without undue risk.

The Stuarts' determination to force the Scots to accept liturgical changes, even at the cost of stirring considerable resistance, was also rooted in a tradition of antipuritan and presbyterian thought that had originated in the late sixteenth century, while acquiring additional layers of meaning since. Like Whitgift, Bancroft, and Patrick Adamson, James regarded puritans in both kingdoms as demagogues who claimed a privileged relationship with God in order to justify their proud defiance of earthly authority. Even if ceremonies like kneeling at the altar were in themselves "matters of indifference," the Scots' refusal to accept such measures reflected a dangerous arrogance that threatened not only the proper regulation of the Kirk but also his authority as king. Charles and Laud added the further belief that a climate of irreverence for authority had recently spread through the British kingdoms. They blamed several kinds of people for this malaise, including debtors who hoped that by sowing chaos they might salvage their finances, lawyers whose captious objections and strained use of precedents obstructed governance, and the MPs whose embrace of "popular" causes had caused the king so much trouble earlier in his reign. But puritan zealots in both kingdoms made common cause with other malcontents, traducing the bishops and loyal servants of the crown. For reasons of state as well as religion, the crown needed to confront these seditious spirits and force them to yield. The campaign to enforce decorum in worship in both British kingdoms served this purpose.

Both Stuart kings had, in addition, absorbed ideas about the fundamental importance of ceremonies in molding spiritual attitudes and behavior first articulated by Richard Hooker, before being further developed in the seventeenth century by Lancelot Andrewes and the Laudian clergy. Their belief in what Laud called "the beauty of holiness" fused with the patterns of thought foreshadowed in Bishop Bilson's 1603 coronation sermon, positing deep connections between the language and symbolism of Christian worship and the institution of kingship. Suggestively, in the same period of 1618–20, in which he struggled to impose the Five Articles of Perth, James wrote and published his *Meditation upon the 27, 28, 29 verses of the XVII chapter of St. Matthew*, which followed the logic of Bilson's sermon by describing Christ's scourging by Roman centurions as an inverted coronation ritual. The Laudians sought even more aggressively to draw analogies between the "beauty of holiness" within English churches and attitudes of reverent submission to kings, as God's representatives on earth. Some elevated the duty of obedience alongside faith as core doctrines of Christianity. From this perspective ceremonial decorum was no longer a matter of indifference, even if specific forms might still be regarded as such. Prescribed forms of worship, involving bodily gestures of submission like kneeling, were essential tools for inculcating habits of obedience, humility, and self-control that underpinned

Christian morality and discipline. They therefore served as crucial ligaments of the state. Forcing people to worship in the proper manner made them not only better Christians but also better subjects. Imposing ceremonial conformity was a way of attacking the problem of spiritual arrogance at its root.

Laud and his followers began the campaign to enforce liturgical conformity in England. The impact of their reforms on parish worship varied a good deal from place to place and historians have disagreed about how much resistance they stirred. A few puritans departed in anger for the New World, while a more sizable number, including a handful of peers, had begun to consider doing so by the late 1630s.[43] Most of the population conformed, although not always happily. But Laud also took a greater interest in the churches of Ireland and Scotland than previous archbishops of Canterbury. He corresponded regularly with Wentworth about recruiting capable clergy for the Irish Church and played an active behind-the-scenes role in shaping policies toward the Kirk, for example by advising on new appointments to the eight episcopal sees that fell vacant in Scotland in the 1630s.[44] In all three kingdoms he and Charles sought to recover Church property, augment collection of tithes, and enhance the prestige of the clergy.[45] English clergy started to serve more frequently on commissions of the peace, while Scottish bishops were also assigned more active roles in secular affairs. Six gained appointment to the Scottish privy council and several also served on commissions of the peace and in other secular capacities.[46]

Far from an isolated act, the new Scottish Prayer Book therefore followed a wider and earlier set of initiatives, stretching back into James's reign but gaining greater momentum after 1625, calculated to enhance the prestige and dignity of the British churches and their royal head. Even before Laud's elevation, Charles had continued enforcing the Five Articles of Perth, while also encouraging Scottish clergy to employ the English Prayer Book and to begin wearing whites. In the mid-1630s he decided to resume the shelved project "to establish a liturgy in Scotland much after the course of ours in England yet with some differences," as Laud put it.[47] The archbishop helped draft a set of Scottish canons in 1636 and the Scottish Prayer Book introduced in July 1637, without seeking authorization from any representative assembly of the Kirk or kingdom.[48] The new liturgy immediately provoked riotous protests and before long more general resistance that built upon networks created by earlier opposition to the Five Articles of Perth.[49] Crowd demonstrations, encouraged by sermons, pasquinades of Prayer Book supporters,

---

[43] Adamson, *Noble Revolt*, 35–6.
[44] Leonie James, *This Great Firebrand: William Laud and Scotland, 1617–1645* (Woodbridge: Boydell, 2017).
[45] Ibid., 70–8.   [46] Ibid., 52–62.
[47] Wentworth Woodhouse Muniments StrP7, fol. 58 (Laud to Wentworth, October 7, 1637).
[48] James, *Great Firebrand*, chapter 3 is the most thorough examination of Laud's role in drafting the canons and Prayer Book.
[49] Stewart, *Rethinking the Scottish Revolution*, 38–9.

and the circulation of political tracts, gave the movement a pronounced popular dimension, which may have encouraged members of the nobility and urban elites to step in and assert their leadership, from fear they would otherwise lose control.[50] Mass signings of a national Covenant, pledging Scots to defend the Kirk, began in February 1638. In November of the same year the first national assembly since 1618 convened, without Charles's authorization, and voted to abolish episcopacy.

Up until this point royal governance in England and Scotland had functioned through unforced obedience, without the need for armed coercion. Unlike the rulers of France, Spain, and the United Provinces, the Stuarts lacked bodies of soldiers capable of enforcing decrees at sword point, except in Ireland. By breaking with this pattern, the Covenanters' defiance threatened to unleash a more fundamental change in the state's machinery and methods of governance that would bring the Stuart kingdoms into closer alignment with continental monarchies like France, in which armed compulsion was more widely used and accepted. For a time, Charles continued to hope that he might negotiate his way out of the crisis after making a show of resolve, but it soon became clear that he would either have to capitulate to the Covenanters' demands or wage war against them.[51] Initially neither side appeared capable of a serious military effort. The only armed forces at their disposal consisted of local militias never designed for long-distance operations, a few armed retainers of Scottish nobles, and small volunteer forces gathered by English courtiers. Both sides would need to build more impressive armies from scratch, while somehow raising the money needed to pay for them. Once the process started, there was no sure way of knowing where it would end, particularly in light of likely English puritan sympathy for the Scots' cause. "I cannot without much regret think of the present condition of these times and the weak constitution of this state to bear those shocks and violent concussions it is like to encounter withal," one informed contemporary mused.[52] The dovish earl of Northumberland lamented in January 1639:

> The discontents here at home do rather increase than lessen, there being no course taken to give any satisfaction. The king's coffers were never more empty than at this time and to us that have the honor to be near about him no way is yet

---

[50] Ibid., 29–32.

[51] The Venetian ambassador reported as late as June 15, 1640 that Charles "adheres to his inclination to try gentle measures" and had sent agents to Scotland "with the principal object of sounding the real sentiments of the people and initiating fresh negotiations for an accommodation, if he finds an opening," but then added: "The queen does not agree with these peaceful counsels" (*CSPV* 25.52). On the other hand, the duke of Hamilton, who had been sent north to negotiate with the Covenanters, had already advised in October 1638 that there was no longer "hope of prevailing any way by treaty" and that if he was determined to resist the Covenanters' demands Charles needed to begin military preparations (Scottish National Archives Mss. GD406/1/570).

[52] Sir William Temple in *Letters and Memorials of State in the Reigns of Queen Mary, Queen Elizabeth, King James, King Charles the First*, ed. Arthur Collins, 2 vols. (London, 1746), 2.592.

known how he will find means either to maintain or begin a war without the help of his people. Several offers have been made his Majesty by particular men to raise both horse and foot at their own charges and to bring them to the rendezvous that the king shall appoint. But they are not persons to be relied upon; or grant the king could be certain of them yet their number is so small that it makes them inconsiderable.[53]

War would once again subject the state—the whole system of institutions, resources, and moral values through which governance functioned—to severe and possibly fatal pressures. But this time the crisis would be a domestic one engulfing the whole of Britain.

The question of how to respond to this challenge split the English privy council between members who thought that trying to subdue Scotland by force was not worth the costs and attendant risks, and those like Laud and his ally, Wentworth, who argued that Charles had no other option because capitulating to Scottish demands would fatally weaken his authority not only there but in England.[54] Laud connected the Scottish resistance to a recent attack on the bishops by William Prynne in England, concluding: "all this comes because we talk still," instead of imposing conformity by "those two able governors," reward and punishment.[55] The Venetian ambassador observed that the riot in Edinburgh against the new Prayer Book had "exceedingly afflicted and depressed the archbishop" because he feared "it may stir up revolutions among the people here, who are no less scandalized and discontented than the Scots," and that his own standing with the king would suffer in consequence.[56] Religious discontents in both kingdoms were a "cancerous malady which possesseth the vulgar at this moment but certainly not the vulgar only...a wolf in the very breast of the kingdom."[57] Wentworth complained that "the reverence and dignity of magistracy is lost amongst us"[58] and argued for using as much force as required "to set up the solid structures of order and government which might remain lasting."[59] Having recently enlarged the army in Ireland, he advised Charles that it was available for use in Britain.

For the moment, the debate about Scotland within the English council turned on issues of practicality rather than religious principle. In some respects, the two sides were not very far apart. Wentworth conceded Northumberland's point that Charles would have difficulty raising military forces. The crisis "happens to the

---

[53] Wentworth Woodhouse Muniments StrP10b, fol. 32.
[54] The debate is analyzed in Malcolm Smuts, "Force, Love and Authority in Caroline Political Culture," in *The 1630s: Interdisciplinary Essays on Culture and Politics in the Caroline Era*, ed. Ian Atherton and Julie Sanders (Manchester: Manchester University Press, 2006), 28–49.
[55] Ibid.   [56] *CSPV* 24.259.
[57] Wentworth Woodhouse Muniments StrP7, fol. 76, Laud to Wentworth, December 19, 1637.
[58] Ibid., fol. 180r, Wentworth to Laud, April 10, 1639.   [59] Ibid.

king in some respects in a very ill conjuncture of time and affairs, it being to be confessed there is neither men to conduct such an action nor money and ammunition to bear it through with that speed and force such an accident as this requires. Again, it is now dangerous because it falls upon us unexpected."[60] He felt sufficiently nervous during the first campaign against the Scots in 1639 to advise Charles to avoid giving battle, from fear that his untested army might disintegrate if put to the test.[61] On the other hand, Northumberland and other councilors who had grave misgivings about Charles's decision to go to war nevertheless continued to serve him. As late as November 1640 the future parliamentarian earl of Leicester had little sympathy for the Covenanters' defiance of royal commands. "I am sure I never could yet believe that the Scots love us when they show so little affection and duty to our king... or that they intend us any good at all, whatsoever they pretend."[62] As early as 1638 a small group of English peers and seasoned politicians, including the earl of Warwick and the future leader of the Commons in the Long Parliament, John Pym, entered into treasonous correspondence with the Covenanters over how to impede Charles's designs.[63] But this group, who were motivated by religious convictions strong enough to override their sense of allegiance, remained a minority. Many people who disapproved of the war continued to act as loyal subjects while they waited to see how it would turn out.

But beneath the surface religious and ideological fissures had begun to appear. Proponents of compromise tended to hold a more latitudinarian view of British Protestantism, which made them skeptical of the dogmatic hostility toward puritans of Laud and his allies. "To think well of the reformed religion is cause enough to make the Archbishop their enemy," Northumberland complained to his brother-in-law, the earl of Leicester.[64] The Covenanters' rebellion presented an opportunity to a Catholic group within the court, encouraged by the queen and the papal envoy George Conn, himself a Scottish Catholic, to argue that subjects of their religion were more loyal to the crown than presbyterians and puritans. They lobbied for an alteration of the Oath of Allegiance to condemn all religiously based resistance to royal authority, rather than the specific doctrine of the pope's right to absolve subjects from their allegiance, and promoted a voluntary collection of money among Catholics to help fund Charles's campaign.[65] When the earl of

---

[60] Wentworth Woodhouse Muniments StrP10b, Wentworth to Northumberland, July 30, 1638.
[61] "The principle which is first and unalterably to be laid at the entrance into this action is in no case to put anything to hazard at land, the whole cause should be entrusted in the hand of some sober staid person, in his nature rather a Fabius than a Marcellus, who following his work constantly and sadly will in three years by the blessing of Almighty God attain and settle all his ends and purposes." Wentworth Woodhouse Muniments StrP10b, fol. 10, Wentworth to Northumberland, August 1, 1638.
[62] *Letters and Memorials*, ed. Collins, 2.660.   [63] Adamson, *Noble Revolt*, 36–40.
[64] *Letters and Memorials*, ed. Collins, 2.623.
[65] Caroline Hibbard, *Charles I and the Popish Plot* (Chapel Hill: University of North Carolina Press, 2nd ed., 2009) remains the most thorough treatment.

Leicester learned that one of these Catholic courtiers, Sir Kenelm Digby, had accused him to the king of being a puritan, he exploded in rage, ranting that Digby was not only the close relative of a Gunpowder Plot conspirator but a man "vehemently suspected of murdering his wife."[66] A not altogether unfounded perception had begun to form that whether or not the Scottish Prayer Book was itself popish, its chief supporters were either papists or people friendlier to papists than to reformed Protestants.

The Covenanters' Revolt had therefore sharpened and realigned religious divisions within England as well as Scotland, not least at the center of power. It began to create a working alliance that had not existed before 1637 between the queen and her Catholic followers, and Laud and his ally Strafford, while threatening to diminish the influence of figures within the court like the earls of Holland, Northumberland, and Leicester whose firm Protestantism and greater sympathy for the Scots opened them to the charge of having "puritan" sympathies. As this happened Charles pressed ahead with efforts to create an armed force with which to compel the Scots. This required him to place new burdens on his English subjects. He first tried to do so without summoning a parliament, by welding together contingents from the county militias and a few auxiliary troops raised by his courtiers into a royal army. But even the strongest supporters of war among the king's advisors, notably Strafford, had little confidence in this ramshackle force, and so advised the king to avoid giving battle and instead wage a contest of attrition, in hopes that the Scottish war effort would collapse before the king's did. This helps explain why Charles accepted an armistice in June 1639 after the English and Scottish armies first came into bloodless contact with each other, postponing the decisive engagement for another year. In the spring he finally summoned the first English parliament to meet in more than a decade. But negotiations over granting him supply broke down, leading to its dissolution within three weeks. Its dismissal touched off a riot by London apprentices outside Laud's palace of Lambeth, while compelling the king and his ministers to find other ways of raising money for a second campaign.

Their efforts to do so fueled fresh fears of arbitrary government. Already in January an anonymous paper had circulated claiming that the king threatened to imprison the lord mayor and aldermen of London over their failure to collect his taxes. Several months later the Chancellor of the Exchequer, Sir Francis Cottington, told the directors of the East India Company that if they were not more cooperative in furnishing the king with money he would speak to them "with louder language from out of the Tower."[67] Rumors circulated that Charles intended to keep some of the cavalry levied for use against Scotland as a permanent royal guard after the war ended, and more ominously that before fighting the

[66] Leicester to king, January 18/28, 1639 (Library of Congress microfilm 041/Camb788/1).
[67] BN Mss. Français 15,916, fol. 279; SNA GD406/1/1231.

Covenanters he might use his newly raised soldiers to "reform" the English parliament.[68] "They are also inquiring here with great diligence into methods calculated to compel the people here to supply the needs of the crown by prompt payments, without having to depend in the future on the decision of parliament," the Venetian ambassador reported, shortly after the dissolution of the Short Parliament. "Some even strongly advise force if the obstinacy of the people does not otherwise permit."[69] A few days later he added, "the king's plan is to go on arming powerfully, without creating alarm, ostensibly in order to subdue the rebellious Scots by force but with the secret intention of using these arms to bridle the insolent demands of parliament."[70] Even if based only on rumors rather than hard information, these reports reveal the level of anxiety that Charles's actions had created. A further development made the king's resort to force appear even more sinister. As his preparations against Scotland moved forward he entered into negotiations for an arrangement with Spain that would allow him to borrow several thousand veterans from the Army of Flanders. He also encouraged the Catholic MacDonnell earl of Antrim to raise forces in his ancestral homelands with which to attack the leading Covenanter earl of Argyll's territories from the rear,[71] and considered Strafford's advice to use the predominantly Catholic royal army in Ireland against the Scots. Although the Scots would have been the primary target for Irish or Spanish soldiers, nothing guaranteed that Charles would not also use them against English subjects who refused to do his bidding.

Not only Scotland but England also therefore appeared at grave risk of suffering a more basic alteration in the state than had occurred ten years earlier, involving a significantly increased use of arbitrary force to compel compliance with the king's commands and religious uniformity. Charles appeared ready to use the sword in ways familiar to inhabitants of Ireland and many continental societies but less familiar in Scotland and unprecedented in recent English experience. This prospect gave added incentives for resistance, further upping the ante for the king, who knew that he would almost certainly suffer a significant loss of power and authority if he did not prevail. The longer the crisis continued the more difficult and unlikely it would become to return to the situation that existed before it began.

To a degree the contest resembled roughly contemporary events in other multiple monarchies, especially Spain, where Catalonia and Portugal revolted at almost the same time as Scotland. Contemporaries noticed the parallel. Charles's ambassador in Madrid reported in November 1640 that the Count Duke of Olivares had sent "a message to me by his secretary saying we ought to meet, if

---

[68] TNA C115/N9/8854; *Archives ou correspondence inédite de la maison Orange-Nassau*, ed. G. Groen van Prinsterer, 12 vols (Utrecht: Kemink et Fils, 1835–45), 3.157.
[69] *CSPV* 25.27.   [70] Ibid., 30.
[71] Jane Ohlmeyer, *Civil War and Restoration in the Three Kingdoms: The Career of Randal MacDonnell, Marquis of Antrim* (Dublin: Four Courts Press, 2nd ed., 2001).

it were only to condole together, our wars being so like, meaning in regard of Scotland and Catalonia."⁷² The following summer Olivares "spoke feelingly" to another British diplomat, "saying that if kings look not to themselves there will be but few kings left in few years."⁷³ Charles had already reached the same conclusion, telling Laud that "the ground of their [the Covenanters'] rebellion is nothing but a mere opposition and hatred to civil and monarchical government, wherein the common interests of all kings are highly concerned."⁷⁴ Twentieth-century historians did not invent the concept of a general seventeenth-century crisis of monarchy in the 1640s; some contemporaries thought they were living through just such an event.⁷⁵ But whereas the Spanish crisis was triggered by resistance to taxation and centralizing policies driven by the demands of foreign war, within a uniformly Catholic collection of kingdoms, the one in Britain stemmed from religious disputes within kingdoms at peace with their neighbors. This gave it a different, more confessional, character.

The so-called Bishops' Wars between Charles's English forces and the Scots also had another destabilizing effect. In 1639 and 1640 many of the tens of thousands of English and Scottish soldiers that over the previous decades had departed for the Continent to serve in European armies, including experienced officers, returned home to fight either for the king or for the Covenanters. Their growing numbers added to the chances that political disagreements would be settled by force rather than negotiation. In the short run the Scots reaped the greatest benefits, since veterans from the Swedish army, led by Alexander Leslie, who had achieved the rank of general, significantly improved the capabilities of their army.⁷⁶ The infusion of hardened veterans and experienced leadership allowed the Covenanters to seize the initiative by invading England in the summer of 1640, after laying the groundwork by making secret contacts with sympathetic English peers and waging a propaganda campaign through print.⁷⁷ After crossing Northumberland without opposition Covenanter forces inflicted a decisive defeat on a contingent of the English army in late August, at the Battle of Newburn. Although Strafford wanted to continue the fight, most of Charles's advisors concluded that it was now hopeless and persuaded the king to conclude an armistice in which he promised to pay the Scottish army's wages until a peace settlement was concluded. Lacking the money to do this he eventually succumbed, after some further delays and maneuverings, to pressure to summon a new parliament.

---

⁷² TNA SP94/42, fol. 73.   ⁷³ Ibid., fol. 199.   ⁷⁴ TNA SP78/109, fol. 170v.
⁷⁵ See, e.g. *The General Crisis of the Seventeenth Century*, ed. Trevor Aston (London: Basic Books, 1965).
⁷⁶ Alexia Grosjean, *An Unofficial Alliance: Scotland and Sweden, 1569–1654* (Leiden: Brill, 2003); Steve Murdoch and Alexia Grosjean, *Alexander Leslie and the Scottish Generals of the Thirty Years War, 1618–1648* (London: Pickering & Chatto, 2014).
⁷⁷ For the contacts see Adamson, *Noble Revolt*, 45–50 and 55–62.

Charles's view of Calvinist Protestantism as an intrinsically seditious religion had therefore become self-fulfilling. By trying to compel obedience to the manner of worship that he and Laud desired, he galvanized resistance that deprived him of control of Scotland and re-energized resistance in England, ultimately leading to a military defeat that discredited him even in the eyes of subjects who had previously remained loyal. Defeat intensified hatred of Laud and other councilors like Strafford, who received the blame for the debacle, while rendering the king dependent on parliament and its leaders for the money needed to pay his obligations. This outcome created a situation in which several members of the privy council believed that they needed to rescue Charles from his own bad judgment and the pernicious influence of a few of their colleagues, by pressuring him to purge his entourage and alter his policies. They worked in tandem with the leadership of both houses of the newly convened parliament to bring these changes about. Charles once again faced the prospect of losing control of his own council and court, and being reduced to "a doge of Venice." The personal stakes were very high because it was clear that if he and hardline advisors like Strafford ever regained control they would try the opposition leaders for treason for their collusion with the Covenanters. Those leaders therefore had every incentive to strike first, as they did by using the parliament to imprison Laud and Strafford on capital charges, and launching investigations of alleged abuses during the 1630s to intimidate other members of Charles's entourage into cooperating with their agenda or vacating the political scene. Secretary Windebanke escaped impeachment for his role in obtaining pardons for Catholics by fleeing to France, while by the spring Sir Francis Cottington was talking of his desire to retire, perhaps by resigning his office of chancellor of the exchequer to John Pym. The queen, who had been thrown into a panic by the collapse of her husband's authority and fear that she might become a target because of her religion and foreign birth, came under intense pressure to serve parliament's leaders and their court allies, by persuading her husband that he needed to compromise. The outcome of the Bishops' Wars revived and expanded parliament's role as an investigative body used to pursue vendettas against fallen politicians, and pressure the king into disposing with ministers who were widely mistrusted and disliked.[78]

The Bishops' Wars had also changed the political environment in other ways. By fueling a backlash already underway against Laud's policies they gave a new lease on life to varieties of Protestant opposition to the established churches in both British kingdoms that Elizabeth and James had worked hard to contain and eradicate. In Scotland this led to the effective replacement of royal governance by

---

[78] This summarizes all too briefly the narratives of Russell, *The Fall of the British Monarchies*, chapters 4–7 and Adamson, *Noble Revolt*. See also R. Malcolm Smuts, "The Court and the Emergence of a Royalist Party," in *Royalists and Royalism during the English Civil Wars*, ed. Jason McElligott and David Smith (Cambridge: Cambridge University Press, 2007), 43–65.

what amounted to a presbyterian confessional state.[79] In England, London crowds and petitions from the provinces demanded the dismantling of the Laudian system and, in some cases, the total abolition of episcopacy, with all its "roots and branches." Because the bishops formed a solid block of support for the king in the House of Lords, the oppositionist coalition had political, as well as religious, incentives to deprive them of their positions. An issue that had appeared settled in both kingdoms by the middle years of James's reign had therefore erupted anew with considerable ferocity. The Bishops' Wars led as well to a revival of entrepreneurial military recruitment by a few noblemen and ambitious gentlemen. This not only challenged the crown's monopoly on violence, most spectacularly in Scotland, but threatened to erode several decades of efforts to curtail and eliminate sources of organized seigneurial violence.

The summoning of what became the Long Parliament in November represented an effort to back away from this cycle of escalating violence and restore royal authority under conditions, through a process of political negotiation. But renewed threats of violence kept intervening in that process itself. Not all involved soldiers: London crowds intimidated bishops from attending Strafford's trial in the Lords in May 1641 and then demonstrated noisily outside Whitehall Palace as the king agonized over whether to sign the earl's death warrant, causing the excitable queen to fear for her life. Although they drew upon a well of public anger, these crowd actions were encouraged by an organized network within the metropolis that kept in touch with the parliament's leaders.[80] Violent intimidation by one side invited an equally violent riposte by the other. Mounting pressure from London crowds induced a group of courtiers, some of whom had only recently sought to promote a compromise settlement, to plan the military coup subsequently known as the First Army Plot. The scheme was leaked, possibly deliberately, before it could be carried out, but its revelation increased suspicions of Charles and the hardliners in his entourage, making a negotiated settlement even harder to achieve.

For some time before an actual civil war broke out, inhibitions against the use of violent threats, in ways that violated the traditional political conventions and procedures, had therefore started to erode. Contemporaries recognized this fact and worried about it. The earl of Warwick claimed to be too busy in May of 1641 to pay a visit to Prince William of Orange, who had come to London to marry Charles's daughter Mary, because of the consuming pressure of "affairs of State and Parliament to avoid civil wars."[81] The continued presence of thousands of veterans of the Thirty Years War contributed to the tense atmosphere. The

---

[79] Stewart, *Rethinking the Scottish Revolution*, esp. chapter 4.
[80] Valerie Pearl, *London and the Outbreak of the Puritan Revolution* (Oxford: Oxford University Press, 1961).
[81] *Archives de la maison Orange-Nassau*, ed. Van Prinsterer, 3.445: "etant toujours en les affaires d'Etat et du Parlement pour nous vider des guerres civiles."

significance of this pool of experienced military manpower should not be underestimated. French ambassadors in London hoped to tap into it if Charles settled his dispute with Scotland. In April 1639 a Scottish captain promised to furnish the French with 6,000 experienced men under "good officers," the moment a truce was concluded in Britain. A few months later the same ambassador commented on the "brave men, old soldiers who search their fortunes," who had come to England to serve in a British war but who would willingly serve France if Charles and the Scots managed to resolve their differences. In June 1641, when a treaty with the Scots finally seemed to allow for the disbanding of the rival British forces, another French diplomat offered to send half the English army to Flanders within eight days.[82] But since the political standoff continued despite the treaty, most of the soldiers remained in Britain.

Even at this stage, most people dreaded the prospect of civil war, in part because they recognized that once it broke out it would be difficult, whichever side won, to restore the traditions of non-violent government under the law that most English people cherished.[83] But since the main protagonists on both sides felt mortally threatened by any settlement that would leave their opponents in control of the state, they had strong incentives to appeal to force if they seemed at risk of losing the political fight. They needed to counter appeals to force by their adversaries by deploying or threatening to deploy force themselves. In the summer of 1641 Charles traveled to Scotland, where he attempted to break Covenanter resistance by arresting the earl of Argyll and his own former representative in Scotland, the earl of Hamilton, on charges of treason. Both escaped after learning of the king's intentions but the Incident, as this episode became known, further poisoned the atmosphere. Shortly after Charles returned to London in the autumn news arrived of a great rebellion in Ireland that was inspired partly by fear that the triumphant "puritans" in the Long Parliament and Scotland would soon launch a campaign of repression against Irish Catholics. Since an army had to be raised to suppress the Irish rebels and neither side in the political contest would trust the other with it, the Irish rebellion brought England even closer to the brink of civil war. Even at this late date, growing support for the king within the parliament, as MPs rallied to him in reaction against what they perceived as the dangerous encouragement of popular violence by his opponents, made it possible that Charles would manage to achieve a political victory. But his failed attempt to seize five of the leaders of the parliamentary opposition by force in January and subsequent departure from London for the North to raise an army finally foreclosed this possibility.

---

[82] BN Mss. Français 15,916, fol. 196v; AMAE, CPA 47, fol. 550v and 48 fol. 325.

[83] John Morrill, *Revolt in the Provinces: The People of England and the Tragedies of War 1630–1648* (London: Longman, 2nd ed., 1999). Although some of Morrill's arguments in this book, especially about the phenomenon of neutralism in the counties, proved controversial the basic point that many and probably most country gentry dreaded the prospect of a civil war coming to their own neighborhood is incontrovertible.

Because most of the political nation still abhorred the prospect of civil war, each side needed to blame its outbreak on the other. As is well known, they did so in large part through opposing narratives of religious betrayals that drew on arguments and memories forged during earlier conflicts. The king and his supporters presented themselves as defenders of an ordered "church established by law," challenged by popular disorder and sectarian radicalism, while the parliament's publicists talked of sinister collusion between Catholics, Arminians, and atheists that imperiled the survival of both English liberty and reformed Christianity. Civil war partisanship therefore took on much of the coloration of a confessional contest between two different concepts of an English Protestant state. This was never perfectly the case, because both sides also appealed for support on more secular grounds, while a significant diversity of religious viewpoints within each camp prevented the pattern from becoming too neat. Although many royalists identified strongly with the episcopal Church and Prayer Book, not all did so, while the Long Parliament was never able to agree on the kind of Church it wanted, once it got rid of the Laudian bishops. Religious values and assumptions—and partisan memories of previous religious crises and conflicts—nevertheless strongly influenced not only original choices of allegiance but subsequent political divisions, especially among the victorious supporters of parliament after their victory in 1646.

In the 1640s problems of religious diversity and animosity therefore finally fractured and destroyed the imperfectly integrated state of Britain and Ireland, leading to civil wars followed by a series of experiments in constructing a new and different kind of state under the Long Parliament, Oliver Cromwell, and Cromwell's successors between 1658 and 1660. There was nothing inevitable about this outcome. If Charles I had been less committed to ceremonial uniformity or more patient and tactful in his efforts to achieve it, he would most likely have avoided the conflict in Scotland that triggered the collapse of his authority. If he had been luckier and more skillful as a military commander, he might have defeated the Scots before he lost control of England and Ireland. In 1643 he and his followers came fairly close to winning a military victory, while even as late as the decisive Battle of Naseby in 1645, the royalists might have won if the king had waited for reinforcements to arrive before engaging in combat. Until late in the day, the triumph and consolidation of a more authoritarian and firmly anti-puritan monarchy remained a possible outcome of the civil wars. But if Charles's defeat was not foreordained, the events of his reign were also far from random. In any number of ways, they were shaped and structured by the fashion in which a Protestant state had developed in Britain and Ireland over the previous two generations, along with the religious and ideological prejudices, arguments, and memories this process had produced. No longer a straightforward confessional clash between Roman Catholics and Protestants, the division now primarily involved different understandings of Protestantism and its relationship to royal authority. But much of the baggage left over from the previous century's religious conflicts appeared to gain a renewed relevance as civic peace grew more precarious. This again illustrates the degree to which religious war remained, not only a recurring reality in parts of early modern Europe but a vexing political problem, acting in constant dialogue with other problems to shape thought and behavior and challenge the orders of command and obedience through which sovereigns ruled.

Bibliography of Works Cited

Manuscripts

Archive du Ministère de l'Europe et des Affaires etrangères (Paris, France)
  Correspondence Politique Angleterre
  Correspondence Politique Hollande
Bibliothèque Nationale (Paris, France)
  Cinq cents de Colbert Mss. 426
  Dupuy Mss. 403
  Manuscrits Français, 1503, 3502, 3503, 3504, 3506, 3509, 3510, 15916, 15972, 15989
Bodleian Library (Oxford)
  North Mss. a.2
Brigham Young University Library (Provo, Utah)
  Vault Mss. 457 (Robert Beale collection of letters)
British Library
  Additional Mss. 4728, 4745, 4757, 5220, 12520, 17677B–K, 18639, 24562, 27962A and B, 32092, 32657, 33594, 34313, 36444, 36316, 39828, 46,369, 47087, 48017, 48027, 48029, 48104, 48116, 48163, 48166, 48167, 74287, 78172, 78178
  Cotton Mss. Caligula BIV, CIII, CVI, CVII, CVIII, CIX, DI, Galba DII, Otho EVIII, Titus BIII, BVI, C VI, Vespasian CVI, Vitellius CXVI
  Egerton Mss. 1694, 2074, 2075, 2598
  Harley Mss. 291, 6854, 6988, 6994, 6999, 7002, 7704
  King's Mss. 123
  Lansdowne Mss. 30, 33, 37, 42, 60, 61, 64, 66, 68, 71, 798
  Sloane Mss. 3199, 3521
  Stowe Mss. 169, 171, 172, 174, 175, 176
Folger Shakespeare Library (Washington, DC)
  L.a. 239, 243, 250, 321, 709, 713, 791, 810, 821
  L.d 2
  X.d 502
  V.a 164
  V.b 5, 214, 215, 291
Hatfield House (Hertfordshire) Cecil Papers, 148, 162
Haus- Hof- und Staatsarchiv (Vienna)
  Belgien PC 21, 44–49
Lambeth Palace Library Mss. 251, 597, 607, 611, 612, 614, 618, 619, 649, 943, 3470, 3471, 3740, 4701
Nationaal Archief (The Hague, Netherlands) Mss. 1.01.01.10/13, 13.01.14.184A, 3.01.14/2005
The National Archives (Kew)
  AO 1/292
  C/115
  E351/2029

E407/12
HC/13/25/141
PRO30/53/2
PRO31/3/27-41, Baschet transcripts of documents related to English affairs in Parisian archives
SP12, State Papers Domestic, Elizabeth I
SP14, State Papers Domestic, James I
SP16, State Papers Domestic, Charles I
SP52, State Papers Scotland
SP63, State Papers Ireland
SP75, State Papers Denmark
SP77, State Papers Flanders
SP78 State Papers France
SP81, State Papers German States
SP84 State Papers Holland
SP94 State Papers Spain
SP99 State Papers Venice
SP105 Archives of British Legations
STAC5/60 Star Chamber papers
Scottish National Archives (Edinburgh)
GD406
Sheffield City Archives
Wentworth Woodhouse Muniments
Staffordshire Record Office
D593/S/4/14/1-20 (Kent militia papers)
D603/K/1/6/1-38, D603/K/1/7/9-75 (Paget papers)
D (w) 1734/2/5/15e-k
Yale University, Beineke Library
Mss. 370

Microfilms

Library of Congress microfilms LC041/Camb194/1-Camb215/1 (The Trumbull Manuscripts)

Printed Primary Sources

Acts and Proceedings of the General Assembly of the Kirk of Scotland, part 3, vol. 1 (Edinburgh, 1845)
Allen, William, *An Apologie and Declaration of the... Two English Colleges* (Reims, 1581)
Anderson, Anthony, *A Sermon at Paules Cross... 23 April 1581* (1581)
Anonymous, *A Sermon Preached in Lent* (1580)
The apologie or defence of the most noble Prince William... Prince of Orange (Delft, 1581)
Ayre, John, *The Works of John Whitgift*, 3 vols, Parker Society Publications, 46-8 (Cambridge, 1851-3)

Bain, J., Boyd, W. K., et al., eds, *Calendar of State Papers Relating to Scotland and Mary, Queen of Scots, 1547-1603, Preserved in the Public Record Office and Elsewhere in England*, 13 vols in 14 (Edinburgh and Glasgow, 1898-1969)

Balesteros Beretta, Antonio, ed., *Correspondencia official de Don Diego Sarmiento de Acuña, Conde de Gondomar*, Coleccion de documentos ineditos para la historia de España, vols 1-4 (Madrid, 1936-45)

Bancroft, Richard, *Dangerous positions and proceedings published and practiced within this island of Brytaine* (London, 1593)

Bancroft, Richard, *A Sermon at Paul's Cross* (London, 1588)

Beccarie de Pavie, Raymond de, Baron de Fourquevaux, *Instructions for the warres, amply, learnedly and politiquely, discoursing the method of militarie discipline*, trans. Paul Ive (London, 1589)

Becon, Richard, *Solon his Follie, or, A Politique Discourse Touching the Reformation of the Common-weales Conquered, Declined and Corrupted*, ed. Clare Carrol and Vincent Carey (Binghamton, NY: Medieval and Renaissance Texts and Studies, 1996)

Bentrinck, G. C. et al., eds, *Calendar of State Papers, Relating to English Affairs Existing in the Archives of Venice, and in other Libraries of Northern Italy*, 38 vols (London, 1864-1947)

Berger de Xivrey, M., ed., *Recueil des lettres missives d'Henry IV*, vol. 6 (Paris: Imprimerie Impériale, 1853)

Berry, Lloyd E., ed., *John Stubbs's Gaping Gulf with Letters and Other Relevant Documents* (Charlottesville: University of Virginia Press for the Folger Shakespeare Library, 1968)

Bidwell, William and Jansson, Maija, eds, *Proceedings in Parliament 1626*, 3 vols (New Haven: Yale University Press, 1992)

Bilson, Thomas, *A sermon preached at Westminster* (London, 1603)

Birch, Thomas, ed., *The Court and Times of Charles I*, 2 vols (London, 1848)

Birch, Thomas, ed., *The Court and Times of James I*, 2 vols (London, 1848)

Birch, Thomas, ed., *An historical view of the negotiations between the courts of England, France and Brussels, from the year 1592 to 1617* (London, 1749)

Birch, Thomas, ed., *The Life of Henry Prince of Wales, Eldest Son of James I* (London, 1760)

Birch, Thomas, ed., *Memoirs of the Reign of Queen Elizabeth from the Year 1581 till her Death*, 2 vols (London, 1754)

Black, Joseph, ed., *The Martin Marprelate Tracts: A Modernized and Annotated Edition* (Cambridge: Cambridge University Press, 2008)

Blok, P. J., ed., *Correpondence inédite de Robert Dudley, comte de Leicester et de François et Jean Hotman* (Harlem: Soosjes, 1911)

Boersma, R. and Busken Huet, G., eds, *Brieven over het Leysterische Tijdvak uit de Papieren van Jean Hotman*, Bijdragen en Mededeelingen van het Historisch Genootschap 34 (Amsterdam: Johannes Müller, 1913)

Bor Christiaenszoon, Pieter, *Oorsprong, Begin, en Vervolgh der Nederlansche Oorlogen*, parts 2 and 3 (Amsterdam, 1680-1)

Bouchier, Elisabeth, ed., *The Diary of Sir Simonds D'Ewes, Journal d'un étudiant Londien sous le règne de Jacques Ier* (Paris: Didier, 1974)

Bradley, William Apsenwall, *The Correspondence of Philip Sidney and Hubert Languet* (Boston: Merrymount Press, 1912)

Brewer, J. and Bullen, W., *Calendar of the Carew Manuscripts Preserved in the Archiepiscopal Library at Lambeth (1515-1624)*, 6 vols (London, 1867-73)

A briefe discovery of the untruths and slanders (against the true government of the church of Christ) contained in a sermon preached the 8. of Feburary1588 by D. Bancroft (Edinburgh, 1590)
Brownlow, Richard, *Reports of diverse choice cases in law* (London, 1651)
Bruce, John, ed., *Correspondence of Robert Dudley Earl of Leicester*, Camden Society Publications, OS 27 (London, 1844)
Bruce, Robert, *Sermons* (Edinburgh, 1617)
Bruce, Robert, *Sermons Preached in the Kirk at Edinburgh* (Edinburgh, 1591)
Brugmans, H., ed., *Correspondentie van Robert Dudley, Graf van Leycester, en andere documenten betreffende zijn Gouvernemente Generaal*, 3 vols (Utrecht: Keminken Zoon, 1931)
Buchanan, George, *De Jure Regnum apud Scotos* (London, 1680)
Burdin, P., ed., *Ambassades de Monsieur de la Boderie en Angleterre... Depuis les Années 1606 Jusqu'en 1611*, 5 vols (Paris, 1750)
Calderwood, David, *The true history of the church of Scotland from the Reformation unto the end of the reign of King James VI* (Edinburgh, 1680)
Camden, William, *Actio in Henricum Garnetum Societatis Jesuiticae in Anglia superiorem, et caeteros qui proditione longè immanissima sereniss. Britanniae Magnae Regem, et Regni Angliae ordines pulvere fulminali èmedio tollere coniurâeunt* (London, 1607)
Camden, William, *The history of the most renowned and victorious princess Elizabeth* (London, 1688)
Cameron, A. I., ed., *The Warrender Papers*, 2 vols (Edinburgh: Scottish History Society, 1931–2)
Campion, Edmund and Hammer, Meredith, *Two Histories of Ireland, The one written by Edmond Campion, the other by Meredith Hammer* (Dublin, 1633)
Carleton, Dudley, *Letters from and to Sir Dudley Carleton, during his Embassy in Holland* (London, 1775)
Castiglione, Baldassare, *The Book of the Courtier*, ed. and trans. George Bull (London: Penguin Classics, 1976)
Cataneo, Giorlamo, *Most briefe tables to know briefly how many footmen... go to the making of a just battaile* (London, 1588)
The Causes of this general fast to begin the first Sabbath of August nixt, 1595 (Edinburgh, 1595)
Cecil, Robert, earl of Salisbury, *An Answere to certaine scandalous papers scattered abroad under colour of a Cathlicke admonition* (London, 1606)
Cecil, William, Lord Burghley, *The Execution of Justice in England*, ed. Robert Kingdon (Ithaca: Cornell University Press, 1965)
Charavay, Étienne, "Le Maréchal de Bouillon à la cour d'Angleterre," *Revue des documents historiques* 1 (1874): 54–9
Charron, Pierre de, *Of wisdome three books written in French by Peter Charro*, trans. Samson Leonard (London, 1608)
Churchyard, Thomas, *A Discourse of the Queen's Majesties Entertainment in Suffolk and Norfolk* (London, 1579)
Churchyard, Thomas, *A Generall Rehearsall of Warre, called Churchyard's Choice* (London, 1579)
Churchyard, Thomas, *Martyne Frobishers Voyage to Meta Incognita* (London, 1578)
Clifford, Arthur, ed., *The State Papers and Letters of Sir Ralph Sadler*, vol. 2 (Edinburgh, 1809)
Clifford, D. H., ed., *The Diaries of Lady Anne Clifford* (Phoenix Mill: Sutton, 1990)

Collier, J. Payne, ed., *The Egerton Papers*, Camden Society Publications, OS 12 (London, 1840)
Collins, Arthur, ed., *Letters and Memorials of State in the Reigns of Queen Mary, Queen Elizabeth, King James, King Charles the First*, 2 vols (London, 1746)
Collinson, Patrick, Craig, John, and Usher, Brett, eds, *Conferences and Combination Lectures in the Elizabethan Church: Dedham and Bury St Edmunds 1582–1590* (Woodbridge: Boydell Press, 2003)
Cosin, Richard, *Conspiracy for Pretended Reformation* (London, 1592)
Courcelles, M., *Extracts from the Despatches of M. Courcelles, French Ambassador at the Court of Scotland, MDLXXXVI–MDLXXXVII* (Edinburgh, 1828)
Cowell, John, *The Interpreter: or Booke containing the signification of words* (London, 1607)
Crosignani, Ginevra, McCoog, Thomas M., and Questier, Michael with the assistance of Peter Holmes, eds, *Recusancy and Conformity in Early Modern England: Manuscript and Printed Sources in Translation*, Studies and Texts 170 (Toronto: Pontifical Institute of Mediaeval Studies, 2010)
Daniel, Samuel, *A Panegyrike congratulatory to the Kings Majestie* (London, 1603)
Dasent, John Roche, et al., eds, *Acts of the Privy Council of England*, 42 vols (London, 1890–1974)
Davidson, John, *D. Bancroft's rashness in rayling against the Church of Scotland noted in an answere to a letter of a worthy person of England* (Edinburgh, 1590)
Davies, Richard, *A Funeral Sermon... at the burial of Walter Earle of Essex* (London, 1577)
Davison, William, *Letters and Papers relating to Patrick, Master of Grey* (Edinburgh, 1835)
Davys, Sir John, *A discoverie of the state of Ireland with the true causes why that kingdom was never entirely subdued* (London, 1613)
Davys, Sir John, *Le primer report des cases & matters en ley* (Dublin, 1615)
A Declaratioun of the Kings Majestis intentioun and meaning toward the late actis of Parliament (Edinburgh, 1585)
Dee, John, *General and Rare Memorials* (London, 1577)
Devereux, Robert, 2nd earl of Essex, *An Apologie of the Earle of Essex* (London, 2nd ed., 1603)
Devereux, Walter Bouchier, *Life and Letters of Robert Devereux second Earl of Essex*, 2 vols (London, 1853)
Digges, Dudley, ed., *The Complete Ambassador* (London, 1655)
Digges, Leonard, *An arithmeticall, militare treatise named Stratioticis* (London, 1579)
Digges, Thomas, *A true Report of the Service in the Lowe countries* (London, 1587)
Duncan-Jones, Katherine and Van Dorsten, Jan, eds, *Miscellaneous Prose of Sir Philip Sidney* (Oxford: Oxford University Press, 1973)
Edes, Richard, *Six learned and godly sermons* (London, 1604)
Emlyn, Sollom, ed., *A Complete Collection of State-Trials and Proceedings for High Treason* (London, 1730)
Estienne, Henri, *Ane Mervellous discours upon the lyfe, deides and behaviours of Katherine de Medicis, Quene Mother* (Paris [for Edinburgh?], 1576)
Evans, John, ed., *The Works of Sir Roger Williams* (Oxford, Clarendon Press, 1972)
Everard, John, *Some Gospel Treasures Opened* (London, 1653)
Fabre, F., "The English College at Eu, 1582–1592," *Catholic Historical Review* 37 (1951): 257–80
Fortescue, Sir John, *De laudibus legem Angliae* (London, 1616)
Fox, John, *Christ Jesus Triumphant* (1579)
Fulbeck, William, *Pandectes* (London 1602)

Furnival, F. J., ed., *Queen Elizabeth's Academy* (London, 1869)
Fussner, F. S., ed., "William Camden's Discourse Concerning the Prerogative of the Crown," *Proceedings of the American Philosophical Society* 101 (1957): 204–15
Fyfe, James Gabriel, ed., *Scottish Diaries and Memoirs, 1550–1746* (Stirling: E. Mackay, 1928)
Gardiner, Samuel Rawson, ed. and trans., *El Hecho de los Tratados del Matrimonio pretendido por el Principe de Gales con la serenissima Infante de Espana Maria/Narrative of the Spanish Marriage Treaty*, Camden Society Publications, OS 101 (1869)
Gardiner, Samuel Rawson, ed., *Letters and other Documents Illustrating the Relations between England and Germany at the Commencement of the Thirty Years War*, 2vols, Camden Society Publications, OS 90, 98 (1865, 1868)
Gardiner, Samuel Rawson, ed., *Parliamentary Debates in 1610*, Camden Society Publications, OS 81 (1862)
Gates, Geffrey, *The defence of the miltarie profession* (1579)
Gentillet, Alberico, *Discours sur les moyens de bien gourverner et maintenir en bonne paix un royame ou autre principauté contre Nicole Marchiavel Florentin* (n.p., 1576)
Gerard, John, *The Autobiography of an Elizabethan* (Oxford: Family Publications, 2006)
Grossart, Alexander, ed., *The Complete Works in Verse and Prose of Samuel Daniel*, 5 vols (London, 1896)
Grossart, Alexander, ed., *The Works in Verse and Prose Complete of the Right Honourable Fulke Greville, Lord Brooke*, 4 vols (Blackburn, 1870)
Hakluyt, Richard, *A Discourse of Western Planting*, ed. David B. Quinn and Alison M. Quinn (London: Hakluyt Society Publications, 1993)
Hammer, Paul, ed., *Letters from Sir Robert Cecil to Sir Christopher Hatton, 1590–1591*, Camden Society Publications series 5, vol. 22 (1999)
Harding, Thomas, *A Confutation of a Booke* (1565)
Hartley, T. H., ed., *Proceedings in the Parliaments of Elizabeth I*, 3 vols (Leicester: Leicester University Press, 1981–95)
Hasler, P. W., ed., *The History of Parliament: The House of Commons 1558–1603* (London: Boydell & Brewer, 1981)
Hayward, Sir John, *The Lives of the iii Norman Kings* (London, 1613)
Hayward, Sir John, *A Treatise of Union of the Two Realmes of England and Scotland* (London, 1604)
Hebel, William, ed., *The Works of Michael Drayton*, vol. 2 (Oxford: Shakespeare Head Press, 1941)
Historical Manuscripts Commission, *Calendar of the Manuscripts of the Marquis of Bath Preserved at Longleat*, 5 vols (London, 1904–80)
Historical Manuscripts Commission, *Calendar of the Manuscripts of the Most Honourable the Marquis of Salisbury... Preserved at Hatfield House, Hertfordshire*, 24 vols (London, 1883–1976)
Historical Manuscripts Commission, *Eleventh Report of the Commission on Historical Manuscripts* (London, 1887)
Historical Manuscripts Commission, *Mar and Kellie Manuscripts* (London, 1904)
Historical Manuscripts Commission, *Report on the Manuscripts of the Duke of Buccleuch and Queensberry*, vol. 1 (London, 1899)
Historical Manuscripts Commission, *Report on the Manuscripts of the Earl of Ancaster* (London, 1907)
Historical Manuscripts Commission, *Report on the Manuscripts of Lord DeLisle and Dudley, Preserved at Penshurst Place*, 6 vols (London: HM Stationery Office, 1925–66)

Historical Manuscripts Commission, *Report on the Manuscripts of the Marquess of Downshire*, vol. 4: *Papers of William Trumbull the Elder, Jan. 1613–August 1614* (London, 1940)
Hooker, Richard, *Of the Lawes of Ecclesiastical Politie, Eight Books* (London, 1598)
Houliston, Victor, Crosignani, Ginevra, and McCoog, Thomas M., eds, *The Correspondence and Unpublished Papers of Robert Persons, SJ*, vol. 1: *1574–1588* (Toronto: Pontifical Institute of Mediaeval Studies, 2017)
Howard, Philip, Earl of Arundel, *Callophisus* (1581)
Howson, *A sermon preached at St. Maries in Oxford* (London, 1602)
Hughes, Paul and Larkin, James, eds, *Tudor Royal Proclamations*, 3 vols (New Haven: Yale University Press, 1969)
An humble motion with submission to the right Honorable LL of Hir Majesties Privie Counsell wherein is laid open to be considered, how necessarie it were for the good of this lande, and the Queenes Majesties safety, that the ecclesiastical discipline were reformed (Edinburgh, 1590)
The Humble Petition of the Communaltie (Middleburg, 1587)
Hume, David, *History of Scotland* (Edinburgh, 1648)
Hume, M. A. S., ed., *Calendar of Letters and State Papers, Relating to English Affairs, Preserved Principally in the Archives of Simancas, Elizabeth*, 4 vols (London, 1896–9)
Hurrault, Jacques, *Politicke, moral and martial discourses* (London, 1595)
James VI and I, *Daemonologie* (Edinburgh, 1597)
James VI and I, *Déclaration du Serenissime Roy Jaques I Roy de la Grand' Bretaigne France et Irlande, Defenseur de la Foy. Pour le Droit des Rois et independance de leurs Couronnes, Contre le Harangue de l'Illustrissime Cardinal du Perron* (London, 1615)
James VI and I, *An Fruitfull Meditatioun* (Edinburgh, 1588)
James VI and I, *His Majesties speech in this last session of Parliament* (London, 1605)
James VI and I, *A meditation upon the Lord's prayer written by the Kings Majesties* (London, 1619)
James VI and I, *A meditation upon the 27, 28, 29 verses of the XXVII chapter of St. Matthew* (London, 1620)
James VI and I, *Ane Meditatioun upon the first buke of the Chronicles* (Edinburgh, 1589)
James VI and I, *A Premonition to All Most Mightie Monarches, Kings, Free Princes and States of Christendom* (London, 1609)
James VI and I, *Regis oratio, habita in postremo regni ordinum convent, Westmonasterii* (London, 1605)
James VI and I, *The Workes of the Most High and Mighty Prince James* (London, 1616)
Jansson, Maija, ed., *Proceedings in Parliament 1614* (Philadelphia: American Philosophical Society, 1988)
Jansson, Maija and Bidwell, William B., eds, *Proceedings in Parliament 1625* (New Haven: Yale University Press, 1987)
Journal of the House of Commons, vol. 1, 1547–1629 (London, 1802)
A joyful song of the royall receiving of the Queenes most excellent Maiestie into her highnesse campe at Tilsburie (London, 1589)
Keeler, Mary Frear, Cole, Maija Jansson, and Bidwell, William, eds, *Proceedings in Parliament 1628*, 6 vols (New Haven: Yale University Press, 1977–83)
Kermaingant, P. Laffleur, ed., *L'Ambassade de France en Angleterre sous Henri IV. Mission de Christophe de Harlay, Comte de Beaumont (1602–1605)*, 2 vols (Paris: Bibliothèque de l'école des Chartes, 1895)

Knox, Thomas Francis, ed., *First and Second Diaries of the English College of Douay*, Records of English Catholics under the Penal Laws, vol. 1 (London: Sagwan Press, 1977)
Knox, Thomas Francis, ed., *The Letters and Memorials of William Cardinal Allen*, Records of the English Catholics under the Penal Laws, vol. 2 (London, 1882)
Kossman, E. H. and Mellink, Albert Fredrik, eds, *Texts Concerning the Revolt of the Netherlands* (Cambridge: Cambridge University Press, 1974)
Kuin, Roger, ed., *The Correspondence of Sir Philip Sidney*, 2 vols (Oxford: Oxford University Press, 2012)
Laing, David, ed., *The Miscellany of the Wodrow Society*, vol. 1 (Edinburgh, 1844)
A Lamentable Complaint of the Commonality, by way of supplication to the high court of parliament, for a learned ministry (London, 1585)
Latham, Agnes and Youings, Joyce, eds, *The Letters of Sir Walter Ralegh* (Exeter: University of Exeter Press, 1999)
Lee, Maurice, ed., *Dudley Carleton to John Chamberlain 1603–1624: Jacobean Letters* (New Brunswick: Rutgers University Press, 1972)
Lemon, R. and Green, M. A. E., eds, *Calendar of State Papers Domestic Series, Preserved in Her Majesty's Public Record Office, Edward VI, Mary I, Elizabeth I and James I*, 12 vols (London, 1865–72)
Lennox, Charlotte, trans., *Memoirs of Maximilien de Bethune, Duke of Sully*, 6 vols (London, 1778)
Leslie, John, *A Treatise of Treasons* (Louvain, 1572)
Lodge, Edmund, ed., *Illustrations of British History, Biography and Manners in the Reigns of Henry VIII, Edward VI, Mary, Elizabeth and James I*, 3 vols (London, 1791)
Lonchay, Henri and Cuvelier, Joseph, eds, *Correspondance de la cour d'Espagne sur les affaires des Pays-Bas au XVIIe siècle* (Brussels: Libraire Kiessling, 1923)
McClure, Norman Egbert, ed., *The Letters of John Chamberlain*, 2 vols (Philadelphia: American Philosophical Society, 1939)
McGinnis, Paul and Williamson, Arthur, eds, *The British Union: A Critical Edition and Translation of David Hume of Godscroft's* De unione Insulae Britannicae (Aldershot: Ashgate, 2002)
McGinnis, Paul and Williamson, Arthur, trans. and eds, *George Buchanan: The Political Poetry* (Edinburgh: Scottish History Society, 1995)
Machiavelli, Niccolò, *The arte of warre* (London, 1588)
McIlwain, Charles, ed., *The Political Works of James I* (Cambridge, MA: Harvard University Press, 1918)
MacMahon, William and Pollen, John Hungerford, eds, *The Venerable Philip Howard, Earl of Arundel, 1557–1559*, Catholic Record Society Publications 21 (London, 1921)
Marprelate, Martin, *Hay any work for the cooper* (1589)
Marsollier, J., *Histoire de Henry de la Tour d'Auvergne, duc de Buillon* (Paris, 1719)
Masson, D., ed., *Register of the Privy Council of Scotland*, vol. 7, 1604–1607 (Edinburgh: H. M. General Register House, 1906)
Melville, James, *The Diary of James Melville, 1556–1601* (Edinburgh, 1829)
Melville, James of Halhill, *Memoirs of his Own Life* (Edinburgh, 1827; facs. repr. New York: AMS Press, 1973)
Mémoires de Maximilien de Béthune, Duke de Sully, 5 vols (London, 1778)
Mendoza, Bernardino de, *Theorique and practise of warre* (London, 1597)
Le mercure françois 1617 (Paris, 1617)
Meteren, Emanuel van, *Historie der Nederlandscher ende haerder naburen oorlogen ende geschieden* (Graven-Hague, 1614)

A most necessary and godly prayer for the preservation of the Earl of Leicester (London, 1585)

Moysie, David, *Memoires of the Affairs of Scotland*, ed. J. Dennistoun, Bannatyne Club Publications (Edinburgh, 1830)

M[unday], A[nthony], *A briefe and true report of the execution of certaine traytours at Tiborne* (London, 1582)

Murden, William, *A Collection of State Papers Relating to Affairs in the Reign of Queen Elizabeth, from the year 1571 to 1596* (London, 1740)

Nichols, John, *The Progresses, Processions and Magnificent Festivities of King James the First*, 2 vols (London, 1828)

Nichols, John, *The Progresses and Public Processions of Queen Elizabeth*, 3 vols (London, 1823)

Nicolas, Nicholas Harris, ed., *Memoirs of the Life and Times of Sir Christopher Hatton* (London, 1847)

Noue, François de la, *The Politicke and militarie discourses of Lord de la Noue* (London, 1587)

Ogle, Octavius, *Copy-Book of Sir Amias Poulet's Letters Written During his Embassy to France (AD 1577)* (London, 1866)

Overton, William, *A Godly and pithie Exhortation made to the Judges and Justices of Sussex* (London, 1579)

Papers Illustrating the History of the Scots Brigade in the Service of the United Netherlands, 1571–1782, Scottish History Society Volumes, Series 1, vol. 32 (Edinburgh, 1899)

Pears, Steuart, ed., *The Correspondence of Philip Sidney and Hubert Languet* (London, 1845)

Pearsall Smith, Logan, ed., *Life and Letters of Sir Henry Wotton*, 2 vols (Oxford: Clarendon Press, 1907)

Peck, D. C., ed., *Leicester's Commonwealth: The Copy of a Letter Written by a Master of Art at Cambridge and Related Documents* (Athens, OH: Ohio University Press, 1985)

Peckham, George, *A true reporte, of the late discoueries by Sir Humfrey Gilbert* (London, 1583)

Penry, John, *Th'appellation of John Penri, unto the highe court of Parliament from the bad and injurious dealing of th'Archb. of Canterb. & other his colleagues of the high commission* (London, 1589)

Penry, John, *A brief discovery of the untruths and slanders (against the government of Christ) contained in a sermon, preached the 8 of Februarie 1588 by D. Bancroft* (Edinburgh, 1589)

Penry, John, *A defence of that which hath been written in the questions of the ignorant ministerie, and the communicating with them* (London, 1588)

Penry, John, *An exhortation unto the governors and people of her Majesties countrie of Wales, to labour earnestly to have the preaching of the Gospell planted among them* (London, 1588)

Penry, John, *An humble motion with submission unto the right Honorable LL of her Majesties Privie Counsell Wherein is to be considered, how necessarie it were for the good of this lande, and the Queenes Majesties safety, that ecclesiastical government were reformed* (Edinburgh, 1589)

Penry, John, *A Treatise Containing the Aequity of an Humble Supplication which Is to be Exhibited Unto Hir Gracious Majesty and this High Court of Parliament in behalfe of the Countrey of Wales* (Oxford, 1587)

Penry, John, *A treatise wherein is manifestly proved, that reformation and those that sincerely favor the same, are unjustly charged to be enemies unto her Majesties, and the state* (Edinburgh, 1590)

Penry, John, *A viewe of some part of such publick wants and disorders as are in the service of God, within her Majesties countrie of Wales together with an humble petition, unto this high Court of Parliament for their speedy redress* (London, 1589)

Persons, Robert, *A brief discours containing certayne reasons why Catholiques refuse to goe to Church* (1580)

Persons, Robert, *The judgment of a Catholike English-man, living in banishment for his religion Written to his private friend in England. Concerning a late booke set forth and entitled, Tripli Nodex, Tripli Cuneus* (St. Omer, 1608)

Persons, Robert, *A treatise tending to mitigation towardes Catholike-subjects in England* (St. Omer, 1607)

Petoe, Henry, *England's Caesar* (London, 1603)

Petti, Anthony, ed., *Recusant Documents from the Ellesmere Manuscripts*, Catholic Record Society Publications 60 (St. Albans: Fisher Knight, 1968)

Prinsterer, G. Groen van, ed., *Archives ou correspondence inédite de la maison Orange-Nassau*, 12 vols (Utrecht: Kemink et Fils, 1835–45)

Q. Z., *A Discovery of Treason* (London, 1584)

Raikes, G. A., *The History of the Honourable Artillery Company of London*, vol. 1 (London, 1878)

Ralegh, Sir Walter, *History of the World*, ed. George Patrides (London: Macmillan, 1971)

Rayon, D. José Sancho and Francisco de Zabalburu, D., eds, *Correspondencia de Felipe II con sus embajadores en la corte de Inglaterra*, Coleccion de documentos ineditos para la historia de España, vol. 91 (Madrid, 1888)

The Reading of the famous and learned Robert Callis... upon the statute of 23 H. 8 (London, 1647)

Reynolds, Matthew, *Godly Reformers and their Opponents in Early Modern England: Religion in Norwich c. 1560–1643* (Woodbridge: Boydell Press, 2005)

Ribaut, Jean, *The whole and true discoverye of Terra Florida* (London, 1563)

Rich, Barnaby, *Allarme to England* (London, 1572)

Rich, Barnaby, *Faults, Faults, Nothing but Faults* (London, 1606)

Rich, Barnaby, *Four bookes of offices* (1606)

Rich, Barnaby, *The Irish Hubub, or, the English Hue and Cry* (London, 1619)

Rich, Barnaby, *A Path-Way to military practice* (London, 1589)

Rushworth, John, *Historical Collections of Private Passages of State*, 8 vols (London, 1721)

Savile, Henry, *The Ende of Nero and Beginning of Galba* (London, 1591)

Sawyer, E., ed., *Memorials of Affairs of State in the Reigns of Queen Elizabeth and King James I*, 3 vols (London, 1725)

Scott, Thomas, *Vox Populi. Or Newes from Spain translated according to the Spanish copies* (London, 1620)

Scott, William, *An Apologetical Narration* (Edinburgh: Wodrow Society, 1846)

Seddon, P. R., ed., *Letters of John Clare Earl of Holles*, 2 vols (Nottingham: Thoroton Society, 1983)

Segar, William, *Honor Militarie and Civil* (1602)

Smith, H. and Baker, G., eds, *Papers of Nathaniel Bacon*, 2 vols, Norfolk Record Society Publications 49 (1982–3)

Smith, Thomas, *De Republica Anglorum* (London, 1583)

Smuts, R. Malcolm, ed., "The Whole Royal and Magnificent Entertainment of King James through the City of London, 15 March 1604, with the Arches of Triumph," in *Thomas Middleton: The Collected Works*, general eds Gary Taylor and John Lavagnino (Oxford: Clarendon Press, 2007), 219–79

Spedding, James, Ellis, Robert Leslie, and Heath, Douglas Denon, eds, *The Works of Francis Bacon*, 14 vols (Boston, 1857–74)
Spenser, Edmund, *A View of the Present State of Ireland*, ed. L. W. Renwick (Oxford: Oxford University Press, 1970)
Spenser, Edmund, *A view of the state of Ireland, written dialogue-wise betweene Eudoxus and Irenaeus, in the year 1596* (Dublin, 1633)
Spottiswood, John, *The history of the church and state of Scotland beginning in the year of our lord 203 and continued to the end of the reign of James VI* (London, 1655)
Stanihurst, Richard, "The Description of Ireland," in Raphael Holinshed, *Chronicles*, vol. 2 (London, 1586)
Starkey, David, "Intimacy and Innovation: The Rise of the Privy Chamber, 1485–1547," in *The English Court from the Wars of the Roses to the Civil War*, ed. David Starkey et al. (London: Longman, 1987), 71–118
Stevenson, Joseph, et al., *Calendar of State Papers, Foreign Series, of the Reign of Elizabeth*, 17 vols (London, 1863–1950)
Stevenson, Joseph, Crosby, A. J., et al., eds, *Calendar of State Papers Relating to Ireland of the Reign of Elizabeth*, 23 vols (London, 1863–1950)
Stow, John, *Annales, or a General Chronicle of England* (London, 1631)
Strype, John, *Annals of the Reformation*, vol. 3 (London, 1728)
Strype, John, *The Life and Acts of John Whitgift*, 3 vols (Oxford, 1822)
Stubbs, John, *A Discovery of a Gaping Gulf Whereinto England is Like to Be Swallowed by an Other French Mariage* (London, 1579)
A Summarie... of Sir Francis Drake's West Indian Voyage (London 1589)
Tacitus, *The Annales of Cornelius Tacitus. The Description of Germany*, trans. Richard Greneway (London, 1598)
Talbot, Claire, ed., *Miscellanea Recusant Records*, Catholic Record Society vol. 53 (1961)
Tanner, J. R., *Constitutional Documents of the Reign of James I, 1603–1625* (Cambridge: Cambridge University Press, 1930)
Taylor, E. G. R., ed., *The Troublesome Voyage of Captain Edward Fenton, 1582–1583*, Hakluyt Society Publications second series 113 (Cambridge: Cambridge University Press, 1959)
Teulet, Alexandre, ed., *Papiers d'état: Pièces et documents inédits ou peu connus relatifs a l'histoire de l'Écosse*, 3 vols (Paris, 1852–60)
Teulet, Alexandre, ed., *Relations Politiques de la France et de l'Espagne avec l'Ecosse au XVIe siècle*, 5 vols (Paris, 1862)
Thevet, André, *The New found worlde, or Antarctike* (London, 1568)
T. P., *The Knowledge and Conduct of War* (1578)
Ungerer, Gustav, *A Spaniard in Elizabethan England: The Correspondence of Antonio Perez's Exile*, 2 vols (London: Tamesis, 1974)
Valdez, Francisco de, *The segieant maijor* (London, 1590)
Vallency, Charles, ed., *Collectanea de rebus Hibernicus*, vol. 1 (Dublin, 1786)
Veenendaal, A. J., ed., *Johan van Oldenbarnevelt Bescheiden Betreffende zijn Staatkundig Beleid en zijn Familie, tweed deel, 1602–1613*, Rijks Geschiedkundige Publicatien 108 ('s-Gravenhage: Martinus Nijhoff, 1962)
Vega, Luis Gutierrez de la, *A compendious treatise entitled, De re militari* (1582)
Verantwoordinge vandeb welgeboren heer Philips grave van Hohenloe (1587)
Wilson, Thomas, *The State of England, Anno Dom. 1600*, ed. J. F. Fisher, Royal Historical Society Camden, fifth series, 52 (1936)

Wither, George, *Britain's Remembrancer, containing a narration of the plague lately past* (London, 1628)
Wotton, Anthony [attributed], *The State of Christendom, or, A most exact and curious discovery of many secret passages and hidden mysteries of the times* (London, 1657)

Secondary Published Works

Acerra, Martine and Matinière, Guy, eds, *Coligny, les protestants et la mer* (Paris: Presses de l'Université de Paris-Sorbonne, 1997)
Adams, Julia, *The Familial State: Ruling Families and Merchant Capitalism in Early Modern Europe* (Ithaca: Cornell University Press, 2005)
Adams, Simon, "'Because I am of that Countrye & Mynde to Plant Myself there': Robert Dudley, Earl of Leicester, and the West Midlands," *Midlands History* 20 (1995): 20-75
Adams, Simon, "The Dudley Clientele, 1553-63," in *Leicester and the Court: Essays on Elizabethan Politics* (Manchester: Manchester University Press, 2002), 151-75
Adams, Simon, "Eliza Enthroned? The Court and its Politics," in *The Reign of Elizabeth I*, ed. Christopher Haigh (Basingstoke: Macmillan, 1984), 55-77
Adams, Simon, "Faction, Clientage and Party: English Politics, 1550-1603," *History Today* 33 (1982): 33-9
Adams, Simon, "Favourites and Factions at the Elizabethan Court," repr. in *Leicester and the Court: Essays on Elizabethan Politics*, ed. Ronald G. Asch and Adolf M. Birke (Manchester: Manchester University Press, 2002), 46-67
Adams, Simon, "The Gentry of North Wales and the Earl of Leicester's Expedition to the Netherlands, 1585-6," in *Leicester and the Court: Essays on Elizabethan Politics* (Manchester: Manchester University Press, 2002), 235-52
Adams, Simon, *Leicester and the Court: Essays on Elizabethan Politics* (Manchester: Manchester University Press, 2002)
Adams, Simon, "The Outbreak of the Elizabethan Naval War against the Spanish Empire: The Embargo of May 1585 and Sir Francis Drake's West Indian Voyage," in *England, Spain and the Grand Armada 1585-1604: Essays from the Anglo-Spanish Conference, London and Madrid 1988*, ed. M. J. Rodriguez-Salgado and Simon Adams (Edinburgh: John Donald, 1991), 45-69
Adams, Simon, "The Patronage of the Crown in Elizabethan Politics: The 1590s in Perspective," in *The Reign of Elizabeth: Court and Culture in the Last Decade*, ed. John Guy (Cambridge: Cambridge University Press, 1995), 20-45
Adams, Simon, "A Puritan Crusade? The Composition of the Earl of Leicester's Expedition to the Netherlands, 1585-6," in *Leicester and the Court: Essays on Elizabethan Politics* (Manchester: Manchester University Press, 2002), 176-95
Adams, Simon, "The Road to La Rochelle: English Foreign Policy and the Huguenots, 1610-1629," *Proceedings of the Huguenot Society of London* 22 (1975): 414-29
Adams, Simon, "Spain or the Netherlands: The Dilemmas of Early Stuart Foreign Policy," in *Before the English Civil War: Essays on Early Stuart Politics and Government*, ed. Howard Tomlinson (Basingstoke: Macmillan, 1988), 79-101
Adamson, John, *The Noble Revolt: The Overthrow of Charles I* (London: Weidenfeld & Nicolson, 2007)
Airs, Malcom, "Pomp and Glory: The Influence of Theobalds," in *Patronage, Culture and Power: The Early Cecils*, ed. Pauline Croft, Yale Studies in British Art 8 (New Haven and London: Yale University Press, 2002), 3-21

Akkerman, Nadine, *Elizabeth Stuart, Queen of Hearts* (Oxford: Oxford University Press, 2021)
Alford, Stephen, *The Watchers: A Secret History of the Reign of Elizabeth* (London: Allen Lane, 2012)
Allen, Paul C., *Philip III and the Pax Hispanica, 1598-1621: The Failure of Grand Strategy* (New Haven: Yale University Press, 2000)
Amussen, Susan, *An Ordered Society: Gender and Class in Early Modern England* (Oxford: Blackwell, 1988)
Andrews, Kenneth, *Elizabethan Privateering: English Privateering during the Spanish War 1585-1603* (Cambridge: Cambridge University Press, 1964)
Andrews, Kenneth, "The English in the Caribbean, 1560-1620," in *The Westward Enterprise*, ed. Kenneth Andrews, Nicholas Canny, and P. E. H. Hair (Liverpool: Liverpool University Press, 1978), 103-24
Andrews, Kenneth, *Trade, Plunder and Settlement: Maritime Enterprise and the Genesis of the British Empire, 1480-1630* (Cambridge: Cambridge University Press, 1984)
Archer, Ian, "The Burden of Taxation in Sixteenth-Century London," *Historical Journal* 44 (2001): 599-607
Archer, Ian, "The City of London and the Ulster Plantation," in *The Plantation of Ulster: Ideology and Practice*, ed. Eamonn Ó Ciardha and Micháel Ó Siochrú (Manchester: Manchester University Press, 2012), 78-97
Armitage, David, *Ideological Origins of the British Empire* (Cambridge: Cambridge University Press, 2000)
Arnade, Peter, *Beggars, Iconoclasts and Civic Patriots: The Political Culture of the Dutch Revolt* (Ithaca: Cornell University Press, 2008)
Asch, Ronald, *Sacral Kingship between Disenchantment and Re-enchantment: The French and English Monarchies 1587-1688* (New York: Berghahn, 2014)
Ash, Eric, *The Draining of the Fens: Projectors, Popular Politics, and State Building in Early Modern England* (Baltimore: Johns Hopkins University Press, 2017)
Aston, Trevor, ed., *The General Crisis of the Seventeenth Century* (London: Basic Books, 1965)
Augeron, Mickaël, "Coligny et les espagnols à travers la course (c. 1560-1572): une politique maritime au service de la cause protestante," in *Coligny, les protestants et la mer*, ed. Martine Acerra and Guy Matinière (Paris: Presses de l'Université de Paris-Sorbonne, 1997), 155-76
Augeron, Mickaël and Vidal, Laurent, "Refuges ou réseaux? Les dynamiques protestants au xvie siècle," in *D'Un Rivage à l'Autre: Villes et Protestantisme dans l'Aire Atlantique (XVIe-XVIIe siècles)*, ed. Guy Martinière, Didier Poton, and François Souty (Paris: Imprimerie Nationale, 1999), 30-61
Bangs, Carl, *Arminius: A Study in the Dutch Reformation* (Nashville: Abingdon Press, 1971)
Bartlett, Thomas and Jeffrey, Keith, eds, *A Military History of Ireland* (Cambridge: Cambridge University Press, 1996)
Bates, Katherine, *The Rhetoric of Courtship* (Cambridge: Cambridge University Press, 1992)
Bauckham, Richard, *Tudor Apocalypse* (Oxford: Sutton Courtney, 1978)
Beik, William, *Absolutism and Society in Seventeenth-Century France: State Power and Provincial Society in Languedoc* (Cambridge: Cambridge University Press, 1989)
Bellany, Alistair, "The Embarrassment of Libels: Perceptions and Representations of Verse Libelling in Early Modern England," in *The Politics of the Public Sphere in Early Modern England*, ed. Peter Lake and Steven Pincus (Manchester: Manchester University Press, 2012), 144-67

Bellany, Alistair, *The Politics of Court Scandal in Early Modern England: News Culture and the Overbury Affair, 1603–1660* (Cambridge: Cambridge University Press, 2002)
Bellany, Alistair, "Railing Rhymes Revisited: Libels, Scandals and Early Stuart Politics," *History Compass* 5 (2007): 1136–79
Bellany, Alistair, "'Raylinge Rymes and Vaunting Verse': Libellous Politics in Early Stuart England, 1603–1628," in *Culture and Politics in Early Stuart England*, ed. Kevin Sharpe and Peter Lake (Basingstoke: Macmillan, 1994), 283–310
Bellany, Alastair, "The Rise of the Howards at Court," in *The Oxford Handbook of John Donne*, ed. Jeanne Shami, Dennis Flynn, and Thomas M. Hester (Oxford: Oxford University Press, 2011), 537–53
Bellany, Alistair and Cogswell, Thomas, *The Murder of King James I* (New Haven: Yale University Press, 2015)
Benedict, Philip, *Christ's Churches Purely Reformed: A Social History of Calvinism* (New Haven: Yale University Press, 2002)
Bitsch, Caroline, *Vie et carrière d'Henri II de Bourbon, Prince de Condé (1588–1646)* (Paris: Honoré Champion, 2008)
Black, Joseph, "The Rhetoric of Reaction: The Martin Marprelate Tracts (1588–89), Anti-Martinism and the Uses of Print in Early Modern England," *Sixteenth Century Journal* 28 (1997): 707–25
Blakeway, Anne, "James VI and James Douglas Earl of Morton," in *James VI and Noble Power in Scotland, 1578–1603*, ed. Miles Kerr-Peterson and Steven J. Reid (London: Routledge, 2017), 12–31
Blet, Pierre, "L'article du Tiers aux États Généraux de 1614," *Revue d'histoire moderne et contemporain* 2 (1951): 81–106
Borja, Francisco de, "Intrigues of a Scottish Jesuit at the Spanish Court: Unpublished Letters of William Crichton to Claudio Aquaviva (Madrid 1590–1592)," in *The Reckoned Expense: Edmund Campion and the Early English Jesuits: Essays in celebration of the first centenary of Campion Hall, Oxford*, ed. Thomas McCoog (Woodbridge: Boydell Press, 1996), 215–45
Bossy, John, *The English Catholic Community 1570–1850* (London: Longman, 1975)
Bossy, John, "English Catholics and the French Marriage," *Recusant History* 5 (1959–60): 2–12
Bossy, John, "The Heart of Robert Persons," in *The Reckoned Expense: Edmund Campion and the Early English Jesuits: Essays in Celebration of the First Centenary of Campion Hall, Oxford*, ed. Thomas McCoog (Woodbridge: Boydell Press, 1996), 141–58
Bossy, John, "The Mass as a Social Institution 1200–1700," *Past and Present* 100 (1983): 29–61
Bossy, John, *Under the Molehill: An Elizabethan Spy Story* (New Haven: Yale University Press, 2001)
Boucher, Philip P., "Revisioning the 'French Atlantic': or How to Think about the French Presence in the Atlantic, 1550–1625," in *The Atlantic World and Virginia, 1550–1624*, ed. Peeter Mancall (Chapel Hill: University of North Carolina Press, 2007), 274–306
Bourdin, Bernard, *La genèse théologico-politique de l'État modern: la controverse de Jacques 1er d'Angleterre avec le cardinal Bellarmin* (Paris: Presses Universitaires de France, 2004)
Bouwsma, William, *Venice and the Defense of Republican Liberty: Renaissance Values in the Age of the Counter Reformation* (Berkeley: University of California Press, 1968)
Boyer, Allen D., *Sir Edward Coke and the Elizabethan Age* (Stanford: Stanford University Press 2003)

Boynton, Lindsay, "The Tudor Provost Marshal," *English Historical Review* 77 (1962): 437–55

Braddick, Michael, *God's Fury, England's Fire: A New History of the English Civil War* (London: Penguin, 2008)

Braddick, Michael, *State Formation in Early Modern England, c. 1550–1700* (Cambridge: Cambridge University Press, 2000)

Bradshaw, Brendan, "The English Reformation and Identity Formation in Ireland and Wales," in *British Consciousness and Identity: The Making of Britain 1533–1707*, ed. Brendan Bradshaw and Peter Roberts (Cambridge: Cambridge University Press, 1998), 43–111

Bradshaw, Brendan, *The Irish Constitutional Revolution of the Sixteenth Century* (Cambridge: Cambridge University Press, 1979)

Brady, Ciaran, "The Captains' Games: Army and Society in Elizabethan Ireland," in *A Military History of Ireland*, ed. Thomas Bartlett and Jeffrey Keith (Cambridge: Cambridge University Press, 1996), 136–59

Brady, Ciaran, *The Chief Governors: The Rise and Fall of Reform Government in Tudor Ireland, 1536–1588* (Cambridge: Cambridge University Press, 1994)

Brady, Ciaran, "From Policy to Power: The Evolution of Tudor Reform Strategies in Sixteenth-Century Ireland," in *Reshaping Ireland 1550–1700: Colonization and its Consequences*, ed. Brian Mac Cuarta, SJ (Dublin: Four Courts Press, 2011), 21–42

Brady, Ciaran, ed., *A Viceroy's Vindication: Sir Henry Sidney's Memoir of Service in Ireland, 1556–1578* (Cork: Cork University Press, 2002)

Breen, Colin, *The Gaelic Lordship of the O'Sullivan Beare: A Landscape Cultural History* (Dublin: Four Courts Press, 2005)

Breen, Colin, "The Maritime Cultural Landscape in Medieval Gaelic Ireland," in *Gaelic Ireland c. 1250–1650: Land, Lordship and Settlement*, ed. Patrick Duffy, David Edwards, and Elizabeth FitzPatrick (Dublin: Four Courts Press, 2001), 418–36

Breen, Colin, "Randall MacDonnell and Early Seventeenth-Century Settlement in Northeast Ulster," in *The Plantation of Ulster: Ideology and Practice*, ed. Eamonn Ó Ciardha and Micháel Ó Siochrú (Manchester: Manchester University Press, 2012), 149–51

Brennan, Michael, *The Sidneys of Penshurst and the Monarchy, 1500–1700* (Aldershot: Ashgate, 2006)

Brenner, Robert, *Merchants and Revolution: Political Conflict and London's Overseas Traders, 1550–1653* (London: Verso, 2003)

Brietz Monta, Susanah, *Martyrdom and Literature in Early Modern England* (Cambridge: Cambridge University Press, 2005)

Brooks, C. W., *Law, Politics and Society in Early Modern England* (Cambridge: Cambridge University Press, 2009)

Brown, Keith, *Bloodfeud in Scotland 1573–1625: Violence, Justice and Politics in an Early Modern Society* (Edinburgh: John Donald, 1986)

Brown, Keith, "Honour, Honours and Nobility in Scotland between the Reformation and the National Covenant," *Scottish Historical Review* 91 (2012): 42–74

Brown, Keith, *Noble Society in Scotland: Wealth, Family and Culture from Reformation to Revolution* (Edinburgh: Edinburgh University Press, 2000)

Bryson, Anna, *From Courtesy to Civility: Changing Codes of Conduct in Early Modern England* (Oxford: Clarendon Press, 1998)

Bryson, Allen, "Elizabethan Verse Libel," in *The Oxford Handbook of the Age of Shakespeare*, ed. R. Malcolm Smuts (Oxford: Oxford University Press, 2016), 477–92

Burgess, Glenn, *Absolute Monarchy and the Stuart Constitution* (New Haven: Yale University Press, 1996)
Burgess, Glenn, "Pocock's History of Political Thought, the Ancient Constitution, and Early Stuart England," in *The Political Imagination in History: Essays Concerning J. G. A. Pocock*, ed. D. N. DeLuna (Baltimore: Owlworks, 2006), 175–208
Burgess, Glenn, *The Politics of the Ancient Constitution: An Introduction to English Political Thought 1603–1642* (University Park: Pennsylvania State University Press, 1992)
Butler, Chris and Maley, Willy, "'Bringing Rebellion Broached on his Sword': Essex and Ireland," in *Essex: The Cultural Impact of an Elizabethan Courtier*, ed. Annaliese Connolly and Lisa Hopkins (Manchester: Manchester University Press, 2013), 133–52
Caball, Mark, "Gaelic and Protestant: A Case Study in Early Modern Self-Fashioning, 1567–1608," *Proceedings of the Irish Royal Academy: Archaeology, Culture, History, Literature* 110 (2010): 191–215
Caldari, Valentina and Wolfson, Sara J., eds, *Stuart Marriage Diplomacy: Dynastic Politics in their European Context, 1604–1630* (Woodbridge: Boydell Press, 2018)
Campbell, Eve, FitzPatrick, Elizabeth, and Horning, Audrey, eds, *Becoming and Belonging in Ireland AD c. 1200–1600: Essays in Identity and Cultural Practice* (Cork: Cork University Press, 2018)
Canning, Ruth, *The Old English in Early Modern Ireland: The Palesmen and the Nine Years' War, 1594–1603* (Woodbridge: Boydell, 2019)
Canny, Nicholas, "The Attempted Anglicanisation of Ireland in the Seventeenth Century: An Exemplar of 'British History'," in *The Political World of Thomas Wentworth Earl of Stafford 1621–1641*, ed. Julia Merritt (Cambridge: Cambridge University Press, 1996), 157–86
Canny, Nicholas, *The Elizabethan Conquest of Ireland: A Pattern Established, 1567–76* (Hassocks: Harvester, 1976)
Canny, Nicholas, *Making Ireland British* (Oxford: Oxford University Press, 2001)
Capp, Bernard, *Astrology and the Popular Press: English Almanacs, 1500–1800* (London: Faber & Faber, 1979)
Carey, Vincent, "Neither Good English nor Good Irish: Bi-lingualism and Identity Formation in Sixteenth Century Ireland," in *Political Ideology in Ireland, 1541–1641*, ed. Hiram Morgan (Dublin: Four Courts Press, 1991), 45–61
Carey, Vincent, *Surviving the Tudors* (Dublin: Four Courts Press, 2002)
Carey, Vincent and Lotz-Heumann, Ute, *Taking Sides? Colonial and Confessional Mentalités in Early Modern Ireland: Essays in Honour of Karl S. Bottigheimer* (Dublin: Four Courts Press, 2003)
Carlton, Charles, *This Seat of Mars: War and the British Isles, 1485–1746* (New Haven: Yale University Press, 2013)
Carluer, Jean-Yves, "L'horizon maritime des protestants Bretons," in *D'Un Rivage à l'Autre: Villes et Protestantisme dans l'Aire Atlantique (XVIe–XVIIe siècles)*, ed. Guy Martinière, Didier Poton, and François Souty (Paris: Imprimerie Nationale, 1999), 101–12
Carroll, Stuart, *Martyrs and Murderers: The Guise Family and the Making of Europe* (Oxford: Oxford University Press, 2009)
Carroll, Stuart, *Noble Power during the French Wars of Religion: The Guise Affinity and the Catholic Cause in Normandy* (Cambridge: Cambridge University Press, 1998)
Cavill, Paul and Gajda, Alexandra, eds, *Writing the History of Parliament in Tudor and Early Stuart England* (Manchester: Manchester University Press, 2018)
Chartier, Roger and Richet, Denis, *Représentation et vouloir politiques: Autour des États généraux de 1614* (Paris: École des hautes études en sciences sociales, 1982)

Childs, Jessie, *God's Traitors: Terror and Faith in Elizabethan England* (Oxford: Oxford University Press, 2014)
Christian, Olivier, *La paix de religion: l'autonomisation de la raison politique au XVIe siècle* (Paris: Seuil, 1997)
Christianson, Paul, "Royal and Parliamentary Voices on the Ancient Constitution," in *The Mental World of the Jacobean Court*, ed. Linda Peck (Cambridge: Cambridge University Press, 1991), 71–95
Clegg, Cyndia, "Print in the Time of Parliaments, 1560–1601," in *Tudor Books and Readers: Materiality and the Construction of Meaning*, ed. John King (Cambridge: Cambridge University Press, 2010), 138–59
Cogan, Susan, *Catholic Social Networks in Early Modern England* (Amsterdam: University of Amsterdam Press, 2021)
Cogswell, Thomas, *The Blessed Revolution: English Politics and the Coming of War, 1621–1624* (Cambridge: Cambridge University Press, 1989)
Cogswell, Thomas, "Underground Verse and the Transformation of Early Stuart Political Culture," in *Political Culture and Cultural Politics in Early Modern England: Essays Presented to David Underdown*, ed. Mark Kishlansky and Susan Amussen (Manchester: Manchester University Press, 1995), 277–300
Cole, Mary Hill, *The Portable Queen* (Amherst, MA: University of Massachusetts Press, 1999)
Cole, Mary Hill, "Religious Conformity and the Progresses of Elizabeth I," in *Elizabeth I, Always her Own Free Woman*, ed. Carol Levin, Jo Eldridge Carney, and Debra Barrett-Graves (Aldershot: Ashgate, 2003), 63–77
Collinson, Patrick, "De Republica Anglorum: Or, History with the Politics Put Back," inaugural lecture as Regius Professor of History in the University of Cambridge, November 9, 1989 (Cambridge: Cambridge University Press, 1990)
Collinson, Patrick, "Ecclesiastical Vitriol: Religious Satire in the 1590s and the Invention of Puritanism," in *The Reign of Elizabeth I: Court and Culture in the Last Decade*, ed. John Guy (Cambridge: Cambridge University Press, 1995), 150–70
Collinson, Patrick, *Elizabethan Essays* (London: Hambledon Press, 1994)
Collinson, Patrick, "The Elizabethan Exclusion Crisis and the Elizabethan Polity," *Proceedings of the British Academy* 84 (1994): 51–92
Collinson, Patrick, *The Elizabethan Puritan Movement* (Berkeley: University of California Press, 1967)
Collinson, Patrick, "The Monarchical Republic of Queen Elizabeth I," *Bulletin of the John Rylands Library* 69 (1987): 394–424
Collinson, Patrick, "Puritans, Men of Business and Parliaments," in *Elizabethan Essays* (London: Hambledon Press, 1994), 52–80
Collinson, Patrick, *The Religion of the Protestants: The Church in English Society, 1559–1625* (Oxford: Oxford University Press, rev. ed. 1984)
Collinson, Patrick, *Richard Bancroft and Elizabethan Anti-Puritanism* (Cambridge: Cambridge University Press, 2013)
Connolly, Annaliese and Hopkins, Lisa, eds, *Essex: The Cultural Impact of an Elizabethan Courtier* (Manchester: Manchester University Press, 2013)
Connolly, S. J., *Contested Island: Ireland 1460–1603* (Oxford: Oxford University Press, 2007)
Constant, Jean-Marie, *La Ligue* (Paris: Fayard, 1996)
Constant, Jean-Maire, *Les conjurateurs: Le premier libéralisme sous Richelieu* (Paris: Hachette, 1987)

Courtright, Nicola, "A New Place for Queens in Early Modern France," in *The Politics of Space: European Courts ca. 1500-1750*, ed. Marcello Fantoni, George Gorse, and R. Malcolm Smuts (Rome: Bulzoni, 2009), 267-92

Courtright, Nicola, "The Representation of the French-Spanish Alliance in the Medici Cycle: 'Concorde perpetuelle'," in *The Age of Rubens: Diplomacy, Dynastic Politics and the Visual Arts in Early Seventeenth-Century Europe*, ed. Luc Duerloo and R. Malcolm Smuts (Turnhout: Brepols, 2016), 39-63

Crawford, John, *A Star Chamber Court in Ireland: The Court of Castle Chamber, 1567-1641* (Dublin: Four Courts Press, 2005)

Crawford, Ross, "Noble Power in the West Highlands and Isles: James VI and the End of the Mercenary Trade with Ireland, 1594-96," in *James VI and Noble Power in Scotland 1578-1603*, ed. Miles Kerr-Peterson and Steven J. Reid (London: Routledge, 2017), 117-35

Cressy, David, *Bonfires and Bells* (Berkeley: University of California Press, 1989)

Cressy, David, *Charles I and the People of England* (Oxford: Oxford University Press, 2015)

Cressy, David, *England on Edge: Crisis and Revolution 1640-1642* (Oxford: Oxford University Press, 2006)

Croft, Pauline, *King James* (Basingstoke: Palgrave Macmillan, 2003)

Croft, Pauline, "Libels, Popular Literacy and Public Opinion in Early Modern England," *Bulletin of the Institute for Historical Research* 68 (1995), 266-85

Croft, Pauline, ed., *Patronage, Culture and Power: The Early Cecils 1558-1612*, Yale Studies in British Art 8 (New Haven and London: Yale University Press, 2002)

Croft, Pauline, "*Rex Pacificus*, Robert Cecil and the 1604 Peace with Spain," in *The Accession of James I: Historical and Cultural Consequences*, ed. Glenn Burgess and Rowland Wymer (Basingstoke: Palgrave Macmillan, 2006), 140-54

Cross, Robert, "'The onely soveraigne medecine': Religious Politics and Political Culture in the British-Spanish Match, 1596-1625," in *Stuart Marriage Diplomacy: Dynastic Politics in their European Context, 1604-1630*, ed. Valentia Caldari and Sara J. Wolfson (Woodbridge: Boydell Press, 2018), 67-78

Cuddy, Neil, "The Conflicting Loyalties of a 'Vulger Counselor': The Third Earl of Southampton, 1597-1624," in *Public Duty and Private Conscience in Seventeenth-Century England: Essays Presented to Gerald Aylmer*, ed. John Morrill, Paul Slack, and Daniel Woolf (Oxford: Oxford University Press, 1993), 122-50

Cuddy, Neil, "The Revival of the Entourage: The Bedchamber of James I, 1603-1625," in *The English Court from the Wars of the Roses to the Civil War*, ed. David Starkey et al. (London: Longman, 1987), 173-225

Cunningham, Bernadette, *Clanricard and Thomond, 1540-1640: Provincial Politics and Society Transformed* (Dublin: Four Courts Press, 2012)

Cunningham, Bernadette, "The English Language in Early Modern Ireland," in *Reshaping Ireland 1550-1700: Colonization and Its Consequences*, ed. Brian Mac Cuarta, SJ (Dublin, Four Courts Press, 2011), 163-86

Cunningham, Bernadette, "Nuns and their Networks in Earl Modern Galway," in *Religion and Politics in Urban Ireland, c. 1500-c. 1750: Essays in Honour of Colm Lennon*, ed. Salvador Ryan and Clodagh Tait (Dublin: Four Courts Press, 2016), 156-72

Cust, Richard, "Catholicism, Antiquarianism and Gentry Honour: The Writings of Sir Thomas Shirley," *Midland History* 23 (1998): 40-70

Cust, Richard, *Charles I and the Aristocracy, 1625-1642* (Cambridge: Cambridge University Press, 2013)

Cust, Richard, *Charles I: A Political Life* (London: Longman, 2005)

Cust, Richard, *The Forced Loan and English Politics, 1626–1628* (Oxford: Oxford University Press, 1987)
Cust, Richard, "Honour and Politics in Early Stuart England: The Case of Beaumont vs. Hastings," *Past and Present* 149 (1995): 57–94
Cust, Richard, "News and Politics in Early Seventeenth Century England," *Past and Present* 112 (1986): 60–90
Dauber, Noah, *State and Commonwealth: The Theory of the State in Early Modern England, 1549–1640* (Princeton: Princeton University Press, 2016)
Daussy, Hugues, *Les Huguenots et le Roi: Le combat politique de Philippe Duplessis-Mornay (1572–1600)* (Geneva: Droz, 2002)
Dawson, Jane, "The Fifth Earl of Argyle, Gaelic Lordship and Political Power in Sixteenth-Century Scotland," *Scottish Historical Review* 67 (1988): 1–27
Dickens, A. G., *The English Reformation* (University Park: Pennsylvania State University Press, 2nd ed., 1989)
Dillon, Anne, *The Construction of Martyrdom in the English Catholic Community* (Aldershot: Ashgate, 2002)
Dodgshon, Robert A., *From Chiefs to Landlords: Social and Economic Change in the Western Highlands and Islands, c. 1493–1820* (Edinburgh: Edinburgh University Press, 1998)
Donaldson, Gordon, "The Attitude of Whitgift and Bancroft to the Scottish Church," *Transactions of the Royal Historical Society*, series 4, vol. 14 (1942): 95–115
Donaldson, Gordon, *The Scottish Reformation* (Cambridge: Cambridge University Press, 1960)
Doran, Susan, "1603: A Jagged Succession," *Historical Research* 93 (2020): 443–65
Doran, Susan, "Juno vs. Diana: The Treatment of Elizabeth I's Marriage in Plays and Entertainments, 1551–1581," *Historical Journal* 38 (1995): 257–74
Doran, Susan, *Monarchy and Matrimony: The Courtships of Elizabeth I* (London: Routledge, 1996)
Doran, Susan and Kewes, Paulina, eds, *Doubtful and Dangerous: The Question of Succession in Late Elizabethan England* (Manchester: Manchester University Press, 2016)
Dovey, Zilla, *An Elizabethan Progress* (Stroud: Sutton Publishing, 1996)
Dubost, Jean-François, *Marie de Médicis: La reine dévoilée* (Paris: Payot, 2009)
Dubost, Jean-François, "Rubens et l'invention d'une image politique: la France personifiée, XVIe–XVIIe siècle," in *The Age of Rubens: Diplomacy, Dynastic Politics and the Visual Arts in Early Seventeenth-Century Europe*, ed. Luc Duerloo and R, Malcolm Smuts (Turnhout: Brepols, 2016), 65–110
Duerloo, Luc, *Dynasty and Piety: Archduke Albert (1598–1621) and Habsburg Political Culture in an Age of Religious Wars* (Farnham: Ashgate, 2012)
Duerloo, Luc and Smuts, R. Malcolm, eds, *The Age of Rubens: Diplomacy, Dynastic Politics and the Visual Arts in Early Seventeenth-Century Europe* (Turnhout: Brepols, 2016)
Duffy, Eamon, *The Stripping of the Altars* (New Haven: Yale University Press, 1992)
Duffy, Patrick, "Social and Spatial Order in the MacMahon Lordship of Aighialla in the Late Sixteenth Century," in *Gaelic Ireland c. 1250–1650: Land, Lordship and Settlement*, ed. Patrick Duffy, David Edwards, and Elizabeth FitzPatrick (Dublin: Four Courts Press, 2001), 115–37
Duffy, Patrick, Edwards, David, and FitzPatrick, Elizabeth, eds, *Gaelic Ireland c. 1250–1650: Land, Lordship and Settlement* (Dublin: Four Courts Press, 2001)

Duke, Alastair, "In Defence of the Common Fatherland: Patriotism and Liberty in the Low Countries, 1555–1576," in *Networks, Regions and Nations: Shaping Identities in the Low Countries, 1300–1560*, ed. Robert Stein and Judith Pollmann (Leiden: Brill, 2010), 217–39

Edwards, David, *Campaign Journals of Sir William Russell* (Dublin: Irish Manuscripts Commission, 2014)

Edwards, David, "Collaboration without Anglicisation: The MacGiollapdraig Lordship and Tudor Reform," in *Gaelic Ireland c. 1250–1650: Land, Lordship and Settlement*, ed. Patrick Duffy, David Edwards, and Elizabeth FitzPatrick (Dublin: Four Courts Press, 2001), 77–98

Edwards, David, "The Escalation of Violence in Sixteenth-Century Ireland," in *Age of Atrocity: Violence and Political Conflict in Early Modern Ireland*, ed. David Edwards, Pádraig Lenihan, and Clodagh Tait (Dublin: Four Courts Press, 2007), 34–78

Edwards, David, "Ideology and Experience: Spenser's *View* and Martial Law in Ireland," in *Political Ideology in Ireland, 1541–1641*, ed. Hiram Morgan (Dublin: Four Courts Press, 1999), 127–57

Edwards, David, "The Land-Grabber's Accomplices: Richard Boyle's Munster Affinity, 1588–1603," in *The Colonial World of Richard Boyle First Earl of Cork*, ed. David Edwards and Colin Rynne (Dublin: Four Courts Press, 2018), 166–88

Edwards, David, *The Ormond Lordship in the County of Kilkenny, 1515–1642: The Rise and Fall of Butler Feudal Power* (Dublin: Four Courts Press, 2003)

Edwards, David, "Out of the Blue? Provincial Unrest in Ireland before 1641," in *Religion and Politics in Urban Ireland, c. 1500–c. 1750: Essays in Honour of Colm Lennon*, ed. Salvador Ryan and Clodagh Tait (Dublin: Four Courts Press, 2016), 95–114

Edwards, David, *Regions and Rulers in Ireland, 1100–1650* (Dublin: Four Courts Press, 2004)

Edwards, David, Lenihan, Pádraig, and Tait, Clodagh, eds, *Age of Atrocity: Violence and Political Conflict in Early Modern Ireland* (Dublin: Four Courts Press, 2007)

Edwards, David and Rynne, Colin, eds, *The Colonial World of Richard Boyle First Earl of Cork* (Dublin: Four Courts Press, 2018)

Elliott, J. H. and Brockliss, L. W. D., eds, *The World of the Favourite* (New Haven: Yale University Press, 1999)

Ellis, Steven, *Defending English Ground: War and Peace in Meath and Northumberland, 1460–1542* (Oxford: Oxford University Press, 2015)

Elton, Geoffrey, *The Tudor Revolution in Government* (Cambridge: Cambridge University Press, 1953)

Enis, Cathryn, "The Dudleys, Sir Christopher Hatton and the Justices of Elizabethan Warwickshire," *Midland History* 39 (2014): 1–35

Enis, Cathryn, "Edward Arden and the Dudley Earls of Warwick and Leicester, c. 1572–1583," *British Catholic History* 33 (2016): 170–210

Everitt, Alan, *The Community of Kent and the Great Rebellion* (Leicester: Leicester University Press, 1966)

Feingold, Mordechai, "Scholarship and Politics: Henry Savile's Tacitus and the Essex Connection," *Review of English Studies* 67 (2016): 855–74

Ferguson, Arthur, *The Chivalric Tradition in Renaissance England* (Washington, DC: Folger Books, 1986)

Ferguson, Arthur, *The Indian Summer of English Chivalry* (Durham, NC: University of North Carolina Press, 1960)

Fernández Álvarez, Manuel, *Felipe II y su tiempo* (Madrid: Espasa, 1998)

Feros, Antonio, *Kingship and Favoritism in the Spain of Philip III 1598-1621* (Cambridge: Cambridge University Press, 2000)
ffolliot, Sheila, "The Italian 'Training' of Catherine de Medici: Portraits as Dynastic Narrative," in *Queens and the Transmission of Political Culture: The Case of Early Modern France*, ed. Melinda Gough and R. Malcolm Smuts, Special Issue of *The Court Historian* 10 (2005): 25-36
Fincham, Kenneth, *Prelate as Pastor: The Episcopate of James I* (Oxford: Oxford University Press, 1990)
Firth, Katherine, *The Apocalyptic Tradition in Reformation Britain* (Oxford: Oxford University Press, 1979)
Fischlin, Daniel, "'To Eate the Flesh of Kings': James VI and I, Apocalypse, Nation and Sovereignty," in *Royal Subjects: Essays on the Writings of James VI and I*, ed. Daniel Fischlin and Mark Fortier (Detroit: Wayne State University Press, 2002), 388-420
Fischlin, Daniel and Fortier, Mark, eds, *Royal Subjects: Essays on the Writings of James VI and I* (Detroit: Wayne State University Press, 2002)
Fissel, Mark Charles, *The Bishops' Wars: Charles I's Campaigns against Scotland 1638-1640* (Cambridge: Cambridge University Press, 1994)
Fitzmaurice, Andrew, *Humanism and America: An Intellectual History of English Colonisation 1500-1625* (Cambridge: Cambridge University Press, 2003)
FitzPatrick, Elizabeth, "Gaelic Service Kindreds and the Landscape of Identity of *Lucht Tighe*," in *Becoming and Belonging in Ireland AD c. 1200-1600: Essays in Identity and Cultural Practice*, ed. Eve Campbell, Elizabeth FitzPatrick, and Audrey Horning (Cork: Cork University Press, 2018)
Fletcher, Anthony, *The Outbreak of the English Civil War* (Caulfield: Anthony Arnold, 1981)
Flynn, Dennis, "Notes on Jaspar Heywood," in *The Reckoned Expense: Edmund Campion and the Early English Jesuits: Essays in Celebration of the First Centenary of Campion Hall, Oxford*, ed. Thomas McCoog (Woodbridge: Boydell Press, 1996), 179-92
Fox, Adam, *Oral and Literate Culture in England, 1500-1700* (Oxford: Oxford University Press, 2000)
Freeman, Thomas and Mayer, Thomas, eds, *Martyrs and Martyrdom in England, 1400-1700* (Woodbridge: Boydell Press, 2007)
Friedburg, Robert von, "'Lands' and 'Fatherlands': Changes in the Plurality of Allegiances in the Sixteenth-Century Holy Roman Empire," in *Networks, Regions and Nations: Shaping Identities in the Low Countries, 1300-1560*, ed. Robert Stein and Judith Pollmann (Leiden: Brill, 2010), 263-82
Gajda, Alexandra, "Debating War and Peace in Late Elizabethan England," *Historical Journal* 52.4 (2009): 851-78
Gajda, Alexandra, *The Earl of Essex and Late Elizabethan Political Culture* (Oxford: Oxford University Press, 2013)
Gajda, Alexandra, "The Earl of Essex and Politic History," in *Essex: The Cultural Impact of an Elizabethan Courtier*, ed. Annaliese Connolly and Lisa Hopkins (Manchester: Manchester University Press, 2013), 237-59
Gajda, Alexandra, "Essex and the 'Popish Plot'," in *Doubtful and Dangerous: The Question of Succession in Late Elizabethan England*, ed. Susan Doran and Paulina Kewes (Manchester: Manchester University Press, 2016), 115-34
Gajda, Alexandra, "Political Culture in the 1590s: The 'Second Reign of Elizabeth'," *History Compass* 8 (2009): 88-100

Gajda, Alexandra, "*The State of Christendom*: History, Political Thought and the Essex Circle," *Historical Research* 81 (2008): 423–46
Gajda, Alexandra, "Tacitus and Political Thought in Early Modern Europe, c. 1530–1640," in *The Cambridge Companion to Tacitus*, ed. A. J. Woodman (Cambridge: Cambridge University Press, 2010), 253–68
Gal, Stéphane, *Charles Emmanuel de Savoie: La politique du précipice* (Paris: Payot, 2012)
Galloway, Bruce and Levack, Brian, eds, *The Jacobean Union: Six Tracts of 1604*, Scottish History Society, 4th series, 64 (Edinburgh: C. Constable, 1985)
Garcia Garcia, Bernardo José, *La Pax Hispanica: Política Exterior del Duque de Lerma* (Leuven: Leuven University Press, 1996)
Garcia Garcia, Bernardo José, "Peace with England: From Convenience to Necessity," in *Material and Symbolic Circulation between Spain and England, 1554–1604*, ed. Anne J. Cruz (Aldershot: Ashgate, 2008), 135–49
Gardiner, Samuel Rawson, *The First Two Stuarts and the Puritan Revolution* (New York: Thomas Y. Crowell, 1970)
Gardiner, Samuel Rawson, *The History of England from the Accession of James I to the Outbreak of the Civil War, 1603–1642*, 10 vols (London: Longman, 1887–91)
Gardiner, Samuel Rawson, *Prince Charles and the Spanish Marriage, 1617–1623*, 2 vols (London: Hurst and Blackett, 1869)
Gaskill, Malcolm, "Little Commonwealths II: Communities," in *A Social History of England 1500–1700*, ed. Keith Wrightson (Cambridge: Cambridge University Press, 2017), 84–104
Gazzard, Hugh, "'Idle Papers': An Apology of the Earl of Essex," in *Essex: The Cultural Impact of an Elizabethan Courtier*, ed. Annaliese Connolly and Lisa Hopkins (Manchester: Manchester University Press, 2013), 179–200
Gelderen, Martin van, *The Political Thought of the Dutch Revolt, 1555–1590* (Cambridge: Cambridge University Press, 1992)
Gibbons, Katy, *English Catholic Exiles in Late Sixteenth-Century Paris* (Woodbridge: Boydell Press, 2011)
Gillespie, Raymond, *Colonial Ulster: The Settlement of East Ulster* (Cork: Cork University Press, 1985)
Gillespie, Raymond, "Gaelic Catholicism and the Ulster Plantation," in *Religion and Politics in Urban Ireland, c. 1500–c. 1750: Essays in Honour of Colm Lennon*, ed. Salvador Ryan and Clodagh Tait (Dublin: Four Courts Press, 2016), 124–36
Gillespie, Raymond, "Success and Failure in the Ulster Plantation," in *The Plantation of Ulster: Ideology and Practice*, ed. Eamonn Ó Ciardha and Micháel Ó Siochrú (Manchester: Manchester University Press, 2012), 98–118
Glete, Jan, *Warfare at Sea, 1500–1650: Maritime Conflicts and the Transformation of Europe* (Abingdon: Routledge, 2000)
Gomez-Centurion Jimenez, Carlos, *Felipe II, La Empresa de Inglaterra y el Comercio Septentrional (1566–1609)* (Madrid: Editorial Naval, 1988)
Gonzáles Cuerva, Ruben, *Baltasar de Zúñiga: Una encrucijada de la Monarquía Hispana (1561–1622)* (Madrid: Ediciones Polifeno, 2012)
Goodare, Julian, "The Attempted Scottish Coup of 1596," in *Sixteenth-Century Scotland: Essays in Honour of Michael Lynch*, ed. Julian Goodare and Alasdair MacDonald (Leiden: Brill, 2008), 311–36
Goodare, Julian, *The Government of Scotland 1560–1625* (Oxford: Oxford University Press, 2004)

Goodare, Julian, "The Octavians," in *James VI and Noble Power in Scotland 1578-1603*, ed. Miles Kerr-Peterson and Steven J. Reid (London: Routledge, 2017), 176-93

Goodare, Julian, "The Scottish Presbyterian Movement of 1596," *Canadian Journal of History* 45 (2010): 21-43

Goodman, David, *Spanish Naval Power: Reconstruction and Defeat, 1589-1665* (Cambridge: Cambridge University Press, 1997)

Gordon, Andrew, "Essex's Last Campaign: The Fall of the Earl of Essex and Manuscript Circulation," in *Essex: The Cultural Impact of an Elizabethan Courtier*, ed. Annaliese Connolly and Lisa Hopkins (Manchester: Manchester University Press, 2013), 153-67

Grafton, Anthony and Jardine, Lisa, "Studied for Action: How Gabriel Harvey Read his Livy," *Past and Present* 129 (1990): 30-78

Grant, Ruth, "Friendship, Politics and Religion: George Gordon, Sixth Earl of Huntly and James VI, 1581-1595," in *James VI and Noble Power in Scotland, 1578-1603*, ed. Miles Kerr-Peterson and Steven J. Reid (London: Routledge, 2017), 57-80

Griffey, Erin, "The Materials of Marital Diplomacy: Henrietta Maria's Trousseau," in *The Age of Rubens: Diplomacy, Dynastic Politics and the Visual Arts in Early Seventeenth-Century Europe*, ed. Luc Duerloo and R. Malcolm Smuts (Turnhout: Brepols, 2016), 197-212

Groenveld, S., *Facetten van de Tachtigjarige Oorlog: Twalf Artikelen over de eriode 1559-1652* (Hilversum: Verloren, 2018)

Groenveld, S., "De Nederlanden en de Gulicks-Kleefse erfopvolging, ca. 1592-1614," in *Facetten van de Tachtigjarige Oorlog* (Hilversum: Verloren, 2018), 206-38

Groenveld, S., "*Verlatinge* en de erkenning van een nieuwe staat," in *Facetten van de Tachtigjarige Oorlog* (Hilversum: Verloren, 2018), 182-205

Grosjean, Alexia, *An Unofficial Alliance: Scotland and Sweden, 1569-1654* (Leiden: Brill, 2003)

Groundwater, Anna, "'He Made them Friends in his Cabinet': James VI's Suppression of the Scott-Ker Feud," in *James VI and Noble Power in Scotland, 1578-1603*, ed. Miles Kerr-Peterson and Steven J. Reid (London: Routledge, 2017), 98-116

Groundwater, Anna, *The Scottish Middle March, 1573-1625* (Woodbridge: Boydell Press, 2010)

Groundwater, Anna, "From Whitehall to Jedburgh: Patronage Networks and the Government of the Scottish Borders, 1603 to 1625," *Historical Journal* 53 (2010): 871-93

Gunn, Steven, *The English People at War in the Age of Henry VIII* (Oxford: Oxford University Press, 2020)

Gunn, Steven, *Henry VII's New Men and the Making of Modern England* (Oxford: Oxford University Press, 2016)

Guy, John, "Introduction: The 1590s, the Second Reign of Elizabeth I?," in *The Reign of Elizabeth I: Court and Culture in the Last Decade*, ed. John Guy (Cambridge: Cambridge University Press, 1995), 1-19

Guy, John, *Politics, Law and Counsel in Tudor and Early Stuart England* (London: Routledge, 2000)

Guy, John, ed., *The Reign of Elizabeth I: Court and Culture in the Last Decade* (Cambridge: Cambridge University Press, 1995)

Guy, John, "The Rhetoric of Counsel in Early Modern England," in *Tudor Political Thought*, ed. Dale Hoak (Cambridge: Cambridge University Press, 1995), 292-310

Habermas, Jürgen, *The Structural Transformation of the Public Sphere: An Inquiry into a Category of Bourgeois Society*, trans. Thomas Burger (Cambridge, MA: MIT Press, 1991)

Haigh, Christopher, *English Reformations: Religion, Politics, and Society under the Tudors* (Oxford: Oxford University Press, 1993)

Haigh, Christopher, *Reformation and Resistance in Tudor Lancashire* (Cambridge: Cambridge University Press, 1975)

Haller, William, *Foxe's Book of Martyrs and the Elect Nation* (London: Jonathan Cape, 1963)

Hamilton, Donna, *Anthony Munday and the Catholics, 1560-1633* (Aldershot: Ashgate, 2005)

Hammer, Paul, "Base Rogues and Gentlemen of Quality: The Earl of Essex's Irish Knights and Royal Displeasure in 1599," in *Elizabeth I and Ireland*, ed. Brendan Kane and Valerie McGowen-Doyle (Cambridge: Cambridge University Press, 2014), 184-208

Hammer, Paul, "The Earl of Essex and English Expeditionary Forces," in *The Oxford Handbook of John Donne*, ed. Jeanne Shami, Dennis Flynn, and Thomas M. Hester (Oxford: Oxford University Press, 2011), 435-46

Hammer, Paul, *Elizabeth's Wars: War, Government and Society in Tudor England, 1544-1604* (Basingstoke: Palgrave Macmillan, 2003)

Hammer, Paul, "Essex and Europe: Evidence from Confidential Instructions by the Earl of Essex, 1595-6," *English Historical Review* 111 (1996): 357-81

Hammer, Paul, "How to Become an Elizabethan Statesman: Lord Henry Howard, the Earl of Essex and the Politics of Friendship," *English Manuscript Studies* 13 (2007): 1-34

Hammer, Paul, "Letters of Travel Advice from the Earl of Essex to the Earl of Rutland, Some Comments," *Philological Quarterly* 74 (1995): 317-25

Hammer, Paul, "Myth-Making: Politics, Propaganda and the Capture of Cadiz in 1596," *Historical Journal* 40 (1997): 621-42

Hammer, Paul, "New Light on the Cadiz Expedition of 1596," *Historical Research* 70 (1997): 182-202

Hammer, Paul, "Patronage at Court, Faction and the Earl of Essex," in *The Reign of Elizabeth I: Court and Culture in the Last Decade*, ed. John Guy (Cambridge: Cambridge University Press, 1995), 65-86

Hammer, Paul, *The Polarisation of Elizabethan Politics: The Political Career of Robert Devereux, 2nd Earl of Essex, 1585-1597* (Cambridge: Cambridge University Press, 1997)

Hammer, Paul, "Shakespeare's *Richard II*: The Play of 7 February 1601, and the Essex Rising," *Shakespeare Quarterly* 59.1 (2008): 1-35

Hammer, Paul, "The Smiling Crocodile: The Earl of Essex and Late Elizabethan Popularity," in *The Politics of the Public Sphere in Early Modern England*, ed. Peter Lake and Steven Pincus (Manchester: Manchester University Press, 2012), 95-115

Hammer, Paul, "Upstaging the Queen: The Earl of Essex, Francis Bacon and the Accession Day Celebration of 1595," in *The Politics of the Stuart Court Masque*, ed. David Bevington and Peter Holbrook (Cambridge: Cambridge University Press, 1998), 41-63

Hammer, Paul, "The Uses of Scholarship: The Secretariat of Robert Devereux, Second Earl of Essex, c. 1585-1601," *English Historical Review* 109 (1994): 26-51

Hassell-Smith, A., *County and Court: Government and Politics in Norfolk, 1558-1603* (Oxford: Oxford University Press, 1974)

Hayden, Michael, *France and the Estates General of 1614* (Cambridge: Cambridge University Press, 1975)

Heffernan, David, *Debating Tudor Policy in Sixteenth-Century Ireland: 'Reform' Treatises and Political Discourse* (Manchester: Manchester University Press, 2018)

Heffernan, David, "Reconstructing the Estate of Richard Boyle, First Earl of Cork," *History Ireland* 23 (2015): 18-20

Heffernan, David, "Theory and Practice in the Munster Plantation: The Estates of Richard Boyle, First Earl of Cork, 1602-1643," in *The Colonial World of Richard Boyle First Earl of Cork*, ed. David Edwards and Colin Rynne (Dublin: Four Courts Press, 2018), 43-63

Heller, Henry, *Anti-Italianism in Sixteenth-Century France* (Toronto: University of Toronto Press, 2003)

Henry, Gráinne, *The Irish Military Community in Spanish Flanders, 1586-1621* (Dublin: Irish Academic Press, 1992)

Hernan, Enrique García, *The Battle of Kinsale* (Madrid: Ministerio de Defensa, 2013)

Herrup, Cynthia, *The Common Peace: Participation and the Criminal Law in Seventeenth-Century England* (Cambridge: Cambridge University Press, 1987)

Hibbard, Caroline, *Charles I and the Popish Plot* (Chapel Hill: University of North Carolina Press, 2nd ed., 2009)

Hindle, Steve, *The State and Social Change in Early Modern England* (Basingstoke: Palgrave Macmillan, 2000)

Holmes, Peter, *Resistance and Compromise: The Political Thought of the Elizabethan Catholics* (Cambridge: Cambridge University Press, 1982)

Holt, Mack P., *The Duke of Anjou and the Politique Struggle during the Wars of Religion* (Cambridge: Cambridge University Press, 1986)

Horning, Audrey, "Shapeshifters and Mimics: Exploring Elite Strategies in the Early Modern British Atlantic," in *The Colonial World of Richard Boyle First Earl of Cork*, ed. David Edwards and Colin Rynne (Dublin: Four Courts Press, 2018), 27-42

Houliston, Victor, *Catholic Resistance in Elizabethan England* (Aldershot: Ashgate, 2007)

Houston, Rabb A., "Custom in Context: Medieval and Early Modern Scotland and England," *Past and Present* 211 (2011): 35-76

Houston, Rabb A., "People, Space and Law in Late Medieval and Early Modern Britain and Ireland," *Past and Present* 230.1 (2016): 47-89

Hudson, Winthrop S., *The Cambridge Connection and the Elizabethan Settlement of 1559* (Durham, NC: Duke University Press, 1980)

Hughes, Anne, *Politics, Society and Civil War in Warwickshire* (Cambridge: Cambridge University Press, 1989)

Hunt, William, The Spectral Origins of the English Civil War," in *Reviving the English Revolution: Reflections and Elaborations on the Work of Christopher Hill*, ed. Geoff Eley and William Hunt (London: Verso, 1988), 305-32

Hunter, Robert J., "Plantation in Donegal," in *Donegal History and Society: Interdisciplinary Essays on the History of an Irish County*, ed. William Nolan, Liam Ronayne, and Mairead Dunlevy (Dublin: Geography Publications, 1995), 283-324

Hutchinson, Mark, *Calvinism, Reform and the Absolutist State in Elizabethan Ireland* (London: Routledge, 2016)

Ingram, Martin, *Church Courts, Sex and Marriage in England* (Cambridge: Cambridge University Press, 1987)

Israel, Jonathan, *Dutch Primacy in World Trade* (Oxford: Oxford University Press, 1989)

Israel, Jonathan, *The Dutch Republic: Its Rise, Greatness and Fall 1477-1806* (Oxford: Clarendon Press, 1995)

James, Alan, *The Navy and Government in Early Modern France 1572-1661* (Woodbridge: Royal Historical Society, 2004)

James, Anne, *Poets, Players, and Preachers: Remembering the Gunpowder Plot in Seventeenth-Century England* (Toronto: University of Toronto Press, 2016)

James, Leonie, *This Great Firebrand: William Laud and Scotland, 1617-1645* (Woodbridge: Boydell Press, 2017)

James, Mervyn, "At a Crossroads of the Political Culture: The Essex Revolt, 1601," in *Society, Politics and Culture: Studies in Early Modern England* (Cambridge: Cambridge University Press, 1986), 416–65

James, Mervyn, "English Politics and the Concept of Honour, 1485–1642," in *Society, Politics and Culture: Studies in Early Modern England* (Cambridge: Cambridge University Press, 1986), 308–415

Jardine, Lisa, "Gloriana Rules the Waves: Or the Advantage of Being Excommunicated (and a Woman)," in *Elizabeth I and the Expansion of England: A Conference Held at the National Maritime Museum Greenwich, 4–6 September 2003* published as *Transactions of the Royal Historical Society*, 6th series, 14 (2004): 210–22

Jeffries, Henry, *The Irish Church and the Tudor Reformations* (Dublin: Four Courts Press, 2010)

Jeffries, Henry, "Tudor Reformations Compared: The Irish Pale and Lancaster," in *Frontiers, States and Identity in Early Modern Ireland and Beyond: Essays in Honour of Steven G. Ellis*, ed. Christopher Maginn and Gerland Power (Dublin: Four Courts Press, 2016), 71–92

Jeffries, Henry, "Tudor Reformations in Cork," in *Religion and Politics in Urban Ireland, c. 1500–c. 1750: Essays in Honour of Colm Lennon*, ed. Salvador Ryan and Clodagh Tait (Dublin: Four Courts Press, 2016), 51–69

Jones, Norman, *Governing by Virtue: Lord Burghley and the Management of Elizabethan England* (Oxford: Oxford University Press, 2015)

Jouanna, Arlette, *Le devoir de révolte: La noblesse française et la gestation de l'État moderne* (Paris: Fayard, 1989)

Jouanna, Arlette, *La France du xvie siècle 1483–1598* (Paris: Presses Universitaires de France, 2nd ed., 1997)

Jouanna, Arlette, *L'idée de race en France au XVIème siècle et au début du XVIIème siècle: 1498–1614* (Paris: Champion, 1976)

Jouanna, Arlette, *Le pouvoir absolu: Naissance de l'imaginaire politique de la royauté* (Paris: Gallimard, 2013)

Jouanna, Arlette, *Le prince absolu: Apogée et déclin de l'imaginaire monarchique* (Paris: Gallimard, 2014)

Kamen, Henry, *Empire: How Spain Became a World Power 1492–1763* (New York: HarperCollins, 2003)

Kane, Brendan, *The Politics and Culture of Honour in Britain and Ireland, 1541–1641* (Cambridge: Cambridge University Press, 2010)

Kane, Brendan, "Popular Politics and the Legitimacy of Power in Early Modern Ireland," in *Becoming and Belonging in Ireland AD c. 1200–1600: Essays in Identity and Cultural Practice*, ed. Eve Campbell, Elizabeth FitzPatrick, and Audrey Horning (Cork: Cork University Press, 2018), 328–43

Kane, Brendan and McGowen-Doyle, Valerie, eds, *Elizabeth I and Ireland* (Cambridge: Cambridge University Press, 2014)

Kane, Brendan and Smuts, R. Malcolm, "The Politics of Race in England, Scotland and Ireland," in *The Oxford Handbook of the Age of Shakespeare*, ed. R. Malcolm Smuts (Oxford: Oxford University Press, 2016), 346–63

Kanemura, Rei, "Historical Perspectives on the Anglo-Scottish Union Debate: Re-reading the Norman Conquest in the 1610s," *History of European Ideas* 40 (2014): 155–76

Kelly, Donald, "Murd'rous Machiavel in France: A Post-Mortem," *Political Science Quarterly* 85 (1970): 545–59

Kelly, James E., "Counties without Borders? Religious Politics, Kinship Networks and the Formation of Catholic Communities," *Historical Research* 91 (2018): 22–38
Kelsey, Harry, *Sir John Hawkins: Queen Elizabeth's Slave Trader* (New Haven: Yale University Press, 2003)
Kerr-Peterson, Miles and Reid, Steven J., eds, *James VI and Noble Power in Scotland, 1578–1603* (London: Routledge, 2017)
Kesselring, Krista, *The Northern Rebellion of 1569: Faith, Politics and Protest in Elizabethan England* (Basingstoke: Palgrave Macmillan, 2007)
Kewes, Paulina, "Henry Savile's Tacitus and the Politics of Roman History in Late Elizabethan England," *Huntington Library Quarterly* 74 (2011): 515–51
Kewes, Paulina, "Roman History, Essex, and Late Elizabethan Political Culture," in *The Oxford Handbook of the Age of Shakespeare*, ed. R. Malcolm Smuts (Oxford: Oxford University Press, 2016), 250–68
Kilroy, Gerard, *Edmund Campion: Memory and Transcription* (Aldershot: Ashgate, 2005)
King, Maureen, "The Essex Myth in Jacobean England," in *The Accession of James I: Historical and Cultural Consequences*, ed. Glenn Burgess, Rowland Wymer, and J. Lawrence (Basingstoke: Palgrave Macmillan, 2006), 177–86
Kishlansky, Mark, *Parliamentary Selection: Social and Political Choice in Early Modern England* (Cambridge: Cambridge University Press, 1986)
Knafla, Louis, *Law and Politics in Jacobean England: The Tracts of Lord Ellesmere* (Cambridge: Cambridge University Press, 1977)
Knights, Mark, *Representation and Misrepresentation in Later Stuart Britain: Partisanship and Political Culture* (New York: Oxford University Press, 2005)
Koopmans, J. W., *De Staten van Holland en de Opstand: De Ontwikkeling hun functies en organisatie in de periode 1544–1588*, Hollandse Historische Reeks 13 ('s-Gravenhage: Stichting Hollandse Historische Reeks, 1990)
Kupperman, Karen, *Providence Island 1630–1641: The Other Puritan Colony* (Cambridge: Cambridge University Press, 1995)
Lake, Peter, *Anglicans and Puritans? Presbyterianism and English Conformist Thought from Whitgift to Hooker* (London: Unwin Hyman, 1988)
Lake, Peter, *Bad Queen Bess? Libels, Secret Histories, and the Politics of Publicity in the Reign of Queen Elizabeth I* (Oxford: Oxford University Press, 2016)
Lake, Peter, *How Shakespeare Put Politics on the Stage: Power and Succession in the History Plays* (New Haven: Yale University Press, 2016)
Lake, Peter, "'The Monarchical Republic of Elizabeth I' (and the Fall of Archbishop Grindal) Revisited," in *The Monarchical Republic of Early Modern England: Essays in Response to Patrick Collinson*, ed. John McDiarmid (Aldershot: Ashgate, 2007), 129–48
Lake, Peter, "The Politics of Popularity and the Public Sphere: The 'Monarchical Republic' of Queen Elizabeth Defends Itself," in *The Politics of the Public Sphere in Early Modern England*, ed. Peter Lake and Steven Pincus (Manchester: Manchester University Press, 2012), 59–94
Lake, Peter, "Puritanism, (Monarchical) Republicanism and Monarchy: or John Whitgift, Antipuritanism and the 'Invention' of Popularity," *Journal of Medieval and Early Modern Studies* 40.3 (2010): 463–95
Lake, Peter, Review of Conrad Russell, *The Causes of the English Civil War*; *The Fall of the British Monarchies, 1637–1642*; and *Unrevolutionary England*, *Huntington Library Quarterly* 57 (1994): 167–97

Lake, Peter, "A Tale of Two Episcopal Surveys: The Strange Fates of Edmund Grindal and Cuthbert Mayne Revisited," *Transactions of the Royal Historical Society* 6.18 (2008): 129–63

Lake, Peter and Pincus, Steven, eds, *The Politics of the Public Sphere in Early Modern England* (Manchester: Manchester University Press, 2012)

Lake, Peter and Pincus, Steven, "Rethinking the Public Sphere in Early Modern England," *Journal of British Studies* 45 (2006): 270–92

Lake, Peter and Questier, Michael, *All Hail the Archpriest: Confessional Conflict, Toleration, and the Politics of Publicity in Post-Reformation England* (Oxford: Oxford University Press, 2019)

Lake, Peter, with Questier, Michael, *The Antichrist's Lewd Hat: Protestants, Papists and Players in Post-Reformation England* (New Haven: Yale University Press, 2002)

Lake, Peter and Questier, Michael, "Puritans, Papists and the 'Public Sphere' in Early Modern England: The Edmund Campion Affair in Context," *Journal of Early Modern History* 72 (2000): 587–627

Langel, Auguste, "Le duc de Bouillon d'après des documents inédits," *Révue des deux mondes* 18 (1876): 897–920

Laoutaris, Chris, "'Toucht with Bolt of Treason': The Earl of Essex and Lady Penelope Rich," in *Essex: The Cultural Impact of an Elizabethan Courtier*, ed. Annaliese Connolly and Lisa Hopkins (Manchester: Manchester University Press, 2013), 201–36

Larminie, Vivienne, "The Jacobean Diplomatic Fraternity and the Protestant Cause: Sir Isaac Wake and the View from Savoy," *English Historical Review* 121 (2006): 1300–26

LaRocca, John, "Popery and Pounds: The Effect of the Jesuit Mission on Penal Legislation," in *The Reckoned Expense: Edmund Campion and the Early English Jesuits: Essays in Celebration of the First Centenary of Campion Hall, Oxford*, ed. Thomas McCoog (Woodbridge: Boydell Press, 1996), 249–63

Law, Ceri, *Contested Reformations in the University of Cambridge* (Woodbridge: Boydell Press, 2018)

Lee, Maurice Jr., *James I and Henry IV: An Essay in English Foreign Policy 1603–1610* (Urbana: University of Illinois Press, 1970)

Lee, Maurice, Jr., *John Maitland of Thirlstane and the Foundations of Stewart Despotism in Scotland* (Princeton: Princeton University Press, 1959)

Lennon, Colm, "Taking Sides: The Emergence of Irish Catholic Ideology," in *Taking Sides? Colonial and Confessional Mentalités in Early Modern Ireland: Essays in Honour of Karl S. Bottigheimer*, ed. Vincent Carey and Ute Lotz-Heumann (Dublin: Four Courts Press, 2003), 197–206

Lestringant, Frank, "Le Drake Manuscript de la Morgan Library: Un document exceptionnel en marge des 'nouveaux horizons' français au Nouveau Monde," in *L'Expérience Huguenote au Nouveau Monde (XVIe siècle)* (Geneva: Droz, 1996), 265–90

Lestringant, Frank, *Le Huguenot et le sauvage: l'Amérique et la controversé coloniale en France au temps des guerres de religion* (Geneva: Droz, 1999)

Levack, Brian, *The Formation of the British State* (Oxford: Oxford University Press, 1987)

Little, Patrick, "The Gerladine Ambitions of the First Earl of Cork," *Irish Historical Studies* 33 (2002): 151–68

Lockyer, Roger, *Buckingham: The Life and Career of George Villiers, First Duke of Buckingham* (London: Longman, 1981)

Loeber, Rolf, "An Architectural History of Gaelic Castles and Settlements, 1370–1600," in *Gaelic Ireland c. 1250–1650: Land, Lordship and Settlement*, ed. Patrick Duffy, David Edwards, and Elizabeth FitzPatrick (Dublin: Four Courts Press, 2001), 271–314

Loo, Yvo van, "Pour la liberté et la fortune: La course néerlandaise pendant la guerre de religion aux Pays-Bas 1568-1609," in *Coligny, les protestants et la mer*, ed. Martine Acerra and Guy Matinière (Paris: Presses de l'Université de Paris-Sorbonne, 1997), 91-107
Love, Harold, *Scribal Publication in England* (Oxford: Oxford University Press, 1993)
Lyttleton, James, *The Jacobean Plantations in Seventeenth-Century Offaly: An Archaeology of a Changing World* (Dublin: Four Courts Press, 2013)
McCaferty, John, "'God Bless Your Free Church of Ireland': Wentworth, Laud, Bramhall and the Irish Convocation of 1634," in *The Political World of Thomas Wentworth Earl of Stafford 1621-1641*, ed. Julia Merritt (Cambridge: Cambridge University Press, 1996), 187-208
MacCaffrey, Wallace, *The Shaping of the Elizabethan Regime* (Princeton: Princeton University Press, 1967)
MacCarthy-Morrogh, Michael, *The Munster Plantation: English Migration to Southern Ireland 1583-1641* (Oxford: Clarendon Press, 1986)
McCavitt, J., "The Flight of the Earls, 1607," *Irish Historical Studies* 29 (1994): 159-73
McCavitt, J., *Sir Arthur Chichester, Lord Deputy of Ireland, 1605-1616* (Belfast: Institute of Irish Studies, Queen's University of Belfast, 1998)
McConica, James, "The Catholic Experience in Tudor Oxford," in *The Reckoned Expense: Edmund Campion and the Early English Jesuits: Essays in Celebration of the First Centenary of Campion Hall, Oxford*, ed. Thomas McCoog (Woodbridge: Boydell Press, 1996), 39-65
McCoog, Thomas, "The English Jesuit Mission and the French Match, 1579-1581," *Catholic Historical Review* 87 (2001): 185-213
McCoog, Thomas, "'Pray to the Lord of the Harvest': Jesuit Missions to Scotland in the Sixteenth Century," *Innes Review* 53 (2002): 127-88
McCoog, Thomas, ed., *The Reckoned Expense: Edmund Campion and the Early English Jesuits: Essays in Celebration of the First Centenary of Campion Hall, Oxford* (Woodbridge: Boydell Press, 1996)
McCoog, Thomas, *The Society of Jesus in Ireland, Scotland and England 1541-1588* (Leiden: Brill, 1996)
McCormack, Anthony, *The Earldom of Desmond, 1463-1583: The Decline and Crisis of a Feudal Lordship* (Dublin: Four Courts Press, 2005)
McCoy, Richard, "Old English Honour in an Evil Time: Aristocratic Principle in the 1620s," in *The Stuart Court and Europe: Essays in Politics and Political Culture*, ed. R. Malcolm Smuts (Cambridge: Cambridge University Press, 1996), 133-55
McCoy, Richard, *The Rites of Knighthood: The Literature and Politics of Elizabethan Chivalry* (Berkeley: University of California Press, 1989)
McCoy, Richard, *Sir Philip Sidney: Rebellion in Arcadia* (New Brunswick: Rutgers University Press, 1979)
Mac Cuarta, Brian, "The Catholic Church in the Ulster Plantation 1609-1642," in *The Plantation of Ulster: Ideology and Practice*, ed. Eamonn Ó Ciardha and Micháel Ó Siochrú (Manchester: Manchester University Press, 2012), 119-42
Mac Cuarta, Brian, *Catholic Revival in the North of Ireland, 1603-1641* (Dublin: Four Courts Press, 2007)
Mac Cuarta, Brian, ed., *Reshaping Ireland 1550-1700: Colonization and its Consequences* (Dublin: Four Courts Press, 2011)
MacCulloch, Diarmaid, Catholic and Puritan in Elizabethan Suffolk: A Community Polarises," *Archiv für Reformationsgeschichte* 72 (1981): 232-89

MacCulloch, Diarmaid, *Suffolk and the Tudors: Politics and Religion in an English County, 1500-1600* (Oxford: Oxford University Press, 1984)

McCullough, Peter, *Sermons at Court: Politics and Religion in Elizabethan and Jacobean Preaching* (Cambridge: Cambridge University Press, 1998)

McDermott, James, *England and the Spanish Armada: The Necessary Quarrel* (New Haven: Yale University Press, 2005)

McDiarmid, John, ed., *The Monarchical Republic of Early Modern England: Essays in Response to Patrick Collinson* (Aldershot: Ashgate, 2007)

MacDonald, Alan R., *The Jacobean Kirk, 1567-1625: Sovereignty, Polity and Liturgy* (Aldershot: Ashgate, 1998)

MacDonald, Alan R., "James VI and I, the Church of Scotland and British Ecclesiastical Convergence," *Historical Journal* 48 (2005): 885-903

MacDonald, Alan, "The Parliament of 1592: A Crisis Averted," in *Parliament and Politics in Scotland, 1567-1707*, ed. Keith Brown and Alastair J. Mann (Edinburgh: Edinburgh University Press, 2005), 57-81

McFarlane, Ian D., *Buchanan* (London: Duckworth, 1981)

McGinnis, Paul and Williamson, Arthur, "Radical Menace, Reforming Hope: Scotland and English Religious Politics, 1586-1596," *Renaissance and Reformation/Renaissance et Réforme* 36 (2013): 101-26

McGowan-Doyle, Valerie, "Elizabeth I, the Old English, and the Rhetoric of Counsel," in *Elizabeth I and Ireland*, ed. Brendan Kane and Valerie McGowen-Doyle (Cambridge: Cambridge University Press, 2014), 163-83

McGrath, Brid, "Electoral Law in Ireland Before 1641," in *Law and Revolution in Ireland*, ed. Dennehy Coleman (Dublin: Four Courts Press, 2018), 265-88

McGrath, Brid, "Ireland and the Third University: Attendance at the Inns of Court, 1603-1649," in *Regions and Rulers in Ireland, 1100-1650*, ed. David Edwards (Dublin: Four Courts Press, 2004), 217-36

McGrath, Patrick, *Papists and Puritans under Elizabeth I: The Early Struggles of the Church of England, the Perils of Moderation* (London: Blandford Press, 1967)

MacGregor, Martin, "Civilising Gaelic Scotland: The Scottish Isles and the Stewart Empire," in *The Plantation of Ulster: Ideology and Practice*, ed. Eamonn Ó Ciardha and Micháel Ó Siochrú (Manchester: Manchester University Press, 2012), 33-54

Macinnes, Allan, *Charles I and the Making of the Covenanting Movement 1625-1641* (Edinburgh: John Donald, 1991)

Macinnes, Allan, *Clanship, Commerce and the House of Stuart, 1603-1788* (East Linton: Tuckwell Press, 1996)

McLaren, A. N., *Political Culture in the Reign of Elizabeth I: Queen and Commonwealth, 1558-1585* (Cambridge: Cambridge University Press, 1999)

MacLean, Sally-Beth, "The Politics of Patronage: Dramatic Records in Sir Robert Dudley's Household Books," *Shakespeare Quarterly* 44.2 (1993): 175-82

McLeod, Neil, "Assault and Attempted Murder in Brehon Law," *Irish Jurist* n.s. 33 (1998): 351-91

McLeod, Neil, "Property and Honour Price in Brehon Law Glosses," *Irish Jurist* n.s. 31 (1996): 280-95

Maginn, Christopher, *'Civilizing' Gaelic Leinster: The Extension of Tudor Rule in the O'Byrne and O'Toole Lordships* (Dublin: Four Courts Press, 2005)

Maginn, Christopher, "One State or Two? Ireland and England under the Tudors," in *Frontiers, States and Identity in Early Modern Ireland and Beyond: Essays in Honour of*

Steven G. Ellis, ed. Christopher Maginn and Gerald Power (Dublin: Four Courts Press, 2016), 147-64
Malone, Nessa, "Henry Burnell and Richard Malone: Lawyers in Civic Life in the English Pale, 1562-1615," in *Religion and Politics in Urban Ireland, c. 1500-c. 1750: Essays in Honour of Colm Lennon*, ed. Salvador Ryan and Clodagh Tait (Dublin: Four Courts Press, 2016), 89-107
Mancall, Peter, *Hakluyt's Promise: An Elizabethan's Obsession for an English America* (New Haven: Yale University Press, 2007)
Manning, Roger, *Religion and Society in Elizabethan Sussex: A Study of the Enforcement of the Religious Settlement 1558-1603* (Leicester: Leicester University Press, 1969)
Manning, Roger, *Swordsmen: The Martial Ethos of the Three Kingdoms* (Oxford: Oxford University Press, 2003)
Marchand, Romain, *Henry de la Tour (1555-1623): affirmation politique, service du roi et révolte* (Paris: Garnier, 2020)
Marks, Adam, "Recognizing Friends from Foes: Stuart Politics, English Military Networks and Alliances with Denmark and the Palatinate," in *Stuart Marriage Diplomacy: Dynastic Politics in their European Context, 1604-1630*, ed. Valentia Caldari and Sara J. Wolfson (Woodbridge: Boydell Press, 2018), 173-85
Marrotti, Arthur, *Religious Ideology and Cultural Fantasy: Catholic and Anti-Catholic Discourses in Early Modern England* (Notre Dame: University of Notre Dame Press, 2005)
Marshall, Peter, "(Re)defining the English Reformation," *Journal of British Studies* 48 (2009): 564-86
Marshall, Peter and Morgan, John, "Clerical Conformity and the Elizabethan Settlement Revisited," *Historical Journal* 59 (2016): 1-22
Martin, Colin and Parker, Geoffrey, *The Spanish Armada* (New York and London: W. W. Norton, 1988)
Martin, Gregory, *Rubens in London* (London: Harvey Miller, 2011)
Mason, Roger, *Kingship and the Comonweal: Political Thought in Renaissance and Reformation Scotland* (East Lothian: Tuckwell Press, 1998)
Masterson, Rory, "The Dissolution of the Monasteries and the Parishes of the Western Liberty of Meath in the Seventeenth Century," in *Religion and Politics in Urban Ireland, c. 1500-c. 1750: Essays in Honour of Colm Lennon*, ed. Salvador Ryan and Clodagh Tait (Dublin: Four Courts Press, 2016), 134-55
May, Steven, *Elizabethan Courtier Poets: The Poems in their Contexts* (Columbia: University of Missouri Press, 1991)
May, Steven and Bryson, Allen, eds, *Verse Libel in Renaissance England and Scotland* (Oxford: Oxford University Press, 2016)
Mayer, Thomas, "Not Just the Hierarchy Fought: The Marian Cathedral Chapters, Seminaries of Recusancy," in *Catholic Renewal and Protestant Resistance in Marian England*, ed. Elizabeth Evenden and Vivienne Westbrook (London: Routledge, 2016), 93-126
Mears, Natalie, "Counsell, Public Debate and Queenship: John Stubbs's *The Discoverie of a Gaping Gulf*, 1579," *Historical Journal* 44 (2001): 629-50
Mears, Natalie, "Love-Making and Diplomacy: Elizabeth I and the Anjou Marriage Negotiations," *History* 86 (2001): 442-66
Mears, Natalie, *Queenship and Political Discourse in the Elizabethan Realms* (Cambridge: Cambridge University Press, 2005)

Meikle, Maureen, *A British Frontier? Lairds and Gentlemen in the Eastern Borders, 1540-1603* (East Linton: Tuckwell Press, 2004)

Merritt, Julia, ed., *The Political World of Thomas Wentworth Earl of Stafford 1621-1641* (Cambridge: Cambridge University Press, 1996)

Meyjes, G. H. M. Posthumus, *Jean Hotman's English Connection* (Amsterdam: Koninglijke Nederlandse Akademie van Wettenschappen, 1990)

Michon, Cédrique, *La crosse et le scepter: les prélats d'état sous François Ier et Henri VIII* (Paris: Tallandier, 2008)

Millstone, Noah, *Manuscript Circulation and the Invention of Politics in Early Stuart England* (Cambridge: Cambridge University Press, 2016)

Millstone, Noah, "The Politic History of Early Stuart Parliaments," in *Writing the History of Parliament in Tudor and Early Stuart England*, ed. Paul Cavill and Alexandra Gajda (Manchester: Manchester University Press, 2018), 172–93

Milton, Anthony, *Catholic and Reformed: The Roman and Protestant Churches in English Protestant Thought, 1600-1640* (Cambridge: Cambridge University Press, 1995)

Milton, Anthony, "Thomas Wentworth and the Political Thought of the Personal Rule," in *The Political World of Thomas Wentworth Earl of Stafford 1621-1641*, ed. Julia Merritt (Cambridge: Cambridge University Press, 1996), 133–56

Morales, Óscar Reio, *Ireland and the Spanish Empire, 1500-1825* (Dublin: Four Courts Press, 2010)

Morgan, Hiram, ed., *Political Ideology in Ireland, 1541-1641* (Dublin: Four Courts Press, 1999)

Morgan, Hiram, "'Tempt not God too long, O Queen': Elizabeth and the Irish Crisis of the 1590s," in *Elizabeth I and Ireland*, ed. Brendan Kane and Valerie McGowen-Doyle (Cambridge: Cambridge University Press, 2014), 209–38

Morgan, Hiram, *Tyrone's Rebellion: The Outbreak of the Nine Years War in Tudor Ireland* (Woodbridge: Boydell Press, 1999)

Morrill, John, *Revolt in the Provinces: The People of England and the Tragedies of War 1630-1648* (London: Longman, 2nd ed., 1999)

Morris, Richard, "'I was never more in love with an olde howse nor never newe worke could be better bestowed': The Earl of Leicester's Remodelling of Kenilworth Castle for Queen Elizabeth I," *Antiquaries Journal* 89 (2009): 241–305

Mortimer, Geoff, *The Origins of the Thirty Years War and the Revolt of Bohemia, 1618* (Basingstoke: Palgrave Macmillan, 2015)

Muldrew, Craig, *The Economy of Obligation: The Culture of Credit and Social Relations in Early Modern England* (Basingstoke: Palgrave Macmillan, 1998)

Muldrew, Craig, "The Middling Sort: An Emerging Cultural Identity," in *A Social History of England 1500-1700*, ed. Keith Wrightson (Cambridge: Cambridge University Press, 2017), 290–309

Murdoch, Steve and Grosjean, Alexia, *Alexander Leslie and the Scottish Generals of the Thirty Years' War, 1618-1648* (London: Pickering & Chatto, 2014)

Murray, Catriona, *Imaging Stuart Family Politics: Dynastic Crisis and Continuity* (London: Routledge, 2017)

Nelson, Eric, "Defining the Fundamental Laws of France: The Proposed First Article of the Third Estate at the French Estates General of 1614," *English Historical Review* 115 (2000): 1216–30

Nelson, Eric, *The Jesuits and the Monarchy: Catholic Reform and Political Authority in France (1590-1615)* (Aldershot: Ashgate, 2005)

Nicholls, K. W., *Gaelic and Gaelicized Ireland in the Middle Ages* (Dublin: Lilliput Press, 2003)

Nicholls, K. W., *Land, Law and Society in Sixteenth Century Ireland*, the O'Donnell Lecture, 1976 (Cork: University College, 1976)

Nicholls, Kenneth, "Woodland Cover in Pre-Modern Ireland," in *Gaelic Ireland c. 1250–1650: Land, Lordship and Settlement*, ed. Patrick Duffy, David Edwards, and Elizabeth FitzPatrick (Dublin: Four Courts Press, 2001), 181–206

Nolan, John C., *Sir John Norreys and the Elizabethan Military World* (Exeter: Exeter University Press, 1997)

Norbrook, David, *Poetry and Politics* (Oxford: Oxford University Press, 1984)

Ó Ciardha, Éamonn and Ó Siochrú, Micháel, eds, *The Plantation of Ulster: Ideology and Practice* (Manchester: Manchester University Press, 2012)

O'Dowd, Mary, "Land and Lordship in Sixteenth- and Early Seventeenth-Century Ireland," in *Economy and Society in Scotland and Ireland, 1500–1939*, ed. Roslaind Mitchison and Peter Roebuck (Edinburgh: John Donald, 1988)

Ó hAnnracháin, Tadgh, *Catholic Europe, 1592–1648: Centre and Peripheries* (Oxford: Oxford University Press, 2015)

O'Neill, James, "Death in the Lakelands: Tyrone's Proxy War, 1593–4," *History Ireland* 23 (2015): 14–17

O'Neill, James, *The Nine Years War, 1593–1603* (Dublin: Four Courts Press, 2017)

O'Neill, James, "'Their Skill and Practice Therein Far Exceeding their Wonted Usage': The Irish Military Revolution, 1593–1603," in *Becoming and Belonging in Ireland AD c. 1200–1600: Essays in Identity and Cultural Practice*, ed. Eve Campbell, Elizabeth FitzPatrick, and Audrey Horning (Cork: Cork University Press, 2018), 293–312

Ohlmeyer, Jane, *Civil War and Restoration in the Three Kingdoms: The Career of Randal MacDonnell, Marquis of Antrim* (Cambridge: Cambridge University Press, 1993)

Ohlmeyer, Jane, *Making Ireland English: The Irish Aristocracy in the Seventeenth Century* (Oxford: Oxford University Press, 2012)

Oosterhoff, F. G., *Leicester and the Netherlands 1586–1587* (Utrecht: HES Publishers, 1988)

Parker, Geoffrey, *The Grand Strategy of Philip II* (New Haven: Yale University Press, 1998)

Parker, Geoffrey, *Imprudent King: A New Life of Philip II* (New Haven: Yale University Press, 2014)

Parker, Geoffrey, *The Military Revolution: Military Innovation and the Rise of the West, 1500–1800* (Cambridge: Cambridge University Press, 1988)

Parry, Glyn, *The Arch-Conjuror of England: John Dee* (New Haven: Yale University Press, 2011)

Parry, Glyn, "Catholicism and Tyranny in Shakespeare's Warwickshire" in *The Oxford Handbook of the Age of Shakespeare*, ed. R. Malcolm Smuts (Oxford: Oxford University Press, 2016), 121–38

Parry, Glyn and Enis, Cathryn, *Shakespeare before Shakespeare: Stratford-upon-Avon, Warwickshire & the Elizabethan State* (Oxford: Oxford University Press, 2020)

Parsons, Jotham, *The Church in the Republic: Gallicanism and Political Ideology in Renaissance France* (Washington, DC: Catholic University of America Press, 2004)

Patterson, W. B., *King James VI and I and the Reunion of Christendom* (Cambridge: Cambridge University Press, 1997)

Pawlisch, Hans, *Sir John Davies and the Conquest of Ireland: A Study in Legal Imperialism* (Cambridge: Cambridge University Press, 1983)

Pearl, Valerie, *London and the Outbreak of the Puritan Revolution* (Oxford: Oxford University Press, 1961)

Peck, Linda Levy, ed., *The Mental World of the Jacobean Court* (Cambridge: Cambridge University Press, 1991)
Peltonen, Markku, *Classical Humanism and Republicanism in English Political Thought 1570–1640* (Cambridge: Cambridge University Press, 1995)
Peltonen, Markku, *The Duel in Early Modern England: Civility, Politeness and Honour* (Cambridge: Cambridge University Press, 2003)
Perry, Curtis, *Literature and Favoritism in Early Modern England* (Cambridge: Cambridge University Press, 2006)
Perry, Curtis, "Seneca and English Political Culture," in *The Oxford Handbook of the Age of Shakespeare*, ed. R. Malcolm Smuts (Oxford: Oxford University Press, 2016), 306–21
Pettegree, Andrew and der Weduwen, Arthur, *The Bookshop of the World: Making and Trading Books in the Dutch Golden Age* (New Haven: Yale University Press, 2020)
Philips, J. E., "George Buchanan and the Sidney Circle," *Huntington Library Quarterly* 12 (1948): 23–55
Philips van Marnix van Sint Aldegonde (Antwerp: Uitgeverij Pandora, 1998)
Platt, Eric, *Britain and the Bestandtwisten: The Causes, Course and Consequences of British Involvement in the Dutch Religious and Political Disputes of the Early Seventeenth Century* (Göttingen: Vandenhoeck & Ruprecht, 2015)
Pocock, John, *The Ancient Constitution and the Feudal Law: A Study of English Historical Thought in the Seventeenth Century. A Reissue with a Retrospect* (Cambridge: Cambridge University Press, 1987)
Pollock, Linda, "The Affective Life in Shakespearean England," in *The Oxford Handbook of the Age of Shakespeare*, ed. R. Malcolm Smuts (Oxford: Oxford University Press, 2016), 437–57
Pollock, Linda, "Honor, Gender and Reconciliation in Elite Culture, 1570–1700," *Journal of British Studies* 46.1 (2007): 3–29
Pollock, Linda, "Little Commonwealths I: The Family and Household Relationships," in *A Social History of England 1500–1700*, ed. Keith Wrightson (Cambridge: Cambridge University Press, 2017), 60–83
Pursell, Brennan, "The End of the Spanish Match," *Historical Journal* 45 (2002): 699–726
Pursell, Brennan, *The Winter King: Frederick V of the Palatinate and the Coming of the Thirty Years' War* (Aldershot: Ashgate, 2003)
Questier, Michael, *Catholicism and Community in Early Modern England* (Cambridge: Cambridge University Press, 2006)
Questier, Michael, *Dynastic Politics and the British Reformations, 1558–1630* (Oxford: Oxford University Press, 2019)
Questier, Michael, "Elizabeth and the Catholics," in *Catholics and the 'Protestant Nation': Religious Politics and Identity in Early Modern England* (Manchester: Manchester University Press, 2005), 69–94
Questier, Michael, "The Politics of Religious Conformity and the Accession of James I," *Historical Research* 71 (2002): 14–30
Questier, Michael, "Practical Antipapistry during the Reign of Elizabeth I," *Journal of British Studies* 36 (1997): 371–96
Quinn, David, ed., *The Voyages and Colonising Enterprises of Sir Humphrey Gilbert*, vol. 2 (London: Hakluyt Society, 1940)
Rapple, Rory, *Martial Power and Elizabethan Political Culture: Military Men in England and Ireland, 1558–1594* (Cambridge: Cambridge University Press, 2009)
Redworth, Glynn, *The Prince and the Infanta: The Cultural Politics of the Spanish Match* (New Haven: Yale University Press, 2003)

Richardson, Lisa, "Plagiarism and Imitation in Renaissance Historiography," in *Plagiarism in Early Modern England*, ed. Paulina Kewes (Basingstoke: Palgrave Macmillan, 2003), 106-18

Rickard, Jane, *Authorship and Authority: The Writings of James VI and I* (Manchester: Manchester University Press, 2007)

Rodger, N. A. M., "Queen Elizabeth and the Myth of Sea-Power in English History," *Transactions of the Royal Historical Society*, 6th series, 14 (2004): 153-74

Rodger, N. A. M., *The Safeguard of the Sea: A Naval History of Britain 660-1649* (New York: W. W. Norton, 1999)

Roux, Nicolas le, "Courtisans et favoris: l'entourage du prince et les mécanismes du pouvoir dans la France pendant des guerres de religion," *Histoire, Economie et Société* 17 (1998): 377-87

Roux, Nicolas le, *Le roi, la cour, l'état: de la Renaissance à l'absolutisme* (Paris: Champ Vallon, 2013)

Roux, Nicolas le, "A Time of Frenzy: Dreams of Union and Aristocratic Turmoil (1610-1615)," in *Dynastic Marriages 1612-1615: A Celebration of the Habsburg and Bourbon Unions*, ed. Margaret McGowan (Farnham: Ashgate, 2013), 19-38

Rowlands, Mary B., "Hidden People: Catholic Commoners, 1558-1625," in *English Catholics of Parish and Town 1558-1778*, ed. Mary B. Rowlands (London: Catholic Record Society, 1999), 36-60

Russell, Conrad, *The Fall of the British Monarchies 1637-1642* (Oxford: Clarendon Press, 1991)

Russell, Conrad, *King James VI and I and his English Parliaments: The Trevelyan Lectures Delivered at the University of Cambridge, 1995*, ed. Richard Cust and Andrew Thrush (Oxford: Oxford University Press, 2011)

Russell, Conrad, *Parliaments and English Politics, 1621-1629* (Oxford: Oxford University Press, 1979)

Ryan, Salvador and Tait, Clodagh, eds, *Religion and Politics in Urban Ireland, c. 1500-c. 1750: Essays in Honour of Colm Lennon* (Dublin: Four Courts Press, 2016)

Ryrie, Alex, *The Origins of the Scottish Reformation* (Manchester: Manchester University Press, 2006)

Salmon, J. H. M., "Seneca and Tacitus in Jacobean England," in *The Mental World of the Jacobean Court*, ed. Linda Peck (Cambridge: Cambridge University Press, 1991), 169-88

Sanz Camañes, Porfirio, *Diplomacia Hispano-Inglesa en el siglo xvii* (Cuenca: Ediciones de la Universidad de Castilla-La Mancha, 2002)

Schneider, Christian, "A Kingdom for a Catholic: Pope Clement VIII, King James VI/I and the English Succession (1592-1605)," *International History Review* 37 (2015): 119-41

Schultz, Jenna, *National Identity and the Anglo-Scottish Borderlands 1552-1652* (Woodbridge: Boydell Press, 2019)

Sessions, W. A., *Henry Howard, the Poet Earl of Surrey: A Life* (Oxford: Oxford University Press, 1999)

Shagan, Ethan, ed., *Catholics and the 'Protestant Nation': Religious Politics and Identity in Early Modern England* (Manchester: Manchester University Press, 2005)

Shagan, Ethan, "The Two Republics: Conflicting Views of Participatory Local Government in Early Tudor England," in *The Monarchical Republic of Early Modern England: Essays in Response to Patrick Collinson*, ed. John McDiarmid (Aldershot: Ashgate, 2007), 19-36

Shami, Jeanne, Flynn, Dennis, and Hester, Thomas M., eds, *The Oxford Handbook of John Donne* (Oxford: Oxford University Press, 2011)

Sharpe, Kevin, *Image Wars: Promoting Kings and Commonwealths in England 1603–1660* (New Haven: Yale University Press, 2010)
Sharpe, Kevin, *The Personal Rule of Charles I* (New Haven: Yale University Press, 1992)
Sharpe, Kevin, *Selling the Tudor Monarchy: Authority and Image in Sixteenth-Century England* (New Haven: Yale University Press, 2009)
Sheils, William, "'Getting On' and 'Getting Along' in Parish and Town: Catholics and their Neighbours in England," in *Catholic Communities in Protestant States: Britain and the Netherlands c. 1570–1720*, ed. Benjamin Kaplan, Bob Moore, Hank van Nierop, and Judith Pollman (Manchester: Manchester University Press, 2009), 67–83
Shell, Alison, *Catholicism, Controversy and the English Literary Imagination, 1558–1660* (Cambridge: Cambridge University Press, 1999)
Shell, Alison, *Oral Culture and Catholicism in Early Modern England* (Cambridge: Cambridge University Press, 2007)
Shepard, Alexandra, *Meanings of Manhood in Early Modern England* (Oxford: Oxford University Press, 2003)
Shriver, Frederick, "James I and the Vorstius Affair," *English Historical Review* 85 (1970): 49–74
Simms, Katharine, *From Kings to Warlords: The Changing Political Structure of Gaelic Ireland in the Later Middle Ages* (Woodbridge: Boydell Press, 1987)
Simms, Katharine, *Gaelic Ulster in the Middle Ages: History, Culture and Society* (Dublin: Four Courts Press, 2020)
Sizer, Jared M. R., "The Good of this Service Consists of Absolute Secrecy: The Earl of Dunbar, Scotland and the Border (1603–1611)," *Canadian Journal of History/Annales canadienne d'histoire* 36 (2001): 229–57
Skinner, Quentin, "A Genealogy of the Modern State," *Proceedings of the British Academy* 162 (2009): 325–70
Skinner, Quentin, "From the State of Princes to the Person of the State," in *Visions of Politics*, vol. 2 (Cambridge: Cambridge University Press, 2002), 368–412
Smith, David Chan, *Sir Edward Coke and the Reformation of the Laws: Religion, Politics and Jurisprudence, 1578–1616* (Cambridge: Cambridge University Press, 2014)
Smith, Frederick E., "The Origins of Recusancy in Elizabethan England Reconsidered," *Historical Journal* 60 (2017): 301–32
Smuts, R. Malcolm, "Concepts of War and Peace in Stuart Court Culture," in *Frieden und Krieg in der Frühen Neuzeit: Die europäische Staatenordnung und die aussereuropäische Welt*, ed. Ronald Asch, Wulf Eckart Voss, and Martin Wrede (Munich: Wilhelm Fink Verlag, 2001), 215–38
Smuts, R. Malcolm, "The Court and the Emergence of a Royalist Party," in *Royalists and Royalism during the English Civil Wars*, ed. Jason McElligott and David Smith (Cambridge: Cambridge University Press, 2007), 43–65
Smuts, R. Malcolm, "Court-Centred Politics and the Uses of Roman Historians," in *Culture and Politics in Early Stuart England*, ed. Kevin Sharpe and Peter Lake (Basingstoke: Macmillan, 1994), 21–44
Smuts, R. Malcolm, "Force, Love and Authority in Caroline Political Culture," in *The 1630s: Interdisciplinary Essays on Culture and Politics in the Caroline Era*, ed. Ian Atherton and Julie Sanders (Manchester: Manchester University Press, 2006), 28–49
Smuts, R. Malcolm, "The French Match and Court Politics," in *Stuart Marriage Diplomacy: Dynastic Politics in their European Context, 1604–1630*, ed. Sara J. Wolfson and Valentina Caldari (Woodbridge: Boydell Press, 2018), 13–28

Smuts, R. Malcolm, "International Politics and Jacobean Statecraft," in *The Oxford Handbook of John Donne*, ed. Jeanne Shami, Dennis Flynn, and Thomas M. Hester (Oxford: Oxford University Press, 2011), 589–99

Smuts, R. Malcolm, "The Making of *Rex Pacificus*: James VI and I and the Problem of Peace in an Age of Religious War," in *Royal Subjects: Essays on the Writings of James VI and I*, ed. Daniel Fischlin and Mark Fortier (Detroit: Wayne State University Press, 2002), 371–87

Smuts, R. Malcolm, "Occasional Events, Literary Texts and Historical Interpretations," in *Neo-Historicism: Studies in Renaissance Literature, History and Politics*, ed. Glenn Burgess, Robin Headlam Wells, and Rowland Wymer (Cambridge: D. S. Brewer, 2001), 179–98

Smuts, R. Malcolm, "Organized Violence in the Elizabethan Monarchical Republic," *History* 99 (2014): 418–44

Smuts, R. Malcolm, ed., *The Oxford Handbook of the Age of Shakespeare* (Oxford: Oxford University Press, 2016)

Smuts, R. Malcolm, "Pirates, Politicians and Urban Intellectuals," in *The Circulation of Culture in the Urban Atlantic World: From Early Modern to Modernism*, ed. Leonard von Morze (Basingstoke: Palgrave Macmillan, 2016), 73–99

Smuts, R. Malcolm, "The Political Thought of Sir John Hayward," in *Doubtful and Dangerous: The Question of the Succession in Late Elizabethan England*, ed. Susan Doran and Paulina Kewes (Manchester: Manchester University Press, 2014), 276–94

Smuts, R. Malcolm, "Prince Henry and his World," in *The Lost Prince: The Life and Death of Henry Stuart*, ed. Catharine MacLeod (London: National Portrait Gallery, 2012), 19–31

Smuts, R. Malcolm, "Religion, European Politics and Henrietta Maria's Circle, 1625–41," in *Henrietta Maria: Piety, Politics and Patronage*, ed. Erin Griffey (Aldershot: Ashgate, 2008), 13–38

Smuts, R. Malcolm, ed., *The Stuart Court and Europe: Essays in Politics and Political Culture* (Cambridge: Cambridge University Press, 1996)

Smuts, R. Malcolm, "Theological Polemics and James I's Diplomacy, 1603–1617," in *Ideologies of Diplomacy: Rhetoric, Ritual and Representation in Early Modern England*, ed. Jane Yeang Chui Wong, special issue of *The Journal of Medieval and Early Modern Studies* 50 (2020): 515–39

Smuts, R. Malcolm, "Varieties of Tacitism," *Huntington Library Quarterly* 83 (2020): 441–66

Soen, Violet, "Reconquista and Reconciliation in the Dutch Revolt: The Campaign of Governor-General Alexander Farnese (1578–1592)," *The Journal of Early Modern History* 16 (2012): 1–22

Sommerville, J. P., *Politics and Ideology in England, 1603–1640* (Harlow: Longman, 1986)

Spence, R. T., "The First Sir Richard Graham of Norton Conyers and Netherby, 1583–1653," *Northern History* 16 (1980): 102–29

Spence, R. T., "The Pacification of the Cumberland Borders, 1593–1628," *Northern History* 13 (1977): 59–160

Spufford, Margaret, *Contrasting Communities: English Villagers in the Sixteenth and Seventeenth Centuries* (Cambridge: Cambridge University Press, 1974)

Stevenson, David, *The Scottish Revolution, 1637–1644: The Triumph of the Covenanters* (Edinburgh: John Arnold, 2nd ed., 2003)

Stewart, Laura, "'Brothers in Treuth': Propaganda, Public Opinion and the Perth Articles Debate in Scotland," in *James VI and I: Ideas, Authority and Government*, ed. Ralph Houlbrooke (Aldershot: Ashgate, 2006), 151–68

Stewart, Laura, "The Political Repercussions of the Five Articles of Perth: A Reassessment of James VI and I's Religious Policies in Scotland," *Sixteenth Century Journal* 38 (2007): 1013–36

Stewart, Laura, *Rethinking the Scottish Revolution: Covenanted Scotland, 1637–1651* (Oxford: Oxford University Press, 2016)

Stewart, Laura, *Urban Politics and British Civil Wars: Edinburgh 1617–1663* (Leiden: Brill, 2006)

Stewart, Richard Winship, *The English Ordnance Office 1585–1625: A Case Study in Bureaucracy* (Woodbridge: Boydell Press, 1996)

Stone, Lawrence, *The Crisis of the Aristocracy* (Oxford: Clarendon Press, 1965)

Stone, Lawrence, *An Open Elite?* (Oxford: Oxford University Press, 1984)

Streatton, Tim, "The People and the Law," in *A Social History of England 1500–1700*, ed. Keith Wrightson (Cambridge: Cambridge University Press, 2017), 199–220

Strong, Roy, "Fair England's Knights: The Accession Day Tournaments," in *The Cult of Elizabeth* (London: Thames and Hudson, 1977), 117–28

Strong, Roy, *Henry, Prince of Wales and England's Lost Renaissance* (London: Thames and Hudson, 1986)

Strong, Roy and Van Dorsten, J. A., *Leicester's Triumph* (Oxford: Oxford University Press, 1964)

Swart, Eric, "'The Field of Finance': War and Taxation in Holland, Flanders and Brabant, 1572–1585," *Sixteenth Century Journal* 42 (2011): 1051–71

Tanner, J. R., *English Constitutional Conflicts of the Seventeenth Century, 1603–1689* (Cambridge: Cambridge University Press, 1928)

Tex, Jan den, *Oldenbarnevelt*, trans. R. B. Powell, 2 vols (Cambridge: Cambridge University Press, 1973)

Thomas, Courtney Erin, *If I Lose Mine Honour I Lose Myself: Honour among the Early Modern English Elite* (Toronto: University of Toronto Press, 2017)

Thurley, Simon, *Hampton Court: A Social and Architectural History* (New Haven: Yale University Press, 2003)

Tighe, William, "Five Elizabethan Courtiers, Their Catholic Connections and Their Careers," *British Catholic History* 33 (2016): 211–27

Tittler, Robert, *The Reformation and the Towns in England, c. 1540–1640* (Oxford: Clarendon Press, 1998)

Tracy, James, *The Founding of the Dutch Republic: War, Finance, and Politics in Holland, 1572–1588* (Oxford: Oxford University Press, 2008)

Trim, David, "Calvinist Internationalism and the English Officer Corps, 1562–1642," *History Compass* 4 (2006): 1024–48

Trim, David, "Calvinist Internationalism and the Shaping of Jacobean Foreign Policy," in *Prince Henry Revived: Image and Exemplarity in Early Modern England*, ed. Timothy Wilkes (London: Paul Holberton, 2008), 238–58

Trim, David, ed., *The Chivalric Ethos and the Development of Military Professionalism* (Leiden: Brill, 2003)

Trim, David, "The Context of War and Violence in Sixteenth-Century English Society," *Journal of Early Modern History* 20.2 (2016): 233–55

Trim, David, "The 'Secret War' of Elizabeth I: England and the Huguenots during the Early Wars of Religion, 1562-1577," *Proceedings of the Huguenot Society of Great Britain and Ireland* 27 (1999): 189-99

Trim, David, "War, Soldiers, and High Politics under Elizabeth I," in *The Oxford Handbook of the Age of Shakespeare*, ed. R. Malcolm Smuts (Oxford: Oxford University Press, 2016), 82-102

Tuck, Richard, *Philosophy and Government, 1572-1651* (Cambridge: Cambridge University Press, 1991)

Tuite, Fionnán, "Family Feud in Early Modern Meath," in *Community in Early Modern Ireland*, ed. Robert Armstrong and Tadhg Ó hAnnracháin (Dublin: Four Courts Press, 2006), 69-90

Tutino, Stefania, *Law and Conscience in Early Modern England, 1570-1625* (Aldershot: Ashgate, 2007)

Tyacke, Nicholas, *Anti-Calvinists: The Rise of English Arminianism c. 1590-1640* (Oxford: Clarendon Press, 1990)

Underdown, David, *Revel, Riot, and Rebellion* (Oxford: Clarendon Press, 1995)

Vanderjagt, Arjo, "The Princely Culture of the Valois Dukes of Burgundy," in *Princes and Princely Culture 1450-1650*, ed. Martin Gosman, Alasdair MacDonald, and Arjo Vanderjagt (Leiden: Brill, 2003), 51-80

Vickers, Brian, "The Authenticity of Bacon's Earliest Writings," *Philological Quarterly* 94 (1997): 248-96

Villiers, Patrick, *Les corsairs du littoral: Dunkerque, Calais, Boulogne de Philippe II à Louis XIV (1568-1713)* (Villeneuve d'Ascq: Presses Universitaires du Septentrio, 2000)

Viroli, Mauricio, *From Politics to Reason of State: The Acquisition and Transformation of the Language of Politics, 1250-1600* (Cambridge: Cambridge University Press, 1992)

Waddell, Brodie, "Governing England through the Manor Courts, 1500-1850," *Historical Journal* 55 (2012): 279-315

Walsham, Alexandra, "Beads, Books and Bare Ruined Choirs: Transmutations of Catholic Ritual Life in Protestant England," in *Catholic Communities in Protestant States: Britain and the Netherlands c. 1570-1720*, ed. Benjamin Kaplan, Bob Moore, Hank van Nierop, and Judith Pollman (Manchester: Manchester University Press, 2009), 103-22

Walsham, Alexandra, *Catholic Reformation in Protestant Britain* (Farnham: Ashgate, 2014)

Walsham, Alexandra, *Charitable Hatred: Tolerance and Intolerance in England, 1500-1700* (Manchester: Manchester University Press, 2006)

Walsham, Alexandra, *Church Papists: Catholicism, Conformity and Confessional Polemic in Early Modern England* (Woodbridge: Boydell Press, 1993)

Walsham, Alexandra, "'Domme Preachers'? Post-Reformation English Catholicism and the Culture of Print," *Past and Present* 168 (2000): 72-123

Walsham, Alexandra, "Supping with Satan's Disciples: Spiritual and Secular Sociability in Post-Reformation England," in *Getting Along? Religious Identities and Confessional Relations in Early Modern England: Essays in Honour of Professor W. J. Sheils*, ed. Adam Morton and Lewine Lewycky (Aldershot: Ashgate, 2012), 29-55

Walsham, Alexandra, "Translating Trent? English Catholicism and the Counter Reformation," *Historical Research* 78 (2005): 288-310

Waszink, J. H., "Henry Savile's Tacitus and the English Role on the Continent: Leicester, Hotman, Lipsius," *History of European Ideas* 42.3 (2016): 303-19

Watts, Sheldon J. with Watts, Susan J., *From Border to Middle Shire: Northumberland 1586-1625* (Leicester: Leicester University Press, 1975)

Wernham, R. B., *The Return of the Armadas: The Last Years of the Elizabethan War against Spain 1595-1603* (Oxford: Clarendon Press, 1994)
Wilks, Tim, "Poets, Patronage and the Prince's Court," in *The Oxford Handbook of the Age of Shakespeare*, ed. R. Malcolm Smuts (Oxford: Oxford University Press, 2016), 159-78
Williams, Patrick, *The Great Favourite: The Duke of Lerma and the Court and Government of Philip III of Spain, 1598-1621* (Manchester: Manchester University Press, 2006)
Williamson, Arthur, "A Patriot Nobility? Calvinism, Kin-Ties and Civic Humanism," *Scottish Historical Review* 72 (1993): 1-21
Williamson, Arthur, "Patterns of British Identity: 'Britain' and its Rivals in the Sixteenth and Seventeenth Centuries," in *The New British History: Founding a Nation State*, ed. Glenn Burgess (London: I. B. Tauris, 1999), 138-73
Williamson, Arthur, "The Rise and Decline of the British 'Patriot': Civic Britain c. 1545-1645," *International Review of Scottish Studies* 36 (2011): 7-32
Williamson, Arthur, *Scotland and the Rise of Social Thought* (forthcoming)
Williamson, Arthur, "Scots, Indians and Empire: The Politics of Civilization, 1519-1609," *Past and Present* 150 (1996): 46-87
Williamson, Arthur, *Scottish National Consciousness in the Age of James VI: The Apocalypse, the Union and the Shaping of Scotland's Public Culture* (Edinburgh: John Donald, 1979)
Wilson, Peter, *The Thirty Years War: Europe's Tragedy* (Cambridge, MA: Belknap Press, 2009)
Withington, Phil, "Plantation and Civil Society," in *The Plantation of Ulster: Ideology and Practice*, ed. Eamonn Ó Ciardha and Micháel Ó Siochrú (Manchester: Manchester University Press, 2012), 55-77
Womersley, David, "Sir Henry Savile's Translation of Tacitus and the Political Interpretation of Elizabethan Texts," *Review of English Studies* 42 (1991): 313-42
Wood, Andy, *Faith, Hope and Charity: English Neighborhoods, 1500-1640* (Cambridge: Cambridge University Press, 2020)
Wooding, Lucy, *Rethinking Catholicism in Reformation England* (Oxford: Clarendon Press, 2000)
Worden, Blair, *The Sound of Virtue: Philip Sidney's* Arcadia *and Elizabethan Politics* (New Haven: Yale University Press, 1997)
Wormald, Jenny, "Bloodfeud, Kindred and Government in Early Modern Scotland," *Past and Present* 87 (1980): 54-97
Wormald, Jenny, "James VI and I, *Basilikon Doron* and *The Trew Law of Free Monarchies*: The Scottish Context and the English Translation," in *The Mental World of the Jacobean Court*, ed. Linda Peck (Cambridge: Cambridge University Press, 1991), 36-54
Wrightson, Keith, "The Decline of Neighbourliness Revisited," in *Local Identities in Late Medieval and Early Modern England*, ed. Daniel Woolf and Norman Jones (Basingstoke: Palgrave Macmillan, 2007)
Wrightson, Keith, ed., *A Social History of England 1500-1700* (Cambridge: Cambridge University Press, 2017)
Wrightson, Keith and Levine, David, *Poverty and Piety in an English Village, Terling, 1525-1700* (London and New York: Academic Press, 1970)
Yates, Frances, "Elizabethan Chivalry: The Romance of the Accession Day Tilts," in *Astraea: The Imperial Theme in the Sixteenth Century* (London: Routledge, 1975), 88-111
Yates, Frances, *The Rosicrucian Enlightenment* (St Albans: Paladin, 1972)

Yellowlees, Michael, *So Strange a Monster as a Jesuite: The Society of Jesus in Sixteenth Century Scotland* (Colonsay: House of Lochar, 2003)
Young, Allen, *Tudor and Jacobean Tournaments* (London: George Philip, 1987)
Younger, Neil, "Drama, Politics and News in the Earl of Sussex's Entertainment of Elizabeth at New Hall, 1579," *Historical Journal* 58 (2015): 343–69
Younger, Neil, "How Protestant was the Elizabethan Regime?" *English Historical Review* 133 (2018): 1060–92
Younger, Neil, "The Practice and Politics of Troop-Raising: Robert Devereux, Second Earl of Essex, and the Elizabethan Regime," *English Historical Review* 127 (2012): 566–91
Younger, Neil, "Securing the Monarchical Republic: The Remaking of the Lord Lieutenancies in 1585," *Bulletin of the Institute for Historical Research* 88 (2011): 249–65
Younger, Neil, *War and Politics in the Elizabethan Counties* (Manchester: Manchester University Press, 2012)
Yun, Bartolomé, *Marte contra Minerva: El Precio del Imperio Español* (Barcelona: Crítica, 2004)
Zaller, Robert, *The Discourses of Legitimacy in Early Modern England* (Stanford: Stanford University Press, 2007)

Electronic Resources

Annals of the Four Masters, Corpus of Electronic Texts online edition at Annals of the Four Masters (ucc.ie)
Holinshed, Raphael, *The first and second volumes of Chronicles* (London, 1587), online edition, http:www.msns.ox.ac.uk/Holinshed/texts.php?text1=1587_9135
Oxford Dictionary of National Biography
Oxford English Dictionary

Unpublished Theses

Adams, Simon, "The Protestant Cause: Religious Alliance with the West European Calvinist Communities as a Political Issue in England, 1585–1630" (Oxford, 1973). Available online at: ORA—Oxford University Research Archive
Cross, Robert, "To Counterbalance the World: England, Spain and Peace in the Early Seventeenth Century" (Princeton, 2012). Available online at: http://arks.princeton.edu/ark:/88435/dsp01hm50tr75s
Fry, Cynthia, "Diplomacy and Deception: King James VI of Scotland's Foreign Relations with Europe (1585–1603)" (St Andrews, 2014). Available online at: Diplomacy & deception: King James VI of Scotland's foreign relations with Europe (c. 1584–1603) (st-andrews.ac.uk)
Grant, Ruth, "George Gordon, Sixth Earl of Huntly, and the Politics of the Counter-Reformation in Scotland, 1581–1595" (Edinburgh, 2010). Available online at: https://era.ed.ac.uk/handle/1842/4508
Juhala, Amy, "The Household and Court of King James VI of Scotland, 1567–1603," (Edinburgh, 2000). Available online at: https://era.ed.ac.uk/handle/1842/1727
Patton, Henry, "'Of Hir Majesties Chappell': Religious Identities in the Elizabethan Chapel Royal" (Oxford, 2021)

Smith, Mark C., "The Presbytery of St Andrews, 1586–1605: A Study and Annotated Edition of the Register of the Minutes of the Presbytery of St Andrews, vol. 1" (St Andrews, 1985). Available online at: https://research-repository.st-andrews.ac.uk/handle/10023/2822

Trim, David, "Fighting 'Jacob's Wars': The Employment of English and Welsh Mercenaries in the European Wars of Religion: France and the Netherlands, 1562–1610" (London, 2001). Available online at: https://kclpure.kcl.ac.uk/

Index

For the benefit of digital users, indexed terms that span two pages (e.g., 52–53) may, on occasion, appear on only one of those pages.

Abbott, George, archbishop of Canterbury
  alerted, and alerts king, about heterodox views of Vorstius 585–6
  excluded from committee considering Spanish match 610–11
  letter attributed to, accuses James of setting up popery 634
  rejoices at Fredericks V's election as king of Bohemia 624–5
  summoned to meet and escort Charles upon his return from Spain 636–7
  tells William Trumbull that some courtiers want to break Parliament 642–3
  thinks Jesuits have a secret treasury in England 558–9
absolute kings and absolutism 18–19, 365–6, 444–5, 462–76
  attempts to constrain, limit or qualify 463–4, 466–7
  encouraged by pressures of war and religious instability 463–4, 467–8
  French, and French concepts of 463–6
  James VI and I's attitudes toward 464–5
  prudential checks on 464–5
  sovereign will and 464–6
  tenures and tenurial obligations under 477–8
  see also common law, royal prerogative
Adamson, Patrick, archbishop of St Andrews 138–9
  arrested and threatened 161
  attacked and humiliated by Andrew Melville and other Kirk leaders 408–9
  communicates with Richard Bancroft 404–5
  helps engineer passage of Black Acts and launches subscription campaign 153
  preaches sermon urging charity toward Queen Mary 164–6
  protests England's sheltering exiled Scottish ministers 154
  solemnizes earl of Huntly's marriage and is suspended from ministry 402–3
  travels to England and appeals to Archbishop Whitgift 152–3
  writes *A Declaration of the Kings Majesties intentioun* 154–5, 403
  see also Beale, Robert; Bancroft, Richard, bishop of London and later archbishop of Canterbury
Aersen, François van 589–90
Albert, archduke and co-ruler of Habsburg Netherlands
  equivocates about whether his army will intervene in France 614–15
  see also Archdukes (Albert and Isabella), the
Allen, William, Catholic leader and cardinal 47, 96–9
  seeks to advance attacks on Elizabeth 48
Álvarez de Toledo, Pedro, marquis of Villafranca and Spanish governor of Milan 612
Amsterdam 273, 286–7
Anderson, Anthony 112–13, 396
Anderson, Edmund 57
Anglo-Scottish alliance negotiations (1584–6) 157–60
  impeded by English mistrust of James VI and Arran 158–9
Anglo-Scottish Union
  ancient Rome as model for 459–61
  celebrated by Samuel Daniel 454
  diversity of social practices complicates 476
  naming the unified kingdom and 460
  poses practical challenges at outset of James VI and I's English reign 458
  problems of religion and 459–60
  promoted, in 1540s 135
  raises questions of priority between royal authority and law 471
  resistance and opposition to 461
  seen as providentially ordained by James VI and I 447
  tracts concerning, at outset of James VI and I's English reign 459
  uniformity of laws and institutions and 460–1
Anjou, duke of, see under Valois, François de
Anjou Match
  initial reactions to 53
  likely impact on religious politics in England 55–6

Anjou Match (*cont.*)
  opposition to 53–4, 59–71, 73–7, 79–80, 82–3
  reasons for collapse of 83–4
  support for 51–3, 78–9, 90
  see also Dudley, Robert, 1st earl of Leicester; Elizabeth I; Radclyffe, Thomas, earl of Sussex; Stubbs, John; Valois, François de, duke of Anjou
Anna of Denmark, queen consort of James VI and I 450–1, 548
  distrusted as pro-Spanish by Henry IV 552
  featured in Ben Jonson's pageant for James I's entry into London (1604) 455–6
  marriage of 167–8, 412
Annals of the Four Masters, The 234–5, 250, 269–70
Anne of Austria, queen consort of Louis XIII of France 608–9
Anne of Denmark, *see under* Anna of Denmark
Anti-Catholic polemics 77
anti-court criticism 638–40
  continuities and discontinuities in, between 1590s and 1620s 641
  corruption and 643–4
  decay of honor and 640–1
  extravagance, venality and 638–40
  opposition to parliament and 642–3
  religion and 643–4
Antwerp 271–3, 278, 305
  surrender of 280–1
apocalyptic thought
  Scottish, focused around godly kings and dynasties 412
  see also Henry, Prince of Wales; providential beliefs
arbitration and compensation, in Irish and Scottish law and society 482–4
Archdukes, (Albert and Isabella), the, rulers of the Habsburg Netherlands
  attitude of, toward James VI and I 550–1
  behavior during first Jülich-Cleves succession crisis 567
  dispatch embassy of congratulations to James VI and I (1603) 547–8
  see also Albert, archduke and co-ruler of Habsburg Netherlands
Arden, Edward 45–6
Arden, Robert 45–6
Armada, the 333–6, 388
  causes members of privy council to close ranks 348–9
  defeat of, interpreted as evidence of God's support for Elizabeth 395
  see also Howard, 13th earl of Arundel

Arminians and Arminianism
  associated with heterodoxy and betrayals of Protestantism 590–1
  Charles I's support for, antagonizes many Protestants 656–7
  House of Commons tries to compel Charles I to abandon (1629) 660
  see also under Arminius, Jacobus; Remonstrant Controversy
Arminius, Jacobus (Hermanzoon, Jacob), Dutch theologian 584–5
Army of Flanders, the 39–40
Art Boys, the 239–40
Ashley, Katherine 189
Association, the (between Mary and James VI) 133, 143, 145
  repudiated by James VI 159
Aston, Roger 425
  blames "secret instruments" for fanning James's conflict with the Kirk (1596) 378–9
  reports to Robert Cecil on David Black's conflict with James VI 426–7
Aston, Sir Walter, Staffordshire landowner 118–20, 124
Aston, Sir Walter, English ambassador in Madrid 632–3
Atlantic voyages and colonization 210–11, 213–14
  assisted by international network of mathematicians, pilots and cartographers 213
  collection of knowledge and 213–14
  effects of war with Spain on 221
  peak and decline, in 1580s 221
  see also under literature on oceanic enterprise; Drake, Sir Francis; Hakluyt, Richard the younger; Lok, Michael; navies; privateers and pirates
Atye, Sir Arthur 330–1
Aylmer, John, bishop of London 71
  orders sermons denouncing *Gaping Gulf* 75

Bacon, Anthony 341, 374
  complains of court's drowsy leaders 380–1
Bacon, Sir Francis 360, 385–6
  accuses crown of acting unlawfully 467–8
  believes he is living in an age of moral decline 637–8
  brought down by charges of bribery and corruption 643
  describes origin of common law in royal decrees 472–3
  dislikes concentration of wealth in hands of nobility 638–9

INDEX 721

objects to a "magistracy enabled to stand by itself," 473–4
tract by, on Anglo-Scottish union 459
Balcanqual, Walter 139–40, 161, 407–8, 417–18
appointed record keeper for Kirk's efforts to monitor Catholics 419–20
exhorts Edinburgh residents to stand for the Kirk against enemies at the court 429
flees to England, following the Tumult 432–3
Bancroft, Richard 396
avoids direct criticism of high-ranking puritan patrons 408
communicates with Patrick Adamson 404–5
constructs intelligence network in Scotland 404–5
Daungerous positions and proceedings of 403–4
implicitly repudiates English support for Scottish presbyterians 403–4
invites Patrick Adamson to emigrate to England 408–9
objects to presbyterian clergy criticizing laymen by name 408
Paul's Cross sermon of (1588) 398–9, 403
shocked at views attributed to Arminius 584–5
stigmatizes puritans as republicans opposed to social hierarchy 403–4
Barnes, George 213–14
Barnewell, Sir Patrick 520–1
becomes popular hero for opposing mandates policy 522–3
heads new delegation of protest to London (1611) 525–6
Bate's Case (1606) 474–5
Beale, Robert 278, 410
protests against Adamson and Whitgift 154–6
Becher, William, British ambassador in Paris 564
Becon, Richard 341–2
Bellarmine, Robert, Jesuit theologian 561–2, 597–8
book of, censored by parlement of Paris 573–4
replies to James in Oath of Allegiance controversy 562–3
Bertie, Peregrine, 13th baron Willougby d'Eresby
inherits command of English forces in the Netherlands (1587) 328
instructed to cooperate with Maurice and Oldenbarnevelt 315
pessimistic about campaigning season of 1588 in the Netherlands 333–4
Bethlen Gabor 623–4
Béthune, Maximilien de, marquis de Rosny and duke of Sully 556–7

concludes James wants a French alliance but Robert Cecil does not 549–51
falls from power 571
fooled by James VI and I 550–1
interviews with James VI and I 549–50
sent as ambassador to James VI and I 548–9
Beutterich, Petrus 290–1
Bilson, Thomas, bishop of Winchester 562–3
coronation sermon of, for James I 443–5, 451–2, 663–4
Bingham, Sir Richard 259–60
Biondi, Giovanni Francisco
has long audience with Charles Emmanuel of Savoy 602–3
sent by James to Huguenot national assembly at Grenoble (1615) 579–80
Black, Patrick 417–18
refuses to answer to king's council for his sermon 425–8
summoned to answer before king's council for inflammatory sermon (1596) 425
Blackwell, George, archpriest of England 561–2
Blair, Patrick 404–5
Blessed Revolution, the 637
Blount, Charles, 1st baron Mountjoy 260–1
Battle of Kinsale and 543–4
disapproves of religious compulsion 516–17
quells rebellion in Cork and other towns (1603) 506–7
Boderie, Antoine le Fèvre de la, French ambassador to court of James I 564, 566–7
Bodin, Jean 321–2
argues that law derives not from reason but the sovereign's will 464
influences thought about Ireland 250–1
paraphrased by Thomas Wilkes in memorandum concerning sovereignty in the Netherlands 320–1
Bohemian crisis, the
erupts 619
generates hopes and excitement in England 623–5
initially viewed as a distraction by major powers 620
issue of whether Bohemia an elective monarchy and 621–2
leads to election of Frederick V as king 622–3
Boisschot, Batta, archdukes' ambassador in London 570–1, 602–3, 605
reports on opposition to a Catholic match for Prince Henry 599–600
reports on progress of Spanish match negotiations 607–8

Boisschot, Batta, archdukes' ambassador in London (*cont.*)
  thinks James underhandedly encouraged Dutch in second Jülich and Cleves crisis 604
Bond of Association 33, 110–11, 125–8, 137
  provokes debate in Parliament 125–7
  targets James VI as well as Mary 156
Borders, (between England and Scotland) 92–3, 489–94
  absence of substantial gentry within parts of 491–2
  feuds within 490–1
  James VI and I attempts to pacify 485, 492
  surnames within 490–1
  wardens and marches within 491
  see also Busy Week; Clifford, George, 3d earl of Cumberland; Graham, Sir Richard; Grahams, Border surname
Bouillon, duke of, *see under* La Tour d'Auvergne, Henri de
Bourbon-Habsburg dynastic alliance 597–8
  deeply concerning to British government 571, 598
  entangled in French factional politics 571–4
Bourbon, Henry II de, prince of Condé 572
  appointed head of French council with extensive powers 580–1
  arrest of, precipitates ministerial reshuffle in France 613–14
  arrested 580–1
  opposes Bourbon-Habsburg dynastic alliance 573–4
  revolts of 576–9
Bowes, Robert, Elizabeth I's ambassador to Scotland 139–40, 147, 155–6, 402–3, 417, 419
  complains carrying out queen's orders cost him friends and contacts 410–11
  instructed to demand that James expel John Penry and suppress works critical of English bishops 410
  receives report of sermon insulting Elizabeth (1596) 425
Boyle, Richard, 1st earl of Cork 232, 501–2, 505
  kinship alliances of, with Irish families 231
Brig o' Dee 414
Briskett, Lodowick 250–1
Brouncker, Sir Henry 519–20
Browne, Anthony, 1st viscount Montague 121
Bruce, Robert
  appointed treasurer of Kirk committee to monitor Catholic activities 419–20
  breaks with James over rehabilitation of earl of Huntly (1596) 424
  flees to England following the Tumult 432–3
  hosts clerical meeting to petition king about earl of Huntly (1593) 420–1
  relationship of, with James VI 413–14
  role of, in the Tumult 429–32
  sermons of 406–8
  writes to Walsingham, demanding repudiation of Bancroft 408–9
Buccleuch, Walter Scot of 491, 550–1
Buchanan, George 137
  ideas of, about kingship, compared to those of James VI 435–7
Burghley, Lord, *see under* Cecil, William
Burke, Richard, 4th earl of Clanricard 522–3
Burke, Ulick, 1st earl of Clanricard 241, 252
Burke, William 241
Burnell, Henry 520–1
Busy Week, the 491–2
Butler, Thomas, 10th earl of Ormond 195
  complains of inadequate support for his military campaign 193
  enumerates losses in his private war with earl of Desmond 238–9
  English factional competition and 241–2
  lordship of 236, 501–2
  protected by relationship with Elizabeth I 261
  pursues campaigns of theft and harassment against rivals 238–40
  sends severed heads to Irish governors 258–9
  suspect because of Catholic friends and clients 260–1
Buys, Paul 280–1, 296–7
  stigmatized by Leicester 304–5
Bye and Main plots 37, 548

Cadiz expedition (1596) 377–8
Calderwood, David 143, 533, 535–7
Calvin's Case (1608) 474–5
Camden, William 560–1
Campbell, Colin, 6th earl of Argyll 134–5
  improves lands 496–7
  loses Battle of Glenlivet (1594) 422
  pacification of the Scottish Isles and 494–6
Campion, Edmund 82–3, 116
Cannock Chase, Staffordshire 118–19
Carew, Sir George, president of Munster 192–3, 268, 365–6
  discusses Irish administration with Elizabeth I 266
Carey, Henry, lord Hunsdon 156
Carleill, Christopher 221
Carleton, Dudley 602–3
  believes France headed for a war of religion 614–15

INDEX   723

comments on Charles Emmanuel of
    Savoy 603-4
comments on military situation in Germany in
    late 1619 625-6
complains that Spanish have duped James VI
    and I 633-4
instructed by James VI and I to press Dutch to
    assist him in restraining French attacks on
    Huguenots and Condé 615
turns against Oldenbarnevelt and supports
    Maurice of Nassau 591-2
Carmichael, James 153-4
    appointed Edinburgh agent of Kirk committee
        to monitor Catholics 419-20
Caron, Noel de, Dutch ambassador to
    England 547-8, 555-6, 574-5, 635-6
    comments on consternation caused by
        Charles's journey to Madrid 636
    discusses Bohemian crisis with James VI
        and I 622
    hears king's complaints about events in
        France 577
    laments that mutual jealousies of James VI and
        I and Henry IV impede their
        cooperation 581-2
    persuades King James to sign letter urging
        states general to quell religious
        controversies (1613) 588
    reassured by James VI and I about his
        friendship for Dutch (1604) 551-2
    reports British court's growing alienation from
        France and tilt toward Spain 607-8
    reports most privy councilors and nobles want
        James to assist Frederick V (1619) 624-5
    reports Prince Charles summoned Archbishop
        Abbot to meet him upon his return from
        Spain 636-7
    reports several British nobles raise volunteer
        soldiers for Continental service (1620) 629
    told of king's support for Charles Emmanuel
        of Savoy 601-4
    tries to negotiate a compromise on
        Vorstius 587-8
Cartwright, Thomas 136, 390-1
    the earl of Leicester and 303-4
Casimir, Johann 79-80, 176-7, 190
Castlenau, Michel de, seigneur de
    Mauvissière 37-8, 43, 71, 73, 80-1, 205
    discusses privateering with Sir Francis
        Drake 206-7
    encourages Catholic revival at English
        court 54
    hears Elizabeth I denounce puritans 80-1
    opposes English aid to Huguenots 79-82

promotes Association between Mary and
    James VI 133
reports Elizabeth's anger over Dutch
    piracy 199-200
reports Elizabeth's hatred of James VI 143-4
reports rumor that James VI will become
    Catholic 82
urges Mary to cultivate Leicester and
    Walsingham 146-7
Catholicism, English, see under Catholic
    recusants and recusancy (in England);
    Catholics, English
Catholic League, in France 47, 464
    Justifies deposition and murder of heretical
        princes 559
Catholic recusants and recusancy (in
    England) 101-2, 105-8, 597-8
    imprisoned without due process 117-18
    in Hampshire 106-8
    in Sussex 62-4
    prosecuted during East Anglian progress of
        1578 57-8
    prosecuted more vigorously after 1578 109-11
    prosecution of, as a means of disrupting
        Catholic political networks 112-13
    recusancy fines 113, 115
    resiliency of, in face of persecution 95-7
    sheltered by landed patrons 103-4
    subjected to bonds restricting
        movements 117-18
    see also Catholics, English
Catholics, English
    communicate with foreign powers 99
    executions and imprisonment of 114-16
    exiled, on the Continent 47-9, 95-8
    historiography concerning 94-6, 98
    individual Catholics, see Allen, William;
        Arden, Edward; Browne, Anthony, viscount
        Montague; Campion, Edmund; Howard,
        Henry lord, later earl of Northampton;
        Howard, Philip, earl of Arundel; Paget,
        Charles; Paget, Thomas lord; Persons,
        Robert; Sander, Nicholas; Tresham, Sir
        Thomas; Tresham, William; Vaux, Henry;
        Vaux, William lord
    intimidate Protestants 102-4
    landed dynasties and households 43-4, 47-8,
        103-8
    loyalty and disloyalty among 99-100
    as magistrates and officials 105-8, 111-12
    networks among, forged by priests 103-6
    occasional conformity among 105-6
    plot against Elizabeth I 87, 92, 108, 125,
        143-4, 164

Catholics, English (cont.)
  reformist impulses and 95–6
  revival of 54–5
  as soldiers 108
  spies target: see Sledd, Charles
  tracts and propaganda by 66–7
  see also Catholic recusants and recusancy (in England); confessional commitments and confessionalization; Jesuits
Catholics, Irish
  active centers of 523–4, 527–8
  assisted by friars 252–3, 255, 523
  attempts to suppress 253–7
  de facto toleration of, by 1620 524–5, 528–9
  entrenched within Dublin administration and among Irish judges 518–19
  growing assertiveness of, in seventeenth century 263–4
  helped by weakness of Irish Protestantism 252, 254
  increasingly organized by end of James's reign 527–8
  in the Pale 263–4
  perceived as growing threat to English rule 251–2
  prosecuted, under James I 519–23
  receive material support from Irish peers and commoners 523
  reinforced by Catholic bishops 263, 523–4
  religious grievances of, fuse with secular issues 252, 254–5, 262–3, 507–8
  role of, in Munster towns rebellion 505–7
  schools and 263
  strength and vigor of 252–3, 522–4
  suspicion of "civil Irish" and 260–1
  in towns 252, 263–4, 268–9, 505–7, 522
  unity among, between localities 255–6
  see also Chichester, Sir Arthur; Desmond's rebellion; Ireland; Irish priests; Irish rebellions
Catholics, Scottish 139–40
  see also Chricton, William
Cecil, Robert, later 1st earl of Salisbury 266, 469, 555–6, 566
  advises Essex to make the queen's "will his perfectest reason," 365
  agrees with James's decision to pardon earl of Huntly 434–5
  describes how to disagree tactfully with the queen 365–6
  publishes An Answere to certaine scandalous papers (1606) 560–1
  relations of, with earl of Essex 348, 353–4, 357–8
  reported to have sent agent to the Netherlands to support Maurice of Nassau against Oldenbarnevelt 590
  upbraided by James before French ambassador 549–50
  worries about renewed rebellion in Ireland (1608) 566–7
  worries Scottish Catholics will link up with Tyrone 422
Cecil, Thomas, eldest son of Lord Burghley, later 1st earl of Exeter 90–4, 400, 447–8
  invests £5000 in his governorship of Brill 284–5
  receives money for Dutch campaign 286
Cecil, William, Lord Burghley 34–6, 276–7
  accused of holding back virtuous men 344
  accused of promoting a regnum Cecilianum 393
  Anjou match and 53
  berated by Elizabeth 343–4
  complains of Whitgift's "Romish inquisition," 400
  complains of Catholics at Cambridge 95–6
  complains of Elizabeth's command to order cease-fire in Dutch wars 325–6
  defends religious compulsion 104–5, 114–15
  determined to prosecute Martin Hackett and his followers 400
  difficulties of, in assuaging queen's fury over Leicester's governor generalship 249
  disapproves of excessive violence in Ireland 248
  drafts legislation to bar Mary from the throne 125
  drafts memoranda concerning Netherlands 271–2
  The Execution of Justice in England 114–15
  favors aiding foreign Protestants 93–4
  has second thoughts about Leicester's Dutch campaign and execution of Mary Stuart 395
  patronizes commercial ventures and exploration 207–9
  promises to throw Job Throckmorton in the Tower, for attacking James VI 394
  quarrels with Leicester over Dutch war (1587) 344, 346–7
  reported to seek Leicester's ruin (1586–7) 347
  resists Scottish demands for more money 147
  seeks to contain military expenditures 379–80
  struggles to obtain supplies for Ireland 193–4
  urges stronger measures against recusants 110–11

INDEX 725

warns Bancroft to stop antagonizing James VI 410–11
wary of Dutch as reliable partners 279–80
worries about crown finances 92
worries about Elizabeth's childlessness 90
cess, the (in Ireland) 194–5, 244, 262
  causes Irish to desert their homes 194
  collected in kind, on *ad hoc* basis 194
  opposition to 244
  in the Pale 195, 244
Champernowne, Henry 189, 200
Chapman, George 360–1
Charles, Prince of Wales and later Charles I
  asks father to break off negotiations for his marriage 628
  attempts to build and maintain a grand European coalition against Spain 653–4
  attempts to build and maintain a "patriot coalition" behind war with Spain 637, 645–6, 652
  compared, as a young and ambitious king, to Louis XIII and Philip IV 647–50
  complains about behavior of his wife's household clergy 656–7
  concern for honor and reputation of 602–3
  confronted by factional conflicts 649
  constrained in negotiating French alliance by worries that James will revive pact with Spain 655–6
  determined to restore vigor and reputation of British crown 647–8
  embarks on ambitious offensive war 652–4
  embarks on second war against France 658
  expresses warm support for Bohemian cause (1619) 624–5, 635–6
  French alliance of 653–4
  justifies war with Spain as fight against universal monarchy 656
  need to demonstrate control of court and council at start of reign 648
  need to mobilize voluntary contributions for war effort 651–2
  pressured by members of his council to change policies (1640) 671
  puts to test old claims that Spanish power will disintegrate if vigorously challenged 654–5
  recalls veteran captains from Dutch service to drill trained bands 654
  relationship of, with duke of Buckingham 648–9, 659–60
  resolves to crush Covenanters and their English supporters by force 668–9
  resumes father's postponed project of creating new liturgy for Scottish Kirk 661–2, 664–5
  seeks to borrow veteran Spanish soldiers for use against Covenanters 668–9
  sees opposition as demagoguery 659–60
  setbacks accumulate for (1625–7) 654
  travels to Scotland and tries to destroy Covenanters (1641) 673
  travels to Spain to woo the infanta 635–7
  wants to lead through actions rather than words 648, 650–1
Charles Emmanuel, duke of Savoy 576–7
  alliances of, with Protestant Union, Venice and other states, promoted by James VI and I 602–4
  assisted by English volunteer soldiers 602–3
  assists Frederick V in Bohemia 603–4
  assists rebellions of Condé and Bouillon 602–3
  defeated by Spanish forces but rescued by generous treaty 612–13
  James VI and I's support for 601–4
  recklessness of 603–4
  seeks alliance with Britain 601–3
  turns against Spain 599
Chichester, Sir Arthur, deputy lieutenant of Ireland 495–6, 498, 503–4
  advocates forcible reformation of Ireland 507–8
  attempts to enforce attendance at Protestant worship 515–16
  attempts to pack Irish Parliament 525–6
  attempts to subdue robbing kern 511–12
  deposes five mayors of Waterford in succession for recusancy 522
  encounters difficulties in finding local officials willing to carry out his religious policies 519
  gathers information while accompanying assizes 513
  keeps secret the English council's orders to relax prosecution of recusants 524–5
  laments inability to suppress public Catholic worship and warns of new rebellion 523–4
  ordered by English council to use restraint in prosecuting recusants 522
  worries about Irish soldiers serving in Spanish armies 524–5
  see also mandates policy
chivalry and the chivalric culture 52, 172–5
  chivalric passions 359
  "chivalric policy" 179

726 INDEX

chivalry and the chivalric culture (cont.)
  courtly love 176–7
  in court culture 176–7
  in descriptions of Elizabeth's East Anglian Progress 59–62
  knight errantry 173
  misleadingly depicted by historians as a fantasy culture 135–7
  supplemented and modified by humanist and biblical learning 178–9
  tournaments and jousts 176–7
Chrichton, William, Scottish Jesuit 135, 142–3
  captured carrying incriminating papers 158–9
Christian IV, king of Denmark 564–5, 568–9
  defeated at Battle of Lutter 658
  promised a subsidy for leading his army into Germany (1625) 653–4
  urges united action in Germany (1620) 629
chronicles 374–5
Church of Ireland
  difficulties of, in collecting tithes 518
  hampered by lack of adequate clergy 517–18
Churchyard, Thomas 219
  celebrates voyages of Humphrey Gilbert and Martin Frobisher 172–3
  commemorates memory of Henry VIII 173
  describes Sir Humphrey Gilbert's methods in Ireland 248–9
  description of East Anglian Progress (1578) 59–60, 75–6
  The Generall Rehearsall of Warre (1579) 175–6, 181
Cicero 187
civility 183
Clifford, Lady Anne 447–8
Clifford, George, 3d earl of Cumberland
  given responsibilities to end crime in the Borders 492
Cockayne project 588–9
coign and livery 194, 481–2
Coke, Sir Edward
  argues cases against officials accused of abusing delegated prerogative powers 469–70
  holds exceptionally reverential and conservative view of the law 473
  invokes concept of immemorial custom as voice of reason 470–1
  Law *Reports* of 473
  loses effort to limit the Council of Wales 474–5
  seeks to turn legal proficiency into a science 473
Coke, Sir John 650–1
Coligny, Caspard de 204–5

Collinson, Patrick 5–6, 24–5, 33–4, 400
Commerce and merchant shipping 207–8
  expansion of 226–7
  joint stock companies and 207–8
common law
  ancient custom and 462–3, 471–2
  as a bulwark against arbitrary power 462–3, 468
  change in, associated with conquest 461–2
  circumvented, in the interest of state security 467
  the common law mind and 462–3
  difficulties of, in dealing with complex hybrid forms of landholding 482
  impedes efforts to solve financial problems through new taxes 475
  insularity of 462–3
  Ireland and 242–4, 504–5, 515–16
  mutability and change in 472
  puritans and 402
  reason and 470–1
  reform, and the union of Britain 460
  see also Coke, Sir Edward; Davys, Sir John; Irish lawyers
commonwealth (as a political concept) 5–6, 137, 229n.4
  Essex accused of "commonwealth courses," 337–8
  Irish "commonwealthmen" 244, 261–2, 504
Concini, Concino, marquis d'Ancre 613–14, 649
  overthrown and murdered 616–17
  seeks to borrow Dutch warships 615
confessional commitments and confessionalization 100–4
  among the landed elite 105–6, 122–3
Conn, George, papal envoy to court of Henriette Marie 667–8
constitutions and constitutional analysis 3–4, 7–8
Conway, Sir Edward, viscount 582–3, 650–1
Cork
  Catholicism and religious resistance in 263, 269, 505
  imprisons crown officials and wages armed struggle against the Lord Deputy 505–7
  resists James's proclamation as king 505
Cornwallis, Charles, English ambassador to Spain 555–6
  sent by James to compose religious conflicts in Ireland (1614) 525–6
Cornwallis, Sir Thomas 46
Cosin, Richard 399–400
Cotton, Sir Robert, approached by Gondomar with proposal for Spanish match 607–8
Couper, John 164–6

coups and royal kidnappings, a feature of early modern politics 384
court, the 343
see also anti-court criticism, court faction
court faction 345–9
   encourages rumors of secret intrigues 347
   events magnify in late 1590s 349
   given a sharper ideological edge by Essex and his circle 357–8
   mid-Elizabethan 345–6
   potential for in late 1580s, defused by events 348–9
Covenanters' Rebellion (1637–1640)
   benefits from return of Scots veterans from the Swedish army 622–3
   breaks with pattern of non-violent governance 665
Cranstoun, Sir William 493–4
Creagh Desmond, Catholic bishop of Cork and Cloyne 263
crisis of the late 1620s 659–61
   accentuates ideological and religious divisions 660, 667–8
   alters conditions at the political center more than in the localities 661
   Charles's escape from 660–1
   remains essentially confined to England 660–1
crisis of 1637–1642
   Charles I's resort to military force during 668–9
   compared to contemporary crises in France and Spain 669–70
   divides English council 666
   helps fuel and renew radical Protestantism 671–2
   increasing resort to force during 673
   London crowds intensify 672
   military weakness of both sides at start of 665–6
   renews fears of arbitrary government and military rule 668–9
   results in Scottish military victory that discredits Charles (1640) 670–1
   revives military entrepreneurship and seigneurial armies 671–2
   in Scotland 661–2, 664–5
   soldiers serving in European armies return to Britain during 670, 672
   spawns competing narratives of religious betrayal, both rooted in past discourses 674–5
   threatens to produce basic alteration in the state 669
   see also under Covenanters Rebellion

Croft, Sir James 325–6, 335–6
crown finances 378–80
   James I's failure to remedy deficiencies of 475–6
   parlous state of, fans worries of arbitrary government, attacks on Parliament, and dependence on Spanish money 643–4
   worries about pressures upon 92
Curtys, Richard 62

D'Albret, Charles, duke of Luynes 616–17, 648–9
   launches offensive against Huguenot strongholds 618
Dacies, Richard 351–2
Daniel, Samuel 15–16, 360–1
   A Panegyrike Congratulatorie to the Kings Majestie (1603) 446, 448, 452–5
Danvers, Charles 383
Davidson, John 410–11
   preaches sermon critical of king's inaction over Catholic earls (1593) 421–2
Davison, Francis 357–8
Davison, William 37–8, 151, 155–6, 277, 283
   complains of opposition to Leicester in the Netherlands 294
   denounces Patrick Adamson 153–4
   procures copy of Tacitus 369–70
   raises money to cover military costs 155–6, 283–4
   seeks to diminish queen's anger over Leicester's governor generalship 294–5
   wounded by Leicester's recriminations 329–30
Davys, Sir John 503–4
   attacks charters of Irish boroughs through *quo warranto* proceedings 525–6
   condemns delegation of peace-keeping to Irish lords 509
   conducts judicial circuit cracking down on recusancy (1606) 522
   expands prerogative powers under Irish law 519–20
   justifies mandates policy by citing medieval precedents 528–9
   sees the common law as an instrument for reforming and Anglicizing Ireland 508–10
   stresses the role of assizes in extending common law rule in Ireland 510–11
   supports Irish challenges to earls of Tyrconnell and Tyrone 513–15
   wants to bring over Protestant jurists from England 519
   see also mandates policy
Dee, John 209

Devereux, Robert, 2nd earl of Essex 174-7
  accuses Elizabeth of undermining her
    state 366-8
  admires Sir Philip Sidney 342-3
  admonishes Elizabeth to act boldly 361-2
  advises Henry IV on how to handle
    Elizabeth 363
  advocates aggressive strategy against
    Spain 378
  analyses effects of peace on the United
    Provinces 363-4
  Apologie of 337-8, 359, 363-4, 367, 370-1,
    381-2
  appears to follow Leicester's example, in
    dealing with court adversaries 347-8
  appointed to command Leicester's
    cavalry 306-7, 342-3
  attachment to the court by 343-4
  believes in risk-taking 339
  blames his misfortunes on envy 381
  complains that Elizabeth mistreats him 345
  composes poem to Virgin Mary 350-1
  concept of nobility of 351-5
  concept of the state of 337-8, 341-2, 355-6,
    363-4, 366-8
  concepts of virtue of 339
  court faction and 345
  cultivates close relation with James VI 349
  denounces court "persuaders," 362-3
  disagreements and conflicts with queen
    358-9, 365-6, 368-9
  enjoys posthumous reputation as godly
    champion 350
  eschews the words commonwealth and
    citizen 5-6
  friendship in the thought of 355-8
  humanist education and interests of 340
  includes Catholics in his entourage 350-1
  indifference to Ireland 363
  legacies of 383-7
  Leicester's political heir 342-3
  less interested in oceanic and colonial projects
    than other swordsmen 340-1
  popularity and 354-5, 381-3
  posthumous reputation of, inspires calls for
    bold action in 1620s 650-1
  predominant concern with war, European
    affairs and intelligence 339-41
  preoccupied by subversion of virtue 377
  quarrels with other swordsmen 380-1
  race and lineage in the thought of 351-2
  rebuked by Elizabeth over close relationship
    with Henry IV 358-9
  recent scholarship on 338-9
  religious attitudes of 350-2
  revolts (1601) 382-3
  sees emotional forces as vital to politics
    358-65
  sent to quell Irish rebellion 269-70
  stresses importance of reputation, in national
    as well as personal life 361-2
  stresses military discipline 184-5
  styles himself a "faithful subject and
    patriot," 337-8
  suspects Cecils of wanting to leave throne to
    Spain 349
  takes minimal interest in parliaments and
    republican institutions 383-4
  thinks the state of England depends on his
    virtues and those of his friends 368-9
  unauthorized return from Ireland by 348
  wants to occupy Cadiz 363, 378
  see also Essex circle, the; passions in political
    life; race and racial theory; *State of
    Christendom, The*; Tacitus
Devereux, Robert, 3d earl of Essex 652
Devereux, Walter, first earl of Essex 344
  funeral sermon for 351-2
D'Ewes, Sir Simonds 635
Digby, George, earl of Bristol
  briefly becomes disillusioned over Spanish
    match 632-3
  complains that members of the council spread
    malicious reports about himself and
    Thomas Lake 609-10
  exchanges accusations of treason with duke of
    Buckingham 649
  obtains secret intelligence of Spanish
    deliberations 606-7
  promises Spanish James will ruin the
    puritans if the Spanish match
    succeeds 610-11
  reports that Lerma interested in negotiating
    dynastic marriage with Britain 607-8
  reports that Spanish want Bohemian crisis
    quickly resolved 620
  tries to keep negotiations over Spanish match
    secret, in case of failure 608-9
Digby, Simon 633-4
Digby, Sir George 308-9
Digges, Leonard 172, 184
Digges, Thomas 125-9, 465-6
  accuses Dutch politicians of corruption 278-9
  inspects fortifications of Ostend 287-8
  muster master under Leicester in the
    Netherlands 198, 298-9
Dillon, Robert 262
Discoverie of a Gaping Gulf, see Stubbs, John

INDEX   729

divine right, *see* hereditary divine right monarchy, absolute kings and absolutism
Dom Antonio, pretender to Portuguese throne 40
  brings Portuguese mariners to England 212
  consults with Drake about privateering 212
  issues letters of mark 212
  passes along rumors of plots against Elizabeth 271-2
Don John of Austria, Spanish commander in the Netherlands 37-8
Douglas, Archibald, earl of Angus 133-4, 137, 150-1, 489-90
  appeals to James VI as godly king 169
  attempts but fails to seize Stirling (1584) 150-1
  discusses *The Arcadia* with Sir Philip Sidney 134-5
  flees to England 142-3
  leads Scottish coup (1585) 159-60, 275-7
  seeks Elizabeth's aid 143-4
  takes refuge in Berwick 156
Douglas, Archibald, Scottish ambassador to England 169-70
Douglas, James, earl of Morton and regent of Scotland 131-2
  antagonizes leaders of Kirk 132, 139
  blames Anjou match for reviving British Catholicism 82
  executed 131-2
  falls from power 41-2, 82
  receives support from Edinburgh 140
  supports Scottish episcopacy 138-9
Dowcra, Sir Henry 196-7
Drake, Sir Francis
  consults with queen about oceanic ventures 211
  discusses collaboration with French corsairs 206-7
  fails to persuade Dutch to join in attack on Portugal 221
  leads Portugal Expedition (1589) 222
  plans expeditions with Dom Antonio 212
  raids Spanish Pacific 211
  resupplies ships during voyage 201-2
  voyage to Panama (1585-6) 221-2, 275-6
Drogheda 527-8
Du Moulin, Pierre 564, 583
  considers emigrating to England to avoid Louis XIII's persecution 630-1
  probable author of tract claimed by James VI and I 578
Du Perron, Cardinal Davy
  embroiled in controversy with French Third Estate, parlement of Paris and James VI and I 577-8

Du Plessis, Armand-Jean, bishop of Luçon and Cardinal Richelieu 613-14, 649
  Charles and Buckingham try to foment rebellion against 658
Du Plessis Mornay, Philippe 564
Dudley, Ambrose, earl of Warwick 44-5, 187-9
Dudley, John, duke of Northumberland 36, 187-9
  supports Muscovy Company and English commerce 207-8
Dudley, Robert, earl of Leicester 37-8, 174-5
  asks Lord Paget to grant a local office to Sir Walter Aston 118-19
  aspires to lead an army to the Netherlands (1578) 39-40
  believes court Catholics want to ruin him 337-8
  death of 335-6, 396
  diverts investments into Dutch campaign (1585) 221-2
  dynastic pretensions of 44-5
  Irish military patronage of 189-90
  manipulates trial of Edward Arden 45-6
  military patronage and leadership of 187-9, 283-4
  misses council meetings 190
  opposes but equivocates over Anjou match 53-4, 73-4
  patronizes oceanic enterprises and privateering 208-10, 213-14
  personality traits of 329-31
  praises Dutch naval strength 293-4
  religious partisanship of 303-5, 350
  secretive relations with James VI 169-71
  suffers period of displeasure over Stubbs's *Gaping Gulf* 74-5
  suspects Roger Williams of disloyalty 329-30
  wants to invest Drake's profits in Dutch war 211
  warns Elizabeth against Mary and James 147
  warns that Parma wants to invade England through Scotland 325-6
  see also under Leicester's expedition to the Netherlands
Dudley family clientele 187-9
  oceanic interests of 208-10
Dury, John 139-42, 145
  foments Edinburgh protest against French embassy 146-7
Dynasties and dynastic politics 23-4, 34-6
  antiquarian research and 44-6
  confessional allegiances and 43-4, 46
  dynastic honor 52, 90-1
  dynastic libels 66-71, 74-5, 86-7

Dynasties and dynastic politics (cont.)
  dynastic sterility and extinction 78, 90
  Tudor successions and 36
  see also under Bourbon-Habsburg dynastic alliance; hereditary divine right monarchy; Spanish match; Stuart dynastic alliances

East Anglia 57
  Queen Elizabeth's progress through, 1578 57–61
ecclesiastical commissions 113–14
Eden, Richard 205–6, 208–9
Edinburgh
  burgesses of, humiliated and cowed by James following the Tumult 432–3
  burgesses of, purged, by Arran 151
  frightened by rumors of Catholic attacks 418–19, 428–30
  Lennox and Arran prepare to seize (1582) 143
  presbytery of, refuses to solemnize earl of Huntly's marriage 402–3
Edmondes, Sir Clement 185–6
Edmondes, Thomas 567–8, 570, 576–7
  accused of fomenting dissidence in France 578–81
  advises support for dissident French nobles 574–5
  instructed to initiate negotiations for a marriage of Prince Charles with Christine de Bourbon (1613) 605
  involved in scheme to deprive Habsburgs of electoral title 616–17
  involves himself in French dispute over censorship of Bellarmine 573–4
  rejoices at Fredericks V's election as king of Bohemia 624–5
  reports growing influence of papal nuncio and Spanish ambassador in Paris (1616) 613–14
  thinks Condé and his allies need Huguenot support to prevail 579–80
  told by king to remonstrate over Marie de Médicis's conduct in controversy over papal deposing power in France (1614) 578
  tries to support duke of Savoy 601
Elizabeth I
  accused of half-hearted conduct of war 385–6
  the Anjou match and 53–4, 80–1
  attempts to remove d'Aubigny and control James VI 132–3
  Catholic threats to 37–8, 49–50
  celebrated as virgin Queen 61
  criticizes James VI for tolerating presbyterians and demands he suppress criticism of English bishops 410
  cult of 89
  dislikes dealing with Dutch merchants and lawyers 279–80
  does not want offensive alliance with James VI 546
  entertained by earl of Arundel. (1579) 80–1
  entertained by earl of Sussex 71–2
  expenditures of, on Dutch wars 285–6, 301, 322–3
  favorites of, see Dudley, Robert, 1st earl of Leicester; Devereux, Robert, 2nd earl of Essex; Hatton, Sir Christopher
  fears and hates James VI 143–4
  foreign ambassadors to, see Castlenau, Michel de, seigneur de Mauvissière; Mendoza, Bernardino de
  furious over Leicester's appointment as governor general of the Netherlands 294–6
  hesitates to challenge Philip II directly 275, 282–3
  invests in purported gold mine in Labrador 210–11
  lacks confidence in Dutch allies 273, 279–80, 319–20
  makes progress through East Anglia, 1578 57–61
  parsimony of 193–4
  pursues negotiations with Parma for Dutch peace 277, 301, 325–6
  reactions of, to the succession crisis of 1553 36
  reacts to Stubbs's *Gaping Gulf* 70–1, 73, 75
  rebukes James VI for inaction against Catholic nobles 420–1
  rejects sovereignty over the Netherlands but agrees to aid them 271–2, 276–7
  relations of, with members of her court and council 343–4
  resists earl of Essex's promotion of his dependents 357–8
  struggles to limit military expenditures 379–80
  target of Catholic libels 87–8
  tries to assume direct control over policy in the Netherlands 296–7
  unrealistic in her management of the Netherlands 331
  wants Hohenlohe arrested and tried for treason 319–20
  see also Anjou Match; Leicester's expedition to the Netherlands
Elizabeth Stuart, daughter of James VI and I 570–1
  negotiations over marriage of 574–5
Elizabethan conformist thought 440–1
  contrasted with ideas of James VI 440–5
  see also Bilson, Thomas, bishop of Winchester

INDEX 731

Elizabethan Exclusion Crisis, the 33, 35–6
episcopacy
  English and Scottish, compared 136–7
  grudgingly tolerated by Edinburgh synod (1576) 161
  jure divino arguments for 398–9
  Scottish 138–9, 530–3, 664
  supplanted in Scotland and attacked in England 671–2
Essex circle, the 274–5
  aggressively promoted by Essex 357–8
  applies story of decline of Roman republic to England 376–7
  consists mostly of young men and political outsiders 339
  importance of ancient historians to 275, 314–15
  produces *The State of Christendom* 340–1
  scholars within 355–6
  see also Devereux, Robert, 1st earl of Essex; Bacon, Anthony; Bacon, Sir Francis; Howard, lord Henry, later 1st earl of Northampton; Perez, Antonio; Tacitus
Estienne, Henri 66–7
Eucharistic celebrations 102–3
European confessional politics
  complexity of 542–3
  grow more polarized, after ca. 1617 613–37
  James VI and I's professed views on 556–9

Farnese, Alessandro, duke of Parma 191–2
  captures Brussels and Ghent 271–2
  offers generous surrender terms to Dutch cities 240
  spreads reports of Anglo-Spanish peace talks 277, 326–7
favorites, royal 649
  see also Devereux, Robert, 2nd earl of Essex; Dudley, Robert, 1st earl of Leicester; Hatton, Sir Christopher; Ker, Robert, earl of Somerset; Stuart, Esmé, seigneur d'Aubigny and later duke of Lennox; Villiers, George, later earl and duke of Buckingham
Fenner, Dudley 391
Fenton, Edward 213–14, 257
Fenton, Geoffrey 250–2
Ferdinand of Styria, later Holy Roman emperor 616–17
  the Bohemian crisis and 619, 623–5, 627
  resists Spanish pressure and transfers Frederick's electoral title to Maximilian 631–2
Field, John 148
  Admonition to Parliament and 391
Fiennes, Edward, earl of Lincoln 208–9

First Army Plot, the 672
Fitzgerald, James, 14th earl of Desmond 82, 90–1
Fitzgerald, James Fitzthomas 269–70
Fitzmaurice, James, nephew of earl of Desmond 39–40, 47–8, 90–1, 255
Fitzpatrick, Barnaby, baron of Upper Ossory 238–9
Five Articles of Perth 534–7, 664–5
  new Prayer Book and 661–3
  reasons for James's commitment to 662–3
flight of the earls (1607) 524–5
Forced Loan, the 658–9
Foster, Sir John 491–2
France
  controversy within, over papal authority and divine right kingship (1614) 577–8
  cooperates with England to counter Spain 40–1
  meddles in Scotland 145–7
  perceived as threat, in the Low Countries 40–1, 93–4
  see also Gallicanism and Gallicans; Guise, Henri I duke of; Henry III, king of France; Henry IV (Henry of Navarre); James VI and I: European Policies of, concerning support for noble opposition to French crown; Marie de Médicis, Queen Mother and regent of France
French dynastic alliance of 1625
  collapses 658
  negotiation of 655–6
  secret marriage articles and 656
Frederick IV, elector Palatine 567–8, 583
  death of 570
Frederick V, elector Palatine 570–1
  accepts offer of Bohemian crown before hearing from James 622–3
  decisively defeated at Battle of White Mountain (November 1620) 627
  refuses to heed advice and make concessions to Habsburgs 631–2
  travels to Sedan to consult about depriving Habsburgs of imperial title 616–17
  worries that civil war in France will spread to the Empire 615–16
  see also Bohemian crisis; Hay, James, viscount Doncaster and later earl of Carlisle; Protestant Union (German)
Freehold tenancies 644–5
  Irish 240–1, 479–80, 499, 515–16
  special position of, in English law and administration 477–8
  undermined by economic change 479–80
Freke, Edmund, bishop of Norwich 57–8

732 INDEX

Frobisher, Martin 172, 205
  claims to discover gold mine in Labrador 210–11

Gaelic languages 134–5, 231–2
Gardiner, Sir Richard, Chief Justice of Ireland 234–5, 258–60
Gallicanism and Gallicans 557, 564
Galloway, Patrick 167, 427–8
  appointed household minister to James VI 413–14
  appointed to committee to monitor Catholic activities 419–20
Garrisons 189–90
  Dutch 278–9
  English, refused quarter in the Netherlands 316–17
  in Ireland 194–5
Garter, Bernard 60–2
Gates, Geffrey 180–6
Gentillet, Innocent 65–6
Gibson, James 162
Gilbert, George 55
Gilbert, Sir Humphrey 172, 179, 205, 209–11
  chivalric policy and 179
  dies during ocean voyage 221
  dislikes leniency in Ireland 234–5
  promotes colonizing ventures 215–16
  ruthless conduct of Irish war 248–50
Gomarus, Franciscus 584
Gordon, George, 6th earl of Huntly 611–12
  attempts to surprise James VI and Maitland 414
  contacts with Spain 164, 402, 420–1
  influence over James's household 166–7
  marries sister of duke of Lennox 402–3
  participates in murder of earl of Moray 419
  rebellion of (1594) 422
  receives pardon and withdraws from active promotion of Catholic plots (1597) 434–5
  relations of, with James VI 416–17
  returns from exile to Scotland and seeks to negotiate rehabilitation (1596) 424
Graham, Sir Richard 493–4
Grahams, Border surname 490–4
grand tours of Europe 340–1
Gray, Patrick Master of 158–9, 169–70, 262–3
  blames Elizabeth for privations of his soldiers in the Netherlands 315–16
  lobbies for English support of Scots exiles 159–60
  raises troops for Leicester's Dutch campaign 159–60, 299–300
Great Contract, the (1610) 570–1

Gregory XV, Pope 631–2
Greneway, Richard
  dedicates translation of Tacitus's *Annals* to Essex 374
  juxtaposes terms "commonwealth" and "state" in translation of Tacitus 375–6
Grey, Arthur lord of Wilton, deputy lieutenant of Ireland 192–3, 251–2
  surveys lands for Munster plantation 257
Grenville, Richard 179
Greville, Fulke 351–2, 360
Grotius, Hugo
  seeks to win support for Remonstrants in England 588
  writes tract defending Vorstius 586
Guise, Charles duke of
  opens communications with James VI and I 573
Guise, Henri I, duke of 41–4, 52, 69–70, 262–3
  assassinated 395–6
  denounced in Scotland 141–2
  hopes for invasion of Scotland 148–9
  patron of Allen and Parsons 108
  plans to invade England 98–9, 120–1, 124, 133–5, 142–3, 164
  resurrects French Catholic League and allies with Philip II 271
  schemes with Lennox and James VI 133
  sends agent to Scotland (1585) 163
Gunpowder Plot, the 450
  blamed by James VI and I on Catholic doctrine and Jesuits 560–1
guns and gunnery 223–5, 446
Guzman, Gaspar de, count-duke of Olivares 612–13, 648
  compares crises in Scotland and Iberia 669–70

Hackett, Martin 399–400
Hackett, Thomas 205–6
Hakewill, George, chaplain to Prince Charles
  preaches sermons and writes book against Spanish match 633–4
Hakluyt, Richard, the younger 205–6, 212, 215–19
  A Discourse of Western Planting 215–17
  discusses strategic value of oceanic exploration 219–20
  influenced by Aristotle and Christian humanism 217
Hamilton, Claude 160–1
Hamilton, John, lord and later 1st marquis of Hamilton 160–1
  declines Presbyterian plea to rise in arms after the Tumult 432
Hamilton, Sir James 498

INDEX   733

Harborne, William 225-6
Harlay, Christophe de, French ambassador to England 547-8, 551-2
  instructed to cultivate Scots at the English court 552
  James appeals to Gallican sentiments of 556-8
  told James wants agreement with France (June 1603) 549
Harpsfield, Nicholas 87-8
Harvey, Gabriel 341
Hatton, Christopher 279-80, 467-8
  helps launch campaign against English presbyterians 396
  likely patron of pamphlets on East Anglian Progress 61-2
  opposes Anjou March 53-4
  rebukes Job Throckmorton for disparaging kings 394
  receives letter of recrimination from William Tresham 85-6
  supports Throckmorton network in midlands 45-6, 345-6
  warns Essex against taking needless risks 339
Hawkins, John 205, 209-10, 217
  suggests creating international privateering fleets based in England 212
Hay, James, lord Doncaster and 1st earl of Carlisle 637
  acts as James's ambassador to mediate crisis in Bohemia 620-2
  advises Frederick V to accept Bohemian crown before hearing from James 622-3
  returns disgruntled from Paris (1617) 607-8
  sent by James as extraordinary ambassador to Paris (1616) 580-1
Hayward, Sir John 15-16
  advocates integration of the laws of England and Scotland 460-1
  draws on Tacitus to embellish story of Richard II's fall 374-5
Heneage, Sir Thomas 294-5, 301
Henriette Marie, queen consort of Charles I 649
  allies with Laud and Strafford against Covenanters 668
  Catholic clergy of 656-7
  pressured to serve leaders of Long Parliament 671
Henry, Prince of Wales, eldest son of James VI and I 486
  apocalyptic hopes surrounding 412-13
  appears to favor French match for himself 598
  baptismal ceremonies of 412-13
  celebrated by Ben Jonson 456-7
  marriage negotiations for 546, 574-5
  memory of, bolsters support for new war with Spain 599-600
  rumored to have turned against a Catholic match at end of his life 599-600
  see also Stuart dynastic alliances
Henry VIII of England 90-1, 173, 175-6, 235-6
  military recruitment under 187-9
  privateering under 199-200
Henry III, king of France
  declines to involve himself heavily in the Netherlands 273-4
  dispatches embassies to Scotland 145-6, 163
  fails to provide counterweight to Philip II 275
  has duke of Guise assassinated and is then murdered 395-6
  religious policies of, compared to those of James VI 171
Henry IV of France (Henry of Navarre) 163, 190, 271
  alarmed by James's expressions of sympathy for Spain 548-9
  allies with England and the United Provinces 395-6
  assassinated 570
  convinced James VI and I shares his mistrust of Spain 551-2
  dealings with James VI as king of Scotland 546
  demands detailed reports on James VI and I (1603) 547-8
  gradually loses confidence in and respect for James VI and I 552
  as Huguenot leader 274-5
  mobilizes for intervention in Jülich-Cleves succession crisis 568-9
  recalcitrant about settling debts to English crown 568-9
  receives presentation copy of James I's *Tripli Nodex* 564
  seeks to dampen controversy between James VI and I and the papacy 564
  supports the Dutch 546-7
  supports privateering (1570s and 1580s) 201, 204-5
Herbert, Henry, 2nd earl of Pembroke 187-9
Herbert, William, 3d earl of Pembroke
  misjudges James's intentions toward crisis in the Empire 625-6
  turns against the duke of Buckingham (1626) 649
hereditary divine right monarchy
  English and French, compared 449-51
  gives rise to veritable cults of royal marriage and procreation 450-7

hereditary divine right monarchy (*cont.*)
  James VI and I sees as means by which God pacifies and unifies kingdoms 451
Hoboque, *see under* Ursel, Conrad van
Hohenlohe, Philip count of 300–1, 334–5
  assaults Edward Norreys 309–10
  co-opts Scottish troops for use against English 315–16
  fears Leicester wants him assassinated 319–20
  initially cooperates with Leicester as governor general 302–3
Holland
  internal politics of 280
  plundered by English troops (winter 1587) 316–17
  provincial particularism within 291–2, 305
  states of, order Maurice and Hohenlohe to drive out English troops 316–17
  staunch opposition within, to Leicester's ban on trade with the enemy 312
Holles, John, earl of Clare 640–1, 658–9
Holt, William 148–9
Home, George, earl of Dunbar
  accused of seeking to undermine the Kirk 533
  delegated task of policing the Borders 492–3
honor 52, 360–1
Hooker, Richard 471
Hotman, Jean, secretary to earl of Leicester 297–8, 304–6
  corresponds with Justus Lipsius 369–70
  reports being hunted by Leicester's Dutch enemies 314
households and householders 477–8
Howard, Lord Henry, later earl of Northampton
  mentor to the earl of Essex 342–3
  praises Essex for supporting young men 357–8
  racialized concept of nobility of 351–3
  secretly converts to Catholicism 54
  seeks refuge with Mendoza 83
  subjected to government harassment 123–4
  tract by, supporting the Anjou Match 78
Howard, Philip, 13th earl of Arundel 80–1, 123–4
  participates in court joust 177
  reacts to news of the Armada 388
Howard, Thomas, 14th earl of Arundel 649
Huddleston, James 286
Hugh, Feagh 258–9
Huguenots 274–5
  appeal for English aid 79–82
  fear being attacked by Spanish and French royal armies (1617) 613–15
  issue of British support for, evaded in negotiations for marriage alliance with France 655–6

lend crucial support to Condé's rebellion (1615–16) 580
privateering and colonial enterprises of 204–6
refugees flee to England from Louis XIII's campaigns 630–1
send emissary to James, to discuss support for Condé 579–80
support for rebellions hardens hostility of French ministers toward 618
threatened by renewed hostility after Henry IV's death 571
Humanism and humanist education
  Christian 217–18
  concepts of the commonwealth and 340
  examination of psychological wellsprings of political action and 375
  fuses with elements of chivalric and medieval culture 174–5, 230–5
  historical readings and 275, 341, 369–70
  influences Irish reform treatises 243
  new vs. old 369, 375, 377
  trains early modern elite 341
Hume, David, of Godscroft 137, 169
Hutton, Matthew, archbishop of York 473

Impropriated benefices 46, 62, 118
In Ireland 518
Ineyeren, Richard 232–3, 250
Inns of Court
  Catholics within 95–6, 103–4
  Irish within 244
Interdict Controversy (between Venice and the Papacy) 564–7
Ireland
  arable farming in 231–2
  assizes in 510–15
  bards and poets of 237–8
  brehon lawyers in 237–8, 482–3
  cattle and animal raiding in 233–4, 238–40
  common law in 242–4, 504–5, 515–16
  drains English resources 92
  English captains in 245, 248–50, 258–9
  English factionalism and 241–2
  ethnic and cultural divisions, stereotypes and interactions within 230–1
  geographic and topographical barriers divide 232–3, 258
  gray merchants in 196
  idle men in 234
  insecurity of 39–40, 91, 528–9, 554, 566–7
  Irish soldiers in 195
  kern and woodkern 234, 238, 511–12, 515–16
  law enforcement in 234–6
  mass executions and killings in 250

Old English inhabitants of 231, 242–3, 250–2, 257–8, 261–4, 266–7
  pastoralism in 232
  prosecution of recusancy in 519–23
  royal armies in 189–90, 193–7, 527–8
  servitor interest within 503–4
  stimulates English political thought 172
  suffers from war, famine and economic dislocation 448–9
  taking of heads in 258–9
  warfare in 192–3, 238–9, 259, 265
  see also Catholics, Irish; cess; coign and livery; common law in Ireland; Church of Ireland; Irish governance; Irish lawyers; Irish lords and lordships; Irish plantations; Irish priests; Irish provinces, counties and regions; Irish rebellions; Irish reform treatises; Irish septs; Irish towns; Kildare, earls of; martial law
Irish governance
  English officials involved in, see Blount, Charles, later earl of Mountjoy, lord lieutenant; Carew, Sir George, president of Munster; Chichester, Sir Arthur, deputy Lieutenant; Davys, Sir John; Grey, Arthur lord of Wilton, deputy lieutenant; Perrot, Sir John; Sidney, Sir Henry
  increasingly conducted by Englishmen 257–8, 264–5
  lenient and harsh approaches to 242
  presidents 244
Irish lawyers 241–2
  compared to Edward Coke and English lawyers 504–5
  cooperate with priests to fuel resistance to crown 264, 505, 507, 523–4
  defend Irish interests and liberties 261–2, 504–5
  opposition to mandates policy and 521
  see also commonwealthmen; Nugent, Nicholas
Irish lords and lordships 235–40
  adaptations and adjustments by, after 1603 501
  coign and livery and other exactions of 238
  drawn into the orbit of the court in London 502–3
  English mediation among 240–2
  Gaelic and Gaelicized 236–8
  galloglass warriors and 238
  individual lords, see Boyle, Richard, earl of Cork; Burke, Richard, 4th earl of Clanricard; Burke, Ulick, 1st earl of Clanricard; Butler, Thomas, 10th earl of Ormond; MacDonnell, Randall, 1st earl of Antrim O'Donnell, Hugh, earl of Tirconnell; O'Neill, Hugh, earl of Tyrone

newly established 498
Old English 236
seigneurial warfare and 238–41
surrender and regrant agreements among 240–1
tanistry and rules of succession and 236–7, 240–1
titles of nobility among, increase after 1603 502–3
towerhouses or castles and 237–8
Uiriaghs 236–8
viewed as oppressive and exploitative 242–3
Irish plantations
  central Ulster 499–500
  eastern Ulster (Antrim) 498–9
  Munster 257
  Other 499–500
  Success or failure of, depends on urban settlements 500–1
Irish Parliament of 1613–1614 526
Irish priests
  accused of spreading libels and rumors 523–4
  encourage people to intimidate Protestants 526–7
  numbers of, increase substantially after 1603 523–4
  present in three-fourths of Ulster parishes by 1620 526–7
  threaten to excommunicate those who do not assist rebels 263–4, 269
Irish provinces, counties and regions
  Antrim 511–12
  Armagh 233–4
  Mayo 233–4, 244, 259
  Meath 235–6, 252–3
  Munster 252, 256–7, 269–70
  Pale, the 252–3, 263–4
  Ulster 234–5, 240, 263, 267, 269–70, 495–6, 498
  Wicklow Mountains 511–12
Irish rebellions
  assisted by priests 263–4
  Baltinglass 251–2
  cost of suppressing 256–7
  Desmond 82–3, 245, 251–2
  encouraged by hopes of foreign assistance 252–4, 523–4
  Munster towns 505–7, 548
  1641 673
  Tyrone's, see under Nine Years War
  see also under O'Neill, Hugh
Irish reformers and reform treatises 229
  blame English misrule for Irish problems 245–6, 248

Irish reformers and reform treatises (*cont.*)
  blame Irish disorder on culture and environment 245-8
  early Tudor 242-3
  Elizabeth's caution concerning 266
  rely on violence and terror 243, 245-7, 249-50
  seek to turn Ireland into a civil commonwealth 250-1, 265
Irish septs 237-8
  McMurroughs, (of Leinster) 239-40
  O'Donnells 240
  O'Neils 240
Irish towns
  elect lawyers as magistrates 268
  resist government demands 268-9
  supply Tyrone's forces 268
  suspected of disloyalty 263-4
  see also Cork, Irish rebellions, Munster towns

Jacobean Peace, the
  blamed for decline in national virtue 637-46
  colors James's historical reputation 447-8, 539-42
  hailed by panegyrists at outset of James's English reign 446
  initial meanings of 447
  James proclaims 447
  paralleled by Ben Jonson to the reign of Augustus 455-7
  perceived as weak and debilitating by some contemporaries 541-2
James VI before 1603, as king of Scotland
  alliance with the Kirk, in the 1590s 169, 403, 409-14, 419
  ambassadors of, *see* Douglas, Archibald; Gray, Patrick Master of; Stewart, William (Colonel Stewart)
  appoints Robert Waldegrave his printer 396-7
  asks Henry III to lend him the *Garde écossais* 150-1
  asserts control over the Kirk, following the Tumult 433-4, 530-1
  attempts to muzzle clergy 140-1
  balances French against English 164
  Catholic earls, complicate relations with Kirk 401-2, 416-17, 419-24, *see also* Gordon, George, 6th earl of Huntly
  Catholics in entourage of 168
  conflict with the Kirk over his right to punish inflammatory sermons 162, 425-8
  continues quarrels with Kirk after English alliance 161
  cooperates with Kirk to secure Scotland from invasion (1588) 166-7
  criticized by Job Throckmorton 393
  cultivates image as a godly king 167-8, 389, 413
  denies writing *A Declaration of the Kings Majesties Intention* 410-11
  does not believe Catholics pose a serious threat to Scotland 417
  early friendship with Huntly and Catholic lords 164-5
  ecclesiastical policies of 388-90
  fears assassination by Morton's relatives and the Hamiltons 156-7
  feels threatened by noble violence 414
  formally complains about Richard Bancroft 410-11
  given adult household (1579) 131-2
  imposes harsh disciplinary measures on clergy and Edinburgh following the Tumult 432-3
  involved in plotting against Elizabeth 143-4, 150-1
  launches rhetorical campaign to affirm his godliness 167-8
  loses confidence of Mary and Philip II 164
  marriage, to Anna of Denmark 167-8, 412
  meets with Jesuits and Catholics 141
  moves against earls of Bothwell, Huntly and Errol 414
  noblemen and other prominent figures involved with, *see* Douglas, Archibald, earl of Angus; Douglas, James, earl of Morton and regent of Scotland; Gordon, George, 6th earl of Huntly; Guise, Henri I, duke of; Hamilton, Claude; Hamilton, John, viscount Hamilton; Mary queen of Scotland; Stewart, Francis, fifth earl of Bothwell; Stewart, James, earl of Arran; Stuart, Esmé, seigneur d'Aubigny and 1st duke of Lennox
  obsession of, with bloodlines and purity of blood 441-3
  orders clergy to pray for Mary 164-5
  orders clergy to stop praying in public for "afflicted brethren" in England 410-11
  pardons Huntly, on strict conditions (1597) 434-5
  perceived as threat to Elizabeth, ally of Mary 92-3, 151, 155-6
  plays double game with papal envoy 422-4, 423n.165
  political theology of 435-43, 470-1
  praises Scottish Kirk and criticizes English liturgy 409-10
  prevented by poverty from raising adequate military forces to control Scotland 415-16

probable advanced knowledge of Essex
   revolt 384
reacts to his mother's execution 166–7
reaffirms his commitment to Protestantism to
   an Edinburgh congregation 166
relations of, with his nobility 484–5
relationship of, with earl of Leicester and
   Walsingham 169–71
relative indifference of, to institutional
   structures 439–40
religious attitudes and ideas of 157–8, 411
rumored to be about to marry daughter of
   duke of Lorraine 42
Ruthven Raiders and 144–5, 147–9
says he relies on soldiers, not nobles 149–51
seeks to rise above and hold balance between
   religious factions 417
tries to counter reports he favors
   Catholicism 141
uncertainties over religious position of 133
the Tumult and 428–31
worries that rigorous treatment of nobles will
   provoke dangerous feuds 417
writes to duke of Guise, after escape from
   Ruthven raiders 148–9
writes letter in support of John Udall at urging
   of Robert Bruce 409
writes paraphrase of Revelation of John the
   Divine 159
see also Kirk, the; Maitland of Thirlestane,
   John, chancellor of Scotland; presbyterians
   and presbyterian clergy in Scotland
James VI and I, 1603 to 1625, as ruler of Britain
   and Ireland
accused of debasing honor 640–1
adopts style of *Rex Pacificus* 446, 541–2,
   see also Jacobean peace
attitudes of, toward religious ceremony, evolve
   during English reign 661–4
cultivates relations with nobility 485–6
difficulties of, in controlling Western Isles of
   Scotland 495–6
enters England and displays military skills 446
enters England to greetings of enthusiastic
   crowds 447
expands peerage in all three of his kingdoms 487
fascinated by supernatural phenomena 439
fills his English bedchamber with Scots 487
governs through personal relationships 485–7
impatience of, with petitions and representative
   assemblies 529–30, 537, 641–2
imposes liturgical innovations on
   Scottish Kirk 534–5, *see also* Five Articles
   of Perth

introduces justices of the peace and constables
   into Scotland 474, 487
moves to restore Scottish episcopacy and
   control Scottish clergy 531–3
plans and makes progress to Scotland
   (1615–17) 534–5
recruits English and foreign writers to refute
   doctrine of papal power to depose kings 564
reputation of, among historians, for shrewd
   flexibility on religious matters 529
resents and tries to suppress criticism of his
   pursuit of the Spanish match 635
resurrects Earl Marshal's Court 474–5
says that since Spanish have Charles they may
   "salt him and eat him," (1623) 636
seeks to spread civility throughout his
   kingdoms 489
settles local feuds and moves to pacify the
   Scottish borders 491
shuts himself in a study to write tracts against
   Bellarmine and Parsons 562–3
views of, about law and lawyers 437–40, 465,
   470–1, 473–4
views of, on royal power and authority 20–1,
   464–5
see also Borders, (between England and
   Scotland); Kirk, the
James VI and I: European Policies 31–2
ambassadors to James's court, *see* Béthune,
   Maximilien de, marquis de Rosny and duke of
   Sully; Boisschot, Batta; Caron, Noel de; La
   Tour, d'Auvergne, Henri de, duke of Bouillon;
   Harlay, Christophe de; Oldenbarnevelt,
   Johan; Leveneur, Tanneguy, count of Tillières;
   Male, Batta van; Salvetti, Amerigo; Sarmiento
   de Acuña, Diego, duke of Gondomar; Ursel,
   Conrad van, baron d'Hoboque
balance of power and 595–6
before 1603 412, 546
challenges Habsburg interests in North Italy
   and Germany 604, 608–9, *see also*
   Charles Emmanuel, duke of Savoy;
   Protestant Union (German)
characterized by dissimulation 545–6,
   559–60, 619–20, 622–3, 625–8
complains of Dutch sea power and commercial
   dominance 588–9
concerning the crisis in Bohemia 620–1,
   621–2, 623, 626–7, *see also* Bohemian crisis;
   Maximilian I, duke of Bavaria; Zuñiga,
   Balthazar
concerning the imperial election of 1618
   617–18, *see also* Ferdinand of Styria, future
   Holy Roman emperor

James VI and I: European Policies (cont.)
  concerning political and religious conflict
    in the Netherlands 581–93, see also
    Arminius, Jacobus, Dutch theologian;
    Grotius, Hugo; Oldenbarnevelt, Johan;
    Maurice of Nassau; Remonstrant
    controversy; Vorstius, Conradus
  concerning relations with France and the
    United Provinces, at start of his English
    reign 547–54, see also Henry IV of France
    (Henry of Navarre)
  concerning Savoy and North Italy 599–604,
    618–19, see also Charles Emmanuel
    duke of Savoy; Interdict Controversy;
    Venice
  concerning support for noble opposition to
    French crown 573–81, 613–16, 618, see also
    Bourbon, Henry II de, prince of Condé;
    Concini, Concino, marquis d'Ancre;
    D'Albret, Charles, duke of Luynes; France;
    Guise, Charles duke of; La Tour
    d'Auvergne, Henri de, duke of Bouillon;
    Marie de Médicis
  concerning truce negotiations in the
    Netherlands 554–6, see also
    Oldenbarnevelt, Johan
  concerning Venice and its quarrel with the
    Papacy 564–7, see also Interdict
    Controversy; Wotton, Sir Henry
  concludes defensive alliance with Protestant
    Union 570–1, see also Protestant Union
    (German)
  conditioned by Britain's relatively marginal
    position in European affairs 544–5
  conducted through rival cohorts of ministers
    and diplomats 609–10
  constrained by poverty of the British
    crown 544–5, see also crown finances
  cooperation with France in 557, 567–70
  cooperation with Spain in 612–13, see also
    Sandoval y Rojas, Francisco de, duke of
    Lerma
  during first Jülich-Cleves succession
    crisis and 567–70, 597–8, see also
    Jülich-Cleves succession crises (1609
    and 1614)
  during second Jülich-Cleves succession
    crisis 604–5, see also Jülich-Cleves
    succession crises (1609 and 1614)
  following Protestant defeats in Germany and
    Bohemia 627–30, 633–5
  French grow disillusioned with 552–3
  has testy exchange with French
    ambassador 578–9
  historians' accounts of 539–41

James's ambassadors to other states, see Aston,
    Sir Walter; Carleton, Sir Dudley;
    Cornwallis, Sir Charles; Cottington,
    Francis; Digby, George, later earl of
    Bristol; Edmondes, Thomas; Hay,
    James, lord Doncaster and later earl of
    Carlisle; Lake, Sir Thomas; Parry,
    Thomas; Spencer, Robert; Trumbull,
    Sir William; Winwood, Sir James; Wake, Sir
    Isaac; Wotton, Sir Henry
  James's professed religious moderation
    and 557–8
  James's *Tripli Nodex* sent to rulers throughout
    Europe 564
  looked to, to spearhead resistance to Spain and
    militant Catholicism 618–19
  motives and calculations behind 548, 593–6
  peace as a goal of 544–5, 595
  Protestant Union and 569–71, 604, 621,
    see also Protestant Union (German)
  publishes and distributes a book against
    Vorstius 587–8
  relations with Spain at start of English
    reign 543–5
  releases Catholics from prison to please Spain
    and Gondomar 610–11
  religious ideas and arguments and 556–64,
    577–8, 583, 585–7
  repayment of debts to English crown
    complicates 568–9, 586
  rhetorical justifications for 554–8, 595–6
  shaped by fears of revival of militant
    Catholicism 559, 571, 595–6, see also
    Jesuits
  see also Archdukes, the (Albert and Isabella),
    rulers of the Habsburg Netherlands;
    Cecil, Robert, later earl of Salisbury;
    Christian IV of Denmark; European
    confessional politics; Frederick V,
    elector Palatine; Henry, Prince; Huguenots;
    Jacobean peace; Neufville, Nicolas,
    seigneur de Villeroy, French foreign
    minister; Philip III; Spanish match;
    Stuart dynastic alliances
James VI and I: published works of
  Basilikon Doron 435–6, 439, 441–4, 446,
    464–5, 495–6, 633–4
  Daemonologie 439
  *Declaration du Serenissime Roy Jacques I Roi
    de la Grand' Bretaigne, France et Irlande...
    Pour le Droit des Rois et independance de
    leurs Couronnes* 578
  *An fruitfull Mediatioun contening ane plane
    and facill exposition of... the
    Revelatioun* 167–8, 411–12

His Majesties speech in this last session of Parliament 560–1
Ane Meditatioun upon the first buke of the Chronicles 167–8, 411–12
A Meditation upon the 27, 28, 29 verses of the XVII chapter of St. Matthew 663–4
A Premonition to all the kings, free princes and states of Christendom 562–3
The True Law of Free Monarchies 435–6, 464–5
Tripli nodex, triplex cuneus. Or An Apologie for the Oath of Allegiance 562–3, 577
see also Bellarmine, Robert; Du Moulin, Pierre; Du Perron, Cardinal Davy; Oath of Allegiance
Jesuits
  black legend of 558–9
  blamed for upsurge in militant Catholic policies in France and the Empire 618–19
  denounced in France after murder of Henry IV 574–5
  disliked by Gallicans 557
  excoriated by lord Burghley 114–15
  French, distance themselves from defenses of papal authority to depose kings 578
  James's antipathy toward 556, 558–9
  mission to England, 1580 55, 82–3
  mission to Scotland 92, 135, 163
  reported to be trying to subvert James's kingdoms 558–9
Jonson, Ben
  alludes to Tudor tyranny 456–7
  Temple Bar pageant for James I's entry into London 455–7
Jouanna, Arlette 463–4
Jülich-Cleves succession crises (1609 and 1614) 567–71
  diplomatic maneuvering over 567–9
  effects of, on strategic power in western Germany 567
  Henry IV's murder and 570
  renewal of in 1614 570–1, 604–5
Junius, Hadrianus 323–4
justices of the peace 469

Ker, Robert of Cessford 491
Ker, Robert, earl of Somerset 575–6
  intermediary in early Spanish match negotiations 607–8
Kildare, earls of 235–6, see also under Fitzgerald
kingdom, as a political concept 4–5
kinship and kinship alliances
  Border surnames and 490–1
  campaigns against and outlawry of kindreds 448–9, 483–4

Irish lordships and 236–8
Scottish nobles and 417
settlements of feuds and quarrels and 482–3
in sparsely populated regions 481–2
Kirk, the 138–9
  angers king by declining to suppress inflammatory sermons 417–18
  appoints standing committee to safeguard its interests in Edinburgh 422
  assists James VI in governing Scotland 413–14, 416
  bishops extend control over 533
  creates network for monitoring Catholic activities 419–20, 424–5
  James VI attempts to bring under control 531–3
  national assembly of, recommends uniform liturgy for Scotland 534
  national assembly of, restores episcopacy 533
  Prayer Book rebellion of 1637 and 661–2
  protests against James VI's lenient treatment of Huntly and other Catholics 417–18
  quarrels with king over episcopacy and other issues (1586–7) 161
  Second Book of Discipline of 138–9
  seeks to create a militia under its own control 422
  standing committee of, votes to defy James's order to disperse 427–8
  weakening support for, provides incentives to cooperate with crown 416
  see also under episcopacy; Five Articles of Perth; presbyterians and presbyterian clergy in Scotland
Knollys, Sir Francis 53–4, 398–9
  accused by Mendoza of being head of the pirates 212
Knox, Andrew, bishop of the Isles and Raphoe 496
  spurs renewed action against Irish recusants (1611) 525–6

Lake, Sir Thomas 548–9, 593
  described as only true friend of Spain on the privy council 609–10
Languet, Hubert 339, 341
La Rochelle 204
  corsairs from, use English ports 630–1
  encouraged to rebel against French crown by British 658
  sends envoy to James 630–1
La Tour d'Auvergne, Henri de, duke of Bouillon 571, 575–6
  fears Spanish will attack his territory of Sedan (1617) 614–15

La Tour d'Auvergne, Henri de, duke of Bouillon (*cont.*)
    international connections and stature of 572–3
    intrigues with duke of Guise and prince of Condé 573
    manages James's intervention in Huguenot assembly (1616) 579–80, *see also* Biondi, Giovanni Francisco
    sends envoy to James to plead for aid to Huguenots 630–1
    sent as ambassador to James I 574–5
    withdraws support for Anglo-French dynastic alliance 605
Laud, William 663–4
    palace of, attacked by a London crowd 668
    sees Covenanters' Rebellion as a threat to monarchy and himself 666
    takes great interest in churches of Ireland and Scotland 664–5
Leicester, earl of, *see under* Dudley, Robert
Leicester's Commonwealth 86–7
Leicester's expedition to the Netherlands (1585–1587)
    achievements and failures of 334–5
    attrition among soldiers during 198–9
    costs and financing of 284–6, 287–8, 298–301, 306, 317–18
    Dutch council of finances and financial disputes during 285, 300–1
    Dutch leaders criticize Leicester in letter to Elizabeth 317
    disputes over military strategy during 305–6
    disputes over trade with the enemy during 310–13, 329
    divisions among English in the Netherlands during 297–8
    early Dutch opposition to Leicester during 294
    Elizabeth's early misgivings over 276–7, 283–4
    Elizabeth's limited objectives for 276–7, 282–3
    English concern over Dutch ports and 305
    final collapse of 325–7
    gravely damaged by William Stanley's betrayal of Zutphen 314–15
    hampered by divisions within military command 310
    Leicester allies with Dutch Reformed Church 303–5
    Leicester blamed for surrender of Graves 301–2
    Leicester blames loss of Sluis on Maurice and other Dutch 325
    Leicester cast in the role of a new prince 332–3
    Leicester complains about and quarrels with Dutch leaders 294, 302–13, 325–7
    Leicester complains of Elizabeth's tepid support for 283–5, 296–8, 344
    Leicester departs from the Netherlands 312–13, 331
    Leicester draws up regulations for his army 198
    Leicester employs force against Dutch opponents 312–13
    Leicester favors English clients in making military appointments 306–7
    Leicester feuds with Count Hohenlohe 310
    Leicester grows touchy and defensive over criticism 297–8
    Leicester has a great seal bearing his arms made 293
    Leicester over-extends resources 306
    Leicester promotes sermons, print and oral reports to defend himself 312–13, 321, 323–5
    Leicester quarrels with Burghley over 344
    Leicester recruits soldiers for 271–2, 299–300
    Leicester tries but fails to pressure Elizabeth to increase her suport for (1587) 323–4
    Leicester urged to redress problems in Dutch government 245, 283, 286–8
    Leicester's court and entourage 286–7, 291–3, 302–3, 306–8
    Leicester's Dutch adversaries consolidate control of armed forces 315
    Leicester's governor generalship 272–3, 288–9, 293–4, 327
    Leicester's partisans accuse Dutch of squandering parliamentary aid 317, 324
    Leicester's personal expenditures on 198–9, 284–5
    Leicester's return to the Netherlands (summer 1587) 317–18, 323–4, 331
    Leicester's vendetta against Sir John Norrey, Thomas Wilkes and lord Buckhurst 319–20, 322–3, 347–8
    military campaigns and troops numbers during 299–302
    military commanders involved in, *see* Bertie, Peregrine, 13th baron Willoughby d'Eresby; Hohenlohe, Philip count of; Maurice of Nassau; Norreys, Edward; Norreys, Sir John; Pelham Sir William; Russell, Sir William; Sonoy, Diederick; Stanley, Sir William
    pageants and triumphal entries during 286–8, 292–3
    support and opposition to, at the English court 295–6, 301

INDEX 741

threatens to ignite civil war in the Netherlands 317, 321
undercut by Elizabeth's negotiations with Parma 277, 301, 323–7
undermined by Elizabeth's fury over Leicester's appointment as governor general 297–8, 302–13
weakened by military retrenchment 314
see also Dudley, Robert, earl of Leicester; Farnese, Alessandro, duke of Parma; Holland; Hotman, Jean, secretary to earl of Leicester; Junius, Hadrianus; military costs, logistics and administration, during Leicester's Dutch campaign; Prouninck, Gerard van; Ringault, Jacques; States General (of the Netherlands); Sackville, Thomas, lord Buckhurst and first earl of Dorset; United Provinces; Wilkes, Thomas
Lerma, see under Sandoval y Rojas, Francisco de, duke of Lerma
Lesley, John, bishop of Glasgow, see under Treatise of Treasons
Leveneur, Tanneguy, count of Tillières, French ambassador to London 623–5
comments on Gondomar's position within British court 632–3
comments on rise of anti-Spanish feeling after Protestant defeat at White Mountain 628
reports protest by English peers against elevation of Scots 640
reports speech by James castigating Charles and Buckingham for going to Spain 636
libels 88–9
see also dynastic libels
Lil, Balthzar de 422–4
Lillingston, Buckinghamshire 103–4, 109
Lindsay, David 413–14, 420–1, 429–30
Lipsius, Justus 369–70
Literature on oceanic enterprises 214–21
advocates good relations with native populations 217–19
analyzes strategic importance of the Atlantic to war against Spain 219–20
connects profit motive to religious conversion and spread of civility 217–19
justifies pursuit of economic gains 215–17
promotes exploration as a tool of commercial expansion and job-creation 215
see also Hakluyt, Richard the younger
local power and authority, differences in, across Britain and Ireland 476–84
blood feuds and 482–3
inflected by patterns of tenure and land use 478–9

inflected through royal agreements with lords and kindreds 484–5
influenced by sparse population in Ireland and upland districts 481–2
lordship and 480
organized in England through spatially defined jurisdictions 476–7
related in England to concepts of credit and neighborliness 478–9
prosecution of crime and 482–4
structured by kinship in Ireland, Scotland and the Borders 480–1
Lok, Michael 209–11
London, tensions in, at the accession of James I 447–8
Lord lieutenants 128–9
Louis XIII, king of France
demands Dutch support against rebel princes (1617) 615
launches military campaign against Huguenots 630–1
Low Countries, the, see under Netherlands, United Provinces
Luynes, duke of, see under d'Albret, Charles
Lyon, William, Protestant bishop of Cork 263

MacDonnell clan 494–5
MacDonnell, Randall, 1st earl of Antrim 498
improves his lordship 498–9
protects priests, friars and Jesuits 523–4
MacDonnell, Sorley Boy 494–5
McGrath, Meiler, Protestant bishop of Cashel 263
Machiavelli and Machiavellianism 374–5
depicted in contemporary treatises 65–9
possible influence on Leicester 332–3
MacKenzie, Colin 496–7
MacKenzies, the 496–7
Maclean, Lachlann Mòr of Duart 495
Madox, Richard 213
Maisterton, Thomas, governor of Wexford 239–40
Maitland of Thirlestane, John, chancellor of Scotland 159–61, 164, 168–70
blamed for retrenchment of James's household 415–16
hated and threatened by Scottish nobility 414, 416
recognizes advantages of James's improved relations with presbyterians 413–14
Malby, Sir Nicholas 187–9, 244–5, 250
warns that Catholicism will unite the Irish 251–2, 255–6

Malcontents 65–6, 68
Male, Batta van, archduke's ambassador in London 609–10
  Reports continuing persecution of British and Irish Catholics 610–11
  mandates policy (in Ireland) 519–26
Manelli, Giovanni Mareia 369–70
Mansfeld, Ernst, count 652–4
  failure of his expedition 654
Marian priests 100–1
Marnix, Philip van, lord of St Aldegonde 280–1
Marprelate tracts, the 396–7, 399–400
Martial law
  in England 129
  in Ireland 234, 258–60
  provost marshals and 467–8
  used to execute a few Irish priests 522
Martial traditions, among the English landed elite 138
Mary, queen of Scotland
  depicted in John Stubbs's *Gaping Gulf* 69–70
  execution of, polarizes Scotland 164–5
  natural head of a reversionary interest in England 42–3
  negotiates with English, over her release 146–7
  professes her desire to cooperate with Elizabeth and retire 145–6
  promotes Catholic seminaries 96–7
  protestant printed attacks on 88–9
  tells Mendoza she hopes to convert James and take England with Spanish help 143
  see also under Association (between Mary and James VI)
Mathematics and military science 178–9, 185–6
Maurice of Nassau 198, 279–80, 604
  accused of reviving designs of earl of Leicester 591–2
  disparaged by lord Willoughby 328
  obtains and modifies letter from James clarifying his views on Dutch religious conflicts 592
  reputed to have quarreled with Leicester 302
  supported by British government against Oldebarnevelt 590–3
  welcomes Leicester to the Netherlands (1585) 286–7
Maximilian I, duke of Bavaria
  army of, seizes Upper Palatinate and other regions (1620) 627
  Protestants prefer to Ferdinand as future emperor 616–17
  receives generous concessions from Ferdinand and Spain in return for military aid 625
Meade, John 256–7

Médicis, Catherine de, attacked in French libels and Stubbs's *Gaping Gulf* 65–8
Médicis, Marie de, Queen Mother and regent of France 649
  initiates negotiations for Bourbon-Habsburg dynastic alliance 571
  James seeks to pressure 574–5
  recognizes that James has encouraged revolt against her 576–7
  talks openly of calling for Spanish military assistance to quell rebellion 614–15
Melville, Andrew 136
  calls James VI "God's silly vassal," 405–6
  commemorates Prince Henry's baptism with Latin poem 412–13
  confronts earl of Arran 142–3
  freed from Tower of London to take a post at the Academy of Sedan 572–3
  imprisoned for defying James's ecclesiastical policies 531–2
  supports David Black's refusal to appear before James's council 425–6
  tells James to confiscate estates of Catholic earls 422
Melville, James. Scottish courtier and memorialist 156
Melville, James, presbyterian minister and nephew of Andrew Melville
  asks presbytery of Edinburgh to pray for "afflicted brethren of England" after receiving news of Hampton Court conference 530–1
  denounces "belly-god bishops" of England 408–9
  imprisoned for defying James's ecclesiastical policies 531–2
Mendoza, Bernardino de, Spanish ambassador to England 43, 49–50, 92
  English Catholic plots and 99
  complains of English spies 122–3
  communications with Mary Stuart 143
  cultivates contacts with English peers and courtiers 83, 108
  finds it increasingly hard to obtain information 123–4
  hopes to co-opt James VI 132
  reports on East Anglian Progress 59
  reports Elizabeth and Leicester want to poison James VI 144
  reports queen's alienation from Protestant councilors 80–1
  reports rumors of the earl of Leicester's designs on the throne 87, 147–8

schemes to assault Elizabeth through
    Scotland 140–1
stokes queen's fears of a Spanish invasion 81–2
thinks earl of Ormond prepared to
    defect 260–1
warns of English privateers in Caribbean
    206–7, 211
mercenaries, *see under* volunteer soldiers
Merchant Adventurers Company 286, 298, 311–12
    connected to presbyterian reformers 390–1
Middleton, Thomas, *A Game at Chess*, contrasted
    with Thomas Scott's *Vox Populi* 644–6
Mildmay, Sir Walter 146–7
Military costs, logistics and administration
    arrears in pay undermine morale 191–4
    contracts with merchants and 197
    corruption in 192, 196–7
    credit and debts to civilians and 191–2, 194–5
    dead pays 192, 195
    death rates, among troops 386–7
    difficulties of captains in sustaining
        finances 190–2, 195
    difficulties of, in Ireland 193–7
    during Leicester's Dutch campaigns 284–8,
        298–300
    Elizabeth's parsimony hampers 192–4, 298–9
    levels of mobilization, under Elizabeth 386–7
    musters and muster masters 195–8
    reformed, in Ireland 197
    soldiers selling arms 196, 315
    soldiers' wages 192
    total financial outlays on Elizabeth's
        wars 386–7
    transport of troops 196–7
    victualling of armies 197
military recruitment 199, 355–7
    Charles I and 651–2
    conscription 177–8, 658–9
    pyramidal structure of 189
military service and experience
    among commoners 178
    among the peerage 177–8
    boom-bust cycles in 192–3
    desertions 191–3, 196–9
    desertions of posts by captains 315
    in Ireland 192–7
military Treatises 180–7
    combat view of soldiers as poor and
        dissolute 180–1
    draw upon ancient histories of warfare 185–6
    emphasize need for godly, learned and wise
        officers 185–6
    enumerate administrative and intellectual
        tasks of officers 185–6

insist on importance of combat
    experience 186
justify military life as godly and
    honorable 181–3
stress importance of training and drill 184–5
view armies as models of civic discipline 184
view military force as bulwark against incivility
    and depravity 181–4
monarchical republic, the 5–6, 337–8
Montague, Walter, English courtier 658
Montgomery, Robert, archbishop of
    Glasgow 141–3
Mountjoy, *see under* Blount, Charles
Morgan, Thomas 187–9, 191–2
Morton, earl of, *see* Douglas, James, earl of
    Morton and regent of Scotland
multiple kingdoms 457–8
    multiplicity of laws within 460–1
Munday, Anthony 174–5
Murray, Thomas, secretary to Prince
    Charles 624–5, 634
Muscovy Company, the 207–8, 210–11
Musgrave, Richard 492

Napier, John 412
Naunton, Sir Robert 404–5, 609–10
navies 207, 209
Netherlands, the
    cautionary towns of 547–8
    presbyterian synod in 390–1
    southern provinces the traditional commercial
        center of 273
    strategic and commercial importance of, to
        England 273–4
    war in 93–4, 198–9
    see also under Leicester's expedition to the
        Netherlands, United Provinces
Netterville, Richard 520–1
Neufville, Nicolas, seigneur de Villeroy, French
    foreign minister 554
    demurs when urged to send forces to
        Jülich 570
    James attempts to topple 582–3
    opposes French support for Savoy 576–7
    resists Edmondes's entreaties to meddle
        in upcoming imperial election 617–18
Nicholson, James 427–8
Nine Years War (in Ireland), the 268–70
    Battle of Kinsale, the 269–70, 543–4
    Irish military methods and tactics in 268
    role of towns in 268–9
    see also O'Donnell, Hugh, earl of Tyrconnell;
        O'Neill, Hugh, earl of Tyrone
Norman Conquest, the 15–16, 246, 461–2

Norreys, Edward 308–10
Norreys, lord Henry 189
Norreys, Sir John 189, 299
　arrears and debts owed to 190
　clashes with William Davison, Leicester and Leicester's followers 308–10
　comments on attrition among troops 196, 199
　commands troops sent to the Netherlands (1585) 271–2
　complains of privations suffered by his soldiers 244
　conducts review of queen's army in the Netherlands (spring, 1587) 318–19
　given divided command over English troops in the Netherlands 313–14
　knighted by Leicester 293
　paid for role in Dutch campaign 285
　participates in Portugal Expedition (1589) 222
　siphons off money intended for Leicester's army 244, 308
　supported by queen in his quarrel with Leicester 310
　threatens to invade Holland if his troops are not fed 316–17
　tries to maintain English position in the Netherlands, during Leicester's absence 315–16
North, Roger Lord 120, 303–4, 306
Northern Rebellion (1569) 106
Nugent, Christopher, fifth baron Devlin 261–3
Nugent family 263–4
Nugent, Nicholas 261–2
Nugent, William 262–3

O'Donnell, Hugh, earl of Tyrconnell 499–500
　see also flight of the earls (1607)
O'Gallagher, Redmond, Catholic bishop of derry 263
O'Neill, Hugh, earl of Tyrone 494–6, 499–500
　adaptability of 267–8, 501–2
　attempts to form alliances with Highland clans 134–5
　claims virtually all of county Tyrone as his demesne 513–14
　discusses renewing his revolt with Spain 524–5
　see also flight of the earls (1607)
O'Neill, Turlough 262
Oath of Allegiance 561–2
　Catholics lobby to modify (1639–40) 667–8
　connected to French debate over authority of kings and popes 577–8
　controversy over 561–4
Oath of Supremacy, used in Ireland to weed out Catholic magistrates 519, 522–3

Octavians, the 422–4, 427–30
Ogilby, John 422
Oldenbarnevelt, Johan van
　agrees to contribute to Portugal expedition 328–9
　appointed as advocate of Holland 280
　asserts Holland's sovereignty, against the states general 592–3
　British undermine in conflict with Maurice of Nassau 590–2
　charged with wanting to introduce popery to the Netherlands 591–2
　cries out against English, after betrayal of Zutphen 314–15
　fall and execution of 593
　inhibits Dutch support for Huguenots and Condé 615
　misconstrues James's views on Remonstrant Controversy 584–5, 588
　negotiates truce with Archduke Albert (1607) 554
　opposes Leicester 312–13
　policies of, toward France, offend King James and Contra-Remonstrants 589–90
　reassured by James during private interview (June 1603) 549
　resists James's demands for dismissal of Vorstius 586
　resists James's request to join with him in mediating French conflict 615
　seeks to contain costs by reducing Dutch army 581–2
　spreads reports of English negotiations with Parma to discredit Leicester 326–7
Ostend, siege of 546–7
Ottoman Empire 225–6
Overton, William 62–4, 75–6

Paget, Charles 120–2
Paget, Thomas lord 111, 118–22
　clerical patronage of, challenged in Norfolk 120
　embarrassed by flight of his brother to France 120–1
　flight into exile 120–1
　humiliated by Staffordshire adversaries 118–20
Paget, William 122
Papacy, the, supports efforts to undermine Elizabeth 49–50
parliaments: general references
　British union debates and legislation in (1604–1606) 461–2, 476
　debate ecclesiastical reforms 388–91
　fear of courtiers sabotaging 641–2

greater emphasis on, in seventeenth century
  discourse 641
 James's reported disgust at 642–3
 printed petitions to 391–2
 revival of impeachment in 643–4
 parliaments: specific sessions
 1584–5 125–8
 1586–7 390–4
 1621 629–30, 640–1, 643
 1625 650–1
 1626 657
 1629 660
 1640 (the Short Parliament) 668
 1641–9 (the Long Parliament) 672
Parma, *see under* Farnese, Alessandro
Parry, Thomas, English ambassador to
  France 547–8
passions in political life 358–65
patriots and patriotism 137
 Dutch 291–2
 Essex and 337–8
 patriot lords 384–5
Paul V, Pope 561–3
 tries to dissuade Catholic princes from
  accepting James's book 563–4
peace negotiations with Spain 274–5, 277, 323–4,
  326–7, 350
Peckham, Sir George 215–19
Pelham, Sir William 194, 250
 mediates feud between earl of Ormond and
  baron of Upper Ossory 238–9
 proposals to reform Ireland 247–8
 reports rumors of foreign aid to Munster
  revels 252
 spends £800 equipping his company for the
  Netherlands 284–5
 splendor of company disgusts Dutch 306–7
 suspicious of earl of Ormond 260–1
Penry, John 392, 396–7, 410–11
 writes tracts against Richard Bancroft 409
Percy, Henry, ninth earl of Northumberland 493
Perez, Antonio 342–3, 350–1, 363–4
Pericles 209
Perrot, Sir John 203–4, 234–5, 247, 263
 proposes to establish Irish industries 247–8
 reported outburst, against Queen Elizabeth 266
 sees Munster famine as providential
  blessing 256–7
Persons, Robert 82–3, 98–9, 562–3
 King James's antipathy toward 558–9
Pembroke, earls of, *see under* Herbert, Henry,
  2nd earl of Pembroke and Herbert,
  William, 3d earl of Pembroke
Percy, Algernon, 10th earl of
  Northumberland 652–3, 666–8

Petrarchan sonnets 176–7
Phelips, Sir Robert 654–5
Philip II, king of Spain
 approves plan to kidnap James VI 92–3, 140
 considers, then abandons plan to invade North
  England 164
 embargoes English ships in Spanish
  ports 273–4
 poses multiple threats to England 273–4
 power and resources of 40, 274–5
 reacts to Ruthven raid 148–9
 tries to claim crowns of England and France
  for his daughter 395–6
Philip III, king of Spain 543–4, 555, 602–3
 death of, precipitates changes at Spanish
  court 612–13
Plowden, William 103–4
Political resistance and resistance theory
 constrained among Elizabethan
  Protestants 138
 in Scotland 137–8
Pont, Robert 407–8
Porter, Endymion 635–6
Portugal Expedition (1589) 222, 380
Potosi 40, 227
Poulet, Sir Amias 50, 71
presbyterians and presbyterian clergy in
  England 148
 exiled, from Scotland 134–5, 152–4
 promote Bill and Book campaign (1586–7)
  390–1
 publicists for, accuse bishops and queen of
  condemning souls to Hell by not promoting
  preaching 392
 puritan conference movement promotes
  388–90
 see also Bancroft, Richard; Cartwright,
  Thomas; Field, John; Fenton,
  Dudley; Penry, John; providential
  beliefs; Schilders, Richard; Waldegrave,
  Robert
presbyterians and presbyterian clergy in Scotland
 alarmed about possible Anglicizing influences
  on the Kirk (1603–4) 530–1
 clash with James VI and his favorites
  (1580s) 132, 139–40
 continue to resist and protest against James's
  policies after 1603 530–1
 criticize James VI over favor to Huntly and
  other matters 402–3, 407–8, 421–2
 development of 136–9
 doctrinal support for 136
 doctrine of the two kingdoms and 405–6
 efforts to rally support for falter (1586) 162
 endangered by Lennox and Arran, 1582 143

presbyterians and presbyterian clergy in Scotland (*cont.*)
   expand their system of presbyteries 413–14
   fail to receive English or Scottish aristocratic support after the Tumult 433–4
   feel a duty to admonish laity for sins 405–8
   feel threatened by Catholic nobles 402
   form a state after 1637 671–2
   in Glasgow 142–3
   individual clergy, *see* Balcanqual, Walter; Black, David; Bruce, Robert; Carmichael, James; Davidson, John; Dury, John; Galloway, Patrick; Melville, Andrew; Melville, James; Penry, John; Ross, John
   oppose appointment of new bishops 141–3
   organize national resistance in Scotland against Catholic earls 419–20
   protest against French embassies 145–7, 163
   regarded as proud demagogues by James I and Charles I 662–3
   resist James's efforts to impose moderators on presbyteries and synods 532–3
   sign declaration condemning episcopacy (1606) 531–2
   six "martyrs" imprisoned for defying James's order not to convene for a national assembly at Aberdeen 531
   stigmatized as enemies of the state 397–9
   support David Black's refusal to appear before James's council to answer for a sermon 396
   tacit English support for 138–9
   see also Kirk; providential beliefs
Print and print culture
   the Anjou Match and 59–72
   attacks on Elizabeth I through 87–8
   Catholic presses and 97–8
   Dutch 290–1, 591–3
   oceanic enterprises and 201, 205–6
   petitioning of parliaments through 391–2
Prince Henry, *see* Henry, Prince of Wales
privateers and pirates 199–207, 207–14
   armaments of 202
   assisted by advances in mathematics, navigation and cartography 213
   assisted by Portuguese mariners 212
   before the Elizabethan period 199–200
   in the Caribbean 225
   in Charles I's reign 651–2
   cooperate to form small fleets 202
   costs, profits and financing of 201–3, 213
   difficulties of, in identifying legitimate prizes 202–3

   Dutch and Huguenot 204–5
   Elizabeth's attitudes toward 201
   encouraged by success of Drake's voyage (1580) 211
   entrenched in some coastal districts 199–200, 203–4
   as examples of "chivalric policy," 214–15
   expand activities after Philip II embargoes English ships (1584) 221
   expand in Caribbean 210–11
   international collaboration and 200–1, 212
   printed literature concerning 205–7
   resupply themselves by plunder 201–2
   size of ships employed in 201–2
   stimulate ship-building, the manufacture of iron guns and commercial enterprise 223–7
   strategic benefits of 223
   strategic planning concerning, under Charles I 652–3
   use network of Protestant ports 201
   Welsh ports and 204
   see also Atlantic voyages and colonization; commerce and merchant shipping; Dom Antonio, pretender to Portuguese throne; Drake, Sir Francis; Frobisher, Martin; Hawkins, John; La Rochelle; literature on oceanic enterprises; navies; Ralegh, Sir Walter
privy chamber servants 187–9
Protestant refugees, in England 134–5, 152–4, 199–200
providential beliefs 235–6, 393, 395
   in Daniel's *Panegyrike* to James I 454
   displayed by James VI and I 439, 451–2, 464–5
   fostered by uncertainties of late 1580s 394
   invoked to explain military defeats and political problems of Charles I's reign 654–5
   link Leicester's Dutch campaign to reform of English worship 390, 394
   see also apocalyptic beliefs
Protestant Union (German)
   concludes defensive alliance with James VI and I 570–1
   disputes over Jülich-Cleves and 567–9
   initially keeps its distance from Bohemian rebellion 620
   prepares an army under command of Frederick V during Bohemian crisis 620
   relations of, with Savoy 602–4
   warned by James that he lacks money to fund an army for their defense 621
Prouninck, Gerard van 288, 302–3, 314–15, 327
   claims Netherlands needs a new prince 332–3

public, the, as an imaginative construction 75–8
public sphere, the 72–9
purveyors and purveyance 469–70

race and racial thought 351–5
  affects views of political corruption 352–3
  James VI and I and 441
  linked to views of the superior virtues of noble lineages 351–2
  "positive racism," 354–5
  and views of the nobleman's military vocation 353–4
Radclyffe, Thomas, earl of Sussex 345–6
  analysis by of Anjou match and Anjou 51–3
  complains of being excluded from negotiations with Huguenots 81–2
  entertains queen at New Hall, Essex 71–2, 75–6, 80n.228
  Irish career of 91
Ralegh, Sir Walter 121, 189
  denounces earl of Ormond 260–1
  extols English valor 385
  leads raid on Caribbean pearl fishery 225
  memorandum attributed to, opposes Savoy match for Prince Henry 599–600
  oceanic enterprises and 209–10, 221
redshank soldiers 494–5
Religious allegiances, see under confessional allegiances and confessionalization
Religious toleration 105–6, 111
Remonstrant Controversy 584
  James's early interventions in 584–5
Resistance theory, see under political resistance
Rich, Barnaby 180–6
Rich, Henry, viscount Kensington and later earl of Holland 637
Rich, Nathaniel 654–5
Rich, Robert, earl of Warwick 603–4
  enters into treasonous correspondence with Covenanters 666–7
  says he is busy trying to prevent civil war (spring 1641) 672–3
Richard II 78
Richelieu, see under Du Plessis, Armand-Jean
Ringault, Jacques 311–13
  driven into exile 313–14
  urges Leicester to establish his sovereignty by armed force 320–1
  wants Leicester to establish lordship over North Sea 312
Rohan, Benjamin de, duke of Soubise 630–1
Roseaus, Henricus 590–1
Ross, John, calls James VI a reprobate 420–1
royal prerogative, the
  abuses of, perceived as threats to liberty 469
  delegates power to royal officials, who can abuse it 469
  efforts to analyze and limit 466–7
  employed under Elizabeth to circumvent law 467–8
  see also absolute kings and absolutism
Rudolph IV, Holy Roman emperor 567–8
Russell, Sir William 258–9, 306–7, 313–14
  encourages mutineers on island of Walcheren 327
  quarrels with lord Willoughby over cooperation with Dutch 328–9
Ruthven Raid 144–5, 147
  eventual failure of 148–9

Sackville, Thomas, lord Buckhurst and first earl of Dorset 304–5
  commissions treatise in defense of the royal prerogative 469
  rebuked by queen, for not taking harder line with Dutch 322–3
  seeks to mediate among Dutch factions, Norreys and Leicester 317–19
  sent to Netherlands by Elizabeth (1587) 317–18
  urges that Norreys remain in his post 318–19
  wants Leicester to return to the Netherlands 319
  warns that Leicester's pursuit of revenge is dangerous 324
Sandys, Sir Edwin 461, 471
Sarmiento de Acuña, Diego, Count of Gondomar 606–7
  believes that James is keeping his options open over the Spanish match 609–10
  Catholic priests released from prison as special favor to 552–3
  comments on James's skill at dissimulation 545–6
  consulted about religious conflicts in Ireland (1614) 526
  distributes pensions among British courtiers 638
  influence at British court reaches new heights 632–3
  launches negotiations for Spanish match 607–8
  receives death threats and suffers attack on his embassy 635
  reported to have said James can rely on Spanish support to break Parliament 642–3
  represented in Thomas Middleton's *Game at Chess* and Thomas Scott's *Vox Populi* 644–6

748 INDEX

Sarmiento de Acuña, Diego, Count of Gondomar (*cont.*)
  told by James that Prince Henry planned to marry Frederick V's sister 599–600
  told James wants to move against Presbyterians but needs Spanish support to do so 610–11
  warns superiors about British sea power 629–30
Savile, Sir Henry 341, 369–70
  appends description of Roman warfare to his translation of Tacitus 372
  composes narrative of Nero's fall to fill gap in Tacitus 372–3
  emphasizes disguise, dissimulation and envy 375
  employed to help translate James's *Tripli Nodex* into Latin 562–3
  footnotes of 374–5
  humanist tutor, with connections to the court and queen, a 371–2
  invites comparisons to contemporary France and religious wars of the Continent in his narrative of Nero's fall 372–3
  translates Tacitus's *Histories* and *Agricola* 370–2
  translation of Tacitus by, used to complicate and enrich stories from chronicle histories 374–5
  translations and compositions describe tactics used by treacherous courtiers 373
  warns against haste in unifying England and Scotland 461
Savile, Thomas 369–70
St. Bartholomew's Day massacres 35–6, 43, 68, 85–6, 575–6
St John, Oliver, viscount Grandison 503–4
St Leger, Anthony 240–1
St Leger, Warham 193–4, 256–7, 263–4, 269
Salvetti, Amerigo, Tuscan ambassador in London 623–7, 630–1
  reports attacks in parliament on Buckingham and the prerogative 640–1
  reports English war fever in 1625 602–3
Sander, Nicholas 47–50
  encourages rebellion in Ireland 252–4
Sandoval y Rojas, Fransisco de, duke of Lerma 543–4
  power declines, after ca. 1615 612–13
  seeks to contain European conflicts 612–13
Sarpi, Paolo 565
  dismayed by James's inaction during Interdict Controversy 566–7

Schilders, Richard 390–2, 396–7
Scone, David lord 532–3
Scotland
  a distorted mirror of English religious politics 133–48
  episodes of instability in 41–2, 92, 160–1
  feudal tenancies and land occupation in 482
  Highlands of, pacified by James VI 497
  pulpit the main medium of public communications in 420
  religious reformation in 136
  threatens to drain English resources 92
  see also James VI before 1603, in Scotland; James VI and I 1603 to 1625, as ruler of Britain and Ireland; Kirk, the; Maitland, John of Thirlestane; Scottish lords and nobles; Scottish (Western) Isles
Scott, Thomas 19–20, 385
  portrays Spanish match as symptom of deeper corruption 644
  Vox Populi of 637–8
Scottish (Western) Isles 494–6
  efforts to colonize 495–6
  improving lords in 496–7
  Isle of Lewis 495–6
  Statutes of Iona, as attempt to civilize 496
Scottish lords and nobles
  attempt to surprise James VI 414–15
  join opposition to king 140–1
  seigneurial armies of, reinforced by shipwrecked Spanish veterans 414–15
Scottish council, the 432
Seminary priests 96–7
Shakespeare, William 354–5, 360–1
Sidney, Sir Henry 91, 187–9, 231–2
  cess, the, and 173
  complains of mistreatment by the queen 344
  factional rivalries and 241–2
  praised for slaughtering Irish 250
  praises restraint of Ulster lords 240
  pursues the commonwealthmen 261
  retains humanist tutor for his sons 341
  seeks to establish an Irish cloth industry 247–8
Sidney, Sir Philip 137, 174–5, 234, 265, 341, 377
  commands garrison of Flushing 306
  cultivated by Master of Gray 159–60
  dies of wounds in the Netherlands 313–14
  invests in New World colony 221
  letter by, opposing Anjou Match 76–7
  receives money for Dutch campaign 286
  recommends Tacitus to Robert Sidney 369–70
  relations with Angus and other Scottish Protestants 134–5, 153–4

INDEX 749

sees English intervention in Dutch wars as God's work 390
seeks to join Anjou's army in the Netherlands 190
spends £7,250 assisting Leicester in the Netherlands 284–5
warned against reckless courage 339
Sidney, Sir Robert, later 1st earl of Leicester 340–1, 355–6, 360, 466–7
receives dedication of Italian translation of Tacitus 369–70
studies under Sir Henry Savile 369–70
Sidney, Sir Robert, later 2nd earl of Leicester 466–7, 666–8
Skidmore, Andrew 263–4
Sledd, Charles 47–50
Sluis 324–5
Smith, Sir Thomas 468, 472
Sonoy, Diederick 310, 328–9
remains loyal to Leicester and Elizabeth 315, 327
resists efforts by Maurice and Hohenlohe to occupy North Holland towns 321
Spanish invasion fleets 543–4
see also Armada, the
Spanish Match, the 605–13
antecedents of (before 1615) 597–8, 605–6
Charles's journey to Madrid and 635–7
criticism and denunciations of 633–5
greater indulgence toward British Catholics a Spanish condition for 610–11
hampered by mutual mistrust 612–13
infighting and instability at English court complicates negotiations for 610
James motives in pursuing 611–12
linked by historians to Bohemian crisis and Thirty Years War 608
negotiations over, complicated by changes in power in Madrid 612–13
negotiations over restoration of the Palatinate and 631–3, *see also* Bohemian crisis; Frederick V elector Palatine
raises concerns over security of British Protestantism 643–4
reception of, in Scotland 536–7
religious differences an impediment to 598, 605–6
Spanish spin out negotiations over, to deter James from supporting Dutch 632–3
Spanish motives for pursuing 605–6
uncertainty and disagreement over 608–10
would not have required complete reversal of Britain's diplomatic position 610–11
see also Charles Prince of Wales, later Charles I; Digby, George, later first earl of Bristol; Porter, Endymion; Sandoval y Rojas, Fransisco de, duke of Lerma; Sarmiento de Acuña, Diego, count of Gondomar
Spelman, Sir Henry 461
Spencer, Robert, sent to participate in negotiations over Dutch truce 555
Spenser, Edmund 245–8, 250
his *View of the Present State of Ireland* 341–2
Spinola, Ambroglio di, overruns Rhineland Palatinate with his army 627
Spottiswood, John, presides over national assembly that restores episcopacy 533
preaches sermon denouncing opponents of Five Articles of Perth 535–6
recommends delaying action over liturgical articles 534
Stafford, Dorothy, mistress of the robes to Elizabeth I 346–7
Stafford, Edward lord, English ambassador to France 271–2
skeptical of Leicester's intervention in the Netherlands 346–7
Standon, Anthony 355–6
Stanihurst, Richard 234
Stanley, Sir William 329
betrays Zutphen to Parma 313–14
runs extortion racket at Zutphen 316–17
state, the
components of 14–15
debased by power of low-born men 352–4
defined by judges, as including the bishops 397–8
definitions and concepts of 13–16
delegated royal authority within 398–9
depends on effective leadership 366–8
depends on its people's moral condition 367–9
depicted as a product of love 452–3, 455
Elizabeth I's view of 365
English 365
fragility and mutations of 13–14, 375–6, 454
frequently referred to by the earl of Essex 337–8
in Ireland 250–1
in multiple kingdoms 458
in the Netherlands 13–14, 319, 364
marital diplomacy and 452–3
an "order of commanding and obeying," 13
Protestantism and 12–13, 16–17, 21–2, 114–15
reason of state 341–2
Samuel Daniel's depiction of, in his *Panegyrike for James I* 452–5
supported by passions 363–4, 453
state formation and state building 18–20

State of Christendom, The 340-2, 350-1, 365, 374
  argues for legitimacy of arbitrary taxation 379
  discusses difficulties of long-distance military operations 380
States General (of the Netherlands) 281-2
  claims to represent the Dutch people questioned by Leicester's partisans 320-1
  declares duty of members to protect Dutch privileges even against the sovereign 320-1
  move to curtail Leicester's authority upon his return to the Netherlands (1587) 324
  propose ban on trade with the enemy (1585) 310-11
  require loyalty oath of troops serving in Netherlands (1586) 315
  resentment of 288, 291-2
  selection of members 289-90
Stewart, Francis, fifth earl of Bothwell 168, 489-90
  attempts to create alliance of Stewart lords 417
  dislikes Maitland of Thirlestane 414
  feared by James VI 416-17
  hopes to exploit tension between James and the Kirk over Catholic earls 420-1
  joins in attempt to surprise James VI 414-15
Stewart, James, earl of Arran
  assures lord Hunsdon that James has not met with Jesuits 157
  blamed by English for murder of Sir Francis Russell (1585) 159-60
  captured in Ruthven raid 144
  emerges as dominant favorite of James VI 149-50
  launches vendetta against Ruthven raiders and other rivals 113, 149-50
  mounting hatred of 150-1
  presented with grievances by general assembly of Kirk 142-3
  reputed greed and dishonesty of 149-50
  role of, in overthrow of Morton 131-2
  threatens to stab minister 140
  travels secretly to Edinburgh 163
Stewart, William (Colonel Stewart) 147, 150-1
  seeks intervention by European Catholics in Scotland 164
  sent by James on mission to German Protestant princes 412
Stewart, William, brother of James Stewart earl of Arran 151
Stuart, Arabella 147-8, 548

Stuart dynastic alliances
  Catholic, promoted by Catholics and Hispanophiles at the court 600-1
  European confessional politics and 597-8
  for Prince Charles 605-13, 628, 637
  for Prince Henry 598
  for Princess Elizabeth 598
  negotiations over, with France 605, 637
  negotiations over, with Savoy 599
  opposition to Catholic 599-601
  pragmatic approaches to 600-1
  see also Spanish match, the; French dynastic alliance of 1625
Stuart, Esmé, seigneur d'Aubigny and later duke of Lennox 41-3, 82
  arrival in Scotland and rise to favor 131-2
  assaults ministers 140-1
  attempts to build a Scottish following 133
  created duke of Lennox 131-2
  death in exile 146-7
  equivocates over his religion 132, 139-40
  expulsion from Scotland after Ruthven Raid 144-5
  offers to lead army to free Mary 142-3
  schemes with duke of Guise and Jesuits 133
Stuart, Ludovic, 2nd duke of Lennox 649
Stubbs, John 64-75
  controversy and demonstrations over 71, 75
  Gaping Gulf 64-71, 73
  ordered punished 75
Stukeley, Thomas 39-40
Suarez, Francisco de 577
successions to the throne 36, 348-9
  imperils Church settlements 389-90
Sussex (county) 62-4
Sussex, earl of, *see under* Radclyffe, Thomas

Tacitus 369-77, 456, 649
  considered a major source of Roman military history 372
  interest of Essex and his circle in 341, 369-71, 374
  links character flaws of Roman emperors to story of the collapse of Republican values 375-7
  lord Henry Howard's early interest in 370
  possible influence of, within Leicester's entourage in the Netherlands 369-70
  psychological subtlety of 315
  read as guide to treachery within courts 373
  readings of sharpened but did not cause Essex's estrangement from the court 377-8

INDEX   751

translations into English of 370–2, 374–6
  see also Greneway, Richard; Lipsius, Justus;
    Savile; Sir Henry
tenant loyalty 178
Thirty Years War, the, historiography of 608
Throckmorton family 44–5
Throckmorton, Job 392–4
  criticizes English court for complacency 393
  disparages European monarchs and advocates
    alliance with Dutch 393
  Marprelate tracts and 396–7
  rebuked by Christopher Hatton for
    disparaging monarchs 394
Throckmorton Plot, see under Catholic plots
Tillières, count of, see under Leveneur, Tanneguy
Topcliffe, Richard 58
Treatise of Treasons (1572) 66–7
Treaty of Hampton Court (1603, between Britain
    and France) 550–1
  James claims to have expired 552
Treaty of Joinville (1584) 271, 274–5
Treaty of Nonsuch (1585) 271–2, 283
  grants English possession of cautionary
    towns 277
  masks disagreements 277
Treaty of Xanten 604–5
Tresham, Sir Thomas 92, 109–10, 115
  complains of imprisonment 117–18
  supports efforts to convert Scotland to
    Catholicism 135
Tresham, William 85–6, 103–4, 109–10
Trollope, Andrew 255–6
Trumbull, Sir William, James I's
    ambassador in the Habsburg
    Netherlands 558–9
Tumult, (December 1596), the 428–32
Turkey (later Levant) Company, the 225–6

Udall, John 397–8
Uitenbogaert, Johannes, Dutch theologian
    584, 588
United Provinces, the
  alarmed by James's apparent sympathy for
    Spain 548–9
  described as an aristocratic polity 289–90,
    321–2
  decentralized and diffused authority
    within 278–9, 289–91
  debts of, to English crown 546–7
  deterioration of British crown's relations
    with 588–9
  dispatches high-level delegation to London
    (1603) 547–8
  Dutch Reformed Church and 583

  Elizabeth seeks indirect influence over 282–3
  establish a council of state 278
  executive authority and sovereignty
    within 281–2, 288–90, 293,
    320–2, 324
  finances of 278–9
  joins alliances of James and Protestant
    Union 570–1
  leaders of, abhor talk of peace 276–7
  Leicester's authority within 282–3, 288–9
  oligarchic leaders of, suspected of
    disloyalty 289–90
  public controversy within 290–1
  regarded as dysfunctional state 278, 280–1,
    283, 288, 331–3, 581–3
  religious conflict threatens to destabilize 590–3
  severely shaken by loss of South 271–3
  urban militias and guilds within 290–1
  see also States General (of the Netherlands);
    Remonstrant Controversy; Vorstius,
    Conradus
Ursel, Conrad van, baron of Hoboken or
    Hoboque, archdukes' ambassador in
    London 554–5
  instructed to discourage plots against British
    crown 559–60
  reports British alarm over prospect of
    Bourbon-Habsburg marriage alliance
    539–40
Utrecht 291–2
  coup in, justified as assertion of popular
    sovereignty 321
  Leicester's capital 292–3
  remains supportive of Leicester 312–13, 325

Valois Dynasty 68–9
Valois, François de, duke of Alençon and
    Anjou 37
  aids Dutch revolt 40–1, 50–1
  consequences of death of 271
  depicted in John Stubbs' *Gaping Gulf* 64–5,
    69–70
  described by Sir Philip Sidney 77
  English captains seek employment under in
    the Netherlands 190
  makes exorbitant demands, during marriage
    negotiations 53–4
  record and reputation of, in France 50–1
  see also Anjou Match
Vaux, Henry 103–4
Vaux, William lord 103–4, 109–10
Venice
  alliance of, with Dutch, promoted by James VI
    and I 603–4

Venice (cont.)
  invited by James to join alliance with Savoy and the Protestant Union 602–3
  see also under Paolo Sarpi
Vere, Edward de, earl of Oxford 54
  reveals conspiratorial activities of court Catholics 83
Vere, Sir Horace, leads soldiers to the Palatinate 626–7
Vere, Sir Francis de 380–1
Villiers, George, duke of Buckingham
  accompanies Charles to Madrid (1623) 635–6
  angered by nobles complaining about inflation of honors 640
  attacked and impeached in parliaments 650
  attacked for debasing honor 640–1
  attempts to build clientage network through marriage alliances and patronge 652
  attempts to build and maintain "patriot coalition" supporting war with Spain 637, 645–6, 652
  attempts to restore his reputation and support through bold action 658
  becomes scape-goat for failures of Charles's early reign 657
  claims not to care about disintegration of alliance with France 654
  constrained in negotiating French alliance by worries that James will revive pact with Spain 655–6
  depicts his relationship with Charles as rooted in love and friendship 659–60
  dominant position of, as royal favorite, at outset of Charles I's reign 648–9
  exchanges accusations of treason with earl of Bristol 649
  grows alienated from Olivares and the Spanish 636–7
  leads expedition to Ile de Rhé 658
  presents himself in a masque as pursued by Envy and the people's barking 659–60
  seeks to deflect criticism by attacking queen's Catholic clergy and attendants 656–7
  sends agent, Watt Montague, to stir rebellions in France 658
  tasked with harnessing voluntary efforts behind war with Spain 652
  tries to construct a Protestant league 654
  urged by lord Doncaster to persuade James to send aid to German Protestants 620
virtue
  connected to ideal of public service 339–40
  different types of 339–40
  juxtaposed to effeminacy and vices of peace 385
  opposed by envy 315
  reinforced and tempered by learning 340
  sometimes associated with risk-taking 339
  subversion of 377
Voluntarism and state formation 18–19
  associated with "noble races," 351–2
  produces conflicts with royal wishes 19–20
  relation of, to godliness 351–2
Volunteer soldiers 38–9, 177–8, 187–90
  English, fight for Savoy 602–3
  French civil war and 615–16
  gentlemen 192
  Irish, in foreign armies 524–5
  numbers of English, serving the Dutch, increases after 1603 553–4
  present in large numbers in Britain on eve of Civil War 672–3
  raised to assist Frederick V 626–7
Vorstius, Conradus 585–6
  exiled to Gouda 588
  James horrified by views of 585–6
  replies in pamphlets to James's attacks 586, 590–1
voyages of exploration, see under Atlantic voyages and colonization
Vranck, François 321–2

Wake, Sir Isaac 603–4
  suspects Franco-Spanish plot against liberties of Italy 618
Wales 243
Wallop, Sir Henry 245, 261
  surveys lands for Munster plantation 257
Waldegrave, Robert
  press of shut down, for printing *A lamentable complaint of the commonality* (1584) 391
  prints apocalyptic works by John Napier and Andrew Melville 412–13
  prints tracts critical of Richard Bancroft and English bishops 409–10
  sets up press in secret, then fleas to Scotland 396–7
  see also Marprelate tracts
Walsh, William, Marian bishop of Meath 252
Walsingham, Frances 342–3
Walsingham, Sir Francis
  advocates spending £400,000 in the Netherlands 275–6
  alarmed by Spanish gains in the Netherlands (1578) 37–8
  anticipates difficulty in overcoming Dutch division 283

assists defense of presbyterian Kirk 153–4
comments on Mary and James VI 146–7
complains of Elizabeth's prevarications over the Netherlands 276–7, 283–4, 315–16
connives over disposal of privateers' prizes 204
despises earl of Arran 156
disapproves of Elizabeth's handling of Scotland 41–2, 160–1, 275–6
encourages resistance to James VI 136
initial reactions to the Anjou match 53
laments queen's churlish treatment of her servants 344
promotes a colonial project 215–16
promotes investments in purported Labrador gold mine 210–11
reacts to Fitzmaurice's landing in Munster 255
recommends removing Norreys from the Netherlands 308–9
suffers period of Displeasure over Stubbs's *Gaping Gulf* 74–5
thinks only hope for Scotland lies with religious minority 147
ties to Muscovy company 208–9
wants to invest profits of Drake's privateering in Dutch war 211
withholds information from queen about costs of Dutch war 287–8
War
 diversionary, at sea 652–3
 exhausts European states by early seventeenth century 448–9
 failure in, produces ideological polarization and search for scapegoats 654–5, 660
 financial and human cost of, under Elizabeth I 386–7, 448–9
 limitations of British resources for 652–3
 viewed as a test of national valor and virtue 654–5
 with Spain, popular at start of Charles I's reign 650–1
Waterhouse, Edward 255
Watts, William 135
Wentworth, Thomas, 1st earl of Strafford 661–2, 664, 666
 advises using Irish army to overcome crisis in Britain 668–9
 eager to wreak revenge on supporters of Scots 671
 nervous about outcome of military campaign against Covenanters (1639) 666–7

Weston, Nicholas 267–8
White, Nicholas 248
Whitgift, John, archbishop of Canterbury 335–6
 accuses puritans and presbyterians of "popularity," 398–9
 dealings of, with Patrick Adamson 152–5
 enjoys good relations with earl of Essex 350–1
 launches campaign against Presbyterians and puritans 281–2
 opposes presbyterians as threat to hierarchy 394
 probably opposed Leicester's expedition to the Netherlands 346–7, 394
Whyte, Sir Richard 263–4
Wilkes, Thomas 13–14, 198–9, 288–9
 accuses the states of Holland of violating Leicester's sovereign authority 320–1
 borrows money on his own credit, to relieve English troops 316–17
 fears Leicester's vindictiveness 329–30
 instructed by Elizabeth to interrogate Dutch about finances 301
 relations with earl of Leicester 297n.138, 317–18
 seeks to rally Dutch support behind Leicester 317–18
William of Orange 190, 201
 assassinated 271–2
 disappearance of, creates leadership vacuum 281–2
Williams, Sir Roger 186–9, 239–40, 308
Willoughby, *see* Bertie, Peregrine
Wilson, Thomas, secretary of state 41–2, 53, 474
Winwood, Sir James 569–70, 609–10
 Accuses Dutch of slighting James's honor over Vorstius 586
 excluded from committee considering Spanish match 610–11
 receives complaints about Dutch excluding English from East Indies trade 588–9
 sent to participate in negotiations over Dutch truce 555
 told to press Dutch to avoid heresy (1609) 584–5
 views Vorstius and Remonstrants as Spanish agents 586–7
 Vorstius affair and 585–6
Winter, William 208–9
Wither, George 639
Wotton, Sir Henry
 instructed by Robert Cecil not to encourage Venetians to expect British military assistance 566

Wotton, Sir Henry (*cont.*)
  rejoices at Fredericks's election as king of Bohemia 624–5
  says news of Dutch truce puts London into a cold sweat 554
  seeks to spread Protestantism in Italy 565
  supports Venice during the Interdict Controversy 564–6

Zuñiga, Balthazar 612–13
  Pushes for Spanish involvement in Bohemian crisis 625
  Seeks to disengage from war in Empire, once Ferdinand's position is secure 631–2
Zutphen and Deventer
  betrayal of and its effects 314–15
  captured by Leicester's forces 306